MAKE Copy
OF TAPE

EDITORIAL ADVISORS

We gratefully acknowledge the participation of the following editorial advisors whose expertise proved invaluable in developing specific content areas of this book:

Thomas Dunfee, University of Pennsylvania—The Wharton School

Lawrence P. Ettkin, University of Tennessee at Chattanooga

David Kroenke, University of Washington

David Ricks, University of South Carolina

William Sandberg, University of South Carolina

Randall S. Schuler, New York University

In addition, we are indebted to the following individuals whose valuable suggestions and constructive comments helped guide the development of the entire manuscript:

Raymond E. Alie, Western Michigan University
Jill Austin, Middle Tennessee State University
Hal Babson, Columbus State Community College
Moshe Banai, CUNY—Bernard M. Baruch College
Allen Bluedorn, University of Missouri
Judith G. Bulin, Monroe Community College
Mary Coulter, Southwest Missouri State University
Joseph De Felippe, Suffolk Community College
Gerald Hollier, Texas Southmost College
Dewey E. Johnson, California State University—Fresno
Pamela Lewis, University of Central Florida
Albert H. Mahrer, Front Range Community College
James C. McElroy, Iowa State University
David Meyer, University of Akron
Edward C. Mirch, West Valley College
Eugene Owens, Western Washington University
Monique A. Pelletier, San Francisco State University
Pat Plocek, Richland College
Scottie Putman, Lansing Community College
Robert F. Scherer, Wright State University
Theresa C. Scott, Community College of Philadelphia
Michael S. Stoll, Genesee Community College
Herman A. Theeke, Central Michigan University
Mary S. Thibodeaux, University of North Texas
Philip A. Weatherford, Embry-Riddle Aeronautical University

Management

Management

Courtland L. Bovée
C. Allen Paul Distinguished Chair
Grossmont College

John V. Thill
Chief Executive Officer
Communication Specialists of America

Marian Burk Wood
President
Strategic Management Services

George P. Dovel
President
Dovel Group

McGraw-Hill, Inc.

New York St. Louis San Francisco Auckland Bogotá Caracas
Lisbon London Madrid Mexico Milan Montreal New Delhi
Paris San Juan Singapore Sydney Tokyo Toronto

Management

1 2 3 4 5 6 7 8 9 0 VNH VNH 9 0 9 8 7 6 5 4 3 2

ISBN 0-07-006831-3

This book was set in Sabon by York Graphic Services, Inc.
The editors were Lynn Richardson, Dan Alpert, and Ira C. Roberts;
the designer was Joseph A. Piliero;
the cover illustration was done by Greg Couch;
the production supervisor was Janelle S. Travers.
The photo editors were Susan Holtz and Elyse Rieder;
the photo manager was Kathy Bendo.
Von Hoffmann Press, Inc., was printer and binder.

Library of Congress Cataloging-in-Publication Data

Management / Courtland L. Bovée . . . [et al.].
p. cm. — (McGraw-Hill series in management)
Includes bibliographical references and index.
ISBN 0-07-006831-3
1. Management. 2. Industrial management. I. Bovée. Courtland L.
II. Series.
HD31.M2887 1993
658—dc20 92-27876

International Edition

When ordering this title, use ISBN 0-07-112944-8.

CONTENTS IN BRIEF

CONTENTS

PART THREE

Organizing

CHAPTER 9 Foundations of Organization Structure 272

CHAPTER 10 Organization Design 302

CHAPTER 19 Foundations of Management Control 600

CHAPTER 20 Operations Management 636

PREPARING THE TWENTY-FIRST-CENTURY MANAGER

The global demand for effective, high-performance managers has never been greater. In large corporations, small businesses, not-for-profit organizations, and government agencies, managers are confronting a wider variety of challenges and opportunities than ever before. Against the backdrop of the continuing globalization of markets, managers in both public and private sectors are driving for improved quality, productivity, and customer/constituent satisfaction. Competition is mounting, and managers must juggle long- and short-term demands as well as the need for innovation to fuel higher performance. As they work toward their performance targets, managers also need to balance critical issues involving social responsibility and ethics. At the same time, contemporary managers are reaping the benefits of advanced technology that enhances the ability to communicate; to manage people and operations; to measure, analyze, and improve performance; and to make timely, well-informed decisions.

Management introduces students to all of these trends and to the theories, tools, and techniques that effective managers need in today's complex, dynamic environment. This is an authoritative, accessible text, well grounded in the classic research and principles as well as the latest developments in theory and practice. In addition to concentrated coverage in dedicated chapters, this text integrates global management, new ventures, and social responsibility and ethics throughout. By devoting an entire chapter to quality, productivity, and customer satisfaction, *Management* goes beyond the buzzwords to explore the relationship among these vital concepts and their influence on organizational performance.

But content is only one aspect of an effective management text. *Management* presents a clear, lively, engaging picture of the art and science of management. It covers the fundamentals and the emerging trends while conveying the excitement and the achievements of contemporary management by including examples from a wide variety of organizations in both the public and private sectors. *Management* also provides a powerful link between concept and application, in which students not only read about management, but experience it first-hand through a variety of highly involving activities. The chapter-opening vignette draws students into the chapter by dramatizing a challenge faced by an actual manager. As students read the chapter, they begin to see the options available to the manager. The chapter-closing case study/simulation shows how the same manager resolved the problem. Students then assume a management role in the featured organization to make decisions in a variety of scenarios.

With these unique case study/simulations, plus thought-provoking video exercises, assignments to improve decision-making and communication skills, research tasks, and a host of other activities, *Management* fosters critical thinking and successfully implements the American Assembly of Collegiate Schools of Business (AACSB) guidelines for undergraduate business programs. For all these reasons, *Management* is unmatched in meeting the needs of today's students and instructors.

OFFERS STUDENTS A BALANCED, INTEGRATED INTRODUCTION TO MANAGEMENT

Management has been carefully structured around the four management functions of planning, organizing, leading, and controlling. An introductory section sets the stage for the in-depth examination of management functions that follows. In contrast to the many texts that include a final catchall section to deal with topics such as international management, entrepreneurship, and social responsibility and ethics, *Management* effectively integrates these topics into the four-function framework. Moreover, we have avoided the common practice of relegating quantitative tools to an appendix, choosing instead to introduce all techniques in the context of their application, so students can understand the theory as well as the practical use of these tools. Here's a brief look at the book's five main parts:

Part One: Understanding Management Today. The text opens with a five-chapter introduction to contemporary management. The first chapter emphasizes the nature and importance of management, the second explores the discipline's theoretical underpinnings, and the third explores the organizational environment. The fourth chapter discusses social responsibility and ethical decision making, and the fifth chapter closes this part with a look at global management. With these concepts as a foundation, students are ready to explore the specific responsibilities and practices of management in today's organizations.

Part Two: Planning. This three-chapter part examines all aspects of management planning. It opens with a chapter on decision making that includes a discussion of individual and group decision making and of key decision-making tools. Next is a chapter on organizational goals and planning, which includes the essential quantitative and qualitative tools and techniques used to support the planning process. Part Two concludes with a chapter discussing strategic management and implementation.

Part Three: Organizing. Five chapters explore the management function of organizing. First is a chapter on the fundamentals of organization structure, followed by a chapter covering organization design. The third chapter in this part focuses on change and innovation in the context of the organization structure, and the fourth chapter examines the organization and management of new ventures, including entrepreneurial and intrapreneurial ventures. The fifth chapter explores the effective management of human resources.

Part Four: Leading. Four chapters analyze various aspects of the leading function within the organization. Opening this part is a chapter on motivation, and next is a chapter on leadership. Following is a chapter on groups within the organization, with a discussion of the growing use of teams (including self-managing teams). A chapter on management and communication concludes this part.

Part Five: Controlling. This part examines the management function of controlling in four chapters, starting with an overview of the key task of managing information resources. In contrast to the traditional MIS approach to this material, *Management* presents information as a strategic resource and explores the importance of information and its uses in the organization before delving into the technical aspects of information management. The second chapter presents and analyzes the fundamentals of management control, and the third chapter is devoted to operations management in production and service organizations. The final chapter links management control and the interrelated concepts of quality, productivity, and customer satisfaction—all critical to organizational performance. Throughout Part Five, *Management* emphasizes the control of processes, not the control of people, giving students a clear picture of how innovative managers approach control.

PUTS STUDENTS ON THE CUTTING EDGE OF CONTEMPORARY MANAGEMENT

In addition to building a solid foundation of management fundamentals, *Management* introduces students to emerging concepts and issues that are shaping the theory and practice of management. Consider the intensifying worldwide quest for quality, productivity, and customer satisfaction. Tomorrow's managers need to understand these related concepts and their application in business, government, and not-for-profit organizations. Although many texts give these areas little coverage or present them only in isolation, *Management* explores the dimensions of quality, productivity, and customer satisfaction throughout the book and caps the discussion with a chapter (Chapter 21) devoted to examining their relationship and their impact on organizational effectiveness and efficiency.

Management also offers fresh insights and discussions about other contemporary topics not covered in depth by most other texts. For example, crisis management is emerging as a key skill.

Students need an appreciation for the variety of crisis problems that can confront organizations, the impact such crises can have on stakeholders, and the ways in which managers can work toward resolving crises. *Management* uses recent examples of crises to show students the distinction between crisis and noncrisis problems (Chapter 6), to examine crisis decision making (Chapter 6), to explore crisis planning (Chapter 7), and to offer insights into crisis communication (Chapter 17).

EXPLORES TODAY'S MOST IMPORTANT MANAGEMENT ISSUES

More than ever before, social responsibility and ethical decision making are critical concerns at every management level and in every organization. Unlike some texts, *Management* draws a clear distinction between ethical dilemmas and ethical lapses. This helps students understand the difference between unresolved ethical questions in which both sides have an arguably supportable position and behavior that is simply unethical. This text covers social responsibility and ethics in three ways: in a dedicated chapter (Chapter 4), in 14 highlight boxes, and in examples throughout the book. Here's a brief sampling of the ethical questions we explore:

- "Regulators Put a Price Tag on Saving Human Life" (Chapter 6) examines the ethical questions raised by valuing human life for the purpose of determining the cost-benefit ratio of federal regulations.
- "When Pyramids Get Flatter, Who Gets Flattened?" (Chapter 9) discusses the implications of downsizing and alternatives to massive layoffs.
- "CEO Compensation: How Much Is Enough?" (Chapter 13) probes the controversy over rising top-management pay and its impact on employee morale, lower-level managers, and shareholders.

Resolving the ethical issues surrounding the right to privacy is another growing concern for today's managers. *Management* presents an overview of the ethical issues of privacy in Chapter 4, Social Responsibility and Ethics, and specific aspects of privacy are explored in four special highlight boxes: "Electronic Communication Raises New Privacy Issues" (Chapter 17), "Your Right to Privacy vs. the Marketing Databases" (Chapter 18), "Cost-cutting at the Expense of Employee Privacy" (Chapter 19), and "Employee Monitoring: Coaching or Spying?" (Chapter 21). This in-depth coverage gives students a realistic glimpse of both sides of the privacy dilemma, and it encourages them to think through the possible alternatives faced by managers and stakeholders.

Here's a brief sampling of the social issues we explore:

- "Ensuring Equal Access to Housing" (Chapter 1) presents insurer Lincoln National's program of donating management skills as well as management funds as part of its social responsibility to the community.
- "Toeing the Line in a Tough Environment" (Chapter 3) offers a look at how the New York College of Podiatric Medicine affirmed its commitment to the community despite the heavy economic burden.
- "Leadership Fights Hunger in Africa" (Chapter 15) shows how rock star Bob Geldof built a socially responsible organization to fight world hunger.

Every "Social Responsibility and Ethics" box ends with two "What's Your Opinion?" questions that encourage students to think about the issues and to draw their own conclusions. These questions can form the basis of class discussions, homework assignments, or student projects.

This text presents a balanced view of management. It fires students' enthusiasm and respect for the profession (see the upbeat coverage of human resource professionals, of intrapreneurs, and of information resource managers, for example), but it doesn't pretend that contemporary management is without its problems or its critics. By pointing out ethical dilemmas and reminding students of the responsibilities that accompany the rights of free enterprise, *Management* helps prepare the next generation of conscientious professional managers.

As the globalization of markets grows in importance, the managers of tomorrow need up-to-date, realistic, comprehensive information that will help put international management into perspective. We positioned a full chapter on global management (Chapter 5) early in the book to set the stage for students' in-depth understanding of the challenges, opportunities, and techniques of managing in the international environment. Because students may work for organizations that operate internationally, compete with global rivals, or obtain resources from other countries, they need such comprehensive coverage of current trends and issues around the world.

In addition, extensive international examples and discussions have been integrated throughout the text, including 11 "Global Management" highlight boxes. In exploring many aspects of global management, these boxes focus on the following real-world management problems: Merck's global push, Unilever's North American challenge, Japanese philanthropy in the United States, Corning's global joint ventures, Marriott's worldwide planning process, Thompson's international strategy, Swissair's global structure, Asea Brown Boveri's international organization design, managing in the Mexican maquiladoras, innovating around the world, and contemporary issues in offshore manufacturing.

OFFERS UNPARALLELED PEDAGOGICAL SUPPORT

Rich pedagogy sets *Management* apart from other texts, and the book includes a number of unique elements.

Facing a Management Challenge

Unique case study/simulations put the student in the manager's shoes to explore a number of decisions related to chapter material. Each chapter opens with a short slice-of-life vignette that draws students into the chapter by vividly portraying a management challenge faced by a real executive. Each chapter then concludes with a section entitled "Meeting a Management Challenge," which describes how the executive met the challenge described earlier and analyzes the results in light of chapter concepts. Then the student takes over, playing a role in the featured organization by making management decisions in a variety of carefully chosen scenarios. Each simulation also contains several traditional case-study questions and a more involved special project (which can also be assigned as a group activity). The 21 management challenges include such intriguing cases as these:

- Microsoft's struggle to survive its own success by creating an organization structure and developing management practices to guide its rapid growth
- Hewlett-Packard's redesigning its decision-making processes to respond to market changes faster and more effectively
- R. W. Frookies' continuing challenge to build market share and fend off larger competitors
- Disney's challenge to reinvigorate the company's creative spirit
- Ford's turnaround in quality and customer satisfaction

Sharpen Your Management Skills

This assignment offers students the opportunity to practice or analyze a particular management skill covered in the chapter. Examples include planning a response to new competition, identifying the environmental forces most likely to affect an acquisition, improving the structure of a student or social organization, and searching for nonfinancial means of motivating public school teachers. By going through the steps needed to solve real-life management problems such as these, students develop a much stronger grasp of the material presented in the text. Each of these exercises includes a decision-making component and a communication component to help students develop these two vitally important skills.

Keeping Current in Management

Each of these library research exercises asks students to find and analyze a recent article about a particular organization that relates to chapter material, such as an article on how a manager assessed the organizational environment and formulated a response, confronted a crisis problem, or increased customer satisfaction through improved quality. These exercises not only keep the student up to date on important issues but also reinforce research and analysis skills.

Highlight Boxes

Management includes three types of highlight boxes. In addition to the "Global Management" and "Social Responsibility and Ethics" boxes discussed earlier, "Managerial Decision Making" boxes explore decisions made by managers or the processes organizations use to reach decisions. Each chapter includes two of the three types, and all boxes provide additional opportunities for class discussion, homework assignments, and student projects.

Integrated Video Exercises

Video provides a powerful and engaging learning experience—as long as the material is relevant, well produced, and clearly tied to the text. In the unique program that accompanies *Management,* each chapter offers a video that integrates material from a variety of organizations, tied together with our own narration to help students make the connection between the chapter's concepts and the ways the featured organizations implemented those concepts. In a section at the end of this book, a brief summary and a variety of student-involvement exercises further enhance the student's opportunity to learn.

Important Additional Features to Help Students Learn

This text includes numerous other student-oriented features:

- Learning objectives in every chapter guide the learning effort, and the chapter summary is arranged in the same order as the objectives to help students gauge their progress.
- The margin glossary quickly reinforces concepts from the text; for easy reference, the entire glossary is repeated at the end of the book.
- Each chapter features a map identifying a country that illustrates a key point covered in the text; these 21 maps enhance the student's sense of geography and highlight the need for a global perspective.
- Hundreds of examples illustrate the management decisions of a diverse collection of managers and organizations.
- Review, analysis, and application questions at the end of each chapter help students solidify their grasp of chapter concepts.
- Uniquely organized case studies at the end of each chapter and integrative case studies at the end of each part give students additional opportunities to analyze and apply management ideas.

The presence of so many features benefits students by giving them multiple ways of learning material. And instructors benefit because preparation time is reduced; discussion questions, activities, and homework possibilities are all presented and ready to be used. Instructors can spend less time creating or finding material and more time teaching and coaching students.

BASED ON FIRST-HAND KNOWLEDGE AND EXTENSIVE, UP-TO-DATE RESEARCH

The superior pedagogy and pragmatic orientation of *Management* is based on the solid foundation of the authors' academic and management achievements. Courtland L. Bovée has for 24 years been a professor at Grossmont College where he has received teaching honors and holds its C. Allen Paul Distinguished Chair. He is the coauthor of six leading texts, including *Business Today* and *Business Communication Today,* and more than 250,000 students a year learn about business from his books. In addition to being a prominent writer and researcher, he is a highly regarded management consultant, known worldwide for his seminars and in-company training programs. He also serves on the board of directors of several corporations.

John V. Thill is the founder and Chief Executive Officer of Communication Specialists of America. Widely recognized for innovations in management education, his organization has become a prominent consulting firm to government and to many of America's largest corporations. He formerly held positions with Pacific Bell, Texaco, and RKO Theaters. A prolific writer, he has presented numerous papers at professional meetings, has been a contributor to a multitude of publications, and is coauthor of five successful textbooks, including *Excellence in Business Communication* and *Marketing.*

Marian Burk Wood is president of Strategic Management Services, a management consulting firm based in Bronxville, New York, that specializes in helping businesses develop plans for strengthening corporate strategy and competitive positioning. Prior to starting her own firm, she held vice-presidential level positions at Chase Manhattan Bank, Citibank, Citicorp Retail Services, and the National Retail Federation. She has also held management positions at Tandy, Sam Goody, and Bloomingdale's and has written extensively for the business press.

George P. Dovel is the founder and president of the Dovel Group, a management consultancy based in Snohomish, Washington, that focuses on the managerial challenges faced by advanced-technology companies. His clients have ranged from Fortune 500 multinationals to entrepreneurial start-ups. His global perspective on contemporary management was fostered during his years at Hewlett-Packard. His responsibilities were as diverse as training sales and engineering personnel in over a dozen countries across Europe and around the Pacific Rim, educating and supporting a worldwide customer base, and leading multidisciplinary product-introduction teams.

In addition to its authors' solid foundation in academic and management expertise, *Management* provides up-to-date coverage in terms of both examples and emerging concepts. The thoroughness of the research is evidenced by the number and currency of source notes in each chapter, with some chapters containing as many as 100 references. A quick scan of any chapter or of the organization/brand/company index will show how many real-life examples have been included, from organizations both large and small, in the United States and in numerous other countries.

KEEPS STUDENTS ENGAGED AND INTERESTED

Every instructor knows that motivating students to read the text is one of the most challenging aspects of teaching. If students find that the time they spend reading is both rewarding and enjoyable, they will read more. This basic premise formed one of the authors' major goals with *Management*: to provide lively, interesting prose.

ENHANCES THE LEARNING PROCESS WITH AN EFFECTIVE DESIGN

The visual appeal of a textbook has a lot to do with the success of the student's learning efforts. *Management* offers a design that is both inviting and contemporary without trivializing the study of management principles and practices. Every exhibit includes a complete caption and is closely integrated with related text. Photos were carefully chosen to demonstrate management in action, rather than simply to entertain the reader. The open, attractive layout complements the lively writing to ensure a high level of interest and retention.

SUPPORTS THE TEACHING PROCESS WITH A FULL COMPLEMENT OF FEATURES

The *Management* text is only one part of a comprehensive teaching package. To meet the challenges of large classes, heavy teaching loads, and limited preparation time, instructors need a complete program of pedagogical resources and support features. Moreover, demands on the student's time call for a textbook that makes the learning process both efficient and effective. Here are the ways *Management* supports both groups.

Instructor Supplements

- *Instructor's Resource Manual.* Each chapter in the Instructor's Manual contains annotated learning objectives, key terms, chapter outline, lecture notes (with references to specific overhead transparencies), and answers to all questions and exercises. In addition, there are numerous lecture update items (all new material, not in the text) for each chapter and numerous suggestions for class discussions.
- *Acetate Transparency Program.* This set of color transparencies presents additional visual material, beyond the exhibits provided in the text. These informative diagrams illuminate text material and give students fresh perspectives on management issues. Each transparency is supported by information in the Instructor's Manual that is integrated into the lecture outlines and includes a discussion of the concept that the transparency illustrates, and class discussion questions (with answers).
- *Test Bank.* This manual is organized by text chapters and includes a mix of true/false, multiple-choice, fill-in, and short essay questions for each chapter—more than 2,000 overall. The questions are coded by question type and text page. The test bank has been carefully screened by reviewers to ensure that questions and answers are correct, relevant, and appropriate for the course. The test bank is available both in hard copy and on disk (Macintosh and IBM formats).
- *Testing Services.* Two major programs are available:

  Computerized Test Bank. A powerful microcomputer program allows the instructor to create customized tests using questions from the test bank, self-prepared items, or a combination. This versatile program incorporates a broad range of test-making capabilities, including editing and scrambling of questions to create alternative versions of a test. This program is available for both Apple and IBM-compatible computers.

Customized Test Service. Through its Customized Test Service, McGraw-Hill will supply adopters of *Management* with custom-made tests consisting of items selected from the test bank. The test questions can be renumbered in any order. Instructors will receive an original test, ready for reproduction, and a separate answer key. Tests can be ordered by mail or by phone, using a toll-free number.

- *Classroom Management Software.* This program helps with grading and recordkeeping.

Student Supplements

- *Study Guide.* Each chapter in the Study Guide includes an outline of the text chapter with learning objectives keyed to the outline, a pretest, a chapter overview, key-term matching, concept application exercises utilizing key terms, a posttest, and skill-practice exercises involving decision making and creativity. The Study Guide provides an effective learning experience that makes the most of the student's time.
- *Software.* To further enhance the student's learning experience, McGraw-Hill provides several software packages for use with *Management.* For further information on prices and availability of our supplements, please contact your local McGraw-Hill representative.

ACKNOWLEDGMENTS

Many colleagues, friends, and family members contributed to the development and refinement of this textbook. We thank them all.

Special thanks to my husband Wally Wood and to my sisters, Isabel Burk and Harriet Burk Goodwin, for their love, friendship, and support. (MBW)

My thanks to Debbie for her wise counsel and sense of humor, and to Andrew for keeping all this in perspective. (GPD)

The authors extend very special thanks to three professionals whose talents and practical inclinations helped give this text its hands-on, real-world feel. Doug Hampton's diverse experiences truly broadened the book's organizational perspective, Colleen Pang's ability to analyze vast amounts of research data and synthesize meaningful information was an enormous help, and Claire Rigodanzo's insights into the close relationship between systems and organizational performance made an invaluable contribution.

Our thanks to Terry Anderson, whose communications abilities and project-management skills ensured the clarity and completeness of this project. Her help and guidance throughout this project is much appreciated. We are also indebted to Jackie Estrada for her specialized knowledge and expert assistance.

Recognition and thanks also go to Philip Perry, Jim Showalter, James Wynbrandt, Joe Glidden, and Robert P. Irwin.

Deep gratitude is expressed to Marie Painter for her expertise in word processing and her work beyond the call of duty.

We also feel it is important to acknowledge and thank the American Management Association, whose meetings and publications provide a useful forum for the exchange of ideas and for professional growth. The staff at the AMA Library was particularly helpful in tracking down some of the classic works in management theory.

We also want to extend our warmest appreciation to the very devoted professionals at McGraw-Hill. They include Seib Adams, June Smith, Alan Sachs, Lynn Richardson, Dan Alpert, Dundee Holt, Kathy Bendo, Susan Holtz, and the outstanding McGraw-Hill sales representatives. A very special acknowledgement to the late Anita Kann, whose commitment and technical skills in the production of this book will long be remembered. Finally, we thank editor Ira Roberts for his dedication and expertise, and we are grateful to copyeditor Carole Schwager, proofreader Joan Bosi, and designer Joseph Piliero for their superb work.

Courtland L. Bovée
John V. Thill
Marian Burk Wood
George P. Dovel

Understanding Management Today

CHAPTER OUTLINE

The Foundations of Management

After studying this chapter, you will be able to

1. Discuss the concept of management and its importance in any organization
2. Differentiate between for-profit and not-for-profit organizations and between the private and public sectors
3. List and briefly describe the four functions within the management process
4. Identify the interpersonal, informational, and decisional roles that managers assume within the organization
5. Describe how managers can be classified according to scope of responsibility and level within the organization
6. Outline the three types of management skills and explain how people can learn to become managers
7. Discuss the key issues in contemporary management

FACING A MANAGEMENT CHALLENGE AT

MICROSOFT

Struggling to Survive Success

Success has brought its own management problems to Microsoft. Shrewd business deals and sheer luck propelled the pioneering software company into a leading role at the center of the volatile, hotly competitive computer industry. But spectacular 50 percent annual growth left Microsoft unwieldy and disorganized, and software companies such as Lotus and Ashton-Tate were coming on strong. Technology continued to evolve at a rapid pace, consumers became more demanding, and rival programmers worked around the clock to create new and better applications. For founder and chief executive officer Bill Gates, just maintaining Microsoft's position required heroic effort.

Gates's visionary leadership was largely the reason for Microsoft's wild success. When Gates dropped out of Harvard to found the company in 1975, personal computers were toys for the "hard-core technoid," as he once described himself. But Gates, barely 20 years old, envisioned a nation with a computer in every home and in every office—and a piece of Microsoft software in every computer. An early alliance with computer giant IBM put Microsoft's basic operating program (MS-DOS) into 80 percent of the nation's 50 million personal computers. Gates boldly led Microsoft into Europe and Asia too. Inspired by Gates's charisma and technical knowledge, Microsoft employees also investigated new data storage technologies and broadened software offerings for home and office. In the future, Gates foresaw handwriting recognition programs, word processing with animation and stereo sound, modular software that lets anyone combine program features, and more.

But good ideas weren't enough anymore. Gates found he was so swamped by new business that he could hardly handle day-to-day operational details, much less develop the vision he needed to beat the competition in the twenty-first century. Coordinating the activities of his many working groups became more difficult, and quality control and planning weren't receiving the needed attention. Time after time his company targeted a new market only to introduce a mediocre product the first time out. Gates took charge of five key product lines but couldn't find time to adequately tailor them to customer needs. Projects died. Customers got angry.

Gates was also worried about something that threatened his leadership of the company. He feared losing touch with his employees, the people who put his vision into action. Microsoft had been fun, a small company where talking shop with the CEO was an important morale booster and a method of indoctrination. Gates still relished personal contact with his people, but their number had grown past 1,000, and they were spread around the world.

Gates had always made the big decisions at Microsoft, but more decisions were needed and he was already working 65 hours or more a week. Now that Microsoft had passed the $1 billion sales mark, Gates couldn't manage the company the same way he had when it was much smaller. Moreover, he was facing the launch of Windows, which had the potential to be one of Microsoft's biggest sellers ever. How could he both plan for the long haul and effectively manage daily affairs? What could he do to stay in touch with his employees and spread his vision? How could he improve quality control? How could he ensure Microsoft's success through the 1990s and beyond?[1]

CHAPTER OVERVIEW

Even for a manager as experienced as Bill Gates, management is a complex, challenging activity. To keep Microsoft on top, Gates needs excellent management skills and a solid understanding of his roles and responsibilities within the company, and he needs to share his goals and his vision with everyone else in the organization. This chapter starts with an examination of the interrelationship between management and organizations. Next is an overview of the four functions that make up the management process and a look at what managers actually do during the workday. Following that is a section on management responsibilities and levels. After a look at the skills all managers need to be effective and at how these skills are developed, the chapter closes with a glimpse of the challenges facing managers today and tomorrow.

MANAGEMENT AND MANAGERS

Only 200 years ago, before the Industrial Revolution, the concept of professional management and managers didn't exist. Today millions of people around the world are managers; in the United States alone, nearly 15 million people, or about 12 percent of the work force, hold managerial positions.[2] These managers coordinate and control organizational resources, lead their people into the future, and help their organizations respond to everything from technological changes to social expectations. Management touches everyone's daily lives in a variety of ways: managers run the largest and the smallest businesses, hospitals and schools, charities and arts organizations, government and military organizations (see Exhibit 1.1).

Who are these managers and what do they do? Thomas C. Theobald, chairman of Continental Bank in Chicago, is a manager who has returned one of the largest banks in the United States to profitability by concentrating on the long-term potential of forging closer relationships with business customers. Anita Roddick, founder of Great Britain's fast-growing retail chain The Body Shop, keeps international employees and customers environmentally conscious while selling personal care products. The president of the United States is a manager, and so is Micky Sadoff, national president of Mothers Against Drunk Driving. Whether the goal is to make money, to save lives, or to serve citizens, management is the key ingredient in achieving any organization's success.

EXHIBIT 1.1

Management Positions in Various Organizations

All types of managers are needed to help organizations achieve their goals.

Management Defined

The art and science of management have developed and changed over the years, and so too have definitions of management. Some early theorists viewed management simply as the ability to work through others. But contemporary managers work with many resources and tools, so this definition of management must be broadened beyond the human aspects. Today, **management** can be defined as the process of achieving organizational goals through planning, organizing, leading, and controlling the human, physical, financial, and information resources of the organization in an effective and efficient manner (see Exhibit 1.2).

management The process of attaining organizational goals by effectively and efficiently planning, organizing, leading, and controlling the organization's human, physical, financial, and information resources

By this definition, management is a distinct *process,* a set of ongoing, coordinated activities that managers engage in as they pursue the organization's goals. Therefore, a **manager** is someone who actively participates in the management process through the four functions of planning, organizing, leading, and controlling the resources of the organization. Managers in various organizations are confronted by different challenges and call on different *resources,* elements such as raw materials, people, information, and money that the organization needs to produce goods or services.

manager Someone who participates in the management process by planning, organizing, leading, or controlling the organization's resources

Depending on their situation and on their resources, managers stress one or another of the four management functions to accomplish their goals. For example, Sharon Foster-Johnson, executive director of the Northside Center for Child Development in New York City, emphasizes planning to keep her not-for-profit center tuned to community needs. Tony M. Hirsch, president of HMV USA, worries about organizing and staffing in order to give the shoppers in his retail subsidiary of Britain's HMV Music the knowledgeable help they want when buying records and compact discs. Harvey Mackay, chairman and CEO of Mackay Envelope, focuses on leading and motivating to build his business. And Brenda Roberts-Branch, executive vice president of Gourmet Companies, monitors the control issues of quality and finance to maintain sales and customer satisfaction in her food-service business.[3] Naturally, all of these executives, and the managers at every level in every organization, shift their focus from one management function to another as conditions dictate.

EXHIBIT 1.2

The Management Process

The management process consists of four interrelated functions: planning, organizing, leading, and controlling.

All organizations, large and small, need management to achieve their goals. Frederick Smith, the founder and chief executive officer of Federal Express, used his management skills to build a tiny start-up into the largest overnight package delivery service in the United States. On its first day of operation in 1973, Federal Express shipped only a handful of packages. Today, the firm serves 1.3 million customers daily and strives to reach Smith's goal of 100 percent on-time performance in every delivery.

The Art and Science of Management

No matter how competent or hardworking these managers are, they understand that no one can achieve an organization's goals alone. Management involves working with and through other people. Because people are unpredictable, and because the interaction between managers and employees is unpredictable, it is impossible to impose a rigid set of rules that will work in every situation. That's one reason management is as much an art as a science.

Consider Lia Manoliu, a former Olympic bronze medalist. As president of Romania's national Olympic committee, she held a pivotal position that affected her country's entry into the 1992 Olympics. She relied on her ability to lead, motivate, and influence people as well as on her technical skills of administration, planning, and budgeting, using both the art and the science of management to deal with a variety of challenges and people. Among other tasks, she recommended the standards for team athletes, facilitated the team's training and travel funding, and recruited coaches and trainers. Her interaction with government officials, members of the International Olympic Committee, coaches, and athletes was as important to Romania's Olympic performance as the prowess of its athletes.[4]

Over the years, many management principles have been scientifically codified for study and application. However, people cannot fully develop their management skills without applying some creative talents. That's why managers draw heavily on their own experience as they balance the demands and opportunities of their jobs. Moreover, the growing body of knowledge about managerial techniques and tools suggests that managers also need to apply invention and intuition, especially when the facts and figures don't paint a clear picture of what to do. So the practice of management includes not only concrete principles that can be objectively studied and taught but also subjective processes that can be difficult to describe and to analyze.

MANAGEMENT AND ORGANIZATIONS

Wherever they live, whatever they do, organizations are part of people's everyday lives. Schools, religious institutions, stores, hospitals, banks, camps, even clubs are organizations. Whether they are run by the government, operated as a business, or devoted to improving society, these organizations have a profound effect on everyone. This section focuses on what organizations are, how they are classified, and management's role in them.

Organization Defined

An **organization** is a group of people working together in a deliberately structured situation to accomplish group goals. Note the two key concepts in this definition: a deliberate structure and group goals. If people have no identifiable common goals, or if they lack a defined structure for achieving goals, then they're just a crowd, not an organization.[5] Obviously, not all organizations are alike, so to distinguish between various types of organizations, it is helpful to classify them according to their primary purpose.

organization A group of two or more people who work together in a consciously structured setting to achieve group goals

Types of Organizations

Organizations can be categorized according to their profit orientation as either for-profit or not-for-profit organizations, and they can be categorized as manufacturing or service organizations. Also, organizations can be categorized according to their ownership as private sector (commercial businesses) or public sector (government) organizations. (Private companies can be further distinguished by type of ownership; some companies sell shares only to selected individuals, and some offer shares to the general public.) Although most organizations can be categorized according to the dimensions of profit goals and ownership, some organizations aren't easily classified because of mixed ownership or multiple goals.[6] For instance, Scandinavian Airline Systems (SAS) is owned jointly by private sector businesses and the governments of Norway, Sweden, and Denmark.

For-Profit and Not-for-Profit Organizations

A **for-profit organization** is an organization that exists primarily to make money for its owners. For-profit organizations range from yogurt stands owned by one person to global corporations owned by thousands of shareholders. Even when they don't actually make a profit, businesses still remain for-profit organizations because their goal is to be profitable. In 1991, General Motors lost nearly $3 billion on more than $100 billion in worldwide sales, but the automaker is a for-profit organization because it seeks to make money.[7]

for-profit organization An organization that sets as its primary goal the achievement of profit

In contrast, a **not-for-profit organization** focuses primarily on social, cultural, or political goals rather than on making profits. Examples of not-for-profit organizations include labor unions, zoos, religious institutions, and charities (see Exhibit 1.3). Even though not-for-profit organizations often sell goods and services and collect money from a variety of donors, profit is not their

not-for-profit organization An organization that does not have profit-making as its primary goal but focuses on social, cultural, or political goals

EXHIBIT 1.3

Types of U.S. Not-for-Profit Associations

A wide variety of national not-for-profit associations in the United States exist to serve other cultural, social, and political purposes.

Type of Association	Number
Trade, business, commercial	3,806
Public affairs	2,292
Health, medical	2,162
Cultural	1,872
Social welfare	1,686
Hobby	1,471
Scientific, engineering, technical	1,363
Educational	1,268
Religious	1,169
Agriculture	914
Athletics, sports	839
Legal, governmental, public administration, military	775
Fraternal, foreign interest, nationality, ethnic	570
Fan clubs	561
Veteran, hereditary, patriotic	404
Greek and non-Greek letter societies	337
Labor unions	254
Chambers of commerce	168
Total	21,911

objective. Money is a means to an end for these groups, and the end is meeting constituents' needs. However, this doesn't imply that the line between for-profit and not-for-profit organizations is absolutely clear. Some not-for-profit companies aggressively compete with for-profit organizations; for example, the American Automobile Association competes with for-profit auto clubs offered by Mobil Oil and others.[8]

Manufacturing and Service Organizations

products Goods or services

A second way to classify organizations is according to their output of **products,** the goods or services they produce (see Exhibit 1.4). Manufacturing organizations use raw materials to produce *goods,* physical items such as pencils, televisions, and candy bars. Goods are tangible, so they can be touched, seen, measured, and otherwise physically evaluated by customers. Further, the customer does not generally have to be present during production; goods can be manufactured in a central location and then stored until needed or shipped to a location where customers can obtain them. In contrast, service organizations produce *services,* activities that provide some value to the recipient such as fi-

EXHIBIT 1.4

A Selection of Major U.S. Manufacturing and Service Corporations

These for-profit U.S. corporations can be categorized in terms of the goods or services they produce; these companies represent some of the largest U.S. firms in their respective categories.

Company	Primary Product Category	Sales/Assets ($ millions)*
American Express	Diversified financial services	137,682.0*
AT&T	Telecommunications	37,479.0
Citicorp	Banking	216,986.0*
Exxon	Petroleum products	103,242.0
General Motors	Motor vehicles	123,780.1
Prudential of America	Life insurance	133,456.0*
Sears, Roebuck	Retailing	55,971.7
Super Valu Stores	Wholesaling	11,160.2
Time Warner	Entertainment	11,517.0
United Parcel Service	Shipping	13,628.6

*For companies marked with an asterisk, this figure represents assets; for all others, it represents sales or total revenue.

nancial, legal, medical, or recreational benefits. Services such as education and health care are intangible, so they cannot be physically examined before they are produced. Moreover, services are generally produced at the same time the customer uses them, so they cannot be stored.[9]

Many organizations offer products that are, in reality, a combination of goods and services. Manufacturing organizations often bundle services along with the tangible items they produce, just as service organizations frequently include goods in their service offerings. Car manufacturers, including Ford and Mazda, offer services such as financing for car buyers; restaurants such as Olive Garden are service businesses because they take orders and prepare meals, but their menu items are tangible goods. The combination of goods and services produced by manufacturing and service organizations determines the unique challenges faced by their managers.

The Public Sector and the Private Sector

Organizations can also be classified by the nature of their ownership. Organizations such as elementary schools and prison systems are considered part of the **public sector** because they are controlled by the government.[10] In fact, many such organizations have the word *public* in their names (such as public schools and public libraries), indicating that they are owned and supported by the government for the use of all. On the other hand, organizations such as manufacturing plants and stores are generally considered to be in the **private sector** because they are under private rather than governmental control. However, in some countries, organizations such as manufacturing plants are part of the public sector rather than the private sector. When East Germany became part of Germany in 1990, German Chancellor Helmut Kohl appointed a government official to *privatize* 8,000 ailing companies by selling the formerly state-controlled businesses to the private sector. And in some cases, private sector organizations operate public sector organizations, such as the private organizations that run the San Diego Zoo and the Philadelphia Zoo, two of the best-run zoos in the United States.[11]

public sector Organizations under governmental control

private sector Organizations under private control

Management and Organizational Goals

Managers in all types of organizations are expected to apply management functions and techniques to achieve their organizations' goals. But the specific actions and responsibilities of managers can differ from organization to organization, depending on the goals of each organization. Because their main goal is profit, the managers of for-profit organizations find that they must pay close attention to the needs and wants of their customers if they wish to make money. **Customers** are the people and organizations who purchase an organization's products, and if managers don't serve their customers, they cannot achieve their goals.

customers Individuals and organizations that buy the goods or services produced by an organization

Even organizations in the public sector have customers in the sense that individuals and other organizations benefit from the services these organizations provide. These public sector customers are called **constituents,** and their needs and wants are as important to public sector managers as the needs of customers are to private sector managers.

constituents Individuals and organizations that are served by organizations in the public sector

Public sector managers sometimes find managing more difficult than private sector managers because their organizational goals are more ambiguous, often debatable, and sometimes conflicting. For example, public sector managers are expected to operate efficiently, yet they are subject to public scrutiny and to laws and regulations that may dictate how certain situations must be handled. For instance, the U.S. Postal Service must serve all the citizens of the United States, even customers who live in isolated, hard-to-reach locations. Also, public sector managers often have difficulty gauging how well they are achieving their goals because some goals, such as public safety or better living standards, are not easily measured.[12] Nonetheless, these managers are responsible for helping their organizations and employees understand and achieve performance, just as their counterparts in the private sector are.

Organizational and Personal Performance

Managers and organizations are continually evaluated to see how well they accomplish organizational goals. Ratings are everywhere: newspapers publish the ranking of teams in the National Football League; *Inc.* compiles a yearly survey of America's fastest-growing private companies; magazines rate international cities according to the cost of lodgings or transportation. Managers and organizations are measured according to their **performance**, the degree to which they attain the organization's goals effectively and efficiently.

performance The degree to which individuals and organizations achieve the organization's goals with effectiveness and efficiency

effectiveness The ability to accomplish the organization's goals

efficiency The ability to minimize waste of the organization's available resources

Effectiveness is the measure of whether an organization is accomplishing its goals. In other words, is the organization doing what it should be doing to achieve its goals? On the other hand, if the organization is effective but does not consider the resources it uses to achieve its goals, then its performance suffers.[13] **Efficiency** is the measure of whether an organization is using the appropriate amount of resources in attaining its goals. Are people's efforts being wasted? Are money and materials squandered to reach the goal? Even when an organization is efficient, it can be ineffective if the focus is on efficiently doing the wrong things. To achieve high performance, the organization must be both effective and efficient.[14]

Of course, individual managers and organizations must be evaluated according to a performance standard that's appropriate for their work. Don McKen-

As president of Mexico, Carlos Salinas de Gortari has set a variety of ambitious goals. He wants to boost Mexico's economy without igniting runaway inflation, and he aims to improve the standard of living throughout the country. Salinas's performance can be evaluated according to measures such as the number of new jobs created annually, the unemployment rate, the rate of economic growth, and the inflation rate.

ney, coach of Northeastern University's hockey team, is rated on the basis of the number of games won or lost. However, Mark Wossner, president of the German-based publishing and recording giant Bertelsmann, is judged on his company's performance in achieving worldwide market share and profits. Top managers are generally measured on the basis of how well their organizations perform overall; managers at lower levels are measured on specific objectives and activities that help the organization achieve overall goals.[15] Performance is personal as well as organizational: managers are responsible for the performance of the people they manage as well as for their own progress toward organizational goals.[16]

When determining how well they have performed, managers must start by understanding what customers or constituents expect. Customers are the ultimate judges of management performance: "Results exist only on the outside," says management expert Peter F. Drucker. If a company's customers are not satisfied, if a team's fans are not happy, or if a city's residents are leaving in great numbers, then management has not performed well.[17]

THE MANAGEMENT PROCESS AND THE NATURE OF MANAGERIAL WORK

As the beginning of this chapter stated, management is composed of four basic functions that help managers achieve organizational goals. Regardless of the kinds of organizations they serve or the level at which they are employed, all managers apply these functions to one degree or another. This section previews the management functions (which will be explored in greater depth in Chapters 6 through 21) and then discusses exactly what managers do and how they do it.

Management Functions

The management process consists of four functions: planning, organizing, leading, and controlling. The functions are not discrete; they often overlap and influence one another. Although society and business have both changed dramatically since these basic functions were first proposed in 1916, with updated interpretations, they remain the most popular approach to studying management.

Planning

The first management function is **planning,** the process of determining the organization's goals and then laying out procedures to attain them. When planning, management looks at where the organization should be in the future, considers alternative strategies for getting there, and then selects and implements the best set of actions. At Lucky-Goldstar, the giant South Korean manufacturer, chairman Koo Cha-Kyung has set up an executive committee to consider the corporation's future direction. From years of experience, these executives have the accumulated wisdom to examine markets around the world, choose attractive opportunities, and marshal the company's resources in pursuit of those opportunities.[18]

planning The process of formulating goals and developing ways to achieve them

The concepts and practices of planning are undergoing dramatic changes as more and more organizations realize that plans conceived in isolation by senior executives are often inappropriate for today's highly competitive, rapidly evolving markets. At Lucky-Goldstar, for instance, chairman Koo Cha-kyung balances the wisdom and experience of the executive planning committee with the hands-on-the-market feel of lower-level managers by spreading decision-making responsibilities up and down the management ranks. This change should help Lucky-Goldstar managers make decisions and plans more quickly to keep up with the fast pace of the competitive environment.[19]

Organizing

organizing The process of creating a framework for developing and assigning tasks, obtaining and allocating resources, and coordinating work activities to achieve goals

The second management function is **organizing,** which involves establishing, maintaining, or changing a structure to accomplish the organization's goals, to define and assign tasks, and to coordinate people and resources. Managers usually move into the organizing phase once they have established their goals and developed plans. When TRW chairman Joseph T. Gorman regrouped the conglomerate's auto-parts business and shifted its managers around recently, he was working within the organizing function to improve the auto group's performance.[20]

Leading

leading The process of using influence to motivate others to work toward accomplishing goals

The third management function is **leading,** the process of influencing and motivating others to work together to achieve organizational goals. Once the organizational structure is in place and people have been assigned their tasks, managers work directly with all members of the organization to help them understand their goals and make their best possible contributions. At Apple USA, president Robert Puette meets frequently with key managers and employees to keep them up to date on the company's results and on any changes in Apple's plans. In this way, Puette keeps everybody driving toward the same goals and boosts the sense of pride in Apple's success.[21]

Controlling

controlling The process of monitoring and regulating the organization's progress toward achieving goals

The fourth management function is **controlling,** which involves setting the standards, monitoring the progress, and making the adjustments needed to keep the organization focused on its goals. Typically, managers anticipate control

When Pizza Hut opened in Moscow in 1990, its general manager Alex Antoniadi had to recruit, hire, and train 60 people; define and assign work tasks; and create an organization structure. His organizing skills enabled him to coordinate both people and materials in pursuit of the restaurant's sales and profit goals. Today, Antoniadi's management duties include maintaining customer service, ensuring a reliable supply of ingredients, and handling complex currency arrangements.

SOCIAL RESPONSIBILITY AND ETHICS

Ensuring Equal Access to Housing

Because of Ian M. Rolland, CEO of Lincoln National Corporation, 150 low-income families have newly refurbished homes in Fort Wayne, Indiana. Rolland heads one of America's largest insurance firms and he has made a difference in Fort Wayne in two ways. First, he commits 2 percent of Lincoln National's annual before-tax profits to community projects, more than the national average of 1.5 percent. Second, he has established Lincoln Life Improved Housing, a program devoted to improving inner-city housing. In fact, the housing program has achieved national acclaim for its results. But Rolland donates more than money to Fort Wayne: he also contributes his firm's management time and skill.

Three Lincoln National managers are paid to oversee the activities of Lincoln Life Improved Housing, which buys and repairs run-down houses. These project managers supervise the choice of properties, the actual renovation, and the selection of families. Once the houses have been renovated, they are rented and later sold to low-income families at affordable rates. The managers check to be sure that the houses are properly maintained and that the tenants pay their bills on time. With these tight controls, the organization has kept its losses to $200,000 a year, and only four families have ever defaulted on their loans. In all, Rolland has spent $2 million to provide affordable housing and help restore Fort Wayne's downtown area.

Even before he was named Lincoln National's president, Rolland was vocal about equal access to housing. But as CEO, his stand on social issues is sometimes controversial. For example, in 1987 he and Lincoln National funded a class-action lawsuit to desegregate Fort Wayne public schools. Some school and public officials angrily accused the insurance company of meddling. Despite the controversy, Rolland persists in his community action, and the company's board of directors has been supportive.

Rolland's philosophy is simple: the role of CEO carries with it an obligation to help the community. To encourage a company to be socially responsible, Rolland says, the commitment must start at the top. If the top manager is truly committed, other senior managers will also become committed. "It is easy to make a contribution to somebody else and let them do their thing. It's a far different matter to develop and manage a program yourself," says Rolland. That may sum up exactly why his pet projects have been so successful: he and his managers have remained actively involved, providing the expertise to set goals and standards, manage the actual work, and monitor all activities. One hundred and fifty families in Fort Wayne certainly agree that Ian Rolland has the management skills to improve housing, reconstruct neighborhoods, and run a large insurance company.

What's Your Opinion?

1. Should corporations lead the fight in such social issues as desegregation?
2. Aside from providing employment, what social responsibilities should an organization take on in its own community?

issues during the planning phase, at which time they determine the appropriate controls for measuring and maintaining performance. For instance, while president of his family's ethnic hair-care business, Johnson Products, from 1989 to 1992, Eric G. Johnson revitalized the company's sales by examining the control elements needed to help keep the company on track. He quickly instituted financial controls that helped the company turn a profit by 1990. His actions included realigning quality-control systems, changing the workweek to manufacture more goods with fewer people, and reassessing the costs of inventory and research.[22] By setting standards, monitoring progress, and making adjustments as needed, Johnson was able to put his company back on track.

The Nature of Managerial Work

Whether they're presidents, deans, or supervisors, all managers perform tasks that can be described and analyzed to one degree or another. On a typical day, managers may actively plan, organize, lead, or control, but these four functions don't really describe what managers *do* during the course of their workdays. During the past two decades, researchers have developed additional frameworks to supplement the traditional four-pronged management model and to clarify the nature of managerial activities. The new research helps explain and differentiate a manager's day-to-day activities.[23]

For instance, researcher Henry Mintzberg once followed each of five U.S. chief executive officers every day for a week so that he could see exactly how these managers spent their time. His findings included the following characteristics of managerial work:[24]

- *Fast pace, long hours.* Managers, especially top managers, work at an unrelenting pace. Many managerial jobs require exceedingly long hours only during peak seasons, but all managers generally have full workdays at any time of year. Microsoft's Bill Gates, whose workweeks usually run to 60 hours or more, is a good example of the busy CEO.
- *Brevity, variety, and discontinuity.* In contrast to the image of managers concentrating on a few key problems, Mintzberg found that management activities are in reality characterized by brevity, variety, and discontinuity.[25] Although additional research has shown that not all managerial jobs fall into this pattern, Mintzberg's description fits the workday of many managers.[26]
- *Calls and meetings.* Most of a manager's time is taken up in oral communication, either face-to-face or on the telephone. Managers favor spoken communication because they can obtain up-to-date information and because many of their contacts do not put all the details on paper.

Managerial Roles

Mintzberg found that regardless of the type of organization or the level of management, managers act in specific ways when they interact with others in the course of performing the four management functions. He argued that all managers take on these behavior patterns, or *roles,* in order to be effective in their jobs. In all, Mintzberg described 10 management roles, which he grouped into interpersonal roles, informational roles, and decisional roles (see Exhibit 1.5).

EXHIBIT 1.5

Mintzberg's Ten Managerial Roles

Henry Mintzberg identified ten managerial roles, which he classified into three categories: interpersonal roles, informational roles, and decisional roles.

Category	Role	Types of Activities
Interpersonal roles	Figurehead	Ceremonial and symbolic duties
	Leader	Hire, train, motivate, and coordinate others
	Liaison	Develop relationships with others outside work unit
Informational roles	Monitor	Gather information from various sources
	Disseminator	Transmit information to other managers
	Spokesperson	Transmit information to people outside the organization
Decisional roles	Entrepreneur	Initiate change to improve units or find opportunities
	Disturbance handler	Make changes to resolve unanticipated problems
	Resource allocator	Decide which managers and projects will receive resources and in what proportion
	Negotiator	Bargain with people outside the unit to support goals

Interpersonal Roles Three management roles flow directly from the authority of the manager's position in the organization. These **interpersonal roles** are roles in which managers develop and maintain relationships. Interpersonal roles include the manager as figurehead, the manager as leader, and the manager as liaison.

interpersonal roles Three roles in which managers develop and maintain relationships: the manager as figurehead, the manager as leader, and the manager as liaison

- *Figurehead.* Because managers are at the head of a unit of an organization, they often represent their organizations in ceremonial and symbolic activities. Serving as a *figurehead,* the manager may present awards or entertain important customers.
- *Leader.* Managers also fulfill the interpersonal role of *leader* when they hire, train, and motivate the people who work for them. As the leaders of Microsoft's work force, Bill Gates and his management team are responsible for influencing the company's employees as they work toward common goals.
- *Liaison.* The third interpersonal role a manager performs is the role of *liaison,* building relationships with people outside the manager's own unit. In the course of their liaison roles, managers may meet with peers, customers, corporate staff, and others.

So important are the interpersonal roles that some managers devote a large portion of their working days to these roles. For example, Peter Schultz, the CEO of Porsche, spends 25 percent of his time as figurehead, leader, and liaison. He meets with car dealers to keep them excited about selling Porsche products, and he meets with Porsche owners to learn more about their needs. Schultz stresses that staying close to his dealers and customers is a good way to avoid management mistakes.[27]

Informational Roles Because managers make interpersonal contacts and build networks of relationships inside and outside the organization, they are in a unique position to send and to receive information. Mintzberg observed that a large part of the manager's job is devoted to **informational roles,** in which the manager acquires, processes, and communicates information. The three informational roles are monitor, disseminator, and spokesperson.

informational roles Three roles in which managers receive and transmit information: the manager as monitor, the manager as disseminator, and the manager as spokesperson

- *Monitor.* Managers continually scan the environment to pick up useful information. They also talk with people they meet in their liaison roles, and they interact with the people who work in their own units. This information-gathering role is the *monitor* role.
- *Disseminator.* In the role of *disseminator,* managers share and distribute the information they have acquired. Managers transmit information from the outside to people within the organization, and they also pass information from one subordinate to another.
- *Spokesperson.* The third informational role is the role of *spokesperson,* in which the manager provides information to people outside the organization. For top managers, this informational role is a key part of their regular management duties as they interact with government officials, consumer groups, and other people who have an influence on or interest in the organization.

For instance, managers at Becton Dickinson, a producer of medical products, used their informational roles to benefit the company operations on two continents. They learned that European manufacturers operate their production lines more slowly than U.S. manufacturers and are thus able to keep product costs low while maintaining high quality. This was useful information because the company was building plants in Spain and Germany where plant managers

As CEO of Southeastern Metals Manufacturing, a $30 million business, Nadine Gramling handles a variety of decisional roles. In her managerial role as entrepreneur, Gramling comes up with new product ideas. In her role as resource allocator, she decides how many people should be in sales, when new plants are needed, and how the budget should be divided among the company's facilities.

could try the new approach. Once Becton Dickinson's European managers confirmed better results with slower production lines, they shared this information with Becton managers in the United States, who then slowed domestic production lines in an attempt to achieve similar results.[28]

Decisional Roles Some of the most important roles that managers play are **decisional roles,** in which they examine alternatives and then make choices and commitments. These decisions range from minor choices that affect only a few people to major strategic decisions that can affect the entire organization. Mintzberg identified four decisional roles: entrepreneur, disturbance handler, resource allocator, and negotiator.

decisional roles Four roles in which managers make choices and commitments: the manager as entrepreneur, the manager as disturbance handler, the manager as resource allocator, and the manager as negotiator

- *Entrepreneur.* In their roles as *entrepreneurs,* managers initiate changes to improve their units or to adapt to shifting conditions in the outside world. These changes may involve new products, new processes, or solutions to problems.
- *Disturbance handler.* Another decisional role that managers assume is that of *disturbance handler.* In this role, managers make changes to solve unanticipated problems that result from forces beyond their control.
- *Resource allocator.* Managers have the responsibility of deciding how to apportion organizational resources. In the role of *resource allocator,* managers make choices about how many people, how much money, and how much of the available materials will be used to achieve the organization's goals. Also, managers are responsible for deciding how much of the organization's time should be devoted to each activity and which activities are most important in reaching the organization's goals.
- *Negotiator.* The *negotiator* role involves bargaining with others to support the organization's goals. Managers often negotiate with suppliers for lower-priced goods and services; they also negotiate contracts with labor unions.

For example, Michael Osbaldeston's skillful use of the decisional roles have been critical to his success directing the activities of Ashridge Management College in Great Britain. As chief executive of the college, he believes that British managers need to prepare for a more global outlook because of changes in the international business and economic environment. Consequently, Osbaldeston has worked as a resource allocator and a negotiator to set up a pan-European course of management study and to persuade the college's board of directors to endorse his plan for a new academic center that will draw more overseas participants.[29]

Managerial Agendas and Networks

Another well-known study of managerial work, by Harvard professor John Kotter, confirmed Mintzberg's findings that sending and receiving information takes up a considerable share of a manager's day. Kotter studied 15 managers and found that each used an **agenda,** a set of goals and plans that addressed the manager's short-term and long-term responsibilities. Early in their tenure in each management position, these managers devoted considerable time to **network building,** activities that put them into contact with people inside and outside the organization, mirroring what Mintzberg observed. Like the managers in Mintzberg's study, the managers Kotter studied built their networks around people who could provide information, support, or action to achieve the manager's goals.[30]

agenda A set of goals and plans that a manager develops to address short-term and long-term responsibilities

network building Management activities that build relationships with people inside and outside the organization

When Pat Riley was named coach of the New York Knickerbockers basketball team in 1991, he established an ambitious agenda that put winning at the top of the list. For the short term, his agenda included both cementing relations with top players to keep the team competitive and considering player changes that would bring more stars to New York. For the longer term, Riley is aiming for the National Basketball Association championship. Riley's network includes the biggest names in basketball, the players and coaches he met during his two decades with the Los Angeles Lakers.[31]

Managerial Demands, Constraints, and Choices

British researcher Rosemary Stewart also studied the nature of managerial work, and she concluded that managers have some flexibility in both *what* they do and *how* they do it. Stewart identified three areas that determine job flexibility: demands, constraints, and choices (see Exhibit 1.6).[32]

- *Demands.* Demands are the activities a manager is required to do and the results that must be achieved. Managers sometimes face specific demands, but at other times the demands are more general. For instance, a specific goal might be to decrease product failures by 10 percent, whereas a more general goal might be to improve employee morale.

EXHIBIT 1.6

Stewart's Areas of Job Flexibility

Rosemary Stewart identified three broad areas that influence how much flexibility a manager has in approaching work tasks: demands, constraints, and choices.

Demands

Overall meeting minimum criteria of performance
Doing certain kinds of work; such work is determined by:
  The extent to which personal involvement is required in the unit's work
  Who must be contacted and the difficulty of the work relationship
  Contacts' power to enforce their expectations
  Bureaucratic procedures that cannot be ignored or delegated
  Meetings that must be attended

Constraints

Resource limitations
Legal and trade union constraints
Technological limitations
Physical location
Organizational constraints, especially extent to which the work of the manager's unit is defined
Attitudes of other people to:
  Changes in systems, procedures, organization, pay, and conditions
  Changes in the goods or services produced
  Work outside the unit

Choices

In *how* the work is done
In *what* work is done
  Choices within a defined area:
    To emphasize certain aspects of the job
    To select some tasks and to ignore or delegate others
  Choices in boundary management
  Choices to change the area of work:
    To change the unit's domain
    To develop a personal domain:
      To become an expert
      To share work, especially with colleagues
      To take part in organizational and public activities

- *Constraints.* Constraints are the internal or external forces that limit a manager's ability to be flexible. Constraints may include scarcity of resources, legal limits, contractual restrictions on labor, technological limitations, and boundaries set by the definition of the manager's work unit.
- *Choices.* Choices describe the range of options managers have when faced with decisions. Although all managers operate under demands and constraints, they also have some leeway in deciding how much time to spend on specific tasks, which tasks to delegate, how to do the work, and whether to share work with colleagues.

Consider how Gary Anderson, president of software maker Execucom Systems in Austin, Texas, has adapted to the changing demands and constraints imposed by four successive company owners. One owner asked Anderson to deemphasize new-product development; another owner wanted higher profitability. Each owner offered different resources and established different goals for performance. Throughout these changes, Anderson stressed flexibility and used his managerial choices to build a top management team that helped bring the company back to profitability.[33]

Implications for Managers

Why are these research studies on management important? Mintzberg noted that managers can become more effective when they have an insight into the way they work. Once they understand the nature of their roles, managers can identify any roles they need to develop further, and they can arrange their workdays to emphasize more of the roles they wish to assume. Kotter's work reinforces the importance of the manager's network. Stewart's research on what must be done (demands), the environmental limits (constraints), and the various ways that managers can approach their work (choices) provides insights into management decisions about specific tasks and work assignments. Further, these researchers have thrown considerable light on the complex environment in which managers operate. Students of management and managers already on the job can apply these observations in order to become more skillful managers.[34]

TYPES OF MANAGEMENT

Although managers use the management process to achieve their organizations' goals, the specific nature of the management task differs according to the manager's scope of responsibility and level within the organization. Of course, job titles and content vary from organization to organization and from industry to industry, but managers can generally be classified according to these two dimensions.

Scope of Responsibility

Depending on the scope of their organizational activities and responsibilities, managers may be called general managers, functional managers, or project managers.

general manager A manager who oversees all the functions and activities in a single organizational unit

- *General managers.* A **general manager** is responsible for all the functions and activities of one unit of an organization. General managers are involved in a wide variety of organizational activities, and their scope of responsibility is the broadest of anyone within the organization. For example, Richard Roodman is the chief executive officer of Valley Medical Center, a hospital in the Seattle area. As a general manager, he plans for the hospital's future, organizes the hospital's personnel to provide good health-care, meets with community leaders to discuss needs, and institutes controls that keep the hospital running smoothly. Roodman is ultimately responsible for every department and employee in the hospital and for the goal of delivering quality health-care services to the community.[35]

- *Functional managers.* In contrast to a general manager, whose scope is broad, a **functional manager** is responsible for only one organizational department. Functional managers head departments such as marketing, engineering, finance, operations, and human resources. For instance, Paul R. Carter is chief financial officer for Wal-Mart, the largest-selling retail chain in the United States. His duties include supervising a team of financial and accounting specialists who use sophisticated computer systems to keep track of store sales, inventory, costs, and other vital financial information.[36]

functional manager A manager who supervises the activities of one organizational department

- *Project managers.* A **project manager** is a manager who coordinates people and activities across several departments in an organization to complete a specific project. Project managers rarely have direct responsibility for the people or resources involved in their projects, but instead must see that the projects are completed and goals attained. As organizations try to respond more rapidly to the changing environment, they are increasingly using project teams led by project managers who can span the organization to accomplish specific goals. For example, William J. McCabe, a project manager with Brown & Sharpe Manufacturing in North Kingstown, Rhode Island, supervised the company's development of a new high-tech manufacturing product. His project was successful because all the departments involved cooperated, sacrificing individual departmental goals so that the company would be able to achieve its overall goals.[37] Even with its increasing importance, however, project management is quite a challenge because it involves crossing organizational territories.

project manager A manager who is responsible for a specific project that involves coordinating people and activities in several departments

Management Level

Managers can also be differentiated on the basis of their position in the organization and their associated responsibilities (see Exhibit 1.7). The military distinguishes management levels based on positions of officers and enlisted personnel; universities distinguish management levels based on position within a department, such as chairperson, and position within the school, such as dean. As they rise to higher levels in the organization's hierarchy, managers assume increased responsibility for projects and people, although all the people may not report directly to them. Large organizations tend to have multiple layers of managers, but many companies have eliminated some of these layers in recent years as they attempt to control costs and increase efficiency. In any event, managers can generally be classified into one of three levels: top managers, middle managers, or first-line managers.[38]

top manager A manager who is part of the small group of people at the highest level of management who bear overall responsibility for the organization

- *Top managers.* A **top manager** is one of a relatively small group of people at the uppermost level of the organization who manage the entire operation.[39] Also known as *senior managers* or *senior executives*, this group includes chairmen, presidents, chief executive officers (CEOs), executive vice presi-

EXHIBIT 1.7

Classifying Managers by Management Level

Managers can be classified according to their level within the organizational pyramid as top managers, middle managers, or first-line managers.

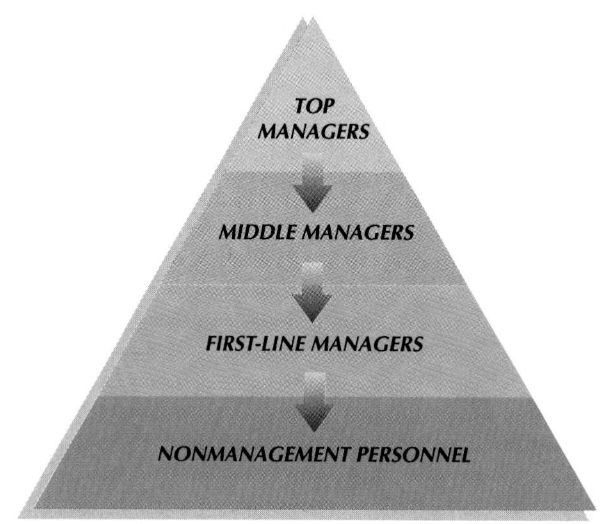

dents, senior vice presidents, and in smaller organizations, vice presidents. In small businesses, the owners are frequently the top managers, assuming most or all of the roles that top managers at larger organizations usually perform.[40] Top managers examine the organization's environment, define goals, establish major strategies, and make decisions that set or change the overall direction of the organization. Top managers also supervise the top layer of middle managers directly below them in the organizational hierarchy, and they instill values that will help create a productive work environment. At the very top, CEOs are well aware that the performance of their organizations depends in large part on their own effectiveness.[41]

middle manager A manager who executes the strategies established by top management and who supervises and coordinates the activities of first-line managers

- *Middle managers.* At the middle of the organizational pyramid is the **middle manager,** a manager who implements the broad strategies devised by top managers and who supervises and coordinates the work of first-line managers. Middle management includes such titles as vice president, department manager, division head, and director. In contrast to the longer-range perspective of top managers, middle managers are more concerned with the near future. Middle managers perform a delicate balancing act because they're caught in the middle between the demands of top managers and the needs of first-line managers. On the one hand, middle managers are expected to implement the strategies defined by top management. On the other hand, they must ensure that the managers below them have the proper resources and the management ability to work with their staffs to produce the organization's goods or services. Moreover, as organizations cut costs and simplify operations, middle managers are being squeezed out in large numbers, a trend that's accelerating because of the accessibility and sophistication of today's information-processing technologies. But with the new leaner middle-management ranks comes an increased opportunity for these managers to develop broader skills while showing how well they can perform.[42]

first-line manager A manager at the first level of management who supervises and coordinates the work of nonmanagerial employees

- *First-line managers.* Closest to the base of the organizational pyramid is the **first-line manager,** someone in the first level of management who supervises and coordinates the activities of nonmanagement operating employees. First-line managers oversee groups of people who produce the goods or services provided by the organization, and they generally carry titles such as supervisor, manager, or foreman. Because first-line managers are involved in the day-to-day operations of the organization, they focus on the concerns of the present and on what their groups will need in the immediate future. Like middle managers, first-line managers must balance the pressures exerted by managers above them and the issues raised by the employees they supervise. Because they are closest to the actual operations of the organization, their management activities are critical to the organization's achievement of its goals.[43]

MANAGERS IN THE MAKING

How do people learn to be managers, and how do they become better managers? Any discussion of what it takes to become a good manager should start with some idea of the attributes that tomorrow's managers will need. Exhibit 1.8 indicates the range of skills and personal attributes that CEOs will need in 2000. Among others traits, twenty-first-century managers will need a visionary sense of where their organizations should be headed, a better communication link with employees, and a commitment to training and developing their successors.[44] The following section takes a closer look at management skills.

Management Skills

Whether they are top managers, middle managers, or first-level managers, working in the private or the public sectors, all managers need specific skills to be effective. Management expert Robert L. Katz identified three basic skills that managers need: conceptual skills, interpersonal skills, and technical skills.[45] Because managers at various levels deal with diverse sets of challenges as they

Personal Behavior	Now	Year 2000	Knowledge and Skills	Now	Year 2000
Conveys strong sense of vision	75%	98%	Strategy formulation	68%	78%
Links compensation to performance	66%	91%	Human resource management	41%	53%
Communicates frequently with employees	59%	89%	International economics and politics	10%	19%
Emphasizes ethics	74%	85%	Science and technology	11%	15%
Plans for management succession	56%	85%	Computer literacy	3%	7%
Communicates frequently with customers	41%	78%	Marketing and sales	50%	48%
Reassigns or terminates unsatisfactory employees	34%	71%	Negotiation	34%	24%
Rewards loyalty	48%	44%	Accounting and finance	33%	24%
Makes all major decisions	39%	21%	Handling media and public speaking	16%	13%
Behaves conservatively	32%	13%	Production	21%	9%

■ Increasing in importance ■ Decreasing in importance

EXHIBIT 1.8

The Successful CEO in the Year 2000

According to a survey of 1,500 corporate leaders around the world, CEOs will need a different mix of abilities to be successful in the year 2000.

EXHIBIT 1.9

How Management Skills Relate to Management Level

Depending on their management level, managers rely more or less heavily on their conceptual, technical, and interpersonal skills.

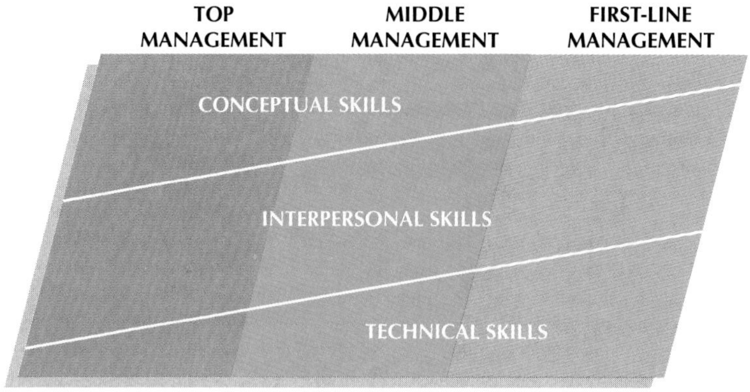

strive to achieve their goals, they apply these skills in differing proportions, depending on their level in the organization (see Exhibit 1.9).

Conceptual Skills

conceptual skills Abilities enabling people to understand the complex interrelationships between the organization's component parts and to see the organization within the context of its environment

Conceptual skills enable the manager to see the organization as a whole, in the context of its environment, and to understand how the various parts interrelate. By applying conceptual skills to recognize the likely consequences of any actions they take, effective managers are able to make decisions that best serve the needs of the organization, not just individual departments. They can recognize which parts of the organization will be affected and think about the ramifications for the organization. They can also envision the impact on their industry and on their community.

Conceptual skills also include the ability to analyze a situation, determine the root of any problems or opportunities, and devise an appropriate plan. Managers need to be able to look at both good and bad situations confronting the organization, whether they are considering increasing or declining sales, or higher or lower enrollment. Once they've assessed why these situations have developed, managers can create plans that will either correct the problems or help the organization capitalize on good situations. The ability to conceptualize is particularly important for top managers who must consider the broad goals and long-term aims of their organizations and plan for the future.[46]

For example, CEO Anthony J. F. O'Reilly revolutionized the way managers operate at global food conglomerate H.J. Heinz by taking a broader view of how various parts of the company could work more closely together to achieve Heinz's goals. He was able to increase the efficiency with which the organization uses its resources by arranging for Heinz managers in different countries to jointly coordinate some of the production and purchasing tasks that had previously been duplicated in country after country.[47] O'Reilly's ability to consider many distinct parts of the company as interrelated components is a good example of the conceptual skills that are needed by managers, particularly managers at his level.

Interpersonal Skills

interpersonal skills Abilities enabling people to work well with and through other people, to communicate effectively, and to work cooperatively within a group

Interpersonal skills, also called *human skills* or *people skills,* allow the manager to work well with and through other people and to communicate effectively within a group. Managers at all levels need good interpersonal skills because they depend on people inside and outside the organization for help in achieving their goals. Managers with good interpersonal skills have the ability to encourage people to freely share their ideas without fear of being criticized or ridiculed. They are also able to understand the needs and motivations of others. Finally, managers who apply interpersonal skills effectively are cooperative members of groups in which they participate.[48]

Excellent interpersonal skills helped Betsy Burton turn the ailing hair salon franchise chain Supercuts into a double-digit-growth success. When Burton took over the helm, the people who owned individual Supercuts franchises were clamoring for a voice in the business and had banded together in a lawsuit against Supercuts. Burton called a meeting with representatives of the franchise owners and forged a new understanding that settled the suit. She also invited franchise owners to join an advisory council that would meet with Supercuts management to discuss operations. Finally, Burton initiated sales of hair-care products in the salons, a strategy that brought the franchise owners higher profits and greater faith in the new management at headquarters.[49]

Technical Skills

Technical skills involve the tools, techniques, and knowledge needed to perform proficiently in a particular field. Managers often develop their technical skills through education and then by working in one or more functional areas of an organization, such as accounting or marketing. First-line managers need particularly strong technical skills because they work directly with people who use the tools and techniques of a specific specialty, such as automotive assembly or classroom instruction.[50]

technical skills Abilities enabling people to use knowledge, methods, techniques, and equipment to perform specialized tasks

As a former singer, Ardis Krainik has the technical skills to handle the artistic affairs of the Lyric Opera of Chicago. She started as a part-time clerk and singer in the company chorus and became the general manager in 1980. Her technical skills in music enable her to lead and communicate with the opera stars who draw sellout crowds. But she also developed the technical skills in business administration that she needs to keep America's fourth-largest opera company operating in the black.[51]

The Development of Management Skills

Considering the range of necessary knowledge and skills and the variety of situations that call for good management, how does someone become an effective manager? Formal education is one way to acquire some of the managerial skills, and specialized training is another. However, managers also need practice and assistance from seasoned managers to gain knowledge about such intangibles as interpersonal and conceptual skills. A study conducted by the Center for Creative Leadership examined the reasons that some managers make it to the top and others derail along the way. The researchers found that successful managers have broad experience, demonstrate performance in more than one functional area, have superior interpersonal skills, and have the guidance of senior managers.[52] This section focuses on the four ways in which people learn to become good managers: education, training, mentoring, and experience.

Education

Formal education is clearly an important element in shaping effective managers for today and tomorrow. Of the CEOs who currently head America's 1,000 largest corporations, over 90 percent hold an undergraduate degree, primarily in

GLOBAL MANAGEMENT

Merck's Prescription for International Performance

How does Dr. P. Roy Vagelos manage 46 manufacturing plants in 18 countries, 17 research laboratories in 7 countries, and 10 experimental farms in 6 countries? The CEO of Merck, the world's largest prescription drug company, faces a challenging but exciting task. As a biochemist and former head of Merck's research group, Vagelos uses his technical, interpersonal, and conceptual skills to manage the global resources and activities of this pharmaceutical giant. During the 1980s, Merck achieved a string of stunning successes, but the 1990s pose a difficult problem for Vagelos as he battles the uncertainties of drug research and the ambitions of rivals Bristol-Myers Squibb and SmithKline Beecham.

Vagelos has built a solid foundation for Merck's success. Since 1985, when he was named CEO, revenues have doubled to over $8 billion—and profits have more than tripled. Among Merck's stable of products are 18 that each contribute more than $100 million a year; of those, 2 pull in $1 billion in annual sales. Proscar, a new drug to fight prostate disease, is in testing and being readied for market. If successful, this new product could sell at the megadrug rate of $1 billion per year by 1998. But Vagelos isn't resting on his new product laurels: he approved a $1 billion research-and-development budget in 1991 to step up the research on tomorrow's potential megadrugs in facilities around the world.

The Merck CEO uses all four management functions to keep his global domain running smoothly. One Vagelos plan is to widen the research targets beyond the obvious ailments, such as expanding heart disease research into less-explored conditions involving the central nervous system. He relies on the organizing function to avoid duplication, especially when assigning research responsibility. For instance, Vagelos has designated the Canadian research labs to investigate treatments for respiratory conditions while the Italian facilities concentrate on viral diseases. To motivate researchers, the CEO offers incentives for scien-

business or related fields. Over the past three decades, the number of students earning bachelor's and master's degrees in business has skyrocketed as more people go to school to learn management. Some graduate schools have enhanced their curricula by including specific issues of interest to business managers. In addition, many college and university deans believe that business administration programs can be improved by placing heavier emphasis on some key areas, including decision-making skills, initiative, interpersonal skills, planning and organizing, analytical skills, computer skills, and risk taking.[53]

Training

Managers must continue learning throughout their professional lives if they are to stay effective in the face of ever-changing management challenges. In fact, if people stop the learning process once they have completed their formal college or graduate education programs, they could soon be considered obsolete professionally. As managers move from one level to another or from one department to another, they must continue developing all four management functions. Moreover, a recent survey shows that training in specific skills is particularly important at certain management levels. For example, although managers at all levels need the opportunity to develop their interpersonal skills, senior managers require more development of the conceptual skills that enable them to plan for the future.[54]

To address such needs, many organizations arrange for training and development programs to sharpen their managers' skills. Sometimes the organizations themselves create and run these training programs, and sometimes they ask universities or professional training organizations to run the programs. Some academic and outside training experts even provide intuition and creativity training.

tists whose research leads to approved drugs. And to keep all these activities on track, Vagelos uses a variety of control activities to monitor performance and make adjustments as required.

With Vagelos at the helm, Merck frequently grabs the top slot in *Fortune*'s survey of "America's Most Admired Corporations," an honor that has also boosted the company's ability to recruit talented people. Moreover, Vagelos has donated free supplies of Merck's Ivermectin to help prevent river blindness, a parasitic illness that affects up to 15 percent of residents in some African, South American, and Middle Eastern villages.

However, there are signs that Merck's competitive headstart over its rivals may be narrowing. Sales of several Merck drugs have flattened; some are even losing ground. The company has grown quickly but its tight controls are starting to slow decision making, a definite threat to the responsiveness the company needs to stimulate innovation. Meanwhile, Du Pont and American Cyanamid are introducing promising new drugs to treat heart disease, memory loss, and childhood meningitis.

Merck is at a critical turning point, and Vagelos has clear organizational goals for the drug giant: he wants to keep profits high; remain number one in market share in the United States, Canada, and Australia; and be among the top three in every other market around the world. Now Vagelos must achieve his goals by applying his considerable managerial abilities to keep Merck ahead of its competitors and to focus research on products that will fuel sales well into the next millennium.

Apply Your Knowledge

1. How might Vagelos play the decisional roles of entrepreneur, disturbance handler, resource allocator, and negotiator in his position as CEO of Merck?
2. Would a research scientist define successful performance in the same way a financial manager would? Should the two employees be measured using the same criteria? What are the implications for organizational and personal performance?

IBM, Xerox, McDonald's, and General Electric are four corporate giants with extensive management development programs. General Electric in particular pays special attention to the development needs of newly appointed first-time managers. Nearly 1,000 GE managers attend the company's annual New Manager's Program in New York, Great Britain, Germany, the Netherlands, Singapore, or Brazil.[55]

Thousands of IBM managers participate in one or more of the firm's variety of management training and development programs offered each year. Some training sessions, like this seminar held in Stamford, Connecticut, focus on the technical tools used in management. Other sessions teach skills such as personnel management and product management or focus on customer satisfaction and quality improvement.

Mentoring

mentor An experienced manager who helps someone with less experience develop better managerial skills, learn specific job functions, and gain an understanding of the organization

Most successful managers will agree that having a mentor is one of the keys to managerial success. A **mentor** is a more experienced manager who helps a lower-level manager or potential manager improve his or her managerial skills, learn particular job duties, and learn more about the organization. Mentors obviously contribute to the professional development of the people they support, and they help smooth the way for these people to advance in the organization. For instance, Judy C. Lewent, vice president for finance and the chief financial officer of drug-maker Merck, credits her mentor, Merck CEO P. Roy Vagelos, with helping her achieve her success. And the benefits of mentoring are not entirely one-sided; the process of teaching someone else the skills of management often helps the mentor understand his or her own skills as well.[56]

Experience

Face it: there's no substitute for hands-on experience. After all the classroom lectures, new managers need the practical experience of applying what they've learned to the challenge of real-life situations. Potential managers can gain this experience in a variety of ways. For instance, some new managers join small businesses rather than larger corporations because they can gain experience in many areas and hold a great deal of responsibility early in their careers. At the same time, large corporations frequently rotate new managers through many departments to broaden their experience. Another key to the executive suite seems to be extensive experience within one organization. By the time they become CEOs, top managers have spent an average of 17 years at their companies; overall, CEOs who head the 1,000 largest U.S. corporations average 22.5 years at their companies when they step into the CEO position.[57]

However, many executives are able to successfully translate their experience from one organization to another. For instance, his experience at Baxter International, a large medical products firm, enabled Henri Termeer to build tiny Genzyme, a start-up biotechnology firm, into a $100 million company. Termeer joined Baxter as a salesperson, rose through the ranks to manage the firm's sales organization in Germany, and then served as executive vice president until recruited as chairman of Genzyme. There, Termeer capitalized on Genzyme scientists' expertise in enzymes and carbohydrates to direct the firm toward a strategy of developing and marketing "orphan drugs" for rare but debilitating disorders.[58]

The Lessons of Success and Failure

Success and failure represent more than just positive or negative results; both offer wonderful opportunities for learning more about management. One of Johnson & Johnson's guidelines for success is that "you've got to be willing to fail," says former CEO James Burke. Over and over again, some of the leading companies in the world encourage their managers to try new ideas and behaviors that may not work out—at least not the first time around. Bechtel, GE, Johnson & Johnson, and other organizations create a supportive environment in which people are allowed to try creative approaches without fear of punishment, to analyze their mistakes, and then to try again until they succeed. Learning from mistakes and from failure has enabled 3M to launch such innovative products as a waterproof suntan lotion and a lawn treatment that slows grass growth.[59]

Entrepreneur Ray Thurston knows full well the value of examining failures, a lesson he learned when he was faced with losing his same-day delivery service, SonicAir. In just seven years, Thurston had built the business into a $7.5 million company. Then customer service started to slide because the company was stressing operational efficiency rather than customer satisfaction. Moreover, Thurston was preoccupied with competition, and he eventually bought out a competitor, only to discover that the acquisition didn't fit well with his current company. Eighty percent of the new firm's salespeople left within three months and SonicAir took a nosedive. Thurston evaluated SonicAir's up-and-down journey and then decided to return to his original goal of total customer satisfaction. He reviewed every service detail and tightened controls to make sure that the company stayed on track. Today SonicAir is again flying high.[60]

Success is also an important factor in a manager's personal and professional development. In one study of top managers, John Kotter observed that these executives were able to gain important knowledge and skills through a series of assignments in which they performed effectively and successfully. Each new success built on the previous success until these senior managers had confidence in their own managerial ability. In fact, each success became the motivation to try another challenge, and each led to another assignment at which the managers again succeeded.[61]

CONTEMPORARY MANAGEMENT CHALLENGES

It's clear that managers face a wide variety of hurdles as they work to achieve their goals. Today and for years to come, management will be confronted with the escalating demands of eight specific issues that have enormous impact on their organizations: productivity, quality, customer satisfaction, innovation, globalization, competition and cooperation, social responsibility and ethics, and long-term and short-term horizons.

- *Productivity.* Managers of large and small organizations around the world today are grappling with the issue of how to improve productivity. Other nations, notably Japan, are outpacing U.S. productivity increases, particularly in manufacturing, so U.S. managers need to keep the pressure on to stay competitive.[62]
- *Quality.* More than just a business buzzword, quality represents the determination of an organization to satisfy its customers or constituents. Unfortunately, U.S. companies have for some time been experiencing a quality crisis, so their customers often turn elsewhere for quality products and services. Steel, automobiles, computer chips, construction, even financial services are among the U.S. industries returning their management attention to quality, in an effort to stave off international competition.[63]
- *Customer satisfaction.* Closely related to quality is customer satisfaction, discussed earlier in the context of performance. For organizations and their managers, no goal is more important; without customers or constituents, organizations have no purpose. In the future, managers will continue to struggle with the issues of defining, measuring, and achieving long-term customer satisfaction.[64]
- *Innovation.* One of today's most pressing problems is how to stimulate and institutionalize innovation in organizations of every type and size. Tiny start-

MANAGEMENT AROUND THE WORLD

Since the 1960s, fast-growing Taiwanese businesses have stepped up their production and export of a variety of manufactured goods, especially home electronics. This aggressive pursuit of worldwide markets has fueled rapid economic expansion within Taiwan. At the same time, Taiwan's emphasis on low-cost production has put pressure on U.S. managers, who must keep manufacturing costs under control and boost productivity to compete more efficiently and more effectively around the world.

Commonwealth Edison CEO James J. O'Connor inspects one of the utility's substations, which route electricity from the generating plants to Illinois customers. To assure long-term quality and customer satisfaction, he is investing $3 billion over five years to expand transmission and distribution facilities and ensure that customers continue to receive power at the flick of a light switch.

up businesses, government agencies, even gigantic international corporations—all need new products and new ways of doing things if they are to survive and ultimately to thrive. Especially critical for managers is the ability to innovate in response to fast-changing events that pose problems or present opportunities for their organizations.[65]

- *Globalization.* All around us, the global marketplace is exploding with promise and competition. Even as American organizations discover the rewards of doing business abroad, overseas challengers are enjoying the opportunities they find in the vast U.S. market. Increasingly, managers must be able to juggle international competition, overseas suppliers, worldwide investments, global customers, and a multinational work force if they are to meet their organizations' goals in the coming years.[66]
- *Competition and cooperation.* Every organization must be both competitive and cooperative to succeed. With the many choices available to customers and constituents today, if an organization isn't continuously and aggressively examining its competitive strategy, it can't hope to be successful. In addition, cooperation is becoming even more critical as organizations forge closer relationships with their suppliers and other organizations to compete more effectively while serving customers in the best possible manner.[67]
- *Social responsibility and ethics.* More and more, constituents and customers are demanding that organizations act in socially responsible and ethical ways. The reasons are all around us: threats to our natural environment, concern for human rights and needs, and the resurgence of values that stress ethical behavior. Whether the lack of social responsibility and ethics is purposeful or due to negligence, organizations are ultimately accountable for their impact on people, on the community, and on society, and managers have a key role to play in this area.[68]
- *Long-term and short-term horizons.* For many organizations, success is measured by the inch rather than by the yard. For example, corporations keep one eye on the daily stock price while trying to maximize the quarterly earnings report. Politicians worry about whether constituents will reelect them after seeing their achievements during their most recent term. Although short-term results are important, managers can't afford to think only of today; they need to prepare for the future and to create a vision of what their organizations should be achieving years from today.[69]

These issues aren't the only challenges facing contemporary managers, but they are some of the most important. Throughout this book, these issues are discussed in the context of the management principles and techniques that managers use to confront and overcome barriers to organizational success.

SUMMARY

Management is the process of achieving organizational goals through planning, organizing, leading, and controlling the human, physical, financial, and information resources of the organization. Without management, organizations would not be able to reach their goals, so management is important to all types of organizations. Organizations can be classified according to their primary purpose, their product offerings, and their ownership.

The management process consists of four functions: planning, organizing, leading, and controlling. Planning involves determining the organization's goals and setting up procedures to achieve them. Organizing includes establishing a structure to achieve the goals, defining and assigning tasks, and coordinating people and resources. Leading is the process of influencing others to work together to attain organizational goals. And controlling involves establishing standards, reviewing progress, and making adjustments to achieve the goals.

Within their organizations, managers assume roles that can be classified as interpersonal, informational, or decisional. Three interpersonal roles are figurehead, leader, and liaison. Three informational roles are monitor, disseminator, and spokesperson. Four decisional roles are entrepreneur, disturbance handler, resource allocator, and negotiator. Depending on the scope of their responsibilities, managers may be categorized as general managers, with the widest scope; functional managers, with narrower responsibilities; or project managers, responsible for one project that spans the organization. According to management level, managers are classified as top managers if they are at the uppermost level of an organization; as middle managers if they are between top managers and the bottom layer of management; or as first-line managers if they directly supervise nonmanagement operating employees.

To be effective, all managers need three sets of skills. They need conceptual skills to see the organization as a whole and understand how the parts interrelate, to analyze situations, and to develop plans. Managers need interpersonal skills so that they can work well with and through other people and can communicate within groups. Finally, managers need technical skills, the tools, techniques, and knowledge to perform in specific fields. People acquire and hone their managerial skills through education, training, mentoring, and experience.

Today and tomorrow, managers face a number of important management challenges. By improving productivity, organizations can use their limited resources more wisely. Quality is an important part of satisfying customers and constituents who use goods or services. Managers also need to define customer satisfaction, measure it, and keep customers and constituents satisfied over the long term. Organizations need to innovate with new products and new ways of doing things to be successful. As more organizations reach out into the global marketplace, managers need an international outlook to achieve their goals. Competition is important, but so is cooperation with suppliers and others in the best interests of customers and constituents. Managers are being held accountable for the social responsibility and ethics of their organizations and for their own managerial actions. Finally, managers need to balance short- and long-term goals if they are to prepare their organizations for lasting success.

APPLYING WHAT YOU'VE LEARNED

Taking what you learn in a management course and applying it to the real world can sometimes be a challenge. Practicing your new skills on a real organization's management situation is a good way to prepare, and each chapter in this book gives you that opportunity. You'll read about the organization's situation at the beginning of the chapter, in a vignette called "Facing a Management Challenge at . . ." For example, at the beginning of this chapter, you read about the challenge Microsoft faced in dealing with explosive growth. After reading the vignette, you can think about the organization's management problem as you read through the chapter and learn the various concepts presented there.

At the end of each chapter is an innovative simulation titled "Meeting a Management Challenge at . . ." In each simulation, you play the role of a management person at the organization introduced in the vignette. You'll face the situation you'd face on the job in that organization. The simulation starts by explaining what the company actually did and whether it worked. Then the simulation presents a series of management scenarios, each with several possible courses of action, and asks you to rank the responses or to select the best alternative from the available choices. Next, several questions about the situation challenge your analytical skills. These scenarios and questions let you explore various management ideas and ask you to apply the concepts and techniques you learn in the chapter. The organization chosen for each simulation uses the same principles you're learning about.

The simulations were designed not as tests but as a means to stimulate your thinking about various management concepts. In fact, some of the questions have more than one acceptable answer, and some have no completely satisfactory answers. That's how it happens for managers on the job, too. The point is to consider the concepts you learn in each chapter and to apply your own judgment.

Now you're ready for your first simulation. Because you've just started learning about management, this simulation is a little different from the rest. It relies on your general knowledge about how organizations operate and on your experience as an employee or a volunteer to give you the insight needed to answer the questions. You'll probably be surprised to discover how much you already know about management.

MEETING A MANAGEMENT CHALLENGE AT MICROSOFT

As his much-anticipated Windows program slipped behind schedule, Microsoft chief executive officer Bill Gates knew he had to take himself out of day-to-day operations. Overall, Microsoft people had great ideas but were less effective in their planning and implementation. Windows was supposed to make personal computers easier to use, but it took Microsoft engineers a year to realize that the software needed more memory than most PCs had. When Windows was finally released—almost two years after it had been announced—mediocre reviews told Gates he had a quality-control problem. Other projects had similar woes. Microsoft's reputation was on the line.

So Gates got help. He turned over daily operations to his new president, which freed Gates for more creative work: envisioning products for the twenty-first century and planning for the company's long-term future. Then he looked at the way activities were grouped and coordinated throughout the company. He split the company into two divisions (one that focused on basic operating systems to control a computer's low-level functions, and one focusing on programs such as spreadsheets) and eventually into 12 business units, each covering a separate type of software. In early 1992, he established the "office of the president" and appointed three leading Microsoft managers to fill the team position.

The new organization improved planning and control because the heads of the two divisions could meet regularly to review progress on product development. Microsoft also set up specific reporting procedures that enabled it to develop up to 10 new products at once without confusion. And business unit managers began to compare their products to the competition by every conceivable measure of effectiveness and efficiency, from the technical sophistication of a program to the amount of labor that went into creating it. Gates received the same information, and he called managers directly if he spotted problems. The new structure allowed Gates to stay

Bill Gates, CEO, Microsoft

involved with managers and projects without having to manage daily operational details.

Gates could now effectively lead his managers, but he was still concerned that his growing work force might lose touch with him and his goals. He didn't have to look far for the solution: computers! When Microsoft established a computer network for its new corporate headquarters, it added an electronic mail system that lets virtually any employee communicate directly with the CEO. Dozens do daily, and Gates tries to respond the same day he receives a message. Employees feel they have direct access to the top. They say Gates's messages are blunt and sometimes sarcastic—but always entertaining. This communication network helps Gates spread his vision and his ideas throughout the company.

Retailers quickly hailed the new-product development systems and the stricter management controls. Gates stuck with the Windows project, fine-tuning it and waiting for the typical PC to catch up with the program's memory needs. The third version of the program, released in mid-1990, was a huge hit and energized the entire computer industry. The program sold 2.8 million copies in less than a year—bringing in more money than the company's total sales of all products five years earlier (when the first version of Windows was released). Current companywide sales, meanwhile, swelled past $1.5 billion, and the staff grew beyond 5,000. But with his new approach to management, Gates is now in a better position than ever to handle the complexities of the top job.

You're the Manager: You're a BUM, one of Microsoft's 12 business unit managers in charge of a particular type of software. Each unit has its own programmers and marketing specialists. Your unit is trying to develop complex software that lets companies tie all their computers together into one network. Although you started out as a programmer, you have been a manager for several years and are no longer an expert on the latest technical developments. You report directly to the vice president in charge of business programs, but it's not unusual for you to interact directly with Gates when he drops by to brainstorm with your engineers.

Ranking Questions

1. You're nearing a critical deadline and one of your employees keeps missing his goals. He promises to do too much, then asks for more time and resources. He's a recent graduate with lots of theory but little practical experience. How do you react? Rank these responses, from best to worst:
   a. You should confront this employee during the next departmental meeting, make an example of his problems, and demand better performance.
   b. The subordinate clearly has enthusiasm and technical skills but may lack the conceptual skills needed to understand his problems and his place in the company. Talk with him privately and share your experience and viewpoint.
   c. Assign another manager to temporarily supervise this employee. Perhaps the change and the new perspective will be more motivating.
   d. Warn the employee that you'll give him what he asks for once more but that he'll be fired if he fails to meet another target date.
2. Gates has just left a meeting with your programmers, and he seems more agitated than usual. During the meeting, Gates wound up in an argument with one of your programmers, and he grilled another about some details that the employee should have known more about. Even worse, Gates called parts of one program "stupid." You're intimidated by the CEO's expertise, you're behind schedule, and you don't need Gates breathing down your neck. What should you do? Rank the following responses from best to worst:
   a. Bone up on your programming so that you can better follow the technical discussion and defend your people more effectively in the next meeting.
   b. Insist that your people adopt a professional air by showing deference to higher-level managers.
   c. Try to get Gates to go through you instead of going straight to your programmers. This would give you more control.
   d. Good managers encourage employees to speak their mind. That's what Gates was doing, and that's what you should do. Talk with your programmers about what they thought of the meeting.

Multiple-Choice Questions

3. Your boss calls and tells you to speak to a reporter about your upcoming PC network program. You know you'll be asked about product development delays in your unit and in Microsoft as a whole. What is your best response?
   a. Don't deny that you've put extra time into your product, but explain that the company has shifted from a focus solely on innovation to also stress quality and customer satisfaction. Express confidence that your product will be a winner from the start.
   b. Don't worry about a thing. If reporters sense that you are too prepared, they'll think you are trying to cover something up.
   c. You have the information the reporter needs, so you are in charge of the interview. Prepare responses that promote your products. Avoid answering questions that are embarrassing.
   d. Develop a friendly relationship with the reporter to ensure that he or she sees things from a favorable point of view. Suggest that you meet for lunch, pick up the tab, and try to avoid talking about product specifics.
4. The division vice president wants you to upgrade a networking program that allows people at company headquarters to communicate with each other and with Microsoft people at other locations. Although your group is working on an improved program, it hasn't yet been tested. Other companies also offer networking software, and you might combine products from several companies to create a new system. You don't want to embarrass yourself (or perhaps the whole company) by installing a system that doesn't work well, or by relying on a rival company's software. What's your best response?
   a. Use the best available resources to set the

network up immediately, and if Microsoft can provide part of the system, so much the better.

b. Use this opportunity to install and hone your own Microsoft software. If problems crop up in the system, fixing them will improve your own product.
c. Seek a delay in installing the networking program until you can test and perfect the software you are currently developing.
d. Agree to immediately install the Microsoft software, then tell your programmers to drop everything else until they've perfected the program.

Analysis Questions

5. Since Gates improved his company's management by removing himself from daily operations, can he still be considered a manager? Was he ever one?
6. How has Gates's intuition been important to Microsoft?
7. How do Microsoft managers ensure that the company is both efficient and effective?

Special Project

A competitor has won a lawsuit that forces you to change your networking program's user-friendly approach to guiding computer operators through the system. Gates has given you two weeks to prepare a report showing the changes that must be made in Microsoft's software. You want the programmers and marketers in your unit to work on this report as a team. In one to two pages, explain how you can use the four management functions to ensure that your group completes this assignment on time.[70]

KEY TERMS

agenda (16)
conceptual skills (22)
constituents (9)
controlling (12)
customers (9)
decisional roles (16)
effectiveness (10)
efficiency (10)
first-line manager (20)
for-profit organization (7)
functional manager (19)
general manager (18)
informational roles (15)
interpersonal roles (15)
interpersonal skills (22)
leading (12)
management (5)
manager (5)
mentor (26)
middle manager (20)
network building (16)
not-for-profit organization (7)
organization (7)
organizing (12)
performance (10)
planning (11)
private sector (9)
products (8)
project manager (19)
public sector (9)
technical skills (23)
top manager (19)

QUESTIONS

For Review

1. What is organizational performance? How does personal performance contribute to organizational performance?
2. How does the management of for-profit organizations differ from the management of not-for-profit organizations?
3. What are the four management functions and how do they interrelate?
4. Why do managers need conceptual skills? Why are technical and interpersonal skills important?
5. How can people learn to be good managers?

For Analysis

1. Which managerial roles would top managers emphasize? Which managerial roles would first-line managers emphasize? Middle managers?
2. Is a manager's scope of responsibility always related to management level? Why or why not?
3. If a manager remains in an organization for six years but is promoted into a new job nearly every year, what are the implications for personal and organizational success?
4. What are the implications of ignoring long-term horizons in everyday management?

5. Why would a seasoned manager act as a mentor for a less-experienced manager? Consider both personal and organizational motivations.

For Application

1. How would a manager apply the four management functions to a volunteer organization such as a local Cub Scout troop?
2. In what ways can the owner of a music store help develop the managerial skills of the managers who supervise employees in each store department?
3. How can the manager of a campus bookstore use agendas and network building to increase the number of students who shop there?
4. How does the issue of customer satisfaction relate to the manager of the after-school recreational program in a high school? To the mayor of a small city? To the manager of a Ford dealership?
5. Can a manager experienced in managing a not-for-profit organization be effective in a for-profit organization? Can a for-profit manager be effective in a not-for-profit organization? Explain your answers.

KEEPING CURRENT IN MANAGEMENT

From recent magazines or newspapers, select an article that describes how a top manager changed the direction of a business, government, or cultural organization. One example might be a story discussing how a government official reformed a particular department or specific government unit; another might be an article discussing the moves of a chairman or CEO confronted with declining market share or lower profits.

1. What is the manager changing? Do these changes help the organization achieve its goals more efficiently or more effectively? What goals did the top manager set for this organization? If these goals are different from the goals previously set for the organization, what specific challenge provoked the change?
2. Is the manager applying all four management functions to change the organization? Or is this manager putting emphasis on only one or two specific functions? What is the manager doing with each function that is particularly effective? How are other members of top management or middle management involved in any of these functions?
3. Which skills is this manager applying to help change the organization's direction? What are the measures of organizational and personal performance?

SHARPEN YOUR MANAGEMENT SKILLS

Few things strike terror into the hearts of small-town retailers like the news that Wal-Mart is planning to open a store on the outskirts of town. Wal-Mart's prices are so low that many local stores have difficulty competing. And now Wal-Mart is coming to the town where you are mayor. Some local stores want to keep Wal-Mart out of town, but many people welcome the retailer because it will bring more tax money and more jobs to the area. Although Wal-Mart will offer your local citizens good merchandise selection at low prices, you know that some downtown stores might not survive.

- *Decision:* As mayor, how can you help local stores work together to compete against Wal-Mart? Using the four management functions as a framework, list as many ideas as you can under each (but don't take any action on these issues). *Planning:* List the events and processes for which you need to have a plan. (Example: The local stores might plan to start a cooperative "Shop Downtown" promotion.) *Organizing:* What organizational issues should you consider? (Example: What tasks are involved in this promotion and who should handle each?) *Leading:* How can you inspire local retailers to compete more effectively? (Example: What should you communicate to everyone involved?) *Controlling:* List the control elements you'll need to consider. (Example: How can the retailers set and meet a target date for launching their promotion?)
- *Communication:* Draft a two-page letter to the Chamber of Commerce explaining your ideas for helping local retailers compete. Discuss why the stores should band together and how their performance may be affected.

No sooner had Sotheby's CEO Michael L. Ainslie guided his international art auction company to stunning profits than the conditions that caused this success changed. Declining economic growth dried up the supply of patrons willing to spend enormous amounts of money on works of art. Ainslie must find new markets and new ways of competing that will keep Sotheby's profits strong.

HISTORY

Sotheby's auctions began modestly in 1744 when London bookseller Samuel Baker began auctioning private libraries, eventually including those of Napoleon and Talleyrand. Nephew John Sotheby inherited the flourishing business in 1778 and changed its name to his own. The auctions expanded into paintings, coins, furniture, jewelry, porcelain, and antiquities during the nineteenth century, and Sotheby's growing reputation for integrity and service increased its market share in following decades. In 1964, Sotheby's created the first international art auction firm by purchasing Parke-Bernet Galleries. The company now has main auction rooms in New York and London, operates in 36 countries, and holds more than 600 auctions a year.

Ainslie was named CEO after investors purchased Sotheby's for $139 million in 1983. The company overextended itself and lost $6.4 million the next year, but in 1988 it netted nearly $62 million on sales of $1.8 billion for a 43.7 percent return on equity. Sotheby's issued its first stock that year. The next year, sales grew 62 percent to nearly $3 billion for a stunning 55 percent return, but business began to slip in 1990.

ENVIRONMENT

Sotheby's faces recession, competition on two fronts, and a turbulent political situation in Europe. The economy is especially bad in the key markets of the United States and Japan. Sotheby's is marketing itself aggressively to win clients away from other art dealers and from its main rival auction house, Christie's. A unified Western European market will finally let foreign auctioneers into France, and the collapse of communism in Eastern Europe will allow capitalist enterprises there.

Within the company, Ainslie saw that Sotheby's management had been emphasizing art expertise but had "minimal interest in budgeting and cost control." So he filled top management posts with experienced businesspeople who now actively budget and plan. This allowed him to use Sotheby's staff of art experts for new client services such as educating prospective buyers and appraising art both for estate auctions and for use as collateral in Sotheby's growing business of lending money to buyers and sellers.

GOALS AND CHALLENGES

Ainslie is committed to increasing sales and profits, so he needs new buyers and more artwork that is attractive to existing customers. One way Sotheby's intends to find new clients is by financing a $142 million joint venture with a potential competitor, a New York art dealer, for the purchase and mutually profitable resale of numerous works by twentieth-century masters collected by the son of Henri Matisse. Sotheby's has already opened a new office in South Korea and strengthened its presence in Singapore, Hong Kong, and Taiwan in an effort to attract Asia's art and some of that continent's great personal fortunes into its auction rooms. The company has opened an office in Berlin; has held discussions in Warsaw, Moscow, and Prague; and has expanded its office in Budapest to take advantage of the newly opened market in Eastern Europe. Just in case sales do decline, management has trimmed office personnel, instituted employee performance reviews, and cut overhead costs in another attempt to achieve Ainslie's goals.

1. Which decisional roles does Michael Ainslie appear to be playing in his search for higher profits? How can he use informational roles to help Sotheby's achieve its goals?
2. Which of the contemporary management challenges is Sotheby's facing? How is the company handling them?
3. How do the business skills of Sotheby's new top managers complement the technical skills of its art experts? How can these top managers use their conceptual and interpersonal skills to improve profits?
4. What performance standards might Ainslie adopt to assess how the client education service is contributing to Sotheby's goal of higher profits?

CHAPTER OUTLINE

Management Theories and Perspectives

After studying this chapter, you will be able to

1. Explain why managers study management theories and how they put these theories into practice
2. Discuss the impact of technological, economic, social, and political forces on the evolution of management theory
3. Explain the theories in the classical management perspective and evaluate their contributions and limitations
4. Describe Fayol's concept of the 6 functions of a business organization and discuss how his 14 principles were intended to be applied
5. Outline the major theories in the behavioral management perspective and assess their contributions and limitations
6. Identify the components of the quantitative management perspective and evaluate their contributions and limitations
7. Discuss the contemporary management approaches of systems theory and contingency theory

FACING A MANAGEMENT CHALLENGE AT

THE BODY SHOP

Putting a New Face on the Cosmetics Business

It was as though a modern Cinderella had gotten away with crashing an exclusive party. Anita Roddick—typically dressed in blue jeans and T-shirts emblazoned with environmental slogans, and wearing little makeup—had opened a store to sell her own line of skin and hair-care products. However, Roddick's approach was unlike any other in the cosmetics industry. She didn't advertise. She didn't use fancy containers and flowery labels. And she didn't promise that her products would fan the flames of romance or slow the aging process. Instead of selling fantasy, Roddick wanted to sell well-being: for her customers, for her employees, and for the world at large.

Roddick started The Body Shop in Brighton, England, in 1976 as a way to support herself and her two young daughters while her husband Gordon traveled in South America. Drawing on her own travels in Third World countries, Roddick created personal-care products that incorporated safe, natural, and effective but unusual ingredients such as Moroccan mud (for shampoo) and jojoba oil (for soap). A peppermint foot lotion, an orchid-oil skin cleanser, and a carroty skin cream became top sellers.

To establish credibility with customers, Roddick offered mountains of information about her products. She wrote fact sheets detailing each product's origin and placed handwritten tags on every product explaining how it was made, how it was tested, and how it should be used. Further, she filled any jar or bottle brought into the store, mainly because she couldn't afford containers. But the founder set The Body Shop apart from traditional businesses in another important way.

Although Roddick started the business to support her family, she also felt that the bottom line should remain at the bottom. In her view, the typical company valued profits more than people and emphasized the needs of the organization over the needs of the people inside and outside. She envisioned her firm as more than a legal framework for buying ingredients, making cosmetics, and selling products for a profit. Roddick wanted to go beyond and build a business dedicated to the betterment of its employees, its customers, its communities, and society as a whole. As the business grew, it would spread the founder's passion for ethical and honest merchandising (no animal testing, no hype). Moreover, The Body Shop would offer employees more than just a job. The business would also become a vehicle for learning about personal health, about other cultures, and about social causes such as environmental protection and human rights.

The first store was a hit. People bought her products, liked her approach, and clamored for more. By the time her husband returned from his South American adventure, Roddick had opened a second store. Soon she was inundated with requests from people eager to operate local outlets of The Body Shop in their own neighborhoods. She wanted to expand, but she could not afford to open a string of stores in rapid succession. And she did not want growth to dilute the excitement of helping customers and employees while helping society.

How could Anita Roddick use her experience to develop The Body Shop into an international chain? What could Roddick do to inspire her employees and to keep their enthusiasm high month after month? How could she communicate with customers to get—then keep—their loyalty and support?[1]

CHAPTER OVERVIEW

Although Anita Roddick has her own unique way of running The Body Shop, she nevertheless confronts many of the same challenges that managers have faced through the ages. Over the years, a wide variety of theories have been proposed to analyze and explain good management practice. This chapter reviews the major developments in management theory, starting with a discussion of historical context and a look at why managers study and apply management theories. Next is an overview of the forces that shape the evolution of management theories. The chapter continues with a brief review of early management practices and an examination of the management ideas introduced by the classical management theorists, the behavioral management theorists, and the quantitative management theorists. The chapter closes with a section about contemporary management approaches.

MANAGERS AND MANAGEMENT THEORY

The past is all around, and managers frequently examine history to learn about the present and to find new ways of addressing the future. The members of the Nordstrom family who run the Seattle-based department store chain constantly refer to the store's roots. For example, when expanding beyond shoe retailing to apparel retailing, Nordstrom's management made a conscious decision to remain committed to the store's traditionally high level of personal service. Management has also maintained the store's 40-year-old practice of having products made to Nordstrom's specifications so that customers can be assured of quality features and good value.[2] The Nordstrom annual reports recount the company's history so that investors, employees, and business analysts can trace the company's development and understand the basis of its achievements.

Philadelphia National Bank looks back on its history in a different way: the bank has cataloged five generations of correspondence so that its senior managers can understand past events and operations. Banking relationships and practices develop and evolve over the course of many years, and having reference points in the past helps the bank's current managers put their own decisions and actions in proper context. In these and many other organizations around the

King Features Syndicate, which distributes comics and columns to U.S. newspapers, celebrated its 75th anniversary by gathering cartoonists, writers, managers, and employees to mark King's past performance and to toast its future. Joined by Stan Drake (of "Blondie" fame), president Joseph D'Angelo (*top*) paid tribute to four cartoonists whose strips had run 30 years or longer: Bil Keane ("The Family Circus"), Hank Ketcham ("Dennis the Menace"), Mort Walker ("Beetle Bailey"), and Dean Young ("Blondie").

world, the past is a valuable source of ideas and warnings that can help managers understand and cope with the expected and the unexpected, the simple and the complex. By reviewing lessons from the past, managers can see patterns and turning points that help them anticipate and meet the challenges of the future.[3]

Through the years, researchers, observers, and managers have offered a variety of theories to explain and illustrate effective management, but these philosophies did not evolve in a vacuum. Each was built on the foundation laid by previous theories and developed within the framework of forces that helped shape management thinking at the time. Despite the years of study, no single, universally accepted theory of management exists today. However, the pioneers of management thought have proposed ideas that offer valuable clues to improving managerial practice.[4]

The Study and Application of Management Theories

Why do managers study management theory? They are seeking ideas that will help to improve their management capabilities and allow them to make better contributions to their organizations. In the same way that people study political or economic history to understand how and why contemporary situations have evolved, students of management look to management theory to provide perspective on today's events. When a Western-style management program was established at the International Management Center in Hungary in 1989, the curriculum included a course on the history of management designed to help Hungarian managers understand how capitalistic business management evolved in Western nations.[5] Even older theories can offer insights that help explain the results of the past and that can be applied to current situations. In fact, many aspects of quantitative management discussed later in this chapter evolved from ideas first proposed decades or even centuries ago.[6]

Management is a dynamic process that defies easy classification, regardless of how tempting it might be to describe management through theories such as quantitative management or classical management. Moreover, applying a neat timetable to the development of successive schools of thought is impossible; theories sometimes emerged concurrently, influencing each other and stimulating research on various tangents that later became key aspects. But by studying the ideas and understanding the evolution of management theory, managers can establish a storehouse of knowledge to use in future situations.[7]

Managers typically draw from a variety of schools of thought as they consider their circumstances and their alternatives for achieving their goals. One way to learn about applying management theory is to study the methods and results of successful managers, keeping in mind that what works in one situation may not in another. Managers must constantly evaluate theories and techniques to see which ones suit their particular organizations or situations. The good news is that researchers and practitioners continue to identify management approaches that help managers improve the practice of management today and in the future.[8]

The Forces That Shape Management Theory

Management thinking evolves through the influence of a variety of forces. Starting in ancient times and continuing today, four forces have influenced the course of management theory: technological, economic, social, and political forces

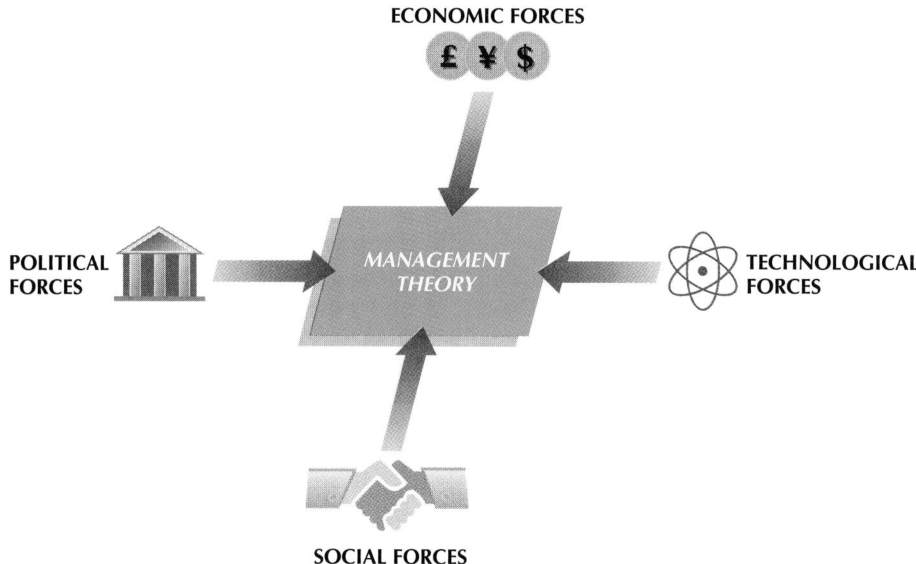

EXHIBIT 2.1
The Forces That Shape Management Theory

Four forces affect the development of management theory: technological, economic, social, and political.

(see Exhibit 2.1). This section examines the nature and impact of each of these forces.

- *Technological forces.* The knowledge, techniques, and activities that lead to profound changes in products or processes are called *technological forces.* Technological forces brought about the Industrial Revolution and made possible the advanced communications and electronics that today support businesses and governments around the world. Advances in technology often lead to social, economic, and political changes, making technology an important influence on management. Among the management areas affected by technological forces are environmental analysis, planning and decision making, organization design, human resource management, leadership, motivation, and control.[9]
- *Economic forces.* Economic trends and the availability of all types of resources (physical, human, financial, and information resources) are called *economic forces.* Scarcity of resources often leads to technological advances, and changes in technology frequently bring about different requirements for various resources, so these two forces are closely related. The economic system of a nation, such as the market economy of the United States and the centrally planned economy of China, can have a profound effect on management, particularly when the economies are evolving from one form to another. Economic forces have influenced management theory in the areas of environmental analysis, decision making and goals, planning, human resource management, control, and organization design.[10]
- *Social forces.* The values, needs, and norms that influence the behavior of people within a culture constitute *social forces.* Among today's major social forces are the interest in preserving the natural environment, the two-career family, and worldwide immigration patterns. Social forces are often influenced by technological and economic forces. For example, when mill and plant owners began buying new, technologically advanced machinery that enabled fewer employees to produce more and better products, the society

began to shift from an agrarian base to an industrial base. City populations expanded as people left the farms and entered the factories, changing the fabric of family life. Professional managers supervised the larger businesses, and the relationship between employees and managers became more distant and more adversarial. As a result, managers have had to apply new theories of employee motivation, organization structure, leadership, and human resource management.[11]

- *Political forces. Political forces* consist of governmental policies and legal institutions. These forces have an impact on organizations in both the private and the public sector, and the political actions of one nation often have a profound impact on organizations in another nation, so organizations are increasingly viewing their situations from a global perspective. For example, if the United States government uses quotas to restrict Japanese car imports, domestic automakers feel the impact—as do German automakers seeking to increase sales in the United States. Political forces influence management theory in the areas of the organizational environment, planning and decision making, organization design, human resource management, and control.[12]

EARLY MANAGEMENT THOUGHT AND PRACTICE

Contemporary management theories are the latest in a long line of management ideas and practices. The application of management principles stretches back to antiquity (see Exhibit 2.2). Even before they could label their actions as "management," ancient leaders practiced some of the management functions still being studied and applied by modern managers.

As early as 5000 B.C., Sumerian temple priests kept written records to control their elaborate tax system, monetary holdings, and lands. The ancient Egyptians were able to erect the pyramids by using management functions to plan, organize, and control these large-scale projects. Later, Hammurabi ruled his kingdom of Babylonia according to a highly developed collection of 282 laws and rules, the Code of Hammurabi. One of the world's oldest nongovernmental organizations, the Roman Catholic Church, also has a long history of management. And yet the exact principles and systems that guide effective managers were not considered within the framework of a formal discipline until the nineteenth century.[13]

MANAGEMENT AROUND THE WORLD

The Industrial Revolution in the eighteenth and nineteenth centuries included the rapid spread of the factory system throughout Great Britain. These larger, mass-production operations could not be managed the same way that owners had operated their small family enterprises. Thus the need to find new methods spurred evolution in management theory and practice.

Before the Industrial Revolution, families owned and operated relatively small businesses that made only one type of good or offered only one kind of service produced under the watchful eye of the owners. However, after the Industrial Revolution, owners assembled larger organizations that could not be managed by the same hands-on techniques used in a small family enterprise. Managers of these large-scale organizations faced new management problems, and it has been argued that the switch from home-centered business to the factory system was in fact a management revolution. Many early pioneers of management thought were practitioners who wrote about their successes in solving the problems of handling large organizations. Three pioneers attracted particular attention: Robert Owen, a British industrialist; Charles Babbage, an English mathematician; and Henry Towne, an American mechanical engineer.[14]

- *Robert Owen (1771–1858).* Both before and after Owen's experiments with human resource practices, factory workers generally suffered under harsh

EXHIBIT 2.2

Management in Ancient Times

As long ago as 5000 B.C., management principles were used in government, religion, and commerce.

Approximate Year	Individual or Ethnic Group	Major Managerial Contributions
5000 B.C.	Sumerians	Used script for recordkeeping
4000 B.C.	Egyptians	Recognized need for planning, organizing, and controlling
2700 B.C.	Egyptians	Recognized need for honesty or fair play in management; used therapy interviews—"get it off your chest"
2600 B.C.	Egyptians	Used decentralization in organization
2000 B.C.	Egyptians	Recognized need for written word in requests; used staff advice
1800 B.C.	Hammurabi	Used witnesses and writing for control; established minimum wage; recognized that responsibility cannot be shifted
1600 B.C.	Egyptians	Used centralization in organization
1491 B.C.	Hebrews	Used concepts of organization, scalar principle, exception principle
1100 B.C.	Chinese	Recognized need for organization, planning, directing, and controlling
600 B.C.	Nebuchadnezzar	Used production control and wage incentives
500 B.C.	Mencius	Recognized need for systems and standards
	Chinese	Recognized principle of specialization
	Sun Tzu	Recognized need for planning, directing, and organizing
400 B.C.	Socrates	Enunciated the universality of management
400 B.C.	Xenophon	Recognized management as a separate art
	Cyrus	Recognized need for human relations; used motion study, layout, and materials handling
350 B.C.	Greeks	Applied scientific method; used work methods and tempo
	Plato	Enunciated principle of specialization
325 B.C.	Alexander the Great	Used staff
321 B.C.	Kautilya (India)	Recognized the science and art of statecraft
175 B.C.	Cato	Used job descriptions
50 B.C.	Varro	Used job specifications

working and living conditions. But in New Lanark, Scotland, Owen's textile mill became a showplace of productivity when he instituted his theories, including a higher minimum age and shorter hours for working children, reduced work hours for all employees, meal facilities, recreation centers, and better employee housing. He scolded his fellow industrialists for spending large sums to improve their machinery and investing nothing in the people they employed. Although few emulated his practices, Owen was one of the earliest to address the social responsibility of businesses.[15]

- *Charles Babbage (1792–1871).* A professor at Cambridge University in England, Babbage was interested in the scientific approach to management. He is probably best known for his work on early computer inventions designed to automate repetitive mathematical computations. In the course of developing his inventions, Babbage visited workshops and factories throughout Europe and became intrigued by the interaction of people and machines. His 1832 book, *On the Economy of Machinery and Manufactures,* focused on general rules for solving management problems in a variety of organizations. Babbage believed that tasks should be analyzed to determine the degree of mental and physical effort required so that work could be assigned to the employees who had the proper skills. He also suggested that employees who found ways to improve efficiency should share in the profits.[16]

- *Henry Towne (1844–1924).* The president of Yale and Towne Manufacturing for 48 years, Towne realized that management techniques could be systematically applied in the factory, and he argued for the recognition of management as a science so that the accumulated knowledge of other practitioners could be studied and shared. Towne also debated the question of effectiveness versus efficiency, and he differentiated between the organization of work tasks and the organization of employees. His 1886 speech before the American Society of Mechanical Engineers in support of management research and education is considered one of the events that spawned the study of management as a discipline.[17]

Other pioneers included Charles Dupin (1784–1873), a French engineer who taught about organizational efficiency; Henry Poor (1812–1905), an editor of the *American Railroad Journal* who developed management principles for large U.S. railroads and advocated organization, communication, and information as the means to manage large businesses; and Daniel C. McCallum (1815–1878), a Scottish-born contemporary of Poor who developed precise operational rules, formal job descriptions, and one of the first organization charts during his tenure as the superintendent of New York's Erie Railroad. Another pioneer, Andrew Ure (1778–1857), was an early instructor of management who lectured on industrial education to factory managers who studied at Anderson's College in Glasgow, Scotland. These and other early management pioneers set the stage for the more formal management theories that followed.[18]

THE CLASSICAL MANAGEMENT PERSPECTIVE

By the end of the nineteenth century, the pace of industrial expansion had picked up, and management was spending more time and money training employees to handle specialized machines and tasks. Despite the rapid advances in technology and mechanization, employee productivity remained relatively low. To increase efficiency, practitioners and academics began to study management more intensely, building on the foundation laid by earlier pioneers. Their theories shed light on the relationship of managers and employees and emphasized the efficient operation of organizations as a whole; collectively these theories are known as the **classical management** perspective. The beginnings of modern management can be traced directly to these classical management theories, and many of the ideas are as useful today as they were when first proposed. The classical management perspective includes two main schools of thought: scientific management and classical organization theory.

classical management A set of management theories that focus on increasing the efficiency of the organization as a whole

Scientific Management

Scientific management is a branch of the classical management perspective that emphasizes the objective, scientific study of work to improve employee efficiency. Contributors to the scientific management school of thought included Frederick W. Taylor, Frank and Lillian Gilbreth, Henry Gantt, and Harrington Emerson.

scientific management A management perspective that focuses on the rational, scientific study of work situations to improve employee efficiency

EXHIBIT 2.3
In Search of Efficiency
Frederick W. Taylor, known as the "father of scientific management," sought the one best way to accomplish a work task most efficiently.

time-and-motion study The examination of the physical movements and the time involved in completing a work task

Frederick W. Taylor and Scientific Management

Frederick Winslow Taylor (1856–1915), a machinist and engineer from Philadelphia, was working for Midvale Steel when he became interested in the problems of managing for increased efficiency and higher productivity (see Exhibit 2.3). He observed *systematic soldiering*, the conscious effort of groups of employees to work at less than full capacity because they feared being laid off when the work was completed. He also saw that management did not clearly delineate the tasks and responsibilities of managers and employees, had no realistic standards for work output, and paid little attention to matching the skills of employees to their assigned tasks. Taylor found that management generally did not understand the connection between rewarding employees and obtaining better results, and he argued for a mental revolution in management and employee relations. He reasoned that if managers understood the "one best way" to accomplish each work task, they would be able to hire, train, and reward employees who could efficiently achieve the expected work output.[19]

Taylor experimented with the ways employees handled materials, machines, and tools, a technique called **time-and-motion study.** At Midvale, and later at Bethlehem Steel and other companies where he served as a consultant, Taylor measured (under controlled conditions) the time it took to complete a particular process using specific materials and techniques. This way, he was able to arrive at a scientific standard for each work task in the manufacturing process; then he planned the work and developed procedures to maintain productivity. So successful was Taylor's work for Bethlehem Steel that it enabled the company to introduce a new product, high-speed steel.[20]

Taylor also clarified the roles of management and employees, giving managers the responsibility for planning, organizing, controlling, and specifying work methods.[21] He instituted such innovations as instruction cards, materials specifications, and inventory control systems to coordinate and control overall factory operations. Taylor advocated a differential piece-rate pay system that rewarded employees who exceeded the standard output. His scientific methods of studying tasks and improving work output in all organizational activities had a far-reaching impact, spreading throughout the United States, France, Italy, Germany, Russia, Holland, and Japan.[22] In 1911 he published *Principles of Scientific Management* to prove that his principles could be successfully applied to any organization.[23] However, Taylor's standardization methods irked many, including union officials who thought he exploited employees and dehumanized work. More than once, Taylor was called to testify at government hearings and questioned about abuses that his scientific management methods were allegedly fostering. Although no solid evidence was ever presented to validate these claims, the notoriety and continued criticism slowed acceptance of Taylor's ideas.[24]

Maids International, a franchised housecleaning service, is one of many service companies that apply modern variations of Taylor's methods. Dan Bishop, CEO of Maids, studied how his employees worked. He broke down each task on a minute-by-minute basis and then simplified each. For instance, employees used to take eight seconds to wind a vacuum cord, but now they take three. Bishop's changes make the job easier on the employees, too. Housecleaners used to bend over 72 times during a cleaning session, but with new routines they bend over just 30 times. Bishop's approach has helped increase productivity and prevent employee fatigue and boredom, so employees stay longer instead of leaving after a few months.[25]

Frank and Lillian Gilbreth and Time-and-Motion Studies

Frank Bunker Gilbreth (1868–1924) and Lillian Moller Gilbreth (1878–1972) were a husband-and-wife team who practiced scientific management at work and at home (see Exhibit 2.4). Frank Gilbreth had the opportunity to examine work practices firsthand when he turned down the chance to attend the Massachusetts Institute of Technology and instead became a bricklayer.[26] He noticed that the bricklayers training him used a variety of motions to complete their tasks, and he wondered which were the most efficient. Using time-and-motion studies, Gilbreth isolated the bricklayers' movements and analyzed them to uncover more-efficient ways to lay bricks. For example, Gilbreth's experiments allowed employees laying interior brick to shave 16 motions from the process, which resulted in a huge productivity increase. He also invented an adjustable stand to hold bricks so that bricklayers would not have to bend over to pick up every brick.[27]

As Gilbreth went on to analyze and then simplify other construction tasks, he invented a variety of tools for time-and-motion studies. For instance, he tried to use movie cameras to capture and examine employee movements. The early cameras, however, were often hand-cranked and did not always run at a constant speed, which would throw off his measurements. In answer to this problem, Gilbreth developed the microchronometer, a clock that records time in 1/2000 of a minute increments.[28]

After his marriage in 1904, Gilbreth worked in concert with his wife, whose background in psychology and management brought another dimension to their work. They used a set of 17 basic motions, each called a *therblig* ("Gilbreth" spelled backward with the "th" reversed), to analyze work tasks in a variety of organizations. Together the Gilbreths developed a management philosophy based on employee individuality, measurement, task standardization, teaching, and incentives. But the Gilbreths didn't leave their scientific management principles at work. The couple ran their household of 12 children according to the same principles of efficiency they advocated for organizations, and two of their

EXHIBIT 2.4

Time-and-Motion Studies at Work and at Home

Scientific management theorists Frank and Lillian Gilbreth, shown with 11 of their 12 children, used time-and-motion studies on the job and at home to build efficiency into routine tasks. Despite their push for standardization, the Gilbreths also emphasized individuality.

children wrote a popular book, *Cheaper by the Dozen,* about their family life. Lillian Gilbreth remained keenly interested in the human aspects of work and continued to consult following her husband's death in 1924.[29]

Central Sterile Supply (CSS), a department of the Manhattan Eye, Ear, and Throat Hospital in New York City, uses many of the Gilbreths' methods to study and improve workflow. Pamela B. Blake, CSS's manager, has four specific goals: to plan activities so that the department is properly staffed, to determine how many people are needed to perform each task, to determine how long each task takes, and to measure the quality of work performance. Blake studied the operating-room preparatory area to determine how long employees took to set up for each medical procedure and how much time was spent on other tasks such as answering telephones. As a result of the changes she implemented following her analysis, the department's scheduling is more efficient and the employees are more productive, which saves critical time during surgery.[30]

Henry Gantt and Pay Incentives

Henry L. Gantt (1861–1919) worked with Frederick Taylor on scientific management experiments over the course of 14 years, before striking out on his own as a management consultant. He originated a unique pay arrangement in which all workers were entitled to a basic daily wage, compared with Taylor's differential piece-rate pay system, which paid according to output. In Gantt's task and bonus system, if employees completed their tasks on time they earned a bonus, and if they performed beyond expectations they were again rewarded, as were their supervisors. Gantt wanted to encourage supervisors to coach employees rather than drive them to perform. Productivity doubled in some organizations after management instituted this pay system, reinforcing Gantt's belief that humanitarian management was the key to achieving organizational goals.[31]

More recently, F. Kenneth Iverson, CEO of the steelmaker Nucor, has initiated a base wage system with bonuses tied to productivity. The base hourly wage is about $8, and bonuses are paid on employees' ability to turn out products in less than the standard time. Employees are very productive and are paid accordingly: in an average week, the bonus makes up more than half of a typical employee's paycheck. Another Gantt innovation was a chart to compare actual output to expected output over time, a useful tool for planning and control functions (see Chapter 7).[32]

Harrington Emerson and Organizational Efficiency

Harrington Emerson (1853–1931) was a consultant who called his specialty *efficiency engineering* because of the emphasis on conserving resources and eliminating waste. Emerson adopted scientific management principles but also viewed work within the context of the organization's structure and its goals. In his view, scientific management concepts were to be justified to the employees, not simply imposed. His 12 principles of efficiency (see Exhibit 2.5) reflect Emerson's dual focus on interpersonal relations and systematic management, with an emphasis on working smarter, not harder. Taken together, his principles were designed to help managers eliminate organizational waste.[33]

classical organization theory A management approach that emphasizes the total organization and ways to improve overall effectiveness and efficiency

Classical Organization Theory

The second branch of the classical management perspective is **classical organization theory,** a management approach that focuses on the organization as a whole

1. **Clearly defined ideal. Managers must know what they want to accomplish, and they must eliminate vagueness and uncertainty.**
2. **Common sense. Managers must develop the ability to differentiate the woods from the trees. They should seek knowledge and advice wherever possible.**
3. **Competent counsel. Managers should actively seek advice from knowledgeable others.**
4. **Discipline. Managers should set up the organization so that employees can obey the rules.**
5. **Fair deal. Managers must seek out justice and fairness.**
6. **Reliable, immediate, accurate, and permanent records. Managers should have the facts available to make decisions.**
7. **Dispatching. Managers should use scientific planning of each function so that the organization as a whole can function smoothly and achieve its goals.**
8. **Standards and schedules. Managers must develop methods for performing their tasks and establish a time to perform each one.**
9. **Standardized conditions. Managers should maintain a uniformity of environment.**
10. **Standardized operations. Managers must maintain a uniformity of method.**
11. **Written standard-practice instructions. Managers must systematically and accurately reduce each practice to writing.**
12. **Efficiency reward. Managers should reward employees for tasks successfully completed.**

EXHIBIT 2.5

Emerson's Principles of Efficiency

When Harrington Emerson formulated his 12 principles of efficiency, he was proposing management practices that are today commonplace. Note the similarity to the management principles in Exhibit 2.6 (developed in France by Henri Fayol).

and on ways to improve its effectiveness and efficiency. Prominent classical organization theorists include Henri Fayol, Max Weber, Lyndall Urwick, Luther Gulick, and Chester Barnard.

Henri Fayol and Administrative Management

Henri Fayol (1841–1925) was a French engineer who developed a systematic method of management that he insisted could be both taught and learned. Fayol refined his methods while a top manager at Commentary-Fourchambault, a large mining company in France that has since been absorbed by Le Creusot–Loire. In contrast to Frederick Taylor's approach of examining the organization from the shop level up, Fayol examined the organization from the top down. He believed in the universality of management, feeling that management principles could be applied to all types of organizations, and he argued for a broad, formal management curriculum to train people in the critical skills they would need to be effective managers. Fayol prepared his management theories for publication as early as 1914, but World War I delayed their appearance until 1916. The second and definitive English translation of his book *General and Industrial Management* was published in 1949, gaining Fayol a much wider audience.[34]

Fayol is best known for his **administrative management** approach, which stresses the functional aspects of the organization structure. In his view, business activities are composed of basic functions that include technical activities such as production, commercial activities such as buying and selling, financial activities such as optimum use of capital, security activities such as protecting property, accounting activities such as costs and balance sheets, and managerial functions (see Exhibit 2.6). Fayol saw management as a five-part function of planning, organizing, commanding, coordinating, and controlling. These functions are the roots of the four-part management process as it is taught today.[35] He also listed 14 rules developed out of his own management experience to help managers run more effective organizations (see Exhibit 2.7). Although the list was not intended to be rigidly applied or to be exhaustive, Fayol's guidelines set the stage for many later theories and practices.[36]

EXHIBIT 2.6

The Functional View of the Business Organization

Henri Fayol identified six basic functions of the business organization.

Technical activities
- **Production**
- **Manufacturing**

Commercial activities
- **Buying**
- **Selling**
- **Exchanging**

Financial activities
- **Searching for capital and credit**
- **Using them optimally**

Security activities
- **Protecting property and persons**

Accounting activities
- **Taking stock**
- **Keeping balance sheets**
- **Tracking costs**

Managerial activities
- **Planning**
- **Organizing**
- **Commanding**
- **Coordinating**
- **Controlling**

administrative management A management approach that stresses the functional aspects of the organization and management by planning, organizing, leading, and controlling

1. **Division of work. Managers use division of work to produce more and better work with the same effort.**
2. **Authority and responsibility. Managers require the right to give orders as well as the power to exact obedience and to establish the degree of responsibility.**
3. **Discipline. Managers establish clear and fair agreements between the organization and the employee and they apply sanctions judiciously.**
4. **Unity of command. Employees receive orders from one superior only.**
5. **Unity of direction. Organizations appoint one head and use one plan for a group of activities having the same objective.**
6. **Subordination of individual interest to the general interest. Personal interests of managers and employees are subordinate to the overall interests of the organization.**
7. **Remuneration of personnel. Employees and managers alike receive fair, reasonable rewarding of effort.**
8. **Centralization. Top managers find optimum degree for a particular organization.**
9. **Scalar chain. Organizations form a chain of superiors ranging from the highest-ranking to the lowest-ranking manager.**
10. **Order. Organizations determine a place for everyone, and everyone understands his or her place.**
11. **Equity. Management requires a combination of kindliness and justice.**
12. **Stability of tenure of personnel. Prosperous firms are generally stable.**
13. **Initiative. Effective managers develop a plan and then execute it.**
14. **Esprit de corps. Harmony among all organization members results in great strength.**

EXHIBIT 2.7

Fayol's Principles of Effective Management

Henri Fayol compiled this list of 14 management principles from his own experience and considered it a starting point for managers seeking guidance about the practice of management.

Max Weber and Bureaucracy

Max Weber (1864–1920) was a German sociologist and scholar who undertook a systematic study of the structure of organizations early in the twentieth century, but his contributions weren't recognized until decades after his death. Weber looked at the internal workings of the organization, and he also considered the structure of society as a whole. He saw that large-scale organizations were becoming more prevalent throughout society: in business, military, government, political, religious, and other organizations. The business world was steadily moving away from the family-based system, and it was no longer feasible to manage on the basis of favoritism or loyalty to a particular person.[37]

bureaucracy A management approach that emphasizes a structured organization in which positions and authority are defined according to formal rules

Weber's theory of **bureaucracy**, a management approach characterized by an organizational structure in which positions and authority are defined according to explicit rules, was meant to rationalize the practice of management in this new order. Weber believed that the authority to manage was exercised by the position a person held, not by the person. No matter who occupied a particular position within the organization, that individual would possess specific managerial authority because of the rules that defined the scope of that job. Using a bureaucratic approach, said Weber, managers would be able to manage complex organizations of all types more efficiently. Although bureaucracy in its most extreme form has become associated with the problems of red tape and layers of rules, the ideal bureaucracy that Weber envisioned has many advantages for managers. Not only do bureaucracies define rational networks of authority and activity that help to achieve organizational goals, they also provide economies of scale in obtaining resources and may therefore promote greater effectiveness.[38]

Managing a bureaucracy can be tricky. Centerior Energy, the utility holding company that serves much of northern Ohio, discovered that its organization contained many duplicative bureaucracies. For example, the utility had separate human resource departments attached to each of its five divisions. CEO Richard Miller recognized that having five departments with five sets of policies was costly and diluted control in the organization, so he decided to reduce the number of departments. In contrast, Reebok encourages its subsidiaries to maintain independent bureaucracies in human resources, sales and marketing, and information services. But Reebok chairman Paul Fireman requires that the human resource managers coordinate their personnel policies so employees won't be confused if they transfer from one subsidiary to another.[39]

According to Max Weber's concept of bureaucracy, management authority is vested in the organizational position rather than in the particular person occupying that position. Joe Gibbs, head coach of the Washington Redskins, holds the authority to drill the players and to develop plays, because of his position in the team organization. Reporting to Gibbs are an offensive coordinator and a defensive coordinator who have been given the authority to direct activities related to their respective specialties.

Chester Barnard and Administrative Systems

Chester I. Barnard (1886–1961) left Harvard before graduating to take a job as a statistician with AT&T, and he rose quickly to become president of New Jersey Bell Telephone, finding time during his career to serve on a lengthy list of not-for-profit organizations. Like Fayol, Barnard developed his management theories during his long tenure as head of a large organization. One of his contributions to classical organization theory was the logical analysis of formal organizations, which he saw as cooperative systems of coordinated groupings of activities. In his 1938 book, *The Functions of the Executive,* Barnard wrote that executives play a key role within an organization because they facilitate communication, acquire resources, formulate organizational goals, and motivate employees to share the vision of the goals and to cooperate in achieving them. Another Barnard contribution was his acceptance theory of authority. He believed that authority depends on the employee's willingness to accept direction rather than on the manager's position of giving direction. This concept will be explored further in Chapter 9.[40]

Lyndall Urwick, Luther Gulick, and the Science of Administration

Lyndall Urwick (1891–1983) was a British army officer turned theorist and consultant whose work integrated the ideas of scientific management with the ideas of classical organization theory. Luther Gulick (1892–1970) served on President Franklin D. Roosevelt's Committee on Administrative Management during the 1930s, and his major interests were political science and public service. Urwick and Gulick edited a 1937 publication titled *Papers on the Science of Administration,* which included articles on organization theory and public administration. Gulick isolated the responsibilities of the chief executive and enumerated them according to the acronym POSDCORB, which stands for planning, organizing, staffing, directing, coordinating, reporting, and budgeting. One of his main points was that well-managed, self-contained organizations or departments are nearly always headed by a single top manager such as a CEO.[41] For his part, Urwick believed that the activities necessary to achieve organizational goals should be grouped and assigned to individuals in an impersonal way, echoing the impartial detachment of Max Weber's bureaucracy. Urwick also wrote about the problems of managing large numbers of employees, identified multiple levels of supervisory management, and used a formula to determine the minimum and maximum number of subordinates a manager can effectively supervise. His work was an important step in synthesizing the principles of scientific management with the thinking of Weber and Fayol.[42]

Assessing the Classical Management Perspective

The classical management theorists established a scientific basis for the study and practice of management, and they gave new momentum to the now commonplace issue of increasing productivity. Moreover, classical management theories helped managers in the public and private sectors effectively manage ever-larger and more complex organizations, and many of these innovations are still used today. However, some of the classical theorists were criticized because they seemed to treat organizations as pieces of machinery and people as cogs in the

GLOBAL MANAGEMENT

Classical Management Goes Global

It's hard to imagine a corporation with a more complex ownership arrangement than Unilever, which serves two masters: Unilever PLC in Great Britain and Unilever NV in the Netherlands. The company started out more than one hundred years ago making laundry soap and now manages a worldwide array of packaged goods products from these two headquarters offices. Sir Michael Angus chairs the British side, and Floris A. Maljers chairs the Dutch side. Together they have crafted a unique organization that has put Unilever way ahead in several product categories. Sixty percent of the company's $34 billion in sales comes from Europe, but only 22 percent comes from North America, where its brands compete with such powerhouses as Procter & Gamble and Colgate-Palmolive. To gain ground in the U.S. market as well as internationally, Unilever is applying management techniques that draw on Henri Fayol's classical organization management theories.

For years, Unilever's multinational management arrangement gave the firm the ability to understand and satisfy the needs of customers in many cultures around the world. Wherever Unilever had a subsidiary, local managers were generally given the responsibility of achieving their goals in their own ways. But Unilever was even more hands-off with its U.S. unit, Lever Brothers, and this management approach backfired, in part because the North American environment was so different from the European environment. Moreover, headquarters set unrealistic profit goals that the Lever managers could achieve only by cutting costs. Lever managers chopped their own advertising budgets and lowered prices, but customers didn't flock to their products because Procter & Gamble and others were spending heavily to tout new products.

At the same time, managers in Lever's food division lacked the funds to upgrade their older margarine manufacturing plants and to change their inefficient distribution system. In light of Lever's $100 million losses from 1981 to 1986, headquarters decided to change the management structure. Angus was sent to

machinery rather than as individuals. Further, the classical management principles were broad and did not always provide specific ideas about how to actually coordinate activities, how to assign functional tasks, or how to carry out other everyday management functions. The classical management perspective tended to focus on the internal workings of organizations rather than considering the influence of the environment around them. In contrast to the notion that management principles are universal, contemporary managers find that many of the original classical management principles must be modified and adapted to today's management needs.[43]

From Classical to Behavioral Management

Although the classical management theories contributed much to the practice of management and to improving productivity, the organizational environment was becoming so complex that these relatively straightforward, somewhat mechanical principles were becoming less useful. Organizations were growing rapidly by merging or buying or expanding, and more professional managers were needed to handle the responsibilities created by this growth. At the same time, labor was in short supply and organizations were more particular about the employees they hired and trained because of the costs. There was also a social backlash against the often deplorable working conditions. As a result, organized labor became stronger and the classical management theorists' mechanical methods of dealing with employees were insufficient. An important theorist whose ideas helped to move management forward into an era of more humanistic perspectives is Mary Parker Follett.[44]

the United States to take charge (he was later followed by Morris Tabaksblat), and the new organization they established carries through many of Fayol's 14 management principles. To start, they got rid of everything but the household products and then bought other businesses that fit well with Unilever's basic product lines and its goals.

Next, they redefined the lines of authority and responsibility so that the U.S. divisions report directly to Europe, rather than to a top manager in the United States. This strengthened the unity of command and also contributed to the unity of direction, especially important for Unilever's ability to share technology and ideas from other worldwide successes. The result: Promise Extra Light was launched in the United States using one of Unilever's European food processes, and the U.S. introduction of Snuggle fabric softener was nearly the twin of the European version, right down to the teddy bear advertising. Snuggle has already captured 21 percent of the U.S. market. In margarines, Unilever is now number one in the United States with a 31 percent share, compared with its number three position and 23 percent share in 1984.

Thanks to these organizational changes, Unilever has begun to clean up in the U.S. household products market, but more management challenges are ahead. One big challenge is to coordinate the activities of its diverse units. For example, in 1989 Unilever acquired Calvin Klein Cosmetics and Elizabeth Arden and immediately ran into a conflict: both launched new men's fragrances that year, and the products wound up competing with each other. Another challenge is to keep competitors at bay while improving profitability. In addition to bringing the U.S. organization under control, Angus and Maljers want to streamline Unilever's European operations by adjusting the degree of centralization to boost efficiency and effectiveness. As Unilever's experience shows, sound management principles such as Fayol's never go out of style.

Apply Your Knowledge

1. What role does subordination of the individual interest to the general interest play in Unilever's revamped U.S. organization?
2. How might Unilever apply Frederick Taylor's principles of scientific management to its U.S. manufacturing plants?

Mary Parker Follett (1868–1933) straddles the spectrum of theory between the classical management and the behavioral management perspectives. Follett brought a background in philosophy, political science, and civic work to her examination of conflict, power, authority, control, and cooperation. She recognized that management as a formal, scientific discipline was necessary for five reasons: (1) organizations could not continue to exploit natural resources forever, (2) keener competition would increase demands on managerial talent, (3) a scarcity of labor would change the way organizations had to treat their employees, (4) a broader view of the ethics of human relations would emerge that encompassed the managerial profession, and (5) business, as a public service, was responsible for efficient utilization of resources.[45]

Most important, Follett believed that the technical, scientific side of management could not be divorced from the human relations side, and her writings continually stressed the importance of the human element, especially the motivating desires of individuals and groups. Because her theories of management control predated the thinking of the systems theorists (discussed later in this chapter), Follett is also considered a bridge to that later management perspective.[46] Follett's viewpoint is clearly reflected in the management practices of Anita Roddick. She operates The Body Shop with evident concern for the natural environment and for ethical relations with her employees and her customers.

THE BEHAVIORAL MANAGEMENT PERSPECTIVE

Even as the proponents of classical management theories argued their views, profound changes continued to transform society. Early in the twentieth century, pressure began building for a new view of the individual and of human behavior in the work setting. Whereas the classical management theorists looked at the total organization and the relationship of managers and employees, the **behavioral management** perspective was concerned with the nature and impact of individual and group behavior within the organization. One of the earliest contributors to this perspective was Hugo Munsterberg, and he was followed in the 1920s by the researchers whose involvement with the Hawthorne studies brought the behavioral management perspective to the forefront of management thinking.

behavioral management A management perspective that focuses on the nature and impact of individual and group behavior in organizations

Industrial Psychology

Hugo Munsterberg (1863–1916) was born in Germany, and at 29 he established the psychological laboratory at Harvard, where he was professor of experimental psychology. Munsterberg believed that psychology could be applied to the practical problems of industry, and in 1913 the English translation of his book *Psychology and Industrial Efficiency* was published. In this book, Munsterberg argued for better understanding and application of psychology in management situations, and he noted that increasing industrial efficiency by applying psychological principles was in the best interests of both managers and employees.[47]

The Hawthorne Studies

The Hawthorne studies involved three management experts: Elton Mayo, F. J. Roethlisberger, and William J. Dickson. Australian-born Elton Mayo (1880–1949) studied the relationship between people who worked together, and he was involved in a series of experiments that helped shape the development of the behavioral management movement. While on the faculty of the Wharton School, Mayo conducted experiments at a Pennsylvania textile mill and found that he could improve employee morale and productivity by introducing rest periods. He joined the Harvard faculty in 1926; the following year he was invited to consult on a project already under way in Chicago at the Hawthorne plant of Western Electric (the equipment-producing arm of AT&T), where Roethlisberger and Dickson were conducting experiments.[48]

The Hawthorne studies were started in 1924 by the National Academy of Sciences in an attempt to learn whether changes in illumination had any impact on employee productivity. From 1924 to 1927, the researchers studied the effect of lighting on the output of women employees who assembled telephone relay equipment. They varied the lighting in one workroom, kept the lighting constant in a second workroom, and then compared the productivity of the two groups. Surprisingly, the researchers found that when they increased the lighting in one workroom, the output of both employee groups increased. Even more puzzling was the finding that when the researchers lowered the lighting, productivity improved in both groups. In fact, productivity didn't drop until the light had been lowered to the level of moonlight. Believing that factors other than lighting were affecting the results, the researchers ended this phase of the studies.[49]

When Mayo came aboard, he joined Roethlisberger and Dickson in resuming the Hawthorne studies. From 1927 to 1932 they conducted experiments in which pay systems, supervision, and other elements were manipulated. In the first phase, known as the Relay Assembly Test Room Study, five women assembled relays in a controlled work environment as the researchers monitored their output every half-hour. The researchers found once again that productivity rose without any clear connection to the physical factors being varied in the experiment, which included the length and timing of rest periods, the length of the workday, and the company-provided lunches and beverages. A number of explanations were proposed for this. One in particular that has received much attention is the possibility that employees treated in a special way will improve their performance precisely because of the attention, a theory known as the *Hawthorne effect.* Researchers have since conducted new experiments and carefully reviewed the Hawthorne methodology but have not been convinced that the Hawthorne effect exists.[50]

In another Hawthorne phase, called the Bank Wiring Observation Room Study, the researchers studied the group behavior that developed among male employees who wired, soldered, and inspected switchboard equipment. This group was isolated in a workroom, and a researcher sat passively observing their activities during the day. This study revealed that the group developed its own informal notion of acceptable productivity and used group pressure to ensure that no one deviated from this norm. Overproducers were branded "rate busters," underproducers were labeled "rate chiselers," and employees who violated the norms were disciplined by sarcasm, ridicule, or a blow on the arm. Mayo and his colleagues concluded that formal organizations also contain informal organizations that have their own social systems. The Hawthorne studies were thus significant because they signaled the importance of interpersonal and group relationships within an organization.[51]

The Human Relations Movement

Despite the controversy surrounding the Hawthorne studies, they prompted a shift in the course of management theory toward the search for a better understanding of human relations. Mayo was concerned that the social order had come unglued by the move from an agrarian, family-oriented society to a more chaotic, technologically-oriented industrial society. He believed that management was more focused on satisfying material and economic needs than on fulfilling the human needs of individuals who work for organizations. To restore meaning to work and to help employees feel more socially satisfied, he believed that organizations needed to consider individuals and their interactions in the workplace. The **human relations movement** that evolved from this thinking is a school of management thought that sees employee behavior as responsive to the interpersonal processes within the work unit. To apply the human relations theories, however, managers would have to act more collaboratively and would need good social skills in addition to their technical skills.[52]

human relations movement A management perspective that views employees as responding to the interpersonal processes within the work unit

Two theorists made particularly important contributions to the human relations movement: Abraham Maslow and Douglas McGregor.

Abraham Maslow and the Hierarchy of Needs

Abraham H. Maslow (1908–1970) was an academic, a plant manager, and a psychologist during his varied career. He proposed the **hierarchy of needs theory,** the idea that people are motivated by the need to satisfy a sequence of human needs, including physiological (the most basic needs), safety, social, esteem, and self-actualization needs. Once people have satisfied their more basic needs, said Maslow, they progress up the ladder to satisfy more advanced needs

hierarchy of needs theory Abraham Maslow's theory that people are motivated to fulfill a sequence of five categories of human needs: physiological, safety, social, esteem, and self-actualization needs such as self-actualization. Because Maslow clarified the importance of motivations other than pay, which had dominated the thinking of the scientific management theorists in search of higher productivity, his contribution to the evolution of management theory was significant.[53]

Anita Roddick's belief that honest merchandising and social activism can motivate The Body Shop employees is an example of Maslow's hierarchy in use. She provides a salary so employees can satisfy their physiological needs for food and shelter, and she encourages long-term employment, which satisfies employee needs for safety. But she also offers membership in an organization renowned for its dedication to social issues, which can satisfy employees' social needs and their needs for self-actualization. Chapter 14 examines Maslow's theory in more detail.

Douglas McGregor and Theory X and Theory Y

Douglas M. McGregor (1906–1964) was a professor, a college president, and later a consultant who specialized in psychology. Searching for a practical management principle that incorporated the social science perspective, McGregor developed Theory X and Theory Y to describe two extreme examples of the ways in which managers can relate to employees (see Exhibit 2.8). His **Theory X** described the traditional management view that employees are lazy and that they dislike work, so they must be driven to perform. In contrast, **Theory Y** managers view employees as willing to accept responsibility, able to be creative in their approaches to work, and without an inherent distaste for work when they are committed to the organization's goals. McGregor favored Theory Y management, saying that managers should rely on employee self-direction rather than external controls to achieve performance, and in fact employees should be able to choose the methods they will use to attain organizational goals. This method implies a trust of employees and an ability to let them fully participate in the organization. But to apply Theory Y, managers must be ready to change their assumptions about human nature and to help employees realize their own potential. McGregor's theories echoed Maslow's ideas about self-actualization, and both presented new concepts of manager-employee relations and the potential contributions of individuals.[54]

Theory X A management philosophy in which employees are seen as lazy, unambitious, and in need of coercion to complete work tasks

Theory Y A management philosophy in which employees are seen as interested in assuming responsibility, capable of innovative approaches to work problems, and having no inherent distaste for work

GenCorp Automotive in Shelbyville, Indiana, is one of many successful organizations that have put Theory Y into practice. The manufacturer of plastic car

EXHIBIT 2.8

Two Management Views of Employees

Douglas McGregor contrasted the traditional management view of employees (Theory X) with his new view of employees (Theory Y). Whereas Theory X assumed that employees must be driven to work, Theory Y assumed that employees were willing and able to guide their own actions.

Theory X	Theory Y
1. Employees want to work as little as possible, so managers must control, direct, persuade, reward, or punish them to get them to work toward achieving organizational goals.	1. Employees do not by nature dislike work.
2. Employees have little ambition and dislike responsibility.	2. Employees can be creative in solving problems and achieving organizational goals.
3. Employees naturally resist change.	3. Employees are willing to seek and accept responsibility.
	4. Employees will commit themselves to organizational goals when they can direct their own efforts and achieve personal goals.
	5. Employees have a potential for development that is generally underutilized by most organizations.

body panels invests heavily in employee and manager training that covers task-specific skills, problem-solving skills, leadership capabilities, and organizational processes. Employees handle much of the manufacturing control responsibilities, and they also periodically switch jobs so that they can bring new insights to the next position and keep enthusiasm high. Far from being seen as lazy and unambitious, GenCorp employees are recognized as active, imaginative participants who can contribute to the company's achievements.[55]

The Behavioral Science Movement

The human relations movement brought the human aspects of management back into focus for industrialized organizations striving mightily for efficiency and productivity. However, critics charged that the movement was based on intangibles rather than on scientific evidence, and they complained that the ideas were more theoretical than practical. Researchers investigating human relations issues found that higher employee satisfaction did not always lead to increased productivity, and they also learned that the nature of the work itself was an important element in productivity. These findings put a new face on human relations theories and showed that interpersonal relationships in organizations were infinitely more complex than originally thought. Researchers from a variety of disciplines joined the search, and the **behavioral science movement** was born, seeking scientific knowledge about human behavior in organizations to help managers become more effective.[56]

behavioral science movement A school of management thought that stresses scientific research about human behavior to guide management practices

The behavioral science movement has attracted a melting pot of researchers from disciplines as varied as cultural anthropology, economics, political science, psychology, sociology, social psychology, and even mathematics. But it's important to note that the study of behavioral science is not the same as the study of physics or chemistry. Because people in organizations often act in unpredictable ways, managers have no ironclad theories that they can universally apply in the way that the established laws of chemistry can be applied, for example. By continuing to study **organizational behavior,** the effect that organizations have on employees, and the effect that employees and groups have on their organizations, behavioral scientists will be able to develop better theories, which managers can adapt to real-life situations.[57]

organizational behavior The study of the effect that organizations have on their members and of the effect that members have on their organizations

Assessing the Behavioral Management Perspective

In contrast to the classical management theorists who generally ignored the individuality and creative abilities of employees, the behavioral management theorists emphasized the importance and the contributions of individuals and groups within organizations. The behavioral management perspective doesn't completely reject the classical management perspective but looks beyond the organization chart, rules, regulations, and rationality to consider how the informal social systems influence the organization. As a result, behavioral management has provided some important clues about how managers and employees at all levels can work together to attain organizational goals and feel good about their personal roles. However, like the classical management theorists, some behavioral management theorists made the mistake of believing that their ideas could be universally applied, and some critics charge that this theory puts too much emphasis on human relations. Perhaps the greatest contribution of this management approach is the realization that people can make a difference, and this perspective led to further research that has changed the way managers think about leadership, motivation, work teams, and the organization as a whole.[58]

NASA's Spacelab Mission Operations Control center in Huntsville, Alabama, uses a variety of management science tools to supervise the activities of scientists in space. This center was first used to direct experiments during a 1990 research mission aboard the Space Shuttle *Columbia.* Supported by mathematical and statistical models, managers make decisions about payload operations and transmit instructions to the crew.

THE QUANTITATIVE MANAGEMENT PERSPECTIVE

By the end of the 1930s, professors were teaching management at Harvard and MIT, and prominent business leaders such as Alfred P. Sloan of General Motors and Robert E. Wood of Sears, Roebuck were practicing management as a discrete discipline. Then World War II broke out, and military officials were suddenly confronted with the massive, complex problems of aligning people and materials all over the globe. To help make these critical decisions, British and U.S. military managers turned to a relatively undeveloped field of management theory, **quantitative management,** an approach that uses mathematical techniques, statistical tools, and information aids to solve management problems. This approach was an outgrowth of the scientific management belief in strict measurement and in using formulas, but it went beyond by involving a variety of disciplines and attacking a variety of problems. Although quantitative management had been explored during World War I (when experts in Great Britain and the United States had studied ways of applying mathematical and statistical models to the problems of war), it wasn't until World War II that managers actively pursued such applications.[59]

quantitative management A management perspective that applies mathematical techniques, statistical tools, and information aids to management situations

After World War II started, mixed teams of researchers representing such diverse disciplines as astrophysics, physics, physiology, and mathematics worked on England's military problems. They contributed to the war effort by improving Britain's early warning radar systems, by helping to determine convoy size, and by helping to plan bombing raids. Within a few years, the United States began to apply similar techniques to naval mining and antisubmarine operations. Because quantitative management was so valuable to the U.S. military during the war, officials continued using these techniques after the war in studying aerial operations and in other applications. Business managers on both sides of the Atlantic became interested in quantitative management after the war. For example, industrial managers in Great Britain today use quantitative management techniques to increase production efficiency and develop new markets in the iron and steel industry, in railways, in textiles, and in other areas, often with government sponsorship. In the United States, managers use quantitative management in a variety of industries, including retailing, utilities, health care, and transportation. And since computers now do most of the computation and statistical work, managers can more easily learn and apply a wide spectrum of quantitative management techniques.[60]

Quantitative management includes three main subfields: management science, operations management, and management information systems.

Management Science

management science A quantitative management perspective that applies mathematical models to management situations

Management science, also known as *operations research,* is a management approach that provides decision makers with a quantitative basis for selecting among alternatives, especially useful in planning. Not to be confused with scientific management, *management science* applies mathematical and statistical models to management situations, whereas *scientific management* focuses on the scientific study of work situations to improve efficiency. Queuing theory (used to analyze waiting lines) and simulation models (used to help predict future situations) are examples of management science tools that managers can apply to support the decision-making process.[61]

For example, Al Boxley, the owner of several McDonald's franchise restaurants in Maryland, uses management science techniques to handle employee scheduling. His restaurant managers used to take more than eight hours to create by hand the weekly employee schedules, which included assigning grill, counter, and drive-through window responsibilities; allowing for employee preferences and absences; and estimating hourly sales projections so that employees could handle the volume. These complex decisions were difficult to make without the aid of quantitative tools. By using a personal computer programmed with some management science tools, Boxley's managers were able to lop off more than six hours from the scheduling process and increased the efficiency of employee staffing.[62]

Federal Express uses operations management techniques to improve productivity and to enhance customer service. When couriers pick up express packages, they use hand-held scanners to enter the origin points and the destination points into the COSMOS package tracking system. This system helps managers determine the most efficient route for each package and pinpoints the exact location of every package until it is delivered.

Operations Management

Operations management is a management approach that uses quantitative methods to improve the productivity and increase the efficiency of goods or services production. Many organizations, particularly manufacturers, use operations management techniques such as inventory management and network modeling to improve decision making about distribution and operational problems. Included in this category are tools that help organizations maintain quality control and scheduling techniques that help managers plan and track production.[63]

For example, when Florida Power & Light received a high number of citations for violating environmental protection regulations, managers analyzed their utility plant procedures with operations management techniques. They used a cause-and-effect model to trace the roots of their operational problems, then they examined the causes to see which were responsible for the highest number of violations. The managers found that more than three-quarters of the violations stemmed from the employees' lack of understanding of hazardous-waste handling. Once the utility instituted annual training on this topic, violations dropped dramatically.[64] Chapter 20 examines operations management in greater detail.

operations management A management approach that uses quantitative techniques to improve the productivity and efficiency of goods or services production

Management Information Systems

Management information systems (MIS) collect, process, and transmit information used to support management functions. Managers use MIS for more than quantitative tasks; for example, they use MIS to keep a mountain of details about their organizations, their customers, and their environment readily available. Because of the wide-ranging benefits of being able to gather and systematically analyze vast quantities of information, MIS has become an integral part of every management function at virtually every management level in most organizations today.[65]

management information systems (MIS) Management tools that focus on the collection, processing, and transmission of information to support management functions

For example, managers at *Reader's Digest* use MIS to capture and store the names and addresses of 50 million U.S. households. By researching customer interests and holding this information in the computer files, the publisher can decide on the appropriate magazine, book, music, and video offers to send to each customer and then track the sales results. Moreover, *Reader's Digest* is currently developing a highly sophisticated MIS system dubbed the Customer

MANAGERIAL DECISION MAKING

Choosing a Management Approach for Smoother Sailing

Can boats, billiards, and bowling balls add up to profits? Brunswick's CEO Jack F. Reichert is working hard to get this equation to come out positive. The international maker of boats, boat motors, and recreational products slid into the red twice in the 1980s as the company battled first a takeover attempt and then the effects of a weakening economy. To prepare Brunswick for the 1990s, Reichert faced some tough decisions.

Although his 30-year experience in the company enabled Reichert to understand its development and its direction, he found as CEO that the rapidly changing environment had a major impact on Brunswick's performance. In its fight against an unwanted takeover, Brunswick had been forced to sell a highly profitable division. Now Reichert had to return Brunswick to profitability. Reichert's contingency management perspective allowed him to fit his management approach to each new situation he faced on the road to higher profits. He decided to manage Brunswick in terms of three Ss: survival, strategy, and succession.

He began by attacking the survival problems. Activities that had been effective in the past were not helping Brunswick's performance in its current situation. Cost-cutting became one of Reichert's top priorities as he systematically examined every business function to see where he could streamline, improve efficiency, and save money. Because each division had a marketing department, Reichert eliminated the corporate marketing department, a transportation department, and other groups that seemed redundant. Today, Brunswick's bureaucracy is less cumbersome, in part because Reichert sliced away several levels, leaving only six layers from the first-line managers to the CEO.

Reminiscent of the behavioral management viewpoint, the CEO consciously turned away from purely mechanistic solutions to Brunswick's problems. He decided to vest each division's employees with the responsibility of doing their jobs and achieving organiza-

Arizona State University has installed a management information system to organize and speed student registration. The computerized Student Information System enables the registrar to efficiently manage enrollments for 42,000 students and more than 6,600 classes per semester. By reviewing registration data on this MIS, university officials can make timely decisions about adding or dropping courses as needed.

Information Management System that will allow company managers to more precisely target direct mail to customers and give faster and more efficient service.[66] Chapter 18 examines the implications of information management in greater detail.

Assessing the Quantitative Management Perspective

In contrast to the more human approach of behavioral management, the quantitative management perspective relies on hard, rational facts and formulas. In particular, managers find quantitative management useful for planning, decision making, and controlling. Because this field is relatively new and has many potential uses for management, its theories are still evolving. Even so, there are obvious limitations. Quantitative management is not helpful for managers seeking a broad framework for analyzing and implementing effective management because it deals primarily with problems and not with management patterns. Some managers claim that particular tools are not applicable to the situations they commonly face. One way around such limitations is to use a technique called *sensitivity analysis,* in which the manager varies elements in the model so that the results reflect what may happen under a variety of conditions.[67]

Also, a study of public sector applications revealed that quantitative management isn't always an effective way to arrive at a real-world solution when political, technical, or timing issues confuse the situation. For example, when the New York City police department wanted to determine the most efficient use of police cars, the initial analysis did not take into account the concerns of the precinct commanders and was not successful as a result. However, after the commanders were invited to participate, they helped find a workable solution. Despite these limitations, organizations can benefit by applying appropriate techniques and tional goals in the ways they think are best. In the past, decisions used to take weeks or even months because division managers had to consult corporate managers before taking action. Today, division managers make their own decisions, so the process takes only hours or days. Reichert also created new pay systems to reward performance. To give employees a sense of pride, commitment, and ownership, he started an incentive program in 1983 that awards employees with shares of Brunswick stock. Moreover, he closed the executive dining room and now all headquarters employees eat in the same cafeteria. This and other actions helped to increase trust and cooperation between management and employees.

For tools to manage the new, more responsive organization, the CEO looked to the quantitative management perspective. He installed an MIS to support managers in every function and he adopted specialized manufacturing techniques to increase productivity. Reichert decided that the future lay in leisure products, and in 1986 he spent heavily to buy leading boat companies that would boost Brunswick's position in the industry. These acquisitions paid off as Brunswick's sales climbed from $1 billion in 1982 to $3 billion in 1987, with marine products leading the way. However, boat buying ran aground during the 1989 recession, and sales retreated to $2.8 billion that year.

In the 1990s, Reichert is turning his attention to expanding the marine lines and penetrating more international markets. His third S is for succession, and he is devoting much of his management attention to developing and training promising employees who will be the company leaders of tomorrow. Even if Brunswick hits more rough waters ahead, Reichert will use every appropriate management technique to make decisions that will keep his organization on course for profits.

Apply Your Knowledge

1. What forces are shaping Jack Reichert's management philosophies and techniques? Be as specific as possible.
2. How can Reichert apply systems theory to Brunswick?

using old-fashioned management judgment to interpret and then implement the results.[68]

CONTEMPORARY MANAGEMENT PERSPECTIVES

The classical, behavioral, and quantitative management perspectives are all being applied today in one form or another. But in recent years, theorists and practitioners have recognized that the environment can also influence organizational management. Therefore, new management approaches have emerged that integrate aspects of each of the three major schools of thought within the context of the organizational environment. As these theories evolve, they are studied, applied, and dissected by researchers and practitioners to see whether they represent true advances in management philosophy. Two contemporary perspectives that have particularly interested theorists and managers are systems theory and contingency theory.

systems theory A contemporary management perspective that views organizations as functioning systems within the environment

system A group of interrelated components that function as a whole to achieve common goals

inputs The human, physical, financial, and information resources used to produce goods and services

transformation process The management, technological, and production operations performed by the organization to convert inputs to outputs

Systems Theory

Systems theory is a management approach that sees organizations as systems functioning in relation to their environment. In this theory, a **system** is defined as a group of interrelated parts that function as a whole to achieve common goals. All organizational systems operate on the basis of four elements: inputs, transformation processes, outputs, and feedback (see Exhibit 2.9). **Inputs** are the physical, financial, human, and information resources that are used to produce the organization's goods and services. During the **transformation process**, the organization uses management, technology, and production operations to con-

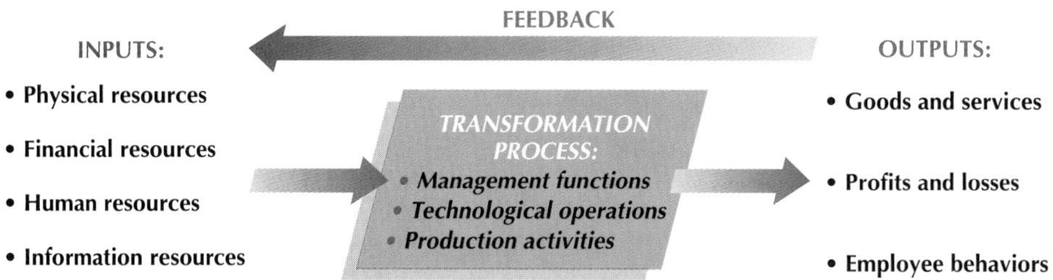

EXHIBIT 2.9 A Systems View of the Organization

According to the systems theory of management, the organization uses a transformation process to convert inputs to outputs. It relies on feedback to monitor results and then modifies inputs and processes as needed. Open systems interact with the environment but closed systems do not.

vert the inputs into **outputs,** which are the goods and services, profits and losses, employee behaviors, and other expected results. These outputs represent the results produced by managers at all levels as they work toward achieving the organization's goals. The environment reacts to these outputs with **feedback,** information that can then be used to modify and adjust inputs and transformation processes to achieve more desirable outputs.[69]

outputs The results, goods, and services produced by an organization

feedback Information about the status and results of organizational activities

subsystem A system within a system, as in the work units within an organization

closed system A system that is self-sufficient, with little or no interaction within its environment

open system A system that interacts with its environment and receives feedback

entropy The tendency of systems to deteriorate over time

negative entropy The capacity to obtain new inputs from the environment to keep the system from falling into decline

synergy The combined activity of two or more subsystems that results in better performance than when the units work in isolation

Systems theory is useful because it helps managers envision the boundaries of their organizations and the ways in which **subsystems,** the various systems within a system, interact with each other. Managers taking the systems perspective also look at their organizations in terms of the amount of interaction with the environment. A **closed system** has no interaction with its environment and is therefore self-sufficient, but an **open system** interacts with its environment and receives feedback. In reality, the most self-sufficient organization cannot be an entirely closed system because it has some interaction with the environment, if only to acquire inputs. So all organizations are really open systems; the concepts of pure open and closed systems are generally used in the relative sense, not as absolutes.[70]

Over time, systems inevitably fall victim to **entropy,** the natural tendency of systems to decay. However, organizations can use feedback to detect entropy and then counter the process with **negative entropy,** the ability to acquire new inputs from the environment to keep the system from deteriorating. Also, systems theory reflects one of the most important reasons for organizations to exist: to take advantage of **synergy,** the idea that the whole is greater than the sum of its parts. Simply stated, people who band together to form an organization can accomplish more than they could working by themselves.[71]

At Detroit Edison, the systems approach helps clarify the relationship of the utility to its environment and the interdependence of the utility's management functions. Managers forge links to the local community, to the state legislature, and to regulatory agencies such as the Public Service Commission, so they can understand and influence the environment outside Detroit Edison. The system may focus on engineering and energy internally, but its inputs, outputs, and transformation process are directly dependent on the environment. For example, if the Nuclear Regulatory Commission modified its guidelines for operating power plants, Detroit Edison would have to change its transformation process to comply. Similarly, if the legislature capped the utility's profit margin, the company's profit output would change.[72]

Contingency Theory

Another contemporary management perspective is **contingency theory**, a management approach that focuses on adapting management behavior to the particular circumstances of the organization and to each given situation. This viewpoint differs from the "one best way" that the classical management theorists sought because they assumed that management principles are *universal,* or applicable in all cases, regardless of the organization's unique circumstances. Of course, most of the classical management theorists didn't intend their principles to be fixed and all-encompassing; recall that Fayol, for one, regarded his principles as general guidelines rather than rigid rules. In the 1950s and 1960s, the research of Joan Woodward, Paul Lawrence, Jay Lorsch, and others revealed that managers act differently depending on the environment, the technology used by the organization, and other factors. Far from rejecting the management perspectives of the past, the contingency theorists embrace any and all appropriate principles that enable managers to manage more effectively. The contingency theory is *integrative* because it serves as a framework within which managers can apply any of the three major management perspectives, be it scientific, behavioral, or quantitative.[73]

contingency theory A management approach emphasizing that appropriate management behavior should be adapted to the unique circumstances of the organization and the specific situation

Regardless of the organizational structure or the obstacles and opportunities they encounter, managers have some leeway in the choices they make and in the actions they initiate. Although some functions such as finance and accounting necessarily operate according to preset rules, managers do have the choice of acting in a variety of ways to achieve the organizational goals, and contingency theory recognizes this individuality. In particular, theorists have applied contingency theory to management problems of leadership, decision making, organization change, employee motivation, human resource management, and organization structure. As a result, managers have a new set of techniques to try, including participative work groups and situational leadership styles. Although critics recognize the benefits of fitting management principles to individual situations, they also argue that contingency theory provides no useful generalizations for managers to apply.[74]

On-site managers of this oil exploration venture in Sumatra conducted jointly by Chevron of the United States and Partamina of Indonesia pay close attention to the resources they input, including human resources, funding, and equipment. They also examine the transformation process and monitor outputs. Feedback from the environment, especially the physical consequences of drilling, can influence this venture's management and the inputs and transformation processes used.

Other Contemporary Management Perspectives

Theory A An idealized management perspective that views U.S. management of organizations as characterized by short-term employment, individual responsibility, and individual decision making

Theory J An idealized management perspective that views Japanese management of organizations as characterized by lifetime employment, collective responsibility, and consensual decision making

Theory Z An idealized blend of U.S. and Japanese management approaches characterized by long-term employment, individual responsibility, and consensual decision making

Within the past twenty years other contemporary management perspectives have emerged. Among the two best-known are Ouchi's Theory Z and Peters and Waterman's search for organizational excellence.

William G. Ouchi developed Theory Z after studying management practices at a variety of Japanese and U.S. firms that operated in both countries. He described one management approach as **Theory A** (for "American") because it typified the U.S. management approach, in which organizations emphasize individualized responsibility and decision making but make no commitment to employment beyond the short term. Ouchi described a second management approach as **Theory J** because it represented the typical Japanese management approach, an approach characterized by lifetime employment, collective responsibility, and consensual decision making. His **Theory Z** is a hybrid, idealized approach that draws from both Japanese and U.S. management techniques, combining a commitment to long-term employment with individual responsibility and consensual decision making (see Exhibit 2.10). The U.S. organizations that Ouchi describes as being managed according to Theory Z have developed a management style that embodies many of the characteristics of Japanese organizations.[75]

Managers in the Water Utilities Department of Fort Collins, Colorado, decided to apply Theory Z concepts to their organization and started by affirming the utility's commitment to its employees. They also invited employees to become involved in problem solving and decision making. When a laboratory pollution group missed an important government deadline, the utility put together a multilevel team of employees to analyze the problem and help correct it. The manager of one unit asked employees what type of equipment they preferred and solicited ideas for finishing the work; as a result of these and other Theory Z innovations, this unit's productivity rose 450 percent over two years.[76]

Of course, one of the appeals of Theory Z is the idea that global managers can successfully borrow good ideas from managers in other parts of the world, and Ouchi's research is one of many studies that shows the power of adapting good ideas regardless of origin. In fact, academics have started examining management styles in Sweden, South Korea, and other countries, to understand how companies there operate and what contributes to their success. Ouchi's studies put the spotlight on Japanese and U.S. management approaches, but some academics have challenged Ouchi's theories, saying they are not supported by sufficient research to prove their value in improving employee productivity. As with the other contemporary management theories, Theory Z is too new to be fairly evaluated and only additional research and examination will prove its long-term worth. Also, critics warn that Japanese management practice is not a panacea for management ills but is only one of many approaches that can be studied and adapted.[77]

Managers at the Nissan truck and car manufacturing plant in Smyrna, Tennessee, blend characteristics of Type A and Type J management styles. Nissan personnel assume individual responsibility for their assigned tasks, but they also work in groups and use consensual decision making to build support for decisions and changes.

In 1982, when management consultants Thomas J. Peters and Robert H. Waterman, Jr., published *In Search of Excellence,* they set managers off on a quest to emulate the best characteristics of Johnson & Johnson, IBM, Hewlett-Packard, Delta Airlines, McDonald's, and other "excellent" firms. Peters and Waterman identified eight attributes that characterized the high-performing companies they studied. These companies display a bias for action, stay close to their customers, foster autonomy and entrepreneurship, support people as the

Characteristics of Type A Organizations (American)	Characteristics of Type J Organizations (Japanese)
1. Short-term employment	1. Lifetime employment
2. Individual decision making	2. Consensual decision making
3. Individual responsibility	3. Collective responsibility
4. Rapid evaluation and promotion	4. Slow evaluation and promotion
5. Explicit, formalized control	5. Implicit, informal control
6. Specialized career path	6. Nonspecialized career path
7. Segmented concern	7. Holistic concern

Characteristics of Type Z Organizations (Modified American)
1. Long-term employment
2. Consensual decision making
3. Individual responsibility
4. Slow evaluation and promotion
5. Implicit, informal control with explicit, formalized measures
6. Moderately specialized career path
7. Holistic concern, including family

EXHIBIT 2.10

Ouchi's Theory Z

William Ouchi's Theory Z is an idealized hybrid of two distinctly different management approaches: Theory A, the U.S. approach, and Theory J, the Japanese approach.

source of quality and productivity, are hands-on and value driven, stick to the businesses they understand, are structured simply with lean staffs, and are both loosely and tightly organized.[78] Excellence as a management precept has, of course, been dissected, praised, and criticized in the same way that all other management theories can and should be examined. But this and other popular perspectives can sometimes provide interesting and practical ideas.

Nearly every year, a new philosophy emerges to capture the imagination by promising insights that will help people manage organizations more effectively. In the end, it is up to each manager to consider the organization's history, goals, and current situation in order to balance the use of the appropriate management theories.[79]

SUMMARY

By studying the past, managers can find ideas for improving their own management capabilities. Understanding how and why management theories and practices evolved gives managers a valuable perspective on current and future events, but managers must also consider their specific situations and adapt the appropriate management theories or techniques.

Management theories are shaped by four forces: technological, economic, social, and political. Technological forces include the knowledge, tools, and actions that profoundly change products or processes, and they generally influence environment assessment, planning, decision making, organization design, human resources, leadership, motivation, and control. Economic forces include economic trends and the availability of resources. These economic forces affect the environment, goals, decision making, planning, human resources management, control, and organization design. Social forces are the values, needs, and norms that affect the behavior of people in a culture, and these forces affect motivation, organization structure, leadership, and human resource management. Political forces include government policies and legal institutions; these forces affect environmental analysis, planning and decision making, organization design, human resource management, and control.

Classical management consists of two schools of thought. Scientific management stresses the objective, scientific study of tasks to improve employee efficiency. Classical organization theory emphasizes the study of the organization as a whole to improve effectiveness and efficiency. The classical management theorists insisted on a scientific basis for the study and practice of management, and they pursued higher productivity. Managers who used classical management techniques were able to effectively manage larger organizations, but the techniques became less practical as organizations and environments became more complex. Also, this approach tended to view employees as cogs in the organizational wheel, and it largely ignored the organizational environment.

Henri Fayol identified six functions of any business organization: (1) technical activities such as production, (2) commercial activities such as buying and selling, (3) financial activities such as finding capital, (4) security activities such as protecting property, (5) accounting activities such as balance sheets, and (6) managerial functions. The managerial functions included planning, organizing, commanding, coordinating, and controlling. Fayol's 14 principles of management were intended as a starting point for managers seeking to run an effective organization, rather than as a comprehensive set of guidelines.

Behavioral management looks at individual and group behavior in organizations. The human relations movement sees employee behavior as responsive to interpersonal processes in a work unit. The behavioral science movement is a multidisciplinary scientific approach to increasing management effectiveness. Behavioral management theorists focused on the importance and the potential of the individual. But they also erroneously believed that their techniques could be applied universally, and they have been accused of overemphasizing human relations in the organization.

Quantitative management relies on mathematics, statistics, and information aids to solve management problems. It includes three subfields: management science, or quantitative techniques that support management decision making; operations management, quantitative methods that help improve operational productivity and efficiency; and management information systems, the use of systems that collect, process, and transmit information. Quantitative management theories help managers make decisions, develop plans, and control operations, but they do not provide a broad framework for effective management, nor do they easily adapt to complex situations. Systems theory portrays organizations as systems functioning within an environment. An organizational system starts with inputs, uses a transformation process to convert inputs to outputs, and relies on feedback to modify the inputs or the process as needed. Systems theory helps managers consider the organization's interrelated parts and the relationship with the environment. Contingency theory rejects the "one best way" idea and focuses on adapting management behavior to each organization's needs and to each situation.

MEETING A MANAGEMENT CHALLENGE AT

THE BODY SHOP

It took Anita Roddick only a few years to expand The Body Shop into an international retail chain. She avoided the financial strain and the risk of rapid expansion by selling franchises (permission to use the name, the operations techniques, and the products) throughout Great Britain, the United States, and more than three dozen other countries. Franchisees and their employees enthusiastically offer information about causes along with the cosmetics—a combination that has been well received by customers. Roddick has accomplished this unique blend of business and social activism by viewing her company as an open system.

On one level, The Body Shop interacts with the environment to buy supplies (inputs), to manufac-

Anita Roddick, founder, The Body Shop

ture skin- and hair-care products (the transformation process), and then to sell them at a profit (outputs). On another level, The Body Shop's transformation process includes raising the social awareness of franchisees, employees, and customers. Roddick provides two forms of inputs: information about social causes and opportunities to volunteer in the community. The transformation process occurs in several ways. When customers visit The Body Shop, they see window displays about social causes and they interact with people in the stores. They leave with more knowledge and often with more determination to make a difference. Similarly, when franchisees and employees do community service work, they become more informed about the world around them and get fired up about working for social change. The output is a better community and, ultimately, a better society, which affects the next transformation cycle.

To make these transformation processes work, Roddick needs people who share her beliefs and enthusiasm for social change. She prefers franchisees who have little business experience, and she screens applicants by asking questions that reveal their personal values. Some typical questions: What's your favorite flower? What heroine do you admire in history or poetry?

Both franchisees and employees can attend training classes at the company school in England. Courses in skin and hair care and in using The Body Shop's products are offered, but other courses cover urban survival, human aging, and the environment. Sales techniques are never mentioned; instead, the school promotes knowledge that is useful to customers and meaningful for employees. When employees go back to their shops, they give customers information instead of a hard sell. Roddick also requires The Body Shop's managers and employees to spend two hours a week on company time in community service or working for a social cause. By participating in such activities, The Body Shop's personnel feel a closer link with the environment.

Roddick's approach to management has had just the effect she hoped to achieve. The Body Shop's employees believe they work for more than company profits. They are earning money to live principled lives, and they are helping educate others about important social issues. Thanks to her honest merchandising and her commitment to society, Roddick has built the world's fastest-growing cosmetics company. With annual sales growth that often exceeds 50 percent, The Body Shop has indeed put a new face on cosmetics.

***You're the Manager*:** You are a new franchisee about to open your first outlet of The Body Shop. You want your employees to project enthusiasm and excitement for store products and for local social causes. But you don't want to overwhelm your customers with "do-gooder" propaganda. Use your knowledge of The Body Shop and of management theories to address the following situations.

Ranking Questions

1. You want to invest in some computerized quantitative management tools to help run your store more efficiently, but you can't afford to immediately buy every program you'd like. Your first priority is to get the store running smoothly, and then you can think about future growth. In what order should you buy the following quantitative management tools?
   a. A queuing theory program to help reduce the time your customers spend waiting in line to check out with their purchases.
   b. A simulation model to help determine how variations in sales or expenses will affect your store's profitability.
   c. An inventory management program to track the number of products in stock and to place reorders so you won't run out of popular items.
   d. A management information system to record the names and addresses of your customers so you can send out notices when you receive products they'd like.
2. The owner of a women's clothing store approaches you and asks you to donate cosmetics for use in an upcoming fashion show. This could

be a good opportunity for publicity but you're not sure it fits with The Body Shop's image. What should you do? Rank these responses from best to worst.

a. Because this store may be able to send you customers, you agree to supply the makeup, but you ask that The Body Shop name not be mentioned.
b. You agree to participate if the fashion show includes a social activism message such as protecting the environment.
c. Fashion is not a concept you want to support, because it encourages people to make unnecessary purchases. You refuse to participate.
d. You agree and ask your employees to do free makeovers for senior citizens in the audience as part of their weekly community service activities.

Multiple-Choice Questions

3. Your store will be open seven days a week and you would like to appoint an assistant manager to supervise operations when you're not there. Although the various management theories offer a wide range of choices for motivating this supervisor, you're not sure which would be most effective and in tune with Roddick's ideas. Which one of these approaches should you choose?
   a. Use Theory Y to show your assistant manager that you believe in her capabilities and that you want to help develop her skills.
   b. Use Gantt's task and bonus system to enable your assistant to earn more if she coaches the other employees about ways to increase sales.
   c. Use Weber's bureaucracy theory to invest your assistant with sizable authority, making her feel important and powerful so she works harder.
   d. Use Emerson's efficiency principles to show your assistant how to work smarter, not harder, so she can cut waste and inefficiency in your absence.
4. One of your employees wants to sell her homemade chocolates in your shop. She argues that social responsibility begins with helping employees improve themselves, and she promises to donate some of her earnings to one of The Body Shop's favorite causes. What is your best response?
   a. If you say yes, then other employees may want to display their handmade items in the store, thus changing the nature of the store. Say no but encourage her to sell chocolates to other employees during her free time, and to donate chocolates or money to any causes she supports.
   b. This is a good way to make money for a cause in which you believe without donating your own money. Say yes and promote her chocolates in the store.
   c. Your employee should enjoy her job and expand her knowledge, so suggest that she find work in a chocolate shop so she can learn more about candy.
   d. Say yes. To encourage all your employees to give money to charity, put on a special "handmade" day to showcase their products in the store window.

Analysis Questions

5. What can Roddick do to counter the effects of entropy?
6. Behavioral management theorists recognized the importance of informal social systems within the organization. Is Roddick actually promoting a kind of social system within The Body Shop? If so, discuss how it affects the organization.
7. How might future social, economic, or political changes around the world help or hurt Roddick's ability to manage The Body Shop in her own way?

Special Project

Roddick is finding that the U.S. public is skeptical about companies that *say* they are environmentally concerned. People in the United States are continually bombarded by such advertising and public relations campaigns, but company actions don't always match company words. As a result, many customers have become cynical about these claims. You have been asked to write a two-page article for the company newsletter about resolving this issue. Should Roddick use the same approach she has in other countries and encourage environmental activism in the United States? Or should she switch to another approach to build credibility and sales more effectively?[80]

KEY TERMS

administrative management (47)
behavioral management (52)
behavioral science movement (55)
bureaucracy (48)
classical management (43)
classical organization theory (46)
closed system (60)
contingency theory (61)
entropy (60)
feedback (60)
hierarchy of needs theory (53)
human relations movement (53)
inputs (59)
management information systems (MIS) (57)
management science (56)
negative entropy (60)
open system (60)
operations management (57)
organizational behavior (55)
outputs (60)
quantitative management (56)
scientific management (43)
subsystem (60)
synergy (60)
system (59)
systems theory (59)
Theory A (62)
Theory J (62)
Theory X (54)
Theory Y (54)
Theory Z (62)
time-and-motion study (44)
transformation process (59)

QUESTIONS

For Review

1. Do experienced managers need to understand the basis and teachings of management theories? Explain your answer.
2. Which forces shape the development of management theories, and what is their impact?
3. What are the major elements in the classical management, behavioral management, and quantitative management perspectives? How are these approaches similar and how are they different?
4. What did Mary Parker Follett contribute to management theory and why is her work considered a bridge between the classical management perspective and the behavioral management approach?
5. When managers apply the contingency theory, how does their practice of management differ from administrative management? From scientific management?

For Analysis

1. Why has Weber's bureaucracy developed a bad reputation? How can modern managers use bureaucratic management to streamline their organizations?
2. Is the scientific management approach still valid? Explain your answer.
3. What influence did early management practices have on the development of contemporary management perspectives such as contingency and systems theory?
4. What impact does the sophistication of computerized management information systems have on the quantitative management approach? On the scientific management approach?
5. Under what circumstances might an organization be considered a closed system?

For Application

1. How could a principal in charge of a local high school apply human relations theories?
2. What are the inputs and outputs of the U.S. Olympic hockey team? What would constitute feedback for the team, and how can this organization achieve synergy?
3. How could the manager of a local bank branch use quantitative management approaches?
4. What lessons of the past has the current U.S. president used to help improve the management of the federal government? Give a specific example.
5. How might Ted Turner, head of Turner Broadcasting System in Atlanta, incorporate Theory Z into his management practices?

KEEPING CURRENT IN MANAGEMENT

Look through recent magazines or newspapers for an article that interviews a manager about the opening of a new manufacturing plant (in any country). Examples might include automotive manufacturing facilities, chemical or drug production plants, food-processing plants, or electronics assembly plants.

1. Does the manager refer to the history of the organization? What is important about this company's past that can help the manager run the new plant more efficiently or effectively? Does the manager mention specific lessons from the past that have led to any changes reflected in the new plant?
2. Are any new management ideas being tested at the plant? Why are they being implemented? What improvements are expected as a result of the new techniques? What do the employees think about the innovation? Are the employees working together with the managers to implement the new ideas?
3. Which management approach (or approaches) does the manager of this plant (or the head of the company) appear to be applying? Why do you think this approach is appropriate? What potential problems might you envision because of this approach? If you think another approach would be more effective, explain why.

SHARPEN YOUR MANAGEMENT SKILLS

Talk about management challenges. Your employer, General Electric, has recently purchased a light-bulb manufacturing plant in Hungary, and you're the new general manager. Even though the Hungarian work force is several steps ahead of those in other Eastern European countries, the people in your plant are generally unfamiliar with the management techniques that GE uses at its plants around the world. GE encourages its employees and managers to work closely as they pursue innovation and efficiency, and these elements of better performance would help your Hungarian plant to compete more effectively in the European market.

The biggest personnel task you face is that most of your employees have been conditioned for years not to take individual initiative. They've come to expect retribution for stepping out of line to suggest new ways of doing things or to criticize current methods. However, you want everyone to innovate, to take risks, and to challenge the status quo, so the factory can attain its goal of improved performance.

- *Decision:* Based on the management theories you've learned in this chapter, how would you solve this problem? Draw up a list of the actions you could take to get people to change their thinking and be willing to suggest and implement new ideas.
- *Communication:* Prepare a brief statement for your first meeting with the Hungarian managers and employees. Limit it to several minutes and assume that introductions have already been made. In your statement, describe why innovation is important, and explain why you feel it's important that factory managers adopt a new management approach.

The self-proclaimed "tightest ship in the shipping business" has sprung a leak in its customer base. United Parcel Service spent so many years concentrating on internal efficiency that archrival Federal Express grabbed the lead on parcel tracking and overnight deliveries. UPS vice president for information services Frank Erbrick must develop a better package-tracking system, focusing on customers as well as on efficiency.

HISTORY

UPS was founded when seven Seattle teenagers with two bicycles and a telephone took the name American Messenger Service in 1917 and started delivering hot meals and messages. They bought a Model T Ford the next year, and soon package deliveries for Seattle retail stores became their main business. The company expanded to other cities, changed its name to United Parcel Service after World War II, and radically changed direction in 1953 by offering two-day air delivery service nationwide and door-to-door parcel pickups for everyone. Next-day air service was offered nationwide by 1982 and now makes up 21 percent of revenues. UPS went global in 1985, operating in more than 180 countries. In 1987 UPS took control of its air operations by paying cash for more than 100 jets worth nearly $2 billion, instantly creating the nation's tenth-largest airline. That year UPS delivered 11 million parcels a day, producing annual profits of $700 million on revenues of $11 billion, which have grown past $13 billion in the 1990s.

ENVIRONMENT

Growth has brought UPS both new kinds of customers and new kinds of competition. When UPS went national in 1953, it broadened its customer base from merchants to all business and residential customers. Its main competition had long been the U.S. Postal Service, but Federal Express exploded onto the scene in 1973 with guaranteed overnight delivery, an ability to track packages en route, and large-volume discounts—all catering to businesses that need to move important documents fast. UPS is now playing an expensive game of catch-up in parcel delivery and tracking capabilities as Federal Express's annual revenues build beyond $7 billion. Technology has provided both companies with another threat: the fax machine, which can transmit documents for pennies over telephone lines. UPS and Federal Express are looking overseas for future market growth, but the huge early investment is depressing profits.

Despite the new threats, UPS has some advantages. It emphasizes economy, rigorous efficiency, and continuous self-criticism and self-improvement; its 1,000 efficiency experts constantly seek to shave seconds off a driver's delivery routine. Moreover, the company motivates employees with high wages and promotions (all the way to top management); in return, employees accept stringent rules on grooming and neatness, strive fervently for efficiency, and often stick with UPS until they retire.

GOALS AND CHALLENGES

Starting as a UPS accounting supervisor, Erbrick rose to his current job as chief of computers and communications and is in the forefront of UPS's goals to focus less on internal issues and more on customer satisfaction. His goal is to blend the old value of efficiency with a new emphasis on customer service; for example, he is monitoring the number of customer calls for help, the amount of time employees spend responding to customer inquiries, and the resulting customer satisfaction. He is also attempting to improve both efficiency and customer service by developing a parcel-tracking system that can outperform Federal Express by quickly finding the origin, destination, contents, and price of any package without referring back to a mainframe computer at headquarters. By giving customers the fast, trackable delivery service they want while improving efficiency in helping customers and using computers, Erbrick hopes to recapture the initiative from Federal Express.

1. How has technological change affected the management of UPS and its predecessor, the American Messenger Service?
2. Can UPS be considered an open or a closed system? Why? How does this affect Erbrick's approach to customer satisfaction?
3. How might UPS learn from past mistakes to deal better with customers and the competition in the future?
4. How might Erbrick apply Theory Y to motivate employees to respond quickly to customer inquiries?

CHAPTER OUTLINE

The Complex Organizational Environment

After studying this chapter, you will be able to

1. Identify the components of the organizational environment and explain their relationship to the organization's boundaries
2. Outline the forces in the general environment and describe how they can affect organizations
3. Discuss the elements in the task environment and explain their impact on organizations
4. Highlight the elements of the internal environment and describe how they influence organizations
5. Identify the characteristics of organizational culture and explain how that culture affects the organization
6. Discuss the frameworks managers use to analyze the dimensions of the organization-environment relationship
7. Explain how managers can respond to environmental pressures by adapting, by influencing the environment, or by using domain shifts

FACING A MANAGEMENT CHALLENGE AT

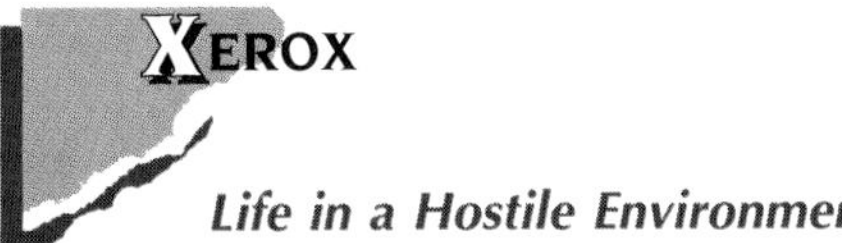

Life in a Hostile Environment

Xerox, one of the great successes in American business, was on the verge of obsolescence not long ago. It had created and dominated the photocopier market for more than a decade but was now being overwhelmed by competitors. *Fortune* magazine called its model 914—the world's first plain-paper copier—"the most successful product ever marketed in America." Then competitors moved quickly to develop new technology, and when Xerox's photocopier patent expired, Japanese companies entered the market with a vengeance. From 1976 to 1982, Xerox's market share plummeted from 82 to 41 percent. Even worse, some analysts thought computers would soon create the "paperless office," making copiers extinct. The future of Xerox looked bleak despite its billion-dollar sales.

Copiers by Canon, Minolta, Ricoh, and Sharp were selling everywhere at prices roughly equal to Xerox's manufacturing cost. Xerox managers suspected these companies were dumping their copiers in the U.S. market at prices below production costs in order to gain market share. But when they examined competitors' methods and products, they learned these firms were actually manufacturing copiers at half Xerox's cost—and the new copiers also were more reliable.

Xerox CEO David Kearns decided to respond by containing costs and focusing on quality and customer satisfaction. However, the company's traditional emphasis on profits was ingrained. Senior managers were satisfied with continuing big profits, and technicians were accustomed to keeping service calls as short as possible, rather than fixing the problem right the first time. Changing such attitudes among 100,000 employees on several continents would be complicated and time-consuming.

The quality of parts bought from suppliers was another difficult problem. The prevailing wisdom held that working with a large number of suppliers promoted competition and ensured the best price for the purchaser. Xerox dealt with 5,000 suppliers, nine times as many as other copier firms. Yet the Japanese companies seemed to be getting better-quality parts. Xerox had been relying on its sophisticated quality-control system to find defects, but even after rejecting 8 percent of its parts as defective at the receiving dock, Xerox still found 5,000 rejects per million on the assembly line. That was too high to be competitive, and Kearns was determined to improve parts quality. However, he knew that his suppliers might be suspicious of the company's new quality emphasis because of their fear that improving quality would cost them money.

Xerox faced challenges near and far. On the horizon was the threat of the "paperless office." Overseas competitors and quality parts threatened organizational performance. Further, years of success had lulled Xerox people into a feeling of complacency. How could David Kearns and his successor Paul Allaire respond to the threat of the paperless office? What was the best way to improve the quality of purchased parts without sending costs (or suppliers) through the roof? And how could these top managers inspire Xerox people to embrace the new emphasis on quality?[1]

CHAPTER OVERVIEW

To manage Xerox most effectively, David Kearns and Paul Allaire needed a thorough understanding of the dynamics of their organizational environment. This chapter opens with an overview of the organizational environment, its importance to management, and its three components. Next comes a closer view of the external environment, which includes the general environment and the task environment. Then the elements within the internal environment and their influence on the organization are examined. After a look at the organization-environment relationship, the chapter ends with a review of some ways in which managers can respond to the environment.

THE ORGANIZATIONAL ENVIRONMENT

organizational environment All forces with the potential to influence the organization and its performance

internal environment Forces inside the organization that can influence the organization and its performance

external environment Forces outside the organization that influence the ability to achieve organizational goals

general environment The part of the external environment composed of forces that have a general influence on the organization

task environment The part of the external environment that includes forces with a direct effect on the organization

Managers in all types of organizations must consider how the environment affects their decisions and activities so that they will be able to react to potential threats, recognize opportunities, and plan for the future. If they ignore their environment, they run the risk of failing to achieve their goals. The **organizational environment** can help or hurt management's efforts to attain organizational goals because it consists of all the forces that influence the organization.

The overall organizational environment is composed of several environments (see Exhibit 3.1). The **internal environment** contains the forces inside the organization, including owners and shareholders, the board of directors, employees, and the organizational culture. In contrast, the **external environment** contains all the forces outside the organization. To distinguish between general forces and more direct forces, it is helpful to further divide the external environment. The **general environment** is the portion of the external environment that contains the external forces that have a more general influence on the organization. These include politicolegal, economic, technological, sociocultural, and international forces. The **task environment,** also known as the *operating environment* or the *specific environment,* contains the external forces that have a more direct impact on the organization, including customers, competitors, suppliers, labor supply, regulators, and partners. However, the forces in the general environment can sometimes have a direct influence on the organization, and the forces in the task

EXHIBIT 3.1

The Organizational Environment

The organization's environment is composed of the internal environment and the external environment. Within the external environment are the forces of the general environment and the forces of the task environment.

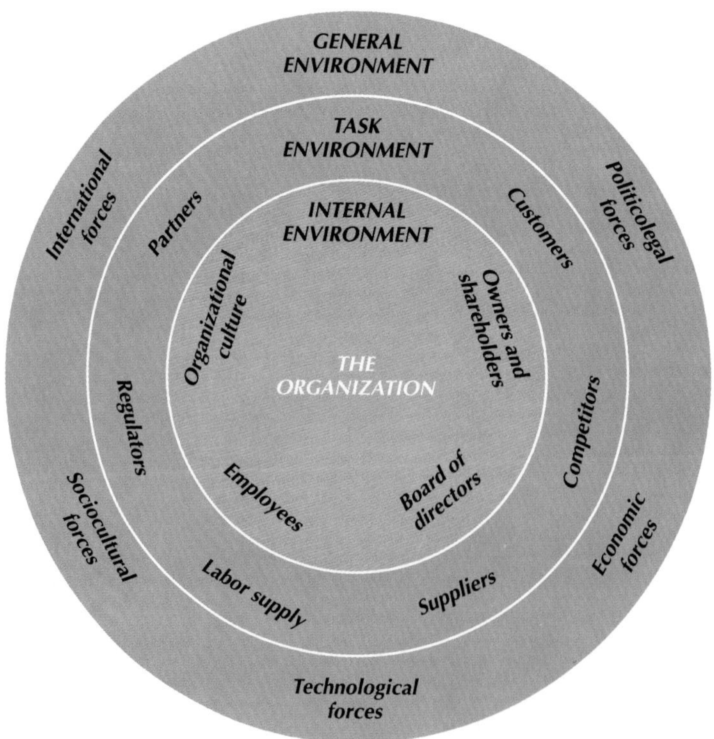

environment can sometimes have a less-direct influence. Environmental forces usually act in concert rather than independently, and their combined influence can have a major impact on organizational performance.[2]

From a systems view of the organization, as explained in Chapter 2, an organization interacts with the various forces in its environment in several ways: by receiving inputs, returning outputs, and using feedback to modify inputs and the transformation process. Thus the organization does not operate in a vacuum but must interact with its environment in order to function. Of course, the interaction may be more extensive in one organization and less extensive in another, and the impact can vary over time.[3] Consider the experiences of two organizations.

When the managers of this Agfa Minilab film processing outlet in Prague, Czechoslovakia, make business decisions, they must consider a variety of forces in the internal environment as well as the external environment. Among the internal forces that may affect this service business are the employees, the owners, and the organizational culture. Among the external forces that can influence the outlet's performance are politicolegal, economic, technological, and international forces, as well as customers, suppliers, competitors, and the labor supply.

Vipul Jain, director of Kale Consultants in Bombay, India, recognized an opportunity in his organization's task environment: no one was addressing the administrative problems faced by hospitals in developing countries. To take advantage of this opportunity, Jain asked his programmers to develop a special software package to help hospital administrators in non-Western countries manage patient billing, inventory, and other functions. By looking carefully at his external environment and using the employees in his internal environment, Jain built a business around satisfying customer needs.[4]

At one time, managers at Seiko, the Japan-based manufacturer, were feeling a lot of pressure from competitors in their task environment: Swiss watchmakers were famous for extremely accurate mechanical watches. Seiko managers decided to finance a concentrated research-and-development effort that would help the company overcome the Swiss competition. Seiko employees, part of the internal environment, worked furiously to perfect quartz wristwatch technology, an approach that rivaled Swiss accuracy. Although quartz clocks had been available for years, the timekeeping mechanisms were typically large and bulky. By using technology to shrink the quartz works to wristwatch size, Seiko was able to make a stylishly slim and extremely accurate watch that rivaled Swiss products. On the basis of this technological breakthrough, Seiko zoomed past its Swiss competitors to become the world's largest maker of timepieces.[5]

However, by the 1980s, an examination of Seiko's task environment revealed that the timepiece market was slowing down. To weather this slump, Seiko managers wanted to lessen the company's dependence on watch and clock sales, so they broadened the organization's scope to include a range of information-related equipment.[6] Like all organizations, Seiko's fortunes have been affected by a variety of environmental forces: employees from the internal environment; customers and competitors from the task environment; and economic, technological, and international forces from the general environment. Because Seiko managers were alert to environmental forces, they were able to sidestep problems and capitalize on opportunities.

The Seiko example also reveals how the boundaries dividing one environment from another are less than distinct. Seiko employees are part of the internal environment, yet they developed the quartz technology, an advance that can be viewed as part of the general environment. Further, people can be employees of an organization (part of the internal environment) and at the same time consumers (part of the task environment and thus outside the organization's boundaries). In the systems view of the organization, managers establish the boundaries that separate the internal and the external environments of the organization when they define the organization's inputs and outputs, its transformation process, and the mechanisms for receiving feedback.[7]

As the managers at Kale Consultants and Seiko know, the organizational environment can create opportunities as well as challenges. But to keep up with today's fast pace and diverse pressures, managers must spend more time now than ever untangling problems caused by external forces and watching for early warning signs about future opportunities. Because it is important to understand the nature and impact of the forces at work in the organizational environment, the following sections examine each environment more closely.[8]

THE EXTERNAL ENVIRONMENT

The forces in the external environment are outside the organization's boundaries and therefore cannot be directly controlled by management. Yet these forces can have a major effect on the organization's ability to achieve its goals. So that they can analyze their impact and respond appropriately, managers at all levels must be aware of the forces in their general and task environments.[9]

The General Environment

The forces within the general environment, including politicolegal, economic, technological, sociocultural, and international forces, have a broad general impact on the organization. Although these forces do not always have a direct influence on the organization's daily activities, they are important for several reasons. First, forces in the general environment can evolve into significant trends with far-reaching effects. A good example is the increasing interest in protecting natural resources and preserving ecological balance. Bowing to public pressure, McDonald's in 1990 abandoned plastic foam hamburger boxes in favor of paper wrappers that may cause fewer waste-disposal problems. Although the foam boxes had been in use for 15 years, McDonald's managers were concerned that environmentally conscious customers would be alienated if the chain didn't switch.[10]

Second, conditions created by forces in the general environment can produce an overall climate that the organization must consider. For example, foodmaker H.J. Heinz did well when inflation allowed it to pass along costs without hurting profits, but when inflation slowed, so did real sales growth. At the same time, Heinz found that a new emphasis on healthy life-styles was changing the food-buying habits of many people. To cope, Heinz cut its costs by 2 percent but diverted the cost savings to build new sales momentum through more efficient product development and promotion for items such as Weight Watchers foods. Finally, forces in the general environment sometimes become more direct over time, influencing the task environment. That's what happened to Marriott when the U.S. economy turned sour in 1990. When the economy was booming, chairman J. W. Marriott went on a hotel-building spree that expanded the chain's room capacity to 150,000 rooms. Then forces in the general environment began to close in on Marriott's task environment. As a result, unfavorable economic forces left consumers feeling too strapped to travel and the supply of investment financing for Marriott hotels dried up.[11]

politicolegal forces Governmental policies, legal policies, laws, and institutions that influence people and organizations

Politicolegal Forces

Politicolegal forces consist of governmental and legal policies, laws, and institutions at the national, state, and local levels. Included in this category are legislation, regulation, taxation, legal decisions, and political policies (see Exhibit 3.2). Politicolegal forces define the business climate by the constraints they impose and by the activities they permit. For example, when the Americans with Disabilities Act went into effect in 1992, many organizations had to review their facilities to be certain that disabled customers were assured ready access. California has had a similar law for many years, prompting Bank of America to install automated teller machines that can be easily operated by people in wheelchairs as well as by people who walk up to the machine. Politicolegal forces also affect the way organizations protect inventions: the patent process for biotechnological products has become so complex that businesses must wait 30 months or more for approval, slowing product introductions.[12]

Of course, politicolegal forces aren't confined to the United States. In Chile, the policies of previous administrations still cause headaches for Alejandro Noemi, the chief executive of the giant state copper company Corporacion Nacional del Cobre de Chile (Codelco). Noemi can't modify Codelco's large and unwieldy organization structure without a change in Chile's constitution, and he depends on the government's Finance Ministry for investment money.[13] In Hong Kong, organizations are concerned about political and legal changes that may occur when the U.K. Crown Colony comes under the control of the People's Republic of China after 1997.[14]

For businesses that operate outside their home countries, politicolegal forces can be felt in the form of trade restrictions or governmental insistence on local suppliers or local materials. Political forces can sometimes result in an organization losing money or property, during a revolution, for example, or because of a change in regime. But politics can also create opportunities. For instance, General Hau Pei-tsun, the premier of Taiwan, is spending $303 billion to revamp the country's transportation, communications, housing, and energy facilities. His "Don't Buy Japan" policy is aimed at avoiding Japanese dominance and his "Buy America" policy is aimed at improving sticky trade relations with the United States. Thus U.S. suppliers have the opportunity to win some major contracts. De Leuw, Cather International, a Washington, D.C. firm, has already

New Iowa tax to affect advertising

By Steven W. Colford

Most everyone agrees Iowa's new 4% tax on "consulting services" will affect advertising. But no one seems to be sure exactly how.

The confusion stems from the vagueness of the ...

pushed through the Democrat-controlled Legislature a measure to extend the 4% state sales tax to dating services, pool-cleaning, taxidermy and consulting services. But late last week ...

Writing Ads to Usher In a New Era in South Africa

Herdbuoys sees itself as uniquely positioned to reach the black public.

By JUDITH D. SCHWARTZ

JOHANNESBURG

It is 5 P.M. on Tuesday, March 17, the historic turning point for South ...

High Court Rebuffs States' Effort To Tax Direct Marketers' Sales

Bill to Codify Baby Bell Order Gains in House

By MARY LU CARNEVALE

WASHINGTON — A House panel approved a bill ...

Immigration act eases foreign transfers

By MARK BECKER

EXHIBIT 3.2

Politicolegal Forces at Work

Organizations are confronted with a wide variety of politicolegal forces in the general environment. These forces tend to restrict and define the organization's activities but also have an impact on the task environment.

won a consulting contract to oversee mass transit construction, and other firms are eying projects such as road construction and commercial incineration.[15] Taiwan's political position on these contracts also affects the economic forces inside the country.

Economic Forces

economic forces The availability of resources and the broad economic trends that affect the organization

Economic forces involve the availability or scarcity of resources and the general economic trends that affect the organization. On the broadest level, economic forces are related to national economic systems. Some nations, including the People's Republic of China and Cuba, have centrally planned economies controlled by the state. In these countries, the government sets the rules for business ownership, manufacturing output, supply purchasing, pricing, and other economic activities.[16] In contrast, the United States and most other countries have adopted a capitalist economy with its free market system, so businesses and other organizations buy and sell according to market values set by supply and demand. An increasing number of countries with centrally planned economies are changing their economic rules and incorporating aspects of free market economies such as private ownership of businesses.[17]

Consider the management challenges that the unification of Germany presented. Previously, East Germany had a centrally planned economy and business managers did not need to consider market concepts such as profit and customer service. In 1990, the third-largest bank in West Germany, Commerzbank, began to establish East German branches. The bank decided to staff its East German branches with West German employees for at least 18 months until East German employees could be trained to understand the bank's service and business standards.[18]

Inflation, interest rates, unemployment, per capita income, consumer purchasing power, and currency exchange rates are other key economic forces that managers must monitor. When inflation runs high, businesses pay more for supplies, and many raise their prices to cover these costs. If inflation runs so high as to threaten economic stability, some governments impose price and wage guidelines or controls that affect all organizations because of their impact on the cost and availability of supplies and on employee and manager salaries. High interest rates can have a disastrous effect on businesses large and small because they cannot afford to borrow for expansion or even to replace equipment, and those that do borrow face higher payments. Eventually, economic pressures can force organizations completely out of existence. For example, many small companies and a few industrial giants in Japan went bankrupt in the early 1990s because of a sustained run-up in interest rates. And Britain's recession was blamed for driving 890 firms out of business every week during the first half of 1991.[19]

Technological Forces

technological forces The knowledge, techniques, and activities that lead to profound changes in products or processes

Technological forces include the expertise, procedures, and systems used by organizations to make profound changes in the transformation process and in goods or services. Fueled by scientific research and industrial breakthroughs, technological forces define new industries and provide organizations with tools and opportunities to compete more effectively. For example, Xerox's competitors used technological breakthroughs to create new copiers that rivaled Xerox copier quality yet were lower in cost. As another example, industrial technology developed by Nucor, a U.S. minimill steel producer, allows the company to produce sheet steel from thin slabs rather than from the conventional fat slabs. This new technology gives Nucor nearly twice the efficiency of the typical mill, and the advance may change the steel industry in the United States or throughout the world.[20]

Computer technology has led to major advances in communications, entertainment, medicine, and transportation as well as to breakthroughs in product design, engineering, production, assembly, and supply. With the latest generation of personal computers, managers can manipulate and interpret mountains of data ranging from financial results to information about consumers and competitors. Computerized communication networks help organizations transact business instantaneously and create new opportunities such as round-the-clock international financial trading.[21] Several years ago, the Internal Revenue Service approved electronic tax filing, and H & R Block recognized that the combination of these technological and politicolegal forces created an attractive opportunity. Co-founder Henry Bloch started a new program called Rapid Refund, which gave customers an instant loan for the amount of their refund when the company filed their taxes electronically. Although competitors jumped in, Bloch's fast reaction to the technological forces gave him 65 percent of this market.[22]

Technological forces have changed the way Boeing designs and manufactures aircraft. Boeing designers and production experts working on the new 777 jet, which is scheduled to enter service in 1995, used a computer-aided design program to draft the plane's components and then to simulate assembly. This advanced technology reduced the possibility of design errors and ensured that parts such as the floor structure shown here fit together properly when produced.

Technological forces can also pose challenges for organizations. To avoid being caught with obsolete equipment or systems and to gain a competitive edge, organizations must stay abreast of developments in technology. For example, when videocassette recorders were introduced, Sony's Beta technology vied with JVC's VHS technology for adoption as the industry standard. Manufacturers and movie makers had to decide which standard to adopt, and the longer-playing VHS format eventually became the dominant technology. Sony's Beta technology never achieved the same widespread acceptance and soon faded as a competitive format. The same standardization race is going on in computer operating systems, high-definition television, laser discs, and other areas.[23]

Sociocultural Forces

Sociocultural forces are defined as the values, attitudes, needs, and demographic characteristics of the societies where the organization operates. The values of a culture are the beliefs that shape individual and group attitudes. Values and attitudes mold people's behavior and influence the needs and wants that they seek to fulfill through interaction with organizations. For example, the values and attitudes of residents of the Canadian province of Quebec have had a major impact on organizations throughout the country. In the 1970s, a nationalist movement to preserve French language and customs swept Quebec. Pressure from constituents led to the government designating French as the primary language in the province. Ultimately, Canada became officially bilingual (English and French). As a result of this shift in values and attitudes and the subsequent political action, organizations are required to print product packages, signs, and other items in both languages. Another sociocultural force, the shift in attitudes toward healthier eating, is sending restaurateurs back to the kitchen for new or modified products. For instance, Arby's has introduced low-fat turkey, roast chicken, and roast beef sandwiches with fewer than 300 calories, and the chain has also started offering salads.[24]

sociocultural forces The values, attitudes, needs, and demographic characteristics of the societies in which the organization operates

Demographic characteristics, another aspect of sociocultural forces, describe the population and its behavior in regions where organizations function. In the United States, major demographic trends include the aging of the population, a declining birth rate, more women in the work force, and a growing minority population (see Exhibit 3.3). For example, by the year 2000, nearly 15 percent of the population will be over 65. These seniors will live longer and will require different products as they age. As an example of a response to this demographic shift, Community Memorial Hospital in Toms River, New Jersey, established an Aging Resource Center that serves as the local hub of an expanding information network for seniors.[25]

At the other end of the demographic spectrum, the shrinking birth rate means fewer high school graduates, a change that colleges must address. Adelphi University in New York recognized the impact of this sociocultural force and targeted adults with "Adelphi-On-Wheels," an outreach program of teaching business courses on commuter trains. Because of the lower birth rate, many businesses that depend on young adults to take entry-level jobs are unable to find enough employees, so the sociocultural forces of the general environment also have a significant impact on the task and internal environments. The demographic trend toward more women in the work force prompted the top leaders of the Girl Scouts to rethink the needs of working mothers with daughters too young to join the Brownies. By examining the environment more closely, Girl Scout executives learned that five-year-olds were ready to take part in small-group activities. So the Girl Scouts created an entirely new Scout category called Daisy Scouts, which now serves 150,000 members.[26]

International Forces

international forces Factors originating outside the organization's home country that can affect how the organization interacts with people and organizations

Forces that originate outside the organization's home country and that influence interactions with people and organizations are called **international forces.** Companies that do business in other countries feel the effects of many international forces, including fluctuations in foreign exchange rates and local and global competition. Moreover, companies may buy materials less expensively from foreign suppliers, or they may assemble products in other countries and then sell the finished products around the world.[27]

International forces also have a major impact on organizations that operate in the United States. For instance, Asea Brown Boveri (an electrical engineering giant based in Switzerland), Philips N.V. (an electronics firm based in the Netherlands), and Northern Telecom (a telecommunications corporation based in Canada) all have significant operations in the United States and all compete

EXHIBIT 3.3

The Growing U.S. Minority Population

The minority population in the United States is expected to grow much more rapidly than the rest of the population, with Hispanics the fastest-growing segment. This sociocultural trend influences the labor supply, customer purchasing patterns, and the ways organizations reach out to their customers.

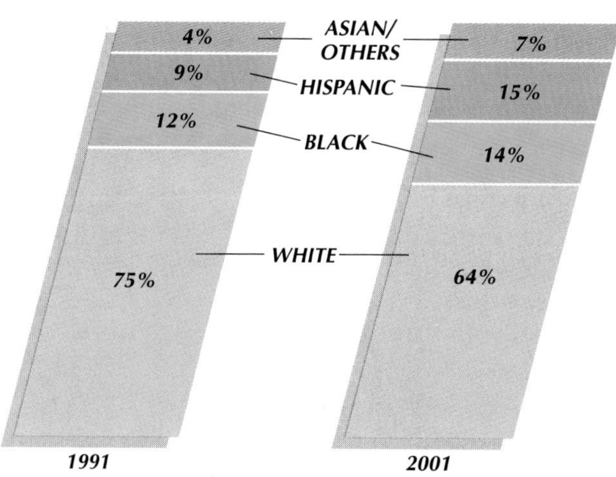

head-on with U.S. companies. Further, U.S. companies that want to operate abroad face many challenges, including the power of the newly unified European Community.[28] Chapter 5 examines global management in greater detail.

Managers of public-sector organizations such as Thomas C. Gooch School in Dallas closely monitor the sociocultural forces that influence the community's demographic makeup and needs. Key trends monitored by school officials include the birth rate, immigration patterns, and population shifts. As a result of sociocultural forces, many schools now serve more diverse student populations.

The Task Environment

In contrast to the forces of the general environment that exert general pressure on organizations, the forces of the task environment more directly influence the organization and its ability to achieve goals.[29] Six forces make up the task environment: customers, competitors, suppliers, labor supply, regulators, and partners. See Exhibit 3.4 for a view of the task environment for Toys 'R' Us.

Customers

Customers and constituents are key forces in the task environment because their purchase or use of goods and services determines whether the organization succeeds or fails. "The purpose of a business is to create and keep a customer," notes marketing guru Theodore Levitt, and this obviously holds true for for-profit and not-for-profit organizations alike.[30] Because customers are not one homogeneous group, organizations need to stay close to their customers to understand their needs and wants—and how these change over time.[31]

Organizations get customer feedback from a variety of sources. One trend gaining favor is the idea of involving customers in the design of the product or service. Advanced-technology companies such as Hewlett-Packard seek out

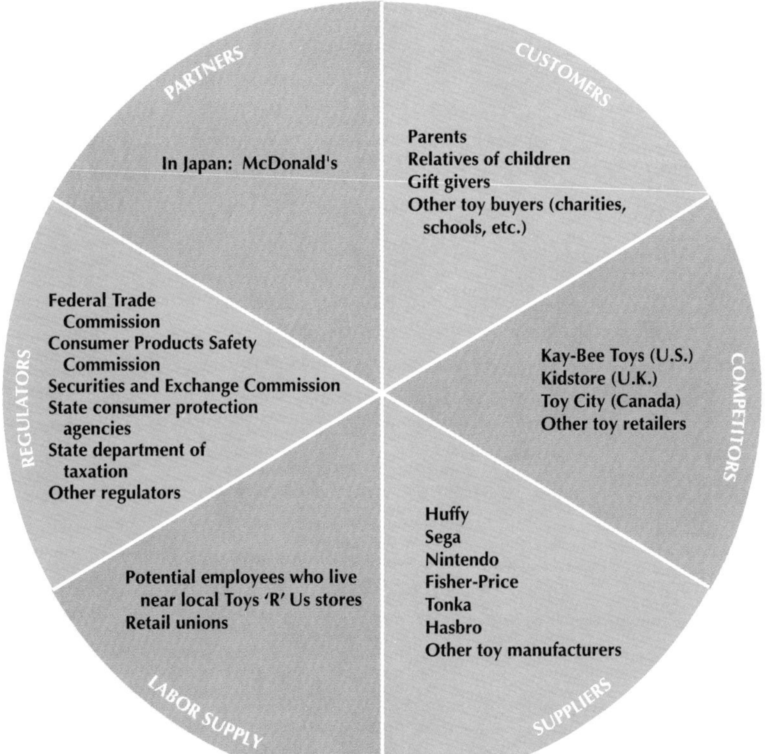

EXHIBIT 3.4

The Toys 'R' Us Task Environment

Because discount retailer Toys 'R' Us operates globally, the task environment that CEO Charles Lazarus faces is varied and challenging.

The U.S. Postal Service uses time-based competition to compete with United Parcel Service, Federal Express, and other delivery services. Express Mail began on a test basis in the early 1970s, and today, customers can use Express Mail for next-day delivery to most U.S. cities and for 2–3 day delivery to 130 countries. Despite fierce competition, the U.S.P.S. has built its yearly Express Mail volume to 58 million pieces.

"user groups" to suggest and evaluate new-product innovations; office furniture manufacturer Steelcase invites customers to participate in product design.[32]

Competitors

Competitors are other organizations that provide goods or services to the same set of customers or that vie for the same resources needed by the organization. Most organizations have at least one competitor (usually more than one) and must consider all potential competitors. For instance, Xerox faces a number of strong competitors in the market for photocopiers. In recent years, *time-based competition* has become a key competitive force. Time-based competition involves delivering what the customer wants on the customer's timetable—and faster than any competitor can deliver. Among the organizations using time-based competition are Federal Express, Domino's Pizza, Sony, Benetton, and Sharp.[33]

Clearly, managers must monitor what their competitors are doing in the way of pricing, products, customer service, supply sources, and other areas. But because competitors are crossing national borders in greater numbers to vie for customers and resources around the world, competitive forces have become extremely tricky to monitor and predict. Methods managers can use to gather information about competitors include going to industry meetings, reading trade publications, checking annual reports, and scanning advertising. By cataloging and analyzing competitive moves, managers can develop plans for competing more effectively.[34]

competitors Rival organizations that provide goods or services to the same set of customers or that vie for the same resources

suppliers People and organizations who furnish the resources that other organizations use to produce goods and services

Suppliers

Suppliers are individuals and organizations who provide the resources used as inputs to produce goods and services. Suppliers are a critical part of the task environment because organizations must have a continuous source of resources in order to serve their customers. A good working relationship with suppliers can also help an organization achieve its goals. For example, when Mazda introduced the wildly popular Miata model, it was able to launch the product early because Mazda's suppliers cooperated with the designers to ensure that all parts fit correctly without the time and the expense of making prototypes.[35]

Moreover, suppliers provide nonphysical resources such as funding, information, and employees. Banks, stockholders, and private investors are some sources of capital for the organization. Magazines, newspapers, and researchers are among the organization's information sources. Employment agencies and college placement offices are two suppliers of human resources.

When organizations such as Maxtor, a computer disk-drive manufacturer in San Jose, California, require sophisticated parts, they may buy from four or five suppliers so that they can be assured of a constant supply. On the other hand, Maxtor buys some customized parts from just one supplier. Dealing with a single source allows the organization to have more control over its materials and may even lower the cost. But when an organization relies on a single source, it can face several risks. If the supplier does not deliver on time, suffers from a shortage of materials, or goes out of business, the organization could have a hard time meeting the needs of its own customers.[36]

labor supply The people who may potentially be employed by an organization

Labor Supply

The people who are available to be hired are collectively known as the **labor supply.** The labor supply is a critical factor in the task environment because it is becoming harder to attract, train, and retain employees who can competently serve customers. In part, this scarcity of labor stems from intense competition among public and private sector organizations that want to hire from the same labor pool. Moreover, demographic trends in the general environment have a lot to do with the people who are in the labor supply at any given time. For example, the number of people aged 18 to 29 who normally take entry-level jobs is dropping, and nearly 20 percent of all 18-year-olds are functionally illiterate. Organizations react to such circumstances in various ways. When U.S. hospitals could not hire locally, many recruited nurses from the Philippines and from Ireland. To cope with the shortage of entry-level employees, Target Stores hires senior citizens and also hires people with disabilities to handle certain store functions.[37]

Labor unions can be a major influence on the labor supply. In the United States, labor unions are confronting for-profit and not-for-profit organizations on a variety of issues, including affordable medical benefits. Of course, many organizations work closely with organized labor on vital issues in the task environment. When General Motors built an experimental factory-of-the-future in Saginaw, Michigan, to test new automated manufacturing technology, managers worked closely with the United Auto Workers to reach key decisions such as the number of employees needed to run the facility.[38] Chapter 13 examines human resources and labor relations in more detail.

Regulators

Regulators include governmental agencies, officials, and special interest groups who create, influence, or enforce legal guidelines and policies that affect organizational activities. Although politicolegal forces are part of the general environment, regulators are part of the task environment because it is their influence that directly determines what immediate impact the legislative and regulatory guidelines will have on the organization. Regulatory agencies and special interest groups are two key regulators in the task environment.

regulators Governmental agencies, their representatives, and groups who influence or enforce guidelines that affect the organization's actions

In the United States, a variety of regulatory agencies monitor how organizations comply with government regulations at the national, state, and local level.

The labor supply is a major force in the task environment of this Ford assembly plant in Kansas City, Missouri. Depending on the demand for the Tempo cars and pickup models produced in this plant, managers may hire additional employees, or they may seek employees with specialized skills. Employees at this plant are represented by the United Auto Workers, and the union can influence how Ford managers handle a variety of personnel issues, including salary, benefits, and work assignments.

EXHIBIT 3.5

How Regulation Affects U.S. Banks

Depending on the industry in which they operate, organizations have to comply with many regulations set or administered by a wide variety of federal regulatory agencies. Depending on whether they hold state or national charters, banks may be regulated by four federal agencies in addition to the state banking commissions in states where they operate.

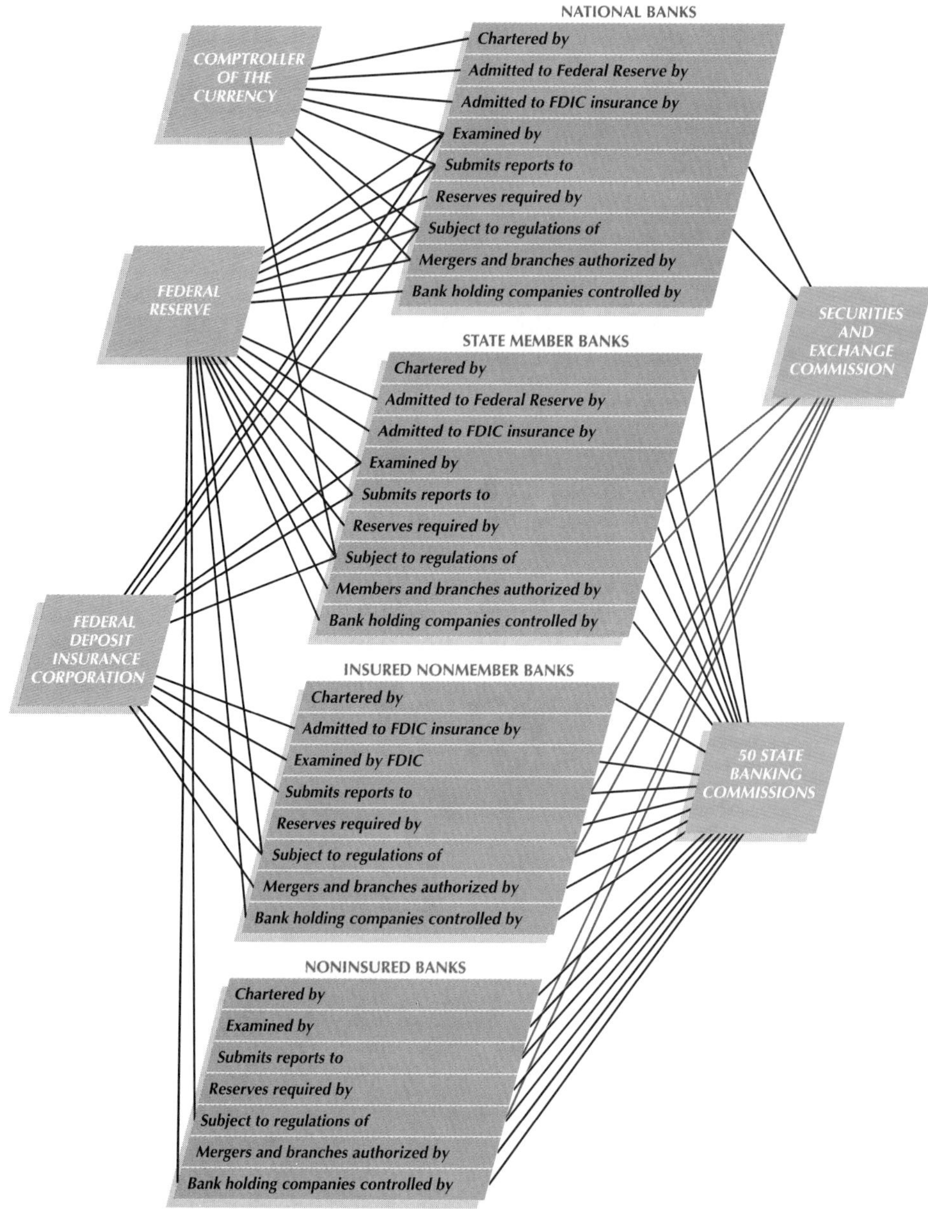

National regulators include the Environmental Protection Agency (EPA), the Occupational Safety and Health Administration (OSHA), the Food and Drug Administration (FDA), and the Internal Revenue Service (IRS). Consider the regulatory situation for the New York Stock Exchange, where chairman William H. Donaldson wants to expand to meet global competition. He would like to invite overseas companies to list their firms on the New York Stock Exchange, but this is against the regulations enforced by the Securities and Exchange Commission (SEC). To move forward, Donaldson will have to convince the SEC and Congress to change the rules.[39] Organizations face many regulatory restrictions around the world, although the trend is toward easing regulation in some industries such as airline transportation and banking (see Exhibit 3.5). For example, Spain is deregulating its financial system, easing restrictions on bank competition. Under deregulation, Britain-based Barclays Bank has been allowed to open branches in Spanish cities, and two large Spanish banks have been permitted to merge so that they can compete more effectively.[40]

Another dimension of regulatory forces involves special interest groups. **Special interest groups** are not formed by the government; they consist of individuals or organizations who voluntarily work together to influence other organizations. Special interest groups may develop on the state, local, national, or international level, depending on their aims and on the organizations they seek to influence. Although these groups have no official authority, they can rally public opinion and pressure governments or businesses into making or changing rules and practices. For example, since 1985, hundreds of special interest groups around the world have been boycotting war toys. Groups such as the New England War Resister's League, Action for Children's Television, and the War Toy Disarmament Project are using petitions, letter writing, lobbying, and publicity to persuade legislators to restrict the sale of realistically detailed toy guns and to dissuade manufacturers, stores, and purchasers from supporting war toys. The groups have succeeded in pressuring several cities and the state of California into banning the sale of realistic-looking toy guns.[41]

special interest groups Groups of people who band together to influence the actions of organizations

Partners

Frequently, the task environment of an organization includes its **partners,** organizations that work together formally or informally so all can pursue their goals more effectively. Organizations seek temporary or permanent partners for a variety of reasons. First, partners can share the risk of a particular project or product. Second, partners can pool their resources and accomplish together what they cannot do alone. Third, partners may have special knowledge of a technology, an industry, or a country where the organization needs to introduce a new product or enter a new market.[42] For example, New York–based Corning Glass has teamed up with European partner Ciba-Geigy to form Ciba-Corning Diagnostics, a firm that designs and produces blood and fluid analysis products for the international market. Although partnerships have many advantages, they also pose potential problems. After some time, organizations may find that their goals have shifted and no longer fit the partnership; or one partner may lose control of its technology or process to the other.[43]

partners Two or more organizations that work together in a formal or informal arrangement that helps them achieve goals effectively

THE INTERNAL ENVIRONMENT

The forces in the external environment can have a strong influence on the organization. But managers must also monitor the impact of forces inside the organization's boundaries. The internal environment contains four forces: the owners and shareholders, the board of directors, the employees, and the organizational culture. This section examines the influence that each force exerts on the organization.

Owners and Shareholders

In a small business, the owner or owners are important influences because they are so involved with all aspects of the organization and its operation. As an organization grows and requires more money, owners often sell shares of the business to other individuals or to other organizations. These investors are

SOCIAL RESPONSIBILITY AND ETHICS

Toeing the Line in a Tough Environment

The New York College of Podiatric Medicine and Foot Clinics of New York had been running a deficit for two years when Louis L. Levine was appointed president in 1991. Levine faced a laundry list of troublesome forces in both the general and the task environments that would continue to make life difficult for the school and clinic. At the top of the list was the dilemma of whether to stay in its Harlem location or to find a new, perhaps less harsh environment that offered more financial promise.

When he joined the college, state funding was in jeopardy because of New York's continuing budget crisis. Moreover, enrollment was dwindling, and the college's facilities needed renovation. Although the clinic had treated 50,000 foot ailments during the previous year and was a major local employer, the institution was little-known outside its Harlem base. There had been opportunities over the years to leave the Harlem site, but the school had always chosen to stay to support the community. In this environment, how could Levine maintain the college's commitments to the community while pulling the school out of the red?

The New York College of Podiatric Medicine is the oldest of seven U.S. institutions that specialize in foot-care training. Although the college had trained one-quarter of the podiatrists who practice in the United States, it lacked the visibility that Levine believed would bring it funding. The school also had a tiny endowment and scholarship fund, yet it operated a foot clinic that never turned patients away, which was a boon to the Harlem community but an expense for the college. The college maintained the clinic because of its commitment to social responsibility, but the clinic's budget gap had been subsidized by college revenues, which were also rapidly dwindling.

The subsidy wasn't the only reason for the school's financial problems. Levine saw sociocultural forces as another cause: he believed that many qualified applicants who would have entered medical and professional schools during the 1980s chose business rather

known as *shareholders*. Large corporations may sell shares to thousands of shareholders, but smaller businesses typically sell shares to only a few. To protect their interests, corporate shareholders elect a board of directors to oversee the organization's management. But shareholders sometimes demand a larger share of the profits and a greater voice in corporate affairs. Consider the plight of Philip Greer, whose investment firm purchased a 20 percent stake of Discovery Toys of Martinez, California, in 1980. Ten years later, the company was selling $70 million worth of educational toys annually. Although Greer held a significant share of the company, he had not received dividends on his investment. Moreover, he was upset that the director he had placed on Discovery's board of directors seemed to be barred from fully participating in company activities. So Greer filed suit against the CEO, Lane Nemeth, seeking dividend payments and more clout over Discovery's management. Soon afterward, the suit was settled out of court. Discovery agreed to repurchase Greer's shares, and in exchange he dropped his suit.[44]

Board of Directors

Corporate shareholders elect a board of directors to represent them in supervising the organization's management and overall performance. A board can appoint or remove top organization managers and approve major goals and plans. Many not-for-profit organizations also have directors or trustees who work in similar fashion, supervising management and guiding the organization's direction, policies, and priorities. A corporate board consists of two types of directors: inside directors, who are full-time organization employees in top management roles, and outside directors, who are not employed by this organization than health care. So the New York College's applications and enrollment declined, and by 1989 the college was losing money. Now that trend seems to be turning around: the college's 1991 applications were up 49 percent over 1990, leading to a larger enrollment and more revenue.

That's a good start, but Levine needs considerably more financial support. He's talking with charitable foundations about obtaining grant money. He's also meeting with school alumni and asking Harlem business leaders for support. If he can find additional classroom space, Levine will be able to bring in more revenue by enlarging enrollment. On the clinic side, the president has come to an agreement with health insurer Group Health Inc. (GHI) to become one of its approved health-care providers. Levine hopes to bring in more revenue by signing agreements such as this, a move that will help the clinic become self-supporting.

Because he was formerly the vice president of governmental affairs for Empire Blue Cross/Blue Shield and held positions in New York State government, Levine has many connections that will help him gather information about the environment and respond appropriately. Of the college, Levine says, "I want to make this the Harvard of the podiatric profession." For Harlem, having the Harvard of podiatry in its midst could give a big boost to local pride and perhaps loosen the purse strings of other organizations interested in the school. But to give the school that kind of prestige and visibility, Levine will first have to educate people about podiatry, about the role that the New York College plays in the profession, and about its socially responsible contributions to the local community. His goals are lofty, but with the college's history, the changes in the environment, and Levine's management skills, he is well positioned to achieve results.

What's Your Opinion?

1. Should the school remain in Harlem if it can find another environment that fosters more opportunities to attract students and funding?
2. What reasons can Levine give business leaders outside of Harlem to convince them that they should support the school and clinic? What kind of support might they provide?

but may be senior managers of other organizations. Directors play an important role by representing the shareholders' views, sharing their own professional expertise, and keeping management on its toes. For example, the board of directors of Bausch & Lomb, which makes health-care and optical products, includes executives from other industries, including banking, publishing, and snack foods. These executives individually contribute their expertise in marketing, finance, strategic planning, technology, and consumer needs. Even more important, the board of directors actively questions management about business activities, and it keeps CEO Daniel Gill focused on company goals.[45]

Employees

Once managers select individuals from the labor supply to work in the organization, these employees become part of the internal environment. In some cases, employees are also owners and shareholders. But in their roles as employees, their impact on the organization differs from their impact as owners because employees conduct the day-to-day affairs of the organization, working in the various organizational functions. Increasingly, organizations are involving employees in decisions and activities that directly affect performance and customer satisfaction. For example, at Nordson, a manufacturer of industrial equipment in Westlake, Ohio, CEO William Madar has set up employee teams with complete responsibility for customer satisfaction. Employees interact with customers in the task environment, review the forces in the external environment, and then make decisions and take action to meet customer needs. The employees enthusiastically support company goals, customers receive excellent service, and sales and profits have dramatically improved.[46]

Organizational Culture

organizational culture The values and norms shared by members of an organization

The internal environment of every organization contains another potent force: **organizational culture,** the set of underlying values and norms shared by members of an organization that form the foundation of the management system and of management and employee practices. In corporations, this force is often referred to as *corporate culture.* The shared values of organizational culture call attention to what is important and shape the patterns of behavior that become norms guiding the way things are done in a particular organization.[47]

The organization's culture is deeply rooted in its past but is also affected by the present and by expectations for the future. For example, everyone at Medtronic, a medical products firm in Minneapolis best known for its heart pacemakers, can recite the story of how Earl Bakken and his brother-in-law founded the company in a garage and had high hopes for applying technology to help humanity. From this idealistic beginning grew a paternalistic company with an emphasis on home-grown scientific ingenuity. As the company expanded, it ran into competition, developed profitability problems, and needed a more consistent method of product development. During the 1980s, Medtronic shifted toward an emphasis on profits and on personal and organizational performance. To combat competitive threats, management pursued controlled but steady growth through diversification and acquisition. Now the organizational culture stresses profitability as well as the founders' passion for improving human welfare.[48]

As Medtronic's experience indicates, culture is a dynamic internal force that not only affects but is affected by the organization and all aspects of its environment. Managers must be aware of this special relationship because the continual give-and-take between the organizational culture and the organization leads to changes in values and norms that become ingrained in the culture and affect all employees. Moreover, various groups within an organization, such as marketing and operations or management and employees, may develop their own subcultures that have a powerful effect on the internal environment. These subcultures sometimes represent competing value systems that can create conflict between employee groups and therefore have a negative impact on performance.[49]

Characteristics of Culture

Underlying any organization's culture are *guiding beliefs,* the values that form the philosophical foundation for the organization's direction. Guiding beliefs generally reflect the personality and goals of the founder and subsequent top managers (see Exhibit 3.6). These guiding beliefs set the norms for everyday behavior within the organization. At United Parcel Service, for example, the guiding beliefs are that the company should maintain an egalitarian workplace where employees are treated fairly and equitably and that employees should be able to earn significant rewards by working hard to meet company goals. Two norms that spring from the guiding belief of the egalitarian workplace are (1) calling UPS employees and executives alike by their first names and (2) having only unreserved parking spots in company lots.[50]

When the cultural values and beliefs are widely accepted throughout the organization and employees act according to these values, the culture is said to be a *strong culture.* Researchers have identified many measures of cultural strength, including the depth of penetration in the organization, how fervently employees embrace the values, the longevity of the culture, and any tangible

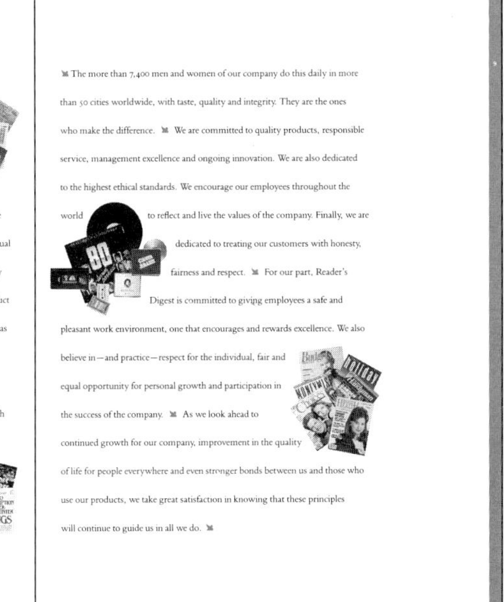

Our Guiding Principles

In 1922, DeWitt and Lila Wallace, founders of The Reader's Digest Association, Inc., did more than start a magazine. They created a new venture that was dedicated to "inform, educate, inspire and entertain" people everywhere. That basic desire to be of service to people is embedded in all that we do at Reader's Digest and is the foundation of the values that drive our company. It seems appropriate in this, our first annual report, that we restate for the new members of our family the "words we live by," the credo that governs how we conduct our affairs, fulfill our obligations to employees, customers and stockholders—as well as to the communities and countries in which we work and live. We believe that we make a difference in people's lives the world over. No matter what the language, the customs, the culture, we are at their side. We grow with them as they raise their families and become contributors to their communities. In every phase of people's lives our products add an extra dimension, open new vistas, make life more pleasant and communicate useful information.

The more than 7,400 men and women of our company do this daily in more than 50 cities worldwide, with taste, quality and integrity. They are the ones who make the difference. We are committed to quality products, responsible service, management excellence and ongoing innovation. We are also dedicated to the highest ethical standards. We encourage our employees throughout the world to reflect and live the values of the company. Finally, we are dedicated to treating our customers with honesty, fairness and respect. For our part, Reader's Digest is committed to giving employees a safe and pleasant work environment, one that encourages and rewards excellence. We also believe in—and practice—respect for the individual, fair and equal opportunity for personal growth and participation in the success of the company. As we look ahead to continued growth for our company, improvement in the quality of life for people everywhere and even stronger bonds between us and those who use our products, we take great satisfaction in knowing that these principles will continue to guide us in all we do.

EXHIBIT 3.6

The Guiding Beliefs of The Reader's Digest Association

When DeWitt and Lila Wallace founded the Reader's Digest Association in 1922, they outlined guiding beliefs that continue to permeate the organization's culture today. After nearly 70 years of private ownership, the company sold shares to the public in 1990, and top management explained the firm's guiding beliefs to shareholders in the first annual report.

evidence of the culture. Stronger cultures influence employees to a greater extent than weaker cultures. Other cultural characteristics include the ability to adapt to environmental change, the degree of employee involvement, and the degree of consistency among the cultural values.[51] Organizations must find ways of sustaining their cultural values and sharing them with others.

How Culture Is Communicated

Culture itself cannot be directly observed and described, but clues to the underlying values can be found in organizational stories, symbols, ceremonies, and slogans.[52] Organizations use these four methods to communicate their cultural values and beliefs to employees, to customers, and to other members of the task environment:

- *Stories* are frequently repeated narratives based on true events. Stories are told to new employees, related during formal training sessions, and repeated to customers as a way of communicating organizational values.[53] The inspirational stories about Chung Ju-Yung, honorary chairman of South Korea's Hyundai Business Group, cover many decades. Some of the stories demonstrate his indefatigable thirst for running a business; others reveal his desire to help reunite Korea. Consider Chung's legendary stamina. Now in his seventies, Chung's 16-hour workdays start at home before 6 a.m., when he talks with Hyundai units around the world. He walks more than two miles to the company headquarters and continues his heavy schedule until dinnertime or later on most days. These stories communicate the hard work and high goals Chung sets for himself and for the company.[54]
- *Symbols* are objects, acts, or events that communicate meaning to others, including employees and customers. Organizational logos, flags, awards, and posters are some examples of symbols. When Maxene Johnston became the CEO of the Weingart Center, a not-for-profit detoxification and rehabilita-

When Tandem Computers was a small start-up, CEO James Treybig could personally share his business philosophy with employees. But when Tandem passed the $1 billion mark, he realized that he had to institutionalize the firm's cultural values. A corporate philosophy group, headed by Susan Hailey, documents and communicates the values to Tandem's 10,000 managers and employees.

tion center in Los Angeles, she installed an aqua-colored flag bearing a giant *W*. Johnston explains: "The *W* stands for more than 'Weingart.' It also means 'Win' to the people who pull themselves up by their bootstraps, find a job, save their money, and move out of Skid Row." To instill a sense of pride, Johnston ordered distinctive aqua aprons for service employees at the center.[55]

- *Ceremonies* are planned activities that mark a special event or occasion. Ceremonies can reinforce organizational values, reward employees who achieve organizational goals, and create a shared experience that will form a bond among staff members. At North American Tool and Die in Oakland, California, owner Tom Melohn once held a ceremony to hand out a one-time award he called "The North American Tool and Die Refrigerator Award," which included a $50 check. The employee being honored had solved a problem ingeniously: parts for a custom-made piece of equipment were too big and fit too tightly, but when cooled in the lunchroom refrigerator, the parts contracted and fit better.[56]
- *Slogans* are phrases that express the organization's key values. Sun Microsystems, a maker of computer workstations headquartered in Mountain View, California, has a number of slogans. One of the company's earliest slogans was "To ask is to seek denial," meaning that employees should be aggressive and take the initiative. However, this shoot-from-the-hip style was modified after Sun posted its first loss. The new slogan, "To ask is not to have read your signature authority policy," indicates that employees must determine who has the authority to make a decision before they press boldly ahead.[57]

When organizations use stories, symbols, ceremonies, and slogans to communicate their beliefs, they help new employees learn about the culture and spread the culture by providing shared feelings and a common language understood by everyone in the internal environment. These methods also reinforce culturally acceptable behavior and discourage unacceptable behavior.[58]

Management and Culture

How does the organizational culture affect management and the organization? The guiding beliefs and norms of a culture have a definite impact on the way employees work and on their ability to achieve organizational goals. Culture can generate a sense of shared identity among employees, foster commitment to greater goals, and enhance the organization's ability to guide and shape employee behavior.[59] When culture has a positive effect on employee behavior it inspires employees to high performance.

Consider the influence of PepsiCo's aggressive, entrepreneurial culture. Prompted by the norms of the company's culture, PepsiCo managers take decisive action, picking up the phone instead of writing a memo, but above all, they get results. Guided by Pepsi values, they are encouraged to take calculated risks so that they can learn from success and failure. Another Pepsi norm involves rotating managers into other positions so they gain experience in a variety of roles. Pepsi takes pride in its culture and in its results and reinforces its culture by offering managers bonuses and other rewards for performance.[60]

At times, culture can cause problems. When top management wants to change the organization's direction or set new goals, the existing culture may be at odds with these changes. Also, the merger of two organizations can cause a culture clash, especially when the organizations operate internationally. For example, when General Electric took over the French medical equipment manufacturer Générale de Radiologie, the newly arrived U.S. managers installed GE flags and posted English-language posters as symbols of the GE culture. They also tried to convert the French employees by intoning "speed, simplicity, and self-confidence," a slogan coined by GE's chairman, John F. Welch, Jr. But the French managers were wary of GE's brash culture, some key French employees left, and the linking of the two organizations has not been as smooth as GE would like.[61] Chapter 11 examines issues that managers face in changing organizational culture.

MANAGEMENT AROUND THE WORLD

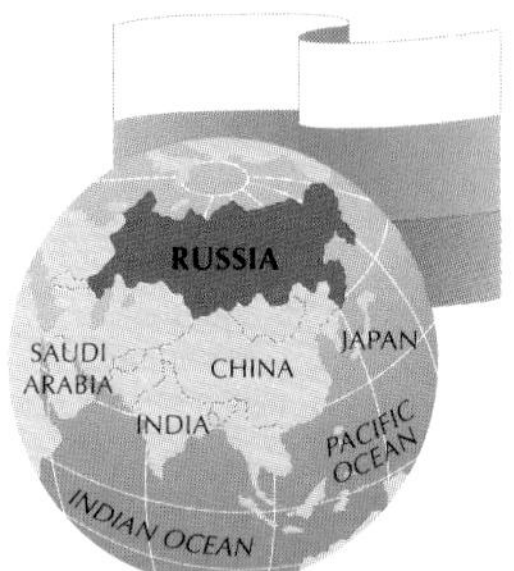

For Western businesses operating in Russia, the external environment has changed dramatically in recent years. Previously, these businesses were not allowed complete ownership of their operations; they had to form joint ventures with local organizations. However, once Russia became independent, the laws on business ownership began to change, and Western managers faced more dynamism and uncertainty.

MANAGEMENT WITHIN THE ORGANIZATIONAL ENVIRONMENT

To remain effective and to continue working toward organizational goals, managers must pay close attention to the extent of environmental influence on the organization. However, organizations are not entirely at the mercy of environmental forces. Managers can and do influence the environment in ways that benefit the organization.[62] This section examines the nature of environmental influence and then looks at a variety of management responses.

How the Environment Influences the Organization

The forces in the organizational environment can potentially affect organizational performance in a variety of ways. Managers must therefore identify the specific forces that influence their particular organization and then determine the nature of their impact. Two frameworks are commonly used to analyze environmental influence: environmental uncertainty and environmental interaction.

Environmental Uncertainty

The first framework of environmental influence is **environmental uncertainty,** a measure of how the combination of environmental change and environmental complexity affects the organization. Environmental uncertainty varies from organization to organization because the elements that have the most impact are not the same for every organization and because the exact influence varies for every organization.

environmental uncertainty How much change and complexity influence the organization and its performance

Environmental change (also known as *environmental dynamism*) describes how stable an organization's environment is. Managers can classify environmental elements according to whether they are *static,* remaining the same over time, or whether they are *dynamic,* changing in ways that are difficult to predict. For example, when Russia had a centrally planned economy, managers faced few unforeseen changes in goods produced or in distribution. But economic reforms have forced the manager of Moscow's upscale MC men's shirt shop to operate under more changeable conditions: the number of shirts sold changes according to customer preferences, and the number of shirts manufactured varies according to demand. Because of these unpredictable changes, MC's environment has become more dynamic, contributing to environmental uncertainty.[63]

environmental change The degree to which an organization's environment is stable or shifting

Environmental complexity refers to the number of elements in the organizational environment and the organization's knowledge of these elements and

environmental complexity The number of elements in the organizational environment and the extent to which the organization understands these elements and their impact their impact. The range of environmental complexity stretches from the simple to the complex. For example, when Citibank began to offer Visa and MasterCard credit cards, its competition included other banks and American Express, and the regulations governing credit card activities were fairly straightforward. But these days Citibank faces a more complex environment because of task environment competition from AT&T, Sears, Prudential, Ford, and other nonbanks that have begun issuing credit cards. Moreover, politicolegal forces in the general environment have changed: the nonbanks are not subject to the same expensive federal capital requirements as the banks. On top of that, customers in Citibank's task environment are finally realizing that they have too many cards. Now Citibank is mounting a series of programs to keep its cards in customer wallets.[64]

Environmental change and complexity can combine to create four possible levels of uncertainty: simple-static, complex-static, simple-dynamic, and complex-dynamic (see Exhibit 3.7). Level 1 has the least amount of uncertainty and level 4 has the most, so managers can respond more easily to level 1 uncertainty than to level 4 uncertainty. Unfortunately, most organizations face uncertainty at level 4, so managers generally must cope with a high degree of change and complexity.[65] On occasion, organizations face environmental turbulence that can alter entire industries and change environmental boundaries. If the turbulence is unexpected and threatens the organization's performance, it can turn into a crisis requiring special management care. When many national governments reduced their regulation of airlines, the domestic and international airline industries were thrown into turmoil. Prices and schedules were no longer standardized but had to be set and changed according to customer demand and competitive pressures, causing unprecedented uncertainty for airline managers. At the same time, domestic and international airlines faced the uncertainty of poor economic conditions in many nations. As a result of this turbulence, some carriers went out of business and others sought partners to bolster their economic and competitive strength.[66]

EXHIBIT 3.7

How Change and Complexity Affect Uncertainty

Environmental change and complexity can combine in four ways to create uncertainty. Level 1 is lowest in uncertainty, and level 4 is highest.

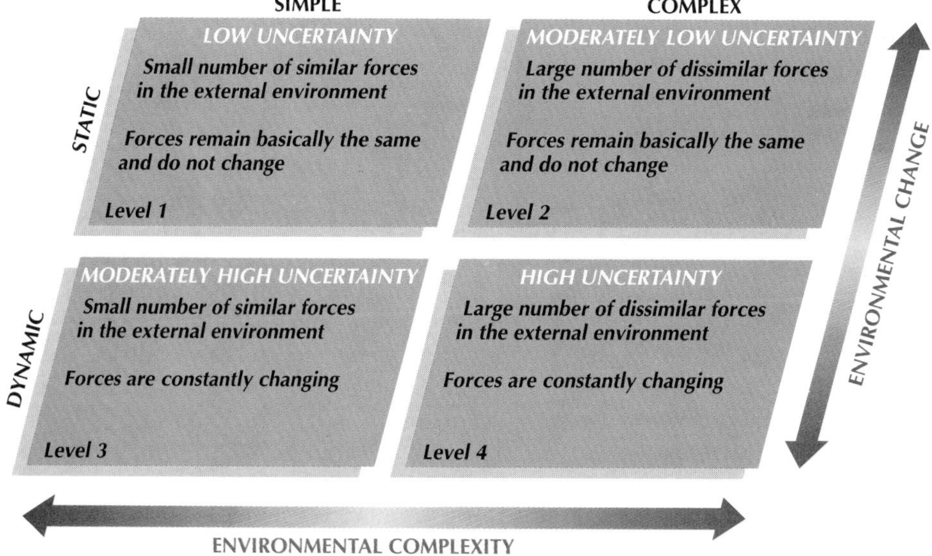

Environmental Interaction

The second framework of environmental influence relates to environmental interaction. In the systems theory of organizations, managers interact with the environment to obtain resources as inputs for the transformation process and to distribute outputs. As they analyze the organization's interaction with the environment, managers consider two aspects: the availability of resources and how dependent the organization is on these resources.

Environmental munificence refers to the level of resources available and the degree of sustained growth and stability that the organizational environment can support. When resources are plentiful, organizations can grow and set aside a cushion of resources such as extra cash or materials to use when resources become scarce. When resources are scarce, organizations must be more innovative in using available resources and often use alliances with other organizations to obtain resources.[67] General Motors' Delco Electronics division, which makes automotive sound systems and engine controls, decided to speed up new-product development on integrated circuits as one way of managing sales and profits during a recent economic recession. Delco cut the development time from 42 to 18 months so it can get new products out more quickly, bringing in faster sales and profits.[68]

environmental munificence The level of resources available in the organizational environment to support prolonged growth and stability

Resource dependence refers to how much the organization depends on resources from the external environment. Because a major environmental change can threaten access to resources, managers seek to control both positive and negative aspects of resource dependence. On the positive side, managers who supply resources can try to increase other organizations' dependence on their products. On the negative side, managers of organizations who need resources can try to minimize their demand or develop alternative sources so that they are not at the mercy of those organizations that produce needed resources.[69] For example, Nalco Chemical, headquartered in Naperville, Illinois, sells chemical products to organizations that must comply with environmental laws by reducing air emissions or purifying wastewater. Although their customers must use fewer chemical products in order to comply with the antipollution laws, Nalco encourages stronger dependence on its services by offering a computer package that automates reorders. This effectively ties the customers to Nalco products.[70]

resource dependence The degree to which the organization depends on resources from the environment

It's not enough for managers simply to monitor their environments for information about uncertainty and interaction. They also need to recognize the direction of environmental trends so that they can predict where the organization is likely to stand in the future and be able to respond to anticipated environmental changes and interaction.

How Management Responds to the Environment

To deal with the impact of environmental forces, managers must gather information about the environment, determine whether to respond, and then decide exactly what action to take.[71] Of course, when an organization faces little environmental uncertainty, enjoys a high degree of munificence, and depends only slightly on outside resources, its managers generally have more room to maneuver. How a manager responds can depend on the degree of environmental uncertainty, the extent of environmental interaction, and the specific forces acting on that organization.

MANAGERIAL DECISION MAKING

Taming the General Environment, Japanese Style

When Morihiko Hiramatsu took office as governor of Oita prefecture in the south of Japan, he knew the area was depressed, but he also knew it had a lot to offer. Oita boasted heavy industry such as oil refining, food processing, and petrochemical manufacturing. Fisheries were an important source of income, and the prefecture had a local forestry industry. But shipyards and coal mines were closing, and jobs were getting scarcer, so residents had to leave to find employment. Faced with a 10 percent unemployment rate, a decreasing population, and a low annual per capita income, Hiramatsu had an important decision to make: should he continue the policies of previous administrations or should he try a new approach that might catapult Oita out of the clutches of the environmental forces that were causing its decline?

Hiramatsu decided that Oita could successfully counteract the forces in its general environment by implementing a new approach. He designed a daring campaign, called "One Village, One Product," to inspire each community to produce one particular specialty. With the resources available to the towns and villages, Hiramatsu reasoned, each could focus on making a single product very well. The plan would encourage self-reliance and would develop the talents of the local citizens. Hiramatsu also wanted to attract new industries that would in turn create new jobs and ultimately bring the jobless rate down and the population back up. Could Hiramatsu achieve such ambitious goals?

From the start, Hiramatsu found that the people of Oita were enthusiastic, but he also found problems. For one thing, he discovered that some areas lacked the resources and the skilled people to create a local specialty. Hiramatsu responded by helping local managers develop new specialties. Also, the farmers and fishermen had little knowledge of how to develop food by-products such as juice, jam, and soups or of how to prepare them for market. So the governor established an Agricultural and Marine Product Processing Research and Information Center to advise on processing, packaging, and selling agricultural and sea prod-

boundary spanning Organizational roles that link and coordinate the organization's plans and activities with the environment

Managers connect the organization with the environment and coordinate interaction with key environmental forces by setting up boundary-spanning roles and activities. **Boundary spanning** involves collecting and processing information about the environment and passing along relevant details to managers inside the organization. In this way, boundary spanners provide a constant source of information that helps to reduce environmental uncertainty. Because boundary spanners also represent the organization to the outside, they help balance environmental constraints and organizational policy.[72] Examples of boundary spanners include strategic planners, market researchers, salespeople, and small-business owners. At Knight Floor Covering in Newark, California, owners Jack Knight and David Fern are both boundary spanners, for example, by staying in touch with property managers who supervise apartment complexes that need the company's carpeting. Knight and Fern learn about customers, suppliers, economic trends, and other external forces as they meet with people outside the firm.[73] By gathering information through boundary spanning and through other information-management techniques, managers can better understand how the environment influences the organization.

The next step is to consider how to respond. According to the systems view of the organization, managers can use a variety of resources and transformational processes to respond to environmental forces and achieve organizational results. This concept, called *equifinality,* suggests that even when the environment has a strong influence on the organization, managers have many options for attaining their goals.[74] In dealing with environmental uncertainty and environmental interaction, managers can choose to respond in one of three ways: by adaptation, by influencing the environment, or by domain shifts.

ucts. Moreover, to develop the professional skills of Oita residents, the governor set up 12 regional schools that offer night courses in word processing, law, accounting, and other skills.

Expanding on his plans to create an environment more favorable for new industry, Hiramatsu created Technopolis, an ambitious project that earmarked land near Oita Airport for industrial development. Hiramatsu realized that companies, especially high-tech firms, need easy access to an airport so that they can receive materials or ship finished goods. By improving the air transportation facilities, Hiramatsu was able to lure so many electronics and software manufacturers to Oita that the city is now known as Japan's Silicon City.

As a result of Hiramatsu's response to the general environment, local unemployment has dropped from 10 percent to under 2 percent in less than a decade. Oita residents now produce everything from prawns and pearls to beef and bamboo crafts. The "One Village, One Product" campaign has been enormously successful: annual per capita income in Oita prefecture has increased by 25 percent over the past decade, and the population has stabilized. Moreover, the top executives of Japan's leading corporations now rate Oita's environment as second only to Tokyo's in terms of economic, political, and cultural vigor. The state of Louisiana, two cities in China, and a city in France are adopting the One Village, One Product concept because of its enormous potential. Los Angeles Mayor Tom Bradley recently honored Hiramatsu's accomplishments with a "One Village, One Product" Day celebration. But the three-term governor couldn't attend the ceremonies: he was on the job in Oita, making decisions that would tame the general environment and bring his prefecture fame and prosperity.

Apply Your Knowledge

1. How did environmental munificence and resource dependence shape Hiramatsu's plans for Oita prefecture?
2. Now that Governor Hiramatsu's decisions have helped Oita prefecture to recover economically, what can he do to monitor future changes to the general environment?

Adaptation to the Environment

One way managers can respond to the environment is through adaptation. When managers decide to adapt, they rearrange internal activities and conditions to make the organization more compatible with the environment. In this approach, managers do not attempt to influence outside forces but concentrate instead on internal elements that can reduce vulnerability to the environment. Boundary spanners play a role in adaptation by providing information that will help shape internal policies regarding environmental elements. Management's role in adaptation can involve changing the organization structure, buffering, forecasting, or smoothing and rationing:

- *Organization structure.* The internal design of the organization can help it adapt to the external environment. In designing the organization structure, managers consider how they will gather information about the environment so that decision makers can act. In highly uncertain environments, it's especially important that organizations be structured to allow managers to get information quickly and have the flexibility to respond, which is why so many organizations are slashing layers and giving local or departmental managers more authority to respond. When environments are simpler and more static, organizations can be more rigidly structured.[75] Chairman Leslie H. Wexner has adapted The Limited to the vagaries of its fashion environment by creating separate store divisions for distinctly different customer segments. Each Limited division can adjust its store look, its pricing, and the merchandise offered to respond to sociocultural, competitive, and other environmental forces.[76]

buffering Either building a reserve or releasing resources and finished goods as a way of adapting to environmental uncertainty

- *Buffering.* Managers can use **buffering** to stockpile or release resources and finished goods as a way of ameliorating fluctuations or adverse conditions in the environment. By storing a reserve of raw materials, cash, or other inputs, managers have ready access to these resources when they need them and can therefore absorb the impact of any environmental shifts. If the organization keeps a supply of its own products, it will have them available for any sudden surges in demand; however, this may be a problem if products become obsolete in the meantime or if they are perishable. Moreover, holding money, physical materials, or products in reserve until needed can be expensive. Nevertheless, Canon accumulates technological resources, routinely investigating a variety of technologies that can be applied to new products, new markets, and emerging opportunities. Although it is based in Japan, Canon received more U.S. patents in 1990 than any U.S. company, outpacing General Electric, Kodak, and IBM. This accumulation of technological resources lets the company react quickly to sudden obsolescence, regulatory changes, and fluctuations in demand.[77]
- *Forecasting.* Most organizations use forecasting to reduce environmental uncertainty by trying to predict what future conditions will be like. Of course, unforeseen elements always crop up. However, forecasting helps managers dig into environmental trends to discover the likeliest turn of events. Then they can prepare for anticipated fluctuations by creating plans and strategies (see Chapters 7 and 8). For example, British Petroleum (BP) uses forecasting to track the global warming trend that could threaten its oil and gas operations in Alaska. BP managers are concerned because long-term warming might melt the permafrost on which its Alaskan facilities rest.[78]
- *Smoothing and rationing.* Even when they use forecasting to predict future conditions, managers still need to respond to the environmental fluctuations they anticipate. Two common techniques are **smoothing,** an approach in which managers make internal adjustments to prepare for expected fluctuations, and **rationing,** an approach in which managers consciously limit their organization's production or distribution of goods and services during times of peak demand. Farm equipment maker Deere uses price incentives to smooth out demand peaks and to keep sales steady even during the fall and winter off-season.[79] Shop Rite, in the Northeast, limits the number of sale items each customer may buy so that the store has sufficient stock to cover demand (a common practice for supermarkets).

smoothing Making internal adjustments in anticipation of expected environmental fluctuations

rationing Deliberately limiting production of goods and services during times of peak demand

Influence on the Environment

A second way that managers can respond to the environment is by influencing it. They can establish a favorable relationship with external elements and work to modify, shape, and control external events. By influencing the environment, managers can reduce environmental dependence, change the interaction with the environment, or improve the impact of a particular element. Boundary spanners can forge personal linkages with the environment that help to influence the elements. But managers can also influence the environment through political and legal activities, joint ventures, and advertising and public relations.[80]

- *Political and legal activities.* Organizations can lobby for or against legal and regulatory issues, and managers can speak out on trade restraints. Managers can also file suit over issues such as patent infringement and antitrust violations. To pool their resources on a political or legal issue, organizations can join or form a *trade association,* composed of organizations that are in the same industry or that are interested in common issues. Also, managers can negotiate with government officials and regulators to enact or change regulations that affect the organization. Brian McAuley, president of Fleet Call, wanted to turn his taxi dispatch service into a mobile radio operation that rivals cellular phone systems. He asked the Federal Communications Commission (FCC) to let him add new technology that would expand his firm's channels and increase calling capacity. Although rivals lobbied against the move, the FCC approved McAuley's request, opening the door to more competition in this growing field.[81]

- *Joint ventures.* An increasing number of companies are teaming up with one or more partners to jointly produce goods or services, and a growing number of joint ventures are springing up across national borders. For example, Gilead Sciences in California works with Britain's Glaxo PLC in a joint venture to research and develop anticancer drugs. And British automaker Rover and Japanese carmaker Honda pool technology, design, and marketing skills. Rover is learning to penetrate international markets and Honda is learning about European car styling and marketing.[82]
- *Advertising and public relations.* A wide variety of organizations (including trade associations) use advertising and public relations to influence the environment. When organizations want to bring in more customers, find new employees, or sway the voting public for or against an issue, advertising and public relations can be powerful tools (see Exhibit 3.8). For example, the American Bankers Association, a trade organization for banks, has advertised to convince the public that it is too costly for the Federal Deposit Insurance Corporation to continue its policy of reimbursing depositors for all deposits held in failed banks.[83]

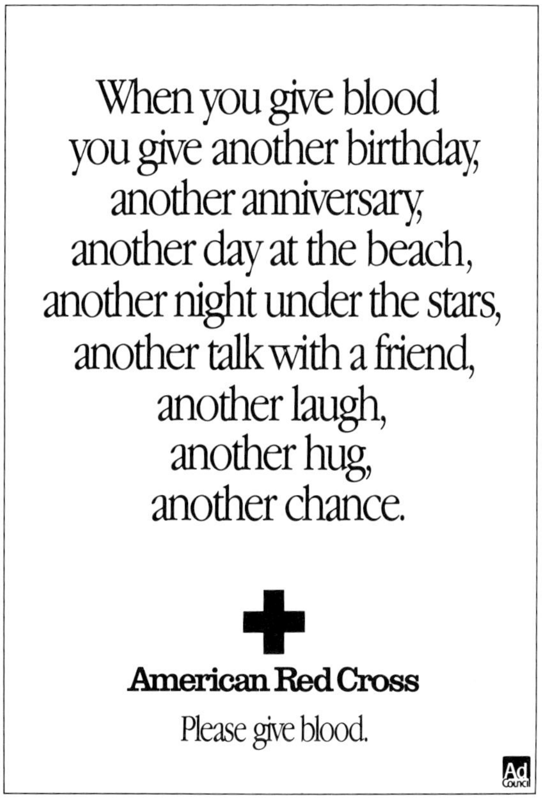

When you give blood
you give another birthday,
another anniversary,
another day at the beach,
another night under the stars,
another talk with a friend,
another laugh,
another hug,
another chance.

American Red Cross
Please give blood.

Ad Council

EXHIBIT 3.8

Advertising to Influence the Environment

One way the American Red Cross influences the environment is by advertising for blood donors. This ad offers a variety of compelling reasons why people should give blood.

Domain Shifts

A third way managers can respond to the environment is through domain shifts. When organizations manage their interaction with the external environment by changing the goods and services they produce, the way they provide their products, or the customers they target, they are making a **domain shift.** If the environment is unfavorable, organizations can drop a product, pull out of a location, or stop serving certain customers. Another domain shift involves adding products and services to diversify beyond the current business.[84] For example, Greyhound started as the operator of the Greyhound Lines, famous for crisscrossing the United States with its bus service. Later the firm diversified into food services, consumer products, and money orders. But during the 1980s, the bus operations faced an uncertain economy, aggressive competition from air travel, and conflicts with employees over wage cuts. Managers decided to use a domain shift to move the firm out of this unfavorable environment. They sold Greyhound Lines, then changed the company name to Dial (the well-known brand name of their soap line) to emphasize the consumer products and the shift out of bus operations.[85]

domain shift A change in the organization's products and services to avoid unfavorable environmental forces or to interact with favorable environmental elements

Managers can adapt to the environment, influence the environment, or use domain shifts to respond to environmental pressures. Depending on the environmental forces, a manager might even combine approaches to achieve organizational goals, adapting to one force while influencing another or while planning a domain shift.

SUMMARY

The organizational environment is composed of all the forces that influence the organization and its ability to achieve organizational goals. The environment is composed of: (1) the internal environment, including those forces within the organization's boundaries, and (2) the external environment, including all forces outside the organization's boundaries. The external environment itself contains the general environment, consisting of five external forces that have a general influence on the organization: politicolegal forces are governmental and legal policies, laws, and institutions; economic forces refer to the availability of resources and broad economic trends; technological forces are the knowledge, processes, and systems used in making changes to the transformation process or to products; sociocultural forces include the values, attitudes, needs, and characteristics of the societies where the organization operates; international forces originate outside the organization's home country and influence interactions with people and organizations in other areas.

The external environment also contains the task environment, which is composed of six forces that have a more direct influence on the organization. Customers receive the organization's outputs and are therefore central to the organization's existence. Competitors are other organizations that vie for the same customers or resources. Suppliers are people and organizations who provide the inputs used in production. The labor supply includes the people available to be hired. Regulators are governmental agencies, officials, and special interest groups who are involved with guidelines that influence organizational practices. And partners are organizations that work together to achieve organizational goals.

The internal environment includes four forces: owners and shareholders, the board of directors, the employees, and the organizational culture. Owners and shareholders influence the organization by actively participating and by electing a board of directors to represent their interests. The board of directors supervises management and guides organizational direction. Employees conduct day-to-day activities. And organizational culture, which includes the underlying values and norms shared by organizational members, forms the foundation of the management system and of manager and employee behavior.

Organizational culture is shaped by guiding beliefs that create the foundation for the organization's direction and that form the basis of the norms that influence employee behavior. Cultures can be strong or weak, depending on whether the values are widely accepted so that employees act according to the values. Because culture brings employees together in pursuit of organizational goals, thus helping guide and shape behavior, it is an important element in the internal environment.

Managers use two frameworks to analyze the influence of the environment. Environmental uncertainty measures how change and complexity affect the organization. Environmental interaction refers to the availability of resources and how dependent the organization is on those resources. By understanding the degree of uncertainty and how the organization interacts with its environment, managers can formulate the appropriate strategy for responding to the environment. To respond to environmental pressures, managers can adapt, influence the environment, or shift domains. Managers adapt by rearranging internal activities to make the organization more compatible with its environment. They can use the organization structure, buffering, forecasting, smoothing, or rationing to adapt. To influence the environment, managers can use political and legal activities, joint ventures, or advertising and public relations techniques. Finally, managers can use domain shifts, changing products and services, to avoid unfavorable forces or to interact with more favorable forces.

MEETING A MANAGEMENT CHALLENGE AT

It was clear to CEO David Kearns that the Xerox of the 1980s was headed for serious trouble. The photocopier company had been without serious competition for many years, and high profits had become a way of life, lulling Xerox managers into complacency. In the meantime, however, manufacturing costs had grown too high, and competitors with more reliable copiers were stealing customers. Moreover, computers were expected to eliminate paper—and the need for copiers—from business offices. What had been a stable environment was becoming terrifyingly dynamic and complex.

Kearns knew he had to shift Xerox's focus from profits to quality. To make quality a goal shared throughout the organizational culture, Xerox spent $125 million and five years retraining every employee. Each manager went through the new training twice, once as a student learning from his or her own manager, and again as a trainer for his or her employees. The company adopted a new slogan: "Xerox is *The Document Company* and our number-one priority is customer satisfaction." Xerox also involved nonmanagers in the quality movement by setting up problem-solving teams that eventually numbered 8,000 (and included 75,000 of its 100,000 employees).

Technicians training to service Xerox copiers

One method the company used to assess its rivals' products and to help establish quality standards was benchmarking. This boundary-spanning technique was performed by teams of technical specialists who studied competitors and quality leaders in all industries to find and emulate the best. With this outside information, Xerox managers were better able to understand how their products measured up and to set new, higher quality goals for their goods and services.

One benchmarking study showed Xerox had far more parts suppliers than Japanese competitors did, so it cut its supplier list from 5,000 to about 300. This reduced the complexity of the company's task environment and gave managers more control over the quality of purchased parts. To ensure price stability, Xerox negotiated price goals for the parts it purchased. As quality improved, materials-related costs fell about 50 percent, assembly line rejects dropped more than 90 percent, and the cost of monitoring supplier quality was slashed by two-thirds.

Another analysis showed that computers were not eliminating paper; in fact, computers were generating more paper. Huge amounts of computer-generated data were now being stored on paper. Xerox responded by shifting outside its traditional copier domain to develop DocuTech, a $200,000 two-ton miniature printshop and editing tool that bridged the worlds of paper and computers. Not only could DocuTech accept computer data and print and bind documents faster and cheaper than conventional printing methods, it could also turn printed documents back into computer text ready for manipulation. Xerox spent 10 years and an estimated $750 million developing DocuTech, and the product sold well when launched in the early 1990s.

By the time Kearns retired and Paul Allaire became CEO in 1991, customers were reporting more satisfaction and profits were rising. Because its managers understood and responded to the environment, Xerox had become the first U.S. company to regain market share from Japanese competitors without government intervention.

***You're the Manager*:** You are Xerox vice president for strategy. It's your job to project the future document-management needs of business and the products Xerox must develop to remain profitable. You also spend much of your time troubleshooting quality problems. Profits are growing, but resources are still tight.

Ranking Questions

1. A paper manufacturer's sales manager says customers using recycled paper are having trouble with the quality of color printing on the DocuTech system. She can't figure out whether the problem could be solved with adjustments to DocuTech or with improvements to the paper. She also says the recycled-paper market is growing too slowly for her company to invest much money in finding a solution, so Xerox should figure out what's wrong. Rank these responses from best to worst.
   a. You don't know enough about the problem to begin considering solutions. Tell the sales manager to call back after she figures out whether the problem is the paper or the printer.
   b. The number of affected customers seems small, and the paper company won't invest much to find a solution, so save your resources and refuse to help.
   c. Propose an informal partnership to consider the problem. Ask some of the affected customers to join in.
   d. Xerox knows DocuTech best, so it should try to solve the problem alone. Order some recycled paper and have your employees try printing in color.
2. The vice president for personnel drops by to ask your advice. He says employees have complained that managers are still being promoted on the basis of short-term profits, even though the company is now stressing customer satisfaction and quality. Rank these actions from best to worst.
   a. Send a memo, to middle and top managers only, stressing that the company's new goals must be a major criterion in all promotions.
   b. Establish a new award to recognize managers whose units show the most improvement in quality and customer satisfaction.
   c. Nip the problem in the bud by supporting your managers. Because the personnel vice president knows who the complainers are, he can explain to them privately that without profits, Xerox couldn't exist.
   d. Profitability is only one of several good reasons to promote people, and the complainers probably don't understand this. Nothing needs to be done.

Multiple-Choice Questions

3. IBM and Microsoft have teamed up to revive the notion of a paperless office by announcing a new line of computers and software. They claim their new system will connect a company's computers throughout the world and organize computerized information into a virtual encyclopedia that can be easily accessed and manipulated. They have announced that this system will eliminate the need for paper documents and copiers. The system will be released in six months. Which is your single best course of action?
   a. Ignore the announcement. The paperless office has already proved to be the forecasting joke of the decade, and the new product isn't even out yet.
   b. Don't make any moves until you talk with technical experts, current and prospective customers, and competitors to find out how useful the new computer system would be.

c. Immediately start an advertising campaign to promote the importance of paper documents and Xerox's experience in document management.
d. Quietly start cutting back speculative research-and-development projects to stockpile resources. You may need all the personnel and money you can muster if a product war develops.

4. An article in the respected British medical journal *Lancet* cites high rates of lung cancer among employees exposed to solvents used in a plastic-molding process. A Xerox factory in New York uses such solvents. Employees at the factory are worried, and several have threatened to sue even though the process is not illegal. What is your single best response?
a. Make your internal environment less complex. You might substitute products from outside suppliers or move the factory to a country that is less sensitive to health issues. The New York plant might have to be closed.
b. Contact federal health and safety officials to see whether anyone is considering a ban on the process. Lobby against any such restrictions.
c. Order employees to wear respirators at work to protect them from airborne solvents. Employees are too valuable a resource to be risked.
d. Ask employees to join managers on a team to study the situation and then propose a solution.

Analysis Questions

5. How did Xerox use boundary-spanning activities to improve its competitive position?
6. How did environmental munificence affect Xerox's quality improvement plans?
7. Explain how environmental dynamism changed in Xerox's task environment.

Special Project

Xerox managers have identified a factory in the United States as one of the company's least-competitive units. They believe Xerox could save $3.2 million a year by closing an entire department, laying off 180 employees, and buying the parts it makes on the global open market. These savings could be crucial to reestablishing the company's competitive position. Now the employees and their union want to set up an employee-management team to study ways of cutting costs without closing the plant. But managers are concerned about disclosing sensitive information on company costs. What would you do? Draft a two- to three- page proposal for Xerox's consideration, relating your response to the principles outlined in this chapter.[86]

KEY TERMS

boundary spanning (92)
buffering (94)
competitors (80)
domain shift (96)
economic forces (76)
environmental change (89)
environmental complexity (89)
environmental munificence (91)
environmental uncertainty (89)
external environment (72)
general environment (72)
internal environment (72)
international forces (78)
labor supply (80)
organizational culture (86)
organizational environment (72)
partners (83)
politicolegal forces (74)
rationing (94)
regulators (81)
resource dependence (91)
smoothing (94)
sociocultural forces (77)
special interest groups (83)
suppliers (80)
task environment (72)
technological forces (76)

QUESTIONS

For Review

1. What impact do sociocultural forces have on the organization?
2. How can managers adapt the organization to the environment?
3. Why is the organizational culture a key part of the organization's internal environment?
4. What effect does environmental complexity have on management?
5. Why is boundary spanning a necessary role?

For Analysis

1. What are the advantages and disadvantages of having inside directors serve on a corporate board?
2. Why should the dean of a not-for-profit college be interested in the technological forces in the general environment?
3. How does a municipal fire company interact with its environment in terms of resource dependence and environmental munificence?
4. Why would the Internal Revenue Service be considered a regulator, a supplier, and a competitor in the task environment of an accounting firm?
5. What domain shifts could a health club use in response to an environment in which men are increasingly interested in health and fitness?

For Application

1. How can the owner of a TCBY yogurt franchise store in a beach resort assess the nature and extent of environmental uncertainty?
2. How would a small business like a neighborhood pharmacy be affected by international forces in the general environment?
3. What can the board of directors of a not-for-profit organization such as the National Dairy Council do to ensure that the organization meets member needs?
4. How can a small-business owner establish and nurture a strong culture that has a positive effect on organizational performance?
5. In what ways can a group dental practice influence the environment through political and legal activities? Joint ventures? Advertising and public relations? Be specific.

KEEPING CURRENT IN MANAGEMENT

Find a recent article that describes how a manager assessed the influence of a force in the organizational environment and then formulated a response. Some examples include how an official in municipal government assessed and managed as a result of shifts in population or industrial development; how the director of a charity or cultural organization planned for or reacted to changes in funding, donations, or need for services; how a business manager discovered shifts in customer demand or faced problems with suppliers and what changes the manager made to prevent future problems or to take advantage of these environmental influences.

1. What is the most important environmental element that challenges this manager? Classify this element as part of the general or the task environment if it is external, or identify its place in the internal environment. What type of force does this element represent? What is its impact on the organization?
2. If the manager wanted to postpone any action to address this key environmental element, what immediate consequences might the organization suffer? How can the manager gauge environmental uncertainty and environment interaction?
3. How is the manager responding to the environment? Is the manager using adaptation, trying to influence the environment, or using a domain shift?

SHARPEN YOUR MANAGEMENT SKILLS

Here's your chance to run a state university for a day. The situation you face is this: your institution is a traditional state university that focuses on undergraduate and graduate degrees for people following a continuous path from high school through college. In other words, you don't put heavy emphasis on educating people who entered the work force right after high school or right after undergraduate school.

The environment is changing, however. Fewer students are entering college directly from high school and continuing through graduate school, and a large number of older students are returning to college after a number of years in the work force. The problem is that you're not set up to handle a lot of students who want to attend part-time, or on evenings and weekends. Furthermore, nearly all your extracurricular activities are geared to 18- to 24-year-olds, but the average age of your returning students is around 30. Overall, your enrollment is dropping because the younger students just aren't as numerous as they used to be, and the returning students are turning to community colleges because of more convenient schedules and better accommodations for older students.

- *Decision:* How should your university respond? What are the benefits and limitations of using adaptation, influence, or domain shifts to meet the university's challenges caused by environmental change?
- *Communication:* Write a paragraph about each approach, outlining its feasibility and suggesting actions you might take in each case. If you think a combination of two or three responses in various parts of the university's operations is best, outline your approach in that manner.

Mighty IBM (nicknamed "Big Blue") has been more humble of late, its profits dampened by price wars and market share losses. Renowned for its quality products and excellent service, IBM has fallen prey to more nimble challengers who wow customers with flexible products, lower prices, and more individualized support. To reverse the profit drain, CEO John F. Akers must win customers back and keep them—no easy task as he leads a behemoth with more than 350,000 people and $70 billion in revenues.

HISTORY

In 1914 Thomas J. Watson, Sr., took over a floundering accounting machine manufacturer, and by 1920 he had tripled sales to nearly $15 million. Expanding overseas, Watson renamed the firm International Business Machines and pushed on to dominate the market for calculating machines and other office equipment. In the 1950s, under Thomas J. Watson, Jr., the company began selling powerful mainframe computers that established IBM's reputation in the computer business. By the 1980s, the company offered a range of computers, including the PC (personal computer) series, IBM's answer to Apple's desktop computers. Over time, IBM so dominated the computer market that its systems were often the de facto industry standards. John Akers became IBM's sixth CEO in 1985.

ENVIRONMENT

During the 1980s and into the 1990s, IBM's environment became more complex and changeable. The U.S. economy was weakening and interest rates were uncertain; demand for mainframes flagged, but sales in minicomputers and PCs surged. At the same time, customers wanted to use existing equipment to handle more applications, and they wanted to link IBM and non-IBM computers. However, most IBM staff lacked the training and the organizational support to solve this type of customer problem. Salespeople who tried to offer feedback about customer needs to the product developers became as frustrated as their customers, who increasingly shopped elsewhere. Throughout the industry, technology was advancing rapidly, and competitors were buying outside expertise, components, and software to build faster, more flexible machines. Worse, many challengers could develop new products nearly twice as fast and sell them for less than IBM, which stubbornly preferred to use homegrown technology. In contrast to younger, hungrier competitors who moved quickly to find new ways of satisfying customers, IBM moved slowly, prisoner of an arrogant culture that celebrated its past success at selling products while ignoring the opportunity of selling specialized solutions to customer problems.

GOALS AND CHALLENGES

Akers is continuing some of IBM's original goals and adding new ones to meet the environmental challenges of the 1990s. Since the beginning, IBM's goals have included excellence in customer service and product design. More recently, Akers has set goals to speed product development so that computers and programs get to market more quickly. He has also established goals to ensure customer satisfaction. Although IBM's revenues have been growing, CEO Akers must stop profits from languishing amidst this environmental uncertainty and complexity. He is adapting by changing the organization structure to bring information on customer needs into the product development cycle much earlier, even inviting key customers to participate. Akers is also chopping management layers, reassigning people to customer-related functions, and thinning the ranks by offering early retirement incentives (moves calculated to lower costs and boost productivity). To influence the environment, Akers has initiated several joint ventures, including an agreement with Apple to develop software and multimedia capabilities for PCs. Further, Akers is insisting on a higher level of employee performance, using training and bonuses to back that expectation. Although he can't eliminate the inevitable impact of environmental forces, Akers hopes his decisions put IBM back on track for future profits.

1. What task environment forces are acting on IBM? What effect has culture had on IBM's competitive position?
2. What roles does Apple play in IBM's environment? What concerns might Akers have about Apple's links with IBM?
3. What information might boundary-spanning salespeople and service technicians bring to IBM? How can IBM use this information to better cope with its environment?
4. How can Akers use forecasting to help the company adapt to environmental turbulence?

CHAPTER OUTLINE

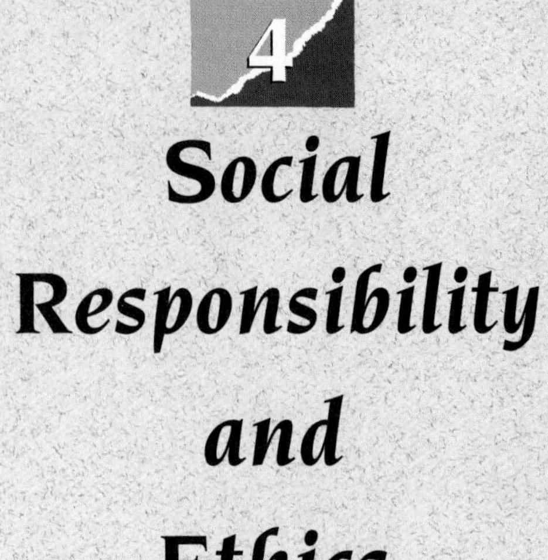

4 Social Responsibility and Ethics

After studying this chapter, you will be able to

1. Discuss the nature of social responsibility and identify the major organizational stakeholders
2. Outline the seven areas of social responsibility
3. Describe the continuum of social responsibility
4. Discuss methods of institutionalizing social responsibility
5. Explain the nature of managerial ethics and distinguish between ethical dilemmas and ethical lapses
6. Highlight the decision-making models managers can use to resolve ethical dilemmas
7. Describe organizational approaches to ethical management behavior

FACING A MANAGEMENT CHALLENGE AT

BEN & JERRY'S HOMEMADE

Balancing Profits and Social Responsibility

Ben & Jerry's Homemade makes more than premium ice cream; it makes an unusual effort to operate a business as a force for social change. The company has earned a nationwide reputation as an organization that stands apart in today's highly competitive business environment, because the founders put a premium on meeting the needs of employees and of the community.

Co-founders Ben Cohen and Jerry Greenfield had intended to start their ice cream parlor in Vermont and then sell it once the business got going. But something always seemed to force them to grow—a new competitor or the need to replace or fix equipment. Almost in spite of itself, the ice cream parlor became a growth company. Growth brought new management challenges, and the fledgling firm hired its first experienced, professional business manager. But Greenfield wasn't interested in building a conventional company, and after four years, he retired from Ben & Jerry's with no intention of ever returning. Cohen shared Greenfield's feelings, so he put the company up for sale.

Before a buyer appeared, however, another Vermont entrepreneur persuaded Cohen to keep the company and to find a way of running it in accordance with his social and ethical goals. Inspired by the challenge, Cohen came up with a plan. The company, he decided, would be a force for social change. He envisioned Ben & Jerry's as being held in trust for the community. Growth and profit, he reasoned, could be a means to increased social responsibility.

Cohen's vision of the company as a force for social change is demonstrated in several ways. Of pretax profits, 7.5 percent is set aside to support social causes (the national average is 1.5 percent). The company is a leader in corporate recycling and environmental programs. Ben & Jerry's uses both its profits and its products to promote the company's vision of peace, justice, and environment. For example, a percentage of sales from Peace Pops goes to promoting world peace, Rainforest Crunch is made with nuts from the South American rain forest (which both supports the native people directly and gives them a long-term financial incentive to nurture the forest), and the brownies mixed into Chocolate Fudge Brownie ice cream are bought from a bakery that employs homeless people.

Today the company is a multimillion-dollar corporation, and double-digit growth is once again challenging the organization's culture and its commitment to social change. Although Greenfield has rejoined the organization to help foster the reignited sense of purpose, Ben & Jerry's now employs hundreds of people, not all of whom share Cohen and Greenfield's idealism. The two founders worry that some managers have lost sight of the firm's social action goals and are concentrating exclusively on profit goals. How can Cohen and Greenfield maintain their ideals as the company grows? How can they share their vision with managers and employees to keep Ben & Jerry's in the forefront of social change? Can a large corporation balance the desire to be socially responsible with the need to be profitable?[1]

CHAPTER OVERVIEW

Since their first day in business, Ben Cohen and Jerry Greenfield have felt an increasing tension between their concept of serving society and the economic necessity of pursuing profits. This chapter opens with a discussion of social responsibility, and it continues with an examination of the organization's stakeholders and of the relationship between social responsibility and organizational performance. After describing the seven areas of social responsibility, the chapter explains the continuum of social responsibility, along with the ways managers can institutionalize social responsibility. Next, the chapter examines ethics in the organization, defining ethics and drawing a distinction between ethical dilemmas and ethical lapses. Following this is a review of the process for developing ethical management practices, including identifying ethical pressures, resolving ethical dilemmas, and institutionalizing ethical behavior.

MANAGEMENT AND SOCIAL RESPONSIBILITY

During this century, managerial decisions and actions have increasingly come under scrutiny as academics, social activists, and managers debate the ideal relationship between the organization and society. One key issue is determining what the organization's responsibility should be for activities that affect society, both positively and negatively. A second key issue is determining how much responsibility an organization should bear for alleviating or solving social problems.[2]

social responsibility The argument that an organization has a greater obligation to society beyond the pursuit of its own goals

These two issues form the core of a concept known as **social responsibility,** which argues that every organization has obligations to society that go beyond pursuing its own goals; organizations should act in a manner that benefits society as well. Social responsibility can be examined at four levels: economic, legal, ethical, and discretionary. First, an organization has an *economic* responsibility to provide products that people want and to sell them at a profit for the company's owners (in the case of for-profit businesses). Management expert Peter Drucker states that organizations should not undertake social actions that are economically untenable or that detract from a minimally acceptable profit level. But economist Milton Friedman and others argue further that the responsibility to maximize profits is a business's only social responsibility. According to this viewpoint, noneconomic activities siphon funds away from shareholders, distracting managers from their primary profit-making goals. Moreover, business managers are not experienced in solving social problems, so their involvement in social causes may create a conflict of interest with ordinary business activities.[3]

The organization's second responsibility is the *legal* responsibility to pursue its activities within the bounds of all laws and regulations. However, laws and

As part of a multifaceted environmental initiative, Du Pont is voluntarily managing 1,000 square miles of corporate land as wildlife habitats. At the Du Pont Fibers plant in Kinston, North Carolina, employees have set up wood duck nesting boxes, created a bass pond, and converted fields to cover areas for sheltering birds and animals. Although Du Pont is not legally or ethically required to conduct these activities, management has made a commitment to the habitats.

regulations can't cover all the possible actions that an organization and its members can take. In numerous instances, from product labeling to employment practices, managers have to choose a course of action from among two or more alternatives, all of which are legal. The question then is no longer "What is legal?" but "What is right?" Determining what is right and acting accordingly represents an organization's third responsibility, its *ethical* responsibility.[4] Ethical decision making is discussed later in this chapter. Finally, the fourth level of social responsibility includes *discretionary* responsibilities, those that are purely voluntary and left to individual judgment and choice. These responsibilities are not required by law or even expected of the organization in an ethical sense.[5]

The four categories are not mutually exclusive; any given organizational activity may have a combination of economic, legal, ethical, and discretionary motives behind it (see Exhibit 4.1 for the relative magnitude of each responsibility). When weighing the interests of several stakeholder groups, managers must avoid letting their economic responsibility to shareholders completely override their legal, ethical, or discretionary responsibilities to other groups.[6]

The motivation to pursue social responsibility can range from pure self-interest to pure altruism. At one extreme, managers may formulate a policy of social responsibility because it seems to be in the organization's best interest to do so. Somewhat less self-serving is *enlightened self-interest,* the belief that the organization will prosper over the long term by undertaking activities that benefit society even if the organization has to bear additional short-term costs. At the other extreme is *altruism,* the desire to act in the best interests of society without considering self-interest. Whereas self-interest means doing good because it is good for the organization, altruism means doing good simply for the sake of doing good. Many organizations use enlightened self-interest to blend concern for their own needs with concern for their customers or others who are affected by their activities. For example, U.S. Bank (based in Portland, Oregon) caused a stir when it spent money on ads encouraging consumers not to overuse their credit cards and not to apply for loans they really didn't need. The ads are part of the bank's philosophy of "consumer advocacy," doing what is best for customers today in hopes of building customer loyalty for tomorrow.[7]

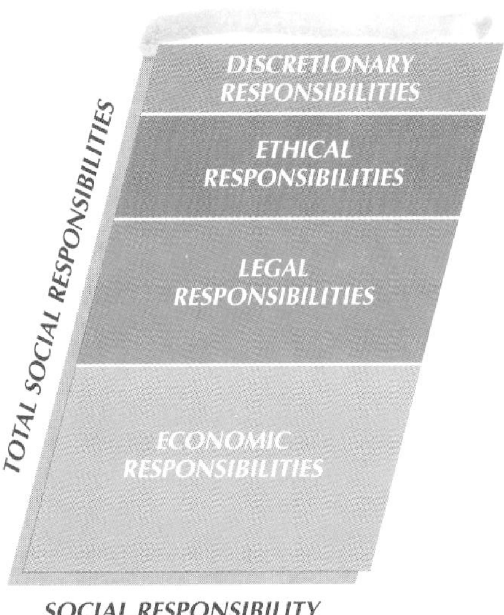

EXHIBIT 4.1

Social Responsibility Categories

An organization's social responsibilities can be viewed at four levels: economic, legal, ethical, and discretionary. The most important is economic responsibility, followed by legal, ethical, and discretionary responsibilities.

EXHIBIT 4.2

The Changing View of Social Responsibility

The nature of social responsibility and the extent to which organizations embrace it have changed significantly over the years. Early views of business involvement in social causes ignored the economic consequences of social activities. In contrast, the contemporary view takes into account the economic rewards (and penalties) of supporting social causes.

CONSEQUENCES
Economic *Social*
Economic
ACTIVITIES
Social

(*a*) 19th-CENTURY VIEW:
Business activities and concerns were purely economic.

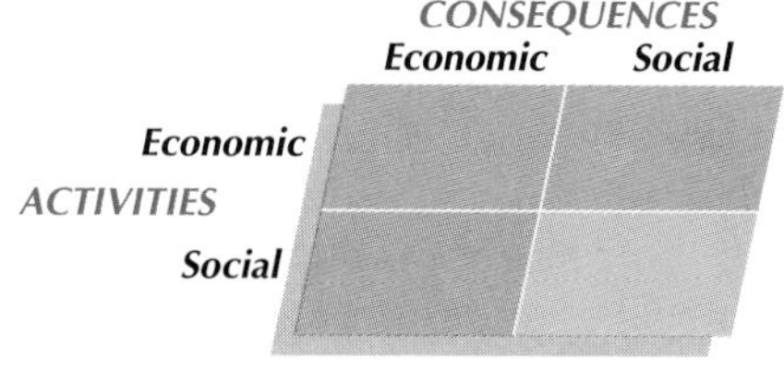

(*b*) EARLY 20TH-CENTURY VIEW:
Business became more charitable but these activities were separate from the firms' economic pursuits.

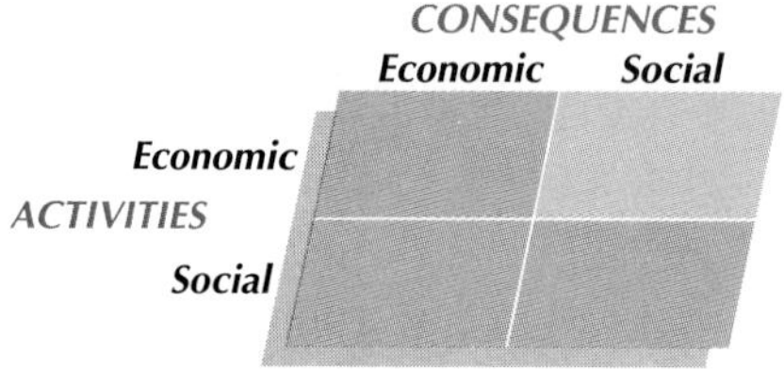

(*c*) 1960s AND 1970s VIEW:
Business was forced to consider the social aspects of its economic activites.

CONSEQUENCES
Economic *Social*
Economic
ACTIVITIES
Social

(*d*) TODAY'S VIEW:
When a firm engages in certain social activities, it can receive economic advantage.

These motivations have transformed the way organizations respond to the demands of society. In particular, businesses in the United States have gone through an evolution in their view of social responsibility (see Exhibit 4.2). From the Industrial Revolution to the early years of this century, businesses focused primarily on economic activities and concerned themselves solely with the economic consequences of their actions. The focus widened somewhat to include social activities, but these were pursued purely for social consequences; in this stage, businesses contributed to social causes strictly to achieve social objectives, quite apart from the economic pursuits of their businesses. From the mid-1960s through the early 1970s, the focus widened again, as social unrest, greater government involvement, and more socially motivated laws and regulations forced businesses to consider the social consequences of their economic activities.[8]

In today's environment, many U.S. businesses have come to believe that commitments to social responsibility and profitability are not incompatible. This view recognizes that social activity can lead to economic rewards. Most recently, the concept of **corporate social performance** evolved as a way to understand how much a business integrates the principles of social responsibility, the process of responsiveness to social issues, and the development of policies to address social issues. However, business executives, not-for-profit managers, government officials, academics, and social commentators are far from reaching complete agreement on the appropriate level of social responsibility for contemporary organizations, and they continue to debate business involvement in societal issues.[9]

corporate social performance A business's degree of integration of the principles of social responsibility, the process of responsiveness to social issues, and the development of policies to address social problems

Organizational Stakeholders

stakeholders Any group inside or outside the organization that can affect or be affected by the organization's activities

A complicating issue in the discussion of social responsibility is the fact that society is made up of many individuals and groups, often with conflicting interests and goals. These **stakeholders** can affect or are affected by the organization's activities. The major stakeholder groups are numerous, and they exist both inside and outside the organization (see Exhibit 4.3). Major stakeholder groups include employees and unions, customers and constituents, shareholders and owners, the government, special interest groups, lenders, suppliers, local community members, and competitors.[10]

Social responsibility involves weighing and balancing the interests of stakeholders to promote the common or social good. (Even the interests of competitors must be considered, to the extent that organizational practices may restrain fair trade.) This responsibility benefits the organization as well, since its very survival depends on the support of these groups and individuals. For instance, AT&T recognized the need to help employee stakeholders cope with increasing family pressures. The nation's largest telephone service supplier agreed to a three-year contract with its two major unions, a contract that emphasized family issues. The contract stipulated that the company would create a $5 million fund to develop community child-care centers and services for the elderly, extend unpaid leave to care for new babies or ailing relatives, and implement flexible schedules so that employees will be able to take off up to two hours on short notice to deal with family problems. Such efforts can be good for the bottom line by improving employee morale and productivity, by making it easier to recruit and retain good employees, and by reducing employee absenteeism.[11]

Marquette University in Milwaukee provides a good example of a not-for-profit organization reaching out to its community stakeholders. Over the last few decades, the neighborhood surrounding the university has steadily declined, amid rising crime rates and deteriorating housing. In response, Marquette recently proposed an ambitious plan to help revitalize the community. The university's president wants to reconstruct housing, to provide a wide range of health and social services, and to encourage employees and middle-class people to move into the area.[12]

Social Responsibility and Organizational Performance

Stakeholders are interested in social responsibility, but they are also interested in organizational performance. In fact, shareholders who invest in a company might be expected to set as their top priority the maximum return on their investments. But when a nationwide study asked people who owned at least 100 shares of stock listed on the New York or American stock exchange to rank their preferences regarding corporate spending, the top two items were (1) cleaning

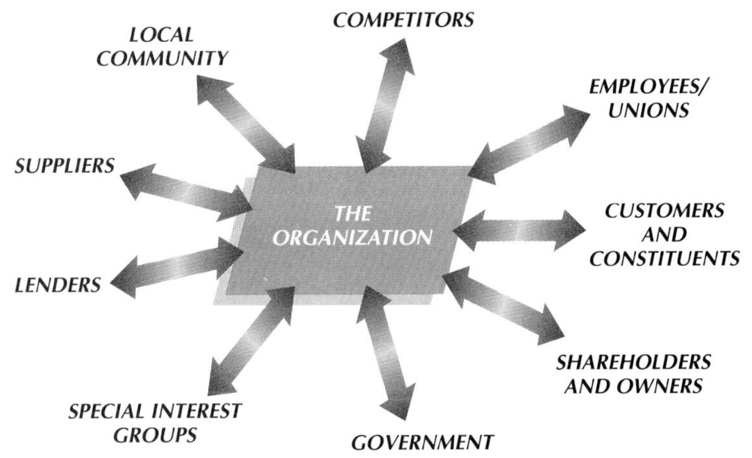

EXHIBIT 4.3

Stakeholder Map

A variety of groups can affect or be affected by an organization's decisions and actions. Managers must keep the interests of their various stakeholders in mind as they go about the daily business of running the organization.

GLOBAL MANAGEMENT

Japanese Adopt U.S.-Style Philanthropy

"We don't want Americans to see us as Godzillas," says Akiko Mitsui, a 26-year-old assistant vice president of Fuji Bank and Trust Company in Manhattan. That's why she and fellow Japanese executives at the bank volunteer their time to renovate buildings in New York City's poorer neighborhoods, turning them into residences for homeless people.

More and more Japanese companies are realizing the need to become good corporate citizens in the United States. Japanese executives have discovered, just as U.S. managers have, that social responsibility can pay off in the long run. Partly to soothe anti-Japanese sentiment, and partly to improve their image, the Japanese are beginning to rethink their relationship with the United States, its people, and its problems. As a result, charitable work by Japanese managers and employees living in the United States has flourished.

Employees of the Bank of California, owned by Mitsubishi Bank, volunteer at shelters for the homeless and at residences for battered women and abused children. The bank supports these efforts with donations to those organizations. In Seattle, spouses of some Japanese executives combine forces with spouses of U.S. employees to work at day-care centers in the inner city. Toyota Motor Manufacturing USA donated $15 million to county schools in Georgetown, Kentucky, after building a plant there (the plant was financed in part by tax-free bonds). Hitachi, the Japanese electronics giant, positions itself as "a truly American corporation," pointing out that 30 percent of the products it sells in the United States are made in the United States, and this percentage will soon be close to 50 percent. To support this position, the company will donate more than 1.5 percent of its pretax profits to community charities, universities, and cultural institutions.

U.S.-style corporate social responsibility is new and strange to Japanese businesspeople, for whom

up plants and ending environmental pollution and (2) making safer products. Higher dividends, which would be income to shareholders, ranked third.[13]

However, research seeking a definite link between social responsibility and company performance has not proved conclusively that socially responsible businesses are more profitable. Many studies comparing various levels of corporate social responsibility with company profitability have found no clear-cut relationship. On the other hand, Johnson & Johnson, the giant of health-care products, wanted to test the belief that the most successful corporations in the country are those that serve the public (in the broadest possible sense) better than their competitors do. With the Business Roundtable's Task Force on Corporate Responsibility and the Ethics Resource Center in Washington, D.C., J&J compiled a list of 15 "public service" companies whose long-term earnings could be compared with those of U.S. corporations in general. The study found that over a 30-year period, a $30,000 investment in a composite of Dow Jones firms (a measure of "typical" industrial performance) would have grown to $134,000. In contrast, if that $30,000 had been invested in the 15 public service companies (a group that includes such well-known firms as American Greetings, Hershey Foods, Matsushita Electric, Maytag, Melville Corporation, and Polaroid), it would have grown to over $1 million.[14]

The performance consequences of socially responsible conduct isn't limited to shareholder returns; it can also boost corporate health. For instance, companies that respond to major social problems and issues tend to keep government regulators at bay. Responsible employee relations garner greater employee cooperation, stronger job loyalty, more flexibility in hard times, and heightened productivity. Community service work reaps public relations advantages. All of these issues illustrate why doing good is often compatible with doing well.[15]

traditional ethics provide no generalized sense of charity. People have a certain duty to help others, but only those with whom they have relationships. In Japan, "corporate social responsibility" means taking care of one's own, the employees. The responsibility to the community at large is left to the government. In the United States, citizens have a clear incentive to make charitable contributions because such expenditures are tax deductible, but citizens of Japan have no such incentives. However, Japan recently doubled a corporate tax deduction for *international* charitable giving. One consultant who tracks corporate philanthropy predicts that this change will increase Japanese international contributions by two-thirds, to $500 million a year.

Support for U.S. philanthropy is especially evident among Japanese executives at the highest level. Sadahei Kusumoto, who heads the Minolta Corporation, spends five hours a week campaigning for United Way of Bergen County, New Jersey. He recently challenged other Japanese companies to contribute one-tenth of 1 percent of all U.S. sales to philanthropy. Matsushita rose to the challenge and pledged to do just that. With estimated sales of $5 billion, that translates to a charity budget of $5 million. Another leadership example was set by Tsuneo Tanaka, the former president of Hitachi America. When he left his position after five years, he skipped a farewell party and instead gave $10,000 "thank you" checks to the volunteer ambulance corps and the fire department in Tarrytown, New York, Hitachi's U.S. headquarters.

Japanese companies recognize that in the long run, failure to play an active role in their overseas communities will hurt their reputations and dim their prospects for the future. As Osamu Yamada, chairman of Bank of California, puts it, "We will not make progress if Japanese goods are no longer thought of as cheap, but Japanese companies are."

Apply Your Knowledge

1. Who are the stakeholders affected by the increase in Japanese philanthropy and how are they likely to be affected?
2. How does Japanese philanthropy relate to the concepts of self-interest and altruism?

Areas of Social Responsibility

Although organizations have come up with many creative ways to serve their various stakeholders, these efforts tend to fall into seven general areas of social responsibility: the community, health and welfare, education, human rights, the natural environment, consumer rights, and culture. Managers often allocate both personal and organizational resources to these causes.

The Community

Socially responsible organizations can make a substantial difference in their communities by providing leadership and assistance in solving pressing needs. Banking executives Mary Houghton, Ronald Grzywinski, Milton Davis, and James Fletcher, for instance, proved that it is possible for a bank to be socially responsible *and* financially sound. When they took over South Shore Bank, the bank and its surrounding community in Chicago's South Shore district were deteriorating. Houghton and her associates made South Shore Bank the first commercial bank in the United States to make community revitalization its primary goal. Unlike many banks that avoid making loans in certain neighborhoods for fear of higher defaults, South Shore makes lending decisions based on each individual's creditworthiness, and the bank now enjoys a repayment rate of over 98 percent. South Shore has an innovative program called Development Deposits, which features checking and savings accounts designed to attract deposits from institutions, not-for-profit corporations, and individuals who want to support worthy causes. As South Shore Bank serves its community, it prospers as well. Today, the bank employs over 100 people, and its assets exceed $163 million.[16]

Xerox emphasizes education as an important part of its corporate social responsibility. In Rochester, New York, engineer Llevelyn Rhone and other Xerox people serve as "Xerox Science Consultants." They visit city schools and teach geology and other science subjects, and they also serve as role models for students considering a career in science.

Ben & Jerry's Homemade supports a variety of socially responsible activities that benefit the local and regional community. The firm donates money to help battered women, homeless people, and other community groups. By making a concerted effort to buy milk from local dairy producers, Ben & Jerry's supports Vermont family farms. And any not-for-profit organization in Vermont that requests it can receive the firm's ice cream—for free.[17]

Health and Welfare

Many organizations believe that investing in community health is not only socially responsible but desirable, valuable, and necessary for everyone—including the company, the employee, and the community at large. These projects range from programs for children (such as Procter & Gamble's $375,000 renovation of community day-care facilities) to programs for the elderly (like the $80,000 worth of time, materials, and money that members of the Northeast Florida Builder's Association donated to turn a private residence into a model day-care center for people with Alzheimer's disease). But the amount of money spent doesn't have to be large. GTE Electrical Products in Danvers, Massachusetts, spent only $600 to reproduce an antismoking film that reached 22 high schools in the Boston area. And without spending a nickel, many organizations support community welfare by offering time off or otherwise encouraging managers and employees to do volunteer work for hospitals and health-care facilities.[18]

The altruistic element of such projects is obvious, but community improvement also gives organizations the opportunity to exercise enlightened self-interest. For instance, health and social welfare projects generate goodwill in the community, which can help companies attract employees and influence potential investors. And in a larger sense, vibrant, growing communities provide better markets for the companies that operate in them.

Education

Organizations of all types have a serious interest in their social responsibility for education. Faced with a shortage of skilled workers, managers realize that they must do something to improve preschool, primary, secondary, college, graduate, and vocational education, not just to be charitable or to generate positive publicity, but to survive. The current shortage of skilled workers may only get worse: researchers predict that the majority of new jobs over the next 15 years will require an education level beyond high school.[19] As much as one-quarter of the work force, or an estimated 20 to 27 million adults, cannot perform the reading, writing, or arithmetic necessary for basic job functions. Some 25 percent of U.S. teenagers drop out of high school, and many graduates have the equivalent of only an eighth-grade education.[20]

In response to these needs, businesses have devoted resources to several aspects of education. The Exxon Education Foundation, the Burnett Tandy Foundation, Westinghouse Electric, Dravo Corporation, and PPG Industries support teachers and principals who employ imaginative teaching methods, such as coaching students to use their intellect, not merely lecturing. In a different vein, Cray Research offers a two-week supplementary training course for 900 math and science teachers every year. And Kentucky's Ashland Oil uses stay-in-school advertising directed at children and their parents to cut the dropout rate.[21]

In the "Pepsi School Challenge," students attending inner-city schools in Dallas and Detroit receive tuition credits of $250 a semester for maintaining at least a C average, for attending school regularly, and for being free of "mood-altering substances." Over four years, the credits can reach $2,000, which are then made available for post–high school education.[22] Soft Sheen, manufacturer of hair-care products and the nation's sixth-largest black-owned company, adopted an elementary school and two public high schools, providing them with materials and equipment. "Our work force comes mainly from Chicago public schools," says Frances Williams Gutter, Soft Sheen's manager of special projects. "So it's important that we do whatever our resources allow."[23]

Human Rights

Some organizations focus their social responsibility efforts on campaigning for human rights. Reebok International, the athletic shoe manufacturer, underwrote Amnesty International's Human Rights Now! concert tour in honor of the fortieth anniversary of the Universal Declaration of Human Rights. Amnesty's objective is to stop torture and execution and to ensure fair and prompt trials for political prisoners and for people who have been detained for their beliefs, color, ethnic origin, language, or religion. Reebok's corporate philosophy, the right to freedom of expression, made it a natural sponsor for the musical tour, which brought the human rights message to 20 locations on 5 continents. Reebok has also established an annual Human Rights Award of $100,000 for one man and one woman younger than 30 who have raised awareness of human rights and freedom of expression.[24]

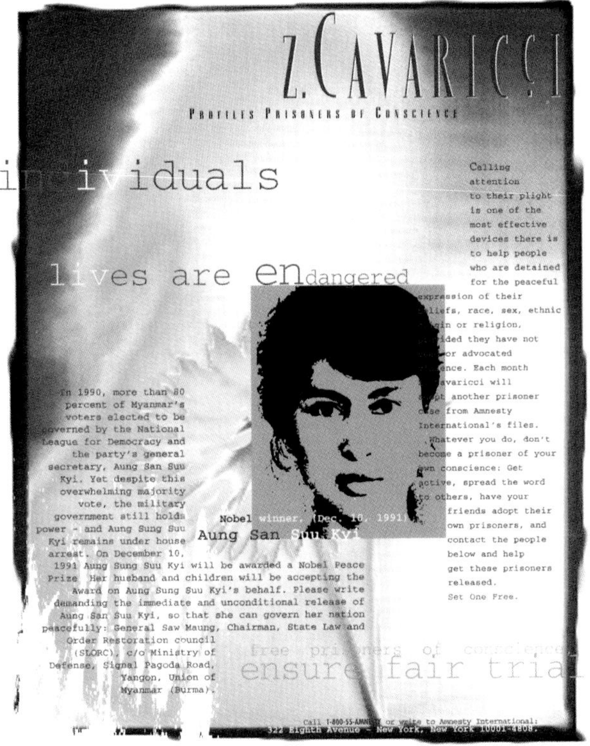

Z. Cavaricci, a Los Angeles, California–based maker of contemporary sportswear for men and women, has thrown its support behind the international struggle for human rights. The company recently ran a series of ads profiling Aung San Suu Kyi and other "prisoners of conscience," all drawn from the files of Amnesty International. The ads urged readers to become active in the fight to free political prisoners.

MANAGEMENT AROUND THE WORLD

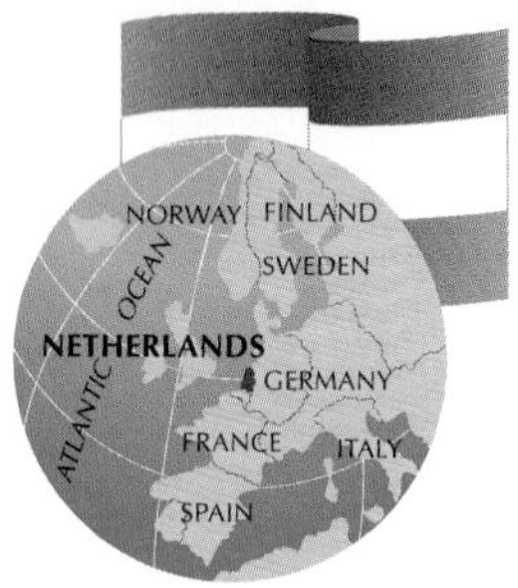

Concern for the natural environment has caused many countries to set stringent auto emission control standards. The Netherlands has one of the strictest regulations in Europe, and carmakers must comply. However, the Netherlands also offers a monetary incentive for manufacturers whose cars meet a higher emission control level. This enables automakers to satisfy economic, legal, and ethical responsibilities.

The Natural Environment

Many organizations choose the natural environment (which can encompass ecology, conservation of natural resources, protection of endangered species, and responsible waste disposal) as their area of social responsibility. Perhaps this isn't surprising: in one study, 77 percent of U.S. adults polled said that a company's environmental reputation influences what they will and won't buy. On a basic level, more organizations are supporting recycling efforts, reducing waste that might otherwise end up in landfills, using biodegradable materials, or switching to recycled materials. For example, the not-for-profit National Wildlife Federation recently began printing its gift catalogs on recycled paper, a move that reflects the organization's concern for the natural environment. Similarly, Apple Computer has switched to brown cardboard to avoid the bleaching agents normally used in white cardboard packaging.[25]

A growing number of businesses are finding ways to capitalize on consumer concerns for the environment by marketing "environmentally friendly" products. The Loblaws supermarket chain in Canada struck gold with its Green brand, promoted as products devoted to environmental preservation. The product line includes more than 100 products such as phosphate-free detergents, Alar-free apple juice, recycled motor oil, rechargeable batteries, and high-efficiency light bulbs. The products are packaged in recycled paper, and they sport lots of environmental or nutritional information. In their first year, Green products generated about $52 million in sales, with profit margins comparable to those of other product lines.[26]

Consumer Rights

Some organizations are particularly conscious of the rights of their consumers, taking great pains to ensure high quality, safety, and truthful advertising. The interests of consumer stakeholders are the top priority of Gillette's vice president of product integrity. This office oversees 29 engineers who use, abuse, and misuse household appliances; test the spraying ability of aerosol products; and double-check the company's quality-control specialists. The company also maintains medical evaluation laboratories where scientists look for ill effects of new Gillette products and check for any allergic reactions to shampoos, antiperspirants, and other Gillette products. Although this massive effort enables Gillette to comply with government regulations regarding product safety, the firm's obsession with effectiveness and quality goes beyond the legal minimum. The approach costs Gillette a lot of money, but top managers believe that a satisfied consumer is a loyal consumer, and that makes it all worthwhile.[27]

Culture

Businesses that support the arts believe that this form of social responsibility promotes awareness of their companies in a positive way. They view their support of cultural events as an investment in a better quality of life for the community. In turn, local customers, employees, and other stakeholders reap the benefits of this community enhancement. Westwood Pharmaceuticals of Buffalo, New York, makes donations to such organizations as the Buffalo Philharmonic. The company considers its support to be vital for these organizations, which, as the backbone of culture in the area, are also an integral part of the economy, bringing in tourists and dollars. By making people aware of the cultural activities available in Buffalo, Westwood believes it will also enhance its own long-term ability to recruit good managers and employees from outside the area.[28]

In the spirit of enlightened self-interest, support for the arts can help the company reach out to a generally upscale audience. When American Express sponsored performances of the National Theater of Great Britain at the Chicago International Theater Festival, it turned out to be a mutually beneficial partnership. The company paid for a brochure to be sent to American Express cardholders, offering tickets a month before they went on sale to the public. A large percentage of tickets were sold through this mailing, and American Express enhanced its upscale image while doing something special for its own customers.[29]

ORGANIZATIONAL APPROACHES TO SOCIAL RESPONSIBILITY

Organizations are remarkably like individuals when approaching the topic of social responsibility; some tend to act responsibly most of the time, others consistently avoid responsibility, and the rest fall somewhere in between. This section explores the range of attitudes and actions that organizations can exhibit, and it discusses strategies for encouraging responsible behavior within the organization.

The Continuum of Social Responsibility

When formulating an approach to social responsibility, an organization's activities can be categorized in one of four ways: opposition, obligation, responsiveness, or contribution to social responsibility (see Exhibit 4.4). These four categories of behavior form the continuum of social responsibility and range from a refusal to meet ethical standards at one extreme (opposition) to actively searching for ways to contribute to society at the other extreme (contribution). However, organizations, like people, don't exhibit consistent behavior day in and day out; generally ethical organizations can suffer temporary lapses, and organizations at the other extreme may perform admirably on occasion. In addition, the lines separating these categories are not always clear; organizational actions may sometimes appear to fall between two categories or defy easy classification.

social opposition The behavior of an organization that must be forced to comply with legal and ethical standards

- *Social opposition.* On one end of the continuum, the organization demonstrates little, if any, commitment to social needs. Organizations exhibiting this pattern of behavior, called **social opposition**, must be pressured into

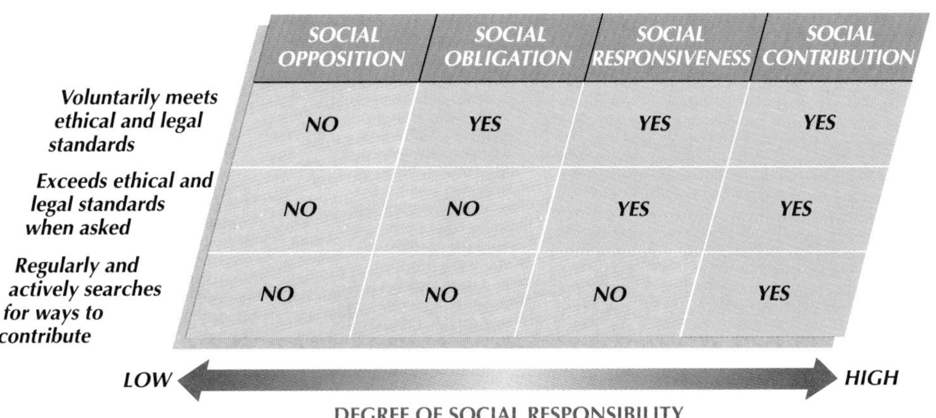

	SOCIAL OPPOSITION	SOCIAL OBLIGATION	SOCIAL RESPONSIVENESS	SOCIAL CONTRIBUTION
Voluntarily meets ethical and legal standards	NO	YES	YES	YES
Exceeds ethical and legal standards when asked	NO	NO	YES	YES
Regularly and actively searches for ways to contribute	NO	NO	NO	YES

EXHIBIT 4.4
The Continuum of Social Responsibility

An organization can react in one of four ways to issues of social responsibility. The lowest level of responsibility is shown by firms that choose social opposition, and the highest level is shown by firms that choose social contribution.

meeting ethical and legal standards, and they sometimes try to conceal their actions. For example, when a government auditor challenged military contractor Sundstrand about improper charges made on government contracts, the company's top managers attempted to slow and then to block the investigation. The auditor ultimately found documents showing that high-level executives ordered employees to falsify reports to the government.[30] Organizations demonstrating social opposition must often be forced by outside parties to meet ethical and legal standards.

social obligation The behavior of an organization that voluntarily conforms with legal and ethical standards but goes no further

compliance Adherence to laws and regulations

- *Social obligation.* Organizations that meet ethical and legal standards voluntarily but that go no further can be described as acting with **social obligation.** These organizations merely conform to legal constraints, ethical standards, and competitive market pressures. Organizations that exhibit this behavior do only what is absolutely necessary, and nothing else. Social obligation, then, is driven by **compliance,** abiding by what is required by law. Tobacco companies, for instance, put the U.S. Surgeon General's warning on their cigarette packages not to demonstrate their concern for consumers' health but because the law requires it of them.

social responsiveness The behavior of an organization that goes beyond legal and ethical standards to respond to some stakeholder needs

- *Social responsiveness.* Further along the continuum, organizations may demonstrate a greater commitment to social issues with behavior that can be described as a **social responsiveness.** These organizations choose to respond to stakeholder needs by assuming obligations beyond their legal and economic responsibilities. They make decisions and engage in activities that benefit society as well as the organization, thus often exceeding legal and ethical standards. Carol Bateson's concern about the environmental hazards of asbestos prompted her to start Dec-Tam, an asbestos removal firm. Dec-Tam has a reputation for going beyond customer and legal expectations. The company was among the first to have its own industrial hygienist check structural safety after asbestos is removed. Moreover, it posts a safety officer on-site during projects, and it alerts customers when their specifications may not be strong enough.[31]

social contribution The behavior of an organization that actively looks for ways to help stakeholders, above and beyond what is normally expected of it

- *Social contribution.* The greatest level of commitment to society can be found at the far end of the continuum. **Social contribution** refers to an organization's efforts to anticipate social issues that may affect the organization, to take preventive action to avoid adverse effects on society, and to regularly and actively search for ways to contribute to society. Consider the social responsibility exhibited by Anita Roddick's international cosmetics chain, The Body Shop. Roddick's concern for the well-being of employees and society permeates her decisions and activities, and she has built her chain on the basis of social contribution. She was an early opponent of testing of cosmetics on animals, and her products use primarily natural ingredients. But her stores are also a soapbox for Roddick's own social agenda. She asks customers to become involved in such diverse causes as Amnesty International and saving the Brazilian rain forests.[32]

The Social Audit

social audit A systematic evaluation and reporting of the organization's performance in the area of social responsibility

An organization that wants to keep social responsibility at the forefront of its strategy and operation can employ a **social audit,** a systematic evaluation and reporting of the organization's current performance in various areas of social responsibility. Some of the more common components of the social audit include the *stakeholder audit,* which helps management understand the interests

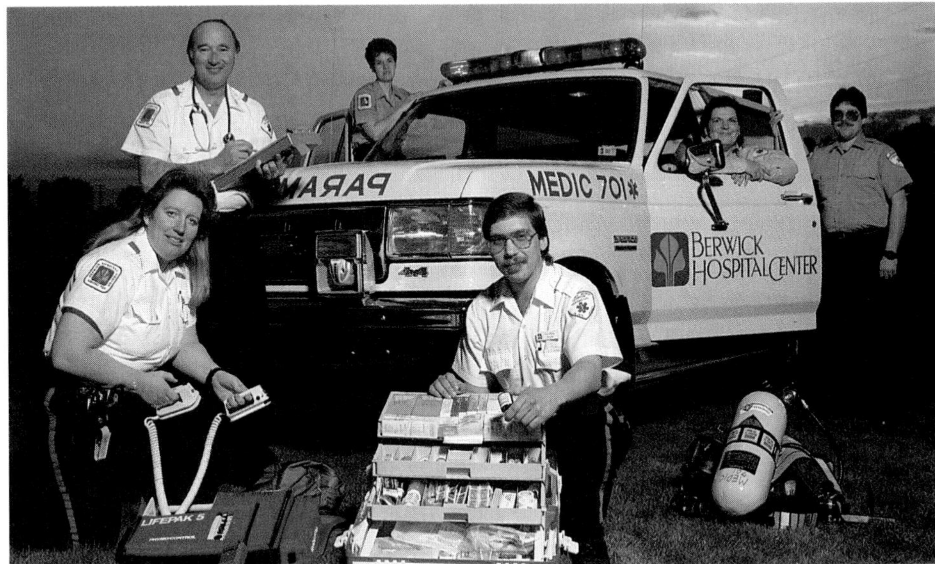

A Borden contribution helped the Berwick (Pennsylvania) Hospital Center launch a 24-hour paramedic service to serve the community, which includes a Wise Foods plant. This is one example of Borden's commitment to social contribution, an approach the firm has pursued for decades. In 1944, top managers created the Borden Foundation to manage corporate contributions, and most of its donations go to charities that help disadvantaged children and homeless families.

of its stakeholders and appraise organizational response; the *safety audit,* which assesses how well an organization is controlling and eliminating work-related hazards; and the *environmental audit,* which pinpoints potential risks to the natural environment, assesses the organization's efforts in this area, and identifies potential solutions. Although a growing number of organizations are preparing and publishing social audits to show the public the extent of their social responsibility, critics charge that many of these reports are incomplete and only cosmetic. However, if used properly, social audits can enable managers to measure organizational progress toward social responsibility goals.[33]

For instance, Ben & Jerry's Homemade conducts a social audit every year, just as it conducts a financial audit, and both are included in the company's annual report to shareholders. The social audit, called a "social performance report," reports on the impact of business activities on the firm's employees, customers, communities, suppliers, and investors, and it shows how well the company has integrated the founders' social vision into daily operations.[34]

Methods of Institutionalizing Social Responsibility

The social audit provides a tool to periodically check the organization's social performance, but it doesn't provide the methods to ensure responsible behavior day in and day out. To help institutionalize responsible behavior—to make it the rule rather than the exception—organizations are taking such actions as setting up public affairs departments, becoming advocates for social causes, establishing partnerships with former adversaries, lending executives to not-for-profit organizations, encouraging philanthropy, and starting cause-related marketing programs.

The Public Affairs Department

The public affairs department, also known as the *external affairs department,* serves as an important link between the organization and key external

Wakefern, owner of Shop Rite supermarkets, pursues corporate social responsibility through its advocacy of the fight against hunger. The firm donates hundreds of thousands of pounds of food every year to the Community FoodBank of New Jersey and to other agencies, and its trucks and drivers help distribute the food to the agencies. Wakefern also loans its expertise in truck maintenance, sanitation, and quality control.

stakeholders such as customers, government agencies, and the media. Its many duties include identifying social issues, forecasting societal trends, analyzing the social environment, communicating this information to the organization's management, and developing programs to meet the needs of specific external stakeholder groups.[35]

For example, many television and radio stations have public affairs departments to keep abreast of their audiences' most pressing concerns. Teri Zeni, public affairs director of KKOB-AM and FM in Albuquerque, learned there were 7,500 reported cases of child abuse in New Mexico each year. Her discovery prompted the AM station to run a week-long news series on child abuse, and the FM station discussed the subject on its Sunday morning public service show. In addition, both stations broadcast daily public service announcements as part of their commitment to social responsibility.[36]

Advocacy

Another way of institutionalizing social responsibility is through **advocacy**, in which the organization adopts a cause to support and throws its financial, material, and managerial resources behind the cause. Pacific Bell, for example, traditionally invisible on controversial topics, has become an outspoken advocate for AIDS education and a leader in addressing AIDS issues. Detecting a rising tide of concern during the 1980s, its director of preventive medicine and health education teamed up with like-minded middle managers to set company policies for handling AIDS issues. The company decided to publish educational articles on AIDS in its monthly newsletter. Soon top-level company officials came to believe that a public stance on AIDS was not only appropriate and politically astute but was also operationally important and morally right. To start, Pacific Bell produced a special video on AIDS issues, and it co-sponsored a statewide "AIDS in the Workplace" conference. Even more public was the company's opposition to proposed legislation that would have backed such measures as quarantining people with AIDS and abolishing anonymous AIDS testing. These and other examples of advocacy have helped Pacific Bell institutionalize the social responsibility for meeting the needs of stakeholders.[37]

advocacy An organization's support of a particular cause, through financial, material, and human resource backing

Partnerships

Partnerships with groups interested in the same cause or with groups that have traditionally been adversaries can help organizations as they seek mutually acceptable solutions to social problems. For example, Pacific Gas & Electric (PG&E) has teamed up with environmental groups (some of whom it used to fight) to conduct joint projects such as a $10 million study of energy efficiency. This cooperation not only helps reduce tensions between the company and special interest groups but also addresses a social problem by tapping into PG&E's expertise, energy production, to seek alternatives to the destruction of the natural environment.[38]

Executive Loans

Many companies allow their executives to take leaves of absence to assume temporary management positions in not-for-profit organizations. This demonstrates corporate commitment to the social causes supported by the not-for-profits, and it offers the loaned managers a new perspective on the issues. Frequently, loaned executives receive part or all of their company salaries while on loan. Asking executives at for-profit organizations to organize fundraising activities on a part-time basis while they remain at their full-time company jobs is another form of executive loan. United Way and other not-for-profits benefit from this common practice.

Philanthropy

Philanthropy is the donation of money, time, goods, or services to charitable, humanitarian, or educational institutions. Corporate philanthropy has traditionally assumed that corporations as citizens of the community (and citizens with greater resources than most) have a duty to make donations with little or no regard for self-interest. But a survey by the Council on Foundations (representing about 1,000 U.S. philanthropic foundations) indicates that the increasingly competitive business environment may be changing the face of corporate giving. Although corporate foundations are not legally allowed to fund programs that benefit their business parents directly, many companies now focus their nonfoundation contributions in more basic areas that potentially have a long-term impact on their own business interests, including developing future employees. Of the large-company CEOs polled recently, 75 percent said they have increased giving to education and have decreased giving to causes such as recreation and the arts.[39]

philanthropy Gifts of money, time, goods, or services to charitable, humanitarian, or educational institutions

For example, Atlantic Richfield in Los Angeles has stopped building museums and endowing symphonies, and it now concentrates on education, especially for Hispanic children who make up the majority of the elementary school population in Los Angeles. Further, overseas markets are playing a greater role in the earnings outlook for U.S. companies doing business abroad, so more firms are using philanthropy as a way of projecting a positive image abroad. Hewlett-Packard recently donated computers to the University of Prague, with the thought that this gesture might ultimately translate into more business opportunities there.[40]

Cause-Related Marketing

The strongest connection linking social responsibility with self-interest is **cause-related marketing,** a company's offer to contribute a specified amount to a designated cause when customers buy the company's goods or services.[41] Once the company has selected a worthy cause, it usually publicizes the issue and shows how contributions will help. At the same time, this association with a worthy cause boosts the firm's public image and its sales. These programs generally supplement but do not replace other organizational promotions (see Exhibit 4.5). For many companies, this form of institutionalized social responsibility complements other socially conscious activities and provides a way for customers to feel good about their purchases.[42]

cause-related marketing An activity in which the company contributes a specified amount to a social cause when customers buy its products

American Express is a pioneer in the use of cause-related marketing. In 1983 the company donated one cent from every American Express card purchase to help refurbish the Statue of Liberty, and it raised $1.7 million for the statue. For its part, American Express garnered free publicity, higher card usage, and a crop of new applicants. The company has since developed more than 60 such cause-related campaigns, and other companies have followed its lead. However, critics question whether the not-for-profit organizations that benefit from these programs feel pressured to make compromises so that their activities will seem more acceptable to the corporation. Some also question whether the funding for not-

EXHIBIT 4.5

Cause-Related Marketing

Cause-related marketing raises money for a social cause while garnering sales and publicity for the sponsoring corporation. Although it is rapidly becoming more popular, cause-related marketing is also controversial.

AN OFFER WORTH THE PAPER IT'S PRINTED ON.

With every new subscription, Business Week will plant a tree in one of America's Heritage Forests.

Every week Business Week brings you up to date on the world of business. We're committed to bringing you coverage of business news that is not only timely but insightful. Now, we're also committed to teaming up with you to make a positive contribution to our environment.

With the help of the Global ReLeaf Campaign of the American Forestry Association (AFA), we will plant a tree in one of America's Heritage Forests with every new, paid Business Week subscription.

Global ReLeaf educates people on opportunities to enhance the environment through improvement of trees and forests. The campaign creates these positive environmental opportunities for individuals, community groups and businesses.

The Heritage Forest Program is one such opportunity. Heritage Forests are special public lands, selected by the AFA as lands where private-sector donations can create new forests, that would not be possible under existing public programs and budgets.

SUBSCRIBE TO BusinessWeek NOW

We'll plant your tree and still offer you substantial savings. At only 89¢ an issue, you save 64% off the $2.50 cover price and make a positive contribution to the environment.

Enjoy the convenience of having Business Week delivered and the satisfaction of having done something to help improve and preserve America's forests.

It's easy to do. Fill out one of the post-paid cards found in this issue and drop it in the mail today or call toll-free 1-800-635-1200.

For more information on the Global ReLeaf Program, call (202) 667-3300 or write to them at P.O. Box 2000, Washington, D.C. 20013.

for-profits should depend on sales campaigns. Finally, should seemingly less-marketable causes such as preventing teenage pregnancy or child abuse be allowed to languish? These and other issues will continue to be raised as cause-related marketing gains momentum.[43]

MANAGEMENT AND ETHICS

The concept of social responsibility is generally applied to the organization, but the organization cannot make decisions; only individuals within the organization can do that. Top managers make decisions that affect the organization's policies and that determine how lower-level managers and employees should react to social issues; lower-level managers confront decisions that involve applying organizational policy to their day-to-day circumstances. Because the decisions that lead to undertaking any social action projects must be made by managers, it is their sense of right and wrong that ultimately determines the extent of any organization's social responsibility and responsiveness. Thus organizational social responsibility can be seen as rooted in managerial ethics.[44]

ethics The study of decision making within the framework of a system of moral standards

ethical behavior Conduct that is considered "right" or "good" in the context of a governing moral code

unethical behavior Conduct that is considered "wrong" or "bad" in the context of a moral code

The study of **ethics** in management addresses individual decisions in the context of certain rules of conduct or moral standards.[45] **Ethical behavior,** then, refers to individual conduct that is considered "right" or "good" in the context of a governing moral code. It conforms not only to the law, but also to a broader set of moral principles expected by all or by a segment of society. In contrast, **unethical behavior** covers any individual conduct that is "wrong" or "bad" within this moral code. It may or may not be illegal, but it falls short of the broader set of moral principles expected by society.

Any examination of ethics immediately encounters two fundamental questions. First, can there be a single fixed moral framework to guide all managerial decisions? Every time managers face ethical decisions, can they refer to one basic set of moral standards to help them decide which path to take? Second, if behavior should indeed be guided by a single set of standards, which is the right set? Many conflicting definitions of what constitutes good versus bad behavior exist;

SOCIAL RESPONSIBILITY AND ETHICS

Walking an Ethical Tightrope

Not long ago, Dayton Hudson, the giant Minneapolis-based retailer, received a blunt reminder of the emotions that underscore decisions surrounding many ethical issues. It all started when the Dayton Hudson Foundation, which handles the company's charitable donations, decided not to fund an $18,000 grant to the local chapter of Planned Parenthood, in response to concerns among the company's employees. This reversal of 22 years of contributions sparked anger among advocates of freedom of choice on abortion, who accused the company of bowing to anti-choice pressure groups. The most vocal opposition came from a statewide coalition of 170 women's groups who argued that the money had always been used for educational programs, not to fund abortion clinics.

The consortium began its attack with a highly publicized planning meeting, followed by a protest rally. Thousands attended the rally, held in front of one of Dayton Hudson's suburban Minneapolis department stores. Some protestors cut their store credit cards in half; one customer canceled a $32,000 order. Hundreds took advantage of the store's liberal return policy and brought merchandise back, complaining about the change in donations.

After a week of bad press, scathing editorials, and credit cards chopped in half, the Dayton Hudson Foundation said it would reconsider, and a few weeks later, an $18,000 grant earmarked for a clearly defined non–clinical education program was in Planned Parenthood's coffers. Then local anti-abortion groups swung into action, picketing the firm's department stores on the Friday after Thanksgiving, one of the biggest shopping days of the year. Although they boycotted many Dayton Hudson stores and conducted a letter-writing campaign to voice their objections, the company decided not to respond. One of these groups suggested that the company fund another educational grant to pay for fetal models to be used in local medical schools, but the foundation declined.

Dayton Hudson's attempts to defuse this emotional issue have not been completely successful. Some protestors still don't shop at the stores, and letters continue to arrive from both sides. Ironically, the Dayton Hudson Foundation gives away $30 million a year, of which the offending $18,000 was a mere pittance. Chairman and CEO Kenneth A. Macke says the incident taught him some hard truths about corporate charitable giving, namely, that good deeds are not necessarily rewarded or even appreciated, especially in today's activist environment. He is concerned that assaults by interest groups will discourage corporate giving or limit it to "safe" causes, to the detriment of society as a whole.

But Macke insists that the experience will not deter Dayton Hudson from future philanthropy. For decades, the company has contributed 5 percent of its taxable income to improving the quality of life in the communities where it does business. Macke views the decision to make charitable contributions as a sound investment in society that has paid off for the community, the customers, the employees, and the shareholders.

What's Your Opinion?

1. Where does Dayton Hudson fall along the continuum of response to social responsibility?
2. How might Macke have applied utilitarian theories and theories of rights to help resolve this ethical issue?

how can a manager determine which set of standards to follow?[46] These two questions are at the heart of every discussion of managerial ethics.

Consider the situation faced by Burroughs Wellcome, the maker of AZT, a drug that slows the development of AIDS. The thorniest problem with AZT is its price; at a cost of roughly $3,000 for one year's dosage, many patients can't afford it. However, Burroughs counters that it has kept the price as low as possible and that it is responsible to investor and employee stakeholder groups in addition to customers. If the company doesn't charge a high enough price to pay dividends to shareholders and to invest in research that will maintain the company's long-term health, wouldn't it be violating its responsibilities to both shareholders and employees? Someone whose value system gives priority to relieving suffering might say that the price should be lowered, but someone who believes a manager is obligated to repay shareholders as handsomely as possible might say that a higher price is more appropriate. As Burroughs Wellcome's situation shows, managers who face ethical issues often feel pulled by conflicting forces.[47]

Philip Morris, maker of Virginia Slims cigarettes, has sponsored championship tennis for more than 20 years, showcasing players like Kimiko Date. Philip Morris says it is promoting entertainment, and it doesn't ask players to smoke or to endorse smoking. But critics charge that linking cigarettes with sports is unethical because it may tempt young people who watch tennis and other sponsored events to start smoking.

Ethical Dilemmas and Ethical Lapses

Ethical questions can be divided into two general categories. The first is the **ethical dilemma,** in which an issue has two conflicting but arguably valid sides. A classic ethical dilemma in business is whether or not tobacco companies should be allowed to advertise. Allowing them to do so encourages unhealthy behavior, but not allowing them to advertise would violate their freedom of speech and hamper their ability to do business.

Here is a small sample of the ethical dilemmas that managers face:

- Employees have a right to privacy, but employers also have a right to expect safe, competent behavior from employees. Should employers be allowed to administer drug tests to their employees? Whose right should take precedence?
- Publicly held corporations have obligations to both shareholders and employees; if money is tight, should a corporation reduce dividends to shareholders or reduce wages to employees?
- Companies can sell more effectively if they collect information about potential customers such as buying habits, income levels, and life-styles. People have a right to privacy, but companies also have a right to conduct business. Whose rights are more important?

The common theme in all ethical dilemmas is conflict between the rights of two or more stakeholders. Managers are held accountable by many stakeholder groups, and the number of potential ethical dilemmas increases with the number of stakeholders.

ethical dilemma An unresolved ethical question in which each of the conflicting sides has an arguable case to make

ethical lapse A situation that occurs when a manager makes an unethical decision or engages in unethical behavior

The second category of managerial ethics covers the **ethical lapse,** which occurs when managers make unethical decisions. It is important not to confuse ethical dilemmas (which are unresolved interpretations of ethical issues) with ethical lapses (which are cases of unethical behavior). For example, the desire of Anheuser-Busch's managers to advertise a product that can result in alcoholism is an ethical dilemma, but the decision by some managers at Salomon Brothers to secretly buy more U.S. Treasury notes than the government normally allows is an ethical lapse.

International Perspectives on Ethics

Ethical standards differ from country to country and from culture to culture. Some of the stickiest ethical dilemmas managers encounter overseas involve bribery, kickbacks, payoffs, political contributions, and other questionable payments to foreign officials in exchange for international business. For instance, if a salesperson gives a potential buyer a gift, such a move would be seen by most U.S. businesses as a bribe. However, in many countries, giving business-related gifts is not only accepted—it is expected.[48] In a number of countries, standards of giving go beyond small gifts and involve cash payments to government officials and kickbacks to important customers.

Responding to cases of U.S. businesses bribing government officials in other countries, the U.S. government passed the Foreign Corrupt Practices Act (FCPA) in 1977 and amended it in 1988. This act imposes strict accounting standards and antibribery prohibitions on U.S. businesses operating overseas and it establishes specific standards for managers to use when determining what is permissible conduct. The law allows payments to officials to expedite routine government actions, such as processing visas and licenses or providing water, electricity, phone service, police protection, and mail delivery. Thus a U.S. manager is allowed to pay a customs officer $25 to expedite the inspection of shipments from overseas, a task that the officer would perform anyway, but the manager cannot pay the official to process the shipment without inspecting it.[49]

Critics of the FCPA say that it places U.S. businesses at a disadvantage in a competitive world marketplace. They argue that this causes U.S. companies to lose export business. Others counter that U.S. exports have not been affected by this law, and that companies can conduct business abroad without violating FCPA regulations. However, until more nations agree on what constitutes corrupt business practices, U.S. companies operating overseas will have to continue to tread lightly around the issue of questionable payments.[50]

Pressure to achieve profit goals and to beat the competition is fierce in the trading pits of the commodities exchanges. In recent years, some traders at the Chicago Mercantile Exchange have been charged with violating regulations in the buying and selling of soybeans and other commodities. To detect fraud and other unethical behavior, the Exchange plans to install a hand-held computer system that will record and track trades.

ORGANIZATIONAL APPROACHES TO ETHICAL MANAGEMENT

Ethical management practices don't just happen; they must be pursued with diligence and persistence. Managers can start by recognizing the pressures that lead to unethical behavior, understanding the decision-making tools that are available for resolving ethical dilemmas, and implementing policies and procedures designed to foster ethical behavior in the organization.

Identifying Ethical Pressures

Considering the complexity and volatility of today's organizational environment, it is no surprise that managers face a variety of intense ethical pressures. These pressures introduce ethical dilemmas in some cases and make unethical behavior seem attractive in others. By recognizing and understanding the pressures, managers better instill a sense of ethical decision making. The major sources of ethical pressure include organizational goals, personal goals, competition, conformity, and fear.

- *Organizational goals.* Ethical dilemmas and lapses can often be attributed to managers feeling pressure to meet their organizations' goals, whether the goal is to get a candidate elected or to sell a certain number of products. This pressure can cause managers to choose certain decisions that may in fact be less ethical than others but that lead to better short-term performance. An organizational culture recognizing that responsible decision making goes beyond immediate goals will encourage managers to ask and answer ethical questions.[51] Exhibit 4.6 lists some questions managers should consider when evaluating a situation's ethics.
- *Personal goals.* Just as organizational goals can distort the decision-making process, so can personal goals. For instance, a salesperson who wants to outsell everyone in the region and be promoted to sales manager might be tempted to overstate a product's benefits in order to close more sales. For

EXHIBIT 4.6

A Checklist for Evaluating Managerial Decisions

Checklists such as this one can help managers make appropriate choices when faced with ethical dilemmas.

1. **Does my decision treat me, or my organization, as an exception to a convention that I must trust others to follow?**
2. **Would I repel customers or constituents by telling them of my decision?**
3. **Would I repel qualified job applicants by telling them of my decision?**
4. **Have I been unduly influenced by peer pressure?**
   (If "Yes," answer questions 4a through 4c; if "No," skip to question 5)
   4a. Is my decision impartial?
   4b. Does it divide the stakeholders of the company?
   4c. Will I have to pull rank (use coercion) to enact it?
5. **Would I prefer to avoid the consequences of this decision?**
6. **Did I avoid any of these questions by telling myself that I could get away with it?**

similar reasons, an employee might try to represent another employee's work as his or her own, or the same employee might pressure others to lower their performance. Because personal performance plays such an important role in compensation and career advancement, personal ambition presents numerous opportunities for unethical behavior.

- *Competition.* The daily pressure of trying to beat the competition can also influence personal and organizational behavior. These situations can be particularly acute when competitors overstep ethical boundaries. In the computer industry, getting to market quickly with advanced products can be crucial to success. This race has spawned a trend in which some companies announce products well before they really exist, in order to preempt the market or to beat competitors to the punch. But the practice can mislead customers and can cause financial damage to businesses that are left waiting for products that arrive late or not at all.[52]
- *Conformity.* Throughout life, both on the job and off, the desire to fit in with one's peer group pressures individuals to act in certain ways. If the group norm on a production line, for instance, is to skip safety tests because they are tedious, anyone who wants to perform the tests is going to feel some pressure not to. The good news about conformity is that it also happens to be a great way to ensure ethical behavior—if employees think they need to act in an ethical fashion in order to be accepted by their peers, they will generally do so.[53]
- *Fear.* In extreme cases, employees sense that they must make unethical decisions in order to keep their jobs. If a building contractor instructs the site supervisor to use materials known to be substandard, the supervisor may see two choices: defraud the customer or find a new job. If the job market is tight and the supervisor has to support a family, the pressure to behave unethically can be overwhelming.

Understanding where potential pitfalls might appear increases an organization's sensitivity to ethics and helps it identify areas that need special attention. Once these areas are identified, managers can then employ a variety of decision-making tools to help address ethical dilemmas.

Resolving Ethical Dilemmas

Ethical dilemmas continue to receive a great deal of attention from philosophers and management experts, who have developed a number of tools to guide managers through the sometimes confusing and always difficult decisions regarding ethical dilemmas. These tools offer frameworks in which to consider the issues involved, and some offer criteria for making decisions. It is important to note that, like ethical issues themselves, these methods for making decisions are not always universally supported. Even the best models rarely lead to a single answer that is absolutely right, just, or fair, but they do point the way to answers that seem more right, more just, or more fair than others.[54]

Principles of ethical analysis have their roots in normative philosophy, the study of *proper* thought and conduct, or how people *should* behave.[55] Five commonly applied normative approaches are the utilitarian theories, deontology, theories of justice, theories of rights, and social contract theories. In addition, managers can temper their ethical behavior by using empathy to consider how other stakeholders might feel or what might happen if questionable organizational actions were exposed to public scrutiny.

Utilitarian Theories

Utilitarian theories support the idea that ethical behavior results in the greatest good for the greatest number. Such theories emphasize the outcome, not the intent, of individual actions. An act or decision is "right" if it results in benefits for people, and it is "wrong" if it leads to damages or harm. So according to utilitarian theories, the most ethical decision creates the greatest degree of benefits for the largest number of people while incurring the least amount of damages or harm.[56]

utilitarian theories Theories that evaluate the ethics of decisions and actions according to the greatest amount of good they generate

Utilitarian theories have several limitations. First, it is impossible to identify and measure all the social and economic benefits that might result from an action. Second, some actions are simply wrong despite great apparent benefits. For instance, embezzling money in order to contribute more to charity accomplishes a noble end with illegal and unethical means. And third, this approach could lead to an unjust distribution of utility, as in decisions that cause severe harm to an individual or to a small group in exchange for small benefits for a large number of other individuals, or as in decisions that sacrifice long-term good for immediate gain.[57]

Deontology

Whereas utilitarian theories emphasize the *outcome* of an action, **deontology** depends on the *intentions* of the person making the decision or performing the act. A deontologist would disagree with the emphasis on outcome as the determinant of moral action because consequences are generally indefinite and uncertain at the time the decision is made. Deontology focuses instead on universal statements of right and wrong, and it concerns the duties and rights of individuals. Immanuel Kant (1724–1804) provided much of the background for modern deontology. He proposed a simple test to evaluate the ethics of a decision: a person should ask whether he or she would be willing to have everyone in the world act in exactly the same way faced with similar circumstances.[58]

deontology A theory that judges the intentions of the person's decision or activities, rather than the consequences

However, this philosophy also has limitations. First, it provides no priorities or degrees of right and wrong, so it cannot offer any guidance when situations aren't clearly black and white. Second, many people insist that universal statements of right and wrong will always have exceptions. Third, this philosophy is too dependent on individual interpretation of the circumstances surrounding a decision; no two human beings are likely to view a given situation in exactly the same light.[59]

Theories of Justice

theories of justice Theories that contend that decisions must be based on standards of equity, fairness, and impartiality

Theories of justice contend that ethical decisions must be based on standards of equity, fairness, and impartiality. This philosophy stresses social justice and the opportunity for all to pursue meaning and happiness in life. The principle is always to act so that the least advantaged members of society will benefit to some extent, for this promotes individual self-respect, which is essential for social cooperation. Critics point out, however, that this theory assumes that social cooperation provides the basis for all economic and social benefits, which may or may not be true. Moreover, it downplays or even ignores individual effort.[60]

Theories of Rights

theories of rights Theories that contend that the most ethical decisions are those that best maintain the rights of the people affected

Theories of rights presume that the most ethical decisions are those that best maintain the rights of the people affected by them. These theories assert that decisions are correct only if all members of society somehow realize greater freedom to develop their own lives in their own way as a result of the decision. Theories of rights, unlike theories of justice, depend on equal opportunities for choice and exchange, not on equal allocations of wealth and income.[61] The limitation of this philosophy arises when rights conflict. For example, how can managers balance an employee's right to privacy and an employer's right to protect the firm by using a lie detector to test the employee's honesty?[62] In such a case, the argument degenerates into a discussion of whose rights are more important.

Social Contract Theories

social contract theories Theories that suggest that individuals as members of communities and of groups agree implicitly to conform to the goals and rules of these groups

Social contract theories hold that by virtue of belonging to a local community, to a larger community, and to groups such as organizations, individuals imply their agreement with the shared values and goals of these groups. By their membership, people are agreeing to conform to the common rules that govern the group's conduct. These rules transcend the moral standards of any individual acting alone and form the social contract that guides all members of the group when making ethical choices that affect other members. In the business world, the social contract maintains that a manager hired by a company is expected to abide by that firm's standards of ethical behavior. However, most people are concurrently members of many groups, including family, employer, local community, and nation, and this overlapping membership may cause conflicts when the social contracts of each group differ. For this reason, critics argue that social contract theories can force managers to weigh the relative morality of one group's rules against another group's rules. Also, these theories do not take into consideration the independent thinker who has a differing opinion about currently accepted group rules.[63]

Empathy

Managers don't have to become philosophers in order to improve the ethical quality of their decisions and actions. Merely practicing empathy can provide vital insights into the potential effects of any decision. Before making decisions, managers should try to imagine what it would be like to be in others' shoes, particularly those who would be directly and adversely affected by the consequences of the decision. By understanding how those people might feel, managers develop empathy with their point of view and can use this insight to temper their ethical decisions.[64]

Another way to use empathy is to try to imagine how colleagues, family members, and friends might react if they were to read about the manager's actions on the front page of the newspaper. Would the manager's peers within the organization approve of the activity or decision? Would family and friends be proud to see the manager's behavior described in public? By asking these hypothetical questions, a manager can consider the potential impact that questionable behavior may have by seeing the results through the eyes of others whose opinions are important.[65]

Institutionalizing Ethical Behavior

Managers can create an ethical organizational culture by introducing and nurturing approaches that emphasize the importance of ethical considerations. The approaches that can instill ethical principles in an organization include strong leadership and commitment from the top, codes and standards of ethics, training in ethics-related issues, ethics committees, ombudsmanship, and ethical audits.[66]

Leadership and Commitment

The move toward an ethical atmosphere must start at the top of the organization, led by the personal influence of top managers. The way the CEO and other executives exercise moral judgment can have more impact on an organization than any written policy. Whether they mean to or not, top managers set examples for the rest of the organization. They indirectly teach others what is forbidden, what is condoned, what is required, and what priorities are important. To be most effective in fostering ethical behavior, top managers should be consistent in their moral philosophy and in their ethical behavior. For example, when a Navy consultant left a confidential report behind after visiting the Bath Iron Works in Maine, chairman and CEO William Haggett scanned a copy, which included data on a competitor's product costs. After he flipped through, Haggett realized that his action was unethical, and he returned the report to the Navy. Soon after, Haggett gave up his CEO position (although he retained the chairmanship), citing his failure to set a proper moral example.[67]

Ethical Standards and Codes

Ethical standards are the guidelines of moral conduct in a given profession or group. One way to maintain the organization's ethical standards is in the employment process. Some firms administer honesty tests to applicants. Others conduct background investigations, with the applicant's permission. Still others require all potential employees to read and sign a statement obligating them to act according to the organization's values and ethical standards.[68]

ethical standards Guidelines governing moral conduct of a particular group

Probably the most visible sign of an organization's ethical philosophy is its **code of ethics**, a formal statement of the organization's values, ethical principles, and specific ethical rules (see Exhibit 4.7). Ethical codes should not be too vague or too detailed for practical use. Codes full of generalizations offer insufficient guidance for day-to-day behavior. However, detailing specific rules to cover every conceivable situation will only substitute rules for good judgment.[69] To be effective, the code must clearly state basic principles and expectations, must realistically focus on potential ethical dilemmas that employees may encounter, must be communicated to all employees, and must be enforced. Ideally, the code of ethics should be drawn up with the cooperation and participation of a cross section of managers and employees.[70]

code of ethics A formal statement of the organization's values, ethical principles, and ethical rules

EXHIBIT 4.7

A Code of Ethics

Defense contractor Raytheon explains its principles of business ethics and conduct in an 11-point code of ethics distributed to all employees. In addition, the company has specific ethical codes that explain the standards for conduct in buying, in labor reporting, and in working with the government.

1. Raytheon continues to adhere to the high ethical standards of conduct that have been with us since the company's founding.
2. Our environment places the strongest possible emphasis on high ethical performance and respect for the law. All employees benefit from Raytheon's reputation for integrity.
3. Every employee is responsible for ethical business conduct. Employees who violate our standards either through their own actions or by not reporting known violations by others will be disciplined (up to and including dismissal).
4. Employees must feel free to report any suspected violations of the Code of Ethics.
5. To be effective, the rules of ethics must be understood by everyone.
6. Raytheon will continue its active communications program about ethical standards to all employees.
7. We will comply fully with federal procurement laws.
8. All of us must avoid conflicts of interest between company business and our personal affairs.
9. The internal audit staff will help the Ethics Compliance Officer make sure we comply with our standards and policies.
10. Raytheon will participate in an annual defense industry "Best Practices Forum" to trade experiences and learn from others.
11. Our Certified Public Accountants will conduct an annual review of how our policies and practices are working.

Ethics Training

Another way to institutionalize ethical behavior is to provide ethics training. Chemical Bank has an extensive ethics-training program, and it starts on the first day of employment. All new employees attend an orientation session at which they read and sign the company's code of ethics. The training program starts with a videotaped message from the chairman emphasizing the bank's values and ethical standards. Chemical also provides in-depth training in ethical decision making for executives, which offers analytical tools to help weigh ethical issues. To make the course as pragmatic as possible, discussion focuses on case studies of hypothetical ethical questions based on interviews with bank managers. Instead of providing solutions to these cases, the trainers pose questions for discussion, such as "Do you believe the individual violated the bank's code?" or "How do you think this person should handle the situation?" As another example, Citicorp supplements its ethical standards book and ethics-training sessions with a board game called *The Work Ethic,* developed to teach the bank's ethical standards and to encourage a continuing dialogue about the ethical issues bank employees and managers frequently face on the job.[71]

Ombudsmanship

ombudsmanship A system of review and evaluation that provides employees with an avenue for airing concerns about ethical conflicts

Ombudsmanship is an informal review process that provides an indirect, nonthreatening means of obtaining a response from senior management about an ethical conflict. An organizational ombudsman may counsel younger employees on sticky career issues, organizational difficulties, and ethical questions; may act as the organizational conscience; may investigate complaints about unethical behavior; and may point out potential ethical lapses or dilemmas to top managers.[72]

Ombudsmanship and other methods, such as telephone hotlines, provide internal methods that allow managers or employees to air their questions and complaints without fear of retribution. But the mere existence of an ombudsman and other channels for reporting or questioning instances of possible organizational misconduct may not go far enough. When organization members are not convinced that unethical activities will be halted even after management has been informed of their existence, they may resort to **whistle-blowing,** the public disclosure of illegal, immoral, wasteful, harmful, or illegitimate practices by the organization. Whistle-blowing brings along with it high costs: the reputation of the organization suffers (whether the organization wins or loses), much time is consumed and money spent as the organization defends itself, and employees' morale may decline as they perceive the organization to be unsympathetic to legitimate concerns expressed by employees. Moreover, whistle-blowers who do not work for the government may very well lose their jobs as a result of their actions, however well-meaning. On the other hand, the U.S. government encourages citizens to uncover government-contract fraud through the False Claims Act, a law that goes back to 1863 and stems from President Lincoln's efforts to halt Civil War profiteering. The whistle-blower who sues to redress defense-contractor fraud, medicare overbilling, and the like can collect a hefty percentage of the damages if the defendant is convicted.[73]

whistle-blowing An employee's public disclosure of illegal, unethical, wasteful, or harmful practices by his or her own organization

Ethics Committees and Ethical Audits

Some organizations establish standing committees of the board of directors to consider ethical aspects of the company's policies and practices. Thus ethics begin at the very top of the organization, communicating to employees and other stakeholders the company's ethics commitment. For example, Boeing has had an ethics committee since 1964 and Xerox established an internal audit committee to monitor ethics.[74]

Dow Corning has used face-to-face "ethical audits" at its manufacturing plants worldwide for over a decade. The evening before the audit, auditors meet with the manager in charge to determine the most pressing issues. The actual questions that the auditors ask come from relevant sections of the corporate code, and they vary according to the audit location. For example, in the sales offices, the auditors may concentrate on kickbacks, whereas at manufacturing plants, the focus may be on environmental issues. Some examples of questions that the ethics auditors may ask Dow Corning are: (1) Has Dow Corning lost any business because of a refusal to provide "gifts" or other incentives to government officials? (2) Do any employees have an ownership or financial interest in any of Dow Corning's distributors? (3) What specific Dow Corning policies conflict with local practices? Dow Corning's manager of Corporate Internal and Management Communications believes the ethical audit makes it virtually impossible for employees to consciously make an unethical decision.[75]

Dow Corning's ethics program is considered one of the most extensive in the country, and it has served as a model for many executives. However, the company's experience with silicone breast implants demonstrates that even the best ethics program doesn't provide an automatic guarantee of ethical behavior. The implants made headlines in 1991 and 1992 when word began to spread that a number of women discovered that their implants had ruptured, causing concern about the silicone's effect on the body's autoimmune system. Concern turned to anger for many people when they learned that a Dow Corning engineer had tried to warn management about the potential for rupture as far back as 1976.[76]

The Arlington, Tennessee, plant that manufactures the implants underwent an ethics audit in October 1990, but no one mentioned the implants. How could a potential problem of this magnitude not show up in the audit? Dow Corning explained that product safety issues are handled through regular management channels, and in the case of the implants, the company decided to conduct further testing but not to stop selling the product. Dow Corning has acknowledged the potential for rupture, but claims that data regarding health problems are inconclusive.[77]

In late 1991, however, the Food and Drug Administration warned the company about misleading women regarding the safety of silicone implants and shortly thereafter issued a temporary ban on implant sales in order to study the problem further. (The FDA has never tested implants in the way it tests other medical products because the implants went on the market before the FDA had such authority.) In the weeks following the ban, dozens of women filed lawsuits against the company which subsequently withdrew from the implant market.[78] Regardless of the outcome of these suits and further scientific investigations, the Dow Corning case clearly demonstrates the challenges inherent in managing organizational ethics.

SUMMARY

The concept of social responsibility argues that organizations have obligations to society beyond pursuing organizational goals and should act in ways that benefit society as well. These obligations can be divided into economic, legal, ethical, and discretionary responsibilities. Social responsibility is undertaken because of motives that range from pure self-interest to enlightened self-interest and further to pure altruism. Every organization affects, and is affected by, a number of stakeholder groups; the major groups are customers and constituents, employees and unions, suppliers, competitors, lenders, shareholders and owners, governments, special interest groups, and local communities.

Social responsibility applies in seven areas: the community, health and welfare, education, human rights, the natural environment, consumer rights, and culture. An organization's social commitment can be viewed on a continuum from doing as little as possible to going above and beyond what is expected. The positions a company can take along this continuum include social opposition, social obligation, social responsiveness, and social contribution. Organizational social responsibility can be institutionalized in a variety of ways: through a public affairs department, through advocacy, through partnerships, through executive loans to not-for-profit organizations, through philanthropy, and through cause-related marketing.

Ethics in management is the study of how closely managerial decisions and actions align with codes of moral standards, which try to distinguish right from wrong. Ethical issues can be divided into ethical dilemmas (a manager has to chose between two or more arguably valid positions) and ethical lapses (cases of unethical behavior). Philosophers have developed a number of models and systems to help people resolve ethical dilemmas. Utilitarianism prompts people to examine the potential outcomes of a decision and then choose the alternative that delivers the most good for the most people. Deontology, on the other hand, places emphasis on the reasons a particular action is taken, rather than on the rightness or wrongness of the outcome. Theories of justice base decisions on the standards of equity, fairness, and impartiality. Theories of rights, in contrast, examine whether decisions and actions leave those affected in positions of greater freedom to live their lives as they see fit. Social contract theories argue that individuals, as members of larger communities and of organizational groups, agree implicitly to conform to the shared values and goals of these groups.

Managers institutionalize ethical decision making and behavior in three ways. First, they try to understand and identify the sources of ethical pressure that pose ethical dilemmas for their employees or that lead some employees into making unethical decisions. Second, they use the decision-making models listed in the preceding paragraph, as well as empathy, to help resolve ethical dilemmas. Third, they introduce and nurture approaches that emphasize the importance of ethical considerations. These include leadership and commitment, ethical standards and codes, ethics training, ombudsmanship, ethics committees, and ethical audits.

MEETING A MANAGEMENT CHALLENGE AT BEN & JERRY'S HOMEMADE

As the size of their company increased, so did the tension that was felt by Ben Cohen and Jerry Greenfield. The reason for the growing tension was simple: the founders now had to deal with multiple stakeholder groups as they balanced the need to make a profit with the desire to be socially responsible. Cohen and Greenfield wanted to translate the company's profits into generous social contributions. Investors, regardless of their personal positions on the company's social stance, wanted to ensure the safety and growth of their investments. Moreover, some stakeholder groups had other concerns. Many managers and employees (and the founders themselves) wanted to maintain the casual, footloose environment that had characterized the company's early days. But others wanted more stability and consistency in their jobs. Although the situation at Ben & Jerry's was more pronounced than at the typical U.S. corporation, the underlying tension was the same: how can managers balance the competing interests of stakeholder groups?

The first step was to recognize that Ben & Jerry's was no longer a tiny partnership that could fly by the seat of its pants. The company was now a public corporation (in Greenfield's temporary retirement, Cohen had sold company stock to the public to fuel further expansion) with hundreds of employees, thousands of stockholders, and annual revenues approaching $100 million. Next, the founders and their management team (with employee participation) defined a mission statement that outlined the company's purpose, areas of focus, and overall goals. This mission statement appears in the company's annual report:

1. *Product mission.* To make, distribute, and sell the finest quality all-natural ice cream and related products in a wide variety of innovative flavors made from Vermont dairy products.
2. *Social mission.* To operate the company in a way that actively recognizes the central role that business plays in the structure of society by initiating innovative ways to improve the quality of life in a broad community: local, national, and international.
3. *Economic mission.* To operate the company on a sound financial basis of profitable growth, increasing value for our shareholders, and creating career opportunities and financial rewards for our employees.

Ben Cohen (*left*) and Jerry Greenfield (*right*), co-founders, Ben & Jerry's Homemade

Ben & Jerry's social mission of actively finding ways to improve the quality of life is the very definition of a company whose approach to social responsibility is one of social contribution. But its economic mission of increasing value for shareholders and creating career opportunities and financial rewards for employees indicates that the company is also seeking to balance the competing interests of various stakeholder groups. Ben & Jerry's employees, suppliers, customers, shareholders, and community now have a clear sense of where the company is going, and each group knows that its interests are important factors in management's decision-making process. For founders Ben Cohen and Jerry Greenfield, profits and products have become the recipe for a unique brand of social responsibility.

You're the Manager: As vice president of Ben & Jerry's and as a member of the board of directors, you are responsible for the day-to-day operations of the company. You need to maintain production and distribution of the ice cream, and you must make sure that the company is managed in accordance with the mission statement. Consider the following scenarios and decide how you will act in each case.

Ranking Questions

1. The national sales manager has just quit, explaining that she can no longer accept the five-to-one salary ratio. This decree, made in the early days of the company, says that the highest-paid person can make no more than five times the salary of the lowest-paid person. So Ben &

Jerry's top managers often make less than they could elsewhere. What can you do to attract highly qualified applicants? Rank these choices from best to worst.

a. Raise the salary of the lowest paid employee in order to offer a more competitive salary for the sales manager position.
b. Examine the local job market and the economy to see whether a higher ratio is truly needed; if the need can be substantiated, recommend a change.
c. Convince the company's directors that salary restrictions are not needed to be a socially responsible company, and suggest that the ratio be eliminated. Good performers are attracted because of the firm's social mission, but the salary restrictions keep the company from hiring the best.
d. Make no attempt to change the ratio. Promote the job opening by stressing the other aspects of the company. The salary will ensure that those who apply are committed to the social goals of the company.

2. A group of the company's employees recently approached you with their concerns about one of the social causes the company supports through its donations. Although you support this cause, some employees are opposed to it and do not want the company to support it through the not-for-profit Ben & Jerry's Foundation, which distributes the company's donations to worthy causes. Rank the following actions from best to worst.
   a. You meet with the concerned employees to say that all employees need not support all the social causes and that the Foundation holds final responsibility for allocating funds to worthy causes.
   b. You decide to take the issue back to the employees, and you convene a meeting of all employees to hold a vote on which causes to support.
   c. You feel obligated to act on employee concerns about this cause. You approach the board and ask them to withdraw support from this cause.
   d. You personally believe in this cause and do not want to change anything, so you use your influence to keep the funds flowing.

Multiple-Choice Questions

3. A new ice cream that would promote a healthy ozone layer has been proposed. Ingredients will be produced by environmentally sound practices, making the product more expensive to manufacture than competitive products. A preliminary review indicates the product would pay for itself but generate no profit at the price currently projected. Which is your best response?
   a. The ice cream meets the company's mission statements. You should go ahead at the proposed price, since other products will make up for the lack of profit, but you should look for opportunities to improve the profit.
   b. You believe you are being disloyal to the shareholders if you do not maximize profits, so you decide to withdraw your support for the product.
   c. You decide to replace some of the environmentally sound ingredients to reduce the cost. This may dilute the social message but you need to keep the shareholders in mind.
   d. You believe people will pay more for a product associated with this issue. You set a higher price to generate profit, and you make the product.
4. Responding to growing public concern about unhealthy foods, a congressional bill has been proposed to limit the fat content of all manufactured foods. Most of your products are high in fat. What can you do?
   a. You should hire a professional lobbyist to block the bill. You believe people must decide for themselves what to eat and which foods to buy.
   b. You share the government's concern for consumer health. You make plans to reduce the fat content of all Ben & Jerry's ice cream products.
   c. To fight the proposal, you organize a coalition of ice cream makers as a special interest group to pressure Congress into dropping the bill.
   d. You support the effort to reduce fat, but you also believe in consumer choice. You propose an alternative bill to require accurate food labeling.

Analysis Questions

5. Was Jerry Cohen right when he concluded that a for-profit company could make acting as a social force its primary goal?
6. Ben & Jerry's ice cream is more costly than some other brands, in part because the company buys from local dairy farmers and from suppliers connected with social causes, whose prices are usually not the lowest. How can Cohen justify higher prices in light of utilitarian theories that seem to suggest that lower prices for thousands of consumers (rather than higher returns to a

few suppliers or contributions to a few social causes) might be the greatest good?

7. How can Ben & Jerry's use a public affairs department to further the achievement of its social goals?

Special Project

An employee has proposed a new idea: to create a separate Ben & Jerry's division specifically to fulfill the company's social goals in supporting the natural environment. The division would be expected to break even but not to generate a profit. In two to three pages, outline your ideas for this division. How could it promote more public and private support for the natural environment? What stakeholders would be affected by this division? What social responsibility goals might Ben & Jerry's set for this division and how might it measure its performance?[79]

KEY TERMS

advocacy (116)
cause-related marketing (117)
code of ethics (125)
compliance (114)
corporate social performance (106)
deontology (123)
ethical behavior (118)
ethical dilemma (120)
ethical lapse (120)
ethical standards (125)
ethics (118)
ombudsmanship (126)
philanthropy (117)
social audit (114)
social contract theories (124)
social contribution (114)
social obligation (114)
social opposition (113)
social responsibility (104)
social responsiveness (114)
stakeholders (106)
theories of justice (124)
theories of rights (124)
unethical behavior (118)
utilitarian theories (123)
whistle-blowing (127)

QUESTIONS

For Review

1. What are ethics and social responsibility and how do they affect management?
2. What are the seven areas of social responsibility? Describe how an organization's stakeholders can benefit in these areas.
3. What is meant by the "continuum of social responsibility," and what are the four organizational positions on this continuum?
4. How do ethical dilemmas differ from ethical lapses?
5. How do utilitarian theories differ from deontology as an ethical philosophy?

For Analysis

1. How are philanthropy and cause-related marketing similar and how are they different? Why is philanthropy more socially acceptable than cause-related marketing?
2. Some people believe that ethics cannot be taught in college because students' moral standards are already formed by then. Should colleges include ethics as part of the curriculum?
3. From the viewpoint of the organization and of society, what are the possible drawbacks to social responsibility?
4. One potential solution to the crisis in public education is to let parents decide which public school their children should attend, allowing free market forces to reform the schools. Which ethical decision-making models might support and which might refute this proposal?
5. Recall some cases in which people acted unethically, and identify some of the pressures that may have contributed to their behavior. How might these pressures have been alleviated without acting unethically?

For Application

1. Corporate leaders often find it difficult to justify philanthropy in times of lower profitability and employee layoffs. Considering the principle of enlightened self-interest, what type of philanthropy program might a publicly owned printer be able to justify to stakeholders?
2. Suppose you are an executive of a large advertising agency. A commercial producer with whom you have worked in the past offers to pay you a "referral fee" for recommending him to other agencies seeking a producer, a common practice in the industry. You would not recommend him unless you believed he was qualified, and you do think he is. What ethical

issues should you consider in making your decision to accept or reject his proposal?

3. How is the issue of random drug testing of company employees an ethical dilemma? What are the two conflicting sides and what decision-making model(s) would be most appropriate in this situation?
4. You're the CEO of an organization in which employees own nearly all of the stock. How should you balance the conflicting interests of *(a)* paying employees higher salaries versus *(b)* paying shareholders higher dividends?
5. How might the director of a local history museum use a social audit to understand its social responsibility performance?

KEEPING CURRENT IN MANAGEMENT

Find an article that describes an ethical lapse in a business, not-for-profit, or government organization. This can cover any ethical topic, as long as the action described was clearly a violation of generally accepted ethical standards. Don't pick an issue in which the moral questions have yet to be resolved to society's general satisfaction (such as abortion, birth control, gun control, and cigarette advertising). Some examples of ethical lapses include instances of securities fraud, deceptive advertising, price fixing, selling dangerous products, and rigging an election.

1. Why did the lapse occur? What pressures may have caused the manager or the employee to behave unethically? Was the lapse disclosed by a whistle-blower?
2. How were the organization's stakeholder groups affected? Did any group benefit as a result of the ethical lapse? Was any group harmed? Could the organization have foreseen this harm by using empathy?
3. What steps could be taken to avoid similar lapses in the future?

SHARPEN YOUR MANAGEMENT SKILLS

How an organization responds when it discovers that managers or employees have crossed an ethical line has a big effect on stakeholders. If top management tries to cover up the wrongdoing until evidence is made public, it may permanently erode stakeholder confidence. At the same time, deciding how and when to disclose an ethical lapse is a delicate task.

You are the director of public relations for Salomon Brothers, a large U.S. government bond dealer. Salomon officials recently admitted that some of the firm's managers had acted improperly by intentionally violating strict bidding rules during some government auctions of Treasury notes. The Securities and Exchange Commission is investigating the potential impact on bondholders, on rival bond dealers, and on Salomon customers. Chairman and CEO John H. Gutfreund has just decided to step aside as a result of his failure to take prompt action when he was notified of the questionable Salomon activities, and your task is to report his departure to the media.

- *Decision:* Although you have not yet notified anyone about Gutfreund's departure, reporters have been calling to ask if and when he plans to resign. You don't plan to formally issue any information for several hours, but you feel the public does have a right to know about this major organizational change. Ethically, how should you respond?
- *Communication:* Draft a one-page press release that breaks the news to newspapers, magazines, and TV and radio broadcasters. Consider the feelings of innocent Salomon employees and managers, of customers who might lose confidence in the firm, of government regulators investigating the incident, and of the community at large.[80]

As consumers grow increasingly concerned about health and the environment, one leading chemical company isn't getting defensive. It's getting on the bandwagon. Monsanto CEO Richard J. Mahoney is voluntarily reducing pollution and moving the company away from bulk chemicals and toward research-based products that promote health. Mahoney believes such socially responsible actions will make his company more competitive and more profitable.

HISTORY

Founded in St. Louis in 1901 by first-generation American John Queeny to produce saccharin, vanillin, and caffeine, Monsanto grew rapidly during World War I, when the United States could no longer get chemicals from traditional sources in Germany. The company entered many chemical businesses but had the greatest success in farm chemicals. When Mahoney was named CEO in 1983 after more than 20 years with Monsanto, he vowed to transform it from a bulk chemical producer into a socially responsible industrial enterprise. Mahoney changed Monsanto's direction by selling off petrochemical, polystyrene, benzene, raw fibers, paper chemical, and oil and gas businesses that produced $4 billion in annual sales. Those businesses have been replaced by more emphasis on farm products (including pesticides), specialty chemicals, and plant and animal genetics, and annual sales have grown to $9 billion with a net income of $546 million. In 1985 Monsanto bought pharmaceuticals company G. D. Searle and picked up Searle's artificial sweetener NutraSweet in the bargain. NutraSweet is Monsanto's hottest item, with sales approaching $1 billion a year. Protein-based NutraSweet replaces sugar in 3,000 products and is the basis of a major subsidiary that plans to be a global leader in innovative foods that contribute to healthier lifestyles.

ENVIRONMENT

Monsanto has pledged to work toward eliminating pollution from its operations, to help achieve environmentally sound agriculture, and to "conduct our business, at all times, in an ethical, lawful, and socially responsible manner." It has reduced its U.S. air emissions of toxic chemicals 58 percent in four years. Its agricultural division has developed insect-resistant cotton that uses less chemical insecticide, and it has offered the industry's first program to assist cleaning up wells in agricultural areas. And even though G. D. Searle has only recently made any profit for Monsanto, it has begun a program that gives away heart-treatment drugs to Americans who have no health insurance. The NutraSweet subsidiary is basing its entire business on health advantages over other sugar substitutes (which are suspected of causing cancer), and it has won approval for a new protein compound, Simplesse, which is designed to replace fat in uncooked products.

GOALS AND CHALLENGES

Some of Monsanto's initiatives create new dilemmas. Monsanto's first biotechnology product is a hormone designed to produce more milk in cows; but dairy farmers are showing resistance because they believe that consumers view milk as a pure product and that sales may plummet if consumers believe, even mistakenly, that this purity is being threatened. The NutraSweet subsidiary's products also are raising some concerns. Although the Center for Science in the Public Interest has no problem with NutraSweet's fat substitute Simplesse, some nutritionists say fat substitutes may actually encourage the consumption of fat; they note that 34 million Americans are overweight and the mean weight of Americans has risen steadily since the introduction of sugar substitutes more than 30 years ago. These concerns complicate Mahoney's drive for social responsibility, a competitive advantage stemming from good public relations, and improvement in short-term and long-term profits.

1. How has Monsanto demonstrated both enlightened self-interest and altruism in its new initiatives under CEO Richard J. Mahoney? Which stakeholders are affected by the company's altruistic actions?
2. Might Monsanto's goals of increasing social responsibility and increasing both short-term and long-term profits create their own ethical pressures?
3. How can Monsanto institutionalize its goal of social responsibility as it develops a new pesticide during a time of growing public concern over farm chemicals?
4. How could Monsanto managers apply theories of rights to determine whether selling Simplesse would be ethical if scientists prove it encourages a small percentage of the population to increase overall fat intake? How could they apply utilitarian theories in such a situation?

CHAPTER OUTLINE

5 Management and the Global Organization

After studying this chapter, you will be able to

1. Contrast domestic business and international business and discuss the difference between multidomestic and transnational management
2. Explain the growing importance of international markets
3. Describe the economic forces that affect global management
4. Discuss the politicolegal forces that influence organizations doing business abroad
5. Outline the sociocultural and technological forces that affect international management
6. Identify the ways an organization can enter the global market
7. Differentiate among ethnocentric, polycentric, and geocentric management and examine the impact of each

FACING A MANAGEMENT CHALLENGE AT

H.J. HEINZ

Cooking Up Global Profits

Anthony J. F. O'Reilly could no longer live on ketchup and beans. Sales of these products had made H.J. Heinz a household name in the United States and England, but food consumption in those markets was increasing at a meager 1 to 2 percent a year. So as CEO of Heinz, O'Reilly was hungrily eyeing sales potential in the People's Republic of China and in the unified European Community—two extremely different types of markets.

China presented an attractive consumer market because it is the most populous country in the world, and it is adding 22 million new mouths to feed every year. Yet it held the prospect of operating amid political upheavals, government interference, low per capita income, and an almost feudal distribution system. Heinz preferred to enter new markets through acquisitions or by forming joint ventures with domestic firms (with Heinz retaining control). But China had traditionally prohibited foreign business ownership, and even though some restrictions were loosening, the government was not inclined to let a U.S. company control a Chinese factory.

Nor would the challenge end even with a successful entry into China. Fear of political unrest kindled by an overheating economy might provoke the government to periodically freeze product prices, which would affect the company's profitability. Moreover, food is of nearly religious importance in China, a culture in which brand names have never been important to consumers.

The changes that were bound to happen in Europe after the 1992 economic unification presented a vastly different and even more immediate opportunity for O'Reilly. The challenge was to get the company in position to take advantage of the single market that encompassed a diversity of tastes and cultures, and to do so in the midst of a furious race for market share involving many aggressive players. Heinz might not get a second chance if it fell behind early. Competition from established companies would be fierce. Although Heinz had a presence in Belgium, France, the Netherlands, Germany, Spain, Portugal, and Italy, its share in these countries was relatively small. Sales in Italy, Heinz's biggest market on the continent, were the equivalent of only a third of the company's sales in England.

The quickest way to capitalize on European unification would be through a merger with or acquisition of a company that was already a major player throughout Europe. This is the approach that the British conglomerate Grand Metropolitan had taken in the United States, when it acquired Pillsbury. But such a strategy would put Heinz into unfamiliar product lines and would surely increase the company's debt load to a point where profits might be eaten away. On the other hand, smaller acquisitions and joint ventures could make Heinz a laggard instead of a leader in the race for the European market. And either solution would likely dilute the power of the Heinz name, since other companies' brands would be involved.

Whether in China or Europe, Anthony O'Reilly's vision of global expansion could easily turn into a nightmare of swollen costs and lost opportunities. Should Heinz explore joint ventures or acquisitions to enter China? Would the status of food in Chinese culture help or hinder his efforts? In Europe, would it be better to quickly establish a strong pan-European presence or to try to build the Heinz name country by country? And how could O'Reilly effectively manage the company's initiatives in these new but potentially major markets? [1]

CHAPTER OVERVIEW

The challenges confronting Anthony O'Reilly stem from Heinz's involvement in the global marketplace, a fast-growing area of opportunity for businesses of all sizes. To tap this opportunity and to be prepared for the issues ahead, managers need a thorough understanding of the nature of global management, the international environment, and the process of entering global markets. This chapter begins by examining the international management challenge, including the rise of transnational management, the growing importance of international markets, and the impact of national competitive advantage. Next is a discussion of the four forces in the international environment, the economic, politicolegal, sociocultural, and technological forces that affect the management of organizations in other countries. Following a review of the ways organizations can enter the global market, the chapter closes with a look at various management approaches to international activities.

MANAGERS AND THE INTERNATIONAL CHALLENGE

Nestlé chocolate on Milwaukee store shelves; Pepsi-Cola for sale in Moscow; Volkswagen cars in Mexico City showrooms—all are familiar brand names on sale far from their home countries, three examples drawn from the cornucopia of international products now available around the world. Buying and selling goods and services across national borders is hardly a new phenomenon; international trade has been in existence for thousands of years. In the past few decades, however, the volume of international trade has risen dramatically. Increasingly, managers in industries ranging from telecommunications, pharmaceuticals, and apparel to retailing, copiers, and automobiles are looking abroad for resources and sales, even as they daily confront overseas businesses entering their own local markets (see Exhibit 5.1). No matter which organization they join, managers in entry-level positions on up will be affected by global management issues in the years to come, either through their purchases of imported products or through transactions with customers in other countries. This globalization of international markets brings challenges as well as opportunities to managers the world over.[2]

The annual Pillsbury Bake-Off, an American tradition since 1949, has taken on a British accent. Grand Metropolitan, the world's largest wine and spirits company, bought Pillsbury in 1988 as a way into foods and restaurants in the U.S. market. The acquisition included Pillsbury baking products, Green Giant foods, and Burger King restaurants.

EXHIBIT 5.1 Hopping National Borders Fuels International Trade

In recent years, an increasing number of businesses have entered global markets or increased their activity in the world marketplace, fueling a dramatic rise in international trade. This is a sampling of manufacturing companies with a minimum $3 billion in annual sales that derive at least 40 percent of those sales from countries other than their home country. It does not include state-owned companies or holding companies.

	Home Country	Sales Outside Home Country	Management Approach
Nestlé	Switzerland	98.0%	CEO is German. Has 10 general managers, of whom 5 are not Swiss
SKF	Sweden	96.0	Foreigners have cracked board and top management group
Philips	Netherlands	94.0	Solidly Dutch company, but number of senior foreign managers is increasing
ABB	Sweden	85.0*	Moved headquarters to Switzerland; managers are Swedish, Swiss, German
Volvo	Sweden	80.0	Solidly Swedish at all top management levels
Michelin	France	78.0	Secretive, centralized, with top management almost entirely French
Unilever	Britain/Neth.	75.0*	Five nationalities on board, thoroughly stateless management
Canon	Japan	69.0	Foreigners run many sales subsidiaries, but none in top ranks
Sony	Japan	66.0	Only major Japanese manufacturer with foreigners on board
BASF	Germany	65.0	Relies on local managers to run foreign operations, but none in top ranks
Colgate	U.S.	64.0	CEO, other top execs have had several foreign posts; many multilingual
Daimler Benz	Germany	61.0	Similar to other German giants
NCR	U.S.	58.9	Nationals run foreign operations, but none in top ranks
Coca-Cola	U.S.	54.0	Thoroughly multinational management group making big international push
Dow Chemical	U.S.	54.0	Out of top 25 managers, 20 have experience outside U.S.
Xerox	U.S.	54.0	Major joint ventures with Rank and Fuji have shaped top management thinking
Hewlett-Packard	U.S.	53.0	Five of top 25 officers not U.S. citizens; many units managed offshore
Corning	U.S.	50.0*	Company is leader in use of joint ventures to penetrate markets
United Technologies	U.S.	49.7	Because of U.S. defense business, few foreigners at top
Merck	U.S.	47.0	Top management is American, but foreign nationals run overseas operations
3M	U.S.	46.0	CEO pushing to raise foreign sales to 50% of total by 1992
Matsushita	Japan	42.0	American named number 2 for North America, but no foreigners in top ranks
P&G	U.S.	40.0	International operations chief recently named CEO

* *Business Week* estimates.

The Rise of Transnational Management

Little more than a century ago, most companies restricted their organizational activities to a single country. They conducted only **domestic business,** activities that take place within the borders of one nation. This domestic business included hiring employees, obtaining a bank loan, purchasing raw materials, selling finished goods, and other business tasks that could be accomplished within the **home country,** the nation where the company was headquartered. The few organizations that operated outside their home countries generally sent locally made goods to countries where those products were unavailable or received needed resources (such as raw materials) from countries where such staples were plentiful.[3]

domestic business Organizational activities that take place within the borders of one country

home country A country where the company has its headquarters

However, as the industrial revolution accelerated and large businesses adopted modern production processes, managers were able not only to make and sell products nationally but eventually to offer them in other countries. By crossing national borders to acquire resources or to sell products, these firms became involved in **international business.** At first, the firms moving beyond national borders to do business in other countries were mainly United States–based companies expanding into attractive European markets. Before World War II, such well-known names as Ford, Gillette, National Cash Register (NCR), Otis, and Western Electric had already developed worldwide markets.

international business Organizational activities that take place across national borders in more than one country

After World War II, more organizations around the world began to cross national borders in search of markets and resources. This movement gave rise to the **multinational corporation (MNC),** or *multinational enterprise,* a company that produces goods or services in several countries and manages its international activities from a single organizational headquarters.[4]

multinational corporation (MNC) A company that produces goods or services in several countries and manages its global activities from one organizational headquarters

multidomestic management A management approach in which a company operating in several countries allows its local units to act independently and does not coordinate its various operations on a global basis

host country Any nation outside the home country where an organization conducts business activities

Multinational corporations have traditionally applied **multidomestic management,** an approach in which a company operating in several countries allows its local units to act independently and does not coordinate its international operations on a global basis. In each country, the local organization is self-contained and acts much like a separate domestic business might act. Multidomestic management allows local managers to be highly responsive to environmental conditions in the **host country,** any nation in which a company conducts business outside the home country. Consider how Toronto-based Bata, the world's largest maker of footwear, operates in 68 countries using multidomestic management. Local managers in each country operate fairly independently of Bata units in other countries. These managers monitor local fashions and customer needs, then manufacture Bata shoes specifically to fit host-country tastes. Recognizing the differences between Malawi, Milan, and Paris has been the key to building Bata's worldwide empire. In general, however, when far-flung businesses act independently, coordinating their activities can be quite difficult, and MNC managers are not always able to respond effectively to the global forces that affect the organization as a whole.[5]

transnational management A management approach in which an organization uses an integrated strategy for achieving organizational goals on a worldwide level while stressing local flexibility in host countries

In recent years, the rapid pace of globalization has caused many MNCs to adopt **transnational management,** an approach in which organizations apply an integrated strategy for achieving organizational goals on a worldwide level, stressing at the same time local management flexibility in host countries. Whereas multidomestic management views the organization as a series of national units, transnational management sees the organization as a whole, with a single system of goals and an organizational culture shared by managers, regardless of their location. By using transnational management, managers can consider the organization's overall resources, challenges, and opportunities, and they can better analyze the impact of both the local and global environments. Guided by this overview of the global situation and by the organization's goals and culture, local managers can handle day-to-day operations in the host countries more effectively.[6]

For example, Honeywell, a multinational corporation based in Minneapolis, makes and sells home temperature, industrial, and aviation controls around the world. Michael Bonsignore, president of the international division, shuttles to Japan, Canada, Germany, France, and elsewhere to share the company's overall strategy with local managers who handle Honeywell operations in the various host countries. Bonsignore carefully considers how local, national, or regional environmental issues affect the entire company, and he is careful to balance organizationwide concerns and goals with the issues and needs of every local operation. For their part, local managers are informed about Honeywell's worldwide operations and goals so that they can make the everyday decisions necessary to keep their operations running smoothly and to enhance the organization's overall performance. This transnational management approach has enabled Honeywell to build a hefty worldwide market share: One-third of all commercial buildings in the world, 85 percent of all single-family homes in the United States, and 70 percent of all single-family homes in the Netherlands use Honeywell thermostats.[7]

The Growing Importance of International Markets

Never before has an organization been able to cross national borders so easily or so inexpensively, thanks to the high speed and low cost of today's communication, transportation, and information systems. Organizations are no longer confined to the resources or to the market potential of a single country. To improve both efficiency and effectiveness, organizations are increasingly looking beyond their home countries for product components, raw materials, and human resources; at the same time, they are working to bring new or existing products to markets in other countries.[8]

Hopping national borders in search of new customers, Mars now sells its candies, ice cream products, rice, and pet foods in more than 25 countries. Moscow residents with a sweet tooth have been able to buy M&M candies since 1986.

The Search for Resources

To remain competitive, organizations need access to the best available inputs (including materials, people, and technology), regardless of the country of origin. Thanks to advances in communication, transportation, and information systems, organizations today can readily hop national borders in search of the resources they need. The Red Lobster chain uses a computerized resource supply program to track the fish and shellfish needs of its 200-plus seafood restaurants in the United States, Canada, and Japan. The chain uses its network to communicate these needs to buyers who travel the world to buy fish in 33 countries and then arrange for the needed fish to be flown or trucked daily to every restaurant.[9]

Some organizations look outside their own countries to strengthen the reliability of resource supplies. Although they may have access to raw materials and to other resources available in the home country, firms frequently need to supplement these supplies with additional amounts brought in from other countries. For example, British Petroleum (BP), headquartered in London, is constantly searching for new sources of crude oil and natural gas, the major inputs for its fuel products. In addition to drilling at home (in the North Sea), BP drills for oil in Papua New Guinea, Alaska, and other areas. Then it refines the crude into fuels to be sold around the world. Many organizations acquire resources by shifting production into other countries where key resources are more plentiful and lower priced. Dominion Textile, one of Canada's largest textile manufacturers, set up a denim manufacturing plant in Tunisia to obtain ready access to that country's pool of employees. Dominion found Tunisia to be a cost-effective source of employees because the payroll costs in Tunisia are lower. Dominion's selection of Tunisia had another benefit: its proximity to Europe helped Dominion bring its products to those markets quickly and easily.[10]

The Search for Customers

Increasingly, organizations find they must reach beyond their home-country borders to build the sales volume they need to operate more efficiently. For instance, the average cost of developing a new drug has risen from about $16 million in the 1970s to $250 million today, and the development process from research to market is twice as long. No single country has enough customers to support such enormous product-development costs, so pharmaceutical companies, and many other firms, are eyeing potential customers outside their home countries. Moreover, some products have so thoroughly permeated home-country markets that their makers must seek overseas customers in order to maintain or increase sales volume. Nike's U.S. revenues recently hit $2 billion, but says the firm's international marketing director, "The kind of meteoric growth we've had in the U.S. can stay at that level for only so long." Looking for sales growth, Nike entered Europe and has already captured the number two slot in running and cross-training shoes, behind market leader Adidas. Nike is also starting to outfit the market of "2 billion feet" in China, where the firm has production facilities and sells a small but growing number of shoes.[11]

Through electronic media and cross-border travel, individuals and organizations are able to learn about and then demand an ever-widening array of goods and services (see Exhibit 5.2). More and more companies want to tap this pent-up demand for products, so they hop national borders to be closer to these customers. In fact, exporters based in the United States are increasingly tapping the demand in developing countries in Asia and Latin America for home appliances, industrial machinery, pollution-control devices, and a wide range of other products. Companies also cross borders to follow their existing customers. The first Japanese credit card, JCB, holds 40 percent of its home market but has expanded its operations around the world to follow customers as they travel or work abroad. Over the past decade, JCB has signed up 1.5 million retailers and hotels in 109 countries to honor its card, allowing customers to use their cards virtually anywhere they go.[12]

However, the international search for customers is not confined to big business. More small businesses are entering global markets to increase their sales, often because many overseas markets need their products. Rather than delay their entry into other countries and take the chance that domestic or international competitors will move into attractive markets with competing products, many small businesses send their products abroad. National Gyp-Chipper, a small manufacturer of gypsum shredders in Pflugerville, Texas, began selling abroad in response to requests from a few overseas customers. Recognizing that other overseas customers would probably be interested in its products, National

EXHIBIT 5.2 The Top 10 U.S. Exporters

Many U.S. companies rely on international markets for a significant portion of their sales; the country's number one exporter, Boeing, gets nearly 60 percent of its revenue from customers in other countries.

Rank (1990)	Company	Primary Products	Export Sales (in $ millions)	Total Sales (in $ millions)	Portion of Total Sales Exported (percent)
1	Boeing	Aircraft	16,093.0	27,595.0	58.3
2	General Motors	Motor vehicles	10,315.9	126,017.0	8.2
3	General Electric	Jet engines, turbines, medical systems	7,128.0	58,414.0	12.2
4	Ford Motor	Motor vehicles	7,098.0	98,274.7	7.2
5	IBM	Computers	6,195.0	69,018.0	9.0
6	Chrysler	Motor vehicles	5,004.0	30,868.0	16.2
7	Du Pont	Chemicals	4,352.0	39,839.0	10.9
8	United Technologies	Jet engines, helicopters, cooling equipment	3,606.0	21,783.2	18.6
9	McDonnell Douglas	Aerospace products, missiles, electronic systems	3,538.0	16,351.0	21.6
10	Caterpillar	Heavy machinery, engines, turbines	3,435.0	11,540.0	29.8

Gyp-Chipper moved quickly to find distributors that could offer its products overseas; ultimately, the firm successfully entered Japan, the Netherlands, the United Kingdom, and other countries. On the other hand, small businesses also go international to stay competitive in their home countries. Crossing national borders allows these businesses to gain firsthand knowledge of the new products being introduced by competitors in host countries, products that are likely to find their way to U.S. markets in a short time. In a recent survey, 30 percent of U.S. manufacturers said that three of their top five competitors for *U.S. markets* are foreign firms.[13]

National Competitive Advantage

A company's ability to compete in global markets is due, in part, to the environmental forces within its home country. Traditional explanations for nations achieving international success in particular industries refer to the theory of **comparative advantage,** the benefit to nations of specializing in the export of products they can produce more cheaply than others because of their existing natural and human resources. However, many nations are now competing successfully on an international level in industries other than those dependent on naturally occurring raw materials or huge labor pools. To explain this, Harvard Business School professor Michael E. Porter points to the theory of **national competitive advantage,** the ability of a nation's industries to innovate and upgrade to the next level of technology and productivity. Porter extensively studied competition in domestic markets (see Chapter 8) and then expanded his research into competition by conducting a four-year study of 10 nations active in international trade. This study of global competition identified four basic elements of national competitive advantage:[14]

comparative advantage The benefit to nations of specializing in the export of products they can produce more cheaply because of their natural and human resources

national competitive advantage The ability of a country's industries to innovate and upgrade to the next level of technology and productivity

- *Company strategy, structure, and rivalry:* The conditions governing how a nation's businesses are created, organized, and managed, and the nature of domestic competition
- *Demand conditions:* The size of the market, sophistication of the customers, and media exposure of the goods, services, and ideas
- *Related industries:* Clusters of suppliers that support a particular industry
- *Factor conditions:* Natural resources, education and skill levels, and wage rates

In contrast to the theory of comparative advantage, which argues that global competitive ability depends on how a country develops its natural and human resources, Porter's theory of national competitive advantage holds that a nation can be competitive in the world market by effectively leveraging innovation and technology. For example, one of the industries studied was the Dutch flower industry. Researchers found that the Dutch did not become international leaders in cut flowers because they have the ideal climate. Their competitive advantage was achieved through the establishment of innovative research institutions specializing in flower cultivation, packaging, and shipping. The Italian shoe industry, on the other hand, achieved international success because of sophisticated consumer demand and rivalry between family-owned companies. Thus they constantly introduce new designs and improve efficiency in order to remain competitive. In the United States, the concept of competitiveness has become such an important issue that Congress proclaimed it the country's dominant economic issue for the remainder of this century.[15]

THE INTERNATIONAL ENVIRONMENT

The entire range of external and internal environmental forces (examined in Chapter 3) can influence the management of organizations that operate in more than one country. However, four forces have a particular influence on the management of operations outside the home country. These four forces in the international environment are (1) economic, (2) politicolegal, (3) sociocultural, and (4) technological.

Economic Forces

Organizations that operate within a country while drawing resources from or selling products to another country can be affected by both national and international economic forces. In addition to understanding the type of national economic system in a particular host country, managers must consider that country's level of economic development, infrastructure (supporting organizational activities), balance of trade, currency issues, and resource availability.

Economic Development

developed countries Nations with a relatively high per capita income and a high degree of industrialization

less-developed countries (LDCs) Nations with a relatively low per capita income and a low degree of industrialization

The level of economic development varies widely around the world. **Developed countries,** also known as *industrialized nations,* are those that have a relatively high per capita income (as measured by the total national production of goods and services divided by total population) and a high degree of industrialization. Countries in this category include the United States, Japan, Canada, Australia, and Western European nations. In contrast, **less-developed countries (LDCs),** also known as *developing countries* and *Third World* nations, have a relatively low per capita income and a lower degree of industrialization. LDCs include African, South American, and some Asian nations. LDCs such as Taiwan, South Korea, and Hong Kong have been driving for extremely rapid economic growth; as a result, they export large numbers of manufactured goods. These countries have become known as the *newly industrialized countries (NICs).*[16]

MANAGEMENT AROUND THE WORLD

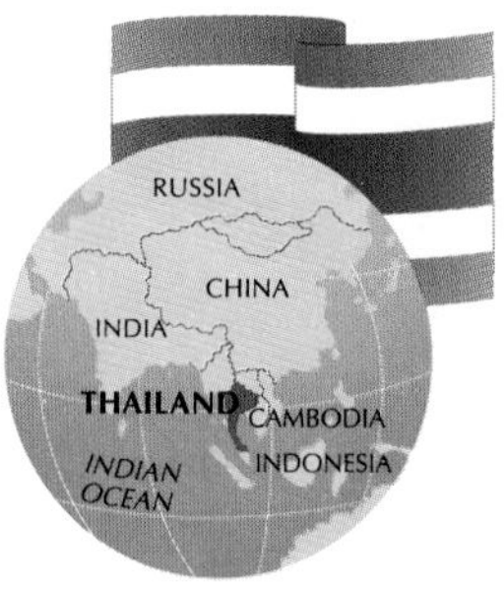

Largely because of its plentiful and willing pool of potential employees, Thailand has enjoyed rapid economic development in recent years. However, this growth has strained the country's infrastructure, which is a concern for multinationals that want to establish factories in Thailand.

For the global manager, the degree of industrialization can affect the organization's ability to obtain natural resources, which may be abundant but largely untapped in LDCs. Also, the labor pool in LDCs tends to be large but less literate than in developed countries, so managers may have difficulty hiring skilled employees. Finally, income level plays a major role in determining how large a market a country will be for an organization's goods and services: the low per capita income in LDCs limits the ability to buy products such as sophisticated electronics or automobiles but opens the market for other products such as basic consumer goods.[17]

Infrastructure

Related to the level of economic development is the development of a country's **infrastructure,** the network of transportation, utilities, housing, education, highways, communication, and other facilities and systems that serve fundamental personal and organizational needs (see Exhibit 5.3). The infrastructure of developed countries is generally more modern and better able to support organizational activities than the infrastructure of LDCs, which often have inadequate or inefficient airports and seaports, rudimentary postal and telecommunications facilities, and insufficient or unreliable electrical and water supplies. The lack of

Country	Highways (paved km)	Railways (km)	Trucks and Buses in Use (000)	Electricity Production (kwh billion)	Newspaper Sales (000)
United States	6,221,000	778,000	34,995	2,367	62,415
Brazil	1,411,600*	30,000	1,144	139	5,094
Japan	1,123,300	53,500	16,146	602	68,142
Colombia	78,200*	3,700	328	27	1,105
Germany	482,000	31,711	1,535	373	25,103
Kenya	64,600*	2,700	87	2	220
Mexico	218,600*	25,000	2,103	82	10,212
Spain	318,549	15,344	1,504	115	2,978

*Includes unpaved and paved.

EXHIBIT 5.3

Infrastructure in Selected Countries

A country's infrastructure influences a business's ability to trade within and across national borders, so managers must gear their activities to the level of infrastructure development in each market.

infrastructure in the LDCs can hinder an organization's ability to transport resources and products, to consistently produce or sell goods and services, and to effectively maintain and coordinate activities that occur within and outside the country's borders.[18]

infrastructure The network of transportation, utilities, housing, education, highways, communication, and other facilities that serve fundamental personal and organizational needs

For example, Honda is one of many companies that have taken advantage of tax and trade incentives to build factories in Manaus, Brazil, a riverfront city surrounded by 1,000 miles of jungle. Brazil is an attractive market because of its large population and the growing buying power of its middle class. Although Manaus has an airport, an upgraded communications system, and one of the most luxurious hotels in South America, local Honda managers daily face other infrastructure problems, especially transportation. The closest source of parts is in São Paulo, over 1,500 miles away, but Manaus is not served by a railroad and is hard to reach overland, so Honda's supplies must be shipped via a two-week cross-country truck trip followed by a one-week boat trip up the Amazon. Finished motorcycles bound for the Brazilian market are shipped out in the same manner. The process is cumbersome, time-consuming, and expensive, and it eats into Honda's Brazilian profits, but the company is counting on the long-term benefits of establishing a presence in this growing market.[19]

Balance of Trade

Also important to managers doing business in other countries is the issue of **balance of trade,** a financial measure of the difference between the value of a nation's imports and the value of its exports. The balance of trade is one of the key ingredients in a country's **balance of payments,** a financial measure of the difference between the outflow and the inflow of a nation's products and funds. When the balance of trade reflects more exports than imports, and the balance of payments shows a net outflow, a country may not want to expand its international trade for fear of worsening these imbalances. Alternatively, the country may try to balance its trade with key trading partners so that exports and imports are more evenly matched. The United States suffered large trade deficits for most of the 1980s, when the value of its imports outweighed the value of its exports. However, U.S. imports and exports were more in balance during the early 1990s, fueled by foreign sales of U.S. chemicals, trucks, industrial and medical equipment, and other products. U.S. exports hit a record $422 billion in 1991, while imports totaled $488 billion, leaving a trade gap of $66 billion, the smallest since 1983. Canada is the largest customer for U. S. goods, followed by Mexico and Japan.[20]

balance of trade A financial measure of the difference between the value of a country's imports and the value of its exports

balance of payments A financial measure of the difference between the outflow and the inflow of a nation's products and funds

In the early 1990s, Chiquita Brands International expanded its distribution of fresh fruits and vegetables into Eastern Europe and Russia. The growth potential in these new markets is enormous. But Chiquita's managers must also contend with the impact of powerful economic forces such as inefficient infrastructures, blocked currencies, and intermittent resource availability.

Imbalances may also lead some governments to place restrictions on an organization's ability to export goods or to transfer money out of the country. For example, Hungary-based Ikarus, one of the largest bus manufacturers in the world, had to adjust its exports when the government decided to shift the balance of trade with certain nations. At one time, a majority of the firm's buses were sold to the former Soviet republics and other nearby nations, but Ikarus was ordered to cut its exports to this region and to replace them with sales to Western nations. The government sees Western nations as more attractive trading partners because they will pay for products in currency that the Hungarian government can use to repay its own debts.[21]

Currency Issues

When an organization sells goods or services in another country, it receives payment in that country's currency and then converts the payment to the home-country currency at the prevailing **exchange rate,** the price at which one country's currency can be exchanged for another country's currency. This rate is important because (1) it influences the prices for supplies, payroll, and other expenses that organizations incur in host countries, and (2) it influences the price of organizations' products in the host country. Exchange rates are volatile and shift constantly, which means that a product's price can seem relatively high or low when the price is translated through the exchange rate into another currency at any given time. This fluctuation can affect an organization's profitability and its ability to sell products abroad.[22]

exchange rate The price at which one country's currency can be exchanged for another country's currency

For example, Suzanne Ridenour, founder of the executive recruiting firm Ridenour & Associates, derives 25 percent of her revenues from international business, and although she deals in services rather than in goods, exchange rates are important to Ridenour's profitability. For every executive placed, her company receives a commission of 30 percent of that manager's total first-year compensation. The commission is paid in the local currency, which Ridenour then converts to dollars. Not long ago, placing an executive with a German firm at a salary of 200,000 Deutsche marks would have generated a fee of $32,856. But one year later, the mark was worth more relative to the dollar, so the same placement would have brought Ridenour a fee of $33,078. However, that same shift in exchange rates would also hurt Ridenour's travel budget, because as the mark rose in value against the dollar, the recruiter would have to spend more to buy the same amount of services when she visited Europe.[23]

Another issue that organizations must consider when they seek payment from activities conducted in host countries is whether the local currency is a **blocked currency,** a currency that cannot be redeemed in the world financial marketplace. Currencies are considered blocked when no exchange rate can be determined and when local governments do not allow their currencies to be taken out of the country or to be traded for *hard currency,* such as dollars, pounds sterling, or yen (all of which are backed by national gold reserves and easily convertible to other currencies). The currency of the People's Republic of China is a blocked currency because the country has not joined the International Monetary Fund (IMF), an organization that manages the international financial system; the value of nonmember currencies is difficult to determine in relation to member currencies. China's blocked currency is clearly one of the problems that Heinz's Anthony O'Reilly would have to resolve before expanding operations there. But even IMF members, including several Latin American nations, have sometimes chosen to block their own local currencies by forbidding the removal of currency from the issuing country. Because businesses that operate in countries with blocked currencies cannot be paid in home-country currency or in hard currencies that are easily traded in world markets, they must find other ways to receive payment.[24]

blocked currency A currency that cannot be redeemed in the international financial marketplace

Resource Availability

Another economic element that affects organizational effectiveness and efficiency in world markets is resource availability. Developed countries generally offer easy access to such resources as skilled labor, financing, and raw materials. Moreover, the natural resources of these countries, such as lumber and minerals, can be offered both domestically and internationally, offsetting the flow of needed imports included in the balance of trade. However, not every country offers easy or consistent access to quality resources, so organizations that enter new global markets need to be flexible and innovative when coping with local availability of resources.[25]

Politicolegal Forces

Within the international environment, governmental and legal policies of the home and the host countries can influence organizational operations. Of particular interest to global managers are political risks, laws and regulations, trade controls, and trade blocs.

Political Risk

Political risk is the likelihood that an organization's overseas goals, operations, or investments will be constrained by a host government's political, legal, or regulatory policies or actions. As mentioned in the opening vignette, this is one of the biggest issues that Anthony O'Reilly had to consider before leading Heinz into China. Because of political actions or public reactions to political policies, an organization may lose the ability to return its profits to the home country, may find its operations, supply, or distribution methods involuntarily changed, or may lose control over its own facilities. Specific threats in some

political risk The likelihood that an organization's international goals, operations, or investments will be threatened by a host government's political, legal, or regulatory policies or actions

MANAGERIAL DECISION MAKING

Taking Advantage of Countertrade

What if a customer can't pay cash? Global managers sometimes find that government and industrial customers in other countries are not allowed to pay cash for purchased goods, either because a national trade imbalance must be corrected or because local laws restrict currency outflows. In such cases, managers may decide to forgo the sale, but another choice would be to use *countertrade,* a trading practice in which local customers offer domestic products instead of cash in exchange for imported goods and services. The U.S. government does not encourage countertrade, but it does not forbid such arrangements, either. Its official position is that countertrade is "contrary to an open, free trading system."

Nevertheless, the decision to countertrade is often the only way an organization can clinch an international sale. Today, as much as 30 percent of all world trade results from countertrade transactions. These transactions are becoming so complex and so commonplace that companies such as General Electric, Monsanto, McDonnell Douglas, Rockwell International, General Motors, and Caterpillar have created special departments, or even separate divisions, just to handle countertrade.

Consider Rockwell International's bid to furnish $8 million worth of printing presses to Zimbabwe. Rockwell initially lost out to a French firm that offered more favorable financing (subsidized by the French government). Rather than lose the contract, Rockwell decided to sweeten the deal by offering to counterpurchase $8 million worth of ferrochrome and nickel, knowing that Zimbabwe had an oversupply. As a result, Zimbabwe awarded the contract to Rockwell, which was able to resell the metal it had purchased as part of the deal.

Countertrade can also be an answer to the problem of accepting payment in a currency that is not generally traded worldwide. For example, Monsanto wanted to sell Fisher control valves to Romania. Rather than accept Romanian currency, the company opted to exchange its valves for Romanian-made ball bearings. Dan West, director of countertrade for Monsanto, arranged to sell the ball bearings in the United Kingdom and then converted the British pounds to U.S. dollars. Deals like this allow Monsanto to sell its products wherever demand arises; during one recent year, the company handled countertrade transactions totaling $200 million.

expropriation The seizure of business assets by a host government, with little or no payment to organizational owners

nationalization The appropriation of one company's operations or an entire industry's operations by a host government for the benefit of the nation

countries include **expropriation,** the host government's seizure of business assets with little or no payment to owners, and **nationalization,** the host government's taking over one company's operations or an entire industry's operations to be run for the benefit of the nation. Moreover, frequent changes in leadership of the host country's government also contribute to the level of political risk that an organization may experience. For organizations selling or manufacturing in another country, the uncertainty of political risk makes management decisions and planning difficult and complex. However, not every organization is affected by political risk in the same way, so managers must assess how the risk affects their individual organizations in a particular country. Although political risk can influence an organization as it enters a market or continues operations abroad, benefits such as opening new markets, finding new sources of supply, and long-term profitability may outweigh the risks.[26]

For example, Whirlpool has confronted political risk when managing its operations in Brazil. When the Brazilian government recently unveiled stronger economic measures such as the end of automatic wage hikes to keep pace with runaway inflation, Whirlpool's local factories were besieged by striking local employees seeking higher wages. Local managers settled the strikes quickly by offering wage increases, but the threat of new strikes for higher wages remains. Despite the political risks and the short-term losses they cause, Whirlpool perseveres, because the country's population of more than 150 million is an attractive source of labor, because the country has abundant natural resources, and because the growing middle class is a burgeoning market for washing machines and other home appliances.[27]

Sometimes managers decide to use countertrade to cover financial obligations that customers can no longer meet. N-Ren International, a small engineering and construction firm based in Brussels, expected to receive $60 million for building a fertilizer plant in Madagascar. However, when the plant was nearly complete, the government of Madagascar said it could no longer pay N-Ren in cash because it had to cover its increasing national debt. To compensate for the shortfall, N-Ren agreed to accept cloves in exchange for its services. N-Ren got to keep the money it made from selling the spice, and the company's exporting success over the next five years earned enough profits to cover the payments not received for the fertilizer plant.

Some companies find that the decision to countertrade is the only way to induce some host-country governments to agree to trade. PepsiCo, for example, was allowed to export to the former Soviet republics only after agreeing to countertrade its Pepsi-Cola soft drink concentrate in exchange for Russian vodka. That countertrade agreement was recently expanded into a $3 billion deal that brings Pepsi commercial ships and vodka in exchange for concentrate. In turn, Pepsi sells or leases the ships in international markets to build foreign exchange credits that can be applied toward opening more Pizza Hut restaurants in the former Soviet republics. By deciding to countertrade, PepsiCo has been able to sell a yearly complement of 40 million cases of soft drinks in the area, and the expanded countertrade arrangement will double regional Pepsi sales within 10 years.

Countertrade is not without an added measure of risk, however. Goods received in trade are sometimes difficult to sell, and facilities set up in other countries can turn into competitors later on. Countertrade agreements can also be extremely complex and time-consuming to arrange and carry out. But for the global manager who decides that countertrade is the best way to overcome economic barriers, this approach can be a competitive advantage in the international marketplace.

Apply Your Knowledge

1. How can an organization selling its products abroad use countertrade to work around a situation in which the exchange rate between the host- and home-country currencies is not advantageous?
2. What factors might Pepsi consider when deciding whether to countertrade soft drink concentrate for cloves in Madagascar?

Laws and Regulations

Whirlpool's Brazilian operations are also affected by local laws and regulations that restrict the company's control over resources and other key elements of its local operations. Host governments frequently pass laws regulating advertising, product and facility safety, product labeling, and other areas, all of which affect an organization's ability to manage its activities in that country. For instance, because the government wants to protect local industry, Brazilian laws require that products made there contain a certain percentage of locally made components. This law prevents Whirlpool from buying components such as electronic controls from suppliers in the United States or in Asia; instead, the company must buy from Brazilian suppliers, who often charge up to six times as much as overseas suppliers. In turn, these costs must be passed along to Brazilian consumers in the form of higher appliance prices.[28]

Legal and regulatory requirements in other countries are closely related to political risk, and trying to comply with local requirements can be a management headache. When Texas Instruments (TI) wanted to build a center in Bangalore, India, to write the programs for its computer chips, the company also sought permission for a private earth station–transmission arrangement to send the programs from India directly to TI's facilities in the United States. TI managers needed two years to obtain the proper approvals from seven regulatory agencies in India. Similarly, Genevieve Gillaizeau wanted to start a silk textile production business in Tianjin, China, as a complement to her small silk weaving business in the United States, but she had to run a gauntlet of legal and regulatory approvals. Rather than work alone to obtain the needed approvals, she found a state-run corporation to work with her. This local partner handled the business applications, land permits, management visas, and other legalities, enabling Tianjin Gillaizeau Silk to be born.[29]

In addition to complying with host-country laws, organizations must consider how home-country laws affect their overseas activities. When U.S.-based companies do business abroad, they are still subject to many provisions of U.S. law, including antitrust regulations and bribery prohibitions. Antitrust regulations seek to prevent any unfair competition in the U.S. market that could result from agreements with other organizations, either here or abroad. If the government determines that one firm's proposed alliance with another firm will create a business capable of dominating the U.S. market in that industry, the government can stop the alliance. In addition, the Foreign Corrupt Practices Act bars U.S.-based companies from offering bribes to government officials in other countries (see Chapter 4). Bribery is an accepted business practice in some areas, so U.S. companies sometimes feel that this restriction puts them at a disadvantage in the global marketplace when other firms are not similarly constrained.[30]

Trade Controls

Even in a global marketplace, every country has the right to control its participation in world trade. Many nations want to protect their domestic industries from international competitors, so they build walls around the local market by establishing mandatory trade controls such as tariffs and import quotas, by seeking voluntary export restraints, and by establishing "buy domestic" policies. **Tariffs** are duties or taxes collected by a government on products shipped into the country. Tariffs can raise money for the local government while discouraging importers from bringing certain goods into the country. Imposing a tariff also increases the final price of products that are imported, so these goods may seem less attractive to customers. The intent is to give domestic businesses an advantage in local markets. For example, the United States currently imposes 3,600 tariffs covering a range of products from peanuts to apparel. In 1991 the United States wanted to encourage domestic manufacture of sophisticated flat-panel liquid-crystal computer display screens, so the government imposed a hefty tariff on any such screens imported from Japan. However, the tariff has encouraged only a handful of U.S. companies to make the investment in research and development necessary to design these screens or others with similar properties.[31]

tariffs Duties or taxes collected by a government on products imported into the country

Another common method of protecting local markets is the use of **import quotas,** legal restrictions on how much of a particular product can be brought into a country. When products from abroad become available in local markets, the government may resort to using import quotas to help domestic companies maintain their market share. During the 1980s, France protected its domestic car manufacturers by restricting Japanese car imports to 3 percent of the French car market; Italy used a stricter import quota to keep Japanese car imports under 1 percent.[32]

import quotas Legal restrictions on the amount of a particular product that can be shipped into a country

When a nation wants to lower the level of imports from another nation, it may ask its trading partner to voluntarily restrict the flow of products, a practice known as **voluntary export restraints.** Although such requests are formal, they do not have the force of law; other countries comply because they prefer to avoid official trade controls such as stiffer quotas or tariffs. For example, the U.S. government protects domestic carmakers and steel manufacturers by asking the Japanese government to voluntarily restrict exports of cars and steel to the United States.

voluntary export restraints Voluntary restrictions in which one nation agrees to limit exports of certain types of products to another nation

Another voluntary method of trade control is to promote "buy domestic" or "buy national" policies that ask organizations in the public and the private sectors, and consumers, to show preference to local suppliers. In the United States, federal and state governments have a wide range of "Buy American" policies that give priority to products with at least 50 percent of their parts made in the United States. Similar policies abroad have held U.S. manufacturers back from gaining contracts for telecommunications projects in many European countries. But the Buy American movement has been confounded by a lack of agreement on exactly what constitutes an "American" product. Can a Honda car made in Ohio be considered American? Can a Ford car made in Mexico be considered American? Products assembled in the United States often use imported parts; what percentage of parts must actually be made in America for the product to be considered American? Such questions are not easily answered, making Buy American policies difficult to enforce.[33]

The European Community has negotiated with Japan for voluntary export restraints that limit the number of imported Japanese vehicles, including these Toyotas. However, if the EC tries to restrict the sales of cars made by Japanese-owned plants in Europe, the automakers may decide to contain their production levels and cut back on new investment in Europe.

Trade Blocs

Countries can restrict trade by using trade controls, but they can also encourage trade by creating *trade blocs,* within which trade barriers hindering member nations are eliminated. Inside a trade bloc, goods and services can flow across national borders without tariffs, import quotas, or other legalities. The United States belongs to a trade bloc that may soon expand to include all of North America; other regional trade blocs include the Caribbean Common Market, the Central American Common Market, the Association of Southeast Asian Nations, the East African Community, the Arab Economic Unity Agreement, and the Latin American Integration Association. Companies operating within these trade blocs have a relatively easy time selling products or buying supplies in any of the member countries.[34]

In the European Community (EC), for instance, the 12 member nations are working to remove national restrictions on the buying and selling of goods and services (see Exhibit 5.4). The founding members include Belgium, Denmark, France, Germany, Greece, Ireland, Italy, Luxembourg, the Netherlands, Portugal, Spain, and the United Kingdom, whose combined populations create an attractive regional market of 325 million consumers. These members have agreed to remove tariffs and other legal controls on products made and sold within the trading bloc; to develop a uniform set of trade controls that governs interactions with nations outside the trading bloc; and to set common standards for regulating product safety, transportation, and other commercial issues. The purpose is to allow European companies to obtain resources anywhere in the trading bloc, then make and sell products throughout the region. The accessibility of the new, larger market should help these firms build volume so that they can reduce unit costs and better compete with non-European companies.[35]

As beneficial as the EC promises to be for the 12 nations in the trading bloc, gaining complete agreement on the hundreds of issues that must be resolved has proved slow and arduous. For example, national representatives wrangled for many months over the necessity (and the mechanics) of a common monetary system. Although the EC members recently approved the concept of a European currency unit, they must still work out the details in advance of issuing the new money, which may be minted in 1997. At the same time, businesses outside the EC trading bloc are concerned about their ability to penetrate "Fortress Europe," fearful that the EC's new controls on trade with nations outside the bloc will make market entry and expansion more difficult and expensive. Both the

EXHIBIT 5.4

The European Community and the European Free Trade Association Trading Blocs

The 12 founding members of the European Community are working to remove their national trade controls to encourage the free movement of goods and services within the trading bloc. A similar organization, the European Free Trade Association (EFTA), began with six nations but now includes all EC member nations as well, making it a market of more than 350 million consumers. (EC countries continue to operate as a distinct trading bloc while enjoying free trade with the EFTA.)

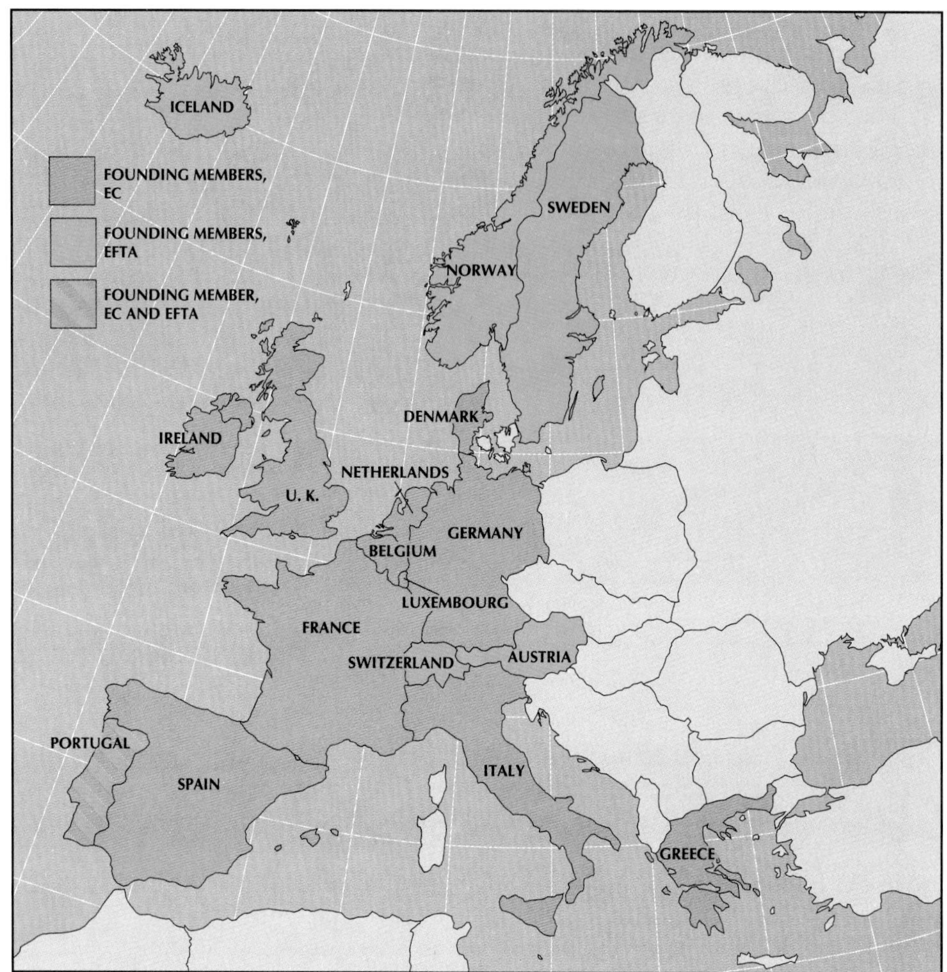

United States and Japan enjoy a sizable merchandise trade surplus with the European Community but may find the doors less open than before when EC rules on import quotas and tariffs are finalized.[36]

In 1989 the United States entered into a free trade agreement with Canada to form a U.S.-Canada trading bloc that phased out tariffs and most other trading controls. The following year, the United States and Mexico began discussions aimed at bringing Mexico into the trading bloc. Already, two-way trade between Canada and the United States totals $170 billion per year; trade between the United States and Mexico tops $50 billion per year. With the addition of Mexico, which may occur in just a few years, the North American trading bloc would contain more consumers than the European Community (364 million versus 325 million). This expanded North American trading bloc should stimulate internal trade and open markets closer to home for many companies doing business in the area.[37]

Sociocultural Forces

In the international environment, the sociocultural forces that affect an organization include the attitudes, values, behaviors, and beliefs of people in various geographic areas. These often differ from nation to nation and from culture to culture, and they can influence the customers, the employees, the suppliers, and even the governmental restrictions placed on organizations operating in a specific area. Dutch researcher Geert Hofstede found that sociocultural differences can be viewed in terms of four dimensions: individualism, power distance, masculinity, and uncertainty avoidance.[38]

- **Individualism** reflects the degree to which people expect to take care of themselves and their immediate families, as opposed to depending on larger social groups for care and protection. In highly individualistic societies such as the United States, Australia, Great Britain, and the Netherlands, people tend to feel freer to move from employer to employer, and they believe that individuals are personally responsible for their own decisions and welfare. On the other hand, Venezuela, Taiwan, Mexico, and Greece are among the countries in which individualism is less important than group cooperation, group loyalty, and dependence on others. In such societies, people often seek group consensus when making organizational decisions, and they generally rely on their employers to provide the training and tools needed to accomplish the work.[39]

individualism The degree to which people expect to take care of themselves and their own families

- **Power distance** is the extent to which people in the society accept the often unequal distribution of power. In high power distance societies such as the Philippines, Mexico, India, and Brazil, individuals of varying social classes rarely interact, and low-status individuals are less able to raise their status. Managers in such societies may be seen as holding much authority over employees, and they may closely supervise their employees, an approach that is accepted by those within the work unit. However, in low power distance societies such as Denmark, Israel, Sweden, and Austria, status differences are minimized, and people of all classes interact more freely. Managers in these societies tend to be more collaborative, involving employees in decision making and asking for their ideas.[40]

power distance The extent to which people in the society accept the often unequal distribution of power

- **Masculinity** is Hofstede's term for the degree to which assertiveness, competitiveness, and materialism dominate the society, as opposed to themes of passivity, cooperation, and personal feelings. Countries considered relatively masculine include Italy, Japan, Mexico, and Venezuela. People in these societies tend to view work in terms of money, recognition, and high job status. In contrast, countries such as Thailand, Finland, Yugoslavia, and Sweden are considered less masculine (or relatively feminine). People in those societies tend to see work in terms of job satisfaction, pleasant working conditions, and security.[41]

masculinity The degree to which assertiveness, competitiveness, and materialism dominate the society

- **Uncertainty avoidance** is the degree to which people feel threatened when confronted with ambiguity or uncertainty, developing beliefs and institutions that avoid such situations. Uncertainty avoidance is generally high in such countries as Greece, Portugal, Peru, and France, where employees seek work security, have many written rules to guide their activities, and develop expertise within narrow work areas. In India, Denmark, the United States, and Great Britain, uncertainty avoidance tends to be low, so employees take more risks, require fewer written rules, and develop a broader range of work expertise.[42]

uncertainty avoidance The degree to which people feel threatened when confronted with ambiguity or uncertainty

Hofstede grouped the 40 countries he studied into country clusters that reflect the interactions of all four dimensions. The societal values, beliefs, and behavior of people within each country cluster tend to be similar (see Exhibit

EXHIBIT 5.5

Hofstede's Country Clusters of Sociocultural Forces

Geert Hofstede, a Dutch social scientist, studied more than 100,000 IBM employees in 40 countries around the world. From this research, he was able to develop a series of eight clusters that group countries according to the four basic dimensions of sociocultural forces: power distance, uncertainty avoidance, individualism, and masculinity.

	Position on Sociocultural Dimensions			
Country Cluster	**Power Distance**	**Uncertainty Avoidance**	**Individualism**	**Masculinity**
Cluster 1: Argentina, Belgium, Brazil, France, Spain	**High**	**High**	**Medium to high**	**Medium**
Cluster 2: Chile, Colombia, Mexico, Peru, Portugal, Venezuela	**High**	**High**	**Low**	**High**
Cluster 3: Japan	**Medium**	**High**	**Medium**	**High**
Cluster 4: Hong Kong, India, Pakistan, Philippines, Singapore, Taiwan, Thailand	**High**	**Low to medium**	**Low**	**Medium**
Cluster 5: Greece, Iran, Turkey	**High**	**High**	**Low**	**Medium**
Cluster 6: Austria, Israel, Switzerland, West Germany*	**Low**	**Medium to high**	**Medium**	**Medium**
Cluster 7: Australia, Canada, Great Britain, Ireland, New Zealand, United States	**Low to medium**	**Low to medium**	**High**	**High**
Cluster 8: Denmark, Finland, the Netherlands, Norway, Sweden	**Low**	**Low to medium**	**Medium to high**	**Low**

*Study was conducted prior to unification.

5.5), an observation that can help global organizations better understand a country's sociocultural environment and the ways sociocultural forces act on competing organizations in that country. For example, Karlheinz Kaske, president of the German electronic and electrical engineering giant Siemens, runs the company with a high uncertainty avoidance approach that is characteristically German. Siemens's high-tech products must be perfected to meet virtually every possible contingency before Kaske will release them for sale. Although the firm has created numerous innovative technologies, this tendency to avoid risks has also led Siemens to be late to market with important competitive products. Clearly, competitors who understand the sociocultural influences on Kaske and his firm can more effectively compete with Siemens anywhere in the world.[43]

Technological Forces

Another aspect of the international environment that affects global management is the impact of technological forces. Organizations in some countries possess more technological capabilities than organizations in other countries. The development and application of more advanced technology (in the form of processes, equipment, and skills) helps an organization compete effectively in the global marketplace and provides an effective competitive tool for fending off overseas organizations attempting to enter domestic markets. For this reason, *technology transfer*, or sharing technology with individuals and organizations who do not currently have it, has become a critical issue. As organizations cross national borders in pursuit of resources and customers, they want to transfer technology to and from local units, but many governments seek to control such transfers.

Home governments frequently argue that sharing technology outside the home country may allow overseas competitors to gain an edge on domestic industries; host governments argue that overseas organizations entering their market should invest in local research-and-development activities that will boost host-country technological know-how. In some cases, governments block the export of technology because of national security concerns.[44]

At the same time, organizations that develop or improve technology want to protect their investment and their competitive advantage, so they seek legal protection such as copyrights and patents to help guard against unauthorized technology transfer. Unfortunately, some countries do not recognize the legal protection afforded by other countries, and they do not act against domestic organizations that illegally transfer technology, for example, by copying products that have been patented or copyrighted by overseas competitors. The lack of patent protection for pharmaceuticals costs U.S. companies an estimated $110 million in lost sales each year in Argentina and Brazil, sales that are being made instead by local organizations that have illegally copied these products for domestic sale.[45]

Great Britain's General Electric Company (known as GEC and unrelated to General Electric in the United States) joined with French partner Générale d'Électricité in 1989 to make and sell generating equipment. Both companies shared their expertise in energy technology, and their joint venture company, GEC Alsthom, is now the largest maker of power systems in Europe.

To overcome barriers to technology transfer that impede global organizations from competing more effectively around the world, managers can join with local partners who are willing to share their technology, or they can contract with the owners to legally license or apply their technology. For example, Hyundai Motors in South Korea initially operated car assembly plants under licenses and technical agreements with Ford. Later, Hyundai licensed more than 30 technologies from companies in other countries and added its own technological discoveries to develop cars for export under its own brand name. Internal technology transfer is equally important to global organizations, and the techniques for internal transfer include locating research-and-development facilities where they can most effectively support local operations; establishing central research-and-development units to develop technology that can be shared among all organizational units and subsidiaries; sending employees to other countries for training; and creating special units that modify existing technology to fit the needs of overseas operations.[46]

ENTERING THE GLOBAL BUSINESS MARKET

Firms can move into the global business market through a range of activities that reflect an increasing level of ownership, financial commitment, and risk. Exporting/importing is often the first entry method businesses use when they decide to expand globally. Three other options involve a higher level of ownership and financial commitment, as well as more risk: licensing, joint ventures, and direct investment.

Exporting and Importing

Many firms entering international markets start by exporting or importing. **Exporting** is selling products outside the country in which they are produced. Typically, businesses choose this approach when they want to minimize their investment and avoid the costs and the risks of maintaining factories or offices in other countries. To be successful, exporters may have to print product brochures in other languages and, in some cases, modify the product to fit local needs. For

exporting Selling products outside the country in which they are produced example, Joanne Henry, owner of Candy Flowers of Mentor, Ohio, eliminated artificial flavoring, replaced plastic with cellophane wrapping, and changed the leaves on her candy roses to make the product more attractive to overseas buyers; then she used trade shows to introduce her products to buyers from retail stores in Italy, France, and Japan. The export process can be complex and sometimes expensive because of tariffs, taxes, transportation, and payment arrangements, but state and federal government specialists and private consultants are available to help companies through the maze.[47]

importing Purchasing products from a supplier in another country

Importing is purchasing products made in another country and bringing them into the organization's home country. The importer may use the products or resell them to other customers. For instance, appliance manufacturers such as General Electric and Whirlpool often buy microwave ovens made by Asian suppliers, attach the GE or Whirlpool brand name, and then sell the ovens in the United States. Importers frequently buy from overseas suppliers specific parts that are then used in the manufacture of finished goods in the home country. This approach allows the company to select from suppliers anywhere in the world to get the best-quality parts and service at the most reasonable price. Electrolux (a Swedish firm) does not make the magnetrons used to power the microwave ovens it sells. Instead, it buys magnetrons from Asian suppliers and installs them in the ovens manufactured and sold in the United States.[48]

Licensing

licensing An arrangement in which one organization sells a second organization the rights to a patent, a brand name, or a product

Another way to enter the global market is through **licensing,** an arrangement in which one organization (the licensor) sells to a second organization (the licensee) the rights to a patent, a brand name, or a product so that the licensee can produce or market the product in another country. A typical arrangement calls for the licensee to pay the licensor a minimum amount, with additional payments based on a percentage of the sales or profits generated by the licensed products. Although the licensor avoids the expense of building factories, hiring employees, and contacting buyers in overseas locations, it does lose some control over how its licensed products are made, marketed, and distributed. Consider how licensing has allowed Dennis Pushkin, founder of Tidy Car in Boca Raton, Florida, to expand his automobile cleaning and polishing business. Rather than personally setting up shop in other countries, Pushkin sold licenses that put Tidy Car Total Appearance Centers into 80 locations in Denmark, Norway, Sweden, and central Europe. Thanks to these far-flung licensing deals, Tidy Car now draws as much as 20 percent of its revenues from overseas sales. Similarly, Walt Disney licensed the Disneyland name and characters such as Mickey Mouse in a 45-year deal with the builders of Tokyo Disneyland, which opened in 1983. Disney initially invested no money but arranged to receive 10 percent of the ticket sales plus 5 percent of the concession sales, worth about $35 million annually.[49]

Seeking to expand internationally, Catesby Jones traveled to Spain as part of a U.S. government-sponsored trade mission. He was interested in finding vendors to license the European rights to his colorful Peace Frogs T-shirts. Jones signed licensees in advance of the Summer Olympics in Barcelona and doubled his profits in 1992.

One of the fastest-growing forms of international licensing is **franchising,** in which the licensor supplies a complete package of goods, services, and materials, generally accompanied by a well-known brand name, to the licensee. Franchising has become so popular that licensees in other countries hold as many as 30,000 franchises from such U.S. licensors as KFC (formerly Kentucky Fried Chicken) and Coca-Cola. Although franchising, like licensing, is a convenient way to expand quickly into global markets, it is not risk-free. Companies may have difficulty evaluating potential overseas franchisees who will be using the brand name and materials, a problem because the franchisor's brand name and reputation are at stake. Further, companies may find that franchisees eventually learn enough about their operations to operate independently or, worse, to become direct competitors sometime in the future.[50]

franchising A licensing arrangement in which the licensor supplies a complete package of goods, services, and materials to the licensee

Joint Ventures

A **joint venture** is an arrangement in which two or more organizations cooperatively develop, produce, or sell goods or services. The parent firms are independent of each other but share control over the joint venture. In some cases, one company supplies the materials and the product expertise, while the other supplies the knowledge to do business in the country they are targeting. This form of joint venture is common in the People's Republic of China and in other regions where the politicolegal environment is complex and the concept of private ownership is evolving. In Moscow, the first two Pizza Hut outlets were joint ventures, 49 percent owned by Pizza Hut parent PepsiCo and 51 percent owned by the city of Moscow. The city contributed two locations, and PepsiCo contributed the recipes, the operational expertise, and the management. Such joint venture arrangements are also common in areas where the culture is unfamiliar to outsiders or where the business environment is so complex that special skills are required. For example, the National Basketball Association has formed a joint venture with C. Itoh of Japan to develop television programming and play basketball games in Japan, where accepted business and regulatory practices often confound firms seeking to enter the market.[51]

joint venture An arrangement in which two or more organizations cooperate to develop, produce, or sell products

In other cases, all the partners contribute materials, skills, and funding to the new organization. Since 1988, for example, GM has participated in a European joint venture with Isuzu to make light trucks in a former GM plant near London. Although the venture has made money, the plant has also had excess capacity. To increase productivity and to cash in on the boom in demand for four-wheel-drive vehicles on the continent, the partners used an Isuzu design and began assembling the Frontera, a utility vehicle akin to the Rodeo model that Isuzu manufactures in the United States. The joint venture helped GM and Isuzu get a jump on competitors who were scrambling to meet demand for four-wheel-drives, and the total cost of adapting the Isuzu design and retooling the GM plant was far less than if the partners had set out (separately or together) to design a vehicle specifically for the European market.[52]

Joint ventures offer more direct control over international operations than licensing or exporting, and they allow organizations to tap the expertise of others as they expand into overseas markets. They also allow organizations to spread the risk of entering a new market, developing a new technology, or building a new plant. But joint ventures do not always perform as expected: according to one study, the average success rate is below 50 percent, and the average life span is under four years. Joint ventures may fail for a variety of reasons, including management disagreements between the partners, operational and personnel problems, incompatible goals and methods, an imbalance in the competence or the investment level of the partners, insufficient sales or profits, and changes in the market.[53]

direct investment An arrangement in which an organization acquires an ownership interest in an overseas company or invests in production and marketing facilities in another country

Direct Investment

The highest level of ownership involvement and control of international operations is **direct investment,** also known as *foreign direct investment,* which occurs

GLOBAL MANAGEMENT

Corning's Joint Ventures Span the Globe

In nearly 70 years, Corning Glass Works has hooked up with more than three dozen partners in a dozen nations, a partnership record that few multinational corporations can match. In all that time, only six of Corning's joint ventures have failed, and today the firm's profits from such partnerships top $100 million. Joint ventures have become a way of life for Corning as the firm uses them to enter new markets and to gain new technology.

What is Corning chairman James Houghton's secret for joint venture success? He sticks to five key rules: (1) seek a compatible partner, one that has a similar organizational culture; (2) build the venture independent of its parents; (3) make the venture a 50–50 partnership; (4) be sure partners agree on long-term goals; and (5) install a strong management team to guide the joint venture organization. On the rare occasion when Corning violates its own rules and rushes into a joint venture arrangement that appears promising, it may find that its partner is incompatible or has long-term goals that do not mesh with Corning's interests. At one time, for example, Corning had a joint venture with Kedaung Group to make dinnerware in Indonesia. The venture was hobbled by government restrictions and by local economic conditions, but more damaging was Kedaung's interest in the profit-enhancing idea of producing and selling a similar product *without* Corning. After five years and numerous clashes, Corning decided that the joint venture was not going to work.

A typical joint venture with Corning starts with careful planning and a long courtship period in which the prospective partners get to know each other. Consider Corning's joint venture with Switzerland's Ciba-Geigy, a global pharmaceutical giant. Corning wanted to gain access to Ciba's research-and-development expertise, and Ciba was eyeing Corning's experience in the growing medical-diagnosis business as well as its 400-member marketing group. Originally, Ciba was not interested in a joint venture; management wanted to purchase the Corning unit to have full control. Negotiations dragged on for two years, but Corning chairman Houghton persisted, and his personal visit with Ciba executive Albert Bodmer convinced the Swiss that the two firms were indeed compatible. A few days after Houghton's visit, Bodmer agreed to the venture, called Ciba-Corning Diagnostics.

Among Corning's worldwide joint ventures are Samsung-Corning, established in 1974 with South Korean partner Samsung; Siecor, established in 1977 with German partner Siemens; and Corning Asahi Video Products, established in 1988 with Japanese partner Asahi Glass. The joint venture with Asahi is a bit out of the ordinary for Corning; it began with Corning owning 67 percent of the venture and retaining management responsibility. Asahi Glass paid Corning to gain access to Corning's existing television-bulb-glass–manufacturing operation, and the Japanese company supplied the technology to manufacture large-sized and high-resolution glass bulbs for televisions and computer monitors. However, their agreement specifies that over time, Asahi's ownership stake will rise to 49 percent.

Corning's strengths in forging successful, long-lasting joint ventures include its diplomatic approach and its managers' ability to compromise. Also important is Houghton's philosophy about trust: "If the partners continually have to look over each other's shoulder, then the offspring venture will have little chance of surviving." Given Corning's worldwide network of joint ventures, Corning's competitors better be looking over their shoulders as Corning gains sales in overseas markets.

Apply Your Knowledge

1. Why would Corning choose a joint venture rather than a licensing arrangement to gain access to another firm's technology?
2. How might a joint venture help Corning overcome potentially adverse politicolegal environmental conditions?

when an organization acquires an ownership interest in an overseas company or invests in production and marketing facilities in another country. Direct investment allows the organization to gain more control over operations, to avoid many problematic trade barriers, and to learn firsthand about the needs of its customers. Moreover, producing goods and services closer to where they will be sold enables the organization to respond more rapidly to environmental changes and, at the same time, keep marketing and distribution costs lower. For example, as an entry to the European market, General Electric bought a controlling

Toymaker Ertl assembles 150 types of trucks, tractors, and other toys in this offshore production plant in Tijuana, Mexico. Based in Dyersville, Iowa, Ertl has fueled expansion by spreading its manufacturing to low-cost offshore production facilities; in addition to the plant in Mexico, the firm operates two in China.

interest in Tungsram, a light-bulb maker in Hungary with a 7 percent share of the Western European market. Because of its majority interest, GE was able to make technological, production, and management changes that boosted productivity by 30 percent and that helped push Tungsram's European sales to double-digit annual growth.[54]

Another method of direct investment is to start up or take total ownership and control of another company, making the second company a *wholly owned subsidiary* of the parent. Having a wholly owned subsidiary involves more investment, ownership control, and risk than having only a partial interest in another company, but it can also allow the parent the freedom to take whatever actions are necessary to make the subsidiary perform as expected and to provide the parent with needed resources to improve its performance. For instance, the British retail giant Marks & Spencer bought New York–based Brooks Brothers in 1988 as a way to expand in the United States through an established network of stores. Marks & Spencer is sharing its operational know-how with Brooks Brothers as a way of improving the chain's profit margins. But Marks & Spencer is also learning from Brooks Brothers about design and manufacturing techniques, helping the parent upgrade the clothing sold in Europe.[55]

Many organizations have established manufacturing or assembly plants in other countries where labor costs are relatively low, a technique known as **offshore production.** Japan-based Hitachi makes color televisions in Taiwan, where labor and facilities are cheaper than in the home country; another Japanese manufacturer, Minebea, makes miniature bearings in Thailand and Singapore for the same reasons. More than a thousand international companies have set up offshore production facilities in Mexico because of that country's *maquiladora program,* which sets aside special duty-free zones where non-Mexican companies can bring in raw materials and assemble products for export (see Exhibit 5.6). The program brings jobs and training for Mexican employees and managers, and it allows companies to manufacture goods cost-effectively close to North American and South American markets. Although some critics charge that these plants, known as *maquiladoras,* are little more than sweatshops for outside firms and that they offer little of long-term benefit to the host country,

offshore production Establishing manufacturing or assembly plants in other countries where labor and resource costs are relatively low

EXHIBIT 5.6

Mexican Maquiladora Exports Multiply

In the last half of the 1980s, the total value of goods produced for export by Mexican maquiladoras has more than doubled.

Industry	Value of Export Goods ($ billions) 1985	1986	1987	1988	1989
Electronics	2,400.0	2,652.0	3,157.0	4,481.0	5,577.0
Transport equipment	1,438.8	1,621.8	2,086.2	2,549.8	3,376.8
General manufacturing	335.5	449.9	681.1	1,066.7	1,367.0
Furniture	110.3	145.5	256.2	414.7	527.7
Textiles	376.6	380.4	409.5	487.9	567.8
Toys	164.8	134.9	152.0	283.5	334.8
Services	75.1	82.6	110.7	112.0	203.3
Tools	61.0	73.0	115.6	168.5	183.6
Other	131.2	105.8	136.7	581.6	287.0
Total	5,093.3	5,645.9	7,105.0	10,145.7	12,470.0

the maquiladora program has gained so much momentum that Honduras, Costa Rica, and other Central American countries have followed suit. However, the savings in labor costs that firms seek through offshore production may be offset by the increased time and higher costs of shipping goods to market, the expense of training local employees, and the risk of changes in trade agreements and foreign exchange.[56]

MANAGEMENT APPROACHES TO GLOBAL ACTIVITIES

No matter which way they choose to enter the global business market, organizations can take one of three distinct approaches to managing their operations in other countries. Depending on whether the organization is oriented toward its home country, toward the countries in which outside activities are based, or toward a more global view, managers can use an ethnocentric, a polycentric, or a geocentric management approach.

Ethnocentric Management

ethnocentric management A management approach in which the values and interests of the parent company in its home country guide the decisions and actions of operations outside the home country

Ethnocentric management assumes that the values and interests of the parent company in its home country should guide the decisions and actions of operations outside the home country. Carried to the extreme, ethnocentric management means that overseas managers have little control over local marketing, finance, human resources, and other key issues. Ethnocentric managers at headquarters try to standardize practices in every location around the world, modeling them after the way things are done in home-country offices and largely ignoring conditions or variations in other countries.[57]

Although this approach helps parent company managers feel more in control over operations outside the home country, it frequently hinders the performance of host-country operations. When Texas Instruments opened a semiconductor production facility in Japan, the company originally sent headquarters managers to run the plant. Instead of adopting traditional Japanese methods of hiring, promoting, and rewarding employees, the TI managers relied on the practices they had used in the United States. Employee morale crumbled and the Japanese plant had difficulty recruiting new employees. The managers then switched to

Japanese methods, which include twice-yearly bonuses, and they eventually turned the plant's management over to Japanese managers. These shifts away from ethnocentric management kept the plant viable, and today TI is the only U.S. chipmaker with memory chip facilities at home and in Japan.[58]

Polycentric Management

Polycentric management allows managers in other countries to make their own decisions according to local needs and environmental pressures. In the extreme, polycentric management results in overseas operations run by local managers, who conduct business largely without any headquarters decisions or approvals. This approach can help the operation run smoothly from day to day, but it prevents the parent from developing and implementing an overall global strategy, which requires coordination among units in other countries. The polycentric approach can also hurt the organization's ability to use its human resources most effectively. Overseas managers are frequently seen by the polycentric managers in the parent company as skilled only at solving problems that arise in their local markets, so they are rarely tapped for senior management roles at headquarters.[59]

polycentric management A management approach in which managers in the home country allow managers in other countries to make their own decisions in response to local needs and environmental pressures

Geocentric Management

Geocentric management involves a global view of the organization's international operations. Rather than orienting themselves toward either the home country or the host country, top managers consider the organization's goals, plans, and performance from a broader, worldwide perspective. The best managers, regardless of their nationality or location, are selected for the assignments that fit their skills and abilities; the various units are connected by a coordinated plan that allows for local needs and actions in the context of overall organizational performance. Although this is the most complex of the three international management approaches, managers who apply geocentric management can make the most effective use of their resources, regardless of origin or location, and achieve the highest possible overall performance.[60]

geocentric management A management approach in which managers take a global view of the organization's international operations

Asea Brown Boveri (ABB), an organization created by the merger of Sweden's ASEA and Switzerland's Brown Boveri, uses geocentric management to achieve consistently high global performance from more than 1,000 companies operating in 140 countries. ABB produces electrical power equipment, robots, locomotives, antipollution control systems, and other industrial goods, and its local operations around the world act both independently and cooperatively. Local managers are free to react to conditions in their countries, but they must also share information and resources with other units and strive to achieve ABB's overall goals. In this way, top ABB managers can balance local needs with the concerns of reaching global goals.[61]

Implications for Managers

Each of these three approaches has specific implications for the management functions of planning, organizing, leading, and controlling. In an organization oriented toward ethnocentric management, primary responsibility for these management functions is typically vested in managers in the headquarters unit of the home country. Although managers in host countries are generally allowed to make decisions about routine matters, decisions that affect the local unit's ability to achieve its goals or to contribute to the organization's overall goals must be referred to the home office.

Similarly, organizations that apply polycentric management allow host-country managers to plan, organize, lead, and control according to local needs and customs, without regard to the organization's overall needs. However, in organizations that use geocentric management, managers in host countries work closely with top managers headquartered in the home country to be sure that their local plans, organization structure, leadership style, and control functions are consistent with the priorities and goals of the entire organization. In this way, geocentric organizations can best prepare for the challenges and opportunities in each of their local markets as well as in the international environment as a whole.

SUMMARY

The volume of international trade has increased as organizations move beyond domestic business activities (conducted within the borders of one nation) and cross borders in search of resources or customers to conduct international business. Early multinational companies with operations in several countries generally used multidomestic management, allowing local units to act independently without coordinating operations on a global basis. But more recently, the rapid pace of globalization has prompted MNCs to apply transnational management, using an integrated strategy to achieve organizational goals on a worldwide level while emphasizing local management flexibility in host countries. Today, organizations can easily and inexpensively cross national borders to enter global markets. They do so in search of the resources and the customers that will improve organizational efficiency and effectiveness in both the home and host countries.

A variety of economic forces affect an organization's entry into international markets. Managers must consider the host country's level of economic development, which can influence resource availability and the ability of local customers to buy goods and services. Also, the host country's infrastructure must be able to support organizational activities. The balance of trade and balance of payments in other countries can influence how their governments regulate the inflow and outflow of products and currency. The exchange rate affects the prices an organization pays for the resources it purchases or the products it sells in a host country, and if a host country has a blocked currency that cannot be exchanged in worldwide financial markets, the organization must find other ways to receive payment. Another economic element that affects organizations doing business internationally is the consistent availability of resources.

Four politicolegal forces influence organizations doing business abroad. First, managers have to consider political risk, the likelihood that their organizations' overseas goals, operations, or investments will be threatened by a host government's political, legal, or regulatory policies or actions. Second, they should be aware of host- and home-country laws and regulations that affect their organization's ability to manage its activities. Third, their products may be subject to trade controls such as tariffs, import quotas, and voluntary export restraints that regulate the flow of trade between countries. And fourth, they may be encouraged to increase overseas activities because of trade blocs that allow the free movement of goods and services within their borders. Sociocultural forces in the international environment differ from nation to nation and can have an effect on an organization's employees, customers, suppliers, and government attitudes. The four dimensions of sociocultural forces that influence global organizations are individualism, power distance, masculinity, and uncertainty avoidance. Technological forces, especially the ability to transfer technology, can have an effect on international competition.

Firms can move into the global business market in several ways, each of which reflects an increasing level of ownership, financial commitment, and risk. Businesses often enter the global marketplace by exporting or importing and then progress to other options, including licensing, joint ventures, and direct investment. Organizations may apply one of three distinct approaches to managing their operations in other countries. If they assume that the values and interests of the parent company in the home country should guide activities in host countries, they are using ethnocentric management, which allows managers in host countries little or no discretion over nonroutine decisions. If managers in the home country allow host-country managers to make their own decisions about local needs and environmental pressures without consulting home-country managers, they are using polycentric management. This approach puts local needs and issues above overall organizational goals and priorities. If organizations take a global view of their international operations and blend an understanding of overall organizational goals and plans with the flexibility to plan, organize, lead, and control on a local level, they are using geocentric management.

MEETING A MANAGEMENT CHALLENGE AT H.J. HEINZ

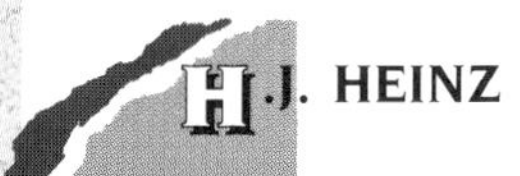

In looking at the challenges and opportunities of the Chinese and European markets, Heinz CEO Anthony O'Reilly saw two distinctly different management scenarios. As a geocentric enterprise, Heinz adapted its strategies and tactics to fit the two vastly different regions while maintaining a consistent organizational vision. O'Reilly and his team succeeded in China because they recognized the unique environment they faced in that market: a government bureaucracy that could be stifling and unpredictable, a shaky infrastructure, and the importance of food and nutrition to people who have experienced malnutrition for centuries.

O'Reilly persuaded government officials that Heinz should have majority ownership in its Chinese operations by proposing to introduce an improved instant rice cereal for infants and children and offering to sponsor a program to fight malnutrition. His proposals were convincing enough to secure 80 percent ownership in a business formed through a joint venture with two Chinese partners. The government also eased export restrictions to allow Heinz products made in China to be exported throughout Asia. All of this was accomplished with a remarkably small investment of only $10 million.

To effectively manage the joint venture, it was crucial for O'Reilly and the other Heinz managers to understand Chinese culture and the Chinese political system. The government had begun a population-control program in which couples would receive higher wages and preference in housing if they limited their families to one child. These incentives created a generation of "Little Emperors," pampered children whose parents wanted to buy—and could afford—higher-quality goods, including Heinz foods. This gave Heinz the market it needed to build brand loyalty.

Heinz cereal products sold in China

Although this policy created an opportunity for Heinz, other policies created problems. Government-imposed price freezes and credit restrictions caused distribution bottlenecks and shortages. Only by arguing that its products were socially beneficial could Heinz gain relief. Understanding culture and politics pulled the company through one crisis after another, so well in fact that the joint venture became profitable less than a decade after start-up, no small feat for a Western company operating in China.

O'Reilly used a completely different approach in Europe. A combination of joint ventures and acquisitions enabled Heinz to prepare for successful operations in the unified market. The question for O'Reilly was scale: would Heinz be better served with one continent-wide operation or with numerous smaller deals focused on particular nations and regions? He decided to pursue a strategy of building "brands that fit specific national markets." In doing so, Heinz chose a route pursued by many multinational corporations: offering many brand names, most of which don't include the parent company's name or logo. Roughly 65 percent of the nearly $7 billion worth of products Heinz sells annually are sold under non-Heinz brand names.

Heinz also built on the European taste for processed tomatoes and seafood. It acquired a leading tomato-processing firm in Spain that had 40 percent of the domestic fried tomato market, and it bought the maker of a popular brand of canned fish products based in Portugal. Together, the plants made Heinz the lowest-cost tomato and fish products manufacturer on the Iberian Peninsula. In southern Europe, Heinz opened a joint venture with a Greek tomato-processing company and upgraded the company's plant to allow it to process fruits in the tomato off-season. With these moves, Heinz gained several leading brands in new markets, strengthened its presence across southern Europe, and improved its ability to sell products across the continent.

***You're the Manager*:** Heinz now has operations in more than 200 countries on six continents, and the company continues to expand. Given the changing nature of the international environment, O'Reilly wants one person to coordinate all strategic decisions that affect global operations, and he's put you in charge.

Ranking Questions

1. The general manager Heinz selects for its Chinese joint venture must balance the company's overall vision and goals with the need to respond to local conditions. Assume that China is a society with high power distance, high uncertainty avoidance, and a low degree of individualism compared to other countries. Rank the following general manager candidates in order of which might be most effective in the Chinese joint venture.
   a. A manager whose entire career has been spent in China, who wants to preserve traditional cultural characteristics, and who has a general disdain for aggressive Western management.
   b. A manager who has spent nearly as much time managing in China as (a), but who has also worked for Heinz in the United States and who sees the value of individual initiative and risk-taking but is cautious about introducing such changes in the factory.
   c. A manager from Denmark who opposes hierarchy and who wants to introduce a job-rotation program in which managers and nonmanagers alike will move through the various jobs in the factory.
   d. A manager who promises to make the plant more creative by encouraging employees to take risks.
2. A small Japanese company has developed a new and more efficient technology for processing and packaging frozen foods. It is a technology that could dramatically help Heinz (and many other food companies) increase productivity and market share around the world. How can Heinz best capitalize on this advance? Rank these ideas from best to worst.
   a. Negotiate a licensing agreement with the Japanese inventor.
   b. Form a joint venture with the Japanese company to develop the technology in cannery and factory equipment that could then be sold to other manufacturers as another source of revenue for Heinz.
   c. Acquire the Japanese company.
   d. Have the Heinz research-and-development department try to develop the technology independently of the Japanese firm.

Multiple-Choice Questions

3. People in Eastern Europe have seen Weight Watchers classes and foods advertised on Western European television, and they seem interested. Weight Watchers is one of Heinz's most profitable subsidiaries, but Heinz has little experience in the Eastern European market. Which of the following might be the best way to enter this unknown market?
   a. Introduce Weight Watchers classes only.
   b. Introduce Weight Watchers classes, then buy Eastern European food companies and convert them to produce Weight Watchers foods.
   c. Introduce Weight Watchers classes and begin exporting Weight Watchers food products into Eastern Europe from existing plants in Western Europe.
   d. Introduce both classes and imported food products into one Eastern European country to learn more about the region, then expand by introducing classes and acquiring food plants.
4. Heinz's Star-Kist unit holds 37 percent of the U.S. market for canned seafood, but its worldwide share is relatively small. For years, Heinz's organization structure has grouped canned seafood products with pet food products under Star-Kist foods. This arrangement has worked

well from a production standpoint because a lot of cat food ingredients come from fish by-products. However, the unified European market may require a different approach to ensure that marketing efforts are responsive to local conditions and focused on customer needs. Which of these organizational approaches would work best?

a. Create a separate Star-Kist Foods unit to market both pet foods and seafood products in Europe.
b. Separate the pet foods and seafood products into two distinct, international companies, each focused on its specific consumer markets.
c. Create a European seafood company only.
d. Change nothing; let each country's management team put its own structure in place.

Analysis Questions

5. How might Heinz handle the issue of China's blocked currency?
6. Why would Heinz prefer to assume control of a joint venture rather than licensing its brand names to an existing Chinese production facility?
7. What issues in technology transfer might Heinz encounter in its entry of Eastern European nations?

Special Project

Infant and child nutrition is an international concern not limited to the People's Republic of China. O'Reilly created the Heinz Institute of Nutritional Sciences to study malnutrition in less-developed countries. Some of these countries present a challenge that is possibly even greater than the challenge of operating in China. In addition to political intricacies, some African nations, for instance, have perplexing and diverse eating customs that often differ from tribe to tribe within a single nation. Draft a general set of guidelines (no more than one page) for entering these complicated—but potentially lucrative—markets.[62]

KEY TERMS

balance of payments (143)
balance of trade (143)
blocked currency (145)
comparative advantage (141)
developed countries (142)
direct investment (155)
domestic business (137)
ethnocentric management (158)
exchange rate (144)
exporting (153)
expropriation (146)
franchising (155)
geocentric management (159)
home country (137)
host country (138)
import quotas (148)
importing (154)
individualism (151)
infrastructure (143)
international business (137)
joint venture (155)
less-developed countries (LDCs) (142)
licensing (154)
masculinity (151)
multidomestic management (138)
multinational corporation (MNC) (138)
national competitive advantage (141)
nationalization (146)
offshore production (157)
political risk (145)
polycentric management (159)
power distance (151)
tariffs (148)
transnational management (138)
uncertainty avoidance (151)
voluntary export restraints (148)

QUESTIONS

For Review

1. Why are international markets becoming increasingly important to managers around the world?
2. How do economic forces in the international environment affect global management?
3. What are ethnocentric, polycentric, and geocentric management approaches?
4. What are trade controls and trade blocs, and how do they influence organizational sales and operations?
5. How can firms enter global markets?

For Analysis

1. How does advanced telecommunications technology improve an organization's ability to apply transnational management?
2. Under what conditions might an organization use ethnocentric management? Polycentric management?
3. Why would a company such as IBM choose direct investment in some countries rather than simply exporting products from the United States?
4. What are the benefits and limitations of using a de-

tailed handbook to establish acceptable practices for employees who work in a country such as the United States, where uncertainty avoidance is low?
5. If Mexico joins the U.S.-Canada trading bloc, what may happen to the maquiladoras?

For Application

1. What political risks might Gannett face today if it started a daily newspaper in Ukraine, which has been undergoing major political changes?
2. How might Levi Strauss conduct business in a country with blocked currency?
3. What effect would a poor infrastructure have on Northern Telecom's ability to sell telephones in a less-developed country?
4. Is the newly unified European Community likely to offer opportunities or threats to the relative competitive positions in Europe of a U.S. computer company such as Digital Equipment Corporation and a German computer maker such as Siemens-Nixdorf? Why?
5. What can McDonald's do to ensure that it is able to transfer its food preparation technology from one country to another?

KEEPING CURRENT IN MANAGEMENT

Find a recent article in which a business manager discusses the company's investment in an overseas firm. Examples include companies based in the United States that buy into Eastern European companies or companies based in Japan that invest in companies located in Europe or the United States.

1. What organizational resources is the parent seeking from its investment? What resources must the parent provide for the overseas unit? How does the parent's investment allow it to better serve local or global customers?
2. Do local managers head the overseas operation or has the parent sent managers from the home country to take charge? Is the parent company's management approach to overseas units ethnocentric, polycentric, or geocentric? What impact does this management approach have on local operations and on the organization's overall performance?
3. What economic and politicolegal forces in the international environment have the most influence on the organization's operations in the other country? How does this organization's investment change its competitive situation at home and abroad?

SHARPEN YOUR MANAGEMENT SKILLS

It's not as if the Fang family hasn't encountered political and economic instability before. The Hong Kong–based group (brothers Kenneth, Lawrence, Vincent, and Jeffrey, and Jeffrey's wife, Christine Ma) is one of the most powerful textile and clothing companies in Asia. The family enterprise was started by the brothers' father and uncle in China before that country embraced communism in 1949. Anticipating the disruption this change would bring, the elder Fangs transferred production capability to Hong Kong. Then in the 1970s, in an attempt to protect its domestic sweater industry, the United States slapped import quotas on low-cost Hong Kong sweaters, which had become a major part of the Fangs' business. In addition, labor costs in Hong Kong had increased. So the brothers built sweater production facilities in other countries.

Several years ago, Jeffrey and Christine opened the Episode clothing store chain, which now has 27 stores in the United States. Most of the clothes sold at Episode, as you might expect, are manufactured by the Fangs in their 20 factories spread around the globe.

- *Decision:* Now the Fangs face another potential political problem: the U.S. government might once again restrict certain clothing imports. This would hurt the brothers' manufacturing business as well as their retailing business. Assume you are Kenneth, the oldest brother; what would you do to limit your family's risk in this situation?
- *Communication:* In a family-owned firm such as this, proposals and ideas are likely to be presented in informal settings, such as over dinner. Once you have decided what the family should do, prepare some brief remarks to introduce your ideas at the next family dinner.[63]

Philips Seeks Global Control

Philips, the world's largest consumer goods company, has recently lost a lot of money despite annual sales of $30 billion. Chairman and president Jan Timmer, who joined Philips's accounting department in 1952, is struggling to consolidate control over Philips's vast global empire. Timmer recently made the Polygram and Sparte entertainment-electronics subsidiaries profitable by cutting costs, but cost cuts alone may not be enough to save Philips.

HISTORY

Philips founder Gerard Philips capitalized on the spread of electricity through Europe by building a light-bulb factory in 1891 at Eindhoven, Holland, where corporate headquarters remains. Foreign sales helped Philips become the third-largest European light-bulb maker by the turn of the century. The company began making x-ray and radio tubes during World War I, set up its first foreign office in Belgium in 1918, and began building plants in other countries during the 1930s to avoid trade barriers and tariffs. It set up hundreds of virtually autonomous subsidiaries and began making televisions and appliances in the boom years after World War II. Philips invented the car radio, audiocassette, videocassette recorder, and laser disc technology, but it lost market share in such products to a flood of inexpensive goods from Japan. During the 1980s, the company struggled to meet its profitability goals; it opened the 1990s with a huge loss. Philips is now trying to consolidate its sprawling international production capacity while abandoning industry segments in which it is not a leader. To cut costs and regain profitability, Philips has closed 75 plants in five years and Timmer has cut the work force from 283,000 to 240,000. The result was a $645 million profit in 1991.

ENVIRONMENT

Philips's empire is far-flung in both geography and products. It is the world's second-largest producer of consumer electronics (Japan's Matsushita is the largest) and the largest in Europe. The company is still the world's largest producer of light bulbs, and the world's third-largest recorded music producer through its 80 percent ownership of Polygram. Strong local managers in 60 countries traditionally have decided what would be produced and how it would be marketed, which has caused a lack of coordination between business units. A joint venture with U.S.-based Whirlpool to sell major appliances in Europe has been hurt by the failure of factories in Italy and Germany to use common parts. The North American division embarrassed its parent by spurning the V-2000 system that Philips developed for VCRs and opting for the VHS standard developed by Matsushita of Japan; Philips has since brought it under tighter corporate control.

GOALS AND CHALLENGES

Timmer knows that Philips needs more corporate direction, but the ability to set a global direction is hampered by a slow-moving bureaucracy at headquarters and by an attempt to focus on too many products. So he is streamlining the topheavy bureaucracy to speed up decision making while retreating on Philips's weakest fronts and advancing on its strongest. Timmer is cutting back on computer chip manufacture, is letting Whirlpool buy out Philips's remaining 47 percent ownership of their European major appliance joint venture, is selling Philips's faltering computer division to Digital Equipment Corporation, and is capitalizing on Philips's recovery in televisions, VCRs, and other consumer electronics. He recently agreed to a partnership with archrival Thomson of France to develop high-definition television, and he has high hopes for a new Philips device that can be programmed to search radio stations and play only certain types of music (from hard rock to light classical) and to automatically interrupt music with timely information—like traffic bulletins—from other stations. Timmer hopes a sleeker bureaucracy and more focused organizational structure combined with continuing product innovations and tighter corporate control will keep Philips profitable.

1. How has Philips's international management evolved? Why did Philips cross national borders?
2. How has Philips responded to economic, politico-legal, and technological forces in the international environment?
3. Assume that Philips has vast resources and that electrical service to homes is increasing in Mexico. What are the advantages and disadvantages of the various methods Timmer could use for entering the Mexican light-bulb market?
4. How might the level of economic development and infrastructure of a developing African nation affect Timmer's analysis of whether to open a plant to assemble radios there?

PART I INTEGRATIVE CASE:
Marriott Registers Long-Term Growth

"Success is never final," says J. Willard (Bill) Marriott, Jr., chairman of Marriott, and that's especially true in the hospitality business. The Marriott empire began with a root beer stand started by Marriott's father and has grown into one of the world's largest lodging and food-service firms. A growth spurt in the 1980s tripled sales from $2 billion in 1982 to $5.8 billion by 1987, and by 1990 Marriott was ringing up $7.5 billion in hotel, restaurant, and contract food services. But Marriott's long-term growth plans for the 1990s seemed stymied by environmental uncertainty and heavy competition.

The chairman faced a key decision between two paths related to its stand-alone restaurant business. He could invest in the restaurant division and build a single, national brand name to try to dominate the market. Or he could shift out of restaurants and commit more resources to hotels, contract food services, and senior living centers. Bill Marriott was keenly aware that either path would significantly alter the corporation's future.

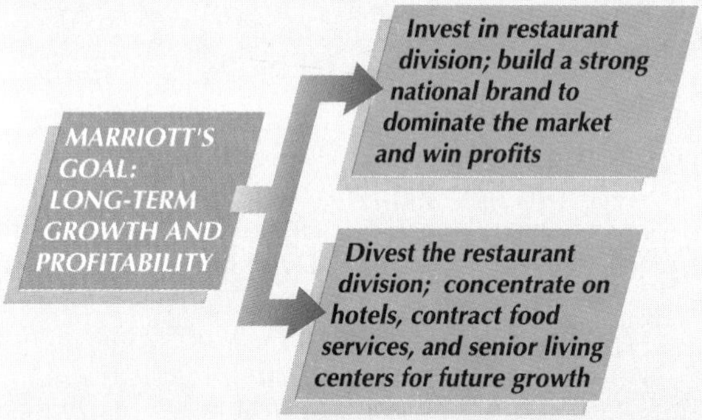

MARRIOTT'S GOAL: LONG-TERM GROWTH AND PROFITABILITY

Invest in restaurant division; build a strong national brand to dominate the market and win profits

Divest the restaurant division; concentrate on hotels, contract food services, and senior living centers for future growth

HISTORY

In 1927 J. W. Marriott, Sr., opened a tiny root beer stand in Washington, D.C. To spark demand during the winter months, he added food and later changed the name to the Hot Shoppe. Eyeing the growth in automobile use, he soon opened the East Coast's first drive-in restaurant, and sales sizzled. During the 1930s, Marriott spotted another opportunity: feeding airline passengers. He approached Eastern and American airlines and arranged to provide on-board meals. For the next decade, catering was the company's main focus.

Marriott kept watching the trends, including a big increase in car ownership, and he saw opportunities beyond food service. In 1957 he opened a motel in Virginia, and the company has been in the lodging business ever since. Today Marriott holds 4 percent of all lodging rooms in the United States. Adding up its worldwide holdings in upscale hotels, resorts, moderately priced hotels, economy lodgings, and extended-stay hotels, the company operates nearly 700 properties. Local managers run their properties according to instruction manuals that outline detailed procedures for virtually every aspect of hotel operations, which ensures uniform quality in every location.

The company branched out into restaurants in 1967 by purchasing the Big Boy chain. The following year, Marriott launched the Roy Rogers fast-food restaurant division, then it bought other fast-food operations and converted many to Roy Rogers units. In 1982 Marriott became the largest operator of airport terminal food and merchandising locations in the United States by acquiring the market leader. Next, the firm made a series of acquisitions that positioned the company as a strong contender in the market for contract food and facilities management services. Marriott now has contracts to operate food facilities for more than 400 U.S. colleges and nearly 1,100 U.S. businesses, and the company manages facilities and housekeeping services for a growing number of health-care institutions. All Marriott kitchens follow standardized recipe and food preparation instructions that take the guesswork out of creating meals in an efficient, cost-effective manner.

Bill Marriott, son of the founder, grew up in the family business. He worked in Hot Shoppes during high school and college and then joined the company full-time in 1956. He became president in 1964, succeeded J. W. Marriott, Sr., as CEO in 1972, and was named chairman in 1985.

ENVIRONMENT

Marriott's environment has become increasingly complex and dynamic in recent years. The Persian Gulf War dampened demand for travel lodgings, and the recessionary economy also kept vacationers and business travelers home. Meanwhile, changes in tax and banking regulations during the 1980s spurred a hotel-building spree, and the number of hotel rooms soon outstripped demand. Many competitors slashed room rates to fill their rooms. But Marriott fought back, mounting aggressive advertising campaigns and positioning its moderately priced Courtyard Hotels and economy-priced Fairfield Inns to attract value-seeking travelers. Despite these moves, Marriott had to cut some rates to stay competitive, which hurt profits.

Marriott typically prefers to build a hotel, sell it to an investor group, and then collect fees for managing the hotel. But as the 1980s came to a close, financing dried up and investors hung back, spooked by the troubled real estate market. Marriott couldn't sell as many of its hotels as planned and had to keep paying interest on those mortgages, a crushing debt load. Late in 1990, Bill Marriott suspended nearly all new-hotel construction, slashed overhead, and delayed some pay increases for top managers as he coped with the uncertain environment ahead.

The outlook for Marriott's in-flight food business also appeared murky. U.S. airlines were in turmoil. Bankruptcies and liquidations had narrowed the field, and many carriers had to cut costs, including food bills, to remain competitive. Deciding that in-flight catering had limited long-term growth potential, Marriott sold this division in 1989. But even as it exited airline catering, the company entered a new business: senior living services. Forecasts showed that the older segment of the population was growing rapidly. Top managers believed that the Marriott reputation for customer service could help the company compete in the large and lucrative market for senior living services. After considerable research, Marriott opened its first full-service retirement community with leisure and medical facilities in 1988, and it started testing other types of limited-service retirement centers.

GOALS AND CHALLENGES

Marriott's mission statement is simple but ambitious: "We are committed to being the best lodging and contract service company in the world, by treating employees in ways that create extraordinary customer service and shareholder value." The mission reflects the founder's belief that if he treated employees well, they would in turn treat customers well. Since the first day, Marriott has focused on hiring good people, clearing avenues to performance, and listening to employee concerns and ideas. Marriott employees receive extensive training, and qualified employees are encouraged to move into management, where they are trained in communications, coaching and counseling, career planning, and more. Further, Marriott has developed a family life program that helps managers and employees locate child care, offers information about care for children and the elderly, and teaches managers to help employees deal with family issues.

Despite its size, Marriott is not a nameless, faceless corporation to its employees. Bill Marriott logs 200,000 miles each year traveling around the world to pump up morale, check on cleanliness, examine kitchen procedures, discuss customer satisfaction, and talk with employees. Employee contact is especially important because, says Marriott, "If you don't do that, you lose touch with what's really happening in the business." Nor does Marriott lose touch with customers' needs and preferences. Customer comments are carefully scrutinized, and the feedback process is computerized at some locations. Guests at the Fairfield Inn economy chain complete a brief computerized form as they check out; this helps managers rate customer satisfaction, pinpoint problem areas, and link employee compensation to guest satisfaction.

One of the biggest challenges has been the drive to compete in the stand-alone restaurant business. Although Roy Rogers eventually carved out a 2.3 percent share of the fast-food hamburger market, market leaders McDonald's and Burger King continued to dominate. After Marriott was outbid in its attempt to buy Denny's, the leading coffee-shop operator, the chain next tried to convert its midprice restaurants into a chain of family restaurants called Allie's. However, latecomer Marriott had difficulty establishing this new brand name. Caught between price-promoting fast-food outlets and high-end tablecloth restaurants, Allie's sales were below expectations. At the end of 1989, Marriott decided that this division had less long-term growth potential than other divisions and put the restaurants up for sale. Today, Marriott sales exceed $8 billion and the chain is concentrating on hotels, contract services, and senior living services to fuel future growth and profitability.

1. Identify the managerial skills and roles that Bill Marriott emphasizes as chairman of Marriott, and cite examples. What specific demands and constraints affect the chairman's work flexibility?
2. Which environmental forces have helped past performance? Which forces may have the most influence on future performance, and why?
3. How does Marriott apply scientific management to effectively manage its operations worldwide? How can Marriott use quantitative management techniques to manage its contract food services in schools around the United States?
4. If Marriott had retained the restaurant business under the Allie's brand and expanded the chain to Mexico and Canada, which forces in the international environment would have had the most influence on Allie's performance in North America? How might Marriott demonstrate its social responsibility to the non-U.S. communities the Allie's chain would be serving?

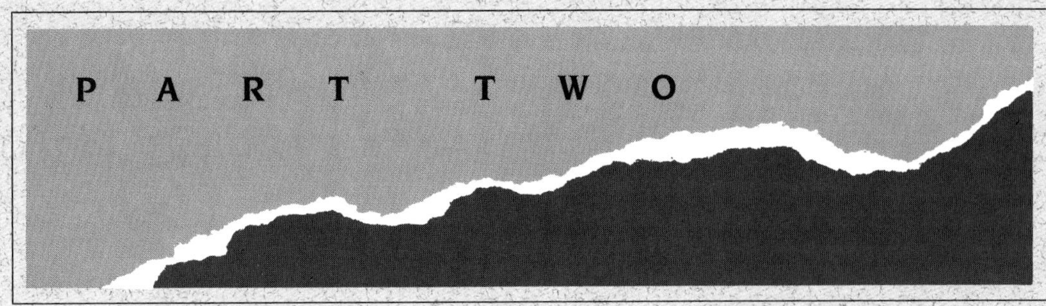

Planning

CHAPTER OUTLINE

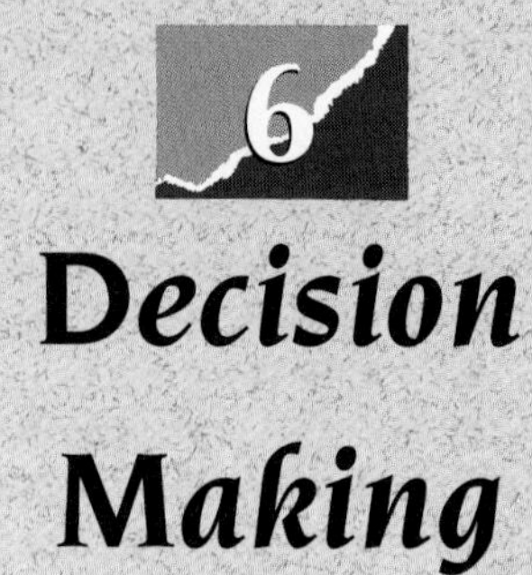

Decision Making

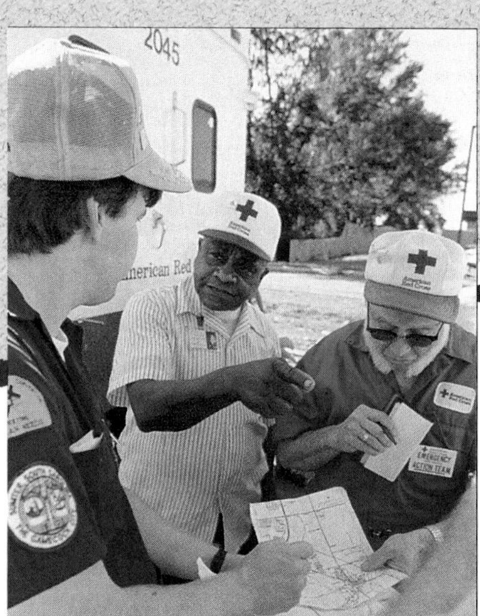

After studying this chapter, you will be able to

1. Discuss the types of problems managers face, the types of decisions they make, and the conditions under which they make these decisions
2. Differentiate between the classical model and the administrative model of managerial decision making
3. Outline the six steps in the rational decision-making process
4. Describe the barriers to effective decision making, and discuss their impact on managers
5. Explain how managers can use behavioral approaches to improve decision making
6. Discuss the payoff matrix, the decision tree, and the simulation model as they improve managerial decision making
7. Identify the benefits and limitations of group decision making

FACING A MANAGEMENT CHALLENGE AT

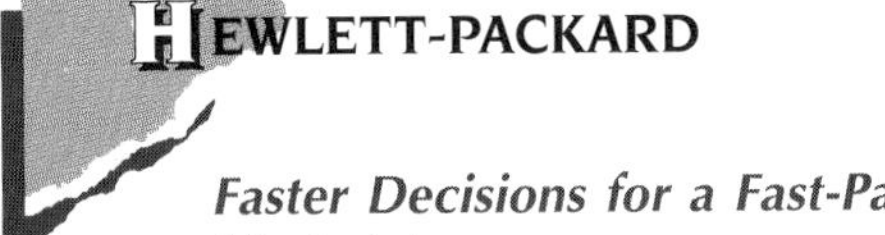

HEWLETT-PACKARD

Faster Decisions for a Fast-Paced Marketplace

Designing new computer products can be both rewarding and frustrating. On the one hand, designers know that astute engineering and programming decisions will lead to satisfied customers and financial success for their companies. On the other hand, computer technology changes so rapidly that many new products are quickly rendered obsolete, sometimes within mere months after introduction. And if a computer manufacturer takes too long to get its products on the market, its new products might be out of date the day they are introduced.

Hewlett-Packard, the electronics manufacturer founded by the now-legendary Stanford University graduate students William Hewlett and David Packard, found itself losing the new-computer race in the late 1980s. Competitors were putting products on the market faster than the venerable Silicon Valley pioneer was able to. By the time some HP products hit the market, customers had already made the move to competitive offerings.

CEO John Young knew that his company was filled with imaginative and highly trained experts who could develop products as quickly as anyone else if given the chance. But why were products so late getting to market? When he discussed the problem with people in the company he heard the same complaint over and over again: engineers and managers were required to obtain too many time-consuming approvals before implementing decisions.

When Young pondered this situation, he realized that a primary cause of the problem was the way in which new-product decisions were being made. Designers were forced to seek consensus across several divisions in the corporation, and top managers were involved in all major decisions, in order to keep the product-development efforts focused and coordinated. In short, HP was spending too much time talking about new products and not enough time designing and manufacturing them.

As is often the case in today's complex management environment, the cause of this decision-making dilemma was actually the solution to an earlier problem. HP had always encouraged an entrepreneurial atmosphere that emphasizes independence from centralized bureaucracies and from strangling corporate policies. However, as the company's business operations grew more complex during the 1980s, the semiautonomous divisions began bumping into each other in the marketplace, creating products that overlapped and competed with each other. Moreover, the company's efforts didn't add up to more than the sum of its parts, because the parts weren't coordinating with each other. In response, top management took control of many key decisions, including new-product development, and required product designers to coordinate their efforts with all concerned parties within the company. This helped solve the coordination problem, but it brought on the decision-making bottleneck that now threatened the company's competitiveness.

The problem was particularly acute in the area of workstations, high-powered desktop computers that offer the performance of minicomputers in packages no larger than traditional microcomputers. Newcomer Sun Microsystems had rocketed to the top of this market segment by avoiding the very same problem that HP was now facing: slow decision making. How can John Young change HP's decision-making process to make the company more competitive? At the same time, how can he ensure that individual product teams don't create overlapping or incompatible products?[1]

CHAPTER OVERVIEW

Hewlett-Packard's John Young was facing one of the most important issues of contemporary management: how to make decisions. This chapter starts by reviewing the fundamentals of decision making, including the types of problems, decisions, and conditions that managers face. Following that is a look at the two managerial decision-making models and an examination of the six-step rational decision-making process. Next is a section on identifying and overcoming the barriers to effective decision making. The chapter closes with a look at decision making in groups.

FUNDAMENTALS OF DECISION MAKING

Can 4 cents make a difference? Before 1991, Penguin USA sold its paperback books for $3.95, $4.95, and up. Now most Penguin books are priced at $3.99, $4.99, and so on. Although the 4-cent increase was small, the decision was a big one for Penguin. Because the publisher sells about 30 million books a year, the 4-cent decision puts over $1 million more into Penguin's pocket each year.[2] So when the issue seems relatively unimportant, like a 4-cent price hike, the consequences can still be considerable. Decision making is a key management element because managers continually face decisions in planning, organizing, leading, and controlling that affect the organization and its performance.

Decision Making Defined

decision The choice made from among available alternatives that is expected to lead to a favorable solution to a problem

decision making The process of recognizing a problem, generating and weighing alternatives, coming to a decision, taking action, and assessing the results

A **decision** is the choice made from among available alternatives that is expected to result in a favorable resolution to a problem. However, managerial decision making does not begin or end with the decision, because there must be a problem posed before a decision can be made, and after that the decision must be implemented. The broader term **decision making** defines the process of identifying problems, considering and evaluating the alternatives, arriving at a decision, taking action, and assessing the outcome. This process, examined in detail later in the chapter, describes how managers should approach the problems they encounter. First, however, it is important to understand the types of problems, decisions, and conditions that managers face.[3]

Types of Problems

problem A situation in which the existing circumstances differ significantly from the preferred situation

A manager uses decision making to solve a **problem,** a condition in which the existing situation differs significantly from the desired situation. Generally, a problem occurs when the current situation does not measure up to the expected situation in achieving organizational goals.[4] For example, in 1991 Henry Breier took the helm of Dellwood Foods in Yonkers, New York, and he faced a double problem: sales were flat and the dairy company was losing money. Part of the problem was an oversupply of milk, which was driving down prices and profits. Breier's alternatives included a massive cost-cutting program or outright withdrawal from the market. Instead, Breier decided to expand beyond the dairy case and become a full-line supplier of refrigerated goods to boost sales. But he also cut costs and streamlined his distribution to improve profitability.[5]

Although Breier's problems at Dellwood Foods were rather large, managerial problems come in all sizes and shapes. Problems can be classified into three categories: crisis problems, noncrisis problems, or opportunity problems. On the problem continuum, crisis problems are the most urgent, and opportunity problems are the least urgent (see Exhibit 6.1).[6]

California Governor Pete Wilson *(center)* faced a crisis when an invasion of whiteflies caused $85 million in crop damage in the state's desert region. After touring the area and meeting with agricultural experts and growers, he declared a state of emergency in Imperial and Riverside counties. This decision allowed growers and employees to receive immediate financial assistance.

Crisis Problems

A **crisis problem** is a critical situation that demands an immediate managerial decision. When managers face a crisis problem, they must consider the threat to the organization and make a decision that will defuse that threat as quickly and effectively as possible.[7] Portman Overseas, a global real estate firm based in Atlanta, faced a crisis while building Shanghai Center in the People's Republic of China. When students clashed with government forces in Tiananmen Square in 1989, Portman's executive vice president A. J. Robinson feared that this might be the beginning of a revolution. Robinson and other top Portman managers had to decide between continuing the project and abandoning it. They decided to continue, but they set specific conditions to safeguard their employees and to show that Portman did not condone the government's actions.[8]

crisis problem A situation that urgently requires an immediate decision

Noncrisis Problems

When managers confront a **noncrisis problem,** they are dealing with a situation that must be resolved but without the urgency and immediacy of a crisis problem. Most of the problems that managers face are noncrisis problems, even when they have potentially significant ramifications. During the 1980s, manag-

noncrisis problem A problem that requires a decision but less urgently than a crisis problem

EXHIBIT 6.1 The Continuum of Managerial Problems

Organizational problems can be viewed on a continuum ranging from crisis problems that require urgent attention to opportunity problems that are less pressing. Although opportunities do not generally demand immediate action, managers cannot assume that the situation will remain favorable indefinitely: opportunities disappear sooner or later as environmental changes occur.

ers at the Ingersoll-Rand plant in Athens, Pennsylvania, spent a great deal of time considering how to resolve two noncrisis problems. First, they had to decide what to do about their old-fashioned plant and outdated equipment; some areas were more than 100 years old. To solve this problem, managers could have decided to scrap the plant. However, they believed it could be a viable plant if modernized, so they decided on a major overhaul. Second, plant employees had never operated computerized equipment, so the managers had to decide whether to hire trained people or retrain their own employees. They decided to offer retraining, and since 1987 plant employees have spent more than 27,000 hours in the classroom. As a result of these two decisions, plant productivity has soared.[9]

Opportunity Problems

opportunity problem A situation that can be dealt with in a way that has a positive effect on the organization and its performance

An **opportunity problem** is a situation that can be addressed in a way that gains the organization some significant advantage.[10] When dealing with an opportunity problem, managers are not trying to defuse a difficult situation. Instead, they are looking for a creative solution that will have a positive impact on organizational performance. The development of a new technology or the sudden availability of new resources often creates an opportunity problem.[11] Although an opportunity problem usually involves less time pressure than a noncrisis or crisis problem, an opportunity may occasionally escalate into a crisis if left unaddressed.

Sometimes noncrisis problems are viewed as opportunity problems by innovative managers who see ways to capitalize on situations that seem burdensome to others. William Ginn was a part-time Maine farmer searching for a source of wood ash fertilizer when he stumbled on an opportunity problem. Ginn had approached a paper company asking for some of its wood ash. Because the company was paying to have the ash hauled away, it was glad to offer him 40,000 tons. Ginn's problem was that he needed some, but not all, of this tonnage. Rather than turn down this supply, Ginn seized the opportunity and arranged for other farmers to receive ash, and he went on to build an entire company around recycling and other environmental services.[12]

Types of Decisions

Day in and day out, managers make decisions about a wide variety of problems. However, not all decisions are alike. Some decisions crop up repeatedly and so can be made without much forethought. Others come up less frequently and are far from routine; such decisions might occur only once in a manager's entire career. In general, decisions can be classified as either programmed or nonprogrammed.[13]

Programmed Decisions

programmed decision A decision made when the situation occurs frequently enough or is sufficiently well-structured to be resolved by applying predetermined decision rules

A manager makes a **programmed decision** when a situation occurs so often or is so well-structured that it can be handled through the use of preset decision rules. In well structured situations, managers need to consider relatively few factors, or they confront relatively clear-cut circumstances surrounding the decision.[14] After repeatedly solving the same kind of problem or meeting the same kind of well-structured situation, managers can develop guidelines for solving that problem in the future. For example, Wal-Mart has set up decision rules to govern the decision to routinely reorder selected merchandise. More than 300

Wal-Mart suppliers are tied into the retailer's electronic cash registers so that they can be notified when products are sold and should be automatically replenished.[15] Of course, decision guidelines must be reexamined regularly to be sure that the rules remain appropriate.

J. C. Penney managers establish credit limits and other rules to guide their decisions in approving or rejecting credit purchases. Following the rules for such programmed decisions, the computerized credit system approves charge sales below the limit and flashes a code to tell the salesperson how to handle sales above the limit.

Nonprogrammed Decisions

In contrast to a programmed decision, a **nonprogrammed decision** is made in a situation that cannot be handled with preset decision rules because the situation occurs infrequently, is unique, or is somewhat unstructured. Because these decisions are less clear-cut than programmed decisions and are not made regularly, managers cannot develop guidelines for handling similar decisions in the future.[16] The critical decisions that top managers make, such as the one that John Young faced at Hewlett-Packard when he needed to revamp the company's decision-making process, are generally nonprogrammed and require much consideration. Consider how Japanese retailer Isao Nakauchi built an empire on a nonprogrammed decision. He had no preset rules to follow when he made the controversial decision to discount merchandise. Japanese retailers rarely discount because manufacturers, who have much influence over the distribution and pricing process, oppose the practice. But Nakauchi persisted, making decisions that challenged prevailing practices, and today his Daiei chain sells $14 billion annually.[17] Because discounting was so rare in Japan, Nakauchi had to make his decision without the benefit of experience and practice.

Conditions of Decision Making

The diverse problems that managers face require that decisions be made under a variety of circumstances. In some cases, managers know so much about the circumstances of a problem that they can make a decision and feel confident about the outcome. In other cases, managers don't have enough information to be sure how a decision will turn out. Depending on the level of information available, decision making occurs under four conditions: certainty, risk, uncertainty, and ambiguity (see Exhibit 6.2).

nonprogrammed decision A decision made in a situation where predetermined decision rules cannot be applied because the situation is less structured, occurs rarely, or is unique

condition of certainty A situation in which the manager has complete information about the problem, the alternatives, and the consequences of a decision

Certainty

A **condition of certainty** exists when a manager has all the information needed to clearly understand the problem, to know all the possible alternative outcomes, and to know all the possible consequences of these alternatives. Of course, few decisions are made under a condition of certainty because it is not realistically possible to accurately predict the future.[18] For example, toymaker Fisher-Price seems to have a sure thing in its line of toys, playhouses, and play figures for tots because demographic trends indicate a sizable preschool population on the way. But this is not an entirely certain situation. Some experts warn that young children are becoming more sophisticated and may soon be clamor-

EXHIBIT 6.2 Conditions of Decision Making

Depending on the amount of information available, managers make decisions under conditions of certainty, risk, uncertainty, and ambiguity.

ing for toys intended for the older set. However, Fisher-Price once dabbled in sophisticated toys and dropped out because of the heavy losses caused by uncertainty in customer tastes. Now CEO Ronald Jackson prefers to focus on basic playthings for preschoolers because a brighter future seems more certain in that market.[19]

Risk

condition of risk A situation in which the manager understands the problem and the alternatives and has only enough information to estimate the probability that the available alternatives will lead to the desired outcome

A **condition of risk** exists when the manager understands the problem and has only enough information to understand the possible alternatives and to estimate the probability that each alternative will result in the desired outcome.[20] Unlike certainty, where the manager has complete information to be sure about the consequences of every alternative, risk entails a chance that the alternative selected will not result in what the manager expects. For this reason, organizations work hard to estimate the risks inherent in their decisions, and they try to increase the probability that the results will be favorable.[21] For example, the U.S.-based chemical firm Monsanto tries hard to assess its risks. In 1990, the growth of Monsanto's herbicide business was slowed by severe drought conditions in California and in Europe. By tracking the risks posed by weather, managers found that the products were hurt by bad weather only 2 years out of 17. As a result, they concluded that the long-term weather odds are in the firm's favor.[22]

Uncertainty

condition of uncertainty A situation in which the manager understands the problem but has incomplete information about the alternatives and the probable consequences of each alternative

A **condition of uncertainty** is a situation in which the manager understands the problem but does not have complete information on the possible alternatives and the likely consequences of each alternative. Whereas managers operating under a condition of risk have enough information to estimate the probable outcomes of each alternative, they have insufficient information to estimate probable outcomes when they operate under a condition of uncertainty. Most of the decisions managers make occur under a condition of uncertainty, primarily because environmental uncertainty makes the future unpredictable.[23] For example, Kodak chairman Kay Whitmore faced considerable uncertainty when he debated whether to authorize the technological development of the compact optical disc, which can store millions of photographic images for viewing on a television screen. Whitmore was uncertain whether consumers were interested in viewing photos on their television screens. He was also uncertain about how customers would react to the new camera systems just introduced by Sony and Canon and about how hard these competitors would push their new products. In this case, Whitmore had enough information to understand the problem but not enough to estimate the likely consequences of the alternatives. Although he could have chosen to postpone or to quash the project, Whitmore decided to introduce Kodak's Photo CD in 1992, betting that the product would give the company's business a boost.[24]

Ambiguity

condition of ambiguity A situation in which the manager has little or no information about the problem, the alternatives, or the consequences of each alternative

Managers make decisions under a **condition of ambiguity** when they have little or no information about the problem, the alternatives, or the likely consequences of each alternative. In ambiguous situations, managers may even lack information about the goals they are to achieve.[25] Consider the ambiguity that Carl Weinrich faced when he became executive director of the YMCA in Sarasota, Florida. He found that the YMCA had no clear goals, and he also lacked information about two key problems: flat membership and burdensome debt.

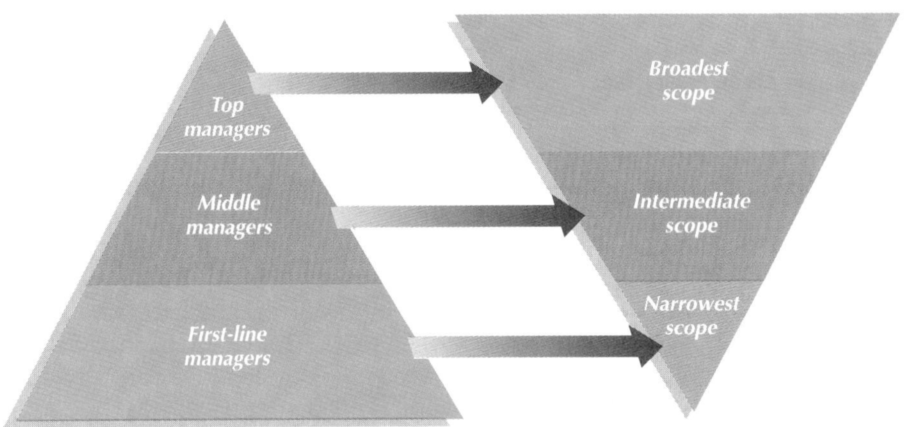

EXHIBIT 6.3

The Level and Scope of Decision Making

Decisions are made at all levels of the organization. Top managers with broad responsibilities tend to make the major decisions that are broad in scope, whereas lower-level managers make decisions that are narrower in scope and more focused on their immediate responsibilities.

Over time, Weinrich reduced the ambiguity by setting clear goals, learning more about member needs, and creatively exploring the alternatives to solve membership and finance problems. He decided to expand programs geared specifically to community needs in order to increase the membership base, and he also untangled the financial situation. Thanks to Weinrich's decisions, the Y now serves more than 2,000 people a day, and its finances are under control.[26]

The Level and Scope of Organizational Decision Making

Just as managerial responsibilities tend to become broader as managers rise from first-line to middle to top management, decisional responsibilities become broader as well (see Exhibit 6.3). Top managers, who are responsible for the overall performance of the organization, make the major decisions that determine its future course. Guided by the goals that top managers set, middle managers are responsible for decisions that are less broad in scope but not so narrow as the nuts-and-bolts decisions that first-line managers face.[27] At Southwest Airlines, chairman Herb Kelleher has made a major decision, setting the tone for the many decisions that lower-level managers must make: he has decided to keep his business simple. "We're the product of 1,000 small decisions, all designed to achieve simplicity," he says. Some of the smaller decisions that support Kelleher's broad decision to keep business simple include serving no meals, forgoing reserved seating, and avoiding connections with other airlines.[28]

MANAGERIAL DECISION-MAKING MODELS

Because decision making is such an integral part of the management function, the process has been the subject of much research and analysis. Two major models of managerial decision making have emerged: the classical model and the administrative model.

The Classical Model

classical model of decision making A model that assumes managers always approach decision making rationally and objectively

The **classical model of decision making** is based on the assumption that managers approach decision making in an objective and rational manner and that they always make decisions that are in the best interests of the organization. According to this model, managers carefully examine every possible alternative and

EXHIBIT 6.4 Differences between Classical and Administrative Decision-Making Models

The classical model of decision making is prescriptive, showing how managers should be able to approach completely rational decision making. In contrast, the administrative model of decision making is descriptive, showing how managers actually approach decision making using bounded rationality.

Classical Model	Administrative Model
1. Managers have complete knowledge and can perfectly anticipate all consequences of each alternative.	1. Managers have fragmentary knowledge of consequences.
2. Managers can competently attach probability values to the consequences of alternatives.	2. Managers are unable to attach probability values to the consequences of alternatives.
3. Managers can generate a complete list of every possible alternative.	3. Managers cannot generate a complete list of alternatives; only a very few come to mind.

consider the wide range of likely consequences for each choice before selecting the alternative that best fits the organization's needs (see Exhibit 6.4).[29] This view was prevalent early in this century when economists took the somewhat simplistic view that managers always make decisions that bring their organizations the optimal economic return.

In order to do this, managers would need to have complete information about the problem, clearly defined goals, all the information about every possible alternative and consequence, and a logical method of weighing each alternative to come to a decision. However, later researchers pointed out that managers do not actually make their decisions this way. Because managers make dozens and sometimes hundreds of decisions in a day, it is impractical for them to approach every decision in the systematic, logical fashion assumed by the classical model, and they frequently don't have enough information to make a thorough analysis, even if they were so inclined. The classical model is therefore *prescriptive*, presenting an idealized approach to guide managers toward better decision making. But tools do exist that help managers make more rational decisions, as shown later in the chapter.[30]

The Administrative Model

Herbert A. Simon was one of the earliest experts to protest that managers cannot actually attain the ideal state of completely rational decision making represented by the classical model. Instead, Simon (who received the Nobel Prize in economics in 1978 for this work) developed a model that examines how managers actually approach decision making. This **administrative model of decision making** is based on the observation that managers do not always approach decision making in a logical, rational way and that they do not always make objective decisions.[31] Because the administrative model shows how managers actually make decisions, not how they should make decisions, it is a *descriptive* model. To support this model, Simon also described two key elements of real-life decision making: bounded rationality and satisficing.

administrative model of decision making A model that assumes managers cannot always approach decision making logically and rationally

Bounded Rationality

The concept of **bounded rationality** suggests that a manager's ability to make completely rational decisions is limited by time constraints and by the cognitive capacity to absorb, retain, and analyze a great deal of information. A number of factors contribute to bounded rationality:

bounded rationality The idea that a manager's ability to make objective decisions is restricted by time constraints and by cognitive limitations

- Managers may have only incomplete information about the problem, the alternatives, the decision criteria, or the impact on the organization.

- Time and money constraints often limit the quantity and quality of information available.
- When more information is available, managers may not use it productively because of the added complexity or because of inexperience.
- Managers may inaccurately assess the importance of the consequences of individual alternatives being considered.
- Human attention and memory are limited, so managers can store only a relatively small amount of information as they consider a problem.
- The ability to weigh and select the optimal choice from among all alternatives is limited by a manager's intelligence and by personal perceptions.[32]

Because of these limitations, managers do not always make rational decisions that represent the optimal choices for their organizations. Instead, they make decisions by satisficing.

Satisficing

When managers stop looking for alternatives as soon as they find one that is acceptable, they are **satisficing.** Rather than searching extensively for alternatives, the satisficing manager selects the first one that meets the minimum criteria of the solution, even if it is not the optimal choice. Managers satisfice because it is a convenient way of simplifying and speeding up the search for alternatives and the evaluation process. For example, when Annette Roux wanted to expand her company, French boatmaker Chantiers Beneteau, she built a new factory in South Carolina to get a toehold in the U.S. market. Roux's decision was influenced by bounded rationality because she was working under the time constraint of finding suppliers as quickly as possible and was limited by her lack of experience with U.S. suppliers. Finding U.S. suppliers wasn't easy at first, and parts were in short supply. Roux therefore satisficed and turned to familiar European suppliers until she could uncover more information about alternative suppliers in the United States. This decision allowed the boatmaker to start production quickly and later mount a more comprehensive search for U.S. suppliers.[33]

satisficing Searching for alternatives only until a satisfactory, not an optimal, solution is found

The Use of Decision-Making Models

Although the classical decision-making model is prescriptive and the administrative decision-making model is descriptive, both offer valuable guidance for managers. By applying the classical model, managers can approach decisions more objectively and systematically. At times, managers are confronted with decisions in such numbers and in such rapid succession that they cannot effectively apply the classical model. The administrative model helps managers understand where their decision making deviates from the rational decision-making process prescribed by the classical model. Moreover, contemporary researchers recognize that managers actually adapt their decision-making methods to the problem at hand. In this way, managers gain the flexibility and responsiveness to resolve problems that range from the simple to the highly complex.[34]

Tom Knapp followed the steps in the decision-making process to build Club Sportswear into a global company. He identified a problem (a need for high-quality volleyball clothing), considered his alternatives, made the decision to produce colorful volleyball shirts and shorts, and started selling. Knapp's feedback: sales have doubled each year since 1986.

THE RATIONAL DECISION-MAKING PROCESS

The rational decision-making process (which follows the classical decision-making model) encompasses six sequential steps. Managers facing either pro-

SOCIAL RESPONSIBILITY AND ETHICS

Regulators Put a Price Tag on Saving Human Life

How much is one life worth? Government regulators are grappling with this question as they provide quantitative information to support decision making on health and safety regulations. In 1981 the Reagan administration issued a rule requiring cost-benefit analysis to show that the benefits of a regulation outweigh the costs of implementation. Because of that rule, regulators must determine the value of a human life so that they can measure the benefits of regulations for saving lives. If the cost of complying with a regulation outweighs the benefit as measured by the value of lives saved, then the regulation cannot be implemented. But valuing human life is not a routine calculation, and each regulatory agency has developed its own guidelines.

For example, the Occupational Safety and Health Administration (OSHA) says that a single life is worth between \$2 million and \$5 million. The Consumer Product Safety Commission says the value is \$2 million. The Environmental Protection Agency (EPA) estimates \$475,000 to \$8.3 million, and the Federal Aviation Administration (FAA) estimates \$1 million. From a rational decision-making perspective, putting a price tag on life could help managers in regulatory agencies objectively determine whether a regulation would cost more than it would save. Take the hypothetical case of a regulation requiring new bicycle helmets. The regulation could cost manufacturers and consumers up to \$70 million, and it might save as many as 75 lives a year. If regulators value each life at \$1 million, that's a yearly life-saving benefit of \$75 million and a net benefit of \$5 million more than the cost.

On the other hand, critics charge that the calculation is a manipulable element that can be used for political maneuvering. When the FAA wanted to require airplane manufacturers to make stronger passenger seats in 1985, the FAA estimated that the rule would save 10 to 50 lives over 10 years. But analysis showed

grammed or nonprogrammed decisions can follow this six-step process for more effective decision making. Of course, there is no guarantee that managers who apply the process will make correct decisions, but they will increase the odds of achieving good results. Also, managers must take into account organizational goals and the broader implications of their own decisions when following the process. Although the steps are generally followed in order, managers sometimes lack the information to continue to the next step, or they uncover information that prompts them to return to earlier steps before the process is complete.[35] The six steps in the rational decision-making process are (1) identify the problem, (2) generate alternatives, (3) evaluate alternatives, (4) make the decision, (5) implement the decision, and (6) evaluate the results and provide feedback (see Exhibit 6.5).

Step 1: Identify the Problem

The first step in the managerial decision-making process is to identify the problem. Managers must be aware of a problem and analyze its scope and nature before they can take any steps to solve it. To identify a problem, managers first

EXHIBIT 6.5

The Rational Decision-Making Process

The rational decision-making process consists of six steps. Although the steps are generally followed in order, managers often uncover additional information that compels them to return to earlier stages.

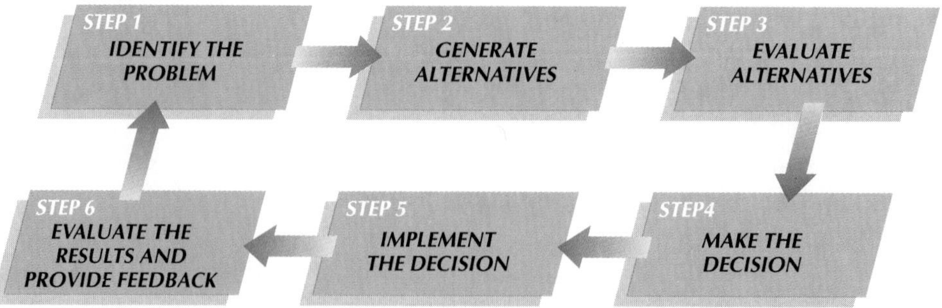

that the benefits did not sufficiently outweigh the costs. So the agency raised its price tag on life, increasing the total benefit calculation, and was then able to implement the rule. Not long ago, a public interest group charged that the federal Office of Management and Budget (OMB) was using cost-benefit analysis to dilute the regulation of ethylene oxide, a sterilizing agent suspected of causing cancer. But the OMB responded that the dangers were being exaggerated.

In another regulatory case, this time involving asbestos, the OMB insisted that the EPA apply a bookkeeping technique called *discounting* in addition to satisfying the cost-benefit analysis requirement. The controversy began when the EPA proposed a rule that would eventually ban asbestos. The asbestos industry vigorously objected and lobbied hard against the rule. The OMB regulatory-affairs division got involved and valued each human life at $1 million. But the OMB also required the EPA to discount the value of the saved lives. Their logic was that asbestos-caused cancer often does not surface for many years, so the immediate benefits of banning asbestos to save lives should not be calculated in the same way. Instead, OMB calculated the discounted value of lives saved at roughly $208,000, and determined that the regulation wasn't justified in terms of cost efficiency. However, members of Congress protested, and the EPA then proposed stronger regulations.

Since the rule was imposed, changes have been made in more than 1,000 proposed regulations, which add up to savings and benefits totaling perhaps $100 billion. But can the valuation of human life and the cost-benefit analyses of saved lives be considered valuable techniques for supporting decision making? No consensus has yet been reached.

What's Your Opinion?

1. Does the public benefit when regulators are required to put a price on human life so that the impact of regulations can be weighed prior to implementation?
2. Should any governmental agencies be permitted to set a price tag on life? Should all regulating bodies apply the same standard of value for human life?

recognize that a problem exists, define it, and then diagnose the situation. These were steps Hewlett-Packard's John Young took when he realized that new-product development teams were taking too long to get products to market.

- *Recognize the problem.* Managers recognize a problem by noticing changes in their organization's performance or changes in their internal or external environment that can potentially affect performance. For example, Volunteer: The National Center (a not-for-profit organization in Arlington, Virginia) had long operated a mail-order business selling gift items to other not-for-profits, which would then give or sell the items to volunteers. The organization first became aware of a problem when it began receiving requests from customers for products offered by a new competitor, the California Association of Hospitals and Health Systems (CAHHS). As Volunteer's sales dropped, management recognized that the CAHHS challenge could seriously threaten its revenue.[36]
- *Define the problem.* Once managers recognize that a problem exists, they need to consider the elements that make up the problem and the relationships among the elements. Managers cannot develop a good solution if the question is not framed correctly, so they try to include the right elements in the problem definition; they try not to exclude anything that may be vital, and they try to be as specific as possible. For instance, by listening to customers who mentioned CAHHS products and by examining the CAHHS catalog, Volunteer was able to precisely define the problem. Now Volunteer managers understood that their problem had three components: their products didn't closely meet customer needs, their catalog was not as attractive as the CAHHS catalog, and their promotion was not as aggressive as CAHHS's.[37]
- *Diagnose the situation.* In this phase, managers gather additional information and consider the causes of the problem so that they can come up with meaningful alternatives. If this part of the process is rushed, managers may

prematurely pounce on a probable cause without looking further for confirmation.[38] In the case of the problem that Volunteer faced, management held a series of meetings with representatives from member associations to discuss the mail-order business. By talking directly to customers, Volunteer was able to diagnose the problems with its product line, learn which products were most and least effective, and find out what customers wanted to see in the catalog.[39]

Step 2: Generate Alternatives

After the problem has been identified and analyzed, managers move to the second step of the decision-making process, generating alternatives. In this step, managers try to develop as many possible alternative courses of action as they can, including the most obvious as well as the most creative, but without passing judgment on any of the ideas. Some alternatives may come from past experiences or from competitive practices; others may be generated by creative techniques such as brainstorming, discussed later in the chapter. Regardless of the methods they use to generate the alternatives, managers can make better decisions when they have a large range of alternatives to consider, because they will not feel pressured to choose an option simply because it seems to be the only available solution.[40] J. Edgar Broyhill II came up with an unusual alternative when his home-decorating center in North Carolina was faltering. He took a chance and ran an ad in an upscale Washington, D.C., magazine, offering quality furniture at discount prices and offering to take collect calls. Although furniture is typically sold through showrooms, Broyhill's ad sold $100,000 worth of furniture long distance, so he closed his store and started a successful catalog business.[41]

Step 3: Evaluate Alternatives

The third step in the process is evaluating the alternatives by considering the implications and the likely consequences of each. In this step, managers assess the attractiveness of each alternative and weed out those that seem unfeasible, inadequate, too expensive, or otherwise unacceptable. Of course, if a solution cannot be effectively implemented, or if it does not help the organization achieve its goals, then it's not a realistic alternative. Moreover, the way a decision might influence other parts of the organization or the environment is another consideration.[42]

For example, Elio Boccitto, president of Berlitz International, wanted to expand his company's services beyond personal language training in order to increase sales revenues. He considered putting the venerable Berlitz name on language books, travel guides, language software, and other goods and services. In addition to assessing potential sales and profitability, Boccitto also evaluated these alternatives according to whether each would enhance or debase the Berlitz brand. He rejected the idea of Berlitz luggage because he felt it would cheapen the name, but he moved aggressively into translation services, achieving sales of $30 million yearly.[43]

Step 4: Make the Decision

After evaluating the alternatives, managers make the decision. They select the best alternative by weighing the risks and benefits of each one. In this step, the

Before opening a new hotel, Hyatt's top managers consider the risk-reward tradeoff of each site. The decision to build the Atrium Hyatt Budapest in 1982 reflected a belief that business and tourist travel in Eastern Europe would soon increase (which it did). After examining the risk-reward tradeoffs, Hyatt recently decided to expand into South America, which has become a major manufacturing center.

manager's *risk propensity,* or willingness to take risks, is a major element. Some managers are more willing to take risks if the potential benefits are greater, so it's important to consider the *risk-reward tradeoff* and understand the benefits that each alternative offers for its associated risk. But alternatives are rarely perfect. That's why managers seek to *optimize* their decisions by selecting the alternative that best solves the problem and most closely meets requirements such as time and cost.[44]

In 1987, when the South Korean apparel manufacturer Trans Pacific Garment was searching for a Central American location to be near the lucrative U.S. market, president Peter Chua wanted to optimize his selection. He considered several alternatives and became interested in Honduras, where he would get special breaks on tax and duty. However, Honduras wasn't a perfect alternative: it lacked the industrial laundry facilities necessary to stone-wash denim for jeans. But Chua believed that the benefits outweighed the drawbacks, so he decided to open a factory in Honduras and then import his own washers and dryers. In addition, he viewed this as an opportunity problem, launching a small sideline business laundering fabric for neighboring manufacturers.[45]

Step 5: Implement the Decision

After they select the best alternative, managers implement the decision. Because decision-making managers generally depend on others to carry out decisions, they must carefully consider how implementation will affect these people and their functions. By openly discussing anticipated changes and expected results, managers can help their employees adjust to any changes that stem from decisions. (Organizational change is discussed in Chapter 11.) An effective way to enlist support in implementation is to involve the affected people in the decision-making process whenever possible. Especially when alternatives are being developed and evaluated, employees can make valuable contributions by spotting hidden difficulties or by uncovering additional resources. In general, successful implementation depends on the manager's communication skills and sensitivity about people's reaction to change.[46]

For example, when he was CEO of Union Pacific Railroad, Mike Walsh learned that 18 percent of the invoices the railroad sent contained errors. He had the errors traced to 20 causes spread across the organization and decided that the mistakes had to be reduced by 50 percent within six months. To implement this decision, he organized a team to attack each cause, appointed one manager to coordinate the 20 teams, and asked for monthly progress reports. Because Walsh had clearly defined the problem and the goal, and communicated with the people involved, each team understood its role and the project was completed successfully and on time.[47]

Step 6: Evaluate the Results and Provide Feedback

The final step is to evaluate the results and provide feedback about the decision and its implementation. This allows managers to see whether the results meet expectations and to make any changes needed to improve the decision or its implementation. If the original decision does not achieve the desired results, then perhaps the problem was incorrectly defined, or perhaps another alternative should be substituted. It is important to give the decision enough time to work before retracing the decision-making process in search of another solution.[48]

The Irish Tourist Board once ran a promotion to attract more travelers, and management was pleased by the initial results, which showed an influx of high-spending tourists. But looking more closely, the board found that these tourists were staying in hotels owned by non-Irish organizations, eating imported beef-steak, and renting imported cars, instead of spending money on uniquely Irish goods and services. Based on this feedback, management realized that they should change the program and aim for thriftier travelers who would stay in locally owned hotels and patronize local restaurants and pubs.[49]

MORE EFFECTIVE DECISION MAKING

As Herbert Simon acknowledged in his administrative model of decision making, managers do not always approach decision making in a completely rational manner. Even when they follow the six steps in the rational decision-making process, managers have no guarantee that their decisions will be successful because they face a variety of barriers that can complicate decision making. Fortunately, managers can take advantage of several behavioral and quantitative tools to improve their decisions.

Barriers to Effective Decision Making

Regardless of the type of problem, managers are often confronted by barriers that work against a rational decision. These barriers include imperfect or incomplete information, inaccurate identification of problems or alternatives, biases, and overcommitment or undercommitment.

- *Imperfect or incomplete information.* Managers rarely have all the information and knowledge they need to solve a problem because gathering perfect information takes so much time and money. Even if managers could obtain complete information, doing so might not be worth the wait or the expense. In some cases, the environment is so dynamic or uncertain that if managers wait for additional information, they may lose important opportunities or fall victim to competitive forces. So managers must be critical users of the information that is available, and they must consider whether the information they have truly fits the situation and whether it is accurate and timely.[50]

- *Inaccurate identification of problem or alternatives.* When managers ask the wrong question, they can't get the right answer. Even worse, managers sometimes fail to search adequately for alternatives. Also, managers can be swayed by *framing,* the wording that describes the alternative solutions in positive or negative terms.[51]
- *Biases.* In the context of decision making, bias refers to situations in which decision-making shortcuts are inappropriately applied. These shortcuts, called **heuristics,** consist of rules of thumb that managers develop to simplify decision making. A banker using a heuristic to simplify the mortgage lending process might follow the guideline that people applying for mortgages should spend no more than 28 percent of their income for housing. One type of heuristic is the tendency to stereotype a situation by comparing it to similar experiences. Another heuristic is the tendency to seek a simple solution by starting with a convenient initial estimate, then adjusting it slightly as time progresses. However, if the original value is inaccurate or inappropriate, adding or subtracting a little from that value will not yield a meaningful solution. Although heuristics can be a practical way of coping with complex problems, they can also lead to traps such as overconfidence, snap judgments, and misconceptions of probability.[52]
- *Overcommitment or undercommitment.* When managers remain committed to a decision long after rational evidence suggests that it should be abandoned, they are exhibiting **nonrational escalation of commitment.** For example, managers may be reluctant to change course because they have already invested money and time implementing a particular decision. But these costs have already been incurred and are therefore irrelevant when making decisions about future actions.[53]

heuristics Rules of thumb that managers use to simplify the decision-making process

nonrational escalation of commitment Staying committed to a previous decision after it should be abandoned

Sheldon Weinig, founder and president of Materials Research Corporation (MRC) in Westchester, New York, was committed to creating high-technology machines that helped semiconductor manufacturers make more-sophisticated chips. His Waferline equipment was a significant technological advance but customers were soon complaining about production glitches. Weinig was reluctant to abandon the equipment because he had invested heavily in the new technology and because he faced devastating losses if the product flopped. If the product was successful, Weinig would enjoy huge rewards. Playing for time, he loaned technicians to his customers worldwide to fine-tune the complex machinery, hoping that this would salvage the situation. After repeated attempts to tweak the equipment failed to solve the problem, Weinig finally cut his losses by buying back the machines or exchanging them for older models.[54]

At the other end of the spectrum, managers may demonstrate their undercommitment through **incrementalism,** selecting the alternative that differs the least from the current situation. This can be particularly troublesome when organizations face a potentially major change but key managers are unwilling to acknowledge the need for taking bold action. However, incrementalism can be a

incrementalism Deciding on an alternative that differs only slightly from the existing situation

MANAGEMENT AROUND THE WORLD

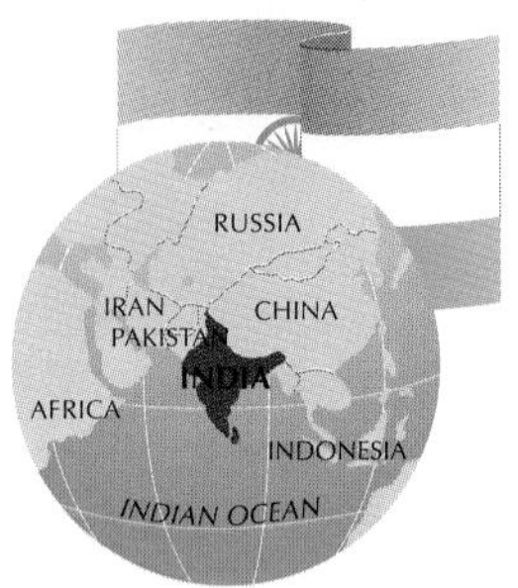

India's 800 million residents present an attractive market to companies selling consumer goods. However, managers doing business in India must weave their way through a maze of government regulations. Multinational firms that plan to build factories in India must often wait months or years to gain approval; moreover, existing regulations can be changed without warning. Therefore, managers seeking access to this market must understand the kinds of constraints posed by government regulations.

legitimate approach for dealing with situations in which managers lack information on which to base a decision or when they must cope with a dynamic or uncertain environment that makes comprehensive, rational decision making difficult or unfeasible. And managers may use incrementalism to implement decisions a step at a time so they can watch the results and then continue to the next action.[55]

Behavioral Tools for Effective Decision Making

Considering the barriers to effective decision making, how can managers make better decisions? Experts suggest a number of ways to improve decision making: know when a decision is necessary, recognize constraints, develop critical thinking skills, apply experience and expertise, and use intuition.

- *Decision timing.* Sometimes the best decision is to postpone making a decision until a situation begins to deteriorate. Generally, managers have to compare the benefits and risks of *action* to the benefits and risks of *inaction* before making a decision.[56] But a manager can often solve a noncrisis problem creatively simply by making a decision in time. When Weyerhaeuser, the wood and paper products giant based in Tacoma, Washington, was searching for ways to cut overhead costs, vice president of employee relations Steve Hill identified a problem. He found that workers' compensation claims were costing almost $30 million a year, and he believed that this cost could be cut through training and tighter controls. Because logging is so hazardous, the proposal might have seemed unrealistic to some, but Hill persisted. Because of his timely decision, Weyerhaeuser cut its annual claims costs by $20 million. More important, Hill's early action saved many employees from possible injury.[57]
- *Realistic decision constraints.* Especially in nonprogrammed problem situations, managers often find few organizational policies to guide the decision-making process. Policies frequently define the limitations of resources (such as the budget or the personnel that managers may use to solve a problem) but go no further. Realistically, managers need to recognize constraints such as physical limitations in production or transportation, government regulations, and standards of quality or time. By understanding the constraints, managers can more realistically select an appropriate and acceptable solution. However, if no alternatives are acceptable after applying tests of constraints, then the manager must search for additional alternatives and must also consider reassessing the constraints.[58]
- *Critical thinking skills.* Another way to improve decision making is to develop *critical thinking* skills, which help managers think clearly, logically, and analytically about the problems they face. Being an effective manager has a lot to do with the ability to take action, but it's equally important that managers be able to recognize and analyze problems, understand their context, and assess the repercussions of various responses before they implement any decisions. Critical thinking helps managers understand and challenge the assumptions that underlie problems and to scrutinize alternatives before making a choice.[59]
- *Experience and expertise.* With decision-making experience comes the ability to make decisions faster because the manager has encountered similar situations in the past. However, managers also need to develop their expertise in

decision making so that they can recognize the key elements in each problem and more accurately identify and evaluate alternatives. By examining the results of decisions, especially mistakes, managers can analyze what went wrong and gain valuable knowledge for future situations. On-the-job experience and classroom learning are both good sources of the knowledge that will help managers make better decisions.[60] Because John Swendrowski, founder and president of Northland Cranberries in Wisconsin, has both experience with and expertise in growing cranberries, he is able to solve a variety of problems that threaten his business, including weather and finances. Despite bad weather and high planting costs, Swendrowski's knowledgeable decisions about buying land and building dams helped Northland increase profits nearly tenfold in four years.[61]

- *Intuition.* Although it must be applied judiciously, intuition is another tool that helps managers improve decision making. *Intuition* grows out of experiences that once called for analytical reasoning but now come to mind when problem patterns recur. However, training and knowledge are also important components of intuition; combined with good analytical skills, they help managers improve their decision-making skills.[62] Consider the problem faced by now-chairman Joseph Antonini when he became K Mart's president in 1987. Compared with discount rivals Wal-Mart and Target, many K Mart stores were small, crowded, and old. Along with his expertise, Antonini used his intuition to transform one new K Mart store by tinkering with its layout, lighting, and decoration. This prototype performed so well that Antonini committed more than $2 billion to overhaul nearly 2,300 K Mart stores by 1996.[63]

Quantitative Tools for Effective Decision Making

Managers can use a variety of quantitative tools to support the decision-making process. These decision tools are especially valuable when planning production, analyzing inventory levels, and considering major budget expenditures. In general, quantitative tools help managers examine alternatives more comprehensively; they also help managers estimate the risks and reduce the uncertainty inherent in the situation. However, quantitative decision aids do not eliminate the need for managerial judgment. At best, they only clarify the alternatives, the consequences, and the probability of expected results so that managers can make a more informed decision.[64] Among the most frequently used tools are the payoff matrix, the decision tree, and the simulation model.

Payoff Matrix

The **payoff matrix,** also known as a *decision matrix,* is a quantitative decision tool that helps managers compare the probable outcomes of two or more alternatives, which can vary according to a variety of future conditions.[65] To use a payoff matrix, the manager first identifies the possible alternatives and the possible future conditions, called *states of nature,* and then arranges them in a matrix. Next, the manager considers the *probability,* or likelihood, that each of the possible future conditions might occur. Probabilities are generally expressed in decimal form or as a percentage: the likelihood that a particular condition might occur could be 1 in 10, expressed as .10 or 10 percent. A probability of 0 indicates that there is no chance that a condition will occur, whereas a probability of 1.00 indicates that a condition will definitely occur. Within the matrix, the

payoff matrix A quantitative tool that compares probable outcomes of two or more alternatives, which can differ depending on various future conditions probabilities of the various states of nature occurring must add up to 1.00.

Once probabilities have been assigned, the value of each alternative's outcome, called the *payoff,* is calculated under each possible state of nature. All the payoffs for a particular alternative are multiplied by the respective probabilities associated with the future conditions, thus arriving at the *expected value.* The manager then compares the expected value of all alternatives and uses the resulting information to make a decision.

To illustrate, imagine that the owner of a commercial bakery is expanding the business and must decide whether to (1) buy one delivery truck, (2) buy two delivery trucks, or (3) buy 3 delivery trucks. These alternatives are displayed on the left side of the rows of the matrix in Exhibit 6.6. The three possible states of nature that have an impact on these alternatives are light customer demand, moderate customer demand, and heavy customer demand (reading across the column headings on the top of the matrix). Based on experience, current trends, and professional judgment, the bakery owner has assigned each future condition a probability of occurrence. Also, the owner has estimated the revenue payoffs of each of the three alternatives under each of the three states of nature. Using the probability assigned to each state of nature and the payoffs possible under each, the owner can calculate expected values as follows:

Alternative (1) .2($30,000) + .3($32,000) + .5($20,000) = $25,600

Alternative (2) .2($24,000) + .3($34,000) + .5($31,000) = $30,500

Alternative (3) .2(−$10,000) + .3($15,000) + .5($40,000) = $22,500

On the basis of this analysis, the manager would get the highest expected value from alternative (2), buying 2 trucks. Of course, it is impossible to accurately predict which future condition will actually occur, and the payoff associated with alternative (2) is not guaranteed if the owner selects this course of action. However, the payoff matrix helps the decision-making process because it guides managers through an examination of the future conditions that influence the outcomes, and it makes managers think about the likelihood of each state of nature occurring. By calculating the expected values, managers can obtain a quantitative assessment of the possible results under varying future states, assuming that the probability values are as realistic as possible.[66]

For example, managers at Hallmark Cards, the greeting card maker in Kansas City, Missouri, use payoff matrices to help manage the purchase and production of novelty gift and party items. Managers develop alternatives representing various quantities to be purchased or produced, estimate levels of demand (cor-

EXHIBIT 6.6

Payoff Matrix for Bakery Truck Decision

The owner of a commercial bakery could use a payoff matrix such as this to determine the expected value of buying one, two, or three trucks.

	States of Nature		
Alternatives	**Light Demand (probability of .2)**	**Moderate Demand (probability of .3)**	**Heavy Demand (probability of .5)**
1: buy 1 truck	**Payoff: $30,000**	**Payoff: $32,000**	**Payoff: $20,000**
2: buy 2 trucks	**Payoff: $24,000**	**Payoff: $34,000**	**Payoff: $31,000**
3: buy 3 trucks	**Payoff: −$10,000**	**Payoff: $15,000**	**Payoff: $40,000**

responding to states of nature), and assign probabilities that are used to calculate expected values. They can then determine the optimal purchase or production level and prevent overruns that exceed demand, or shortages where quantities do not meet customer demand.[67]

Decision Tree

The **decision tree** is an analytical tool that graphically illustrates the logical sequence of alternatives and decisions involved in a problem, including the probabilities and payoffs associated with each alternative.[68] Decision trees can be used to graphically depict the same information found in payoff matrices. But they are particularly valuable when managers face problems that lead to a series of future decisions. The branches of the decision tree that emanate from a square represent a decision point from which alternative courses of action can be traced. The branches that emanate from a circle depict possible outcomes that arise from varying states of nature, and these outcomes are labeled with their respective probabilities and payoffs.

decision tree An analytical tool that graphically portrays the logical series of actions and decisions in a problem situation

The decision tree in Exhibit 6.7 illustrates the bakery owner's problem, based on the alternatives, states of nature, probabilities, and payoffs shown in the payoff matrix in Exhibit 6.6. However, this decision tree shows additional decisions that the owner faces, including whether to sell or to lease one or two trucks if customer demand is not heavy. The decision tree reflects this second decision point after alternative (2) or (3). Because the consequences of every possible course of action can be traced on a decision tree, it is a valuable tool for helping managers think through problems involving sequential decisions. For managers faced with complex decisions—whether to acquire another company or how to price products, for example—the decision tree can be particularly useful.[69]

Simulation Model

A **simulation model** is a mathematical depiction of a situation that expresses the relationships between the elements and that can be used to predict the outcome of various courses of action. Frequently, managers use computer-based simulation models because these can be easily manipulated once they are set up. To create a simulation model, managers start with information about the current situation, add details about each alternative, and include data about the

simulation model A mathematical representation of a problem that reflects the relationships between the elements and is used to project the results of certain actions under various circumstances

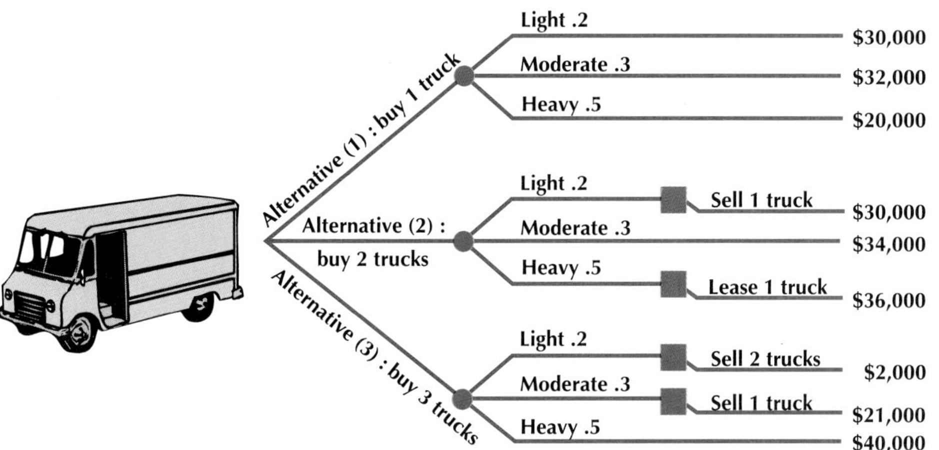

EXHIBIT 6.7

Decision Tree for Bakery Truck Decision

The bakery owner has three alternatives in the problem of how many delivery trucks to buy. This decision tree graphically illustrates the alternatives, the states of nature, and the payoffs for two consecutive decision points so that the owner can see the consequences of each course of action.

MANAGERIAL DECISION MAKING

Crisis Decision Making: Quick, Reasoned, and Decisive

When Chuck Martin received an urgent call from a worried pet owner in February 1990, he wasn't thinking "crisis." As secretary-treasurer of Martin Feedmills (based in Elmira, Ontario, Canada), Martin was covering all the bases while his father, the president, and his brother, manager of the pet food division, were away. The caller told Martin that his dog had gotten sick from eating the firm's Techni-Cal Growth pellets. In a few short minutes, Martin found himself enmeshed in a crisis problem that threatened not only the unblemished 20-year reputation but also the future sales of a company worth $100 million (Canadian).

Martin recognized that he had a problem on his hands as soon as the caller began to describe the situation. To pinpoint the problem, Martin sent samples of the customer's bag of pellets to the Ontario Ministry of Agriculture for testing. When the Ministry reported that the pellets contained traces of a poultry medication that is toxic to dogs, Martin had to consider his next move. He still didn't know whether the problem was due to widespread sabotage or whether it was confined to only one bag, so his decision entailed considerable risk. "We could have ignored the situation or dealt with it out of the public eye on a case-by-case basis, I suppose," says Martin. "But the rumors would have gone out, and that would have hurt us even more."

Martin Feedmills was not going to stonewall or to delay action. Within 24 hours of learning of the toxic traces, Martin decided to notify dealers and distributors that the company was voluntarily recalling the entire batch of pellets. Two days later, two more dogs turned up sick, and Martin now knew that more than one bag was affected. He also learned that all the bags were from the same batch. And according to his deal-

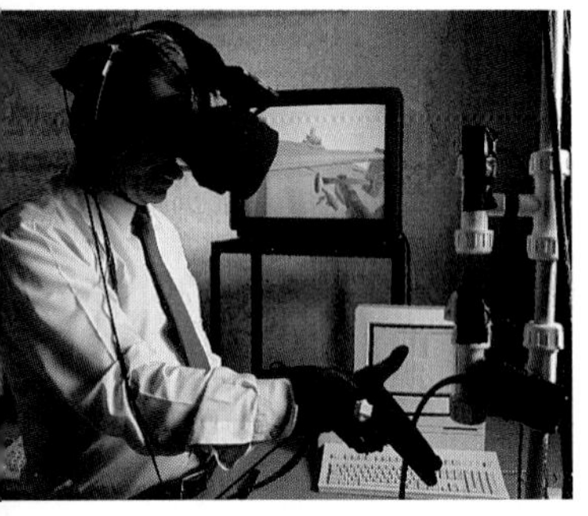

Donning special goggles and gloves, Boeing executive Keith Butler interacts with a simulation model to "fly" the hypothetical tilting-rotor airplane shown on the computer screen. Boeing is experimenting with simulation models that harness the three-dimensional view and realistic touch of *virtual reality* to improve manufacturing processes.

past and about possible future conditions. Once the mathematical relationships between the elements have been determined, managers can run the simulation to examine expected outcomes. Then they can substitute other data to see how the results are affected.[70]

Building a simulation model can be challenging, time-consuming, and costly, because it is difficult to express real-life problems in formulas and to quantify the relationships between the elements. Properly used, such models are valuable tools that allow managers to consider many alternatives and possible outcomes. They also help reduce the risk of adopting an unworkable approach.[71] Moreover, once they have been built, simulation models can be used over and over again. For example, American Airlines worked with the Federal Aviation Administration to develop a computerized simulation model of air-traffic control to diagnose the elements that contribute to air-traffic congestion anywhere in the world. After the model had been created, it was made available to other airlines and individuals interested in analyzing air-traffic problems and alternative solutions. Managers at American and at other airlines can use the model to simulate a variety of air-traffic situations and to see how changes affect congestion.[72]

Other Tools

A variety of other decision aids are available to help managers cope with complex problems. These tools include linear programming, game theory, queuing theory, forecasting, and decision support systems.

- *Linear programming* seeks to minimize or maximize a dependent variable (such as delivery time) that is a function of several independent variables (such as staffing level and equipment availability). Using linear programming to consider all possible combinations of the independent variables helps managers make decisions about allocating their resources in ways that yield the optimal outcome. Managers can also use this tool to allocate resources ers, more than half of that batch was already in the hands of dog owners. This information increased the time pressure on Martin; he had to move quickly if he hoped to prevent more dogs from becoming ill.

The top managers of Martin Feedmills generated and evaluated alternatives and decided on a course of action. They called a press conference quickly to alert dog owners and breeders to the potential danger. During the presentation, company officials displayed the pellets and the bags, showed where to read the lot number on the bag, and announced a toll-free consumer hotline that dog owners could call for more information. The company further demonstrated its concern by mailing letters to thousands of veterinarians and dog breeders to explain the symptoms and recommend treatment. Not long afterward, the company withdrew all remaining Techni-Cal Growth bags from store shelves (even though they were not contaminated) and relaunched the product in brand new packaging easily distinguishable from the packaging that had been recalled.

The total cost, says president Don Martin, was as high as $500,000 (Canadian), including the cost of the recall, the relaunch, and the settlements with dog owners and breeders. Of course, costs might have reached that level anyway if Martin Feedmills had decided to wait for government action instead of voluntarily withdrawing the product. But the president also notes that most of the breeders who have settled with the company are continuing to use the product. Considering the customer feedback that the company has received, the Martins are convinced that their decisions were sound solutions to an unprecedented crisis.

Apply Your Knowledge

1. What quantitative decision aids might the top managers of Martin Feedmills use to help solve future crisis problems?
2. Which barriers to effective decision making did the Martins encounter? What behavioral techniques could they have used to improve the chances of making a better decision?

among many product lines or to determine the least costly method of shipping products from many plants to many markets.[73]

- *Game theory* helps managers analyze competitive situations involving conflicting interests. Originally developed for use in games of strategy, game theory can be applied to economic, business, and military problems. When a situation can be influenced by the actions of two or more competitors, game theory is a good tool for studying possible competitive reactions to the various alternatives a decision maker is considering.[74]
- *Queuing theory* helps managers consider the waiting-line problems and possible solutions in production and in service organizations. Whether the bottleneck involves multiple lines or a single line, or *queue,* queuing theory is a practical tool for studying the balance between waiting time and changes in service or production capacity.[75]
- *Forecasting* is a planning and decision-making tool that helps managers predict future events and trends that can affect organizational decisions and activities. By using forecasts, managers hope to lower the level of uncertainty in many of the problems they encounter.[76] Forecasting is further examined in Chapter 7.
- *Decision support systems* are used by a growing number of managers to help analyze nonprogrammed, complex decisions. Like other quantitative tools, decision support systems are designed to supplement, not replace, managerial judgment.[77] Chapter 18 examines decision support systems in greater detail.

GROUPS AND DECISION MAKING

Decision making is often an individual activity but there are many times when groups become involved in the process. For example, groups can be effective during the second step of the process when management wants to generate many

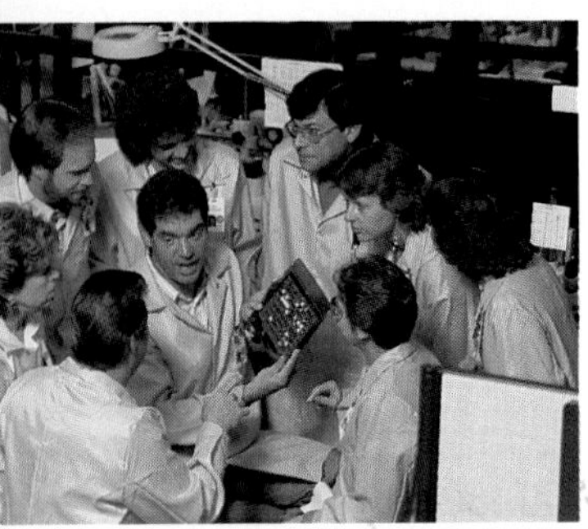

This employee group at Westinghouse's circuit board plant in College Station, Texas, is an interacting group that meets once a week to consider ways of improving production quality. Group members work together to identify problems, to generate and evaluate alternatives, and to recommend solutions to management or, when appropriate, to approve their own decisions.

alternative solutions to a problem. In some cases, groups are involved in every step of the process, from problem recognition through implementation and feedback. When and how should employees be included in the decision-making process? The Vroom-Yetton-Jago Model is one tool that managers can use to determine the extent of employee participation.

Employee Participation in Decision Making

Managers have a great deal of latitude when deciding whether to handle decision making alone or to involve others in the process. Some problems can be more effectively resolved when employees participate with managers in group decision making. An important step in group decision making is determining the relative levels of management and employee participation in the process. In some cases, it is best for managers to make decisions with relatively little participation by their employees; in other cases, the employees are in a better position than the manager to make the decision.

A model developed by Victor H. Vroom and Philip Yetton, and enhanced by Vroom and Arthur G. Jago, can be used to determine the appropriate level of participation. Managers apply the model by answering a series of questions about factors that affect the decision: decision quality, decision acceptance, concern for employee development, and concern for time. Depending on the answers to these questions, managers select the appropriate level of employee participation, including direct participation in decisions regarding the work; consultative participation, in which employees voice opinions; short-term participation focused on specific projects; informal participation; or representative participation, in which elected employee representatives are involved in the decision-making process.[78] Although participation in group decision making enhances the participants' satisfaction with the decision, the effect on productivity has not yet been proven.[79] The Vroom-Yetton-Jago Model is discussed in greater detail in Chapter 15.

Group Decision-Making Formats

Just as managers have a variety of choices for involving others in the decision-making process, they also have a variety of choices for group decision-making formats. Three of the most common formats are interacting groups, nominal groups, and Delphi groups.

Interacting Groups

interacting group A decision-making group in which people meet personally to solve a problem

An **interacting group** brings people together face-to-face to consider a particular problem. Some interacting groups are convened specifically to solve one problem and may include people from a variety of departments or locations. On the other hand, some groups already exist, such as members of a committee or a specific work unit. Interactive groups generally start with a statement of the problem and include a discussion of the problem and its cause. Group members collectively generate and evaluate alternatives and finally come to a decision.[80] This face-to-face interaction often triggers creative ideas and helps air the various alternatives thoroughly. However, a disadvantage is that the group may be dominated by one or more members who prevent others from participating.

When Republic Engineered Steels faced a difficult distribution problem, it turned to an interacting group composed of union and management members.

The railroad cars used for shipping steel from Republic's plant in Canton, Ohio, were dirty, creating a hazard for workers and damaging the products. Although the problem was caused by the railroad, Republic needed a short-term solution until the railroad could permanently solve the problem. The union-management team considered the problem and came up with a solution that Republic implemented: designing and building a crane-operated machine to scrape debris from the cars.[81]

Nominal Groups

A **nominal group** approaches decision making in a highly structured format, emphasizing individual thinking and active group participation. Meeting face-to-face, nominal groups follow a specific format. To start, the group leader presents the problem and then asks the group members to silently and independently write down their ideas. Then members present their ideas, but none are discussed until all ideas have been considered by the group. Next, the group discusses each idea in turn, and once all ideas have been considered, members vote by written ballot, ranking the ideas in order of priority. Although this format can be time-consuming, it often generates more alternatives than interacting groups.[82]

nominal group A decision-making group that uses a formal structure to facilitate individual thinking and active group participation

Delphi Groups

A **Delphi group** is composed of experts who respond to written questionnaires about problems. The experts' answers are summarized and reported back to the group, and new answers are requested until consensus has been reached. Delphi groups do not meet face-to-face but instead pool their ideas by mail, eliminating some of the problems that can plague interacting groups. Originally developed during an Air Force–sponsored study by the Rand Corporation in the 1950s, the Delphi technique has been adapted for use in many management situations where expert opinions would be helpful in considering long-term future situations. For example, when the U.S. State Department was considering a budgetary problem concerning benefit and cost analysis, managers could find no other comparable cases to stimulate thinking about creative alternatives. Using the Delphi technique, managers were able to identify and evaluate a number of alternatives.[83]

Delphi group A consulting group of experts who respond to circulated questionnaires and offer ideas about a problem until a consensus has been reached

Impact of Group Decision Making

Regardless of the format used or the tools employed, group decision making has both benefits and limitations, as compared with individual decision making (see Exhibit 6.8). In some cases, individual decision making is necessary; in other cases, managers want or need to involve groups in the decision-making process. However, managers can improve group decision making by understanding the limitations and planning accordingly.

Benefits of Group Decision Making

When attacking a problem, group members are able to contribute more knowledge and information than individuals. Moreover, the group can bring a broader perspective to problem definition, alternative generation, and evaluation of possible solutions. Another benefit of group decision making is that the people who participate in the process generally feel more satisfied and are more likely to accept the decision and to support its implementation. Finally, group

EXHIBIT 6.8 Advantages and Disadvantages of Group Decision Making

Compared with individual decision making, group decision making has benefits but also limitations that managers must carefully consider.

Benefits	Limitations
1. Groups can accumulate more knowledge and facts.	**1. Groups tend to work more slowly and to take more time to reach a decision.**
2. Groups may have a broader perspective and consider more approaches and alternatives.	**2. Too much dependence on group decision making may limit a manager's ability to act quickly and decisively when necessary.**
3. Individuals who participate in group decision making are more likely to be satisfied with the decision and to support its implementation.	**3. Groups may be dominated by one individual or a small clique.**
4. The group decision-making process serves as an important communication device.	**4. Group effort frequently results in compromises that may not be optimal for organizational effectiveness or performance.**

decision making fosters good communication about the decision. In Japan, group decision making has been codified into the ritual of *ringi,* a process in which a decision must be approved by managers from the top to the bottom of the organization. By the time all the official comments and approvals have been completed, a collective consensus has been reached, which serves to commit the participants to supporting the decision.[84]

Limitations of Group Decision Making

Although group decision making has many benefits, it also has several limitations. First, group decision making usually takes more time than individual decision making. This is one of the key problems Hewlett-Packard faced when it tried to reach consensus on new-product development decisions. Second, managers who rely on group decisions must guard against losing the ability to act quickly and decisively when necessary. Third, groups may be dominated by one or more individuals who prevent others from participating. And fourth, the group process may result in compromises that do not represent the optimal decision from the organizational perspective.

groupthink The tendency of members deeply involved in a group to pursue harmony and agreement rather than realistically considering the problem and the alternatives

This last limitation is the result of **groupthink,** the tendency of members in cohesive groups to avoid conflict and to reach agreement quickly, often at the expense of realistically evaluating the problem and the alternatives. When groupthink occurs, members of a closely knit group feel pressured to avoid topics that can cause conflict and threaten unanimity, so they do not discuss every possible alternative. They end up selecting a course of action preferred by the majority, but without carefully considering its risks. To reduce the impact of groupthink, managers should push for a thorough examination of every alternative and encourage freewheeling discussion of problems and solutions.[85]

Reebok chairman Paul Fireman has been a firm believer in involving employees in decision-making situations, and he encourages employees at the Stoughton, Massachusetts, headquarters to participate in corporate planning sessions. However, when more than a dozen employees started attending advertising planning meetings to voice their individual opinions, it was difficult and time-consuming to reach a decision. Because of this limitation, Reebok's president John Duerden now allows only a handful of managers to participate in such planning sessions.[86]

Cathy Hendrie *(left)*, editor-in-chief of *The Daily Aztec*, the student newspaper at San Diego State University, conducts brainstorming sessions with her editors to come up with ideas for future articles and photographs. Once the editors have generated a large number of alternatives, they select the best and assign reporters and photographers.

Tools for Effective Group Decision Making

Groups have a variety of tools available that can enhance and facilitate the decision-making process, helping managers overcome the barriers to effective group decision making. To spark creativity in generating alternative solutions, many groups use the brainstorming technique. To stimulate more rigorous examination and evaluation of the alternatives, groups can turn to such tools as the devil's advocate and the dialectic process. One or more of these tools can be used during the group decision-making process, and they can even be adapted for individual decision making.

- **Brainstorming** is an informal interactive group technique in which people freely generate ideas that are not evaluated until all ideas have been presented. Because ideas are not judged until later, group members can relax and spontaneously offer as many ideas as possible. During brainstorming sessions, groups can come up with a large number of imaginative and high-quality solutions.[87]
- **Devil's advocate** is a technique in which one or more group members assume the role of challenging the overall group's problem analysis, alternatives, and evaluation. In this way, the group is forced to carefully examine its assumptions and to thoroughly critique the alternatives before coming to a final decision.[88]
- **Dialectic process** is a technique in which two or more individuals or groups are asked to present and defend opposing proposals for solving the problem. Whereas the devil's advocate approach focuses on the flaws and limitations of the group's assumptions and alternatives without presenting better alternatives, participants in the dialectic process revise their assumptions and present new proposals for group consideration. This confrontation of conflicting viewpoints pushes the entire group to consider various ways of approaching the problem, and often the new proposal is better than the existing alternatives.[89]

brainstorming An informal interactive group technique in which members generate many alternatives without passing judgment on their value

devil's advocate A technique in which one or more group members deliberately challenge the group's view of the problem, the alternatives, and their evaluation

dialectic process A technique in which individuals or groups present and defend opposing solutions to a particular problem to derive an improved solution

Both the devil's advocate technique and the dialectic process use structured conflict to force managers to carefully and critically examine their assumptions and their alternatives. This inherent scrutiny helps managers make higher-quality decisions than if they attempted to bypass the conflict and make decisions by group consensus. On the other hand, participants generally accept group decisions more readily when they are made by consensus; they may feel less satisfied or less committed to decisions that involve the use of the devil's advocate or the dialectic process techniques. For this reason, managers must consider how the quality of the decision and the group's commitment to the decision will ultimately affect the actions taken.[90]

SUMMARY

Managers confront three types of problems: crisis problems are critical situations that require urgent decisions; noncrisis problems present challenges to the organization but don't need to be resolved immediately; and opportunity problems are positive scenarios in which the organization might reap significant advantages. Regardless of the type of problem, the decision can fall into one of two groups. Programmed decisions are made in routine, well-structured situations or in situations that can be resolved by applying preset decision rules. Nonprogrammed decisions are made when preset decision rules cannot be applied. With any decision, the information that managers have available affects the quality of their decision making. A condition of certainty occurs when the manager has complete information about the problem, the alternatives, and the consequences. A condition of risk occurs when managers understand the problem and have sufficient information to understand the alternatives and to estimate the probability that each alternative will lead to the expected outcome. A condition of uncertainty occurs when managers understand the problem but have incomplete information about the possible alternatives and the probable consequences of each alternative. Finally, when managers have little or no information about the problem, the alternatives, and the consequences, they are operating under a condition of ambiguity.

The classical and the administrative models of decision making differ in several ways. The classical model is prescriptive, setting out an ideal process for making rational decisions, whereas the administrative model is descriptive, showing how managers actually make decisions. Also, the classical model assumes that managers approach decisions rationally, but the administrative model acknowledges that decision making is not always rational. Finally, the classical model makes no allowances for managerial limitations, whereas the administrative model describes the bounded rationality that exists because of management limitations and the satisficing that managers engage in.

The rational decision-making process consists of six steps. First, managers identify the problem, define it, then diagnose it. Second, they generate alternatives. Third, they evaluate the alternatives and the consequences. Fourth, managers make the decision. Fifth, they implement the decision. Sixth, managers evaluate the results and provide feedback about the outcome. In nearly every decision situation, managers face one or more barriers to effective decision making. One barrier is imperfect or incomplete information. Managers rarely have perfect information; moreover, complete information costs time and money to obtain. Another barrier is inaccurate identification of the problem or inaccurate identification of the alternatives. Also, biases caused by the inappropriate application of heuristics that simplify decision making can be a barrier. A final barrier is overcommitment or undercommitment to decisions.

Managers can use five behavioral approaches to improve decision making. First, know when a decision is necessary. Second, recognize constraints that limit the range of possible solutions. Third, develop critical thinking skills. Fourth, apply experience and expertise. And fifth, use intuition when appropriate. Quantitative decision aids help managers make more-informed decisions. The payoff matrix helps managers compare the results of probable outcomes of alternatives in various future states. The decision tree illustrates the logical sequence of alternatives and decisions involved in a problem, as well as the probabilities and payoffs. The simulation model mathematically expresses the relationships between the elements and helps predict the outcomes of various alternatives.

Group decision making, which includes interacting groups, nominal groups, and Delphi groups, has a number of benefits. When they participate, group members can contribute more knowledge and information than individuals alone, and they bring a broader perspective to the decision. Group members feel more satisfied and tend to accept the decision. Finally, group decision making fosters good communication. However, group decision making can take more time than individual decision making, and groups may be dominated by one or more members. Moreover, managers who depend on group decisions must be careful not to lose the ability to act quickly and decisively. Because of groupthink, group decision making may result in compromises that are not optimal for the organization. Tools that managers can use to enhance group decision making include brainstorming, devil's advocate, and the dialectic process.

MEETING A MANAGEMENT CHALLENGE AT HEWLETT-PACKARD

John Young had a classic decision-making predicament on his hands. In the earlier attempt to improve the *quality* of the decision-making process (by involving more people and placing more decisions under top management control), the company had inadvertently damaged the *efficiency* of that process. And now products were late, profits were slipping, and customers were increasingly turning to competitive products. Donald Purkey, a California workstation dealer, summed up much of the market's sentiment at the time: "I'm moving away from Hewlett-Packard now." Purkey switched and started selling computers made by HP competitors.

Young analyzed the problem and uncovered two reasons for the slow decisions. First, too many decisions were referred up the management chain, slowing product development as engineers waited for answers. Second, divisions working on related products took too much time reaching consensus, a potential problem whenever groups are involved in decisions. The consensus process, designed to tap the creativity of a broad base of people and to ensure better coordination, threatened HP's position in the market.

The problem was clear, but the solution—which would mean changing the way that many of the company's 90,000 employees did their jobs—was far from simple. Young faced a major nonprogrammed decision that would dramatically affect the company's future. He had to speed up decisions,

Hewlett-Packard computers and workstations

perhaps by shifting away from consensual decision making, but he couldn't stifle creativity or demotivate employees. And Young couldn't be sure that any changes would help until they were implemented and given a chance to work, so the decision carried a high degree of uncertainty as well.

Young's first step was to improve communication among the people who had a stake in important product decisions. He did this by aligning teams that worked on similar products under common managers, which preserved the creative interaction among engineers while speeding up the flow of information needed to make decisions. In addition, he put strong leaders in charge of product development, leaders with the authority to make unilateral decisions if they believed consensus building and group decision making would take too long. Finally, Young gave the development leaders the authority to manage their products without constantly asking for top-level approval, as long as they understood and supported HP's overall vision and stayed within the bounds of their own divisional product missions.

Once Young modified the organization's decision-making process, results began to show very quickly. Some of the best evidence of HP's new decision-making capability is the Series 7000 family of workstations. The company beat the competition to market with these products; one of the new HP computers is nearly twice as fast as a comparable machine from IBM and more than twice as fast as its Sun Microsystems counterpart. Donald Purkey, the dealer who had begun to move away from HP, sold more HP systems in eight weeks than he had in the previous year and a half. HP has always had the technical capabilities to create breakthrough products, and it has now streamlined the decision-making process to get those products to market ahead of the competition.

***You're the Manager*:** You have joined HP as the vice president of engineering, reporting to CEO Lewis Platt, who replaced Young in 1992. You plan to leave individual product decisions to the product-development teams; the decisions that you'll get involved in are mostly research and development and arbitration of internal product conflicts. Consider the following questions and determine how you would make these decisions.

Ranking Questions

1. One of your researchers has developed a new computer screen that shows colors more vividly than competing products. Three divisions want to use this screen in new products, but only one can have it. You also know you must get this product to market quickly. How should you approach this decision? Rank the following ideas from best to worst.
   a. Have each division describe the profit they expect to make with products using this screen. Use a payoff matrix to determine which division would make the most money in various situations, then make the decision yourself.
   b. Send a Delphi questionnaire to the division heads, asking for their opinions about the most profitable markets to enter. Report their answers back and ask for new estimates until you get a consensus about the most profitable market. Select the division most familiar with this market.
   c. Bring the division heads together in an interacting group and ask for their ideas. Summarize the options in a decision tree, and then ask the division heads to jointly decide which should have the screen.
   d. Build a simulation model that shows how each division's products would sell with the screen, and project the effects of aggressive competition and a bad economy. Choose the division that the model projects will be most profitable under the least favorable conditions.
2. An inventor in Montana has created a data storage device that holds twice as much data as HP's best product. You think this development could have an impact on your business, but the device is experimental and no patent has been granted. What should you do? Rank the following from best to worst.
   a. If you don't act quickly, HP's data storage products will be obsolete. Immediately buy the rights to the product before a competitor grabs it.
   b. You have time, but if you don't watch the situation carefully, HP will lose out to a more aggressive competitor. Offer to underwrite the inventor's research in exchange for the option to buy the device once it is perfected.
   c. Hire the inventor so that the device becomes HP's exclusive property and you can use it in HP products.
   d. Do nothing until the invention has been perfected and the patent granted. Then you can buy the device with more certainty that it will work.

Multiple-Choice Questions

3. Although product-development leaders can act independently when they feel that consensus will take too long, you occasionally have to arbitrate conflicts between divisions that are developing products that might compete with each other. You've just learned that four divisions are developing instruments to measure air pollution. You meet with the four managers and tell them that you're going to pick the product that promises the lowest level of risk and uncertainty. Which of these would you choose?
   a. Product A uses a measurement device that promises to be more accurate than any other on the market. However, the manufacturer that supplies these devices hasn't gotten a prototype to work correctly.
   b. The engineers on Product B discovered that with a few minor changes they can convert

an existing medical instrument to the air-pollution application.

c. Product C will use technology licensed from a French company. However, the licensing fee is too high, so division managers are visiting Paris next week to see if the company will lower its fee.

d. Product D is being developed entirely by the HP team, but two key engineers from the project left the company last week without warning. The manager is reviewing the pair's notes to see how the design works.

4. You want to reduce the negative impact of the bounded rationality that affects decisions made by engineers and product development leaders, but you know that some options are less practical than others. Which of these plans is most sensible, in terms of cost, time, and employee relations?

   a. Ask project managers to check each other by studying the same information and reaching conclusions independently, then comparing decisions.

   b. Since mental capacity contributes to bounded rationality, you should hire only the smartest people who apply for each engineering and management job.

   c. All employees may not have the basic skills needed for effective decision making. You should therefore offer extensive training in decision making.

   d. Laziness and carelessness can also contribute to faulty decision making, so the best approach to this problem is to penalize people for making poor decisions by taking away vacation days or other benefits.

Analysis Questions

5. How can Lewis Platt and the other executives at HP monitor the company to make sure that new barriers to effective decision making don't appear?
6. Which of the six steps of the rational decision-making process did Young use when he changed the decision-making process at HP?
7. How did Young's changes affect the level and scope of organizational decision making at HP?

Special Project

The decision-making process that HP uses to select new-product development projects is one key to its long-term success. The company needs a process that minimizes mistakes (such as launching a new-product project based on technology that proves impractical or introducing a product that the market doesn't want) without screening out so many ideas that the company misses good opportunities. Draw up some brief guidelines (no more than two pages) for generating and evaluating new-product ideas.[91]

KEY TERMS

administrative model of decision making (178)
bounded rationality (178)
brainstorming (195)
classical model of decision making (177)
condition of ambiguity (176)
condition of certainty (175)
condition of risk (176)
condition of uncertainty (176)
crisis problem (173)
decision (172)
decision making (172)
decision tree (189)
Delphi group (193)
devil's advocate (195)
dialectic process (195)
groupthink (194)
heuristics (185)
incrementalism (185)
interacting group (192)
nominal group (193)
noncrisis problem (173)
nonprogrammed decision (175)
nonrational escalation of commitment (185)
opportunity problem (174)
payoff matrix (187)
problem (172)
programmed decision (174)
satisficing (179)
simulation model (189)

QUESTIONS

For Review

1. What are programmed and nonprogrammed decisions, and why do top managers usually tackle the nonprogrammed decisions?
2. What are bounded rationality and satisficing, and how do they influence rational managerial decision making?
3. What are the six steps in the rational decision-making process?
4. In what ways can a payoff matrix, a decision tree, and a simulation model help managers improve their decision making?
5. What three formats can groups use to enhance decision making?

For Analysis

1. What can managers do to determine whether a decision is programmed or nonprogrammed?
2. Are heuristics and overcommitment always barriers to effective decision making?
3. If a manager cannot quantify the probability of risk for each alternative under consideration, how can a decision tree be useful?
4. In what ways can managers use realistic decision constraints during the six steps of the decision-making process to improve decision making?
5. How can managers reduce the uncertainty they perceive in crisis situations?

For Application

1. How can a not-for-profit organization such as the Cleveland Museum use a Delphi group to solve an opportunity problem?
2. What can a restaurant owner do to discourage the chef from satisficing?
3. If a hotel manager wanted to generate and evaluate alternatives for solving the problem of dwindling room-service revenues, what tools might be used?
4. How can a recent college graduate acquire experience, expertise, and intuition to improve decision making as a retail store manager?
5. How might a high school student adapt brainstorming, devil's advocate, and the dialectic process to make a more effective individual decision about applying to particular colleges?

KEEPING CURRENT IN MANAGEMENT

Find a recent article that discusses how a manager confronted a crisis problem that required a difficult decision. Examples might include an athletic coach who must decide which player to substitute after a star athlete has been injured, a plant manager who faces a wildcat strike by employees, or a supplier whose biggest customer has just declared bankruptcy.

1. Is this decision to be made under a condition of certainty, risk, uncertainty, or ambiguity? Can this problem be handled as a programmed decision? Why or why not?
2. How does the manager define the problem and what alternatives does the manager consider? How are the alternatives evaluated? Does the manager use heuristics in the decision-making process?
3. Which tools, if any, does the manager use to support the decision-making process? If the manager involves a group in the decision-making process, what techniques does the group use to reach a decision? How might the manager have improved the decision-making process in the crisis situation described in this article?

SHARPEN YOUR MANAGEMENT SKILLS

Black & Decker's 1989 purchase of Emhart seemed like a great decision at the time. Emhart made several product lines that dovetailed nicely with Black & Decker's own products. The plan was to join Emhart's locks and plumbing products with Black & Decker's tool and appliance lines to create a more nearly complete offering for home owners. Other Emhart businesses were to be sold to repay the debt Black & Decker racked up in purchasing Emhart.

After the acquisition, the product lines fit well, but the external environment didn't cooperate. Black & Decker could not quickly sell off the unwanted businesses. Then a prolonged economic slump slowed home building and remodeling, which hurt Black & Decker's product lines. In the meantime, rivals introduced new tools that competed directly with Black & Decker products. CEO Nolan Archibald wound up juggling a difficult financial and competitive situation, with little certainty about the environment and the company's future.

Suppose Archibald wants to make another acquisition decision. You are called in as a management consultant to evaluate the acquisition of a manufacturer of car accessories.

- *Decision:* Identify the environmental forces most likely to affect the outcome of this acquisition. Determine whether you can obtain enough information to predict the future state of each force, or whether the decision must be made under conditions of risk, uncertainty, or ambiguity.
- *Communication:* Report your findings to Archibald in a two-page memo. Next, recommend any decision support tools you think will help Black & Decker make a better decision, and explain why these tools would be helpful.[92]

CASE

Kellogg Has an Appetite for Market Share

A week of hard decisions starts with a good breakfast at Kellogg, the world's leading ready-to-eat cereal company. Former chairman and CEO William A. LaMothe instituted the Monday morning taste test, in which the company's top executives gather at 7:30 A.M. to sample bowls of cereal from the company's factories. The executives add milk and assess the taste, "bowl life," and "mouth feel" before rushing off to decide whether to diversify, when to raise prices, and how to convince adults to eat more cereal.

HISTORY

The creation of wheat flakes in 1894 delighted hungry patients at the vegetarian sanitarium run by the Kellogg brothers in Battle Creek, Michigan. The brothers soon perfected corn flakes and sold cereal by mail to former patients. One brother, W. K. Kellogg, set up his own firm to produce corn flakes in 1906, and a *Ladies Home Journal* advertisement increased demand from 33 cases a day to 2,900 cases a day by the end of the first year. Enduring advertising images such as Rice Krispies' "Snap, Crackle, and Pop" helped Kellogg secure 41 percent of the U.S. market by 1988. Then a sudden consumer passion for oats caught Kellogg unawares; profits declined in 1989 for the first time in 37 years, and Kellogg's market share eroded below 35 percent.

ENVIRONMENT

When cereal market growth slowed as the baby-boom generation grew up and turned away from traditional childhood breakfast cereals, Kellogg appealed to adult sensibilities by positioning fiber-filled All-Bran as a cancer preventive. Annual growth in U.S. ready-to-eat cereal sales shot from 2 percent to 5 percent as cereal moved beyond simple nutrition to become a factor in the fight against cancer, heart disease, and constipation. When news reports touted the special advantages of oat fiber, consumers jumped for oat cereals, which Kellogg lacked.

Kellogg was able to respond quickly to market changes because it focused on the cereal business, despite periods of slow market growth, whereas less patient competitors diversified into restaurants, fashion, and other areas. LaMothe had lost faith in diversification while working as an assistant to a previous chairman, and his decision to stick to the business Kellogg knew best helped the company's executives recognize opportunities and make decisions about new cereal products before competitors made a move. Now, as competitors shed unrelated businesses to sharpen their focus on cereals, Kellogg already offered health-conscious consumers Nutri-Grain, Nutrific, Cracklin' Oat Bran, and Common Sense Oat Bran cereals.

GOALS AND CHALLENGES

LaMothe's successor, Arnold G. Langbo, knows that a quick response alone will not secure the goal of increasing market share; products must also be reviewed for quality, customer need, and price. For instance, Kellogg might pull its belated, struggling oat products off the shelves unless consumers show more interest, and the company is trying to stimulate consumer interest in all cereals through ads stressing convenience, nutrition, and nostalgia for childhood breakfasts. Kellogg's largest seller has remained Corn Flakes, but annual 7 percent price increases have pushed the price to twice the level of rival brands. So the company halted price increases to keep Corn Flakes competitive. As a result of all these decisions, Kellogg has increased sales of cereal to Americans 25 to 49 years old by 26 percent, its U.S. market share has risen to 39 percent, and Kellogg has begun the 1990s earning more than $500 million a year on annual sales surpassing $5 billion. International sales will surely remain a priority for Langbo as well; before assuming his current positions, he was president of Kellogg International, and he continues to be the executive responsible for international sales.

1. What types of problems does Langbo grapple with in managing Kellogg? What nonprogrammed decisions does Kellogg face in resolving those problems?
2. How has Langbo used his experience and expertise to reach decisions that advance organizational goals?
3. How might Langbo use the decision-making process to determine whether to pull slow-selling oat cereals from the shelves?
4. What quantitative tools would most appropriately support a decision about the proper price of a box of Corn Flakes?

CHAPTER OUTLINE

7

Organizational Goals and Planning

After studying this chapter, you will be able to

1. Explain the relationship and importance of organizational plans, goals, and missions within the planning process
2. Outline the levels of goals and discuss the hierarchy of goals
3. Highlight the characteristics of effective goals and describe the goal-setting process
4. Identify the three levels of planning and discuss the importance of coordinating multilevel planning
5. Distinguish among single-use plans, standing plans, and contingency plans, and describe when each is appropriate
6. Explain the process, benefits, and limitations of management by objectives
7. Discuss the two types of forecasts, and show how break-even analysis and project planning tools support the planning process

FACING A MANAGEMENT CHALLENGE AT

THE U.S. DEPARTMENT OF LABOR

Preparing Tomorrow's Work Force

One doesn't have to look far for gloomy news about education in the United States: SAT verbal scores in 1991 were at their lowest level in 20 years; SAT math scores, which had shown some signs of hope, dropped for the first time in 11 years; and the chairman of Ford says that today's high school graduates have lower math and reading skills than they did 50 years ago. Nor are negative reports of U.S. industrial competitiveness in short supply: Japanese automakers continue to gain U.S. market share, and other Japanese companies already dominate consumer electronics, semiconductors, photography, and other businesses; emerging Asian nations such as South Korea and Taiwan are building significant market presence; and numerous European countries continue to produce high-quality goods and services.

These two themes point up an issue that has been on a lot of minds lately: the decline in the skills that people need to succeed in today's complex work environment. One study estimates that 60 percent of people aged 21–25 don't have the reading and writing skills required for today's jobs, and a startling 90 percent lack the necessary math skills. U.S. businesses can't hope to compete in the international marketplace if the U.S. work force can't perform basic tasks.

Work skills are also a very personal issue for millions of Americans, particularly for the 40 percent of all high school graduates who move directly into the work force with no additional training or education. The high-paying manufacturing jobs that many of their parents rode to financial security are harder and harder to find. And all too frequently, young people fortunate enough to land these jobs don't have the skills required to be successful. Harold Poling, the Ford chairman who compared today's graduates with those from 50 years ago, emphasized the irony of the situation. Yesterday's students had the basic skills, but many jobs back then didn't require them. And now that most jobs do require basic skills in reading, writing, and arithmetic, graduates no longer have them. This situation is compounded by the fact that many jobs require not only the basics but also some level of advanced skills in computer applications, technical reading and writing, and a variety of interpersonal skills such as team relations.

Why is one of the world's wealthiest and most technologically advanced nations facing such a problem? Elizabeth Dole, a former secretary of the U.S. Department of Labor, said in 1990 that much of the problem lies with the educational goals of the U.S school system. When she headed the Department of Labor, Dole launched a study to identify the skills that U.S. schools should be imparting to today's—and tomorrow's—students. The Secretary's Commission on Achieving Necessary Skills, SCANS for short, was established in 1990, with the mandate to explore the workplace and highlight the skills that U.S. businesses require their employees to have if the companies are to succeed in the competitive global marketplace. The skill needs that the commission identified would then serve as educational goals for the country's schools.

What is the best way for Dole's successor, Lynn Martin, to approach this complex issue? Should Martin try to identify specific skills or should she concentrate on general skill areas? What steps should she take to ensure that educators and others involved in the school system support these educational goals and work to meet them?[1]

CHAPTER OVERVIEW

The efforts of Elizabeth Dole and Lynn Martin to define work-force skill goals started with a clear mission of pursuing educational excellence and then used a process of planning to set goals and to prepare a course of action that would focus local and national activities on those goals. This chapter examines organizational goals and planning, starting with the organizational mission and the connection with goals and with the overall planning process. Next is a review of organizational goals, including their purpose, the levels of goals, characteristics of effective goals, and goal commitment. Then organizational planning is explored in more detail, including the levels of planning, time frames, types of plans, responsibility, and ways to plan more effectively. The chapter closes with a look at the concept of management by objectives and an examination of various planning tools.

FUNDAMENTALS OF ORGANIZATIONAL PLANNING

Planning, the first of the four functions that make up the management process, is defined in Chapter 1 as the process of determining where the organization should be in the future and then selecting and implementing the most effective set of actions to achieve that future state. Because the other three management functions (organizing, leading, and controlling) all involve efforts to achieve the goals set in the planning process, planning is the most fundamental part of the management process.[2] Managers plan because they understand that the future results represented by their organizational goals can be achieved only by making decisions about current actions. Very simply, if no action is taken today, the organization cannot achieve its desired results tomorrow.[3]

For example, Taiwanese shipping magnate Chang Yung-fa planned for two years before launching his new airline, EVA Airways, in 1991. He wants to build EVA into a major Asian airline, an ambitious undertaking considering that he is competing directly with the world's most profitable air carriers, Cathay Pacific and Singapore Airlines, which together dominate the regional skies. Before the first airplane took off from Taipei, Chang had to secure landing rights at capitals throughout southeastern Asia, Australia, and Austria, and he had to hire qualified personnel. He also had to arrange financing and order 28 airplanes (a $3.6 billion investment). Ultimately, Chang wants EVA to fly to more European countries and to the United States. But to make that future a reality, he will have to concentrate on the goal and on the activities that will keep EVA flying high.[4]

goal A target or future state that an organization strives to achieve

A **goal** is the target or future state an organization wishes to achieve. Goals are important for four reasons. First, they define the organization and justify its existence by specifying the ends it hopes to achieve. Second, they are clear targets that motivate and guide managers and employees in their daily activities. For instance, the educational goals that Elizabeth Dole hoped to identify would be targets for teachers and school administrators. Third, goals direct organizational decision making, focusing attention on the desired future state and ways to reach that future state. And fourth, the desired outcome specified by organizational goals serves as a standard against which performance can be measured. Although definitions vary according to scope and timing, the word *goal* is commonly used interchangeably with the word *objective*.[5] For consistency, *goal* is used throughout this text.

plan The means of pursuing goals

To achieve the ends represented by organizational goals, managers prepare a **plan** to identify the means by which goals are pursued. A plan helps management bridge the gap from the current state to the future state. Managers must choose among many alternatives in their daily activities, so a plan is a way of anticipating the actions necessary to reach goals, allowing managers to make decisions in advance about the actions to be taken. At every level of the organization, plans are used to direct and to coordinate activities so that goals can be achieved both effectively and efficiently.[6]

When James Busby *(seated)* founded QMS, he used an informal process to develop his mission, goals, and plans for designing printer circuit boards. However, rapid growth outstripped Busby's informal process. He hired Charles Daley *(standing)*, who initiated the formal planning process that enabled QMS to develop this color printer for Japanese characters.

THE ORGANIZATIONAL PLANNING PROCESS

The planning process includes developing the organizational mission, setting goals, and devising plans (see Exhibit 7.1). Managers begin the planning process by creating, modifying, or reaffirming the mission, which is the topmost goal in the organization and which describes the organization's purpose. Next, managers use the mission to guide the development of organizational goals. Then they outline and implement the plans necessary to achieve those goals. This planning process is as important for organizations that operate in a relatively simple and stable organizational environment as it is for those that operate in a more complex and dynamic environment. By applying the planning process, managers are better able to cope with environmental changes, large or small, because the process forces them to focus on relevant results rather than considering daily activities in isolation.[7]

Although the planning process is concerned with predetermining courses of action that will achieve organizational goals, it is also closely linked with the management function of control. Managers use control methods and measures to trace progress toward achieving the goals they have set, and they use this feedback on performance to make any necessary changes. Further, they use control to ensure that their plans are properly implemented and to maintain consistency of activities and decisions at every organizational level.[8]

The Organizational Mission

The first step in the organizational planning process is to formulate or to review the organizational **mission,** the basic purpose for and driving force behind the organization's existence. The mission incorporates top management's *vision,* a vivid picture of where the organization should be in the future, what it should be, and whom it will serve. The mission communicates a compelling vision of the organization's long-term future state, helping managers inspire employees and enlist their enthusiastic support toward fulfilling the aspirations described in the vision. The mission is generally described in terms of the organization's philosophy, self-concept, public image, location, technology, concern for survival, customer targets, and products.[9]

mission The basic purpose for and driving force behind an organization's existence

Once the top managers (with the board of directors, if the organization has one) have established the mission or, in the case of existing organizations, revised the mission, they must communicate it to the rest of the organization. By sharing the mission, they provide employees with a sense of common understanding that helps unify the goals, the decisions, and the actions of everyone in the organization. As managers set goals, confront decisions, or outline courses

EXHIBIT 7.1

Mission, Goals, and Plans in the Organizational Planning Process

The organizational planning process starts with a mission that drives the development of goals and plans to achieve performance.

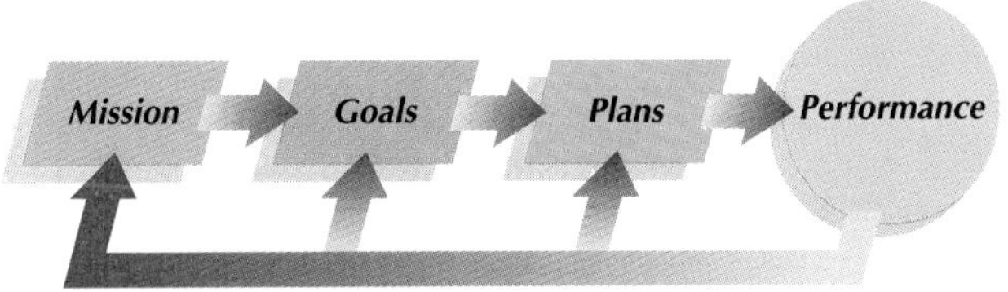

of action, they can look back to the mission to see whether their decisions are consistent with the organization's purpose. The mission also communicates the organization's direction, purpose, and vision to stakeholders outside the organization.

For example, the top managers of Tokyo-based Dai-Ichi Kangyo Bank (DKB), the world's largest bank, are concerned about the role that banks play in society. DKB's mission incorporates their vision of addressing customer needs, meeting international obligations, and providing for employees. The mission is to help raise the standard of living by providing the best possible service to the public, to play a positive role in the development of a wide spectrum of businesses by providing them with funding, and to contribute to the development of domestic and overseas economies. DKB also seeks to create a workplace where employees can enjoy fulfilling work and develop their individuality and ingenuity.[10]

However, no organizational mission is static. Even the most successful mission becomes obsolete sooner or later because of changes in the environment or because of changes in the needs or the influence of stakeholders. For this reason, top managers and boards of directors must go beyond asking "What is our purpose?" and anticipate longer-term environmental changes by asking "What will our purpose be?"[11] For example, the not-for-profit Atlanta Historical Society (AHS) was established in 1926 to cater to the interests of Civil War scholars. But by the 1980s, Atlanta had evolved into a major urban center, an environmental shift that prompted the AHS board and director John Ott to reexamine the stakeholder groups and the original mission. After considering current and expected changes in Atlanta, they decided to broaden the AHS mission beyond its scholarly focus on the Civil War. The AHS mission is now to present the entire story of Atlanta's history to a wider public audience, including schoolchildren and international visitors.[12]

mission statement A declaration of the organization's purpose and scope of operations

To effectively convey the organization's purpose and thrust, top managers develop a **mission statement,** a declaration of the organization's underlying purpose and unique scope of operations that distinguishes it from similar types of organizations. In recent years, a growing number of organizations have expanded their mission statements to include a statement of commitment to stakeholders (see Exhibit 7.2). Regardless of their length or complexity, mission statements help top management articulate what the organization stands for and where it should be going. In smaller, entrepreneurial organizations, the mission statement may be implicit in the decisions and actions of the founder. But many organizations, particularly large ones, prefer written mission statements that can guide managers throughout the planning process.[13]

EXHIBIT 7.2 The CSX Corporate Mission Statement

Top managers at CSX have developed this mission statement as a public expression of the organization's purpose. It guides managers as they set goals and prepare plans that will help fulfill the mission. It also communicates CSX's commitment to the firm's three major stakeholders: customers, employees, and shareholders.

CSX is a transportation company committed to being a leader in railroad, inland water, and containerized distribution markets. To attract the human and financial resources necessary to achieve this leadership position, CSX will support our three major constituencies:

- **For our customers, we will work as a partner to provide excellent service by meeting all agreed-upon commitments.**
- **For our employees, we will create a work environment that motivates and allows them to grow and develop and perform their jobs to the maximum of their ability.**
- **For our shareholders, we will meet our goals to provide them with sustainable, superior returns.**

Organizational Goals

Once the top managers have determined the basic purpose of the organization, the next step in the planning process is to establish goals, which will direct organizational resources and efforts toward fulfilling the mission. Goals specify exactly where the organization wants to go and what must be achieved, thus allowing managers to develop the plans that will translate the mission into reality.[14] Although top managers and the board of directors are responsible for establishing the mission as the topmost goal, goals are also set and used by lower-level managers to guide the planning process throughout the organization.

Levels of Goals

Goals are needed at three specific levels in the organization: the strategic, the tactical, and the operational levels. At each level, the goals focus attention on responsibilities and activities that move the organization toward the desired state described by the mission statement.

Strategic Goals **Strategic goals** are set by top management and are broadly defined targets for the organization's overall results. Also known as *official goals* or *corporate-level goals,* strategic goals are formal statements of the organization's major intended achievements. Management expert Peter Drucker recommends that businesses develop strategic goals in eight key areas that affect performance and survival: marketing, innovation, human resources, financial resources, physical resources, productivity, social responsibility, and profitability (see Exhibit 7.3). For example, Canadian National, the Montreal-based rail freight company owned by the Canadian government, has set a clear mission and multiple strategic goals. CN's mission is to meet customers' transportation and distribution needs by being the best at moving goods on time, safely, and damage-free. To support this mission, its strategic goals are to understand and meet customer needs; to be first in service, quality, and safety; to be environmentally responsible; to be cost-competitive and financially sound; and to create a challenging and fulfilling place to work.[15]

strategic goals Broadly defined targets for the organization's overall future results

tactical goals Targets to be achieved by the divisions or units of the organization

Tactical Goals **Tactical goals** are set by top and middle managers and are targets for future results to be achieved by specific divisions or functional units

EXHIBIT 7.3

Strategic Goals for Businesses

To be effective, businesses should set strategic goals in these eight key areas.

Marketing Goals
- Market share
- Customer service
- Product and market development

Innovation Goals
- Innovation in goods and services
- Innovation in organizational skills and activities

Human Resources Goals
- Management development and performance
- Employee skills and attitudes

Financial Resources Goals
- Development of sources of funding
- Efficient use of financial resources

Physical Resources Goals
- Development of sources of supply
- Efficient use of physical resources

Productivity Goals
- Efficient use of resources to yield results

Social Responsibility Goals
- Responsibility for impact on community and society

Profit Requirement Goals
- Profitability to support the pursuit of all goals
- Profitability to support organizational survival and growth

of the organization. These goals, also known as *business-level goals* when they pertain to individual business divisions, define what each unit must accomplish to support the strategic goals of the organization. At Canadian National, tactical goals are set for the individual business divisions. The railway business has two tactical goals: first, to pursue productivity gains through cost control and technological advancement, and second, to increase revenue through aggressive marketing efforts that differentiate the product, increase market share, and provide appropriate profitability. CN's nontransportation division handles energy exploration, construction, and contracting and strives to meet its tactical goal of maximizing the value and earning potential of its assets so it can contribute to the organization's financial performance.[16]

operational goals Targets to be achieved by departments and individuals

Operational Goals **Operational goals** are set by middle managers and first-line managers as specific targets for results to be achieved by departments and individuals within the functional units or the business divisions. These goals, also called *functional-level goals* when applied to functional units, generally cover particular short-term results needed to support the organization's tactical and strategic goals. Canadian National's recent operational goals included (1) purchasing 30 new fuel-efficient locomotives to increase equipment productivity and deliver higher-quality transportation service, (2) developing and testing more sophisticated railway-control equipment to enhance safety and customer service, and (3) eliminating redundant facilities by selling certain track systems.[17]

MANAGEMENT AROUND THE WORLD

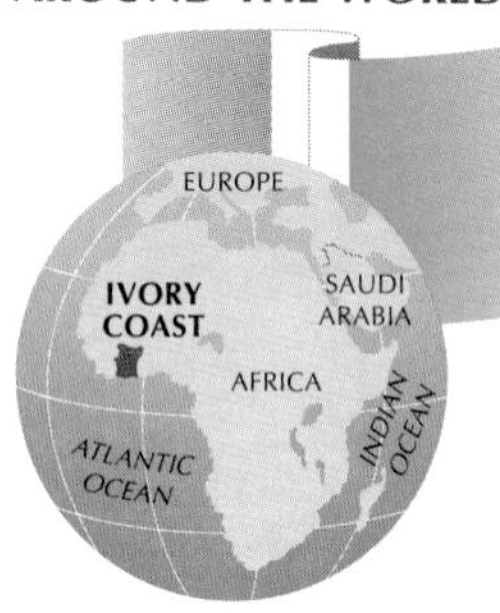

Developing countries frequently set strategic goals for higher domestic production in order to boost economic growth. The Ivory Coast has successfully increased per capita income by encouraging agricultural production. Thanks to its agricultural goals, the Ivory Coast is now the world's largest cocoa exporter, Africa's largest coffee exporter, and the continent's third-largest cotton producer. To achieve another goal, reducing food imports, the country has also set ambitious production targets for both rice and corn.

Hierarchy of Goals

In any organization, the wide range of goals form a *hierarchy of goals* in which the goals on a higher level form the basis of the goals on the next lower level (see Exhibit 7.4). In effect, the goals of the lower level become the means by which the goals of the level above are attained. For example, the *ends* of the strategic goals have as their *means* the tactical goals set for the next lower level; the strategic goals cannot be attained if the tactical goals are not achieved. In Exhibit 7.4, the strategic goal of increasing net income by 15 percent per year cannot be met if the tactical goals of opening 150 hotels over 2 years, increasing revenue by 20 percent over 3 years, and earning a 6 percent yield on investments are not achieved. Known as the *means-ends chain,* this link between levels must be carefully coordinated because of the cascading relationship between the successive levels.[18]

Characteristics of Effective Goals

To be effective in guiding the decisions and actions of organizational members, goals must be more than abstract statements of future results. Managers should be sure that the goals they set are challenging, attainable, specific and measurable, time-defined, and relevant.

Challenging Goals Goals that present an interesting and demanding challenge motivate managers to achieve results while developing and improving their own managerial skills. For example, Darla Mendales is vice president of corporate quality management for Fidelity Investments in Boston, and she is responsible for setting standards for quality service delivery. When she was named to this position, customer problems were being resolved in an average of 11 days. Mendales set a goal of solving problems in one day or less within three years. Al-

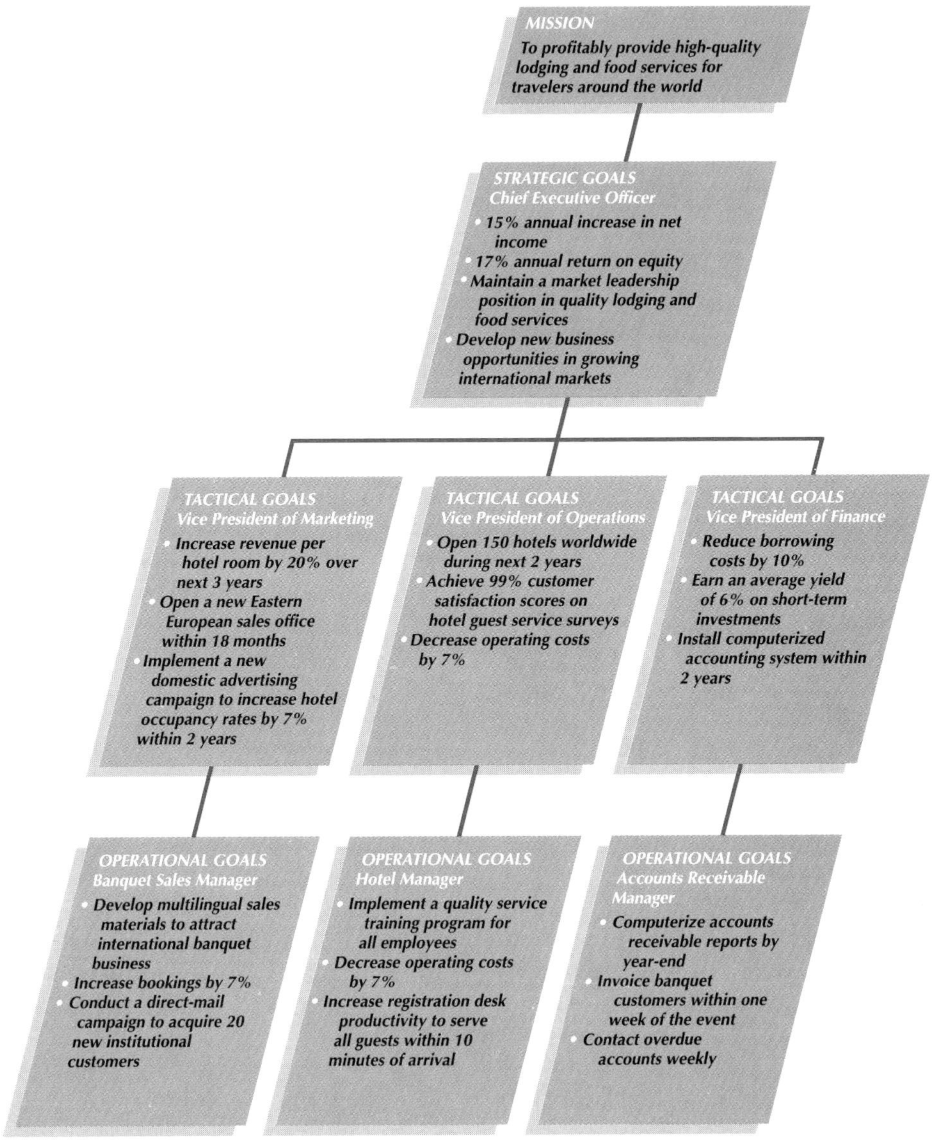

MISSION
To profitably provide high-quality lodging and food services for travelers around the world

STRATEGIC GOALS
Chief Executive Officer
- 15% annual increase in net income
- 17% annual return on equity
- Maintain a market leadership position in quality lodging and food services
- Develop new business opportunities in growing international markets

TACTICAL GOALS
Vice President of Marketing
- Increase revenue per hotel room by 20% over next 3 years
- Open a new Eastern European sales office within 18 months
- Implement a new domestic advertising campaign to increase hotel occupancy rates by 7% within 2 years

TACTICAL GOALS
Vice President of Operations
- Open 150 hotels worldwide during next 2 years
- Achieve 99% customer satisfaction scores on hotel guest service surveys
- Decrease operating costs by 7%

TACTICAL GOALS
Vice President of Finance
- Reduce borrowing costs by 10%
- Earn an average yield of 6% on short-term investments
- Install computerized accounting system within 2 years

OPERATIONAL GOALS
Banquet Sales Manager
- Develop multilingual sales materials to attract international banquet business
- Increase bookings by 7%
- Conduct a direct-mail campaign to acquire 20 new institutional customers

OPERATIONAL GOALS
Hotel Manager
- Implement a quality service training program for all employees
- Decrease operating costs by 7%
- Increase registration desk productivity to serve all guests within 10 minutes of arrival

OPERATIONAL GOALS
Accounts Receivable Manager
- Computerize accounts receivable reports by year-end
- Invoice banquet customers within one week of the event
- Contact overdue accounts weekly

EXHIBIT 7.4

Hierarchy of Goals for a Hotel Chain

The hierarchy of goals for this hypothetical hotel chain is driven by the organizational mission and covers the strategic goals, the tactical goals, and the operational goals. As shown, goals for the lower levels become the means for achieving the goals of the higher levels.

though the goal was ambitious, before the second year Fidelity managers and employees were able to resolve 70 percent of customer complaints in a day and shorten the average turnaround to three days.[19]

Attainable Goals Although goals should be challenging, they should also be realistic and attainable with the resources available. If goals are too difficult or are set without regard to environmental constraints or managerial capabilities, managers and employees can become frustrated and discouraged, leading to lower or inappropriate performance. Consider the strategic goals set by Lawrence J. Ellison, founder of Oracle Systems, a computer software maker in Redwood City, California. In 1988, when Oracle was booking $280 million in annual sales, Ellison established a goal of $5 billion in sales by 1993 and growth of 50 percent annually. In pursuit of these goals, the sales department buckled

H. Wayne Huizenga, CEO of Blockbuster Entertainment, has built an empire of more than 2,000 video rental stores using an integrated hierarchy of goals. Operational goals include opening, on average, a new store every day; tactical goals include boosting rental revenue at all stores; and strategic goals include expanding sales and profits worldwide.

down, selling $971 million in 1990. However, nearly half of these sales were only on paper: salespeople were taking orders on products not yet released so that they could meet their goals. Because customers would not pay until they had received the product, sometimes a year after the sale was recorded, Oracle suffered a severe cash flow problem. Ellison had to revise his goals to a more realistic 25 percent annual growth rate—and he also tightened up the sales process.[20]

Specific and Measurable Goals Goals must be specific and measurable so that managers understand exactly what is expected and exactly how progress will be evaluated. Whereas many goals are quantitative and can be expressed and measured numerically, others are qualitative and require subjective judgment regarding performance. For example, E.P.S. Logistics Management, one of the United Kingdom's largest packing businesses, has both quantitative and qualitative goals. The quantitative goal is to increase net income by £500,000 within three years without an increase in costs. The qualitative goal is to establish, within three years, a basis of sustainable future growth in its logistics management service. One way managing director John Hillidge will assess performance is by periodically reviewing the customer base to be sure that the types of customers being served can fuel the firm's long-term growth.[21]

Time-Defined Goals So that progress can be measured, goals must include an explicit definition of when results are to be achieved. This helps focus and coordinate organizational activities during the appropriate period and provides a deadline for performance. For instance, Haruo Yamaguchi, president of Nippon Telegraph and Telephone, is committed to developing a new integrated communications network that will bring voice, picture, and data transmission services into Japanese businesses and homes via one supercharged telephone outlet. To accomplish this goal, he set a series of tactical goals with specific time requirements. By 1988 the service had to be installed and available to NTT subscribers in Tokyo, Osaka, and Nagoya; by 1989 all major Japanese cities had to be wired; and by 1995 subscribers would number 1 million and produce $2 billion in annual revenues.[22]

Relevant Goals If managers are to make a meaningful contribution to organizational performance, their goals must be directly relevant to the mission and to higher-level goals, and they should be appropriate to the manager's scope of responsibility and skills. Consider the goals set by the management of the Alaska Air Group, an airline based in Seattle. One strategic goal is to achieve profitable growth, and one tactical goal is to deliver consistently higher-quality customer service every year. The tactical goal is directly related to the strategic goal, because satisfied customers are loyal customers who will choose Alaska Air rather than competitors.[23]

American National Can produces over 1 billion beverage cans each year at this manufacturing facility in Chicago, Illinois. Plant managers set specific production goals for particular periods and then (1) measure their progress toward those goals and (2) review the impact on plant performance.

Goal Setting and Commitment

Goal setting involves establishing, coordinating, and prioritizing goals for work groups, managers, and employees throughout the organization. Although top managers establish the mission and the strategic goals, lower-level goals can be assigned or, more often, are developed jointly by the managers who must achieve those goals and the level of management above them. Thus top managers and middle managers work together to set tactical goals, and middle managers and first-line managers work together to set operational goals. In this way, lower-level managers can propose goals that are realistic and consistent with their work unit's capabilities and with the manager's own personal skills and abilities. The supervising managers review and approve these goals, ensuring that they directly support the organization's higher-level goals.[24]

This process of goal setting and approval helps managers maintain consistency and coordination among goals throughout the organization so that goal conflicts do not occur. When balancing multiple goals, managers cannot focus on one to the exclusion of others that are important to the organization's long-term performance. Therefore, when managers set and review goals, they also consider how the goals will affect long-term and short-term results and then balance the goals accordingly.[25]

For goals to have the optimal effect on organizational performance, managers must gain the commitment of the people who will work to achieve them. In many cases, this can be accomplished by invoking managerial authority and assigning employees the task of achieving a particular goal. Research shows that when managers support their employees and when employees trust their managers, the individuals in a work group are more likely to be committed to achieving the assigned goals. Also, the influence of peer and group pressure can help forge commitment, especially when members of the work group set an example by making a commitment to goals. And individuals tend to show more commitment when they are offered incentives and promised rewards for performance.[26]

When individuals believe that they can successfully achieve their goals, they feel a stronger commitment than when they think the goals are too difficult to be attained. In addition, when people understand their goals and how to perform the tasks involved in achieving the goals, they are more likely to be motivated to work toward the goals. Finally, commitment may be strengthened when employees participate in the goal-setting process, helping establish the goals that they then must achieve; see Chapter 14 for more detail on employee motivation.[27]

Organizational Planning

With the mission and the goals in place, the next step in the planning process is to prepare plans to achieve the desired results. Because a variety of paths can lead to any goal, planning helps focus organizational decisions and actions on the path that management has selected as the most effective and efficient means of achieving the desired ends. Regardless of the number or types of goals, planning is a managerial activity that takes place throughout the organization.

Levels of Planning

Just as goals are developed on three organizational levels, so plans are developed on three levels: strategic, tactical, and operational. This multilevel planning allows managers at each level to consider the actions necessary to achieve their goals so that the mission can be fulfilled.

Strategic Plans **Strategic plans** are the means used to achieve strategic goals. Developed by top managers, strategic plans generally cover resource allocations and define a broad scope of longer-term organizational actions designed to attain strategic goals. Because of this wide scope, strategic plans usually have a significant impact on the organization. For example, Snap-on Tools, a manufac-

strategic plans The means of pursuing strategic goals

turer and distributor of tools for professional mechanics and technicians, wants to grow globally. To achieve this growth, top managers designed a strategic plan that expands the company's sales beyond the automotive market to the broader market of other industrial tool and equipment users. The strategic plan includes long-term investments in warehouse and manufacturing facilities to serve the new markets.[28]

tactical plans The means of pursuing tactical goals

Tactical Plans **Tactical plans** outline the means for achieving the organization's tactical goals. Typically, top and middle managers work together to create tactical plans, which cover shorter periods than strategic plans and which directly support the implementation of strategic plans. Tactical plans consist of specific actions to be taken by business divisions or individual groups and are therefore narrower in scope than strategic plans. One tactical goal of Snap-on Tools is to be the most reliable tool supplier to its newly designated industrial markets. To this end, Snap-on's tactical plan for the sales department includes installing a new computer system that allows representatives to locate any product in the company's inventory in any U.S. location and ship it directly to the customer.[29]

operational plans The means of pursuing operational goals

Operational Plans **Operational plans** describe the means for achieving the organization's operational goals. Such plans support the implementation of tactical plans, and they specifically define necessary decisions and actions to be taken by divisions or functional departments. Operational plans cover briefer periods than tactical plans, and they include the day-to-day operations of the organization. Snap-on develops operational plans to achieve operational goals of creating tools needed by the new industrial customer groups. For example, the center for manufacturing special tools used an operational plan to guide the design and production of a unique 5.5-foot stainless steel wrench for aluminum smelter employees.[30]

The U.S. Bureau of the Census counts the entire U.S. population once every decade. In addition to long-range planning for the next census (in 2000), managers conduct intermediate- and short-range planning to achieve tactical and operational goals (such as the operational goal of entering all census data into the bureau's computers for analysis and reporting).

Planning Time Frames

Organizational planning covers a variety of time frames. *Long-range planning* encompasses strategic goals and plans that may extend more than 5 years into the future, although the exact time horizon varies from organization to organization. When Elizabeth Dole and the Department of Labor wanted to identify future work-force skills, for instance, they had to look many years into the future to ascertain the skills that tomorrow's graduates will need. In dynamic, complex environments, managers may not be able to plan for a period as long as 5 years, so their strategic plans may cover shorter periods. In simpler, more stable environments, a strategic planning time horizon of 10 or even 20 years is possible. Managers at Xerox used long-range planning to create an entirely new product line that would support the company's strategic goal of becoming the world's premier document-processing firm. For 10 years, they planned the development and marketing of the DocuTech, a digital imaging machine that allows users to create documents on their desktop computers and then reproduce high-speed, high-quality copies.[31]

Intermediate-range planning generally covers time spans from 1 to 5 years and involves tactical goals and planning. Again, the exact time frame depends on the circumstances of each organization. To cover operational goals and plans and to manage activities that span periods of 1 year or less, organizations use *short-range planning*. For British Petroleum, both intermediate-range and short-range planning are vital to reaching the company's profitability goals. BP uses intermediate-range planning to guide its energy exploration and development efforts in Papua New Guinea, in the North Sea, and in other regions. Plans cover the period from drilling to full production and can cover as many as 4 years. Short-range planning helps BP manage the daily operation of its global network of gas stations.[32]

One of the major challenges facing managers today is the pressure to achieve immediate results while ensuring the long-term viability of the organization. In particular, business managers are concerned about the quarterly earnings and stock price expectations of shareholders even as the organization develops plans for a future that is 5, 10, or 20 years away. Not-for-profit and governmental managers bear similar burdens, especially when they have limited or reduced funding to service their constituents' needs. Despite the clamor for immediate results, managers must balance their time frames to avoid shortchanging activities that support long-term organizational health and growth.[33]

Types of Plans

Managers match the type of plan they use to the situation they face. Generally, plans are needed to handle three types of situations: one-time situations not likely to recur, situations that recur regularly, and situations less likely to occur. The types of plans managers use in these situations are single-use plans, standing plans, and contingency plans.

Single-Use Plans A **single-use plan** is specifically prepared to fit a one-time situation. Because the situation does not recur, a single-use plan becomes obsolete when its one-time goals have been achieved. Two common types of single-use plans are programs and projects.[34]

single-use plan A plan designed to fit a one-time situation

A **program** is a complex set of interrelated actions aimed at achieving a major goal that will be pursued only once. To develop a program, managers (1) divide the course of action into steps, (2) determine the logical sequence of steps, (3) decide who will be responsible for each step, (4) establish and provide the resources necessary to complete each step, (5) gauge the time needed to finish each step, and (6) prepare a schedule for implementation. When the Mud Creek Clinic in Grethel, Kentucky, burned down, founder Eula Hall put together a program with a single, one-time aim: to build a new clinic for this rural coal-mining community. Her program consisted of several steps, including finding a temporary site to house the clinic until a permanent site could be built, raising money from government and private sources, contracting for construction, and moving into the new facility. The not-for-profit clinic now serves 8,000 patients annually.[35]

program A complex single-use plan consisting of a set of interrelated actions aimed at achieving a one-time major goal

A **project** is a less complex single-use plan that is narrower in scope than a program and aimed at achieving a specific one-time goal. Projects integrate fewer activities and resources than programs and are often developed as subunits of programs. For example, Eula Hall's program for a new clinic included a fundraising project that solicited donations and grants from a variety of sources. One step in the project was an application to the Appalachian Regional Commission requesting federal development money to support the clinic. The commission agreed to supply \$320,000 if Hall raised \$80,000, so the next step in the project was to hold quilt raffles, radiothons, and other events to attract individual donations. Hall exceeded her goal by \$40,000, raising \$120,000, and she received the federal funding that enabled construction to start.[36]

project A single-use plan that is narrower in scope than a program and that is aimed at achieving a specific one-time goal

Habitat for Humanity, a not-for-profit group that builds decent housing for needy families, uses both single-use plans and standing plans to reach its goals. Volunteers building this house in Lexington, Kentucky, followed a single-use plan for construction. The organization's standing plans guided the selection of the housing site, the materials, and the family who will own the house.

Standing Plans Many organizations pursue ongoing goals that require managers to address the same type of situation over and over. When a situation recurs repeatedly, managers use a **standing plan** to guide management decisions and activities. Three commonly used types of standing plans are policies, procedures, and rules.[37]

standing plan A plan for guiding management decisions and activities in situations that recur repeatedly

policy A standing plan that provides broad guidelines for directing managerial activities in pursuit of organizational goals

A **policy** provides managers with general guidelines for action to achieve organizational goals. Policies define broad boundaries for managerial actions in recurring situations so that managers have some flexibility in responding to each situation. For example, chairman Robert E. Allen has established a policy of allowing AT&T business managers the freedom to buy technology from outside firms when this approach makes sense. Rather than relying exclusively on internally developed technology, AT&T managers can now buy externally developed technology when the purchase will help achieve AT&T goals. This policy enabled AT&T managers to buy software from an outside supplier so they could quickly launch the VideoPhone 2500, a home telephone with a tiny video screen (even though internal researchers have been investigating similar technology for 30 years).[38]

procedure A standing plan encompassing a series of detailed steps to be followed in particular recurring situations

A **procedure** outlines specific steps to be followed in particular recurring situations. Compared with the use of policies, procedures are more detailed and allow less leeway in responding to individual situations. Many organizations rely on *standard operating procedures,* or *SOPs,* to guide managers and employees through situations that recur repeatedly. For instance, fashion retailer Merry-Go-Round of Joppa, Maryland, handles hundreds of apparel and accessory products and relies on an SOP to determine when merchandise should be marked down. If an item sells more slowly than expected within a given period, managers must slash the price to speed sales and make way for new merchandise.[39]

rule A standing plan specifying the circumstances in which certain activities can or cannot be performed

A **rule** details the specific circumstances under which certain activities are to be performed. The narrowest type of standing plan, rules relate to one specific action that can or cannot be performed, whereas procedures relate to a series of steps undertaken in particular situations. Because rules are so precise, they substitute for managerial decision making in repetitive situations and therefore allow managers little flexibility. When Malgorzata Daniszewska became president and part-owner of *Firma,* a Polish business magazine, only one or two ads were being sold per issue. Daniszewska needed to build profits, but she also believed that readers would feel cheated if they saw too many ads. To avoid losing readers, Daniszewska established a rule that no more than 25 percent of one issue's pages can be advertising.[40]

Contingency Plans Rarely do situations unfold exactly as managers have planned. At times, unexpected environmental shifts such as economic recession or severe weather conditions can cause serious problems that require managerial response if goals are to be achieved. Therefore, managers also develop **contingency plans,** alternative courses of action to be followed in the event of influential environmental shifts that were not considered in the original plan. Whereas most managerial planning deals with situations considered likely to occur, contingency planning covers less-likely events. For example, the Los Angeles Department of Water and Power (LADWP) has contingency plans for dealing with emergencies that interrupt power transmission to the utility's customers. The plans detail assigned responsibilities, emergency equipment to be used, safety procedures, supplier contacts, and procedures for communicating with all personnel. When a major storm ripped through the Owens Valley region of California in 1988 and damaged 24 transmission towers, LADWP implemented its contingency plans and quickly restored full service.[41]

contingency plans Alternative courses of action to be followed if unforeseen environmental shifts occur

PLANNING AND MANAGEMENT

Planning begins at the top when senior managers (often in conjunction with the board of directors) develop the organizational mission. But responsibility for other planning activities is not confined to upper management. Moreover, managers at every level must be aware of barriers to effective planning so that they can overcome these potential threats.

Responsibility for Planning

In some organizations, particularly large ones, planning may be the responsibility of one or more planning specialists on staff, or it may be conducted by a planning task force. In smaller organizations and in a growing number of large organizations, individual managers are responsible for specific aspects of planning.

The Role of the Planning Specialist

Top managers sometimes rely on *planning specialists,* groups of professionals on staff who help develop organizational plans. Planning specialists generally report directly to the president or the CEO. They plan for the entire organization and supervise the planning for divisions or departments. In some organizations, each division has its own specialists to plan only for that unit. Wherever the specialists report, they are responsible for monitoring environmental shifts, examining internal capabilities, suggesting changes or new directions for goals and plans, and coordinating plans to avoid conflict or overlap.[42]

For example, the Royal Dutch/Shell Group has a central group of planning specialists responsible for examining environmental changes and for helping

MANAGERIAL DECISION MAKING

How to Plan for the Worst

Can managers plan for a crisis? Seemingly a contradiction in terms, crisis planning allows managers to lay out, in advance, the steps they will take to cope with a crisis situation. Crisis planning is a form of contingency planning because managers consider how to deal with future situations that would be clearly out of the ordinary yet within the realm of possibility (no matter how remote). What makes crisis planning so important—and so effective—is its role in removing the element of surprise that often paralyzes managers in the grip of a sudden, unexpected disaster. Instead of panicking when a crisis looms or trying to deny the gravity of the problem, managers can look to the crisis plan for guidance on defusing the threat. Companies such as Campbell Soup, Niagara Mohawk Power, Johnson & Johnson, H.J. Heinz, United Airlines, and Dow Chemical already practice crisis planning, and in the complex, ever-changing business environment of the 1990s, more will surely follow.

Consider how Campbell Soup handled a 1987 crisis precipitated by a caller claiming to have poisoned several cans of tomato juice in a New England supermarket chain. When managers at corporate headquarters learned about the situation, they immediately assembled their newly formed crisis planning and management team. The team quickly decided on a regional recall of the product, received top management approval, and dispatched Campbell employees to pull tomato juice cans from every store in the chain. In less than six hours, they had yanked two truckloads of cans from 84 supermarkets. Fortunately, the crisis turned out to be a hoax, but Campbell managers were able to respond quickly and appropriately because of their crisis planning.

The Campbell experience highlights some of the decisions managers face when preparing a plan for handling crises. One decision that managers must make is to select who will be involved in managing the actions taken during a crisis. Dow Chemical and United Airlines, among others, have designated corporate SWAT teams to take charge of catastrophes; other firms simply identify key managers who should be notified in the event of specific emergencies. These managers are often drawn from diverse parts of the organi-

company managers to incorporate these changes into the planning process. The planning specialists develop detailed scenarios of the external environment 10 years in the future, enabling Shell managers to plan for the wide variety of potential problems and opportunities shown in the scenarios. Because they had planned for a similar situation, Shell managers were ready with alternative sources when the 1991 Persian Gulf War interrupted the flow of oil from Kuwait and Iraq.[43]

The Role of the Planning Task Force

Another approach to planning is to use a *planning task force,* a temporary group of managers, drawn from various areas of the organization, who are responsible for developing a plan. The task force includes managers whose units will be affected, so the plan can be geared specifically to their needs and resources. Moreover, participants are able to coordinate the activities of their own units with those of other work groups, so implementation is smoother. And by participating in the planning process, these managers develop a commitment to the goals, to the plan, and to its implementation.

The Role of the Individual Manager

Although planning specialists and planning task forces play valuable roles in developing organizational plans, the individual manager remains the key to effective planning. Every manager faces decisions about actions that contribute to the organization's ability to achieve its goals. To guide these decisions and activities, managers use the organizational mission and higher-level goals to set divisional or departmental goals and to make plans that pertain to their particular zation and are selected because of their specific skills. Organizations generally need to communicate with the public during a crisis, so a second decision is the choice of spokesperson, which is especially critical. In some cases, the CEO personally meets the media to reassure people about the company's commitment to investigating and solving the problem.

A third decision involves determining exactly which calamities might be likely to touch off a crisis. Says George C. Greer, vice president and coordinator of the crisis management program at H.J. Heinz, "We try to say, 'What would we do if the president of the company were kidnapped, if a plant burned down, if somebody alleged tampering with a product?'" Once managers have identified the range of potential threats and considered the influence that each might have on the company, they can decide which should be the focus of the crisis planning process.

Next, managers must decide on a course of action for dealing with the potential crises they have identified. The contingency plan should give managers the kind of guidance they need to react quickly and efficiently yet allow them the flexibility to respond to the unseen events of an actual emergency. Managers at H.J. Heinz decided to develop plans keyed to specific types of crises and then stage mock disasters to test their ability to respond. This crisis planning paid off when managers suspected product tampering at a Heinz food-processing plant in Australia only one day after staging a simulated incident on the site. Following the contingency plan they had tested, managers notified corporate headquarters and local authorities, then launched an investigation. Although this proved to be a false alarm, managers breathed easier because the plan had enabled them to react quickly and confidently to what could have been a disastrous situation. And that, after all, is what crisis planning is all about.

Apply Your Knowledge

1. What kinds of goals might the H.J. Heinz crisis management team set for the plans they develop to deal with crises?
2. How might Campbell involve planning specialists, planning task forces, and individual managers in the crisis planning process?

work group and their own managerial responsibilities. As part of the planning process, individual managers generally prepare financial plans or budgets that reflect their need for and use of funding (see Chapter 19). Individual managers are also valuable sources of information about environmental conditions that can affect the organization's overall goals, plans, and implementation. In many cases, lower-level managers formulate and execute the single-use, standing, and contingency plans that actually accomplish organizational goals. With the guidance and support of top managers, individual managers can make a big difference in their organization's performance.[44]

More Effective Planning

Several barriers can potentially threaten the effectiveness of the planning process as a means to achieving organizational goals. By understanding the impact such barriers may have on the planning process, managers can plan more effectively. One barrier is a rapidly changing, complex environment that can render part or all of a plan inoperable in a short time. In such situations, managers may feel that planning is useless. To overcome this barrier, managers should prepare contingency plans that address a wide range of possible situations. Just as important, they should review their plans frequently and maintain flexibility to adapt to the environment.[45]

Another barrier may go up when planning specialists dominate the planning process and downplay the needs and concerns of the managers who must implement the plans. In the extreme, this can lead to unrealistic or inappropriate plans that are not suitable for implementation. This barrier can be overcome by relying on specialists to support the planning process rather than to develop the plans that others actually execute. Planning specialists have the expertise to aid managers who are ultimately responsible for performance, and they can create a planning process that reflects organizational realities.

For example, Tougaloo College in Tougaloo, Mississippi, is a small, private college with a tradition of educating African-Americans. The college needed a more structured planning process to ensure that financial and educational goals were met. Adib A. Shakir, Tougaloo's president, called in a consultant to establish a systematic planning process. Although the consultant outlined the process, faculty members, department heads, and administrators actually participated in planning and then evaluating performance. With the president's commitment and involvement, the participants continued to contribute their ideas, carry out their plans, and evaluate performance long after the consultant had left.[46]

As more organizations try to blend the expertise of planning specialists with the hands-on knowledge of managers who implement the plans, individual managers may face the barrier of planning inexperience. Managers who have never been directly responsible for monitoring their environment or applying planning tools and systems may require training and the support of the planning specialists. Probably the single most influential element in overcoming any planning barrier is the degree of commitment of top managers. When the CEO and other top managers demonstrate their support by personally participating and by creating the expectation of effective planning, they send a powerful signal about the value they place on planning.[47]

MANAGEMENT BY OBJECTIVES

management by objectives (MBO) A collaborative process in which managers and employees set mutually agreeable goals, define the responsibility for results, and determine the means of evaluating individual and group performance

Once they have defined their goals and plans, managers use these to direct the activities of the entire organization. One method often used to link goals and plans with everyday actions is **management by objectives (MBO)**, the process by which managers and employees jointly define their goals, the responsibility for achieving these goals, and the means of evaluating individual and group performance. Popularized by management expert Peter F. Drucker, MBO provides a systematic method of setting goals for work units and for individuals so that all their activities are directly linked to achieving organizational goals.[48]

A wide variety of for-profit organizations have adopted the MBO process, including General Electric and General Motors, two early adherents. In the public sector, schools, universities, and government agencies have also applied MBO. The Holt public school system in Michigan, the Canadian Post Office, and many other nonbusiness organizations have implemented the MBO process. For example, Planned Parenthood Federation of America uses MBO to connect management and employee activities with the attainment of organizational goals and with continued professional development. Each year, Planned Parenthood employees establish goals that are assigned a percentage weight to determine their relative importance. Supervisors measure progress against each goal and award salary increases based on how employees have performed.[49]

The MBO Process

The MBO process consists of a cycle of four steps: setting goals, planning action, implementing plans, and reviewing performance (see Exhibit 7.5). Because

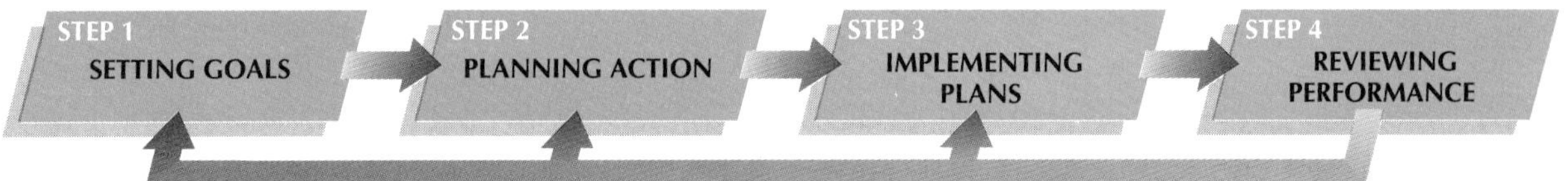

EXHIBIT 7.5 The Management by Objectives Process

The MBO process is an ongoing cycle of four steps: setting goals, planning action, implementing plans, and reviewing performance.

MBO links individual actions to the achievement of organizational goals, the specific goals, plans, implementation, and reviews differ from individual to individual and from level to level.

- *Setting goals.* In the first step, top managers formulate the overall organizational goals and plans and then work with middle managers to develop goals for the organizational divisions or units they manage. In turn, middle managers work with first-line managers to set goals for their departments or groups. During this process, managers and employees at all levels, in collaboration with their supervisors, also set individual goals for performance. Because managers establish mutually agreeable group and individual goals, this step strengthens organizational teamwork and commitment, and it keeps the focus on achieving the organization's overall goals. Like the goal-setting process described earlier in the chapter, these MBO goals should be as specific as possible so that performance can be evaluated according to appropriate standards. Because organizational members participate in the goal-setting process, they understand the results expected and how performance will be measured.[50]
- *Planning action.* In the second step, managers determine exactly how their individual and group goals will be accomplished. During action planning, managers decide on the "who, what, when, where, and how" details needed to achieve each objective. Managers also prepare a schedule for the action plan to ensure that goals are reached on time, and this schedule is reviewed when individual performance is being evaluated.[51]
- *Implementing plans.* Once managers have made a commitment to achieve specific goals and have received approval for their plans, the third step is implementation. To control their own performance, managers must be allowed to implement their plans in their own way. This element of self-control allows managers to channel their expertise for the benefit of the organization while allowing them to develop their professional skills more fully as they tackle the challenges of implementation. Of course, managers need information about their progress so that they can adjust their plans and stay on track toward the goals they are committed to achieve.[52]
- *Reviewing performance.* In the last step of the MBO process, managers periodically review the performance of the people they supervise and evaluate how well the plans are working in achieving group and individual goals. During reviews, managers and their personnel identify any obstacles to performance. They discuss how these obstacles can be overcome, and they discuss any corrective action necessary to put the plan back on track. Depending on environmental changes, MBO goals may be modified or new goals set during this step. In appraising performance, managers assess progress to-

ward goals, and when necessary they explore why expected results have not been achieved, so that their people can make changes to improve performance. Generally, managers appraise MBO performance on a yearly cycle that is tied to recognizing and rewarding achievement.[53]

Benefits and Limitations of MBO Programs

Although many organizations have instituted MBO programs, not every organization has found that MBO improves individual performance. Like any management tool, the MBO concept has benefits and limitations that must be considered before implementation.[54]

- *Benefits.* One major benefit of the MBO process is its ability to focus management and employee attention on specific activities that directly influence performance and goal attainment. Also, MBO ties the goals of each manager to the goals of managers on levels above and below, acting as a coordinating system and facilitating teamwork throughout the organization. Thanks to these links and to the periodic reviews, managers communicate more clearly and more frequently about goals, plans, and results. Further, the MBO process fosters participation, which can encourage stronger commitment and motivation. MBO also encourages managers to exercise self-control in implementing their action plans, which can help develop personal and professional skills. Finally, MBO provides an unbiased and systematic way to measure the contribution of managers and employees.[55]
- *Limitations.* Although the MBO process offers many benefits, it also has a number of limitations. Without consistent involvement and commitment from top management, an MBO program can prove ineffective. Another limitation is the difficulty of setting specific MBO goals for particular jobs and areas of performance. Also, an MBO program may overemphasize short-term goals and performance, postponing or ignoring activities needed to maintain long-term organizational health. Moreover, individuals may emphasize their own MBO goals to the detriment of the goals of other individuals and groups. The efficiency of the process (and employee motivation) can also be limited by the mandate to complete forms about goal setting, performance standards, and reviews. Finally, if the MBO process is administered too rigidly, managers may lose the flexibility to effectively respond to environmental changes.[56]

Although MBO may not be right for every organization, those that want to take advantage of the benefits and minimize the limitations can tailor the process to meet their own needs. When implementing an MBO program, top managers can ease the transition by providing information and training about goal setting, evaluation, and coaching for improved performance.[57]

TOOLS FOR PLANNING

Whether they are planning for their own units or for the organization as a whole, managers have a variety of tools available that can enhance and facilitate the planning process. The general decision-making tools described in Chapter 6 can certainly be applied to the decisions made during the planning process.

Managers also use forecasts, break-even analysis, and project planning tools to support the planning process.

Forecasts

To guide organizational actions and decisions during the planning process, a manager can make a **forecast,** a prediction or an estimate of future conditions or events. **Forecasting** is the process of predicting future environmental conditions based on current data, research, and past experience. Forecasts support planning in every function:[58]

forecast A prediction or an estimate of future events or conditions

forecasting The process of predicting future environmental conditions based on current data, research, and past experience

- *Marketing.* Forecasting helps managers predict sales by product, by geographical area, and by customer. It is also used to estimate competitors' future sales and to predict costs and pricing trends.
- *Operations.* Managers use forecasts to predict demand for goods and services and to assess the impact on production or service capacity. Forecasts are also used to manage inventory and work schedules.
- *Finance and accounting.* Some uses of forecasts in finance and accounting include projections of sales revenue, operational costs, and taxes. Forecasts of economic conditions help managers plan their future cash flow and project the cost and availability of funds for expansion.
- *Human resources.* Managers use forecasts to plan for hiring and training, for turnover and retirement, for maintaining appropriate salary levels, and to predict employment trends.
- *Information resources.* Forecasting helps managers project the need for expanded management information systems and other information-processing and delivery systems that support organizational decision making.
- *Research and development.* Managers use forecasts to predict future technological trends and their impact on every part of the organization. In this way, R&D managers can plan to incorporate new technology in new products, new facilities, and new processes throughout the organization.

Top managers at Southern California Edison, an electric utility, use forecasts of future energy needs and environmental conditions to support long-range planning. By considering economic trends, oil availability, and other environmental forces, managers can build more flexibility into their plans and prepare generation plants to increase or decrease capacity as needed.

Taisei, a Japanese construction company, used a variety of forecasts to develop its long-range plan for the company's position in the year 2000. These forecasts included future economic trends, forecasts of consumer life-style and values, forecasts of construction trends, and forecasts of resource availability. In general, managers use two forecasting approaches in their planning: quantitative and qualitative forecasting.[59]

Quantitative Forecasting

quantitative forecasting A mathematical method of analyzing historical data to determine a pattern that can be projected into the future

Quantitative forecasting is a mathematical method of analyzing the results of historical data (values previously recorded) to determine a pattern that can be projected into the future. Because of its applicability to a broad spectrum of planning situations, including marketing and financial planning, quantitative forecasting is widely practiced. Two common forms are time-series methods and causal models.[60]

time-series method A quantitative forecasting tool used to identify patterns in historical data and predict how these are likely to recur in the future

Time-Series Methods Managers use the **time-series method** to identify historical patterns and sequences and to predict how they are likely to recur in a future period. The time-series model assumes that a historical pattern or combination of patterns will repeat over time, so if managers plot the sequence of events during a previous period, they can mathematically project how the sequence might recur in a future period. Time-series methods can be used to describe four types of patterns: trends, seasonal patterns, cyclical patterns, and random patterns (see Exhibit 7.6).[61]

A *trend* describes a steady upward or downward movement in a pattern of events taking place over an extended period. For example, the not-for-profit Seattle Emergency Housing Service (SEHS) has set its mission as "serving homeless families." Since SEHS's founding in 1972, the number and needs of home-

EXHIBIT 7.6

Four Types of Time-Series Patterns

When using time-series methods to forecast events, managers find that events form one of four patterns: a trend, a seasonal pattern, a cyclical pattern, or a random pattern.

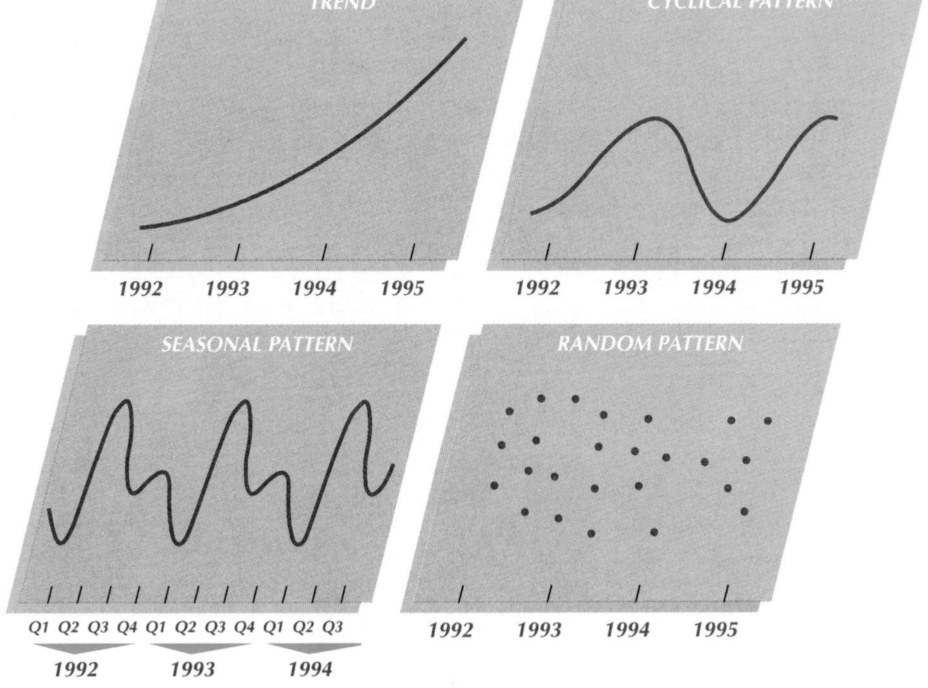

less people in Seattle have both increased. Today, families make up half of Seattle's homeless population, and their needs have expanded beyond housing to include food, child care, and other services. To be effective in fulfilling its mission, SEHS directors must understand these trends so that they can respond with appropriate services.[62]

A *seasonal pattern* reflects fluctuations in data that recur periodically, coinciding with particular times or seasons of the year. Seasonal patterns may vary monthly, quarterly, or annually, but they may also vary weekly, daily, and even hourly. Based in Phoenix, the Pizza Now! chain uses seasonal forecasting to determine pizza demand and to avoid waste. Each outlet has a computer that tracks the number and type of pizzas sold every hour and projects hourly demand, by product, for the same day the following week. Using this forecast, managers can make enough pizzas to satisfy forecasted demand but discard only a few unsold pizzas.[63]

A cyclical pattern describes fluctuations that occur over a period longer than one year. Consider how the long-range cycle in worldwide climatic conditions can affect organizations. Weyerhauser, the lumber and paper company based in Tacoma, Washington, must plan 30 to 60 years ahead for planting, growing, and harvesting the trees it needs. In reaction to a weather forecast for lower rainfall, the company is planting more drought-resistant saplings and developing tree strains with increased drought resistance.[64] Fluctuations due to political crises, strikes, and other unpredictable events fit no discernible pattern and are therefore part of a *random pattern*. Generally nonrecurring and quite transitory, random patterns are not suitable for forecasting.[65]

Time-series methods require managers to systematically record and analyze events. Moreover, time-series methods are applicable only when patterns are likely to remain relatively stable, providing a good indicator of the future. But because such methods rely on the patterns of the past to forecast the future, they are not useful for predicting what may change (or when) as a result of managerial decisions and actions.[66]

Causal Models A **causal model** helps managers predict the behavior of one variable, known as the *dependent variable*, on the basis of the past interaction of other variables, known as the *independent variables*. By understanding the historical relationship between the dependent and the independent variables, managers are able to predict how changes in the independent variables are likely to influence the dependent variable. Three frequently used types of causal models are regression analysis, econometric models, and leading indicators.[67]

causal model A quantitative forecasting tool that helps managers predict the behavior of one variable on the basis of past interaction with other variables

Regression analysis uses mathematical equations to predict the behavior of the dependent variable on the basis of the current fluctuation of one or more known independent variables. This method can also be used to analyze the impact of potential changes in the independent variables on the dependent variable. The manager of a plate glass manufacturing firm might use regression analysis to predict sales on the basis of factors that cause glass sales to increase or decrease, such the rate of automobile production and the number of building permits issued. By substituting higher or lower values for automobile production or building permits, the manager can see how the forecast of plate glass sales changes and can prepare contingency plans for use if those situations occur.[68]

regression analysis A quantitative forecasting tool that uses mathematical equations to predict the behavior of one variable on the basis of the fluctuation of one or more known variables

econometric model A quantitative forecasting tool comprising a series of regression equations that together predict how interrelated variables will affect the economy, the organization, and the organization's industry

An **econometric model** is a system of regression equations that together predict how interrelated variables will affect the economy, the organization, and the organization's industry. Although econometric models are useful for under-

GLOBAL MANAGEMENT

Managing Multinational Planning

For more than 65 years, the name Marriott has been synonymous with hospitality. With revenues approaching $10 billion and operations in 50 states and 17 countries, the giant hotel and catering chain has aggressively pursued global growth. Marriott's rapid expansion has been guided by a clear-cut corporate vision, specific goals, and a carefully orchestrated planning process that coordinates corporate and divisional planning in the United States and around the world.

Marriott didn't go global until 1966, nearly 40 years after it was founded, when it acquired an airline catering kitchen in Venezuela. The chain entered the international hotel market in 1975 with the opening of the Amsterdam Marriott. In recent years, the company has opened hotels in Poland, Hong Kong, and other locations around the world, and it plans to double the number of Marriott hotels within the next few years. This global growth is guided by an overall corporate vision: to create the best lodging and food service company in the world. In each business, Marriott strives to become (1) the preferred employer with the best management team, (2) the preferred service provider, and (3) the most profitable.

Each business, be it catering, hotels, or retirement properties, makes plans to meet the key goals set by J. Willard Marriott, Jr., and his top management team. One important but challenging financial goal set by these top managers is a 15 to 20 percent annual return on equity. To support the planning process, the corporation develops forecasts on a three- to five-year time frame, examining market conditions in North America and on other continents.

The hotel market differs from country to country, and Marriott's planning process recognizes and maximizes these variations. Because the United States presents the best growth opportunity, that's where the chain plans to build most of its hotels in the coming years. However, unfavorable economic conditions and a glut of hotel and motel rooms in the United States has led the firm to reexamine growth goals and plans for each of its four lodging operations: upscale resorts

standing complex relationships among multiple variables, they are difficult, expensive, and time-consuming to develop, so they are not generally developed by individual managers. Instead, organizations turn to firms such as American Business Econometrics, which specialize in developing such models for economic forecasting applications.[69]

leading indicators Variables that are correlated with the movements of a broad economic phenomenon but that tend to occur in advance of the phenomenon

Leading indicators are variables that are correlated with the movements of a broad economic phenomenon, but they tend to occur in advance of that phenomenon. The United States government tracks more than 10 variables that tend to be leading indicators of economic conditions such as recession. Because the economy can exert a powerful influence on sales and other organizational activities, many managers consider changes in these leading indicators to be predictors of future movement in the economic climate. However, economic movement may occur immediately after a change in the leading indicators or after many months, so leading indicators are not precise predictors of the timing of economic change.[70]

Qualitative Forecasting

qualitative forecasting A forecasting method based on individual judgments or committee agreements about future events or conditions

The second type of forecasting frequently used by managers is **qualitative forecasting,** or *judgmental forecasting,* a method based on individual judgments or committee agreements about future events or conditions. This is the most frequently used type of forecasting, and it relies less on mathematical analyses than does quantitative forecasting. Because qualitative forecasting depends on the knowledge and expertise of the managers involved, it is generally less systematic and less objective than other methods, and its effectiveness can be diminished by the types of decision-making biases discussed in Chapter 6.[71]

and hotels, moderately priced hotels, extended-stay hotels, and economy lodgings. Marriott's international plans are closely tied to market conditions in each country and in each region. Company plans call for luxury hotels for London, Paris, Vienna, and Amsterdam, but Marriott is also targeting growing cities in the Pacific Rim.

Forecasts for specific market segments help the chain determine whether to enter, exit, or remain in particular businesses. Not long ago, for instance, Marriott was weighing whether to enter the retirement residence market. After reviewing population forecasts and assessing the needs of potential users, top managers believed that a large and lucrative market in senior living services could be developed. They decided to launch a new type of full-service retirement community with leisure and medical facilities as well as a prototype limited-service retirement property; in all, 150 retirement communities are planned for the 1990s. Marriott's planning process has already paid off: 80 percent of the first two retirement communities were snapped up on the first day of business.

At the local level, hotel managers have some leeway in setting prices and controlling costs, and they use this autonomy to help achieve operational goals. They are, however, expected to run their hotels according to the corporation's many standing plans, which cover virtually every hotel function, including the right way to clean bathroom sinks. These standing plans help Marriott ensure that every one of its hotels maintains uniformly high standards for quality and customer service. For example, housekeeping personnel must follow 66 specific procedures for tidying guest rooms. No leeway here: these standing plans can't be altered without corporate approval. With a clear vision, challenging goals, and coordinated planning geared to local and global conditions, Marriott is able to continue growing and spreading its special brand of hospitality around the world.

Apply Your Knowledge

1. How might contingency planning help a local Marriott hotel manager in Vienna deal with an extended electrical power outage? Be specific.
2. What types of quantitative forecasts might be useful to Marriott's corporate planners as they assess the opportunity for new hotels in France?

The Delphi group technique (see Chapter 6) can be used to obtain a qualitative consensus among experts about the most likely pattern of future events. Three other commonly used qualitative forecasting approaches are technological forecasting, the jury of executive opinion, and the sales force composite.

Technological Forecasting **Technological forecasting** focuses on long-term predictions of the environment and technology. Technological forecasting is often used when no direct history of patterns or relationships exists or when change has disrupted the patterns and relationships among environmental variables. For this reason, managers who use technological forecasting to predict long-term changes in technology must have foresight, judgment, and considerable knowledge of the variables.[72]

technological forecasting A qualitative forecasting method that focuses on long-term predictions of the environment and technology

Technological forecasting is used to predict possible new developments and advances in a specific field or to estimate when a technological advance might become widespread. Also, managers use this method when they want to understand the types of changes, future patterns, and relationships that may emerge from a current or anticipated environmental shift. However, technological forecasting can be tricky because of the difficulty in accurately predicting long-term changes. So managers often consider such forecasts a way of understanding potential technical changes rather than as a definitive prediction of specific events.[73]

James Clark, chairman of Silicon Graphics in Mountain View, California, uses technological forecasting to consider the future of *virtual reality*, a computer application created by a display mechanism and a control technology that seems to surround the user with an artificial environment that emulates reality.

He predicts that after the middle of this decade, people will be able to slip an attachment onto personal computer screens that will allow them to see graphics in a virtual reality state, which is more realistic than the flat figures displayed on today's computer screens. This forecast helps Clark plan how and when his company, which manufactures powerful graphics workstations that run virtual reality programs, will respond to such a future development.[74]

jury of executive opinion A qualitative forecasting technique in which organizational executives meet and decide as a group on their best estimate for the forecast

Jury of Executive Opinion One of the simplest qualitative forecasting methods is the **jury of executive opinion,** in which organizational executives meet and decide as a group on their best estimate for the forecast. This approach is most effective when participants receive background information in advance of the meeting. However, because this method involves group decision making, it is susceptible to the influence of groupthink and other limitations of the group decision-making process discussed in Chapter 6.[75]

sales force composite A qualitative forecasting method that combines estimates provided by salespeople, sales managers, and distributors in order to derive a prediction about future sales

Sales Force Composite Another qualitative forecasting method is the **sales force composite,** which combines estimates provided by salespeople, sales managers, and, on occasion, distributors about the organization's future sales outlook. Because salespeople generally work closely with customers, they learn about marketplace changes and trends that can be incorporated into their sales estimates. However, they often lack knowledge of the broader conditions that affect sales, so managers may have to provide information on general economic trends as background.[76]

Break-Even Analysis

break-even analysis A quantitative tool that helps managers understand the relationship among costs, sales volume, and sales revenues

break-even point The point at which sales volume produces sales revenues equal to total costs

To create plans that lead to achieving organizational profitability goals, managers frequently need to consider how certain decisions will affect profits. In such situations, they can use **break-even analysis,** a quantitative tool that helps managers examine the relationship among costs, sales volume, and sales revenues. By manipulating these elements, managers can determine the **break-even point,** the level of sales volume that produces sales revenues equal to total costs. As the name suggests, the break-even point occurs when the organization neither loses money nor makes a profit but merely breaks even. At sales volume above this point, revenues more than cover costs, so the organization makes a profit. But revenues from a sales volume below this point do not cover costs, so the organization suffers a loss.[77]

In applying break-even analysis, managers determine their *fixed costs,* costs such as rent or mortgage that remain the same regardless of the level of sales. Fixed costs are shown as a horizontal line on the graph in Exhibit 7.7. Managers also calculate their *variable costs,* such as labor and raw materials, which fluctuate according to the number of units produced. Adding fixed and variable costs together (for a given level of sales) yields *total costs,* seen as an upward-sloping line on the graph in Exhibit 7.7. Next, managers calculate the total revenues at each level of sales volume, represented by the steeply sloped line. The total revenue line crosses the total cost line at the break-even point. In this example, if fixed costs are $500, if variable costs are $7.50 per unit, and if price per unit is $10.00, the break-even point is 200 units. At the level of 200 units sold, the total revenue is 200 × $10.00, or $2,000. Total costs include $500 (fixed costs) plus 200 × $7.50 (variable costs), for a total of $2,000. Therefore, total revenues equal total costs at the break-even point of 200 units sold.

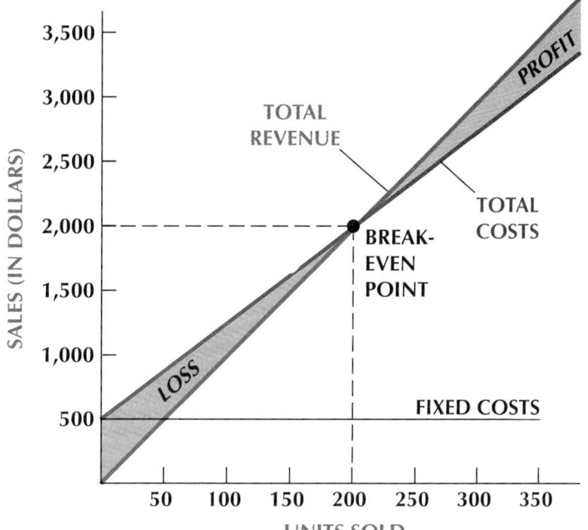

EXHIBIT 7.7
The Break-Even Point
The break-even point is the level at which sales revenues equal total costs. On sales above that point, shown in orange, the organization makes a profit. But on sales below that point, shown in green, the organization loses money.

Managers find break-even analysis a useful way to calculate how many units must be sold before the product returns a profit. This planning tool also helps managers consider how profitability is influenced when costs or prices are changed or when fewer units are sold because of increased competition or other environmental influences. Once they have calculated the break-even point, managers need to key their sales goals to the level of sales that will yield the desired profitability.[78]

Large and small organizations can apply break-even analysis. Zully Alvarado is using it to run Janette Franch, her small custom-made orthopedic footwear business in Chicago. Since starting the small business in 1989, Alvarado has carefully analyzed her fixed costs, which include a rented facility, and her variable costs, such as making a plaster cast of each customer's foot. Her stylish custom-made shoes sell for $275 and up, and by carefully managing costs and pricing, Alvarado broke even in 1991 on total sales of $70,000. Similarly, Stride Rite, a major manufacturer of children's footwear, also watches the relationship of its costs, prices, and sales volume. Compared with previous years, the company ended 1990 with higher total costs, higher unit prices, and increased sales volume. To keep profitability under control, Stride Rite kept a close eye on its costs and allowed only those increases that were lower than the growth in sales volume.[79]

Project Planning Tools

Large organizational projects often involve many steps or complicated activities that must be carefully sequenced and coordinated. Giant single-use plans can be designed and controlled using project planning tools such as Gantt charts and the Program Evaluation and Review Technique (PERT).

Gantt Charts

Gantt chart A project planning tool developed by scientific management theorist Henry L. Gantt to show the planned duration and current status of all activities in a project

The **Gantt chart,** developed by scientific management theorist Henry L. Gantt, is a project planning chart that shows the separate activities, their duration, and the current status of each activity in a given project. The entire project's time period is shown along the horizontal axis of this bar chart, and project

EXHIBIT 7.8

Using a Gantt Chart for Project Planning

In this Gantt chart for a hypothetical project to prepare and mail a newsletter, the tasks are listed on the left and the time is shown across the top. To indicate how much of each task has been completed, managers darken the appropriate portion of the corresponding bar. In this project, the printing of newsletters and envelopes is behind schedule.

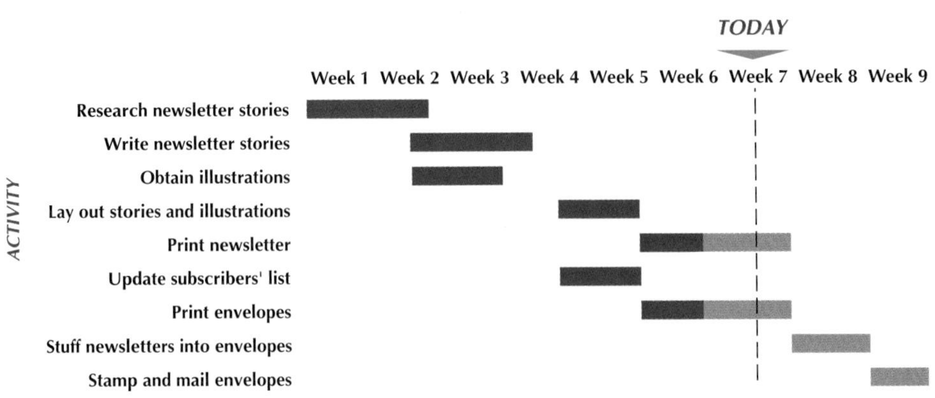

activities are listed on the left (see Exhibit 7.8). The beginning, duration, and end of each scheduled activity is shown on the bar chart and a graphical device (shading or colors) allows managers to see at a glance the progress in each activity.[80]

Gantt charts help managers plan projects with many steps and allow them to easily track the completion of individual steps. By checking the chart, managers can quickly tell whether the organization is behind or ahead of schedule, and which activities have not yet been completed. A variety of computer software programs are now available to help managers develop and maintain Gantt charts. However, this planning tool does not take into account the interrelationships among activities. For this reason, complex projects may require more sophisticated planning techniques.[81]

Program Evaluation and Review Technique

Program Evaluation and Review Technique (PERT) A project planning tool that helps managers identify the optimal sequencing of activities, the expected time for project completion, and the best use of resources within a complex project

The **Program Evaluation and Review Technique (PERT)** is a planning tool that helps managers identify the optimal sequencing of activities, the expected time for project completion, and the best use of resources within a complex project. This tool was developed in 1957, when the U.S. Navy was grappling with the enormous task of coordinating the thousands of suppliers and activities needed to build the Polaris submarine fleet. By using PERT to view this giant project as a network of related activities rather than as a list of separate, sequential activities, Navy managers could see the potential impact of delays on their projected completion dates.[82]

To use PERT, the manager must (1) identify the activities to be performed, (2) determine the sequence of activities, (3) establish the time needed to complete each activity, (4) draw the network, (5) calculate the longest path through the network that leads to project completion (this is known as the *critical path* because the project cannot be completed in less time), and (6) refine the network's timing or use of resources as activities are completed.

Consider how PERT might help a retailer plan and control a new store opening. In this simplified example, the retailer starts by listing all the activities needed to build and open a store, such as locating a site, obtaining building and business permits, hiring a construction firm, handling construction, hiring personnel, training personnel, stocking merchandise, and trimming windows and putting up displays (see Exhibit 7.9). After arranging these activities in sequence,

EXHIBIT 7.9 Activity and Time Estimates for Building and Opening a Store

In this hypothetical illustration of building and opening a store, the retail manager first identifies the key activities, then determines which must take place before others. Next, the manager estimates the optimistic, the most likely, and the pessimistic times for completing each activity and calculates the expected time for each. This information is used to draw a PERT network diagram of the project (see Exhibit 7.10).

Activity	Predecessor Activity	Estimated Optimistic Time (in weeks)	Estimated Most Likely Time (in weeks)	Estimated Pessimistic Time (in weeks)	Calculated Expected Time (in weeks)
A. Locate site		4.0	5.0	6.0	5.0
B. Get building, business permits	A	2.0	4.0	5.0	3.8
C. Hire a construction firm	B	2.0	3.0	4.0	3.0
D. Build the store	C	9.0	11.0	15.0	11.3
E. Hire personnel	B	3.0	5.0	6.0	4.8
F. Train personnel	E	4.0	5.0	6.0	5.0
G. Stock merchandise	D, F	1.0	2.0	3.0	2.0
H. Trim windows, put up displays	G	1.0	1.0	2.0	1.2

the retail manager determines the expected time to complete each activity. This is a calculation involving the optimistic time, which assumes nothing will go wrong; the pessimistic time, which assumes that problems will cause delays; and the most likely time, which is the period that the activity will probably require to complete. The retailer uses the following formula to find a weighted average of the three time estimates, with the most likely time given the most weight:

$$\text{Expected time} = \frac{(\text{Optimistic time}) + 4\,(\text{Most likely time}) + (\text{Pessimistic time})}{6}$$

Next, the retailer draws the network (see Exhibit 7.10) and traces the longest continuous path through the activities in the network. This critical path is the total time needed to complete the project. Now the manager knows that if an

EXHIBIT 7.10 A PERT Network for Building and Opening a Store

Constructed from the information in Exhibit 7.9, this PERT diagram portrays the interrelationship of activities and the expected number of weeks needed to build and open a new store. The critical path (the longest path through the project network) is 26.3 weeks, as shown by the heavier lines. If any of the predecessor activities in this critical path are delayed, later activities will be delayed unless the manager uses additional resources or other methods to stay on schedule.

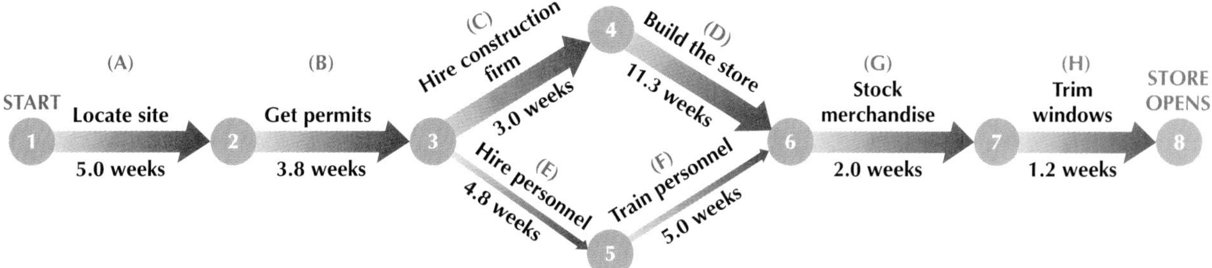

individual activity is not completed on time, the project is likely to run longer than the time indicated by the critical path. But the PERT network also shows how the manager can refine the network and adjust for delays by speeding up later activities, starting some activities concurrently with others, or using additional resources to make up for unexpected delays. Any of these will shorten the critical path, allowing the retail manager to shorten the schedule or to finish on time.[83]

Managers in many organizations, including construction, manufacturing, and government organizations, use PERT when planning complex projects and tracking results. As with Gantt charts, software programs can help managers compute the time estimates, diagram the project network, and make any scheduling changes needed to cope with unforeseen events.

SUMMARY

The planning process includes the organizational mission, goals, and plans. The mission defines the organization's basic purpose and serves to unify organizational goals and plans. Goals are the results an organization wishes to achieve, and they provide targets for employees, guide decision making, and set standards for performance. A plan is the means of pursuing goals, bridging the gap between the organization's current state and the desired future state. Plans help managers anticipate the actions needed to achieve goals and to coordinate organizational activities.

Goals are needed at three organizational levels. Strategic goals broadly define overall organizational targets for future results. Tactical goals set targets to be achieved by business divisions or units. Operational goals set targets for departmental and individual performance. The three levels create a hierarchy of goals in which higher-level goals dictate the goals below them, and lower-level goals are the means of attaining the goals above.

To effectively guide the organization, goals must be challenging, attainable, specific and measurable, time-defined, and relevant. Goal setting involves establishing, coordinating, and prioritizing goals. Plans are developed on three levels. Strategic plans are the means to be used in achieving strategic goals. Tactical plans support the implementation of strategic plans and describe how tactical goals will be achieved. Operational plans support the implementation of tactical plans and describe how operational goals will be achieved. Plans at all levels must be coordinated because the combination enables managers to fulfill the organizational mission. If lower-level managers do not achieve their goals, then higher-level managers may not be able to achieve their goals.

Managers prepare single-use plans when they face a one-time situation. When the same type of situation recurs repeatedly, they use standing plans, and when environmental shifts may affect organizational performance, managers prepare contingency plans to outline alternative courses of action. To link goals and plans with everyday actions, organizations can establish management by objectives (MBO) programs. The MBO process consists of four steps: (1) setting goals, (2) planning action, (3) implementing plans, and (4) reviewing performance. MBO focuses on activities that affect goal attainment, and it helps coordinate multilevel goals by fostering cooperation and communication. Moreover, MBO provides an unbiased, systematic way to measure performance. However, MBO needs top management support to succeed, and it can be difficult to set MBO goals for some jobs. Also, individuals may concentrate on their own goals, ignoring the goals of others. Managers may be frustrated by MBO paperwork, and they can lose the flexibility to respond to the environment if the program is too rigid.

Managers can use two types of forecasts to support the planning process. Quantitative forecasts are mathematical methods of analyzing the results of historical data to determine a pattern that can be projected into the future. Qualitative forecasting is based on individual judgments or committee agreements about the future. Break-even analysis supports the planning process by helping managers understand how pricing, cost, and sales decisions affect profitability. Gantt and PERT are planning tools that help managers schedule activities and track progress toward project completion.

MEETING A MANAGEMENT CHALLENGE AT THE U.S. DEPARTMENT OF LABOR

When she was U.S. labor secretary, Elizabeth Dole launched the Secretary's Commission on Achieving Necessary Skills (SCANS) to identify the skills that the U.S. work force should have. These skills would in turn become goals for the country's educators. Dole resigned to become head of the American Red Cross before the commission's study was completed, but her successor, Lynn Martin, continued the project.

The commission presented its report to Martin and to education secretary Lamar Alexander in July 1991. The report first identified a three-part foundation of skills and personal qualities:

- *Basic skills,* including reading, writing, mathematics, listening, and speaking
- *Thinking skills,* which include creative thinking, decision making, problem solving, visualizing, and reasoning
- *Personal skills and qualities,* which include responsibility, self-esteem, social skills, integrity, and self-management

These goals lead to five specific competencies:

- *Resources,* such as the management of time, money, materials, and people
- *Interpersonal skills,* allowing students to work in teams, to both lead and follow others, and to work with people from diverse backgrounds
- *Information,* including the ability to collect, evaluate, and interpret data, to communicate findings, and to use computers in this process
- *Systems,* specifically social, organizational, and technical systems and processes
- *Technology,* particularly the skills involved in selecting and using technologies

These skill needs are intended to serve as strategic and tactical goals for the nation's schools, and Martin and SCANS commission chairman William Brock, himself a former secretary of labor, encourage local school officials to go into their own communities to identify the specific operational goals that students need to succeed on the job. The commission proposes to measure success in meeting the goals with a national skills assessment test.

Lynn Martin, Secretary of the U.S. Department of Labor

The commission's goals have met with mixed reviews. Albert Shanker, president of the powerful American Federation of Teachers union, called it a "first-rate plan" and "the first concrete sense of what employers want." The support of teachers is critical to the plan's success, so Shanker's assessment is certainly encouraging. On the other hand, Shanker and others have criticized the federal government for not backing up the new ideas with additional funding. Martin and Brock recognize that identifying goals is not the end of a process but the beginning of a long, difficult period of implementation. In fact, Martin told an interviewer that this report is no different from the many other education-improvement studies conducted in recent years "if it all goes on the shelf. It becomes another book." To make sure this doesn't happen, Martin is committed to, in her words, "taking it from inside the Beltway [Washington, D.C.] to Main Street USA."

You're the Manager: Lynn Martin has appointed you assistant secretary of labor for work-force skills. Your job is to lead and coordinate continuing efforts to improve the work skills of students throughout the country. Consider the following situations and decide how you will respond.

Ranking Questions

1. The educational process directly involves millions of people across the country and indirectly affects and involves many millions more. You know that people are more likely to reach goals if they have a say in setting those goals, but you also know that it would be impossible to involve millions of people. You do want as much participation as possible, however. Rank the following approaches in terms of overall effectiveness.
   a. So that you can involve all interested parties in one manageable group, randomly pick one representative school anywhere in the country and invite the students, parents, administrators, and teachers to participate.
   b. Because employers are most affected by poor job skills, they should have the most input. Consequently, you should ask business organizations such as the Chamber of Commerce to help.
   c. Teachers will ultimately be responsible for the successful implementation of education plans, so they should participate in the planning process. Contact the national teachers' unions and invite them to get involved.
   d. Establish a committee that represents all of the interested parties. Have state education officials nominate people from their states, then select the committee members for one- or two-year terms.
2. Monitoring and feedback are vital parts of the planning process because they allow managers to see whether goals are being met and to pinpoint changes if goals are not being met. However, in a process that involves so many people and is so loosely structured, formal managerial control would be hard to implement. Given this situation, how would you rank the effectiveness of the following ideas if the department's goals are not met?
   a. Hold state education officials responsible for meeting the goals; periodically test students in each state, then publish performance reports on the states that are not meeting the goals. By publicly chastising them, you'll encourage higher performance.
   b. Modify the idea presented in (a) to make it more positive; rather than singling out failing states, highlight successes. Encourage people from those states to explain how they were able to meet the goals.
   c. Ask teams of teachers and school officials from high-performing states to work closely with their counterparts in low-performing states to share ideas about plans that will effectively raise performance.
   d. Bring the education system under national control; unless teachers across the country are directly accountable to the secretary of education, there can be little hope of meeting national educational goals.

Multiple-Choice Questions

3. The competencies outlined in the SCANS report are closely tied to future development in science and technology; for instance, one of the goals is for students to use computers to process information. To keep goals current, you'll have to ensure that educators understand future developments. Which of the following will do the best job of identifying future developments?
   a. Use time-series analysis to project the number of new technologies that will appear in future years, based on historical patterns.
   b. Periodically survey business leaders about which technological issues are no longer relevant, then drop those topics from the school curriculum.
   c. Assemble a panel of scientists and engineers and have them periodically publish reports on current and expected developments.
   d. Appoint a technological consultant to examine technical literature and report back on developments that are likely to affect the workplace.
4. Martin has asked you to develop a program for implementing MBO in the educational process. Which of these four ideas is most likely to succeed?
   a. Because parents play such a key role in education, the MBO chain should include teachers and parents.
   b. The only place to apply MBO is between teachers and students.
   c. Use MBO at the school district level, involving the school board, superintendents, school principals, and teachers.
   d. Recommend a comprehensive system that starts with students and reports all the way up to Martin herself. This way, the department could monitor every student's progress toward meeting the skills goals.

Analysis Questions

5. Comment on the hierarchy of goals as this concept relates to the department's skills goals. Who is responsible for defining the operational goals that will support Lynn Martin's tactical and strategic goals, and who is responsible for implementing all aspects of the plan?
6. Are the goals identified by the SCANS report consistent with the characteristics of effective goals? What improvements can you suggest?
7. Why do you think this program was conducted by the Department of Labor, rather than the Department of Education? What are the ramifications of this circumstance, in terms of successfully implementing the plans?

Special Project

Local school districts may have a tough time making plans to achieve the education goals that the Department of Labor advocates. Although the goals are clear, the means to achieve the goals on a local level (and over the long term) are less clear. What role should planning specialists, planning task forces, and administrators from individual school districts play during the local planning process? Draft a two-page letter to Lynn Martin suggesting how local districts might use each of these resources to plan more effectively. If you believe the Department of Labor can assist local districts by offering services such as training for planning specialists, include your ideas in this letter.[84]

KEY TERMS

break-even analysis (226)
break-even point (226)
causal model (223)
contingency plans (215)
econometric model (223)
forecast (221)
forecasting (221)
Gantt chart (227)
goal (204)
jury of executive opinion (226)
leading indicators (224)
management by objectives (MBO) (218)
mission (205)
mission statement (206)
operational goals (208)
operational plans (212)
plan (204)
policy (214)
procedure (214)
program (213)
Program Evaluation and Review Technique (PERT) (228)
project (213)
qualitative forecasting (224)
quantitative forecasting (222)
regression analysis (223)
rule (214)
sales force composite (226)
single-use plan (213)
standing plan (214)
strategic goals (207)
strategic plans (211)
tactical goals (207)
tactical plans (212)
technological forecasting (225)
time-series method (222)

QUESTIONS

For Review

1. Why does an organization need a mission statement?
2. What are the characteristics of effective goals?
3. How are single-use plans, standing plans, and contingency plans used?
4. What are the steps in the MBO process?
5. How do managers use break-even analysis and Gantt charts in the planning process?

For Analysis

1. Would a small-business owner such as an architect need strategic, tactical, and operational goals? Why or why not?
2. How can the U.S. government apply long-range planning despite the four-year cycle of presidential elections?
3. Why are technological forecasts important for public sector organizations such as local school systems?
4. If an organization meets its operational and tactical goals, is it likely to meet its strategic goals? If it meets its strategic goals, is it assured of meeting its operational and tactical goals? Why or why not?
5. How can not-for-profit organizations apply Drucker's eight areas for strategic goals?

For Application

1. How might the manager of a Winn-Dixie supermarket design an MBO program to meet storewide and departmental sales and productivity goals?
2. What kind of mission statement might the general manager of a local radio station prepare?
3. How can contingency planning help the head of the U.S. National Park Service protect park visitors?

4. What policies, procedures, and rules might Hyatt Hotels establish to ensure a consistent level of quality and service at its hotels around the world? Give a specific example of each.
5. How might PepsiCo use quantitative forecasting to support planning for its Taco Bell fast-food restaurant chain?

KEEPING CURRENT IN MANAGEMENT

Find a recent article in which a top manager discusses his or her organization's mission and announces quarterly or year-end results in achieving organizational goals. Examples would be a corporation that has recently launched a major new product; a not-for-profit organization that is seeking to find a cure for a disabling disease; a small business completing its first year of operation; or a multinational firm establishing a branch outside its home country.

1. How does the manager describe the organizational mission? How does this mission translate into organizational goals? What are the goals on the strategic, operational, and tactical levels?
2. How is performance being measured? How has performance varied since the last time results were announced? If results are below expectations, what single-use or standing plans is the manager using to improve performance?
3. Who is responsible for organizational planning? How are plans linked to the organizational mission and goals? How does the manager communicate the mission, goals, and plans to employees and to other organizational stakeholders?

SHARPEN YOUR MANAGEMENT SKILLS

The Seattle Mariners have never been one of professional baseball's shining stars. In fact, until 1991, the team never had a winning season. One continuing problem area is hitting; even with rising stars such as Ken Griffey, Jr., the Mariners simply don't produce enough runs day in and day out to be a pennant contender. In an attempt to turn things around, the team has called you in as a management consultant. Although you were initially skeptical that a management expert could help a baseball team, you now realize that managing is exactly what the coaches and team executives do. You start your assignment by thinking about the Mariners' goals and performance.

- *Decision:* What strategic, tactical, and operational goals will help turn the club into a batting powerhouse within three years? If you're not a baseball fan, team up with a classmate who is, and consider your options—bringing in new players, scouting the farm teams, improving the skills of existing players, and so on. Then identify three strategic goals for the team president, three tactical goals for the team manager, and three operational goals for the batting coach. Be sure the goals support each other.
- *Communication:* Draw a chart of the nine goals you have identified, showing the linkages among the three levels. Then prepare a two-minute speech to the Mariners' management and players to explain the new goals and to discuss how performance will be measured for each goal.

After becoming CEO in 1986, Allen Jacobson contained the soaring costs that threatened 3M's long-term health while preserving the uniquely innovative corporate culture that built an empire out of sandpaper and tape. Jacobson, who started in 3M's tape lab in 1947, streamlined production, reduced spending by more than a third, and sped up development of new products. But just as he was getting ready to retire, recession threatened to undo the progress he'd made toward 3M's long-term goals.

HISTORY

The Minnesota Mining and Manufacturing Company was founded in 1902 to mine grinding wheel abrasives on the shores of Lake Superior. But the mine was a bust, so 3M moved to nearby Duluth to produce sandpaper. There, it struggled with supplies and quality until investor Louis Ordway moved it to its current home in St. Paul. Sandpaper improvements turned the company around, and it paid its first dividend in 1914. 3M had its first major success early the next decade with the invention of waterproof sandpaper, which reduced the dust from dry sanding (and eased associated health problems). The company diversified for the first time in 1925 with the invention of masking tape, the first in 3M's line of Scotch brand tapes. Cellophane tape kept 3M sales growing during the Great Depression, and numerous innovations—from videotape and dry-silver microfilm to digital sound recording and Post-it brand note pads—have kept the company growing ever since. 3M now has 60,000 products and introduces 200 new ones a year. The company operates in 37 states and 53 countries, with international sales accounting for half its business. Sales reached $13 billion in 1990, but the recession sent profits tumbling.

ENVIRONMENT

3M stakes its future on continuing innovation, which its corporate culture encourages by rewarding innovators, fostering cooperation between divisions, and limiting rigid rules that would stifle experimentation. An internal grant program gives researchers up to $50,000 to take a project past the idea stage, and people with ideas are encouraged to use whatever employees and other resources they can find inside the company. A 3M employee with an idea for a new product forms an action team by recruiting full-time members from technical areas, including manufacturing, marketing, and sometimes finance. The team is in charge of its own planning and execution from product design through manufacture and marketing, and members get raises and promotions as the project advances. Almost any 3M employee is allowed to spend up to 15 percent of the workweek on any desired project, as long as it is product-related; one employee used this policy to find an adhesive of less than standard weight to keep a bookmark from falling out of his hymnal, resulting in development of Post-it note pads, which now bring in as much as $300 million a year.

GOALS AND CHALLENGES

3M needs constant innovation to meet its stiff financial goals of 10 percent minimum growth in earnings per share and 20 to 25 percent return on equity per year. Another goal requires each division to get at least a quarter of its revenue from products developed within the last five years. As a result, 3M plans to continue investing 6.6 percent of its sales revenue in research and development, despite recession. Another goal is to reduce manufacturing costs 10 percent per unit in five years; therefore, even though the recession has forced 3M to scrap plans to boost capital spending 10 percent, the company still plans to spend $1.3 billion to modernize its 101 factories worldwide. 3M's avid pursuit of innovation has seen some failures, including liquid gloves and paper brassieres. But Jacobson's successor, Livio "Desi" DeSimone, plans to improve product success ratios by linking marketing more closely with research and development, rather than continuing to create products before determining the market potential.

1. How well do 3M's strategic goals match the characteristics of effective goals? How might 3M's short-term goals conflict with its long-term goals?
2. How could 3M use planning specialists to help launch new products?
3. Assume that 3M has developed a unique new abrasive cleansing cream that would be sold by prescription to people with acne. What types of plans might 3M managers adopt to reflect and preserve 3M's corporate culture in the new program?
4. How might a marketing manager use forecasting to improve the chances of a revolutionary new superinsulated house siding system?

CHAPTER OUTLINE

8 Strategic Management and Implementation

After studying this chapter, you will be able to

1. Discuss the role of strategic management and list the steps in the strategic management process
2. Differentiate among corporate-level strategy, business-level strategy, and functional-level strategy, and describe the four components of strategy
3. Explain how situation analysis incorporates internal and external assessment within the SWOT analysis
4. Outline the three grand strategy options and explain the two major tools for formulating portfolio strategy approaches
5. Explain how managers can use the adaptation model and Porter's generic competitive strategies to develop business-level strategy
6. Identify the major functional strategies and show how they relate to business-level strategy
7. Discuss the implementation and control aspects of strategic management

FACING A MANAGEMENT CHALLENGE AT

Generating Paper Profits

It was a retailing concept waiting to be discovered: the office-supply superstore. Thomas Stemberg stumbled across it at a general merchandise wholesale club store in 1985, while rummaging through the office-supplies aisle. Already a highly regarded supermarket industry executive, Stemberg was searching for a new retailing challenge, and he became convinced the answer was discount office supplies.

Office supplies was a $100 billion business, but its antiquated distribution system left most consumers—and even most small businesses—paying full retail prices. All the ingredients were here for a successful "category killer," a retailer that dominates a product category through heavily discounted, high-volume sales conducted in a highly efficient, low-cost, no-frills shopping environment. What supermarkets were to food, what Toys 'R' Us was to toys and games, Stemberg wanted his chain to be to office supplies. He named the new company "Staples," and he defined the company's mission as "giving Staples' customers the best price, selection, service and convenience in office supplies."

Now Stemberg had to analyze his situation, define goals, and formulate and implement a strategy for a merchandising category that didn't yet exist. His situation analysis outlined the challenge. Internally, Staples' major strength would be low merchandising costs, allowing the chain to offer low prices on a large selection of merchandise. Its weaknesses included the lack of an infrastructure and the high operating costs in the Northeast, where Stemberg planned to open. Externally, Staples faced the threat posed by indifferent consumers and, even more dangerous, the category copycats certain to follow. But the nation's voracious appetite for pens, paper, and office paraphernalia provided an opportunity that couldn't be ignored.

Stemberg formulated a strategy of rapid growth. He would blitz a well-defined market, open as many as a dozen stores in a year, and build leadership through market domination, a tactic that he believed "keeps competitors at bay." He quickly raised $18.5 million in private financing and assembled a first-rate board of savvy investors and retail executives, all solidly committed to implementing his plan for lightning growth. In 1986 the flagship Staples store opened. By the end of the year the company had 3 outlets, and there was talk of having 20 by the end of 1988 and 100 locations across the Northeast by 1990.

However, Stemberg was increasingly worried about copycats. By May 1987, venture capitalists had seeded at least five competitors, and more start-ups were on the way. The discounters were separated geographically, but it was only a matter of time before they grew, expanding into one another's markets. The inevitable result would be an industry shakeout.

Internally, Staples' own growth plans were on schedule, its sales goals were on target, and the strategy of dominating markets with sales outlets was on track. Therefore, members of Staples' board were baffled when Stemberg suddenly proposed suspending construction of outlets in favor of building a $6.5 million regional distribution center, something unheard of in the fledgling industry. Stores received merchandise shipped directly from manufacturers, so a distribution hub seemed unnecessary. Was Stemberg abandoning his strategy? Could there be a flaw in the strategy formulation or implementation? What was so important about a distribution center? And should the board agree to his proposal?[1]

CHAPTER OVERVIEW

Strategic management is at the heart of Thomas Stemberg's quest to promote the growth of Staples. Stemberg follows a well-coordinated process to examine the company's situation and then formulate, implement, and control strategy. This chapter begins with an overview of the strategic management process. The steps in the process are examined in order, starting with the purpose and practice of situational analysis. Following that is a look at how organizations formulate organizational strategy on the corporate, business, and functional levels. After exploring how organizations implement strategies and coordinate across organizational levels, the chapter concludes with an examination of strategic control.

FUNDAMENTALS OF STRATEGIC MANAGEMENT

The organizational mission and goals discussed in Chapter 7 give managers at every level a specific focus for their plans and decisions. But to be able to attain the organization's overall objectives effectively and efficiently, top managers need a structured way of guiding and integrating their long-term and short-term planning. To accomplish this, organizations rely on **strategic management,** the ongoing process of formulating and implementing comprehensive plans that help the organization fulfill its mission and achieve strategic goals. The strategic management process enables top managers to consider the organization's long-term situation from a broad perspective, and it helps them align the internal capabilities and resources with the demands of the external environment.[2]

strategic management The ongoing process of formulating, implementing, and controlling broad plans to guide the organization in achieving its strategic goals, given its internal and external environment

By following the strategic management process, managers are able to design an organizational **strategy,** a large-scale overall plan of action designed to help achieve the organization's goals within a specified time. A strategy is not a static planning document that is developed once and then implemented. Rather, strategy is adjusted and honed over time to ensure that this guiding plan remains in tune with the environmental changes that challenge the organization's ability to achieve its goals. Strategy is the cornerstone of the strategic management process, so it is important to understand its components and the levels at which strategy is formulated and implemented.[3]

strategy A comprehensive plan aimed at helping the organization achieve its goals

Organizational Strategy

Strategy sets the organization's direction and provides the framework that management will use to achieve its goals through strategic, tactical, and operational planning. When developing a strategy, managers answer such questions as "What products should we make?" "What markets should we serve?" "What operations should we use?" "How should we compete?"[4] To effectively answer these questions, managers consider four elements when they create organizational strategies.

Components of Strategy

Organizational strategy contains four elements: scope, distinctive competence, resource deployment, and synergy. By considering their own unique circumstances, weighing alternative courses of action, and making decisions about each of these four components, managers develop a strategy that is appropriate to their organization's situation. Combined, these four elements form a comprehensive, unifying strategy that directs the organization's planning efforts toward fulfilling the mission and achieving the strategic goals.

scope The spectrum of products offered, operations performed, markets served, or supplier relationships specified in a strategy

- *Scope.* The **scope,** or *domain,* of a strategy specifies the range of goods and services offered, the operations performed, the markets served, or the supplier relationships maintained. By defining the scope of their strategy, managers are consciously choosing their competitive arena. For example, Continental Bank in Chicago focuses its energies on serving the financial needs of businesses, thus competing against Citicorp and other banks that serve commercial customers. Dayton Hudson, based in Minneapolis, confines itself solely to retailing and competes against May Department Stores and other retail organizations.[5]

- *Distinctive competence.* An organization's **distinctive competence** is its competitive superiority or unique capability in one particular skill (such as customer service or manufacturing) that directly relates to the organization's chosen scope. To be effective, this distinctive competence must be sustainable over the long term. For example, Nike's distinctive competence has long been its ability to engineer and manufacture high-performance athletic footwear; Avon's distinctive competence is its 1.5 million sales representatives worldwide who sell cosmetics and accessories.[6]
- *Resource deployment.* The way management uses the available human, physical, financial, and information resources is **resource deployment.** Organizations distribute their resources according to the scope of the strategy they are pursuing and the distinctive competencies they are using to compete. For example, United Way recently developed a strategy that changes its resource deployment to emphasize a broader scope of family and health-related services. The not-for-profit charitable organization has reduced its funding of the Red Cross and the Scouts, increasing its support of programs that provide family and health-related services.[7]
- *Synergy.* Synergy describes the way various parts of the organization combine to complement or enhance each other. For example, by concentrating on products that can be manufactured in shared production facilities, managers may be able to lower overall manufacturing costs and achieve higher profit margins. But there are other ways of increasing synergy. For example, Campbell Soup played on its marketing competency to create synergy when the firm acquired Pepperidge Farm, which makes cookies and breads that appeal to upscale consumers. Campbell was able to use its marketing expertise, especially its connections with retailers across the country, to launch Pepperidge Farm into national distribution, thereby increasing Campbell's overall sales.[8]

Tandy chairman John V. Roach crafts strategy around the distinctive competencies of designing and selling consumer electronics. In recent years, Tandy has narrowed its scope (by selling foreign stores), changed its resource deployment (by increasing production capacity), and improved synergy (by selling products through many retail formats).

distinctive competence An organization's competitive superiority in a given skill

resource deployment The way the organization apportions its human, physical, financial, and information resources

Levels of Strategy

Just as they develop goals and plans at a variety of levels, managers also need to plan strategy at a variety of levels because decisions are made and actions are taken throughout the organization. Therefore, the total strategy of an organization is composed of strategies defined at three levels: the corporate level, the business level, and the functional level. Strategies at each level are affected by strategy formulation and implementation on the other levels, creating an interconnected network of decisions and actions that help the organization achieve the hierarchy of goals set during the planning process (see Chapter 7). By coordinating strategies on all three levels, managers gain a powerful method of guiding actions for consistency throughout the organization.[9]

- **Corporate-level strategy** sets the overall direction for the organization, defines the businesses in which a company will compete, and determines how resources will be allocated. Corporate-level strategy drives the strategic goals

corporate-level strategy The level of strategy that guides the organization's overall direction, defines the businesses in which a company competes, and specifies how resources are allocated and plans at the top of the hierarchy in the organizational planning process, determining the broad path for managers throughout the organization to follow in achieving the organization's mission. Top managers are responsible for formulating corporate-level strategy, which generally looks ahead three to five years or longer.

business-level strategy The level of strategy that determines how a company will compete in each of its business units

strategic business unit (SBU) A separate business, with its own set of managers, products, resources, customers, and competitors, that is managed independently of a company's other organizational units

- **Business-level strategy** is derived from corporate-level strategy and defines how a company will compete in each of its chosen businesses, including the product and market choices. When a company is composed of numerous businesses, managers decide which should be designated as a **strategic business unit (SBU)**, a separate business that has its own set of managers, products, resources, customers, and competitors, and that is managed independently of the other businesses. Because each of these SBUs has the ability to decide how to approach its own markets, where to obtain its supplies, and how to make other key decisions, the top managers of each one must develop a business-level strategy for that SBU.[10] If an organization operates only one business, then the top level of middle managers works with top managers to develop business-level strategy, which generally looks ahead one to three years. From the perspective of each SBU, business-level strategy may drive strategic goals and plans, but from the perspective of the SBU's parent, business-level strategy drives the tactical goals and plans that are the means for achieving the organization's overall strategic goals and plans in the planning process.

functional-level strategy The level of strategy that determines how activities in each of the organization's functional areas will support business-level strategy

- **Functional-level strategy** supports business-level strategy by specifying activities in each of the functional areas within an organization, such as marketing, finance, and other functions. Functional-level strategy generally drives the operational goals and plans that are the means for achieving the tactical goals in the hierarchy of goals of the organization's planning process. Strategies on the functional level are typically developed by middle managers who head up each functional area, and they tend to focus on the short term, up to one year.

For example, managers at computer manufacturer Digital Equipment Corporation (DEC) use strategy on the corporate, business, and functional levels to synchronize worldwide business activities. All strategies are based directly on the corporate mission and are keyed to the corporate strategy of growth through increased sales and improved profitability. DEC's previous business-level strategy stressed the development of proprietary minicomputer networks. Now the firm has switched its emphasis, offering hardware, software, and services that allow customers to link together computers of virtually any type or brand. To support this new business-level strategy, DEC is making changes in its functional-level strategies, such as speeding up new product design. Internationally, DEC's various geographic groups (Europe, for example) adopt their own specific missions and goals to guide managers in each country as they formulate and implement their business-level strategies and functional-level strategies.[11]

The Nature and Importance of Strategic Management

As the broadest application of the planning process within the organization, strategic management provides a framework for thinking about the organization's situation and for creating and applying strategy. The strategic management process starts with a thorough understanding of the organization, its mission and strategic goals, its strengths and weaknesses compared with competitors. Strategic management also involves detecting those environmental forces and changes that organizations should or must respond to. Moreover, strategic management must seamlessly link strategy formulation and implementation. A clever strategy that cannot be implemented in the real world is doomed to fail, just as a workable strategy that is badly executed will fall short of achieving organizational goals.[12]

Strategic management is important for several reasons. It helps managers systematically examine the organization's basic problems and capabilities, and it helps them anticipate changing conditions. For instance, defining a strategy of rapid growth and keeping close watch for copycat competitors helped Staples plan for the challenges that lay ahead. Also, the process results in setting a clear direction for employees, and it makes the organization more responsive to the environment and to the internal and external stakeholders who can influence the organization's performance. Finally, strategic management can improve the coordination of activities and the allocation of resources on all levels. For maximum effect, the process demands that managers juggle focus and flexibility to give the organization a sense of direction without stifling the ability to respond to unpredictable environmental changes.[13]

Seeing an opportunity to reach young male readers 14–21, publisher Bobbie Halfin *(right)* and the editorial staff launched *Dirt* magazine in 1991. As the magazine grows, Halfin will be using the steps of the strategic management process to watch for competition from larger publishers and to formulate an appropriate strategy for maintaining profitability.

The Strategic Management Process

The strategic management process shown in Exhibit 8.1 consists of four steps, encompassing most of the organizational planning concepts outlined in Chapter 7. In the first two steps, managers assess their environmental situation, review the mission and goals, and create strategic plans, a process known as *strategy formulation.* In the last two steps, managers execute these strategic plans and maintain control, a process known as *strategy implementation.* Managers generally follow the sequence of the four steps but may return to earlier steps to reshape strategy formulation or implementation in response to unexpected problems that confront the organization.[14] The four steps are

1. *Conduct a situation analysis.* Managers review the mission and goals; then they scan the internal and external environment to identify elements and stakeholders with the ability to influence organizational performance.
2. *Formulate the organizational strategy.* Based on the results of the first step in the process, managers develop corporate-level, business-level, and functional-level strategies.

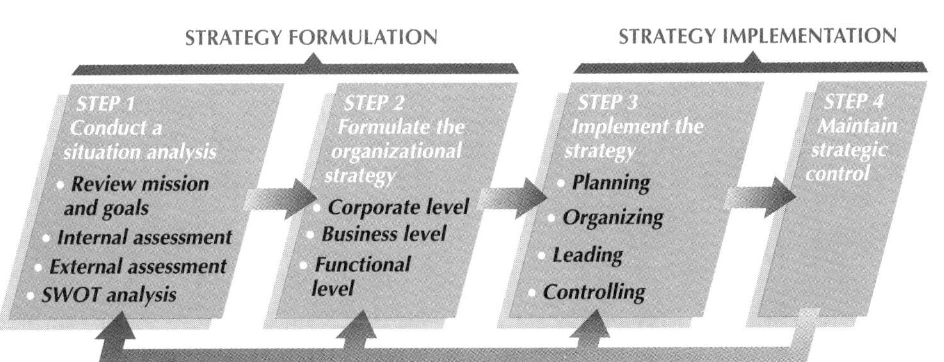

EXHIBIT 8.1

The Strategic Management Process

The four-step strategic management process provides a planning framework for managers to follow when formulating and implementing strategies for achieving organizational goals.

3. *Implement the strategy.* Once the strategies have been formulated, managers carry them out, using a combination of long-range, intermediate-range, and short-term plans.
4. *Maintain strategic control.* The final step is to monitor progress, evaluate results, and make any necessary corrections. This step provides feedback to every step in the process, allowing managers to reconsider their mission, goals, situation, strategy, and execution on an ongoing basis.

STEP 1: CONDUCT A SITUATION ANALYSIS

The first step in the strategic management process is to conduct a situation analysis. In this step, managers start by reviewing their current mission, their current goals, and the results of previous strategies. Next, they consider their organization's overall situation. In particular, they review the organization's context in terms of the internal and external environmental forces (described in Chapter 3) and the stakeholders (described in Chapter 4). To determine the potential impact that internal and external factors may have on the organization, its mission, and its ability to achieve goals, managers often practice SWOT analysis.

SWOT analysis A situation analysis tool that helps managers identify internal strengths and weaknesses, external opportunities and threats, and the potential impact of these factors on organizational performance

SWOT Analysis

SWOT analysis is a method that helps managers identify their organizational strengths *(S)*, organizational weaknesses *(W)*, environmental opportunities *(O)*, and environmental threats *(T)*. Each analysis helps them understand how these elements may influence organizational performance. An organizational *strength* is an internal capability that can be exploited to achieve goals, whereas an orga-

With monster competitors like Tower Video and Blockbuster Entertainment, Guy Hanford *(left)* has to continually be on the lookout for environmental threats and opportunities that may influence Kensington Video, the San Diego store his family owns and operates. To compete more effectively in a crowded market, the store has built its strategy around its key strength, a good selection of foreign and classic films.

nizational *weakness* is an internal characteristic that may undermine performance. An environmental *opportunity* is a situation that offers potential for helping the organization achieve its goals. In contrast, an environmental *threat* is an external element that can develop into a noncrisis or crisis problem and potentially prevent the organization from achieving its goals.[15]

SWOT analysis encompasses a wide range of issues. (See Exhibit 8.2 for a sampling.) By identifying the organization's strengths, weaknesses, opportunities, and threats, managers have the background to formulate strategies that build on their strengths and that take advantage of environmental opportunities. They are also better able to formulate strategies that aim to overcome or to minimize internal weaknesses and environmental threats.[16] To conduct the SWOT analysis, managers make both an internal assessment and an external assessment.

Internal Assessment

This part of the SWOT analysis involves examining internal resources and capabilities to identify organizational strengths and weaknesses. Primary sources of

EXHIBIT 8.2

Components of SWOT Situation Analysis

Managers examine their internal and external environments to identify strengths, weaknesses, opportunities, and threats that may influence their organizational performance.

Internal Environment	
Strengths	**Weaknesses**
A distinctive competence?	No clear strategic direction?
Adequate financial resources?	A deteriorating competitive position?
Good competitive skills?	Obsolete facilities?
Well thought of by buyers?	Subpar profitability because . . . ?
An acknowledged market leader?	Lack of managerial depth and talent?
Well-conceived functional area strategies?	Missing any key skills or competences?
Access to economies of scale?	Poor record of implementing strategy?
Insulated (at least somewhat) from strong competitive pressures?	Plagued with internal operating problems?
Proprietary technology?	Vulnerable to competitive pressures?
Cost advantages?	Falling behind in R&D?
Competitive advantages?	Too narrow a product line?
Product innovation abilities?	Weak market image?
Proven management?	Competitive disadvantages?
Other?	Below-average marketing skills?
	Unable to finance needed changes in strategy?
	Other?

External Environment	
Opportunities	**Threats**
Enter new markets or segments?	Likely entry of new competitors?
Add to product line?	Rising sales of substitute products?
Diversify into related products?	Slower market growth?
Add complementary products?	Adverse government policies?
Vertical integration?	Growing competitive pressures?
Ability to move to better strategic group?	Vulnerability to recession and business cycle?
Complacency among rival firms?	Growing bargaining power of customers or suppliers?
Faster market growth?	Changing buyer needs and tastes?
Other?	Adverse demographic changes?
	Other?

GLOBAL MANAGEMENT

A Strategy That Stretches around the World

From electrical cable and light bulbs to semiconductors and videocassette recorders, the saga of Thomson S.A. reads like a history of electrical power and electronics products. Founded in 1893 as a manufacturer of power generation equipment, the French manufacturer grew by diversifying into a dizzying array of related businesses such as x-ray equipment. But by the early 1980s, Thomson's financial condition had slipped out of control, and the embattled company (on the verge of collapse) was nationalized by the French government. In 1982, when Alain Gomez was appointed chairman and CEO, he set two goals for Thomson: to restore profitability and to successfully expand into the global arena. Gomez needed a new strategy to achieve these long-term goals and to position Thomson for international competition through the 1990s. He started with a situation analysis.

Assessing Thomson's internal capabilities, the CEO believed that the expertise in electronics manufacture was a strength he could capitalize on. From its roots in electrical equipment, the firm had moved into washing machines and other household appliances and had developed a sideline manufacturing home entertainment products such as radios and televisions. Moreover, the company had a thriving defense electronics business. However, one weakness was its semiconductor business, which had missed out on a decade of growth opportunities. The company owned a market share too small to be considered a serious competitor, even within the European market.

Externally, Gomez recognized two prime opportunities: a booming international market for consumer electronics products and a promising French market for defense electronics. But there were threats as well. Entrenched competitors were fighting hard over market share, a battle that threatened the potential profitability of consumer electronics. Moreover, Japanese firms were racing ahead with powerful new technology standards such as VHS videocassette recorders that effectively locked out competing formats around the world. To achieve his profitability and global expansion goals, Gomez needed a new strategy that would use company strengths to exploit opportunities, defuse threats, and minimize weaknesses.

Formulating and implementing an effective strategy meant making hard decisions about many of Thomson's traditions. Gomez considered the scope,

information for an internal assessment are the organizational MIS systems that cover functional areas such as finance, marketing, and operations. Additional sources of information about strengths and weaknesses include company patents, distribution procedures, marketing activities, financial results, and executives and employees. Also, managers examine the organization's historical performance to understand the circumstances and results of previous strategies.[17]

For example, the not-for-profit World Wildlife Fund United Kingdom (WWF) annually conducts an internal assessment to understand which key organizational areas have the potential to profoundly affect performance. Managers recently identified 10 key areas that are important to WWF's ability to achieve its goals of raising money and funding projects that conserve international natural resources. These included awareness by the general public and by conservation groups of the WWF's existence, and the use of human and physical resources. Assessing these key areas, managers concluded that WWF's good financial standing and its scientific authority were strengths, whereas its lack of campaigning activities was a weakness.[18]

External Assessment

By scanning the external environment, managers can detect opportunities and threats to organizational performance. Elements of both the general and the task environments are evaluated as part of the external assessment. Sources of information about the external environment include business publications, trade as-resource deployment, distinctive competencies, and synergy that would comprise his new strategy. Moving away from the company's roots, he narrowed his scope to consumer electronics, defense systems, and electronic components and sold unrelated businesses such as lighting, telecommunications, cables, and medical systems. In their place, Thomson established joint ventures with global competitors such as RCA (consumer electronics) and the Italian firm IRI (semiconductors). These alliances allowed Thomson to overcome its weaknesses by learning from its partners and by deepening its reach into products and markets within the new scope.

In line with this scope, the CEO redeployed his financial resources to acquire consumer electronic, semiconductor, television, and defense businesses from European and U.S. competitors. This move gave Thomson a strong presence outside its home markets in France and in Europe. Gomez viewed his company's skill in consumer electronics technologies as a distinctive competence and decided to license VHS and television picture tube technologies that would build on Thomson's capabilities. Finally, he fostered synergy by encouraging the exchange of management techniques among the many home-grown and acquired divisions. He deliberately complemented the flexibility and responsiveness of Thomson's French management team with the systematic decision-making processes practiced by the U.S. managers of the acquired consumer electronics divisions.

Today, Thomson's revenues have grown to $15 billion, and its activities have expanded to more than 50 countries. In an important step toward perfecting high-definition television technology, the company recently introduced a 34-inch stereophonic television system. Because the global outlook for the defense business is not encouraging, Gomez plans to move into consumer phone equipment and related areas. Moreover, a profit-sapping price war in consumer electronics looms in Europe, where Japanese competitors want to protect market share. So to stay on course toward his long-term goals throughout the 1990s, Gomez will have to stay ready to react to environmental changes with a strategy that stretches around the world.

Apply Your Knowledge

1. How can Gomez create synergy among the various parts of Thomson so that they complement or enhance each other?
2. If Gomez wants to sell televisions in Australia, what should he know about the external environment before crafting a strategy for that market?

sociations, industry suppliers, government and regulatory agencies, annual reports, and the organization's employees in sales, service, research, and other areas. Because of the pressures of formulating strategies under increasingly complex and uncertain environmental conditions, some organizations have set up special environmental scanning departments to gather and analyze information about the external environment. Moreover, it is important that managers place as high a priority on recognizing opportunities as on spotting potential threats; both play key roles in planning for the organization's future.

In the World Wildlife Fund U.K.'s external assessment, managers identified legislation, competition, and the economic climate as three significant environmental threats to marketing the organization. But the organization also uncovered a wealth of opportunities, including a growing public interest in nature conservation, a variety of untapped funding sources, and current events that prove the need for conservation. As a result of examining the internal and external environments, managers not only determined WWF's current situation but also examined the organization's relationship to other scientific and conservation organizations as part of the groundwork for identifying appropriate paths to the future.[19]

STEP 2: FORMULATE THE ORGANIZATIONAL STRATEGY

The second step in the strategic management process is to formulate organizational strategy. Strategy formulation at every level is guided by the organiza-

As chancellor of the University of Michigan at Dearborn, Blenda J. Wilson *(left)* uses strategic management to meet the goals of satisfying student needs and the needs of businesses that hire graduates. To stay abreast of environmental changes, Wilson regularly meets with students, faculty, and business leaders and examines the impact of trends such as the changing demographics of the student body and the level of state funding.

tional mission and by the results of the situation analysis. Managers start with their corporate-level strategies, which are used to develop business-level and functional-level strategies.

Developing Corporate-Level Strategy

At the corporate level, managers have two types of decisions to make when formulating strategy. First, they must decide on the overall direction for the organization by preparing a grand strategy that will serve as the master plan. Second, they must decide on a portfolio strategy that will determine the types of organizational activities and will establish how resources will be allocated among the businesses. The next two sections examine the elements of grand and portfolio strategies.[20]

Grand Strategy

grand strategy A comprehensive general strategy formulated to direct the major actions that will help the organization achieve long-term goals

Grand strategy is a comprehensive general strategy designed to guide the major actions that will accomplish the organization's long-term goals.[21] When selecting and implementing a grand strategy, managers are seeking to maintain or to improve the organization's performance in achieving its goals, making the most of environmental opportunities and internal strengths while minimizing external threats and internal weaknesses. Grand strategies include three types of strategies: growth, stability, and retrenchment (see Exhibit 8.3).

growth strategy A grand strategy involving expanding the organization along one or more dimensions

Growth Strategy Many organizations choose to define their targets in terms of increased sales, profits, market share, or similar measures, as Thomas Stemberg did when he outlined the strategy for Staples. When managers see opportunity on the horizon and believe their organizations have the internal capabilities to achieve higher goals, they formulate a **growth strategy** that will expand the

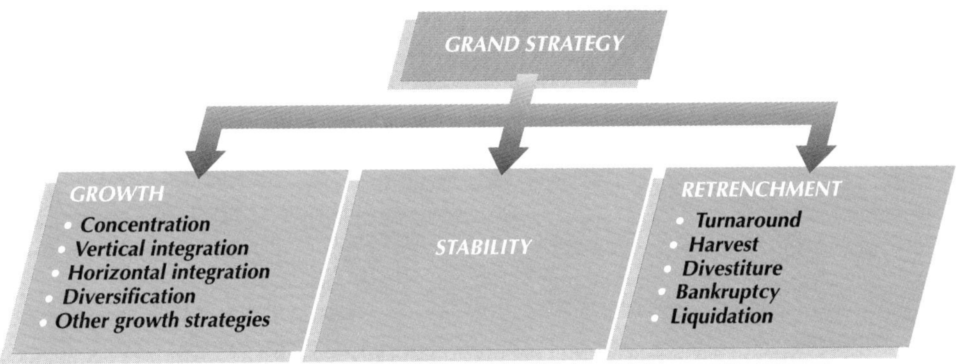

EXHIBIT 8.3

Selecting a Grand Strategy

When formulating corporate-level strategy, managers choose among three master plans for the organization's direction: growth, stability, and retrenchment.

organization along one or more of these dimensions. Among the possible growth strategies are concentration, vertical or horizontal integration, diversification, and other approaches.[22]

- *Concentration.* To direct their organizational resources toward the growth of a single product in a single market or of a small group of related products, managers rely on a **concentration** strategy. Also known as a *market penetration strategy,* this approach is a good way for organizations to improve their market position. McDonald's, Deere, and Apple have all used concentration to achieve market share goals.[23]

concentration A growth strategy that involves focusing organizational resources on the growth of one product or on a small group of related products

- *Vertical integration.* **Vertical integration** is a growth strategy that involves acquiring or starting up one or more organizations that supply resources, serve as customers, or serve as conduits to deliver the firm's products. Acquiring or establishing a supplier is *backward integration;* acquiring or establishing a customer or a distribution channel to customers is *forward integration.* Chiquita Brands applied forward integration when the company acquired North American and European fresh-produce distribution operations as well as a major Chilean exporter of fresh fruits and vegetables. These acquisitions support the company's position as the world's largest producer and marketer of bananas.[24]

vertical integration A growth strategy that involves the acquisition of one or more organizations that are suppliers, distributors, or customers of the firm's products

- *Horizontal integration.* When managers expand their organizations by acquiring one or more competitors, they are applying **horizontal integration.** In contrast to vertical integration, which involves expansion through the supply chains or the distribution channels that serve the organization, horizontal integration involves expansion by broadening the reach of the current product lines and eliminating the threat presented by the acquired competitor's operation. Horizontal integration is generally a step toward increasing organizational sales, profits, and market share. For example, when Giddings & Lewis, a machine-tool manufacturer based in Wisconsin, acquired rival Cross & Trecker, the combination resulted in a much stronger global presence and higher sales.[25]

horizontal integration A growth strategy that involves the acquisition of one or more competitors

- *Diversification.* Organizations that pursue growth through the acquisition or start-up of operations in other industries or in other lines of business are using a **diversification** strategy. Whereas horizontal integration involves broader expansion of current product lines, diversification involves expansion into differing product lines. One reason to diversify is to counter the effects of external environmental conditions such as economic changes and

diversification A growth strategy that involves the acquisition of organizations in other industries or in other lines of business

MANAGEMENT AROUND THE WORLD

Makers of consumer goods are increasingly interested in reaching the 150 million people in Brazil. One way to tap this market is to take advantage of the concentration of people in São Paulo and Rio de Janeiro, which together are home to nearly 30 million. This concentration presents a good opportunity for implementing a growth strategy by efficiently reaching customers in these huge cities.

seasonal changes. For instance, Head Ski originally diversified into summertime sports equipment and apparel to balance the seasonality of its winter business in ski goods. For other organizations, diversification is a way of acquiring product lines to replace products at the end of their life cycle, or of immediately acquiring a resource such as innovative technology.[26]

- *Other growth strategies.* To create an organization capable of competing more effectively, managers can choose to *merge* their organizations with another organization, creating an entirely new organization. Another option is to enter a joint venture to develop a specific product, technology, or market position. This option is increasingly attractive for companies that operate internationally, because it brings managers into contact with local partners who have intimate knowledge of the local environment and experience implementing business-level strategies for more effective competition.[27]

Growth strategies are dynamic, and managers may shift from one to another over a period of time. Consider the growth strategies of PepsiCo. Originally a soft-drink manufacturer, the corporation diversified during the 1960s by buying Frito-Lay snack foods, which now contribute more than $5.5 billion of Pepsi's $20 billion–plus annual sales. During the 1970s, the corporation bought Pizza Hut and Taco Bell, a vertical integration strategy because the restaurants provided new fountain outlets for PepsiCo drinks (as well as the opportunity to cash in on the fast-food boom). Today, the restaurant division (which includes KFC, acquired in 1986) rings up $7 billion annually. During the 1980s, PepsiCo's growth by horizontal integration included the addition of popcorn snack Smartfoods, a fast-growing Frito-Lay competitor in the United States, plus Smiths Crisps and Walkers Crisps, two leading snack makers in the United Kingdom. By adjusting his growth strategies to suit the organization's environment and capabilities, CEO Wayne Calloway can keep PepsiCo on the road to higher sales and profits.[28]

stability strategy A grand strategy that involves maintaining the status quo by continuing to offer the same goods or services and continuing to serve the same markets

Stability Strategy When an organization neither grows nor retrenches but continues to offer the same goods or services, to serve the same markets, and to perform the same functions over a period of time, it is pursuing a **stability strategy,** in which management consciously maintains the status quo, making only small, incremental changes. But stability is far from an inactive strategy. For example, managers can increase profits through productivity gains achieved by developing more business from existing customers, a move that exploits environmental opportunities or internal strengths revealed by the SWOT analysis. Or they can use stability to protect against environmental conditions that threaten market share or profits.[29]

Managers may adopt a stability approach when they believe that their organizations are doing well, when they perceive that changes may entail considerable risk, or as a break after a period of rapid growth. Rhys Eyton, president and CEO of PWA, is switching to a stability strategy now that he has built the Vancouver-based airline group into Canada's second largest airline, serving the United States, Europe, Asia, and South America. After years of explosive growth by acquisition, Eyton is turning his attention to customer service and systematic efficiencies to retain customers and rebuild his cash position.[30]

retrenchment strategy A grand strategy that involves reducing organizational operations

Retrenchment Strategy The third category of grand strategy is a **retrenchment strategy,** also known as *a defensive strategy,* in which management needs or wants to reduce organizational operations. When an organization is in financial trouble, is threatened by new competitors or by other environmental changes revealed in the situation analysis, or can be made more profitable by reducing operations, managers may choose retrenchment. Retrenchment strategies include turnaround, harvest, divestiture, bankruptcy, and liquidation.

- *Turnaround.* To reverse a negative trend and regain profitability, managers can launch a **turnaround.** In turnaround situations, management may reduce the payroll or trim employee benefits, cut the number of operating facilities, or eliminate unprofitable products and markets. But turnaround managers also try to increase customer satisfaction and to adjust pricing for better profitability. David Stern accomplished a major turnaround after becoming commissioner of the National Basketball Association (NBA) in 1984. When he took over, 17 out of 23 teams were losing money as a result of high costs and the public's image of drug-abusing players. Stern reversed the slide by strictly enforcing NBA antidrug regulations, capping salaries and other costs, and embarking on a full-court press to attract fans. Six years later, all but two NBA teams had become profitable—and those two were poised to move into the black when the multimillion-dollar prime-time television contract Stern negotiated with NBC starting filling the coffers.[31]

turnaround A retrenchment strategy intended to reverse a negative trend and regain profitability

- *Harvest.* When an organization is in decline, managers may adopt a **harvest** strategy, putting little money into and wringing the most cash out of the operation in the short term and, at the same time, planning to sell or liquidate in the long term. Using this strategy, management may increase prices to get maximum profits at the same time that advertising or marketing efforts are reduced or eliminated to cut costs.[32]

harvest A retrenchment strategy that involves minimizing investment and maximizing short-term profits while planning to sell or liquidate in the long term

- *Divestiture.* Managers use a **divestiture** strategy to sell all or part of an organization's operation. When a unit fits poorly with the remainder of the organization or does nothing to help achieve long-term organizational goals, divestiture is one solution that enables the unit to continue to exist but under another owner or as an independent business. Immediately after he was named chairman of Occidental Petroleum, Ray R. Irani unveiled a divestiture program calculated to bring organizational focus back to energy and chemical products and to help lower the company's debt level. Included in the list of operations on the selling block were a majority stake in a meat-processing company and part of a coal-mining venture in China.[33]

divestiture A retrenchment strategy that involves selling all or part of an organization

- *Bankruptcy.* At times, an organization degenerates into such deep financial distress that management decides its best alternative is **bankruptcy,** a form of court protection in which an organization unable to meet its obligations is allowed time and opportunity to prepare for a turnaround. Generally, managers choose bankruptcy only after they have failed to reverse a long period of decline. After Continental Airlines filed for bankruptcy protection in 1990, CEO Hollis L. Harris saved $54 million by suspending airplane lease payments, received a $20 million cash infusion from a major bank, renegotiated some airplane lease arrangements, and expanded Continental's schedule at New York airports. Harris hoped these moves would help the struggling airline regain financial stability and win back customers.[34]

bankruptcy A retrenchment strategy in which an organization unable to meet its obligations seeks court protection to gain time and opportunity to attempt a turnaround

- *Liquidation.* **Liquidation** is a retrenchment strategy that involves selling or dissolving an entire organization, ending its existence in the current form. Some small-business owners choose liquidation when they believe that their organization's future is bleak. However, organizations of any size can be

liquidation A retrenchment strategy that involves dissolving or selling an entire organization forced into liquidation because of their weakened financial condition. Eastern Airlines, the venerable U.S. carrier that was established in 1928, was liquidated in 1991 when all other remedies to reverse the airline's huge losses failed.[35]

Diversified organizations are likely to employ a combination of grand strategies, selecting an appropriate strategy for each individual division. For example, Henri Blanchet and Christian Moretti, the co-founders of the French conglomerate Dynaction, are using a combination of grand strategies to support ambitious profit goals for their 10 subsidiaries. Dynaction specializes in buying family-owned companies where succession is a problem and divisions of large firms that are being spun off. The co-founders use growth strategies to expand sales of the healthy businesses, preferably into international markets. But they also snap up troubled divisions and use retrenchment strategies to nurse these businesses back to health.[36]

Portfolio Strategy

portfolio strategy An approach to corporate-level strategy that involves analyzing the relationships and positions of an organization's SBUs to create the mix that will best support organizational goals

The second component of corporate-level strategy is portfolio strategy. Whereas grand strategy sets the organization's overall direction, portfolio strategy is concerned with the types of activities an organization will engage in and how resources will be allocated. Using a **portfolio strategy,** managers analyze the relationships and positions of an organization's SBUs to create the mix of businesses that will best support overall organizational goals. In this way, they can assemble a group of SBUs that takes advantage of synergies between the individual businesses and allows for better coordination of SBU goals and strategies. Portfolio strategy also helps managers compare differing businesses and decide how to allocate resources among them.[37]

Two major techniques managers can use to develop portfolio strategy are the BCG growth-share matrix and the GE business screen.

BCG growth-share matrix A four-cell matrix that categorizes SBUs in the organizational portfolio according to market growth and market share

BCG *Growth-Share* Matrix The Boston Consulting Group (BCG), a leading management consulting firm, developed one of the earliest tools for understanding the position of businesses within the corporate portfolio. The **BCG growth-share matrix** helps a manager classify the SBUs within the organization's portfolio according to market growth and market share (see Exhibit 8.4). *Market growth* is defined as the annual rate of growth within the SBU's market; *market share* is the relative market share held by the SBU when its sales are compared with the largest competitor. The result is a four-cell matrix divided by the measures of high and low. Managers plot the position of each SBU and then examine how well the portfolio is balanced in terms of users of resources and contributors of resources. Depending on their position on the matrix, SBUs can be categorized as question marks, stars, cash cows, or dogs.[38]

- *Question marks* hold a low share of a high-growth market. Many SBUs begin as question marks by entering high-growth markets in which market leaders are already established. Question marks, also known as wildcats, are aptly named because they have an uncertain future. Such businesses require substantial cash infusions if they are to attain higher market share, but they may never gain enough share to grow into stars. The decision here is between growth and retrenchment.
- *Stars* hold a high market share of a high-growth market. The star is a key category because of its future profit and cash potential. But it does not neces-

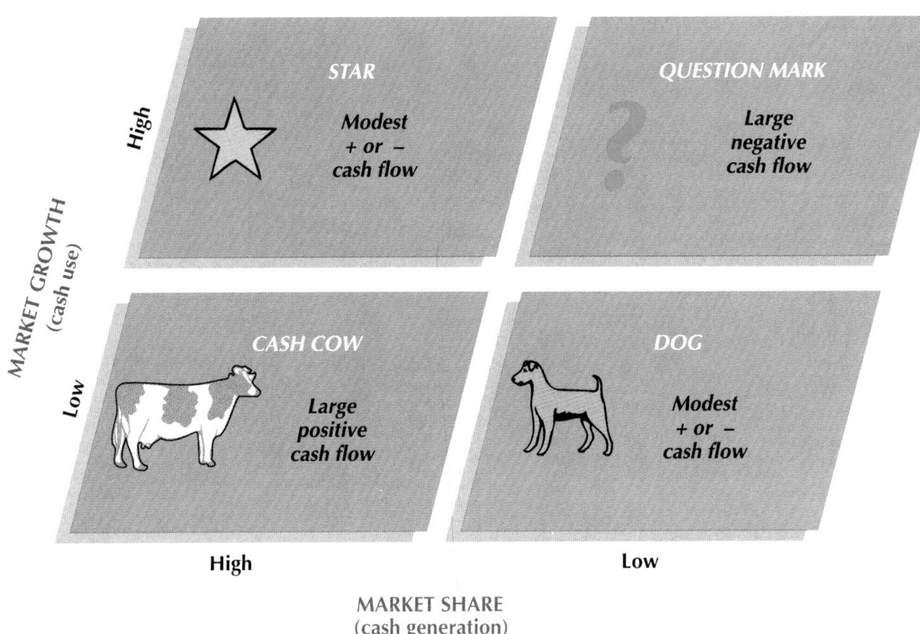

EXHIBIT 8.4

The BCG Growth-Share Matrix

The Boston Consulting Group developed this matrix to help managers analyze the relative market growth and market share positions of SBUs within the corporate portfolio. Once they have pinpointed SBUs on this matrix, managers have a better understanding of cash flow and cash requirements, and they can make more informed resource allocation decisions.

sarily produce much current cash flow and in fact often requires investment to keep up with the rapid pace of market growth. Managers generally use a growth strategy to develop a star into a cash cow.

- *Cash cows* hold a high share of a low-growth market. Cash cows are generally well-established businesses in mature markets. Because high cash investment is no longer required to establish and nurture this type of business, a cash cow can yield high profits. The cash from cash cows can be invested in the development of SBUs in other categories, such as stars and question marks.
- *Dogs* hold a low share of a low-growth market. Such businesses typically produce low profits and little cash, but they may absorb large amounts of cash and management time. Faced with a dog, managers usually consider a retrenchment strategy such as divestiture, harvest, or turnaround.

Although the BCG growth-share matrix is a technique that helps managers understand and balance cash flows, as well as providing general guidance on strategy formulation, it also has several weaknesses. First, this analysis assumes that market growth and market share are good measures for determining investment and cash flow, an assumption that is not universally valid. Second, the matrix does not help managers compare SBUs within the same category, such as two question marks. Third, slotting SBUs into a convenient matrix is not a substitute for a thorough analysis of each business, each market, future prospects, and competitive position. Finally, the matrix ignores factors such as competition, which are important in strategy formulation.[39]

GE Business Screen When General Electric was faced with the problem of evaluating strategies for its portfolio of more than 40 SBUs, it turned to management consultants McKinsey and Company for help. Together they developed the **GE business screen,** a nine-cell matrix that is used as a tool to help managers

GE business screen A nine-cell matrix that classifies SBUs according to industry attractiveness and business strength

EXHIBIT 8.5

The GE Business Screen

To evaluate a portfolio of businesses, managers can use this three-by-three matrix developed by General Electric in conjunction with prominent management consultants McKinsey and Company. Depending on where each SBU is positioned on this matrix, managers can choose a growth, stability, or retrenchment strategy.

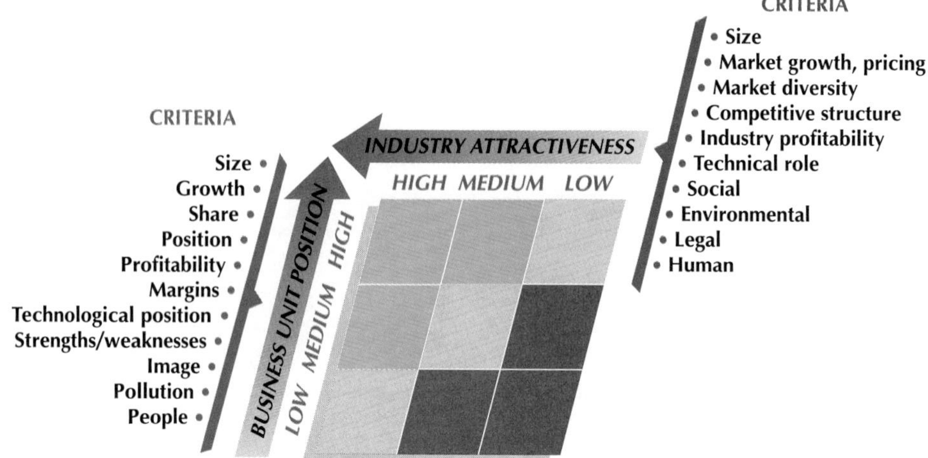

analyze SBUs according to industry attractiveness and business strength. This model relies on the manager's ability to identify the specific factors that contribute to success in a particular industry. For example, the criteria for evaluating industry attractiveness include the size of the market, market growth, and the competitive situation (see Exhibit 8.5). The criteria for evaluating business strength include market share, profitability, and business size. However, managers may choose different factors for each SBU in the corporate portfolio. Next, each SBU and its industry is rated as high, medium, or low on the two matrix dimensions, and its position is plotted on the matrix. Once the entire portfolio has been plotted, managers can check the balance, plan strategy, and use the position of each SBU to determine corporate investment and resource allocation.[40]

According to this model, the most attractive businesses are those in which the SBU holds a strong position in a highly attractive industry. The three green boxes of the matrix represent such businesses, and managers typically follow a growth strategy for those, making them a high priority for investing corporate funds and allocating resources. The yellow boxes represent less attractive businesses, and managers generally choose selective growth or stability for these, depending on the characteristics of the individual businesses. The red boxes represent the least attractive businesses because the businesses have low competitive strength in unattractive industries. In these situations, managers choose retrenchment strategies and limit corporate investment and resources.[41]

By balancing the potential and the investment needs of all SBUs in the corporate portfolio, managers can allocate resources to the businesses that are most likely to succeed and minimize investment in businesses that are marginal or performing poorly. Compared with the BCG growth-share matrix, the GE business screen is a more sophisticated technique to use in formulating portfolio strategy, because it encompasses many more of the factors that are critical for business success. However, the screen shares some of the same drawbacks as the BCG growth-share matrix, including the lack of specific recommended strategies for individual businesses.[42]

Both the BCG growth-share matrix and the GE business screen are useful tools for planning portfolio strategy, but they do have limitations. Especially when the external environment is unstable, these approaches may be difficult to

(Skip)

apply because market or competitive boundaries can change quickly or become blurred. Moreover, the internal environment can also change, and managers must be alert to the impact of these shifts on the SBUs and on their position within the overall organization. Nevertheless, portfolio planning can provide useful insights if managers recognize the underlying assumptions, carefully select the key factors, adjust to the changing demands of the environment, and use good judgment.[43]

In addition to helping managers assess their current portfolios, portfolio strategy can help managers assess the potential impact of acquiring businesses. For example, Jose Concepcion III, president of the Philippine firm RFM, wants to improve the balance of food products in his portfolio. Originally a flour-milling concern, RFM also offers chicken and meat products, but all of these foods are subject to government price controls that can potentially damage RFM's profits and cash flow. For that reason, Concepcion recently acquired an ice cream manufacturer and a soft-drink bottler. These acquisitions have helped Concepcion balance his corporate portfolio in two ways: first, they provide RFM with a presence in lucrative markets, and second, they establish RFM in product lines that are not subject to government price controls.[44]

Developing Business-Level Strategy

After determining corporate-level strategy, managers formulate business-level strategy. If the organization has more than one business, managers need to develop a business-level strategy appropriate for each business. Guided by the direction set by the corporate-level strategy, business-level strategy is concerned with the way each business approaches its marketplace.[45] Managers can use three tools as frameworks to analyze and to support their development of business-level strategy: Miles and Snow's adaptation model, Porter's generic competitive strategies, and the product life cycle model.

Miles and Snow's Adaptation Model

After studying the practices of organizations in four industries, Raymond E. Miles and Charles C. Snow developed the **adaptation model,** a framework that helps explain how managers relate business-level strategy to their organizational environment. According to this model, organizations meet the challenges of uncertainty and change in the external environment through adaptation. This process of adaptation involves aligning strategy and the internal environment to the external environment. Miles and Snow identified four business-level strategies that managers use to adapt to the environment: the defender strategy, the prospector strategy, the analyzer strategy, and the reactor strategy.[46]

adaptation model A strategy analysis tool based on the relationship of business-level strategy to the internal and external environments

- *The defender strategy* involves defining a narrow market niche that the organization can thoroughly penetrate with a limited number of goods or services. Having attained market share, the organization focuses on defending its domain and pursuing internal efficiencies rather than worrying about the external environment. The defender strategy is most effective in a stable environment, where it can lead to high profitability, but this approach may leave the organization vulnerable in the case of a major environmental shift. For example, the Morrison chain of cafeterias based in Mobile, Alabama, tradi-

EXHIBIT 8.6

The Adaptation Model of Business-Level Strategy

Because organizations confront varying degrees of environmental uncertainty and change, managers can adapt to the external environment by applying one of four business-level strategies.

Strategy	Approach to Environment	Risks
Defender	In a stable environment, defender selects a limited domain to penetrate and defend. Relies on strict controls to ensure efficiency.	Defender may be unable to respond to major shifts in the environment or to quickly switch technologies, products, or markets.
Prospector	In a dynamic environment, prospector seeks out and exploits new product and market opportunities. Remains flexible and responsive to environmental changes.	Prospector may yield low profitability due to costs of overextension of the resources needed to innovate in a changing environment. Prospector also faces risk of inefficiencies due to the multiplicity of technologies in use.
Analyzer	In an environment with both stable and changeable characteristics, analyzer pursues innovation while protecting current customer base. Requires a balance of flexibility and stability.	Analyzer risks both inefficiency and ineffectiveness because of inability to respond fully either to total stability or to a major environmental shift.
Reactor	In any type of environment, reactor acts without a consistent strategy. Reactor responds inappropriately and in an ad hoc fashion.	Reactor risks poor performance because of inability to react appropriately or consistently to any environmental situation.

tionally followed a defender strategy, concentrating on Southern shopping centers and offering low-priced home-style meals. However, the chain saturated its market, and when shoppers deserted the malls during the 1990–1991 recession, Morrison ran into trouble.[47]

- *The prospector strategy* is nearly the opposite of the defender strategy, being concerned with identifying and exploiting new product and market opportunities. Organizations that follow the prospector strategy carefully scan their environment for signs of change and tend to be flexible, innovative, and dynamic when exploiting these changes. The prospector strategy is therefore well suited to uncertain, changeable environments, but it can be a costly strategy to pursue. As one example, 3M, headquartered in St. Paul, Minnesota, uses a prospector strategy to continuously study its environment for signs of new opportunities. This strategy enables 3M to develop, perfect, and market a steady stream of innovative products in each of its four business sectors.[48]
- *The analyzer strategy* combines elements of the defender and prospector strategies. Using this strategy, the organization maintains a firm base of traditional products and customers while simultaneously watching its competitors and searching for new products and markets that appear to be viable. Thus, the organization must have the flexibility to respond to environmental change but must also have the stability to profit from a stable environment. However, if managers cannot keep flexibility and stability in balance, the result can be inefficiency and ineffectiveness. One example of the analyzer strategy in use is EgyptAir, which is protecting its profitable Cairo-based transportation and tourism business while expanding in promising new areas such as specialized packaging and soft drinks, two markets not being pursued by its competitors.[49]

- *The reactor strategy* is not a proactive response to the organizational environment and so is not really a strategy at all. Unlike organizations that follow the defender, prospector, and analyzer strategies and actively form a consistent pattern of adjustment to their environments, organizations that fall into the reactor category lack a set of consistent mechanisms for adaptation. Such organizations respond in ad hoc fashion to environmental change and uncertainty, thereby achieving only poor performance.[50]

These business-level strategies are summarized in Exhibit 8.6. In the view of researchers Miles and Snow, an organization must constantly reevaluate its mission, redefine its interaction with the environment, identify and maintain a viable market for products, and arrange internal alignments to mount a successful business-level strategy. Although the external environment can restrict management's ability to maneuver, the adaptation model argues that top managers can pursue strategies that allow their organizations to successfully adapt and perform well.[51]

Porter's Generic Competitive Strategies

The second analytical framework for formulating business-level strategy was developed by Harvard Business School professor Michael E. Porter, who studied the interplay of forces within the competitive marketplace and their effect on profitability. **Porter's generic competitive strategies** are cost leadership, differentiation, and focus, three broad business-level strategies that organizations can adopt to achieve competitive advantage within their industries. The strategies are considered generic because they can be applied in a variety of situations. Each requires particular skills, resources, and organizational characteristics (see Exhibit 8.7).[52]

- *Cost leadership strategy.* In following a **cost leadership strategy,** the organization consciously works at keeping costs as low as possible, appealing to a

Porter's generic competitive strategies Three business-level strategies—cost leadership, differentiation, and focus—that help organizations attain competitive advantage

cost leadership strategy A generic competitive strategy that keeps costs as low as possible to attract a broad market and to yield high profits

EXHIBIT 8.7

Porter's Generic Competitive Strategies

Harvard professor Michael E. Porter has identified three generic competitive strategies that organizations can use to achieve competitive advantage on the business level. If an organization does not make a clear choice about which strategy it will follow, Porter warns that it will be "stuck in the middle" and unable to achieve high profitability.

Strategy	Commonly Required Skills and Resources	Common Organizational Requirements
Cost leadership	Sustained capital investment and access to capital Process engineering skills Intense supervision of labor Products designed for ease in manufacture Low-cost distribution system	Tight cost control Frequent, detailed control reports Structured organization and responsibilities Incentives based on meeting strict quantitative targets
Differentiation	Strong marketing abilities Product engineering Creative flair Strong capability in basic research Corporate reputation for quality or technological leadership Long tradition in the industry or unique combination of skills drawn from other businesses Strong cooperation from channels	Strong coordination among functions in R&D, product development, and marketing Subjective measurement and incentives instead of quantitative measures Amenities to attract highly skilled labor, scientists, or creative people
Focus	Combination of the other two policies directed at the particular strategic target	Combination of the other two policies directed at the particular strategic target

MANAGERIAL DECISION MAKING

BankAmerica Turnaround Puts Money in the Bank

When A. W. (Tom) Clausen retired for the second time from BankAmerica, he was able to look back with satisfaction on two separate careers as chairman and CEO of the second-largest bank in the United States. During Clausen's first tour as CEO, he pursued a rapid growth strategy, moving aggressively into real estate and international loans. The second time around, Clausen took the helm of a troubled bank in need of a carefully crafted retrenchment strategy. From 1985 through 1987, BankAmerica lost nearly $2 billion, and bank regulators were concerned about its rapidly deteriorating condition. Moreover, a much smaller rival nearly succeeded in a hostile takeover attempt. Reeling from the combined effects of bank deregulation, fierce competition, bad loans, and an unsettled world economy, BankAmerica was on the brink of disaster.

When the board invited Clausen back in 1986, the survival of BankAmerica was in question. The two-time CEO took a long, hard look at the situation and realized that the bank no longer had the resources to be all things to all people. Instead, he set two new goals: to become the major provider of bank services in the western United States and to be a major player in international wholesale banking. Then Clausen made five decisions that would shape BankAmerica's future.

First, he recognized that the bank's external environment had irreversibly changed and that his management team would have to key its strategies to today's challenges, even if that meant restructuring the organization of the entire bank and changing its approach to banking. Second, Clausen decided to rebuild his management team with experienced bankers who had the ability to implement the new strategy. Third, he decided that profitability had to be improved. Fourth, he decided to concentrate on actions that would bring immediate results but not at the expense of BankAmerica's future. And fifth, Clausen resolved to proactively communicate about the bank's performance inside and outside the organization.

Implementing this turnaround strategy involved

Yves Saint Laurent creates stylish and distinctive apparel as part of a differentiation strategy that sets his fashion designs apart from Ungaro, Christian Dior, and other competitors. His most exclusive fashions must be made to order in Paris, which further emphasizes their uniqueness.

differentiation strategy A generic competitive strategy in which an organization crafts a product that customers perceive to be distinctly different from the competition

broad market, and pursuing high returns. Managers who adopt a cost leadership strategy actively control costs such as labor, raw materials, and marketing while pursuing efficiencies in production, purchasing, and other areas. By becoming the industry cost leader, managers can price their products below the competition and gain market share and higher profits. However, if an organization is not consistent in pursuing a strategy of cost leadership, its success can potentially be challenged by competitors who imitate its moves or use improved technology to achieve even more cost efficiencies. Wal-Mart has parlayed cost leadership into a $32 billion retailing empire that is now the nation's largest. Wal-Mart managers keep a tight lid on merchandise and store operating costs so that they can offer low prices, and they continue to work on additional warehouse and distribution efficiencies.[53]

- *Differentiation strategy.* A company is using a **differentiation strategy** when it creates a product that customers perceive to be unique when compared with the competition. Managers can differentiate their products on the basis of technology (Intel microprocessors), customer service (American Express credit cards), product design (Sony's Walkman), distribution (Caterpillar tractors), and other dimensions that are meaningful to customers. When customers believe that these products are indeed different from competing products, they are generally willing to pay premium prices. The benefits of differentiation are customer loyalty and higher profits. But organizations following this strategy also face challenges from competitors who imitate or improve on this differentiating characteristic, which can erode its importance to customers.[54]
- *Focus strategy.* An organization that concentrates its efforts on a narrow portion of the market, such as a particular customer segment, part of a prod-

decisions that affected every corner of the bank. For example, BankAmerica had traditionally protected the jobs of its employees, but Clausen cut more than 21,000 from the payroll over a four-year period. He also closed enough BankAmerica branches in California to save almost $100 million in yearly expenses. Clausen recruited Richard M. Rosenberg, president of BankAmerica's SeaFirst Bank subsidiary, to run the branch system and to introduce new products, which brought in hundreds of thousands of new accounts.

Moreover, Clausen involved the entire bank in the turnaround, asking every employee—even those not normally involved with selling—to bring in one new customer. Employees responded by making 18,000 referrals in a three-month period. To boost productivity and to reward employees who exceeded their goals, Clausen and Rosenberg installed an incentive system linking pay to performance. The bank shrank its international loan portfolio and chopped away incessantly at its bad-debt problem. Thanks to smart marketing, higher employee productivity, and improved cost controls, the bank began to leave its money-losing days behind. In a dramatic turnaround, BankAmerica racked up $1.1 billion in net income two years in a row, outpacing the earnings of every other bank in the country.

Although Clausen retired in 1990, the legacy of his successful turnaround lives on. Richard Rosenberg now heads a BankAmerica that is back on the trail of aggressive growth. In addition to the acquisition of rival Security Pacific, the bank has acquired smaller banks in Oregon, Washington, Nevada, Arizona, Texas, and New Mexico. Now the bank operates more than 1,300 branches that serve over 5 million households, and the CEO is eyeing the 187 million customers currently beyond the reach of BankAmerica branches, especially in East Coast markets. As he makes the decisions that will bring his goal of nationwide banking closer, Rosenberg tempers his growth strategy with the memory of BankAmerica's recent turnaround.

Apply Your Knowledge

1. How can Rosenberg apply Porter's theories of generic competitive strategies to make decisions about business-level strategy?
2. How can the GE business screen help Rosenberg manage the banks in BankAmerica's portfolio?

uct line, or a specific geographic area, is using a **focus strategy.** The organization gears every aspect of its operation toward serving its narrow target through either cost leadership or differentiation. When following a focus strategy, the organization is seeking to be rewarded with the higher profitability of dominating a smaller market that is not intensely competitive. As with the other two generic strategies, if an organization does not maintain its focus, it faces risks. For example, broad-targeted competitors may overwhelm the market, or a competitor may subsegment the market to focus on a narrower target. White Castle is a fast-food restaurant chain that follows a focus strategy. The company operates in only 25 markets with a stripped-down menu featuring tiny, low-priced hamburgers. Unlike competitors who have broadened their menus, the 70-year-old chain has consistently maintained its focus on hamburgers and has built up a devoted following that gobbles up $319 million worth of White Castle food products each year.[55]

focus strategy A generic competitive strategy in which an organization concentrates on a limited part of the market, a limited product line, or a confined geographic area

Although Porter contends that organizations can only rarely be successful in pursuing both differentiation and cost leadership simultaneously, this has been disputed by other researchers. Some studies have uncovered a variety of situations in which differentiation and cost leadership seem to be compatible. Therefore, managers must take a contingency viewpoint and consider their own situation before selecting a business-level strategy.[56]

Product Life Cycle

The third analytical technique that managers can use to support their formulation of business-level strategy is the **product life cycle,** which describes the passage of goods and services through a sequence of marketing stages (see Ex-

product life cycle The passage of goods and services through a progression of market acceptance stages

EXHIBIT 8.8

The Product Life Cycle

Every product, whether it is a tangible item or a service, passes through a series of marketing stages that make up the product's life cycle. At each stage, managers must consider how to allocate resources to maximize sales and profits.

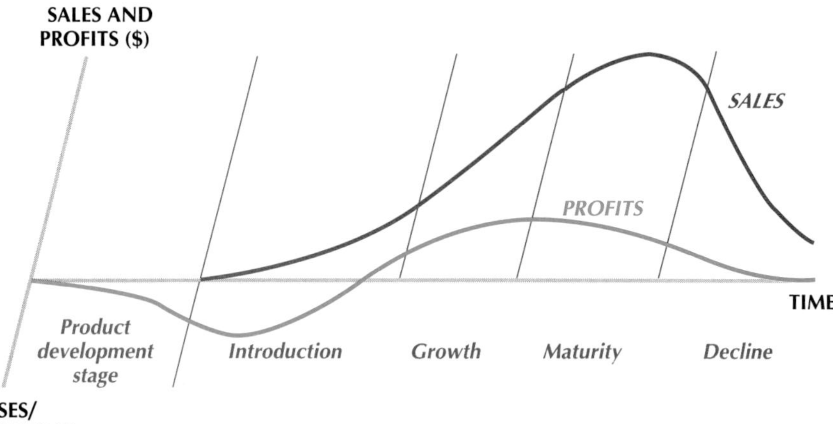

hibit 8.8). Sales and profits vary from stage to stage, so by understanding and anticipating these stages, managers can apply appropriate business-level strategies. When the product is under development, the company makes an investment but sees no sales in return. In the introduction stage, sales for the new product build slowly, providing low or no profits because of the expense of development and introduction. Next, the product passes into the growth stage, in which sales and profits improve substantially. In the maturity stage, sales and profits peak and slowly decline. Finally, the product slips into the decline stage, in which sales drop off and profits erode. How long it takes for a product to pass through these stages depends on the product and on the market; products such as rock music CDs move through the cycle more quickly than staple products such as refrigerators.[57]

Managers can coordinate their business-level strategies with the stages of the product life cycle to maximize sales and profits. For example, during the introduction and growth stages, managers frequently use differentiation or prospector strategies to exploit their innovations. During the maturity and decline stages, managers may shift gears, investing organizational resources to pursue cost leadership or defender strategies that boost efficiency and to sustain profits.[58] Product life cycle is important for the furniture retailer Bombay, which operates more than 300 mall-based stores in the United States and Canada. Chairman Robert Nourse and his wife Aagje Nourse carefully exploit the product life cycle to fuel their growth strategy. To keep merchandise fresh and to attract impulse buyers, the Nourses change 25 percent of the furniture, 50 percent of the wall decor products, and 75 percent of the home accessories every year. With this understanding of product life cycle, Bombay has been able to ring up retail sales per square foot that are four times that of the average furniture store.[59]

Deaf Life, a national magazine for deaf people, reached the growth stage of the product life cycle after a year in development and 2 years in the introduction stage. Publisher Matthew Moore launched the monthly magazine in 1987, built the subscription base to 3,000 within 3 years, and will continue growing by adding new features to appeal to younger readers.

Developing Functional-Level Strategy

The third level of organizational strategy involves developing the functional-level strategy. Managers formulate functional-level strategies to support the execution of their business-level strategies. A functional-level strategy is narrower in scope than a business-level strategy because each strategy deals only with the part of the business-level strategy that relates to each of the six organizational functions: marketing, finance, operations, human resources, research and development, and information resources. Although each functional area follows its own strategy, all must be coordinated with each other and integrated with the business-level strategy they support.[60]

- *Marketing.* The marketing function supports every type of business-level strategy through its focus on customer needs and through the use of product, price, distribution, and promotion strategies. In an analyzer strategy, marketing would be involved in maintaining the current customer base while reaching out to new markets. For instance, when Coca-Cola implemented its business-level strategy of expanding into the Japanese market, the company relied on a wide range of marketing strategies, including establishing a distribution sales force, deploying a complement of vending machines, and using extensive promotion. As a result, Coke was able to grab 70 percent of the Japanese market for soft drinks.[61]
- *Finance.* The finance function supports business-level strategy through finding and funneling financial resources, analyzing costs and profits, handling the organization's assets, and managing tax and accounting requirements. In a cost leadership strategy, for example, the finance function would project sales volumes and monitor costs and profits. Finance managers are also involved in obtaining capital from sources such as stock offerings, loans, and private investment. When Sweden-based Saab's aircraft-manufacturing division wanted to increase production of its 50-seat commuter airplane to keep up with orders from American Airlines and others, financial managers obtained financing from the Swedish government and from other sources.[62]
- *Operations.* The operations (or production) function is concerned with obtaining raw materials, developing appropriate production processes, producing goods or services, maintaining inventory, and making adjustments in plant or service capacity. In a prospector strategy, for example, operations may build or lease additional plants or service facilities to take advantage of a new product or a new market opportunity. The Finnish shipbuilder Oy Wartsila Ab has used its production flexibility to build competitive advantage. The company adapted its production capabilities to be able to build smaller specialized ships, which other shipbuilders avoid. In this way, it has carved out a profitable niche and become a major international supplier.[63]
- *Human resources.* To support business-level strategies, organizations develop human resources strategies that cover issues such as number of employees required, skill levels, training needs, motivation, salary and benefits, and labor relations. For example, an organization might require the human resources function to attract and train more salespeople at the start of the product life cycle but fewer when the product goes into decline. Human resources made a major contribution to Seagate Technology's strategy of relocating its manufacture of computer memory devices in Thailand. Starting there eight years ago with 50 employees, the company now has over 15,000 Thai employees and is one of the country's two largest employers. Seagate managers cite human resource availability, trainability, and low turnover as key reasons for their success.[64]
- *Research and development.* When business-level strategy involves innovations or improvements in goods or services, the research and development (R&D) function supports these needs. R&D is concerned with uncovering new advances, improving current products or processes, and developing new ways to apply technology. For instance, in a prospector strategy, the R&D

GM's R&D functional-level strategy stresses sharing technology among GM units to support business-level and corporate-level strategies. To reach the goal of developing a viable electric car, GM coupled the talents of its Hughes Aircraft subsidiary and alternative energy experts Howard Wilson, Paul MacCready, and Alec Brooks of AeroVironment (partly owned by GM).

function would aggressively search for new products and new technologies. At Corning, the specialty glass manufacturer in Corning, New York, the R&D functional strategy calls for identifying, developing, and sharing new products and new technologies among SBUs throughout the organization. A central R&D function serves all business groups, and technologies are shared and recycled throughout the organization. For example, a ceramic material that the firm originally developed for dinnerware has become the basis for a computer memory disk.[65]

- *Information resources.* The information resources function supports business-level strategy by providing information to support all functional areas and all levels of management, along with the means of gathering data, storing and analyzing them, and presenting results. Included in this function are transaction-processing systems, management information systems, and decision support systems. The information resources function has helped Jackson Hewitt, a tax preparation firm based in Virginia Beach, to compete against industry giant H&R Block in the growing market for electronic tax transmission, which enables customers to receive refunds faster. CEO John Hewitt's information resources support a sophisticated computer system that allows Jackson Hewitt tax preparers in 12 states to fill in an electronic tax return that is ready for immediate transmission to the IRS.[66]

STEP 3: IMPLEMENT THE STRATEGY

In the previous steps, managers established the mission and goals, reviewed their situation, and developed one or more courses of action to achieve organizational goals. To have an effect on organizational performance, the strategy must be implemented. In this step, managers create the conditions under which a strategy can be successfully set into motion by applying the four functions in the management process.[67]

- *Planning.* In the context of strategy implementation, planning involves setting goals and integrating and coordinating activities at all organizational levels. This ensures that managers on each level and in each function understand the direction and the timetable. Because managers at higher levels set the guidelines for plans that implement strategy at lower levels, they can coordinate implementation at the various levels. Moreover, managers review implementation plans to be sure they are consistent with the organization's overall strategy and allocated resources and to resolve any overlaps or conflicts between levels or functions.[68]
- *Organizing.* To implement strategy, managers need to define exactly what must be done and then assign resources and responsibility for specific tasks to individuals and to groups within the organization. The organizing function involves identifying specific tasks, matching the skills of people and groups within the organization to these tasks, and coordinating and integrating the use of resources to achieve performance. Moreover, any changes that are made to ease implementation may affect (or be affected) by the organization's culture. For this reason, managers must consider how the culture helps or hinders implementation, then take steps to ensure that the culture is in tune with the strategic direction they want to take.[69]
- *Leading.* The leading function is concerned with providing direction for the organization at all levels, communicating the strategy, and motivating em-

ployees. In many but not all cases, successful implementation depends on the skills of the managers who execute the strategy. Also, the leading function includes communicating so that employees understand the strategy and are motivated to perform in ways that support the implementation process.[70]

- *Controlling.* To manage the organizational resources and the processes involved in implementing the strategy, managers apply the controlling function of the management process. This function also monitors and measures whether the organization makes progress in implementation and whether the actions taken are helping to achieve goals. Using control techniques allows managers to understand whether the strategy is being implemented correctly and whether changes are necessary.[71]

When Rochelle Zabarkes opened Adriana's Bazaar, a gourmet shop in New York City, implementation was the key to carrying out her growth strategy. Zabarkes set out to establish a one-stop food shop where her sophisticated Manhattan clientele could buy professionally prepared entrées as well as the authentic ingredients to cook in 15 international cuisines. She set \$300,000 to \$350,000 as her first-year sales goal and was aiming for sales of \$500,000—and profitability—by the third year of operation. To implement her strategy, she developed detailed operational plans covering every minute detail, including store operation, advertising, and accounting. She defined the specific duties of her salespeople; then she recruited, hired, and trained the three employees who wait on customers. Her enthusiasm and extensive knowledge of her environment, her market, and her products has helped Zabarkes motivate and communicate with her salespeople. Moreover, she uses control methods to keep costs such as inventory in check and to set appropriate prices, both of which affect profitability. These control techniques allow Zabarkes to determine whether her plans are achieving the goals she set, and they allow her to identify whether her actual results vary from the expected results. Zabarkes was struggling during the recessionary period in 1992, but if she continues to implement her strategy, and if the economy cooperates, she should be on her way toward meeting her yearly goals.[72]

STEP 4: MAINTAIN STRATEGIC CONTROL

Strategic control is the fourth and final step in the strategic management process. Most of the time, managers implement strategy and then wait, sometimes for a lengthy period, until they can see the expected results. In the interim, both the internal and the external environments on which the strategy has been based continue to evolve. Managers use strategic control to track the progress of the strategy, assess whether the changing environment poses current or future problems that would interfere with achieving goals, and make any necessary adjustments to put the strategy back on track toward planned goals. In this step, managers identify the critical areas to be monitored and then develop methods for measuring results. Often, managers use a computerized MIS to collect, store, analyze, and report the details they need to maintain strategic control.[73]

If strategic control is too rigid, it can stifle the flexibility that managers need to cope with environmental uncertainty. If it is applied too soon or too late, it may be ineffective in detecting deviations from strategy or in adjusting to environmental changes. For these reasons, strategic control is a delicate balancing act in which managers juggle the methods and timing of feedback, evaluation, and corrective action. But if strategic control has been properly planned, it strengthens management's ability to recognize the need for change, to assess the alternatives, and to react by making the change. Of course, when SBUs pursue differing strategies, the strategic controls for each must take into account their varying resource allocations as well as their individual strategies. Global organizations must be particularly sensitive to the degree to which strategic control hampers or helps local managers implementing strategy within varying local environments.[74] Control is discussed in more detail in Chapter 19.

Consider the key role that strategic control plays in keeping the global strategies of two giants of food marketing on track. General Mills and Nestlé have created a joint venture called Cereal Partners Worldwide (CPW), which is using a growth strategy to aim for 20 percent of the European cereal market by the year 2000, and which has also set a goal of attaining profitability within five years. CEO Charles Gaillard is monitoring progress toward these twin goals at key milestones. By the end of the first year, stores in Spain and Portugal already sold the cereals, and the firm had persuaded 80 percent of the food retailers in France to carry its products. Although Gaillard is pleased that CPW's strategy is on track and on schedule, he knows that the venture still has far to go to achieve its long-term goals.[75]

SUMMARY

Strategic management is the ongoing process of formulating and implementing comprehensive plans that help organizations fulfill their missions and achieve their strategic goals. This process provides a framework for examining the organizational environment, for developing and implementing strategies, and for responding to environmental changes. Strategic management consists of four steps: (1) conduct a situation analysis, (2) formulate the organizational strategy, (3) implement the strategy, and (4) maintain strategic control.

Managers formulate strategy at three levels: at the corporate level, at the business level, and at the functional level. Top managers formulate corporate-level strategy to set overall direction for the organization. Business-level strategy guides the activities of each strategic business unit. Functional-level strategy for each of the organizational functions supports the execution of business-level strategy. Strategy is composed of scope, distinctive competence, resource deployment, and synergy. Scope specifies the range of goods and services offered, operations performed, markets served, or supplier relationships maintained. Distinctive competence is an organization's superiority or capability in one particular skill. Resource deployment is the way management uses the available human, physical, financial, and information resources. Synergy is the way the parts of the organization combine to complement or enhance each other.

Situation analysis involves reviewing the mission and goals and then examining the internal and external environments to uncover factors that can influence the organization's performance. Managers use SWOT analysis to examine the strengths and weaknesses in the internal environment as well as the opportunities and threats in the external environment. SWOT analysis helps managers formulate strategies that build on strengths, overcome weaknesses and threats, and take advantage of opportunities.

At the corporate level, managers can select one of three grand strategy options, or they can implement a combination. Growth strategies, including concentration, vertical or horizontal integration, diversification, mergers, and joint ventures, expand the organization along one or more dimensions. Stability strategies maintain the status quo. Managers use retrenchment strategies such as turnaround, harvest, divestiture, bankruptcy, and liquidation to reduce organizational operations. Another component of corporate-level strategy is portfolio strategy, in which managers analyze SBUs to create the unit mix that best supports organizational goals. The BCG growth-share matrix is a tool that helps managers analyze the organization's SBUs according to market growth and market share. The GE business screen is a tool that helps managers look at SBUs in terms of industry attractiveness and business strength.

The Miles and Snow adaptation model is a tool that helps an organization consider and adapt its business-level strategy to the challenges of uncertainty and change in the external environment. This process of adaptation involves aligning strategy and the internal environment to the external environment. The Miles and Snow model identifies four business-level strategies that managers can use to adapt to the environment: the defender strategy, the prospector strategy, the analyzer strategy, and the reactor strategy. Porter's generic competitive strategies for developing business-level strategy are based on the interplay of forces within the competitive marketplace and their effect on profitability. Managers use Porter's framework to choose among three broad-based business-level strategies (cost leadership, differentiation, and focus) to achieve competitive advantage within the industry. The major functional strategies developed by an organization include (1) marketing, (2) finance, (3) operations, (4) human resources, (5) research and development, and (6) information resources strategies. Each functional area follows its own strategy, but all must be coordinated with each other so they are consistent with the business-level strategy they support.

Implementation and strategic control are necessary if the strategy is to achieve organizational goals. Strategy is implemented using the four management functions. The planning function involves integrating and coordinating activities to ensure that implementation follows the proper direction and stays on schedule. The organizing function involves defining tasks and assigning responsibilities to individuals and groups. The leading function provides leadership for the organization, communicates the strategy, and motivates employees. The controlling function is involved with controlling resources and tracking results. Managers use strategic control to monitor the progress of the strategy, to assess whether environmental forces may interfere, and to make any needed adjustments.

MEETING A MANAGEMENT CHALLENGE AT

Thomas Stemberg's 1987 proposal to halt Staples' expansion in favor of building a regional distribution center was greeted with immediate opposition. But Stemberg wasn't abandoning a strategy, he was exercising strategic control in support of the corporate mission, that of giving Staples' customers the best price, selection, service, and convenience in office supplies.

An updated SWOT analysis clarified the issues. Staples' major strengths remained low costs and wide merchandise selection. The company's weak infrastructure was being addressed with an ambitious management training program and new outlets to flesh out the company's lean and mean management frame. Externally, the company wasn't counting on \$100 billion worth of sales opportunity just yet, but operating results already showed encouraging potential. The company was implementing plans to deal with threats, as well. Consumer indifference was being battled with advertising and with promotional campaigns, including pen set giveaways, telemarketing, even offering selected office managers \$25 to spend at Staples.

Thomas Stemberg, CEO, Staples

But the major threat to Staples over the long haul remained category copycats. As these competitors appeared, Stemberg paid close attention to their operations as part of his ongoing strategic control process. He noted that they were opening in markets with much lower operating costs; for example, rents were less than half of the $18 to $19 per square foot Staples was paying in the Northeast. Competitors' stores were also about a third larger than Staples, with the extra space used for inventory storage.

At the time, discounters' only competition came from traditional stationery stores. But the real test would begin when discounters battled each other in one market. Stemberg believed price would be the primary weapon, which made cost control a key strategic goal. "In competition with the clones," he said, "it will come down to who has the lowest costs and the best in-stock position."

When viewed from this perspective, the distribution center made perfect sense as a means of achieving those goals. It would reduce inventory costs and eliminate the need to use expensive retail space for storage. And since labor costs were cheaper outside metropolitan areas, a suburban distribution location would cut inventory-handling costs. This strategy would make Staples much stronger in the event of a price war. Staples could enter a competitor's market (where consumers were probably already educated to the concept) and capture market share based on price. Clearly, building the distribution center wasn't a strategy reversal but a logical course correction to support the corporate mission.

Stemberg's proposal for a distribution center was approved, and within a year of its completion, board-room skeptics had been converted. "On a long-term basis, Tom has been right," said one board member. "The average dollar value of Staples' store inventory is the lowest in the industry. That means Tom has a major long-term competitive edge in pricing his merchandise." For Stemberg, the board-room brouhaha was business as usual: "If you're a CEO, it's your job to make those kinds of strategic decisions."

You're the Manager: Since the completion of the company's distribution center, growth has exploded. By 1991 Staples had 97 outlets and annual sales of $500 million. One-fifth of the Staples stores were in southern California, where the chain could maintain its low-cost structure. However, opening in this market meant competing directly with other office-supply discounters such as Office Club. As an assistant to Louis Pepi, executive vice president of operations, your assignment is to participate in developing corporate, business, and functional strategies that deal with both competitive concerns and the company's own growing pains.

Ranking Questions

1. Staples wants to increase its sales of office electronics such as copiers and fax machines. These sales have been particularly listless at one new location in southern California, and you have been asked to formulate a strategy to remedy the situation. List the following objectives in the order in which you plan to accomplish them, and identify which step of the strategic management process each represents.
   a. Analyze the office electronics equipment market in the target store's vicinity.
   b. Collect feedback from the task environment.
   c. Get the staff to agree to specific goals.
   d. Consider possible strategies that might improve the store's office equipment sales.
2. As part of your regular program of monitoring the external environment, you've recently uncovered evidence that several companies might be planning to enter the discount office-supplies fray. Based on the following descriptions of their respective strengths and weaknesses, rank these competitors in terms of their threat to Staples.
   a. The B. Dalton book chain, which you've heard is considering converting some bookstore locations into discount office-supply outlets; its biggest problem is being "landlocked" in the malls, with no room to expand.
   b. A large office-supplies manufacturer with a well-known brand name but no experience in wholesaling or retailing.
   c. Wal-Mart, which is the undisputed physical distribution leader in the retailing world; however, customers might not consider a general merchandise retailer such as Wal-Mart to be a "real" office-supplies retailer.
   d. A start-up firm that has a lot of capital but no experience in office-supply manufacturing, wholesaling, or retailing.

Multiple-Choice Questions

3. You are conducting a situation analysis to analyze the market demand for high-end, executive office furniture and to determine whether Staples should enter this market, which is currently served by specialty showroom dealers and interior designers. Which of the following would you be least likely to consider during the initial phase of this assessment?
   a. A suspected weakness in your marketing support.
   b. The opportunities in spin-off services for the high-end executive market.

   c. A program to capture market share from existing furniture dealers.
   d. The impact of your company's superior management training program.
4. You have been asked to suggest vertical integration strategies to help Staples increase its share of the market. Which of the following ideas makes the most sense to you?
   a. Buy a well-known but financially weak manufacturer of office supplies.
   b. Buy out weaker competitors in appropriate markets.
   c. Start your own office-supplies manufacturing operation.
   d. Expand into other discount product areas, such as clothes and consumer electronics.

Analysis Questions

5. What effect did SWOT analysis have on Stemberg's strategy?
6. Office-supply superstores have captured only about 3 percent of the $100 billion annually spent on office supplies. One area where the category has made little penetration is in the purchasing departments of major corporations. This market could not be exploited by Staples' current retail structure, because corporate purchasing agents do not generally visit stores to make their purchases; instead, they invite suppliers to the corporate offices to discuss office-supply needs and to bid on purchasing contracts. Is pursuing this market, and making the adjustments required, consistent with the company's mission? Why or why not?
7. How would you explain the reasons for Staples' success so far, using the theories of Michael Porter?

Special Project

The company offers customers a free Staples Membership Card, which it describes as the centerpiece of Staples' marketing approach. The application form contains questions about the applicant's type of business, number of employees, and purchasing habits. The card entitles cardholders to additional discounts on selected merchandise, and purchases made by cardholders are tracked electronically, yielding valuable marketing information. Eighty percent of customers use the Staples Card when making a purchase. The company wants to increase the card's use and penetration further and has set store-level and chainwide goals for higher usage by current customers and for enrolling new members. You have been asked to develop ideas for maintaining strategic control so these goals are achieved. List four ways you might review performance at the store level and for the chain overall. Then explain how you might use the feedback you obtain to improve performance at each store and throughout the chain.[76]

KEY TERMS

adaptation model (253)
bankruptcy (249)
BCG growth-share matrix (250)
business-level strategy (240)
concentration (247)
corporate-level strategy (239)
cost leadership strategy (255)
differentiation strategy (256)
distinctive competence (239)
diversification (247)
divestiture (249)
focus strategy (257)
functional-level strategy (240)
GE business screen (251)
grand strategy (246)
growth strategy (246)
harvest (249)
horizontal integration (247)
liquidation (249)
Porter's generic competitive strategies (255)
portfolio strategy (250)
product life cycle (257)
resource deployment (239)
retrenchment strategy (248)
scope (238)
stability strategy (248)
strategic business unit (SBU) (240)
strategic management (238)
strategy (238)
SWOT analysis (242)
turnaround (249)
vertical integration (247)

QUESTIONS

For Review

1. What are the four components of strategy?
2. Why is strategic management important? How does it differ from other planning processes?
3. Under what conditions do managers select a stability strategy? When is a growth strategy appropriate? A retrenchment strategy?
4. What are the four approaches, as described by the

adaptation model, that managers can use to formulate business-level strategy?
5. How do managers apply the four functions of the management process to implement strategy?

For Analysis

1. How does the product life cycle relate to the BCG growth-share matrix used as a tool for developing portfolio strategy?
2. When might managers prefer to take the steps of the strategic management process out of sequence?
3. If an entrepreneur were conducting a situation analysis of a soon-to-be-launched business, how could the organization's internal environment be assessed?
4. Does a government agency need a business-level and a functional-level strategy? Explain.
5. What impact would an organization's portfolio strategy have on its structure?

For Application

1. If Sony wanted to use the GE business screen to evaluate its compact disc player business, which factors could be considered critical to determining industry attractiveness and business strength?
2. Under what circumstances might the apparel retailer The Limited apply stability and retrenchment strategies to some of its divisions?
3. How can the publisher of Rand McNally road maps apply Porter's generic competitive strategies to help set business-level strategy?
4. In what ways would strategic control methods and timing be different for the not-for-profit American Cancer Society compared with the bookstore chain Waldenbooks?
5. If Mobil Oil wanted to open a new self-service gas station in downtown Pittsburgh, which specific internal and external forces should managers examine in a SWOT analysis?

KEEPING CURRENT IN MANAGEMENT

Check recent issues of business publications for an article in which a business leader discusses his or her organization's competitive position and plans for the future. Examples might include an automobile manufacturer that has designed a new type of car, a computer manufacturer that has developed an innovative technology, a restaurant chain entering a new market, or a hotel chain building a new resort or hotel facility.

1. What are the organization's strengths and weaknesses? Describe the organization's environmental opportunities and threats. What tools does the manager use to conduct a situation analysis?
2. What is the corporate-level strategy? The business-level strategy? In what ways are the functional-level strategies supporting the business-level strategy? How have these three strategies changed over time?
3. Is the organization taking advantage of the product life cycle to achieve its goals? Which adaptation approach does this organization appear to be applying to its business-level strategy?

SHARPEN YOUR MANAGEMENT SKILLS

Colleges and universities in the United States operate within a dynamic and uncertain environment: demographic shifts are changing the size of the market for undergraduate education; employers are demanding that graduates have up-to-date job skills; and funding from government and private sources is becoming more difficult to obtain. Despite these challenges, few colleges have developed formal, systematic scanning methods to conduct an internal and external assessment of their situation. Planners in higher education often do not understand how they might organize such a scanning effort or what information sources might be used to support their strategic management process.

Your college wants to implement a formal environmental scanning system to support strategy formulation. You and a classmate are appointed to a committee of instructors, students, and administrators who will recommend how this system might operate.

- *Decision:* Who should participate in environmental scanning? What sources should be used? And what information should the college collect to determine its strengths, weaknesses, opportunities, and threats? With your classmate, determine your answers to these questions.
- *Communication:* Working with your classmate, draft a two-page report to be submitted to the head of your committee. Include your recommendations for the people who should be involved in environmental scanning. Also list the types of information the college will need to conduct a SWOT analysis and show next to each type your suggestions about where the data can be obtained.[77]

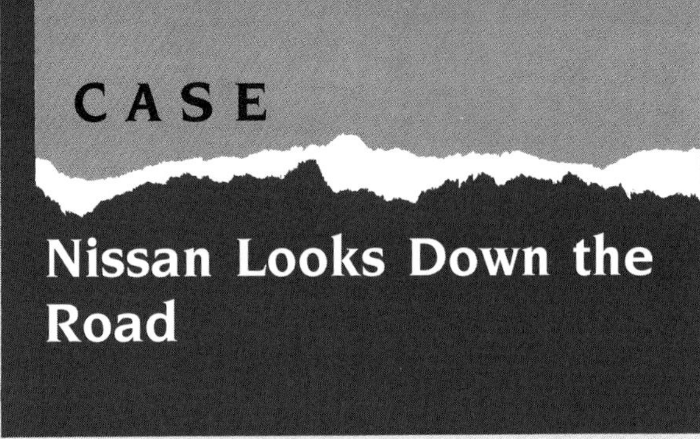

Nissan Looks Down the Road

After spinning wildly through the 1980s, Nissan has stabilized enough for its managers to contemplate strategy for the next century. The Japan-based automaker sees mature markets in industrialized countries and great potential in Asia. Its chief North American strategist, senior vice president Katsua Yamada, must adopt both a regional and a global point of view.

HISTORY

In one form or another the Nissan Motor Company has been around since 1911. In 1913, it produced its first Dat (Japanese for "fast rabbit"). In 1931, "son of Dat" was built, with the spelling changed slightly to "Datsun," the brand under which Nissan's cars were introduced to the United States in 1958. The introduction of the 240Z sports car in 1969 gave the company a big sales boost in the United States. (The 240Z has since evolved through several versions into today's 300ZX.)

It seemed Nissan could do no wrong as it entered the 1980s. The Datsun line of cars and trucks won a following among Americans for their engineering and performance and nearly toppled Toyota as the top U.S. import. Nissan moved aggressively, becoming the first Japanese automaker to manufacture in the United States, first at Smyrna, Georgia, in 1983. Shortly thereafter Nissan opened factories in Europe and Asia, but then the company stumbled. It confused consumers in 1984 by dropping the Datsun name in favor of the corporate name, and it bored young buyers with a steady flow of boxy vehicles. Its share of the U.S. market fell from 5.3 percent to 4 percent as Honda roared ahead into second place. Nissan's U.S. woes mirrored the company's troubles in Japan, where its historic 30 percent domestic market share shrank to less than 24 percent by 1987. Moreover, worldwide sales dropped 8 percent to $33 billion. Nissan responded by changing its president and by changing direction; it moved from an inward, hierarchical focus to an outward focus that was responsive to customers and changing market conditions. It started introducing exciting new cars like the 300ZX, which had Yamada as principal project designer. Nissan's world sales are up 16 percent from its 1987 low, and its U.S. market share is approaching 6 percent.

ENVIRONMENT

The automobile market has matured in industrialized nations and is expected to grow there only with the population. However, developing Asian countries are expected to push global demand from about 50 million cars a year to 60 million cars a year by the end of the century. Nissan plans to capitalize on the market growth, but volatile currency exchange rates are hurting profits in Japan (where Nissan manufactures two-thirds of its cars), and consumer reaction against imports is hurting Nissan sales in other countries. Another problem is that the developing markets themselves may be able to produce cars more cheaply than Nissan.

GOALS AND CHALLENGES

Nissan's goal is to increase its global market share from 6 to 8 percent and to raise annual production from 2.8 million vehicles to 4.8 million vehicles by the turn of the century. To do this, the company has adopted a three-part strategy that responds to both regional and global concerns. The strategy aims to (1) increase from 60 to 85 percent the amount of domestically made components used in cars manufactured in U.S., European, and Asian factories, (2) eventually establish 60 percent of Nissan's production capacity overseas, and (3) link all of Nissan's operations with a single computer network. Increasing the percentage of domestically made parts per vehicle would enhance local economies and reduce consumer resistance to imports. Increasing manufacture overseas would minimize the havoc wreaked by exchange rate fluctuations and would increase customer satisfaction by allowing factories abroad to respond more quickly to their customers' desires. A global computer network would improve efficiency by integrating previously independent marketing, manufacturing, and parts supply operations; it would also improve employee morale by making problems with orders easier to detect, and it would please customers by giving their special orders top priority from manufacture to final delivery. The strategy also promotes economies of scale by allowing factories to specialize in parts that could be shipped around the world whenever they are needed.

1. What are the scope, resource deployment, and synergy components of Nissan's strategy?
2. Which growth strategy is Nissan using in its effort to reach market share and production goals?
3. What would a SWOT analysis tell Yamada about the competitiveness of his North American operations?
4. How might Yamada apply Miles and Snow's adaptation model to assess Nissan's current business-level strategy in the North American market and to set strategy for the future?

PART TWO INTEGRATIVE CASE
PepsiCo Plans for Peak Performance

PepsiCo has been in a food fight for nearly 100 years. The company has been battling Coca-Cola since the first Pepsi-Cola soft drink was quaffed in 1898. In the fast-food arena, McDonald's still outsells all the Pepsi restaurants combined. But Pepsi has persisted and built powerful food-related brands that draw customers back again and again. As a result, sales and profits have exploded in the past decade. In 1980, PepsiCo's total sales were $5 billion and net income was $260 million. By 1987, sales had more than doubled to $11 billion, and they jumped again in 1990 to $18 billion, when net income topped the $1 billion mark for the first time.

As the 1990s began, CEO Wayne Calloway was set to build on PepsiCo's skills in food processing, marketing, and distribution to continue expanding sales and profits. He could concentrate on Pepsi operations in the United States, where market share was highest, and use price promotions to battle competitors. Or he could buy businesses outside the United States to gain an immediate position in international markets while expanding his U.S.-based businesses to other countries. Calloway's decision was difficult because each alternative would have a major impact on the direction Pepsi took to increase sales and profits in the years ahead.

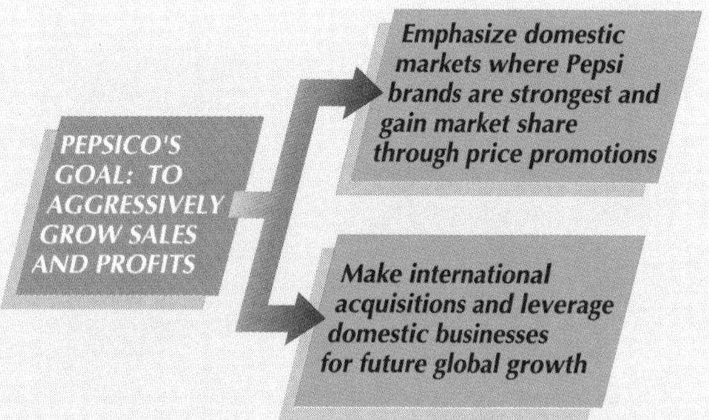

HISTORY

In 1898, pharmacist Caleb Bradham invented a drink he called Pepsi-Cola, and he promoted it as a cure for dyspepsia (indigestion). Following Coca-Cola's lead, he franchised the bottling rights and by 1915 he had 300 franchisees. Financial difficulties forced Bradham to sell the company in 1923, and Pepsi floundered under several owners until the Loft candy company acquired the firm in 1931. In 1934, Pepsi began offering twice as much soft drink for the same 5-cent price, and sales soared. Loft merged with its Pepsi subsidiary in 1941 to form the Pepsi-Cola Company.

Pepsi started offering its soft drinks in cans in 1948. During the 1960s, Pepsi president Donald M. Kendall scored a public relations coup by convincing Soviet premier Nikita Khrushchev to drink a Pepsi in front of the cameras at the Moscow Trade Fair. Not long afterward, Kendall signed an agreement allowing Pepsi to distribute Pepsi-Cola in the Soviet Union in exchange for distributing Russian vodka in the United States. Under his direction, the company also began to promote its soft drinks more heavily to teenagers and young adults, which helped propel Pepsi into the number two slot behind Coca-Cola. When Pepsi acquired Frito-Lay in 1965, it gained a shelf-full of popular snack foods, including Lay's potato chips, Fritos, and Chee-tos. That year the company name was officially changed to PepsiCo.

Pepsi expanded beyond soft drinks and snacks during the 1970s and 1980s. The 1977 acquisition of Pizza Hut was Pepsi's first foray into restaurants, and the firm strengthened its position by buying Taco Bell in 1978 and Kentucky Fried Chicken (now called KFC) in 1986. Today, Pepsi scores its biggest sales in soft drinks but enjoys its biggest profits in snack foods. Although domestic markets still provide the bulk of its sales and profits, Pepsi has been growing more quickly overseas than at home.

Wayne Calloway succeeded Kendall as CEO in 1986. Calloway started at PepsiCo in 1967 as director of corporate profit planning and control. He headed the company's Canadian operations for several years and then moved over to lead the Frito-Lay division, where his aggressive introduction of new brands catapulted divisional sales from $700 million in 1976 to over $2 billion in 1982. Calloway was named chief financial officer in 1983 and moved up to the presidency before being named CEO.

ENVIRONMENT

Competition is a key environmental force affecting all PepsiCo businesses. Although Taco Bell, Pizza Hut, and KFC are all market leaders in their segments, the combined sales of company-owned and franchised PepsiCo restaurants doesn't approach McDonald's systemwide total of $20 billion in annual sales. McDonald's wields a huge advertising budget, but cash-strapped customers have not been happy with its higher prices, and Taco Bell has used careful pricing to woo these customers. Rather than simply discount, the chain revamped its entire menu structure in 1988 to emphasize value-priced items starting as low as 39 cents. Simultaneously, managers pursued cost reductions and productivity increases that slashed overhead to keep profits healthy. McDonald's responded with discount promotions that attracted customers but put a dent in profits.

Competition is also fierce in the soft drink segment, where the cola wars with Coca-Cola have been unrelenting and often costly. Coca-Cola is the undisputed market share champ both in the United States and overseas. Pepsi has used innovative (and expensive) promotions and advertising programs to successfully gain share in the United States, but Coke continues to dominate. Moreover, Coke has long been number one in Europe, where it outsells Pepsi 2.5 to 1. Despite the competitive challenges, the global opportunities for soft drink sales seem almost limitless, which whets Pepsi's appetite for a larger stake. Per capita soft drink consumption in the United States grows every year. Overseas, consumption is far less than in the United States, but it would increase faster if soft drinks were more available, according to Pepsi experts.

Frito-Lay is a major player in the snack category. Its brands account for about 13 percent of all snacks sold in the United States, including nearly half of all salty snacks. Of the 10 best-selling chips in U.S. supermarkets, 8 are Frito-Lay brands. Coming up fast, however, is Anheuser-Busch's Eagle Snacks division, whose Eagle Thins Potato Chips grabbed the number 10 slot on the best-selling chips list. Frito-Lay sliced prices to stay competitive, but the discounting hurt profits, and in 1991 top management embarked on a program of cost-cutting and productivity improvement to tighten operations and improve performance.

GOALS AND CHALLENGES

PepsiCo's goal, says CEO Calloway, "is simply to be the best consumer products company in the world." To reach this goal, the company will have to fend off powerful rivals, cope with economic uncertainty, and overcome slower growth in domestic markets. Calloway has therefore put the company on the road to global growth by pursuing international acquisitions and by bringing its restaurants and foods to other countries. In addition to the 1989 acquisition of Smiths Crisps and Walkers Crisps, top snack makers in the United Kingdom, Pepsi bought Gamesa, Mexico's leading cookie maker, in 1990. Gamesa may ultimately account for more than one-third of Pepsi's snack business in Mexico, and managers are exploring how the operational synergies between chips and cookies can boost Frito-Lay's results.

On the soft drink front, Pepsi wants to raise overseas sales volume by 150 percent within five years. To reach that goal, divisional managers are preparing programs to (1) encourage higher soft drink consumption and (2) take share from smaller competitors. Pepsi's fast-food restaurant formats are also becoming globetrotters. Whereas there is approximately one fast-food restaurant in the United States for every 1,400 people, the international ratio is one restaurant for every 100,000 people, leaving PepsiCo lots of room for expansion. Opening fast-food restaurants at an average rate of three per day, Pepsi is moving into Ireland, Israel, and other markets. The KFC chain is now the second-largest restaurant system in the world; Pizza Hut is the market leader in 53 countries; and Taco Bell, which is just starting its international expansion, has units in 8 nations.

The profit potential is enormous—the return on overseas operations can be 50 to 100 percent higher than in domestic markets—but Pepsi may have to wait a long time to see those kinds of figures. Real estate and labor costs can be high in other countries, and if local suppliers can't meet Pepsi's quality standards, the company must pay to bring in its own materials. Despite these concerns, Calloway is counting on Pepsi's marketing, manufacturing, and distribution strengths to blaze the trail to international sales and profits. It's a future that will be built chip by chip, taco by taco, and gulp by gulp.

1. Identify PepsiCo's distinctive competences and strategic goals. What kinds of MBOs might Pepsi seek from its restaurant managers to support overall corporate goals?
2. How does Pepsi use standing and single-use plans to achieve its goals? What contingency plans might the company make to deal with a possible price war initiated by Eagle Snacks?
3. Was Calloway's decision to expand internationally programmed or nonprogrammed? Which group decision-making methods might he use to resolve problems with the help of PepsiCo executives located in other countries?
4. What threats and opportunities does Pepsi face in its global campaign to sell soft drinks abroad? How can Calloway use the product life cycle framework to support Frito-Lay's international growth?

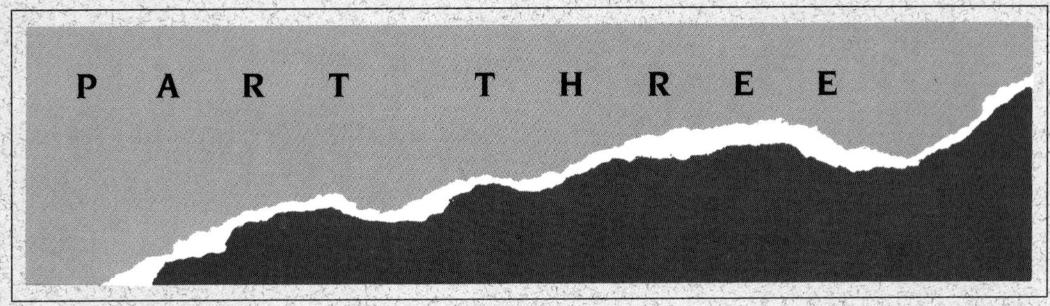

Organizing

9 Foundations of Organization Structure

CHAPTER OUTLINE

After studying this chapter, you will be able to

1. Discuss how managers use organization structure to achieve organizational goals and explain the basis of work specialization
2. Outline how managers use the chain of command to distribute authority
3. Describe the barriers to effective delegation and show how managers can overcome these barriers
4. Contrast the organizational impact of centralization and decentralization
5. Explain how the span of management affects tall and flat structures
6. Identify four common forms of organizational departmentalization and discuss the nature of horizontal coordination
7. Distinguish between the formal organization and the informal organization

FACING A MANAGEMENT CHALLENGE AT

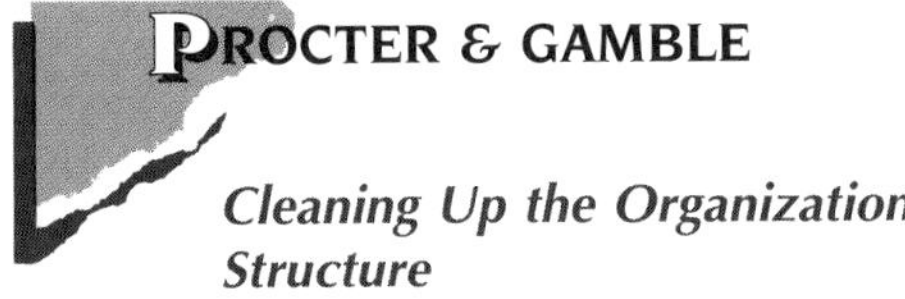

PROCTER & GAMBLE

Cleaning Up the Organization Structure

One of the largest and most successful business enterprises in the world, Cincinnati-based Procter & Gamble has long been a symbol of effective management. Ninety-five percent of all U.S. households have at least one P&G product on their shelves, whether it's Crest, Pampers, Oil of Olay, or one of the company's many other famous brand names. A P&G product is the top seller in 21 of the 39 product categories in which the firm competes.

However, in the mid-1980s the company ran into trouble. Profit slipped for the first time in over three decades. Some of its most famous brands, including Crest and Pampers, were losing market share. Competitors were becoming more efficient in getting products to market.

What was wrong? In approaching the problem, then-CEO John Smale took a closer look at the corporation's brand managers, key marketing personnel in the P&G organization. Each brand manager develops a marketing plan for a single product, a plan that includes the product design, the target consumer, the advertising message, and even the packaging. Smale could see that the brand managers were still bringing the same level of enthusiasm and creativity to their tasks, but he was dismayed at how difficult it had become for the brand managers to interact with other company managers. Poor communication was causing numerous delays and false starts.

Smale realized that rapid growth had strained managers' ability to exchange information, get urgently needed answers, and make decisions. Division managers, who oversee the brand managers, were taking too long to approve marketing plans. P&G had added products and people so quickly that each division manager was now supervising over a dozen brand managers.

The brand managers, who numbered more than 90 by this point, were also causing delays in engineering, research, product design, and manufacturing. Faced with a cascade of work orders from the brand managers, the other departments couldn't keep up with the pace of requests and had trouble coordinating their diverse projects throughout the organization. Furthermore, some brand managers weren't consulting with experienced hands in other departments before finalizing their plans. Unworkable ideas were being discovered late in the product-development cycle, which created delays when the brand managers had to rework their plans.

Division managers were having difficulty coordinating the activities and decisions of the brand managers, who had traditionally developed their products in isolation. Various P&G products had competed with each other since 1923, when the company introduced Camay to compete with Ivory. This worked well as long as the market was expanding, but that was no longer the case. With many consumer markets maturing, P&G brands were starting to steal sales and profits from each other.

Smale realized that he needed to get the departments talking with each other. They needed to share ideas and to coordinate their work so P&G would meet its profit goals. How could Smale speed up the approval of brand managers' decisions without sacrificing control over strategic direction? How could he get brand managers to share market information without sacrificing the pride of achievement that came from managing a market-leading brand? How could he speed up the work from the other departments without sacrificing quality? And how could he get more input from other departments early in the development of marketing plans without challenging the independence of the brand managers?[1]

CHAPTER OVERVIEW

John Smale and his successor at Procter & Gamble, Edwin Artzt, recognize the profound impact that organization structure has on performance. This chapter explores the basic principles of organization structure, starting with a look at the purpose of organization structure, the organization chart, and the concept of work specialization. Next is a glimpse inside the vertical organization, including the chain of command, the delegation of authority, centralization and decentralization, the span of management, and line and staff roles. Following that, the horizontal organization is examined, including the four major methods of departmentalization and horizontal coordination. The chapter concludes with a look at the formal organization, formalization, and the informal organization.

MANAGEMENT AND ORGANIZATION STRUCTURE

organization structure A formal system of interaction and coordination that links the tasks of individuals and groups to effectively achieve organizational goals

The management function of organizing involves defining and assigning tasks and responsibilities, coordinating people and resources, and establishing or changing the organization structure to accomplish organizational goals. Managers design the **organization structure,** a formal system of interaction and coordination that links the tasks of individuals and groups to help achieve organizational goals. The organization structure is a *formal* system because top managers officially create the structure. An *informal* system also exists, and it is discussed later in the chapter. During the planning process (see Chapter 7), managers set goals and develop the strategies to achieve them. Then they design the organization structure to support the implementation of their strategic plans so that their goals can be achieved.[2]

organization chart A diagram of the positions and relationships within the organization structure

One purpose of the organization structure is to channel information to the appropriate managers so that their level of uncertainty is reduced when they make decisions. Another is to effectively distribute the authority to make decisions so that organization members can implement their plans smoothly and cohesively at every level. Finally, the organization structure defines and governs the relationships among the various work units, ensuring that all work is assigned and completed in an orderly fashion, which contributes to overall organizational performance.[3]

After General Electric acquired a majority interest in Tungsram, a Hungarian lighting manufacturer, George Varga *(right)* was named CEO and given the task of redefining the organization's structure. He created a structure that clearly delineated the tasks and responsibilities needed to improve efficiency and expand sales in Europe.

Structure and the Organization Chart

In some organizations, such as football teams, the formal system of task assignments and interactions is clear. Football players all understand their assigned tasks and know how they must interact with each other so that the team can score points, defend against opponents, and win games. But in other organizations, the organization structure is less clear. To help organization members and stakeholders visualize the structure, top managers create an **organization chart,** a diagram that maps the positions and relationships within the organization structure.[4]

Traditional organization charts are schematic diagrams in which a box represents an organizational position and a solid line represents a reporting relationship between two positions. Such charts show the top management positions at the upper part of the chart and indicate how positions and reporting relationships extend to the lower-level positions at the bottom of the chart (see Exhibit 9.1). However, some organizations use other types of diagrams to map their positions and interactions between levels. For example, department store retailer Nordstrom uses an inverted triangle to represent its organization structure. At the base, which appears on the top of the chart, are sales positions and sales support positions that serve the customer. Below these positions are department

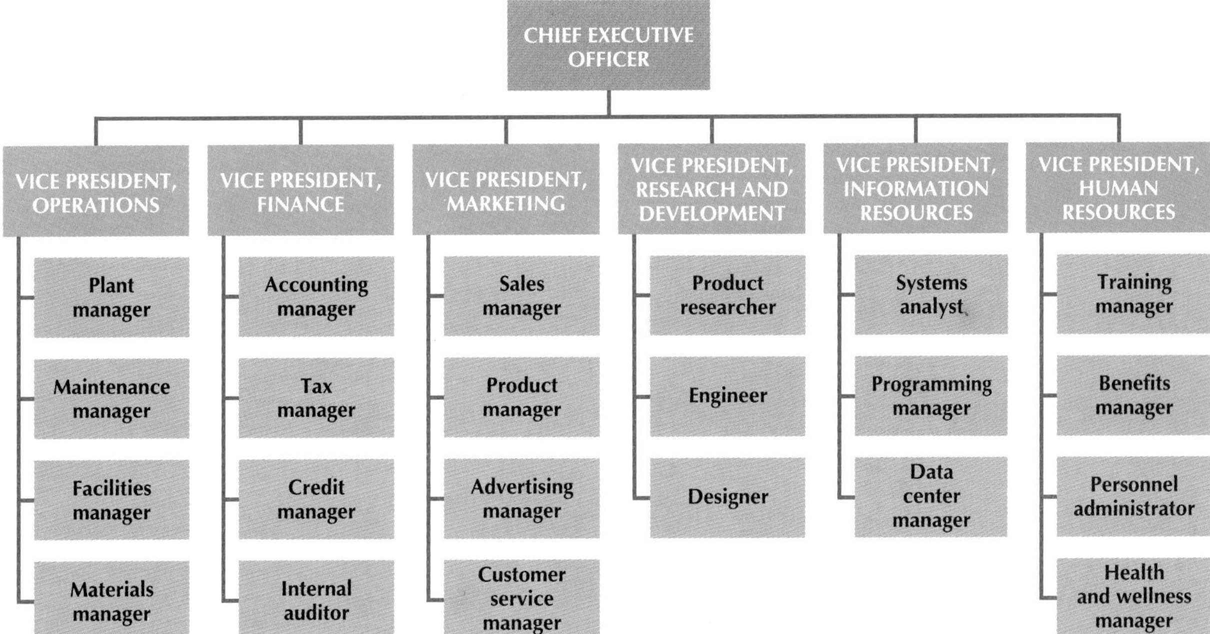

EXHIBIT 9.1

The Organization Chart

The organization chart maps the positions and relationships in the formal organization. This chart represents the top- and middle-management positions in a manufacturing organization.

managers, and below them are a level of store managers, buyers, and merchandise managers. At the very bottom of the inverted triangle (the narrowest point) are the positions on the board of directors. Nordstrom's management uses this organization chart to convey the idea that higher management levels exist to support the efforts of the employees who directly serve the organization's customers.[5] Some organizations take the inverted organization chart a step further and show customers at the top, in order to emphasize the organization's real mission.

Another nontraditional approach is the circular organizational chart. Semco, a Brazilian manufacturing company, uses a circular chart consisting of three concentric circles. A tiny circle at the center contains the five people who integrate all company activities—the president and four other senior managers. Surrounding this is a second circle that contains the heads of Semco's eight divisions. Around the second circle is a third, the largest of the three, which contains all employees who handle the research, design, sales, and manufacturing tasks. Whether the shape is traditional or nontraditional, organization charts are useful tools for depicting the individual tasks that must be completed by organization members and for visually expressing the relationships among organization members.[6]

Work Specialization

In a one-person business, the owner personally performs all the work necessary to achieve the organization's goals. However, as the business expands, this arrangement becomes less practical, and the founder soon hires other people to handle specific tasks. Similarly, no manager in a large organization is capable of carrying out all the work outlined in the organization's plans, so it is necessary to carve out individual tasks that others will tackle. Therefore, managers apply the principle of **work specialization,** also known as *division of labor* or *division*

work specialization The degree to which an organization's work is divided into smaller parts that constitute separate jobs

Before filming *Roger and Me,* director Michael Moore *(right)* defined the specific tasks involved in making the movie, then hired skilled technicians to handle sound recording, camera work, and other jobs. As the top manager on the set, Moore had to ensure that the employees understood their roles and coordinated their efforts to complete the movie on time.

of work, the degree to which organizational work is divided into smaller parts that constitute separate jobs. By dividing the work into separate and differentiated tasks, managers and employees can concentrate on specific areas and develop the expertise to handle these more efficiently.[7]

One of the earliest proponents of work specialization was the eighteenth-century economist Adam Smith. He observed that a pin maker working alone, performing every manufacturing task, could make only 20 pins per day. However, a group of 10 pin makers working together, each specializing in one aspect of the manufacturing process, could turn out 48,000 pins per day. Smith recognized that work specialization vastly improved individual and group productivity, and it also helped workers clearly understand and master their respective jobs.[8]

Consider how work specialization helped the U.S. Bureau of the Census achieve its 1990 goal. It would have been extremely difficult, not to mention very time-consuming, to train every worker in every task necessary to complete the census, much of which took place on a single day (April 1). So the director, Barbara Bryant, assembled a 9,500-person organization, assigning each person a particular task (such as developing census questionnaires, checking on unreturned questionnaires, or recording data found on completed questionnaires). Each job covered a segment of the total work, so the combined efforts of everyone in the organization enabled Bryant to complete the entire task and achieve her goal of counting the 248,709,873 people in the United States on that day.[9]

Although work specialization improves organizational efficiency, it also creates an interdependency among the various component jobs. Thus, managers need to carefully design and coordinate the jobs so that all contribute to achieving organizational goals. Some jobs will necessarily be more complex than others, some will need to be finished before others can be started, and some will require specific skills that others do not demand. The boundaries of jobs must be clearly defined so that each covers a meaningful segment of the work and so that organization members understand their duties. However, if jobs are defined too narrowly or too rigidly, employees and managers can become bored and lose motivation once they master the necessary skills.[10] Chapter 13 explores job design in more detail.

THE VERTICAL ORGANIZATION

Once the work has been subdivided into meaningful and differentiated tasks, employees are responsible only for their individual jobs. How then can managers effectively coordinate these component jobs at every organizational level so that goals are achieved? Early in the development of management theory (see Chapter 2), managers saw the need for a vertical structure to link the job activities of various levels and to facilitate the flow of information among the levels. They identified five basic elements within this vertical organization: the chain of command, the delegation of authority, centralization and decentralization, the span of management, and line and staff positions.

chain of command The unbroken line of authority that extends from the bottom to the top of the organization and defines reporting relationships

Chain of Command

Within the vertical organization, employees and managers are connected by the **chain of command,** the unbroken line of authority that extends to the top level

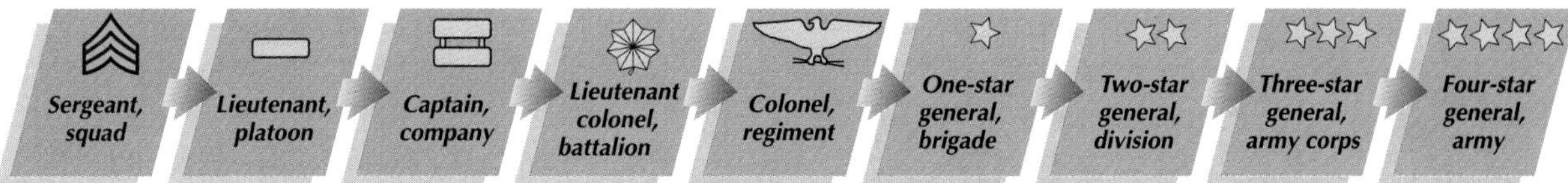

EXHIBIT 9.2 The Chain of Command in the U.S. Army

The chain of command of the United States Army illustrates the scalar principle, the concept of a clearly defined chain of authority extending through successive layers of management. The arrows indicate the reporting relationships, illustrating the unity of command principle that every individual reports to only one superior.

of the organization and defines who reports to whom. In a traditional chain-of-command sequence, employees report to managers who in turn report to higher-level managers, and so on until the reporting link reaches the top manager (see Exhibit 9.2). The chain of command is based on two underlying principles. The first is *unity of command,* the idea that each employee should report to one, and only one, direct supervisor. The second is the *scalar principle,* which states that there should be a clearly defined line of authority that extends through successive layers of managers and employees, from the highest to the lowest level.[11]

Because the chain of command creates a direct link from each job to the level above and to the level below, no role is left unsupervised or uncoordinated. Organization members can also use the chain of command to identify their direct superiors, to trace the line of authority upward and downward, and to understand their own position within the hierarchy. As organizations grow increasingly larger and more complex, however, their structures do not always reflect the unity of command or the scalar principle.[12] In fact, in some organization structures, these principles have become the exception rather than the rule. Chapter 10 discusses these and other variations to organization structure.

Delegation of Authority

Because top managers cannot personally perform all the tasks needed to achieve their goals, they must use the chain of command to distribute authority among other organizational members to ensure that the work is completed. **Authority** refers to the right to make decisions, to perform or supervise activities, and to allocate resources in order to accomplish tasks that will achieve organizational goals. Authority flows down the chain of command, so higher-level positions have a wider scope and therefore more authority than lower-level positions. However, as the classical management theorists first pointed out, formal authority is vested in the position, not the person. For example, when John F. McGillicuddy retires as CEO of New York-based Chemical Bank, he will no longer have the right to decide on the bank's strategic goals or to approve new products. This top management authority belongs to his successor, Walter V. Shipley, once he becomes CEO in 1994.[13] The formal authority resides in the office of the CEO, not in the person who happens to be occupying that office.

authority The right to make decisions, to perform or supervise activities, and to allocate resources in order to achieve organizational goals

Employees play a key role in the manager's exercise of authority. The **acceptance theory of authority** argues that authority is meaningful only when employees accept a manager's legitimate right to direct their activities. But if employees

acceptance theory of authority The notion that authority is meaningful only when employees accept the manager's legitimate right to direct their activities believe their manager's directions are outside the boundary of legitimate authority, they may choose not to accept these directions, and the manager's authority is diminished. Closely related to authority is the concept of **responsibility,** the obligation to perform the assigned tasks or activities. Every organizational position carries with it the responsibility for achieving specific goals by performing specific duties. To carry out these responsibilities, every position also requires the appropriate authority.[14]

responsibility The obligation to perform assigned tasks or activities

Once organization members have accepted the authority and the responsibility of their jobs, they are subject to **accountability;** they must achieve the expected results or justify their deviation from the expected results to managers higher in the chain of command. For example, Sir Peter Abeles owns Eastwest Airlines, the third-largest carrier in Australia. Below him in the chain of command is Neil Berkett, Eastwest's general manager, whose job is to achieve the strategic goals of improving revenues and profitability. Since 1987, Berkett has been responsible for the entire airline operation, with authority to make plans that will achieve the strategic goals. Eastwest has been steadily increasing both revenues and profits since 1988, but Berkett is bound by accountability to explain to Abeles any downward trend in revenues or profits, should either occur. If Beckett's authority to act were not equal to his responsibility for carrying out organizational plans, he could not be held accountable for attaining Eastwest's goals. This is why Abeles uses **delegation;** that is, he transfers part of his total work load to others, including the necessary authority and responsibility. Through delegation, Abeles transfers to Berkett the authority and the responsibility for increasing airline revenues and profits, and Berkett becomes accountable for the expected results.[15]

accountability The requirement that managers achieve the expected results or justify any deviation to managers higher in the chain of command

delegation The process of transferring to others a part of a manager's total work load, including the appropriate authority and responsibility

This pattern of transferring authority from one level to the next lower level occurs throughout every organization, enabling work to be accomplished and goals to be achieved at every level. In this way, authority can be distributed to the lowest possible level in the organization where employees and managers must make decisions and exercise judgment about the day-to-day operations that contribute to performance. Even when managers delegate work to their employees, they are ultimately held accountable for the expected results.[16]

Barriers to Effective Delegation

Although delegation enables managers to complete their work assignments and achieve results without having to handle every task personally, managers sometimes face barriers to effective delegation. Especially when the stakes are very high, some managers view delegation as too risky. In such cases, managers may not trust their employees to complete delegated tasks competently, so they resort to *micromanagement,* an excessive degree of personal involvement in and control over the daily decisions and actions of their employees. Managers also may be reluctant to share authority, may believe they can do a better job than employees, or may fear an employee's performance will outshine their own. Further, some managers may delegate responsibility but not the authority to complete the assigned tasks. On the other hand, employees may fear failure and therefore be unwilling to accept delegated authority, thus creating another barrier to effective delegation.[17]

When managers do not delegate effectively, they risk creating bottlenecks for both decisions and actions, which hinders the work unit's ability to perform. Moreover, by not letting go of tasks better handled by others, managers may be unable to focus on more important decisions and activities. Employees may become demoralized when their managers show insufficient trust and confidence by refusing to delegate. Finally, organizations would be unable to function effectively if managers tried to personally complete every task rather than using delegation.[18]

Overcoming Barriers to Effective Delegation

To overcome these barriers, managers must recognize the long-term benefits of delegation as an efficient method of completing organizational work, accomplishing results, and developing future managers. Because an employee's achievements reflect a manager's ability to manage, it is in the manager's best interest to develop employees' skills—thereby preparing them to step in when the manager is promoted. Managers can delegate effectively by carefully matching the employees to the tasks, delegating well-defined tasks, setting specific performance goals, communicating with employees, monitoring progress, and providing coaching and support as needed. When delegation is seen as a chance to develop new skills and demonstrate competence, employees may be more motivated to accept increased authority and responsibility.[19]

Consider how President George Bush handled the delegation of authority during the 1991 Persian Gulf War. He set the goal of winning the war quickly and with a minimum loss of life, and he delegated the authority for planning the tactical and operational strategies to General Colin L. Powell, chairman of the Joint Chiefs of Staff. In turn, Powell delegated authority for military action to General H. Norman Schwarzkopf, who was in charge of the allied military commanders. The chain of command in the field was as international as the allies: for example, a British general commanded the U.S. Marines on the Kuwaiti front, and a Saudi lieutenant general commanded the Egyptian, Saudi, Moroccan, and Syrian forces. Bush also set performance goals, monitored progress, and frequently communicated with his staff to provide support and clear direction.[20]

Centralization and Decentralization

Although top managers distribute some authority for decisions and actions throughout the vertical organization, they also retain a certain amount of authority. **Centralization** is the extent to which authority remains concentrated at the top management levels. The opposite of centralization is **decentralization,** delegating authority to lower management levels. Centralization and decentralization are the two extremes of a continuum: more authority delegated downward reflects a higher degree of decentralization, whereas more authority retained by top managers reflects a higher degree of centralization.[21]

centralization The extent to which authority is concentrated at the top management levels

decentralization The extent to which authority is delegated to lower management levels

Some organizations centralize strategic decisions that affect the overall organization but delegate authority for tactical and operational decisions and activities to lower-level managers. For example, Frito-Lay CEO Roger Enrico decentralized the company by delegating more authority to sales and marketing managers in regional offices. This streamlined the decision-making process for addressing tactical and operational problems, and it gave those managers closer to the customer more authority to respond to environmental changes such as growing local competition. However, a decision to centralize or to decentralize can be reversed. For example, Honda's top managers centralized control of the carmaker's Japanese automotive operations in 1991, seeking to speed decisions and boost sales growth. But in 1992, Honda shifted toward higher efficiency

Nordstrom has decentralized many functions to allow store employees and managers the flexibility to respond to local needs and conditions. Unlike most competitors, who maintain a centralized shoe buying staff, Nordstrom has a shoe buyer in every store to watch over inventory and to tailor the selection to the local climate, fashion trends, and the needs of the community.

rather than rapid sales growth, so some authority was delegated back to the middle managers. At times, organizations may centralize some functions while decentralizing others. For example, Marriott's centralized room-reservation function frees its resident hotel managers from decisions that influence room sales so that they can focus on decisions that affect customer service.[22]

Centralization offers several benefits. When top managers make the major decisions, they can coordinate activities and balance the needs of the various parts of the organization. Centralization can also reduce expenses because resources and activities need not be duplicated on lower levels. Finally, centralization ensures that the most experienced top managers will make the big decisions, an important consideration when critical problems arise.[23]

Decentralization offers a variety of benefits as well. Top managers in a decentralized organization do not get overburdened by decision-making chores and can therefore concentrate on issues that affect the entire organization. Also, decentralized organizations can respond quickly to environmental changes because local managers familiar with conditions in their areas are authorized to make decisions, rather than having to wait while problems and decisions travel up and down the chain of command. Lastly, decentralization allows lower-level managers to gain experience in decision making, motivating these managers to perform well and preparing them for the decisions they will make at higher levels.[24]

When top managers consider whether to move toward the centralized or the decentralized end of the spectrum, they must weigh a variety of factors, including size, environmental dynamism, and interdependency. Often, an organization grows so large that decentralization is the most efficient way to manage daily decisions and activities. For other organizations, the pace of environmental change is so rapid that it forces speedier exchange of information and quicker decision making, which is difficult under centralization but easier under decentralization. When decisions in one organizational unit depend on decisions in other units, centralization helps managers coordinate these interdependencies. Today's highly developed information and communication networks can give managers at all levels the information they need to make decisions, so top managers can use these tools to support both centralization and decentralization.[25]

Span of Management

span of management The number of people who report directly to one manager

The fourth basic element of the vertical organization is the **span of management,** also known as the *span of control,* which refers to the number of people who report directly to a single manager. The span of management is a key determinant of how closely managers can interact with and supervise their employees. Although the manager with few employees is able to work closely with each and to effectively coordinate their activities, this manager may also supervise too intensely, interfering with the way employees complete their tasks. In contrast, the manager with many employees cannot spend much time supervising each and may also have difficulty coordinating the various activities of the unit.[26] This was the problem encountered by division managers at Procter & Gamble, who had too many brand managers reporting to them.

Factors Affecting the Span of Management

Over the years, the question of how many employees an individual manager can effectively manage has been much debated. Classical management theorists insisted that the optimal span of management was no more than six employees per manager, allowing for close supervision. However, as organizations grew increasingly large and complex, many managers began to realize that they could effectively supervise dozens of employees. Indeed, Seiuenon Inaba, president of the Japanese robotics firm Fanuc, has 60 people reporting to him.[27] In general, the span of management may be wider (more subordinates) or narrower (fewer subordinates), depending on a variety of factors, including the following:

- *Complexity of work.* More complex tasks typically require greater supervisory attention, leading to a narrower span of management.
- *Standardization of work.* Managers can supervise more employees when those people perform routine, repetitive tasks that rarely change or when formal procedures and rules are available to guide employees' activities. However, new employees or employees handling new assignments may require closer supervision.
- *Location of employees.* When employees and their manager are together in the same location, the span can be wider than when employees are dispersed and the manager must travel to supervise their activities.
- *Skill level.* When employees are highly trained and experienced, they require less supervision, so the span can be wider. Similarly, skilled, seasoned managers can usually supervise more employees.
- *Nonsupervisory activities.* Managers who must perform many nonsupervisory activities have less time to devote to employees, so their span should be narrower.
- *Management support.* Managers who have secretaries and assistants to help can generally manage more employees than managers who have less support.
- *Personal preferences.* Managers who interact frequently with their employees favor narrower spans. Similarly, some employees prefer the relative autonomy of wider spans.[28]

Increasingly, organizations are finding that they can efficiently handle large spans of management through the use of *self-managing work teams.* For instance, a manager who supervises 20 employees could divide them into four teams of 5 employees each, then ask each team to manage its own affairs as much as possible. Such a move would have the effect of decreasing the span (since the manager would be overseeing four teams instead of 20 individuals) while maintaining the same manager-to-employee ratio.

Tall and Flat Organization Structures

The width of the span of management determines the number of hierarchical levels in an organization. On average, a **tall structure** has a narrow span of management, so the organization has more hierarchical levels. In contrast, a **flat structure** has fewer hierarchical levels because the average span of management is wide. Even when two organizations have the same number of members, their vertical structures look vastly different when each applies a different span of management (see Exhibit 9.3).[29]

tall structure An organization structure characterized by a narrow span of management and many hierarchical levels

flat structure An organization structure characterized by a wide span of management and few hierarchical levels

These differences can have profound effects on the organization. In a tall structure, communications and decisions may be slower because of the many levels. In addition, the higher number of managers may raise overall costs. In a flat structure, managers are challenged by comparatively more responsibility and authority, but the outlook for upward movement is dimmer because the hierarchical levels are fewer. Still, organizational effectiveness may be enhanced

SOCIAL RESPONSIBILITY AND ETHICS

When Pyramids Get Flatter, Who Gets Flattened?

Downsizing and demassing are two terms with one result: flatter structures with fewer bodies. Seeking lower costs and higher productivity, Chrysler, General Motors, Campbell Soup, IBM, Eastman Kodak, and many other companies have reduced their management ranks in recent years. Undeniably, cost containment and improved productivity are critical issues in today's highly competitive business environment. But when they flatten the pyramid, top managers face a difficult dilemma: how to balance the push for increased efficiency with the human impact on those managers who go and on those who remain.

Consider the dilemma at Hewlett-Packard, where CEO John Young took dramatic steps to flatten the organization structure before his retirement in 1992. The number of management layers once slowed decision making, a decided liability in the fast-paced electronics world. For example, a manager needed eight higher-level management approvals to launch a marketing program. Then Young changed the management structure and removed some middle-management layers, so now the same marketing program needs only two approvals. Hewlett-Packard revenues per employee are up substantially, and the company has been able to avoid laying off people just to save money. However, the company has offered early retirement programs to entice people to voluntarily leave, and people can be "excessed," meaning that they would have three months to find another position within the company. If they don't find a job on their own during that period, they are assigned one, although it may be lower in the hierarchy or in another location. As a result, many at Hewlett-Packard are wary because they feel the company no longer has their interests at heart.

Similar scenes are being played out at organizations across the country and around the world as structures get flatter, leveling the careers and the hopes of managers and employees caught in the squeeze. When people are cut or displaced despite their performance, they are often disillusioned, bitter, and disheartened about future prospects. Moreover, the company loses the benefit of their knowledge and their experience. But those who remain on the job also suffer. Their confidence in the company is shaken, and they worry about job security, the collapse of the ca-

downsizing Flattening the organization structure selectively by cutting middle management layers, expanding spans of management, and reducing the size of the work force

in a flat organization because fewer layers separate managers from the customer and from the external environment, allowing managers to monitor customer needs and environmental changes more closely.[30]

To take advantage of the benefits, an increasing number of organizations are flattening their structures by **downsizing,** selectively cutting middle management layers, expanding spans of management, and reducing the size of the work force.

EXHIBIT 9.3

Tall and Flat Organization Structures

Managers in a tall organization *(a)* have a narrower span of management than managers in a flat organization *(b)*. Although these two organization charts include the same number of people, the tall structure has more hierarchical levels.

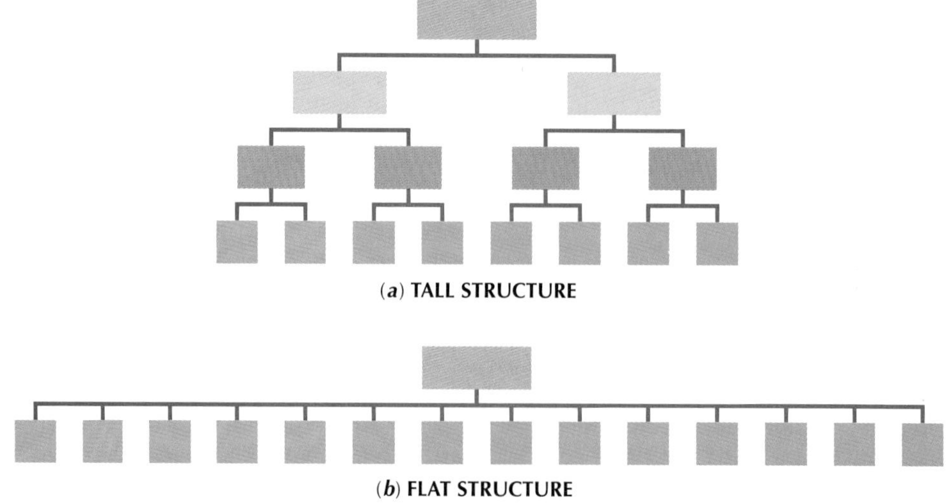

reer ladder, and the amount of work they must now shoulder. Thus, the human cost of flatter pyramids can be quite high, magnifying top management's dilemma over who, when, and how to cut.

How can top managers flatten the pyramid without flattening the people? Experts advise top managers to apply the following guidelines:

1. *Start with strategy.* Consider where the company is going, what it wants to achieve, and how structure can help them reach those targets.
2. *Plan for the long term.* Rather than demass in one gigantic step, judiciously plan and prune the organization structure on an ongoing basis so that long-term goals can be achieved.
3. *Pinpoint unnecessary positions and work.* Carefully consider which positions can be trimmed, targeting extraneous or redundant positions rather than eliminating a percentage or a specific number of people. Reevaluate the work done by those who remain, both to eliminate nonessential tasks and to be sure that essential tasks are covered.
4. *Look beyond layoffs.* Flattening the structure can be accomplished in many ways, and layoffs are only one. Often, people can be shifted to functions where additional help is needed, or they can be retrained in skills that the organization needs for future growth. When work-force costs must be cut, early retirement packages and other voluntary methods are alternatives.
5. *Communicate with stakeholders.* Downsizing affects not only organization members but also customers, shareholders, and other stakeholders. All need to be kept abreast of the organizational changes, and top management should be as candid, as specific, and as accurate as possible.
6. *Show sensitivity.* Plan carefully so that people who lose their jobs are treated humanely and are allowed to retain their dignity and self-respect. At the same time, those who remain must be sensitively managed so that they maintain their morale, their performance, and their commitment.

What's Your Opinion?

1. Should one or more members of top management be cut when organizations flatten the structure? Why or why not?
2. How can top managers avoid overloading the remaining organization members after hierarchical levels are removed?

When top managers go beyond downsizing to cut large numbers of managers from the payroll in widespread cutbacks that affect nearly all departments and levels, they are **demassing.**[31]

demassing Flattening the organization structure by widespread cutbacks of managers in nearly all departments and at several levels

Consider how Nucor, one of the most efficient steel manufacturers in the United States, operates with a flat organization. Nucor has only four hierarchical layers because of its wide span of management at the plant level: the foreman supervises many employees and reports to a department head, who reports to the general manager of the facility, who reports directly to top management. Within this structure, information can be relayed quickly, the organization can be responsive to environmental change such as competitive threats, and managers at all levels can understand the scope of their authority, responsibility, and accountability.[32]

Line and Staff Positions

The fifth element of vertical organization is the differentiation between line and staff positions. A manager in a **line position** makes decisions and supervises activities that directly affect the organization's ability to achieve its goals. In contrast, a manager in a **staff position** supports the people in line positions by providing information and guidance and by performing specialized or technical tasks that line managers lack the skills (or the time) to perform. To signify this difference, staff positions on the organization chart are connected to the line positions they advise by dashed lines, rather than by the solid lines that connect line positions in the direct chain of command. Depending on the degree of de-

line position A position in which managers and employees make decisions and supervise activities that directly contribute to the performance of the organization

staff position A position in which managers and employees assist line positions by providing information and guidance or performing specialized tasks

EXHIBIT 9.4

Line and Staff Positions in a Centralized Organization

Staff positions in a centralized organization report to the CEO and provide advice and assistance to a variety of line positions. Because staff positions are not in the direct chain of command, they are linked by dashed lines to the line positions they support.

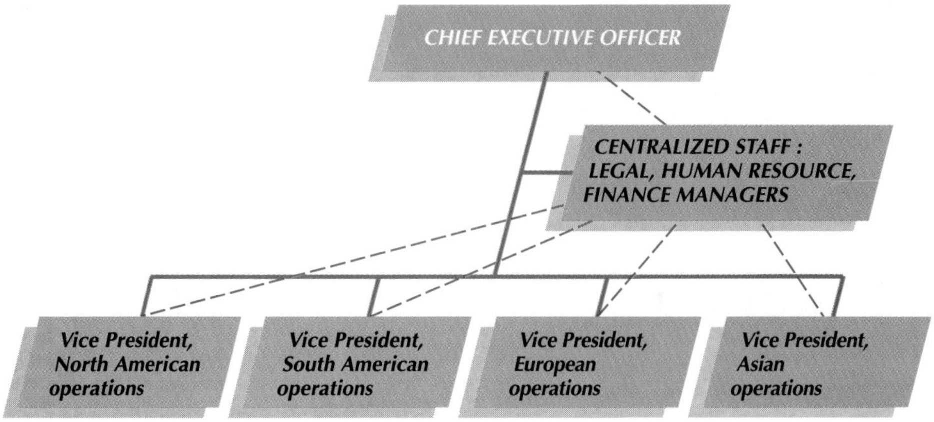

centralization, staff positions may report to the CEO or to the heads of organizational units (see Exhibit 9.4).[33]

Types of staff positions vary widely; among them are administrative assistants, purchasing agents, lawyers, research-and-development engineers, human resource specialists, and public affairs representatives. An increasingly important staff function is helping organizations adhere to the ever-growing set of government regulations that affect both domestic and international business operations. And the definition of a staff position can differ from organization to organization. For example, in a manufacturing firm such as Ford, lawyers are in staff positions because they advise line managers but do not make the final decisions. However, in a law firm such as Jacoby & Meyers, lawyers are in line positions because their decisions and activities contribute directly to the organization's performance.[34]

line authority Formal authority based on the hierarchical positions in the chain of command

staff authority The authority to provide advice and to direct activities within a particular functional area of expertise

Managers in line positions hold **line authority,** formal authority based on their hierarchical positions in the chain of command. This allows them to make decisions and to supervise employees in the line who perform the duties that lead to achieving organizational goals. Managers in staff positions hold **staff authority,** the authority to provide advice and to direct activities within their functional area of expertise. However, staff authority is not the same as line authority, and the difference sometimes leads to conflicts between line and staff. Staff managers can make recommendations to line managers about key issues and activities that influence the organization's performance, but because line managers make the final decisions (accepting or rejecting staff recommendations), staff may disagree with decisions that run contrary to their advice. Also, staff managers frequently have the authority to request that line managers prepare reports about activities that pertain to the staff manager's specialty. Although line managers may see these reports as unproductive paperwork, staff managers may use them to spot problems and to formulate new ideas that can be implemented in many organizational departments.[35]

Linking Pin Roles

Finally, it's important to recognize that nearly every manager in the organization structure is simultaneously involved with at least three groups: a group of employees who report to the same manager, a group of peers at the same level, and the manager of a group of managers or employees. Because they straddle three

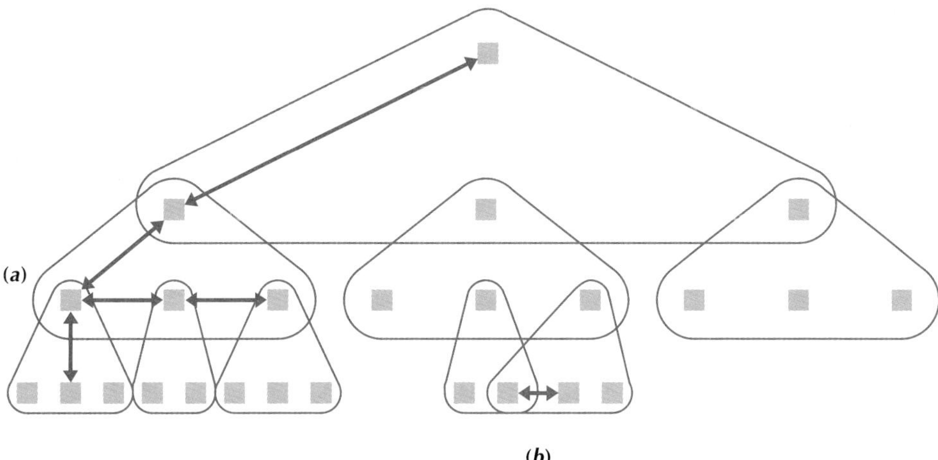

EXHIBIT 9.5
Linking Pin Roles
Managers in linking pin roles such as *(a)* hold a triple affiliation that enables them to facilitate communication and decision making vertically and horizontally, in their own groups and in linked groups. In *(b)*, the employee who belongs to two groups performs a linking pin role by exchanging information that enhances horizontal coordination.

groups, managers serve as important links between the groups to which they belong (see Exhibit 9.5). Managers in such *linking pin roles* facilitate the flow of information between peers and between higher and lower hierarchical levels. They also help coordinate activities within the linked groups to manage interdependencies more effectively. Some employees in linking pin roles are simultaneously part of two groups or units, such as a member of a product group and a member of a marketing group. Although people in linking pin roles do not have formal authority to make decisions that affect other departments, their ability to exchange information between departments enhances overall coordination.[36]

THE HORIZONTAL ORGANIZATION

Just as the organization requires a vertical structure to link the jobs within the hierarchy and to coordinate activities between the levels, the jobs on each level must also be linked and coordinated so that tasks can be efficiently completed. To accomplish this, managers use departmentalization and horizontal coordination, two basic elements of the horizontal organization.

Departmentalization

Once managers have used work specialization to carve out the component jobs needed to accomplish all the organization's work, they must arrange and cluster these jobs. **Departmentalization** is the arrangement of individual jobs and activities into logical groups and the clustering of groups into larger departments and units that combine to form the total organization. Four common methods are functional departmentalization, product departmentalization, geographical departmentalization, and customer departmentalization (see Exhibit 9.6).[37] Managers typically choose the type of departmentalization that will best support the organization's efforts toward reaching its goals.

departmentalization The arrangement of individual jobs and activities into logical units and then combining these units to form the total organization

Functional Departmentalization

Functional departmentalization is the basis for grouping together jobs that relate to a single organizational function or specialized skill, such as marketing,

functional departmentalization Grouping of jobs dedicated to a single organizational function

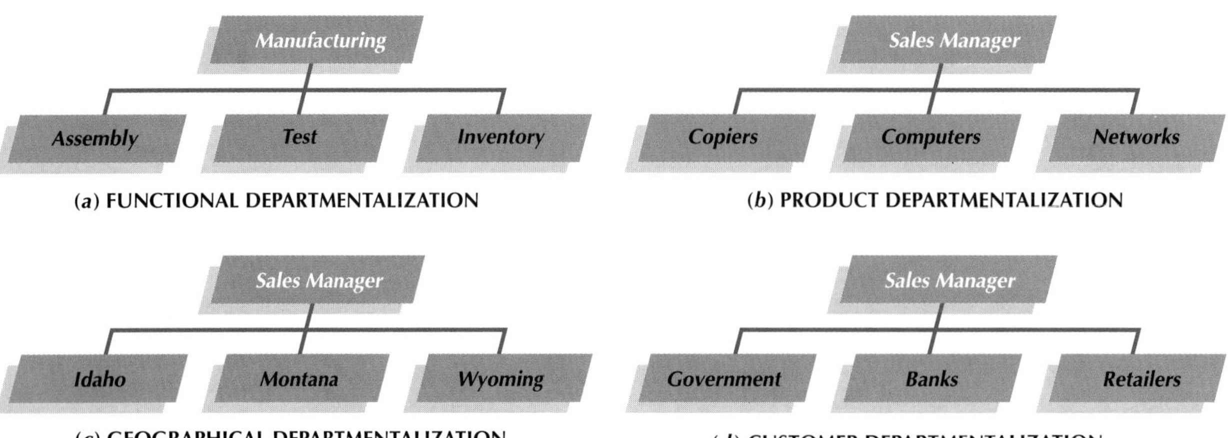

EXHIBIT 9.6 Types of Departmentalization

The four most common approaches to departmentalization are based on functions, products, geography, and customers.

finance, operations, human resources, information resources, and research and development (see the organization chart in Exhibit 9.1). Depending on the type of organization and its size, other functions such as purchasing and legal may be added or substituted. For example, the United Kingdom government agency of Customs and Excise organizes its 28,000 employees into functions such as collections, investigation, finance, human resources, revenue duties, and tax control. This helps the agency use its resources efficiently and provide better service. Similarly, General Motors maintains centralized functional departments such as design and engineering to serve all of its North American brands. Buick and other GM divisions maintain functional departments such as marketing to serve their own needs.[38]

Functional departmentalization has several benefits and limitations. One benefit is increased efficiency; the people grouped together have similar skills and can communicate and work together easily to complete tasks. Also, functional departments form pools of expertise that can be tapped to develop the organization's distinctive competence, such as outstanding proficiency in marketing or manufacturing. But there are several limitations to functional departmentalization. Members of each functional unit may become more concerned with their specialty than with the needs of the organization overall. Moreover, organizational barriers (ranging from physical barriers such as walls to informational barriers such as separate group meetings) can impede communication with colleagues in other functional areas. Finally, functional departmentalization encourages narrow specialization that does not adequately prepare people for management roles at higher organizational levels.[39]

Product Departmentalization

product departmentalization Grouping of jobs according to the products offered by the organization

When managers apply **product departmentalization,** they group jobs according to the goods and services offered, enabling members of each group to concentrate on the activities that produce their respective goods or services. Ericsson, an international telecommunications supplier based in Stockholm, Sweden, departmentalizes according to six product lines: public switches, private branch exchanges, radio communications, defense systems, components, and cable and networks. Despite this product departmentalization, president Lars Ramqvist insists that Ericsson must present a unified front to its buyers. In the past, major customers such as British Telecom had to meet individually with representatives of all six Ericsson groups when they needed a range of equipment and services. Now British Telecom managers discuss their needs with a single Ericsson team, the members of which can cross departmental lines to secure the appropriate products from anywhere in the Ericsson organization.[40]

One benefit of product departmentalization is the ability to develop considerable expertise in producing particular products, leading to ever-more-efficient and effective methods of production. Another benefit is the ease of coordinating all activities relating to the product. But as Ericsson's president recognized, product departmentalization also has limitations. One limitation is the confusion that can occur when customers must deal with more than one department to purchase a variety of goods from the same organization. Also, employees in one group may be so focused on their own product that they lose sight of the organization's broader activities. Moreover, it can be expensive to have duplicate support functions for each product group.[41]

Geographical Departmentalization

In **geographical departmentalization,** jobs are grouped according to defined locations. Although it can also refer to the locations of major organizational facilities, geographical departmentalization generally follows the pattern of customer location. For example, Toys 'R' Us uses geographical departmentalization to group jobs into two regions: Toys 'R' Us United States, operating more than 400 toy stores in the 50 states, and Toys 'R' Us International, operating nearly 100 locations around the world. The international group is further subdivided by individual overseas locations, including Italy, Germany, France, Canada, Taiwan, Hong Kong, Singapore, and the United Kingdom.[42]

geographical departmentalization Grouping of jobs by defined locations

Among the benefits of geographical departmentalization are (1) the ability to respond quickly and efficiently to environmental conditions in a variety of locations and (2) the ability to effectively manage operations scattered over a wide area. However, one limitation is that resources must often be duplicated in each of the various locations, driving up expenses. Moreover, coordination among the various geographic groups can be difficult.[43]

Customer Departmentalization

In **customer departmentalization,** jobs are grouped according to the unique needs of specific groups of customers or constituents. For example, Boeing uses customer departmentalization to arrange activities into such customer groupings as commercial airplanes and military airplanes. This departmentalization increases the company's efficiency in three ways: it can target customer needs, manufacture similar products, and market products to be sold to the same type of customers. A variation is departmentalization by market or distribution channel, in which an organization groups jobs according to the way goods or services reach the final customer. Thus, a food manufacturer might group jobs according to wholesale and retail channels, or according to supermarket, convenience store, and restaurant outlet sales.[44]

customer departmentalization Grouping of jobs that meet the unique needs of customers or constituents

The major benefit of customer departmentalization is the increased responsiveness to the diverse needs of a variety of customer groups. However, customer departmentalization can also be expensive because of the duplication of resources needed to serve each customer group. Another limitation is the difficulty

Jaguar uses process departmentalization to group manufacturing jobs according to the assembly process used. In this plant in Brownslane, England, the work of 3,500 employees has been organized according to the specific operation each employee performs. All the employees in this section of the plant use the same operations to assemble components for car door panels.

of coordinating activities between groups. A final limitation is the tendency to concentrate more on the needs of individual customer groups than on overall goals.[45]

Other Approaches to Departmentalization

In addition to the four common forms of departmentalization, organizations sometimes use other methods to group jobs. Three approaches are process departmentalization, project departmentalization, and time departmentalization.

process departmentalization Grouping of jobs dedicated to a single operational process or technique

Process Departmentalization Managers use **process departmentalization** to group jobs that relate to a single phase of an overall process. A manufacturer of electronic equipment, for instance, might divide its production process into departments that handle component insertion (putting the electronic parts onto the circuit boards), soldering, final assembly, and performance testing. Often used within an operating department or division, rather than at the top hierarchical level, process departmentalization may be organized around a specific technology or a specific type of machine. For example, Archer Daniels Midland, a major processor of agricultural products, uses process departmentalization to organize the activities of its various businesses. Its divisions include oilseed processing, corn processing, grain processing, dry milling, and feed processing.[46]

One benefit of process departmentalization is increased efficiency; managers and employees are able to concentrate their efforts on particular areas of expertise. Another is additional opportunities for promotion: within a specialized process area, more high-level technical or specialized jobs are available than would be possible in product or customer departmentalization. However, process departmentalization has several limitations, including the potential of concentrating on the process to the exclusion of the external environment and the organizational goals. Also, as with functional departmentalization, organizational barriers can cause communication problems in process departmentalization, and coordination of the entire organization's work becomes more complex. Finally, because managers in these groups are highly specialized, they may not be able to move into positions either in other groups or in the organization's top management level.[47]

project departmentalization Grouping of jobs according to the skills needed to complete a specific project

Project Departmentalization Also known as *team departmentalization,* **project departmentalization** is the basis for grouping organization members with a variety of skills into a team designated to work on one specific and well-defined project. Each project team is composed of a diverse group of employees and managers chosen for the knowledge and skill they can bring to that project's tasks. Becton Dickinson used project departmentalization to launch a new medical diagnostic instrument for processing blood samples. Called the Bactec 860, the instrument was developed by a project team of engineers, marketers, manufacturers, and company suppliers.[48]

Because these projects have clear goals, each team member has a well-defined role in achieving that goal, so project departmentalization can be both effective and efficient. Also, team members can quickly adapt if the scope or goal of the project changes, because they are dedicated exclusively to the project. However, one limitation to project departmentalization is the potential isolation from the rest of the organization, making communication difficult. And as with any type of departmentalization, team members may tend to concentrate on their own project rather than on the overall organizational goals.[49]

Time Departmentalization When managers group jobs according to the time of day those jobs are performed, they are applying **time departmentalization.** This method can be useful for organizations such as hospitals and factories that operate on more than one shift or even around the clock; time departmentalization permits them to include in each grouping just those jobs needed during that period. The most obvious benefit of this approach is that managers can efficiently group the jobs that are needed during specified periods. Also, organization members working during each period clearly understand the time restrictions on their activities and responsibilities. However, communication may be difficult between groups working at various times. Finally, groups may not get a sense of the organization's overall goals and progress because of the multiple time periods during which work is performed.[50]

time departmentalization Grouping of jobs according to the time of day they are performed

Alabama-based Birmingham Steel has successfully used time departmentalization to group jobs into 12-hour shifts at its manufacturing plants. Employees work three 12-hour days one week and four 12-hour days the next, so little time is lost in shift changes and productivity is soaring. Similarly, Sankyo Seiki Manufacturing, the world's largest producer of music boxes, uses time departmentalization in its highly automated assembly plant located on Lake Suwa in Japan's Nagano Prefecture. Employees work 11 hours and 30 minutes on three consecutive days, then take three days off before returning to work another three-day cycle.[51]

Although entire organizations can be departmentalized in one way, some organizations prefer to departmentalize various units in different ways. Sometimes organizations will apply one form of departmentalization to higher levels and one or more to lower levels. For example, a manufacturer may use functional departmentalization to group jobs at the level just below the CEO but may use time departmentalization to group jobs at individual plants. Regardless of the method used, managers also apply the second element of the horizontal organization: horizontal coordination.

Horizontal Coordination

Once organizational work has been departmentalized and spread across work groups, managers must integrate the various activities. **Horizontal coordination** links activities across departments so that organizational goals are achieved. Whereas the vertical organization facilitates the flow of information between hierarchical levels, horizontal coordination facilitates the flow of information across the lines of departments or units. Highly interdependent organizational units require more horizontal coordination than other units. Three types of interdependencies may exist between organizational departments or units: pooled, sequential, and reciprocal.[52]

horizontal coordination The linking of activities across departments so that organizational goals can be achieved

- *Pooled interdependence* exists when the results of independently operated departments must be pooled (combined or added together) to achieve organizational goals. Although top managers allocate resources to each department (so that no group depends on any other for inputs or outputs), the organization as a whole depends on the combined results of the individual units. Because the daily activities of each unit have little or no impact on other units, this is the simplest type of interdependence. For example, Banc One (based in Columbus, Ohio) pools the results of its 51 affiliated banks to achieve overall organizational performance. At the same time, each bank in the network pools the results of its many branches to achieve individual bank performance.[53] Resource allocation is another key aspect of such arrangements; Banc One has to choose which one of its affiliates gets which resources and in what quantity. On the other hand, pooled interdependence also means that lower performers probably benefit from the financial results realized by higher-performing affiliates.

- *Sequential interdependence* is a more complex type of interdependence that exists when the output of one department becomes the input for another, continuing in a sequence until all tasks have been completed. In effect, each department becomes a customer of the department that is ahead of it in whatever process (anything from preparing a Big Mac to building a house) the organization is engaged in. This interdependence is generally one-way, so that the department that produces the output is usually not dependent on the department that receives the output. For example, each of the companies within Integrated Waste Services (based in Amherst, New York) supplies output that in turn becomes input for another. One company demolishes buildings, the next collects trash, one operates transfer stations and recycling activities, and yet another operates a landfill.[54]
- *Reciprocal interdependence* exists when departments both provide output and receive input from other departments. This is the most complex of the three types of interdependence because the output and input flow in two directions. For example, the Internal Revenue Service (IRS) and the United States Postal Service (USPS) are involved in reciprocal interdependence. The IRS gives its output of tax forms to the USPS to deliver to taxpayers. But the IRS also depends on the USPS to return the tax forms mailed by taxpayers.[55]

Exhibit 9.7 illustrates these interdependencies. Managers can apply a variety of horizontal coordination techniques to manage these organizational interdependencies, including information systems, slack resources, and lateral relationships.

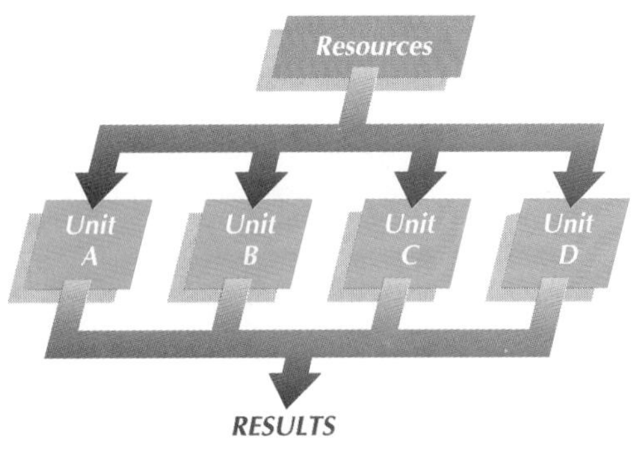

(a) POOLED INTERDEPENDENCE

(b) SEQUENTIAL INTERDEPENDENCE

(c) RECIPROCAL INTERDEPENDENCE

EXHIBIT 9.7 Types of Interdependencies

In pooled interdependence *(a)*, the four units receive resources and operate independently, but their results are pooled together to achieve organizational performance. In sequential interdependence *(b)*, the output of unit A becomes the input for unit B, and this sequence continues until all tasks have been completed and organizational performance achieved. In reciprocal interdependence *(c)*, unit B receives input from unit A and produces output that becomes input for unit A, which produces output that leads to organizational performance.

Information Systems

Without information about the activities in every department, managers cannot effectively coordinate across departments. Information systems allow managers to collect, store, and communicate information about departmental activities. The simplest types of information systems are paper-based methods, such as memos comparing a department's progress toward achieving planned goals and explaining any variations. The greater the interdependency, the more frequently managers need reports on departmental results. Information systems allow managers to monitor the timing of outputs, to adjust the schedules for departments expecting inputs (if necessary), or to revise other plans so that overall organizational goals can be met. Increasingly, managers are using computerized information systems, discussed in more detail in Chapter 18.[56]

Slack Resources

Another technique for horizontal coordination is the use of **slack resources,** a cushion of resources that can be made to help departments cope with environmental changes. Managers can create slack resources in a variety of ways, such as stocking additional inventory or spare parts, allowing for overtime pay, buying additional equipment, or inserting extra time into the output schedule. Slack resources can be used when the task environment changes, such as when a supplier cannot deliver needed inventory on time, or they can be used when the internal environment changes, such as when an employee falls ill and others must work overtime to stay on schedule. Although organizations can operate without slack resources, they help safeguard the coordination of interdependent activities in various departments. However, investing in slack resources raises organizational costs, so managers must carefully weigh the benefits of using this technique.[57] For instance, a clothing retailer might decide to stock up on a popular item in case the manufacturer has trouble delivering enough of them. But if consumer tastes change quickly, the retailer might be caught off guard, with excessive inventory that it can't sell.

slack resources A cushion of resources that help departments cope with environmental changes

Miguel Rincon, president of Grupo Durango, a fast-growing pulp and paper supplier based in Durango, Mexico, uses slack resources to stay prepared for future increases in demand. In anticipation of the need for more sack and grocery bag paper, he opened a new facility and limited its production to only 60 percent of its total capacity during the first year. Another plant devoted to the manufacture of tissue, printing, and writing paper has the flexibility to switch from one type of paper to another, in case demand shifts. By using slack resources such as extra capacity and flexible manufacturing processes, Rincon avoids any last-minute coordination problems and enables his company to respond quickly to environmental changes.[58] There is a price to pay for this preparedness, of course; Rincon must sacrifice some efficiency in the short term.

Lateral Relationships

When two departments report to the same manager, it is possible to coordinate their activities by referring conflicts or problems up the chain of command to the next managerial level. But when many departments are involved or when interdependencies are especially complex, another solution is to develop *lateral relationships,* personal links across departments that allow individuals and groups to communicate and to make decisions, thus maintaining departmental coordination. Managers can often resolve problems faster by using lateral relationships than by relying on the elements of the vertical organization, because information need not travel up and down the hierarchy before a decision can be made. Four types of lateral relationships are commonly used: direct contact, liaison roles, task forces and teams, and integrating roles.[59]

Direct Contact The simplest type of lateral relationship is *direct contact,* the direct, spontaneous communication between two interdependent departments involved in a problem. Because the people within the departments are the most knowledgeable about the situation and can exchange information to make decisions jointly, problems can be quickly resolved at the middle or lower levels of the organization, rather than being referred up the chain of command.[60]

Liaison Roles Unlike the less formal spontaneity of direct contact, *liaison roles* are formal positions for channeling information between departments that must maintain frequent or constant communication to coordinate interdependent tasks. A liaison role is a position filled by a specific individual through whom an entire department communicates with other departments. Like direct contact, liaison roles keep problem solving at the middle and lower levels of the organization, rather than being referred upward, so problems can be quickly solved. For instance, managing director Michio Naruto plays a key liaison role at Fujitsu, the Japanese high-tech manufacturer. Because Fujitsu's partners in Europe and in the United States operate autonomously, Naruto must carefully coordinate their activities to avoid conflict and duplication throughout the organization.[61]

Task Forces and Teams *Task forces and teams* are groups of people drawn from interdependent departments who meet to discuss their common concerns and to find acceptable solutions to problems. Participants representing each affected department exchange information about a particular problem and either recommend a solution that higher-level managers must approve or agree on a solution that the group is authorized to implement. Teams are usually permanent and meet on an ongoing basis to discuss frequently occurring problems. Task forces are often temporary groups formed in response to a specific problem, so members disband once the problem has been solved.[62]

Federal Express uses teams to find and fix problems, such as incorrect bills and lost packages, that cross departmental boundaries. This team of Memphis-based employees (from billing, quality control, and other departments) identified a billing problem, tracked it to its source, and implemented a solution that saved the company $2.1 million a year.

For example, Xerox formed a task force of people from accounting, sales, distribution, and administration to coordinate the flow of materials through the various manufacturing departments. The task force discovered that each department was ordering extra supplies to avoid being caught short, which was costing Xerox dearly in added inventory expenses (a good example of the risks inherent in using slack resources). The group set up procedures to ensure that each department received its supplies at the appropriate time during the manufacturing process, and the solution saved Xerox $200 million a year.[63]

Integrating Roles *Integrating roles* are formal, full-time positions filled by people who coordinate the decision-making process and who solve problems that arise between interdependent departments working on large, complex tasks. Integrators are not members of the departments whose activities they coordinate, and they generally do not have formal authority over those departments. Their role requires considerable expertise and excellent interpersonal skills because they must resolve conflicts that arise among interdependent departments, and they must facilitate decision making so that major tasks can be completed as expected.[64]

Some common integrating roles are product manager, brand manager, project leader, and materials manager. These roles reflect the kinds of large-scale tasks that require coordination across many departments. For example, to develop new products and to build product sales, the brand managers at Procter & Gamble work with people at many levels in the organization and in a variety of departments, including marketing, product development, engineering, manufacturing, purchasing, and sales. In addition, they travel to the production facilities to discuss any manufacturing issues that affect their brands, and they incorporate those concerns into any decisions they make about product improvements and sales goals. Because P&G brand managers know more about their products than anyone else in the hierarchy, they can effectively coordinate the activities that affect their products. However, traditional brand management cannot always prevent the occasional conflicts that occur among competing brands marketed by a single producer.[65] "Meeting a Management Challenge at Procter & Gamble" at the end of this chapter explains how P&G was able to solve this particular coordination problem.

At times, these lateral relationships are not sufficient to ensure effective horizontal coordination, in part because they often lack the force of formal authority. So managers create a matrix organization, a formal organization structure in which employees and managers are accountable to their departmental heads *and* to the managers in a horizontal chain of command. Because of these dual reporting relationships, information flows vertically and horizontally so that managers can effectively coordinate and integrate activities across departments. Matrix organizations are discussed in more detail in Chapter 10.[66]

FORMAL AND INFORMAL ORGANIZATIONS

The elements of the horizontal and vertical organizations relate to the **formal organization,** the planned structure and relationships officially established by top managers. Managers create the formal organization as a general framework for implementing decisions about how activities should be divided, coordinated, and integrated in order to achieve organizational goals.[67]

formal organization The planned structure and relationships officially established by top managers

GLOBAL MANAGEMENT

Worldwide Horizontal Links

Every top manager faces the dual challenge of efficiently arranging activities and coordinating the component jobs so that strategic goals can be achieved. Even more daunting is the task confronting top managers of international service organizations, who must manage and integrate operations in far-flung locations. Consider the horizontal organization needed by Swissair, a Zurich-based airline that serves the European continent and selected global capitals. The airline boasts consistent profits for more than 30 years, and it enjoys a worldwide reputation for reliability and quality. But Swissair president Otto Loepfe is anything but complacent. He knows how difficult it can be to orchestrate the activities of the 18,000 employees and managers who serve Swissair's yearly complement of 8 million passengers.

For years, Swissair operated a centralized organization, using functional departmentalization to manage planning, scheduling, and other activities. In addition, the airline used geographical departmentalization to organize its worldwide sales force. However, no one was directly responsible for the flight routes, and decisions often moved slowly when issues had to be hashed out between departments. Unlike the days when the airline was smaller and nearly everyone had customer contact, Loepfe saw that comparatively few managers now met the customer. To solve these problems, Loepfe changed his organization structure.

The new horizontal Swissair organization establishes route managers in key integrating roles. These route managers are responsible for meeting customer needs on several routes, and they influence but do not have direct authority over the types of aircraft used on their routes, the meals served, the schedules, and even the hotels where the crews stay. Although route managers are accountable for the overall cost of their routes, Loepfe does not measure their performance based on profitability. This is because many Swissair routes are interdependent, feeding traffic to and from key destinations, and the company sometimes elects to maintain certain routes even if they are temporarily unprofitable.

Given their responsibilities, route managers must frequently consult with top managers in Zurich, and Loepfe has smoothed this process by flattening the organization. In the old organization, a country manager was separated by three layers of management from the president. In the new organization, a route manager is only one layer away from the president. But Loepfe didn't simply transfer managers into these new positions. Instead, he required people to apply for these positions; the manager of North America had to apply for the position of route manager of North America, even though the new position included many of the tasks already handled under the old position.

Loepfe knows that some difficulties may lie ahead, including increased competitive pressure and the worldwide impact of airline deregulation. But his new organization structure should help the airline serve passengers effectively and efficiently on every route, positioning Swissair for high-flying customer satisfaction and profits throughout the 1990s.

Apply Your Knowledge

1. How might Loepfe use functional departmentalization to organize activities conducted at Swissair's central headquarters?
2. How can Swissair use information systems to improve horizontal coordination?

Formalization

formalization The use of written documents to systematize, link, and control the activities of organization members

Within this formal organization, managers need to maintain reasonably consistent employee behavior so that they can predict and control both how individuals conduct themselves throughout the workday and how they complete their assigned tasks. Managers also need to manage the flow of work and information according to the formal relationships defined by the formal organization. They accomplish this through **formalization,** the use of written documents to systematize, link, and control the activities of organization members. Nearly every organization applies formalization to a greater or a lesser extent, relying on standing plans such as policies, procedures, and rules, and on other written documents such as job descriptions.[68]

Consider how the East Bay Asian Local Development Corporation (EBALDC) uses formalization. EBALDC is a not-for-profit organization com-

Recognizing the importance of the informal organization, Toyota wants to encourage cross-cultural interaction among employees in its U.S. plants. At the Georgetown, Kentucky plant, Toyota pays part of the cost when U.S. and Japanese employees bowl together. Such activities help employees build a network of contacts in other departments.

mitted to housing and commercial development in the Chinatown district of Oakland, California. When the organization was smaller, few written regulations were needed because the executive director could communicate directly with every employee. But now that the number of employees has grown, formalization helps standardize activities and work behavior. Two examples of formalization at EBALDC are its financial control manual, which explains how all financial transactions must be handled, and its personnel manual, which contains policies governing employee behavior.[69]

Although formalization enables organizations to run smoothly, excessive formalization can be a burden when fast or flexible action is important. If tasks must always be completed "by the book," organizations may find it difficult to speed up or modify activities in response to environmental changes, so they must be aware of the impact of formalization measures. Although apparel manufacturer Levi Strauss uses formalization, managers and employees are also encouraged to focus on ways of achieving goals. Rather than spend their time rigidly enforcing work rules and regulations, Levi Strauss managers are expected to help employees identify and respond to opportunities and challenges. In this way, corporate goals can be achieved, and employees can become more involved in goal setting and decision making while strengthening their skills.[70]

MANAGEMENT AROUND THE WORLD

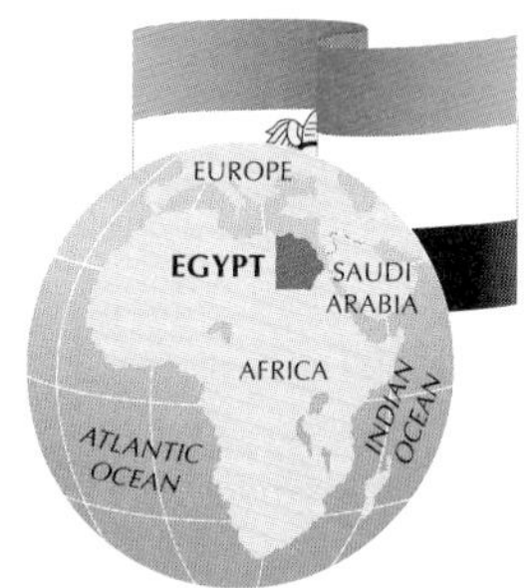

Organization structures and organizational behavior in Egypt and other countries in the Middle East tend to have a strong emphasis on formalized structure and process; control is usually focused among a handful of top executives.

The Informal Organization

Despite formalization, many interactions among organization members are not written into the structure of the formal organization. These interactions make up the **informal organization,** the unofficial and unwritten system of relationships that develops spontaneously in the course of organizational activities. In contrast with the officially planned structure of the formal organization, the informal organization reflects the flow of communication and authority that actually exists among organization members (see Exhibit 9.8). Chester I. Barnard (discussed in Chapter 2) and Herbert A. Simon (discussed in Chapter 6) were two of many management experts who observed that these informal relationships affect many organizational decisions and activities. They concluded that both the informal and the formal organizations influence the organization's ability to achieve its goals.[71]

informal organization The unofficial, unwritten system of relationships that develops spontaneously within the organization

EXHIBIT 9.8

The Informal Organization

Relationships in the informal organization (indicated by red lines) develop spontaneously and often cross the formal boundaries that delineate authority and departments.

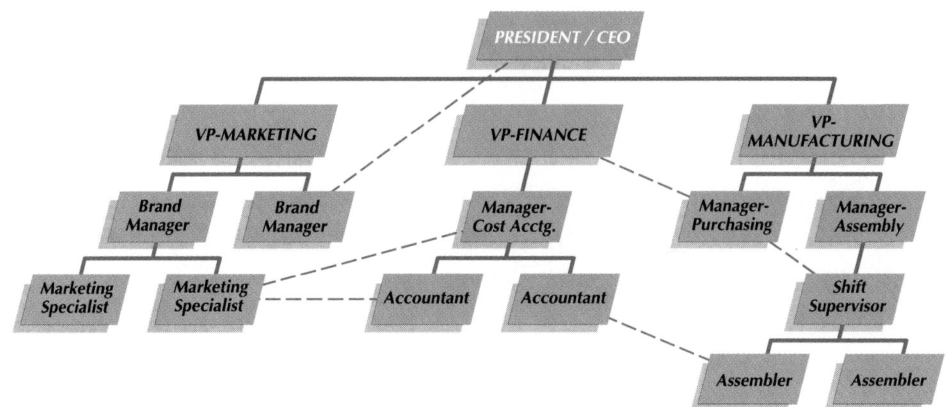

When managers and employees are confronted with nonprogrammed decisions or crisis situations that demand fast action, they often turn to their contacts within the informal organization. These informal contacts frequently cross the formal lines of departments and authority, providing information, advice, assistance, and even materials to solve problems or complete tasks. Thus, the informal organization may be more expeditious than the formal organization, and informal interactions often satisfy the social needs of participants as well.[72]

SUMMARY

The organization structure is a formal system of interaction and coordination that links the tasks of individuals and groups. Managers start with the goals and strategies they have established during the planning process, then they design the organization structure so that these plans can be implemented and the goals achieved. Managers use work specialization to carve the organization's work into smaller components. Work specialization allows managers and employees to concentrate on specific areas and to develop the skills to handle these areas more efficiently.

The chain of command is the unbroken line of authority that extends from the top to the bottom of the organization, and it is based on unity of command and on the scalar principle. Managers distribute authority through the chain of command to give other organization members the right to make decisions, to perform or supervise activities, and to allocate resources. Along with the authority to accomplish a task comes responsibility, the obligation to perform the task. This transfer of authority in the chain of command is known as delegation. Once organization members have accepted authority and responsibility, they are subject to accountability, the obligation to perform or to explain nonperformance to higher-level managers.

Managers face a variety of barriers to effective delegation, including their fear that employees may not complete delegated tasks capably, their reluctance to share authority, their belief that they can do better than employees, and their fear that employees can perform better than they can. To overcome these barriers, managers must recognize the benefits of delegation, and they must realize that employees' achievements reflect well on managers. Also, delegation helps prepare employees to step in when managers are promoted, and employees may be more motivated to perform when they are delegated challenging tasks.

Centralization, the extent to which authority is concentrated at the top management level, allows top managers to coordinate activities, to balance the needs of the various parts of the organization, to reduce expensive duplication, and to make major decisions. In contrast, decentralization is the extent to which authority is delegated to lower management levels. Decentralization relieves top managers of making many small decisions and allows them to concentrate on strategic issues. Moreover, local managers in decentralized organizations can respond quickly to environmental changes, and decentralization provides lower-level managers with valuable decision-making experience.

The span of management is the number of people who report directly to one manager. The width of this span determines the number of hierarchical levels. In a tall structure, the average span of management is narrow, so the organization has more hierarchical levels. But in a flat structure, the average span of management is wide, so the organization has fewer hierarchical levels.

Departmentalization is the grouping of individual jobs into logical units and the grouping of units to form the total organization. Four common methods are (1) functional departmentalization, grouping jobs according to their function; (2) product departmentalization, grouping jobs according to the goods and services offered; (3) geographical departmentalization, grouping jobs according to defined locations; and (4) customer departmentalization, grouping jobs according to customer needs.

Horizontal coordination links activities across departments. It facilitates the flow of information to manage interdependencies.

The formal organization is the planned structure and the relationships officially established by top managers. It serves as a framework for implementing decisions about how activities should be divided, coordinated, and integrated. In contrast, the informal organization is the unofficial and unwritten system of relationships reflecting the interactions that actually occur among organization members.

MEETING A MANAGEMENT CHALLENGE AT PROCTER & GAMBLE

John Smale recognized in 1985 that he had to revise the organization structure of Procter & Gamble if his company was to regain the degree of profitability it had enjoyed for decades. Brand managers needed to share information with each other and coordinate their product development with other departments. However, Smale knew he ran the risk of demoralizing his company's aggressive brand managers if he introduced structures that would limit their traditional independence.

Smale solved the coordination problem by creating category managers between brand and division managers. Category managers can share information learned from one brand manager with the others, while carefully avoiding the dissemination of information that a brand manager might view as proprietary. Because their span of management is much narrower than that of division managers, category managers are able to approve marketing plans faster. Each category manager is responsible for a group of related products. As a result, they guide the marketing plans of the brand managers so that brands do not cannibalize each other's profits by competing for the same customer group or shelf position. Brand managers are still encouraged to aggressively pursue the success of their products since

Selling Procter & Gamble's Head & Shoulders shampoo in China

category managers are responsible for the success of individual brands as well as of overall categories.

Smale's second step was to improve horizontal coordination by creating the position of product supply managers, reporting to category managers. Product supply managers coordinate work orders from category managers so that departments such as distribution, manufacturing, engineering, design, research, and purchasing are not overwhelmed with requests from every direction. To do this they brought department heads together into teams that coordinate work flow in order to develop products faster.

Smale improved horizontal coordination in an

other important way as well. The category and product supply managers organized business teams consisting of brand managers and representatives from other departments. These teams began to work together to develop new products. The team approach gets products to market faster because it anticipates problems from the departments—such as an unwieldy package design—that were appearing only later in the development process and causing costly delays when marketing plans had to be redone. The teams also provide vehicles for experienced personnel in the departments to provide creative ideas.

Within a few years, the new organization structure had brought about its intended effect. With better communication and closer coordination, the company was reporting double-digit increases in its earnings as sales topped $20 billion by the end of the decade. Smale's successor, Edwin Artzt, is strongly inclined to continue making structural adjustments as required. By his own description, Artzt is "a wrecking crew. If it doesn't work right, I break it down and build it up again." Given this mindset and P&G's success with the changes instituted by Smale, one can be sure that P&G will continue to adapt its structure as internal and external conditions dictate.

***You're the Manager*:** Recognizing the importance of organization structure to his company's performance, Artzt has brought you in as a consultant to monitor the organization, to suggest structural modifications as needed, and to help him troubleshoot specific situations.

Ranking Questions

1. A Procter & Gamble packaging scientist has formulated a new packaging material that is easily biodegradable, cheaper than current materials, and applicable to a wide range of products, but it has to be formulated slightly differently for beverages, laundry detergent, and shampoo—the three groups most interested in it. Resource constraints are preventing the packaging group from developing all three versions simultaneously. How would you resolve this problem?
   a. The three category managers should pitch their causes to the packaging department manager, who will then decide which package to pursue first.
   b. It is likely that one of the three package types can be developed faster than the other two, and that is the one that should be developed first.
   c. Artzt and his staff should make the decision without input from the category managers to avoid any appearance of favoritism.
   d. Each category manager should present his or her case to top management, and the packaging team should explain the implications of pursuing each of the three packages. Then Artzt and his staff should pick the course of action that best supports the company's strategic goals.
2. Some brand managers are talking about quitting, complaining that the changes have given category managers too much of the authority for brand management and not enough of the responsibility for brand success. What would you do to retain these brand managers and make them feel valuable?
   a. Meet one-on-one with the brand managers. Communicate your understanding that a change in organization structure means a shift in some authority. Emphasize that the changes are nothing personal and ask for their understanding.
   b. Issue a memorandum that the company will terminate anyone discovered talking with headhunters about leaving P&G.
   c. Shift some of the decision-making authority back into the hands of the brand managers by allowing them to make the final decision about which market niche their products will target.
   d. Schedule joint meetings with the category and brand managers to chew over some of the issues that are troubling the brand managers. Search for ways to let authority and responsibility for product success be shared without losing the coordination needed to keep products on schedule and profitable.

Multiple-Choice Questions

3. P&G has placed both toothpaste and mouthwash products under the guidance of a single category manager. Now the brand managers in this category are complaining that the category manager has too much to handle and approvals are taking too long, even for minor decisions such as a change in package color. What would you recommend?
   a. Narrow the category manager's span of management by appointing a new category manager to one of the product groups.
   b. Create another level of management with approval authority between the category manager and the brand managers.
   c. Allow the situation to remain as it is, since

longer approval times may be required for these particular product categories.

d. Allow the category manager to delegate some of the decision making to the brand managers.

4. Two brand managers who want to use the same package designer are complaining because often they both need the services of the designer at the same time. This has become a chronic problem and is slowing the pace of product development. The product supply manager, through whom requests for the designer's services proceed, says that the brand managers do not place their requests far enough in advance to allow for smooth scheduling. The designer concurs in this. The brand managers say that the product supply manager is just getting in the way. They would rather deal directly with the designer. What suggestion would you make to improve horizontal coordination?
   a. Hire another designer, using the technique of slack resources. Let the brand managers review and approve of the work of the designer prior to hire.
   b. Taking advantage of the company's information systems, have the brand managers present the product supply manager with work request memos a specified number of days prior to the time designs must be completed.
   c. Allow for overtime pay for the designer so that all of the work can be done on time.
   d. Use the technique of lateral relationships by allowing the brand managers to place their work orders directly with the designer.

Analysis Questions

5. How does the introduction of category managers affect the ability of brand managers to make decisions and take actions to increase product sales?
6. Which of the lateral relationships do the company's new product supply managers represent?
7. Can you identify any potential drawbacks to P&G's new structure?

Special Project

The brand management structure used at P&G (and many other companies) has two important drawbacks: brand managers rarely have the time or opportunity to become experts in any of the marketing specialties that affect their success (such as advertising, marketing research, and pricing), and they typically have no formal authority over the people who work in those functions. Consequently, the brand managers must rely on the experience and judgment of others, and they have to count on persuasion and horizontal coordination to get work done through these specialists. Draw an organization chart that would fix both problems and briefly describe how the new organization would work. Be sure to point out both the strengths and the weaknesses of your proposal.[73]

KEY TERMS

acceptance theory of authority (277)
accountability (278)
authority (277)
centralization (279)
chain of command (276)
customer departmentalization (287)
decentralization (279)
delegation (278)
demassing (283)
departmentalization (285)
downsizing (282)
flat structure (281)
formalization (294)
formal organization (293)
functional departmentalization (285)
geographical departmentalization (287)
horizontal coordination (289)
informal organization (295)
line authority (284)
line position (283)
organization chart (274)
organization structure (274)
process departmentalization (288)
product departmentalization (286)
project departmentalization (288)
responsibility (278)
slack resources (291)
span of management (280)
staff authority (284)
staff position (283)
tall structure (281)
time departmentalization (289)
work specialization (275)

QUESTIONS

For Review

1. What are the benefits and limitations of work specialization?
2. How do line positions differ from staff positions?
3. Why do organizations departmentalize, and what are the four major forms of departmentalization?

4. What impact does the chain of command have on the distribution of authority?
5. How do information systems, slack resources, and lateral relationships contribute to horizontal coordination?

For Analysis

1. How does the acceptance theory of authority apply to volunteers working in an organization such as the Little League? To a military organization such as the U.S. Air Force?
2. What types of interdependencies might occur in a school newspaper office?
3. What are the arguments for and against centralization in an organization with facilities around the world?
4. Why does direct contact help create the informal organization?
5. How do customers benefit when organizations have flatter structures?

For Application

1. What roles might line and staff managers play in an organization such as H & R Block, the tax preparation chain with offices throughout the country?
2. How can a local television station use time departmentalization to coordinate and integrate its broadcast activities?
3. When might a not-for-profit organization such the ASPCA use slack resources for effective horizontal coordination? What would be the benefits and limitations of this approach?
4. In what ways might General Mills use formalization in its cereal-production facilities?
5. How would a small 7-Eleven convenience store use an organization chart?

KEEPING CURRENT IN MANAGEMENT

Find a recent article in which a manager announced a significant change in the organization's structure. Examples might include a corporation that expanded its span of management to create a flatter organizational structure, a government agency that switched from geographical departmentalization to product departmentalization, or a not-for-profit organization that centralized or decentralized its funding activities.

1. Why did the organization change its structure? How does the new organization structure affect work specialization? What impact does the change have on the chain of command?
2. What types of interdependencies will exist in the new organization? How is the organization using horizontal coordination techniques to manage these interdependencies?
3. How does the new structure affect line and staff positions in this organization? What is likely to happen to the informal organization as a result of the new organization structure?

SHARPEN YOUR MANAGEMENT SKILLS

As a student, you are undoubtedly a member of several organizations. Part-time jobs, campus clubs, sports teams, not-for-profit groups, fraternities/sororities, musical groups, student chapters of professional groups—all of these involve membership in an organization. Even with just the information you learned in this chapter, you now have some important insights into how people and jobs should be organized to achieve maximum performance. Remember that even the simplest organization can benefit from the right structure.

- *Decision:* Pick one of the organizations you belong to and identify the ways in which the organization's structure helps or hinders the attainment of the organization's goals. This should include both the formal and informal organizations. For instance, let's say you belong to the student chapter of the Institute of Electrical and Electronics Engineers (IEEE). There is both a formal organization (president, vice presidents, etc.) and an informal organization (networks of juniors and seniors who've been in the chapter for several years, star students who influence the group's direction, and so on). If you've uncovered any serious hindrances, devise a structural change that would overcome them.
- *Communication:* Prepare a brief presentation to the organization (or selected leaders in the organization if that is more appropriate) to explain your findings and make the presentation if circumstances allow. Present your proposed structural change if you've designed one. Be sure to consider the interpersonal dynamics of your audience (e.g., don't single out someone in the audience as the source of the organization's difficulties).

AT&T Organizes for Global Conquest

Telephone pioneer AT&T is struggling to stay profitable in an unfamiliar world of competition after relinquishing its most lucrative units and its guaranteed profits. Robert E. Allen, who rose from head of AT&T Information Services to president and then chairman in just two years, has pared the payroll and must now organize for competition on a global scale.

HISTORY

Alexander Graham Bell invented the telephone in 1886, and the Bell Telephone Company was founded the next year. The bankers who controlled the rapidly expanding company renamed it American Telephone and Telegraph when it moved its headquarters from Boston to New York in 1899. After Bell's original patents expired in 1893 and 1894, thousands of independent telephone companies sprang up from coast to coast. AT&T bought some of them, underpriced others, and refused to let outside companies connect to Bell System lines. Federal antitrust efforts in 1913 forced AT&T to sell off the Western Union telegraph company and give local phone companies access to its lines, but the company retained a virtual telephone monopoly. Attacks on AT&T's monopoly never ceased, and it finally agreed to divest itself by 1984 of its profitable regional telephone holding companies. By 1986 AT&T was losing $1 billion a year, but Allen reduced its work force from 373,000 to 272,000, and in 1990 AT&T earned $2.7 billion a year on revenues of $37 billion.

ENVIRONMENT

Divesting the local phone companies cost AT&T three-quarters of its $150 billion in assets but left it with a long-distance telephone system, an equipment manufacturing division, and a laboratory that had developed such technological milestones as sound motion pictures, the transistor, and lasers. Divestiture also freed AT&T to compete in the $600 billion-a-year global telecommunications industry, which is becoming a free-for-all with corporate customers demanding global telephone networks, with developed countries encouraging competition, and with developing countries seeking communications as a prerequisite for attracting business investment.

Competition is a new game for AT&T. Before the breakup, AT&T didn't have to compete to sell $14 billion worth of phone equipment each year, it had little competition for local and long-distance phone service, and it was regulated by state and federal agencies that guaranteed it a profit of 10 to 15 percent above its costs. But these days expenditures no longer guarantee profits, so AT&T has trimmed payroll and eliminated duplication in accounting, data processing, and even internal telephone systems. The corporation has been reshaped as a decentralized organization of strategic business units focused on a type of product or a type of customer; the business equipment manufacturing subsidiary AT&T Information Systems, for example, has separate divisions for large business systems, consumer and small systems, and computer systems, with another division for installing and servicing products sold by the other three divisions.

GOALS AND CHALLENGES

Allen is moving to turn AT&T into a global power by pledging to increase foreign revenues from 16 percent of total sales to 50 percent by the turn of the century, by increasing overseas staff, and by taking over computer manufacturer NCR, which has 62 percent of its sales abroad. AT&T wants to revamp NCR's European sales and distribution network to push its telecommunications gear there. In the meantime, AT&T's major international business is coming from its Network Services division (which makes telephone switches) through both outright sales and a host of joint ventures with foreign companies and governments. To oversee the international efforts of all AT&T divisions, Allen has appointed Randall Tobias to the new job of vice chairman for international activities.

1. Why might Tobias favor a narrow span of management for his job as he organizes for global expansion? What could he do to maximize the number of direct subordinates he could effectively manage?
2. What type of departmentalization is AT&T using today? Could AT&T use geographical departmentalization as part of its global expansion strategy? Why or why not?
3. How could horizontal coordination among AT&T's managers in Europe help Tobias meet goals for European performance? What role would elements in the vertical organization have in the effort to achieve Tobias's goals?
4. If Tobias decides he must cut European costs 20 percent in three months, what kinds of lateral relationships among European managers would be most effective in helping them respond? Should these relationships be formal or informal?

10

Organization Design

CHAPTER OUTLINE

After studying this chapter, you will be able to

1. Discuss the nature of organization design and explain the three theoretical approaches
2. Describe the relationship between strategy and organization design
3. Discuss how the environment affects organization design
4. Contrast unit technology, mass-production technology, and continuous-flow-process technology
5. Explain the relationship between organization size and life cycle and outline their impact on organization design
6. List and discuss four common types of organization designs
7. Describe Mintzberg's five structural configurations and explain when each is appropriate

FACING A MANAGEMENT CHALLENGE AT

CAMPBELL SOUP

Cooking Up a New Organization

Despite a solid reputation for quality and a dominant presence in the U.S. market, Campbell Soup found itself losing market share in the latter half of the 1980s. Nimbler competitors had begun to recognize and cater to the growing interest in foods geared to regional tastes. They served up Cajun gumbo in the Mississippi delta region and spicy hot chili in the Southwest, but Campbell had stuck with its one-taste-fits-all approach. A separate sales force was assigned to each product group, with each salesperson selling a single product line to a large number of stores. It was up to CEO R. Gordon McGovern to examine the company's organization structure to see whether anything could be done.

To pursue its nationwide approach to sales, the company had developed an organization structure composed of experts grouped according to functions such as marketing, finance, research, and operations. Within each function there existed a hierarchy of managers, culminating in a functional head who reported to a corporate manager. Top managers coordinated all of the functional activities, and decisions were centralized. This functional departmentalization allowed managers to focus on their areas of expertise and thereby develop considerable skills in their specialties. For decades, this structure had worked well: thanks to the expertise developed by division managers, the company was able to roll out products and promotions like a great carpet from one coast to the other.

However, the market was changing, as shoppers clamored for foods that catered to their specific taste buds. Campbell's strategy of thinking nationally no longer seemed appropriate when the giant U.S. market for prepared foods was shifting toward a series of smaller regional markets. McGovern needed a new organization structure if he was to successfully target regional consumers with specially formulated products and marketing activities geared to their needs, with the ultimate goal of allowing Campbell to compete more effectively. He knew the functional approach could not respond as quickly or as effectively to regional differences, so he decided to redesign the structure to follow his new strategy.

McGovern concluded it was time to abandon the functional approach and switch to a structure that would move rapidly and flexibly in response to market needs. He had to redesign the structure by splitting Campbell into autonomous regional divisions. The decentralization of decision making would allow the divisions to be sensitive to and responsive to local tastes. And smaller divisions would be able to make decisions more quickly.

McGovern recognized that change would not come easily. Going regional would involve assigning factories to local output, finding new regional supply sources, and retraining some regional personnel from being salespeople to thinking like strategic marketers. Because of the need for personnel in the regions, some people would need to change positions and even move to new parts of the country.

Never before had a food industry giant attempted to organize geographically on such a large scale. How could McGovern restructure the organization to allow his managers to respond quickly to regional consumer preferences? And how could the structure avoid the slow decision-making process characteristic of large corporations without sacrificing top management's control over corporate direction?[1]

CHAPTER OVERVIEW

As R. Gordon McGovern knows, managers must consciously combine and juggle the elements of structure to allow the organization to reach its goals efficiently and effectively. This chapter builds on the fundamentals of organization discussed in Chapter 9 and shows how organizations put these concepts to work. It starts with a discussion of the nature of organization design and the theoretical approaches to designing organization structures. Next, the factors affecting organization design—strategy, the environment, technology, organization size, and life cycle—are explored. After the common forms of organization design are described, the chapter ends with a look at the application of organization design principles, exemplified by Mintzberg's structural configurations.

MANAGEMENT AND ORGANIZATION DESIGN

To create a workable organization structure, managers arrange the basic elements of the organization described in Chapter 9 into a meaningful pattern. They can develop one structure for the overall organization or vary the arrangement of structural elements for individual organizational units. Whether they are running a business, a not-for-profit clinic, or a government agency, top managers face many decisions in the process of creating an organization structure to achieve their goals.

The Nature of Organization Design

organization design The process of developing and implementing an appropriate organization structure

Organization design is the process of developing and implementing an appropriate organization structure. This process involves an ongoing series of decisions about the combination and application of structural elements that are used to form the organization structure. In the course of its life, an organization's structure rarely remains constant; it can change any number of times as its managers continually make decisions about the structural elements in an effort to improve performance and to achieve organizational goals.[2]

Management expert Peter Drucker observed that organization design is concerned with four questions:

1. What should the units of organization be?
2. Which units should be grouped together, and which should be kept separate?
3. What size and shape should the various units assume?
4. What is the appropriate placement and relationship of the various organizational units?

To determine the units and their grouping, said Drucker, managers must specify the results needed to achieve their goals and consider how each unit contributes to those results. To determine the size, shape, placement, and relationship of the units, managers must analyze how decisions and unit relations affect the needed results.[3] Campbell Soup, for instance, began to suspect that its monolithic nationwide structure was hampering its ability to compete in diverse regional markets. Although Drucker's approach recognizes that the combination and alignment of structural elements can differ from organization to organization, this contemporary perspective has its roots in earlier views that stressed the universal aspects of organization design.

Theoretical Approaches to Organization Design

Over the years, scholars and practitioners have explored the principles of organization design and considered how they can be applied to achieve organizational goals. Of the diverse management perspectives described in Chapter 2, three have had a significant influence on the development of contemporary organization design principles: the classical approach, the behavioral approach, and the contingency approach.[4]

As CEO of R. R. Donnelley, the world's largest printer, John Walter reviews organization design and realigns the company's structure to support his ambitious global expansion strategy. Donnelley is moving deeper into satellite delivery of information and has acquired printing plants around the world, so its organization design must evolve to accommodate these changes.

The Classical Approach

The classical management theorists generally sought to identify a set of rational principles that could be applied to all types of organizations. Henri Fayol, Lyndall Urwick, Luther Gulick, and Chester Barnard are among the many who contributed to the classical approach to organization design, but one of the most enduring concepts was presented by Max Weber (see Chapter 2). His theory of bureaucracy, a design in which tasks, authority, and reporting relationships are formally defined, was meant to bring order and reason to the organization while eliminating favoritism and other inequities. Although bureaucracy is today often associated with red tape and rigidity, Weber's ideal form of bureaucracy was intended to enhance organizational efficiency.[5]

Bureaucracy is characterized by six elements: (1) a clear-cut division of labor that allows managers to employ experts, (2) a chain of command that distributes authority through defined hierarchical channels, (3) a formal set of rules and regulations that makes decisions and actions predictable and consistent, (4) an administrative staff that maintains communication and coordinates organizational activities, (5) an impersonal and unbiased interaction between managers on differing hierarchical levels as well as with customers or constituents, and (6) an advancement system based on merit and on the achievement of technical skills.[6]

As Weber intended, bureaucracy's major benefit is efficiency. A large organization is bound to run more smoothly when individual tasks are logically defined, when specialists proven to be skilled in their work are employed, when organization members understand the scope and limits of their authority, and when everyone is treated in the same manner. Indeed, the U.S. Army and many governmental agencies are operated according to bureaucratic principles. Generally, government positions are clearly defined, require Civil Service examinations as proof of competence, are vested with authority appropriate to their hierarchical level, and are administered impersonally. These characteristics of bureaucracy are designed to allow the government to operate efficiently and impartially.[7]

However, bureaucracy has several limitations. First, reliance on rules and regulations inhibits bureaucratic organizations' flexibility and responsiveness to environmental changes. Second, strict adherence to the chain of command can slow communications, a particular threat when organizations operate in dynamic environments. Third, organization members may be discouraged from accepting individual responsibility because their defined positions do not explicitly cover every conceivable situation. And fourth, bureaucracy fails to take into account the influence of the informal organization and the needs of organization members. This last limitation was addressed by the behavioral theorists when they investigated how organization design affects the individual organization members.[8]

The Behavioral Approach

Whereas classical theorists concentrated on the rational and systematic aspects of organization design, later theorists recognized the importance of the human side. Theorists who advocated a behavioral approach to organization design did not completely ignore the earlier theories. Instead, they used the classical approach as a base for their *behavioral models* and incorporated the influence of human behavior and attitudes. Two behavioral models of organization design are Likert's systems and the sociotechnical systems theory.[9]

System 1 A traditional organization design that relies heavily on formal authority and the hierarchical chain of command

System 4 An ideal form of organization design that relies on manager-employee collaboration, uses a wide array of motivational processes, and encourages freer interaction among organization members

Likert's Systems When he was the director of the Institute for Social Research at the University of Michigan, Rensis Likert studied the link between organization design and organizational effectiveness. He analyzed organizations in terms of eight dimensions: leadership, motivation, communication, interaction, goal setting, decision making, control, and performance goals. As a result of this research, he developed a continuum of four organization types. At one extreme is the traditional organization that relies heavily on formal authority and the hierarchical chain of command, which Likert called **System 1.** At the other extreme is the organization that relies on manager-employee collaboration, uses a wide array of motivational processes, and encourages freer interaction, an ideal form he called **System 4.** In between are System 2 and System 3, organizations that represent intermediate stages between emphasizing managerial authority and emphasizing employee-manager collaboration.[10]

In a System 4 organization, members are encouraged to communicate freely with the people above, below, and on the same hierarchical level, both to coordinate activities and to provide information for better decision making (see Exhibit 10.1). Because of this reliance on interpersonal and intergroup communication, Likert identified the linking pin roles (see Chapter 9) as essential System 4 elements. Moreover, System 4 managers use a variety of motivational techniques to stimulate employee performance, and they involve employees in the goal-setting and performance measurement processes. In contrast to the one-to-one delegation typical of a classical bureaucracy, Likert's systems stress the importance of using organization structure to facilitate group decision making and group responsibility.[11]

According to Likert's research, traditional bureaucratic organizations are less effective and less efficient than organizations with designs more in tune with the social and behavioral processes of organization members. By gradually shifting toward the ideal represented by System 4, managers should be able to increase productivity, lower costs, boost performance, increase employee satisfaction, and improve labor relations. Although System 4 is intended to be appropriate for any organization, it does not take into account an organization's specific circumstances.[12] (Chapter 14 covers Likert's systems in more detail.)

sociotechnical systems theory The concept that organization design must take into account the interaction of the organization members, the technological system, and the degree of environmental interaction

Sociotechnical Systems Theory The **sociotechnical systems theory** argues that organization design must take into account the interaction of the organization members, the technological system used to produce goods or services, and the degree of interaction with the external environment. Eric Trist, K. W. Bamforth, and other researchers who advanced this theory recognized that every organization contains a social system that transcends the formal organization, encompassing individual and group interactions, behavior, and attitudes. They also realized that the operational technology has a profound effect on the social system because the people must interact with the technology to produce the organization's goods and services. Whatever the nature of this interaction—whether running factory equipment, using a computer keyboard, or stitching apparel—the technological system can affect employee attitudes, ideas, and satisfaction.[13]

EXHIBIT 10.1 Comparison of Likert's System 1 and System 4

Rensis Likert's behavioral model of organization design covers a continuum of four organization types. System 1, at one extreme, builds on the classical elements of managerial authority, whereas System 4, at the other extreme, builds on the social and behavioral processes that emphasize manager-employee collaboration.

Characteristic	System 1	System 4
Leadership	Managers do not trust subordinates, rarely support their efforts, and do not involve subordinates in problem solving.	Managers trust subordinates, support their efforts, and encourage interchange of information. They also involve subordinates in problem solving.
Motivation	Top managers feel the responsibility for achieving goals; managers motivate by using threats, fear, and punishment.	All organization members feel responsible for achieving goals; managers motivate employees by offering participation and rewards.
Communication	Information flows downward, so managers know little of the problems faced by subordinates. Managers and subordinates rarely communicate about organizational goals.	Information flows upward, downward, and horizontally, so managers understand the problems faced by subordinates. Managers and employees communicate frequently about organizational goals.
Interaction	Organization members have little interaction outside their department and rarely participate in cooperative teamwork. Also, subordinates have little influence over departmental activities and goals.	Organization members interact frequently with people outside their departments and often engage in cooperative teamwork. Subordinates have much influence over departmental goals and activities.
Decision making	Decisions are centralized at the top, and subordinates do not participate in decision making.	Decisions are decentralized and made with the participation of subordinates.
Goal setting	Goals are assigned by top managers and resisted by subordinates.	Subordinates participate in goal setting and therefore fully accept their goals.
Control	Control is centralized at the top; data collected through the monitoring process are used to police and to punish poor performance.	Concern for performance is felt throughout organization; data are used to support self-guidance and problem solving.
Performance goals	Managers seek and set average goals and do not receive the training they need to develop their skills.	Managers seek and set extremely high goals and receive management training to help develop their skills.

Because the organization design influences how and when employees interact with technology, the social system and the technological system are inextricably interrelated. The remaining element is the organization's level of interaction with the external environment, which can in turn affect both the technological and the social systems. Seen from this perspective, organization design is a delicate balancing act in which the three elements must be carefully juggled.[14]

Not long ago, for example, Campbell Soup's Toronto plant operated less efficiently, and at a higher cost, than the U.S. plants. David Clark, CEO of the Canadian division, looked to the plant's production employees for ideas that would improve productivity. The employees altered much of the human interaction with the technological system, including work schedules and staffing levels, and within a year, output was up and costs were down. Campbell managers will continue to face the challenge of balancing the social and the technological systems with the environment as they introduce automated soup-blending machinery in North American plants during the coming years.[15]

The people who run the equipment at Chaparral Steel are most affected by the impact of new technology, so CEO Gordon Forward *(right)* invites their involvement in buying new production machinery. This team of employees traveled the world to research and evaluate sophisticated new machinery. Once top management approved the model they selected, the team negotiated the purchase contracts and supervised the installation, which ran smoothly.

In contrast to the classical approach, sociotechnical systems theory reflects an astute awareness of the relationship among the formal organization, the informal organization, and technology. The benefits include increased employee satisfaction and improved productivity. However, the theory does not explain the origins and causes of events within the social system or the interaction among the social system, the technological system, and the environment, so its practical application is sometimes limited. But because sociotechnical systems theory acknowledges that no single approach is appropriate for all organizations, it has foreshadowed the development of the contingency approach.[16]

The Contingency Approach

The contingency theory of management (explored in detail in Chapter 2) applies to organization design in two ways: (1) there is no single best way to design an organization's structure, and (2) the alternative ways to organize may not be equally effective. Whereas the classical approach stresses universally applicable organization designs, the contingency approach suggests that no one design is appropriate for every type of organization. Moreover, the internal and the external environments of organizations vary, as do their goals, so a design that is effective for one organization may not be appropriate for another. Therefore, the choice of design is contingent on the organization's specific situation.[17]

For instance, Gannett and *The Source* are both in the media business, but their internal and external environments differ, so their organization designs must also differ. Gannett employs more than 36,000 people and reaches millions worldwide with its diverse media vehicles. Its organization design integrates and coordinates the domestic and overseas activities of its newspaper publishing, television and radio broadcasting, and outdoor advertising divisions. On the other hand, *The Source* is a monthly magazine that employs a handful of people to cover hip-hop music, culture, and politics for 55,000 U.S. readers. Whereas

CEO John Curley cannot personally manage the extensive list of tasks that must be completed to achieve Gannett's goals, *The Source*'s owners David Mays and John Shecter personally coordinate the tasks that get their magazine written, printed, and sold. For these organizations, as for every organization, the appropriate design depends on the circumstances.[18]

FACTORS AFFECTING ORGANIZATION DESIGN

Drawing on the contingency approach, researchers have recognized that managers can design the organization structure in a variety of ways to achieve organizational goals. Which structure is most appropriate depends on five contingency factors: (1) strategy, (2) the environment, (3) technology, (4) organization size, and (5) organization life cycle.[19]

Strategy

Historian Alfred D. Chandler, Jr., studied the relationship of strategy and structure in large U.S. corporations, including Du Pont, General Motors, Standard Oil of New Jersey (now Exxon), and Sears. In his landmark 1962 book *Strategy and Structure,* Chandler wrote about strategy as a major determinant of structure. As organizations grow and increase the number and diversity of their strategic goals, their strategic plans call for increasing output, opening new offices or factories, adopting new operating technologies and new functional skills, locating new sources of supply, and other activities designed to achieve the new goals. In particular, when organizations pursue growth by vertical or horizontal integration, managers face increased demands on their ability to define work specialization, assign responsibility, and coordinate all tasks.[20]

For example, when organizations decide to grow by diversifying into unrelated products, managers must undertake such challenges as obtaining new types of resources, arranging appropriate distribution, and selling to new customers. Because these activities are not included in the current structure, management must make structural adjustments to carry out the new plans. If the structure is not altered, the new activities cannot be integrated and coordinated with other activities. Without the appropriate structure to pursue the new strategy, the organization will be unable to achieve its goals, and effectiveness and efficiency will be impaired.[21]

When the U.S. Air Force changed its strategy toward air defense, secretary Donald Rice announced sweeping changes in the organization structure that were designed to support the new air power strategy. Originally, the Air Force maintained a separate unit, the Strategic Air Command (SAC), to manage an arsenal of long-range bombers and missiles. However, because of the new post–Cold War strategy, officials decided to integrate these activities by dismantling the SAC and transferring its crews and planes to a new centralized unit, the Air Combat Command. To ensure better coordination of airlift operations anywhere in the world, the Air Force established a second centralized unit, the Air Mobility Command. Further, the new structure requires fewer staff positions, so a large number of senior officers were reassigned to line positions that involve flying and commanding aircraft. These changes help top officials to more tightly control international intelligence gathering, air power logistics, and military communications.[22]

The principle that new strategies require structural accommodations also holds true for companies that operate internationally. When top managers first decide to expand overseas, their current structure is generally constraining rather than facilitating because it is not geared to the activities and processes needed to succeed in the new markets, especially when the markets are geographically removed. Managers must therefore consider the unique problems of international operations when they design a global organization structure.[23]

The Environment

A second contingency factor is the environment. Environmental munificence, resource dependence, and environmental uncertainty (discussed in Chapter 3) are three powerful influences on organization design. For example, when resources are plentiful, managers can use a decentralized structure, but when resources are scarce, they often centralize to tighten control over the available resources and to better coordinate all organizational activities. Centralization is CEO Carl Reichardt's response to resource scarcity at Wells Fargo. Pursuing a cost leadership strategy at the California-based bank, Reichardt keeps a tight rein on costs and loans. At times, he has personally approved all major expenditures, and he still reviews loans of $5 million or more.[24]

Managers can also use organization design to cope with the uncertainty of changeable and complex environmental conditions. Depending on the level of uncertainty, managers can choose a mechanistic or an organic organization structure. Further, they must consider how the environment affects the responses of each organizational unit and then use organization structure to more effectively coordinate these responses.

Mechanistic and Organic Structures

How do organizations use structure to respond to the environment? British researchers Tom Burns and G. M. Stalker investigated the link between environment and organization design in 20 U.K. companies drawn from various industries. First, they classified each company's environment as either static (relatively little change over time) or dynamic (relatively rapid and constant change), then they studied how each company used organization structure to respond to its environment. They found that the companies were using two distinctly different structures to cope with their environments and that the choice of structure varied according to the degree of environmental change.[25]

mechanistic structure A relatively inflexible organization structure characterized by centralized decision making, narrow work specialization, and hierarchical delegation and communication

Those companies operating in a static environment tended to have a **mechanistic structure,** a relatively inflexible structure characterized by centralized decision making, narrow work specialization, and hierarchical delegation and communication (see Exhibit 10.2). Similar to a bureaucracy or a System 1 design, a mechanistic organization is designed to move information upward to top managers, who make the decisions and then coordinate activities via the chain of command and formalized rules and instructions. Because of its relative tightness, a mechanistic organization structure is most effective when environmental conditions rarely change and managers face little uncertainty.[26]

organic structure A relatively flexible organization structure characterized by decentralized decision making, fluid work definition, and horizontal and vertical communication

However, those companies operating in a dynamic environment tended to have an **organic structure,** a relatively flexible structure characterized by decentralized decision making, fluid division of labor, and both horizontal and vertical communication. In organic organizations, decision-making authority is delegated to those with specialized knowledge of the tasks at hand. For this reason,

EXHIBIT 10.2 Comparison of Mechanistic and Organic Structures

Tom Burns and G. M. Stalker found that organizations tend to use one of two types of structure to respond to their environments. In a static environment, organizations use a mechanistic structure, whereas in a changeable environment, organizations use an organic structure.

Mechanistic Structure	Organic Structure
Work is subdivided into specialized tasks that do not change except when managers make formal changes.	Work is defined in terms of tasks needed to achieve goals, and tasks are continually adjusted to manage interdependencies.
The role of each organization member is precisely defined in terms of rights, obligations, and technical methods.	The role of each organization member is loosely defined in terms of responsibility for task completion.
Authority, control, and communication are structured hierarchically.	Authority, control, and communication are based on commonality of interest.
Information flows vertically.	Information flows vertically and horizontally.
Managers direct activities and make decisions that subordinates implement.	Managers act as consultants, offering information and advice to employees.
Loyalty to the organization and obedience to managers are emphasized.	Commitment to organizational goals is emphasized.

information flows horizontally as well as vertically, and people at all levels can be consulted about a problem. The nature and content of individual tasks change according to environmental conditions, so specialists continually redefine their roles and their interaction with others in the context of the overall work that must be completed. Thanks to this looser structure, organic organizations are most effective in rapidly changing or unpredictable environments.[27]

For example, Kyocera, a Japanese supplier of industrial ceramics for high-tech applications, uses an organic structure to keep up with the fast pace of change in the business equipment and consumer electronics industries. When a task arises, a manager assembles a team of employees with the needed skills. This team, which CEO Kazuo Inamori calls an "amoeba," operates autonomously from other amoebas. Each amoeba decides how to use its allocated resources, and when the project is finished, employees disband to join another amoeba.[28]

Differentiation and Integration

Paul R. Lawrence and Jay W. Lorsch, two Harvard professors, took the concept of environmental influence on organization structure a step further. They examined the sales, operations, and research-and-development functions of 10 U.S. companies in three industries to determine how each unit reacted to its firm's environment. The researchers found that each functional unit developed its own method of coping with environmental uncertainty, and these responses differed on the basis of work specialization, work techniques, goals, and other elements. Lawrence and Lorsch called this pattern of differences **differentiation,** the degree of variation in structure, behavior, and orientation among organizational units.[29]

differentiation The degree of variation in structure, behavior, and orientation among organizational units

In this study, companies facing a high level of environmental uncertainty tended to exhibit greater differentiation than companies facing more certain environments. However, the researchers found that the greater the differentiation, the greater the need for structural elements to coordinate the activities of the various units so that the organization as a whole can reach its goals. Lawrence and Lorsch called this degree of coordination and collaboration among

GLOBAL MANAGEMENT

The ABCs of ABB's Organization Design

What kind of organization structure is appropriate for a corporation with more than 1,000 business units and 210,000 employees spread around the world? Percy Barnevik faced this challenge when he engineered the merger of Sweden's ASEA and Switzerland's Brown Boveri into Zurich-based ABB Asea Brown Boveri, a global organization producing electrical power equipment, robots, locomotives, antipollution systems, and other industrial goods. Barnevik needed an organization design that would allow the business units to execute his marketing-driven strategy of meeting customer needs. At the same time, the organization structure would have to enhance corporate and business unit performance in diverse global environments.

To start, Barnevik embraced decentralization with a vengeance. He quickly pushed responsibility, authority, and accountability as far down as possible in the organization to put decision making in the hands of the ABB people closest to the customers they served. On top of the traditional functional and product departmentalization, he carved out a series of 100 national companies. The top managers of each national company were directed to act as though they managed a domestic company, and they assumed the responsibility for dealing with their own local governments, unions, and customers. Manufacturing was also decentralized, so that products would be manufactured in the customer's country whenever possible.

Barnevik's unique corporate structure has allowed each national company to develop a local identity that attracts domestic orders as well as export orders. For example, ABB's Combustion Engineering unit, headquartered in the United States, serves many U.S. customers and also serves customers abroad. In South Korea, where it is building nuclear power plants, Combustion Engineering operates as a U.S. company and must comply with U.S. legal and regulatory guidelines. Further, despite its Swiss ownership, the unit enjoys the support of the U.S. government, which can be particularly helpful in trade negotiations.

Thanks to this organization design, the ABB units have been able to reap the benefits of acting locally while taking advantage of the parent company's resources. Although decentralization has helped business units focus on executing customer-oriented strategy, Barnevik has also applied centralization to coordinate and to integrate activities that cut across company (and country) lines. He has designated key research-and-development labs in Germany, Switzerland, and Sweden as "centers of excellence." Rather than duplicate many research activities in individual business units, Barnevik has assigned these labs to conduct basic research that will support product innovation throughout the corporation. The money he saves as a result of such efficiencies is plowed right back into research so that overall R&D expenditures remain sufficiently high to fuel long-term growth.

Barnevik developed his organization structure in record time, announcing the new design some five months after the merger was announced. He hasn't slowed since, and his subsequent acquisitions and joint ventures have only contributed to ABB's explosive growth. By 1991, ABB was ringing up $30 billion in yearly worldwide sales as Barnevik pushed boldly ahead to engineer more growth for the 1990s.

Apply Your Knowledge

1. How can Barnevik use his organization structure to manage differentiation and integration among ABB's business units?
2. If ABB's strategy changes, must Barnevik change the organization's structure? Why or why not?

integration The degree of coordination and collaboration exhibited among organizational units

organizational units **integration.** The companies operating in a relatively certain environment used rules, regulations, and the formal chain of command for effective integration, whereas the companies operating in a relatively uncertain environment used lateral relationships such as integrating roles and teams.[30]

Increasingly, organizations are using their information resources to improve the integration between various departments. For example, Xerox installed sophisticated computer programs that allow product designers, engineers, materials purchasers, and manufacturing personnel to collaborate on the design-to-production sequence. Despite its uncertain environment, Xerox can develop new products more quickly than before because functional experts are better able to coordinate their activities.[31] Chapter 18 examines information resources in greater detail.

Technology

A third contingency factor influencing organization design is **technology**, the expertise, equipment, and procedures used by organizations to transform resource inputs into outputs of goods or services. Technology covers both tangible elements (such as machinery and tools) and intangible elements (such as the sequence of activities in the work flow and employee skills). Moreover, service providers and manufacturers apply technology differently. For example, Hyatt's technology includes its reservation system, its housekeeping procedures, and its food preparation systems; Sterling Drug's technology includes its laboratory tools, its scientific knowledge, and its manufacturing equipment.[32]

technology The expertise, equipment, and procedures used by organizations to transform resource inputs into outputs

British researcher Joan Woodward was one of the earliest to identify the link between technology and organization design. During the 1950s, she led a team that studied the technological processes, span of control, centralization, staff and line positions, formalization, and performance of 100 British manufacturers. The study revealed significant differences in organization structure, but the reason for these differences did not become clear until Woodward isolated technology as a contributing factor. By grouping the firms according to the type of technology employed, she discovered that technological complexity directly influenced organization structure. Woodward's research identified three broad categories of technology. In ascending order of complexity, these categories are (1) unit and small-batch technology, (2) mass-production and large-batch technology, and (3) continuous-flow-process technology.[33]

- **Unit and small-batch technology** is a type of technology in which products are custom-produced to customer specifications or produced in small quantities by skilled technicians. Examples of organizations that use this technology include the Custom Shop Shirtmakers, which makes shirts to the customer's measurements, and Sikorsky, which makes helicopters for government customers worldwide.
- **Mass-production and large-batch technology** refers to a type of technology in which products are manufactured in large quantities, often on an assembly line. This more complex type of technology is used by Ford, General Motors, and Chrysler to produce automobiles.
- **Continuous-flow-process technology** is a type of technology in which products are manufactured through an uninterrupted series of transformation processes. This technology, more complex than the other two types, is used by Du Pont to produce chemicals and by Mobil to produce gasoline.[34]

unit and small-batch technology A type of technology in which products are custom-produced to customer specifications or produced in small quantities by skilled employees

mass-production and large-batch technology A type of technology in which products are manufactured in large quantities, frequently on an assembly line

continuous-flow-process technology A type of technology in which products are manufactured through a continually linked series of transformation processes

As the level of technological complexity increases, the machinery becomes more intricate, the process becomes more standardized, and the need for constant human interaction drops. Whereas unit technology requires personal attention from skilled specialists who customize the products or work one at a time, continuous-flow-process technology demands less personal attention because it is more automated, so employees intervene only when maintenance or repair is required.[35]

Moving toward more complex technology meant a structural change but also rapid growth for Larson, a company in Tucson, Arizona, that makes artificial rocks, trees, and other nature items for zoos, parks, and resorts. For years, the company had used unit technology, with each employee completing an entire piece. When new owners took over, they introduced mass-production technology in which one person created the product's frame, another applied the cover-

The Union Carbide plant at Seadrift, Texas, uses continuous-flow-process technology to produce plastics (used in products such as lawn furniture) and chemicals (used in products such as soap). Production engineers monitor the production cycle at regular intervals to be sure that the transformation processes are operating correctly. This plant's organization design differs from that of plants using unit or mass-production technology.

ing, and a third applied the paint. This change in technology required a new structure because of the more narrowly defined work specialization and the need for increased integration. But with mass production, the company was able to manufacture products more quickly, so sales grew from $5 million yearly to $20 million in five years.[36]

Woodward's study was significant because it revealed that the most successful firms in each technology category followed a similar structural pattern; the less successful firms deviated from this structure. Therefore, to achieve performance, managers have to establish a structure that is appropriate for the organization's technology (see Exhibit 10.3). In general, the study found that technology influences the degree of formalization and centralization, the span of management, the number of hierarchical levels, and other elements of organization structure. For example, Woodward observed that the best-performing mass-production firms had a traditional, relatively mechanistic organization structure. In these firms, the span of management of first-line managers was significantly higher on average than that of their counterparts in firms using unit

EXHIBIT 10.3

Technology and Organization Structure

Joan Woodward found that the technology used in an organization's production process influenced its structure. For large firms, this influence was reflected primarily at the lower levels, but for smaller firms, this influence was reflected in the overall structure.

	Type of Technology		
Structural Characteristic	**Unit**	**Mass-Production**	**Continuous-Flow-Process**
Degree of formalization	Low	High	Low
Degree of centralization	Low	High	Low
Span of management of first-line managers	23	49	13
Span of management of top managers	4	7	10
Number of hierarchical levels	3	4	6
Type of organization	Organic	Mechanistic	Organic

Structural Characteristic	Small Organizations	Large Organizations
Work specialization	Broadly defined jobs	Narrowly defined jobs
Degree of differentiation	Low	High
Need for integration	Low	High
Use of staff positions	Minimal	Greater
Degree of formalization	Low	High
Decision making	Centralized	Decentralized

EXHIBIT 10.4

The Effect of Organization Size on Organization Design

Structural characteristics in small organizations are distinctly different from structural characteristics in large organizations. However, as small organizations add employees, they need to reconsider their organization design to retain effectiveness and efficiency.

and continuous-flow-process technology (primarily because of the standardization of work activities). In addition, these firms relied heavily on formalization and centralization, compared with firms using other technologies.[37]

Technology affects the structure of large organizations differently than it affects the structure of small organizations. In large organizations, technology often influences only the lower levels, where employees and managers are directly concerned with production. In contrast, the overall structure of smaller organizations can be influenced by technology. Regardless of size, all organizations should reassess their structures as new technologies emerge; however, size also influences organization design.[38]

Organization Size

Joan Woodward and other researchers have studied the relationship of organization size (as measured by the number of organization members) and organization design. Although Woodward found that technology has a greater influence on structure than does size, other researchers observed that size does affect specific elements of organization design. These elements include work specialization, differentiation and integration, staff positions, formalization, and centralization and decentralization.[39]

In smaller organizations, fewer people are available to complete the organization's work (see Exhibit 10.4). By necessity, work specialization is often broad and differentiation minimal, so integration is more readily achieved. The small organization needs few staff managers to coordinate and advise line managers, and the organization generally operates with few, if any, written rules and regulations. Because resources are generally scarce, decision making in small organizations is typically centralized.[40]

However, as organization size increases, more employees and managers are hired to perform specific tasks, leading to well-defined work specialization. In turn, these specialized work units exhibit greater differentiation, so larger organizations require greater efforts to achieve integration. Larger organizations also tend to use more staff managers, and they generally apply a larger number of formalized rules and regulations to guide decisions and activities. To avoid decision bottlenecks, larger organizations frequently decentralize decision making.[41]

Organizational growth brings specific management challenges. For example, top managers find it more difficult to stay in touch with customers and with employees at all levels. Also, sheer size and burgeoning bureaucracy may slow an organization's response to its internal and external environment, which can ultimately hurt effectiveness and efficiency. To solve such problems, top managers often cleave large organizations into smaller units. For example, Parker Hannifin, a \$2.3 billion producer of industrial parts, is divided into some 80 divi-

When Kim Byung Yul opened the Busan Restaurant in Los Angeles, he had few employees and he was involved in every aspect of the business. Two years later, he moved his Korean restaurant to a new location and added employees to perform specialized tasks as a way of increasing efficiency. As his business grows and moves through its life cycle, he will continue to add specialized employees and to adapt his organization structure to cope with changes and increases in the work load.

sions and more than 200 plants. When the manager of a division or a plant is unable to understand all aspects of the business and the needs of customers, CEO Paul G. Schloemer splits that unit in two.[42]

At birth, most organizations have few employees, but as organizations age, they generally add employees. Because size and life cycle are so closely related, managers must consider both when designing an appropriate organization structure.

Organization Life Cycle

organizational life cycle A series of four developmental stages through which every organization passes

Organizations evolve from small to large by passing through a series of four developmental stages known as the **organizational life cycle.** Although organizations progress through the four stages at their own pace, each stage has an identifiable influence on organization design, and this influence is closely related to size. In the first stage, the organization is founded by an entrepreneur who works alone or with a handful of employees to launch the product. Because the new organization has few employees, it exhibits the structural characteristics of a small organization, with few formal rules, broad work specialization, and centralized decision making.

Typical of this stage is Belinda Hughes's experience in launching Boo-Boo Baby, a children's apparel company. At the beginning, Hughes personally designed, stitched, and sold her product line, but soon orders multiplied, so she had to contract out the actual manufacturing. Retaining centralized control, Hughes also hired an assistant and a shipper to help build her young firm.[43]

Once the organization evolves into the second stage, it is growing more rapidly; it must expand its use of resources and add employees and managers to complete the work necessary to achieve goals. In this youthful stage, the organization hires specialists to perform specific functions and establishes formal rules to coordinate and integrate activities. Although a few top managers may share decision-making authority with the founder, the organization remains relatively centralized. For instance, soon after he founded Wall Street Games to market mock stock market tournaments, growth was so robust that owner Timothy A. DeMello had to hire more managers and employees to handle specialized duties. Within four years, he had built a centralized structure that included a new president and 135 employees, 10 full-time and 125 part-time.[44] Cypress Semiconductor, one of the fastest-growing electronics companies in the country in recent years, had two and a half times as many employees in 1990 as it had in 1987.[45]

By the third stage, the organization has evolved into middle age and has grown much larger. In this stage, managers subdivide tasks for a finer division of labor, apply formalized rules and regulations to guide activities and decisions throughout the organization, and add staff positions to advise line managers and to coordinate activities. Top managers also decentralize decision-making authority in the third stage to speed response to environmental changes. Microtek International, a $100 million electronics manufacturer operating both in Taiwan and in the United States, has reached this stage. President Bobo Wang uses a decentralized organization structure to speed decision making. He also relies on finely defined work specialization to accomplish the complex and technical tasks needed to design and manufacture Microtek's products.[46]

As the organization matures and enters the fourth stage, growth is usually slower. Managers still require flexibility, so splitting the organization into units is frequently a good structural solution. But managers also need to balance and integrate activities without imposing a stifling bureaucracy, so they generally increase their reliance on lateral relationships such as teams, integrating roles, and linking pin roles. In a mature, large organization, managers often formalize these lateral relationships, delegating authority and responsibility for coordination and integration. For example, Hughes Aircraft is in the fourth stage, and it has established an office of the chairman to be shared by the CEO and five top managers. This enables the top managers to more easily coordinate and integrate Hughes's diverse activities. Moreover, the firm has broken its commercial activities into separate operating units and decentralized decision-making authority to allow these units more flexibility.[47]

In addition to these five objective factors, organization design is influenced by the values and management styles of the organization's top managers. For instance, some leaders are more inclined by nature toward centralized control, whereas others start with the assumption that power and control should be dispersed throughout the organization. Similarly, some leaders are comfortable with wide spans of management; others prefer to have fewer people reporting to them. A manager's positive and negative experiences with various organization structures also play a big part in structural decisions.

FORMS OF ORGANIZATION DESIGN

Top management can select from a variety of organization designs, depending on the organization's strategy, environment, technology, size, and life cycle as well as on their own preferences and inclinations. The most common forms can be classified as one of four categories: (1) functional, (2) divisional, (3) conglomerate, or (4) matrix. Each design has benefits and limitations, and the organization's situation at any time may require a change to another form or to a hybrid form of organization design.

EXHIBIT 10.5

The Functional Organization

In the functional organization, units are formed around specialized skills, and each unit is managed by a functional head who reports to the top manager.

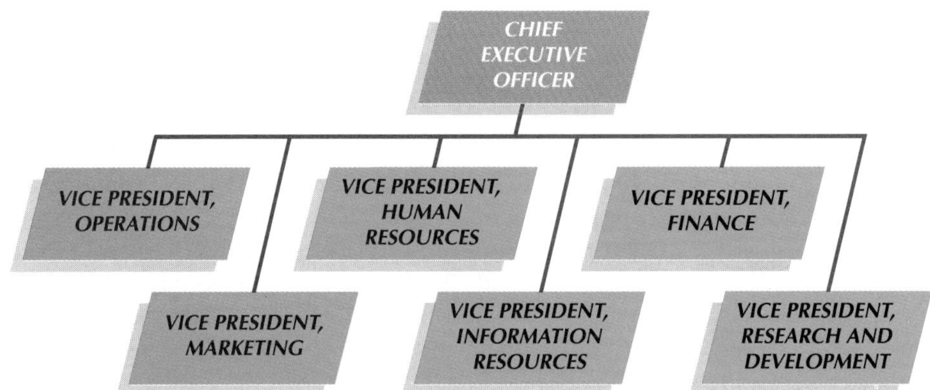

The Functional Organization

functional organization An organization design based on employee function or specialized skill

The **functional organization** is a design based on employee function or specialized skill (see Exhibit 10.5). The functional organization features separate hierarchies for each function, creating a larger-scale version of the functional departmentalization discussed in Chapter 9. The chain of command in each function leads to a functional head, who in turn reports to the top manager. In this design, the top manager coordinates and integrates all organization activities, so decisions are generally centralized. For example, the not-for-profit Interlochen Center for the Arts (in northern Michigan) has a functional organization. Directors for its camp operation, for its academy of arts, and for its finance, human resources, public affairs, and funding development functions report directly to president Dean Boal, who works closely with Interlochen's board of directors to coordinate and integrate all activities.[48]

One benefit of a functional organization is the ability to develop and reinforce expertise in specialized functions. This design can also enhance organizational efficiency, because resources are allocated by function rather than being duplicated or diffused throughout the organization. Moreover, functional managers can easily coordinate the decisions and actions that relate to their functional areas. Finally, the centralization inherent in this design helps unify all organizational efforts so that organization goals can be achieved.[49]

However, the functional organization has several limitations. First, coordination and integration of activities that cross functions become more difficult as organizations grow and spread geographically. The top manager's attention may be stretched too thin to effectively coordinate activities or to allocate resources appropriately. Second, this design encourages functional specialization rather than general management skills, so managers are less prepared for top management positions. And third, people in the functional units may concentrate on their specialties and be less responsive to the needs of the organization overall.[50]

For many smaller organizations, the benefits of functional organizations outweigh the limitations, especially during the early stages of their life cycles. As organizations grow, the limitations become more apparent, and eventually, the functional organization may actually restrain performance. For this reason, larger organizations often switch from the functional to the divisional organization design.[51]

The Divisional Organization

The **divisional organization** is a design in which separate but related units are created by departmentalizing by product, geography, customer, or other methods (see Exhibit 10.6). In this design, also known as the *self-contained structure,* the divisions operate much like small organizations under a large organizational umbrella, meeting divisional goals that contribute to organizational performance. Each division contains the diverse functions needed for its daily operations, and decisions are generally decentralized so that the divisions guide their own activities. However, the organization's top managers coordinate decisions and activities that affect all the divisions, and they also monitor progress toward achieving divisional and organizational goals.[52]

divisional organization An organization design in which separate but related units are established according to product, geography, customer, or other departmentalization method

For example, Motorola established a divisional organization design based on product departmentalization. The company's six divisions focus on related electronics products, including communications, semiconductors, general systems, information systems, government electronics, and automotive and industrial electronics products. The firm also maintains a new-enterprises division that manages Motorola's entry into completely new businesses related to its main product lines. Each division, which Motorola calls a sector or a group, is self-contained and functions as a separate business to serve its own customers.[53]

A primary benefit of the divisional organization is effective coordination of activities within each division. Especially important for large organizations, decisions about day-to-day activities can be made quickly and knowledgeably because each division is self-contained and authority is decentralized. And when environmental changes require a quick response, divisions are empowered to react without waiting for centralized approval from top management. In such a design, top managers are not overburdened with decisions about divisional activities, so they can concentrate on strategic planning and rely on divisional managers who have the responsibility for achieving divisional goals. Finally, top managers can allocate resources according to divisional performance.[54]

However, the divisional organization has several limitations. A major limitation is the expense and inefficiency of duplicating resources for each division. In some cases, divisions find themselves aggressively competing with each other for

EXHIBIT 10.6 The Divisional Organization

In the divisional organization, self-contained units that focus on related products or customers are formed by departmentalization. The divisions each contain the various functions needed to operate, and they pursue divisional goals that contribute to achieving organizational goals.

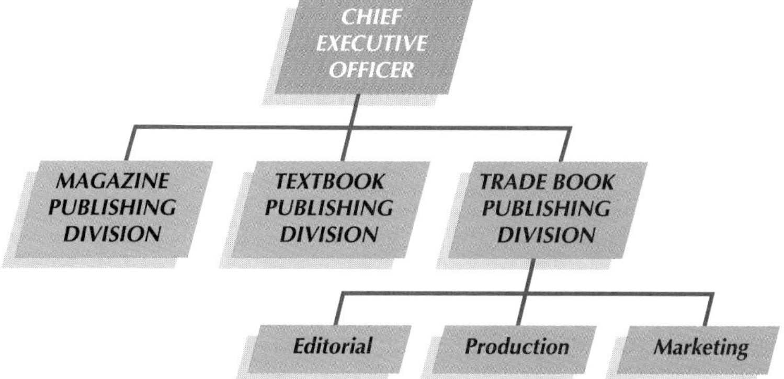

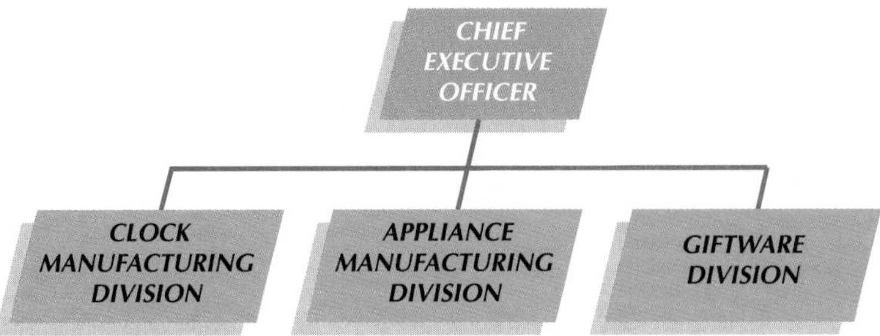

EXHIBIT 10.7 The Conglomerate Organization

In the conglomerate organization, divisions focus on an unrelated group of goods and services. Because the divisions are self-contained, their activities are rarely interdependent, but top managers must take care to balance divisional performance so that organizational goals are attained.

resources allocated by top managers, causing the divisions to lose their focus on overall organization goals and concentrate on individual division goals. Another limitation is the difficulty of providing adequate staff assistance to support the divisions when needed. Moreover, coordination between the divisions is much more difficult than coordination within each division.[55]

The Conglomerate Organization

conglomerate organization An organization design in which the divisions are largely unrelated

A third commonly used form of organization design is the **conglomerate organization,** a design in which the divisions are largely unrelated (see Exhibit 10.7). In contrast to the divisional organization, where divisions may be related by technology focus, customer focus, product focus, or other common elements, divisions in the conglomerate organization have little in common. Each self-contained division is delegated the authority to choose and serve its own customers, using its own technology to produce its own goods or services. Because of this diversity, the conglomerate organization creates fewer interdependencies among divisions. However, the diversity also requires that top management use a portfolio strategy to plan for balancing the allocation of resources among the divisions and to monitor divisional performance so that overall organizational goals are achieved.[56]

For example, Bernard Arnault has built a Paris-based conglomerate of international businesses unrelated except for the sense of luxury associated with each. His holdings include LVMH Moët Hennessy Louis Vuitton (luggage, leather goods, champagne, and cognac); Christian Dior, Givenchy, Christian Lacroix (fashion); and Bon Marché (retailing). Although the divisions operate fairly autonomously, Arnault is setting up an in-house agency to buy advertising space for all divisions, and he is building a common system for managing information resources. Moreover, he wants to enhance synergy by building clusters of luxury stores to sell his various upscale brands.[57]

Managers in conglomerate organizations have the ability to juggle their varying resource requirements and divisional outputs to weather challenges posed by environmental uncertainty, an important benefit. The same environmental conditions will affect the divisions in varying ways, so managers can switch resources and boost or slash production where needed. In this way, the organization can achieve its overall goals, despite challenges to individual divisions. The major limitation is that top management may be unable to effectively manage

MANAGEMENT AROUND THE WORLD

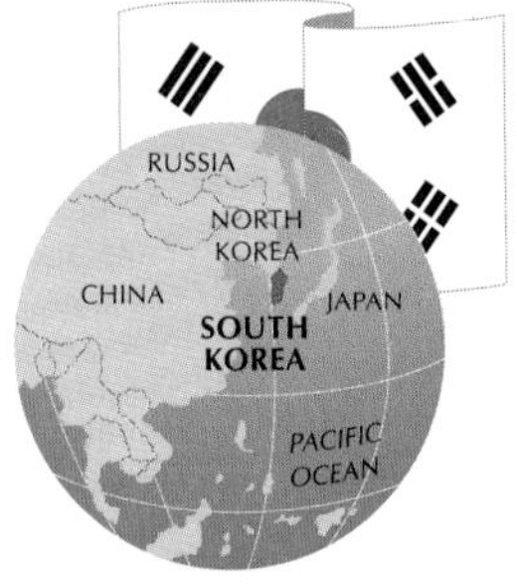

Huge conglomerates called *chaebol* dominate the economy of South Korea. In fact, the five largest conglomerates account for about one-half of the nation's entire economic output.

these diverse divisions and may therefore be unable to achieve overall organizational performance.[58]

The Matrix Organization

The **matrix organization** is a design in which management superimposes a divisional organization design onto a functional organization, creating two simultaneous chains of command (see Exhibit 10.8). Although the dual-chain-of-command structure may not be applied everywhere in the organization, many individuals in a matrix organization report to two people. One of their managers belongs to the functional chain of command, which runs vertically; the other belongs to the divisional chain of command, which runs horizontally; and both have equal authority over the *two-boss employee.* Each chain of functional and divisional command is headed by a manager known as the *matrix boss.*[59]

The matrix organization emerged as a formal organization design during the 1960s, when firms in the aerospace industry faced an organizing dilemma. To quickly and efficiently develop materials for space exploration and for defense, they needed the depth of technological expertise inherent in a functional organization, but they also required the tighter coordination and product focus inherent in a divisional organization. Rather than reduce reliance on specialized tech-

CEO Beverly F. Dolan must balance the contributions and resource needs of the diverse businesses in Textron, a conglomerate. In addition to owning financial services firms, the conglomerate makes defense products and commercial products. As the defense industry shrinks, Dolan can shift emphasis to nondefense products.

matrix organization An organization design that overlays a divisional organization design onto a functional organization design, forming two chains of command

EXHIBIT 10.8 The Matrix Organization

In the matrix organization, a divisional design is overlaid on a functional design, creating two simultaneous chains of command. Plant manager A is a two-boss employee who reports to the vice president of operations (a functional manager in the vertical chain of command) and the vice president of the North American division (a divisional manager in the horizontal chain of command), both of whom are matrix bosses.

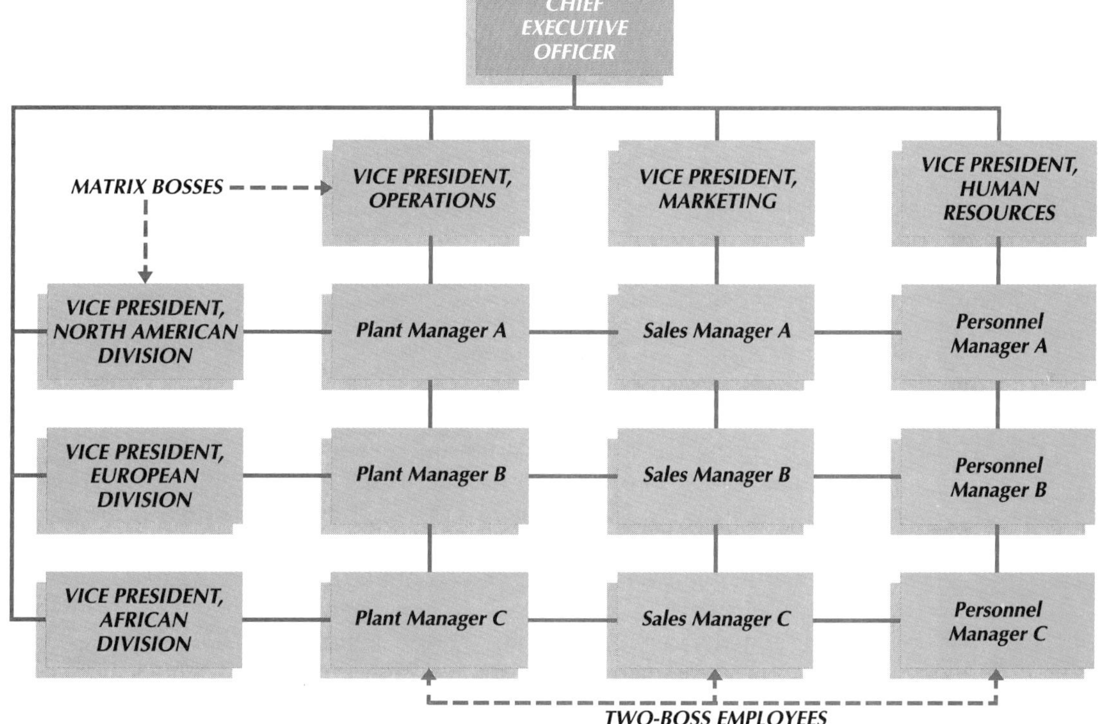

MANAGERIAL DECISION MAKING

Organizing the Lattice and the Network

Decisions, decisions: organization design requires an ongoing series of decisions to keep up with the challenges posed by new strategies, the environment, more complex technology, and organization size and life cycle. In recent years, an increasing number of managers have responded to these challenges by combining structural elements in nontraditional ways. Two unique organization designs that have emerged from these structural decisions are the lattice and the network.

W. L. Gore, the late founder of W. L. Gore & Associates, the maker of Gore-Tex and other specialty materials, started with a strategy of fostering creativity to fuel company growth. To support this strategy, he decided to bypass the traditional hierarchical pyramid in favor of a structure criss-crossed with horizontal and vertical connections. In this organic structure, which he called a *lattice,* anyone in the organization can directly interact with anyone else. Missing from Gore's structure are the vertical elements of the chain of command and multiple levels of management. In fact, Gore has no managers at all: every employee is an "associate," and a new hire works with a "sponsor" who trains the associate and monitors his or her contribution to organizational goals.

Work assignments in the lattice are voluntary, made when associates join the teams that evolve to tackle specific tasks and achieve specific goals. Associates often participate on several teams and may take a leadership role in one or more. This series of lateral relationships helps coordinate the interdependent tasks that must be integrated to complete a particular project. Decisions in the lattice organization are decentralized and generally made by individuals who must implement the action. Using the lattice design, Gore has fostered the creativity to develop innovative products that have pushed company growth to approximately $300 million in annual sales.

Lewis Galoob Toys in California has taken another approach to organization design, deciding to use a network organization structure to build a multimillion-dollar toy business. The network, tightly coordinated by Galoob managers and employees, consists of outsiders who perform selected organizational functions. Independent inventors, designers, and engineers develop many products, and overseas plants manufacture the toys on a contract basis. The toys are then shipped to the United States and distributed to stores through independent representatives, so Galoob doesn't need a warehouse. Moreover, Galoob uses an outside firm to collect from its retail customers.

This network design allows Galoob (with a few hundred employees and a single company-owned plant) to compete with Hasbro, Mattel, and other industry giants. By relying on outsiders, Galoob gains the flexibility to respond quickly to environmental changes, which can be fast and furious in the faddish toy industry. Galoob carries a leaner payroll and requires little capital investment, so it can operate less expensively than traditional competitors. Moreover, the company's powerful network plays on the synergy of its suppliers' unique skills and strengths, making the choice of suppliers a critical decision. In fact, the real test of a network organization lies in its supplier relationships. Although Galoob has used the network design effectively for nearly 40 years, this structure isn't for everyone: if suppliers don't deliver exactly as promised, network organizations can suffer badly.

Apply Your Knowledge

1. At what stage in the organization life cycle might the network be most effectively introduced? Why?
2. Is Gore's lattice design closer to Likert's System 1 or System 4?

nical skills by using a purely divisional organization, and without sacrificing close coordination and product orientation by using a purely functional organization, the aerospace firms combined the designs. The resulting intersecting chains of command in the matrix organization allow organization members to share information both vertically and horizontally and to coordinate more effectively activities that cross functional lines while maintaining the depth of expertise in their functional organizations. Dow Chemical and Lockheed are two firms that adopted the matrix organization design to increase responsiveness to environmental change and to customer needs.[60] An increasing number of organizations now rely on matrix structures for more effective project management, with one chain of command driving the project toward completion and the other focusing on functional specialties such as engineering and marketing.

However, the shared responsibility for achieving specific goals creates a web of interdependencies that spans the functional and the divisional chains of command. Because the matrix organization violates the classic principle of unity of command, it is a complex design that demands excellent interpersonal skills on the part of the two-boss employee and the managers in both chains of command. The two-boss employee must share information with two managers and is accountable to both for results. At the same time, neither of the managers has the authority to unilaterally make decisions, so they must jointly decide how to resolve any problems that arise. When a problem cannot be resolved by the matrix bosses, it is referred to top management for a decision.[61]

The matrix organization has several benefits. This design strengthens horizontal coordination by formalizing the lateral relationships that cross functional lines. In addition, the lateral relationships and the frequent communication enhances organizational responsiveness, a major benefit in a complex and changeable environment. The organization can also use its personnel more efficiently, because in each functional specialty managers maintain a pool of skilled people who can be assigned to support specific product or customer projects. Many matrix organizations gain additional flexibility by reassigning specialists when projects are completed or when other operations need their expertise. And the interaction with specialists from other parts of the organization helps employees and managers develop their technical, conceptual, and interpersonal skills.[62]

The matrix organization has limitations as well. When two managers hold equal authority over a shared subordinate, this two-boss employee may feel confused and pulled in different directions, which can hurt morale and ultimately affect productivity. Also, the decision-making process is slowed because the matrix bosses and, in many cases, their shared subordinates must meet and discuss the issues until they agree on appropriate solutions. If the managers and employees lack good interpersonal skills, this design can quickly become unworkable, and it can lead to major decision bottlenecks if top management must continually resolve conflicts arising from the dual authority. Another limitation is the need to provide a functional specialist to every divisional project or department, which means employing a large pool of specialists. Similarly, by creating a divisional chain of command in addition to a functional chain of command, the organization increases the total number of managers, an added expense.[63]

Hybrid Organization Designs

Although the functional, conglomerate, divisional, and matrix organizations are commonplace, not all organizations adopt these pure design forms. Instead, some top managers combine elements of two or more organization designs to create a hybrid organization design. Managers may choose one form for the topmost organization level and another (or more than one) for other levels, or they may combine two designs at the same level.[64]

For example, Champion International uses a hybrid of divisional and functional organization forms at the top management level. The firm's divisional design is based on both product and geographic departmentalization. Separate

Champion divisions focus on distinctly different product lines, including printing and writing papers, publication papers, newsprint, kraft paper, and forest products. In addition, the company operates two geographic divisions, Weldwood of Canada and Papel e Celulose in Brazil. The functional organization is responsible for centralized corporate services such as finance and accounting, legal, and human resources.[65]

APPLICATION OF ORGANIZATION DESIGN PRINCIPLES

Managers select from and combine a variety of structural elements in response to the contingency factors that influence organization design, because some structures are more effective than others in specific situations. Researcher Henry Mintzberg identified five common structural configurations and described the design characteristics that make each effective under certain conditions. Mintzberg's configurations are (1) the simple structure, (2) the machine bureaucracy, (3) the professional bureaucracy, (4) the divisionalized form, and (5) the adhocracy (see Exhibit 10.9).[66]

simple structure An organization design characterized by centralization of authority, minimal work specialization, minimal differentiation, and minimal formalization

The Simple Structure

The **simple structure** is a design based on centralization of authority, minimal work specialization, minimal differentiation, and minimal formalization. One example of a simple structure is an automobile dealership whose owner is ag-

EXHIBIT 10.9 Mintzberg's Structural Configurations

Henry Mintzberg identified five common configurations of organization structure and determined the conditions under which each is appropriate.

	Structural Configuration				
Characteristic	Simple Structure	Machine Bureaucracy	Professional Bureaucracy	Divisionalized Form	Adhocracy
Structural element					
Centralization	Centralized	Centralized	Decentralized	Decentralized	Decentralized
Work specialization	Broadly defined	Narrowly defined	Defined by knowledge and skills	Narrowly defined	Defined by knowledge and skills
Formalization	Low	High	Low	High	Low
Typical design	Functional	Functional	Functional or hybrid	Divisional, conglomerate, or hybrid	Matrix
Contingency factor					
Environment	Simple and changeable	Simple and stable	Complex and stable	Simple and stable or diversified	Complex and changeable
Technology	Simple, custom	Standardized, mass production	Complex and standardized but not automated	Simple or complex but segmentable into units	Sophisticated, complex, automated
Size	Small	Large	Varies	Large	Small or medium-sized
Life cycle	Young	Mature	Varies	Mature	Young

gressive and entrepreneurial. This highly integrated, organic organization appears to have no structure because it sidesteps most formal elements of design. It contains few (if any) staff specialists, and information flows informally among all organization members. The structure is flat, with virtually everyone reporting to the top manager, who makes or approves all major decisions and coordinates all activities. Mintzberg found that this configuration is appropriate for small organizations, especially those in the early stages of their life cycle. Moreover, it is most effective when the organization uses relatively simple technology and operates in a simple but changeable environment where flexibility and quick response are important.[67]

Machine Bureaucracy

The **machine bureaucracy** is a design based on relatively centralized authority, narrow and precise work specialization, functional departmentalization, and high formalization. Examples include McDonald's and the U.S. Postal Service. Only slightly less centralized than the simple structure, the machine bureaucracy is a mechanistic organization that relies on standardization of work processes for coordination. Information flows through the formal chain-of-command channels, and rules and regulations developed by staff specialists guide the decisions and activities within each functional unit. The machine bureaucracy is typically a tall structure with narrow spans of control and larger work units than the simple structure. In Mintzberg's view, this configuration is best suited to large and mature organizations with standardized operations such as mass-production technology. He found that the machine bureaucracy is most effective in a simple and stable environment because this inflexible design responds slowly to change.[68]

machine bureaucracy An organization design characterized by relatively centralized authority, narrow and precise work specialization, functional departmentalization, and high formalization

Professional Bureaucracy

The **professional bureaucracy** is a design based on decentralized authority, functional or hybrid departmentalization, a large core of skilled professionals, a technical support staff, and little formalization. Examples include hospitals, consulting firms, and law firms. In contrast to the machine bureaucracy, where the employees have little discretion over their tasks or how tasks are performed, the professionals in a professional bureaucracy operate more autonomously within the confines of their technical, standardized roles, and they require little coordination. These professionals are responsible for achieving organizational goals, so managers delegate to them a considerable amount of decision-making authority and support their efforts with staff specialists. The professional bureaucracy is most effective when standardized technologies are used and when the environment is complex but static.[69]

professional bureaucracy An organization design characterized by decentralized authority, functional or hybrid departmentalization, a large core of skilled professionals, a technical support staff, and little formalization

Divisionalized Form

The **divisionalized form** is a design based on relatively decentralized authority, divisional or conglomerate organization, standardized outputs, and high formalization. Examples include General Motors and the University of California. In this configuration, top management delegates considerable decision-making authority to the heads of each division, but decisions within each division may be

divisionalized form An organization design characterized by relatively decentralized authority, divisional or conglomerate organization, standardized outputs, and high formalization

Surgical teams are professional bureaucracies because they are composed of trained specialists who function fairly autonomously, relying on hospital staff for administrative support. Subject to hospital budget approval, these teams often make their own decisions about purchasing new equipment. Here, technicians from United States Surgical show surgeons how to use new staplers in bowel and esophageal procedures.

either centralized or decentralized. Divisions typically exhibit a high degree of formalization for coordinating internal activities and for standardizing their outputs. Moreover, the structure of each division may be divisional or another design. Because the divisions are self-contained, they are not interdependent and therefore require little coordination from top management. However, top managers monitor divisional performance, and staff specialists support such divisional functions as legal and human resources. Mintzberg found that the divisionalized form is most appropriate for older, larger organizations operating in diversified markets. When the environment is simple and stable, the divisionalized form can assume the shape of many machine bureaucracies under a single umbrella. However, when the environment is complex and changeable, the divisionalized form can use a hybrid organization for more flexibility.[70]

Adhocracy

adhocracy An organization design characterized by a matrix organization, relatively decentralized authority, considerable work specialization, and little formalization

The **adhocracy** is a design based on matrix organization, relatively decentralized authority, considerable work specialization, and little formalization. One example is the National Aeronautics and Space Administration (NASA). A complex configuration, the adhocracy is an organic organization in which skilled experts are grouped together to tackle specific projects and these group activities are coordinated by a contingent of functional and divisional managers. Decision-making authority is dispersed selectively to managers and nonmanagers rather than being concentrated at the top management level. Because specialists can be assigned to projects as needed and because information is shared constantly and informally, the adhocracy can produce rapid and significant innovation. According to Mintzberg, this configuration is most effective in a complex and changeable environment. Generally, young organizations using sophisticated, even highly automated, technology can successfully adopt the adhocracy.[71]

Each of Mintzberg's structural configurations represents a pure form that is modified by the organization in response to the four contingency factors. And because organizations frequently adopt differing structures in their various units, these configurations often appear in combination rather than in their single, pure forms. But the five configurations are useful for understanding how organizations combine structural elements in response to the influence of various contingency factors.[72]

SUMMARY

Organization design is the ongoing process of developing and implementing an appropriate organization structure. By making decisions about the combination and application of structural elements, managers create an organization design to achieve organizational goals. The classical management theories stressed universal organization design principles. One of the most enduring of these classical theories is bureaucracy, an ideal form intended to enhance organizational efficiency. Behavioral theorists developed behavioral models that incorporated the influence of human behavior, including Likert's systems and the sociotechnical systems theory. The contingency approach stresses that no one design can be universally applied, so the choice depends on each organization's situation.

Strategy is a major determinant of structure. Organizations that pursue growth strategies make strategic plans that call for increasing activities and their diversity. Therefore, managers must adjust the structure to coordinate and integrate these new activities. Environmental munificence, resource dependence, and environmental uncertainty also influence organization design. Depending on the level of environmental uncertainty, managers can choose a mechanistic structure, appropriate for a static environment, or an organic structure, appropriate for a dynamic environment. Moreover, they must consider how the environment affects the level of differentiation in organizational units, increasing or decreasing the need for integration.

Unit and small-batch technology is the least complex type of technology, in which products are custom-produced to customer specifications or produced in small quantities. In mass-production and large-batch technology, products are manufactured in large quantities. Continuous-flow-process technology is the most complex type of technology, in which products are manufactured through a series of transformation processes. As the level of technological complexity increases, the machinery becomes more intricate, the process becomes more standardized, and the need for constant human interaction drops.

Organization size and life cycle are two related factors that influence organization design. Young organizations have fewer employees, but as they pass through their life cycle, they hire more employees, thus increasing their size. Among the structural elements affected by organization size are work specialization, differentiation and integration, staff positions, formalization, and centralization and decentralization. The organizational life cycle is a series of four developmental stages through which organizations evolve as they grow. Similar to the influence of organization size, each stage is characterized by specific structural elements.

Four common forms of organization design are the functional, the divisional, the conglomerate, and the matrix organization. The functional organization is based on employee function or specialized skill. The divisional organization is based on separate, related units created by departmentalization. The conglomerate organization is based on largely unrelated divisions. The matrix organization is based on two simultaneous chains of command created by superimposing a divisional organization onto a functional organization.

Henry Mintzberg's design configurations are (1) the simple structure, (2) the machine bureaucracy, (3) the professional bureaucracy, (4) the divisionalized form, and (5) the adhocracy. The simple structure includes centralization, minimal work specialization, differentiation, and formalization. This configuration is appropriate for young, small organizations operating simple technology in a simple, changeable environment. The machine bureaucracy includes relative centralization, narrow work specialization, functional departmentalization, and high formalization; it is appropriate for large, mature organizations operating standardized technology in a simple, stable environment. The professional bureaucracy includes decentralized authority, functional or hybrid departmentalization, skilled professionals, a technical support staff, and little formalization. This design is appropriate when using standardized technology in a complex, static environment. The divisionalized form includes relative decentralization, divisional or conglomerate organization, standardized outputs, and high formalization; it is appropriate for older, larger organizations operating in diversified markets. The adhocracy includes matrix organization, relative decentralization, considerable work specialization, and little formalization; it is appropriate for younger organizations using sophisticated technology in a complex, changeable environment.

MEETING A MANAGEMENT CHALLENGE AT CAMPBELL SOUP

Campbell Soup Company was experiencing an erosion of its market share because many U.S. consumers were no longer satisfied with standardized, nationwide products. In many cases they were choosing the diversity offered by Campbell's regional competitors. No longer could Campbell sell the same can of soup from one coast to the other.

To play in this new game, Campbell Soup had to change its strategy and its structure. To support the effort, CEO R. Gordon McGovern had to redesign Campbell Soup's division structure from functional to regional. McGovern decentralized sales efforts by dividing the selling organization into 22 regions. Each region was then assigned a brand sales manager responsible for tailoring national marketing efforts to his or her region, for planning and implementing regional promotions and advertising, and for collecting information about the region's markets for the company. To capture as much market share as possible, the regional brand sales managers were told that their performance would be assessed by volume increases, not by profit.

Where sales reps were once assigned specific brands, they are now told to sell all of the company's products. This also means that each rep calls on a much smaller number of stores, giving them the time to learn more about their territories. They pass such knowledge on to the regional brand sales managers, who use it to fine-tune regional marketing. McGovern added four new managers at headquarters to coordinate the efforts of the regional brand sales managers.

David W. Johnson, R. Gordon McGovern's successor as CEO of Campbell Soup

McGovern also sliced up Campbell to create business units that concentrate on specific groups of products, such as beverages or soups. Each unit, headed by a category general manager, is encouraged to innovate in fulfilling customer needs and to capitalize on the market information passed up from the regional brand managers. To free the category general managers from the time-consuming layers of centralized approvals, McGovern gave them considerable autonomy to reach decisions in areas such as finance, manufacturing, logistics, and marketing.

To better allocate production resources, McGovern also regionalized the company's several dozen domestic manufacturing plants, grouping them into five manufacturing regions. Because each manufacturing region is now dedicated to a certain group of sales regions, the plants can more efficiently manufacture the products each region needs. In addition, plant managers are expected to come up with new product ideas and to share them with the sales region staffs. Under the company's previous functional structure, manufacturing, sales, advertising, and other divisions held separate meetings to plot strategy. Now coordination is encouraged as representatives from all of the formerly separate functions attend the same meetings.

These structural changes allow Campbell to compete more effectively and to produce food specially formulated to appeal to local tastes. In the years following the structural changes, Campbell reported a 12 percent increase in operating earnings on sales increases of 7 percent. The reorganization had helped push Campbell's annual sales to $6 billion. The company's structure is now in the hands of CEO David W. Johnson, who has made additional changes to improve operational efficiency, such as increasing control over the firm's fast-growing European operations by having executives there now report directly to him. It's a sure bet that Campbell will continue to adapt its structure in order to stay responsive in an ever-changing market.

You're the Manager: As the vice president of human resources, your responsibilities include adjusting and tuning the organization structure to keep it responsive to both consumer demands and competitive threats and advising David Johnson on overall strategy.

Ranking Questions

1. One year after the regional structure was implemented, the sales region in the Southwest is reporting higher profit than others. The computer printouts show this is because the manufacturing plants have been better able to produce goods in quantities sufficient to meet consumer demand. The Southwest regional brand manager attributes this to a team of sales reps that meets every two weeks and distributes market information to the plant managers, allowing them to plan production in ways that reflect sales trends and consumer preferences. No other sales region is using this approach. How would you rank these techniques for capitalizing on the Southwest region's experience and success?
   a. Insist that all sales regions use the same approach.
   b. Gather information on additional ways the sales regions are responding to the changing market environment at the corporate level, and disseminate these ideas to all sales regions.
   c. Establish a team that represents each region and meets regularly to integrate the best ideas developed in all regions.
   d. Install a computer communications system that allows all of the regions to discuss this team idea and other techniques they might be using.
2. Because each manufacturing plant now produces on a regional basis, it can no longer be counted upon to assist other plants in producing their goods when consumer demand surges in another part of the country. In deciding how to solve this problem, rank the following solutions from best to worst.
   a. Accept this risk as necessary for the company, given its new organization structure.
   b. Have plants exchange recipes so that any plant is ready to start producing a certain food with minimum delay.
   c. Have each plant produce a limited number of each of the regional foods, even those normally produced outside its assigned sales regions. This will ensure that its assembly lines are already in place when a shortage of food items occurs in another manufacturing region.
   d. Establish a department of production resource management at headquarters, which is responsible for maintaining communications among the plants, recording their production levels, and tracking patterns of consumer demand from regional brand managers' reports. When it appears that consumer demand is outstripping supply of a product, this department will assign a production order to another plant and provide the necessary recipes.

Multiple-Choice Questions

3. The regional brand managers are exhibiting more success with modifying older Campbell products to suit regional tastes than they are

with launching new products. Of the following suggestions for improving the success rate of new product launches, which is best?

a. Create the position of "new-products manager," and fill this post in each of the 22 regions. Establish a matrix reporting structure so that the new-products manager reports to the regional brands manager and to a category general manager at the home office.
b. Investigate the situation in each region before making any moves to reorganize; you might be able to solve the problem without the expense and disruption of reorganizing.
c. A company should always stick to what it does best. Since the regions have been successful at fine-tuning older products for regional tastes, recommend that the corporation shift its product strategy to deemphasize or perhaps even stop development of new products.
d. Establish a new-product division at the home office that runs market tests in the regions and then directs the regions on new-product decisions; this will allow functional specialists to determine exactly what each region needs.

4. The regional divisions have aggressively introduced the various product lines geared to local tastes. As a result, regional sales volume has soared and market share has increased. However, not all products have been equally profitable. For instance, some that are very popular with customers don't turn a profit because the cost of their ingredients is high. Others require an inordinate amount of advertising and sales promotions in order to be competitive. How can Campbell assure that the effort to satisfy local tastes will be more profitable?
   a. Create a financial unit at the regional level. The regional financial manager will coordinate decision making with the regional brand sales manager and with the corporate VP of finance.
   b. Have financial specialists at the corporate office assess the financial performance of each brand and then provide each region with a list of the products that should be dropped due to poor profitability.
   c. Replace the regional brand managers with financial personnel who are better equipped to manage financial concerns.
   d. Modify the criteria by which brand sales managers are measured; include profitability in addition to sales volume as a measure of performance.

Analysis Questions

5. How did the new Campbell Soup structure affect differentiation and integration in the firm's response to the changing environment?
6. Of the five key factors that affect organization design, which was the most influential in the Campbell situation? Did others play roles?
7. Suppose Campbell Soup were to use only the classical approach to organization design. What would be the key drawback?

Special Project

In an effort to diversify, Campbell Soup has purchased a manufacturer of dishes, pots and pans, and kitchen utensils that sells its wares primarily through general merchandise stores. The acquired company has always operated with functional divisions on a nationwide basis. Marketing research shows you that housewares do not exhibit the same degree of regional market differences as food products do; in fact, people all over the country use basically the same products. David W. Johnson plans to have his regional divisions sell the new lines of housewares along with the company's regionalized food items. Prepare a letter to Johnson describing possible difficulties with this proposition and suggesting an alternative way to structure the acquired division.[73]

KEY TERMS

adhocracy (326)
conglomerate organization (320)
continuous-flow-process technology (313)
differentiation (311)
divisionalized form (325)
divisional organization (319)
functional organization (318)
integration (312)
machine bureaucracy (325)
mass-production and large-batch technology (313)
matrix organization (321)
mechanistic structure (310)
organic structure (310)

organizational life cycle (316)
organization design (304)
professional bureaucracy (325)
simple structure (324)
sociotechnical systems theory (306)
System 1 (306)
System 4 (306)
technology (313)
unit and small-batch technology (313)

QUESTIONS

For Review

1. What is the contingency approach to organization design?
2. How do mechanistic and organic organizations differ?
3. What is the relationship between differentiation and integration?
4. What are the four common types of organization decisions?
5. Under what circumstances is each of Mintzberg's five structural configurations most effective?

For Analysis

1. How can organizations overcome the limitations of bureaucracy?
2. Must a not-for-profit organization with few employees but many volunteers consider the impact of organization size on organization design? Why or why not?
3. Should an organization change its structure when it changes its strategy? Conversely, should an organization change its strategy when it changes its structure?
4. How does an organic structure resemble Likert's System 4?
5. How does the matrix organization differ from the lateral relationships needed to coordinate and integrate activities in any organization?

For Application

1. How might a local print shop use the results of Woodward's research to design an appropriate organization structure?
2. In what situations could the Red Cross most effectively apply Mintzberg's adhocracy configuration?
3. Which structural elements should the owner of a pizza parlor review when designing the appropriate organization structure to open a second location?
4. What two organization designs might the Gap combine to form a hybrid design to manage its national chain of GapKids stores?
5. Would an accounting firm be more likely to adopt Mintzberg's professional bureaucracy or his machine bureaucracy? Why?

KEEPING CURRENT IN MANAGEMENT

Find a recent article in which a manager discusses how an organization changed its structure to cope with the challenges of more complex technology. Possible examples are a small manufacturer that switched from unit technology to mass-production technology and a chemical producer that built a new automated plant based on continuous-flow-process technology.

1. Is the organization's entire structure affected by the technology? If not, what part or parts are affected? How do employees interact with the new technology? Is work specialization affected by the change?
2. Did management change the span of management, the number of hierarchical levels, or the degree of centralization when the new technology was instituted? Is management applying more or less formalization in response to the new technology?
3. What elements of bureaucracy can be seen in the new organization? Is the new organization design more mechanistic or more organic? Is the new organization design a functional, divisional, conglomerate, matrix, or hybrid form?

SHARPEN YOUR MANAGEMENT SKILLS

Talk about sending a shock wave up and down Wall Street. Westinghouse Electric has long impressed investors and analysts, particularly with its performance during rough market conditions, so the news that its finance subsidiary, Westinghouse Credit, was writing down (declaring uncollectible and writing off as losses) $2.7 billion of its $10 billion portfolio of loans came as a nasty surprise.

At the end of 1991, fully 85 percent of Westinghouse Credit's loans were high-risk, high-interest affairs in such shaky arenas as shopping centers, junk bonds, and leveraged buyouts. Some analysts predict that the losses may eventually exceed even the $2.7 billion figure. Both insiders and outsiders say the problem was caused by sloppy controls at Westinghouse and inattention from corporate headquarters. Complicating matters is the fact that the Westinghouse corporation is run by a former engineer with no operating experience in financial services.

Ironically, throughout the 1980s, Westinghouse Credit provided the growth to keep Westinghouse moving forward. During that time, Westinghouse executives were preoccupied with building the perfect conglomerate. They bought and sold a staggering number of companies—selling 70 companies in one three-year period—while searching for a profitable and stable mix. All the while, income from Westinghouse Credit's ever-growing stable of loans kept Westinghouse healthy. Or so it seemed at the time.

- *Decision:* Structurally speaking, what should be done with Westinghouse Credit? Let the company continue to run as a fairly independent entity and rely on new management to clean it up, or put it under the direct control of Westinghouse executives, even though those executives have little experience in financial services? (If you need more information, your library undoubtedly has several articles on Westinghouse's plight.)
- *Communication:* Draft a one-page press release outlining your plans for Westinghouse Credit. Rest assured that Westinghouse shareholders, unhappy about the 36 percent hammering their stock has received, will be quite interested in what you have to say.

CASE

Kodak Focuses Its Organization

Four reorganizations in six years have given Eastman Kodak an identity crisis, but chairman and CEO Kay R. Whitmore sees a solution. Whitmore, who directed the chemicals and imaging divisions before becoming president in 1983 and chairman in 1989, wants Kodak to focus on its basic purpose, reproducing images.

HISTORY

The company that would become Kodak arose from a bank clerk's frustration about not having enough room in his luggage to pack the liquid chemicals necessary for taking photographs on his Caribbean vacation. George Eastman canceled his vacation, developed a method for dry-plate photography, invented flexible photographic film, and in 1884 established the Eastman Dry Plate and Film Company in Rochester, New York. Eastman invented the name Kodak because he liked the strong sound of the letter *K*. Kodak introduced its first camera in 1888 and 12 years later brought out the highly successful Brownie camera, which sold for $1 and used 15-cent rolls of film. Kodak moved into home-movie cameras and x-ray equipment, but its greatest success, introduced in 1963, was the Instamatic camera, which used a film cartridge that eliminated the need to load film in the dark. By 1976 Kodak had sold 50 million Instamatics, five times as many cameras as all its competitors combined.

The company's success attracted film and camera competitors, especially in the 1980s. Revenues have steadily risen, but profits fell from $1.1 billion to $529 million during the 1980s, recovering to $703 million on sales of $118.9 billion in 1990. Kodak recently has held 80 percent of the U.S. film market and 50 percent of the market elsewhere in the world.

ENVIRONMENT

Whitmore's predecessor responded to lagging profits and growing competition by putting Kodak through four reorganizations; he cut 25,000 jobs and diversified into such new areas as electronic publishing and batteries. Increasing complexity required faster decision making, so he abandoned Kodak's functionally organized structure in favor of a decentralized, divisional structure that brought decision making down to appropriate levels within its four divisions (chemicals, health, information systems, and imaging).

But Kodak is still struggling. The chemical division, which has expanded far beyond photoprocessing to include such products as plastics and polyester, is hurting from a cyclical downturn in the chemical market. The health division, created in 1988 by the acquisition of Bayer aspirin maker Sterling Drug, is hurting as consumers turn to painkillers based on ibuprofen. The information systems division's mainstay photocopiers and microfilm are performing below par. The photography business of Kodak's imaging division, which is bigger than all other divisions combined, is hurt by film and camera competition and by the declining size of U.S. families (because children are one of the biggest reasons for taking pictures).

GOALS AND CHALLENGES

Whitmore has decided to sharpen Kodak's focus on its distinctive competence, production of images, whether they are photographs, photocopies, or x-rays. He has sold off computer floppy-disk maker Verbatim and eight smaller information system units, and he has hinted that he may sell off Sterling if a joint venture with big French drug company Sanofi doesn't pay off. Whitmore also recognizes that Kodak is not a growth company these days; in the photography business, for example, development of successful new cameras is years away and the major film markets of the United States, Japan, and Western Europe are mature, though sales are still growing in Latin America and potential exists in Asia and Eastern Europe. Therefore, he is boosting profit margins by slashing costs (including payroll) and by improving efficiencies; for example, a new computerized information network has dramatically reduced customer ordering time and order error rates for Kodak's Business Imaging Systems unit.

1. How have strategy and environment affected Kodak's organization structure?
2. How has Kodak's organization design changed through its life cycle, and how is this related to organizational performance?
3. How might Whitmore use Likert's systems to structure his health division for improved employee participation?
4. Which of Mintzberg's five structural configurations would be appropriate for a business unit that uses standardized processes to develop and print a large number of photographs?

CHAPTER OUTLINE

Organizational Change and Innovation

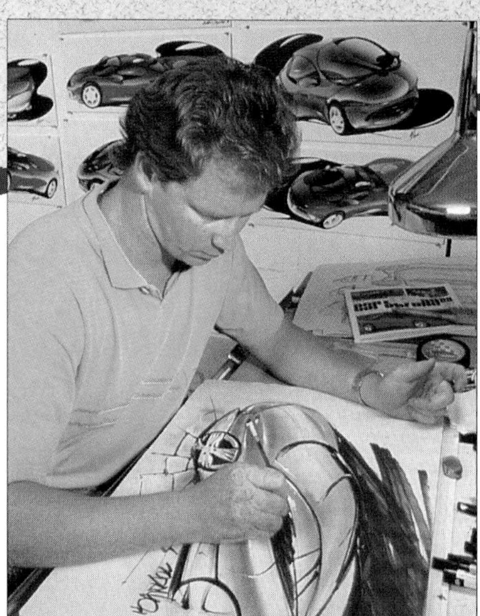

After studying this chapter, you will be able to

1. Explain the relationship among organizational change, creativity, and innovation, and discuss the forces for change
2. Describe the stages in Lewin's organizational change process
3. Identify the most common reasons for resistance to change and explain the use of force-field analysis
4. Discuss the methods managers can use to overcome resistance to change
5. List and describe the four areas of planned change
6. Discuss the nature of organizational development and outline the steps in the organizational development process
7. Explain the role of planning, organizational culture, and organization structure in institutionalizing creativity and innovation

FACING A MANAGEMENT CHALLENGE AT

Turning the Magic Kingdom into an Entertainment Empire

When Michael Eisner was appointed chairman and CEO of Disney in 1984, he took charge of a company that had become little more than an uninspired memorial to the legacy of founder Walt Disney. Walt himself was a true original. He had charmed audiences by populating his cartoons and movies with eccentric and endearing animals—talking mice were followed over the years by chuckleheaded dogs, irascible ducks, and hippos in tutus. In an era when amusement parks were considered tawdry and disreputable, he succeeded in presenting Disneyland as a wholesome destination for a family vacation. A marketing genius, Disney was quick to appreciate the power of the small screen, quietly promoting his movies and theme parks on his weekly TV show.

But when Walt Disney died, the innovation, creativity, and quality that animated everything he touched began disappearing from the Magic Kingdom. Before Eisner arrived, Disney executives had been terrified of tampering with Walt's winning formula. When contemplating new ideas, they continually wondered aloud, "What would Walt have done?" Eisner inherited a movie studio that specialized in outdated family flicks and aging theme parks that were battling new competition around the country. The weekly television show had even been canceled. As president of Paramount Pictures, Eisner had the creative foresight to support such hits as *Saturday Night Fever*, *Raiders of the Lost Ark*, and *Terms of Endearment*. Now at Disney, he found himself at the helm of a drifting company whose last successful movie had been *The Love Bug*, a 1969 comedy about a Volkswagen named Herbie.

Eisner realized immediately that Disney possessed more than enough raw material to make a successful comeback. The company owned more than 29 years' worth of "Wonderful World of Disney" TV shows, hundreds of cartoons, and nearly 200 feature movies. Disney's three existing hotels at Disney World in Orlando were probably the most profitable in the United States, with unheard-of occupancy rates of 92 to 96 percent (when the industry average was 66 percent). And Orlando offered plenty of room for expansion. Disney World and the three hotels occupied just a small fraction of Disney's Orlando holdings of 31,000 acres, an area twice the size of Manhattan.

The prescription for reversing Disney's decline was obvious: exploit the company's existing assets while creating new properties for the future. But implementing this strategy was another matter. In many ways, the challenge facing Eisner was even larger than the challenge that Walt himself had faced. Disney had to bring his cartoon characters to life; Eisner had to reanimate an entire corporation. In order to turn Disney around, Eisner had to exorcise Walt Disney's ghost while revitalizing his spirit.

How could Eisner mobilize Disney, mired as it was in the 1960s, to take advantage of opportunities in the 1990s? How could he return the company's movie business to competitiveness? And what role should Eisner himself play at Disney? Should he try to step into Walt's shoes or take on an entirely new role?[1]

CHAPTER OVERVIEW

To get Disney back on creative track, Michael Eisner had to revitalize the company and set the stage for renewed growth. To accomplish this, he had to understand the nature of organizational change, and he had to institutionalize creativity and innovation. This chapter starts with a look at the relationship among change, creativity, innovation, and the forces for change. Next, planned organizational change is examined, including the change process, reasons for resistance to change, and methods for overcoming resistance. After reviewing the four areas of planned change, the chapter explores organizational development and closes with a section on managing creativity and innovation.

MANAGEMENT AND ORGANIZATIONAL CHANGE

change Any alteration in the organization's existing situation

creativity The process of generating novel ideas

innovation The transformation of creative ideas into goods or services that meet customer needs or solve customer problems

Even in the most stable environments, change is a constant, no matter how slight. **Change** is any alteration of the organization's current situation. One specialized type of change is **creativity,** the process by which novel ideas are generated. A related type of change is **innovation,** the transformation of creative ideas into goods, services, or processes that meet customer needs or solve customer problems. Innovation is a deliberate process that requires organizational resources and must therefore be introduced from within the organization. However, the creativity that sparks an innovation can originate either inside or outside the organization.[2] Creativity and innovation are explored in more detail later in this chapter.

Although creativity and innovation both alter the existing situation and therefore always involve change, change does not always involve either creativity or innovation. For example, the Justice Department mandated change when Fleet/Norstar acquired Bank of New England, a failed bank in Boston. Enforcing antitrust regulations, the Justice Department ruled that the merged bank's concentration of market share in Maine was too high, so Fleet/Norstar had to sell some operations, a structural change that was neither creative nor innovative. On the other hand, Lew Frankfort, president of Coach Leatherware in New York, recently set up a new-product development group that uses unique designs and innovative marketing methods to launch products such as luggage and fashion accessories. This change involved both creativity and innovation, and it helped Frankfort expand his customer focus beyond the women's market to target men as well. Whether the change involves creativity, innovation, or another type of change, managers must be aware of the forces for change that can influence the organization.[3]

The Forces for Change

Various environmental forces influence organizational change. For example, suppliers stop making certain parts, an economic recovery fuels demand for goods and services, and employees and managers leave or join the organization. Some of these forces emanate from the external environment, and some emanate from the internal environment. Although managers have no direct control over the external forces, they can make internal organizational changes in an attempt to influence these forces, to adapt to these forces, or to shift domains.

External Forces

External forces for change arise from both the general and the task environments, but regardless of origin, such external forces can affect the organization's ability to achieve its goals. Even though general environment forces such as politicolegal, economic, technological, sociocultural, and international forces frequently affect organizational change less directly than the forces in the task environment, they must not be discounted. For example, Richard R. Wackenhut, president of security service provider Wackenhut, sensed opportunity in the confluence of a variety of sociocultural, politicolegal, and economic forces: crime rates are soaring, bulging prisons are under court order to reduce overcrowding, and state budgets are withering. With more criminals to house but less money to build and operate prisons, state and federal agencies are seeking ways of reducing the pressure on the penal system. Although these forces did not

One of the external forces for change faced by U.S. carmakers is California's mandate that 2 percent of the cars sold in 1998 emit no pollutants. In response, Chrysler teamed up with Westinghouse Electric to develop a propulsion system for commercially viable, nonpolluting electric vehicles, including the Epic model being shown by Chrysler's Jean Mallebay-Vacquer *(left)*.

immediately affect his security business, Wackenhut decided to establish a subsidiary to enter the private prison business. This fast-growing unit now operates prisons, jails, and detention facilities in Louisiana and in other states.[4]

The forces in the task environment, including customers, competitors, suppliers, the labor supply, regulators, and partners, affect organizational change much more directly (see Exhibit 11.1). Consider the forces that influence Polskie Linie Lotnicze (LOT), the national airline of Poland. Bronislaw Klimaszewski, who heads the airline, faces rising customer demand for air travel into and out of Warsaw, and he faces increased competition from Western European and U.S. carriers. Klimaszewski also faces problems servicing his fleet, which consists largely of Soviet-made planes. Because these planes do not use standardized parts, the airline cannot simply order replacement parts from suppliers. In response to these customer, competitive, and supplier forces, Klimaszewski has made several changes. He initiated nine weekly flights to U.S. destinations using Boeing 767 jets, and he began searching for a buyer for his older planes. Once the old planes are sold, he plans to order new jets, but until then, he must use internal workshops to make replacement parts, and he sometimes winds up stripping other planes to keep the fleet flying.[5]

MANAGEMENT AROUND THE WORLD

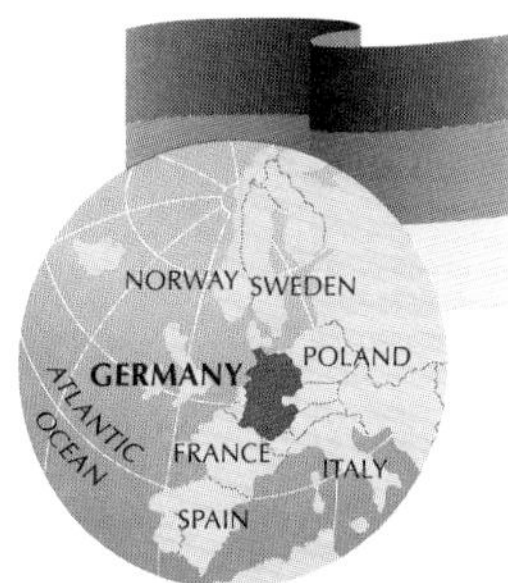

Political changes in Eastern Europe during the early 1990s also brought on economic changes. The former East Germany, once the world's tenth-largest exporter with captive markets in the former Soviet bloc, saw its export business collapse when coveted goods from the West and Asia began arriving in Eastern Europe. The unified Germany now exports to markets in the West as well as to those in Eastern Europe.

Internal Forces

In the internal environment, forces for change can come from owners and shareholders, boards of directors, employees, or organizational culture. In addition, strategy, management decisions, and organizational activities can all be forces for change. Often, the internal forces for change are affected by external forces, such as when shifts in the composition of the labor supply affect the makeup, behavior, and attitudes of the employee population, or when economic forces affect the inputs needed to implement strategic plans. For example, the San Francisco Education Fund (SFEF) is a not-for-profit organization founded to reward the creativity and motivation of teachers in the city's public school system. At first, the organization provided teachers with small grants, but it later

EXHIBIT 11.1

Competitors as an External Force for Change

As part of the task environment, competitors can directly influence organizational change. For example, one way that Visa responded to competition from American Express was by becoming a sponsor of the 1992 Olympic Games.

1. Worldwide Acceptance.
2. Hand-Delivered Refunds.

expanded its activities in response to the external economic pressure of procuring funding. Soon SFEF was receiving funds to operate the San Francisco Math Collaborative (a joint undertaking with high schools, colleges, and area companies), as well as two other collaboratives. Then internal forces came to the fore: the board of directors became concerned about pursuing activities far afield from SFEF's original mission. After much discussion, the directors decided to refocus the organization's primary thrust on the grants program, and this change prompted additional internal changes so that the board and SFEF employees could focus on funding and administering the teacher grants.[6]

Planned and Reactive Change

reactive change Change that is undertaken piecemeal to resolve specific problems as they occur

The constant forces for change that buffet every organization can have profound effects on the organization's ability to remain competitive, to maintain productivity, and to perform in general. Managers can respond to these forces in one of two ways. One response is **reactive change,** change that is undertaken piecemeal to deal with specific problems as they arise. Managers may be forced into reactive change by sudden and unanticipated crises. Under such circumstances, they usually have little time to analyze the situation and make plans before responding, so their actions may be potentially inappropriate or ineffective, and the results may not meet their expectations. Reactive change is also a way to resolve the many noncrisis problems that crop up. For example, Svetislav Stamenovic, a manager for the Yugoslavian construction firm Generalexport, is in charge of building the Holiday Inn Chinggis Khaan in Mongolia. As he completes the 184-room hotel (which has fallen months behind schedule), reactive change is Stamenovic's daily response to recurring power outages and unexpected shortages of cement and other materials.[7]

planned change Change that is deliberately designed and implemented in anticipation of future environmental threats and opportunities

A second response to the forces for change is **planned change,** change that is deliberately designed and implemented in anticipation of future opportunities and threats. Managers use planned change to intentionally alter the organization

in advance of a problem or an opportunity, with the aim of improving efficiency and effectiveness. With planned change, managers can spend more time considering their response to environmental forces, so their actions are more likely to be appropriate and effective, and the results are more likely to be closer to their expectations.[8]

Even in complex and changeable environments, effective managers strive toward planned change over reactive change. For example, carmakers around the world see tougher regulation of air pollution and fuel economy coming in the not-so-distant future. The advent of such regulations presents new opportunities for making cars that run on alternative fuels, but it also threatens the sales of current models that don't meet the stricter standards. Faced with the inevitability of these government actions, the automakers are responding with planned change. Fiat has designed and produced the Elettra, a $22,000 battery-powered car being sold in Italy; Chrysler has redesigned its LH sedan to run on gasoline, methanol, ethanol, or a blend of fuels; and Honda has created a solar-powered car prototype called the RaRa.[9]

In a perfect world, all managers would guide their organizations with carefully planned changes. However, all managers are affected by forces beyond their control or anticipation, so the process of managing change is a combination of both reactive and planned change. Even as he proceeds with carefully laid plans for constructing the Mongolian hotel, Svetislav Stamenovic is forced to resort to reactive change in response to unanticipated and uncontrollable forces in his environment.

The San Diego County Water Authority uses planned change to ensure the long-term reliability of the county water supply. The agency started planning a 7,000-foot pipeline extension in 1988, and broke ground to start construction in 1992. As a result of this planned change, aging aqueducts will be replaced with a new pipeline to the Sweetwater Reservoir.

MANAGING PLANNED ORGANIZATIONAL CHANGE

To enable organizational goals to be achieved despite the unrelenting pressures exerted by the forces for change, managers must continually make changes. Thus, planned organizational change is an ongoing process, not a journey with a final destination; every organization can be seen as evolving from its present state to a state that will facilitate performance in the environment of the future.[10] To manage planned organizational change effectively, managers must start by identifying the need for change.

The Need for Change

When is organizational change needed? The need for change can surface during the strategic management process. During the strategic control phase of this process, managers compare their organization's current performance to the targets described in their strategic goals. If they find discrepancies, they may need to make changes that will bring performance into line with their vision of the ideal future state. Similarly, in the situation analysis phase, managers may uncover external or internal forces that can potentially affect the organization's performance (either positively or negatively). Depending on the nature of these forces and the severity of their impact, change may be needed to keep the organization on the track of achieving its goals.[11]

For example, Warren Featherbone is a small business in Gainesville, Georgia, that has survived for more than 100 years by recognizing and responding to the early warning signs of needed change. The firm originally made corset stiffeners, notions, and fashion accessories, but top managers soon realized that trends in women's fashions were changing, posing a threat to their main product lines. They also became aware of a new material, plastic, that could potentially offer a variety of benefits, all largely untapped by other manufacturers. As a result of this situation analysis, company officials recognized the need for organizational change. So they expanded their product line to add plastic baby pants (to be worn over cloth diapers), and later they began making plastic cover-ups for disposable diapers. Warren Featherbone stopped making corset stiffeners more than 30 years ago, but the company continues to prosper because its top managers monitor performance and the environment, and they stay alert for signs of needed change.[12]

The Change Process

Once the need for change and the goals of that change have been established, managers can start to implement the change. Managers need to realize, though, that it is not always easy to make changes stick. Organizational theorist Kurt Lewin observed that organization members tend to make changes for a short time and then drift back to the former, more familiar way of doing things. To overcome this tendency for change to be short-lived, Lewin proposed a three-stage process (later elaborated by Edgar H. Schein) for implementing permanent change that moves the organization toward the desired future performance: (1) unfreezing, (2) moving, and (3) freezing (see Exhibit 11.2).[13]

- *Stage 1: Unfreezing.* Before the change is introduced, organization members who will be affected by the planned change are made aware of the need for change and are motivated to accept the change. This stage thaws their behavior, values, and attitudes in anticipation of the coming change. At Disney, Michael Eisner used brainstorming meetings, company celebrations, and other techniques to get creative juices flowing again and to change attitudes and performance expectations.

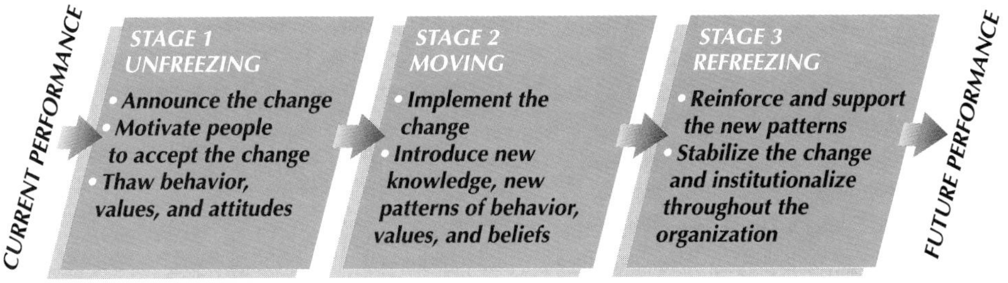

CURRENT PERFORMANCE

STAGE 1
UNFREEZING
• Announce the change
• Motivate people to accept the change
• Thaw behavior, values, and attitudes

STAGE 2
MOVING
• Implement the change
• Introduce new knowledge, new patterns of behavior, values, and beliefs

STAGE 3
REFREEZING
• Reinforce and support the new patterns
• Stabilize the change and institutionalize throughout the organization

FUTURE PERFORMANCE

EXHIBIT 11.2

The Three-Stage Change Process

The change process proposed by Kurt Lewin consists of three stages: unfreezing, moving, and freezing. The actions in each stage are designed to promote permanent (rather than temporary) change, in order to move the organization from its current performance toward the desired future performance.

- *Stage 2: Moving.* The change occurs, introducing new patterns of behavior, new values, new knowledge, and new attitudes in order to move organizational performance toward the goal.
- *Stage 3: Refreezing.* After the change has been introduced, management reinforces and supports the new patterns so that the change is frozen in place. At this point in the change process, the change can be institutionalized, and performance can be stabilized at the desired level.

As the events in each stage of the change process unfold, organization members individually and collectively react by understanding and adjusting to the change in their own ways. These individual interpretations can affect the outcome of the change, so the process is not complete until the results have been evaluated to determine whether the desired performance has been achieved and can be sustained. However, when organization members resist change, managers may experience difficulty in unfreezing, moving, and refreezing both behavior and activities.[14]

Resistance to Change

No matter what type of planned change managers want to implement, it is not uncommon for organization members to show resistance. After all, people have become accustomed to their existing behavior, tools, and techniques for solving daily problems and achieving current performance. Even when the change is obviously in their best interest and will clearly improve their situation, people often resist. To successfully implement organizational change, knowledgeable managers understand the reasons for resistance, analyze the forces for and against change, and make plans to overcome resistance.

Reasons for Resistance

No matter who is initiating the change, no matter what the impact, some people may resist change. Among the reasons for resistance to change are self-interest, lack of understanding and trust, uncertainty, and differing perceptions.

Self-Interest How vigorously organization members resist needed change often depends on the extent to which they believe their self-interests are threatened. When people fear that a change will threaten their status, their turf, their pay, their relationships with co-workers, or other aspects of their work, they are more likely to resist change. For example, some physicians felt their self-interests were threatened when Pacific Presbyterian Medical Center in San Francisco proposed opening a new unit in which patients would be encouraged to participate in their treatment, including being allowed to read and comment on their medical records. Although the physicians resisted this change because they didn't welcome patient participation or comments, the new unit, Planetree, eventually opened and quickly became a valuable testing ground for innovative medical treatment ideas.[15]

Lack of Understanding and Trust People often resist change when they do not understand its purpose or its impact. Moreover, organization members may resist change when they do not trust its intent—or the intent of the managers who initiate the change. For example, when General Motors proposed converting its Buick City plant to a new, more participative management style, Buick managers balked. Distrustful of the change, they didn't believe they could ever apply the new management approach in real-life situations. But top management persisted, and soon the Buick managers were using the new styles to encourage employee participation in improving the production process.[16]

Uncertainty When people have little information about a proposed change, they may resist because they are afraid of the unknown. This is especially true for organization members who have a particularly low tolerance for change and therefore feel anxious about the rate of change or about the new tasks, the new skills, or the new demands for performance that the change entails. Few industries have experienced the turmoil felt in the U.S. banking industry in recent years. Many weak institutions have been purchased by stronger competitors, sold at government auctions, or shut down entirely. Even for the survivors, the level of uncertainty can be high. Over a four-year period in the 1980s, Illinois-based Boulevard Bancorp purchased two banks and started a third independent operation, leaving it with essentially four different corporate cultures. Employees, many of whom were told they would be transferred from one unit to another, didn't know what to expect and so began to resist the changes. CEO Dick Schroeder's successful strategy for addressing this uncertainty centered on a clearly stated list of corporate values for all four units. This strategy reduced the uncertainty surrounding a transfer from one unit to another and helped employees overcome their resistance to such changes.[17]

Differing Perceptions Those who will be affected by a proposed change often have perceptions that differ significantly from the perceptions of those initiating the change. Some may complain that its drawbacks outweigh its benefits; others may argue that the initiators have set an unrealistic timetable for implementation. Also, people in organizational units frequently pursue differing tactical and operational goals, so they may not agree on the value of a particular change or on its implementation. For example, top managers at RCA's Consumer Electronics Division decided not long ago to change their product development procedure to better compete with overseas producers. Because the people in engineering and manufacturing concentrated on specific aspects of product development rather than on the entire process, their departmental goals and expectations differed and they initially resisted the change. When it was implemented, the change ultimately cut product development time and costs and improved quality.[18]

To successfully implement change, managers must analyze any resistance to understand why the individuals feel as they do. Next, they must determine how this resistance can potentially affect the desired future performance. One commonly used method of assessing resistance to change is force-field analysis.

Force-Field Analysis

Kurt Lewin developed **force-field analysis** as a technique for analyzing the overall impact of the various forces that support and oppose change (see Exhibit 11.3). Any situation into which change will be introduced contains both *driving forces* that push for the change and *restraining forces* that resist the change. By diagraming these forces and analyzing their impact, managers can better understand how to proceed. For example, change is easiest when the driving forces outweigh the restraining forces. On the other hand, when the restraining forces are stronger than the driving forces, managers seeking change have several choices. They can reduce the restraining forces, increase the driving forces, or both. However, increasing the driving forces tends to cause a corresponding rise in the intensity of the restraining forces, so managers are usually more successful in implementing change when they work to remove or to minimize the restraining forces.[19] When Michael Eisner set about reinvigorating Disney, for instance, his driving forces were facing well-entrenched restraining forces, primarily the organizational paralysis caused by the "I wonder what Walt would have done?" mindset.

force-field analysis A technique for analyzing the overall impact of the various forces that work for and against change

Techniques for Overcoming Resistance to Change

Once managers understand the reasons behind any resistance and have analyzed the driving forces and the restraining forces that affect their situation, they can make plans to overcome people's resistance to change. Researchers have identified six methods for effectively overcoming resistance: (1) education and communication, (2) participation and involvement, (3) facilitation and support, (4) negotiation and agreement, (5) manipulation and co-optation, and (6) explicit and implicit coercion (see Exhibit 11.4).

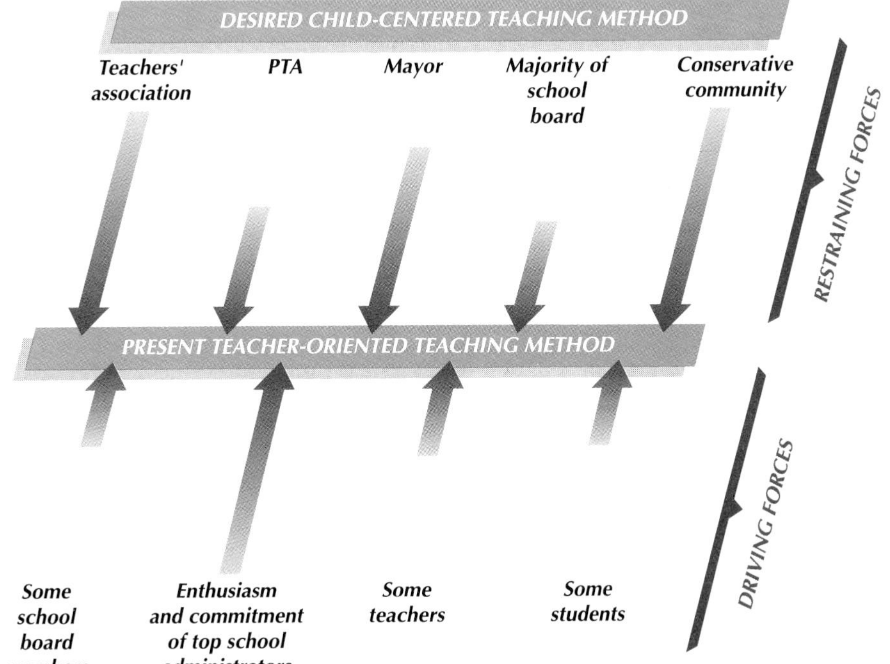

EXHIBIT 11.3

Force-Field Analysis

This example of force-field analysis shows the restraining and driving forces that a school administrator might encounter when attempting to change from teacher-centered to child-centered teaching methods. As shown by the number and length of the arrows, the restraining forces in this example are stronger in total than the sum of the driving forces, so change will be difficult.

EXHIBIT 11.4 Ways of Overcoming Resistance to Change

Managers can use one or more of six methods to overcome people's resistance to change. This chart indicates when each is appropriate and shows their benefits and limitations.

Approach	Common Situations	Advantages	Drawbacks
Education and communication	When there is a lack of information or inaccurate information and analysis	Once persuaded, people will often help with implementing the change.	Can be time-consuming if lots of people are involved
Participation and involvement	When the initiators do not have all the information they need to design the change, and when others have considerable power to resist	People who participate will be committed to implementing change, and any relevant information they have will be integrated into the change plan.	Can be very time-consuming if participators design an inappropriate change
Facilitation and support	When people are resisting because of adjustment problems	No other approach works as well with adjustment problems.	Can be time-consuming, expensive, and still fail
Negotiation and agreement	When someone or some group will clearly lose out in a change, and when that group has considerable power to resist	Sometimes it is a relatively easy way to avoid major resistance.	Can be too expensive in many cases if it alerts others to negotiate for compliance
Manipulation and co-optation	When other tactics will not work or are too expensive	It can be a relatively quick and inexpensive solution to resistance problems.	Can lead to future problems if people feel manipulated
Explicit and implicit coercion	When speed is essential, and when the change initiators possess considerable power	It is speedy and can overcome any kind of resistance.	Can be risky if it leaves people angry with the initiators

Education and Communication One way that managers commonly overcome resistance is by communicating with everyone involved in the change and educating them about the reasons for the change, the methods to be used, the schedule, the people involved, the desired result, and the expected benefits. This can be especially useful when dealing with uncertainty and lack of understanding. When electronics manufacturer Motorola embarked on an ambitious program of change aimed at boosting quality, slashing costs, and grabbing market share, CEO Robert W. Galvin and his successor, George Fisher, headed off resistance caused by uncertainty by launching a massive educational program. All Motorola managers and employees have been invited to take courses that range from global competitiveness and risk-taking to operations control and product development processes. Although this program costs a hefty $60 million annually, it helps Motorola's people understand the need for change and learn new ways of achieving their goals.[20]

Participation A second way that managers can overcome resistance is to involve the people who will be affected by the change. Although participation can be a time-consuming process, people are more likely to accept and support change when their ideas have been solicited and incorporated. Moreover, the ideas that emerge from such participation may improve the plan, the implementation, and the results of the change.[21]

Consider Steve Fox's situation at Amot Controls, a family-owned industrial controls manufacturer located in Richmond, California. Taking over the top slot from his father, Fox realized that Amot would need to change in order to continue its international expansion. But union employees were hostile and mistrustful, suspecting Fox of manipulation. He and his top managers overcame this resistance by involving employees in the change process. They actively sought employee ideas for improving the manufacturing process, encouraged them to accept more responsibility, and rewarded people who went the extra mile to please customers or to save money. In changing Amot's manufacturing process from a traditional assembly-line to a more participative approach, Fox increased sales and improved the relationship with union members.[22]

Facilitation and Support A third way of overcoming resistance is to facilitate the change by providing support for those who will be affected. Top managers can set the tone for the organization and demonstrate the importance of the change by visibly displaying their commitment to the change. Managers can also facilitate the change by offering training in new skills and procedures and by providing sufficient time for people to adjust. Just as important, managers can provide the moral support that organization members need to feel comfortable with the change.[23]

When CEO John Thompson wanted to change IBM Canada's focus from technology to customers, he faced considerable resistance from managers and employees who had been through countless change programs and mistrusted management's long-term commitment to the latest change. Further, many IBM employees did not believe that management would actually delegate the responsibility and the authority necessary to carry out the new mandate. To overcome this resistance, Thompson and his top managers traveled to locations across the country to discuss the changes personally, and they created leadership-training courses to teach managers the new skills that would be needed to fulfill customer needs. Top managers also showed their support by allowing the lower-level managers the time and the opportunity to gain experience in their new decision-making roles.[24]

Negotiation A fourth way of overcoming resistance is to negotiate with resisters and come to agreement about the change. This can be particularly effective in overcoming the resistance of people in an organizational group who perceive that they will lose significantly as a result of the change and who are sufficiently powerful as a group to successfully resist. Seeking changes that would improve productivity, seven steel companies (Armco, Inland, Bethlehem, LTV, Wheeling-Pittsburgh, Cleveland-Cliffs, and Acme) have used negotiation to avoid resistance from unionized employees. After obtaining agreement from the powerful United Steelworkers of America, these companies formed joint labor-management participation teams that search out ways to save money and boost efficiency.[25]

Halfway around the world, Toys 'R' Us had to use negotiation to overcome resistance to its plan to open stores in Japan. Local toymakers had resisted the Toys 'R' Us invasion because the company's discount format and direct connections with manufacturers are contrary to the Japanese tradition of full-price retailing and extensive wholesaling networks. After negotiating for two years, Toys 'R' Us was able to overcome resistance and establish relationships with key manufacturers such as Nintendo and Bandai in preparation for opening a string

To overcome resistance to provisions in a new union contract, Navistar International negotiated with officials of the United Auto Workers (who represent more than 8,000 Navistar employees in six states). After 14 consecutive days of negotiation, the two sides agreed on a contract that limited layoffs, boosted retirement benefits, increased pay, and improved health-care benefits.

MANAGERIAL DECISION MAKING

GE's Welch Decides to Work Out

One of GE's biggest-ever changes was born in a helicopter bound for General Electric headquarters in Fairfield, Connecticut. On board were CEO Jack F. Welch, Jr., and James Baughman, head of GE's Management Development Institute. They were discussing how to tap the enthusiasm and ideas bottled up inside the company's 298,000 managers and employees. Seeking improved synergy and performance, Welch had recently changed the business unit portfolio, flattened the management structure, shuttered some facilities, and reduced the number of staff positions. But after all the businesses had been juggled and many lines redrawn on company organization charts, Welch realized his aggressive growth plans depended on shaking up GE employees and managers to get the energy and ideas flowing again, creating even more changes that would help GE achieve its goals.

Less than a week after their helicopter discussion, Baughman hatched the Workout concept. Workout operates as an open forum where a cross section of GE managers and employees collaborate on planned change by devising and implementing solutions to a wide range of noncrisis problems and opportunities. A typical Workout involves 40 to 100 people drawn from various levels and functions in a GE facility, who assemble at a nearby conference center or hotel for three days of meetings and discussions. The facility's top manager kicks off the Workout by explaining the problem-solving agenda. Next, the group is divided into five or six teams, and each meets separately to tackle a specific portion of the agenda.

Over a two-day period, the teams identify problems, swap ideas, evaluate alternative solutions, and prepare proposals for change that management should consider. On the third day, the top manager returns and listens as each team presents its proposals. At this point, the top manager is allowed to respond to each proposal in only one of three ways: with an immediate approval, with an immediate rejection, or with a request for additional information. If the manager requests more data, a date must be set for receiving this information so that a prompt decision approving or rejecting the proposal can be made.

of stores in major urban areas. The agreements allow the retailer to obtain needed merchandise, the toymakers can continue to use traditional wholesaling networks if they choose, and they are not locked into offering discount prices.[26]

Manipulation and Co-optation A fifth method, albeit one of questionable ethical merit, that managers can use to overcome resistance to change is manipulation and co-optation. By releasing information selectively and by carefully orchestrating their activities, managers can try to manipulate people into accepting the change. A specialized form of manipulation is *co-optation,* which involves giving key people a visible, desirable role in the design or in the implementation of the change. The initiators of the change do not really want these key resisters to participate in the change; they merely want them to endorse the change and to use their influence to help overcome other people's resistance. The ethics of this method are questionable, and if people become aware that they have been manipulated or co-opted, the method can backfire.[27]

Coercion A sixth method for overcoming resistance is coercion. By explicitly or implicitly using the threat of penalties such as a cut in pay, a transfer, or even the loss of their jobs, managers can force resisters to accept change. Especially when a change is expected to be unpopular in any form, coercion may be the only effective way of overcoming resistance, although it should generally be used only as a last resort. Coercion is not a positive move, however, and managers who use coercion run the risk that resisters may become more frustrated and resentful, ultimately threatening the success of the change.[28]

For example, CEO Michael Cornelissen used coercion to overcome resistance at Royal Trustco, a Canadian financial services company. Cornelissen

What can one Workout do? A Workout can create change but it can also overcome resistance to change. Of the 108 changes proposed by a Workout held by the GE Aircraft Engines factory in Lynn, Massachusetts, 100 were approved and implemented, saving the plant over $200,000 in a single year. Before the Workout, employees had been angry and mistrustful of GE management because 6,000 jobs had been cut at this plant over five years. But the participative nature of the Workout, and its results, has opened a new avenue for employees and union officials to find ways of saving existing jobs, thus rebuilding the trust between employees and management. At the Workout, employees argued for—and received—permission to bid against an outside supplier for a contract to make new protective shields for the plant's grinding machines. The employees quoted $16,000, the supplier quoted $96,000; GE saved $80,000 by keeping the contract in-house, and its employees gained an outlet for their skills.

Of course, even as the employees are becoming energized and enthusiastic about their new, more active roles, managers are facing changes of their own. Instead of planning, directing, and controlling employee efforts, managers are expected to coach and counsel, to provide resources, and to help employees develop and implement their own ideas. CEO Welch may come up against some management resistance to Workout, but he is prepared to overcome the resistance through education and communication, through facilitation and support, and through coercion (in the form of performance reviews). Given Welch's ambitious growth strategy for the 1990s, there's no turning back: he wants, and needs, every good idea that the organization can develop, and Workout is the cornerstone of his change program.

Apply Your Knowledge

1. What facilitation and support techniques can Welch use to overcome some managers' resistance to this radical change in manager-employee relations?
2. How can Welch refreeze and institutionalize the changes that emerge from Workout sessions?

wanted his divisional top managers to think more like owners, so he flattened the organization structure, decentralized authority, and changed the executive compensation program. Instead of receiving a salary, managers would have to buy shares in their divisions and then receive part of the profits. Although some managers resisted initially, Cornelissen told them that they would be replaced if they did not accept the change, so they relented. However, Cornelissen didn't rely on coercion alone to overcome resistance; he also used education and communication, as well as facilitation and support, and today Royal Trustco's managers actively seek new and innovative ways of serving customers.[29]

Areas of Planned Change

Although planned change can alter virtually any aspect of the organization, managers generally make changes in one or more of four broad areas: strategy, structure, technology, and people and culture. These areas are interrelated, so a change in one area often requires a change in some or all of the other areas.[30]

Changes in Strategy

One type of planned change involves alterations to organizational strategy. Many changes to the transformation process involve technological changes. To better exploit environmental opportunities and organizational capabilities or to defend against environmental threats and organizational weaknesses, managers can alter the organization's mission or its strategic goals. They can also change corporate-level strategy, by switching from a grand strategy of growth to a retrenchment strategy, for example, or by altering their business portfolio and selling an unprofitable operation or altering the business-level or functional-level strategies. Finally, managers can make changes in the four components of strategy, expanding or narrowing their scope of products or markets, changing their resource deployment, developing some other distinctive competence, or enhancing organizational synergy for improved efficiency and effectiveness. For example, Scandinavian Airlines System (SAS) chief Jan Carlzon recognized that intense competition, dwindling demand, and rising fuel prices posed critical environmental threats. He identified business travelers as a lucrative but underserved market segment, so he changed the SAS strategy to focus on this opportunity. Carlzon then changed structure, technology, and people and culture to support his strategic change. He switched from a centralized to a decentralized organization; ordered new, more technically advanced aircraft suited to the needs of business travelers; and retrained all managers and employees to reinforce the service orientation.[31]

Changes in Structure

A second type of planned change involves altering the organization structure. This type of change, known as *reorganization,* can take a variety of forms. Depending on their goals, managers can reorganize by changing the design of the various tasks that make up the organization's work, or they can change the delegation of responsibility and authority for some or all of these tasks. Reorganization can also cover changes in centralization, line and staff positions, horizontal coordination structures, and departmentalization. Or managers can reorganize by changing their organization design and switching from a functional organization, for example, to a matrix organization.

Consider how British Petroleum (BP) instituted structural change. Top management believed that BP needed more flexibility and responsiveness to deal with such opportunities as the burgeoning Eastern European market. Working with a team of middle managers, top managers developed a reorganization plan that included a flatter headquarters structure, a team approach to horizontal coordination, and more extensive delegation of authority and individual accountability. With these structural changes came changes in BP's business portfolio, work processes, and job assignments.[32]

Seeking improved efficiency and effectiveness, the Matsushita subsidiary National Bicycle Industrial changed the technology in its Kokubu, Japan, factory by altering the production process, the order of operations, and the level of automation. No longer are frames welded by hand; computer-driven robots custom-fit and weld each bicycle frame to meet individual customer specifications.

Changes in Technology

A third type of planned change involves altering organizational technology. To increase organizational efficiency or effectiveness, managers may want to change the equipment, the expert skills, the processes, or the sequence of activities used to produce goods and services. Technological changes in information resource management can help organizations survive and succeed by making information available to decision makers throughout the organization and by providing data that employees need to serve customers or constituents. Further, changes in strategy (such as diversification into new products) may require changes in technology. Defense contractor Lockheed recently decided to speed its production of aircraft parts, so it changed its technology and introduced a computer-integrated manufacturing system. To help employees understand their new roles, management facilitated the change by showing employees the manufacturing process from start to finish. Then to accommodate the new technology, they invited employees to participate in teams to redesign individual jobs and work flows. As a result, a part that once required 52 days to move through the process now requires only 2 days.[33]

Changes in People and Culture

A fourth type of planned change involves changing people and culture. Managers seeking to improve performance and to compete more effectively can change people and culture by altering the skills, the knowledge, the values, the attitudes, or the behavior of organization members. A change in people and culture is often precipitated by a change in another area, such as the introduction of new technology or a change in the delegation of authority, both of which require new skills and behaviors. To change people and culture, organizations frequently use hiring, training, and development programs as well as motivational techniques. For example, the American Bankers Association (ABA), a not-for-profit association in Washington, D.C., wanted to change its culture so that the organization could respond more effectively and flexibly to the challenges presented by rapid changes in the banking industry's environment. After

An increasing number of organizations are using training programs to change managers' and employees' behavior and attitudes toward sexual discrimination and harassment. In Du Pont's training program, called "A Matter of Respect," male and female managers and employees work through a series of role plays that simulate work situations involving discrimination and harassment.

analyzing the organization's culture, executive vice president Donald G. Ogilvie and other top managers pinpointed areas that needed change, such as people's attitudes, values, and behavior regarding risky new ideas and collaboration. After developing their vision of the new organization culture, top managers invited employee participation in the implementation, and they also arranged for all managers to receive training in the skills they needed to be effective in the new culture.[34]

ORGANIZATIONAL DEVELOPMENT

The three-stage change process discussed earlier is based on the recognition that people's skills, knowledge, values, attitudes, or behaviors must be unfrozen, moved, refrozen, and institutionalized if a change made in any area is ultimately to result in more-effective personal and organizational performance. Although achieving large-scale, comprehensive change in people and culture is generally not easy, it is especially critical when the health and effectiveness of the entire organization are at stake. Faced with the need for such change, some top managers turn to a specialized approach known as organizational development.

The Nature of Organizational Development

organizational development (OD) A long-term, organization-wide planned change effort that is managed from the top and that aims to improve organization effectiveness and health by using behavioral science techniques to intervene in organizational processes

change agents Specialists with the behavioral science skills to guide organizational change

Organizational development (OD) is a long-term, planned change effort that is organization-wide, managed from the top, and aims to improve organization effectiveness and health by using behavioral science techniques to deliberately intervene in organizational processes. However, OD is not a narrowly focused, short-term, or one-shot attempt at immediate change. Short-term change may occur as a result of OD, but the approach is based on a series of actions planned as part of a broader long-term change process designed to affect most or all of the organization. For such change to be effective, top managers must acknowledge the need for change and be committed to working through internal or external experts known as **change agents,** or *change facilitators,* who have the behavioral science skills to intervene in the organization's processes and guide the change process. To bring about change that will enhance organization effectiveness and health, change agents must be aware of environmental influences and must also be able to analyze and improve the working relationships among organization members.[35]

Organizations such as General Motors, Polaroid, and the 82nd Airborne Division of the U.S. Army have used OD to solve a variety of problems, as have organizations in Canada, Sweden, the Philippines, Holland, Japan, and other countries. One situation in which OD can be helpful is when frequent or profound environmental changes demand that organizations (and their managers and employees) change to become more adaptable and innovative. A second situation in which OD may be used is when the organization is stagnating or in decline and managers fail to anticipate entropy (the natural tendency of organizations, as systems, to decay) or when managers cannot agree on how to solve organizational problems, make faulty decisions, implement decisions poorly, or experience a major crisis that threatens the organization's existence. OD can help management revitalize the organization by combating the problems of stag-

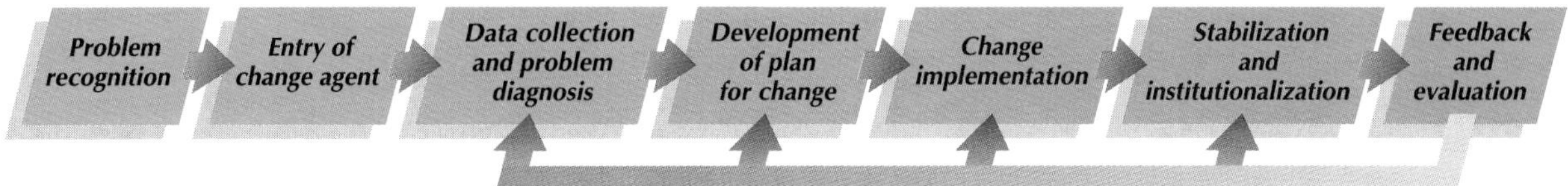

EXHIBIT 11.5

The Organizational Development Process

Organizational development follows a seven-step process: problem recognition, entry of change agent, data collection and problem diagnosis, development of the plan for change, change implementation, stabilization and institutionalization, and feedback and evaluation. The final step of feedback and evaluation can help organizations improve the problem diagnosis, the plan for change, its implementation, or the stabilization and the institutionalization of change.

nation and decline, which include lower morale, higher turnover, increased interpersonal conflict, and personal stress. A third situation in which OD may be helpful is when the organization must work closely with another organization, such as in a joint venture, merger, or acquisition. Here, OD can help overcome the resulting anxiety, conflict, and stress so that resistance to the interorganizational change is reduced.[36]

Steps in the OD Process

As a specialized process of organizational change, OD is based on Kurt Lewin's three-stage change process, but it also incorporates the use of the change agent, data collection and diagnosis, and formal feedback and evaluation of the results. The OD process consists of seven steps (see Exhibit 11.5):[37]

- *Step 1: Problem recognition.* To start, top managers must recognize that the organization has a problem and that change can solve the problem. Once they are willing to take action that will lead to change, the unfreezing process begins.[38]
- *Step 2: Entry of change agent.* A trained change agent from inside or outside the organization is asked to help the organization solve the problem.[39]
- *Step 3: Data collection and problem diagnosis.* Working with organization members, the change agent reviews organization documents and uses interviews, questionnaires, and observations to collect data about the organization and its problems. Next, the change agent and selected managers examine the data and develop a preliminary diagnosis of the cause, the nature, and the extent of the problem. The change agent may also ask some managers to provide feedback on this preliminary diagnosis.[40]
- *Step 4: Development of the plan for change.* The change agent works with key managers to establish goals for the planned change, to generate and evaluate alternative courses of action, and to select the most appropriate alternative.[41]
- *Step 5: Change implementation.* The selected action is implemented and change occurs. This step corresponds to the moving stage in Lewin's change

process, and it can involve changes in structure, people, culture, or other areas. Techniques for implementing change can take a variety of forms; the most common techniques are discussed in the following section.[42]

- *Step 6: Stabilization and institutionalization.* The change resulting from the intervention is refrozen and then perpetuated by making it part of the organization's daily activities.[43]
- *Step 7: Feedback and evaluation.* Months or even years after the change has been institutionalized, the change agent again collects data, compares them to the data gathered when the diagnosis was originally made, and then evaluates the results. What emerges from this step can be used to improve any of the other steps in the change process. Although uncontrollable environmental forces may influence the outcome, the ultimate test is whether top managers believe that the organization's health and effectiveness have improved as a result of the OD change.[44]

OD Techniques

After diagnosing the organization's problems and setting goals for the change, change agents can use one or more OD techniques to implement the change. Some OD techniques focus on individuals, some on groups, and some on interpersonal and intergroup processes. There are six commonly used OD techniques:[45]

- *Survey feedback.* In this technique, the change agent distributes a questionnaire to organization members, asking about their attitudes, perceptions, and other areas under investigation. Once the survey responses have been tabulated, the change agent meets with managers and employees to provide feedback about the results. Organization members then work together to solve the problems uncovered by the survey.[46]
- *Training.* Change agents can use training (conducted individually or in small groups or large groups) to help employees and managers improve their technical, decision-making, planning, or interpersonal skills, and they can also use it to help participants understand the process of change. Examples include sensitivity training workshops (known as *T-groups*) and educational seminars. For example, more than half of the Mercedes-Benz dealerships in the United Kingdom are family owned and operated. Because the owners' children feel the dual pressures of preparing to run the business and simultaneously managing family relationships, Mercedes-Benz offers a seminar program that covers not only management and business subjects but goes beyond to examine topics such as sibling rivalry and parental relations.[47]
- *Coaching and counseling.* Conducted on an individual level, coaching and counseling is designed to help selected organization members adjust to changes. When key individuals are unaware of how their job performance relates to organizational performance, coaching and counseling can help them understand their roles and develop new, more effective behavior patterns.[48]
- *Team building.* Also known as *group development,* this technique focuses on working relationships in groups, on decision-making skills, or on work activities, and it is used to help work groups improve communication, collaboration, and effectiveness. Change agents can use team building with manager-subordinate groups, functional teams, project teams, or peer groups. For

example, when International Harvester was on the brink of bankruptcy, one of the ways it cut costs was by selling part of the business, dramatically downsizing the remaining operations, and renaming itself Navistar International. Management used team building to help the survivors reestablish feelings of harmony and teamwork and to renew organizational vitality.[49]

- *Third-party intervention.* When conflict between individuals or groups threatens performance, a change agent can intervene as a neutral third party and help make peace. Whether used with small or large groups, third-party interventions generally start with a frank discussion of each side's point of view and then move on to negotiate the points of difference until the conflict has been resolved.[50]
- *Process consultation.* In process consultation, the change agent observes the dynamics and quality of interaction among organization members and provides feedback about the effectiveness of processes such as decision making, communication, and leadership. Used with small and large groups, process consultation serves managers and employees as feedback for understanding group dynamics and for changing their behavior so that group processes operate more smoothly.[51]

Change agents often use more than one technique to accomplish large-scale organizational change. For example, changes at the Communications and Electrical Division of the City of San Diego involved several OD techniques. The unit's top managers asked OD specialists from the city's OD and Training Section to find ways of boosting productivity, increasing job satisfaction, and maintaining or improving customer satisfaction. The change agents worked with both employees and managers on team-building exercises, individual counseling, process consultation, and skills training. Months later, the change agents collected additional data, compared the results with the situation prior to the intervention, and discovered (1) that productivity and job satisfaction had both improved and (2) that customer satisfaction had not deteriorated.[52]

Benefits and Limitations of Organizational Development

Organizational development can be a useful tool when organizations want to improve working relationships by strengthening collaboration, reducing conflict, improving communication, and improving decision-making processes. It can also help organizations make changes that result in more viable, flexible structures that are better suited to their missions, strategies, and environment. The chance for success is highest when OD is applied in organizations whose top managers are committed to and willing to be involved in such a systematic change, have realistic expectations for long-term results, and value the personal and professional satisfaction of their employees and managers.[53]

Organizational development does have several limitations. First, it may not be universally applicable. Studies suggest that change agents must consider the organizational and national culture if OD is to have any chance of success. When an OD intervention attempts a change that goes against the grain of cultural values, attitudes, and beliefs of organization members, the managers involved may find it difficult to achieve any long-lasting effect. Second, given the variety and scope of OD techniques, the complexity of the problems they are used to resolve, the influence of environmental forces, and the sometimes lengthy period between the intervention and the evidence of permanent and

SOCIAL RESPONSIBILITY AND ETHICS

Taking Sides: Change Agents Face Five Dilemmas

As a management-directed phenomenon, planned organizational change is geared toward improving effectiveness and efficiency. However, without the acceptance and support of organization members, change simply cannot endure. Thus, to achieve long-lasting results, change agents have to become involved with managers and with employees. At the same time, change agents have their own personal needs (such as professional status) that are satisfied through their work. In such complex situations, they may feel the pull of conflicting needs and desires, and the change process can potentially be inappropriately or unethically planned and implemented. Change agents generally face five types of ethical dilemmas:

1. *Misrepresentation and collusion.* For personal reasons, a manager may misrepresent the true nature of the need for (or the goal of) change, inducing change agents to undertake programs that are not in the organization's best interest. Also, the change agent or the manager may try to exclude other parties, such as other change agents or other members of management, and this exclusion can hurt the change process. Moreover, if change agents identify too strongly with organization members, they can lose their objectivity and consciously or unconsciously collude (conspire) to obstruct or distort needed changes.
2. *Misuse of data.* Change agents collect a great deal of data before and after the change, and ethical dilemmas surround its collection and use. Ordinarily, when participants voluntarily agree to provide information, they rely on promises of anonymity and confidentiality. Mandatory participation or the release of information in order to punish organization members can hurt the participants and damage the change process. If data are distorted or omitted by either the change agent or the organization members directly involved in the change, this can also have a negative impact on the eventual success of the change.
3. *Manipulation and coercion.* Another dilemma

positive change, it is difficult to derive every expected benefit. And third, OD presumes that top managers want to encourage an atmosphere of open communication, trust, and participation; to the extent that these elements are not valued, OD change is likely to have limited success.[54]

MANAGING CREATIVITY AND INNOVATION

Creativity and innovation are special breeds of planned change that organizations actively seek to promote. Creativity, the process of developing a novel idea or a new way of approaching an old idea, is the spark for innovation, the transformation of creative ideas into products or processes that fulfill customer needs. Organizations can approach innovation from two main perspectives. **Product-oriented innovation** involves developing goods and services that incorporate entirely new and novel breakthrough advances, and **process-oriented innovation** involves making improvements to existing products and production or other organizational processes. For instance, 3M's breakthrough Post-it note pads are a product-oriented innovation, and the company's overhaul of the industrial-tape manufacturing process (rearranging equipment and changing key activities) is a process-oriented innovation. 3M devotes 50 to 60 percent of its $890 million research-and-development budget to product-oriented innovation, between 20 and 30 percent to process-oriented innovation, and roughly 15 percent to leading-edge technological research designed to find creative ideas that will form the basis for innovations far in the future. As 3M knows, both types of innovation are needed if organizations are to succeed in today's increasingly complex, changeable environment.[55]

product-oriented innovation The development of goods and services that incorporate novel breakthrough advances

process-oriented innovation Incremental improvements to existing products and production or other organizational processes arises when a proposed change forces organization members to alter their personal values or needs involuntarily. Participants who are required to participate in training sessions tend to feel manipulated and coerced, thus threatening the management-employee relationship as well as the participants' right to self-respect and dignity.

4. *Value and goal conflict.* Whose values and goals guide the change effort? Whose needs are really being met by the proposed change? If managers and change agents are not clear about or do not agree on the values and goals, the change may be inappropriately designed, targeted, or implemented.
5. *Technical deficiencies.* On occasion, change agents may be unqualified to diagnose certain types of organizational problems, may have little experience with the specific technique needed to effect the change, or may be unable to select the appropriate targets for change. If the change agent does not disclose and prepare to overcome these deficiencies, the change process is destined to be, at best, ineffectual. Like a doctor not qualified or experienced in diagnosing or treating a patient's symptoms, the change agent must also know when to call for assistance.

Perhaps the most wrenching ethical dilemma is also the most basic. Even the most well-meaning change, a change carefully designed and appropriately implemented to increase productivity, can hurt those whose jobs are lost or profoundly altered. What is the change agent's responsibility to organization members, to management, and to himself or herself? For everyone involved, there are no easy answers, and many questions, throughout the organizational change process.

What's Your Opinion?

1. Should change agents consider how the results of their activities will affect all organizational stakeholders rather than just managers, employees, and themselves? Why or why not?
2. How would organization members be likely to respond to frequent and differing OD interventions? What are the implications for managers?

The Importance of Creativity and Innovation

Although a wide variety of forces can affect organizational change, four are exerting an increasingly powerful influence in today's economy: the intensified pressure of competition, the internationalization of the marketplace, the accelerated pace of technological advancement, and the rapid change in consumer values and life-styles. Jolted by the combined impact of these and other environmental forces, more managers are taking a closer look at how creativity and innovation can help their organizations adapt to the environment, influence the environment, or shift domains, both today and tomorrow. In addition to helping organizations respond to the environment, the opportunity to pursue creative and innovative changes can provide individual and group challenges that motivate employees and managers alike to higher performance.

Consider how creativity and innovation affected the motivation and performance of Corning scientist and manager David Morse. He was aware that the company had long sought a nonstick version of its Visions glass cookware line, so he tinkered with glass formulas, developed a new one he was convinced could be bonded to nonstick materials, and tirelessly pursued top management approval. As a result of Morse's creativity and motivation, the idea formed the basis of an innovative line of Visions products that has positioned Corning to grab a big piece of the lucrative U.S. market for nonstick cookware.[56]

Institutionalizing Creativity and Innovation

Creativity and innovation often begin spontaneously, sparked by a particular organizational problem or an insight into an organizational opportunity. Such changes may be planned and implemented through informal, episodic activities. However, to consistently contribute to organizational performance, creativity and innovation must be systematized and incorporated into the organization's daily activities. A variety of factors are involved, but three key elements are particularly crucial for institutionalizing creativity and innovation: planning, organizational culture, and organization structure.[57]

The Role of Planning

The road to consistent creativity and innovation starts with planning. Managers draw on the organization's mission and strategic goals to set the targets and the agenda that will guide creative and innovative change. By using situation analysis, they examine the environment for signs of threats and opportunities and for clues about organizational strengths and weaknesses that can potentially be overcome or exploited through the use of creative and innovative change. Then they craft their strategies around the distinctive competencies and resources needed to initiate and sustain creativity and innovation. For example, Applied Immune Sciences (AIS) founder and CEO Thomas B. Okarma established the firm's mission as finding new therapeutic approaches to battling cancer and AIDS. When the company was just starting out, he gave twice-weekly lectures to his scientists on applied medical research to focus their attention on the innovative yet feasible aspects of their research (rather than on exciting but unrelated or impractical breakthroughs). Today the researchers who attended those lectures are in management positions, guiding other AIS scientists as they pursue research projects with promising clinical applications.[58]

Organizational plans must be aggressive, realistic, and flexible to pave the way for the ultimate innovation, and yet they must allow for the unforeseen problems that often crop up during the creative and innovative process. After all, creativity involves something that has never before been produced or perhaps even defined; thus, no plan can anticipate every contingency. Moreover, managers need to understand the constraints that apply to their plans for creative and innovative change, and they need to use strategic control to check on interim results, keeping the process on target to achieve the stated goals.[59]

A special set of tools are often used to help systematize the planning process for creativity and innovation. In addition to brainstorming, organizations have successfully applied synectics, storyboarding, and matrix analysis, among other techniques, to generate and evaluate ideas that may subsequently be considered appropriate for implementation.

synectics A technique for stimulating creativity and innovation in which participants consider a broadly worded problem, generate ideas using analogies and metaphors, and agree on a single, radically new solution

storyboarding A technique that stimulates creativity and innovation by asking participants to focus on a well-defined problem, jot down their ideas, and then combine and reorder the ideas to uncover promising solutions

matrix analysis A technique to stimulate creativity and innovation in which managers use a two- or three-dimensional matrix to identify new-product ideas

- **Synectics** is a group technique (developed by William J. Gordon of Arthur D. Little, a management and consulting firm) in which participants are presented with a broadly worded problem, discuss the problem from a variety of perspectives, generate ideas using analogies and metaphors, and then settle on a single, radically new approach.[60]
- **Storyboarding** is a group technique (originated by Walt Disney) that stimulates creative thinking by asking participants (1) to focus on a well-defined problem, (2) to quickly write their ideas on cards, and (3) to pin the cards on the wall according to various categories. By shifting the cards between categories, group members can see relationships forming, and they are ultimately able to select the most promising ideas arranged in the most appropriate order.[61]
- **Matrix analysis** is an individual or group activity that involves identifying the

	Markets		
Packaging Products	**Food**	**Chemicals**	**Health Care**
Adhesives	**Reclosable cereal boxes**	(*a*)	(*d*)
Laminating	**Water-resistant labels for beverage containers**	(*b*)	(*e*)
Foam	**Insulating packages for fresh fish**	(*c*)	(*f*)

EXHIBIT 11.6

Matrix Analysis for Creativity and Innovation

This matrix analysis could be used to help an organization innovate by considering new packaging products for specific markets. The ideas in the food column are possible new products based on adhesives, laminating, and foam packaging. Managers would fill in the cells *(a)* through *(f)* with ideas for packaging products designed for chemicals and health-care applications.

various market needs, technologies, or product benefits and then using them to head the columns and rows in a two- or three-dimensional matrix. This focuses the search for innovative products and processes on the intersections that form each cell in the matrix. For example, a packaging manufacturer seeking innovations to offer customers might construct a market-product matrix (see Exhibit 11.6) and fill in the cells with one or more ideas for applying packaging to those markets.[62]

These are only three of the many techniques managers can use to guide and focus the creativity and innovation planning process. However, institutionalizing these and other activities can be difficult if the organizational culture does not welcome creative and innovative change.

The Role of Organizational Culture

Innovation and creativity can be discouraged, suppressed, or even extinguished by a hostile organizational culture; however, according to Harvard professor Rosabeth Moss Kanter, a "culture of pride" contributes significantly to institutionalizing these specialized types of change. When top managers take pride in their organization members' creativity and innovations, they reinforce higher performance, leading to an upward cycle of performance–pride–performance. In fact, when creativity and innovation are *expected* from employees and managers, this expectation permeates the culture and creates a climate supercharged for such changes. For example, 3M insists that 25 percent of its sales come from products that were introduced in the past five years; Rubbermaid goes further, seeking 30 percent of its sales from such products. Employees and managers of both organizations consistently strive to meet or exceed these expectations by unleashing their creativity to produce marketable innovations that will bring in sales dollars.[63]

An important aspect of aggressively seeking creativity and innovation is tolerating failure. Every creative and innovative change carries with it the possibility of failure, so the organizational culture must not only encourage managers and employees to try something new but also encourage them to learn from their mistakes. For instance, Johnson & Johnson's culture is legendary for its tolerance of failure, which starts at the top. Current chairman Ralph S. Larsen is following in the tradition of former chairman General Robert Wood Johnson, who 40 years ago told his people, "If you are making mistakes, that means you are making decisions and taking risks. And we won't grow unless you take risks." Even standardization-oriented McDonald's has loosened up its formerly rigid culture: CEO Michael R. Quinlan is giving employees and store operators more freedom to try innovative new store formats and menu items. However, his new cultural orientation avoids the all-too-common problem of sacrificing long-term gains for short-term results: Quinlan is encouraging changes that will boost profits today but at the same time, he's planning for the innovations that will fuel McDonald's sales and profits several years in the future.[64]

The Role of Organization Structure

Managers can use organization structure to institutionalize creativity and innovation in a number of ways. One way is to use work specialization, formalization, and delegation to empower managers and employees to be creative and innovative. People are generally more creative and innovative when they perform jobs that are broadly (rather than narrowly) defined, when they use a range of skills to accomplish a variety of tasks, when they have fewer formal rules to govern their work, and when they are evaluated on results (rather than on methods). In such an environment, managers and employees alike are stimulated (and have the knowledge and the tools) to step out of their routines to solve everyday problems more creatively and innovatively. Further, when people are delegated the responsibility and authority for achieving goals, they often make innovative changes that allow them to work more efficiently or to accomplish their goals more effectively.[65]

For example, United Electric Controls, based in Watertown, Massachusetts, makes industrial temperature and pressure controls. The family-owned firm turned red ink into profits by allowing its employees more leeway in completing their work and by sharing more information on goals and results. Invited to be creative when meeting goals, employees responded with a flood of innovations. One employee invented a simple method of ensuring that the equipment he assembled was 100 percent leakproof, an important quality concern. He worked with United Electric's model shop to build a modified aquarium so that he could plunge completed assemblies into the water and correct any problems immediately. The rising tide of seemingly small, daily innovations such as this have helped the firm improve its on-time delivery record, cut costs, and increase sales and profits.[66]

Managers sometimes set up a separate unit to isolate certain creative and innovative activities from other organizational units. The purpose is to allow the isolated unit to concentrate on developing creative ideas into product innovations without the distractions of other goals, tasks, or rules. However, people working on innovations usually get more ideas (and informal feedback on their ideas) by being around and involved with people outside their own unit. Raytheon, for example, has a separate New Products Center that services several

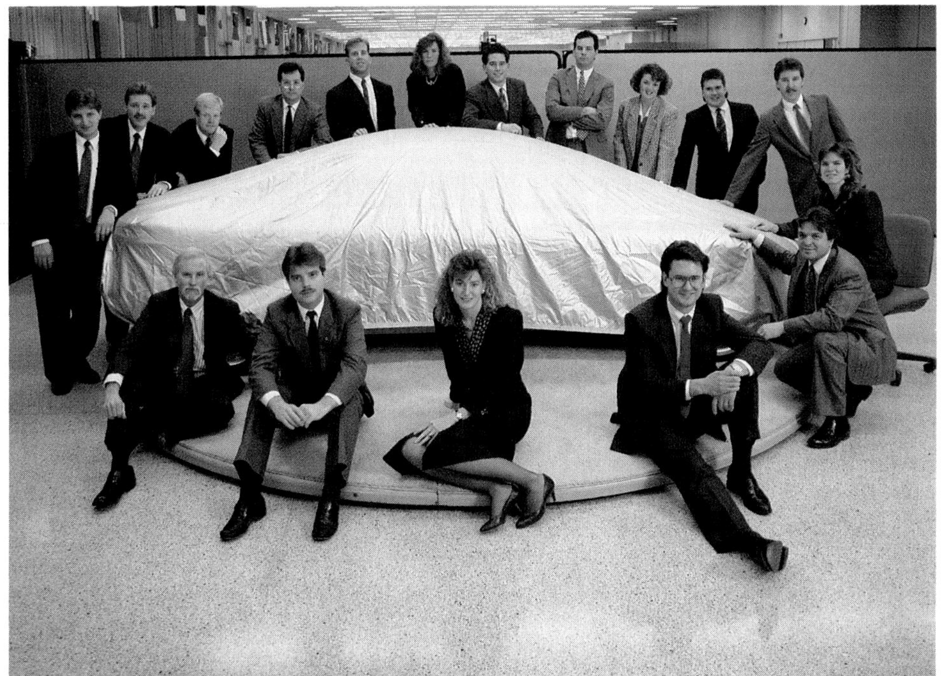

Rather than develop the 1995 Mustang model using its conventional automotive design and production process, Ford assigned this task to a cross-functional team of talented young designers, engineers, and planners. To spur innovation, speed communication, cut costs, and reduce confusion, the group was brought together in a single, separate location.

divisions, but the technical people who develop the new products circulate freely among other Raytheon units and talk to customers and suppliers in their attempts to generate ideas. Similarly, Hallmark Cards has set aside a special facility, separate from but adjacent to its corporate headquarters, called the Innovation Center. Here, a diverse group of researchers, designers, artists, and other specialists share their ideas and help one another devise, evaluate, and ultimately produce innovations. Some people are permanently assigned there; others rotate in from other units and leave after a few months, primed to make creative and innovative contributions to their own units.[67]

An increasingly popular structural method for institutionalizing creativity and innovation involves the use of interdisciplinary teams composed of people from marketing, operations, R&D, and other functional areas. The team approach can be used to encourage collaborative creativity and innovation throughout the organization, not just in designated units. Moreover, because team members represent a variety of functions and are versed in a range of skills, they can help organizations anticipate and solve the problems that often accompany the development and launch of a new product or process. For instance, at General Motors, Kenneth R. Baker has put together a 200-member team of managers and employees from engineering, marketing, design, production, and other areas to achieve GM's goal of developing and producing the Impact, the country's first mass-market electric car. Like GM's Saturn project, the Impact is a team effort that seeks to cut the time and costs for new-product development by having people from many functions work together throughout the process (instead of moving the product sequentially through the various functions). And like the Saturn project, the Impact team approach is designed to harness team members' creativity and innovation to produce a novel yet practical car that will capture the public's imagination.[68]

SUMMARY

Change refers to any alteration of the organization's existing situation. Creativity, a specialized type of change, is the process by which novel ideas are generated. A closely related type of change is innovation, the transformation of creative ideas into goods or services that meet customer needs or solve customer problems. A variety of forces affect organizational change. In the general environment, politicolegal, economic, technological, sociocultural, and international forces often influence change less directly than the forces in the task environment, which include customers, competitors, suppliers, labor supply, regulators, and partners. In the internal environment, forces for change can come from owners and shareholders, board of directors, employees, organizational culture, strategy, management decisions, and organizational activities.

Lewin's organizational change process consists of three stages. In the unfreezing stage, organization members are made aware of the need for change and are motivated to accept the change by thawing their behavior, values, and attitudes in anticipation. In the moving stage, new patterns of behavior, new values, new knowledge, and new attitudes are introduced to change organizational performance. In the refreezing stage, management reinforces and supports the new patterns so that the change is stabilized and institutionalized at the desired level.

The most common reasons that organization members resist change include self-interest, lack of understanding and trust, uncertainty, and differing perceptions. Force-field analysis is a technique for analyzing the overall impact of the driving forces that support change and the restraining forces that oppose change. Change is easiest when the driving forces outweigh the restraining forces. When the restraining forces outweigh the driving forces, managers must reduce the restraining forces, increase the driving forces, or do both in order to implement change. Managers use six methods to overcome resistance: (1) education and communication, (2) participation, (3) facilitation and support, (4) negotiation, (5) manipulation and co-optation, and (6) coercion.

Changes are generally made in one or more of four broad areas: strategy, structure, technology, and people and culture. Strategic change involves changes in mission; strategic goals; corporate-level, business-level, and functional-level strategy; and overall strategy. Structural change involves changes in task design, delegation, centralization, line and staff positions, horizontal coordination, departmentalization, and organization design. Technological change involves changes in equipment, skills, processes, and activity sequencing. Changes in people and culture involve changing the skills, knowledge, values, attitudes, or behavior of organization members.

Organizational development (OD) is a long-term, planned change effort that is organization-wide, is managed from the top, and aims to improve organization effectiveness and health by using behavioral science techniques to deliberately intervene in organizational processes. The seven steps in the OD process are (1) problem recognition, (2) entry of change agent, (3) data collection and problem diagnosis, (4) development of the plan for change, (5) change implementation, (6) stabilization and institutionalization, and (7) feedback and evaluation.

To institutionalize creativity and innovation in support of organizational performance, managers can use a variety of elements, but planning, organizational culture, and organization structure are among the most important. Planning helps managers set goals and plans to guide creative and innovative change, establish constraints, and systematize idea generation and evaluation using synectics, storyboarding, matrix analysis, and other techniques. A supportive organizational culture encourages creativity and innovation, tolerates failure, and values long-term and short-term results. Managers can use organization structure to institutionalize creativity and innovation through broadly defined jobs, low formalization, and increased delegation of responsibility and authority. In addition, some organizations set up separate units for people working on creative and innovative projects so that they can focus on their work, and many organizations encourage their new-product development people to circulate inside and outside the organization in search of creative ideas. Increasingly, managers are using interdisciplinary teams to harness the creativity and innovation in people throughout the organization.

MEETING A MANAGEMENT CHALLENGE AT

DISNEY

In the decades following Walt Disney's death, the leaders of the Magic Kingdom shunned innovation and shut themselves away from their audience. A lethargic shadow of the company that had produced *Fantasia, Snow White,* and a string of other brilliant animated films, Disney was under-licensing its cartoon characters, underutilizing its filmmaking capabilities, and underpricing its theme parks (in other words, considering consumer demand, it could've been charging a good deal more).

After analyzing the situation, Michael Eisner devised a plan that would restore the openness to change that had brought Disney such great success. Rather than attempt to change Disney's corporate culture, which centered on a strong creative leader, he stepped right into Walt's shoes. This approach was risky, but it was exactly what Disney needed. Eisner became not a reincarnation of Walt, but a living, walking embodiment of all that Walt stood for. He set a creative example for his staff, suggesting ideas for Disney ad copy, new health-food restaurants, and the next Disney comedy. He even appeared on a weekly TV show the company launched.

Eisner used a number of tactics to encourage, even induce, creativity in others. To kick off planning for the $2 billion Euro Disneyland, he met with 12 of the world's most respected architects in a wildly creative session, which became so heated that two architects almost came to blows. "I'll use meetings, company anniversaries, anything to create some kind of catalyst to get us all going," he said.

Instilling the creative spirit throughout the Disney organization became one of Eisner's top priorities. As part of their management training, employees develop innovative ideas and practice presenting them to top management. He also established an "I Have an Idea" program to reward employees who submit original creative ideas (with checks of up to $10,000).

Eisner guided the revival of Disney's fortunes by communicating clear strategic goals to his staff, including an ambitious growth plan. Although Disney World at Orlando was already on its way to becoming what it is today—the most popular vacation destination in the United States—one business niche had been neglected: hotels. Eisner ordered an ambitious $1 billion hotel expansion plan. Disney has doubled its room count to over 20,000, becoming a midsize hotel group on a par with the Ritz Carlton chain.

Michael Eisner, CEO, and Roy Disney, vice-chairman of the board, Walt Disney Company

Another Eisner priority was revitalizing Disney's movie business, the creative fount for its theme parks, its licensing activities, and its retail stores. By maintaining tight budgets, hiring talented but inexpensive actors, and working with adventurous scripts, Eisner and his team transformed Walt Disney Studios from a break-even operation to a dominant force in U.S. moviemaking. Disney scored with such hits as *The Dead Poets Society, Dick Tracy, Good Morning, Vietnam, The Little Mermaid, Pretty Woman, Ruthless People, Splash, Beauty and the Beast,* and *Who Framed Roger Rabbit?*

Michael Eisner has proven that creativity and innovation pay. From 1984 to 1990, Disney's sales increased from under $1.7 billion to more than $5.8 billion. With theme parks in Japan and France, comic books in 12 languages, a chain of 100 Disney retail outlets in the United States and England, two book-publishing groups, two film companies, and a record label—Eisner has revitalized Disney and transformed the Magic Kingdom into an entertainment empire.

***You're the Manager*:** Michael Eisner has hailed the 1990s as the Disney Decade, a period of vigorous growth for the Disney operations around the globe. Eisner fully appreciates that success will require changes even greater than those that produced the dramatic turnaround of the 1980s. Eisner likes to surround himself with brash, energetic people who can translate his ideas into effective strategies. He's hired you as his troubleshooter.

Ranking Questions

1. On an inspection tour of Euro Disneyland, which opened outside Paris in 1992, Eisner begins to feel uneasy. Some sections of Euro Disneyland feel like uninspired copies of Disney's U.S. parks. Eisner asks you to step in and decide what to do. Rank the following possible courses of action.
   a. Use matrix analysis to determine the basic features that the theme park should contain.
   b. There is no sense in going ahead with the project if Eisner doesn't feel comfortable with it. Tear up whatever has been constructed so far and have the French team start over again.
   c. The members of the French Imagineering team (Imagineers are Disney's in-house designers) need someone to tell them what to do. Bring over a powerful U.S. manager who is highly experienced in theme park operations to lead the team.
   d. Assemble a team of artists, engineers, animators, and other specialists to examine Euro Disneyland and several competitive parks now under construction. Ask the team to propose ways to inject some creative sparks into the existing plan.
2. Eisner believes that the essence of a guest's experience at Disney's theme parks is joy and happiness. His employees are trained to extend themselves in an effort to make visitors feel welcome. But Eisner worries that as Disney World grows during the Disney Decade, its guests will find the Disney experience increasingly impersonal. He jots down a series of ideas and asks you to rank them for his further consideration.
   a. Add additional periodic training sessions that would help employees rededicate themselves to customer service.
   b. Develop new rides that are more exciting.
   c. Divide the employees into smaller work groups and give these groups more autonomy to initiate customer-relations efforts.
   d. Cut back on funding for expansion.

Multiple-Choice Questions

3. Disney's Touchstone Pictures has been a tremendous success, turning out movies with adult themes (such as *The Color of Money* and *Ruthless People*) to supplement such traditional Disney fare as *The Little Mermaid.* Disney's newly formed book-publishing division has been less successful. Although Disney has produced a series of hits for children, most of the division's adult titles have been panned by critics as tame and boring. After interviewing several managers in the book division, you realize that they have not yet shaken off the ghost of Walt Disney. In an effort to emulate Walt's creativity, they have reduced it to a simplistic formula. You tell them that being creative "by the numbers" is a contradiction. Cultural change is in order. What should you do?
   a. Assign an executive from Touchstone to write a manual detailing how Touchstone selects a picture for the adult market. Make this required reading for all book division management.
   b. Encourage those book division employees who are bucking the old culture and have ideas for a better one.
   c. The book division needs a shake-up; change can help unfreeze management behavior. Rotate the managers into new positions, to give each a fresh perspective.
   d. Arrange coaching and counseling for individual managers and then offer a team-building program that helps the managers work together to learn to try new ideas.
4. Eisner wants to capitalize on Disney food-service expertise by opening a new chain of fast-food restaurants called Mickey's Kitchen. The menu would feature low-fat, low-salt, low-cholesterol meals and reflects Disney's commitment to healthful eating. However, some executives in Disney's consumer products division feel that Eisner's decision is a mistake. They point to the fierce competition that characterizes the United States' $65-billion-a-year fast-food restaurant industry. This is not the time, they argue, to enter the fray with an unproven concept. The consumer products division should concentrate on expanding its line of Disney Stores, an area in which Disney faces no competitors. Eisner is convinced that Mickey's Kitchen will be successful, but only if the consumer products division stands behind it. He asks you to devise a plan to gain their support without jeopardizing the other activities of the division. Which of the following should you choose?

a. Coercion is the best approach. Explain to the consumer products executives that the real issue is whether they support the company's chairman and CEO. If they don't, they have no place in the company.
b. Invite the resisters to participate in designing and implementing plans for opening Mickey's Kitchens in Disney Stores. Ask them to analyze the strengths and weaknesses and offer ideas for improvement.
c. Appoint an executive who strongly opposes Mickey's Kitchen to its advisory board. Eisner will appear to humor the directives of the advisory board while keeping his own counsel.
d. Negotiate with the resisters. Tell them that you will offer more funding for Disney Stores if they agree to support Mickey's Kitchens.

Analysis Questions

5. How important is Michael Eisner's role in the creative process? Would the reenergized Disney still be as effective with a different CEO?
6. What are the internal and external forces for change that rendered the old Disney a moribund creative force?
7. How did Eisner's changes to company strategy necessitate new ways of managing people?

Special Project

Disney's board of directors has suggested a change of strategy for Touchstone Pictures. Rather than continuing to focus on action, adventure, and romantic comedy films, the board wants to enter the increasingly popular horror genre, represented by such films as *The People under the Stairs* and *Children of the Corn.*

You immediately realize that such a shift is likely to meet tremendous resistance both inside Touchstone and throughout the Disney corporation. Using force-field analysis, identify and diagram the driving and restraining forces that might come to play in a situation like this. [69]

KEY TERMS

change (336)
change agents (350)
creativity (336)
force-field analysis (343)
innovation (336)
matrix analysis (356)
organizational development (OD) (350)
planned change (338)
process-oriented innovation (354)
product-oriented innovation (354)
reactive change (338)
storyboarding (356)
synectics (356)

QUESTIONS

For Review

1. What internal and external forces affect organizational change?
2. What are the most common reasons that people resist change?
3. How can managers use force-field analysis to understand organizational change?
4. What are the four areas of planned change that managers can implement?
5. How can managers use planning to institutionalize creativity and innovation?

For Analysis

1. How can managers use interdisciplinary teams to overcome resistance to change?
2. Why do changes resulting from organizational development occur slowly and over a long period?
3. Can managers use process-oriented innovation in such nonproduction areas as accounting?
4. Must large-scale organizational change always be planned? If not, can reactive change be accomplished using OD techniques?
5. How does Lewin's three-stage change process apply to creative and innovative changes?

For Application

1. How can John Sculley of Apple Computers use force-field analysis to understand the impact of the forces that might support and oppose an organizational

change such as creating a separate organizational unit to develop a pocket-sized computer?
2. If Sculley encountered resistance from Apple employees and managers who had differing perceptions about the value of the change, what methods might he use to overcome this resistance?
3. What external and internal forces for change might Kellogg experience in the process of exporting sugared, ready-to-eat cereal products to China?
4. What changes in people and culture might the Internal Revenue Service make if its top managers wanted to create a new unit devoted to auditing the tax returns of self-employed people?
5. How might Toshiba use organization structure to institutionalize creativity and innovation if it wanted to develop a new large-screen television for the U.S. market?

KEEPING CURRENT IN MANAGEMENT

Find a recent article in which a manager discusses how an organization planned and implemented a major technological or strategic change. Examples would include a company that has adopted new technical processes or installed new production equipment to improve productivity and a university that has changed its strategy to target nontraditional student populations.

1. What external and internal forces contributed to the need for change in this organization? Was the change planned or reactive?
2. What were the driving forces for change? What were the restraining forces opposing change? What resistance to change did management encounter? How did management overcome this resistance?
3. How did the managers unfreeze, move, and refreeze behavior, values, and attitudes? Were any organizational development techniques applied to ease the change process? What was the effect of these techniques?

SHARPEN YOUR MANAGEMENT SKILLS

It's a fact of life: creativity and innovation usually imply some degree of risk. The result is a recurring management dilemma. On the one hand, if you don't apply some degree of control and oversight, you might have so many people taking so many risks that the company's very existence is jeopardized. On the other hand, you can be so risk-averse that you don't give your people enough leeway to experiment and innovate.

Consider the example set by Kendrick Melrose, CEO of Toro, a lawn equipment manufacturer based in Bloomington, Minnesota. A team of engineers at Toro once installed an innovative metal-molding technique on the company's riding mower production line. Unfortunately, the process didn't work well when the line was operating at full speed, and Toro lost a year's worth of sales as a result. The engineers thought they were history, but Melrose instead threw them a party in his office to celebrate the fact that they had taken the risk. Melrose probably earned the respect and loyalty of those engineers for life, and Toro certainly survived the setback, but what if the company *repeatedly* encountered setbacks of the same magnitude?

- *Decision:* Develop a "creative control" checklist that managers can use to make sure that their employees have plenty of creative freedom without taking risks so large that the company is put in jeopardy.
- *Communication:* Divide into groups of three to five students. Have each member of a group present his or her checklist to the rest of the group, then have the group discuss the merits of each idea and see whether the group can reach consensus on the best idea.

No Small Change at Woolworth

The company that invented the five-and-dime variety store evolved into an international specialty retailer to survive economic hard times—but hard times press again. Woolworth chairman and CEO Harold E. Sells knows from his days as vice president for store development and corporate development that creativity is required to design successful store formats. Sells hopes that changes in the planning process will pull Woolworth through its latest difficulties.

HISTORY

Frank W. Woolworth built a retail empire on small change. After a false start at Utica, New York, he moved his Great Five Cent Store to Lancaster, Pennsylvania, and was so successful selling toys, whistles, kitchenware, and other items costing five cents or less that he raised the price limit to a dime, moved headquarters to New York, bought up rival dime-store chains, and expanded into Canada in 1897. Twelve years later, Woolworth opened a chain of stores in England. The company added a 20-cent line of goods in 1932, abolished price limits in 1935, and stayed competitive after World War II by offering credit and by increasing merchandise selections. In the early 1960s, Woolworth began to diversify, opening a chain of Woolco discount stores to compete with stores such as K Mart and moving into specialty retailing by acquiring the family-shoe-store chain Kinney.

During the recession of the early 1980s, profits evaporated, and Woolworth undertook a major restructuring, shutting down all 372 Woolco stores in the United States, selling off Woolworth interests in England, and shifting corporate strategy away from general merchandising toward specialty stores. Some 1,400 Woolworth variety stores are still in business, but more than half the corporation's operating profits now come from 7,000 specialty stores selling shoes, clothes, athletic equipment, costume jewelry, discount drugs, and home furnishings. Forty-three percent of profit comes from international operations. Highly successful specialty stores like Foot Locker reversed the company's fortunes, and earnings grew at a rate of 15 percent a year for much of the decade. Unfortunately, the 1990s also opened with a recession; net income declined slightly to $317 million on sales of $9.8 billion, and in the first nine months of 1991 it plummeted 55 percent.

ENVIRONMENT

In the 1980s Woolworth sought flexibility by decentralizing store operations. The company adopted a mission of providing customers value through distinct but complementary retail stores, and it opted to do that by encouraging creativity in the development of such stores. As a former Kinney assistant manager in Fort Smith, Arkansas, Sells knows that store managers have keen insights into customer needs and organizational strengths, so he reaches to the lowest levels of the organization to find ideas for specialty stores. Managers encourage creative ideas from employees, and no one is penalized if these ideas fail.

Another change Sells made was to standardize space requirements for all stores so that unsuccessful units can be closed and switched to a new format in a few months, making failure less painful. However, even more creativity is needed to deal with current difficulties: the U.S. sneaker market is saturated, and Foot Locker's annual sales growth has fallen from 23 percent to 10 percent. Among other woes, Woolworth's 428-store Kids Mart is being battered by a children's clothing price war with Kids 'R' Us and with department stores.

GOALS AND CHALLENGES

In response to these environmental forces, Sells is expanding aggressively and relying on revenues from general merchandise operations to support specialty stores. Athletic footwear is just catching on in Europe, and Sells thinks he can increase Foot Locker's presence there from 61 to 1,000 stores by the year 2000. In the United States, Sells wants to put 5 to 10 stores in each of the nation's 1,400 shopping malls. He plans expansion for Foot Locker and may quadruple Champs Sports' 250-store sporting goods chain.

1. Which environmental forces have affected Woolworth and what changes has the company made in response?
2. How has Sells made planned changes in Woolworth's strategy, culture, and structure to encourage creativity?
3. What resistance might Woolworth face if the corporation converts one store format to another and then asks the manager of the original store to manage the new format? How could Woolworth overcome this resistance?
4. How might the manager of the Foot Locker chain use organization structure to institutionalize creativity in product displays at individual stores?

12 Organizing New Ventures

CHAPTER OUTLINE

After studying this chapter, you will be able to

1. Describe the economic and social contributions of new ventures
2. Outline the characteristics of entrepreneurs
3. Discuss the three new venture strategies and their implications for entrepreneurs
4. Describe the five factors to consider when initiating a new venture
5. Identify the criteria for entrepreneurial success
6. Explain how intrapreneurship fosters innovation in a large organization and outline the intrapreneurial process
7. Discuss two major issues faced by new ventures and small businesses

FACING A MANAGEMENT CHALLENGE AT

R.W. FROOKIES

Putting a Sweet Idea on the Shelf

Richard S. Worth has always done things his own way. Son of a well-to-do Boston family—and a former hippie—Worth's first managerial experience was on a blueberry farm in Canada. He tried to grow everything his family needed, and he worked at odd jobs to buy what he couldn't grow. His reason for moving to the farm was to get away from money, and he was certainly successful at that: the farm pulled in around $3,500 a year. However, the birth of his son changed his financial outlook, and to increase his income, he began selling the all-natural jams that he and his then-wife had been cooking up on the farm. The jam business was an entrepreneurial success, and sales eventually climbed to $3 million a year.

Then somebody convinced him that the jams needed to be produced on a larger scale with national distribution. Lacking the resources to step right into the big time, Worth sold his jam business to a company called Allied Old English. In addition to getting a job at Allied Old English, he received a cash payment and 3 percent of the jams' future revenues.

But with his products now under someone else's control, Worth grew restless and began casting around for another new-product idea. While he had been building the jam business, all-natural products had moved into the mainstream of the contemporary diet. Consumers had grown wary of additives, preservatives, and anything else that didn't sound like it belonged in food. Worth searched grocery stores and found quite a variety of all-natural products, from hot dogs to dog food. What he didn't find were all-natural cookies, and that sparked his next business idea. He would make cookies that contained no artificial ingredients and that were sweetened with fruit juice (hence the name Frookies), not processed sugar.

Confident that his success at selling all-natural jams would lead to success with all-natural cookies, Worth approached the management at Allied Old English with the idea. His new bosses weren't interested, so Worth found himself in the role of entrepreneur once again. After several thousand test batches in his kitchen, he had a mix that was healthier than regular cookies but that didn't taste "healthy," the perfect combination for consumers who wanted to give up chemicals without giving up taste.

But as every successful entrepreneur knows, it takes more than a great product. In the case of food, the name of the game is shelf space. Food companies introduce thousands of new products every year, but there are only so many shelves in the nation's grocery stores. If a store decides to sell a new brand, then another brand has to suffer—and giants like Keebler and RJR Nabisco weren't about to give up space without a fight. With manufacturers and distributors competing for shelf space, most grocery stores have begun charging slotting fees—which basically amount to rent payments for shelf space. But Worth already had a daunting list of things to pay for, from baking cookies to telling the world about Frookies.

Against odds that some experts considered insurmountable, how could this one-time blueberry farmer get Frookies out of his kitchen and into consumers' mouths? Should he give up on the idea of selling through supermarkets and settle for specialty stores, thereby avoiding slotting fees and the giants of the cookie business? Where could he get the money he would need to expand nationwide? And how should he manage the growing company if and when the product becomes a hit?[1]

CHAPTER OVERVIEW

Richard Worth's success with Frookies combines all the elements of entrepreneurial drama, from dreaming up a new idea to scraping up enough money to share the idea with the world to structuring the organization as the company grows. This chapter begins with a discussion of the impact that the organizational environment has on new-venture opportunities and the contribution that

A magazine story about the destruction of rain forests prompted California entrepreneur Lisa Conte to found Shaman Pharmaceuticals, a new venture devoted to the discovery and development of drugs derived from rain forest plants. Conte's training in pharmacology, biochemistry, and business enables her to effectively handle the technical and managerial aspects of the operation.

new ventures make to society. Next is an overview of personality characteristics common to founders of new ventures and the strategies used by successful new businesses. Following that is a description of how new ventures are formed and how they are organized for growth, including the criteria for success. After a look at how large organizations can continue to be innovative, the chapter closes with a discussion of several vital issues that new ventures and small businesses face.

MANAGEMENT AND NEW-VENTURE FORMATION

The dream of owning and operating a business is shared by almost half of all Americans and a growing number of people around the world. Motivated by the potential for profit, the independence of being their own bosses, and the ability to focus their efforts on what they truly enjoy, entrepreneurs continue to strike out on their own. Some entrepreneurs leave successful careers in other organizations to start or to buy small companies; others see entrepreneurship as an attractive option after experiencing a disruption in their lives, such as losing a job. In either case, people who choose to start their own ventures take many financial risks and work harder and longer than the average employee in an established organization, but they are driven by the potential rewards and the great personal satisfaction that comes with business ownership.[2]

Who are these successful business owners and what do they do? Alan Sugar began the London-based Amstrad as a wholesale distributor of stereo equipment for cars. By manufacturing electronic and computer equipment for European and U.S. markets, Sugar's business has grown to generate $1 billion in annual revenue.[3] Sandra Kurtzig established her software company, ASK, as a home-based venture that soon moved to larger quarters and now has annual sales over $186 million.[4] Stew Leonard decided to stop delivering the milk his cows produced and open a store to sell it. Having recently opened a second store—the first set records as one of the most profitable retail businesses in the country—Leonard's annual sales are in the neighborhood of $100 million.[5] But entrepreneurial success doesn't always mean multimillion-dollar ventures; thousands and thousands of entrepreneurs chase their dreams and reach their goals on much smaller scales. And new ventures aren't always started by individuals; many of the world's largest corporations launch entrepreneurial organizations to develop new products and reach new markets.

Entrepreneurship and New Ventures

new venture An organization still in its formative stages

A **new venture** is any organization still in its formative stages. A new restaurant, a new biotechnology research firm, and a new residential community are all examples of new-venture activities. Although many new ventures grow into very large organizations, during their formative stages they face unique risks and present special challenges to their owners.

entrepreneurship The process of launching a new venture, organizing the resources it requires, and assuming the risks it entails

Entrepreneurship is the process of initiating a new venture, organizing the resources it requires, and assuming the risks it entails.[6] Katha Diddel launched her new venture, called Twin Panda, when she began importing embroidered bed linens from China shortly after that country opened its borders to trade with the United States. By working closely with the managers and artisans in the Chinese factories, Diddel created a quality product with broad appeal in the

Industry	Number of Employees	Yearly Sales (in millions)
Manufacturers		
Furniture and fixtures	Fewer than 500	
Electronic computers	Fewer than 1,000	
Petroleum refining	Fewer than 1,500	
Wholesalers		
Automotive parts and supplies	Fewer than 500	
Dairy products	Fewer than 500	
Sporting goods	Fewer than 500	
Retailers		
Bakeries		Less than $13.5
Restaurants		Less than $10.0
Grocery stores		Less than $13.5
Services		
Beauty shops		Less than $3.5
Computer processing services		Less than $7.0
Passenger car rental and leasing		Less than $12.5

EXHIBIT 12.1

Small Business Administration Definitions in Selected Industries

Small Business Administration standards are used to determine an organization's eligibility for financial, procurement, management, and other assistance programs. Organizations are deemed small businesses based either on the number of employees (for some industries) or on the annual sales revenue (for other industries).

United States. Her timing was perfect, since the home-furnishings market was exploding, and her entrepreneurial venture flourished.[7] Diddel is an excellent example of an **entrepreneur,** someone who takes the initiative to start an entrepreneurial venture, organizes the resources it requires, and assumes the risks it entails.[8]

entrepreneur A person who takes initiative for a business project, organizes the resources it requires, and assumes the risks it entails

Since most entrepreneurial ventures start small, they fall into the category of **small business,** businesses that are independently owned and generally employ no more than a few hundred people. However, the U.S. government's official Small Business Administration (SBA) definition depends on the industry (see Exhibit 12.1).

small business An independently owned business, generally employing fewer than 500 people

Environmental Factors Affecting New Ventures

Changes in the external environment often cause problems for established businesses and create opportunities for the entrepreneur. For instance, the technological developments that made the personal computer possible launched such companies as Apple Computer and Microsoft while putting competitive pressure on existing manufacturers of larger computers, which personal computers have replaced in many cases. Economic changes benefited many new companies when a sharp rise in energy costs popularized wood-burning stoves, chain saws, and solar energy while crippling sectors of the U.S. industrial base that operated on the assumption of cheap energy. A change in social values regarding health and physical fitness created markets for exercise centers, exercise clothing, and healthier foods while damaging the tobacco industry. Consumer interest in healthier foods is the key trend on which Richard Worth is betting Frookies's fortunes. And deregulation of airline travel, financial services, and telecommunications in recent decades sparked competition and gave many entrepreneurial ventures a chance to enter new markets.[9]

The airline industry provides a good example of the cycles of opportunity and risk created by changes in the organizational environment. Until the late 1970s and early 1980s, air travel in the United States was under close government control. The Civil Aeronautics Board (CAB), an agency of the federal

SOCIAL RESPONSIBILITY AND ETHICS

Education Alternatives for Profit

Should the public school system be an arena for profit-driven entrepreneurs? John Golle, founder of Education Alternatives, plans to replace bureaucratic public school systems with a highly efficient teaching system characterized by lean management, quality service, satisfied customers, and return on investment. Although Golle is focused on providing affordable, quality education for preschoolers through sixth graders, he is also focused on a 15 to 20 percent pretax profit.

As an industry, public education is in desperate need of reform. When compared with other industrialized countries, U.S. eighth-grade math scores were ranked 13 out of 15. The majority of high school graduates are unprepared for entry-level jobs, and the students who drop out of school in just one year cost the country more than $240 billion in lost wages and productivity.

Entrepreneurs may just have the necessary creativity, drive, and enthusiasm to alter the public school system. Golle's work with two private schools brought about small class sizes, individualized instruction, computer classes, and students who outperform the national average by almost two grade levels. His aggressive financial proposal details how educational innovations can be implemented for a national average of $5,100 per student. Allocation of these funds would be quite different from current practices. The average public school spends 37 cents of every budget dollar on students, but Golle expects to spend 80 cents. His plan is based on the following changes:

1. Reduce the administrative positions by almost half.
2. Eliminate stand-alone positions, such as physical education instructor and librarian, by giving those responsibilities to classroom teachers.
3. Put contracted services (such as food and janitorial services) out for bid.
4. Purchase supplies, from pencils to desks, from discounters rather than from expensive school-supply distributors.
5. Hire union teachers at the agreed salary with concessions such as the right to offer three teaching

MANAGEMENT AROUND THE WORLD

Prospective entrepreneurs in Bulgaria feel stymied by the lack of private property rights. As the country moves toward capitalism, the government must decide whether people who owned property before the Communist takeover should get it back and whether former Communist officials should be able to own property. Until these questions are settled, budding entrepreneurs are reining in their creative impulses.

government, decided which airlines could be in the air, where they could fly (including routes the government said needed service, even if the airlines didn't want to fly them), and how much they could charge for tickets. Airlines enjoyed healthy profits, and airline operators could rest easy, assured of a stable marketplace and steady incomes.

But public pressure concerning airfares led the government to abolish the CAB and deregulate the industry. In the 10 years that followed, more than *100* new airlines were started in the United States. Few survived this entrepreneurial explosion. With so many competitors in the market, aggressive price wars were inevitable, and many carriers failed—both new and old. With the industry continuing to consolidate into the 1990s (with big names like Pan Am, Eastern, and TWA falling from the sky), the huge supply of excess aircraft continues to grow. This oversupply of jets has pushed down the price, attracting another generation of entrepreneurs who are taking advantage of the lower cost of entering the air-travel market. Baltia Air, for instance, has exclusive rights to fly passengers from New York to Leningrad and Riga, and Reno Air is meeting customer demand for routes into Reno from various cities in California and on the East Coast.[10]

Economic and Social Contributions of New Ventures

The changing external environment in the United States and other countries continues to provide new opportunities for entrepreneurs and, as a result, entrepreneurship has altered the economy and society. For example, as the demand for services continues to grow, entrepreneurs continue to innovate to meet the unfulfilled needs. Innovative services such as home delivery of restaurant food, fast automobile tune-ups, overnight delivery of packages, and home medical

levels in the classroom and the right to remove teachers who fail to perform.
6. Efficiently invest money from school districts and manage cash flow.

Based on experience and an aggressive financial proposal, Education Alternatives recently won a five-year, $1.2 million contract from the school district in Dade County, Florida, to manage the new South Pointe Elementary School. Although Education Alternatives has innovative teaching concepts and efficient management techniques, can business be accepted as a partner in public education? With a public school tradition that is 150 years old, can teachers, teacher unions, principals, school boards, parents, and business leaders alter their ingrained beliefs that the public sector is responsible for public education?

In fact, 34 states have restrictions on how public money can be spent, eliminating the ability to contract with an educational management company. Working with unions to accept the new teaching responsibilities and evaluations is bound to be difficult. Getting school boards and parents to accept an educational management company that intends to profit from their children's education may be insurmountable. The infrastructure of the public school system and the convictions of all involved must be overcome to introduce such a radical concept.

All eyes will be on the success or failure of the Dade County experiment. Education Alternatives and John Golle have the opportunity to demonstrate the benefits of a business-education partnership. Although Dade County views success as increasing standardized test results and improving the quality of education (as determined by a questionnaire to parents), Education Alternatives's views on success ultimately come down to profit.

What's Your Opinion?

1. Should educational management companies be used to increase the quality of public education in the United States?
2. Based on your understanding of new ventures and entrepreneurship, what entrepreneurial strategy is being employed by Education Alternatives? Explain whether this strategy will be successful and why.

care are examples of creative new services that fuel the economy, increase employment, and, in some cases, better the health and welfare of our society. Here are some other important contributions of the entrepreneurial spirit:

- *Sparking innovation.* New ventures play an important role in introducing new goods and services to the economy. In the last 50 years, small firms and creative individuals contributed nearly half of all innovations, including the Xerox copier, the Polaroid camera, and the personal computer. In the service sector, entrepreneurial innovations include warehouse stores such as Costco and Staples, franchising of a variety of businesses, diet centers, and the dry-cleaning process.[11]
- *Enhancing health and welfare.* Innovative new ventures can better society by decreasing suffering, discomfort, and loss of life. Personal experience often leads entrepreneurs to create products that can help others. When individuals experience personal pain or tragedy, they may discover a need for a product that isn't being met. For example, Robert H. Petit lost his six-month-old son to sudden infant death syndrome. After his son's death, Petit gave up his aerospace career to launch Healthdyne, a new venture dedicated to designing and manufacturing a home machine that monitors infant breathing and heartbeat. He struggled in the early years, but Petit finally built a workable home model that was similar to the machines found in hospitals. The company went on to manufacture other health-care equipment and to provide home-care medical services, including antibiotic therapies and obstetrical care. Today, Healthdyne has annual sales over $150 million.[12]
- *Fueling economic growth.* Economists view a healthy small-business community as the best way to fuel economic growth, preserve competition, prevent monopolistic control of industries, and assure competitive prices for quality products.[13] Small businesses have been star performers at creating new jobs.

For instance, over a recent 10-year period, small U.S. manufacturers added 1.3 million jobs during a time when their larger counterparts cut 100,000 jobs.[14] Small businesses now employ over 60 percent of the U.S. work force, and they are expected to generate more than half of all new jobs between now and the year 2000 (although after the high-growth 1980s, some economists worry that the small-business job boom might be permanently slowing down.)[15]

- *Creating ownership opportunities.* Entrepreneurship offers people an alternative to the traditional career path. In recent years, minorities and women have been particularly aggressive in following the entrepreneurial path to success. Over 4 million women in this country own their own businesses, representing 30 percent of all U.S. businesses, and the Small Business Administration estimates that by the year 2000, some 38 percent of U.S. firms may be owned by women.[16]

Many businesses owned by minorities and women make a special effort to provide opportunities to other people who aren't following traditional careers in corporate America. For example, Wallace Stephens, an African-American and the owner of a computer and facilities management company called Stephens Engineering, is committed to hiring and promoting minorities and women. Stephens's firm employs 125 people and far exceeds the staff diversification guidelines that all federal contractors must meet. In his words, "This country has afforded my family an excellent living, but that is no good if you can't share."[17]

THE ENTREPRENEURIAL ORGANIZATION

New ventures do provide a wealth of benefits for owners, employees, and society at large, but they are not without risk, and new ventures exhibit high failure rates. According to the Small Business Administration, within 2 years of inception, 24 percent of new ventures will fail; within 10 years, 60 percent will be gone.[18] In some industries the figures are even more daunting; in the restaurant business, for instance, 85 percent of new establishments close within just five years, and nearly half don't even survive the first year.[19] The potential entrepreneur's first step should be to understand the characteristics of successful entrepreneurs, the organizational strategies they employ, and the challenges they face when launching and managing new ventures.

Entrepreneurial Characteristics

Entrepreneurs have been studied at great length to identify the personality characteristics that drive them to pursue their innovative goals. Although the conclusions are quite diverse, six characteristics appear to be common:[20]

- *Energy level.* To be successful, a new venture requires hard work and dedication. In a recent survey, over half of the business owners reported that they worked over 60 hours per week, and 25 percent reported working 70 hours or more. Entrepreneurs need an unusually high energy level in order to meet the demands of launching and running a business.
- *Need for achievement.* Entrepreneurs exhibit a high need for achievement, which accounts for their seemingly endless drive. High achievers set ambi-

As general manager of a foundry in Orrville, Ohio, Indian-born Vinny Gupta *(in white shirt)* saw an opportunity to strike out on his own by buying the unprofitable plant from its conglomerate owner and implementing his own ideas. Gupta renamed the foundry Technocast and put in long hours working with his employees to boost quality and productivity. His entrepreneurial efforts soon paid off: sales quadrupled and profits soared.

tious short-term and long-term goals that challenge them and that provide great personal satisfaction when achieved.

- *Level of risk.* Although entrepreneurs are typically characterized as risk-takers, successful entrepreneurs actually tend to take moderate risk rather than little risk or excessive risk.
- *Self-confidence.* Entrepreneurs are confident in their own abilities to make both strategic and day-to-day decisions regarding technical matters, marketing, and overall business strategy. They also feel capable of overcoming any future, unanticipated problem. In a recent study, over 80 percent of entrepreneurs believed they were very likely to succeed, and 33 percent were convinced they would succeed.[21] Richard Worth certainly fits this category; his confidence in the potential of Frookies provided the drive behind his start-up efforts.
- *Locus of control.* Entrepreneurs tend to believe they have a high degree of control over their lives, as opposed to believing their lives are influenced by luck, fate, or other external sources. Because they feel in control of their lives, they are able to strike out on their own and take the future into their own hands.
- *Tolerance for ambiguity.* Entrepreneurs are comfortable with and capable of making decisions based on little information. This is a critical trait for entrepreneurs, who face a great deal of uncertainty when starting new ventures.

Starting an innovative new venture takes a great deal of planning, investigation, organization, and perseverance. Consider the not-for-profit operation called We Can, which has a goal of cleaning up the environment while helping poor and homeless people. Founder Guy Polhemus was volunteering at a church soup kitchen when a homeless bottle-and-can scavenger explained how difficult it was to return bottles and cans to the various retailers all over town to receive the 5-cent refunds. By beginning with a business plan, working with a law firm that arranged incorporation and tax-exempt status, and receiving donations from foundations and individuals, Polhemus opened his first center on the West Side of Manhattan in an empty lot temporarily loaned to him by a developer.

Even with all its planning, We Can faced a terrible cash flow shortage. It pays out a nickel deposit for each of the thousands of containers collected by destitute New Yorkers. Then it collects 5 cents from the beverage distributor plus a 1.5-cent processing fee that distributors are required to pay to retailers and collection agencies that act as middlemen. At first, the distributors often took 30 to 60 days to pay the required 6.5 cents. This huge cash flow deficit is being eased by distributors that are beginning to pay for redemptions in advance.[22]

Entrepreneurial Strategies

Just as the personality of entrepreneurs can be characterized, the strategies they implement for creating viable new ventures can be identified as well. Initiating a new venture is a decision that must be considered carefully (see Exhibit 12.2), but an innovative idea and a strategy for implementing that idea can easily tip the balance in favor of the new venture. Peter Drucker has studied many entrepreneurs and has identified three broad entrepreneurial strategies: new-market leadership, creative imitation, and entrepreneurial judo.[23]

New-Market Leadership

new-market leadership An entrepreneurial strategy that aims to create and implement products faster and better than anyone else, thereby leading and dominating the new market

In this strategy, entrepreneurs aim at leadership and dominance in an emerging market or industry by implementing a new idea faster and better than anyone else. The **new-market leadership** strategy, referred to as "fustest with the mostest" by Drucker, is the biggest gamble any entrepreneur can make because, to be successful, there can be no allowances for mistakes and no second chances. Once the innovation becomes a viable business, the entrepreneur must focus on retaining a leadership position in the market or industry and on discouraging competitors. This is the situation Frookies faces today, now that its innovative products have caught on around the country, and the established cookie companies are casting an eye on the market.

EXHIBIT 12.2

Deciding to Start a New Venture

Entrepreneurs view the rewards of starting their own business as more important than the costs, especially if they have an innovative idea.

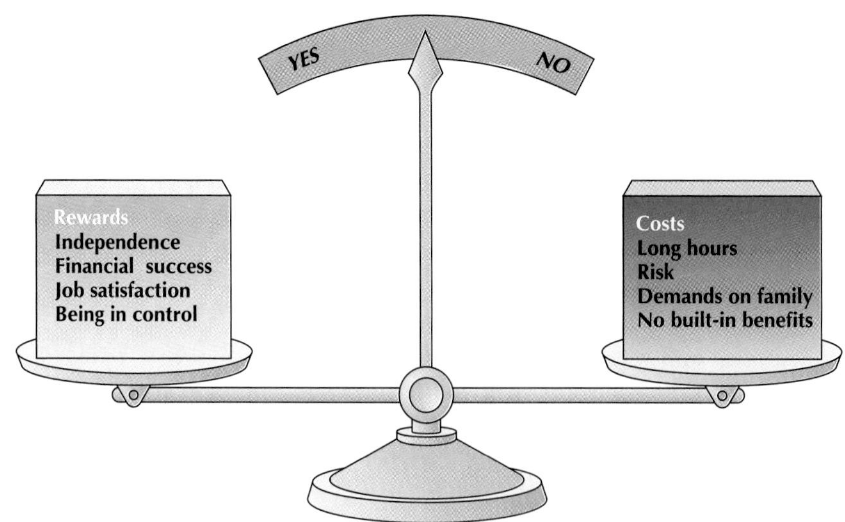

Henry Yuen and Daniel Kwoh, both Ph.D.s from the California Institute of Technology, invented a product that created a new market, and their strategy for delivering this innovation to the new market ensures their dominance of that market (at least in the foreseeable future). The product is called VCR Plus, a remote-control device that allows VCR owners to record TV shows without the usual hassle of programming a VCR. Viewers simply key in a short code number for whatever show they wish to record; the codes are located in their television program guide. VCR Plus then signals the VCR to record the program at the correct time, and it even changes the channel on the cable box if necessary. The new venture, backed by Hong Kong investors, is called Gemstar Development and is located in Pasadena, California. Its sister company in Hong Kong handles engineering and manufacturing. Newspapers, cable guides, and *TV Guide* buy the numbers from Gemstar. The VCR Plus remote control retails for around $60, and first-year sales far exceeded the predicted 1 million units. Gemstar also receives royalty and license fees from VCR manufacturers that incorporate VCR Plus into their machines.[24]

Rémi Gaston-Dreyfus and his partners used entrepreneurial judo to find and fill a niche in home horticulture. They learned that only 11 common varieties make up 80 percent of the house plants sold in France. To capture a piece of that market, the partners developed a small treelike plant that blooms all year. Their company, Tropical Green, now rings up $10 million in worldwide sales.

Creative Imitation

The entrepreneur implementing **creative imitation** capitalizes on an existing innovation through a better understanding of what the innovation represents and how it can be marketed. By the time the creative imitator comes along, the original innovator has already established the market and reduced the level of uncertainty. But the original innovator has overlooked something crucial about the product, its features, or the market. The creative imitator steps in and dominates the market by perfecting the product or its positioning in the marketplace. The creative imitator satisfies an existing demand that has not been fulfilled by the original innovator.

Entrepreneurial Judo

By creating new methods of filling niches left by others in the industry, entrepreneurs utilize the strategy called **entrepreneurial judo**. This strategy focuses on segmenting the market and finding attractive areas missed by the original innovator. Small businesses may never reach a leadership position in an industry, but they can find areas that have been overlooked by larger companies and capitalize on these opportunities. For example, artist Alex Corbbrey from Tulsa, Oklahoma, established Shades of Black to create greeting cards for African-American customers. After some research, Corbbrey determined that African-Americans were spending over $320 million yearly on greeting cards even though few were focused on African-American culture and experiences. The demand for Shades of Black cards has been overwhelming, especially in major cities, and Hallmark is now stocking the cards in its stores that have large African-American clienteles.[25]

creative imitation An entrepreneurial strategy that aims to do a better job of bringing an existing idea to market and satisfying customers

entrepreneurial judo An entrepreneurial strategy in which an idea is aimed at filling holes left by others in the industry

Starting New Ventures

Selecting an entrepreneurial strategy is just the first of many crucial decisions made during the early stages of new-venture formation. This section considers the other major choices entrepreneurs make, including the approach used to get into the market, the form of ownership the new organization will adopt, the development of the business plan, and sources of funding and managerial support.

Approaches to New Ventures

Starting a new venture from scratch is the entrepreneur's first choice in many cases, but it is not the only choice. Some entrepreneurs opt to purchase an existing business enterprise, such as a store that is already in operation, or to purchase a franchise. To determine which is the best for a given situation, entrepreneurs need to consider the benefits and limitations of the three approaches.[26]

start-up A new venture created by an entrepreneur

Starting a New Business A **start-up** organization is one created by the entrepreneur. A start-up gives the entrepreneur greater freedom in selecting goods or services, location, facilities, equipment, suppliers, and professional services. Similarly, a start-up is not bound by the established procedures or legal commitments that an existing business often carries, and a start-up avoids the possibility of inheriting problem customers, problem suppliers, or problem employees. However, the limitations of the start-up option are quite pronounced as well. These can include the difficulty of getting bank loans or lines of credit, the need to find employees who can be trained to run the operation, the need to design the organization structure, a shortage of good locations in many towns and cities, and the challenge of attracting customers to an unknown enterprise.

Purchasing an Established Business Although an existing business has some limitations, with careful examination and professional assistance, purchasing an existing business can have many benefits. The existing firm has already invested the time and effort required to choose a good or service to produce, select a location, establish a customer base, hire employees, select suppliers, design the organization structure, and create operating procedures. The track record of the business can be evaluated and compared with competitors in the industry. However, the entrepreneur is also buying all the problems that the business may have, such as poor location, poor reputation, outmoded facilities, obsolete inventory, and unfavorable contractual agreements.

Consider Andy Halsey, who was dissatisfied with his job making sails for a company in Old Saybrook, Connecticut, and purchased an existing business that had both positive and negative points. With $30,000 in savings and a $60,000 bank loan, Halsey bought an ailing sailmaking company, renamed it Halsey Sailmakers, and turned the company around. The new emphasis for the company became making top-quality sails with an emphasis on service. By capitalizing on the company's existing employees and equipment and by recruiting talented colleagues from his old firm, Halsey Sailmakers doubled volume in both the first and second years. By the third year, volume was up another 40 percent and still climbing.[27]

Buying a Franchise Some entrepreneurs opt for the benefits of franchising, which include an established brand name and company identity, well-defined policies and procedures, and assistance in both starting up and managing the enterprise. Examples of franchises include Imposters stores, which sell excellent imitations of expensive jewelry (sale of a good), One Hour Martinizing (use of a dry-cleaning process), and Arthur Murray Dance Studios (delivery of a service).[28] For the entrepreneur, franchising affords the opportunity to reduce the risks of starting a business by using proven methods and selling goods or services that have an established image in the minds of customers.

In recent years, franchising has increased dramatically. With over 2,000 U.S. companies offering franchises, franchised businesses number 500,000 and account for over $550 billion in sales (a third of all retail sales in the United States).[29] Many large organizations, such as Prudential Insurance and Pillsbury, are entering the profitable franchise business either by acquiring franchise companies or by franchising a concept of their own. Prudential, for example, recently invested $40 million to franchise over 320 real estate brokerage offices throughout the country, and Pillsbury (which is owned by a British firm, Grand Metropolitan plc) acquired the franchise company Burger King back in 1973.[30]

However, franchises can limit the entrepreneur's freedom. The franchise fee, start-up costs, and royalty fee, normally paid whether the franchise makes a profit or not, can be quite a hardship for a small business, especially if revenue is lower than expected (see Exhibit 12.3). And even if a concept is franchised, it can still fail. For example, Rick Taylor bought three Videos 1st franchises, which provided drive-through video rentals. But within three years, the parent company folded, along with the 10 Videos 1st stores scattered throughout the country. The company's failure was attributed to inadequate understanding of customer needs—especially for drive-through service. If he were trying to do it again, says Taylor, "I'd spend more time analyzing the market and the product. I'd talk to competitors rather than rely on the information provided by the franchisor. I was so enamored of the concept that I jumped; then looked."[31]

Jacqueline Clark, president and founder of A Choice Nanny, started her franchise business because she saw a need for qualified child care. Based in Columbia, Maryland, the growing chain has 30 franchisees. Clark estimates that opening a local franchise of A Choice Nanny generally costs the franchisee between $37,000 and $41,000.

Ownership Form

Deciding on the form of ownership is a key step in the organizing process and a crucial decision for every entrepreneur. Each form has distinct benefits and limitations (see Exhibit 12.4). Attorneys, accountants, and the Small Business Administration can help guide entrepreneurs through the many complex legal issues needed to implement an ownership form that matches the type of business to be established.[32]

Sole Proprietorship The most common form of business ownership is an organization that is owned by a single individual, known as a **sole proprietorship.** Approximately 70 percent of all businesses in the United States are owned by individuals. This form of ownership is popular with entrepreneurs because it is the easiest and least expensive form to establish and the owner has all decision-making responsibility. All profits, taxed as ordinary income, belong to the owner, for personal use or for reinvestment into the business. However, establishing a sole proprietorship has some limitations. The first and major drawback is termed *unlimited liability,* which means that the individual owner and the

sole proprietorship A form of business ownership in which the organization is owned by one individual

EXHIBIT 12.3

What Franchises Cost

The costs of franchises differ greatly, as shown by data collected from 10 well-known franchises.

Franchise	Franchise Fee	Start-Up Costs	Royalty Fee
Domino's Pizza	$6,500	$50,000–$100,000	8%
ERA Real Estate	$13,900	$10,000–$25,000	Varies
Jazzercise	$500	$1,500–$2,000	20%
Mail Boxes Etc.	$19,500	$35,000–$75,000	5%
McDonald's	$22,500	$450,000–$475,000	12%
Meineke Discount Mufflers	$22,500	$31,500 and up	7%
Novus Windshield Repair	$2,900	$3,600	6%
Sir Speedy Printer	$40,000	$75,000	4–6%
Sleep Inns by Quality International	$30,000	$1.2–$3.0 million	4%
Subway	$7,500	$35,000–$60,000	8%

SOLE PROPRIETORSHIP		PARTNERSHIP		CORPORATION	
PROS	CONS	PROS	CONS	PROS	CONS
• Simplicity. • Income or loss is taxed as owner's personal income or loss. • No legal fees or other administrative costs to form.	• As owner, you're personally liable for business debts. • Difficult to transfer ownership. No continuity of operation after owner retires or dies.	• Partnership generally pays no tax. Each partner's share of income or loss is taxed as his or her personal income or loss.	• General partnerships are personally liable for debts of the partnership. • Legal and administrative costs to form. • Partnership must file its own tax return. • Death of partner may end partnership.	• Shareholder's personal liability is usually limited to corporation's assets. • Qualifying small corporations can elect to be S corporations, which are taxed much like partnerships.	• Both corporation and shareholders pay tax on distributed income. • Additional tax return form required. • Must pay legal expenses to incorporate, along with filing fees. • Must conform to corporate structure (board of directors, record of minutes, etc.).

EXHIBIT 12.4 Structuring a New Business

When starting a new business, entrepreneurs can choose from three basic forms of ownership, each with benefits and limitations that must be considered.

business are considered one legal entity. In this arrangement, business debts or lawsuits can result in the loss of personal assets. In addition, financing and growth may be limited; the business ceases to exist with the death of the sole owner; and the sole owner must be capable of handling all business functions.

partnership A form of business ownership in which the organization is owned by two or more individuals

Partnership The least popular form of ownership is a **partnership,** in which the organization is owned by two or more people. *General partners* have unlimited liability, so their personal assets are at risk to business debts and lawsuits. The liability of *limited partners,* on the other hand, is limited to the amount each one invested in the partnership. There is no limit on the number of general or limited partners, but each partnership must have at least one general partner. Partnerships have the benefit of being easy to form, and they also provide shared responsibility, more help with the workload, and ongoing moral support. Financially, partnerships find it easier to raise capital than sole proprietorships, and business profits are still considered personal income for the partners and are therefore taxed as ordinary income. The limitations of partnerships include unlimited liability (for general partners), the liability of all partners for the actions of one partner, and the common occurrence of disagreements or tensions among partners.

corporation A form of business ownership in which a legal entity, chartered by the state, has an existence separate and apart from that of its owners

Corporation Large organizations usually choose to form **corporations,** creating a legal entity that has an existence separate and apart from its owners. For the most part, the advantage of incorporating is the protection of personal assets, since the assets of individuals are legally separate from the assets of the corporation. However, in many start-up corporations, the entrepreneur still must personally guarantee business loans, often using personal assets as collateral. If the corporation cannot repay the debt, the entrepreneur may then lose those personal assets. In essence, entrepreneurs cannot realize the benefit of limited liability until the business is financially self-sufficient. Other advantages of corporations include the ability to raise capital by selling stock and the continued existence of the organization in the event of death or retirement of a principal. On the downside, start-up costs are higher, and the process is more complex; the amount of ongoing paperwork required with incorporation is also a large burden for many small businesses. Moreover, incorporating means double taxation; the company must pay income taxes based on net income and shareholders must pay income taxes based on dividends paid out of net income.

An **S corporation** is a special form of a corporation with all the benefits of a corporation, including limited liability. However, the company has the advantage of being taxed at personal tax rates rather than the higher corporate tax rate. Even though S corporations have some limitations, they are popular with small businesses since personal assets are protected and taxation is at a lower rate.

S corporation A special form of a corporation that allows the profits and losses of the company to be taxed at personal tax rates while still providing the advantages of a corporation, notably limited liability

The Business Plan

Once the entrepreneur has decided on a form of ownership, the new venture must establish a presence in the target market, understand the characteristics of the market and its competition, and effectively implement strategies and tactics that will establish the new venture as a permanent force in the marketplace. Prior to initiating the new venture, an entrepreneur creates a **business plan,** which documents the results of the strategic management process and lays out the strategies and tactics that the venture will implement. The business plan contains several important elements: a statement of goals; a description of feasibility of the product(s) that will be sold; the selection of target markets; timetables for start-up activities; site selection; and projections regarding human, physical, and financial requirements. The plan also discusses strategic issues that will affect the new venture's chances of survival and examines the distinctive competencies that will set the venture apart from its competitors. Finally, the plan covers financial analyses and projections.

business plan A document detailing business strategies and tactics prepared by an entrepreneur prior to opening a new business

The business plan has two distinct purposes. First, since many entrepreneurs need to borrow money for their new ventures, they use the business plan to persuade investors and lenders to fund the new business.[33] Second, and more important, entrepreneurs rely on their business plans to monitor ongoing progress of new ventures. Essentially, the business plan guides the new venture through its early phases. Bill and Julie Brice of Dallas, Texas, didn't write a business plan when they used $10,000 of their own savings to buy two foundering frozen yogurt stores. After expanding to four stores, the difficulty of managing the business without a plan led Julie to sign up for an entrepreneurial class at a nearby university. By the end of the semester, she had written a business plan that became the foundation for ongoing planning and control. Today, the brother-and-sister team preside over a nationwide franchise network of more than 120 I Can't Believe It's Yogurt stores.[34]

Sources of Funding

Generating capital, both to start the business and to keep it going until it is self-sufficient, is another crucial step for entrepreneurs. Many new ventures fail because of insufficient capital. Often, personal savings can provide the entrepreneur with sufficient funds. However, many entrepreneurs must raise funds by obtaining loans (debt capital) or by sharing the ownership of the firm with investors (equity capital).[35] Exhibit 12.5 shows the sources of financing that entrepreneurs rely on, both for start-ups and for the purchase of existing businesses. Many entrepreneurs use a combination of sources. For example, entrepreneur Mary Ann Lombard used both personal savings and $60,000 in bank loans to launch BePuzzled, a business that produces a series of murder mystery jigsaw puzzles.[36]

EXHIBIT 12.5

Sources of New-Venture Capital

Financing for entrepreneurs to either start their own business or purchase existing businesses comes primarily from personal savings, banks, and friends and relatives.

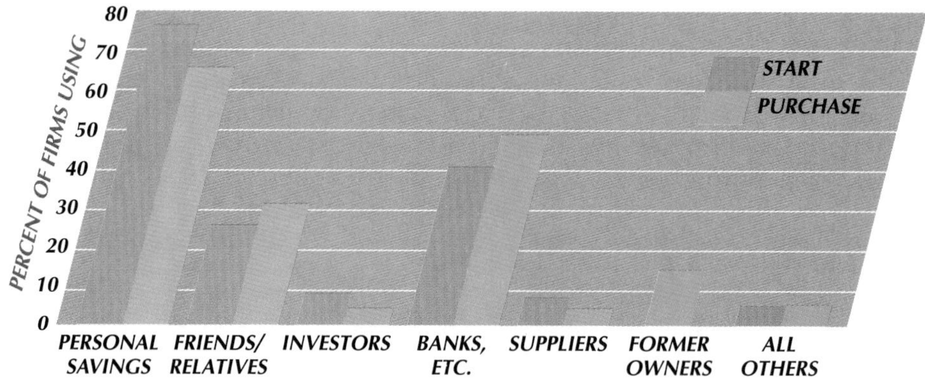

debt capital A form of financing in which the funds received by an organization must be repaid

Debt capital refers to funds that a firm borrows and must repay in the same way that consumers get loans for cars and houses. Entrepreneurs who finance with debt capital retain full ownership and control of their firms, although the loans are based on the assets of the firm and perhaps on the assets of the entrepreneur. The primary benefit that debt financing has over equity financing is the opportunity to maintain control over management of the firm and over the firm's profits.

On the other hand, debt financing usually involves making regular payments to lenders, which can restrict the firm's financial flexibility. In times of slow sales, for instance, a firm that is heavily debt financed may find that most of its cash must go toward debt payments, leaving little or no money for advertising, new-product development, or other vital functions. Another drawback of debt financing is that the value of the firm's assets and its profit potential limit the amount of debt that can be incurred.[37]

equity capital A form of financing in which the funds received by an organization are exchanged for part-ownership in the organization

Equity capital refers to the funds received by a business in exchange for part of the ownership in the organization. Firms can use equity financing only if they are structured as partnerships or corporations. For a partnership, adding new partners that contribute capital to the firm is a form of equity financing. For a small business structured as a corporation, it is most common for shares of company stock to be sold to friends, family, private investors, larger businesses, or government-subsidized businesses that specialize in furnishing equity capital to small firms.[38]

The benefits and limitations of equity financing are the reverse of those of debt financing. With equity financing, the firm does not take on additional debt, which keeps cash available for various business purposes. The downside is that the entrepreneur begins to lose a portion of the ownership of the firm and thus some control over its management. And the more capital that is raised through equity financing, the more control the entrepreneur loses.

private stock offering Equity financing in which shares in the company are offered only to selected investors

public stock offering Equity financing in which shares in the company are offered for sale to the general public

A **private stock offering** is an equity-financing technique in which shares in the company are offered only to selected individuals and cannot be purchased by the general public. Richard Worth, for instance, eventually sold a third of Frookies to some of his suppliers and distributors. On the other hand, a **public stock offering** makes shares available to the general public. Most small-business equity capital is raised through private offerings, since the general investing public is usually too concerned about the high failure rates and the sparse profits of small businesses in their early years to invest a great deal of money in them.[39]

Mel Coleman, founder of Coleman Natural Meats, is a fourth-generation Colorado rancher who built a $25 million business with the help of venture capitalists. Coleman started his business in 1979, but the turning point came in 1989, when he obtained $2.5 million from three venture capital firms (in exchange for more than 50 percent of the equity) to fund the advertising campaign that launched his meat products into supermarket distribution.

An important source of small-business financing is **venture capitalists,** individuals or companies that invest in new or growing businesses. They generally seek out businesses that have a potential for success but that are considered too risky for commercial lenders. In the United States, venture capital firms typically invest in a small number of businesses that show potential for rapid growth and strong return on investment. Because few small businesses can meet venture capitalists' investment criteria, this method of financing is not available to every entrepreneur.[40]

venture capitalists Individuals or companies that invest in new or expanding businesses

Particularly in industrial and high-technology areas, however, venture capital is spurring the formation of new ventures in many countries throughout the world. In Poland, for example, a venture capitalist named Jan Bednarek, a 51-year-old engineer who heads a state-owned synthetic fiber company, is striving to reshape the Polish economy. Rather than lay off employees in his overstaffed factory, Bednarek uses the profits of the state-owned company to set up employees and others in new businesses, which will provide jobs and help revive the ailing economy. Of the 18 start-ups that Bednarek is responsible for, his most successful offspring is a venture that specializes in factory automation and industrial processing equipment that helps Polish companies upgrade their plants.[41]

Sources of Support

In addition to capital, new ventures often need other forms of support, and most entrepreneurs can tap into several different sources. The first type involves **incubators,** business-development facilities that help young companies get on their feet and grow past the start-up phase (see Exhibit 12.6). Incubators offer a variety of services and benefits, including management advice, information on financing, reduced rent, flexible office and factory space, and shared administrative services that let growing companies minimize their expenses. Diane and Paul Santille utilized an incubator for Pasta Mama's, a retail food company, shortly after they moved the operation out of their home. They leased 6,000 square feet at the Tri-Cities Enterprise Center in Richland, Washington, at a very attractive

incubators Business-development facilities designed to help young companies grow beyond the start-up phase

EXHIBIT 12.6

Incubator Statistics

The number of business incubators has increased from 15 in 1980 to 422 nationwide. More than 6,500 small businesses are currently incubator tenants.

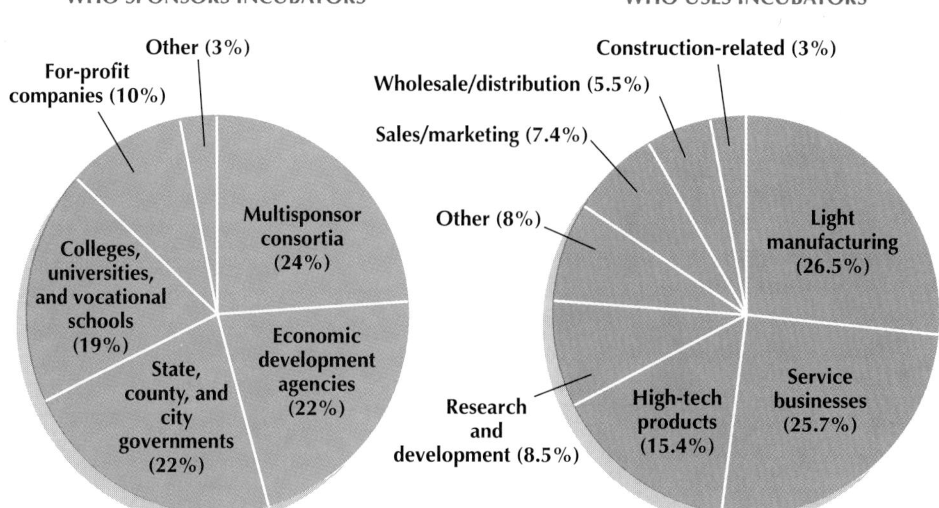

rate that included the use of office machines, support staff, and business counseling. Says Paul Santille, "We felt like we had a brand-new facility, and it wasn't costing us an arm and a leg."[42]

A second source of support is the Small Business Administration, which offers free counseling and financial support to qualifying entrepreneurs. One of the SBA's most important efforts involves the Small Business Institutes located on several hundred college campuses around the country. The SBA can also help entrepreneurs secure bank loans by guaranteeing 90 percent of the loan amount, up to a maximum of $750,000. Moreover, the SBA loans money directly to new ventures that are owned by veterans, minorities, and entrepreneurs in high-unemployment areas.

Other sources of support include consulting and accounting firms that provide low-fee advice to new ventures in exchange for future business.[43] Paul A. Kittle hired the management consulting and accounting firm of Arthur Andersen as a resource, which helped his new chemical firm, Rusmar, reach revenues of $1.5 million.[44] Accounting and consulting firms usually have a wide range of experience with finance, operations, and growth-management issues, so they are in a good position to help new ventures sort through their various business options, obtain financing, and organize for sustainable growth.

Growth of the Entrepreneurial Organization

Once the entrepreneur has formed the business, developed a business plan, and obtained funding, he or she must then focus on surviving and managing toward success. Understanding the general growth patterns of new businesses enables business owners to diagnose problems and implement solutions that address the needs of an organization in a specific stage of growth. Making sure that the organization structure evolves along with the organization's growth is a key management challenge, considering that many new ventures start with no organization structure at all and must define and develop structures as they grow. The evolution of a small business falls into five general stages:[45]

- *Stage 1: Existence.* In this stage, the organization focuses on finding customers and selling products. The start-up must find enough customers and sell enough to remain viable. The owner is constantly concerned whether there is enough money to cover the considerable cash demands of the start-up phase. The organization is struggling just to stay alive at this point.
- *Stage 2: Survival.* At this stage, the new venture is a viable organization, with a customer base and the means to meet their needs well enough to retain them. The entrepreneur's focus begins to shift toward managing cash to break even and finance growth. The returns on investment of money and time are still quite slim at this stage, and the goal is still just to remain viable, not to realize long-term goals just yet.
- *Stage 3: Success.* When the new venture grows in size and profitability, owners must decide whether they want their organizations to capitalize on the success and continue expansion or whether they want to keep the organizations stable and profitable. Owners choose to keep the organization stable and profitable when they see that the market they are in cannot grow sufficiently or they want to finance other ventures. If owners choose growth, they must focus all cash resources and borrowing power on financing growth. In both situations, this is the stage in which hiring professional managers and implementing formal systems for strategic and operational planning are essential for keeping the organization profitable. Selecting an appropriate organization structure and tuning it in response to both internal and external changes is a key step in this phase.
- *Stage 4: Takeoff.* If owners choose expansion and are successful, the organization reaches the takeoff stage, characterized by delegating the decision making, using formal control systems, and often incurring a high amount of debt necessary to fund continued expansion. Organization structure remains a key factor, since the firm must be structured properly in relation to the type of growth and management style that its owners wish to pursue. This is where Richard Worth and Frookies are today; he is now wrestling with the issues of managing a successful, nationwide company that grew faster than he expected.
- *Stage 5: Resource maturity.* The organizations that reach resource maturity are concerned with the consolidation and control of the financial success gained from rapid expansion. Even though an organization that has reached resource maturity may have managerial talent, financial resources, and well-developed systems, the organization must strive to retain its entrepreneurial spirit to remain a formidable player in the market.

Dairy Queen is an older company that is deeply in the resource maturity stage. The Minneapolis-based franchiser has kept investors happy with a high stock price, good returns on sales, and great market share. To keep the company successful against stiff competition in the fast-food industry, Dairy Queen recently introduced grilled-chicken sandwiches and frozen yogurt to entice health-conscious customers. And to encourage the franchisees to spruce up some of the older outlets, Dairy Queen is offering below-market loans and a temporary reduction of franchise fees. When Jack and Donna Van Tilburg of Steator, Illinois, utilized the program to build a drive-through window, add a sloping roof, and expand the parking lot of their 1948 vintage Dairy Queen, sales more than doubled, with half their orders coming from the drive-through window.[46]

MANAGERIAL DECISION MAKING

City Year Innovates for the Public Good

Alan Khazei and Michael Brown are entrepreneurs who measure success in terms of citizenship, rather than profit. Their venture, called City Year, is a not-for-profit organization that will take youngsters from all walks of life to form a national youth service corp. By working together on societal problems, they will develop a heightened sense of citizenship, which they might be inclined to exercise for the rest of their lives.

Although the organization is not-for-profit, the management of the venture is as professional as it gets. Khazei and Brown both have Harvard law degrees, and they have hired other Harvard students or graduates, some with business backgrounds. After establishing their vision, they launched their new venture in a well-planned, organized fashion.

1. *Conducting marketing research.* Rather than start their venture based on a simple concept, Khazei, Brown, and their colleagues decided to prove the project's feasibility by operating a nine-week pilot program in Boston.
2. *Creating the business plan.* Included in the business plan are City Year's concept, strategy, goals, and projected budgets for both the Boston pilot program and the Boston full-time operation. The plan also stated that after the first year of full-time operation in Boston, they would focus on national expansion.
3. *Locating sources of funding.* Unable to qualify for federal funding, City Year targeted the private sector, operating on the belief that corporations, like individuals, have civic responsibilities. Armed with their business plan, City Year raised more than the $200,000 needed to run the pilot program; by the end of summer, it had raised all of the $1.5 million budgeted for the first year of full-time operation. Says William W. Bain, Jr., chairman and founder of the management consulting firm Bain & Company, "They had a long-term vision of where things could go and practical ideas of how to get there. They understood that even lofty goals require planning and work." Their corporate sponsors include Bank of Boston, The Equitable, General Cinema, Bain & Company, Reebok International, General Atlantic Partners, and New England Telephone.
4. *Recruiting employees.* Khazei and Brown knew that to be successful they had to convince youngsters with a wide variety of backgrounds to participate in the program. They hired Kristen Atwood, who systematically traversed the city and suburbs, tailoring her pitch to each segment of youths. In city schools, she emphasized the program as a jobs program to help students gain valuable experience; in the suburbs she discussed service to the commu-

Roberto J. T. Arguello, on the other hand, provides a good example of an entrepreneur who has reached the success stage but hasn't yet decided whether to expand his current business or use it to finance new business ventures. Arguello was a successful business owner in Nicaragua, but he and his family fled when the Sandinistas took control of the government in 1979. Since most of his assets were tied up in Nicaragua, Arguello and his family began a new life in New York City with just a few hundred dollars. After being turned down for loans by various banks and by the Small Business Administration, Arguello decided to enter the grocery business since, at the time, it required relatively little capital. Arguello's company, Matlyn-Stofel Foods, quickly passed through the existence and survival stages. The company now owns two grocery stores with sales of $22 million and is well established in the success stage. Arguello would prefer to expand his grocery business but believes that current prices for existing supermarkets are too high and that building a new supermarket would cost even more. Arguello is considering a number of new business ventures, including brokering the works of South American artists, renovating apartment buildings in Brooklyn, or brokering food products for South America or Eastern Europe. Whether Arguello's grocery business will expand or will fund the development of new business ventures remains to be seen.[47]

nity, because the students there seemed to feel sheltered from real issues. Youngsters were also recruited with a small stipend and scholarship funds. In the first year, City Year accepted one out of every three applicants.

5. *Implementing the plan.* With the business plan guiding implementation, both the summer program and the first-year program were successful. The customers were happy with the free services, the participants learned about issues facing the community and about their own abilities, and the sponsors believe City Year provided just what was promised—increased citizenship and community service. The City Year projects included renovating a long-neglected park and ensuring future maintenance by nearby residents, designing and operating an after-school program at a housing project, and working at an elderly housing project to clean away years of accumulated filth.

The observations of customers, participants, and corporate sponsors summarize what City Year is all about. Mel Reicher, former director of the Boston Living Center, a drop-in residence for people with AIDS, relates how the City Year team members would thank him for giving them the opportunity to work with AIDS patients. Kenny Lopez, who joined the program with no direction in his life, learned that life is "about what you can do for yourself and others." Lopez decided to enter college and later work in child care. Susan Flaherty, former director of corporate contributions at New England Telephone, notes, "We give a little money to City Year and they give priceless support to other institutions we're interested in [like] the Boston Food Bank."

Future challenges for City Year include securing necessary funding and long-term expansion. Some existing sponsors are interested in start-up funding only, but others are interested in a long-term partnership. Although only one corporate sponsor declined to help out for the second year, Khazei and Brown believe that some government funding may be necessary. However, they are concerned that basic goals or premises might be compromised if government funding were offered and accepted.

The founders have changed their plans for nationwide expansion. After their first successful year and discussions with sponsors, Brown and Khazei believe that long-term expansion will be more successful if the Boston program is well established with a wide variety of supporters and sponsors. In essence, City Year is facing the traditional entrepreneurial challenge of how to move from a start-up venture to a successful organization with enough funds to grow and expand.

Apply Your Knowledge

1. How have the founders of City Year demonstrated entrepreneurship?
2. How are the start-up challenges faced by City Year similar to those faced by for-profit ventures?

Factors for Entrepreneurial Success

There are many ingredients necessary for the success of a new venture. Innovative ideas alone cannot build a new venture. In fact, over 90 percent of new-business failures result from poor management. Since many successful business owners have experienced one or more business failures at some point in their careers, entrepreneurs learn from their mistakes.[48] For example, Wendall Ward began a new venture in Dallas, Texas, selling country sausages. This business did not succeed, however. Ward pondered the failed sausage business and applied the lessons he learned to a new opportunity, tortilla chips made from white corn, which enabled him to utilize his previous experience as manager of mechanical engineering and research at Frito-Lay. With a $10,000 loan, research to get the chips just right, and a rented truck, he established Gourmet Foods. When Kroger's and Safeway agreed to stock the chips, Gourmet Foods became a hit.[49]

Small business experts consider the following factors to be essential in the success of new ventures:[50]

- *Managerial expertise.* Knowledge of a variety of managerial functions gained through the combination of education and experience has proved essential in successfully launching and managing a new venture. Creating a business plan can help the entrepreneur assess the potential of the new venture. And effective delegation enables the entrepreneur to focus on critical decisions. For example, Blackstone Bank & Trust, a Boston-based bank, was faced with $2.2 million loan losses on a $50 million portfolio approximately four years after start-up. A co-founder and consultant to the ailing bank, Daniel J. Dart admits that the bank made loans before drafting definitive approval procedures. The co-founders were involved in designing the logo, developing plans for office space, purchasing furniture, drafting personnel policies, and a variety of other minor and major decisions that new ventures face. But failure to focus on key managerial responsibilities caused the bank's financial crisis and its ultimate failure.

- *Flexibility.* Entrepreneurs must be able to recognize and react to completely unpredictable events, both small and large. Flexibility means being able to revamp operations and shift domains if the company is selling to the wrong customers, is distributing through the wrong wholesale or retail channels, or is simply in the wrong business. Buddy Systems originally manufactured medical computer systems that allowed cardiac patients to monitor their vital signs at home. When its original target market, hospitals and home-care nursing companies, failed to purchase many of the systems, Buddy Systems began providing the same clinical services offered by its original target customers. Using the computer system as a competitive advantage, the company now has service contracts with clinics in Cleveland and Chicago.
- *Product objectivity.* Many entrepreneurs initiate a business venture because they are fascinated by an innovative idea but have little information about the viability of the product in the marketplace. Successful entrepreneurs assess the need for their product before launching new ventures. A company called VideOvation recently came up with the idea of producing video yearbooks. Rather than blindly jumping into the business, however, the founder showed admirable objectivity and spent more than a year testing the production process, the customer demand, and the company's ability to execute the project.
- *Industry experience.* Entrepreneurs usually do better if they start new ventures in industries in which they already have some experience. If entrepreneurs don't know their business, they should hire someone who does. Consider the company Plastic Lumber, which manufactures plastic products such as speed bumps and picnic tables. With limited technical knowledge, the founder immediately hired a specialist in plastics manufacturing. In its second year, the company exceeded sales projections by more than $500,000.
- *Regard for competitors.* Successful entrepreneurs realize that competitors are to be respected. Even if the entrepreneurial product is an improvement, competitors already have a viable business with a loyal customer network. Entrepreneurs should not automatically assume that a new venture has a better chance than an existing company. For example, the founders of Keener-Blodee in Holland, Michigan, estimated they could sell $1.7 million worth of chairs in their first year of business. One analyst thought this was a gross miscalculation, because the company would have to take 7,100 chair sales away from competitors in order to meet the goal. As the analyst predicted, the new start-up did indeed fail to meet the goal. The business was recently closed and its assets liquidated. By studying the competition more carefully to better understand the marketplace, Keener-Blodee might have been successful.

THE INTRAPRENEURIAL ORGANIZATION

Few organizations start out with a plan to stifle creativity or to make slow decisions. Unfortunately, all too many previously entrepreneurial organizations become ponderous and bureaucratic as they expand, making it more difficult for innovation to flourish. However, creative ideas are just as vital for large, established organizations as they are for nimble, entrepreneurial ventures, and managers in many large organizations are now working hard to reintroduce the innovative spirit so common in their smaller counterparts. These efforts involve breaking down formal organizational barriers and control mechanisms that have begun to stifle creativity and creating environments that allow people with an entrepreneurial bent to be successful inside the organization.

Championing Innovation within the Organization

intrapreneur A person who promotes innovation and creativity within a larger organization

An **intrapreneur** is an individual who promotes innovation within a larger organization (see Exhibit 12.7). In fact, entrepreneurs and intrapreneurs have very similar outlooks and capabilities: both are highly creative with a strong need to accomplish specific goals. Indeed, many entrepreneurs start as would-be intrapreneurs, become frustrated with the larger organization's inability to handle creative and innovative thinkers, and take their ideas outside the organization. For example, Steve Wozniak couldn't get Hewlett-Packard to support his idea for personal computers. He reluctantly left the company to form Apple Computers with Steve Jobs, who had been unable to sell a similar idea to Atari. Both HP and Atari belatedly entered the personal computer market and, presumably, wish they had listened to the two entrepreneurs when they were trying to be intrapreneurs.[51]

The importance of intrapreneurship is evident in failure as well as in success. Texas Instruments studied more than 50 of its successful and unsuccessful new-product introductions and reached the startling conclusion that every failed

EXHIBIT 12.7 Are You an Intrapreneur?

If you answer yes more often than no to these questions, the chances are good that you have solid intrapreneurial instincts.

1. **Does your desire to make things work better occupy as much of your time as fulfilling your duty to maintain them the way they are?**
2. **Do you get excited about what you are doing at work?**
3. **Do you think about new business ideas while driving to work or taking a shower?**
4. **Can you visualize concrete steps for action when you consider ways to make a new idea happen?**
5. **Do you get in trouble from time to time for doing things that exceed your authority?**
6. **Are you able to keep your ideas under cover, suppressing your urge to tell everyone about them until you have tested them and developed a plan for implementation?**
7. **Have you successfully pushed through bleak times when something you were working on looked like it might fail?**
8. **Do you have more than your share of both fans and critics?**
9. **Do you have a network of friends at work whom you can count on for help?**
10. **Do you get easily annoyed by others' incompetent attempts to execute portions of your ideas?**
11. **Can you consider trying to overcome a natural perfectionist tendency to do all the work yourself and share responsibility for your ideas with a team?**
12. **Would you be willing to give up some salary in exchange for the chance to try out your business idea if the rewards for success were adequate?**

product lacked an intrapreneur to guide the innovation from idea to a specific product delivered to the marketplace.[52]

The Intrapreneurial Process

For innovation to flourish in an established organization, intrapreneurs and their managers must keep the guiding vision on track while allowing others to contribute to it, which can be quite a balancing act. The intrapreneur is responsible for an informal process that, if followed, will enable the vision to take form, to gather support, and eventually to be fully developed. There are four stages in this intrapreneurial process.[53]

- *Stage 1: Going solo.* An intrapreneur generally builds the initial innovative vision while working alone. The solo stage allows for the vision to grow in the mind of the intrapreneur, avoiding the inevitable ego clashes or differing goals that occur when people work together. Nebulous and unformed ideas are difficult to describe to people, which also makes it hard to solicit suggestions from others. Therefore, intrapreneurs must wait until the vision is cemented before sharing it with others in the organization.
- *Stage 2: Networking.* An intrapreneur shares the vision first with trusted colleagues in the organization and perhaps with open-minded customers. In the network stage, intrapreneurs attempt to receive casual feedback on the idea to learn more about the benefits and limitations of the vision. Even individuals who are not well known by the intrapreneur can be included in this stage. Many people would feel honored to have an intrapreneur consider them knowledgeable enough to give advice, and they willingly help. By informally testing the waters, an intrapreneur can gain supporters for the vision and work out problems that advisers may have pointed out.
- *Stage 3: Bootlegging.* During the networking stage, the intrapreneur will identify individuals who are excited enough about the vision to begin assisting in the development of the product idea or in the exploration of market potential. During the bootlegging stage, the intrapreneur becomes the leader of an informal team focused on improving the vision, even though the vision has not yet been accepted by the organization. The team generally gathers after work hours at a restaurant or a team member's home. By meeting off-premises, the official work roles are left behind. The bootleg stage allows the intrapreneur to test the waters of leadership and examine the abilities of others who may eventually be part of the official development team.
- *Stage 4: Creating the formal team.* Once the developed idea has been accepted by the organization, a formal team must be put together. The intrapreneur needs to gather others of similar intrapreneurial, innovative inclinations who are committed to the vision. Some are participants from the bootleg phase, but others may be recruited from various parts of the organization. To form an effective team, the intrapreneur must balance the abilities and characteristics of all members of the team.

Because intrapreneurial efforts by definition go against the organizational grain, managers need to take special care so that the sparks of innovation aren't stamped out by the pressures of conformity and tradition. The following section examines the factors that need to be in place for intrapreneurship to thrive in a large organization.

These Rubbermaid managers helped adapt an existing production process to make a new product for a new market. While visiting a Rubbermaid picnic-cooler plant, a senior executive realized that the same plastic molding technique could be used to make a sturdy but lightweight line of office furniture. Building on his vision, the intrapreneurial manager spearheaded a development program that created this WorkManager System product line.

Factors for Intrapreneurial Success

There are many obstacles to the success of intrapreneurial ventures. Being new and unproven, such ventures are likely to be criticized by members of the organization, and they are easy targets for budget cutbacks during financial crises. They also provoke jealousy from managers of established programs within the organization because of the amount of attention and resources they may receive from top management. Managers can use the following guidelines to overcome obstacles to innovation in their organizations.[54]

- *Establish appropriate rewards and punishments.* Rather than offer large rewards for success and impose big career risks on employees, it is more effective to offer modest rewards that are balanced with minimal career setbacks for failure. The goal of intrapreneurship, after all, is to encourage ongoing innovative activity. At both IBM and Texas Instruments, for instance, the major reward for excellence in new-product development is increased freedom to explore new-product ideas.
- *Recruit interested, enthusiastic personnel.* Just as entrepreneurs must be motivated and dedicated, members of a new-product development team must be excited and enthusiastic about the project. Some managers and employees appointed to intrapreneurial, risky ventures will have mixed feelings about the project and may not be dedicated to its success. By asking for volunteers instead of appointing people, IBM successfully recruited enthusiastic personnel for its proposed personal computer project. When employees were asked to express interest in the project, IBM received 5,000 applications for 50 positions. Not only was IBM able to staff the project with enthusiastic employees, but managers were convinced they had a winning idea.
- *Manage new ventures and established businesses differently.* Requiring new ventures to follow the strict operating and reporting procedures of established businesses may limit creativity. By loosening the reigns and managing both the people and the businesses differently, organizations will see intrapreneurial behavior rise (see Exhibit 12.8).

EXHIBIT 12.8

Managing for New Venture Success

Large organizations generally organize their new-venture units differently from other operating units to encourage intrapreneurial behavior and innovation.

Organizational Dimension	New-Venture Unit	Operating Unit
Span of management	Wide	Narrow
Job descriptions	Loose	Detailed
Planning frequency	Frequent	Infrequent
Planning time frame	Long	Short
Planning detail	Low	High
Controls	Loose	Tight
Investment hurdle rates	Low	High
Goals	Global	Specific/precise
Performance criteria	Innovation and risk taking	Current profits
Frequency of performance reviews	Infrequent	Frequent
Reward frequency	Low	High
Reward type	Recognition	Promotion
Compensation	Deferred	Current
Size of reward	Large	Small

CONTEMPORARY CHALLENGES IN SMALL-BUSINESS MANAGEMENT

Aside from the entrepreneurial and intrapreneurial processes, a number of management issues affect small organizations in unique ways or to different degrees than they affect large organizations. For instance, both large and small companies face myriad government regulations concerning employment, safety, and the environment, but large companies can more easily afford the specialized staffing needed to handle such concerns. Cash flow is another acute concern of small businesses; with smaller customer bases and fewer established sources of funding, small businesses have fewer options when it comes to maintaining positive cash flow. If managed inappropriately, these and other issues can slow the growth of a new venture or even cause its failure. Although the challenges confronted by entrepreneurs are numerous, providing health-care benefits and managing the crises of growth are two of the most important.

Providing Health-Care Benefits

All organizations are concerned about the staggering costs of health care and health insurance, but the pain is particularly acute for small businesses because they don't have the purchasing power and negotiating clout that larger organizations enjoy. Out of financial desperation, many small businesses have canceled health-care insurance for their employees or never even established such programs in the first place. Nearly 20 million employed people in the United States are without health-care coverage, and half of these are employed in small businesses.[55]

Small companies are at a disadvantage precisely because they are small. Insurance companies monitor the health of individual employees at small companies, where a single serious illness can wipe out an insurer's profit on a policy. Consequently, insurance companies reject coverage for approximately 15 percent of small businesses and force others to pay up to four times the standard rate for coverage. De Best Manufacturing in Los Angeles provided coverage for its employees for over 30 years. When two employees were treated for cancer, de Best's insurer tripled its premiums overnight. Although it would have wiped out the company's profits, de Best accepted the new rate because not doing so would have left the two cancer-stricken patients helpless. Then, even after raising de Best's premium, the insurer canceled the policy within a month.[56]

To overcome their insurance problems, many small companies are banding together to seek the advantages enjoyed by larger companies. The Cleveland Chamber of Commerce formed an association of 8,000 small businesses to purchase insurance. With the power of numbers, the association saves its members 35 to 50 percent over the cost of obtaining coverage on their own.[57]

Another dilemma in the small-business insurance situation is the question of just what health insurance should cover. In recent years, many state legislatures, in good-intentioned attempts to broaden employees' coverage, mandated so many points of coverage that they drove the price of insurance beyond the reach of many employers. For instance, mandating that health insurance provide for psychiatric hospital stays adds nearly 13 percent to the cost of the insurance. To bring basic insurance back into the range of affordability, 11 states now allow small businesses to cover their employees with stripped-down policies that address only basic health-care needs.[58]

Managing the Crises of Growth

All organizations experience crises related to growth. In new ventures, for instance, a major crisis often occurs after the company experiences its initial, rapid growth. While toiling to gain acceptance in the marketplace, the new venture focuses purely on developing innovative products and creatively developing its markets. Because of the fast pace and excitement of the start-up activity, the new venture gets by without formal control systems or organization structures. Ventures can experience four crises as they grow from start-up to established enterprise:[59]

- *Crisis of leadership.* The initial growth phase in a new venture is marked by creativity, in both developing products and finding markets. The founding entrepreneurs are likely to wake up one morning and realize that they have a sizable organization to lead, with responsibilities ranging from production techniques to personnel policies. This is a critical juncture in a new venture's life because it marks the point at which the entrepreneurial drive needs to be balanced with stable, day-to-day leadership. Entrepreneurs often find that their skills and interests are ill-suited to this new reality. Successful ones, such as Microsoft's Bill Gates, recognize that their organizations need strong management and so appoint experienced executives to guide the company.
- *Crisis of autonomy.* With the introduction of mainstream management, the new venture takes on formal organization structures and control systems. While they are clearly needed to help rein in the creative chaos of the early days, the formality and structure can start to demoralize lower-level managers and employees, particularly those who were around in the rough-and-tumble days.
- *Crisis of control.* In response to the lack of autonomy that many members in the organization begin to feel, company leaders often decentralize, putting decision-making authority down on the front lines. However, letting go of the steering wheel is often very hard for an entrepreneur to do. Some may try to recentralize to restore a sense of control.

- *Crisis of red tape.* The centralization issue is often solved with coordination programs and policies that try to seek a comfortable medium between control and chaos. This is the stage at which red tape and bureaucracy begin to creep in.

As managers begin to realize that the organization has become too bureaucratic, they respond with simplified controls, matrix organization structures, and other efforts to make the organization leaner and more efficient. Many leading-edge companies are just now responding to the red tape crisis, so researchers aren't entirely sure what the next crisis stage might involve.

SUMMARY

New ventures bring innovative new products to market, fuel the economy, increase employment, and improve the health and welfare of our society. New ventures are agents of change, and they have contributed nearly half of all product and process innovations in the last 50 years. Many of the innovations introduced have enhanced society's health and welfare by decreasing suffering, discomfort, or loss of life. Economic growth is provided by the existence of a healthy small-business community that ensures competition by improving product quality and by keeping prices fair. New ventures are responsible for creating many of the new jobs in the United States and other countries; between now and the year 2000, new ventures could generate more than half of all new jobs. Lastly, entrepreneurship creates career alternatives for people who may be dissatisfied with traditional career paths.

Entrepreneurs have distinct personality characteristics that drive them to pursue their innovative goals. The first is a high energy level, which allows the entrepreneur to work the long hours necessary for the new venture to be successful. Next, entrepreneurs exhibit a high need for achievement, which allows them to set ambitious goals and to receive great satisfaction when those goals are achieved. Characterized as moderate risk-takers, successful entrepreneurs neither avoid risky situations nor take excessive risks. Another trait possessed by entrepreneurs is their high level of confidence in their own abilities to overcome any obstacle and achieve success. Entrepreneurs also believe they have control over their lives (rather than believing in luck or fate). Finally, entrepreneurs are comfortable making decisions with little information, a trait critical for entrepreneurs who face so much uncertainty when starting a new venture.

The three strategies for starting new ventures are new-market leadership, creative imitation, and entrepreneurial judo. New-market leadership is a strategy to gain leadership and dominance in an emerging market or industry by implementing a new idea faster and better than competitors. Entrepreneurs must structure their products and organizations to discourage competition. The strategy of creative imitation focuses on dominating the market by perfecting an existing product or its positioning in the marketplace. Entrepreneurs who utilize this strategy succeed by improving on the strategies and tactics of the original innovator. Entrepreneurial judo is a strategy employed by entrepreneurs to fill the holes left by competitors in an existing marketplace. This strategy works well for small business ventures since it enables entrepreneurs to focus on one segment of the market and grow at a comfortable pace.

When initiating a new venture, entrepreneurs must consider five factors. First, they must decide whether they want to start a new business, purchase an existing business, or buy a franchise. Second, they must decide whether the new venture will be a sole proprietorship, partnership, corporation, or S corporation. Third, entrepreneurs must create a business plan that details business strategies and tactics. This plan is used to procure capital and to guide the new venture through the start-up phase. Fourth, entrepreneurs must acquire capital through personal funds, by taking out loans, or by selling a portion of ownership in the business. And fifth, entrepreneurs need to consider support from business incubators, the Small Business Administration, entrepreneurial centers at universities, and accounting firms that provide low-fee consulting to new ventures.

Entrepreneurial success can be attributed to a sound knowledge of business and managerial functions, flexibility in adapting to a changing environment, objective rather than emotional views of products, previous experience in the industry, and respect for competitors who have a loyal customer base.

Intrapreneurship is the process of promoting innovation within a large organization. An organization that provides an atmosphere for creative individuals will be rewarded with innovative new products. The four steps in the intrapreneurial process are (1) going solo, in which the intrapreneur works alone to build his or her vision; (2) networking, in which the intrapreneur seeks feedback and support by sharing the idea with others; (3) bootlegging, in which the intrapreneur becomes the leader of an informal team that is excited about the idea; and (4) creating the formal team after the organization has accepted the idea. For intrapreneurship to grow, organizations must establish modest rewards for success and minimal career setbacks for failure, recruit product-development teams (rather than merely appointing employees), and manage intrapreneurial new ventures with looser controls.

Two significant issues faced by small businesses are the high price of health care and health-care insurance and the management of growth with emphasis on the transition to professional management.

MEETING A MANAGEMENT CHALLENGE AT

R.W. FROOKIES

Richard S. Worth could never be accused of doing things the easy way. When he decided to sell his all-natural, fruit juice–sweetened cookies in grocery stores instead of through his own chain of independent specialty shops, he automatically took on the largest companies in the industry: RJR Nabisco, Keebler, and Sunshine Biscuits. He also put himself at the mercy of grocery store slotting fees, or at least that's what the common wisdom in the industry figured.

One of Worth's more unusual moves helped solve several problems at once. First, he needed money, plain and simple, and he's never been too fond of debt financing. Second, he needed support from customers, which include both grocery stores and grocery distributors (who buy products from food companies such as Frookies, then sell them to independent grocers and small chains). And third, he needed suppliers who were willing to be flexible about getting paid.

His bold stroke was selling one-third of the company in a private stock offering aimed at his customers and suppliers. By selling shares in the company, he raised much-needed capital, and by selling those shares to the outside groups that would have the greatest impact on his success, he turned them into partners. For instance, Consolidated Biscuit, which bakes all of Worth's cookies, is one of the largest

Richard S. Worth, founder, R.W. Frookies

shareholders and gives Worth months to pay his bills. And Shur-Good Biscuit, a distributor that is also a shareholder, works extra hard to sell Frookies because as Frookies's financial fortunes rise, so do Shur-Good's.

The same ingenuity helped Worth conquer his biggest challenge—getting adequate shelf space in major grocery chains. To persuade store managers to give his product a try without pulling establishing products from their shelves, he provided his own shelves—cardboard shelves in freestanding displays that doubled as in-store advertising. He also agreed to stage promotional events that helped draw people into the stores. The colorful purple and green displays attracted enough attention for store managers to notice not only the cookies but also the number of customers who were buying them. Demand shot up. One grocery chain after another opened up shelf space, pushing aside the name brands of industry leaders. Cash flow turned positive, enough to finance limited and highly targeted advertising, usually in newspapers. As for slotting fees, Worth's tough stance against paying them combined with the sudden demand for his cookies forced managers either to reduce the charges or to forgo collecting them altogether.

Frookies were so successful that Worth encountered an unexpected problem: actual sales made a mockery of his business-plan projections. He had expected to sell about 139,000 cases of cookies for $1.6 million by his second year. But before that second year was through, more than 1.5 million cases had been sold for $17.5 million—so much that Consolidated Biscuit had to bake around the clock to supply enough cookies. That rapid growth not only put Frookies on store shelves in all 50 states, Canada, and France but also led Worth to the next stage of entrepreneurship: managing a maturing start-up. He still works 12 to 16 hours a day, and he's still reluctant to delegate responsibilities in daily management. But Worth is preparing for one more challenge—indeed, he's been aware of it since his first day in business—the inevitable competition from RJR Nabisco, Keebler, and Sunshine. He's already working on ideas for new products.

You're the Manager: Richard Worth realizes that his company is growing fast and that some important decisions need to be made to ensure its continued success. He hires you as executive assistant. Although Worth has final authority, it is your job to help him manage the explosive growth of Frookies and guide the company to its peak potential.

Ranking Questions

1. Frookies has reached the stage at which a business either keeps growing at its phenomenal rate or begins to slow because of changes in its internal and external environment. You are particularly concerned about anticipating what those changes might be and deciding how to respond to them promptly and effectively. Rank from most to least important the possible changes that could affect the short-term performance of Frookies.
   a. Competitive products introduced by industry leaders RJR Nabisco, Keebler, and Sunshine Biscuits
   b. A leveling of demand, which might induce some grocery store chains to get adamant about slotting fees
   c. Worth's refusal to limit himself to certain aspects of the business and to allow professional management to steer the company
   d. The development of too many new products for introduction, which could distract management from its primary product focus
2. Selling shares to suppliers and distributors seems to have been very effective so far, but the tactic is not without risk. Rank the following potential ramifications of the private stock offering, from most likely to happen to least likely.
   a. Grocery stores will stop buying from Frookies's shareholder distributors if they think there is some sort of collusion going on.
   b. Suppliers who own shares might assume that they have Frookies over the proverbial barrel, since Frookies isn't likely to use nonowners as suppliers. The shareholder suppliers might think they can get away with increasing the prices they charge to bake, package, and transport Frookies.
   c. What if a dealer who owns a significant portion of shares runs into competitive trouble in a given market area? The shareholding arrangement might stop Frookies from finding a better distributor.
   d. New distributors might be reluctant to sign up with Frookies if they know that their own sales efforts might help their competitors who own shares in Frookies.

Multiple-Choice Questions

3. A rule of thumb in the industry is that it costs about $10 million to produce an effective national advertising campaign for a major food product. Worth's goal is to transform R.W. Frookies into a truly national company, and doing that will require an appropriately sizable and aggressive marketing program. Yet despite Frookies's success, the company is still far from being able to justify a large marketing budget. Given the circumstances, how should the business plan be changed?
   a. Raise the necessary capital by becoming a publicly traded company and selling shares on the stock market.
   b. Change nothing in the current marketing strategy.
   c. Try to negotiate an increase in the company's credit line to allow for greater debt capitalization.
   d. Budget for a limited advertising campaign conducted on a regional basis, thus limiting

marketing expenditures while testing the marketing strategy.

4. One aspect of Frookies's first few years in business that was anything but smooth was Worth's relationship with the people he hired to help lead the company. In fact, he has already gone through three company presidents, all of whom had experience at successful food companies. He says they weren't entrepreneurial; they say he wouldn't relinquish control and let them manage what they were hired to manage. (The current president, with whom Worth is pleased, is his cousin, who helped write the initial business plan.) Given the company's current situation and prospects, which of the following managers would be the most attractive choice as Worth's second-in-command?
   a. A manager who isn't intimately familiar with the food industry but who has successfully guided a company through the transition from start-up to nationwide sales.
   b. Someone with qualifications similar to the candidate in (a), but who served as second-in-command in the organization, not as the CEO.
   c. An aggressive, no-holds-barred entrepreneur who will push the company to grow as fast as possible.
   d. A career consultant with a thorough understanding of the food business.

Analysis Questions

5. Which of Drucker's three broad entrepreneurial strategies is Frookies pursuing? Explain your answer.
6. How is Frookies contributing to the economy and society overall?
7. Which element of the external environment has had the most impact on Frookies so far? Why? Will this same element continue to be the leading external factor into the future?

Special Project

Consolidated Biscuit officials met recently with several of the other minority owners in Frookies, including the largest and most important distributors. You and Worth have just been informed of this meeting, at which it was agreed that the minority owners should exercise more influence over major management decisions concerning the direction of the company. It appears that Worth's ingenious idea to sell shares in Frookies to suppliers and distributors is turning out to be a double-edged sword. The minority owners realize that they have two things in their favor: it was their equity investments that financed the growth of Frookies, and they are the key businesses in the chain, controlling the manufacture and distribution of Frookies. They are making two demands. First, they want Worth to hand over all management functions to professional managers and confine himself to new-product development. Second, they want to begin a major marketing program immediately, financing to a great extent with debt capital. What is the best way to respond? Outline your ideas on a page or two for Worth.[60]

KEY TERMS

business plan (379)
corporation (378)
creative imitation (375)
debt capital (380)
entrepreneur (369)
entrepreneurial judo (375)
entrepreneurship (368)
equity capital (380)
incubators (381)
intrapreneur (387)
new-market leadership (374)
new venture (368)
partnership (378)
private stock offering (380)
public stock offering (380)
S corporation (379)
small business (369)
sole proprietorship (377)
start-up (376)
venture capitalists (381)

QUESTIONS

For Review

1. How do entrepreneurial new ventures affect society and the economy?
2. What are the common personality traits of entrepreneurs?
3. What are the three new-venture strategies?
4. What are the major issues that entrepreneurs need to consider before launching new ventures?
5. What are the factors that lead to entrepreneurial success?

For Analysis

1. How can environmental factors affect entrepreneurship?
2. What are the major differences between establishing a start-up and becoming a franchisee?
3. Why might a small business established as a sole proprietorship change to an S corporation form of ownership?
4. How does the entrepreneur's role change as the organization grows?
5. How are entrepreneurship and intrapreneurship similar? How are they different?

For Application

1. Where could a new McDonald's franchisee turn for assistance and support?
2. What factors should IBM consider if it is contemplating spinning off its laptop PC operation into an independent business?
3. The owner of a small manufacturing firm with a serious cash flow shortage wants to expand operations. Should she choose debt or equity financing? Why?
4. Could a major automaker such as Ford or General Motors set up an entire intrapreneurial organization to design and build a new car? Why or why not?
5. Would it be a good idea for a large company such as Exxon to hire several successful entrepreneurs in an attempt to instill an intrapreneurial spirit in the corporation?

KEEPING CURRENT IN MANAGEMENT

From recent magazines or newspapers, select an article that discusses an entrepreneur who initiated a new business venture using a specific entrepreneurial strategy. One example might focus on an entrepreneur who introduced a new product aimed at a gap in an existing market. Another example might involve an entrepreneur who created an innovative product that creates a new market.

1. What entrepreneurial strategy did the new-business owner implement? Was the strategy successful? Explain.
2. How did the entrepreneur initiate the new venture? Discuss the entrepreneur's decisions about the approaches to new ventures, ownership forms, the business plan, sources of funding, and sources of support.
3. What factors for entrepreneurial success were utilized by the business owner? Did they help to increase the entrepreneur's chances for success? How?

SHARPEN YOUR MANAGEMENT SKILLS

Pretend that you're about to launch a small community newspaper. You need $100,000 to buy equipment and set up your operations. You have $15,000 in savings and a $20,000 home equity line of credit, which you've already decided to use.

- *Decision:* Decide whether you want to raise the remaining $65,000 through debt or equity financing, then decide which potential source of funds you'll approach first.
- *Communication:* Write a one-page letter to the best potential source of funds you can think of. (For the purposes of this exercise, make up any details you like, such as the existence of a wealthy uncle who's been sailing the South Pacific for the last five years.) Introduce yourself (if the person you're writing to is a stranger), explain your business idea, and explain/describe your need for capital.

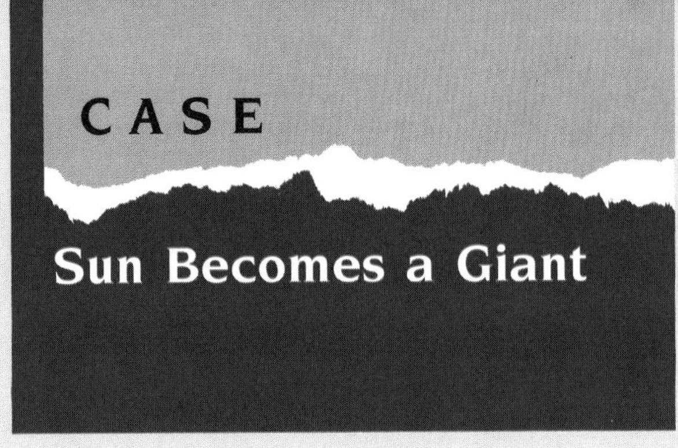

Sun Microsystems, founded by four talented 27-year-olds, has quickly become the world's leading supplier of the powerful compact computers known as workstations. But the gung-ho independence that built sales to 135,000 units a year has also made Sun difficult to manage. As founding partner and CEO Scott McNealy meets new competitive and marketing challenges, he must keep control of his organization.

HISTORY

Sun was founded in 1982 when McNealy and a fellow Stanford MBA were excited by a workstation that had been built from spare parts by a Stanford engineering graduate student. The three formed a partnership with a Berkeley computer whiz who specialized in Unix, an operating system popular with the scientists and engineers who made up the potential market for workstations. The main competition was workstation pioneer Apollo (later bought by Hewlett-Packard), but Sun had key advantages: it could offer lower prices because it used existing technologies, and its adoption of Unix allowed Sun workstations to easily communicate with the hardware and software of other vendors.

Sun sales exploded past $1 billion in its first six years as its work force rose from 90 to 10,000, but the organization couldn't keep up. In the spring of 1989, as computer glitches shut down manufacturing systems and market share fell, Sun posted a $20 million quarterly loss. McNealy reversed the situation by centralizing and focusing his company. Over the next year, sales of Sun workstations shot up to $2.7 billion, net income nearly doubled to $111 million, and Sun recaptured the lead in the $7.3 billion global workstation market. Sales have since surpassed $3 billion, income is growing even faster, and Sun's share of the market has grown to 32 percent, well ahead of second-place Hewlett-Packard's 21 percent.

ENVIRONMENT

Sun's early success was built on an aggressive organizational culture that encouraged employees to take the initiative. But the resulting rapid-fire decision making spawned dozens of projects and sent Sun in contradictory directions. For example, the company developed three separate product lines based on different computer chips, which confused customers about which was the best. McNealy centralized the organization and virtually eliminated two of the product lines. He also stopped customizing workstations for individual orders and instead chose to concentrate on high-volume manufacturing. That let Sun simplify its tasks by choosing to assemble and test components made by outside suppliers.

GOALS AND CHALLENGES

With Sun back under control, McNealy can concentrate on finding opportunities in the fast-changing environment. Sun is running out of engineers to sell to, so McNealy is targeting commercial operations such as brokerage houses and airlines. But selling to buyers who are less technically sophisticated than engineers and scientists has forced Sun to change both its hardware and its software. The company has rewritten its manuals and designed computers to be easier to install and maintain, and it has added features to make the software easier for nonengineers to use.

Sun has also changed its distribution tactics to appeal to commercial users by relying less on direct sales and convincing major retailers to offer Sun systems. Sun is trying to lure commercial customers away from high-end personal computers by bringing out a string of low-end products, but this strategy carries some risk: lower-cost products mean lower gross margins, so volumes must be high to keep revenues up. High volumes, however, should make it more attractive for software companies to write programs for Sun systems, and that would make Sun more competitive against PCs, which have many more programs available. Sun has recently convinced software giants Lotus, Ashton-Tate, and WordPerfect to adapt their programs to Sun's systems.

1. What entrepreneurial strategies has McNealy used for Sun, and how has he implemented them?
2. What factors for entrepreneurial success has Sun exhibited?
3. If McNealy decides that Sun needs a subsidiary to develop business application software for commercial buyers, how should he start this new venture to balance risk, cost, and control?
4. McNealy is likely to encounter managerial crises during rapid expansion in the commercial computer market. How might his future response to such crises compare with his response to the crises experienced when Sun's main buyers were scientists and engineers?

CHAPTER OUTLINE

13 Human Resource Management

After studying this chapter, you will be able to

1. Explain the basis of human resource management and discuss how it supports organizational goals
2. Describe the five environmental influences on human resource management
3. Identify four key issues that organizations face in international human resource management
4. Outline the steps in the human resource management process
5. Discuss the five tools managers can use to select qualified people to fill available jobs
6. Explain the role of training and development in human resource management
7. Highlight the role of performance appraisals in facilitating employee development and movement within the organization

FACING A MANAGEMENT CHALLENGE AT

JOHNSON & JOHNSON

Keeping Employees in the Pink and the Company in the Black

By the time James E. Burke had taken over as chairman and CEO of Johnson & Johnson, the baby-boom generation had matured—and with it the company's baby-products business. To keep the New Brunswick, New Jersey, giant in a leading position in the worldwide health-products business, Burke knew he had to follow the aging baby boomers into new, more sophisticated markets. So in the span of four years, Johnson & Johnson bought 25 companies, and it now produces a huge range of products, from the venerable Band-Aids and Tylenol to advanced medical instrumentation and surgical implants.

As a result of growth in its existing businesses and the addition of the new units, Johnson & Johnson also became the country's largest health-care employer, with more than 80,000 employees. Burke knew that, as always, employees were the key to making the complex organization work. Ever since its founding in the 1880s, the company has demonstrated a commitment to the people on its payroll. The Johnson & Johnson Credo, which articulates the company's values and mission, has this to say about employees:

> We are responsible to our employees, the men and women who work with us around the world. Everyone must be considered as an individual. We must respect their dignity and recognize their merit. They must have a sense of security in their jobs. Compensation must be fair and adequate, and working conditions clean, orderly, and safe. Employees must feel free to make suggestions and complaints. There must be equal opportunity for employment, development and advancement for those qualified. We must provide competent management, and their actions must be just and ethical.

Coupled with this genuine concern for the well-being of their employees, Johnson & Johnson executives also knew that employee productivity was key to the company's continued success. People play a vital role in the research, production, and marketing of Johnson & Johnson products, and the more productive these people are, the more profitable the company will be.

With these two concerns in mind, James Burke faced some challenging human resource issues. For example, smoking affects both the well-being and productivity of employees. Studies showed that over 30 percent of Johnson & Johnson's employees were smokers, and an internal report revealed that the smokers' absenteeism rate was 45 percent higher than that of nonsmokers. Furthermore, major medical expenses for smokers average 30 percent higher than for nonsmokers, an ominous statistic at a time when health-care costs were rising at nearly twice the rate of inflation.

Poor health wasn't the only issue facing management. Company employees increasingly fell into one of three groups: they were in two-career couples with children; they were responsible for aging parents; or they were single parents. Most had become frustrated by their inability to meet all their obligations to their families and to their employer. Many had trouble finding and affording day care. To compound the situation, most employees said that their managers were unsympathetic about the dilemmas they faced.

How should James Burke meet these important challenges? How can he improve the health of his employees? How can he help them balance work and family obligations? And how can he ensure the company's continued success while meeting the longstanding commitment to his employees' well-being?[1]

CHAPTER OVERVIEW

James Burke, and his successor at Johnson & Johnson, Ralph S. Larsen, know that any organization is only as good as its people. Finding, developing, supporting, and keeping those people is the essence of human resource management. This chapter explains the basis of human resource management and discusses how it supports organizational goals. The chapter then describes the five environmental influences on human resource management, followed by the steps in the human resource management process. After that is a list of the five core dimensions in the job characteristics model and an explanation of how each relates to job design. The chapter also discusses five tools managers can use when selecting qualified people to fill available jobs. Finally, it explains the role of performance appraisals in employee development and movement within the organization.

HUMAN RESOURCE MANAGEMENT AND THE ORGANIZATION

Every organization, whether it's a multinational conglomerate, a small business, a religious institution, or a government agency, depends on people. Appropriate candidates for each job from chairman of the board to night shift janitor must be located, either inside or outside the organization, and they must be convinced by pay, benefits, and working conditions to take and keep the job. They must also be trained and motivated. Handling these functions is part of the human resource management process.

human resource management A comprehensive, integrated system for effectively managing the work force in the effort to achieve organizational goals

Human resource management is a comprehensive, integrated system for effectively managing the work force in the effort to achieve an organization's goals.[2] This system has traditionally included hiring, firing, and payroll, which are essentially reactions to problems or organizational goals that already exist. But since World War II, the business world has grown more complex and human resource management has grown to include introducing new technology to the workplace, arranging work tasks, and communicating with employees. With the great increase in global competition, in government regulation, and in the need for skilled labor, human resource managers are increasingly invited to participate in strategic planning (see Exhibit 13.1) and organizational goal setting. They have also become involved in personal and career development (to prevent stagnation and to develop talent), in interpersonal relations (to assure teamwork

EXHIBIT 13.1

Strategic Human Resource Management

The human resource management process leads to productivity by balancing personnel availability and requirements in accordance with the organization's resources and strategic plans; human resource managers may contribute to organizational strategic plans as well as reacting to them.

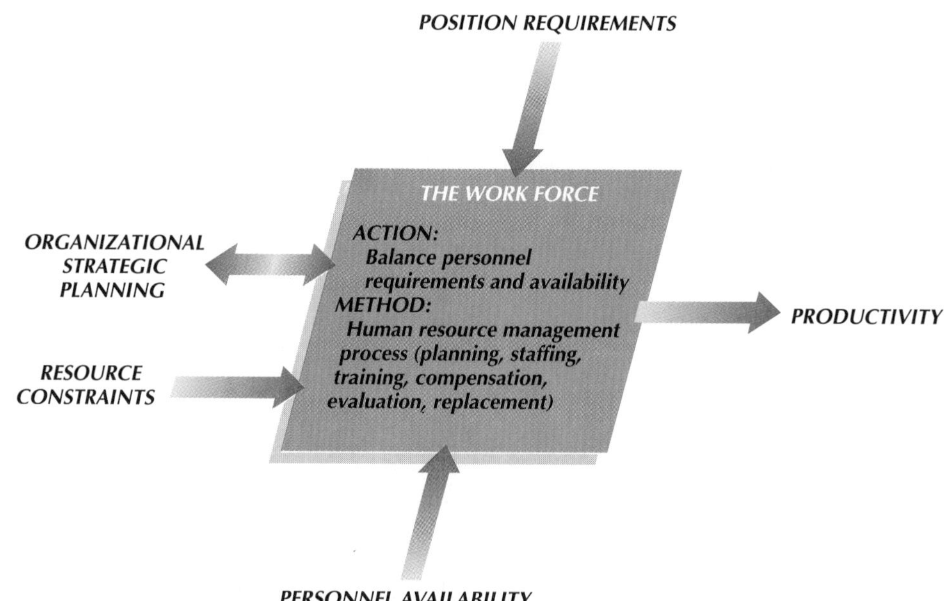

and accurate communication), in attending to employee needs (to demonstrate the organization's concern for them), and in employee participation in work life (to help employees perform at their full capacity).[3]

The dedicated instructors at the Institute for Effective Education in California are the key to ensuring that this not-for-profit organization reaches its goals. Executive director Kenneth Traupmann *(front row, left)* provides training and coaching to support the instructors as they work with students who have learning or developmental disabilities or other problems.

Meeting Organizational Goals

The human resource function plays a vital role in any organization's ability to meet its goals. Like other organizational managers, human resource managers must consider their organization's environment, resources, and goals. For example, take the human resource function of compensation as it relates to the company's economic environment and resources. A new, cash-poor company might offer employees company stock as part of its compensation plan in order to keep immediate expenditures low, whereas an established competitor might try to attract the best employees with higher salaries.

Moreover, an organization's efforts to implement its strategy often involve a highly interrelated set of human resource actions. Downsizing efforts, for instance, integrate the human resource functions of employee movement (for outplacement, retirement, and management succession), compensation (for severance pay), and better human resource planning (to reduce the need for further downsizing). Similarly, decentralizing integrates the human resource functions of training (to develop leadership skills and foster decision making), evaluations (for new performance appraisal methods), and compensation (for changes in wage structure).[4]

Developing Future Managers

An important function of human resource management is developing future managers. These key professionals can be recruited from within the organization, recruited away from other organizations, or even recruited fresh out of school. Like other employees, managers must often be educated in the organization's culture and trained in people-handling skills and legal requirements. General Electric annually trains about 1,000 employees through its New Manager's Program, which encourages first-time managers to seize the initiative, take risks, and even challenge their supervisors, all while respecting the company's culture and goals.[5]

Although GE has decided to develop dynamic, innovative, risk-taking management as a way to stay flexible and competitive in an ever-changing business environment, this emphasis is not the only appropriate style of management training. In organizations that favor stability over growth, a traditional caretaker style of management may be preferred, as it has been in many businesses since World War II. But rapid changes in the organizational environment are prompting many organizations to develop a new kind of manager that is more in the GE mold: flexible, innovative, and able to share power with employees.[6]

A variety of human resource functions are helping develop this new breed of manager. Compensation plans increasingly reward actual performance instead of longevity or rank. New-management training programs emphasize problem solving and creativity, and job rotation is broadening managers' experience and perspectives.[7]

A major environmental factor that is forcing the development of flexible managers is global competition, which is forcing prices and profits down in many industries. Companies are trying to cut costs and speed decision making by reducing the number of middle managers and transferring more decision-making power to lower-level employees and self-managing work teams. The managers in such companies must be comfortable with letting subordinates make decisions and receive sensitive information. For instance, Procter & Gamble eliminated a layer of middle management at each of its plants by turning half its production employees into salaried technicians charged with making and implementing most day-to-day operating decisions.[8]

THE HUMAN RESOURCES ENVIRONMENT

Human resources is a complex field that is affected by numerous external forces. Managers need to recognize the influence of these environmental forces as they develop human resource strategies and tactics for meeting organizational goals. The forces in the human resource environment can be divided into five general categories: competition; labor relations; laws and regulations; international scope, and a collection of broad technological, economic, and social influences that affect employees' expectations, performance, and well-being.

Competitive Influences

Organizations often compete with each other for available employees. In some industries, shortages are so extreme that organizations occasionally must go to great lengths to satisfy their work-force needs. Seattle-based airplane manufacturer Boeing once experienced a skilled-labor shortage so acute that its human resource managers had to solve the problem by arranging to borrow 670 trained employees for six months from a Georgia-based competitor, Lockheed.[9] Competition has been increasing because labor, especially skilled labor, is in short supply.

In industries where they occur, labor shortages (1) give employees more power over what jobs they will take and under what conditions and (2) force employers to look to nontraditional sources such as retirees and part-time employees to fill open slots. For instance, employees over 65 make up 25 percent of Days Inns' reservation sales staff, and drastically lower turnover among these older employees has reduced the company's training and recruitment costs by 40 percent.[10]

Skilled employees are demanding more of a chance to direct their own careers, the ability to fit jobs around their life-styles and home obligations, and the opportunity to pursue their personal goals while at work. Human resource managers are responding by giving employees greater responsibility, more flexible work arrangements, and novel training and incentive packages designed to retain their loyalty (see Exhibit 13.2).[11] This approach, as well as a good compensation package, can both attract job applicants and keep current employees on the job.

Retaining Employees

Organizations usually try to avoid employee turnover because it is expensive. It may cost $1,000 to replace a data-entry operator when hiring, training, and lost productivity are considered, and replacement of a specialized professional or executive may cost $50,000.[12] A major factor in retaining employees is **job satisfaction,** the positive emotional state resulting from performance of a job.

job satisfaction The positive emotional state resulting from performance in a job tion and 2-4 years supervisory experience. You must be able to code data for inputting into computer system, contact customers on past due accounts, reconcile reports, review credit ratings and establish credit limits. You will plan and coordinate all work assignments for an accounting clerk.

We offer a flexible benefits program including 401(k) participation and pleasant working conditions. Starting salary is in mid 20s. Please call for appointment, or send resume

PROGRAMMING

SENIOR PROGRAMMING/ANALYST

Largest independent gasoline retailer has immediate need for a Senior Programmer/Analyst. Qualifications include 5-7 yrs in experience. Excellent communication skills while interfacing with all levels of mgmt., good skills in RPG programming environment are also required. Knowledge of retail operations, and PC programming in Foxbase desirable.

Our company offers a competitive salary and fringe benefits package including 401(k), along with a non-smoking computer center env. If interested, please mail or fax resume with cover letter

SENIOR BUYER

(Pomona)

Loral Electro-Optical Systems has an immediate opening for a Senior Buyer in our Pomona facility.

The successful candidate will be responsible for purchasing casting and machine parts. Must be experienced with all Government Specifications (DAR/FAR) requirements consisting of castings and machine parts. Must be able to document P.O. file to satisfy Government Audit system. A BS degree in Business or Engineering is preferred and a minimum of 4 years of experience.

Loral offers excellent benefits, including dental, medical, 401K, educational reimbursement and Christmas shutdown, etc. Please mail resume to LORAL EOS, 300 N. Halstead St., Dept. A/5-10A, Pasadena, CA 91107.

Loral EOS supports a drug-free work environment. Pre-employment drug screening will be conducted.

Equal Oppty Employer MFHV
Minorities & Females Are
Encouraged To Apply

- Know what it's like to give outstanding customer svce
- Have excellent phone skills.
- Can handle customers.

WE OFFER:
- The chance to make $19-$24K per year.
- A great group of people to work with.
- A competitive benefits package (Dental ins. incl.).
- All the training you'll need to be successful with us.
- Flexible hours.

For More Information & Application, appy in person: SFV Tues & Thurs. 8:30 ONLY

INSURANCE

Marketing Reps
Los Angeles Area

With over 110 offices nationwide, General Rehabilitation Services is rapidly growing as an industry leader. If you have sales exp. and knowledge of casualty insurance, come share in our success. Insurance rehab background a plus. Enjoy an excellent salary and bonus, company car, a 401(k) plan, profit sharing and life and LTD insurance. Forward your resume to: GENERAL REHABILITATION SERVICES,

PAYROLL ASSISTANT

IN-N-OUT BURGER, a growing, high profile food service leader, is looking for a someone with 2 years general office or accounting experience to fill this full-time position.

We require good math skills, data entry, 10-key by touch, and light typing. Payroll experience preferred.

Our outstanding benefits package includes:

- Flexible starting salary commensurate with qualifications
- Paid health insurance
- Company sponsored retirement plan
- Paid vacations and sick days

If you have high personal and professional standards and enjoy a challenging atmosphere, please apply in person or forward your resume to:

Accounts Receivable Supervisor

EXHIBIT 13.2

Employees Want More Than a Paycheck

Today's employees are increasingly demanding jobs that offer flexibility and self-fulfillment, in addition to income.

Satisfaction results when human resource managers design work activities with built-in motivating factors such as achievement, recognition, responsibility, and growth or advancement.[13] Turnover, on the other hand, is associated with low job satisfaction, low pay, lack of clarity about the job, low unemployment rates, and job alternatives outside the organization.[14]

Attracting Employees

Another concept that can be as important in attracting employees as in retaining them is avoiding *job dissatisfaction.* A variety of factors lead to job dissatisfaction, including employee concerns about work policies, interpersonal work relationships, working conditions, pay, status, and job security.[15] Many federal government managers report it is difficult to attract and retain good employees because pay is poor, work is hampered by numerous regulations, and advancement is limited because some of the best jobs go to political appointees.[16] Jobs that appear low in dissatisfaction potential and high in satisfaction will be attractive to job applicants. Human resource departments can take a variety of positive steps to make jobs attractive and satisfying, from ensuring fair compensation and benefits to helping employees prepare for and adjust to changes in technology.

Labor Relations Influences

Another important force influencing human resource management is organized labor. Unions help employees both in negotiating employment contracts and in enforcing their terms. **Labor relations** is the conduct of relations between management and labor unions. Unions play a smaller role in U.S. business than they once did (in recent years, union membership has sunk below 20 percent of all employees from a peak of 35 percent in 1954), but they remain an active force wherever employees believe that unions can improve compensation, working conditions, job security, chances for promotion, or treatment by managers.[17] In addition, some observers point out that the changes brought on by company restructurings, massive layoffs, and the increased role of foreign companies in

labor relations The conduct of relations between management and labor unions the U.S. economy create fertile ground for unions, particularly among white-collar employees.[18]

Unions and management have traditionally been rivals. But today's highly competitive business environment is prompting management and unions to try to work together, and some organizations are even sharing power with unions. For example, at United Press International (UPI), the Wire Service Guild convinced member journalists to accept pay cuts, and in exchange, the union increased its power and access to information by receiving two seats on the company's board of directors.[19]

The Role of Unions

labor union A group of employees that collectively bargains on behalf of employees and oversees their interests in the workplace

A **labor union** is a group of employees that collectively represents employees and oversees their interests in the workplace. Employees have the freedom to decide by secret ballot whether they will affiliate with an established union, form their own, change unions, or end any union affiliation. An election is called if at least 30 percent of the eligible employees sign cards requesting one. The only employees eligible to vote are members of the proposed *bargaining unit,* which is a logical grouping of employees who would be represented by the union, such as all clerical employees or all nonmanagement employees. The most visible role of unions is negotiating employment contracts and bringing pressure on management to change compensation and work conditions through strikes, informational pickets, and appeals to public sentiment. But an equally important task that relates directly to management of human resources is administration of employment contracts through formal *grievance* procedures (see Exhibit 13.3), arbitration, and even lawsuits.

The U.S. labor movement has its roots in associations of skilled artisans such as printers and shoemakers who were threatened by mass production and who slowly won the right to organize and to strike beginning in 1842. Unenlightened management practices were also a major force behind the rise of unionism. The modern labor movement arose after the Civil War, when price declines prompted railroad, steel, and oil companies to consolidate into huge, powerful combinations as a way to control costs and reduce competition. Trade unions also banded together in an effort to negotiate more effectively with the new giants. The labor movement was consistently hurt by economic downturns and failed strikes, and only 3 percent of the nation's employees were union members at the turn of the century.[20] The Great Depression of the 1930s saw passage of federal laws that encouraged unionization and restricted management rights. Congress then limited union rights after a wave of 4,985 strikes resulted in an unprecedented 116 million workdays of lost production in 1946 alone.[21] Labor-management relations today are still governed by laws from that era.

MANAGEMENT AROUND THE WORLD

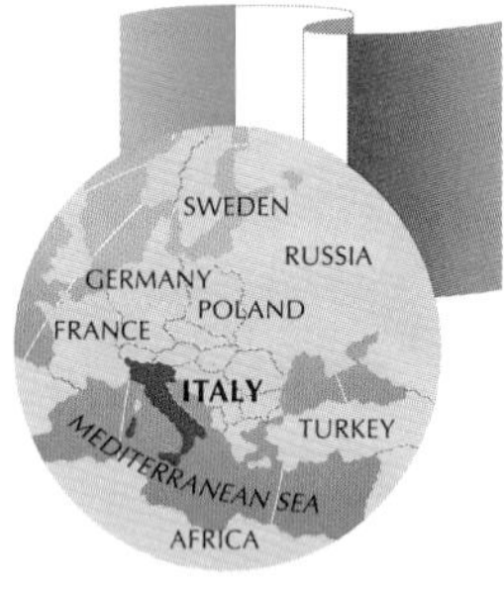

Strikes are a larger part of the business environment in some countries than in others. Over a recent 15-year period, for instance, Italy witnessed 1,337 days lost in strikes per 1,000 employees. In contrast, the Netherlands lost only 33 days, and Switzerland lost only 1 day. The United States was roughly in the middle, with 511 days, although strikes have decreased in the United States over the last several years.

Balancing Labor and Management Concerns

Negotiation can be an effective means for management and labor to balance their concerns, but the process is often confrontational and can lead to strikes that hurt both productivity and morale. Human resource managers and union officials therefore increasingly balance their concerns through cooperation, which can transfer some decision-making power to employees and improve profits. For example, the United Auto Workers Union joined General Motors and the Toyota Company to create New United Motor Manufacturing. The plant has generated the highest quality and productivity levels in the General Motors system, comparable to Toyota plants in Japan. Management's emphasis

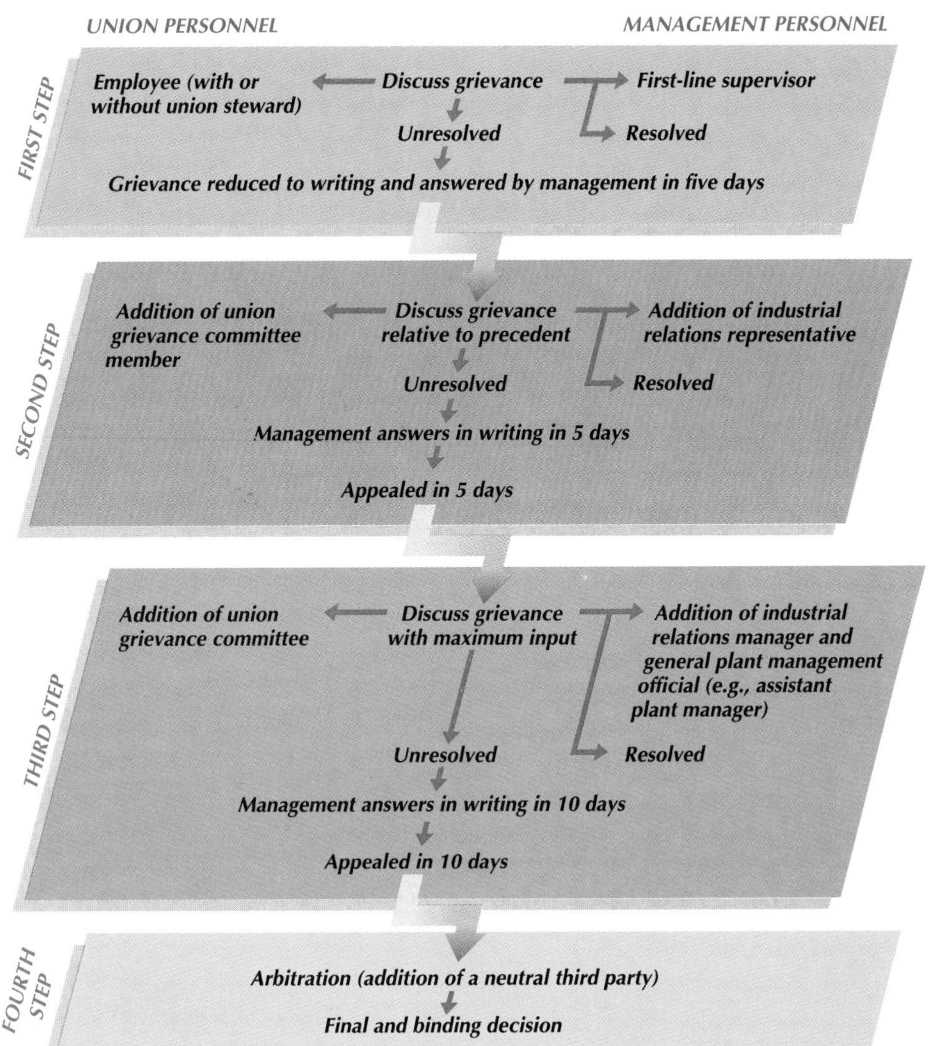

EXHIBIT 13.3

Typical Grievance Procedure

A typical grievance procedure starts with the employee discussing the situation with his or her direct supervisor and can lead all the way up to arbitration involving a neutral third party if the problem is not resolved at earlier stages.

on teamwork and flexibility transfers responsibility for some decisions to its diverse work force, which is 28 percent Hispanic, 24 percent black, and 22 percent female. According to union official Bruce Lee, "Having people from diverse cultures with differing ideas is a plus in the team concept process."[22]

Legal and Regulatory Influences

Human resource management is restricted and guided by a host of laws and regulations. Federal and state laws forbid employment discrimination on the basis of sex, race, or religion; set minimum wages; oversee labor relations; impose safety standards; and forbid sexual harassment (see Exhibit 13.4).

Equal Employment Opportunity and Affirmative Action

The Civil Rights Act of 1964 outlawed discrimination on the basis of race, religion, sex, and national origin. As later amended by Congress, the law prohib-

EXHIBIT 13.4 Major Federal Laws Governing Human Resource Management

The federal laws governing human resource management are complex and numerous. These are but a few.

Law	Description
National Labor Relations Act (Wagner Act) of 1935	Establishes employees' right to organize and bargain collectively; prohibits interference with unionization and other unfair labor practices by management; and establishes the National Labor Relations Board.
Labor-Management Relations Act (Taft-Hartley Act) of 1947	Forbids unfair labor practices by unions, such as charging excessive dues, demanding that employees be paid for services that are not performed ("featherbedding"), refusing to bargain collectively in good faith, coercing employees not to exercise their rights, encouraging work stoppages to force an employer or self-employed person to join the union or to force an employer to stop doing business with any person.
Equal Pay Act of 1963	Requires employers to provide equal pay for men and women performing "substantially" equal work.
Civil Rights Act of 1964	Title VII of the act prohibits discrimination because of race, color, religion, sex, or national origin in all employment practices, including hiring, firing, promotion, and compensation. The law has been amended to prohibit discrimination against people with physical and mental disabilities, pregnant women, AIDS and cancer patients, and treated and recovering substance abusers. The law applies to all organizations with 15 or more employees.
Executive Orders 11246 of 1965 and 11376 of 1967	Require most federal contractors to take affirmative action to ensure equal employment opportunity to people regardless of race, color, religion, sex, and national origin.
Age Discrimination Act of 1967	Prohibits discrimination in terms, conditions, and privileges of employment on the basis of age for employees and job applicants aged 40 through 69 (there is no upper age limit for federal employees).
Occupational Safety and Health Act of 1970	Imposes a wide range of requirements on employers relating to safety of working conditions, operating practices, staffing, and training and may cause changes in job design.
Equal Employment Opportunity Act of 1973	Makes it unlawful to fail to hire, refuse to hire, discharge, or otherwise discriminate against a person based on race, color, religion, sex, age, or national origin. Established the Equal Employment Opportunity Commission, which can file suit against employers to enforce provisions of the act.
Employee Retirement Income Security Act of 1974	Establishes standards for employer-sponsored benefit programs such as pensions and may affect human resources planning by regulating aspects of termination, retirement, and reemployment.
Immigration Reform and Control Act of 1986	Imposes fines against employers that hire illegal aliens and requires employers to verify within 24 hours of hiring that a job applicant is a U.S. citizen, registered alien, or illegal alien.
Americans with Disabilities Act of 1991	Prohibits discrimination based on disabilities and requires employers to make workplaces accessible and usable by persons with disabilities, integrating people with physical and mental disabilities into the workplace.
Civil Rights Act of 1991	Reverses a number of Supreme Court decisions considered to have undermined the protections created by the Civil Rights Act of 1964. Among other actions, extends civil rights protections to employees of U.S. companies stationed in other countries. Allows plaintiffs under both the Civil Rights Act of 1964 and the Americans with Disabilities Act to seek compensatory damages in cases of allegedly intentional discrimination.

its discrimination against people with physical or mental disabilities, people with AIDS or cancer, and people being treated for or who are recovering from substance abuse.[23] The law applies to all organizations with at least 15 employees, including government agencies, labor unions, and charities. It requires most employers to offer equal employment opportunity to women and members of minority groups on a passive basis. However, any organization holding a major contract with a federal agency must undertake **affirmative action,** which is a process of taking active steps to hire and retain members of minority groups that are underrepresented in its work force. An outstanding example is Xerox, which increased the number of African-Americans in management jobs by basing 20 percent of each senior manager's performance evaluation on success with

affirmative action A process of active steps to hire and retain members of minority groups that are underrepresented in the work force human resources management, including affirmative action. Members of minority groups, who make up 21 percent of the work force, now account for 16 percent of Xerox management and 18 percent of its professional posts.[24]

U.S. Supreme Court decisions have recently weakened some civil rights requirements. The Court has backed away from its rigorous 1972 ruling that hiring and promoting relatively few women or minority members is allowed only if the organization proves such practices are a strict business necessity. The new rule is that such practices are permissible if they are supported by "legitimate business reasons." This means that an organization no longer must prove that a potentially discriminatory practice (such as hiring mainly friends or relatives of current employees) is absolutely necessary for finding qualified employees; the organization now could assert merely that such a practice identifies reliable employees.[25]

On the other hand, employees with physical or mental disabilities recently won significant new protections under the Americans with Disabilities Act. The law was designed to help the more than 40 million U.S. residents with disabilities move into the work force and into jobs for which they are qualified. The essence of the law is removing barriers to successful employment, which can range from physical barriers (such as a lack of stairway ramps or elevators for people using wheelchairs) to employer attitudes (such as the assumption that disabled people can't perform certain tasks or need special protection). More than one million businesses are affected by these new regulations, and many managers are concerned about the costs involved and the procedural changes required, although a presidential commission says that 88 percent of U.S businesses can comply for less than $1,000.[26] The potential benefits of making the talents of this many people more readily available to U.S. organizations are enormous. No longer will organizations have to forgo the contribution of an employee just because he or she isn't able to function effectively in a traditional job environment.

Wages and Benefits

The Great Depression resulted in laws that still regulate how human resource managers handle the payment of wages today. The Davis-Bacon Act of 1931 and the Walsh-Healy Act of 1936 require organizations to pay at least the prevailing industry wage rate for work performed under most federal contracts. The Fair Labor Standards Act of 1938 sets minimum wages and requires payment of overtime rates for work in excess of 40 hours a week, although salaried professionals and managers are exempt from minimum wage and overtime provisions. The act was amended in 1963 to require that men and women receive equal pay for equal work, provided that working conditions, seniority, performance, and qualifications are the same.

Federal and state laws also require employers to make contributions to the Social Security retirement system, to unemployment compensation insurance for laid-off employees, and to employees' compensation insurance for employees injured on the job. Pension plans are regulated by the Employee Retirement Income Security Act of 1974, which sets standards for funds and insures against bankruptcy. Human resource managers in not-for-profit organizations must also take care not to construct compensation plans that inadvertently transfer profits to employees; doing so would jeopardize their organizations' tax-exempt status.[27]

Labor Relations Laws

collective bargaining The process by which representatives of employees negotiate an employment agreement with the employer

In addition to protecting wages, federal legislation during the Great Depression also assured employees the right to unionize. The 1935 Wagner Act affirms employees' right to **collective bargaining,** the process by which representatives of employees negotiate an employment agreement with the employer. The process allows either side to bring or threaten economic pressure, such as a strike by employees. The act also prohibits "unfair labor practices" by employers (such as firing union sympathizers) and set up the powerful National Labor Relations Board to oversee the collective bargaining process. After a series of strikes following World War II, the Taft-Hartley Act of 1947 outlawed unfair labor practices by unions (such as harassing managers).

In the 1980s, the layoff of millions of employees prompted enactment of the federal Worker Adjustment and Retraining Notification Act. The act requires all businesses with more than 100 employees to provide at least 60 days' advance notice to employees subject to a mass layoff or a shutdown lasting more than six months.[28]

Handling layoffs in a fraudulent manner can subject companies to serious legal penalties. When Atari laid off more than 500 employees without notice at its Sunnyvale, California plant, the employees sued, claiming that management had told them their jobs were secure virtually up to the moment the layoffs were announced. Atari admitted it had been planning to relocate operations to Asia for as long as three years and agreed to a multimillion-dollar settlement benefiting the released employees.[29]

Increasingly, human resource managers and union officials are relying less on legal prerogatives and contract rights and are cooperating to preserve jobs and increase performance. For example, unionized production employees at Union Camp's Savannah, Georgia, mill have agreed to work outside their traditional areas; union members have helped Copeland managers redesign and choose equipment for their Sidney, Ohio, refrigeration plant; and Thomson Consumer Electronics of Bloomington, Indiana, has reduced absenteeism 26 percent by working with its union to develop attendance policies.[30]

Safety and Health

In 1970, Congress moved to protect employees by setting up the Occupational Safety and Health Administration and giving it authority to set safety standards and to conduct surprise inspections. OSHA also requires employers to train employees who will handle hazardous materials, and courts have held that employees have the right to refuse work if they have reason to believe that the work would represent a danger of death or serious physical harm. But many human resource managers don't wait for legal problems to develop before they improve their organization's safety standards. Even though OSHA's guidelines for design of meatpacking equipment were only voluntary, meatpacker IBP hired a consultant to improve knife designs and even agreed to try slowing the work pace if engineering changes didn't reduce injuries.[31]

Sexual Harassment

Sexual harassment is the newest area of civil rights law and one that jumped to public prominence following the 1991 confirmation hearings of Supreme Court Justice Clarence Thomas. Courts have determined that sexual harassment is a violation of the Civil Rights Act of 1964. As defined by the Equal Employment Opportunity Commission in 1980, unwanted sexual advances, remarks, or

Safety is one of Alcoa's highest priorities, and employees and managers alike are involved in the drive for an injury-free workplace. Here, a specially trained employee *(with clipboard)* watches as his colleague monitors aluminum being poured into a crucible. Afterward, the observer and the employee discuss any deviations from OSHA safety regulations, and individual names are removed before managers receive the safety reports.

acts become sexual harassment when (1) their acceptance is a condition of employment or advancement, or (2) they interfere with work performance or create an intimidating or offensive work environment. Courts have favored a liberal interpretation of sexual harassment. A judge in Jacksonville, Florida, ruled in July 1991 that pictures of nude and seminude women displayed at Jacksonville Shipyards was sexual harassment of a female welder.[32]

Studies indicate more than 40 percent of working women are victims of sexual harassment.[33] Jury awards to victims of sexual harassment often exceed \$180,000.[34] Even worse, the nation's largest companies annually lose more than \$6.7 million on average due to decreased morale and production as well as increased absenteeism and turnover caused by sexual harassment.[35] As a result, many human resource managers have drafted policies prohibiting sexual harassment and establishing formal systems to handle complaints. At Douglas Aircraft of Long Beach, California, equal employment opportunity manager Kristine Robinson investigates sexual harassment complaints, confronts alleged harassers if warranted, and tells their managers to monitor future behavior.[36]

International Influences

Managing on an international scale introduces another level of issues to the challenge of human resource management, whether (1) managing employees in other countries or (2) being employed by managers or owners from another country (several hundred thousand U.S. citizens are employed by firms based in other countries). Here's a quick look at some of these issues:[37]

- *Working for foreign owners.* Working for managers and owners who are either from another country or still working and living in another country can be difficult. For example, some U.S. executives in Japanese-owned companies operating in the United States express frustration with being "watched over" too closely by top management in Japan.
- *Compensation and benefits.* Laws and customs related to compensation and employee benefits can vary greatly from country to country, a fact that multinational organizations must take into account.

- *The impact on families.* Families often face a large adjustment during international assignments. Spouses may have to leave careers, children have to change schools and activities, and everyone has to leave friends and relatives behind. Employees involved in these assignments have to adjust as well, of course, but they have the organization's support mechanisms to help.
- *Locating suitable employees for international assignments.* Multinational organizations often post employees on temporary assignment in other countries, either to bring special expertise to operations in those countries or to expose the employees to conditions in other markets. However, the ideal employees for these assignments can be hard to locate because they need to be flexible, be willing to travel and relocate, be open-minded concerning other cultures, be especially good with people, and accept everything from new food to new banking procedures.

Technological, Economic, and Social Influences

Human resource management is being revolutionized by the continuing advances in technology, by economic constraints imposed by an era of fierce competition and tight budgets, and by changes in the composition and expectations of society. Automation and other technological developments may reduce the number of employees needed for production, but they also increase the level of skill needed by employees who operate the new machines or systems. Economic factors, such as unemployment rates and local wage rates, affect the compensation packages and recruiting strategies that human resource managers must design.

Impact of Technology

Technology brings both opportunities and challenges to the human resource areas of staffing, training, and job design. Automation in manufacturing plants has allowed companies to trim their work forces. But it has also created a demand for more highly skilled employees to run the new machines and has changed manager-employee relationships in many cases. Technology is allowing employees to access the office computer from home—Mutual of New York found that productivity gains far outweighed its costs for the telephone lines and terminals that let employees work from home at any hour of the day. However, allowing employees to work at home via computer hookups (a practice known as *telecommuting*) requires managers who are comfortable outside the traditional boundaries of face-to-face contact and direct authority.[38] Managers who are accustomed to a great deal of control over their employees are less likely to accept advances such as telecommuting, in spite of the benefits.

When Baldor Electric installed a new system to allow the manufacture of several motors on a single assembly line in its Columbus, Mississippi plant, the company found that the change in technology created a need for additional employee training in reading and other skills. Trainer Karen Overstreet explained the new equipment and helped production employees learn the system.

Impact of the Economy and Rising Health-Care Costs

Even after two decades of stagnation in real wages (defined as the effective purchasing power of a person's income, after taking inflation into account), health-care costs continue to accelerate faster than the nation's gross national product.[39] National spending on health care recently passed $600 billion, accounting for 11.6 percent of the entire gross national product and increasing at an average rate of 11 percent per year.[40] In addition to direct physiological problems, job stress and mental illness cost U.S. business $150 billion a year in health insurance and disability claims, lost productivity, and other expenses.[41]

Many executives consider health-care costs to be one of the most critical issues facing management today.

Another health-care concern is the growing need for employees of the baby-boom generation to care for their aging parents. Human resource managers have designed some kind of elder-care assistance at 20 percent of major U.S. corporations, including AT&T, which recently began offering unpaid leave and nursing referral services.[42] These and other health-care issues were at the root of Johnson & Johnson's decision to reexamine its employee health programs.

Impact of Society

Many social influences affect human resource managers. The increasing entrance of women and minorities into the work force will make white males a minority work-force group by the turn of the century.[43] Like the rest of society, managers are increasingly worried about substance abuse, AIDS, and other widespread health issues, all of which affect individual performance, morale, and privacy. Two-career families and nontraditional family structures present challenges as well as opportunities to innovative human resource managers who can fit jobs around the people who do them.

Work-Force Diversity The number of women, African-Americans, Hispanics, and Asian Americans entering the work force is increasing so fast that white males will make up just 45 percent of all employees not long after the turn of the century.[44] Organizations that ignore any of these groups may find themselves at a competitive disadvantage in today's tight labor market. According to Stona Fitch, vice president of manufacturing for Procter & Gamble: "The first companies that achieve a true multicultural environment will have a competitive edge. Diversity provides a much richer environment, a variety of viewpoints, greater productivity. And not unimportantly, it makes work more fun and interesting."[45] Human resource managers are responding by working to remove the "glass ceilings" that prevent women and minorities from advancing to the top management levels, which are dominated by white males, and actively seeking to attract women and minorities at all organizational levels.

Globalization of markets is also making the work force more diverse. Knowledge of multiple languages and of diverse cultures is required by the creation of a single Western European market, the dissolution of Soviet power in Eastern Europe, and the transfer of Hong Kong to the People's Republic of China in 1997. International organizations must adapt management styles and job designs to various cultures. For example, research shows that the dominant culture in Mexico is strong in hierarchical differences and is very assertive. Thus a participative management style would probably not work there, and Mexican employers and employees would probably expect managers to rely heavily on the chain of command and formal authority.[46]

Lotus Development, a software company in Cambridge, Massachusetts, works hard to attract and retain talented employees regardless of background and actively seeks to make the most of employee diversity. One way the firm fights negative stereotypes is by running diversity awareness workshops in which heterosexual and homosexual employees share their fears and thoughts.

Substance Abuse Substance abuse on and off the job has become a concern of human resource managers because an impaired work force is less able to achieve organizational goals. Alcoholism costs the United States $86 billion a year, and a quarter of all accidents at work involve people who are intoxicated. An estimated 10 percent of the work force, including senior executives, experiences problems with alcohol.[47] On-the-job drug abuse presents similar costs. Studies show drug abuse costs up to $60 billion a year in decreased productivity, acci-

MANAGERIAL DECISION MAKING

Organizations Learn the Value of Diversity

Successful organizations realize that work-force diversity presents an opportunity to expand the pool of people who can contribute to the organization, but managing diversity sometimes requires managers to take extra steps. For example, human resource managers might try to improve the performance of certain employees; Sheraton Hotels did this in Hawaii, where employee-education programs improved the reading and writing skills of Philippine and Samoan immigrants and helped them understand policies and manuals. Or managers might try to improve organizational performance by helping valuable employees move into influential roles; *The Wall Street Journal* production manager Karen Kennedy did this when she established an informal coaching network for women and minority employees, several of whom advanced into management jobs. But diversity is also a feature of organizations' *external* operating environment. It is in the external environment that organizations interact with customers, regulators, and the general public. Managers who respect and address diversity outside the boundaries of the organization can improve their organization's performance.

Consider the case of Nadia Ali, newly appointed southwest district manager for the gift and engraving company Things Remembered. Ali quickly determined that ethnocentric hiring practices by the organization had resulted in a mismatch between her customers and her work force. Half of the chain's local customers spoke Spanish, but many of the store's employees spoke only English and could not communicate with these customers. Corporate headquarters seemed unaware of the problem.

Ali responded by instituting new hiring and training practices that valued the diversity of her customers and increased the diversity of her employees. Within 30 days, she made the ability to speak conversational Spanish a hiring criterion for new recruits from part-timers to store managers, and she arranged for existing employees to take free Spanish lessons. Corporate headquarters readily gave financial support for the training once Ali made her needs known. Ali's decision helped increase district sales by 13 percent. It also helped reduce employee turnover in her region to 7 percent, compared with a company average of 30 percent. Ali's experience shows that hiring a diverse staff that matches the demographics of the customer base can help the work force both understand and respond to the market. Or, as Ali put it, "You don't get the potential out of the business unless you're attuned to your customers."

Apply Your Knowledge

1. Is it fair to require that U.S. citizens speak Spanish? Could this requirement amount to illegal discrimination against English-speakers?
2. How did Ali consider her company's environment and resources in her effort to improve organizational performance?

dents, absenteeism, medical claims, and thefts.[48] As a result, more than one-third of companies in the United States and Canada require or are considering drug testing as a condition of employment.[49] Motorola, a $10 billion electronics manufacturer, plans to save $190 million a year by ridding itself of drug abusers, and it expects its drug testing program to find at least 3,000 of its 60,000-member U.S. labor force out of compliance with its policy against drug use.[50]

Employees may object to drug tests because they may violate privacy rights and are sometimes inaccurate. The tests may also hurt morale among drug-free employees who are humiliated by the experience.[51] One alternative is performance testing. Jim Davison takes a computerized performance test every morning before starting work as a sightseeing tour driver for Old Town Trolley of San Diego. If he successfully finishes the test (a 30-second video game), the computer issues a pass allowing him to work that day. Performance tests may improve safety by detecting employee impairment for lack of sleep or emotional problems as well as drug use.[52] R. F. White, a California petroleum distributor, registered a 67 percent drop in accidents after it began using eye-hand coordination tests to determine acceptability for work.[53]

AIDS, Health, and the Workplace AIDS presents several challenges to human resource managers, including issues of privacy, problems with morale, and rising medical costs. The U.S. death toll from AIDS topped 100,000 through 1990, and another 200,000 are expected to die by 1993.[54] AIDS is killing people in the prime of their work lives, and its long incubation period will cause higher medical costs for employers than any other acute epidemic.[55] Courts have held that employees with AIDS can be terminated once they can no longer perform the job, but a simple diagnosis of AIDS is not grounds for dismissal.[56] AIDS patients have sued employers for breach of confidentiality when co-workers learned about their condition. Fear of AIDS infections may also cause morale problems among co-workers; one employee survey indicated 35 percent did not believe findings that AIDS cannot result from casual contact.[57]

Quality of Work Life Today's employees are increasingly dissatisfied with narrow jobs that underutilize their capacities and knowledge. Merging the organization's need for productivity with employees' desires to humanize the workplace has produced a new human resource philosophy that seeks to fulfill both objectives. This is called **quality of work life,** a philosophy of improving productivity by providing employees with the opportunity to use their special abilities, pursue self-improvement, and identify with the organization. At the lowest level, this can mean sponsoring blood drives or charitable payroll deductions. Human resource managers can develop the philosophy further to involve joint management-union problem-solving task forces, self-managing work teams, and even programs that reflect management's concern with competition and profits as well as employee concerns of job security, economic well-being, dignity, and respect.[58] Quality of work life has implications for **job design,** which is the effort to organize and specify the tasks, duties, and responsibilities of a job in order to advance organizational goals.[59] A common result of quality-of-work-life job designs is **empowerment,** which means giving employees discretion, authority, and some powers of self-management.[60]

quality of work life A philosophy of improving productivity by providing employees with the opportunity to use their individual abilities, pursue self-improvement, and identify with the organization

job design The effort to organize and specify the tasks, duties, and responsibilities of a job in order to advance organizational goals

empowerment Giving employees discretion, authority, and some powers of self-management

One approach to improving the quality of work life is **job enlargement,** which is the horizontal expansion of employee tasks to offer variety and make the job more challenging. At Texas-based Chaparral Steel, for example, night security personnel are qualified emergency medics, do data entry on the day's quality statistics, and may take on some accounting work during their shifts.[61] Another method of making work more interesting through horizontal expansion is **job rotation,** which is the lateral transfer of employees to various jobs to broaden their focus and increase their knowledge.[62] Job rotation is often used in training managers because it gives them a broader perspective of the organization. Another approach is **job enrichment,** which is the vertical expansion of jobs by increasing the responsibilities associated with a given position.[63] This often involves self-managing work teams that give employees more power to make decisions about how their jobs will be done.[64]

job enlargement The horizontal expansion of employee tasks to offer variety and make the job more challenging

job rotation The lateral transfer of employees to various jobs to broaden their focus and increase their knowledge

job enrichment The vertical expansion of jobs by increasing employee responsibilities associated with the positions

Two-Career Families The increasing entrance of women into the work force has resulted in more families in which both parents hold jobs. In fact, the stereotypical family where the father holds a job and the mother stays home with the children makes up only 15 percent of U.S. households today.[65] Some human resource managers have viewed this as an opportunity. More than three decades ago, Merck implemented a liberal child-care-leave policy after its managers noticed an increasing number of women entering its work force. The policy assured employees the chance to return to a good job and let the company escape the high costs of recruiting and training replacements for talented employees.[66]

Flexibility in the human resource functions of compensation, scheduling, and job design can have direct effects on the bottom line when dealing with two-career families who can't always work full schedules. When Midwest window and door manufacturer Rolscreen started letting two employees share a single full-time position, absenteeism improved immediately. This job-sharing program also reduced overtime and eliminated the need to overstaff in order to compensate for absenteeism.[67]

The two-career family has spawned a growing trend in people seeking the flexibility of working at home. Sunny Bates, who runs an executive recruiting firm from her New York City kitchen, observes, "If you do the job and do it well, then it doesn't matter where you work." Working with an assistant, Bates *(feeding her daughter Lola)* can run her business and still have time for family.

Managers can address these diverse issues and guide their organizations more effectively if they approach human resource management as a process that is linked to organizational goals and strategy. The next section describes the steps in this process.

THE HUMAN RESOURCE MANAGEMENT PROCESS

The human resource management process consists of six distinct steps: human resource planning, staffing, training and development, compensation management, employee evaluation, and employee movement. One step leads naturally to the next, and the process is somewhat circular: analysis of the final step of employee movement can help improve the first step of human resource planning, as seen in Exhibit 13.5. Note that in larger organizations, functional specialists handle most of these human resources management tasks; in smaller organizations, the tasks are usually divided among the whole management team.

Step 1: Human Resource Planning

human resource planning The process of analyzing an organization's needs for various employees in accord with its goals, and devising activities to meet those needs

Human resource planning is the process of analyzing an organization's needs for various employees in accord with its goals and devising activities to meet those

EXHIBIT 13.5

The Human Resource Management Process

The human resource management process leads from planning to staffing, training, compensation, evaluation, and replacement, then back to planning; this makes the process circular.

needs.[68] This planning consists of forecasting an organization's needs for employees in accordance with organizational goals and determining both the components of each job necessary to meet those goals and the characteristics of the people needed to fill each job. In simplest terms, human resource planning is about filling jobs. A **job** is defined as the array of tasks and responsibilities given to an employee in order to meet organizational goals.

job The array of tasks and responsibilities given to an employee in order to meet organizational goals

Forecasting Human Resource Needs

When forecasting human resource needs, an organization must determine the number of employees required, the skills they must have, and when they will be required. These needs are affected by personnel changes within the organization, by changes in organizational plans or structure, and by variations in the organization's demand for human resources or in the supply of job candidates both inside and outside the organization.

- *Personnel changes.* Even if an organization's strategy and staffing levels remain static, managers must still anticipate the human resource demand caused when employees take new positions within the organization, retire, leave voluntarily, or are fired. One way to find qualified job candidates within the organization (and help forecast the need for hiring from outside the organization) is a **skills inventory,** which lists each employee's skills, knowledge, and other job-related personal information.[69] Filling the vacancy created by the departure of an employee is called **succession.** Succession needs can be forecast with a **replacement chart,** which is an organization chart showing each key management position, who occupies it, when a vacancy may occur, and the names of potential replacements.[70]
- *Organizational changes.* Changes in organizational goals and strategies create new positions and change old ones. As mentioned earlier, for example, automation reduces the need for some skills and increases the need for others. Changes such as downsizing, flattening organizational structures, diversifying, or decentralizing reduce demand for some jobs and may increase demand for others. For example, the lifting of Western Europe's internal trade barriers prompted electronics giant Groupe Bull to replace its national managers for maintenance, sales, and marketing with a single management structure for all of Europe.[71]
- *Supply and demand.* Organizations must also determine the number of jobs required to meet organizational goals (demand) and the number of people who will be available to fill those jobs (supply). Many organizations forecast short-term personnel demand through the budgeting process, in which managers estimate the number of employees demanded by their units' goals. For long-term forecasting of up to 10 years, organizations must anticipate demands posed by strategic organizational plans in relation to labor supply trends affected by population, technology, and competition.[72]

skills inventory A list of each employee's skills, knowledge, and other job-related personal information

succession Filling the vacancy created by the departure of an employee

replacement chart An organization chart showing each key management position, who occupies it, when a vacancy may occur, and the potential replacements

Job Analysis

A basic tool of human resource planning is **job analysis,** a systematic process of collecting information about jobs, including the purpose of each job, its duties, its place in the organizational hierarchy, its working conditions and environment, and employee requirements.[73] Job analysis is often undertaken to check compliance with civil rights hiring requirements, but it is also useful in other human resource areas, such as job design. Managers at Nissan Manufac-

job analysis A systematic process of collecting information about jobs, including the purpose of each job, its duties, its place in the organizational hierarchy, its working conditions and environment, and employee requirements turing's plant in Sunderland, England, for instance, modified an employee's job following a costly mistake by making the job's environment less confusing. The employee had mistakenly filled numerous windshield washer fluid bottles with the wrong liquid, which came in a similar drum. Managers reduced the chance for future errors by ordering that various fluids be placed in drums with different colors, sizes, and connectors.[74]

Job analysis can also be helpful because it sorts information into job specifications and job descriptions. **Job specifications** list the knowledge, skills, and abilities needed by an employee to successfully perform each job.[75] **Job descriptions** list duties, working conditions, hierarchical relationships, equipment, and other requirements of the job itself (see Exhibit 13.6). Job specifications help employers identify potential candidates, and they also help those candidates assess their own fit with various positions. Job descriptions then give current and potential employees an idea of what's expected of them in each position.

job specifications A list of the knowledge, skills, and abilities needed by an employee to successfully perform each job

job description A list of duties, working conditions, relationships, equipment, and other requirements that define a particular job

In an effort to improve both the quality of work life and the organization's utilization of its work force, jobs are often designed on the basis of **job characteristics,** the theory that employees will be satisfied if they can assume adequate responsibility, can believe their jobs are meaningful, and can receive feedback regarding their performance (see Exhibit 13.7).[76] This theory holds that employees will be satisfied, motivated, and effective if their jobs include five specific **core job dimensions:**

job characteristics The theory that employees will be satisfied if they can assume adequate responsibility, can believe their jobs are meaningful, and can receive feedback regarding their performance

core job dimensions According to job characteristics theory, the job aspects (skill variety, task identity, task significance, autonomy, and feedback) that are necessary for employees to be motivated, satisfied, and effective

- *Skill variety.* This is the requirement that employees use a variety of different activities, talents, and skills to successfully complete their jobs.
- *Task identity.* This means allowing employees to complete whole tasks from start to finish, rather than limiting them to disjointed portions of the job.
- *Task significance.* An employee's belief that the job significantly affects the lives of others within and outside the workplace has a great deal to do with overall job satisfaction.
- *Autonomy.* A degree of autonomy gives employees freedom in planning, scheduling, and choosing methods to complete the job.
- *Feedback.* Feedback means that the job itself provides employees with clear, direct, and understandable knowledge of their performance.

EXHIBIT 13.6

Job Description

Job descriptions set out the abilities, knowledge, and experience required of the person who will fill a given job.

C, generate computerized ıecks, answer vendor inquiries, ıd provide routine clerical assisınce. Previous payables experınce, knowledge of PC/DE and ood communications skills reıired. Lotus would be a plus. ompetitive hourly rate plus paid ıcation, holidays & sick time. ease mail/fax resume to:

H.R Director, Fax 212-967-7161

AULKNER & GRAY, INC.

leven Penn Plaza, NY, NY 10001

n Equal Opportunity Employer

PART TIME

ADMINISTRATIVE ASST

exec reqs P/T Asst. 3+ days per Must be detail-oriented, efficient. communctns exp a must. word essing, phones, hvy follow-up . Mac exp prefd. Send resume w/ eqs to: F4623 TIMES 10108

PERSONNEL

BENEFITS ASSISTANT

University

Excellent opportunity to learn all aspects of Personnel/Benefits. Diverse duties include: process monthly insurance bills; assist in benefits orientations; assist in employment recruitment; update and maintain manual and automated personnel records; and general clerical duties. Strong computer background, proficiency in Word-Perfect 5.1. Knowledge of LOTUS & DOS preferred. 2-3 years relevant work experience, preferably in Personnel, and excellent organizational and interpersonal skills required. Excellent benefits include free tuition, one month vacation, and comprehensive health insurance. Salary: mid-twenties. Send resume and cover letter to: Shari Dross, Benefits Coordinator, Personnel Dept., NEW SCHOOL FOR SOCIAL RESEARCH, 66 West 12th Street, New York, N.Y. 10011. Affirm action/equal oppty employer.

and applications is required. Ex lent salary and benefits. Send c fidential resume and salary requ ments to: Patty, P.O. Box 8546, B salem, PA 19020. EOE, M/F.

PHARMACEUTICAL

Quality Assurance Inspect

College grad(Chem courses), will t Send resume or call Mr Heend or Green, Forest Laboratories Inc, Prospect St., Inwood, NY 11696. 371-1155 or 718-471-8000

PHARMACISTS

Elmhurst Hospital Center, the m teaching affiliate of Mt. Sinai Scho Medicine, has excellent opportun available in our progressive pharm for New York State Registered P macists. Selected candidates will vide UD, IV and outpatient serv Some hospital experience preferre

We offer competitive salaries & b fits. Send resume to: Judith Alvarez

Core Job Dimensions	Critical Psychological States	Outcomes
Skill variety Task identity Task significance Autonomy Feedback from job	Meaningfulness of the work Responsibility for work outcome Knowledge of actual results of the work	High internal work motivation High growth satisfaction High general job satisfaction High work effectiveness

EXHIBIT 13.7

Job Characteristics Model

Job characteristics theory holds that proper job design incorporating the five core job dimensions will increase the meaningfulness of jobs and lead to satisfied and effective employees.

Step 2: Staffing

Staffing is the process of attracting and selecting employees for positions in accordance with organizational goals. This is done by recruiting job applicants and then selecting the best applicants for the available jobs.

staffing The process of attracting and selecting employees for positions in accordance with organizational goals

Recruiting

Recruiting is the process of attracting qualified people to apply for positions with an organization. This can be done internally (among an organization's current employees) or externally (outside the organization). One disadvantage of internal recruiting is that the employees who take the new jobs must themselves be replaced, unless their own jobs are being phased out. But a policy of internal promotions can improve employee morale and keep good employees from seeking work elsewhere. A key disadvantage of external recruiting is that new hires must undergo orientation, organizational socialization, and possibly other training.

recruiting The process of attracting qualified people to apply for positions with an organization

Human resource managers focus recruiting efforts to help meet organizational needs for certain kinds of employees. For example, foreign organizations find it relatively easy to recruit highly motivated women in Japan because career opportunities for women are very limited in Japanese companies, where women hold just 0.3 percent of managerial positions.[77]

A common technique used by human resource specialists during the recruiting process is the **realistic job preview,** in which a representative of the organization tells job applicants both the good and bad aspects of the organization and the jobs they seek. For example, human resource employees at Diamond-Star, a joint venture between Chrysler and Mitsubishi Motor, tell applicants they must learn several jobs, change shifts, give and take criticism, and work overtime; "You've got to ask yourself if you're willing to dedicate yourself to the Diamond-Star team," a company video warns.[78] Realistic job previews may cause some qualified applicants to decide against taking the job. Research confirms that realistic job previews lower applicants' initial job expectations, but that such previews also increase the organizational commitment, satisfaction, performance, and ultimate longevity of applicants who join the organization.[79] In turn, increased commitment, satisfaction, performance, and longevity help human resource managers by minimizing morale problems and turnover.

realistic job preview A recruiting technique in which a representative of the organization tells job applicants both the good and bad aspects of the organization and the jobs they seek

Selection

Selection is the process of choosing the applicants who best suit vacant positions and organizational needs. The best selection methods are ones that have

selection The process of choosing the applicants who best suit vacant positions and organizational needs

One way organizations can recruit people with specific skills or work experience is to set up a table at a specialized job fair and meet face-to-face with the attendees, who are seeking new jobs. Here, Motorola representatives at a Los Angeles job fair sponsored by the National Society of Black Engineers discuss career opportunities and company policies with potential candidates.

the most *validity,* which is the degree to which the selection method accurately predicts future job performance. Common selection methods are:

- *Applications.* The first thing a job applicant normally does is fill out a job application, listing education and previous work experience. Applications can be a quick way to compare applicants and determine whether an individual applicant meets minimum job requirements. On the downside, applications don't provide much insight into personality, attitude, ambition, or other important attributes.
- *Interviews.* The most widely used selection method is the interview. But some researchers say it often has low validity because interviewers make the mistake of prejudging applicants on the basis of prior information or judging them based on only one or two key traits. Interviews can be most effective if the interviewer establishes rapport with applicants and puts them at ease and reviews all information available about applicants and the positions sought.
- *Reference checks.* Reference checks are also a popular selection method, in part because of the false information buried in many job applications, and in part because the potential hiring manager can often get a realistic assessment of the candidate from a managerial peer in another organization. Fear of defamation lawsuits has prompted many employers to restrict information about former employees to dates of employment, although growing numbers of executives are willing to be candid in informal conversations. Gregory M. Jenks, operations manager for Eldon Group America's Thule division in New York, started giving candid references after a supervisor whom he had hired on good references was caught stealing; his previous employer had not revealed that the person had a police record.[80]
- *Testing.* Human resource managers use a variety of tests to determine whether applicants have the characteristics required for jobs. *Ability tests,* like the spelling tests common in the publications industry, have recently lost favor because they may work against some minority applicants who haven't been exposed to mainstream educational opportunities. If carefully related to job requirements, however, tests can have both high validity and minimal adverse impact on minority applicants. *Personality tests* are controversial because of doubts about their relationship to job performance. But Massachusetts retailer Morse Shoe reduced its losses to theft by one-third after introducing a test designed to predict whether a job applicant would be honest, punctual, and conscientious.[81] *Performance tests,* in which an applicant manipulates an object or equipment such as a word processor or flight simulator, can have high validity. A similar technique uses *assessment centers,* where management candidates are tested on such things as decision making and interpersonal skills while handling simulated work assignments in an officelike setting. If properly designed, assessment center tests can be of high validity. *Physical examinations* are sometimes overlooked, but they have high validity and can be valuable if physical attributes such as strength or endurance are important.

Step 3: Training and Development

The shortage of skilled employees and their increasing demands for personal fulfillment on the job make training and development an essential area of human resource management. In one recent year, IBM invested $2 billion in employee training, an amount equal to one-third of its after-tax profits for the year.[82] Overall, businesses in the United States spend somewhere between $30 billion and $60 billion a year on training. This money goes for orientation and socialization for new employees, training for employees taking new jobs or whose jobs have changed, career development for professionals, and coaching for all employees.

- *Orientation and socialization.* If employees selected for vacant positions come from outside the organization, they must undergo orientation and socialization to become effective members of the organization. **Orientation** is a short-term process of introducing employees to their jobs, their peers and managers, and the organization's structure and hierarchy. For instance, new employees at Mazda Motor Manufacturing's assembly plant in Flat Rock, Michigan, undergo weeks of technical and philosophical training, including three days on *kaizen,* the concept of continual improvement that is valued by Mazda's Japanese-influenced corporate culture.[83] **Socialization** is a longer process of making an employee aware of the organizational culture, including such issues as on-the-job behavior and attitudes toward customers and suppliers.
- *Training.* **Training** is the process of teaching employees the behaviors, knowledge, and skills necessary for performing their jobs successfully or of reinforcing existing abilities to improve job performance. Employees can be trained in various ways. Videotapes, reading assigned for home or work, hands-on work with new equipment or simulators, and role playing or other problem-solving games are all used in training. Manufacturing managers who once operated under Communist regimes in Poland and Hungary have been trained in capitalist finance, product development, and employee motivation by visiting Japan, where government and business leaders offered lectures, plant tours, and personal contact with successful businesspeople.[84] The most common training method is **on-the-job training,** in which a manager trains employees while they are at their work assignments. This is efficient because trainees receive immediate feedback and are producing while being trained. Apprenticeship programs are one of the oldest types of on-the-job training.
- *Career development.* When applied to managers and professionals, training is often called **career development,** which prepares those key employees for present and future jobs. Career development is driven by two needs: (1) the organization's need for future managers and leaders and (2) the employees' and managers' need for increased knowledge and opportunities that will advance their careers. Organizations have responded by offering career development programs that identify the organization's career advancement paths or that consider individual skills and desires in light of job opportunities inside and outside the organization. Organizations may also help develop motivated employees' careers by giving them specialized training or by sending them to seminars to improve their skills and perspectives or to learn from other professionals. The Clerical and Secretarial Employee Advancement Program established by the state of New York and its civil service union helps develop nonprofessionals into professionals. The program has expanded administrative and technical career opportunities in the health and

orientation A short-term process of introducing employees to their jobs, their supervisors, the organization's structure, and its hierarchy

socialization A relatively long-term process of making an employee aware of the organizational culture

training The process of teaching employees the behaviors, knowledge, and skills necessary for performing their jobs successfully or of reinforcing existing abilities to improve job performance

on-the-job training A training method in which a manager trains employees while they are at their work assignments

career development Preparing key employees for present and future jobs

SOCIAL RESPONSIBILITY AND ETHICS

CEO Compensation: How Much Is Enough?

The last decade was a time of great increase in compensation for the chief executive officers of U.S. corporations. The amount of money paid to CEOs through salary, stock options, and bonuses more than tripled during the decade, while teacher pay merely doubled and the average factory worker realized a 53 percent increase. The ranks of the poor and the working poor rose, and hundreds of thousands of well-paying jobs were eliminated. By the end of the decade, the average chief executive of a major U.S. corporation made 85 times the pay of a typical U.S. factory worker, 5 times the pay disparity found in Japan. As the 1990s dawned, investors and employees were charging that U.S. CEO pay had become excessive and demoralizing to both lower-level managers and employees.

Not all of the top organizational leaders were making huge salaries, and the level of pay often seemed divorced from organizational performance. Contrast United Air Lines Chairman Stephen M. Wolf with U.S. Army General H. Norman Schwarzkopf. While UAL's profits fell by 71 percent in 1990, Wolf collected $18.3 million in salary, bonuses, and stock-based incentive plans, 1,200 times the wage rate for new flight attendants, whose pay had been frozen for five years. That same year, General Schwarzkopf was paid $104,000 (less than 1 percent of Wolf's pay) for commanding 250,000 subordinates and vast assets in the highly successful Operation Desert Storm in the Persian Gulf.

One CEO who faced shareholders' wrath was Rand V. Araskog of ITT. At a shareholder meeting, owners of ITT stock repeatedly questioned why Araskog's pay doubled to $11.4 million in 1990 when corporate profits rose only 4 percent. The California Public Employees Retirement System, which held 1 percent of ITT's shares, earlier voted against reelection of company directors to protest Araskog's pay. At the meeting, Araskog said shareholders were unfairly singling out CEOs and ignoring the hefty compensation drawn by athletes and entertainers. (The same year, Boston Red Sox pitcher Roger Clemens landed a $5 million annual contract, and rock star Madonna took in $25 million.) Araskog also noted that he had received few stock options on his way to the top during his 25-year career with ITT.

Araskog's compensation was later defended by Robert Burnett, who serves on ITT's board of directors, chairs its compensation committee, and is himself CEO of Meredith Corporation. Bennett noted that Araskog's compensation also reflected his crucial role in selling ITT assets that earned the corporation $186 million after taxes. "He did an outstanding job in a very important area," Burnett said. A CEO may be the best judge of another's CEO's performance and value to an organization, but critics say the presence of CEOs on each other's compensation committees creates a conflict of interest. They say it is in any CEO's interest to push for higher compensation for their peers because that raises the average rate of CEO pay and increases pressure for a raise in their own compensation. CEO compensation promises to remain an issue as employees, shareholders, and the general public all learn more and begin to scrutinize CEO salaries more closely.

What's Your Opinion?

1. Who should control the salary of top executives?
2. Is it ethical for a CEO to receive 1,000 times as much compensation as a new employee? 100 times as much? 10 times as much? Is focusing on ratios such as these even a proper response to the problem?

legal fields and has helped move clerical and secretarial employees into professional budgeting, counseling, investment, and administrative positions.[85]

coaching A one-on-one relationship in which supervising managers or more experienced employees give other employees continual guidance and feedback about their performance

- *Coaching.* An important type of on-the-job training is **coaching,** a one-on-one relationship in which supervising managers give employees continual guidance and feedback about their performance.[86] Coaching can be effective because it is continuous. General Electric found that its annual employee appraisal program was hurting productivity by making criticized employees feel defensive, so it improved performance by emphasizing daily coaching and more frequent meetings for employees and their managers to mutually set goals and discuss performance and career plans.[87]

Step 4: Compensation Management

One of the most important human resource tasks is setting levels of compensation. **Compensation** includes the direct wages, benefits (insurance, vacation time, and so forth), and incentives (such as merit pay, stock options, and bonuses) given to employees in exchange for their work. **Benefits** are parts of the compensation package provided by the employer other than direct wages, such as health insurance and pension plans. Benefits exceed 30 percent of payroll costs in some organizations.[88] An example of an incentive is the employee suggestion program at Johns Hopkins University Hospital in Baltimore, Maryland, under which an employee who suggests a money-saving idea receives 10 percent of resulting savings.[89]

compensation The direct wages, benefits, and incentives given to employees in exchange for their work

benefits Parts of the compensation package provided by the employer other than direct wages, such as health insurance

If compensation levels are too low, an organization will have trouble attracting qualified candidates, holding onto its best employees, and keeping morale and productivity high. Excessive compensation levels, on the other hand, reduce profitability. A balance was struck at Hungary's Ganz-Hunslet locomotive and metals company, a joint venture with Great Britain's Teflos group, in which pay raises improved employee performance to such a degree that production increased and profitability became possible despite the layoff of half of the 1,400-person work force.[90]

For maximum effectiveness, employees must perceive compensation levels as equitable both outside the organization when compared with industry and regional averages, and inside the organization as compensation changes for various jobs. Compensation rates also vary according to the economic sector in which the organization operates; professionals in the for-profit sector can earn as much as 20 percent more than professionals in the same jobs with not-for-profit organizations.[91]

The main tool human resource managers have in setting compensation levels is the **job evaluation,** a process of ascertaining how much each job is worth to the organization and assuring that the pay level for various jobs is fair.[92] In small organizations, this may be done by simply ranking jobs from most important to least and assigning compensation on the basis of prevailing local levels. A more complex organization might assign points for various job factors such as danger, responsibility, physical difficulty, and required skills, and then base wage levels on the total of points per job (see Exhibit 13.8). This *point method* is a popular way to determine wage structure.[93]

job evaluation A process of ascertaining how much each job is worth to the organization and assuring that the pay level for each job is fair

Other concepts also guide human resource managers in designing compensation plans. The notion of *comparable worth* holds that jobs of equal value to an organization should be compensated at the same level, which promotes a feeling of pay equity within the organization. This issue has been raised frequently in recent years, as many women have found themselves performing the same functions as men but receiving lower pay. Another concept is to peg pay to performance (by the organization as well as the individual) through merit awards, bonuses, and profit sharing. First Service Bank of Massachusetts reduced turnover 50 percent and increased productivity 25 percent by tying paychecks and bonuses directly to performance.[94] An organization that rewards performance through merit pay or advancement is called a **meritocracy,** and the use of incentives tied to organizational performance is called *gain sharing.* Gain sharing is addressed in detail in Chapter 14.

meritocracy An organization that rewards individual performance through merit pay or advancement

EXHIBIT 13.8

Point Method Job Evaluation

The point method is a way of comparing organizational jobs to determine their pay. Management first determines the maximum number of points possible for any job's primary factors, based on each factor's difficulty or importance. Then each job is awarded points according to the factors required; the highest-scoring jobs will carry the highest pay.

Primary Factor	Subfactor	Points	Percentage
Skill	Education	70	14
	Experience	110	22
	Initiative and ingenuity	70	14
	Subtotal	250	50
Effort	Physical	50	10
	Mental	25	5
	Subtotal	75	15
Responsibility	Equipment process	25	5
	Material or product	25	5
	Safety of others	25	5
	Work of others	25	5
	Subtotal	100	20
Job conditions	Working conditions	50	10
	Hazards	25	5
	Subtotal	75	15
Grand total		500	100

Step 5: Employee Evaluation

It is difficult for people to know where they are going if they don't know where they've been. This is why it is important for an organization to have a formal system of evaluating employees, their managers, and even the organization itself. Employee evaluation is the process of assessing the quality of an employee's job performance and communicating those findings to the employee. This is accomplished through a **performance appraisal,** which is the process of evaluating employee performance in relation to expectations and providing feedback. Most often the performance appraisal consists of an annual meeting in which a manager tells an employee how well the employee is doing the job.

performance appraisal The process of evaluating employee performance in relation to expectations and providing feedback

Appraisals can improve performance and provide a basis for promotions, transfers, demotions, and terminations. Great Britain's Rentokil Group improved employees' performance by combining its appraisal program with management development efforts and changing its evaluation emphasis from past financial performance to employees' needs, abilities, and performance over the next 12 months.[95] Appraisals can also have dramatic effects on organizational performance. For example, Bedford Vans of Great Britain had lost money for a decade, but three years after Isuzu bought a 40 percent share the joint venture finally became profitable by establishing work teams and requiring performance appraisals for all 1,750 employees.[96] In some organizations, employees also appraise their managers. Researchers warn, however, that management often hurts the integrity of such appraisals by ignoring results and by failing to communicate findings to employees.[97]

A novel approach to appraising performance was used by Bemis of Minneapolis, Minnesota. The company hired a cultural anthropologist for 30 days to observe employees in work and social situations, which provided a more in-depth and accurate assessment of the organization's culture and daily climate than standard appraisal methods could. The anthropologist discovered that top management did not delegate responsibility well; when supervisors and craftspeople were reluctant to make decisions, top management moved in quickly and made the decisions for them. As a result of the anthropologist's study, the company began coaching top managers to help them overcome the temptation to do the work they had delegated to others.[98]

Step 6: Employee Movement and Replacement

Employees who leave jobs within the organization must be replaced unless the organization is downsizing. Employees who are leaving are a valuable source of feedback about the organization itself, and the entire process of employee movement provides information for assessing the organization's job analysis. Employees leave their jobs in one of five ways:

- *Promotion.* The happiest way for employees to leave their jobs is through **promotion,** which is the elevation of an employee to a different job that pays better or is higher in the chain of command.
- *Transfer.* Employees may also leave their positions through **transfer,** which is a lateral move to a different job of similar pay and responsibility within the organization.
- *Demotion.* Employees who do not perform their jobs adequately or who are dissatisfied with the amount of work or responsibility required by their position are candidates for **demotion,** which is moving an employee to a lower-status position. This isn't always viewed as a negative outcome, however; in a few cases, employees appreciate the opportunity of trying a higher-level job and returning to a lower-level position if they find that the job isn't a good match for their skills and interests.
- *Voluntary severance.* Managers also have to provide for the loss of employees who voluntarily leave the organization. Employees can leave because a spouse has been transferred, because they've found more attractive jobs in other organizations, because of serious illness or injury, or for other personal reasons.
- *Termination.* Employees may leave an organization involuntarily if they are surplus to the organization's needs or if they are unacceptable to the organization because of discipline or performance problems. Any dismissal of an employee is called a **termination.** Terminations of employees for strategic reasons that are not connected with employee performance are called **layoffs.** Layoffs can be permanent (when caused by reorganization or by elimination of surplus employees—hired as a result of poor planning, for example) or temporary (when caused by economic factors such as recessions or by seasonal factors such as winter in a summer resort).

promotion The elevation of an employee to a different job that pays better or is higher in the chain of command

transfer A lateral move to a different job of similar pay and responsibility within the organization

demotion Changing an employee's job to a lower-status position

termination Any dismissal of an employee

layoffs Terminations of employees for strategic reasons that are not connected with employee performance

The last step in the human resource management process leads back to the first two steps because replacing organization members involves planning and staffing functions. Finding replacements for organization members can be difficult, and an inability to replace organization members could require changes in strategic planning.

If employees are leaving the organization voluntarily, it is important to know why. An organization can get valuable feedback about employees and its own performance through an **exit interview,** which is a formal conversation with a departing employee to learn why the employee is leaving the organization. Exit interviews can help the organization find and correct problems with employee morale, job design, planning, and other aspects of the human resource management process. In the case of involuntarily terminated employees, exit interviews offer human resource managers the chance to clarify the employee's rights of

exit interview A formal conversation with a departing employee to learn why the employee is leaving the organization appeal, to head off or gauge the potential for a future wrongful discharge lawsuit by the employee, and to help avoid strong negative feelings among employees who remain at the organization.[99] Because they can provide candid feedback about employment situations, exit interviews (and performance evaluations with current employees) are a valuable source of information for job analysis and the overall task of human resource management.

SUMMARY

The basis of human resources management is finding, developing, supporting, and retaining a work force that helps meet organizational goals. This process includes motivating employee performance and developing future managers and leaders in an ever-changing environment. Human resource management supports organizational goals by providing a motivated, satisfied work force and by meeting the work and family needs of these employees wherever possible. Particular functions include downsizing, out-placement, retirement, management succession, compensation, evaluations, and resource planning.

Five environmental areas influence human resource management. The first influence is competition for employees, especially for the skilled employees who are in increasingly short supply and are therefore able to exact better compensation packages and working conditions. A related influence is labor relations, in which employees join unions to negotiate their employment contracts. The most restrictive influences are the laws and regulations that cover discrimination against women and minority group members, wages and benefits, labor relations, safety, and sexual harassment. Four key issues that managers face in international human resource management are working for foreign owners, facing differing compensation and benefit laws and practices, dealing with the impact on families of employees taking international assignments, and locating suitable employees for international positions. Finally, one of the most important influences is the emergence of human issues in the technological, economic, and social spheres.

The work force is assembled and maintained by a six-step process of human resource planning, staffing, training and development, compensation management, employee evaluation, and employee movement and replacement. Planning is facilitated by a careful job analysis, the effort to find the people to fit the available positions. Increasingly, organizations are also trying to fit the *positions* to the *people* by redesigning jobs.

To select employees for jobs, managers can use applications, interviews, reference checks, tests, and physical examinations. Applications provide a quick and easy way to compare objective qualifications, but they typically can't address subjective issues such as attitude and ambition. Interviews are very common, and they provide the benefits of interpersonal contact and subjective evaluation. On the other hand, they don't usually replicate real-life job situations, so a person's performance in an interview may not correlate with his or her performance on the job. Reference checks (with previous employers and other acquaintances) can provide additional information on candidates, but many managers fear defamation lawsuits and are reluctant to discuss (particularly in writing) the performance of former employees. Finally, a variety of tests, including ability, personality, and performance tests, can be used to assess various attributes.

Once selected, employees must often be trained in job skills and organizational culture. Major categories of training include orientation and socialization; training in specific behaviors, knowledge, and skills; career development aimed at professional and managerial employees; and continual, on-the-job coaching by experienced employees.

The appraisal of employees by their superiors can improve individual performance and can provide a basis for promotions, transfers, demotions, and terminations. The performance appraisal, an informal or formal process of evaluating employee performance in relation to expectations and providing feedback, is a key tool here. Appraisal of managers by employees can assist the human resource planning process as well, but it is far less common.

MEETING A MANAGEMENT CHALLENGE AT JOHNSON & JOHNSON

The effort to keep Johnson & Johnson at the forefront of the world health-products market has been a success up to this point, and the company shows no signs of slowing down. Aside from its skills in research, technology development, manufacturing, and marketing, Johnson & Johnson continues to demonstrate particular skills in the management of its human resources, the people who make the various functions work.

To meet both the employees' need to balance work and family pressures and the company's need to have a productive, healthy work force, James Burke and his management team instituted several key programs. One of the most important for two-career and single-parent families was the opening of on-site day-care centers. Employees' child-care expenses at these centers are limited to 10 percent of their disposable income, in order to keep the benefit accessible to as many people as possible. Another work/family initiative is a liberal policy on family-care leave. Employees may take family leave of up to one year after the arrival of a newborn or adopted child and may arrange a flexible work schedule to attend to an ailing family member.

To ensure the success of these initiatives, Johnson & Johnson sent its managers to a training program to sensitize them to work and family issues. And it underscored its commitment to family interests by adding a new sentence to the company credo: "We must be mindful of ways to help our employees with their family responsibilities."

Johnson & Johnson's commitment to helping employees become better family members boosted productivity by reducing absenteeism, tardiness, and stress. In addition, its work and family initiatives helped attract and keep qualified employees in a tightening labor market.

The other major issue that Burke addressed was employee health and its ramifications, including job satisfaction, performance, and costs. He established a wellness program, Live for Life, which emphasizes steps employees can take to maintain and improve their health. The program sets four straightforward goals for employees: to quit smoking, to eat more fruit and fewer fatty foods, to exercise regularly, and to use their seatbelts. At company headquarters in New Brunswick, New Jersey, for instance, employees can work out in the company gym, select "healthy heart" foods in the cafeteria, and check their weight in restrooms. Signs in hallways and brochures promote Live for Life activities, and participants win prizes for meeting their goals.

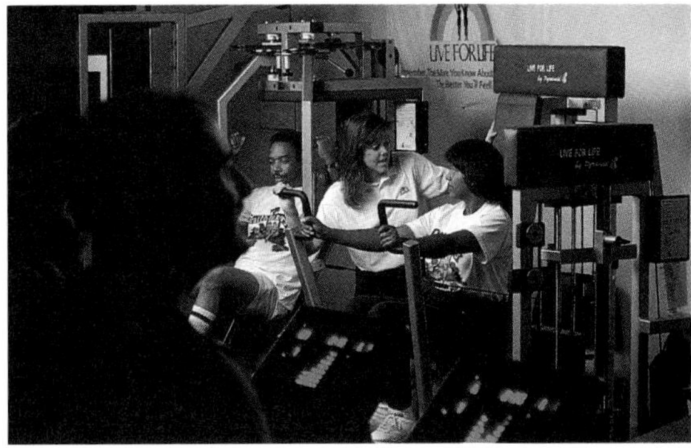

A Johnson & Johnson Live For Life fitness center

Over 35 Johnson & Johnson locations now have fitness centers and wellness programs, and the results are impressive. Smoking by employees has been reduced by more than one-third, to less than 20 percent of the work force. According to company estimates, even though Live for Life costs $200 a year for each employee, the program saves nearly twice that amount by lowering absenteeism and by slowing the rise in health-care expenses. Employees who participate in Live for Life have hospitalization costs that are 40 percent lower than those of nonparticipants.

In fact, Live for Life has been so successful that Johnson & Johnson formed a new company, Johnson & Johnson Health Management, to market it to other employers. The new company also assists with fitness center design and management, and it orchestrates health promotion campaigns in the areas of smoking, nutrition, and stress management. Live for Life is now available at 60 leading corporations and medical centers that together employ more than 850,000 employees.

***You're the Manager*:** James Burke's successor, Ralph Larsen, is intent on continuing the successful drive toward a work force that is satisfied and productive. As the vice president for human resources, your job is to initiate and manage programs that help the company meet both its strategic goals and its commitment to its employees.

Ranking Questions

1. The people who sell Johnson & Johnson prod-

ucts to pharmaceutical distributors and healthcare professionals play a big role in the company's success. They are of course motivated by financial rewards, but satisfaction with their jobs is a key factor as well, both in their productivity and in their commitment to staying with the company over the long haul. You recognize that job design can dramatically affect productivity and satisfaction. A task force looking for ways to improve sales force satisfaction and productivity has presented you with four proposals for modifying the job design of salespeople; rank them from best to worst.

a. The more standardized the job is, the more efficient the salespeople will become, and the more efficient they are, the more they'll sell. Consequently, instruct the task force to begin a standardization program for sales presentations, customer service, and related elements.
b. Give individual salespeople as much control over their jobs as possible, without giving them so much freedom that they start to impede each other's efforts or otherwise run counter to company goals.
c. Rather than focusing on just empowerment, broaden the job redesign to include a range of quality-of-work-life issues, which would be identified by the salespeople themselves.
d. Set each salesperson up as an independent entrepreneur making all decisions with complete freedom, including everything from which products to sell to where to find new customers.

2. Johnson & Johnson's Acuvue disposable contact lenses have become the leading soft contact lenses in the United States for new users and for those switching from other lenses. They are so successful that the company plans to double the size of its production facility in Jacksonville, Florida. You've been asked to recommend a process for selecting more production employees. The facility will need people with manual dexterity and assembly-line experience. In what sequence should the company use the following tools?
   a. Job applications.
   b. Interviews.
   c. Reference checks.
   d. Performance tests.

Multiple-Choice Questions

3. Acuvue lenses emerge from the assembly in a soft, wet state. They must be protected in a sterile environment in order to protect the customer from infection. Assume that you've received reports of on-the-job employee drug abuse that have raised concerns of careless behavior that might contaminate the work area. You obviously don't want to jeopardize the health of your customers or subject the company to product liability lawsuits. The plant manager wants to conduct some level of drug testing. What would you recommend?
   a. Test only those employees who are suspected of substance abuse.
   b. Test only those employees whose performance could put the company and the customer at risk.
   c. The only fair way is to test everyone in the plant. The plant manager should set an example by taking the test first.
   d. Whatever the risks, drug testing will offend innocent employees. Don't test anybody.
4. An important priority for Larsen is cost containment. He asks you to review the Live for Life program and the work/family initiatives to see if there are any areas where the company can realize even greater savings. Your staff has compiled a list of four options; which one would you recommend to Larsen?
   a. Live for Life nets nearly $200 for each person enrolled; make it compulsory for all employees.
   b. There are too many potential problems in trying to force employees into Live for Life. Instead, increase the incentives to join, such as greater recognition for meeting health goals.
   c. Raise the cap on on-site child-care fees to 25 percent of the employee's disposable income.
   d. Maternity expenses are a big part of the cost of Live for Life. During the hiring process, ask female candidates whether they intend to have children within the next few years. In those instances where you have a choice between otherwise equally qualified candidates, give preference to applicants who don't have immediate plans for children.

Analysis Questions

5. How might Live for Life affect Johnson & Johnson's efforts to recruit new employees?
6. How did social elements of the general environment affect Burke's decisions regarding the work and family initiatives and Live for Life?
7. What are some possible ways that the wellness

and fitness programs might play a role in the company's human resources planning process?

Special Project

The 75 million Americans born between 1946 and 1964—the baby-boom generation—are working their way through their careers, and their aging will not necessarily be a happy one. Because the baby-boom generation is so populous—and because many organizations are reducing the number of available management positions—competition for middle and top management spots will be fierce, and many capable and ambitious people simply will not have the career opportunities they would like. Your job is to help Johnson & Johnson find ways of increasing job satisfaction so that the company can head off the frustration that is likely to occur when baby boomers find themselves stuck on the career ladder. Draft a one-page memo to Larsen outlining your ideas.[100]

KEY TERMS

affirmative action (406)
benefits (421)
career development (419)
coaching (420)
collective bargaining (408)
compensation (421)
core job dimensions (416)
demotion (423)
empowerment (413)
exit interview (423)
human resource management (400)
human resource planning (414)
job (415)
job analysis (415)
job characteristics (416)
job description (416)
job design (413)
job enlargement (413)
job enrichment (413)
job evaluation (421)
job rotation (413)
job satisfaction (402)
job specifications (416)
labor relations (403)
labor union (404)
layoffs (423)
meritocracy (421)
on-the-job training (419)
orientation (419)
performance appraisal (422)
promotion (423)
quality of work life (413)
realistic job preview (417)
recruiting (417)
replacement chart (415)
selection (417)
skills inventory (415)
socialization (419)
staffing (417)
succession (415)
termination (423)
training (419)
transfer (423)

QUESTIONS

For Review

1. What is human resource management, and how does it help an organization meet its goals?
2. How can human resource managers both attract and retain good employees?
3. What implications do changes in technology, economy, and society have for human resource management?
4. What are the six steps in the human resource management process, and how is the process circular?
5. What is the job characteristics model? Describe the model's five core dimensions.

For Analysis

1. Can human resource managers improve relations with the work force once employees have decided to unionize?
2. What are the implications if a major defense contractor ignores cultural diversity?
3. Would it be important for the owner of a small or moderate-sized general construction company to develop a skills inventory?
4. Why would a law firm go to the trouble and expense of training a researcher in basic skills such as English grammar instead of simply hiring someone who already has such skills?
5. Why should a department store manager bother to give an exit interview to an employee fired for low productivity?

For Application

1. How might global competition affect human resource management at a tire manufacturing company that sells only in the United States?
2. What steps might a manager take to orient new employees at a Subway fast-food restaurant?
3. How might a human resource manager design volunteer tour guide jobs for a state historical society under the quality-of-work-life concept?

4. What selection methods would a county garbage-hauling supervisor use to fill a low-skill position requiring strength but little experience?
5. How would a vice president for human resources use performance evaluations to improve organizational performance at an international toy retailer such as Toys 'R' Us?

KEEPING CURRENT IN MANAGEMENT

From recent magazines or newspapers, select an article that describes how a union has expressed dissatisfaction with a business or group of businesses. The article might describe a strike, an attempt to unionize a company, or another confrontation between union and management.

1. Why is the union dissatisfied? What has management done or not done that might have led to the situation as it now stands?
2. What role is the union playing in the dispute? Is it representing employees through collective bargaining or the grievance process? Is it trying to unionize the organization? What tactics is the union using to apply pressure—pickets, strikes, strike threats, appeals to the public, legal action, or some combination of these? What are management and union leaders doing to solve the problem?
3. What is the reaction of affected employees? Do the employees' and union's goals coincide? Do the employees believe the union can improve compensation, working conditions, job security, chances for promotion, or treatment by managers?

SHARPEN YOUR MANAGEMENT SKILLS

Ted Turner, chairman and president of Turner Broadcasting Systems (TBS), puts special emphasis on recognizing cultural diversity, both inside his company and in communications in general. In fact, he established a policy whereby TBS employees can be fined up to $100 for using the word *foreign* when referring to other countries. (He prefers *international.*)

Turner's efforts at cultural sensitivity would apply equally well in any organization, even one without the global reach of his Cable News Network (CNN) and other broadcasting and business ventures. For instance, virtually every organization has employees that are offended by many common jokes, anecdotes, and word usages, and the more diverse the work force is, the greater the chance of offending someone's sensitivities becomes.

- *Decision:* Identify all the members of a diverse work force who could be offended by various uses of language, including jokes, innuendo, slurs, and so forth, and compile a list of words and phrases that are likely to cause offense.
- *Communication:* Put yourself in Ted Turner's position and assume you are writing a letter to all TBS employees. Explain the need for increased sensitivity in a diverse work force, and outline the language that should be avoided. As you draft the letter, keep in mind that you are dealing with sensitive and potentially embarrassing language.[101]

CASE

Merck Emphasizes the Human in Human Resources

Merck's human resource managers have proved that nice guys can finish first. They have helped make Merck one of the most admired companies in the nation by building work policies around employees' needs. Human resources vice president Steven Darien knows the complexity and makeup of the work force are changing as fast as society, and Merck can't rest on past successes.

HISTORY

Merck was founded in 1887 as the American subsidiary of the German drug and chemical company E. Merck, and in 1903 it opened a factory at Rahway, New Jersey, where it still has its headquarters. During World War I, George Merck gave the U.S. government the 80 percent of the Merck shares owned by his family in Germany (keeping the remaining 20 percent for himself), and after the war, the government's shares were sold publicly. The U.S. and German companies never reunited, and Merck is now three times the size of the German firm that created it. Merck grew through mergers with rivals and through joint marketing ventures with Johnson & Johnson and Du Pont to become the world leader in prescription drug sales with 4 percent of the market. Merck manufactures drugs in 24 countries and makes nearly half its sales outside the United States. It manufactures products to control livestock parasites and specialty chemicals to improve industrial processes, but more than 80 percent of its $7.7 billion in sales comes from human health products. Eighteen of Merck's drugs have annual worldwide sales of more than $100 million each. Vasotec, a treatment for hypertension and congestive heart failure introduced in 1985, is Merck's first drug to reach annual sales of $1 billion.

ENVIRONMENT

Merck has long believed that promoting human health and supporting its 31,000 employees are good business practices. The company pays well and is regarded as a mecca for ambitious researchers because of the collegial spirit and the high caliber of its people (five Merck scientists have received Nobel prizes). It provides 18 months of parental leave, allows flexible work hours, funds an employee-operated day-care center, and has maintained flexible leave policies for 30 years. But surveys have found that many employees still have problems balancing family and work responsibilities, and some managers are unaware of the problems or refuse to implement policies that would ease them. Merck is responding by training managers to be sensitive to family issues. Recent surveys show that most employees now give their managers high ratings for flexibility.

GOALS AND CHALLENGES

Darien views the human resource function as protecting shareholders' assets in addition to supporting employees, and he thinks both goals can be pursued aggressively without conflict. Darien knows Merck gains a competitive advantage when it attracts and retains good employees through its programs for job sharing, flexible work hours, and child care. But he sees other ways to enhance productivity and performance. He supports linking salaries to performance by using a personnel evaluation process that requires managers to identify both their top and their bottom performers (to overcome the tendency of many managers to lump all employees in the middle). Annual turnover runs 3 percent in the top categories and 23 percent in the bottom categories, so Merck retains the best employees and loses (usually voluntarily) the worst. Merck is also seeking to improve the work environment (1) by instituting a structured orientation program in which key executives introduce new employees to the organization and to its benefits package, and (2) by training managers in interviewing job applicants, in affirmative action planning, and in avoiding sexual harassment.

1. How have competitive influences affected Merck's human resources policies? How do these relate to societal influences?
2. How does Darien use training and employee evaluations to protect shareholders' assets while supporting employees?
3. Should Darien be concerned if employees claim that their manager ignores complaints about sexually insulting talk in the lunchroom, even though no one has quit because of it?
4. How could Darien use elements of the job characteristics model to design jobs in a cholesterol-control-drug factory employing highly specialized technicians?

PART THREE INTEGRATIVE CASE

Alcoa Organizes for the Long Term

In the boom-or-bust world of aluminum production, profits can vary widely, and top managers of the Aluminum Company of America (better known as Alcoa) have struggled with this cyclicality for decades. Aluminum demand and prices are at the mercy of economic cycles, mashing profits in unpredictable ways. From 1980 to 1986 Alcoa's sales hovered around $5 billion while net income bounced in and out of the red. CEO Paul H. O'Neill arrived in 1987 and pushed sales over the $10 billion level by 1989. Net income was nearly $1 billion in 1989, but Alcoa's 1990 income of $295 million was disappointing.

To counter cyclicality and keep Alcoa profitable, the CEO had to choose between an abrupt break with the past and a gradual movement toward long-term prosperity. He could delegate more authority to business managers, allowing them the freedom to meet customer needs but holding them accountable for performance. Or he could work through the hierarchy to pursue continuous incremental improvements that would slowly but steadily increase efficiency, lower costs, and hike profits. No matter which path he chose, O'Neill knew this decision would influence Alcoa's performance for many years to come.

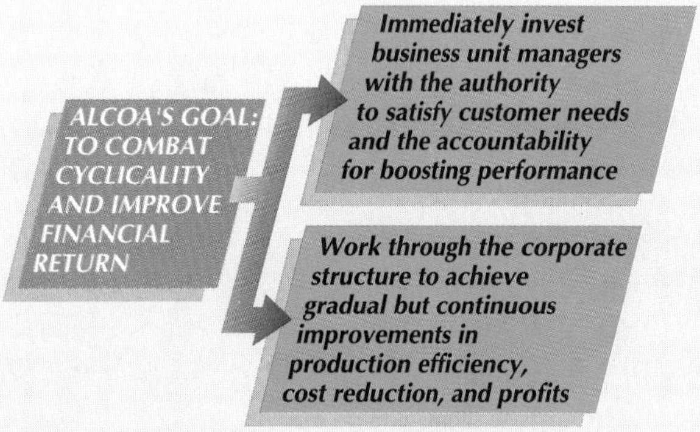

ALCOA'S GOAL: TO COMBAT CYCLICALITY AND IMPROVE FINANCIAL RETURN

Immediately invest business unit managers with the authority to satisfy customer needs and the accountability for boosting performance

Work through the corporate structure to achieve gradual but continuous improvements in production efficiency, cost reduction, and profits

HISTORY

Charles Martin Hall, a 22-year-old Ohio chemist, discovered an inexpensive aluminum smelting process in 1886. He obtained a patent and found backers to help launch the Pittsburgh Reduction Company (later renamed Aluminum Company of America) in 1888. Working with a small group of researchers, Hall concentrated on refining the smelting process to bring costs down and increase output; he left most management decisions to collaborator Arthur Vining Davis. Hall and Davis pushed hard to develop a market for aluminum in emerging industries such as electrical transmission, automobile manufacturing, and airplane manufacturing. Not only did the firm mine its own bauxite (a rich source of aluminum), it also operated factories to make a wide range of aluminum products such as cooking utensils.

For years, Alcoa was the largest—indeed, the only—aluminum producer in the United States. Demand soared during World War I, and the company started feeling the effects of rapid growth. Although one engineer traveled between the far-flung units to help solve technical problems, no one had the authority to set or enforce standards for the quality and the flow of materials moving through the production process in the vertically integrated operations of Alcoa's plants in Pennsylvania, Canada, Tennessee, North Carolina, and New York. Moreover, other inventors were developing new alloys, a threat that could potentially lessen Alcoa's dominance of the U.S. market.

In 1919, the company reorganized around five basic functions (finance, production, purchasing, sales, and engineering) and established a central research-and-development laboratory. Over the years, the lab created many innovative alloys and materials, fueling company (and industry) growth. Alcoa's alloys were used extensively in U.S. planes during World War II, and demand for aluminum was so strong that the federal government helped boost output by financing the construction of new Alcoa plants. After the war, many of these plants were sold to rivals Reynolds and Kaiser as part of an antitrust settlement, but Alcoa's market share remained over 50 percent.

Alcoa changed its organization design again in the 1950s. Although some managers defected to competitors rather than accept the change, the company shifted from a functional design to a divisional design geared to product applications. In 1962 Alcoa introduced the easy-open aluminum can and won a large share of the beverage container market. The firm diversified into nonaluminum products in the early 1980s in an effort to counter the effects of aluminum's cyclicality. But Paul O'Neill reversed that strategy and declared that Alcoa's future lay in aluminum. O'Neill had been deputy director of the Office of Management and Budget under President Ford, and he then served as president of International Paper until becoming the first CEO ever hired from the outside to lead Alcoa.

ENVIRONMENT

Alcoa faced the uncertainty of a complex and dynamic external environment. No one could predict future economic conditions, and the economy influenced the volume of housing starts and car sales. Housing and automobile manufacturing were two key Alcoa markets, so every twist of the economic cycle meant a turn in demand, prices, and profits. Further, the company was feeling mounting pressure from more efficient overseas competitors, and others were trying to lure customers away from aluminum by offering substitutes such as plastic.

Analyzing the external environment, O'Neill saw an opportunity to make new inroads into an old market: automobiles. Gasoline prices were rising and tougher fuel economy standards loomed, so some observers predicted that car makers might use lighter weight aluminum to replace steel components, despite aluminum's higher price tag. To take advantage of this opportunity, Alcoa teamed up with Audi to develop the "aluminum-intensive vehicle," a cast- and extruded-aluminum car frame that weighs 250 pounds less and uses fewer parts than conventional frames.

The internal environment was also dynamic. The organizational culture was inwardly focused; many in the company remembered how Alcoa had singlehandedly built the aluminum industry, and they didn't believe they could learn much by looking outside. Researchers in Alcoa's product development labs received little feedback about customer needs or wants. Then Alcoa switched from a product-oriented divisional structure to a market-oriented divisional structure in 1986. In making this change, the company decentralized decision making to give divisional and unit managers the flexibility to respond more quickly to environmental threats and opportunities.

Each division designated teams of people from sales and marketing, engineering, research, and production to study customer needs and competitive offerings. The teams met with people in each customer organization, asking about their immediate needs, their projections for the future, and what their own customers wanted. Over time, this information helped Alcoa managers see how well their current products met customer needs and helped them spot market opportunities. The information was also fed back to researchers to guide their product development efforts.

GOALS AND CHALLENGES

In his quest to combat cyclicality and improve performance, O'Neill has set a variety of ambitious goals. Although the company has the best safety record in the industry, O'Neill is driving toward an injury-free workplace for Alcoa's 63,000 employees and has already reduced the number of serious injuries by 25 percent. The focus on safety shows employees that they matter, but it also means that employees must understand how their activities relate to the overall production process: this fosters a focus on quality and productivity. For example, when employees take shortcuts, one of the leading causes of work accidents, they may actually be trying to avoid inefficient procedures. This new emphasis on safety has helped Alcoa lower its operating costs and dramatically improve efficiency and product quality.

With aluminum consumption in the United States growing only 2 percent a year, O'Neill is targeting Europe and Asia where consumption is rising 3 to 5 percent a year. If Alcoa can grab a worldwide market share as large as its domestic share, the company could grow as much as 50 percent. O'Neill also wants each Alcoa business to achieve a 15 percent return on equity.

To attain these goals more quickly, O'Neill recently decided against a slow but steady approach and instead unveiled a massive structural overhaul. The CEO lopped off the top two management layers, and he gave business unit managers much more authority to run their operations. These 25 managers now report directly to O'Neill and they are being held accountable for achieving dramatic performance gains within two years. Teamwork is key: every business unit is expected to exchange information and work more closely than ever before to battle competitors, increase efficiency, and build profits. O'Neill is counting on this new approach to boost profits by $1 billion by 1995.

1. How has Alcoa's vertical integration approach affected interdependencies among the units over the years? How have Alcoa managers dealt with these interdependency issues?
2. Trace Alcoa's organization design changes. What prompted these changes? What impact did these changes have on the vertical organization? How might such changes affect job analysis, staffing, and other human resource management activities?
3. Can the original Alcoa structure be characterized as mechanistic or organic? What about the latest Alcoa structure? What is the likely impact on innovation and intrapreneurship?
4. Just before O'Neill announced his reorganization, Alcoa's president retired abruptly. Other Alcoa managers may resist the drastic changes imposed by O'Neill's reorganization. What steps can O'Neill take to overcome resistance and encourage managers to stay rather than moving to rivals?

Leading

Management and Motivation

After studying this chapter, you will be able to

1. Discuss the role of motivation in increasing employee performance and explain the manager's role in motivating employees
2. Identify the major motivation challenges that managers face today and describe the process of motivation
3. Outline the four major need theories and discuss their implications
4. Identify two major process theories and explain their contributions and limitations
5. Relate the reinforcement theories to the law of effect and to behavior modification
6. Identify the four forms of reinforcement and explain the use of reinforcement schedules
7. Highlight how merit, pay-for-knowledge, and other reward systems can motivate employee performance

FACING A MANAGEMENT CHALLENGE AT

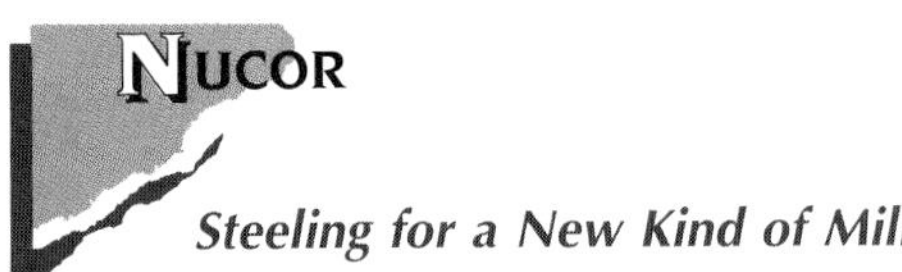

Steeling for a New Kind of Mill

Employees and managers were at loggerheads. Employees resented the way executives enjoyed special perks such as country club memberships, separate cafeterias, and private rest rooms. Supervisors charged that unions were pampering employees who were more concerned about racking up their paid sick leave than about the quality of the product going out the factory doors. This would hardly be a promising environment for anyone starting a new enterprise. But it describes conditions that were widespread in the U.S. steel industry in 1968 when F. Kenneth Iverson broke ground on his first mill.

Iverson had to act fast. His company was a successful maker of steel roof joists (beams used to support roofs). But his main supplier, United States Steel (now called USX), had raised prices so much that Iverson was paying more for steel than he could get for his finished joists. Iverson couldn't afford to stay in business very long with that arrangement, so he decided to open his own mill, a decision many criticized as unwise.

Since the end of World War II, the U.S. steel industry had boomed until it was larger than all other nations' steel industries put together. How could a tiny firm like Nucor produce material more cheaply than so-called Big Steel? Skeptics pointed out that Iverson faced an even more formidable challenge: expensive labor. In the typical steel mill, union contracts guaranteed wages that were half again higher than those in other industries. It would be hard for Iverson to hire and retain skilled employees when they could work elsewhere for higher pay.

But Iverson saw things differently. He looked closely at Big Steel and saw complacent operations trapped in webs of bureaucracy. Management rewarded itself with favorable employment contracts, often ignoring the needs of shop employees. The employees resented managers who insulated themselves from mill operations with layers of supervision and who preferred to rule by decree. So employees turned to unions, which negotiated good salaries and benefits but demanded restrictive work rules that drove up the final cost of steel.

Iverson concluded that the problem with the steel industry was not the high cost of labor. It was the declining productivity of an alienated work force. If employees could be managed by people who were sensitive to their needs, they might be motivated to perform more enthusiastically and more productively. Then Nucor could afford to make its own steel and be able to sell its roof joists at a profit. Furthermore, Iverson believed that if employees were motivated and rewarded properly, they would be less inclined to seek union representation.

Iverson had to attract employees with nothing more than a promise. Then he had to convince them he was sincere about a new approach to managing steel production. How could Iverson attract and retain employees when experienced people could earn higher wages at union shops? How could he motivate his employees to produce steel at rock-bottom cost when they traditionally viewed such efforts as benefiting only management?[1]

CHAPTER OVERVIEW

Kenneth Iverson recognized the vital role that motivation plays in the success of any organization, and he knew that the ability to motivate employees is a key attribute of effective managers. This chapter discusses the manager's role in motivating employees to reach new levels of performance. After outlining the motivational challenges that confront managers, the chapter examines the process of motivation and historical approaches to motivation. Next, the three groups of contemporary theories—need theories, process theories, and reinforcement theories—are presented. The chapter concludes with a look at reward systems, which are fundamental to motivation.

EXHIBIT 14.1

The Components of Performance

Performance is determined by three factors: the ability to perform the job, the organizational environment, and the level of motivation.

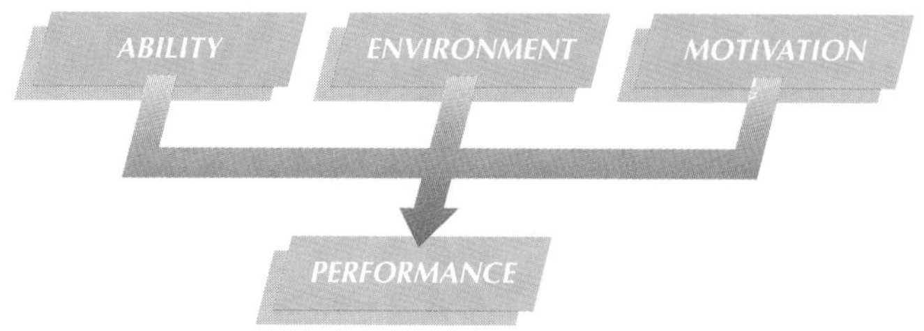

FUNDAMENTALS OF MOTIVATION

Understanding the forces that shape employee performance is no simple task. Why does one employee tackle every project with enthusiasm and consistently succeed, when another grumbles at every new task and often fails to meet minimum expectations? What causes an employee with a record of low performance to suddenly catch fire and become an important contributor in the organization? Why does a star employee lose energy and begin to lack commitment to the organization?

Performance depends on three factors: ability, environment, and motivation (see Exhibit 14.1).[2] If employees have the necessary abilities, are supported by their organizational environments, and are adequately motivated, they have the best chance of meeting their goals. If one of these factors is absent or weak, organizational performance is likely to suffer. In many cases, managers can help individuals develop their abilities through training and coaching. Similarly, managers can often cope with the environmental conditions that prevent performance by improving lighting and safety, among other elements. However, managers often find that dealing with a lack of employee motivation is more difficult.

Motivation factors differ from person to person, and because motivation is an internal force, it cannot be empirically observed, measured, or analyzed in quite the same way that staffing, funding, or other management concerns can be. Moreover, a particular act or decision may be the result of one of many different motives, just as a variety of motives may cause people to act in similar or identical ways. Nonetheless, one of a manager's most important responsibilities—and one of the most challenging tasks—is to enable employees to perform at the highest possible level in order to achieve the organization's goals.[3]

The Nature of Motivation

motivation The force that moves people to initiate, direct, and sustain behavior and action

Motivation is the force that initiates, directs, and sustains personal behavior and action.[4] In other words, it is the force that moves employees and managers to higher performance. Motivation can take a variety of forms. Sometimes, as in the case of Kemmons Wilson, the founder of Holiday Inn, motivation is fueled by the promise of nonfinancial, personal rewards. Nine years after he had suffered a massive heart attack at age 66, Wilson launched a new chain of budget-priced hotels named Wilson Inns. At a time when most retirees—especially those worth $160 million—would be content to play an occasional round of golf or join in a hand of bridge, the multimillionaire was active in over 90 companies and business ventures. Wilson's explanation reflects his high degree of internal motivation: "I just love to build and I love to create."[5]

On the other hand, motivation can also result from external factors that stimulate the inner drive to perform. Darlene Schultz, a night-shift employee at Andersen, the leading U.S. manufacturer of window and door units, hasn't missed a day of work in the two years she's been with the company. She is part of a six-person crew that exceeded its production goals by 132 percent, earning her $3.65 an hour in incentive pay in addition to her base pay of $11.41 per hour. At the end of the year, Schultz received another bonus: a profit-sharing check for $15,000. Schultz says she intends to stay at Andersen until she retires, sometime after the turn of the century. Unlike Wilson, whose motivation is linked to the internal rewards of accomplishment and creativity, Schultz's motivation comes from the desire for an external reward, the higher pay she receives.[6]

Motivating the people who handle such demanding tasks as anchoring skyscraper walls to the ground poses a particular management challenge. During the building of 500 Boylston Street in Boston, Bond Brothers and Dugan & Myers balanced the need for productivity with the need to motivate construction personnel who completed potentially dangerous jobs. The employees who drilled tie-backs were members of the Sand Hogs Union, which negotiated pay and benefits to reward members' efforts.

The Motivation Challenge

As the cases of Kemmons Wilson and Darlene Schultz illustrate, motivation is not a simple subject; no two people respond to precisely the same set of motivators. Managers in the 1990s face several pressing issues that complicate the challenges of motivating their employees:

- *Work-force diversity.* In the United States and in many other countries, the composition of the work force is becoming less homogeneous (see Chapter 13). This diversity complicates the task of motivating employees because managers must consider so many more motivational variables.[7]
- *Organizational restructurings.* The wave of mergers and acquisitions in the 1980s, followed by the massive layoffs that continue in the 1990s, presents another challenge. Employees who have been let go for reasons unrelated to their performance may question whether initiative and creativity are now less important than political survival skills. And employees who have seen colleagues lose their jobs may concentrate on keeping their own jobs and may stop taking risks—risks that might lead to new products, new markets, or other advances.[8]
- *Fewer entry-level employees.* In the 1990s, the labor force is growing at half the rate of the previous decade, and with 25 percent of all teenagers dropping out of high school, the number of qualified candidates for most entry-level positions is decreasing. In such a tight labor market, managers face new challenges in attracting, retaining, and motivating qualified entry-level employees. Managers must also determine how to motivate underqualified candidates to upgrade their skills and education so that they can handle entry-level tasks.[9]
- *An oversupply of managers.* In the middle and top ranks of management, quite a different phenomenon is causing organizational headaches. The sheer size of the baby-boom generation means that many of its members will not be able to move up as quickly as they would like. The number of senior management positions is far fewer than the number of deserving candidates, and the trend toward flatter organizations only makes matters worse for people who want to climb the hierarchical ladder. Stalled careers have begun to demoralize baby boomers as well as younger employees, who fear that their own aspirations will not be realized.[10]

As managers in for-profit and not-for-profit organizations come to grips with these increasingly urgent challenges, they must understand the forces that drive employee actions, how employees channel their actions toward goals, and how high-performing behavior can be sustained. These elements are all part of the process of motivation.[11]

The Motivation Process

need A perceived deficiency

In its simplest form, the motivation process begins with a **need,** an individual's perception of a deficiency (see Exhibit 14.2). For instance, an employee might feel the need for more challenging work, for higher pay, for time off, or for the respect and admiration of colleagues. These needs lead to thought processes that guide an employee's decision to satisfy them and to follow a particular course of action. If an employee's chosen course of action results in the anticipated outcome and reward, that person is likely to be motivated by the prospect of a similar reward to act the same way in the future. However, if the employee's action does not result in the expected reward, he or she is unlikely to repeat the behavior. Thus, the reward acts as a feedback mechanism to help the individual evaluate the consequences of the behavior when considering future action.[12]

intrinsic rewards Internally experienced rewards that result directly from a person's behavior

extrinsic rewards Rewards that are provided by others as a consequence of a particular behavior

Rewards fall into two categories. Kemmons Wilson, who founded a new hotel chain at the age of 75, is motivated by **intrinsic rewards,** rewards that are internally experienced as the direct consequence of a particular action. The inner sense of accomplishment Wilson expects to gain from starting and building new ventures is an intrinsic reward that motivates him more than the money he might make. Darlene Schultz, the window maker, is motivated more by **extrinsic rewards,** external rewards that are provided by others as a consequence of an action. Schultz has chosen to work for Andersen rather than another company because she knows that if she performs well, the company will reward her with a substantial bonus. In this case, Andersen managers are offering an external reward (money) as an inducement to motivate employees to perform.[13]

Early Approaches to Motivation

Throughout the twentieth century, researchers and practitioners have sought to understand exactly how the motivation process operates. As the large-scale corporation became more important in the world economy, and as managers began

EXHIBIT 14.2

A Basic Model of Motivation

The basic steps in motivation include (1) recognizing a need, (2) selecting ways to satisfy that need, (3) engaging in behavior with the goal of satisfying the need, and (4) assessing the outcome and reward of the chosen behavior. The individual's assessment of the reward influences the decision to act when the need next arises.

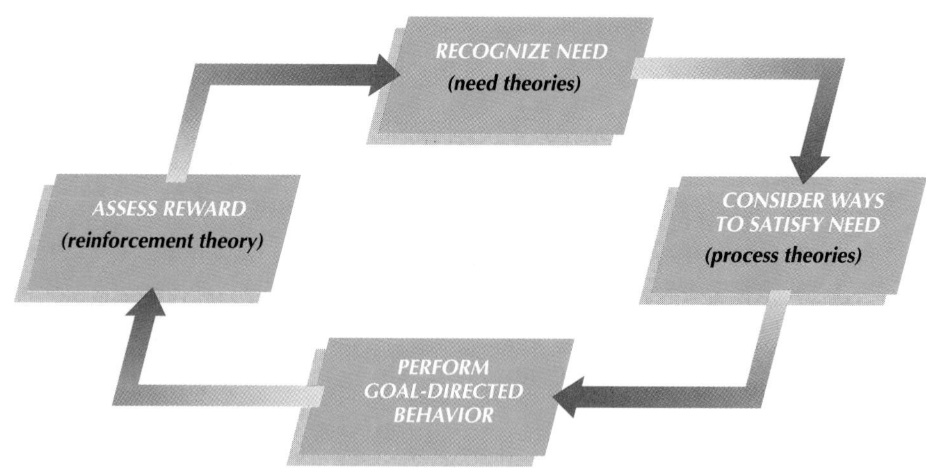

working with larger numbers of employees to accomplish more-complex goals, the question of effective motivation became increasingly urgent. Theorists in the scientific and behavioral management schools (see Chapter 2) were among the first to examine the nature and impact of motivation.

The Scientific Management Approach to Motivation

Frederick W. Taylor, the "father of scientific management," was keenly interested in employee motivation. Using time-and-motion studies, Taylor first determined the most efficient way for employees to perform various tasks. Then he turned his attention to motivating them to perform these tasks exactly to his specifications. Believing that people were motivated almost exclusively by money, Taylor advocated the use of incentive pay systems, which paid employees more when they produced more. Another member of the scientific management school, Lillian M. Gilbreth, also studied the use of incentives to inspire performance. She noted that promotions, higher pay, shorter hours, and holidays were all powerful motivators, especially when they were tailored to the individual's needs and interests. Scientific management theorists did take into account the differences among individuals, but because they focused almost exclusively on monetary rewards, they failed to examine how other elements (such as opportunities for individual initiative) affect employee motivation.[14]

The Behavioral Management Approach to Motivation

Whereas proponents of scientific management emphasized the impact of financial rewards, the proponents of behavioral management theorists focused on how behavioral factors affect motivation. Stimulated by the findings of the Hawthorne studies performed by Elton Mayo and others at Western Electric, behavioral management researchers began to examine the role that human relations play in motivation. On the basis of these early studies, managers who wanted to apply behavioral management techniques tried to increase their employees' sense of importance and involvement. However, organizations often went through the motions without actually increasing employees' power or responsibilities; typically, these organizations tried to communicate more effectively with employees, paid more attention to the dynamics of work groups, and invited participation in decision making only on mundane matters. By and large, managers continued to reserve most of the power for themselves, and employees were allowed little latitude in the methods they could use to accomplish their goals.[15]

In later years, behavioral management theorists such as Douglas McGregor offered other insights into the motivation process. McGregor's Theory X represented the traditional management view that employees were lazy, were uninterested in work, and needed to be prodded to perform. In contrast, his Theory Y viewed employees as creative, complex, and mature individuals interested in meaningful work. McGregor believed that under the right circumstances, employees would willingly contribute their ingenuity and their talents for the benefit of the organization. He suggested that managers motivate employees by giving them the opportunity to develop their talents more fully and by giving them the freedom to choose the methods they would use to achieve organizational goals. In McGregor's view, the manager's role was not to manipulate employees but to align their needs with the needs of the organization so that employees would regulate their own actions and performance.[16] These insights led researchers to investigate the origins and processes of motivation more closely.

MANAGEMENT AROUND THE WORLD

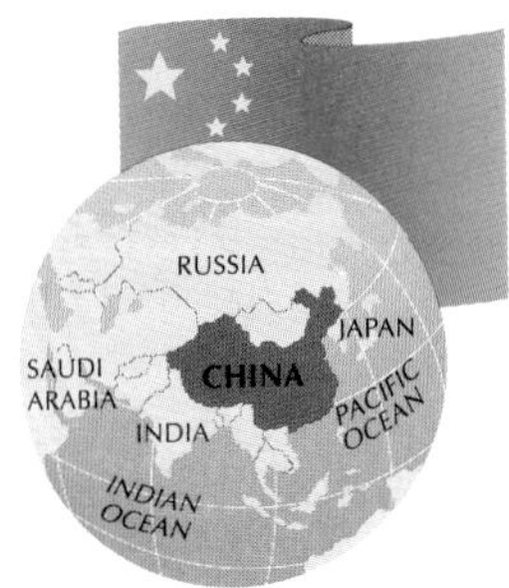

State-owned enterprises in the People's Republic of China, which are responsible for most of the country's industrial output, apply a variety of motivational methods. Factory managers can use financial incentives to some degree, and the slogan "To be rich is glorious!" was widespread during the 1980s. However, employees have little leeway in performing their tasks; they must follow management-set rules and directives, a requirement that became even stricter after the political unrest in 1989.

CONTEMPORARY APPROACHES TO MOTIVATION

Contemporary approaches to motivation can be divided into three schools of thought, each of which addresses a particular concept within the motivation model. Need theories examine the internal needs that drive people to take action. Process theories consider the thought processes that people use when deciding how to act, rather than the needs that stimulate action. Reinforcement theories are concerned with how and why rewards and punishments influence behavior. These three schools of thought are discussed in detail in the following sections.

Need Theories of Motivation

need theories Theories of motivation that focus on the needs that cause people to act in certain ways

Need theories examine the internal deficiencies that drive people to act. According to these theories, people are stimulated to act in certain ways because they are trying to fulfill particular inner needs or deficiencies. Need theories are also called *content theories* because they concentrate on the content of the underlying needs that motivate behavior.[17] Four well-known need theories are Maslow's hierarchy of needs, Alderfer's ERG theory, Herzberg's two-factor theory, and McClelland's acquired-needs theory.

Maslow's Hierarchy of Needs

Abraham Maslow's hierarchy of needs, introduced in Chapter 2, was an important step forward in understanding the complexity of human needs. Maslow argued that people are universally motivated to satisfy a sequence of five categories of needs; they start by addressing the basic needs and then they advance up the hierarchy as they seek to satisfy each progressively higher need (see Exhibit 14.3). The five categories are physiological, safety, social, esteem, and self-actualization needs.[18]

physiological needs The lowest-level needs in Maslow's hierarchy, including the elements that ensure basic human survival

safety needs Needs related to a safe, secure life

- **Physiological needs** are the needs for elements that ensure basic survival, such as food, clothing, and shelter. In the workplace, physiological needs are reflected in the desire for adequate pay, breaks to rest and eat, and protection from harsh weather conditions.
- **Safety needs** refer to the needs that ensure a safe, secure life that is free from harm. In an organizational setting, these needs are expressed as desires for such elements as safe working conditions, job security, medical insurance,

EXHIBIT 14.3

Maslow's Hierarchy of Needs

Abraham Maslow theorized that human needs can be divided into five categories and that people progress up the needs hierarchy as each level is satisfied. Employees seek a variety of rewards to satisfy these needs on the job.

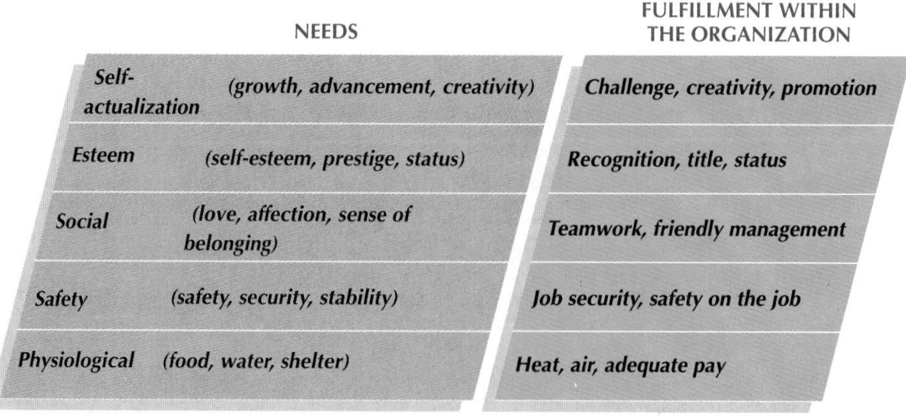

and retirement plans. At Nucor, for instance, physical safety needs are a critical balancing issue in the company's motivational programs because of the emphasis on production and the inherently dangerous nature of steel mill work.

- **Social needs** arise from the need for a sense of belonging and for social interaction; they include the need for love, affection, and acceptance. In private life, family and friends help fulfill the social needs. On the job, people try to fulfill such needs by building friendly relationships with others.
- **Esteem needs** are the needs for self-respect and for personal recognition. Within the organization, people try to satisfy these needs by seeking commendations, awards, promotions, and other tokens of recognition.
- **Self-actualization needs** include the need to realize one's full potential and to further develop personal capabilities. Self-actualization needs can't be completely satisfied, said Maslow, because as people develop their talents, the ability and the desire to grow becomes stronger. On the job, people strive to fulfill self-actualization needs by participating in training programs and by tackling demanding tasks. Someone like Angela Azzaretti, who handles a wide variety of communication tasks at Caterpillar's engine plant in Mossville, Illinois, is motivated by self-actualization. She turned down two promotions (and higher pay) because, she says, "In those other jobs, I would have had less responsibility, less of a challenge."[19]

social needs The need for love, affection, acceptance, and a sense of belonging

esteem needs The need for self-respect and for personal recognition

self-actualization needs The highest-level needs in Maslow's hierarchy, reflecting the need to realize one's full potential

According to Maslow, people must satisfy their lower-level needs before they can progress up the hierarchy to satisfy higher-level needs. As needs are satisfied, they no longer motivate behavior. Higher-level needs emerge as the main motivators once lower-level needs have been fulfilled. However, when people again feel a deficiency in connection with a previously fulfilled lower-level need, that need will take precedence over higher-level needs.

Although Maslow's hierarchy of needs continues to be a popular tool for thinking about motivation, researchers have found little support for this theory. They have also raised serious questions about the number of categories and their hierarchical arrangement. Maslow did note that the categories were not necessarily rigid or distinct, but later research suggested that people may very well attend to higher needs before completely satisfying lower needs, or that they may try to satisfy higher- and lower-level needs at the same time. These criticisms pointed the way for more research into the nature and the sequence of human needs.[20]

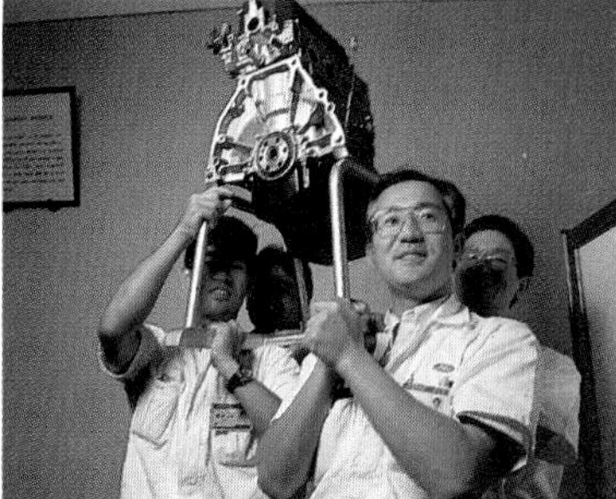
Higher-level needs such as esteem and self-actualization needs motivated these Honda engineers to develop a lean-burn car engine that didn't sacrifice power for fuel efficiency. They started without any formal authorization and persisted through 7 years of breakthroughs, changes, and setbacks until the engine, the first of its type, was perfected.

Alderfer's ERG Theory of Motivation

Researcher Clayton Alderfer shared Maslow's belief in a needs hierarchy, but his studies in the late 1960s and early 1970s suggested a slightly different set of categories. He proposed the **ERG theory,** a modification of Maslow's hierarchy that condenses the five categories of needs into three: existence needs (E), relatedness needs (R), and growth needs (G). Alderfer differentiated between the lower-level needs and the higher-level needs according to how concrete the needs seemed to be. In his theory, *existence needs* are the lowest-level needs and the most concrete; these include Maslow's physiological and some safety needs, all of which can be examined and verified. *Relatedness needs* are less concrete and include Maslow's social needs plus parts of the safety and the esteem needs. *Growth needs* are the highest-level needs in Alderfer's hierarchy, and the least concrete; these include parts of Maslow's self-esteem needs plus the self-actualization needs.[21]

ERG theory A need theory that refines the hierarchy of needs by reducing the number of categories to three: existence needs, relatedness needs, and growth needs

Alderfer did not believe that people had to completely satisfy one level of needs before they progressed to another level. Instead, he found that people could be simultaneously motivated by needs on more than one level. For example, the need to earn an adequate salary (an existence need) can occur at the same time as the need to be appreciated (a relatedness need) and the need to be creative (a growth need). Moreover, Alderfer discovered that the order of the categories can vary from individual to individual; an entrepreneur might seek recognition (a relatedness need) or creative expression (growth need) before worrying about more concrete needs such as hunger and thirst (existence needs).[22]

Alderfer also expanded on Maslow's theory by considering how people react when they can or cannot satisfy their needs. He developed the *satisfaction-progression principle* to describe the way people progress up the needs hierarchy as they satisfy lower-level needs. On the other hand, his *frustration-regression principle* explained that when people remain frustrated in their attempt to satisfy a higher-level need, they will stop trying to fulfill that need and will revert to trying to satisfy a lower-level need. Thus, ERG theory recognizes that people can move both up and down the needs hierarchy, depending on whether they are able to satisfy their lower-level or their higher-level needs.[23]

For example, officials at Willow Run High School in Ypsilanti, Michigan, recognized that achievement alone may not motivate all students. So the school adopted a program that appeals to lower-level needs by offering students concrete rewards for higher grades. Students with straight-A grades get free reserved parking spots and free or discounted merchandise at nearby stores, and they are allowed to skip two exams each semester. Students who earn a mix of A, B, and C grades receive fewer discounts and fewer free items but do get free tickets to some sports and social events as well as an annual pizza party. Even students who simply improve their grades are rewarded with a few freebies and discounts. Critics charge that such incentives devalue the goals of learning and are only a short-term solution. But since the program started in 1989, school attendance is up and standardized test scores have improved, a turnaround for a school that previously had poor records of attendance and achievement.[24]

Alderfer's theory, like Maslow's theory, is difficult to prove empirically. But both theories suggest that managers may want to develop flexible reward systems aimed at helping employees and managers satisfy a wide variety of needs on several levels. The theories also highlighted the powerful motivational potential of higher-level needs. For example, the Leeds family, owners of CMP Publications in Manhasset, New York, were concerned about retaining and motivating several superstar managers who ran the company's magazines. Although the organization was growing more than 30 percent a year, it was still relatively small and had few top management positions in relation to the number of deserving superstars. Founders Gerard and Lilo Leeds recognized that the superstars might become frustrated in their attempts to fulfill growth needs, so they created separate magazine divisions and delegated each superstar more authority and additional resources to expand individual divisions. The Leedses also invited these managers, called group publishers, to join a new committee that would formulate the company's overall strategic goals. This arrangement encouraged the group publishers to satisfy their higher-level needs by assuming more challenging responsibilities and by stretching their capabilities, a combination that has fueled high performance.[25]

Herzberg's Two-Factor Theory

In the late 1950s and early 1960s, less than a decade after Maslow first presented his needs hierarchy, Frederick Herzberg developed another perspective on the relationship between need and behavior. He asked hundreds of Pittsburgh accountants and engineers to think about times when they were satisfied with their jobs and felt motivated to perform, then he asked them to discuss the times when they were dissatisfied with their jobs and felt unmotivated. The factors his subjects mentioned when discussing their satisfaction differed from the factors they associated with dissatisfaction, leading Herzberg to conclude that they did not consider satisfaction and dissatisfaction to be opposite ends of a single continuum. Instead, his subjects seemed to see "no satisfaction" as the opposite of "satisfaction," and "no dissatisfaction" as the opposite of "dissatisfaction." On the basis of these findings, Herzberg proposed the **two-factor theory**, a theory that suggests that job dissatisfaction and lack of motivation are derived from factors entirely separate from the factors that affect satisfaction and motivation.[26]

two-factor theory A need theory arguing that job dissatisfaction and lack of motivation are derived from factors separate from those that affect satisfaction and motivation

The set of factors that influence dissatisfaction Herzberg called **hygiene factors** or *dissatisfiers.* Hygiene factors relate to the lower-level needs and include elements in the work environment such as company policies, knowledgeable supervision, interpersonal relations, working conditions, and pay (see Exhibit 14.4). For example, employees in Nucor's steel mills would probably feel a sense of dissatisfaction if they believed that working conditions were unsafe or if they found the company's policies overly restrictive. When managers improve hygiene factors, they lessen dissatisfaction, but they do not influence satisfaction.[27]

hygiene factors Factors that influence dissatisfaction

Motivators, also known as *satisfiers,* are the set of factors that influence satisfaction. Motivators appeal to higher-level needs and include work content, achievement, recognition, responsibility, advancement, and personal growth. If motivators are not available, employees will not feel either motivated or satisfied; only by providing motivators can managers help employees feel motivated and ultimately satisfied. Herzberg believed managers could provide motivators by using job enrichment techniques (see Chapter 13). For example, Yulia Kajakova is a manager trainee at the Moscow McDonald's, the busiest restaurant in the chain. Although employee turnover is a problem for most U.S. fast-food restaurants, the turnover rate at the Moscow McDonald's has been much lower. Kajakova enjoys the company's base pay and bonus system, hygiene factors that reduce dissatisfaction. But she is motivated by the opportunity for advancement and recognition for a job well done. Of her plans for the future, Kajakova says, "If I can prove to everybody that I am good and if I'm promoted, I'll stay."[28]

motivators Factors that influence satisfaction

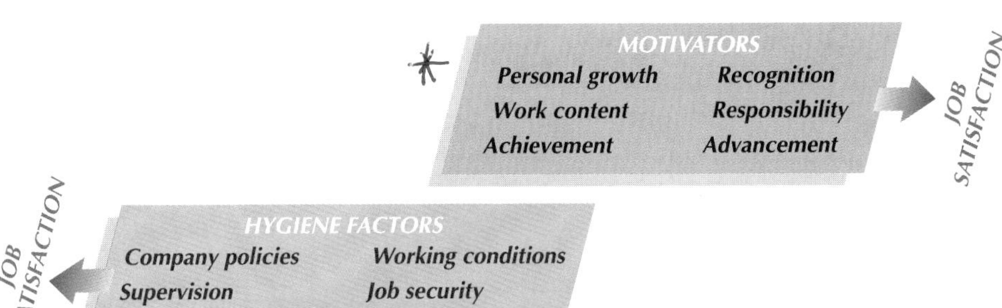

EXHIBIT 14.4

Herzberg's Two-Factor Theory

Frederick Herzberg suggested the existence of two distinct sets of motivational factors: hygiene factors, which influence dissatisfaction, and motivators, which influence satisfaction.

Although a number of studies (in the United States and abroad) have provided some support for Herzberg's two-factor theory, its validity has been questioned by researchers who are critical of the original methodology and who believe that some hygiene factors may in fact lead to satisfaction. Moreover, critics point out that a particular factor may influence dissatisfaction for one person but influence satisfaction for another person. Another criticism is that the theory seems to oversimplify the relationship between (1) motivation and satisfaction and (2) the factors that lead to satisfaction and dissatisfaction. Despite these limitations, the theory is significant because it offers valuable insights into the nature and the impact of motivators.[29]

McClelland's Acquired-Needs Theory

Another needs theory, developed by psychologist David C. McClelland, argues that needs are neither inherent in all people nor the same from person to person, as Maslow, Alderfer, and Herzberg presumed. McClelland's **acquired-needs theory** suggests that needs are acquired or learned as people move through life and that some people are more oriented to certain needs than to other needs. McClelland and his associates focused on three needs in particular: the need for achievement, the need for affiliation, and the need for power.[30]

acquired-needs theory A need theory suggesting that needs are acquired or learned through life and that some people are more oriented to certain needs than to other needs

need for achievement The desire to reach goals, to assume challenges, and to excel

The **need for achievement** is the desire to reach goals, to tackle challenges, and to excel. People with a high need for achievement are generally competitive, set moderately difficult goals, and actively seek feedback about their performance. Moreover, they tend to want total responsibility for their projects and are reluctant to give up control. For people with a high need to achieve, satisfaction comes from accomplishing the task; any monetary rewards they receive serve as an objective measure of their accomplishment, not as the motive for their efforts.[31]

People with a high need for achievement frequently become successful entrepreneurs. However, they prefer to handle tasks personally, so they are not always successful in a large organizational setting where they must manage through others to complete tasks. For example, entrepreneur Bill Gates sought challenging computer programming assignments when he was in college. He harnessed his need for achievement to found and build Microsoft into an international software powerhouse. As the company grew, Gates realized that his sense of accomplishment was fed more by developing innovative new products than by handling the everyday details of running the company. So as CEO, he delegated operational management responsibilities to other managers and retained the vital tasks of spotting product opportunities and focusing all Microsoft's resources on outthinking, outprogramming, and outselling the competition. Similarly, Gates recruits his programmers by stressing the opportunity to work on exciting new projects. Most new recruits take a pay cut to work at Microsoft, but they enjoy the creative atmosphere and the chance to grow; the payoff comes later, when many receive stock options and other rewards.[32]

need for affiliation The desire to form personal bonds with others

McClelland's work also examined the **need for affiliation,** the desire to make friends and to form personal bonds with others. When people have a high need for affiliation, they seek the approval and the reassurance of others, and they are also interested in how other people feel. Such people are likely to seek jobs where they can work with others and can build strong interpersonal relationships. Managers can stimulate motivation in employees who have a strong need for affiliation by creating a work environment that emphasizes cooperation and teamwork. For instance, at the GE Appliance Service Center in Louisville, Kentucky, customer service representatives recognize their colleagues' achievements by nominating deserving peers for monthly awards ranging from certificates to \$300 checks. "It's good to get recognition from a manager," says Sally Johnson, program manager for team development, "but it has a greater impact on motivation to know your work is appreciated by fellow reps."[33]

In addition, McClelland and his associates studied the **need for power,** the desire to influence or to control others. This need takes two forms: personal power and institutional power. People who exhibit a high need for personal power tend to seek power for its own sake. On the other hand, people with a high need for institutional power (also known as social power) are more concerned with organizational problems and with influencing others to achieve group goals. These people are willing to make some sacrifices for the sake of the organization, and they like the discipline that work provides. Not surprisingly, McClelland argued that when people with a high need for institutional power hold management positions in large organizations, they are more effective than people with a high need for achievement.[34]

need for power The desire to influence or to control others

McClelland called his theory the acquired-needs theory because of his belief these needs can be learned. Most people learn them as children, but McClelland's theory maintains that these needs can also be learned by adults. In one experiment, McClelland taught businesspeople in India the characteristics of high achievers. A follow-up study revealed that the participants in McClelland's 40-day seminar became more entrepreneurial than those who had received no training. McClelland learned that those who had acquired the need for achievement had started new businesses, sought out new customers, found new sources of funding, and made significant contributions to the local economy. This suggests that managers and employees can learn the need for achievement and build on that need to motivate higher performance.[35]

Managerial Implications of Need Theories

Taken together, Maslow's hierarchy of needs, Alderfer's ERG theory, Herzberg's two-factor theory, and McClelland's acquired-needs theory focus attention on the range and kinds of needs that motivate individuals (see Exhibit 14.5). The frustration-regression principle that Alderfer highlights in his ERG theory and the distinction Herzberg makes between hygiene factors and motivators seem to indicate that if people are unable to meet higher-level needs, they may turn to satisfying the more concrete lower-level needs. As a result, the organization might lose the benefit of these people's creativity and talents, which would hurt the organization's ability to reach its goals. The ERG and the acquired-needs theories both underscore the complexity of human motivation by suggesting that needs differ from person to person. Further, McClelland's work in other countries and his view that needs are acquired offer the possibility that needs may be changed through training, which can greatly influence organizational and even national performance and competitiveness. However, the needs theories do not adequately explore how individuals make the decision to act.

Process Theories of Motivation

Need theories describe the desires that propel behavior by examining *what* motivates people. **Process theories,** on the other hand, explain the thought processes that guide the decision to act on needs and to follow a particular path in satisfying them; that is, these theories explore *how* people are motivated. Process theo-

process theories Theories of motivation focusing on the thought processes that guide people as they act to satisfy their needs

EXHIBIT 14.5

Comparing the Major Needs Theories

The four major needs theories cover the range of human needs, but each takes a different approach in terms of categorization and hierarchy.

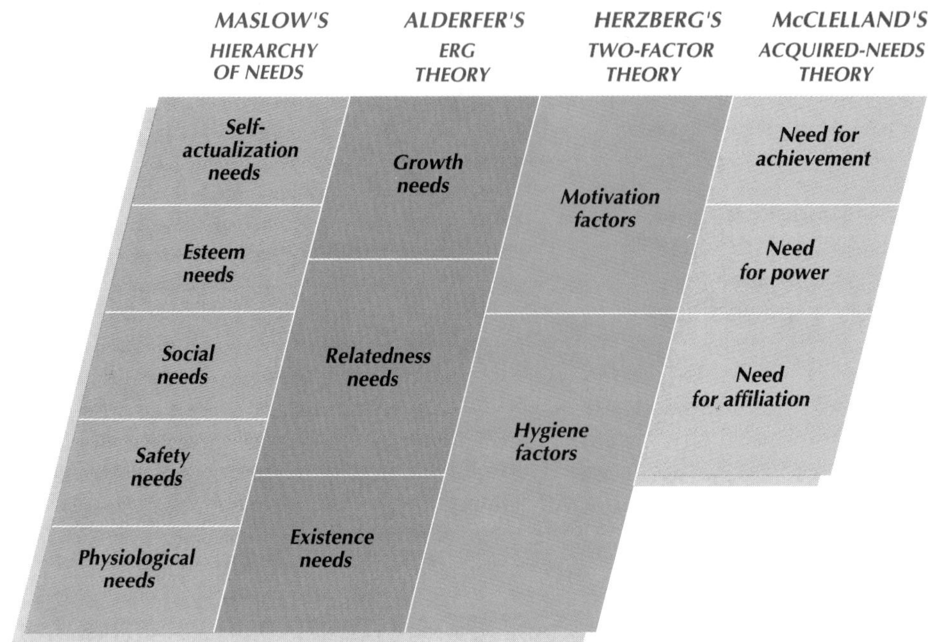

ries are also called *cognitive theories* because they look at the mental processes that shape human responses to needs. Two important process theories are expectancy theory and equity theory.

Vroom's Expectancy Theory

expectancy theory A process theory suggesting that before people act, they consider whether they have the ability and whether their effort will bring about the desired results

Expectancy theory contends that before people are motivated to act, they consider whether they have the ability and whether their effort will bring about desired results. The building blocks of this theory, which is generally associated with the work of Victor Vroom, are threefold: (1) the individual's perception that effort will lead to performance, (2) the perception that performance will lead to a particular result, and (3) the desirability of the rewards related to the result.[36]

effort-performance expectancy The perceived relationship between the effort required and the performance that is likely to result

Effort-Performance Expectancy **Effort-performance expectancy,** the first part of the expectancy equation, involves a process of self-assessment related to future performance. Employees consider whether they have the necessary abilities, tools, and resources to achieve the desired performance by investing the personal effort. In effect, they ask themselves, "Can I succeed?" If they do not believe that their efforts will lead to high performance, then their effort-performance expectancy is low. To encourage high effort-performance expectancy, effective managers set realistic, well-defined goals for performance, provide employees with the necessary training, equipment, and support to enhance their performance, and match the employees' skills to the requirements of the task.[37]

performance-outcome expectancy The perceived relationship between a person's performance and the possibility that various outcomes will result

Performance-Outcome Expectancy The second part of the expectancy equation is **performance-outcome expectancy,** which involves an assessment of the work environment and the reward system. Employees consider what outcomes (or results) are likely to occur if their actions lead to performance. In effect, they ask themselves, "If I succeed, will I be rewarded?" As with effort-performance expectancy, when people perceive that their efforts will not lead to desirable outcomes, they do not feel motivated to act. To boost performance-outcome expectancy, managers should make clear the explicit connection between performance and outcome, and they should deliver rewards on time and as promised—but only to those who perform.[38]

For example, managers at United Controls wondered why employees rarely used the employee suggestion box. The company intended to reward employees whose ideas resulted in significant savings, but for 20 years the box was nearly always empty. Before management would reward an employee for making a suggestion, the idea had to wend its way through a lengthy review process that involved calculating how much the company would save if it adopted the idea. Because the process seemed complicated and the rewards were slow in coming, employees felt that good ideas were not appreciated. Then company executives simplified the program to more quickly evaluate suggestions and to reward employees much faster than under the old system. Performance-outcome expectancy went up, and employee involvement soared. Welder Mike Vailliant, who submitted 45 ideas in one year, says that the challenge of improving performance makes him look forward to doing his job.[39]

To improve overall productivity, managers at the IBM plant in Austin, Texas, have shifted the responsibility for testing product and process quality from plant engineers to a small group of assemblers, who receive special training before they assume their new positions. The training strengthens the link between effort and likely results, boosting the assemblers' effort-performance expectancy.

Outcome Valence Each action an organization member takes can lead to a number of outcomes. However, not all outcomes are equally attractive; someone may look forward to a particular outcome but dread another. Employees ask themselves, "Will this outcome be satisfying?" Thus, people attach a value, or **valence,** to the anticipated satisfaction of each outcome. When the outcome is desirable, the valence is positive; when the outcome is undesirable, the valence is negative; and when the outcome is neither desirable nor undesirable, the valence is zero (see Exhibit 14.6).

valence The value of the anticipated satisfaction that each possible outcome of an action represents

For instance, a first-line manager might work hard and in return be promoted quickly or receive a pay raise. These two outcomes are desirable and have a positive valence for this individual. However, as a result of this hard work, the manager might be asked to transfer to another plant or to take on more stressful tasks. The manager attaches a negative valence to these two outcomes because they seem undesirable. At this point, the manager looks at the sum of the positive and the negative valences. If the sum of the valences is positive, the manager will feel motivated to invest the effort to perform; but if the sum of the balances is negative, the manager will not feel motivated to act.[40]

As Alderfer and McClelland suggested, needs vary from person to person, and consequently the valences people assign to different outcomes will vary as

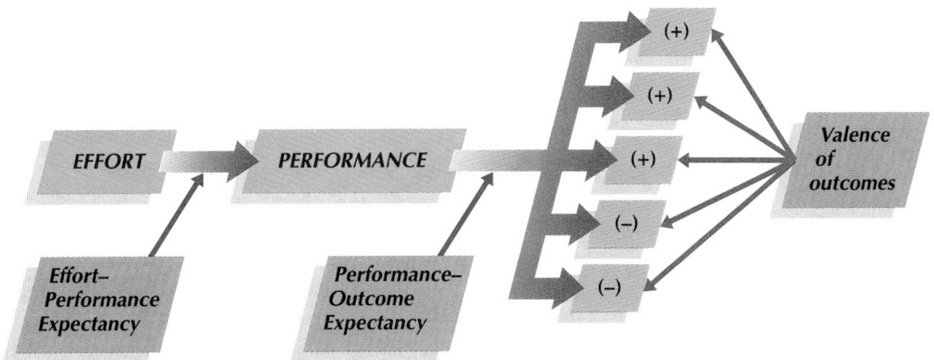

EXHIBIT 14.6

Expectancy Theory

Expectancy theory suggests that people will act to satisfy their needs if (1) they think their efforts will lead to performance, (2) they think performance will lead to a specific outcome, and (3) they value the anticipated satisfaction (the valence) of the outcome.

GLOBAL MANAGEMENT

Rethinking Motivation in Maquiladoras

In 1965 the Mexican government established the maquiladora program in hopes of encouraging foreign firms to establish assembly plants in Mexico and to employ Mexican workers. The Mexican government offered foreign companies exemption from tariffs, exemption from ownership restrictions, and access to inexpensive Mexican labor. U.S. firms responded enthusiastically. More than 1,500 maquiladora plants are now in operation, and they employ more than 500,000 people in all. General Motors has 29 Mexican maquiladoras; other major U.S. firms with a presence include General Electric, Zenith, Rockwell International, A. O. Smith, and Texas Instruments.

Although more maquiladoras are now being run by local managers, many plants are still headed by managers transferred from the United States. These managers sometimes have difficulty retaining and motivating their Mexican employees. Employee turnover occasionally runs as high as 135 percent, which means that maquiladoras sometimes hire and train their entire work force more than once a year.

Local employees and managers may not take the same path to reach their performance goals as their U.S. counterparts would take. For instance, the U.S. manager of a maquiladora producing automotive parts was pleased that his plant received 99 percent ratings on its product quality inspections. He was mystified, though, by inexplicably high costs for raw materials. He later learned that plant supervisors snuck into the plant every night and threw out the rejects. They didn't want to disappoint their U.S. manager by admitting that they didn't know how to adjust malfunctioning equipment.

Such misunderstandings are costly and can lead to poor quality, high absentee rates, and low morale. Clearly, U.S. methods of motivation—and the values and assumptions on which they are founded—can't always be easily transferred to other countries. In the case of maquiladoras, U.S. managers can't effectively motivate employees unless they understand the values and culture of those employees.

Studies have found that Mexican organizations—government, business, and religious—are frequently modeled after the family. When employees join these organizations, they often feel that they are joining a

well. Because of the diversity of today's work force, the possible variations in outcome valences are also diverse. For this reason, managers must consider how their employees perceive outcome valences and then tailor the outcomes to meet the expectations of their employees.[41] But for employees to feel motivated, all three building blocks of the expectancy theory must be in place. For motivation to occur, people must perceive (1) that their actions will lead to performance (effort-performance expectancy), (2) that their performance will lead to certain results (performance-outcome expectancy), and (3) that the results will be desirable (positive sum of the outcome valences). When all three conditions are met, people are motivated to invest the effort toward achieving performance.[42]

Although expectancy theory has not been proven to be applicable to all individuals or in all situations, its principles offer valuable insights into the motivation process. As a result, the theory has been enormously influential, both in management research and in practice, despite the shortcomings identified by later investigators. Since Vroom originally proposed his theory in the 1960s, a number of researchers have expanded on the basic theory in an attempt to develop a more complete and applicable motivation model.[43] One interesting extension was proposed by Porter and Lawler.

The Porter-Lawler Extensions Expanding on Vroom's expectancy theory, Lyman W. Porter and Edward E. Lawler III added several key elements, including the influences of individual abilities, personal traits, and role clarity, which contribute to the potential for job performance. Their findings confirmed that motivation alone cannot improve performance if people lack the ability to do the job or family, and they expect to be treated as family members. In return, they are prepared to be loyal and to work hard. Mexican employees are inclined to see their jobs as a personal relationship with their employers, and they work for more than just a paycheck. For example, at Hamill de Mexico, after an attendance bonus failed to reduce the 20 percent absentee rate, the plant manager pinned photographs of employees with outstanding attendance records on company bulletin boards. Employees responded enthusiastically to the recognition program, and absenteeism dropped to 5 percent.

Mexican organizations also tend to be openly hierarchical, with clear distinctions between the various levels. For this reason, many employees feel uncomfortable when U.S. managers try to minimize the hierarchical distinctions by wearing casual clothes and by conducting conversations on a first-name basis. In one maquiladora where automotive parts were made, a U.S. manager even tried to create closer bonds between hourly employees and supervisors by locking the supervisor's lunchroom in hopes the two groups would at least eat together. But rather than eat with the hourly employees, the supervisors started eating their lunch beneath a tree outside the plant.

Temsa, an electronics assembly subsidiary of U.S. manufacturer Allen-Bradley, is one maquiladora that gears its motivation efforts to the culture. High turnover was one of the managers' greatest concerns. To reduce the turnover rate and to motivate those who remained on the job, Temsa managers decided to create more of a family feeling within the organization. They established a variety of employee activities, including a Christmas dinner, a sports club, employee recognition programs, and a Temsa anniversary program. They also created a two-tier hierarchy for assemblers that rewarded employees with higher wages and higher status for learning new skills. Thanks to these steps, turnover has dropped. Temsa's experience suggests that the language of motivation, like the language of a country, can be learned.

Apply Your Knowledge

1. How can U.S. managers apply Herzberg's two-factor theory to reduce dissatisfaction and increase satisfaction? What nonfinancial rewards might be effective?
2. How might the U.S. manager of a maquiladora draw on expectancy theory to make the plant's motivation programs more effective?

if they are unclear about their roles. Porter and Lawler also theorized that people distinguish between the intrinsic and the extrinsic rewards that result from various outcomes and that they compare the rewards they actually receive to the amount of effort they invest, the level of performance they attain, and the rewards they think are fair. If employees believe that their efforts have led to high performance, they will expect higher rewards than if they believe their performance was low. They will feel satisfied if the rewards seem equitable in relation to the effort and the performance, but they will feel less satisfied if the rewards are lower than they believe to be equitable. Moreover, if employees are rewarded despite low performance, they may feel satisfied but they will not be motivated to improve, because the reward was not tied to their actual effort or performance level.[44]

Porter and Lawler probed deeper into the relationship between performance and satisfaction and proposed the idea that high performance can itself lead to satisfaction and provide motivation for future action. When employees achieve high performance, they receive the intrinsic rewards of doing a good job and accomplishing their goals as well as the extrinsic rewards such as bonuses or time off. These outcomes have positive valences, so employees feel satisfied, which in turn motivates them to expend the effort for future performance. Thus, managers who want to encourage high performance should offer equitable and timely rewards, and they should not reward low performance. Although Porter and Lawler's extension was criticized on several grounds (including the technique they used to measure satisfaction), their ideas expanded the usefulness of expectancy theory.[45]

Adams's Equity Theory

equity theory A process theory suggesting that people are motivated to seek equitable treatment compared with others in similar situations

Expectancy theory generally assumes that people want to maximize the rewards they receive. **Equity theory,** on the other hand, assumes that people are primarily concerned with being treated fairly in relation to others. First described by J. Stacey Adams, equity theory argues that people will act on their needs if the outcome for a given effort is comparable to the outcomes that others receive for similar effort. Thus, people compare the ratio of their inputs (such as the number of hours worked, experience, and training) and their outcomes (rewards such as salary, promotions, and vacation time) with the ratio of inputs and outcomes of people believed to be in similar situations.[46]

A state of equity exists when the employee believes that the ratio of inputs to outcomes is equivalent to the input/outcome ratios of other employees who have similar responsibilities or of people who do the same job in other organizations. But when the ratios do not seem equivalent, the employee feels underrewarded or overrewarded. Either of these states of inequity creates an inner tension that the employee feels driven to relieve. The greater the inequity, the greater the tension and the stronger the motivation to reduce it. For example, Nucor's CEO F. Kenneth Iverson was concerned that he couldn't attract or retain employees if they perceived inequity when they compared their base salaries to the higher base salaries offered by unionized steel mills.

People can reduce inequities in several ways. First, they can change their inputs. An employee may decide to work fewer hours in order to reduce the level of inputs and thereby achieve perceived equity with fellow employees. Second, they can change their outcomes by pushing for raises, promotions, or bonuses. Third, they can alter their own perceptions. If efforts to change inputs and outcomes fail, employees may reassess their estimation of both inputs and outcomes to bring them into line with other employees. Or they may reassess the input/outcome ratio of the comparison group so that it approximates their own. Fourth, employees can change the object of comparison by deciding that special circumstances skewed their original view and that another person or group would provide a more valid comparison. Finally, they can transfer to another job, or if no other method resolves the inequity they feel, they can resign.[47]

Managers of the Cummins Engine factory in Columbus, Indiana, where 5,000 are employed, must be sensitive to how assembly-line employees perceive the equity of their pay relative to the work they perform. If some employees believe that they are working harder but receiving less pay than others doing equivalent assembly-line work, this perceived inequity will influence their motivation and, ultimately, their performance.

One of the problems in applying equity theory is that the estimation of equity is subjective, not objective. People have their own personal methods of evaluating inputs and outcomes and of comparing their own ratios to those of others. Moreover, an employee may feel equity in comparison to others even when the inputs and outcomes are not identical. The key is that the employee believes that the *proportion* of inputs and outcomes is equitable. For example, employees working 20 hours a week may believe it is equitable for 40-hour employees to earn twice as much as long as the ratio of inputs to outcomes is the same. This implies that managers must clarify the relationship between inputs and outcomes. If all assembly-line employees reach their production targets, for example, all must be rewarded equitably. Most important, as managers develop their reward systems, they should try to understand what employees consider "equitable" in relation to their effort and performance.

Researchers have found conflicting evidence to support the validity of equity theory, but it can be useful for managers who couple it with expectancy theory. For example, Corning pays bonuses of 3 to 6 percent of pay to individuals who do an outstanding job. This outcome has a positive valence and rewards high performance, which leads to additional effort and performance. However, Corning managers are aware that the bonus system sometimes stirs a sense of inequity within the ranks. Although the company doesn't publicize the names of people who receive bonuses, word sometimes leaks out, with both good and bad results. "The good news is that people can get one," observes Corning executive Peter Maier. "The bad news is if I've been doing good work and I didn't get one." So Corning managers work hard to clarify the relationship between performance and reward and to outline as specifically as possible the bonus criteria.[48]

As discussed in Chapter 13, the issue of equity has come to the fore as lower-level managers and employees eye the generous compensation packages that many U.S. CEOs have received in recent years. The perceived inequity of exorbitant top-management compensation creates a demoralized, cynical work force. According to industrial psychologist Elaine Sloan, once the link between pay and effort (between outcomes and inputs) is broken, employees look for other factors to explain the inequity. Many employees angrily cite office politics as a key determinant of compensation. Others try to equalize their input/outcome ratios by stealing office supplies or by taking long lunches. Such perceptions of inequity between top management pay and the pay at other levels make it harder for managers to use intrinsic rewards to motivate employees' performance. In Sloan's words, "How can you ask someone to do something for the sheer satisfaction of doing the work if you're not doing the same?"[49]

Managerial Implications of Process Theories

Process theories help managers understand how employees take action to respond to their needs. Expectancy theory suggests that managers must give employees the tools to succeed, that they must clearly link rewards to employee performance, and that they must select rewards that are meaningful to their employees. To motivate employees, managers should help sustain their employees' view that their efforts will lead to performance, that performance will lead to specified rewards, and that these rewards are attractive. The Porter-Lawler extensions point out the importance of rewarding high performance, because this can lead to satisfaction and renewed effort toward reaching goals. Equity theory suggests that individuals take the expectancy equation and apply it to

Don Carlton, president of Texas-based Radian, uses positive reinforcement to encourage behaviors that contribute to higher performance. He recognized the efforts of Allana M. Coffey, manager of facilities administration, by presenting her with the firm's Corporate Achievement Award in honor of the initiative she displayed in finding ways to save money.

others as well as to themselves. If employees believe that others are being rewarded in ways that are proportional to the inputs they bring to the organization, then they are likely to remain well motivated and enthusiastic.[50]

Reinforcement Theories of Motivation

According to the motivation equation, needs trigger behaviors, which in turn lead to outcomes. Need theories look at what motivates people, and process theories examine the thought processes that are triggered in responding to needs. Another category of motivation theories examines *why* people continue to behave as they do, and why they change their behavior. **Reinforcement theories** suggest that people's behavior is directly related to the consequences of their actions. Pioneered by psychologist B. F. Skinner during the 1930s, these theories draw heavily on the *law of effect,* which states that the consequences (effect) of a behavior determine whether the behavior will be repeated. According to this law, people are likely to repeat behavior that results in enjoyable or positive consequences, whereas they are likely to abandon behavior that results in unpleasant—or no—consequences.[51] Reinforcement theorists contend that the law of effect holds true no matter what a person's needs or thought processes may be.

Reinforcement theories assert that an initial stimulus causes an individual to respond by taking action. If the consequences of that action are pleasant, the person will probably choose to repeat the same behavior when the stimulus recurs. But if the consequences are unpleasant, the person is likely to act differently the next time the stimulus occurs.[52]

reinforcement theories Motivation theories that suggest that people's behavior is directly related to the consequences of their actions

behavior modification The deliberate use of techniques to change human behavior

reinforcement The use of techniques that cause a behavior to be repeated or abandoned

positive reinforcement Strengthening behavior by offering pleasant consequences for a particular action

Forms of Reinforcement

Skinner's work on reinforcement has been the basis for **behavior modification,** the deliberate use of techniques to change (modify) human behavior. Skinner believed that behavior can be modified by applying **reinforcement,** the use of techniques that cause a behavior to be repeated or abandoned. Reinforcement theory includes four methods of behavior modification: positive reinforcement, avoidance learning, extinction, or punishment (see Exhibit 14.7).

Positive reinforcement strengthens behavior by offering pleasant consequences for a specific action. One example of positive reinforcement is praise for employees who finish their work on schedule. Because these employees receive praise (pleasant consequences), their behavior (finishing work on time) is reinforced, and they are more likely to complete future projects on time. Pizza Hut uses another form of positive reinforcement in its Boston outlets to reduce the high rate of employee turnover. Employees who work more than 200 hours a quarter earn credits toward tuition reimbursements for themselves, their children, or their grandchildren. The credits they are eligible to earn—that is, the level of positive reinforcement—increases with the length of employment. The longer employees remain with the company, the more credits they can earn, which reinforces their continued employment.[53]

avoidance learning Strengthening one behavior by allowing people to avoid the negative consequences of not exhibiting that behavior

Sometimes employees act one way because they know that if they act differently, they will invite negative consequences. Their behavior is thus reinforced by **avoidance learning,** which strengthens the behavior that people exhibit when they want to avoid the negative consequences of not exhibiting that behavior. Also known as *negative reinforcement,* avoidance learning works because people want to avoid unpleasant consequences, so they behave in ways that will not

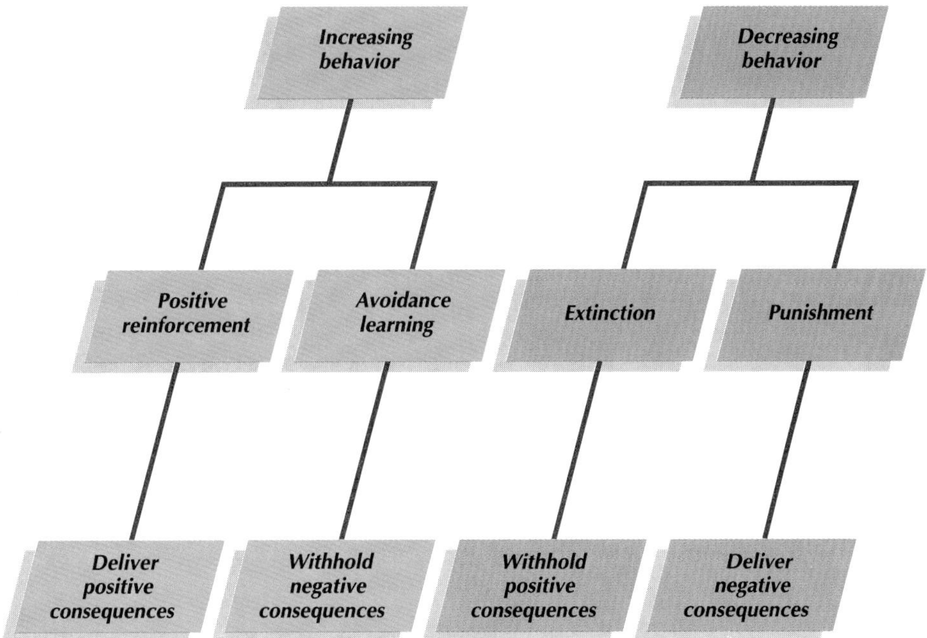

EXHIBIT 14.7

Approaches to Reinforcement

According to reinforcement theories, managers can respond to employee behavior in one of these four ways: with positive reinforcement, with avoidance learning, with extinction, or with punishment.

invite such consequences. For instance, if employees know that their manager will ask them to work late if they don't finish their assigned projects, and if they also know that the manager won't do so if they complete the projects on time, they can avoid working late by punctually completing their assignments.

Extinction discourages a specific behavior by withholding the positive consequences that have been associated with that action. This reinforcement method works by eliminating the pleasant consequences that previously served as positive reinforcement for a particular behavior, so the behavior eventually disappears (becomes extinct). For instance, managers who want their employees to work less unpaid overtime by working more efficiently may choose to stop thanking employees for staying late and for working on weekends. This removes the pleasant consequences of working overtime. Once employees realize that their overtime hours are not appreciated, they will not be motivated to continue this behavior.

extinction Decreasing a specific behavior by withholding positive consequences that were once associated with that behavior

Another reinforcement method used to discourage behavior is **punishment,** which decreases behavior by providing unpleasant consequences. Managers at China's Xian Department Store use punishment to change the behavior of sales clerks. Each month, the managers review customer complaints and select employees for the "40 Worst" list. These employees' undesirable behaviors range from ignoring customers to throwing things at them. Managers then post plaques above the selected employees' stations, proclaiming them the worst clerks in the store.[54] Punishment has been criticized as a form of reinforcement because it does not present any acceptable alternative forms of behavior. And although punishment is usually successful in eliminating unwanted actions, it does not necessarily produce long-term improvements in behavior. When punishment is used, it should be used sparingly and judiciously.[55]

punishment Decreasing a behavior by providing unpleasant consequences

Although reinforcement can be a powerful method of shaping employee behavior, managers sometimes send the wrong signals through their own behavior.

According to motivation expert Ferdinand F. Fournies, managers can inadvertently use extinction or punishment when they mean to offer positive reinforcement. He cites the example of an employee who complains, "I worked late last night to finish a report, but the boss didn't even look up when I handed it in this morning." Without the positive reinforcement of acknowledgment, this employee is less likely to work late in the future. Managers may unintentionally punish their high achievers who complete challenging assignments by giving them even more difficult work. These employees may see the new assignments as negative consequences, so they may change their future behavior to avoid such unpleasant results.[56]

Schedules of Reinforcement

The timing or schedule of reinforcement also has an important impact on motivation. Managers can use either continuous or partial schedules of reinforcement to influence employee behavior. In a *continuous schedule,* every instance of a particular behavior is reinforced. Steven Ettridge, president of Temps & Company in Washington, D.C., uses a continuous schedule to reinforce his salespeople's efforts. Each time a salesperson makes one call to find new customers for the temporary-help agency, he or she receives 50 cents. Ettridge calculates that after 200 calls, the salesperson will earn $100, will find five people who are interested, and will actually close one sale. He had previously paid $100 for each new account, so the new system doesn't increase Ettridge's costs, and he believes that the new system encourages salespeople to continue making sales calls even when they do not get that one sale. However, a continuous schedule is less effective when used over a long period, and employees quickly stop the behavior when the schedule is withdrawn.[57]

Because maintaining a continuous schedule of reinforcement can be tedious as well as time-consuming, many managers rely on a *partial schedule* of reinforcement, in which only some instances of the behavior are reinforced. Partial schedules of reinforcement include fixed-interval, fixed-ratio, variable-interval, and variable-ratio schedules.[58]

- A *fixed-interval schedule* reinforces employee behavior at set intervals of time. A weekly paycheck is an example of reinforcement delivered on a fixed-interval schedule. When fixed-interval reinforcement is used, performance is only average and tends to peak right before the reinforcement is administered, because employees know they will be paid despite variations in their performance. Furthermore, when fixed-interval reinforcement is withdrawn, performance rapidly declines.[59]
- A *fixed-ratio schedule* reinforces employee behavior after the desired behavior has been exhibited a specific number of times, rather than at specific time intervals. Managers who treat their employees to dinner after they have signed 10 new customers are using a fixed-ratio schedule to reinforce the behavior of signing new customers. The employees are motivated because they know that each new customer they sign brings them closer to the next free dinner. Fixed-ratio schedules can lead to higher and more consistent performance than fixed-interval schedules, but when fixed-ratio schedules are withdrawn, performance drops rapidly.[60]
- A *variable-interval schedule* reinforces behavior when some variable but average period has passed between instances of reinforcement. For example, a manager may inspect each department once a week on average, but employ-

ees can't predict the exact day on which the manager will appear in any given week. This schedule promotes moderately high but more consistent performance than under a fixed-interval schedule, and when reinforcement is withdrawn, performance declines less rapidly.[61]

- A *variable-ratio schedule* reinforces behavior after a variable but average number of occurrences of the behavior. For example, a manager who uses a 15-to-1 variable-ratio schedule might praise employees first after they submit 10 cost-cutting ideas, next after they submit 20 ideas, and so on. This schedule can lead to the highest consistent levels of performance because employees can't foresee exactly when the next reinforcement will occur, so they maintain their performance. As with the variable-interval schedule, when the variable-ratio schedule is withdrawn, performance declines more slowly than when fixed schedules are withdrawn.[62]

Managerial Implications of Reinforcement Theories

Managers can use reinforcement theories to motivate higher employee performance in a variety of ways. Many organizations use a combination of reinforcements and schedules to reach their goals. Positive reinforcement is an extremely powerful way of encouraging performance, especially when coupled with the appropriate reinforcement schedules. Continuous reinforcement helps strengthen employee behavior when learning a new skill; once the training period is over, managers will want to switch to partial reinforcement to keep performance high. To discourage particular behaviors, managers should consider extinction rather than punishment; if punishment is used, it should be offered as soon after the behavior occurs as possible, to link the negative consequences to the action.

REWARD SYSTEMS

In their quest for higher levels of performance and productivity, managers can build on insights gained from motivation theory to design effective motivation programs for their employees. With a better understanding of (1) the needs that stimulate an individual to take action, (2) the cognitive processes that shape an individual's decision to act to satisfy these needs, and (3) the effects that reinforcement can have on behavior, managers can create motivation programs that mesh with organizational and personal goals. One of the first steps in the process is identifying these goals and setting standards for performance (see Chapter 7). Next, managers develop a reward system to encourage employees to achieve these goals and standards.

Rewards can be either intrinsic (such as an inner sense of accomplishment) or extrinsic (such as a bonus check), and many organizations try to reinforce appropriate behavior by setting up conditions that allow employees to receive both types. One of the first steps in the process is to identify these goals and set performance standards. Next managers develop a reward system to encourage employees to achieve the goals.

Types of Reward Systems

Reward systems come in a variety of sizes and shapes. For any reward system to work well, it must address Maslow's and Alderfer's lower-level needs as well as

MANAGERIAL DECISION MAKING

Motivating Government Employees

During the 1980s, a stream of computer and electronics firms moved to Chester County, Pennsylvania, drawn by its beautiful, rolling countryside and its proximity to the research universities in nearby Philadelphia. Business in the county flourished, but county government suffered. The new companies—and those that arose to support them—contributed millions of dollars to the local economy, but they siphoned off skilled employees just as the demands on county government hit new highs. Finding qualified employees for jobs in county government became difficult, in part because base pay was low, but keeping them once they were hired proved even more difficult.

Much of the problem could be traced to the county's antiquated pay-for-performance system. Introduced in 1974, the system allowed six 5 percent salary increases within the salary range assigned to each of the county's 480 positions. Each year at appraisal time, managers met informally with their employees to review each employee's performance during the year. If employees performed satisfactorily, they received salary increases of 5 percent. As a result, almost all employees received a yearly 5 percent merit increase and reached the top of their salary range in the minimum of six years.

To make matters worse, the program actually discouraged superior performers, because managers could not reward them. Managers could only approve or disapprove a merit raise. No matter how hard these star employees worked, they received the same raises as everyone else. Moreover, those who had less seniority but higher performance than their colleagues might still be paid less until their sixth year, when they finally reached the top of the pay scale. Few had the patience to wait.

(Chester County was not alone in its problems. A poll of 4,000 managers in the federal government found that they were strongly committed to public service but were dissatisfied with their financial rewards. More than 70 percent felt that their pay was inadequate, and 74 percent complained that the government's merit pay system did not recognize individual achievement.)

Realizing that their reward system was not encouraging performance, the Chester County commissioners directed the personnel department to devise a system

Herzberg's hygiene factors. The managers who create these reward systems must also recognize that, as McClelland suggested, individuals have different needs and may therefore require different rewards. To be effective, the systems should also apply both the effort-performance expectancy and the performance-outcome expectancy, offering outcomes that are meaningful to employees. Furthermore, reward systems must pass the test of the equity theory, both in comparison to other organizations and within the organization itself. Then reinforcement theory comes into play: managers should use rewards to reinforce only the appropriate behaviors. Organizations generally use one or more reward systems, including merit and pay-for-knowledge systems.[63]

Merit Systems

merit system A system in which employees receive rewards as their performance improves

A **merit system,** also called a *pay-for-performance system,* is a system in which employees receive rewards such as salary increases as their performance improves. When managers apply merit systems conscientiously, they are generally able to motivate employees to higher performance. But the link between performance and reward is undermined when managers fail to apply merit-pay systems rigorously. Merit systems may not succeed if the performance standards are not clearly explained, if the standards can't be objectively measured, or if the merit rewards don't vary according to performance. The compensation consulting firm Towers Perrin reports that merit increases during the early 1980s varied widely, from 0 to 17 percent of salary, suggesting that they were used to reward differing levels of performance. However, by 1988, merit increases were concentrated between 4 percent and 5 percent; nearly everyone, regardless of perfor-

that would encourage initiative, motivate employees, and reduce turnover. The first step was to develop job descriptions for all 480 positions in the county government, from county supervisor to clerk typist. Job descriptions would remedy a defect in the old system: poorly defined criteria for performance appraisals.

The new job descriptions were assigned no more than six key goals per position and included specified measurements to be used in assessing whether the person holding that position had accomplished each goal. For instance, one of the goals for an environmental health supervisor in the Chester County public health department is to train, motivate, and supervise lower-level employees. The data used to measure this objective include training records, skill certifications, productivity statistics, and employee morale figures derived from attitude surveys.

Under the old system, managers could only approve or disapprove an employee for a merit raise. The new system allows a manager five ratings, ranging from provisional to outstanding. But Chester County officials knew that just presenting more appraisal options would not solve the problem. They examined the federal government merit system, which has five performance levels, and learned that fewer than 1 percent of federal employees were rated in the lower two categories. Chester County avoided this problem by assigning point values to the measurements used to evaluate each objective. Managers tabulate the point totals for each employee and compare the results to the minimum values established for each level in the rating system. Merit raises are awarded on the basis of these values.

The Chester County merit system is still too new to be judged, but participants are enthusiastic. County officials invited employees from throughout the government to participate in drawing up the job descriptions so that they would understand how the descriptions were created and what the revamped merit system was expected to accomplish. Employees now have a clear understanding of performance expectations, and managers have a more objective method of evaluating employee performance.

Apply Your Knowledge

1. How might Chester County administrators use nonfinancial rewards to reinforce high performance?
2. What role does equity theory play in the new system?

mance, received similar pay increases. In such a situation, employees see no meaningful relationship between their performance and their salary increases, so merit pay loses its ability to motivate.[64]

Pay-for-Knowledge Systems

A **pay-for-knowledge system** rewards employees as they learn to perform additional tasks or as they acquire new skills. For example, employees in Northern Telecom's Santa Clara, California, assembly plant earn pay raises when they learn new "skill blocks" such as circuitboard preparation. Although pay-for-knowledge systems can be complex to establish and administer, they can improve productivity and can help organization members develop the experience, the flexibility, and the skills to handle future challenges. Organizations that use pay-for-knowledge systems to increase their employees' versatility may even be able to operate with fewer people. Employees generally like pay-for-knowledge systems because they satisfy higher-level needs (such as building competence) as well as lower-level needs (such as security).[65]

pay-for-knowledge system A system in which employees receive rewards as they learn to perform additional tasks or acquire new skills

Other Reward Systems

Many organizations want to reward their employees on the basis of their proportional contributions to overall organizational performance. Reward systems linked to overall organizational performance include profit sharing, gain sharing, and employee stock ownership plans.

profit sharing A reward system in which employees receive bonuses based on the organization's profitability

- **Profit sharing** is a reward system in which employees receive bonuses based on the organization's profitability. Many for-profit companies, including

General Motors, Ford, Hewlett-Packard, and USX, have profit-sharing plans. Alcoa has instituted a program that is activated when operating profits exceed 6 percent of assets—a target well above the industry average. When the target is reached, 20 percent of the profits above the threshold are distributed in bonus form.[66] Advocates of profit sharing note that it boosts employee motivation to increase performance and to eliminate waste. However, in terms of expectancy theory, the link between effort and performance is often weak. Jerome M. Rosow, president of Work in America Institute, a not-for-profit research firm, observes that a number of factors affect profits, and many of them are unrelated to employee effort, such as pricing policy, market environment, and taxation. He notes that "one financial decision, such as taking on a lot of debt or making an acquisition, can wipe out anything the worker can do."[67]

gain sharing A reward system in which employees receive bonuses based on their unit's performance

- **Gain sharing,** a system that was devised to meet some of the shortcomings of profit sharing, rewards employees with bonuses based on the performance of their unit (or group, division, or team). Unit performance targets can include better productivity, lower costs, higher quality, and better customer service. By linking employees' rewards to the performance of their individual unit, managers strengthen the link between effort and performance. Darlene Schultz, the window maker at Andersen, participates in a gain-sharing plan. When her six-person team exceeds their production target, they receive a bonus. Under gain sharing, group pressure encourages employees to cooperate and to work harder. Gain sharing also encourages experienced employees to boost the unit's performance by sharing their skills with less experienced employees.[68] However, gain-sharing plans do have limitations. Managers must carefully establish group goals so that employees don't slight other important organizational goals. For instance, overall quality should not be ignored in the drive to meet production quotas. Another limitation is that companies may find themselves awarding gain-sharing bonuses for group performance even when the organization overall is not profitable.[69]

employee stock ownership plan (ESOP) A reward system in which managers encourage employees to own stock in their own companies, providing an incentive for employees to increase the value of that stock through higher performance

- **Employee stock ownership plans (ESOPs)** reward employees by encouraging ownership of stock in their own companies; employees then have an incentive to increase the value of that stock through higher performance. Although some large corporations have started to adopt ESOPs, this technique has been popular with small businesses for some time as a way of aligning the interests of management and employees for the benefit of the organization. As shareholders, employees directly benefit when the company does well, so they are motivated to improve productivity and profitability. For example, the 240 employee-owners of Reflexite, a high-tech manufacturer based in New Britain, Connecticut, receive monthly bonuses based on profitability. If there are no profits, there are no bonuses. In addition, Reflexite employees receive an annual dividend check representing their proportional share of the pretax earnings. The ESOP program helps the company attract and retain good people, and it motivates all employees to do their best. One limitation of the ESOP system is that the company may be required to repurchase the shares of employee shareholders who retire or resign to join other organizations, which can be a financial burden.[70]

flexible reward system A reward system that offers employees the option of selecting the rewards they consider most valuable

A less traditional way of motivating employees is to use a **flexible reward system,** which builds on the idea of outcome valence by allowing employees to select their own rewards from a menu of choices. For instance, an employee with a family might choose additional medical benefits or more vacation days, whereas an unmarried employee might choose a lump-sum bonus. Flexible systems are more complex to plan and administer than traditional reward systems, but the option of being able to choose their rewards can improve employees' motivation.[71]

Managerial Implications of Reward Systems

Establishing reward systems requires that managers understand their employees' needs; understand their organization's short- and long-term goals; be able to apply motivation theories effectively; and understand the benefits and limitations of various reward systems. Managers must also be prepared to adjust and refine their motivation programs as the composition of the work force changes and as the market environment evolves. Two points are especially important:

- *Keep performance goals in perspective.* Many managers have the advantage of using quantifiable measurements to assess performance. However, overemphasis on operational goals and performance standards, which are relatively easy to define and to track, can obscure overall organizational goals. For instance, soon after Solar Press introduced a new reward system in its 75-person mail room, many employee teams doubled their production. But as they pursued higher production figures, the teams neglected routine equipment maintenance and did not share ideas with other teams. Overall performance suffered and company morale plummeted; managers finally scrapped the plan.[72]
- *Pay attention to higher-level needs.* Not every system has to revolve around large sums of money; managers can provide motivational opportunities by appealing to higher-level needs such as self-esteem and self-actualization. For example, GTE Data Services honors its top-performing 100 employees by sending them (along with their spouses) to a conference at a luxury resort, by presenting them with a plaque and a $500 check, and by trumpeting their achievements in the company magazine. Some motivation programs don't

When furniture maker Herman Miller's earnings plunged late in the 1980s, managers took a closer look at their reward systems. Bonuses had been based on productivity and cost-cutting achievements; managers added two additional measures, customer satisfaction and return on assets. This change made employees more aware of the firm's overall goals, and coupled with an aggressive sales campaign, the new system boosted earnings.

rely on financial incentives at all. Warren Trucking in Martinsville, Virginia, tried to restore employee motivation after a debilitating strike and a wage rollback. Strapped for cash, top management decided to create a community feeling within the company by helping employees load trucks. They also reduced the stress on drivers and their families by scheduling trips so that drivers could return home several nights a week, and they invited 10 employees to join management in looking for ways to make Warren Trucking more efficient. Thanks to these moves, the company's sales doubled within two years.[73]

SUMMARY

Motivating employees to perform at the highest possible level in order to achieve organizational goals is one of management's most important responsibilities and one of its most difficult tasks. Motivation is the force that initiates, directs, and sustains personal behavior and action. A manager's role is to determine the factors that stimulate employee motivation and to channel that motivation in ways that serve organizational goals. However, managers today face several pressing issues that complicate the challenge of motivation. These issues include work-force diversity, organizational restructurings, fewer entry-level employees, and an oversupply of managers.

The process of motivation starts with a need. That need triggers an individual examination of whether particular behaviors will result in rewards that satisfy the need. If the chosen behavior results in the anticipated reward and satisfaction, then the individual is likely to act the same way in the future. But if the action does not lead to the expected reward, the person is unlikely to repeat the behavior.

Theories of motivation are clustered around three ideas: the nature of human needs and desires, the thought processes that people adopt to satisfy those needs, and the reasons that people repeat or change their behavior. Need theories assume that people act to reduce deficiencies in various areas. The four major need theories are Maslow's hierarchy of needs, Alderfer's ERG theory, Herzberg's two-factor theory, and McClelland's acquired-needs theory. These theories explore the range and kinds of needs that motivate people but do not explain how people decide to behave in a particular way to satisfy their needs.

Process theories explain the thought processes that guide the decision to act on needs and to follow a particular path in satisfying them. Two important process approaches are Vroom's expectancy theory and Adams's equity theory. Although these theories help managers understand how employees take action to respond to their needs, they do not examine why people continue to behave in a particular way. Reinforcement theories examine the influence of consequences on behavior and suggest that people's behavior is directly related to the consequences of their actions. The law of effect states that behavior with enjoyable consequences is likely to be repeated, whereas behavior with unpleasant consequences (or no consequences) is likely to be abandoned. Reinforcement theories are the basis of behavior modification, the deliberate use of techniques to change behavior. Managers can use four methods of reinforcement to modify employee behavior: positive reinforcement, avoidance learning, punishment, and extinction. Reinforcement can be delivered according to continuous or partial schedules of reinforcement; partial schedules of reinforcement include fixed-interval, fixed-ratio, variable-interval, and variable-ratio schedules.

Managers design reward systems to encourage employees to achieve short-term and long-term goals. In a merit system, employees receive salary increases and other rewards as their performance improves. In a pay-for-knowledge system, employees are rewarded as they learn to perform additional tasks or as they acquire new skills. Other reward systems include profit sharing, gain sharing, and employee stock ownership plans. In addition, some organizations opt for flexible reward systems that allow employees to pick the rewards that they find most meaningful.

MEETING A MANAGEMENT CHALLENGE AT NUCOR

People shook their heads when F. Kenneth Iverson opened his first steel minimill in 1969. Cynics said Iverson's company, Nucor, would collapse under the weight of the industry's sky-high wage scale. But Iverson believed he could succeed by paying careful attention to employee motivation. Iverson opened state-of-the-art mills in rural areas where industry was still largely nonunion, allowing him to avoid the high union wage structures. He hired people from nearby farms who lacked knowledge of steel but made up for it with ambition, and he assigned each to a small work group dedicated to a specific task required for making steel.

Iverson encouraged employees to think of their work groups as small businesses of their own. The financial reward for each employee included gain-sharing bonuses scaled to production targets achieved by each work group. Although the base pay for a typical plant might be $8 an hour, employees in teams that produced more than the standard amount of steel could earn twice the going wage through performance bonuses. These production bonuses were posted daily on bulletin boards and paid weekly to reward performance as quickly as possible. Ten percent of all the pretax earnings were paid to employees in a profit-sharing plan, and the company offered tuition assistance for employees' children. Moreover, Nucor's medical benefits were generous, and its personnel policies were geared to employee needs as revealed through employee attitude surveys.

But Nucor also introduced punishments. An employee who arrived 15 minutes late lost a whole day's production bonus. The whole week's bonus was lost if the employee was a half hour late. Moreover, employees were not paid if their group's machinery broke down. Employees supported such rules because they helped groups earn their maximum bonuses.

Iverson minimized the number of management layers to keep top management in close touch with managers and employees on every level. Nucor used four layers of management in an industry that traditionally used eight, and Iverson encouraged people at every level to share their ideas. As supervisors walked through plants they solicited ideas; managers called group meetings to hash out problems. Further, Iverson cut management pay faster than employee pay when times were slow. Managers and employees had the same vacation time, enjoyed the same insurance program, and even wore the same color hard hats.

F. Kenneth Iverson, CEO, Nucor

Nucor today is a $1.4 billion company producing 980 tons of steel per employee per year, far more than the industry average of 420. Including bonuses, Nucor's average employee compensation of $32,000 is higher than the average in unionized steel shops. Iverson's views on the vulnerability of Big Steel have also proven correct. Nucor's new production processes, narrower product line, and innovative motivation programs helped the company remain highly profitable even as larger steel companies were undergoing painful downsizing. During the 1980s Nucor doubled in size while Big Steel laid off 70 percent of its work force and reduced its annual capacity by 50 million tons.

From one small mill in 1969, Iverson has built Nucor into the nation's ninth largest steel producer. The company is known around the world for its motivation techniques. Nucor's success proves that motivated employees make a difference.

***You're the Manager*:** You have joined Nucor as the vice president for human resources. Your responsibilities include helping managers and supervisors keep their employees motivated and establishing programs and policies that encourage a motivated work force.

Ranking Questions

1. Nucor has grown both by building new mills and by acquiring existing mills. Employees at one of these existing mills are upset. Until Nucor

replaces the old equipment in a few months, these employees can't produce as much steel. Much of Nucor employees' compensation is based on production levels, so these employees sense inequity when they compare their pay with that of employees at newer mills. How would you handle the situation?

   a. Until new equipment is installed, temporarily raise the base pay of these employees to cover the bonus shortfall caused by old equipment.
   b. Stop releasing performance data so that employees can't compare their production levels and bonuses with those of other mills.
   c. Temporarily reduce the bonuses available to employees in newer mills so that their newer equipment won't give them an unfair advantage.
   d. Employees in the older mills really shouldn't have to suffer because of circumstances beyond their control. Compute the average production bonus companywide and award the same amount to all employees.

2. One of the mill supervisors asks your help in solving a problem. An employee who was hired last month refuses to do more than the minimum effort required to complete his tasks. He lives with his parents and is concerned only with earning enough to pay his modest rent. The other members of his work team see him as jeopardizing their own income. What do you recommend?
   a. Fire the man immediately for underperforming. He understood how the bonus system operated when he came aboard.
   b. Send the employee a book about high performance and suggest that he apply some of the principles.
   c. Transfer the man to another department such as clerical, data processing, or mail delivery, where the production bonus system is not in effect.
   d. Hold a team meeting to allow teammates to tactfully express their concerns. If the employee isn't motivated to perform once he realizes that others depend on his efforts, he will have to be fired.

Multiple-Choice Questions

3. A rift is developing in one plant between the young, single employees and the married employees, particularly those with children. The single employees want to work overtime to boost the plant's production for higher bonuses, but the married employees value time off with their families and want to limit their overtime. What do you suggest the plant manager do?
   a. Search for a way to satisfy both groups, such as working with a scaled-down crew on weekends, which would allow the single people to work overtime but wouldn't require the married people to do so.
   b. Let the employees vote on whether to work overtime (assuming that either decision is compatible with demand for the company's products).
   c. Stay out of the disagreement; there's no way you can solve this without alienating one of the two groups.
   d. Side with the employees who want to work harder; everyone will benefit from increased production.
4. You recognize that employees need a sense of belonging when they're part of a team. However, the working conditions inside a steel mill aren't conducive to many of the rapport-building activities that occur in an office setting—chatting by the water cooler, attending meetings, and so on. In the steel mill, employees often work alone at their stations; the noise level is high, so normal conversation is impossible; and the situation is potentially dangerous, so employees have to concentrate on their work. How could you help foster team feelings?
   a. Publish a newsletter that profiles several employees each month, both on and off the job; this will help employees learn more about each other and thus develop feelings of empathy.
   b. Encourage employees to visit at each other's stations so they can get to know one another.
   c. You can't force teamwork on people; if they need to get along on the job, they'll find a way to do so.
   d. Arrange social activities away from the stress and danger of the mill, such as picnics, parties, and softball games.

Analysis Questions

5. How is Iverson's motivational approach similar to that advocated by scientific management theorists? How is it different?
6. What nonfinancial rewards does Nucor offer its employees? Do they seem to be effective in motivating performance? Why or why not?
7. How might the emphasis on production targets work against Nucor's overall business interests?

Special Project

For managers at Nucor, the work has become harder and the hours have become longer as the company grows. The company is profitable, but managers are concerned about their compensation. During an economic downturn, a manager's salary may drop as much as 75 percent, while a foreman's salary might drop only 25 percent. The manager's base salary is only 70 percent of the pay offered for similar positions at other steel firms. Assume that apart from production bonuses, managers receive no discretionary bonuses and are not covered by a pension program. Outline an equitable reward system to more effectively motivate these managers.[74]

KEY TERMS

acquired-needs theory (444)
avoidance learning (452)
behavior modification (452)
effort-performance expectancy (446)
employee stock ownership plan (ESOP) (458)
equity theory (450)
ERG theory (441)
esteem needs (441)
expectancy theory (446)
extinction (453)
extrinsic rewards (438)
flexible reward system (458)
gain sharing (458)
hygiene factors (443)
intrinsic rewards (438)
merit system (456)
motivation (436)
motivators (443)
need (438)
need for achievement (444)
need for affiliation (444)
need for power (445)
need theories (440)
pay-for-knowledge system (457)
performance-outcome expectancy (446)
physiological needs (440)
positive reinforcement (452)
process theories (445)
profit sharing (457)
punishment (453)
reinforcement (452)
reinforcement theories (452)
safety needs (440)
self-actualization needs (441)
social needs (441)
two-factor theory (443)
valence (447)

QUESTIONS

For Review

1. How does the behavioral management approach to motivation differ from the scientific management approach?
2. What are the four need theories?
3. What are the contributions and limitations of the two process theories?
4. How can the four schedules of reinforcement influence behavior?
5. What major motivation challenges do managers today face?

For Analysis

1. If an organization starts to recruit senior citizens for entry-level jobs formerly filled by young people just entering the work force, should its managers rethink the motivation programs? Why or why not?
2. Some airlines have instituted two-tier salary programs in which they pay new employees less than the employees who held those jobs several years ago. Considering the equity theory of motivation, what are the likely implications of this practice?
3. Can the motivation programs adopted by an organization affect the composition of its work force? Use need theories to explain your answer.
4. When recruiting to fill a position as head of nursing for a critical-care medical facility, how would the personnel director be likely to view a candidate with a high need for affiliation? A candidate with a high need for personal power? Explain your answers.
5. Which is more likely to lead to feelings of equity: pay-for-performance systems or pay-for-knowledge systems? Why?

For Application

1. How might the celebrity director of a children's charity use reinforcement schedules to plan her trips to thank the volunteers who work in local chapters around the country?
2. Assume that a slump in auto buying has forced Chrysler to lay off employees at its most efficient factory. How might the factory's general manager motivate the remaining employees and improve morale during the weeks following the layoff?
3. What might be the most significant hygiene factors for a college professor?
4. What can the manager of a Thom McAn shoe store do to boost salespeople's effort-performance expectancy? Be specific.
5. How can a newspaper editor make use of the ERG theory to motivate reporters?

KEEPING CURRENT IN MANAGEMENT

Find a magazine or newspaper article that discusses a new motivation program or a new reward system that an organization is about to introduce. The organization can be a company, a government agency, or a not-for-profit group, and the program can involve either monetary or nonmonetary rewards.

1. Why is the organization establishing the new motivation program? Did the organization previously use a formal motivation program to improve employee performance? What were its strengths and weaknesses?
2. Which theories of motivation did the managers draw on when designing the new program? What performance goals is the plan trying to accomplish? How are the managers demonstrating their commitment to making this program a success?
3. How are employees reacting to the program? If you were an employee, would you be motivated by the program? Would the program be attractive to a diverse work force? Would members of different age groups react positively to it? Do you think another type of program would be more effective?

SHARPEN YOUR MANAGEMENT SKILLS

Attracting and motivating public school teachers is one of the greatest management challenges in the United States. State and local governments are hard-pressed to find money to raise salaries, so teachers continue to be motivated by intrinsic rewards and, to a lesser extent, by a variety of nonfinancial extrinsic rewards. However, many critics believe that teachers should not be forced to rely only on the satisfaction they receive from teaching as a substitute for better pay.

- *Decision:* Put yourself in the role of a state superintendent of public education. Outline a motivation program that will do the best possible job of attracting new teachers and retaining current teachers. Assume that the state faces a budget shortfall, so there is no chance for raising teacher salaries. Take advantage of any insights offered by need, process, and reinforcement theories.
- *Communication:* You've been asked to appear on a local television talk show to explain your plan. You have three minutes for your opening remarks before you'll have to answer phoned-in questions from the audience. Write the notes you'll need to explain your plan in the time you'll have.

CASE

American Airlines Innovates to Motivate

American Airlines emerged from the turbulence of federal deregulation and of its internal overhaul as the largest airline in the world. But profits have been slipping, and CEO Robert Crandall must once again transform American if it is to survive the tumultuous 1990s.

HISTORY

American Airlines was formed in 1934 when a Fairchild Aviation subsidiary sold off the unconnected coast-to-coast network of small aviation companies that it had consolidated under the name of American Airways. Under president C. R. Smith, the fledgling airline lost money until 1936, when it introduced passenger service on the relatively large, 21-seat DC-3 airplane. It offered the first nonstop, coast-to-coast flights in 1953 aboard the 80-seat DC-7, and six years later the company ushered in the jet age with the Boeing 707. American declined after Smith stepped down in 1968, and in the early 1970s the company sent notes to 140,000 regular passengers apologizing for poor service.

Crandall joined American in 1973 as chief financial officer and introduced many innovations. His computerized reservation system earned hundreds of millions of dollars from travel agents. Moreover, the system enabled American to track and fill empty seats (by offering discount fares) and to reward steady customers with the industry's first frequent-flyer bonus program. After becoming president in 1980, Crandall promised job security and profit sharing to convince employees to ratify a lower wage scale for newly hired employees despite union opposition; new employees now must gradually work up to parity with veterans. American entered the 1980s losing $75 million a year, but it expanded rapidly both in the United States and abroad, and it ended the decade with annual profits of nearly half a billion dollars. Then in the wake of the Persian Gulf War and economic recession, all major airlines lost money and American began the 1990s with a $40 million deficit.

ENVIRONMENT

These days American often ranks tops in U.S. customer service and employee satisfaction in part because it trains managers to delegate authority and it trains employees to take the initiative when solving problems. For example, American managers at Los Angeles International Airport have saved $400,000 by turning over budgets for ramp and passenger services to employees who implemented their own ideas. In Odessa, Texas, 14 American agents have developed their own performance feedback system with regular reports on customer satisfaction. In both cases, morale has improved because employees feel they have significant control over their jobs. American also motivates employees by rewarding good ideas and performance with travel and merchandise. American's employee suggestion program saved the airline $31 million in a single year. The program promotes a sense of involvement by giving suggesters rewards and prompt reports on the status of their ideas. Under American's employee recognition programs, managers give employees points toward merchandise for good work such as helping a passenger with an emergency. Frequent flyers recognize superior service by awarding cards that can be redeemed for travel or merchandise.

GOALS AND CHALLENGES

The 1990s opened with airline layoffs, liquidations, and bankruptcies, and Crandall thinks the industry will remain in turmoil through the decade. Problems include declining growth in domestic traffic and in economies around the world, as well as the increasing strength of airline unions. Crandall wants to cut costs and improve productivity through automation, but the pilots' union is pushing for salary increases that would raise costs. Crandall also wants to expand overseas and is training employees to provide yet a higher level of service demanded by international flyers, but good service depends on good morale and his flight attendants are upset over regulations governing female attendants' weight. American has liberalized the rules while insisting that weight limits help keep attendants fit and are good for safety. The attendants say the regulations are sexist and they are asking Congress to abolish them.

1. How does American Airlines address employees' needs, as identified by Maslow's hierarchy?
2. What would McClelland's acquired-needs theory tell Crandall about American's decision to delegate authority and to encourage employees to take the initiative in solving problems?
3. How could Crandall use Herzberg's two-factor theory to help resolve his problem with flight attendants' opposition to weight rules? How does the issue of weight rules relate to organizational goals and societal trends?
4. How would Vroom's expectancy theory guide Crandall in designing a profit-sharing plan that would reward American baggage handlers for improving customer service?

CHAPTER OUTLINE

15 Leadership in Organizations

After studying this chapter, you will be able to

1. Explain the relationship between leadership and power
2. Describe the types and sources of leadership power
3. Discuss the trait theories of leadership
4. Outline the behavioral theories of leadership
5. Contrast autocratic and democratic leadership behavior
6. Discuss the contingency leadership theories and their application
7. Differentiate between transactional and transformational leadership and explain when each is appropriate

FACING A MANAGEMENT CHALLENGE AT

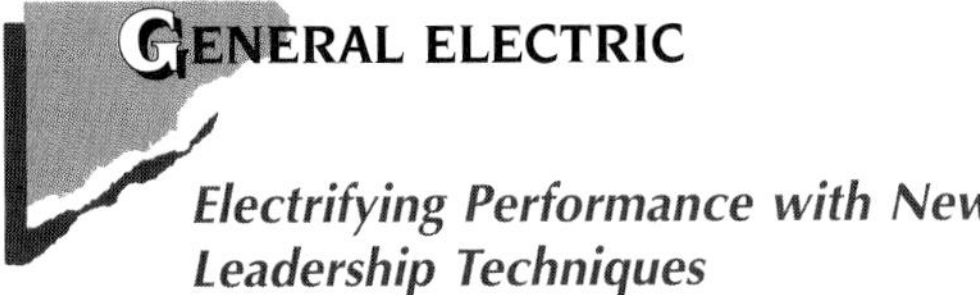

GENERAL ELECTRIC

Electrifying Performance with New Leadership Techniques

Aircraft engines, major appliances, broadcasting, financial services, medical systems—in these areas and in many others, General Electric businesses held first or second place in worldwide market share. The huge conglomerate employed 300,000 people and earned income of $3.4 billion on revenues that topped $50 billion. Some units, such as Kidder, Peabody, were struggling, but overall profits rose year after year. In short, GE looked for all the world like the very epitome of business success.

As the 1980s came to a close, GE's situation satisfied its employees, its customers, its shareholders, and just about everyone else except for one person: its chief executive officer John F. (Jack) Welch, Jr. Welch had been largely responsible for restructuring the firm into a global powerhouse, but he realized that his job was not yet done. Although his managers had been effective in meeting past challenges, Welch believed they needed a new management approach if GE was to enjoy continued success into the twenty-first century.

During the go-go growth years, GE managers were able to hand down orders without inviting employee comment or discussion. As long as organizational goals were met, management methods weren't questioned, even when they intimidated employees or discouraged people from contributing their ideas. However, after decades of expansion, many GE businesses were facing the profit-flattening challenges of economic recession and aggressive competition. In the short run, GE was healthy; but in the long run, Welch knew that GE had to score large productivity gains to keep profits on track.

Welch reasoned that the only way to do this was to harness the creativity and the talents of every man and woman who worked at GE, managers and employees alike. But inviting this participation would require a fundamental change in management style. No longer would managers be judged solely on their ability to achieve GE's short-term goals regardless of their management methods. They needed to support and to trust their employees rather than order them around, and they would have to find ways of involving employees in the decision-making process at every level.

Welch wanted to create, in his words, "a more stimulating environment, a more creative environment, a freer work atmosphere, with incentives tied directly to what people do." He wanted to instill "speed, simplicity and self-confidence" in every person in the organization. People need "the freedom to be creative" and to work in "an open, fair place" that "brings out the best in everybody." In short, Welch wanted his managers to rethink their leadership styles.

Welch realized that the attitude of GE managers was only one side of the coin. Employees, too, needed a new way of thinking. Some lacked the self-confidence to speak up or to question their managers, and others had become so intimidated by management's reactions to employee initiatives that they simply stopped making the effort. They seemed to lack the fire and zest Welch believed was necessary to propel GE into a $60 billion behemoth.

How could Welch bring about such a major break from the management traditions of the past? How could he help managers change their attitudes so that they inspired rather than drove their people? How could GE employees be motivated to speak up and to take active roles in the company's future?[1]

CHAPTER OVERVIEW

General Electric stands to gain a great deal from the effective leadership style advocated by CEO Jack Welch. Without these leadership skills, GE might not be able to achieve its long-term goals. This chapter first looks at the nature of leadership and then explores the nature of power, including the sources of power, its application, and its relationship to organizational politics. Next is a review of trait theories, behavioral theories, and contingency theories of leadership. The chapter closes with an examination of transactional and transformational leadership within the organization.

LEADERSHIP AND POWER

One of the four basic functions of management is leading, defined in Chapter 1 as the process of influencing and motivating others to work together to achieve organizational goals. Because overall performance can be achieved only when goals at every organizational level have been met, the ability to lead others is a critical skill for middle managers, first-line managers, and even entry-level employees, as well as for top managers. Widely researched and discussed, leadership is especially important in today's increasingly complex and dynamic environment.[2] To lead effectively, managers need to understand the nature of leadership and of power.

The Nature of Leadership

leadership The ability to influence and to motivate others to achieve organizational goals

leader Someone who advances organizational goals by influencing the attitudes and actions of others

Leadership is the ability to influence and to motivate others to achieve organizational goals. The leadership process involves using authority to help determine group or organizational goals, motivating organization members to work toward achieving those goals, and influencing group dynamics and organizational culture. A **leader** is someone who advances organizational goals by influencing the attitudes and actions of others. Leadership and motivation go hand-in-hand: just as employees draw inspiration from leaders, leaders are not considered leaders unless they can motivate others. Generally, organizational leadership is a continuous process rather than a one-time event, providing the means to one end: performance. The reason leaders at any organizational level (with or without formal authority) are able to influence people to perform is that leadership is related to power.[3]

The Nature of Power

power The capacity to affect the decisions, attitudes, and behavior of others

Power is the capacity to affect the decisions, attitudes, and behavior of others. Leaders apply power within the organization to influence individuals or groups of employees, peers, and managers, and they also use power outside the organization to sway customers and suppliers, among others. However, leaders do not always have to exercise their power in order to influence others. Often, the possession of power and the potential of using it can be as effective as the power itself.[4]

For example, Leonard Roberts didn't have to actually exert his power to get others to cooperate in putting Arby's back on track. A fast-food franchiser that was fading fast under the weight of operational neglect and competitive pressures, Arby's needed a wake-up call that Roberts was brought in to sound. As the new CEO, he chose not to fire anyone who was underperforming; instead, he influenced managers and employees by communicating a new "culture of achievement" in which high performers were rewarded, and low performers felt uncomfortable and soon left. Nor did Roberts have to wield his power over franchisees. When one franchisee balked at contributing the required amount of advertising money to support a system-wide promotion (because he felt his Midwest locations would not benefit), Roberts argued the merits of showing support for the entire restaurant system and dropped hints about the legal implications of noncooperation. Rather than face the loss of his franchise licenses, this franchise owner chipped in a fair share—for the first time in four years.[5]

Mayor Wellington Webb is using the legitimate power drawn from his position as the top elected official in Denver to work toward ambitious goals. During his term, Webb's top priorities include reducing the city's debt, helping local businesses survive, and attracting firms from outside Denver to add jobs and boost tax revenues.

Sources of Power

Although a number of frameworks have been proposed over the years, one of the most widely accepted classifications of power was developed by John R. P. French, Jr., and Bertram H. Raven, who identified five types: legitimate, reward, coercive, expert, and referent power. Later, Raven collaborated with Arie W. Kruglanski to add informational power as a sixth type. These six classifications of power are drawn from two sources. Legitimate, reward, coercive, and informational power are derived from the manager's position in the organization structure. This means that as managers climb higher in the organization, they usually acquire more of these types of power. On the other hand, expert and referent power are derived from the individual rather than from the office, so people anywhere in the organization can apply these forms of power.[6]

- **Legitimate power** is the authority vested in a specific organizational position, such as production manager or vice president of finance. Because their positions within the organization structure give them this formal authority, managers are able to legitimately direct their employees' activities; the employees, in turn, understand that they are expected to accept this direction. Legitimate power therefore derives from the organizational position or level, not from the actual person occupying the position. For example, Eugene Proctor, executive director of the not-for-profit Baxter Community Center in Grand Rapids, Michigan, can influence paid employees and volunteers alike by applying his legitimate power as head of the organization.[7] If Proctor left Baxter, his legitimate power would pass to the next person appointed as executive director.

legitimate power Power derived from a specific position in the organization structure and the formal authority vested in it

- **Reward power** is the ability to provide others with valued rewards such as pay raises, bonuses, promotions, special training, recognition, and coveted job assignments. Generally, the greater a manager's control over bestowing or modifying rewards, the greater that manager's reward power. Conversely, when employees perceive that a manager has little or no control over valued rewards, that manager has little reward power. At Baxter Community Center, Proctor can use his reward power to give salary increases, to send people to training courses, and to provide public recognition of people's outstanding performance.[8]

reward power Power derived from the ability to provide valued rewards to others

- **Coercive power** is the ability to reprimand, to demote, to withhold pay raises, to fire, or to use other means of penalizing people. In contrast to reward power (the ability to provide valued rewards), coercive power is the ability to take rewards away or to reduce their value. The greater the leader's control over punishments, and the more powerful the value of the punishments in the eyes of employees, the greater the coercive power. When Proctor first took over as executive director at Baxter Community Center, he used his coercive power to fire 13 employees who were "doing absolutely nothing." This decisive action showed the remaining employees that Proctor was serious about his performance expectations and that he would not hesitate to use his coercive power when necessary.[9]

coercive power Power derived from the ability to penalize others

- **Informational power** is the ability to control access to important information

informational power Power derived from the ability to control access to important information about organizational operations and plans, organization members, and the external environment. As managers rise through the organizational ranks, they typically gain more access to key information, and they also gain more control over the distribution of that information. The greater the leader's ability to restrict access or to determine how information is disseminated, the greater that leader's informational power. At Baxter Community Center, Proctor shares his informational power with the not-for-profit's board of directors. Together, they decide how and when to disseminate information (to employees and to outsiders) on the performance of the organization's programs and on Baxter's strengths, weaknesses, and opportunities.[10]

expert power Power derived from the manager's personal skills, technical knowledge, and experience

- **Expert power** is the leader's personal skills, personal knowledge, and experience. Whereas informational power relates to the access and control of information, expert power relates to the individual's ability to understand or to use information. People at any organizational level have expert power when they acquire special knowledge and technical skills that can benefit their work groups. For managers, expert power is greater when employees recognize the value of the manager's competence and expertise and when they require assistance in solving problems or completing tasks. Eugene Proctor's knack for fundraising and his experience with a variety of not-for-profit, religious, and political groups have proven invaluable sources of expert power. Because of his background, Baxter's board and its employees turn to Proctor for advice and action when problems arise.[11]

referent power Power derived from the ability to inspire respect, admiration, and loyalty

- **Referent power** is the leader's ability to inspire respect, admiration, and loyalty. Referent power stems directly from the individual's personal qualities, which evoke a response in others. The stronger an employee's desire to identify with a manager, to emulate that manager's characteristics, or to be accepted and liked by that manager, the stronger is the referent power. Managers and employees respond to Proctor's admirable qualities of industriousness, humility, savvy, and deep personal commitment to his clients. Business leaders in the community also respect his abilities, and they feel motivated to donate their time and their corporate funds because they believe in Proctor.[12]

Expert power is central to Dr. Jay Kranzler's ability to lead scientists working at Cytel, a California-based firm that develops drugs to fight inflammatory diseases and hepatitis. CEO Kranzler's background in pharmacology and his innovative approach to biotechnology influence Cytel's scientists as they work on new drug formulas and new ways of modulating the immune system to combat disease.

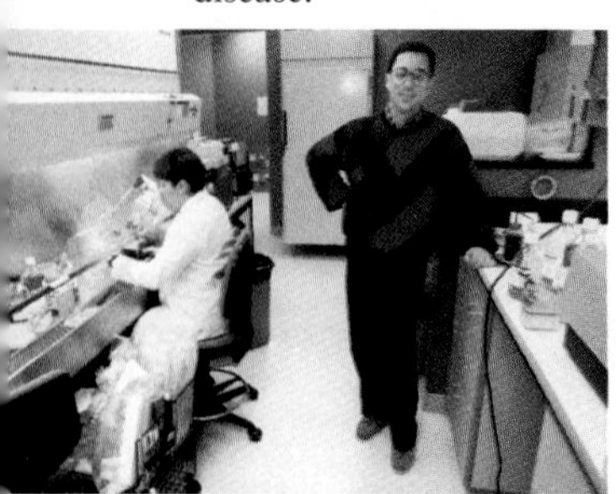

Of course, managers at every organizational level can effectively influence others by leveraging the powers they derive from their positions as well as their personal powers. But even nonmanagers can use the powers they derive from their personal skills and abilities to influence others. For example, Josh Block, a high school senior in Chappaqua, New York, wanted the local Board of Education to establish a formal policy advocating paper recycling. As part of his senior project, Block researched paper use in the school district and presented his findings to the Board. Noting that the district had bought 30 tons of copier paper during the previous year, he demonstrated that if recycled paper had been used, the Board would have saved 510 trees, 210,000 gallons of water, and 123,000 kilowatt hours of energy. Then Block suggested specific policies that the Board might implement, including buying recycled paper exclusively, photocopying on two sides of the page, and using half-sheets of paper for handouts whenever feasible. Impressed by Block's command of the facts and by his fervor for the subject, which reflect his expert and referent power, the Parent-Teacher Association and other groups backed his suggestions. Block's efforts aren't the only example of student power: elementary, middle, and high school students have successfully persuaded schools and companies around the United States to act in more environmentally conscious ways, driving for such changes as a ban on foam food containers.[13]

The Application of Power

When leaders apply power to influence or to affect the attitudes and behavior of the people who report to them, these employees may react in one of three ways. Those who show *commitment* enthusiastically accept their leaders' goals and work hard to achieve them. Those who show *compliance* are unenthusiastic, even passive, and they exert only minimal effort to carry out their leaders' instructions. Employees who show *resistance* oppose the leaders' goals and actively try to avoid completing their assigned tasks.[14]

Which reaction an employee offers depends on the source of the leader's power and the way the power is applied. Research suggests (1) that employees tend to react with commitment to the use of referent or expert power and (2) that employees are more satisfied and tend to perform better when directed by managers using referent or expert power. However, when legitimate, informational, or reward power is used, employees are more likely to react with compliance; when coercive power is used, employees are more likely to react with resistance (see Exhibit 15.1). For this reason, effective leaders try to use coercive power only when absolutely necessary, such as in situations where people's behavior or attitudes are detrimental to others or to the overall group and its performance. Moreover, leaders who exercise power in an arrogant or manipulative manner are more likely to encounter resistance than those who are courteous and who protect their employees' interests.[15]

Leaders are also finding that they can build their power by sharing their power. Discussing the application of power, Colgate-Palmolive CEO Reuben Mark says, "The more you have, the less you should use. You consolidate and build power by empowering others." Adds Ralph Stayer, CEO of Wisconsin sausage-maker Johnsonville Foods, "Real power is getting people committed. Real power comes from giving it up to others who are in a better position to do things than you are." Power alone won't move the organization forward; along

EXHIBIT 15.1 Power and Reaction

Employees may react with commitment, compliance, or resistance to a manager's attempts to influence their performance, and the type of power the manager uses determines which reaction is most likely. When managers use referent and expert power, they are more likely to gain employee commitment than when they use other types of power.

	Employee Reaction		
Type of Power	**Commitment**	**Compliance**	**Resistance**
Referent	Likely if the request is believed to be important to the leader	Possible, if the request is perceived to be unimportant to the leader	Possible, if the request is for something that will bring harm to the leader
Expert	Likely if the request is persuasive and if employees share the leader's task goals	Possible, if the request is persuasive but employees are apathetic about task goals	Possible, if the leader is arrogant and insulting or if employees oppose their task goals
Legitimate	Possible, if the request is polite and appropriate	Likely if the request is seen as legitimate	Possible, if the leader makes arrogant demands or if the request appears improper
Informational	Possible, if the leader has the data to justify the request	Likely if the request is supported by reasonable data	Possible, if the leader conceals or distorts data
Reward	Possible, if used in a subtle, personal way	Likely if used in a mechanical or impersonal way	Possible, if used in a manipulative, arrogant way
Coercive	Highly unlikely	Possible, if used in a helpful, nonpunitive way	Likely if used in a hostile or manipulative way

SOCIAL RESPONSIBILITY AND ETHICS

Leadership Fights Hunger in Africa

Persuading Sting, Phil Collins, U2, Duran Duran, George Michael, and other popular British rockers to reserve a day in their busy schedules to make a record without pay is not an easy leadership task. Nor is the task of convincing Elton John, the Beach Boys, Paul McCartney, Peter Townshend, Bob Dylan, Mick Jagger, Tina Turner, and Lionel Richie, among others, to play a concert for free and even to pay their own expenses. The leader who organized both Band Aid (the record) and Live Aid (the concert) had no formal leadership training or experience, but he was driven by a special goal: to save lives. Bob Geldof, lead singer of the Boomtown Rats in Great Britain, became Bob Geldof, leader of an international movement to feed the hungry, literally overnight after watching a television show about the millions who were starving in famine-struck Ethiopia.

Haunted by the faces and bodies shown in a news report, Geldof could not sleep. He believed that he, and everyone else, had a personal responsibility to help. By the morning, he had hatched the idea of making a fundraising record to benefit the starving Ethiopians. Geldof reasoned that his Band Aid record (so named because it would patch but not heal the wound of hunger) could be an effective vehicle for channeling the efforts of those who wanted to help but felt unable to help as individuals. He envisioned Band Aid as a concentrated, short-term effort that would complement the charity and relief organizations already at work in Africa. As the leader of a grassroots fundraising organization, Geldof would have the legitimate power to raise money, to deliver food and supplies, and to challenge the government practices that threatened to slow the relief effort.

The rock singer did not have the resources to personally manage the mechanics, so he convinced the record label Phonogram to handle the record's manufacture and distribution without profit. He also persuaded donors to provide a long list of free goods and services from the record jacket artwork to the vinyl. Geldof invited prominent rock stars to join his effort, stressing that the Band Aid record was the most important record they would ever participate in making. The recording took place late in November 1984 and within days, "Do They Know It's Christmas" was in stores in the United Kingdom and in the United States.

In newspaper, radio, and television interviews, Geldof talked about how each person should do some-

with the power must come the responsibility, the authority, and the accountability for achieving results. Once people throughout the organization have experienced the sensation of using this power to perform better, they feel more powerful and capable of undertaking even greater challenges. This is the situation that GE's Jack Welch wanted to create to propel GE toward achieving its long-term goals. By sharing with others the power to make decisions, to take actions, and to motivate themselves and those around them, Welch knew that his managers would increase the total amount of power within the organization and increase the commitment that people at all levels felt toward attaining organizational goals.[16]

Stayer has shared his informational power with Johnsonville Foods managers and employees from the top to the bottom levels. Now volunteers from the shop floor have the information to develop the manufacturing budget for the company's four plants, with assistance from a financial executive (who is less and less active in the process every year). Because employees set the financial guidelines, they are committed to staying on budget. Moreover, because Stayer has spread his legitimate power throughout the organization, his people set and meet ambitious goals that he would not—and could not—have imposed on them. One year when the sales department wanted to increase sales volume by 40 percent, the manufacturing group set and attained the additional production level, even as it held the increased costs to just 20 percent. Another time, Johnsonville had the opportunity to land a huge contract that would have meant a punishing seven-day-a-week production schedule. Stayer turned the decision over to his people; department by department, managers and employees held thing, no matter how small, to help save lives. Urging the purchase of the Band Aid record, he said, "It's only £1.30. That's how cheap it is to give people the ultimate Christmas gift—their life." The rock singer released just the right amount of information at the right time to keep the media interested, to keep them covering the progress of Band Aid, and to whip up public support. Under Geldof's leadership, Band Aid raised more than £5 million in three weeks. He then organized a committee of charity and relief organizations to devise the most effective ways of using the money, and he set up a board of trustees to oversee Band Aid's finances. Even as tankers and convoys made their way to Ethiopia with grain, oil, drugs, and other supplies, Geldof battled government officials who tried to tax the record's proceeds (the tax money was ultimately spent on African aid) and lectured politicians who put obstacles in the way of speedy action.

Band Aid inspired similar efforts in other countries, including USA for Africa, which raised money through its star-studded recording of "We Are the World." Although Geldof had created an international outpouring of compassion and money to benefit Ethiopia, the rocker wanted to do more. He came up with the idea of two simultaneous concerts, one in the United States and one in England, linked by satellite over the course of 16 hours. To make this Live Aid concert a reality, he had to persuade the biggest musical names on two continents to participate for free. Using his now-considerable referent power, he attracted dozens of acts; some canceled lucrative concerts so that they could appear with Geldof.

On July 15, 1985, Live Aid played to a worldwide audience of 2 billion and brought in a total of \$100 million to relieve hunger and suffering for victims of the Ethiopian famine. At the end of 1986, Geldof turned over permanent responsibility for distributing the funds to a committee of charity and relief representatives, but his leadership legacy lives on in the hearts of those he has helped and in the memories of the people who saw Band Aid and Live Aid as a way to make a difference.

What's Your Opinion?

1. Should Geldof be drafted to lead the fight when an effective fundraising effort is needed to combat famine or disease? Why or why not?
2. Can college students successfully apply power to supply the leadership needed to fight local hunger and homelessness? If so, which types of power might be most effective in such a situation?

meetings to consider the issue and then decided to commit themselves, and the organization, to the challenging production goals (which they handily achieved). As a result of sharing power, Stayer and his staff have increased Johnsonville's annual sales by nearly 20 percent and pushed profits up even higher.[17]

Although power properly applied or shared enables leaders to motivate and influence others to work toward achieving organizational goals, misused power can hurt the organization and its performance. For example, when managers misuse information power by withholding vital data, they may effectively stop or slow the effort to achieve organizational goals. Similarly, managers who misuse legitimate power by denying others access to resources (such as employees, facilities, or funds) can also harm performance. Once misuse is uncovered, it breaks the bond of trust and shared values that draws organization members together in pursuit of group goals. Because employees look to their leaders for indications of the beliefs and values that guide an organization, leaders must be role models in the proper use of power.[18]

Power and Organizational Politics

Organizational politics is the pursuit, protection, and use of power to enhance or to protect the self-interest of individuals or groups whose goals may or may not be directly related to organizational goals. Political actions may be carried out by organizational units or by informal groups as well as by individual managers using their legitimate, informational, and other sources of power. However, the political system operates independently of the organization's system of formal authority, which typically results in a power shift that benefits

organizational politics The pursuit, protection, and use of power to achieve individual or group goals not necessarily directly related to organizational goals some individuals or groups at the expense of others or often at the expense of the organization. With political power, managers may obtain scarce resources that would otherwise have been allocated to another manager or another unit, or they may influence the development and implementation of important plans that would otherwise have proceeded in a different direction.[19]

Managers can gain power politically in several ways. First, by gaining control over organizational decision processes, or by influencing them indirectly, managers can use these decisions to gain legitimate power. Second, when one person acting alone does not have sufficient power, building a coalition or an alliance with others helps to pool power for a specific purpose. Third, co-optation enables a manager or a group to gain the influence and the commitment of one or more people whose power is needed for a particular project. Co-optation involves turning potential resisters into allies by inviting them to join in making and carrying out decisions and by rewarding them publicly for supporting the project (see Chapter 11). Fourth, people can use their informational power to withhold information, to distort information, or even to overload others with a volume of data they cannot analyze or understand. And fifth, people at all levels may blame or attack others in order to discredit them. Once they have increased their power, managers (or groups) are in a better position to influence organizational activities.[20]

Organizational politics can help a manager or a unit consolidate power to achieve legitimate goals, such as when an intrapreneur puts together a coalition to help develop and market a new product. But politics can also cause problems. Sometimes the group or individual goals of those seeking power through politics are in conflict with stated organizational goals. Another problem is that the use of political power may stir resentment in less-powerful people, who may then actively work against the interests of the politically powerful. Therefore, managers at all levels must be aware of the political system of power and how it affects organizational performance.

For example, when David Johnson became CEO of Campbell Soup, he inherited some of the best-known food brands in the business as well as an organizational culture rife with political problems. The U.S. plants kept to themselves and did not exchange information and technology with Campbell's Canadian or Mexican plants. Moreover, product groups focused more on their own performance than on overall corporate performance. One example: when the soup products group organized a soup-and-crackers promotion, the group passed up Campbell's own Pepperidge Farm products and instead joined with Nabisco, a competitor. To counter these and other problems with organizational politics, CEO Johnson reorganized the plants in the United States, Canada, and Mexico into a single North American division and charged their managers with sharing technology, knowledge, and resources. He also used his reward power to redefine the basis for management bonus payments. Before, the bonus had been based solely on the results of the manager's own unit; now, 20 percent of the bonus depends on overall company performance. As a result of these changes, Johnson has significantly improved Campbell's performance.[21]

THEORIES OF LEADERSHIP

Over the years, researchers and practitioners have developed a variety of views on leadership. Three major theories have emerged from these ongoing studies.

Two types of theories view the principles of effective leadership as being universally applicable to any situation and to any organization: Trait theories deal with the personal characteristics of leaders, and behavioral theories deal with the behavior of leaders. The contingency theories deal not with universal applicability but with leadership in the context of specific situations.

Trait Theories of Leadership

Some of the earliest studies of leadership led to the development of trait theories, which emphasize the identification and measurement of the **traits**, or the personal characteristics, that distinguish effective leaders. During the first half of the twentieth century, researchers studied ways to predict leader effectiveness based on personal traits such as personality, skills, and physical attributes (including height and appearance). Examining the traits of well-known leaders, many studies found that the most effective leaders generally possessed intelligence, alertness to the needs of others, understanding of the task, good communication skills, initiative and persistence in dealing with problems, self-confidence, and a desire to accept responsibility and to occupy a position of dominance and control.[22]

traits An individual's personal characteristics

However, no single list of traits predicting leadership success emerged from these early studies, because the traits identified as contributing to leader effectiveness differed from study to study. Also, researchers were able to show only a weak link between these personal traits and leader effectiveness. Moreover, later researchers noted that the various leadership traits were not of equal value in every situation.[23]

Despite these criticisms, contemporary researchers have used more sophisticated research and analysis techniques to affirm that leaders who possess certain traits and skills are more likely to be effective (see Exhibit 15.2). Among the personal elements that both early and contemporary researchers agree can influence leadership ability are intelligence, self-confidence, the drive to accept responsibility, good communication skills, and education. And recent findings indicate that effective leaders generally have a high energy level as well as good interpersonal skills.[24]

The newer studies also suggest that leadership traits are not universally applicable to every situation or to every organization. In addition, some researchers

EXHIBIT 15.2

Characteristics of Effective Leaders

Recent studies have shed new light on the role of leadership traits. Using sophisticated techniques, researchers have confirmed that effective leaders do tend to possess certain traits and skills such as those listed here.

Traits	Skills
Adaptable to situations	Clever (intelligent)
Alert to social environment	Conceptually skilled
Ambitious and achievement-oriented	Creative
Assertive	Diplomatic and tactful
Cooperative	Fluent in speaking
Decisive	Knowledgeable about group task
Dependable	Organized (administrative ability)
Dominant (desire to influence others)	Persuasive
Energetic (high activity level)	Socially skilled
Persistent	
Self-confident	
Tolerant of stress	
Willing to assume responsibility	

have determined that leader effectiveness depends on the balance of specific traits rather than the possession of any particular trait or skill. Although personal traits are now believed to play a role in leader effectiveness, another school of thought emphasizes the way leaders behave as an important element in leader effectiveness.[25]

Behavioral Theories of Leadership

Given the shortcomings of early trait studies, researchers turned to examining the *behaviors* or actions that separated effective leaders from ineffective leaders. Like the trait theories, these behavioral theories have been seen as universally applicable regardless of the specific situation facing a leader in a particular organization. Behavioral theories include studies of autocratic and democratic leadership behavior, leadership research conducted at the University of Michigan and at Ohio State University, and Blake and Mouton's managerial grid.

Autocratic and Democratic Leadership

autocratic leader A manager who tends to centralize authority and to make unilateral decisions

democratic leader A manager who tends to delegate authority and to encourage participation in decision making

One way to view leadership is in terms of autocratic and democratic behavior. An **autocratic leader,** also known as an *authoritarian leader,* generally centralizes authority and makes unilateral decisions. Autocratic leaders tend to rely on legitimate, reward, and coercive power to motivate others. In contrast, a **democratic leader** generally delegates authority and invites participation in decision making. Democratic leaders tend to use referent and expert power to influence others. Among the earliest to research autocratic and democratic leadership behavior was Kurt Lewin, who in the late 1930s and onward worked with colleagues to examine the performance of groups under both types of leaders. Lewin found that groups led by democratic leaders generally produced the same quantity of work as groups led by autocratic leaders, but members led by democratic leaders expressed more satisfaction with their work. Although subsequent studies did not always find that autocratic leadership and democratic leadership produced the same level of performance, they did confirm that group members were consistently more satisfied under democratic leadership.[26]

Researchers Robert Tannenbaum and Warren H. Schmidt expanded the view of autocratic and democratic leadership from a simplistic choice between two distinct behaviors to a continuum of seven behaviors (see Exhibit 15.3). Autocratic behavior is at one extreme of the continuum and democratic behavior is at the other extreme. Between the two extremes is a range of behaviors representing varying degrees of employee participation. However, the researchers stopped short of prescribing the best leadership behaviors for specific situations. Instead, they advocated selecting the appropriate leadership behavior by examining the forces that influence the manager (such as the manager's confidence in employees), the forces that influence the employee (such as the employee's need for autonomy), and the forces inherent in the situation (such as time constraints). This approach set the stage for later theories that viewed leadership in terms of the manager's particular situation.[27]

As CEO of Flagship Express, an air freight firm in Ypsilanti, Michigan, Judith Rogala uses democratic leadership to encourage the participation of all 700 employees. She freely shares company data, invites employees to phone in ideas and complaints on a 24-hour hotline, and ensures that employees understand their goals and the limits within which they can perform their tasks.

In Tannenbaum and Schmidt's framework, managers with little confidence in employees would probably adopt a behavior closer to the autocratic leadership extreme. Managers whose employees have a high need for autonomy might adopt a behavior closer to the democratic extreme. And managers facing time constraints might adopt a behavior closer to the autocratic leadership extreme. By matching the level of autocratic or democratic behavior to the situation,

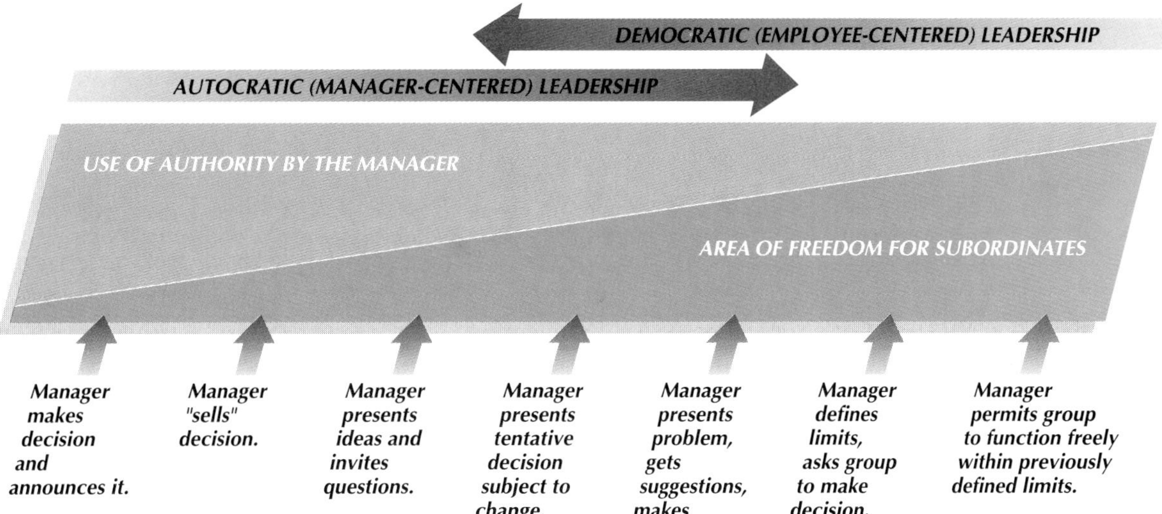

EXHIBIT 15.3

The Continuum of Autocratic-Democratic Leader Behavior

Managers can select from seven behaviors along the continuum from autocratic to democratic behavior. At one extreme, the leader makes all decisions and tells employees how to implement the decisions. At the other extreme, the leader allows employees to make decisions and also allows employees to choose how to meet their goals.

managers gain the flexibility to analyze and then to adapt their leadership behaviors as needed.[28]

Consider Marisa Bellisario, managing director and CEO of the state-owned telecommunications utility Italtel in Italy. She adapts her leadership behavior to the various challenges she faces. When she found managers spending more time writing and approving the minutes of their meetings than they spent either in the meetings themselves or in carrying out the actions discussed in the meetings, Bellisario acted quickly to stop the waste of time. Adopting an autocratic leadership approach, she declared that the system was going to change. From now on, managers would either dispense with the minutes or rely on only one person to make an official record. In other situations, her leadership behavior is more democratic. She carefully recruits capable and efficient managers, sets high but attainable goals, then allows her people enough freedom to make decisions that contribute to achieving those goals. Once Bellisario has delegated responsibility and authority for a unit, she avoids changing any decision made by that unit's manager.[29]

The Michigan Studies

A few years after Lewin and his associates began their studies of autocratic and democratic behavior, Rensis Likert and other researchers at the University of Michigan started to investigate how leadership behavior relates to organizational performance. As a result of studying effective and ineffective supervisors, the Michigan researchers identified two distinct leader behaviors. The first, **employee-centered leader behavior,** emphasizes interpersonal relationships, teamwork, and employee participation. Leaders who exhibit employee-centered behavior are generally supportive of their employees, show appreciation for their ideas, and allow their employees more leeway in determining how their goals should be accomplished. The Michigan studies found that employees working under employee-centered leaders were generally more satisfied, and these organizations were generally higher performing. The second behavior, **job-centered leader behavior,** emphasizes the technical aspects of the job and the tasks that must be accomplished to achieve group goals. Leaders who are job-

employee-centered leader behavior A behavior pattern emphasizing interpersonal relationships, strong teamwork, and employee participation

job-centered leader behavior A behavior pattern emphasizing the job's technical aspects and the completion of the tasks to achieve group goals centered concentrate on the mechanics of accomplishing their assigned goals, and they pay close attention to work specialization, to planning and scheduling work, and to coordinating employee efforts. In the Michigan studies, those who worked under job-centered leaders were typically less satisfied and often less productive.[30]

Building on these studies, Likert went on to develop his continuum of four organization types, known as System 1, System 2, System 3, and System 4 (see Chapter 10). At one extreme of the continuum, System 1 is more hierarchical and its leaders are more job-centered, relying heavily on formal authority and the chain of command. At the other extreme, System 4 is more participative and its leaders are more employee-centered, relying on teamwork, group decision making, and freer interaction among organization members. On the basis of his research, Likert believed that organizational performance would improve if leaders shifted their behavior to become more employee-centered by encouraging better teamwork, by involving employees in decision making, and by showing concern for individuals at all levels. In advocating a more democratic leadership style for his managers, Jack Welch of GE was seeking to move toward an organization much like Likert's System 4.[31]

The Ohio State Studies

While the University of Michigan researchers conducted their studies, a group at Ohio State University was beginning an intensive investigation into the dimensions of leader behavior. Using questionnaires to survey employees about their managers' behavior, the Ohio State researchers found that leader behavior could be described in terms of two dimensions. **Initiating structure,** the first of the two dimensions, describes the extent to which leaders define their own roles and their employees' roles to achieve organizational goals. Leaders do this by clarifying the specific tasks and responsibilities of organization members, setting standards of performance, coordinating employee activities, and emphasizing the importance of deadlines. **Consideration,** the second of the two dimensions, is the extent to which leaders show concern and respect for employees. Leaders who exhibit consideration behavior develop relationships of mutual trust with their employees, encourage employee suggestions and participation, and show appreciation for good work.[32]

initiating structure The extent to which leaders define their own roles and their employees' roles to achieve organizational goals

consideration The extent to which leaders show concern and respect for employees

Initiating structure is similar to the job-centered leader behavior observed by the University of Michigan researchers, and consideration is similar to the employee-centered leader behavior. However, the behaviors identified by Ohio State researchers are separate, independent dimensions (not two ends of a continuum as are the behaviors studied by University of Michigan researchers and the range of autocratic-democratic leader behaviors). This means that a leader's initiating structure behavior is unrelated to his or her consideration behavior, and a leader may be rated high or low on either dimension without affecting the rating on the other dimension (see Exhibit 15.4).[33]

For instance, Dorothy Roberts, CEO of family-owned Echo Scarves, rates high on consideration. She is scrupulous about remembering her employees' birthdays and employment anniversaries, she offers supportive comments to help her managers develop their skills, and she uses group decision making to deal with issues that affect several departments. As considerate as her behavior may be, Roberts is also a stickler for performance, and her behavior reflects a moderate amount of initiating structure. She carefully defines areas of responsibility but allows her managers considerable freedom to choose how they will

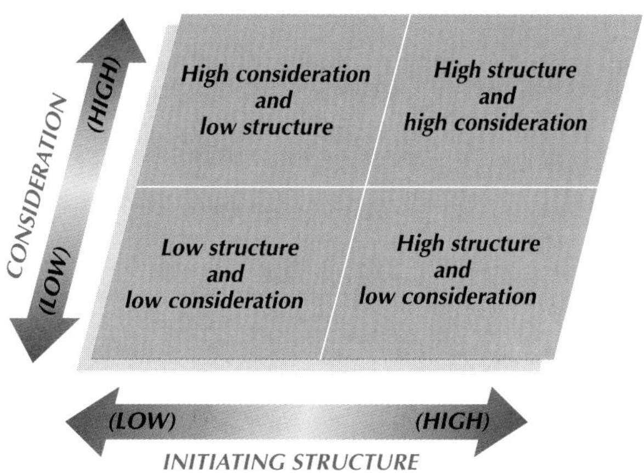

EXHIBIT 15.4

Ohio State Leader Behaviors

Whereas autocratic and democratic behaviors are extremes within a continuum, consideration and initiating structure are separate, independent behaviors. Thus, a manager who is high in one can be either high or low in the other, yielding four possible combinations of leader behaviors.

achieve their goals. Echo's employee turnover is unusually low, and when a vacancy pops up, the first qualification Roberts seeks in a job candidate is "niceness." Her combination of consideration and initiating structure behavior has helped build Echo into a $44 million company.[34]

In the Ohio State research, a leader who exhibited a high degree of both behaviors (called a "high-high" leader) usually, but not always, motivated employees to higher performance. Although the finding that employees of leaders rated high on consideration are more satisfied than employees whose leaders are rated low on consideration has largely been confirmed, the conclusion that high-high leader behavior is predictive of high performance has not been supported by other researchers. In fact, later studies found that behavior high in initiating structure could lead to more grievances, absenteeism, and turnover among employees performing routine tasks; moreover, the performance of leaders who exhibited a high degree of consideration was often rated lower by their managers. As a result, the Ohio State two-dimensional behavioral framework, like the University of Michigan continuum and the autocratic-democratic dichotomy, is now seen as too simplistic to be universally applied to all leadership situations.[35]

Blake and Mouton's Managerial Grid

The **managerial grid,** developed by Robert R. Blake and Jane Srygley Mouton, is a method of analyzing leader behavior using a two-dimensional grid in which the axes are concern for people and concern for production. The horizontal axis measures concern for production, which is similar to job-centered leader behavior and to initiating structure. It emphasizes achieving organizational goals, work output, and efficiency standards. The vertical axis measures concern for people, which is similar to employee-oriented leader behavior and to consideration. It emphasizes personal relationships, personal commitment, and the human aspects of the organization (see Exhibit 15.5).[36]

managerial grid A method developed by Blake and Mouton to analyze leader behavior using a grid with two axes, concern for people and concern for production

Of particular interest to Blake and Mouton were the leader behaviors represented by the four corner positions (9,9; 1,9; 9,1; and 1,1) and the center position (5,5), where the interplay of concern for people and concern for production resulted in distinctive leader behaviors. Team management (position 9,9), which balances high concern for people and high concern for production, is seen as the most effective leader behavior (similar to the conclusions of researchers from Ohio State who advocated high-high leadership), although research has not confirmed this view. Like other behavioral theories, the managerial grid does not

EXHIBIT 15.5

The Managerial Grid

Blake and Mouton's managerial grid charts leader concern for production on the horizontal axis and leader concern for people on the vertical. Each axis has nine positions, ranging from 1 as the lowest level of concern to 9 as the highest. Key management positions studied by Blake and Mouton are at the four corners and in the center of the grid.

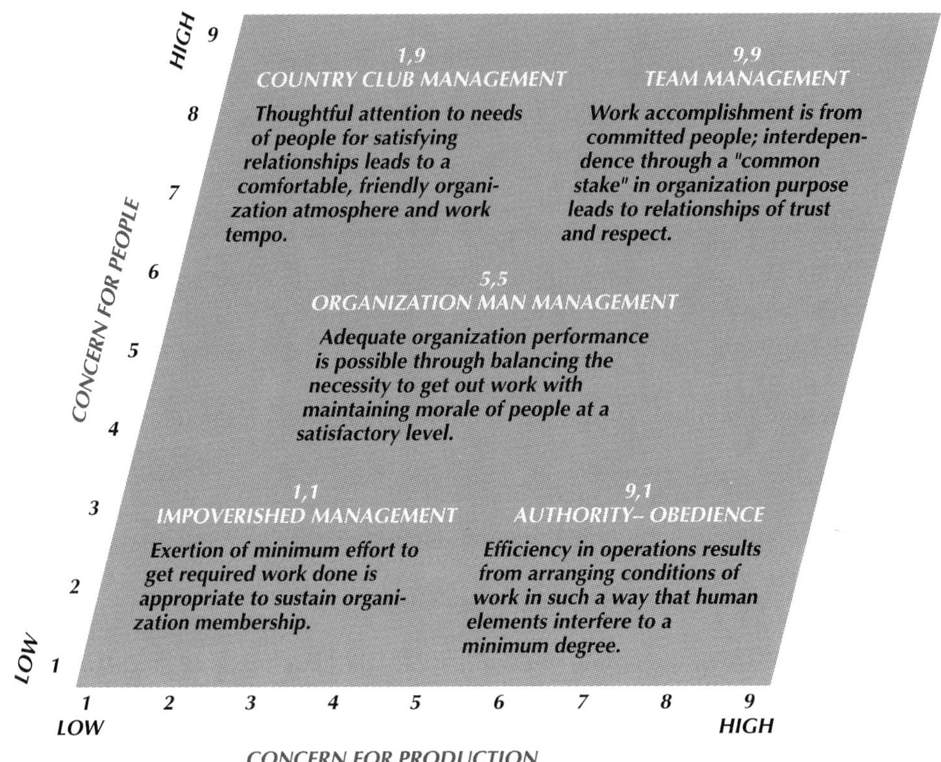

consider any variation in leader ability, in the organizational environment, or other factors that differ from situation to situation, so its applicability is limited.[37]

Contingency Theories of Leadership

The failure of trait and behavioral theories to consistently predict leader effectiveness made it apparent that leadership involves more than personal traits or behaviors. Researchers turned next to studying how situational variations affect leader effectiveness. These *contingency theories of leadership,* also known as situational theories of leadership, suggest that effective leadership is dependent on (or contingent on) the specific variables in each situation. Contingency leadership theories include the Fiedler contingency model, path-goal theory, the Vroom-Yetton-Jago model, the Hersey-Blanchard situational leadership theory, and the substitutes for leadership theory.

The Fiedler Contingency Model

Fiedler contingency model A model that relates leadership style (as determined by manager reaction to the least preferred co-worker) to the favorability of situational variables to determine the appropriate leadership approach

least preferred co-worker (LPC) scale A questionnaire that scores managers' descriptions of the one person they have least enjoyed working with

The first comprehensive contingency leadership model was developed by Fred Fiedler. The **Fiedler contingency model** is a model that relates the situation's favorability toward various leadership styles, to help leaders determine the best approach in a given situation. Fiedler assessed leadership style by asking managers to complete a brief questionnaire about the one person they least enjoyed working with. This questionnaire, known as the **least preferred co-worker (LPC) scale,** contains a series of positive and negative adjective pairs. Fiedler argued that managers with high LPC scores, who used positive adjectives to describe their least favorite co-worker, were more concerned with good interpersonal relationships, whereas those with low LPC scores, who used negative adjectives to describe their co-workers, were more concerned with completing work tasks.[38]

Situational Favorability The Fiedler model, like other contingency theories, assumes that the appropriate leadership approach varies according to the situation. In Fiedler's view, people cannot change their leadership styles, so his model helps match leaders with the situations most favorable for their styles.[39] Three variables define the favorability of a situation for leadership:

- *Leader-member relations.* This is the degree of mutual trust and support between employees and the leader. It indicates the willingness of employees to respond to leader guidance. According to Fiedler, it is the single most important situational variable that must be considered in matching leader style to situation. When employees and leaders trust each other and are mutually supportive of work efforts, leader-member relations are good; when employees and leaders distrust each other and are not supportive, leader-member relations are poor.[40]
- *Task structure.* This is the degree to which a job's goals, methods, and standards of performance are clearly specified. Routinized, well-defined jobs such as those on an assembly line have a high degree of structure, whereas creative, more loosely defined tasks such as strategic planning have a low degree of task structure. Fiedler considered this variable the second most influential in determining situational favorability.[41]
- *Position power.* This is the degree of authority granted by the organization to the leader to hire, reward, and discipline employees. When leaders have little authority to select employees, to grant salary increases, or to fire employees, position power is considered to be weak, whereas when leaders have the authority to handle such tasks, position power is considered to be strong. Although position power plays a role, Fiedler considered this the least important situational variable.[42]

At Emerson Flag in San Francisco, each of the 24 employees has been assigned a specific task in which the goals, the standards of performance, and the work methods are clearly defined. These production jobs are routinized and highly structured, an important element to be considered when company managers match their leadership styles to situational favorability.

EXHIBIT 15.6

Matching Leader Style with Situational Favorability

Fiedler found that three variables, leader-member relations, task structure, and position power, form eight possible combinations of situational favorability, ranging from most favorable to most unfavorable.

Overall Situational Favorability	Leader-Member Relations	Task Structure	Position Power	Most Effective Leader
Most favorable	Good	Structured	Strong	Low LPC
Favorable	Good	Structured	Weak	Low LPC
Moderately favorable	Good	Unstructured	Strong	Low LPC
Moderately favorable	Good	Unstructured	Weak	High LPC
Moderately favorable	Poor	Structured	Strong	High LPC
Moderately favorable	Poor	Structured	Weak	High LPC
Unfavorable	Poor	Unstructured	Strong	High LPC
Most unfavorable	Poor	Unstructured	Weak	Low LPC

These three variables, in combination, establish a situation as either favorable or unfavorable for leadership. To apply Fiedler's model, the leader first examines the impact of these three variables, reviews the favorability of the situation, and then determines the leadership style most appropriate for that situation.

Matching Situations and Leader Styles The three variables that contribute to situational favorability form eight possible combinations (see Exhibit 15.6). To apply the Fiedler model, a manager would see which situations are most favorable for his or her own leadership style. Low-LPC leaders, who are task-oriented, are likely to be most effective in either highly favorable situations (those with good relations, highly structured tasks, and strong position power) or highly unfavorable situations (those with poor relations, highly unstructured tasks, and weak position power). High-LPC leaders are relationship-oriented and are likely to be most effective when the situation is neither highly favorable nor highly unfavorable.[43]

Inevitably, organizations face situations in which a manager's leadership style is mismatched with the situational favorability. In such an instance, the current manager might have to be replaced with another manager whose LPC scores and leadership style better fit the situation. Or the manager can change one or more of the variables that contribute to situational favorability. By altering the favorability, the manager can assure a better fit with his or her own leadership style.[44]

The Fiedler model has drawn criticism over the years. Some researchers question precisely what the LPC scale measures, and others charge that the scale ignores the leadership style of managers who score in the middle. Also, some researchers believe that Fiedler's conclusions about situational favorability and the match with leader style are open to other interpretations. But as the first comprehensive contingency theory of leadership, the model unquestionably broke new ground with its contributions to the understanding of leader effectiveness in various situations.[45]

path-goal theory A contingency theory of leadership which holds that leader effectiveness depends on the ability to motivate and to satisfy employees so they will perform

Path-Goal Theory

Another important contingency theory of leadership is **path-goal theory,** which argues that leader effectiveness depends on the ability to motivate and to satisfy employees so that they will perform. Most closely associated with Martin G. Evans, Robert J. House, and others who expanded and clarified its elements, path-goal theory has its roots in the expectancy theory of motivation (see Chapter 14). Employees are motivated to perform if they believe that their efforts will lead to successfully completing assigned tasks and if they believe that completing their tasks will result in the expected rewards. Building on these concepts, path-goal theory suggests that the leader's primary motivational functions are to make attractive rewards available, to guide employees through the path to these rewards by clarifying the behavior that will achieve goals, and to remove any obstacles that prevent goal attainment.[46]

Leader Behavior Depending on the situation, a leader can adopt one of four leader behaviors: directive, supportive, participative, or achievement-oriented.

- *Directive leadership* is telling employees exactly what they should do and how they should do it by preparing detailed work assignments and schedules and by defining specific standards of performance. This behavior is similar to initiating structure and task orientation, discussed earlier.
- *Supportive leadership* shows concern for employee needs and well-being by treating employees as equals and by creating an open and friendly work environment. Similar to consideration behavior and relationship orientation, supportive leadership behavior involves taking an interest in employees as people.
- *Participative leadership* is consulting with employees, seeking their ideas, and encouraging participation in decision making.
- *Achievement-oriented leadership* sets clear and challenging objectives for employees. Leaders who are achievement-oriented seek continuous improvement in group performance while displaying the confidence that employees can meet these high standards.[47]

Unlike Fiedler's model, which assumes that leadership styles are unchanging, path-goal theory suggests that leaders can modify their behavior to affect employee performance and satisfaction. Thus, leaders are not presumed to be locked into one consistent behavior but can shift among the four behaviors depending on the situational variables they face.[48]

Situational Variables The leader's choice of behavior is affected by a variety of situational variables. These variables can be grouped into two general categories: environmental factors and subordinate characteristics. The first category, environmental factors, includes task structure, the organization's formal authority system, and the work group itself. These factors are not easily influenced by employees but contribute to their ability to perform satisfactorily and to feel satisfied in their work. As one example, directive leadership may be too overbearing and even redundant when employees are working on a highly structured, routine task, so motivation and performance may suffer. However, when the task is unstructured and ambiguous, employees may welcome the specificity of directive leadership and therefore perform better.[49]

The second category of situational variables is subordinate characteristics, including employee skills and needs. Managers generally adjust their leadership styles in line with their employees' capabilities. For instance, employees whose abilities are less developed may respond better to directive leader behavior. On the other hand, those who are highly skilled and experienced may perform better under an achievement-oriented leader who sets challenging goals and shows confidence in employee abilities.[50]

Michael Dell, founder of Dell Computer in Austin, Texas, explains his achievement-oriented leadership approach this way: "We don't want to be number two. I don't believe in setting goals that are limiting. If you are going to set in place a strategy, it should be a strategy to lead." Dell leads by setting clear and challenging goals, motivating employees to perform and to feel satisfied as annual sales soar beyond $650 million.

EXHIBIT 15.7

Path-Goal Theory

A supportive leader can use path-goal theory to improve employee performance and satisfaction in two ways. One way is to focus on environmental factors, increasing the intrinsic rewards. A second way is to focus on subordinate characteristics, boosting the employees' feelings of being able to complete their tasks.

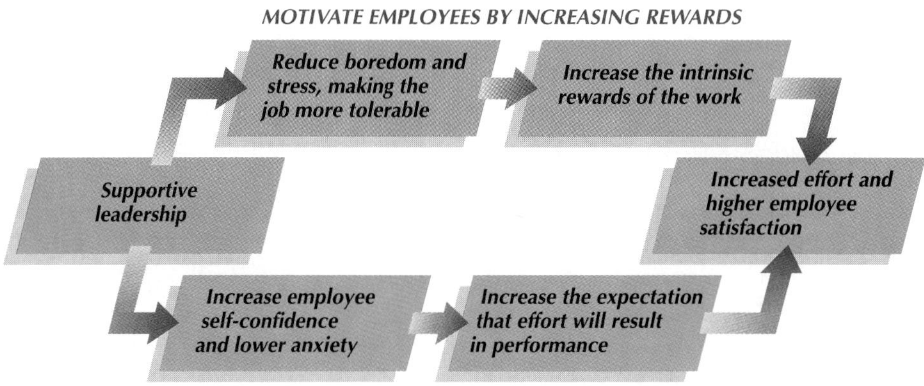

Selecting Leader Behavior Directive, supportive, participative, and achievement-oriented leader behaviors clear paths to goals and rewards in different ways, so the choice of behavior depends on how the situational variables influence employee motivation. When a task is stressful (environmental factor) and employees lack confidence (subordinate characteristic), for example, supportive leadership can provide two motivational paths to goals and rewards (see Exhibit 15.7). First, the leader can make the job seem more tolerable by creating a friendly, open work environment, which leads to the intrinsic reward of more pleasurable work. To reach this reward, employees are motivated to work harder and therefore achieve their goals and feel more satisfied while doing it. Second, when employees under stress believe that their managers support their efforts, they have more confidence that their hard work will actually lead to successful completion of the task. By boosting their belief that work will lead to performance, the supportive leader encourages employees to increase their efforts to reach the goal and helps employees feel more satisfied.[51]

Similarly, the other leader behaviors clear other paths to goals and to rewards, motivating employees to increase their efforts. For example, Grace Pastiak is director of manufacturing at a division of Tellabs, which makes sophisticated telephone equipment. Pastiak uses participative leadership at her factory in Lisle, Illinois, to guide plant employees toward paths that lead to higher performance. Not long ago, the factory received a large order that could be completed on schedule only by putting in a lot of overtime work, an environmental factor that influenced Pastiak's choice of leader style. Although the order was an important one, Pastiak was concerned because the overtime crunch coincided with the holiday season and could add a lot of stress to her employees' lives. Rather than apply a directive style and simply assign overtime, Pastiak used a participative style and asked the employees to help solve the problem. At an employee meeting, she laid out several possible paths to the goal: the plant could go on overtime as needed, the plant could add contract employees to help with production, production could be shifted elsewhere, or the marketing department could be told that only half the order would be filled. Her employees voted to produce the order without outside help, and committed to their decision, they worked overtime to finish on schedule.[52]

Because path-goal theory is complex, managers may find it difficult to apply in everyday situations. As a theoretical tool, path-goal theory has stimulated much research into the relationship of situational variables, leadership, employee motivation, and performance. These studies have generally supported the theory, but they have also identified conceptual limitations that require further investigation.[53]

The Vroom-Yetton-Jago Model

Another contingency theory of leadership, the **Vroom-Yetton-Jago model,** also known as the *normative decision model* or the *normative leadership model,* analyzes how situational factors affect the degree of employee participation in decision making. Initially developed by Victor H. Vroom and Philip Yetton, this model was enhanced by Vroom and Arthur G. Jago. Unlike other contingency theories, the scope of the Vroom-Yetton-Jago model is relatively narrow; it focuses only on a range of five leader styles that can be applied according to the manager's need to share decision making with employees.[54]

Vroom-Yetton-Jago model
A contingency theory of leadership that examines how situational factors affect the degree of employee participation in decision making

To determine the most effective style, managers follow a decision tree that guides them through a series of questions about the decision to be made (see Exhibit 15.8). Vroom and Jago have developed a series of decision trees to help managers consider a wider variety of problems. The questions in these decision trees examine four types of situational factors that affect the decision: decision quality, decision acceptance, concern for employee development, and concern for time.[55]

- *Decision quality* refers to the concern that the technical quality of the decision may or may not be critical to the achievement of organizational goals. If all the possible solutions to the problem are about equal in their ability to bring the organization closer to its goals, then decision quality is not a factor in that situation. However, when employees have relevant information about the problem or the decision and when they share their managers' goals, the model assumes that a consultative or a group style will result in a higher-quality decision.[56]
- *Decision acceptance* relates to the likelihood that employees will accept the decision and be committed to its implementation. As discussed in Chapter 6, employees generally accept a decision and implement it more readily when they have been involved in the decision-making process. Thus, decision acceptance is highest with a group style, lower with a consultative style, and lowest with an autocratic style.[57]
- *Concern for employee development* refers to the manager's interest in helping employees improve their technical and decision-making skills. Many situations present opportunities for one or more employees to learn new skills or to sharpen existing skills if the employees are involved through a consultative or a group style in the decision-making process.[58]
- *Concern for time* is a situational factor that takes into account whether the speed of decision making is important to the achievement of organizational goals. Too often, the concern for time conflicts with the concern for employee development, and the manager must sacrifice one or the other. When a situation involves a critical deadline that must be met if goals are to be achieved, the manager may have to use an autocratic or a consultative style for faster decision making, even though employees will lose the opportunity to practice or improve their skills.[59]

Based on the answers to questions about these situational factors, the manager traces the path along the decision tree to find the recommended style, which can be an autocratic, a consultative, or a group leadership style. Unlike Fiedler's

EXHIBIT 15.8

Leader Styles in the Vroom-Yetton-Jago Model

The Vroom-Yetton-Jago model poses a series of questions about the decision to be made, which leads the manager through a decision tree to determine the most appropriate of the five styles of leader-employee participation in organizational decision making. AI and AII are autocratic styles, CI and CII are consultative styles, and GII is a group style. This decision tree illustrates a group problem in which time is a major situational factor.

QR	Quality requirement:	How important is the technical quality of this decision?
CR	Commitment requirement:	How important is subordinate commitment to the decision?
LI	Leader's information:	Do you have sufficient information to make a high-quality decision?
ST	Problem structure:	Is the problem well structured?
CP	Commitment probability:	If you were to make the decision by yourself, is it reasonably certain that your subordinates would be committed to the decision?
GC	Goal congruence:	Do subordinates share the organizational goals to be attained in solving this problem?
CO	Subordinate conflict:	Is conflict among subordinates over preferred solutions likely?
SI	Subordinate information:	Do subordinates have sufficient information to make a high-quality decision?

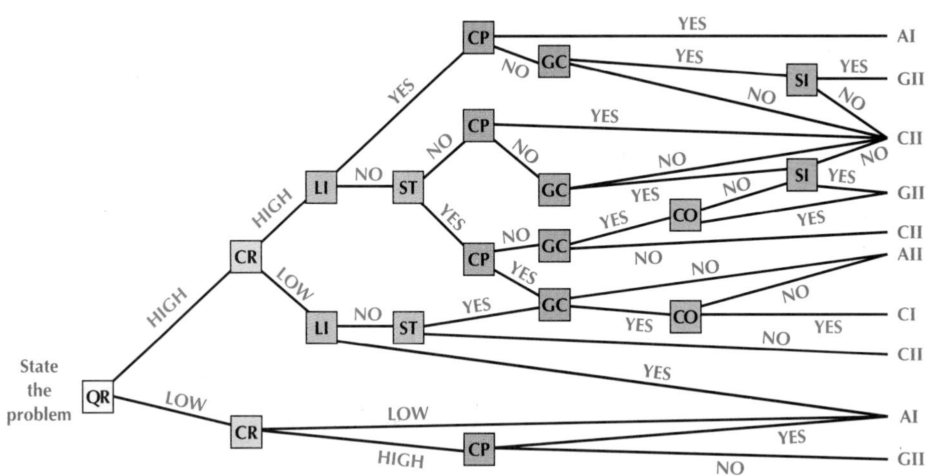

AUTOCRATIC LEADERSHIP STYLES **AI (Autocratic I): Leaders make the decision themselves, using information available at the time.**

AII (Autocratic II): Leaders obtain necessary information from employees and then make a unilateral decision. Employees may or may not be told about the decision.

CONSULTATIVE LEADERSHIP STYLES **CI (Consultative I): Leaders share the problem with certain individuals, getting their ideas and suggestions without bringing them together as a group. The leaders make the decisions themselves, and these decisions may or may not reflect the employees' influence.**

CII (Consultative II): Leaders share the problem with employees as a group, collectively obtaining their ideas and suggestions. Leaders make the decisions, which may or may not reflect subordinates' influence.

GROUP LEADERSHIP STYLE **GII (Group II): Leaders share the problem with employees as a group, and together the leader and the employees generate and evaluate alternatives to reach a consensus decision.**

model, which assumes that managers cannot change their styles, the Vroom-Yetton-Jago model is geared toward helping managers change their styles when appropriate. However, the Vroom-Yetton-Jago model has been criticized for oversimplifying the contingency factors that influence leader style, and the model itself is so complex that managers may find it too difficult and too time-consuming for everyday use. To facilitate the use of this model, a computer program is now available. The program guides managers through the questions in the decision tree and then automatically determines the optimal leader style.[60]

Hersey-Blanchard situational leadership theory A contingency theory of leadership that contends that leader behavior should be altered according to the employees' readiness to perform tasks

Hersey-Blanchard Situational Leadership Theory

The **Hersey-Blanchard situational leadership theory** argues that leader behavior should be altered according to the employees' readiness to complete tasks. This theory was developed by researchers Paul Hersey and Kenneth H.

Blanchard to help managers adapt their leadership style to their employees' readiness level, which may vary from task to task. Employee readiness (which Hersey and Blanchard called *follower readiness*) is a function of two factors: (1) ability (such as skills, knowledge, and experience), and (2) willingness (such as confidence, commitment, and motivation). The combination of these two factors yields four possible states of employee readiness to accomplish a particular task: unable and unwilling or insecure (labeled R1), unable but willing or confident (R2), able but unwilling or insecure (R3), and able and willing or confident (R4).[61]

The Hersey-Blanchard theory recognizes two independent leader behaviors, task behavior and relationship behavior, which are similar to the two dimensions of leader behavior in the Ohio State studies. Task behavior, as the name implies, occurs when leaders spell out the specific work responsibilities of an individual or a group. Relationship behavior is the extent to which leaders listen to and communicate with employees, coupled with the degree of support they show for employee efforts. Because these behaviors are separate and distinct, a leader can be high on one and low on another, high on both, or low on both, allowing managers a choice of four possible leader styles to adapt to employee readiness. Hersey and Blanchard termed these leader styles telling, selling, participating, and delegating (see Exhibit 15.9).[62]

- *Telling* (high task, low relationship). The leader carefully defines employee tasks and explains what to do and how to do it. This leader style works best

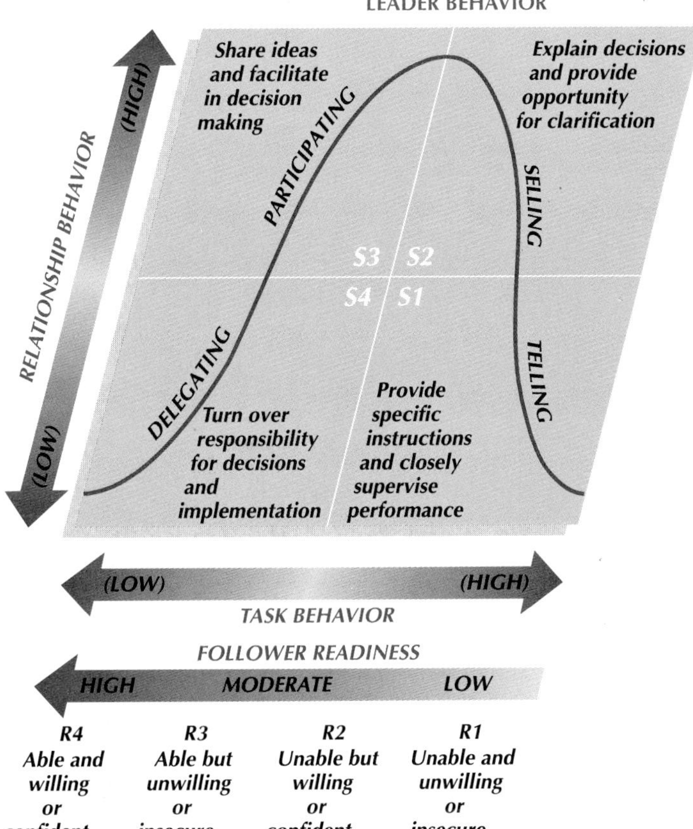

EXHIBIT 15.9

Situational Leadership Theory

Hersey and Blanchard's situational leadership theory argues that managers should adjust their leadership behavior, choosing from a total of four behaviors, to deal with situations in which employee willingness, ability, and confidence may vary.

with employees who are both unwilling and unable (by lack of competence or confidence) to perform tasks.

- *Selling* (high task, high relationship). The leader is directive about tasks and, at the same time, supportive of employee needs. This style is most effective when followers are willing to work but lack the appropriate skills.
- *Participating* (low task, high relationship). The leader stresses communication and support and downplays specific directions for completing tasks. A participating style is appropriate when followers have just gained the skills but lack the confidence to accomplish tasks on their own.
- *Delegating* (low task, low relationship). The leader provides little direction or support, allowing employees to complete tasks on their own. This style works best with followers who are both able and motivated.[63]

Although research has shown only partial support for its validity, the Hersey-Blanchard situational leadership theory is popular among managers because of its intuitive appeal and ease of application. However, some researchers find the readiness levels to be ambiguous. Critics have also challenged the theory on the grounds that employee readiness is not always the single most important situational variable that determines leader style.[64]

Substitutes for Leadership Theory

The contingency theories just discussed indicate when some leader behaviors are ineffective or inappropriate, but they do not indicate when leader behavior may be redundant or negated. In contrast, another contingency theory, the **substitutes for leadership theory,** states that some situational variables can actually substitute for leader behavior or render leader behavior ineffective. According to this theory, which is associated with the work of Steven Kerr and John Jermier, **substitutes** are situational variables that make leader behavior unnecessary or redundant. Substitutes can include any characteristics of the employees, of the task, or of the organization or group that enable employees to clearly understand their roles and their tasks and that motivate them to work toward group goals without formal leadership. For instance, when employees are trained professionals such as doctors, pilots, and accountants, they generally have the expertise to accomplish their tasks without close supervision; in this situation, skills and training substitute for leader behavior. Sometimes one member of the group will act as the informal leader, but no formal manager is needed to help the group complete its everyday tasks.[65]

substitutes for leadership theory A contingency theory of leadership that argues that certain situational variables can substitute for leader behavior or can render leader behavior ineffective

substitutes Situational variables that make leader behavior unnecessary or redundant

Situational variables that cancel out leader behavior or prevent leaders from exhibiting certain behaviors are called **neutralizers.** Neutralizers can include employee or group characteristics. When the employee doesn't value the rewards offered or when the manager is not in a position to offer rewards, leader behavior has little impact on employee performance. By understanding the effect of substitutes and neutralizers, managers can create or alter situations so that leader behavior can have the desired effect on performance.[66]

neutralizers Situational variables that negate leader behavior or prevent leaders from exhibiting particular behaviors

In an increasing number of organizations, work groups are deliberately structured to substitute for leadership, allowing the members to follow a focused path to an established goal. For instance, Robert Hershock, group vice president at 3M, encourages new-product innovation by harnessing the individual and group creativity of 10 self-managing cross-functional teams. Each team is composed of 8 to 10 people drawn from manufacturing, marketing, and other departments, and all are trained and highly skilled people capable of working effectively on new products and ideas without day-to-day management direction. As a result of using substitutes for leaders to spur product development, this unit is today one of 3M's fastest growing and most innovative. Although research into leader substitutes has focused attention on situations in which leadership may be neutralized or may simply not be needed, the theory is still relatively new and has received limited but encouraging support from subsequent studies.[67]

MANAGEMENT AROUND THE WORLD

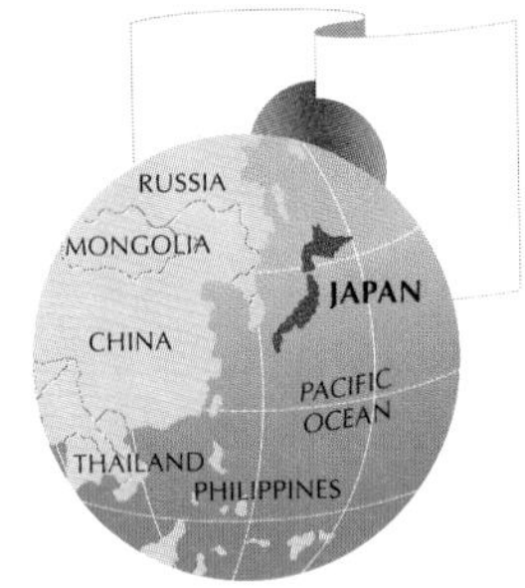

Managers in Japanese firms use participative leadership styles and invite considerable employee involvement in organizational decisions to build commitment. They also promote harmony among organization members by emphasizing personal relationships rather than maintaining a strictly task orientation. A growing trend in Japan is the careful design of work groups to substitute for leadership, especially in technical units such as research-and-development departments.

CURRENT TRENDS IN LEADERSHIP

Contemporary researchers continue to conduct studies that expand and revise the trait, behavioral, and contingency theories of leadership. In addition, researchers are looking more closely at the role of managerial leadership in today's increasingly complex and dynamic organizational environment. One issue that has received considerable attention in recent years is the distinction between transactional and transformational leadership.

Transactional Leadership

Traditionally, the leading function has been seen as **transactional leadership,** a term developed by political scientist and historian James MacGregor Burns to describe an approach in which managers motivate employees to perform as expected by clarifying task requirements and by providing rewards in exchange for employee efforts toward achieving the goals. The reciprocal exchange of work for pay and other exchanges that occur throughout the organization help all organization members feel satisfied about working together toward attaining everyday goals. Except for trait theories, the theories discussed earlier in this chapter all relate to transactional leadership.[68]

transactional leadership An approach in which managers motivate employees to perform as expected by clarifying task requirements and by providing rewards in return for employee efforts to achieve the goals

Transactional leadership is often considered synonymous with everyday management because it can be highly effective in a relatively stable environment where the emphasis is on maintaining current organizational performance or on dealing with well-structured problems. When managers apply transactional leadership, they are staying on course toward established goals by handling routine tasks efficiently and effectively. However, many researchers argue that this leadership approach alone may not be enough to bring an organization through the challenges wrought by an increasingly complex and dynamic environment.[69]

Transformational Leadership

When the organizational environment undergoes profound or rapid change, or when it becomes much more complex, another leadership approach is needed. **Transformational leadership** is Burns's term for an approach in which leaders motivate employees to do more than is expected and therefore achieve superior performance. Transformational leaders are charismatic and motivate their employees in several ways. First, they communicate a clear and compelling vision of where their organization or unit should be in the future, and they show how this vision is important. Second, they appeal to higher-level personal motivations such as self-actualization by offering employees the opportunity to learn new skills and to participate in projects that lead to the important outcomes de-

transformational leadership An approach in which leaders motivate employees to do more than is expected to achieve superior performance

MANAGERIAL DECISION MAKING

Putting Teeth into a Paper Tiger

What a difference a decade can make. The Food and Drug Administration of the 1980s was a shell of an agency, with too few inspectors, too slim a budget, and nearly anemic powers to carry out its mandate to protect the public from unsafe foods, drugs, and cosmetics. Without a clear sense of direction, the agency moved slowly to prosecute lawbreakers, to seize contaminated drugs and foods, and to evaluate new drugs. Contrast that sluggish performance to the FDA of the 1990s, which has moved decisively to crack down on fraud, to force more accurate labeling of foods, and to speed up approvals of drugs to treat life-threatening diseases. This transformation is the handiwork of Dr. David A. Kessler, a pediatrician and law school graduate who has used his leadership skills to put teeth into the paper tiger.

Dr. Kessler took office as FDA commissioner in December 1990, and he immediately established priorities for agency managers and employees by announcing his intention to vigorously enforce compliance with the Food, Drug and Cosmetic Act. By clarifying this strategic goal and making his performance expectations explicit, the commissioner used an achievement-oriented leadership style to send a signal throughout the agency and to the industries he regulates that the FDA was determined to regain its credibility as an enforcement agency. In motivational terms, this public announcement of goals and expectations gave agency members a shot in the arm, helping them feel that the commissioner had confidence in their abilities and that their work would result in more effective enforcement.

To keep the agency running smoothly on a day-to-day basis, Kessler decided to appoint five deputy commissioners to manage functions such as strategic planning and operations. In line with his vision, the commissioner also decided to overhaul the enforcement process. Before, an FDA inspector's report on contaminated food or mislabeled drugs had to pass through 15 management levels before it reached the Justice Department, a process that could take several months. Today, the report passes through just 5 levels and takes 25 days to reach the Justice Department, which has the legal jurisdiction to go after offenders. Now inspectors who identify potential lawbreakers know that their work will be backed up by swift legal action.

scribed in the vision. Employees are motivated to work harder when they believe that their extra effort will enable the organization to accomplish great things. And third, they build mutual trust and encourage employee confidence by personally modeling positive, ethical values. Through these behaviors and attitudes, transformational leaders inspire employees to look beyond their own immediate self-interests and to become committed to working even harder to make the leader's vision a reality.[70]

Transformational leadership complements rather than supplants transac-

As head of automated teller machine (ATM) operations for NCR in Dundee, Scotland, James Adamson *(center)* provided the transformational leadership that changed an old plant with demoralized employees into a world-class manufacturer. Employees were motivated by his vision of quality, his focus on customer needs, and his confidence in their abilities, and together they turned the plant into a showcase that challenged IBM's global ATM dominance.

Kessler took the initiative and made other decisions that affect the agency's goals and operations. In the past, FDA medical officers considering new drug applications typically saw themselves as the shield protecting patients from drug manufacturers. Mindful of the pressing need to find treatments for AIDS and other devastating diseases, Kessler's current goal is not only to prevent unsafe drugs from being sold but also to help safe drugs get onto the market. To this end, he had agency staff develop a new series of measures to speed drug approvals without compromising safety. Kessler has also hired additional criminal investigators, field inspectors, and drug advertising examiners to chop away at the backlog of FDA work and to help the agency move quickly to stop illegal or unsafe practices.

The commissioner's medical training has been an important ingredient in his ability to command the respect of FDA managers and employees. And his willingness to delegate gives his people plenty of opportunity to build their professional skills and to gain satisfaction from a job well done. In addition, the time Kessler spent (from 1981 to 1984) drafting food and health legislation for Senator Orrin G. Hatch of Utah has proved valuable, because the political savvy he picked up during those years has helped him negotiate the maze of Washington politics to boost agency power and funding. He has also used his knowledge of politics and publicity to show the agency's improved performance to best advantage. During his first year, Kessler drew the attention of legislators and press to such high-profile enforcement achievements as the FDA crackdowns on false cholesterol claims, mislabeled foods, and questionable pharmaceuticals promotion practices.

Under Kessler's transformational leadership, the FDA is now much more effective at policing food, drug, and cosmetic safety. But Kessler sees still more work on the horizon, including increased attention to over-the-counter drugs (drugs sold without a prescription). With its commissioner's combination of transformational and transactional leadership, the FDA's fangs promise to stay sharp for a very long time.

Apply Your Knowledge

1. Which types of power might Kessler use to influence legislators to increase funding for the FDA?
2. How might Kessler apply path-goal theory to understand the situational variables that influence his leadership of the FDA?

tional leadership, because organizations require leaders who can motivate everyday performance as well as leaders who can inspire the extraordinary efforts that are needed in uncertain or unstable environments. In fact, transformational leaders must work with transactional leaders or they must have the appropriate transactional leadership skills to keep their organizations or units running smoothly.[71]

For instance, Anita Roddick is a transformational leader who has built The Body Shop into an international chain that does more than fulfill customers' needs for cosmetics and personal-care products and satisfy employees' needs for monetary rewards. She has created a vision of using the store network to raise consciousness about the natural environment, human rights, and other social causes. Employees are energized by her leadership, and they work hard to fulfill the twin goals of profitability and social responsibility. Roddick's transformational leadership is balanced and complemented by the transactional leadership skills of her husband, Gordon Roddick, who handles the operational side of the business, including managing the finances and the many other daily activities that keep the company running smoothly.[72]

By taking an organization through significant changes, a transformational leader can effectively transform it. At the same time, this leader can transform employees by helping them build their capabilities and confidence. But transformational leadership alone will not build an organization or achieve its goals. Both transactional and transformational leadership are needed to strengthen the organization and its members and to contribute to high performance.

Consider how John Ott, executive director of the Atlanta Historical Society (AHS), used transformational leadership to shift the organization and its board of directors into high gear. Ott had a vision of the not-for-profit organization as more than just a museum dedicated to Civil War minutiae. He wanted to expand the organization's mission to present the entire story of Atlanta's history (not just the Civil War era) to a broad audience of local adults, schoolchildren, and out-of-town visitors. He painted a picture of this vision for board members, who were excited by the prospect of reaching this larger constituency. Spurred on by Ott's fervor and his supportive behavior, the board was transformed from a largely social group into a more hands-on, professional board that is highly motivated to invest the time and effort to manage key functions such as strategic planning. Because of Ott's transformational leadership and the renewed commitment of the board to transactional management, AHS doubled its membership rolls during Ott's first five years as executive director.[73]

Are transformational leaders found only at the top management levels? Studies have found that managers at lower levels can be charismatic and can inspire people to superior performance because of their unusual creativity and their ability to visualize a future that differs significantly from the present. To be effective, these transformational leaders generally have to exhibit personality and behavior patterns that vary from those used by the highly visible leaders at the top. As they move upward in the organization and meet a wider variety of challenges, such leaders become more skillful in their management abilities. At the same time, they are personally changed by their experiences, so they vividly recall and later use the lessons of the past when confronting current issues. Combined with their personal traits and talents, this experience and seasoning helps build the leadership skills of the transformational leaders who will head tomorrow's organizations.[74]

SUMMARY

Leadership is the ability to motivate and to influence others to achieve organizational goals. Leaders influence people to achieve performance through power, which is the capacity to affect the decisions, attitudes, and behavior of others. Power can be of six types. Four types are drawn from the manager's position in the organization structure: legitimate, reward, coercive, and informational power. Legitimate power is the authority vested in a particular position, reward power is the capacity to offer valued rewards, coercive power is the ability to penalize people or to withhold rewards, and informational power is the ability to control access to data. Expert and referent power are two types of power drawn from the individual rather than from the position. Expert power is the manager's own skills, knowledge, and experience; referent power is the manager's ability to inspire respect, admiration, and loyalty.

Trait theories emphasize the identification and measurement of the manager's traits or personal characteristics such as personality, skills, and physical attributes. Although trait theories have been criticized on a number of grounds, contemporary researchers have affirmed that certain traits and skills do seem to make a leader more effective. However, trait theories cannot be applied to every situation and to every organization. Behavioral theories of leadership emphasize the behaviors or actions that separate effective leaders from ineffective leaders. Included in the behavioral school are studies of autocratic and democratic leader behaviors, the University of Michigan studies of employee-centered and job-centered leader behaviors, the Ohio State studies of initiating structure and consideration behavior, and Blake and Mouton's managerial grid.

Autocratic and democratic behavior can be seen as two ends of a continuum. Autocratic leaders generally centralize authority and make unilateral decisions, and they often rely on legitimate, reward, and coercive power to motivate others. Democratic leaders generally delegate authority and invite participation in decision making. Democratic leaders often use referent and expert power to influence others, and organization members tend to be more satisfied when they work under democratic leaders.

The contingency theories of leadership examine how situational variations influence leader effectiveness, and they contend that leaders must adapt their styles to fit each situation they face. The Fiedler contingency model relates the favorability of a particular situation to the specific leadership style likely to be most effective. Path-goal theory argues that leader effectiveness depends on the ability to motivate and to satisfy employees so they will perform. The Vroom-Yetton-Jago model analyzes how situational factors affect the degree of employee participation in decision making. The Hersey-Blanchard situational leadership theory stresses that leader behavior should be altered according to the employees' readiness to complete tasks. The substitutes for leadership theory argues that some situational variables can be substituted for leader behavior or can negate leader behavior.

The managerial function of leading has traditionally been seen as transactional leadership, in which managers motivate employees to perform as expected by clarifying task requirements and providing rewards in exchange for employee efforts toward achieving the goals. Transformational leaders motivate employees to do more than is expected so that they achieve superior performance. Transactional and transformational leadership are complementary, and organizations need both types if they are to maintain everyday performance and attain the extraordinary efforts needed in uncertain or unstable environments.

MEETING A MANAGEMENT CHALLENGE AT GENERAL ELECTRIC

CEO Jack Welch feared that managers at General Electric were mired in the autocratic management style of the past. Although GE was profitable, Welch realized that he needed to encourage a more democratic leadership style if he was to unleash the creativity and enthusiasm of everyone in the company to improve productivity and profits in the long term.

Preparing for a GE Workout session

Welch started by flattening the organization structure to bring top managers closer to middle managers, first-line managers, operational employees, and ultimately to customers. Whereas corporate executives used to manage 6 or 7 middle managers, each would now manage up to 15. To handle the wider span of management, these managers had no choice but to let their managers and employees make and implement their own decisions.

Next, Welch launched a program called the Corporate Executive Council (CEC). Every three months, the 13 business unit leaders meet to discuss their units' successes and failures. The meetings foster trust among the leaders and enable them to learn from each other's mistakes as well as to benefit from their good ideas. Managers and employees at lower organizational levels meet regularly to discuss many of the same issues covered in the CEC meetings. Moreover, each business unit has an operations committee made up of managers and employees—experts in manufacturing, engineering, marketing, and other functions—who meet quarterly to thrash out operational issues and to share new ideas. These structures provide a solid foundation for the more democratic leadership approach Welch favors.

To encourage a more productive employee-management relationship, Welch introduced the Workout program. Several times a year, the heads of each GE facility meet with up to 100 people drawn from various levels and functions. The facility's top manager outlines the key challenges, then the group works without the manager to develop ways of meeting those challenges. Although the top manager must approve these ideas before they are implemented, most are innovative, so few ideas are rejected. Welch especially wants employees to question any unnecessary practices that inhibit performance. Challenging the boss, says Welch, clears out fossilized methods of doing things and increases the employees' self-confidence.

Finally, Welch provided extensive leadership training to help GE managers learn and practice new leadership skills and approaches, and then he changed the manager evaluation process to reflect the new emphasis. Business unit managers now rate the top corporate officers on how well their actions exemplify the new GE values of encouraging managers to share ideas with and from employees, to be self-confident enough to delegate work, to be honest in their communications, and to make and implement decisions more quickly. Managers who use these values and whose groups achieve their goals will be promoted; managers who achieve their goals by forcing performance out of people rather than by inspiring it will not be.

Welch understands that transforming GE managers into more participative leaders will take time. Already, he reports a change in spirit among General Electric personnel at all levels, and a rise in productivity. Welch notes that if GE had shown the same productivity growth in 1991 as in 1981, earnings would have been closer to $3 billion, rather than the $4.4 billion actually achieved in 1991. Armed with this new energy and enthusiasm, GE is well positioned for the challenges of the 1990s.

***You're the Manager*:** As one of General Electric's vice presidents, you are concerned about leadership skills—your own skills, the skills of those executives you report to, and the skills of the middle managers who report to you. Decide how you would handle the following situations.

Ranking Questions

1. When a technician in the broadcasting division challenged an unnecessary procedure in front of other employees, his manager fired him. Employees are upset, claiming that the employee was only carrying out the democratic vision articulated by Jack Welch. The company has already decided to review the termination, but a decision must be made about the manager's future. How would you rank these techniques for handling this situation?
   a. Except for the fairness review already noted, take no action that may cause the manager's power to be eroded. Although GE wants to change managers' leadership styles, their decisions must be supported by the corporation if discipline is to be maintained.
   b. Hold a Workout session during which the workers can directly challenge this and other decisions of the manager.
   c. Target the manager for special leadership training so that he can more readily accept criticism from his employees.
   d. Reassign or terminate the manager and assign a new leader experienced in participative leadership approaches.
2. A long-time manager is complaining because deep cuts in the staffing of his department have forced him to work 70-hour weeks to keep an eye on his employees' work and make sure tasks are accomplished. He wants more pay to compensate for the extra work. Rank these possible responses.
   a. In an informal gathering of his peers, have the other managers exchange ideas with this manager about how they have handled such staff cuts without stretching out their work weeks.
   b. Increase the number of people reporting to this manager so that he will be forced to stop supervising his employees so closely.
   c. Tell him that no one else in his position has asked for a raise, even though many of them face the same cuts; furthermore, none of them consistently work 70-hour weeks.
   d. Work with the manager to identify responsibilities that can be delegated to his employees, thereby decreasing his own work load.

Multiple-Choice Questions

3. A competitor recently hired away the top three managers from GE's home appliance business. The person you want to put in charge is knowledgeable in manufacturing and marketing but doesn't have much general management experience. However, there is a freeze on outside hiring, and in a limited field of internal candidates, this manager is the most attractive. Acknowledging his lack of management experience, he reluctantly takes the job but doesn't feel confident. From a path-goal perspective, which of these ideas would help him get started with his new responsibilities?
   a. Because the unit is an important part of the company's revenues, you can't afford to let this manager slip up. You should use a directive style, clearly explaining what he and his people should do.
   b. Invite the manager to participate in your own decisions.
   c. Immediately set demanding goals for the manager, giving him a target to focus on and not allowing him any time to get worried about his own perceived weaknesses.
   d. You need to support this manager as he moves into the new role. Share your own views of the satisfaction that comes with

and help remove obstacles to his success.

4. A manager has turned around a previously unprofitable segment of the company's medical systems division. In doing so, she concentrated on the tasks that had to be accomplished and ignored her employees' personal ambitions and needs. Morale is low. Which of the following solutions might be best for the division now?
   a. Assign a new manager with a style oriented toward personal relationships rather than toward tasks.
   b. Reassign the employees who are exhibiting a bad attitude before they threaten the profitability of the division.
   c. Reward the manager for turning the division around, discuss the need for a new style now that circumstances have changed, and offer to help with training and coaching. If she doesn't want to change, or if she finds she is unable to, discuss reassignment, perhaps to another turnaround situation.
   d. Take no action, but let the manager stay to ensure that the segment stays profitable. After the progress that has been made, it would be a big mistake to bring in another manager who might let things slide back down.

Analysis Questions

5. How are the sources of power at General Electric undergoing change?
6. What leader substitutes are present in GE's Corporate Executive Council and operations committees that replace formal leadership?
7. How is Welch's approach to changing the existing leadership styles likely to influence organizational politics at GE?

Special Project

When a highly regarded manager with a democratic and employee-centered leadership style was installed in the research division with its veteran team of experts a year ago, Jack Welch expected productivity to boom. The manager had little technical experience but did have a good track record of motivating employees. One year later, performance is high but the department has introduced few efficiencies. In a memo to the CEO, analyze the possible reasons.[75]

KEY TERMS

autocratic leader (476)
coercive power (469)
consideration (478)
democratic leader (476)
employee-centered leader behavior (477)
expert power (470)
Fiedler contingency model (480)
Hersey-Blanchard situational leadership theory (486)
informational power (469)
initiating structure (478)
job-centered leader behavior (477)
leader (468)
leadership (468)
least preferred co-worker (LPC) scale (480)
legitimate power (469)
managerial grid (479)
neutralizers (488)
organizational politics (473)
path-goal theory (482)
power (468)
referent power (470)
reward power (469)
substitutes (488)
substitutes for leadership theory (488)
traits (475)
transactional leadership (489)
transformational leadership (489)
Vroom-Yetton-Jago model (485)

QUESTIONS

For Review

1. What are the two sources of the six types of power?
2. What are trait theories of leadership and behavioral theories of leadership?
3. What is organizational politics, and how does it affect the organization's ability to meet goals?
4. How do transactional leadership and transformational leadership differ?
5. What are substitutes and neutralizers, and how do they affect leader behavior?

For Analysis

1. How do the path-goal theory and the Vroom-Yetton-Jago model address the autocratic-democratic behavior continuum?
2. In what ways are Blake and Mouton's 9,9 team management leadership style and the Ohio State high-high leadership similar? In what ways are they different?

3. Does transformational leadership have any limitations that might interfere with an organization's ability to reach its goals? Does transactional leadership have any limitations that might interfere with reaching organizational goals?
4. How can a manager be concerned about production and concerned about people at the same time (team management, 9,9 leadership style)? How might employees and superiors react to such a leadership style?
5. If no formal manager must lead a group because leadership substitutes are present, how might the group account for its activities and performance? To whom?

For Application

1. How can a Burger King manager apply the Hersey-Blanchard situational leadership theory to determine the appropriate leader style for a store with an enthusiastic but inexperienced work force?
2. When dealing with suppliers, what sources of power might the manager of an electrical generation plant find most effective? When dealing with union representatives?
3. How might the head of a local public library, who manages a group of highly trained professional librarians, apply path-goal theory to motivate employees despite a state-mandated salary freeze and recent layoffs?
4. Might the executive director of a Girl Scout chapter be able to apply autocratic leader behavior when dealing with the need for more volunteers to assist during Girl Scout events? Why or why not?
5. How would a leader in student government use the results of the Ohio State studies to determine the appropriate level of initiating structure and consideration to use when working with committee members to plan the next student dance?

KEEPING CURRENT IN MANAGEMENT

From recent magazines or newspapers, find an article that describes how a transformational leader overcame difficult obstacles to achieve organizational goals. Examples might be a corporate executive who successfully returned a company to profitability despite competitive pressures or a not-for-profit director who expanded the organization's activities despite economic hardships.

1. Why can this manager be considered a transformational leader? What changes has this manager made that probably could not have been made by another type of leader? Does this leader also act as a transactional leader or does another transactional leader help manage the organization on a day-to-day basis? How effectively does this arrangement work? Why?
2. What are this leader's sources of power? Which power sources might be most effectively used with this organization's members? Which might be used with suppliers of resources such as funding and raw materials?
3. What situational variables might the transformational leader have encountered before making the change? How did these variables change afterward? How has this leader altered his or her leadership style to fit the situational variables encountered?

SHARPEN YOUR MANAGEMENT SKILLS

Love him or hate him, everybody who knows T. J. Rogers seems to have a strong opinion about the hard-charging CEO of Cypress Semiconductor. Older managers in the electronics industry call him naive and unaware of what it's like to compete in the big leagues. A former Cypress executive, on the other hand, says he builds "a winning team" and that his people respect him. *Business Week* describes his management style as "tough, frugal, and highly aggressive." He races through 13-hour workdays and is demanding and unforgiving with his employees. He has been known to yell and to pound on the table when he isn't pleased with someone's performance. People who apply for work at Cypress are subjected to "pack of wolves" interview sessions in which technical experts ask candidates questions that they probably can't answer, just to see how they handle the pressure.

So far, anyway, Rogers can certainly make a case for his leadership style: his company's sales shot up 31 percent during a recent period when the industry's overall growth was about 5 percent.

- *Decision:* As a first-line manager in Cypress's research-and-development department, you've seen how effective Rogers's autocratic leadership style can be. However, you also know that his style has scared away talented people who might have made valuable contributions. You wonder if you should emulate his approach to boost performance in your department, where creativity and innovation are key elements.
- *Communication:* Draft a two-minute speech to the people who work for you, explaining the approach to leadership that you decide to take. Cite any appropriate theories and discuss how your leadership style will benefit the unit and the organization.

CASE

Stew Leonard Inspires Fun and Profits

Fun has become serious business at Stew Leonard's Dairy Store in Norwalk, Connecticut. Leonard's vision of a store where shopping is fun and the customer is always satisfied has been so successful that a long series of expansions has hardly kept up with the growing demand. Leonard's huge sales volume, zany showmanship, and customer-oriented business practices have attracted national attention, new customers continue to discover the store, and a second, larger store has been opened 30 miles away at Danbury, Connecticut.

HISTORY

Stew Leonard's customer base keeps growing because the store has low prices, offers fresh products, and features a customer-oriented philosophy that turns shopping from drudgery into fun: robots sing in the produce section, animated butter sticks dance in the dairy case, and employees (sometimes Leonard himself) wander the aisles dressed as cows and chickens. Leonard has also built his business by inspiring his employees with his vision of customer satisfaction and by using his expertise as a dairyman.

Leonard started business as a milkman with a small dairy, a home delivery route, and dozens of satisfied customers—until 1968 when the state decided to build a highway through the middle of his farm. Leonard obtained a bank loan and built a small store around a milk-processing plant that remains the focus of his operation. The store originally sold only eight items, but it has expanded into a 110,000-square-foot facility with bakery, fish market, butcher shop, 660 employees, and 25 checkout counters that handle $100 million in annual sales and 100,000 customers a week. Leonard has turned management of the business over to sons Stew, Jr., and Tom.

ENVIRONMENT

Expansion of floor space and product lines has already brought Stew Leonard's into competition with nearby supermarkets. Leonard prospers by being unconventional. Supermarkets stock an average of 15,000 separate items and try to offer a wide selection of products to prevent customers from having to shop at competitors. In contrast, Stew Leonard's stocks only 750 items and doesn't carry products such as flour or toothpaste, which forces his customers to do some shopping elsewhere. But selective merchandising makes Stew Leonard's more profitable; with 33,000 square feet devoted to selling, the store averages $3,000 in sales per square foot, compared with an industry average of $300 to $500.

Leonard's employees must be especially motivated to accept the additional responsibilities and accent on humor that his vision requires. He inspires them by paying better than other retailers for comparable work, advancing top performers into better jobs, and publicly recognizing employees' achievements. Many of the store's first-line managers, middle managers, and even top executives got their start at the bottom of the ladder, which makes them familiar with the jobs of the people they manage. Co-workers elect a "Superstar of the Month" in each department, plaques are displayed publicly to honor employees who submit money-saving ideas, and T-shirts emblazoned with the letters "ABCD" are presented to recognize employees who go "above and beyond the call of duty."

GOALS AND CHALLENGES

Leonard's strategic goal of customer satisfaction is literally written in stone. A three-ton chunk of granite at the front door of the Norwalk store proclaims: "Rule 1: The customer is always right. Rule 2: If the customer is ever wrong, reread Rule 1." To this end, Leonard authorized every employee to issue refunds on the spot to any dissatisfied customer, no questions asked.

A tactical goal is to stock only items that will ring up at least 1,000 sales a week. Large volume allows the store to bypass intermediaries and buy 90 percent of its items directly from farmers and manufacturers. Customers benefit because products are fresher and priced 10 to 20 percent lower than competitors' products, although some complain about lack of selection. The new store in Danbury may have a wider selection, which would allow Leonard to expand his strategic goal to pursue customer satisfaction by offering even more items.

1. How does Leonard use his sources of power to influence employees?
2. To what extent is Leonard a transformational leader? To what extent is he a transactional leader?
3. How can the Leonards encourage the same high level of commitment and motivation among employees who work at the second store?
4. How can the Leonards apply democratic leadership behavior to decisions about customer service policy?

CHAPTER OUTLINE

16 Groups in Organizations

After studying this chapter, you will be able to

1. Explain the role of groups within the organization and identify the various types of groups
2. Describe how roles, norms, and cohesiveness affect individual and group performance
3. Identify the reasons people join groups
4. Outline the five stages of group development
5. Explain why improving teamwork is important, and describe how managers can encourage effective teamwork
6. Discuss the causes of conflict and explain how constructive and destructive conflict can influence organizational effectiveness
7. Describe how managers can deal with conflict in the organization

FACING A MANAGEMENT CHALLENGE AT

FEDERAL EXPRESS

Delivering the Goods a Million Times a Day

Football coaches are famous for drawing elaborate diagrams with little *x*'s and *o*'s to describe a play—a play that typically involves one or, at most, two handoffs, a single football, and a team of 11. Imagine the coaches' frustration if they were asked to design a play covering five or six handoffs, over a million footballs, and a team of 95,000. And if that didn't prove sufficiently daunting, imagine them having to come up with a new play every day. Yet this is the challenge that faced Frederick W. Smith, founder and chairman of Federal Express.

Federal Express handles over 1.3 million packages daily. Local couriers bring customers' packages to a field office, then the packages are sent to nearby Federal Express sorting hubs or to the central hub in Memphis, Tennessee. There, they ride down a conveyer belt into one of the company's 380 airplanes. The packages are flown to a field office near their final destination, and local couriers deliver the packages to the recipients. Each of these millions of handoffs must be performed perfectly: Smith's goal is 100 percent customer satisfaction. And Smith won't tolerate any fumbles: he insists that Federal Express never lose a package, and each package must be delivered on time.

From 1974 to 1987, Federal Express's package volume has increased an average of 52 percent a year. As volume grew, Smith realized that standardized procedures and intensive training could not guarantee perfect performance. No one play would fit every situation or meet every contingency. Smith also saw that the rigid, hierarchical management structure found in other companies could deprive Federal Express managers of the ability to make decisions quickly and correctly. The predicament that Smith faced was compounded by Federal Express's impressive growth. Its revenues rose from $1 billion in 1983 to $3.2 billion in 1987. The company became the nation's largest overnight carrier, capturing more than 45 percent of the U.S. market for fast delivery services.

As Federal Express grew, however, its exposure to unforeseen events such as snowstorms and fuel price hikes grew as well. At the same time, the market opportunity attracted aggressive competition from companies such as United Parcel Service and Airborne Express. To head off the competition while maintaining profitability, Federal Express had to increase efficiency and lower costs. Smith's challenge was to push authority down the hierarchy, giving local managers and employees the power to make decisions quickly and then to act on them. Moreover, Smith had to create a corporate culture in which each player shared some of the coach's responsibility.

How could Smith create within Federal Express the feeling of an efficient, tight-knit group working toward corporate goals? How could he encourage Federal Express people at all levels to take the initiative when problems arise, to develop cost-cutting measures, and to feel responsible for company performance? And how could Smith foster a new spirit of teamwork among the employees without antagonizing the company's managers?[1]

CHAPTER OVERVIEW

Fred Smith knows that the continued success of Federal Express depends on the ability of his people to work well in groups. This chapter begins with a discussion of the nature of groups and of how individuals relate to each other in group situations. Following that is an overview of several types of groups and how they operate within organizations. After highlighting the characteristics of groups, the chapter presents the reasons people join groups and the stages of group development. Next, the chapter examines methods of managing groups, concluding with a discussion of conflict and ways to manage it.

FUNDAMENTALS OF INTERPERSONAL PROCESSES

People relate to one another in a multitude of ways within the organization. Their interactions, known as *interpersonal processes*, are shaped by the combination of personalities, relationships, and situations. Interpersonal processes are a key influence on performance because nearly every organizational task involves some interaction with others. Thus, performance ultimately depends on the ability of individuals to work with others. People in organizations often operate as members of one or more groups, pooling knowledge, ability, and effort to achieve organizational goals (see Exhibit 16.1).[2]

Groups Defined

group Two or more people who interact interdependently in the pursuit of a common goal

What makes one collection of people a group and another only an anonymous, disorganized crowd? In organizational settings, a **group** consists of two or more people who are interdependent and who interact in the pursuit of a common goal or purpose. The interdependency, interaction, and shared purpose separate a group from a random collection of people.[3] Thus, fans standing in line together waiting to purchase concert tickets may have a common goal, but they are not interacting and they do not depend on each other's actions to achieve their common goal, so they do not constitute a group.

Groups are integral to the success of the organization, and today the need to create and manage groups effectively is urgent: competitive realities demand that employees work closely in ongoing efforts to improve efficiency and effectiveness. Changes in the work force are bringing men and women from a variety of backgrounds together within the organization, so managers must be able to build and lead work groups that transcend gender, culture, and race. When organizations merge, two formerly separate work forces must learn to work as one. At the same time, many organizations are cutting costs by laying off personnel, so fewer employees are left to cover the work once handled by a larger contingent.

EXHIBIT 16.1

Groups in Organizations

Groups in organizations constantly change and require careful management to assure continued productivity and performance.

GM to emphasize profits, not market share

"Your corporation's North American focus has moved ... 'market share

Janitors join CEOs in gain-sharing programs at more companies

Firms reap bonuses in happier workers, productivity boost

By HANK EZELL

ATLANTA — Gary Sorrell, the operator of a paper-slicing machine at a printing plant in Norcross, got an extra ... for $60 ...

"If you're making a product, you can measure how many you made, how fast you made them, how many were rejected, what it cost to make them," said David Jones, an Atlanta-based compensation consultant with William M. Mercer Inc.

ment plans.

The company matches employee contributions at a minimum of 30 percent. When Engraph's return on equity goes ...

I'd like to have a little money."

workers. Engraph's boosted retirement plan, for example, helps the company hire and then retain highly skilled employees, said Dan Tuttle, the company's vice president for human resources.

panies are looking into ways to reward employees when they take an interest in the company's performance, and take the trouble to improve it.

"I think people love to be involved," said Jerry McAdams, vice president of St. Louis-based Maritz Inc., a consultant in performance improvement. "For too ... we've asked people ... brains at the

END OF AN ERA

GenDyn sale seen grounding once high-flying Convair

By S. LYNNE WALKER

John McSweeny was stunned when he heard the news. General Dynamics' Tomahawk missile division, a unit McSweeny had nurtured and developed during his eight years as general manager of Convair, was being sold.

He knew sales at Convair were declining long before he retired last November from his position as the division's top executive. "But to sell the business?" McSweeny said. "I would never have expected that."

San Diego Aerospace Museum. "From the beginning, they were very innovative, very daring in design."

Six years after the company came to San Diego, Consolidated Aircraft merged with Vultee Aircraft Corp. and the new firm — nicknamed Convair — started turning out B-24 bombers for the war effort.

New bomber every 58 minutes

The Pacific Highway plant ran 24 hours a day to turn out a new bomber every 58 minutes. In those days, the company employed more than 44,000 people in San Diego to build war planes that served on every front in World War II.

The production line moved so quickly, that "when the whistle blew, the first shift guy hand ... the second shift guy waiting behind him

At Polaroid, pleasing boss no longer enough

NEW YORK TIMES NEWS SERVICE

The quest for a customer-oriented culture is one factor driving Polaroid in an ambitious effort to apply a version of knowledge-based pay to all jobs — from the factory to the board room.

Winning over a boss is no longer enough to move to the next level. Instead, an employee and a supervisor must convince a new board that the employee's internal customers that he demonstrated the requisite skill for his next position.

The challenge in a pay-for-skills program is to keep ... who are more used to competition than on ... the team's needs rather than ...

To successfully adapt to these challenges, organizations are rethinking their traditional approaches to interpersonal processes, group structures, and group operating procedures. Consider how Granite Rock, a $90 million concrete and asphalt supply firm in Watsonville, California, has used groups to increase its market share every year since 1987. Despite aggressive competition, stringent government regulation, and demanding customers, co-CEOs Bruce and Steve Woolpert have expanded the business their grandfather founded by relying heavily on groups. In fact, the company has more than 100 small work groups involved in everything from truck purchases to quality control. In every plant and on a companywide basis, groups meet regularly to solve problems, suggest improvements, and make decisions that keep Granite Rock growing. This degree of involvement takes time and effort, but the Woolperts believe that without this group approach, Granite Rock wouldn't be able to compete effectively.[4]

Recognizing that interpersonal processes and work groups influence corporate performance, top managers at British Airways require nearly all managers and employees to attend training programs that enhance their ability to work together. In this group exercise, first-line managers play tiddlywinks as part of a team (rather than as individuals) to reach the group goal of winning.

Granite Rock isn't an isolated case; even large organizations are rethinking their approaches to groups. The Denver-based telecommunications company U.S. West has a director of pluralism, who is responsible for ensuring that company groups at all levels reflect the diversity of society. Managers believe that encouraging diversity in the workplace will help the company understand, anticipate, and then respond to the telecommunications needs of their diverse customers. At Cadillac, managers have redefined the nature of work groups to include not only internal but external members as well. The luxury automaker's product-development and improvement process now incorporates employees and managers from all company functions as well as from outside suppliers, providing a wider range of perspectives on product issues. Another example: a company aerobics class at a plastics division of General Electric ends with a 10-minute freestyle modern dance, reinforcing the message that, like professional dancers, groups must strive for teamwork and self-expression while enhancing individual empowerment and creativity.[5]

The Nature of Groups

Groups serve both survival and socialization needs. People in groups can accomplish tasks that an individual alone cannot; a task may require more expertise than any one individual possesses, it may require physical strength or geographical coverage that one individual is incapable of, or it might require a consensus for action that one person cannot provide. Groups also provide members with an identity, and they codify rules of conduct that enable the group to function as a unit.[6]

The size of a group directly influences the complexity of its interpersonal processes and, ultimately, the group's performance. Moreover, the interactions of individuals within the group and between individuals and the group as a whole add another dimension to the effect that groups have on organizational performance.

Group Size

The number of members in a group can vary. A two-person unit, or *dyad,* is the smallest group size. A dyad provides only one possible channel of communication, and if both members do not agree, coming to a decision can be a frustrating process. The small size of a dyad minimizes one of the major strengths of a group: the potential for sharing information and exchanging ideas.[7]

Adding a third person creates a more complex social system. A group of three can come to a decision by majority agreement, avoiding the deadlocks that dyads sometimes face. Also, each group member can interact with the other two, creating three channels of communication for exchanging information. For many tasks, 5 to 12 members is regarded as the ideal group size: the group gains the benefit of a wider variety of member skills and insights while remaining small enough to permit a lot of personal interaction.[8] For example, Bill Gates has purposely kept Microsoft's design teams small to nurture the creativity he credits with driving the company's success. "You can't just put more people onto a development project to get it done faster," says Gates. Citing the demands of Microsoft's growth and global span, Gates has also created a three-person office of the president to oversee product development, sales, and operations worldwide. Members of this group, which reports to Gates, have the talents and the experience to coordinate the company's activities while focusing on opportunities and challenges that need top-management attention.[9]

As Gates recognizes, managers cannot improve group performance simply by adding more group members. Depending on the diversity of tasks and the need for coordination, adding members does not increase—and may actually decrease—group performance (see Exhibit 16.2). In general, the larger the group, the more difficult the leadership task faced by its manager in directing and coordinating the group's activities. Moreover, when groups are large, members may have difficulty coming to agreement and may also feel less committed to group goals, which can hurt performance. Members sometimes form smaller subgroups, complicating both communication and decision making within the group as a whole. Because they have fewer opportunities to actively participate, members of larger groups may also feel less satisfied than members of smaller groups, which can influence their motivation and, ultimately, both group and individual performance.[10]

Groups and the Individual

Groups and their members influence each other in a complex and ongoing relationship. Individual members influence each other and the group process; the group as a whole influences individual behavior and performance. Thus the performance of the members and of the group, as well as the behavior and attitudes of the members, may vary. Researchers studying the interactions between groups and individual members have examined a variety of issues, including the types of people who make the best members for various kinds of groups,

EXHIBIT 16.2

Group Size and Performance

The size of a group has a definite impact on performance. When groups are very small, they may lack the expertise and the diversity to enhance performance. However, when they are too large, the problems of communication and coordination can bring performance down.

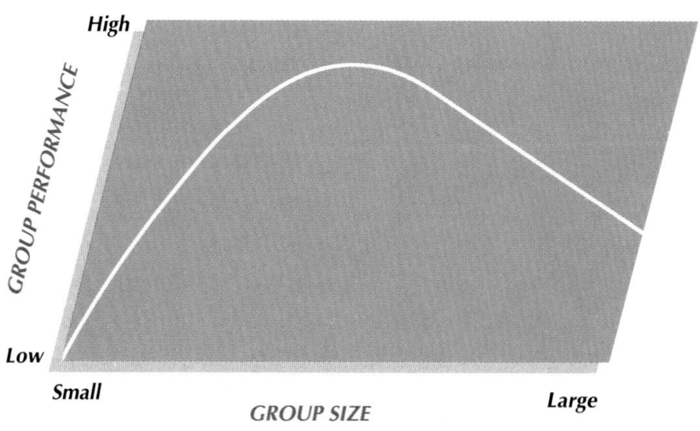

the most effective methods for stimulating group productivity, and the group structures that are most conducive to high performance.[11]

Attempts to understand these issues have taken experts from football fields (where they study the ways of winning coaches) to aircraft carriers (to see how groups operate in stressful and potentially dangerous environments). Seeking ways to improve group performance, executives have climbed mountain slopes (where they face physical challenges with group members) and have experimented with a variety of group management techniques (including leader substitutes).[12] Inquiries into the complex dynamics of groups have even penetrated the college classroom. A five-year Harvard University study found that undergraduate students do best when they are in small classes where they can freely interact with each other and with instructors, and when they participate in small study groups outside the classroom.[13]

TYPES OF GROUPS

Organizations contain many different kinds of groups, which can be categorized by common characteristics such as how the group forms, what the group does, and who its members are. The most basic distinction is between formal groups that are formed by the organization and informal groups that are not officially part of the organization structure.

Formal Groups

A **formal group** is created by the organization to carry out a specific set of tasks related to official organizational goals. Such groups are part of the formal organizational structure, and they appear on the organization chart as part of the hierarchy. One type of formal group is a **command group,** or *functional group,* a group consisting of a manager and all the employees who report directly to that manager. The goals of command groups are not usually confined to one project, and members' work is ongoing. For example, a museum curator plus all the people who report to that curator are considered a command group. In a traditional command group, one member (the manager) supervises the others and provides the link in the chain of command through which organizational communication and authority flow.[14]

formal group A group created by the organization to carry out specific tasks related to organizational goals

command group A group composed of a manager and all employees who report directly to the manager

At times, organizations confront issues that require more sharply focused attention or more highly diverse expertise than a command group can provide. In such situations, managers may designate a **task group,** a group created to handle a narrower range of tasks in connection with solving a particular problem or accomplishing a specific goal. Also known as a *task force,* this group's members are typically drawn from two or more command groups and may continue their roles in the command groups even as they serve on a task force. Whether they are called task groups, task forces, committees, or other names, such groups are all part of the formal organization; organizations often have their own names for the formal groups they establish.

task group A group created to handle a narrow range of tasks related to a specific issue or goal

Task groups may be temporary or they may be permanent. Once temporary task groups complete their work and achieve their short-term goals, they disband. For example, when Norman P. Blake, Jr., took over as chairman of the Baltimore-based insurance firm USF&G, he appointed employees to five task groups and gave them four months to study company operations with an eye toward cost-cutting and attracting new customers. After the groups presented their recommendations to Blake, they disbanded.[15]

Permanent task groups such as *standing committees* conduct ongoing work and rarely disband. For instance, in many corporations, members of the board of directors serve on a variety of standing committees that meet regularly to monitor the organization's affairs. Except for the chairman, Sara Lee's directors each serve on two of the company's six standing committees, which include the executive committee, the audit committee, the board affairs committee, the compensation and employee benefits committee, the employee and public responsibility committee, and the finance committee.[16] New members are sometimes added and members who leave are replaced, but despite such changes, permanent task groups usually continue their work dealing with recurring issues.

Informal Groups

informal group A group formed voluntarily by its members rather than by the organization

An **informal group** is a group voluntarily formed by its members rather than by the organization (see Exhibit 16.3). Members form these groups to serve social needs or to pursue common interests that may or may not relate to organizational goals. Informal groups often arise spontaneously in the normal course of interactions among group members, and employees and managers may be members of several informal groups.[17]

interest group An informal group created by members with a common purpose, agenda, or concern

friendship group An informal group that forms spontaneously in response to a social attraction among members

One type of informal group is the **interest group,** a group created by members with a common purpose, agenda, or concern. These concerns may or may not be related to organizational goals. For example, women executives at AT&T in New Jersey formed an interest group to share ideas about the common issues and opportunities they face as women in management.[18] Another type of informal group is the **friendship group,** a group that arises in response to a social attraction among members rather than from a unifying interest. Friendship groups often develop spontaneously when individuals work together, and a friendship group linking members of a formal group can improve interpersonal communications while making work more enjoyable.

EXHIBIT 16.3

Command, Task, and Informal Groups

Command groups, formally designated on the organization chart, include all the people who report to a particular manager. Task groups are formal groups that contain people from more than one command group. Members of informal groups may be drawn from any command or task group.

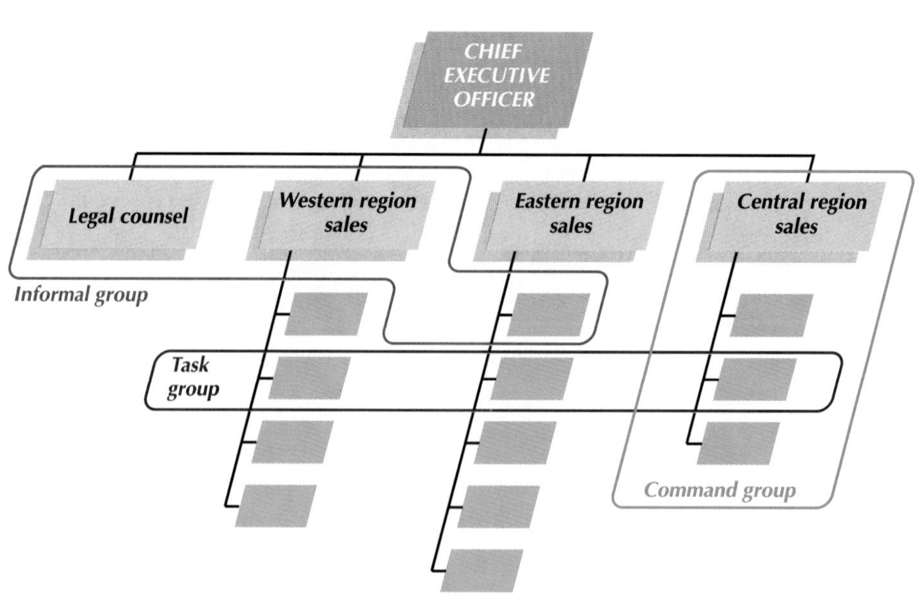

Avon, the international cosmetics firm, encourages employees to form or join interest groups. One such group is the Avon Asian network, which helps members develop their professional skills and make contacts throughout the company. The network also sponsors Avon Asian Day, an annual event that showcases Asian art, history, and poetry and helps to break down cultural stereotypes held by non-Asian personnel.

Teams

In many organizations, the traditional structure of formal command groups is being replaced by groups emphasizing greater group autonomy and employee participation. Called a **team,** these formal groups encourage member participation in management and decision-making activities as a means of maximizing performance and productivity. Three types of teams increasingly popular in the United States are problem-solving, special-purpose, and self-managing teams (see Exhibit 16.4).[19]

team A formal group characterized by relative autonomy and active employee participation in management and decision-making activities

A *problem-solving team* consists of a group of employee and manager volunteers who meet regularly to discuss methods for solving problems with products, processes, quality, or the work environment. Problem-solving teams generally make recommendations but cannot make changes without management approval. Many organizations create problem-solving teams as the first step toward encouraging greater employee participation. In a survey of nearly 500 large companies, the U.S. General Accounting Office found that by the end of the 1980s, 70 percent had formed such teams.[20]

A *special-purpose team,* also called a *cross-functional team,* is made up of members with diverse levels of experience and knowledge who work together on a specific activity. For example, Cadillac uses special-purpose teams composed of members drawn from every area of the company to improve and speed up the product-development process. Special-purpose teams with union employees and officials working alongside management are becoming more common in many industries as companies seek closer cooperation on a variety of issues that affect organizational competitiveness, productivity, and profitability. In many plants, such teams work on ways to improve product quality; in other plants, they consider how to improve workplace conditions.[21]

The **self-managing team** is a team in which members are responsible for virtually all aspects of an operation or production process. The team operates fairly autonomously, without a management-designated leader, and members

self-managing team A team in which members are responsible for virtually all aspects of an operation or a process

EXHIBIT 16.4 The Evolution of Teams in the United States

The team concept is spreading rapidly in the United States. Three types of teams are common in U.S. organizations.

	Problem-Solving Teams	Special-Purpose Teams	Self-Managing Teams
Structure and function	**Teams consist of 5 to 12 volunteers, managers and employees, drawn from different areas of a department. They meet one to two hours a week to discuss ways of improving quality, efficiency, and work environment. They have no power to implement ideas.**	**Duties may include designing and introducing work reforms and new technology, meeting with suppliers and customers, linking separate functions. In union shops, labor and management collaborate on operational decisions at all levels.**	**Teams usually consist of 5 to 15 employees who produce an entire product instead of subunits. Members learn all tasks and rotate from job to job. Teams take over managerial duties, including work and vacation scheduling, materials ordering, and so on.**
Results	**Teams can reduce costs and improve product quality, but they do not organize work more efficiently or force managers to adopt a participatory style. They tend to fade away after a few years.**	**Teams involve employees and union representatives in decisions at ever-higher levels, creating atmosphere for quality and productivity improvements. They create a foundation for self-managing work teams.**	**Teams can increase productivity 30 percent or more and substantially raise quality. Teams fundamentally change how work is organized, giving employees control over their jobs. They create flatter organizations by eliminating supervisors.**
When introduced	**Teams used in small-scale efforts in 1920s and 1930s; widespread adoption in late 1970s based on Japanese quality teams.**	**Teams grew out of problem-solving approach in early-to-middle 1980s; still spreading, especially in union sectors.**	**Teams used by a few companies in 1960s and 1970s; began rapid spread in middle-to-late 1980s and appear to be the wave of future.**

MANAGEMENT AROUND THE WORLD

Sweden's tradition of service excellence, its literate and skilled work force, and its cultural values have fostered the widespread adoption of work teams. Employees working in such teams are more motivated to contribute creative ideas, are more satisfied with their participation, and work more productively.

generally handle a variety of team tasks, sharing collective responsibility for the group's work. For example, at Chrysler's components plant in New Castle, Indiana, 77 self-managing teams are responsible for everything from hiring and disciplining team members to dividing tasks, setting work hours, and contacting customers. Thanks to the team approach, product defects are nearly nonexistent, product costs are down, labor relations have improved, and absenteeism has dropped. At Goodyear Tire and Rubber Company's plant in Mount Pleasant, Iowa, team members evaluate each other's performance, set salaries, and take turns serving as coordinator of the group's operations.[22]

Self-managing teams have taken hold in other countries as organizations pursue higher performance. The Swedish manufacturer Almex, which makes ticket-taking machines, uses self-managing teams throughout its plant. Each team elects a contact person to act as liaison with management, and team members have the opportunity to learn all the skills needed to complete the group's tasks. Leveraging the performance of its self-managing teams, the highly profitable Almex now exports its products to more than 40 countries. Self-managing teams are spreading to service organizations as well. At AT&T Credit, 11 teams of 10 to 15 employees perform all the functions required to serve the credit needs of the firm's small-business customers. The teams arrange members' vacation schedules, assign work to cover for absent members, and interview candidates to fill vacancies. Productivity has skyrocketed, but team members report feeling pressured by colleagues to produce more. However, the concept has been so successful that AT&T Credit is creating teams throughout the company.[23]

CHARACTERISTICS OF GROUPS

Bringing together a suitable number of people with the appropriate skills to pursue a shared goal is not sufficient to create an effective group. As groups are created and mature into viable working units, they develop characteristics that affect the way members work together. These characteristics include roles members assume within the group, the norms that set the standard for behavior in the group, and the level of cohesiveness that determines member commitment to the group.

When managers at the Veteran's Administration hospital in Canandaigua, New York, meet to discuss health-care programs, each understands his or her role within the group. One group member acts as the recorder (by creating agendas, taking notes, summarizing decisions, and reviewing the minutes of previous meetings), a task role that helps move the hospital toward its goal of quality health care for U.S. veterans.

Roles

A **role** is a set of behaviors expected of a member who holds a particular position within the group. Managers fill a variety of roles in their organizations, including interpersonal, informational, and decisional roles (see Chapter 1). In a smaller work group, members also play roles. Some of these roles are formally assigned by the organization, such as data analyst, general counsel, and account executive. But members assume additional informal roles that influence group performance.

role A set of behaviors expected of a member who holds a particular position within a group

Researchers Kenneth D. Benne and Paul Sheats described a variety of informal roles members may assume, categorizing them as one of three types: (1) task roles, (2) group building and maintenance roles, or (3) individual roles (see Exhibit 16.5). Task roles move the group toward its goals. Members who fulfill these roles help the group define its goals, reach decisions on how to accomplish them, and deal with roadblocks that impede progress. Group building and maintenance roles are those that facilitate interpersonal interactions and strengthen the social glue that binds the group together. Individual roles fill personal rather than group needs, and they sometimes hinder rather than help group performance.[24]

In high-performance groups, the formal roles are clearly defined and readily accepted. Even within groups that encourage autonomy and initiative, member roles are clear and compatible. For example, as he considered how to make Federal Express nimbler, founder Fred Smith wanted to establish roles that were defined clearly enough to guide employees in their daily activities without cramping their ability to make fast decisions. When roles are less clearly defined, are unacceptable, or are unachievable, members may experience role ambiguity, role conflict, or role overload, which can cause performance and member satisfaction to decline.

Role Ambiguity

Role ambiguity occurs when individuals are unsure about what is expected of them. Members may experience role ambiguity when they don't understand the goals of their role or when they don't know how to achieve those goals. New employees may experience role ambiguity if they haven't received an adequate orientation about their roles or if their managers have assigned roles with vague goals. Organizational changes wrought by mergers, restructuring, layoffs, and other workplace upheavals also create uncertainties that lead group members to experience role ambiguity. Higher levels of role ambiguity are associated with lower job satisfaction, lower job involvement, and lower commitment to the organization, as well as a decrease in productivity. Because their roles are often

role ambiguity The uncertainty created by lack of understanding of a role or how to perform it

EXHIBIT 16.5 Roles in Formal Groups

In addition to their assigned roles, individuals often take on one or more informal roles in groups. Some of these roles help the group meet its goals, some help the group develop as a cohesive unit, and some advance the individual's own position.

Types of Roles	Purpose	Examples
Task roles	Help advance the group toward its goals	Initiator-contributor: Provides ideas, vision, direction Information seeker: Finds facts on which to base decisions Opinion seeker: Determines members' views on issues Information giver: Contributes expertise Elaborator: Explains and expands on the ideas of others Coordinator: Reconciles possibilities and realities Orienter: Keeps the group on track toward its goals Evaluator-critic: Provides a critical analysis of group ideas Energizer: Stirs group members to take action Procedural technician: Handles administrative tasks Recorder: Preserves the group's documents and records
Group building and maintenance roles	Help establish and maintain the group's interpersonal processes	Encourager: Supports and reinforces other members' ideas Harmonizer: Dispels tension and resolves conflicts Compromiser: Forges acceptable solutions Gatekeeper and expediter: Promotes equal participation Group observer: Assesses group operation and behavior Follower: Defers to the will of the group
Individual roles	Seek to satisfy personal needs rather than the needs of the group	Aggressor: Criticizes others to enhance own status Blocker: Refuses to cooperate Recognition seeker: Cites own past achievements Self-confessor: Expresses personal but irrelevant feelings Joker: Exhibits nonserious and unprofessional behavior Dominator: Attempts to monopolize the group's agenda Help seeker: Tries to win sympathy and assistance Special-interest pleader: Tries to pursue private agenda

loosely defined, higher-level managers may feel more role ambiguity than managers or employees in lower-level positions.[25]

Role ambiguity can be reduced by setting clear, consistent expectations for the roles and the performance of group members and by offering training or counseling to help members meet those expectations. For example, when they switched to flexible work teams, Eastman Kodak's top managers worked to reduce role ambiguity by defining new roles for foremen (now called team advisers) and other managers. This reduced confusion over the change in emphasis from a directive style of leadership to a supportive style of leadership more suited to team performance.[26]

Role Conflict

role conflict A conflict caused by contradictory or incompatible expectations associated with a particular role

Role conflict arises when the expectations associated with a particular role are contradictory or incompatible. In such a situation, the individual who assumes that role can fulfill one expectation only at the expense of another. Common forms of role conflict include intrasender, intersender, interrole, and person-role conflict.

- *Intrasender role conflict* occurs when two or more contradictory expectations come from one individual or source. This could occur if a team leader in a manufacturing operation is requested by a manager both to increase productivity and to take manufacturing equipment out of service for routine maintenance.

- *Intersender role conflict* arises when contradictory expectations come from two or more individuals. For example, intersender role conflict might occur when a team leader is ordered to increase productivity by one manager and to take manufacturing equipment out of service for routine maintenance by another.
- *Interrole conflict* occurs when an individual must perform in two or more roles with conflicting demands. If a manager charged with assuring product quality is given the added responsibility of increasing production, interrole conflict could result. Many parents trying to juggle the responsibilities of career and family have also experienced considerable interrole conflict in trying to meet the demands of each.[27]
- *Person-role conflict* occurs when the attitudes and beliefs of the individual in the role are incompatible with role expectations. If a manager is told to increase production or profitability by unethical or illegal means, person-role conflict might result. This conflict can also prompt an executive to give up a respected and well-paid position for a less lucrative but more personally fulfilling career.[28]

Role conflict can lower performance, decrease satisfaction with co-workers and managers, and raise employee turnover rates. Additionally, people are more likely to feel underrewarded, to take less interest in their work, and to be less loyal to their organizations when they feel a great deal of role conflict.[29] To counter these problems, effective managers should consider and try to resolve any potential sources of conflict in the roles that group members are expected to perform.

Role Overload

Role overload occurs when role expectations exceed the abilities of the person filling the role. Role overload can be caused by excessive work loads, unrealistic demands, inadequate resources, or personal lack of skills. Managers and employees who attempt to cope with budget cutbacks and larger work loads often feel role overload. It is also common when insufficient time is provided to complete assigned tasks.

role overload The inability of an individual to perform up to the expectations of a particular role

Role overload, like role ambiguity and role conflict, can have a negative impact on performance, morale, and satisfaction. Research suggests that people who feel role overload may also experience serious health problems.[30] Managers can avoid setting up situations that result in role overload by matching the members' abilities and limitations to their role responsibilities and by considering the resources available to accomplish the tasks they assign.

Norms

Over time, groups develop **norms,** which are informal standards of behavior that govern member actions. Whereas roles define behaviors that differentiate group members, norms define behaviors that are common to all. Not all behaviors are regulated by norms (only those most critical to the group's goals and operations), but norms are important because they help define the group's productivity levels, its operating procedures, and prescriptive rules for work-related

norms Informal standards of behavior that govern member actions in a group

SOCIAL RESPONSIBILITY AND ETHICS

Ben and Jerry's Pushes Group Norms

The commitment to social goals demonstrated by Ben & Jerry's Homemade, the Vermont ice cream maker, generally gets positive reviews from people both inside and outside the business community. The company demonstrates its social responsibility in a variety of ways, such as encouraging the preservation of South American rain forests, supporting the efforts of local farmers, donating a considerable portion of its profits to charity, capping executive salaries at a relatively small multiple of the salary of the lowest-paid employee, and assisting in voter registration and voter awareness programs.

However, there is one fundamental aspect of this commitment that troubles some observers. Is it appropriate for founders Ben Cohen and Jerry Greenfield to expect all their employees to share their personal values and social goals? Conversely, do employees have an obligation to share those values and goals? As Cohen himself commented, "I think it would be a mistake for a right-of-center person to work at a left-of-center company."

Efforts to preserve the company's position on social responsibility begin in the personnel office. Employees are asked to endorse a "Statement of Mission" regarding the company's philosophy of social issues and corporate responsibility. Some call the practice "Orwellian," referring to George Orwell's novel *1984*, in which citizens of a mythical police state are not allowed to think any thoughts not approved by their leaders.

The salary cap in particular has made it difficult to attract and then retain qualified managers. Although the cap has been raised to seven times the lowest-paid employee's wages, managers still earn considerably less than they could earn elsewhere. This doesn't sit

actions. Norms are often unwritten and may even be unspoken.[31] For example, the norm in a packaged foods company may be to present no more than one new-product idea per member at any group meeting. If a member presents two ideas, others may make sarcastic comments or ridicule the member's ideas.

Group members exert pressure on each other and on new members to conform to the group norms. Those who conform may be rewarded by a pat on the back or another symbol of acceptance; those who do not conform may find themselves ostracized or ignored. Group norms that run counter to organizational goals sometimes develop or persist. For example, most organizations have explicit policies that define and prohibit sexual harassment. However, some managers have been lax in enforcing these policies within their groups, allowing harassing behavior to become or remain the norm.[32]

Norms typically evolve through one of four methods: explicit statements, critical events, primacy, or carryover behavior.[33]

- *Explicit statements* by leaders or group members formalize expected norms. A handbook given to management trainees, a "no smoking" sign in a company cafeteria, and an employment contract are examples. Explicit statements can be delivered orally (such as when a manager lays out a new employee's responsibilities) or in writing (such as AT&T's policy statement prohibiting sexual harassment).[34] Explicit statements are among the most effective methods for changing performance-hindering norms in an existing group. Although explicit statements are often issued by managers, members may also make such statements, as is done by Goodyear Tire and Rubber Company's employees in Mt. Pleasant, Iowa, who decide on vacation schedules and pay raises for team members.[35]
- *Critical events* are key events in the group's history that shape norms by setting precedents about acceptable behavior. The group's response to the

well with everyone in the company. Jim Rowe, the company's director of retail operations, believes the cap does not recognize his professional training or his aspirations. "I, for one—I'm materialistic," he says. "I'm also a career person. I've trained for years and years and years." When a manager leaves, or when Ben & Jerry's needs a new manager to help handle the continued growth, the head of human resources spends a lot of time searching for a candidate who is willing to accept the pay scale *and* is committed to the company's social agenda. Those requirements are not easy to fulfill, and executive searches sometimes continue for months without success.

Teamwork plays a central role at Ben & Jerry's, but it isn't at all clear just how socially committed the employees must be to perform as effective team members. Nor is it clear just how far a company should go to enforce its norms. When the company refuses to hire employees who do not subscribe to the prevalent group norms at Ben & Jerry's, is the company treating all of its stakeholders fairly?

For instance, assume that a particular managerial candidate has the potential to greatly increase returns for shareholders but that this candidate doesn't give voter registration or rain forest preservation programs high priority. By not hiring this person, would Cohen and Greenfield be failing to meet their responsibilities to shareholders? With socially active companies such as Ben & Jerry's, The Body Shop, and Smith & Hawken becoming increasingly visible, the issue of conformity to group norms promises to become a major issue in contemporary management.

What's Your Opinion?

1. It is appropriate for the leaders of a for-profit company to encourage group norms that extend beyond the operational issues of running the business?
2. What effect might the disagreement over social values have on the cohesiveness and the performance of employee groups inside the company?

past event can become a model for dealing with similar situations that arise in the future. A critical event can also be a crisis that spurs a group to change its existing norms. For example, after the regional telephone company Nynex was rocked by charges of questionable transactions between suppliers and company purchasers, the company established an ethics office to handle reports of misconduct and added training sessions to carry the message to every employee and manager. The ethics office logs more than 1,000 calls each year about unethical behavior, and the company's disciplinary measures have helped establish a more clearly defined norm for ethical behavior.[36]

- *Primacy* is the tendency of a group to adopt the first behavior pattern as the norm. Once behaviors become entrenched, they may be difficult to change even if they inhibit performance. However, primacy can also be used to foster positive expectations among group members by establishing a precedent for behavior and performance. For example, taking time off to attend to family or personal concerns was established as the norm when Benneville Strohecker first started Harbor Sweets, a candy company in Salem, Massachusetts. His help-wanted ads proclaim "Schedules to fit your needs," and managers and employees are encouraged to adjust their work hours to fit their other demands. This norm reduces role conflict and motivates the people at Harbor Sweets to achieve higher performance.[37]
- *Carryover behavior* refers to norms that are inherited from other groups or organizations. When group members have worked together in other groups or in other organizations, they may bring with them the norms of those situations, which are then incorporated into the new group. Like primacy, that can slow the adoption of changes when organizations try to alter their traditional structure or operations by shuffling personnel. But carryover behavior can also rapidly spread norms that improve performance to additional groups when people shift from unit to unit.[38]

Cohesiveness

cohesiveness The extent to which members are loyal and committed to a group and its goals

Another characteristic of groups is **cohesiveness,** the degree of loyalty and commitment members exhibit to the group and to group goals. When members are strongly committed to the group and its goals and are motivated to remain in the group, the group is more cohesive than when members are less committed and want to leave. Compared with members of less-cohesive groups, members of more-cohesive groups tend to have higher morale, to be more satisfied, and to agree more with group norms and roles. In groups where high productivity is the norm, cohesiveness will encourage members to perform at high levels. Likewise, if low productivity is the norm in a highly cohesive group, new members who perform energetically will usually reduce their output, because cohesiveness creates pressure to conform.[39]

Among the factors that can influence group cohesiveness are external threats, group history, interdependent goals, and accomplishment.

- *External threats.* Cohesiveness increases when groups perceive an external threat to their existence or their esteem. When Ingbert Blüthner-Haessler bought back his family's piano company during the East German government's privatization campaign in 1990, he faced the challenge of turning a state-subsidized company into one that could be profitable in a market economy. Employees knew their jobs were at risk and they knew many Europeans regarded East German workmanship as inferior. These external threats increased the employees' cohesiveness and paved the way for them to accept the changes needed to enhance performance. "We are highly motivated, partly by fear of losing our jobs, but even more so by pride," Blüthner says.[40]
- *Group history.* Common experiences and challenges faced over time instill a sense of heritage, which increases cohesiveness. Group and organizational traditions tend to perpetuate group history, so members need not have been participants in the original events to feel part of the experience. For example, managers and employees at Medtronic, a medical products firm in Minneapolis that makes heart pacemakers, can all tell the story of how Earl Bakken and his brother-in-law founded the company in a garage and had high hopes for applying technology to help humanity. This sense of shared history has enhanced cohesiveness and helped the company weather both aggressive competition and profitability problems.[41]
- *Interdependent goals.* Sharing common goals, which increases the dependence of group members on each other's performance, can heighten group cohesiveness. Creating such goals where none exist can also build cohesiveness. To lower costs and reduce toxic wastes, corporate planners at the Northrop Corporation wanted to replace the conventional photography system their engineers used with an electronic system, but the engineers didn't support the conversion. Once the planners showed the engineers the benefits of the new technology, the two groups were drawn closer by agreeing on the interdependent goal of installing the electronic system.[42]
- *Accomplishment.* When group members share the sense of accomplishment that comes from effective performance, group cohesiveness increases. For example, the "Post-Holiday Soiree Fund-Raising Council" is a volunteer group of 10 young professionals who run an annual party to benefit the Seattle Emergency Housing Service, a not-for-profit organization that helps homeless families. The group's first party in 1986 was so successful that the

Interdependent goals enhanced the cohesiveness of the printer department development section at NEC Tohoku, a computer equipment maker in Japan. When Akio Abe *(left)* was a section team leader, his group worked to upgrade operations as part of a company plan for winning the Deming Prize for quality, a goal set by president Hisaei Kikuchi *(right)* and supported by director Kikuo Suzuki *(center)*. The cohesive group met its goals, and the firm won the coveted award.

group was encouraged to try for more attendees—and more donations—the following year and every year since. Because of their success, group members feel a stronger sense of commitment to the yearly event.[43]

Members of highly cohesive groups tend to feel more satisfied and to conform more to group norms than members of less-cohesive groups. However, high cohesiveness does not necessarily lead to high performance (see Exhibit 16.6). Even highly cohesive groups can perform poorly if norms encourage members to restrict their output. But when members share high-performance norms, high cohesiveness can help members achieve and maintain high performance.[44]

GROUP FORMATION AND DEVELOPMENT

Groups are constantly forming and evolving within the organization. Managers may create a new unit, split a larger unit into two or more smaller groups, or

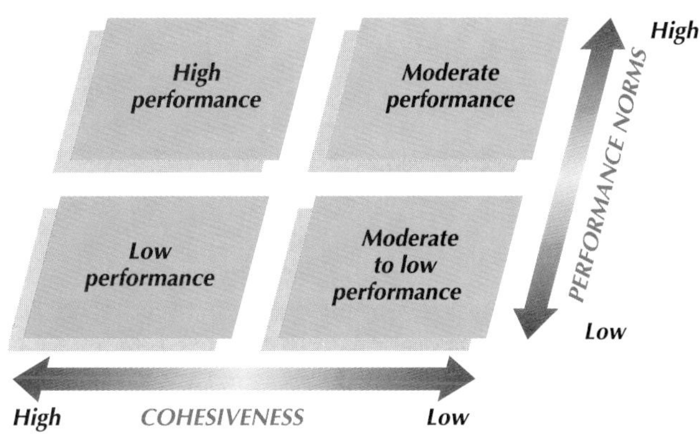

EXHIBIT 16.6

How Cohesiveness and Norms Affect Group Performance

Both a high degree of cohesiveness and high performance norms are required for high levels of group performance.

merge two or more units into one. Over time, members join new or existing groups, and current members leave. People have a variety of reasons for joining groups.

Joining a Group

Individuals cite a variety of reasons for joining groups in the workplace: to earn money, to learn new skills, to work with respected colleagues, to assume increased responsibility, or to take a position that's more personally fulfilling. They may volunteer for a task group because they believe in its goals or because they want to associate with the other members. The many reasons cited overlap in a complex web that spans the range of motivations identified by researchers who developed the need theories of motivation (see Chapter 14). However, the most common reasons for joining groups include the needs for security, for status, for self-esteem, for a sense of belonging, for power, and to achieve goals.[45]

When they join a work group, people feel less vulnerable, stronger, and more capable of confronting challenges than when they work alone. In the workplace, employees derive a sense of security from feeling that their colleagues will help out if needed, that a paycheck will cover their financial needs, or that their health-care benefits will pay most of the bills if they become ill. When people join an organization seeking status, they want the prestige of public recognition. The status may come from being able to land a job at an important company, from the title and level associated with the job, or from the glamorous nature of the job duties.

People also join groups to enhance their sense of self-worth and their confidence. When an employee is invited to serve on an elite special-purpose team, joining that group boosts the employee's self-esteem. Joining a group also fulfills the need to belong and to engage in social interaction. For example, some of the older employees who take jobs as reservation agents at Days Inns are seeking the social interaction more than the paycheck, so they tend to stay longer than younger employees who more quickly move on to other jobs.

Sometimes the power to be gained by joining a particular group can be a strong inducement to join. A member may want to wield influence over a process, a policy, a project, or other people or may even want to escape the abuse of power. For example, self-managing teams at some General Mills factories enjoy considerable autonomy. Team members have more say in how they complete their tasks, which provides an incentive to join and to participate while at the same time increasing satisfaction and performance.[46] Finally, the desire to see goals achieved can be a strong magnet that attracts members to a group, because many goals that can't be attained by an individual working alone can be achieved by a group.

Stages of Group Development

Groups typically undergo an evolutionary process of group development, a life cycle that many researchers argue is fairly predictable and consistent from group to group. New members may be added to a group at any stage of its life cycle, which may alter the cycle and prompt a return to an earlier stage. In newly formed groups, the process of group development can be viewed in five stages: forming, storming, norming, performing, and adjourning (see Exhibit 16.7).[47]

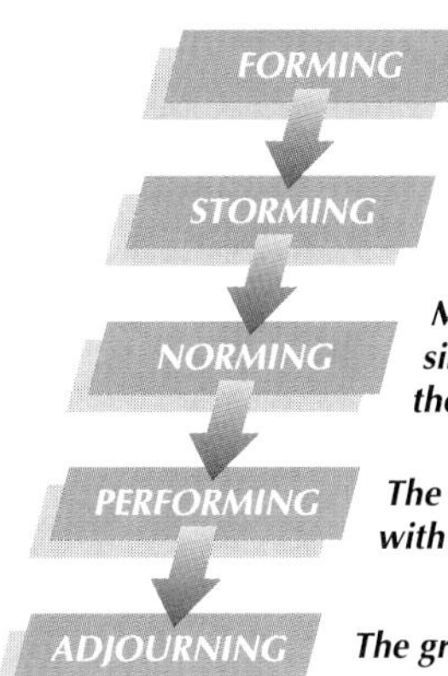

Members meet and lay the foundation for the group's goals, structure, and tasks. Members assume initial roles and responsibilities and monitor the group's reaction.

Members clarify their roles and responsibilities, and they may clash as they come to terms with issues such as dissatisfaction with the emerging leadership, structure, or norms.

Members come to understand and to accept their roles and responsibilities. They agree on the goals and on how to achieve them, and they begin to conform to group norms.

The group is fully functional. Members fill their roles and interact with other members to keep the group moving toward its goals.

The group completes its work and then disbands.

EXHIBIT 16.7

Stages of Group Development

Groups, especially those that are newly formed and relatively unstructured, progress through a predictable five-stage process of group development.

- *Stage 1: Forming.* During the **forming** stage, group members meet and lay the foundation for the group's purpose, structure, and activities. This is a period of uncertainty and testing as members assume initial roles and responsibilities and monitor the group's reaction. By the end of this stage, members have become acquainted both with each other and with the goals and tasks ahead.

forming The first stage of group development, during which group members meet and lay the foundation for the group's purpose, structure, and tasks

- *Stage 2: Storming.* In the **storming** stage, members clash with each other as they attempt to clarify their roles and responsibilities and come to terms with group issues. The name of this stage reflects the stormy interactions that often occur as members begin to assert themselves or to express dissatisfaction with the emerging leadership, structure, or norms of the group. Disagreements may replace the cautious reservations voiced during the forming stage. Even when titles and responsibilities are clearly defined, members may jockey for position within the group. Special-interest groups and coalitions may form, participation may be unequal, and the group may exhibit a general lack of unity.

storming The second stage of group development, during which members clarify their roles and responsibilities and come to terms with group issues

- *Stage 3: Norming.* The group moves into the **norming** stage as members come to understand and to accept their roles and responsibilities. Members agree on the goals and the methods for achieving them; they begin to conform to group norms of performance and interpersonal relations. As a result, the group becomes more cohesive.

norming The third stage of group development, during which members come to understand and to accept their roles and responsibilities

- *Stage 4: Performing.* In the **performing** stage, the group is fully functional and moving ahead to achieve its goals. Members fill their roles and interact with other members to keep the group on track toward its goals. Group members can also effectively deal with any problems or conflicts that threaten to sidetrack performance. This is the most productive stage of group development.

performing The fourth group development stage, in which the group is fully functional and able to move ahead toward its goals

- *Stage 5: Adjourning.* Once the group has completed its work, it enters the **adjourning** stage, during which the group disbands. Many formal groups have a finite life. Doctors may gather to study the outbreak of a rare disorder; a charitable organization's fundraising committee may stage one annual event. But with the task accomplished, priorities shift and the group's final goals become the evaluation of its work and the orderly dissolution of the group itself. Members may feel a sense of accomplishment over the goals they have achieved, but they also feel sad about the end of the group's activities. The organization often holds a ceremony to mark the adjourning of a formal group.

adjourning The fifth stage of group development, during which the group disbands after completing its work

When General Motors organized a team of engineers, designers, production experts, and other specialists to plan, design, and produce its Saturn model, the newly formed group developed its own performance norms. By the time the first Saturn car was unveiled, the team had reached the performing stage, and members were feeling both pride and accomplishment at producing this much-awaited new model.

Not all researchers agree on the exact number or content of the stages in the group development process, nor do they agree that every group goes through these stages. Some studies suggest that these stages are more applicable to new, relatively unstructured groups than to groups that have been in existence for some time. Moreover, the exact moment when a group passes from one stage to the next is not always clear. But understanding the issues likely to emerge in each stage helps a manager to anticipate and to plan for the issues that may arise within a particular work group.[48]

MANAGEMENT OF GROUPS

To build effective work groups, managers must have the cooperation of all participants, but antagonism between management and employees, especially unionized employees, sometimes makes this difficult. Some union officials are openly skeptical of the move toward work teams. For example, the president of United Steelworkers local says of the concept, "We don't think there's any benefit to cooperation. No way will we ever take part." Others argue that teams pit employee against employee and ultimately eliminate jobs. Pockets of antagonism persist, and some employees who have worked in teams say that the concept is just another management tool for pressuring employees to increase output. However, some union officials see teamwork as a way of making union members' employers more competitive, which in turn makes jobs more secure. At the United Auto Workers, union leaders are strongly committed to the team efforts mounted by General Motors, Ford, and Chrysler.[49]

To gain the cooperation of members in forming effective and productive work groups, managers must first build a foundation of trust. Only after trust has been established can managers encourage teamwork and build high-performing groups.

Building Trust

Before groups can work together effectively, members must feel a shared confidence in each other's willingness and ability to pursue a common goal. Without this relationship of trust, productive norms cannot be established and maintained. Members have to agree with and support both group and organizational goals, and leaders have to exhibit similar faith in their employees (see Exhibit 16.8).[50] The issue of trust was central to Fred Smith's struggle to encourage Federal Express employees to take the initiative and creatively solve customer problems, and many organization managers recognize its importance.

For example, Microsoft CEO Bill Gates credits this bond with allowing him to rely on small teams that work autonomously. "You've got to pick a few people and really trust them," he observes. Employees and managers at Republic Engineered Steels, in Canton, Ohio, saved their plant by buying the company when it was put up for sale. Saving jobs and turning the company around required close cooperation between managers and employees, who were previously often at odds. To make this cooperation possible, CEO Russell Maier set as one of his top priorities "to build the one ingredient without which you fail. Trust."[51]

1. Am I willing to listen to others without judgment or preconceived notions about what they should or shouldn't say? Do I listen less carefully if someone looks unattractive or seems to be in a class or a position that's different from mine?
2. Do I genuinely like the people with whom I'm dealing? Or would I prefer to spend my time with my own social group?
3. Even when other people disagree with me, am I able to show respect for their opinions?
4. Do I always want things to go *my* way before I start a conversation? Do I feel strangely awkward if I do not have control over a conversation? Does silence in an interaction or a group meeting disturb me? Do I have an intense, uncontrollable desire to fill up silences with my remarks or humor so as to end the lull?
5. Do I intend, or need, to exploit others? Do I hope to control situations or to get "something for nothing"?

EXHIBIT 16.8

A Self-Test for Manager Trustworthiness

Organizational psychologist Marsha Sinetar developed a five-question self-evaluation to assist managers in assessing the attitudes that affect their ability to form bonds of trust with employees.

Trust is critical in today's group environments because members must often fulfill roles and complete tasks that may be perceived as threatening or beyond the scope of their traditional responsibilities. Under such circumstances, employees have to be willing to retrain, to learn a variety of skills, and to take the initiative. Effective managers also understand that a successful group effort means sharing responsibilities and decision-making authority. However, downsizing and other upheavals that often accompany these group restructurings serve to reduce trust, creating a barrier to the adoption of planned changes.[52]

Consider how Union Pacific handled the issue of trust. The railroad was among the many that streamlined and cut costs by laying off thousands of employees during the 1980s. When Michael Walsh arrived as CEO in 1986, he aggressively implemented a looser and more autonomous management structure that required close cooperation from union employees. But how could he build trust and cut the payroll simultaneously? As part of the effort, the company provided generous assistance to employees who had to relocate to retain their jobs. Employees who worked together were moved to the same place so they wouldn't feel isolated, and the company threw welcoming parties for them. These efforts eased the transition and earned high marks from employees, who felt that the railroad was "going the extra mile" for them. Walsh built an atmosphere of trust that helped make the group restructuring successful, laying the foundation for the company's continued success under Richard Davidson, who took over as CEO in 1991.[53]

Growing recognition of the importance of trust is reflected in the rise of internal ethics groups within many organizations. These ethics groups are charged with overseeing ethical issues, conducting awareness training, and investigating internal complaints of misconduct. Creating these groups helps assure employees that management is concerned with protecting the best interests of employees and other stakeholders. By the early 1990s, more than 15 percent of companies with 50,000 or more employees had such groups.[54]

Developing trust takes time. Managers must balance the interests of the organization and the group with those of employees, and they must find common ground from which to pursue common goals. But managers must also become personally involved, through such actions as taking a real interest in group members as individuals, openly sharing information, and demonstrating their own honesty and integrity. A manager can express sincere commitment to employees, but if employees do not have confidence in the ability of the manager, trust may never develop.[55]

GLOBAL MANAGEMENT

Importing Japanese Teamwork

When Japanese automakers decided to build automobile manufacturing plants in the United States during the early 1980s, they knew they'd have to build a new kind of work environment as well. Although the Japanese carmakers used advanced manufacturing technology to build quality cars, their real edge over U.S. automakers came from the way the people who built the cars worked together. The Massachusetts Institute of Technology recently conducted a major study of the world's auto companies, and researchers confirmed that Japan's car manufacturing advantages came from teamwork, efficient use of resources, and a tireless commitment to improving quality.

Japanese managers seeking to re-create their team success when they opened plants in the United States began by defining the jobs. Instead of the narrow job classifications found in many U.S. auto plants, the Japanese manufacturers defined assembly-line jobs more broadly. At Honda, production employees were called "associates"; at Nissan, they were "technicians"; and at Mazda and Toyota, they were "team members." In the plant, teams of employees would be responsible for assuring quality and improving production methods on the assembly line, so the companies had to search for people with the right talents who also worked well in groups. For example, Toyota screened applicants with a battery of tests covering general knowledge, work attitudes, assembly skills, and problem-solving ability, then followed up with an in-depth interview and a physical exam.

Once they hired employees, the companies provided extensive training. Mazda developed training sessions to prepare employees for their involvement in shop decisions, and Toyota sent promising employees to Japan for several weeks of training in specific manufacturing techniques. Team leaders who returned from their Japanese training tour enthusiastically spread the word about the techniques they had learned, and they helped build excitement within their own work teams.

The team production process in these Japanese-owned plants required close cooperation between managers and employees, a dramatic departure from the traditionally adversarial relationship between labor and management in many U.S. plants. To foster closer relations in the Japanese plants, the man-

Encouraging Effective Teamwork

The effectiveness and efficiency of a group or team can be measured by the same performance standards applied to organizations: the ability to achieve goals through the productive use of resources. Managers can set the stage for perfor-

Managers of Westpac Bank in Australia learn about group leadership, trust, and teamwork during their Outward Bound training program. Over the course of several days, these managers learn to work more closely and to maintain a positive attitude as they confront—then overcome—physical challenges such as climbing rocks or crossing rivers. Each manager has the opportunity to take the lead in one or more activities, and their shared achievements enhance group cohesiveness.

agers and employees shared the same dining facilities and often wore the same company-issued uniforms. Activities like Toyota's "personal touch" program, which subsidizes after-hours socializing between Japanese and U.S. employees, encouraged the development of friendship groups, enhancing organizational performance. Although Nissan employees don't punch a time clock, the firm boasts one of the best attendance records of any auto plants in the United States. But most Japanese plants in the United States do not maintain a relief crew, so when employees are ill, team members have to cover those duties as well as their own, which can add pressure and stress to their already challenging jobs.

Some Japanese team protocol has been modified to be more acceptable to U.S. employees. At Nissan's U.S. plants, for example, employees do not have to wear the company uniform, and the morning exercise program has been dropped. But key elements of the team approach have not been changed. Managers in the Japanese-owned plants consult with the people on the line when considering production issues, and employees have more input into plant processes. At Honda, top managers hold a banquet every other month to honor employees in the U.S. plants who submit the best suggestions. And by paying above-average wages and actively supporting teamwork and cooperation, many Japanese manufacturers have warded off unionizing activities by the United Auto Workers.

There are now more than 10 Japanese-owned plants in what is called "Japan's Auto Alley," a stretch from Michigan to Tennessee with a combined manufacturing capacity of over 2 million vehicles a year. Since the first Honda facility opened in Marysville, Ohio, the benefits of the transplanted team approach have been evident: the quality of Hondas made in the United States rivals—or exceeds—the quality of the same models built in Japan. However, the real sign of the success of the Japanese approach to teamwork can be seen in U.S.-owned auto plants: many have restructured their assembly processes to resemble the Japanese system, and about one-third of UAW members working in these plants now belong to some type of team.

Apply Your Knowledge

1. How does the Japanese team concept affect group roles, norms, and cohesiveness?
2. What kinds of conflict might Honda managers encourage at the Marysville plant to boost quality and efficiency?

mance through better teamwork by selecting group members with appropriate skills, providing an optimal environment for their work, and providing positive leadership to keep the group moving toward its goals.[56]

Creating Groups

A group cannot be successful without members who are able to perform the assigned tasks. Therefore, selecting appropriate team members is a basic requirement for creating effective groups. Individuals should have the proper qualifications to join the group, and the group should be attractive enough that people want to become members. Even as organizations seek diversity in their employee population, too much diversity can make coordinating the variety of input difficult, while too little diversity can result in a kind of consensus-seeking groupthink that can inhibit creativity and stifle decisions that take the group toward new directions (see Chapter 6).[57]

A particular group becomes attractive to prospective members through the elements it offers in addressing the reasons why they join. One of the most obvious considerations is typically the size of a paycheck, but for many this issue is becoming less important than quality-of-life concerns. For example, most of the 1,000 or so white-collar employees counseled each year at the Center for Career and Life Planning at New York University say they want to move to smaller companies where they hope to achieve more control over their careers.[58] For these people, organizations that address quality-of-life issues are the most attractive places to work. Likewise, managers who address employees' needs will be more successful at recruiting qualified individuals as well as at motivating high performance.

Groups and the Environment

In a group, the environment includes all the materials, personalities, policies, and other influences that affect its performance or operation. Office layout, the availability of parking, and other physical aspects of the workplace are all part of its environment, but intangibles such as the organizational culture in which the group operates are also important.

Organizations characterized by high effectiveness and efficiency create an environment in which superior performance can be achieved. Studies have identified several key elements required to create such an environment. These include clear goals, a structure that fosters competent work, a culture that reinforces excellence, the availability of expert coaching and assistance, and adequate resources.[59] Managers can arrange these elements in a variety of ways to create an environment where group performance can flourish. Among the most basic resources required to create a high-performance environment is a suitable place for the group to work. For example, after reorganizing its headquarters personnel into self-managing teams, Aetna Life installed a new line of "team" office furniture that created workspace "neighborhoods," making it easier for members to communicate and to work together.[60]

Groups and Leadership

Creating an environment that encourages teamwork and participation requires a different management approach than that used in traditional formal groups. As members of a team, managers act as coaches, advisers, consultants, and liaisons rather than as directive leaders, because responsibility is shared with employees and their participation is encouraged. Although managers share power in a team environment, they still must provide the leadership that moves the group toward its goals. One way to do this is by providing vision. This can be especially important for managers who direct not-for-profit organizations, where vision must sometimes compensate for lack of physical or financial resources in creating a high-performance environment. These managers must often build coalitions of diverse interests united behind a single cause, requiring members' commitment and time without providing large financial rewards.

For example, Astin Jacobo, a Dominican-born school custodian in the Bronx, New York, envisioned reducing crime and providing a healthy outlet for local youths by transforming a garbage-strewn empty lot into a baseball field, a dream that sprang from his own childhood memories. He remembered that when he and his friends played baseball, the parents would also come to the park and play games, hold a barbecue, and watch each other's children. He wanted to bring this sense of family and community to the Bronx neighborhood. By rallying others to his vision, he gained the support of community groups and then persuaded the city to donate both the lot and the money to turn it into a ballpark equipped for night games.[61]

Managers also lead by example in establishing group norms of attitude and performance. Iva Wilson, an electrical engineer and manager at a division of the Dutch multinational N.V. Phillips, used this principle to create a supportive, high-performance group environment after she was named president of the unit. Wilson believes that a group must be supportive and sensitive to all its members.

One of her first acts was to assemble a group of top managers who shared her philosophy. "If top management acts like a team, then this type of behavior can trickle down through the ranks," she says. By setting a good example of teamwork and high performance, Wilson helped her unit's revenues increase 40 percent in four years.[62]

Leaders must also know when group principles must be modified or overhauled. Groups do not exist in a vacuum, and the environment in which they operate is constantly changing. Managers must continually evaluate the external and internal environments and be able make adjustments in order to survive changing conditions. Compaq's CEO Rod Canion created and led one of the most successful start-ups in corporate history for nearly a decade, and his consensus style of management was hailed for helping spur the company's growth. He was ousted after the company reported its first quarterly loss in 1991, because his consensus-seeking style was seen as an impediment to making the rapid changes needed to meet the growing challenge posed by competitors making low-priced computer clones. "We needed quick decisions and a single leader," one board member said after they voted to replace Canion as CEO.[63]

GROUPS AND CONFLICT

No group exists in which members all share the same attitudes, behaviors, expectations, and opinions. When differences become extreme, the resulting clashes can influence effectiveness and efficiency. Conflict has threatened the performance of government agencies and small partnerships, but it has also reenergized complacent firms. Indeed, because of its impact on groups and organizations, the ability to constructively channel conflict has become a key skill in the manager's toolbox.[64]

The Nature and Importance of Conflict

conflict Disagreement resulting from differences between two or more individuals or groups

Conflict is a disagreement that results from the differences between two or more individuals or groups. In organizational conflict, an individual or a group opposes the goals or the activities of another. *Interpersonal conflict* occurs when there is conflict between individuals. Management experts attributed the demise of Eastern Airlines in part to interpersonal conflict between Frank Lorenzo, who headed Eastern's parent company, and Charlie Bryan, who headed Eastern's machinist's union. Their profound disagreements prevented these two leaders from developing a rescue plan that could have saved the air carrier, which was ultimately liquidated.[65]

Intergroup conflict involves disagreements between two or more groups. This type of conflict sometimes occurs when two groups compete on the same assignment. For example, Ingalls, Quinn & Johnson, a Boston-based ad agency, assigned two competing groups to independently develop an entirely new advertising campaign for Converse, the sneaker manufacturer. The practice of assigning two groups to a task and then using the work of only one is common in advertising, because the disagreement between the groups often stimulates creativity and productivity.[66]

Conflict can have a positive impact on a group, as in *constructive conflict,* or a negative impact, as in *destructive conflict.* Constructive conflict energizes members to explore their differences, examine many alternatives to problems, and pursue a group goal. At Ingalls, Quinn & Johnson, the constructive conflict between competing groups motivated members to work harder and more creatively in the hope of having their group's work selected for the campaign. On the other hand, destructive conflict creates tension and dissension that can hurt group effectiveness. For example, when managers at Converse were unhappy with both campaigns developed by Ingalls, Quinn & Johnson, the two creative groups were asked to work together to develop an alternative campaign, but they couldn't agree on a direction. A new campaign could not be created without the intervention of a senior manager, who resolved the conflict.[67]

How did a conflict that initially benefited the organization become a conflict that threatened its ability to achieve an important goal? Although a definitive model of conflict has not been developed, researchers suggest that a moderate amount of conflict can improve group performance; too little or too much conflict can actually hold groups back from performing optimally. Conflict can stimulate creativity, encourage innovation, and lead to increased cohesiveness and higher morale. Problem solving is also enhanced in groups whose members have conflicting points of view. These groups examine more alternatives and create a greater number of innovative solutions than groups whose members think alike. However, when the intensity of conflict is too high, it has a counterproductive influence on group performance.[68]

The Causes of Conflict

Because of its powerful impact, channeling conflict is a management priority. But before managers can effectively handle conflict, they must understand its sources. Conflicts in organizational settings may be caused by competition for resources, group interdependence, interpersonal differences, goal incompatibility, communication issues, or inappropriate reward systems.[69]

- *Competition for resources.* A shortage of resources frequently provokes conflict. Competition for office space, budget, raw materials, or information is a common cause of conflict among individuals and groups.
- *Group interdependence.* Whether the interdependence is pooled, sequential, or reciprocal, intergroup conflict can occur whenever one group's work depends on the activities and decisions of another (see Chapter 9). Sequential and reciprocal interdependence are particularly difficult to coordinate. When one group cannot complete its tasks because it must first wait for another group to finish, or when one interdependent group sends or receives poor-quality work, conflict is often the result.
- *Interpersonal differences.* People with dissimilar backgrounds, personalities, or values are more likely to clash with each other in an interpersonal conflict.
- *Goal incompatibility.* Individuals or groups within an organization sometimes pursue differing goals, which also causes conflict. Because goals are set on many levels, managers may not always be aware of inconsistencies unless they actively coordinate goals throughout the organization (see Chapter 7).
- *Communication issues.* Lack of communication, or distorted communication, can be a source of conflict. If information is not freely shared and available to all members of a group, conflict may arise between group members or between the groups that must communicate to achieve goals. Communication is discussed in more detail in Chapter 17.

- *Inappropriate reward systems.* Managers may create conflict when they inadvertently design a reward system that rewards one group or one individual for achievements that can be attained only at the expense of the goals or activities of other groups or individuals. Although managers often intend to foster cooperation rather than competition, inappropriately designed reward systems can create destructive rather than constructive conflict.

Managing Conflict

Given its potential benefits, managers would not want to eliminate conflict entirely even if it were possible. Indeed, sometimes the task of managing conflict involves *creating* it. Thus, managers must be able not only to resolve destructive conflict but to stimulate constructive conflict when appropriate.

Bearing in mind that too much or too little conflict can hurt performance, managers can create conflict in several ways. Competition is commonly used to stimulate performance through conflict, such as in pitting creative teams against each other or having sales groups vie for performance honors. Changing the group's processes or procedures also creates conflict. Changing the group composition can also cause conflict: when performance lags, personnel may be shifted, new members may be added, or a leader may be replaced. For example, managers sometimes bring in "new blood" to shake up a stagnant or complacent group.

Managers have several tools at their disposal for reducing or resolving conflict. They may create a **superordinate goal,** one that cannot be achieved without the support and cooperation of all group members. Such superordinate goals reduce conflict because members must submerge their differences in the course of pursuing the more important collective goal. Thus, when managers at Ingalls, Quinn & Johnson explained to their creative personnel the urgency of delivering an alternative campaign to the client, the groups cooperated to produce this new campaign.[70]

superordinate goal A goal whose achievement requires the cooperation of all group members

Conflict can also be resolved through negotiation or bargaining, discussions aimed at reaching an agreement or understanding between the individuals or groups in conflict. *Mediation* is a conflict-reduction method in which an impartial third party is asked to listen to both sides, then helps the dissenting parties craft a solution to their conflict. When both sides cannot agree on a solution, one way of resolving the conflict is to invite a third party to make a decision that is binding on both sides, a process called *arbitration.*[71]

SUMMARY

Organizational performance depends on the ability of managers and employees to work together as a group. A group is two or more individuals who interact interdependently in the pursuit of a common goal. Groups can be classified as either formal groups, which are created by the organization, or informal groups, which are formed voluntarily by their members. Two common formal groups in organizations are command groups and task groups. In many organizations, traditionally structured formal groups are being supplanted by teams that emphasize group autonomy and active employee participation in decision making.

Group members act according to one or more roles, behaviors expected of group members who hold specific positions. Roles differentiate group members, and if they are not understood or cannot be fulfilled, role ambiguity, role conflict, or role overload may result, which can have a negative impact on individual and group performance. Groups also develop norms, informal standards of behavior that govern member actions and can influence performance. Cohesiveness is the degree of loyalty and commitment members exhibit to the group and to group goals. Highly cohesive groups with high-performance norms tend to perform better than either highly cohesive or less cohesive groups with low-performance norms.

Groups evolve through a five-stage development process of (1) forming, (2) storming, (3) norming, (4) performing, and (5) adjourning. In the forming stage, group members lay the foundation for the group's goals, structure, and tasks. In the storming stage, members clarify their roles and responsibilities and come to terms with group issues such as leadership, structure, and norms. In the norming stage, members come to understand and accept their roles and responsibilities. In the performing stage, the group is fully functional and able to work toward its goals. In the adjourning stage, the group has completed its work and disbands.

Managers can use their knowledge of interpersonal processes and group dynamics to create and manage effective and efficient groups. Groups cannot operate effectively unless a bond of trust exists between employees and managers. To encourage effective teamwork, managers start by selecting group members who are qualified for their tasks and able to work with others. Managers can also encourage teamwork by setting clear goals, establishing a structure that fosters competent work, creating a culture that supports excellence, making available expert coaching and assistance, and providing adequate material resources.

Conflict is a disagreement that results from the differences between two or more individuals or groups. Competition for resources, group interdependence, interpersonal differences, goal incompatibility, communication issues, and inappropriate reward systems are some of the causes of conflict. Constructive conflict can have a positive effect on organizational performance; destructive conflict can have a negative effect. Managers sometimes encourage conflict to improve group performance, using methods such as competition, changing group processes or procedures, and changing the group composition. To reduce or resolve conflict, managers can use methods such as creating superordinate goals, negotiation, bargaining, mediation, and arbitration.

MEETING A MANAGEMENT CHALLENGE AT FEDERAL EXPRESS

Federal Express grew at an enviable rate in the 1980s, extending its network of stations and doubling its package volume every two years. CEO Fred Smith was quick to understand that such rapid growth could be dangerous. It could lead to logistical bottlenecks that would slow operations, and it could increase the company's vulnerability to unforeseen emergencies such as strikes, fuel shortages, floods, and snowstorms. Both situations would frustrate Federal Express's goal of 100 percent customer satisfaction.

Unloading Federal Express packages in Anchorage, Alaska

Smith realized that a rigid hierarchy of command groups would only heighten delays and magnify errors. To give his personnel the flexibility they needed to move quickly and help Federal Express remain the dominant overnight delivery service in the United States, Smith organized employee teams. He empowered these groups by giving them the authority and the responsibility to make the changes needed to improve productivity and to satisfy customers throughout the Federal Express system.

Typical of the Federal Express approach is the Quality Action Team that employees in Springfield, Virginia, formed to overhaul their package-sorting techniques. The improvements they introduced put couriers on the road 12 minutes earlier than before and halved the number of packages they delivered late. Smith also assigns employee teams to company-wide projects. In 1988, facing growing competition from United Parcel Service and Airborne Express, Federal Express organized its 1,000 clerical employees into "superteams" of up to 10 people. These teams cut service glitches, such as incorrect bills and lost packages, by 13 percent. One team spotted—and worked until they eventually solved—a billing problem that had been costing the company $2.1 million a year.

Federal Express teams work because Smith sets norms and reinforces them. He spread the idea of the "golden package," the idea that every package Federal Express handles is critical and must be delivered on time. Whenever there's a crisis, whether due to competitive pressure or to Mother Nature threatening to ground the company's planes, the team with the golden package takes charge to figure out how to make the delivery on time. Smith reinforces group performance by presenting a monthly Circle of Excellence award to the best Federal Express station. And he encourages innovative thinking by creating a "job-secure environment." He insists that "if you hang people who try to do something that doesn't quite work, you'll get people who don't do anything."

Managers are by no means obsolete at Federal Express. Smith has redefined their roles. Managers are expected to formulate clear, attainable goals for their groups, to solicit employee ideas, and to act on the best employee suggestions. Federal Express managers are not coaches, they're facilitators—and sometimes they're players. During emergencies at the Memphis hub, senior managers hurry down from the executive suite to help load packages onto the conveyer belts that feed the company's planes.

Federal Express continues to satisfy its 1.3 million daily customers by relying on the collective strength of employee teams. The sense of group responsibility Smith fosters throughout the organization has helped the company remain the leader in overnight package service. It is also one of the reasons that Federal Express has earned high marks as one of the top 10 companies to work for in the United States.

***You're the Manager*:** James Perkins, senior vice president for personnel at Federal Express, has the job of translating Fred Smith's vision of teamwork into action. As Perkins's special assistant, you monitor the various facets of Federal Express's effort to encourage effective teamwork, and you stand in for Perkins when necessary.

Ranking Questions

1. Federal Express's annual Quality Achievement Award is presented to the group of employees who best exemplify effective teamwork in action. Perkins asks you to rank these top four nominees.
   a. A Federal Express station that has been ranked in the 95th percentile in its performance and customer satisfaction ratings each quarter for the past three years, a feat no other Federal Express station has ever achieved.
   b. A team of couriers who used quality improvement techniques to make the package-sorting process more efficient. Working at night, they designed a new sorting table, built it, installed it, and tested it. The result: reduced training time, quicker sorting, and annual savings of $32,000.
   c. A courier who drove across a hurricane-swollen stream to deliver a heart pump to a hospital in time to save a patient's life.
   d. A technical team of flight schedulers and mathematicians who established a routing system that enabled Federal Express to schedule its aircraft more efficiently, saving it hundreds of thousands of dollars each year.
2. Federal Express is having difficulty in its latest big venture: cracking the overseas market. Although it has poured over $1.5 billion into international expansion, Federal Express makes just one of every ten express deliveries in Europe. Perkins asks for your recommendation on the type of group that should be used to investigate the problem. Rank these options.
   a. Use an informal group to build on the knowledge that already exists at Federal Express. At Memphis headquarters, an interest group meets to discuss international trade. You think this group could handle the task.
   b. Turn to an existing command group. International operations are the responsibility of the international division. Ask the head of this division to work with his people to develop a new overseas strategy.
   c. Create a task group of people from domestic and international operations to study the problem and recommend a new strategy.

d. Organize a self-managing team and charge it with identifying ways to confront the obstacles that block Federal Express's international operations. Then allow this group the authority to carry out their solutions.

Multiple-Choice Questions

3. Cooperation occasionally breaks down among some employee groups. Suppose pilots and mechanics have been at odds. Pilots blame mechanics for delays; mechanics blame pilots for failing to give them adequate feedback about the planes. The conflict has led to delays and redundant repairs. Perkins asks you to step in and make a proposal to get operations running smoothly again.
   a. Don't fight this conflict. Manage it by channeling the conflict that both groups feel for each other into constructive competition. Pit the mechanics against the pilots in a race to reach efficiency targets.
   b. Problems between groups are often started by individual troublemakers. Identify the employees who are causing trouble and suggest they be fired.
   c. Appeal to both groups' overriding sense of loyalty to Federal Express and its mission. Stress that cooperation between the two groups is needed more than ever as Federal Express battles for market share.
   d. Create small teams of pilots and mechanics who together will be responsible for a specific group of airplanes. You could build camaraderie (and efficiency) by having these mixed teams compete against each other.
4. Federal Express's courier vans are aging, and senior management has decided to replace them. Perkins asks you to head a seven-member task group to choose a new model. You're excited about the assignment, but you're discouraged after the first meeting because the group didn't seem to make any progress. What should you do?
   a. Don't worry. Groups always take a little while to gel. Just give the group development process a few weeks to run its course.
   b. Prepare an agenda that focuses on the group's task, send it to group members for comment, and send out a final agenda just before the next meeting.
   c. Call the committee members and find out what they think went wrong.
   d. Your experience at the meeting just confirms your belief that meetings are a waste of time. List six criteria for evaluating new vans, assign one to each team member, and ask each to submit a report to you in two months.

Analysis Questions

5. What effect might the approach of emphasizing groups have on management recruiting throughout Federal Express?
6. In the hypothetical conflict between pilots and mechanics described in Question 3, what steps could Federal Express take to build trust between the two groups?
7. How do group cohesiveness and norms affect performance at Federal Express?

Special Project

Sometimes a group can function more efficiently if it is formed with a group leader already identified. Such leaders might be technical specialists who have important insights into a problem that a problem-solving team is being asked to solve, or they might be people who simply have a strong interest in the group's function and success. An employee at the Memphis hub has expressed interest in leading a group of people to start a recycling program throughout the facility. This person has a strong interest in recycling and the environment and also wants to develop as a managerial candidate.

You support the employee's wish to form and lead the group, but you want to make sure that this employee has the right skills and temperament to be the group leader. Identify the group roles this person should be able to play, and give examples of how these roles would help the group create and manage the recycling program.[72]

KEY TERMS

adjourning (515)
cohesiveness (512)
command group (503)
conflict (521)
formal group (503)
forming (515)
friendship group (504)
group (500)
informal group (504)
interest group (504)

norming (515)
norms (509)
performing (515)
role (507)
role ambiguity (507)
role conflict (508)
role overload (509)
self-managing team (505)
storming (515)
superordinate goal (523)
task group (503)
team (505)

QUESTIONS

For Review

1. What is a group? Why do people join groups?
2. How does size affect group performance?
3. How do norms, roles, and cohesiveness affect individual and group performance?
4. What are the five stages of group development?
5. Why does conflict occur in groups? When should it be encouraged?

For Analysis

1. What positive and negative effects can friendship groups that form among employees have on group and organizational performance?
2. What are the implications for individual and group performance if role responsibilities and expectations are not clearly expressed to group members?
3. If membership in a team is highly stable, what are the potential consequences for the performance?
4. What may happen when an organization tries to simultaneously increase productivity and eliminate jobs?
5. Can a team manager be effective in an organization with a traditional command-group structure? Can a traditional command-group manager be successful in a team environment? Explain your answer.

For Application

1. What can the manager of a weekly student newspaper do to reduce role ambiguity, role conflict, and role overload for the volunteer reporters?
2. How might the U.S. Secretary of Commerce make management positions in the Commerce Department more attractive to qualified candidates?
3. How can the management of Chemical Bank and Manufacturers Hanover Trust, which have been merged, assure that the consolidated group will perform optimally?
4. How does the creation of effective teams relate to academic environments? How does it relate to a small business?
5. How can a Nordstrom department store manager promote conflict to boost sales and productivity?

KEEPING CURRENT IN MANAGEMENT

From recent magazines or newspapers, find an article that describes how a manager is leading a group, an organization, or an institution undergoing rapid change. One example might profile an executive overseeing a reorganization in the wake of a recent merger. Another might highlight a manager who helped return a poorly performing group to high performance. A third example might focus on a top manager who takes a position directing a not-for-profit organization facing critical challenges.

1. What changes is the manager making to the groups within the organization, and how are these changes likely to affect the organization's performance? Do the manager and the group members seem to trust each other? What steps has the manager taken to strengthen this trust?
2. What norms seem to be operating within individual groups or within the organization? How have roles, norms, and cohesiveness been affected by changes in the group? Has the manager tried to clearly define new roles and then establish productive norms?
3. Did conflict precipitate any changes in the group or organization? Is the conflict constructive or destructive? How is the manager managing conflict?

SHARPEN YOUR MANAGEMENT SKILLS

In their efforts to help support Olympic athletes, companies such as J.C. Penney, Anheuser-Busch, and Hyatt are moving into new territory in the management of organizational groups. Through the U.S. Olympic Committee's Olympic Job Opportunities Program (OJOP), these companies hire Olympic hopefuls, with the understanding that the athletes can take time off for training. Since the program's inception in 1984, roughly 150 companies have hired nearly 400 athletes, including fencer Michael Lofton (who works for the accounting firm Ernst & Young) and luger Bonnie Warner (a pilot with United Airlines). The athletes get full salaries and benefits, which help defray the tremendous costs of training and traveling.

The program is also a hit with employers, who get free publicity and tickets to Olympic events, as well as the satisfaction of supporting the team. Fellow employees seem to enjoy working with these celebrity athletes. However, managers may face some important group-related issues, such as handling the absence of an employee who is a key member of one or more formal groups and dealing with the full-time employees who have to keep working while a colleague jets away to compete.[73]

- *Decision:* Assume that you are the personnel manager at a company that is about to hire its first OJOP athlete. Make a list of all the group-related issues that your firm will need to consider.
- *Communication:* Draft a two-page memo to all employees, explaining that an OJOP athlete is about to join the firm (make up any details you like). In this memo, you are to set the stage for issues related to group dynamics that are likely to affect the company.

Corning Has Team Spirit

Corning fended off competition with automation and a strong emphasis on quality, and the company is seeking further advantage by using self-managing teams as urged by manufacturing expert Norman E. Garrity. After initial success at new factories, Garrity, now executive vice president, must oversee the difficult transition from traditional command groups to self-managing teams at 27 existing plants.

HISTORY

The direct descendants of founder Amory Houghton still manage the firm that began in 1851 as the Houghton Glass Company and that became the Corning Glass Works in 1868 after moving from Massachusetts to Corning, New York. Corning has capitalized on innovation to achieve steady growth, $292 million in annual profits, and $2.9 billion in sales. The company supplied the glass for Thomas Edison's first light bulb in 1880, and it launched the Pyrex brand of oven and laboratory ware in 1915. By 1945 Corning was the undisputed world leader in specialty glass, and today it produces over 40,000 products used in all major world industries. Applications for Corning's glass technology include television tubes, sealed-beam car headlights, and optical fibers. The company has expanded globally (tripling foreign sales between 1966 and 1970) and is now involved in biotechnology, emission control, and video displays.

ENVIRONMENT

Corning changed direction in the mid-1980s when markets matured for its television tubes and light bulbs and competition increased from foreign competitors that could operate at lower costs. Top management decided to respond by emphasizing quality, adding automation, and improving inventory controls. But a study led by Garrity found that half the potential benefits of such moves would be lost unless the company eliminated layers of management and empowered production employees to make decisions. Garrity urged creation of self-managing teams, and he put his recommendations into practice when Corning reopened a plant in Blacksburg, Virginia, to produce high-quality automobile filters.

With union approval, Corning reduced job classifications from 47 to 4, enabling production employees to rotate jobs upon learning new skills. The company hired 150 people with good problem-solving abilities and organized them into 14-person teams to make managerial decisions, to discipline fellow employees, and to learn new skills. One result of their skill and job flexibility is that these highly trained employees can retool a line to produce a different type of filter six times faster than employees in a traditional filter plant. The employees say they like the additional responsibilities and they believe they can improve their job security by turning out quality products. The plant turned a $2 million profit in its first eight months, instead of losing $2.3 million during start-up as projected. Corning had similar success with flexible, highly trained, self-managing teams at a new ceramic filter plant, which production employees helped to design. Teams of production employees (called "ceramics associates") work with teams of engineers and maintenance specialists to continually improve the production process, which has dramatically reduced error rates and improved delivery times.

GOALS AND CHALLENGES

Corning wants to convert its other plants to self-managing teams. But managers worry that the success at Blacksburg and Corning will be difficult to duplicate at plants that are already built and staffed. Although Corning could hire whomever it wished, two-thirds of Corning's 20,000 current employees are weak in reading and math and need remedial education in addition to job training. In response, Corning plans to devote 5 percent of all work hours to classroom training, up from 4 percent. Garrity must also decide what to do with the supervisors that self-managing teams will supplant. They could be moved into advisory and coaching roles, but in the meantime first-line managers worry whether they will have jobs after the transition to teams.

1. How do the roles and norms in Corning's self-managing teams improve organizational performance?
2. What motivates the members of Corning's work teams to remain with those teams?
3. What problems might Corning face at its existing plants if it attempts to establish new norms in changing from traditional command groups to self-managing teams? How could these problems be overcome?
4. How could Garrity convince first-line managers to support the transition?

CHAPTER OUTLINE

17

Management and Communication

After studying this chapter, you will be able to

1. Highlight the importance of organizational communication to managerial functions
2. Distinguish among the various types of communication
3. Describe the communication process
4. Contrast interpersonal and group communication and explain the implications of communication networks
5. Differentiate formal from informal communication
6. Discuss the use of internal and external communication
7. Identify the interpersonal and organizational barriers to effective communication

FACING A MANAGEMENT CHALLENGE AT

GENERAL MOTORS

Tuning Up Corporate Communication at the World's Biggest Automaker

General Motors skidded into the 1980s with an unresponsive and top-heavy bureaucracy, a complacent and poorly motivated work force, and an autocratic management style. Its efforts to introduce a small car to counter competition from Japan had produced one costly flop after another. The world's biggest automaker lost $726.5 million in 1980, and the Japanese companies gained an unprecedented 19.6 percent of the U.S. market.

In response, top GM managers had ordered a massive overhaul of the troubled company. They restructured GM's North American car and truck operations, built new plants and modernized others (at a cost of almost $50 billion), made huge investments in advanced technology (including the acquisitions of Hughes Aircraft and Electronic Data Systems), reduced the number of nonproduction employees, and cut operating costs by $10 billion. But they made one serious omission: they neglected to communicate the company's new direction to GM employees.

As director of corporate communication, Alvie Smith was asked to muster employee support for the company's reorganization, opening new lines of communication and conveying the purpose of new directives. Smith faced a daunting challenge. GM employees were in shock. As one GM manager observed, "We changed all of our cars. We downsized them twice, changed from rear-wheel drive to front-wheel drive, changed all the systems of the company, changed all the factories, and *then* told almost every employee in North America, 'You've got a new job.'" Employee attitude surveys revealed that employee loyalty was strained and that managers were alienated. Established lines of communication were disrupted, and worthwhile initiatives (such as Pontiac's campaign for quality) were abandoned.

GM's size complicated the situation. GM is not merely the largest automaker in the world, it is the world's largest industrial corporation. It has roughly three-quarters of a million employees and more than 200 plants in 33 countries. It has also struggled under the weight of a complex corporate hierarchy, with 21 layers between the chief executive and the people on the assembly line.

Smith quickly conducted a number of internal surveys. They revealed that one of GM's most serious problems was the "frozen middle"—the reluctance or inability of a disaffected middle management group to communicate upward or downward. Even worse, GM management lacked credibility in the eyes of its employees. The employees didn't believe top managers when they described the extent of GM's losses and explained how the sweeping changes they advocated would solve GM's problems.

Smith understood that fostering communication through the many hierarchical layers was only the first step in mobilizing the entire corporation in support of the needed restructuring. Once he established lines of communication, he would have to train everyone at GM, from the assembly-line employee to the top manager, to be a better communicator. How could Smith improve communication throughout the company? How could he convince GM's 60,000 middle managers that good communication could improve their ability to achieve their business goals? And how could he tailor his communication program so that employees regained their trust in management and supported the company's goals?[1]

CHAPTER OVERVIEW

As in every organization, communication plays a critical role in the management of General Motors. This chapter relates communication to the four management functions, defines communication, discusses the various types of communication, and details the process of communication. The patterns of organizational communication are described, followed by discussions of internal and external

Many businesses use market research as a communication vehicle for soliciting information about customer needs and attitudes. The Fox Hills Mall in Los Angeles periodically hires interviewers to ask shoppers about its stores, facilities, and activities. By listening to customer reaction and ideas, mall managers are better able to plan future expansion and create special events that attract shoppers.

communication. The chapter concludes with suggestions for improving organizational communication by overcoming both interpersonal and organizational barriers, by creating an open communication climate, and by committing to communication that is both ethical and efficient.

FUNDAMENTALS OF COMMUNICATION

The most effective managers are those who understand communication and its use in the organizational setting. Communication is the vehicle that allows managers to fulfill each management function. To plan successfully, managers must be able to effectively communicate their vision to the rest of the organization. To organize successfully, managers must allow for and encourage free-flowing communication both up and down the hierarchy, as well as between departments and colleagues. To lead successfully, managers must clearly communicate organizational goals to employees and, through that communication, inspire employees to trust in their leadership and to perform at the highest levels possible. To control successfully, managers must effectively communicate with employees to monitor progress, to reemphasize organizational goals, and to correct ongoing processes.

Harvey Greenberg, now senior technical manager at Polaroid, was responsible for improving communications at R-2, the largest plant in Polaroid's Integral Film Assembly division. "When I arrived here," says Greenberg, "the most common complaint at all levels was, 'Nobody ever gets back to us.'" For four years, Greenberg focused his efforts on informing employees through monthly "What's Happening" meetings, emphasizing clarity in communications, providing the means for improving communication skills at all levels, encouraging two-way communication, and persuading all levels of the organization to participate. Why would a manager put so much time and effort into improving communications? Because, in today's organizations, "It's communication, communication, communication, says Greenberg."[2]

What Greenberg means is that communication is more than simply talking, writing, reading, and listening. Effective communication is the key to successful management (see Exhibit 17.1). It allows managers to share goals with stakeholders both inside and outside the company. It permits managers to stimulate behavior changes in employees and suppliers. It enables managers to inspire loyalty from employees and customers. It allows managers to convince employees and unions to abandon counterproductive practices. It enables managers to persuade lenders to provide financing. And it permits managers to calm angry customers and to impress new ones.[3]

Managers must be effective communicators to function. But what makes managers successful communicators? First, they must understand what communication is. Next they must understand how communication works, on both an interpersonal and an organizational level. And finally, they must understand what barriers can impede communication so that they can overcome such impediments and improve communication throughout the organization.

The Types of Communication

communication The exchange and comprehension of information

Communication is sharing. It is what enables managers and employees to cooperate and organize.[4] **Communication** is the exchange and comprehension of

EXHIBIT 17.1 Communication and Managerial Roles

Although only 3 of Henry Mintzberg's 10 managerial roles (see Chapter 1) are labeled as "informational," communication is a vital element in all 10 roles, as these examples demonstrate.

Interpersonal Roles	Informational Roles	Decisional Roles
Role: Figurehead Function: Performs ceremonial duties Examples: A CEO represents the company at major events, such as the opening of new facilities or the introduction of new products. A sales manager takes an important customer to lunch.	Role: Monitor Function: Scans environment for information Examples: A president asks staff members for their opinions on a new product. An accountant reads a newspaper article on proposed changes in the tax law.	Role: Entrepreneur Function: Sifts through facts to identify changing conditions and new ideas and then launches projects to capitalize on opportunities Examples: A director of human resources develops seminars to help managers deal with stress in the workplace. An office manager spots a bottleneck in interoffice mail delivery, so she revises schedules and reassigns personnel.
Role: Leader Function: Directs work of subordinates Examples: A CEO holds employee briefings to coach and motivate employees. A supervisor shows a new employee how to do a job.	Role: Disseminator Function: Processes information and passes it on to subordinates Examples: A CEO explains the company's financial performance to employees at a briefing. A sales manager hears that a new brand of clothing is hot and suggests that clerks rearrange displays.	Role: Disturbance Handler Function: Responds to pressures Examples: A general manager learns that construction costs are skyrocketing on a new plant and instructs the contractor to revise the budget. A buyer lines up an alternate vendor when a major supplier reneges on a contract.
Role: Liaison Function: Makes contacts outside the vertical chain of command Examples: A president sees a top executive of another company at a party and gossips about the industry developments. An engineer attends a professional conference and catches up on the latest technical developments.	Role: Spokesperson Function: Sends information to people outside the organizational unit Examples: A president gives a speech on a takeover attempt to a group of securities analysts. A director of environmental affairs meets with officials from the Environmental Protection Agency.	Role: Resource Allocator Function: Decides who will receive what Examples: A CEO authorizes a budget for launching a new product. A manager takes paperwork home at night in order to free more time during the day for meetings.
		Role: Negotiator Function: Persuades people to agree to things Examples: A CEO convinces foreign government officials to permit the company to distribute products abroad. A supervisor resolves a grievance with the shop steward.

information; for managers, this exchange is usually to influence decision-making behavior and employees.[5] Whether nonverbal or verbal, whether oral or written, communication is what enables managers and organizations to achieve high performance.

Nonverbal Communication

Nonverbal communication expresses information without words, through gesture and behavior. It is often unplanned, even unconscious, and it is governed by few rules. Nonverbal cues carry more than 90 percent of the emotional meaning of a message, which is why these cues have a greater impact than verbal communication. In fact, people tend to believe nonverbal messages over verbal ones when the two conflict.[6] The variety of nonverbal cues is vast, and by ob-

nonverbal communication
The expression of information through gesture and behavior

MANAGEMENT AROUND THE WORLD

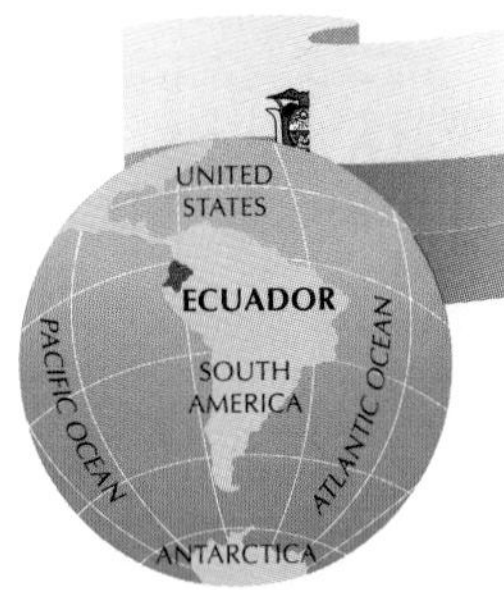

The importance and use of nonverbal gestures vary from country to country. Visitors to Ecuador, for instance, are advised to avoid nodding or shaking their heads to indicate "yes" or "no." Ecuadorian custom is to communicate verbally when a "yes" or "no" answer is required.

serving them and interpreting them correctly, managers can learn much about the meaning of a message and about the person sending that message. However, nonverbal cues do vary from culture to culture, and they are easy to misunderstand or misinterpret. In the United States and in some other Western cultures, nonverbal communication can convey the following meanings:

- *Gestures and postures.* Leaning forward and maintaining eye contact shows interest. Leaning toward another person or assuming a relaxed posture usually indicates liking for that person.[7] Body carriage can convey a person's status because more powerful people tend to relax their hands and legs, lean forward, and position their shoulders directly, whereas less powerful people cross their arms, lean back, and bow their heads more frequently.[8]
- *Facial expressions and eye movements.* Faces reveal both the type and the intensity of an emotion. A genuine smile indicates warmth or approval, but when forced, a smile can cause people to doubt the bearer's sincerity. Similarly, infrequent eye contact can often make a person appear "shifty" and untrustworthy. Of course, people sometimes use facial expression to portray an emotion they don't feel or to mask an emotion they do feel.
- *Vocal cues.* A person's voice can represent as much as 38 percent of the information received from the sender. Voice characteristics include volume (how loud the voice sounds), pitch (how high or low the voice sounds), tone (the modulation of the voice), rate (how fast or slow the speaker talks), enunciation (how clearly the speaker pronounces words), and expression (the inflection in the voice)—all of which can be used to emphasize points, maintain interest, and convey personality or behavior traits such as introversion, extraversion, anxiety, intelligence, and leadership potential. Voice characteristics can also influence the perception of a speaker's credibility. Too many pauses, repetitions, and meaningless words (such as *uh, you know*) can undermine any speaker's credibility.[9]
- *Touch.* Touching can have both positive and negative connotations. It can communicate caring and support as well as intimidation and intrusion.[10] Touch can suggest dominance, so a higher-status person might be more likely to touch a lower-status person than the other way around. However, touching can sometimes be interpreted as sexual harassment; thus, physical contact in certain organizational situations can be controversial.
- *Use of space.* How close people position themselves to each other during conversation can reveal their relationship or the nature of the message. Most people have a comfort zone around them (which varies from culture to culture), so people standing too close or too far away can make others feel uncomfortable. Space can also be used as a symbol of status; the environment surrounding a person (the size of an office and how it's decorated) can send messages about the occupant.
- *Use of time.* The way people use their time also sends messages. Although attitudes toward punctuality are cultural, consistent tardiness might be interpreted in the United States as meaning that the latecomer doesn't care much about the appointment or about the people involved. However, in some cultures, keeping people waiting is a sign of status.
- *Dress and personal grooming.* Appearance communicates style, personality, and status. In most organizations, a professional image is important, and adopting the style of the people one wants to impress goes a long way toward acceptance, even respect.

Placement services often offer counseling on how to communicate effectively with prospective employers. During her meeting with a placement service that specializes in finding jobs for high school students, this Texas teenager receives pointers on both nonverbal and verbal communication techniques, including tips on dressing for interviews, on appropriate facial expressions, and on writing letters and résumés.

Effective managers are aware that reading other peoples' nonverbal messages correctly allows them to interpret underlying attitudes and intentions so that they can respond appropriately.[11] Managers who are good communicators also understand how careful they must be to avoid sending nonverbal signals that conflict with or distract from the messages they are trying to get across (see Exhibit 17.2). For example, managers emphasizing teamwork and togetherness belie that message by using private dining rooms and heated garages when employees must eat in the cafeteria and park in outdoor lots several blocks from the office. When Union Carbide restructured its class-defining headquarters (where each rank had its own offices, furniture, and even ashtrays) to create an environment of equality (with similar offices, no executive parking, and no executive dining room), employee productivity and satisfaction increased substantially.[12]

Verbal Communication

Verbal communication expresses information through the use of language, which is composed of words and grammar. To create a thought, words are arranged according to the rules of grammar so that the various parts of speech are in the proper sequence. Then the message is communicated either in oral form or written form.

verbal communication The expression of information through language, using words and grammar

Oral Communication **Oral communication** expresses ideas through the spoken word. Managers communicate with colleagues and employees using such oral media as face-to-face conversations, telephone calls (including messages left on answering machines), private meetings, group meetings, teleconferencing (the use of telephone equipment to allow people in differing locations to take part in

oral communication The expression of ideas through the spoken word

EXHIBIT 17.2 Negative Nonverbal Cues for Managers to Avoid

Managers who send signals like these are perceived as unapproachable, and they rarely have the trust and support of their employees.

Manager's Behavior	Signal Received	Receiver's Reaction
Looking away when talking to employee	I do not have this person's undivided attention.	Believes manager is too busy to listen or simply doesn't care.
Failing to acknowledge greeting from fellow employee	This person is unfriendly.	Believes manager is unapproachable.
Ominous glaring	This person is angry.	Experiences reciprocal anger or fear, depending on who is sending the signal.
Rolling of the eyes	I am not being taken seriously.	Believes manager thinks he or she is smarter or better.
Deep sighing	This person is disgusted or displeased.	Thinks, "My opinions do not count. I must be stupid or boring to this person."
Heavy breathing	This person is angry or under heavy stress.	Avoids person at all costs.
Not maintaining eye contact	I should be suspicious or uncertain about this person.	Wonders what manager has to hide.
Crossing arms and leaning away	This person is apathetic and closed-minded.	Thinks, "This person has already made up his or her mind; my opinions are not important."
Peering over glasses	This person is skeptical or distrustful.	Assumes manager does not believe what person is saying.
Continuing to read report while employee is speaking	I do not have this person's undivided interest.	Thinks, "My opinions are not important enough to get the manager's undivided attention."

the discussion), and videoconferencing (the use of voice and video transmission to allow people in various locations to take part in the discussion). Oral communication is generally easier and more efficient than written communication. It allows the audience to discern added meaning through nonverbal cues, and it allows for immediate feedback. Managers tend to rely more heavily on oral than on written communication for sharing information on a day-to-day basis, although they generally put important messages in writing.[13] A major limitation of oral communication is that, even though it provides a personal and dynamic form of expression, its transitory nature makes it subject to misinterpretation and misremembering.[14]

written communication The expression of ideas through words that are meant to be read

Written Communication **Written communication** expresses ideas through words that are meant to be read. Managers use such written media as memos, letters, reports, electronic mail (messages conveyed via computer network), and facsimile machines (which transmit an exact duplicate of any written communication) to communicate with employees and colleagues. Written communication allows people to absorb information at their own speed and to review any parts that may be difficult. Even though it lacks nonverbal cues and any chance for immediate feedback, written communication has the advantages of stability, permanence, and formality.[15]

In a recent nationwide survey, executives rated writing skills high in terms of their importance to productivity and career advancement. Yet 79 percent of the executives surveyed said that writing was one of the most neglected skills in business. Poor writing ability has a negative impact on an organization's effectiveness. Consider collective bargaining agreements between labor and management. These documents have traditionally been extremely difficult to read and nearly impossible for most employees to understand, which creates apprehension and distrust among employees, further antagonizing what may already be an adversarial relationship with management.[16] In an attempt to clarify technical subjects and to make complex material easier to understand, more approachable, and less intimidating, some Japanese companies have begun using comics. A four-volume primer on economics, *A Cartoon Introduction to the Japanese Economy*, has been issued (1.8 million copies sold), and Honda published a comic version of its corporate history for job-seeking graduates (see Exhibit 17.3).

Electronic Communication Technology is changing the way people communicate in organizations. The latest developments have opened up even more options for

EXHIBIT 17.3

Comics as Written Communication

Comics turn what can be dry, technical subjects into lively and readable stories. Some Japanese companies, including Honda, have used comics to communicate with prospective employees and other stakeholders. Honda published its company history in comic form as part of its recruitment drive to attract high school and college students who were starting to look for jobs.

managers to communicate effectively using both oral and written media. Traditional methods of face-to-face conversations, group meetings, telephone calls, and written correspondence are now supplemented by the many forms of **electronic communication:** computer modems, facsimile machines (popularly known as fax machines), voice mail, electronic mail, teleconferencing, videocassettes, private television networks, and other advanced techniques. In fact, Japan has earmarked telecommunications as the key strategic industry for the twenty-first century.[17]

electronic communication The transmission of information using advanced techniques such as computer modems, facsimile machines, voice mail, electronic mail, teleconferencing, videocassettes, and private television networks

These communication techniques have several advantages. A greater volume of information can be accumulated and transmitted through computer-based systems. Information can be sent faster and to more people through faxes and electronic mail. Voice mail cuts down on the time spent placing and returning telephone calls. Teleconferencing and private television networks can bring people in many locations together without travel costs and time.

For instance, Federal Express uses its private network to broadcast to its 800 installations daily weather, air-traffic updates, and news of any delivery problems that may have arisen the night before. Local buyers for J.C. Penney now select most of their merchandise by viewing internal video broadcasts rather than traveling to headquarters, which gives them a longer lead time for placing orders and allows them to take advantage of fast-breaking consumer trends. Merrill Lynch uses its private television network to broadcast its weekly show "Action Line," which features employees talking about how they have succeeded in selling particular products; it also allows those employees to take questions from colleagues around the country.[18]

Personnel in the Boston headquarters of Fidelity Investments use electronic communication to stay in touch with colleagues throughout the country without the expense or inconvenience of travel. These Boston-based managers are using teleconferencing via a video hookup to meet with managers in Dallas. They can also display written information *(see the right-hand monitor)* simultaneously in both offices.

Even with all its advantages, however, electronic communication is not without its limitations. The speed and efficiency of this communication method makes it easy to send unnecessary information, and the accessibility of such technology allows both managers and employees to grow careless about the quality of the information they send. Pertinent information and high-quality messages come from human beings, not from the machines they have access to. Thus, in addition to understanding the types of communication and the communication media that are available, effective managers strive to understand the communication process.

The Process of Communication

Whether nonverbal, oral, or written, communication is not a single act but a dynamic process. Managers may communicate one-on-one or in a group, but the communication process is the same. The dynamics are complex, but the process of communication may be thought of as being circular and including five phases (see Exhibit 17.4):

1. *The sender has an idea.* One person conceives an idea and wants to share it.
2. *The idea becomes a message.* A **message** is a symbolic representation of the idea the sender wants to communicate.[19] The process of putting the message into a form the receiver will understand is called **encoding:** the sender decides on the message's form (word, facial expression, gesture), length, organization, tone, and style—all of which depend on the idea to be transmitted, the audience to be reached, and the sender's personal style or mood. Then the sender chooses verbal and nonverbal symbols that best present the content.[20]

message The symbolic representation of an idea the sender wants to communicate

encoding The process of putting an idea into a message form that the receiver will understand

EXHIBIT 17.4

The Communication Process

An analysis of the various components in the communication process can help managers become aware of where communication breakdowns can occur.

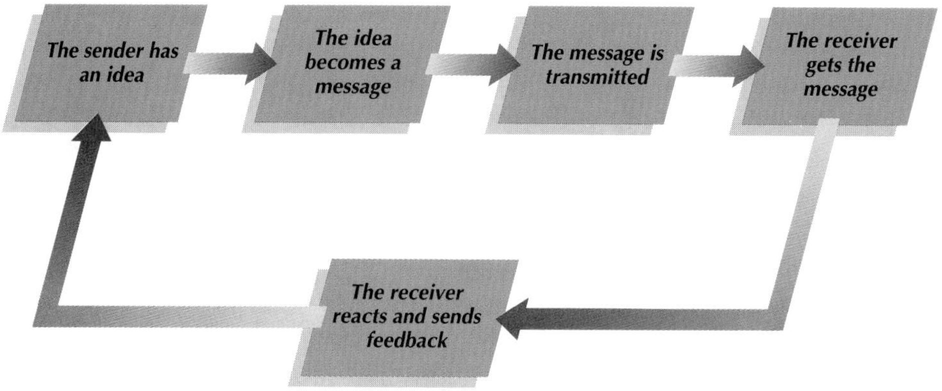

The sender has an idea → The idea becomes a message → The message is transmitted → The receiver gets the message → The receiver reacts and sends feedback → (back to) The sender has an idea

channel The means of transferring a message from the sender to the receiver

3. *The message is transmitted to the receiver.* The transmission **channel** is the means of transferring the message from the sender to the receiver. The choice of channel depends on the organizational structures available, and the choice of medium can be anything from traditional face-to-face conversations, telephone calls, and letters to the more modern methods of electronic communication. The sender adds meaning to the message by the choice of channel and medium; some channels and media communicate formality, others may indicate bad news, and still others may signal urgency.[21]
4. *The receiver gets the message.* The receiver must physically receive the message (if nonverbal, the message must be observed; if oral, the message must be heard; if written, the message must be read). Then the receiver must interpret the message, a process known as **decoding.** If all goes well, the receiver assigns a meaning to the words that matches the meaning the sender intended and then responds in the desired way.[22]
5. *The receiver gives feedback to the sender.* **Feedback** is a response from the receiver that informs the sender how the message is being interpreted and how the communication is being received in general. Senders use this feedback to verify similarities and differences in meaning and to adjust their message strategies to clarify the communication.[23]

decoding The process of interpreting a message to arrive at the sender's meaning

feedback A response from the receiver that cues the sender as to how the message is being interpreted and how the communication is being received in general

When communication is one-way, it doesn't allow for feedback. A speech, an advertisement, and a policy manual can be examples of one-way communication if the speaker doesn't allow the audience to ask questions, if the advertisement doesn't contain a toll-free number or an address for requesting more information, and if the policy manual is not accompanied by a questionnaire soliciting employee reactions. The danger of one-way communication is that without the benefit of feedback, the sender has no way of knowing whether the receiver understands the intended meaning.

In two-way communication, the sender explicitly seeks feedback. Managers who listen to feedback from employees, customers, suppliers, and other important groups can gain valuable information that will enhance their decision making. Moreover, they can elicit cooperation, communicate respect for the perspective of others, and use the feedback to improve their messages.

Ronald W. Watkins, president and CEO of Nebraska Public Power District, uses customer and employee surveys to get needed feedback. Says Watkins, "As I go out and meet with employee groups, I really encourage two-way conversation—not just me talking to them but also them talking to me." Watkins believes that managers who sit in their offices and carefully plan goals and strategies are wasting their time if they can't communicate those ideas and get feedback from all their employees.[24]

Beatrice A. Fitzpatrick, founder and CEO of the not-for-profit American Woman's Economic Development Corporation in New York, uses two-way communication extensively as she trains and counsels women entrepreneurs. In one-on-one discussions and in group meetings, Fitzpatrick actively seeks feedback to determine whether the meaning of her message has been received as it was intended.

COMMUNICATION IN THE ORGANIZATION

Managing communication in an organization requires more than an understanding of the communication process. Managers must be effective communicators themselves, and they must also encourage employees to communicate effectively. Moreover, they should consider the amount of information to be communicated, the number of people who need to communicate with one another, and the complexity of communication patterns in an organization.

Patterns of Communication

Organizational communication can take several forms. It may be one-on-one with another individual, or it may take place in a larger group. Organizational communication may be confined to members of the organization, or it may be directed to individuals or groups outside the company.

Interpersonal Communication

Interpersonal communication takes place between two people, enabling individuals to establish and maintain relationships and to coordinate decisions and activities. Managers spend between one-third and two-thirds of their time communicating with employees, and the dominant medium of interaction is face-to-face discussion. The relationship between employees and their managers presents one of the most important communication opportunities in the organization. This relationship influences how employees identify with the organization and how satisfied they are with their jobs. Thus the employee-manager relationship is strongly related to job performance, absenteeism, turnover, and the tendency to unionize.[25]

Feelings of discomfort and defensiveness can result from interpersonal communication when either the content of the message or the way the message is presented makes people feel they are being judged, manipulated, tricked, lectured, treated impersonally, or treated as inferior. So to be effective, managers must be sure their communication is objective (rather than evaluative), focuses on working together to solve problems or achieve goals, is an honest expression of their attitudes (rather than an attempt to manipulate), reflects the belief that employees are capable and competent, and expresses the appropriate degree of approachability (openness to questioning). This kind of supportive communication encourages employee trust.[26]

Interpersonal communication is effective when it contributes to personal insight and when it helps employees communicate more effectively in the future. Effective communication provides both managers and employees with information about what is expected of them and about their success in meeting those expectations.[27] To accomplish such supportive communication, effective managers tend to ask or persuade (rather than tell or demand). They are also sensitive to their employees' feelings and needs, and they tend to share information by giving advance notice of changes and by explaining the reasons for policies and regulations.[28]

For example, Duke Power Company emphasizes the importance of good interpersonal communication throughout the organization. The company trains both managers and employees in supportive communication through a program that lets participants observe and role-play effective interpersonal communication in situations that could occur in the workplace. This lets the Duke Power people to see good interpersonal communication in action and to improve their own communication skills.[29]

Group Communication

Communication roles in organizational groups are related to the three types of group roles: (1) task roles (focusing on group goals), (2) group building and maintenance roles (promoting social support), and (3) individual roles (supporting individual goals that may or may not coincide with group goals). Although most members engage in a variety of roles, effective managers analyze the group's needs and then use communication to help members establish the roles that will achieve group goals (see Chapter 16). Managers can support effective group communication through these activities:

- Preparing for group participation.
- Valuing diverse opinions and people.
- Contributing ideas and seeking information.
- Stressing group productivity.
- Avoiding individual roles that serve only their own self-interests.
- Recognizing and managing conflict.
- Supporting leadership.
- Building group pride.
- Producing results (by taking responsibility for group performance).[30]

As organizational groups pursue their goals, they generally face a series of decisions. Groups engage in complex interactive processes when making decisions, but whether they reach a decision by following logical steps, by passing through descriptive phases, by brainstorming, or by haphazard discussion, leadership in communication plays an important role in the process. Effective leaders (whether managers or employee facilitators) are the links among groups and among organizational units, tying them together by communicating information back and forth to various members. Leaders develop relationships with group members to help gather this information and to elicit member cooperation. Moreover, leaders gather and provide information to transform potentially destructive conflicts into opportunities for improving organizational relationships and for achieving organizational goals. Thus, leaders and groups can use communication to achieve information exchange and to manage conflict. To use communication effectively, group leaders and members must also support productive communication networks.[31]

Communication Networks

communication network The pattern of communication within a group and among groups

A **communication network** is the pattern of communication within a group and among groups. Organizations can use such networks to direct information to those who need it and to withhold it from those who don't (see Exhibit 17.5).[32] The flow of information through these structures affects the efficiency and effectiveness of the group's performance.

Centralized networks such as the wheel, the Y, and the chain funnel information to and through a key individual. These patterns work best in groups that

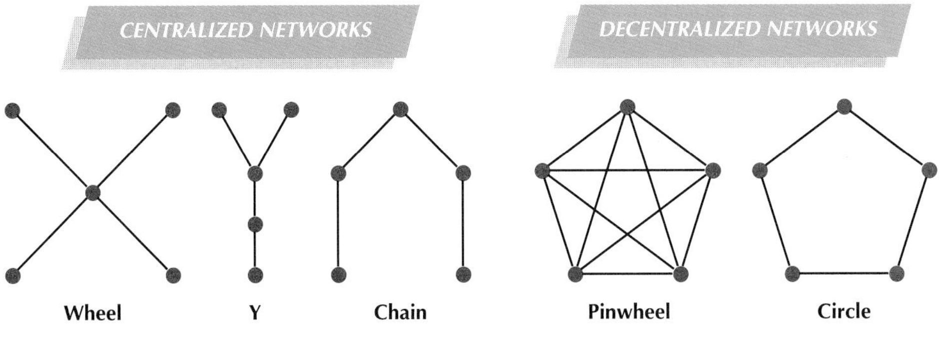

EXHIBIT 17.5
Communication Networks

In these group communication networks, dots represent an individual or work unit, and lines indicate the flow of information. Decentralized networks such as the pinwheel and the circle perform better when the decision to be made is complex and nonroutine. Centralized networks such as the wheel, the Y, and the chain are more efficient in solving routine problems.

must solve simple, routine problems quickly and efficiently. Centralized networks clearly define the function of the leader and of each member, and because of this clarity, they may help control costs. However, managers must be aware that members of centralized networks are often dissatisfied: peripheral members can feel uninvolved in the process, and central members can become overloaded with information or overburdened with feeling responsible for the group's success or failure. Moreover, centralized networks are inflexible, so they are more difficult to adapt to changing task requirements, and they can stifle creativity.

Decentralized networks such as the pinwheel or the circle tend to work best in groups that must solve complex, nonroutine problems. Decentralization allows all members to share their expertise, which can foster creativity and innovation. Accuracy may be enhanced in decentralized structures because members can correct the errors of other members. Moreover, members generally feel more satisfied when they participate.

Japanese automakers operating plants in the United States rely on decentralized communication. Honda, Toyota, and Nissan production employees actively participate in group decision making (especially on such issues as rotating jobs and scheduling overtime). This participative and egalitarian atmosphere is maintained with decentralized communication networks, which reinforce cooperation between production employees and managers.[33]

Internal Communication

internal communication The exchange of messages among organization members

Internal communication is the exchange of messages among organization members. It is the means of assigning tasks, coordinating activities, and accomplishing goals.[34] In the past, managers strove to limit employees' access to organizational information. But today, open internal communication is seen as the way to release creativity within an organization. Managers are using it to build trust, respect, and cohesiveness among employees. They turn to internal communication to discover and then develop the best ideas, and effective managers use it to instill pride in employees and to strengthen their commitment to the organization.[35]

For example, the various divisions of Massachusetts Mutual Life Insurance (Mass Mutual) issue weekly newspapers to share information about the company's accomplishments, to trumpet new ideas, and to disseminate other news. This is one way a large company can keep in touch with employees in far-flung locations. But Mass Mutual also uses two-way communication to get feedback from employees about a variety of issues, including human resource issues. When the company was considering changes to its group health plan, managers

Improved internal communication helped Kodak boost productivity and quality in the precision component manufacturing division, where x-ray film products are made. Rather than work as individuals on isolated tasks, assembly-line employees work as a team, pooling problem-solving ideas and discussing quality issues that affect output. Now, one shift can produce as much as three shifts formerly produced.

asked 50 employees drawn from throughout the company to react to the planned changes, and they later asked for ideas about establishing a group dental plan. This internal communication helped managers understand their employees' needs and also enabled the participants to feel satisfied with their involvement.[36]

Internal communication is the flow of information that can help a manager identify and attack problems quickly.[37] To be effective, managers must make sure that internal communication flows freely, both through the organization's formal channels—up and down the hierarchy (vertical) as well as across and within departments (horizontal)—and through its informal channels.

Formal Channels

formal communication A flow of information that is dictated by the organization's official structure

Every organization has a **formal communication** system in which the flow of information is dictated by the official organization structure. Formal channels follow the organization's arrangement of the various levels, divisions, departments, and job responsibilities.[38] In an organization chart, the lines of authority that link the chain of command are the formal channels managers and employees use to transmit official information. Formal communications can take many forms, including phone calls, memos, reports, staff meetings, department meetings, seminars, company newsletters, and official notices.[39] As suggested by the layout of traditional organization charts, the flow of formal communication may be either vertical (up and down) or horizontal (across and within departments).

vertical communication A flow of information up and down the organization's hierarchy

Vertical Communication **Vertical communication** is the flow of information up and down the organizational hierarchy. Vertical communication supports all managerial functions, and it follows the chain of command, connecting all levels in the hierarchy and enabling managers and employees to share information from bottom to top for better decision making. Effective vertical communication provides people on lower levels with information about plans, schedules, policies, and procedures to help them accomplish their work, and it provides upper-level management with feedback to determine the responses to messages sent downward. However, vertical communication can be distorted by the number of organizational levels, the rigid enforcement of status differences, and delays in transmitting information between levels.[40]

Downward communication is the flow of information from higher to lower levels in the organizational hierarchy. Managers use it to accomplish a variety of key organizational functions:

downward communication A flow of information from higher to lower levels in the organization's hierarchy

- *To clarify and build support for the organization's mission.* Explaining goals, strategies, and plans helps build employee loyalty, cohesiveness, and performance.
- *To instruct employees.* Identifying what needs to be done and outlining the options for completing these tasks helps employees focus on the activities necessary for high performance.
- *To provide job rationale.* Explaining how specific jobs relate to other tasks in the organization helps employees coordinate activities to achieve organizational goals.
- *To explain policies and practices.* Explaining rules, procedures, and schedules provides employees with a basis for decision making and planning.
- *To provide feedback.* Informing employees about how well they are performing improves individual and organizational efficiency and effectiveness.
- *To share information about the organization's health and about key elements in the external environment.* Informing employees about the state of the company and about market conditions that might affect their work or their jobs helps build commitment and team spirit.[41]

For instance, at Kentucky's Winchester Farms Dairy, personnel manager Gerry Boocock believes that employees are committed to company goals because managers keep them informed about conditions inside and outside the company. When Winchester experienced a severe water shortage a few years ago, management urged employees to conserve water to help both the city and the company. Their response was wholehearted cooperation, and they cut the company's water usage by 30,000 gallons in the first month.[42]

Upward communication is the flow of information from lower to higher levels in the organization. Managers encourage upward communication to perform these important functions:

upward communication A flow of information from lower to higher levels in the organization's hierarchy

- *To gather valuable information.* Tapping into the knowledge of employees (who are often the best source of information about problems and issues in the organization's operation) helps managers make better decisions.
- *To find out when employees are ready for information from management.* Timing downward messages correctly can make a difference in how employees accept them.
- *To give employees the opportunity to air grievances.* Knowing what bothers employees allows managers to take steps to correct problems.
- *To provide employees the opportunity to ask questions.* Having access to employee questions and ideas helps managers improve operations and exploit business opportunities.
- *To get feedback.* Soliciting employee feedback helps managers know whether their downward messages have been effective.
- *To get information about work problems.* Sharing information with managers helps employees reduce conflict, allows managers to correct problems quickly, and cements employee feelings of belonging.[43]

EXHIBIT 17.6

Directions of Communication in a Typical Organization

Formal communication can flow upward, downward, and horizontally in an organization.

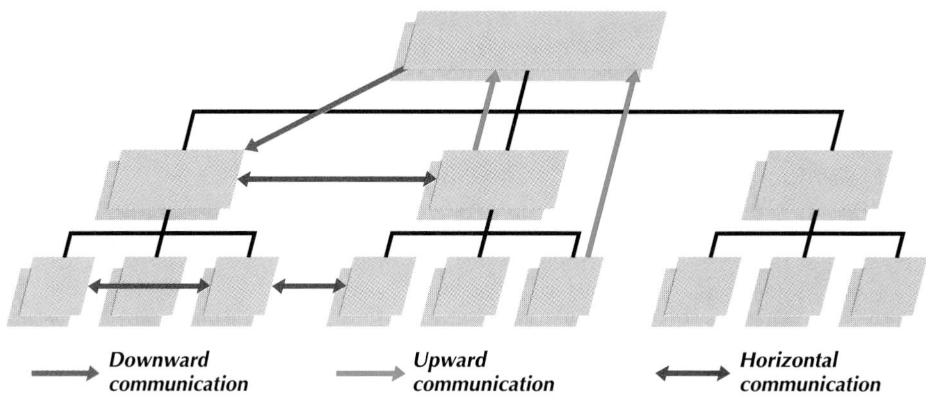

James A. Perkins, senior vice president for personnel at Federal Express, believes that treating employees fairly leads to greater productivity and profit for the organization, and he encourages upward communication to ensure equitable treatment. He pioneered a five-step employee complaint and grievance process that allows employees to protest what they consider to be unfair treatment on the job. Perkins also conducts a series of internal employee surveys to ask employees whether they believe they are being treated fairly by their supervisors and whether they feel they are being adequately compensated.[44]

Effective managers are receptive to open and honest upward communication, and they plan workable upward communication programs that operate continuously. Through routine channels, they elicit feedback from employees who have firsthand knowledge of the organization's operation, and they entertain any and all ideas with receptivity and sensitivity. They listen well, and they use the knowledge they gain to direct the organization's activities toward high performance.[45]

horizontal communication A flow of information across departmental boundaries, either laterally or diagonally

Horizontal Communication **Horizontal communication** is the flow of information across departmental boundaries, either laterally or diagonally (see Exhibit 17.6). Managers themselves use and encourage their employees to use horizontal communication to perform these vital functions:

- *To coordinate activities.* Coordinating work assignments among departments or within groups helps managers and employees accomplish specific tasks and achieve interdependent goals.
- *To share information.* Exchanging information about plans and activities among departments or within a department allows employees and managers to benefit from the ideas of more than just one person.
- *To solve problems.* Cooperating with other departments or with members of a group reduces costs, prevents overlapping work tasks, and reduces difficulties in arriving at solutions.
- *To promote understanding.* Encouraging common understanding across departments and groups helps employees and managers focus on specific tasks without distractions.
- *To minimize destructive conflict.* Communicating horizontally is often the best way to resolve disagreements and to coordinate priorities.
- *To develop interpersonal support.* Strengthening interpersonal relationships helps managers and employees increase rapport and cohesiveness.[46]

Eugene A. De Fouw systematizes horizontal communication at Alofs Manufacturing Company, where he is president. The company makes and assembles automotive parts and other metal products. De Fouw wants his employees to understand how communication and interrelationships between departments contribute to high quality. Thus, employees in the factory use a work-order sheet to record comments about a task, both while in progress and after completion. Inspection employees add their comments, and members of all departments ultimately review the work-order sheets, noting what improvements can be made based on the critiques of others.[47]

Informal Channels

Informal communication is the flow of information without regard for the formal organizational structures, hierarchical levels, or reporting relationships. Informal communication structures have no set direction, and they evolve from employees' interpersonal and social interactions. Compared to formal channels, informal channels are apparently less susceptible to distortion, and research shows that they are generally accurate more than 75 percent of the time. Informal channels are shorter than formal ones, they allow for more feedback opportunities, they have fewer status discrepancies among the communicators (making requests for feedback less risky), and they allow organization members to compare the same information from several sources.[48]

informal communication A flow of information without regard for organizational structure, hierarchical levels, or reporting relationships

Informal communication moves primarily through word-of-mouth, and one common form is the **grapevine**, an informal channel of person-to-person communication that is not officially sanctioned by the organization. Grapevines usually follow one of four structures (see Exhibit 17.7). In the single-strand chain, each person passes the information on to one other person. The longer this chain, the more the information is prone to distortion. The gossip chain moves information slowly because it depends on one person telling everyone else. The probability chain has no definite pattern of communication; one person passes along information at random, and receivers in turn pass it randomly to others—so some people hear the information, and others do not. In the most predominant pattern, the cluster chain, information is passed along selectively. One employee passes information to co-workers, who pass it along to other co-workers. In this grapevine structure, people relay information to those with whom they feel most comfortable.[49]

grapevine An informal interpersonal channel of information not officially sanctioned by the organization

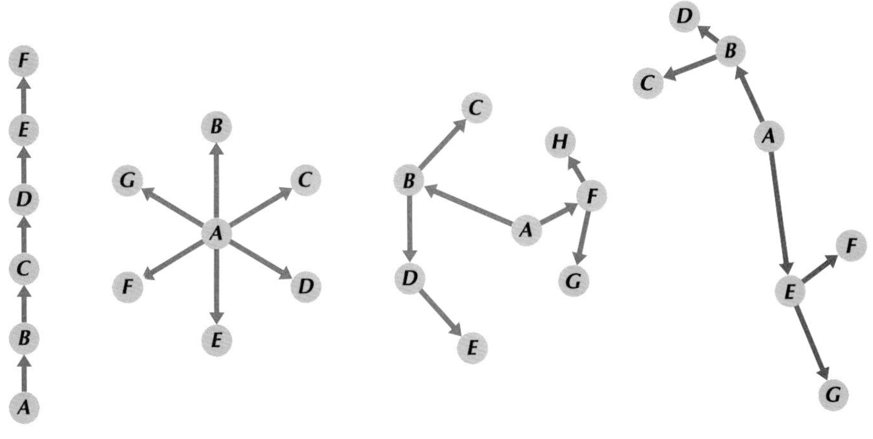

EXHIBIT 17.7

Types of Grapevine Structures

Grapevines most commonly form one of four structures of informal communication.

Consider how the informal communication structure at Ballard Medical Products helps the company thrive in the competitive hospital-supply industry. Continuous innovation and a steady flow of new products keeps Ballard competitive, and the catalyst for these new ideas can be traced directly to the company's grapevine, which carries information about product design, marketing, sales, service, refinement, and other aspects of the company's operations. The easy communication between sales representatives in the field and product designers at the plant enables the company to act immediately on suggestions or problems that come directly from customers, resulting in higher customer satisfaction. Moreover, new products are developed quickly because the informal communication channels at Ballard circumvent all the time-consuming coordinating activities that other companies have to contend with, such as review committees and project reports.[50]

When managers and employees don't receive what they consider to be full information from formal channels, they seek it from informal sources. The more the formal communication system withholds relevant information from employees, the more employees seek to develop informal communication networks, which can often work against the purposes of the formal organization.[51] However, efforts to get rid of the grapevine often make it even more powerful. As informal communication is restricted, the need for relevant information increases. Grapevines flourish in climates of high uncertainty, when information from formal channels is especially scarce.[52]

However, when grapevines pass inaccurate or unconfirmed information, especially about rumored layoffs or other stressful events, employees who cannot verify the truth may feel demoralized. Some companies have set up formal communication channels to defuse the anxiety caused by grapevine rumors. For example, Mass Mutual has installed a telephone line known as the "rumor hot line." Employees can call anonymously to ask whether a rumor is factual, and they are assured that if the person handling the call does not know whether a rumor is true, it will be verified within 24 hours. Instead of fighting the grapevine, effective managers make it work for them. Employees consider the grapevine a highly credible source, so managers should not ignore the information that flows through it. The grapevine can provide a wealth of information about employee attitudes, performance, and morale. Managers can use it to unofficially propose new ideas and monitor employees' reaction to them. The responses give clues to how the proposal could be revised for better acceptance.[53]

External Communication

external communication A flow of information between the organization and outside individuals or groups

External communication is the exchange of information between the organization and outside individuals or groups. Such external networks include customers, suppliers, distributors, government organizations, the media, financial organizations, the community, and other groups that can have significant influence on the organization. Messages are sent outside to influence the way external groups perceive and react to the organization. At the same time, messages received from the outside provide the organization with information about how well current activities are meeting the needs of external stakeholders.[54]

Rosemary B. Greco, president of Fidelity Bank in Philadelphia, takes external messages seriously and has devoted herself to handling complaints and other inquiries. She reads all complaint letters and lets customers know that management is personally involved with their problems. Her hard work has paid off. In just two years, Fidelity customers who say they are satisfied or highly satisfied with the bank's service jumped from 57 percent to 87 percent.[55]

To improve external communications, managers can design formal organization structures and assign representatives or formal contacts, such as marketers, public relations experts, and crisis teams, to communicate with external stakeholders. Also valuable to the organization are the informal contacts managers establish as they network with colleagues and others outside the company.

Formal Contacts

Organizations initiate a variety of formal contacts with stakeholders. Marketing managers send messages to customers, identifying and positioning products through face-to-face or telephone conversations, direct-mail, television and radio commercials, newspaper and magazine ads, product brochures, and mail-order catalogs. They also solicit messages from customers through surveys and research to develop products that meet customers' needs. This exchange of information between marketers and outside stakeholders is crucial for developing organizational strategies and for implementing them to achieve goals.[56]

Public relations is the ongoing management of communications related to the organization's reputation with employees, customers, shareholders, government agencies, and the general public. Through external communication, public relations people (1) create and maintain organizational identity, (2) identify potential threats to the organization and enlist the aid of external agents to develop plans for avoiding those threats, and (3) enhance organizational effectiveness by tracking trends and by identifying and creating markets for organizational products.[57]

Crisis communication managers plan for and respond to serious problems and disasters. Well-publicized crises in the last decade (Johnson & Johnson's cyanide-laced Tylenol capsules; Union Carbide's gas leak in Bhopal, India; and the Exxon *Valdez* oil spill) illustrate how these events and the way they were handled have had long-lasting effects on public perception of the organizations involved. The challenge to managers in such situations is twofold: (1) managing the crisis itself and (2) managing the external communication involved in the crisis.

Effective crisis communication involves two stages: preparation before the crisis occurs and decisive action during the crisis. Successful crisis communication must be planned, and the plan must be regularly updated and carefully tested to make sure it will work under actual conditions. The plan should consider a number of possible events, ranging from industrial accidents and major product defects to terrorism and embezzlement.[58] Ketchum Public Relations recommends using a message action plan that covers target audiences, message elements, communication method, responsibilities, and time and schedule commitments in a single, easy-to-read document that shows at a glance what must be accomplished, how, when, and by whom.[59]

During the crisis, managers must act quickly to take charge of the news flow; the organization's immediate and appropriate response can make or break how it is perceived. A spokesperson should make a statement right away, or at least within a few hours, and the CEO usually takes charge and personally manages the crisis. This sends the clear message that the organization considers the crisis a serious concern. The spokesperson should share as much information as possible with everyone involved, should be honest about the situation, and should choose language that explains the situation (rather than inflaming it).

MANAGERIAL DECISION MAKING

Turning Disaster into Public Support through External Communication

It's hard to imagine that the employees of Solid State Circuits were ever at odds with the residents of South Golden Road in Springfield, Missouri. The two groups play softball and have picnics together. They hold twice-a-year Red Cross blood drives. The neighborhood association hosts its annual holiday social in the Solid State cafeteria, and it holds its giant rummage sale in the company's parking lot.

But the relationship between Solid State and South Golden residents was not always so amicable. From the moment Solid State moved into the neighborhood, residents made it clear that they did not want the plant next to their homes. As one resident put it, "Residential neighborhoods and industry are like oil and water, they don't really mix!" Another said, "I don't care for chemicals in my neighborhood or near my family!"

As if Solid State didn't have enough problems, only six months after the company moved into the area, one of the storage tanks at the plant began leaking chlorine. When attempts to stop the leak failed, firefighters were called in and police evacuated 3,000 residents from their homes in the surrounding neighborhood. All of this, along with the fear, anger, and frustration felt by the residents, was recorded by the local television stations and appeared on the evening news. The reports did little to help Solid State's image. They mentioned delayed evacuations, insufficient protective gear for the firefighters (resulting in minor chemical burns), and chlorine vapors (which damaged clothing and may have killed a pet dog). Even though no residents were injured, some began to talk about getting compensation for their inconvenience and for the possible decline in their property values. A new neighborhood homeowners' association was formed to file suit if local property values declined.

Solid State could have faced eternal hostility from its residential neighbors, had it not been for a companywide community relations campaign that the company mobilized immediately after the leak. With director of human resources Bob Stephens in charge of the effort, which emphasized open and honest external communication, relations between the plant and the neighborhood began to improve within days as representatives from Solid State met with the neighborhood homeowners' association, listened to their concerns, and answered their questions. Questions that couldn't be answered immediately were recorded so that company representatives could respond to them at a later date.

A slow or inappropriate response to a crisis can hurt an organization's image. For example, Exxon's handling of the *Valdez* oil spill has been heavily criticized. Information from the company was sketchy, scarce, and contradictory early in the crisis. Chairman Lawrence G. Rawl did not comment for six days, and when he finally did, he seemed defensive. He blamed the Coast Guard and Alaska officials for the slow cleanup, and he didn't visit the spill site until three weeks after the spill.[60]

In contrast, when one million gallons of diesel fuel spilled into the Monongahela River from one of Ashland Oil's storage tanks, CEO John R. Hall's response won praise. As soon as he realized that the situation was critical, he flew to the disaster scene to personally take responsibility. Against the advice of his lawyers, he apologized and admitted that the company had made some mistakes. Hall offered to pay for the damage, he pledged to support an independent investigation of what really happened, and he made himself available for questions.[61]

Informal Contacts

All employees and managers are informal conduits for communicating with individuals and groups outside the organization. Through networking, managers have a special reliance on informal contacts with outsiders to exchange information that might be useful to their organizations. Managers obtain relevant and needed information from contacts such as customers, suppliers, vendors, professional organizations, and community service organizations.

To keep the entire community informed, Solid State's Bob Stephens and the neighborhood association's president Chuck Puskus discussed the issues. Stephens provided detailed, step-by-step information on what had happened and what had been done to correct the situation. He pointed out that the company was providing the fire department with four "moon suits" for greater protection should any future chemical problems occur. He explained that Solid State would replace the one-ton chlorine tanks with several smaller ones. To emphasize Solid State's commitment to the residents' safety, he explained how the company had gone beyond legal requirements to voluntarily contact the Department of Labor and ask that a Safety and Industrial Hygienist independently examine the plant on a consulting basis. Later on, Solid State invited residents to tour the facility.

These steps and the company's continuing emphasis on communication and good community relations have cultivated an atmosphere of close cooperation and involvement between the plant and the neighborhood. Each quarter, members of the environmental concerns committee of the homeowners' association meet with the company's human resources director and the safety manager to discuss issues that are important to the property owners. The company's technical experts (such as its chemical engineers and quality managers) often join the meetings to answer questions from association members. The meetings allow Solid State to supply information about what the company is doing and to build rapport with the residents.

Solid State intends never to be in a reactive situation again. At least one person on each shift at the plant goes through Red Cross disaster training. The company is also prepared to provide special emergency help to those people in the neighborhood who have been identified as being bedridden, needing wheelchairs, or having visual or hearing impairment.

Effective external communication and community relations helped Solid State turn disaster into strong local support. Chuck Puskus, initially one of the most vocal opponents of the plant, says, "It's hard to get mad at someone if they have opened their place to you or if you've been in their home, attended social gatherings with them, or played softball with them. It's hard to be hostile toward someone you know on a first-name basis."

Apply Your Knowledge

1. What elements in Solid State's external communication were most successful in turning around the community's attitude toward the company?
2. What could Solid State have done to prepare for a disaster before it actually occurred?

But the information exchanged with informal contacts isn't only one-way. Whenever managers encounter "outsiders," they represent their organization, whether giving speeches to community groups or to professional associations, whether talking sports with fellow tennis-club members or with vendors, whether handling complaints from customers or from competitors. Successful managers recognize the value of keeping in touch with the "real world." Thus Rubbermaid's chairman asks travelers in airports for ideas about new products, Hyatt Hotel executives serve as bellhops, and Disney managers all take their turn in character costumes at one of the theme parks.[62]

IMPROVING ORGANIZATIONAL COMMUNICATION

Noise is any interference in the communication process that distorts or obscures the meaning intended by the sender. Effective managers are concerned with reducing interference in physical transmissions (bad connections, poor acoustics, and illegible written copy), so they exercise as much control as they can over physical transmission links. They can do this by making sure that everyone can hear during a speech, for example, or by checking that a document's appearance doesn't detract from the message. But beyond purely physical problems, other barriers can block communication. Effective managers help their organizations decrease noise and improve communication by overcoming such barriers on both the interpersonal and organizational levels.

noise Any interference in the communication process that distorts the meaning intended by the sender

Interpersonal Barriers

Even though messages are intended to convey meaning, they don't really contain it. Meaning exists only in the minds of the sender and the receiver. To interpret the sender's meaning accurately, the receiver must understand the words, gestures, and other symbols a sender uses in a given situation.

Differences in Perception

perception The way individuals process information to comprehend the world around them

selective perception The process of focusing only on details that are pertinent to an individual's present circumstances and consistent with personal views and preferences

perceptual organization The process of organizing selected details into some meaningful order and filling in the gaps with assumptions

Perception is the way individuals process information to comprehend the world around them. Rarely will one person's perception of a situation be the same as another's; each person draws on a personal frame of reference that includes the experiences, values, and beliefs particular to that individual.[63] To create order out of the chaos that surrounds them, receivers pay attention to details that are pertinent to their present circumstances and consistent with their views and preferences, a process called **selective perception.** Then because they have elected to focus on only certain details, receivers use **perceptual organization** to arrange these details into meaningful order and to fill in any gaps with assumptions, based on logic, judgment, and experience (see Exhibit 17.8).[64] Overcoming perceptual barriers can be difficult, but effective managers are able to predict fairly accurately how their message will be received because they anticipate reactions and shape the message accordingly, constantly adjusting to correct any misunderstanding.

Incorrect Filtering

filtering The process of screening out or abbreviating information before passing a message to someone else

Filtering occurs when some information is screened out or abbreviated before a message is passed on to someone else. Organizational communication requires some filtering; individuals must interpret the messages they receive and send only what is necessary and relevant. However, the wrong kind of filtering can have negative effects. Employees may withhold information from managers in an attempt to please or to conceal unfavorable circumstances. Managers can overcome filtering by establishing more than one communication channel so that information can be verified through multiple sources, by eliminating intermediaries, and by condensing information to the bare essentials so that distortion-proof messages can be created.[65]

EXHIBIT 17.8

Selective Perception

Different people may perceive different images in this picture as a result of selective perception. Similarly, selective perception can cause people to disagree on what was said during a communication.

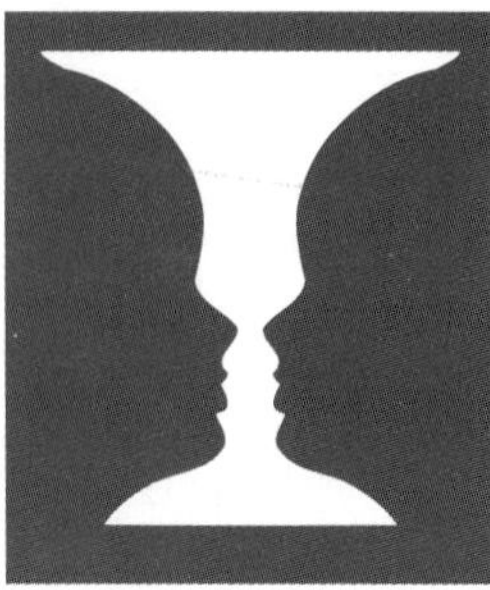

Language Problems

With its finite number of words, language is limited in its ability to accurately represent the unlimited shades of meaning and constantly changing events in the world. But more than that, word meaning (semantics) and term definition can vary from person to person and from department to department in an organization. Managers can increase the accuracy of information exchange by using language that describes rather than evaluates and by presenting observable facts, events, and circumstances. By using concrete language, managers can heighten the clarity of a message and reduce the distortion of meaning between the sender and the receiver.[66]

Managers who understand language are able to use it both skillfully and creatively. When Reatha Clark, executive director of the General Mills Foundation, was called on to raise funds for a Minneapolis day-care center, she toured the center. There she saw healthy babies (who responded to a finger placed in their hands by grasping it) and cocaine-addicted babies (who had no grasping response). In her appeal to the Business Economic Education Foundation, Clark wanted to communicate the profound needs of the children involved, so she painted a vivid picture of the healthy babies and of the unhealthy ones who "don't have a firm grasp on life." By urging the potential donors to "come to grips" with the situation, Clark got her message across clearly and urgently, and the day-care center received its grant.[67]

Poor Listening

Listening goes beyond the purely physical process of hearing and extends to the assignment of meaning, which must take place in order for any receiver to begin the decoding process. Too few people listen well. Immediately after hearing a 10-minute speech, people typically remember only half of what was said. Three days later, three-quarters of the message is gone.[68]

Effective managers practice active listening by verifying interpretations (which increases the accuracy of message reception), by empathizing with other people and viewing the world through their eyes, by resisting the impulse to jump to conclusions or make assumptions, and by paraphrasing what they have understood (to allow any inaccuracies to be corrected). They ask nonthreatening questions to clarify meaning, they listen without interrupting, and they don't respond until they have summarized the main points and evaluated the available facts and evidence.[69]

When Clinton Wharton, Jr., made major changes to improve the Teachers Insurance and Annuity Association–College Retirement Equities Fund, which is the largest private pension fund in the world, onlookers were stunned by the speed of the turnaround. Some say that Wharton's secret is listening. "He listens to people at every level of this organization," says one employee, "and based on what he hears, he mobilizes people to change." Wharton counsels managers to listen to find out what the problem is and then find out whether there's a better way of handling the situation. As a result of Wharton's emphasis on listening skills and two-way communication, the organization now receives higher marks on participant satisfaction surveys.[70]

Differing Emotional States

If certain words or subjects arouse strong feelings in a receiver, the rest of the message may not be heard through the barrier of emotion. Criticism, for example, can create enough emotion in the receiver to block any helpful suggestions or advice on how to improve performance. Wording criticism constructively is helpful, but emotions are unavoidable. Effective managers reduce the possibility of negative reactions by being alert to the greater potential for misunderstanding that accompanies emotional messages, and by avoiding attitudes, blame, and other subjective or vague concepts.[71]

People are more receptive when they are unemotional, relaxed, and attentive. That's why some organizations have hired humor consultants to bring levity to the workplace. Humor can be used to send messages that are socially risky, for example, testing responses through humor before openly opposing a co-worker or manager. Moreover, humor can enhance learning and retention. Humor relieves the stress that people feel when they are learning something new by making them more receptive and heightening their awareness.[72]

Cultural Diversity

Because people assign meaning to messages based on their backgrounds, cultural differences in both verbal and nonverbal symbols make it more difficult

Cultural diversity is a way of life for Hewlett-Packard. Although its headquarters is in Palo Alto, California, the firm operates internationally, and its 90,000 employees come from a variety of ethnic backgrounds. At the H-P plant in Penang, Malaysia, Malay employees *(center)* and Chinese employees work side by side; communication is critical if they are to work effectively with each other and with their managers.

to communicate successfully. Managers must deal with cultural diversity on several levels. If an organization has global interests, managers should learn how to conduct business abroad. Beyond the expected language differences, global managers also face cultural values, attitudes, and customs that are unfamiliar. They must study the cultures they come in contact with so they can improve communication and avoid mishaps.

For example, chipmaker Intel started an intercultural training program to reduce the decision-making time that was lost in miscommunication between its Japanese subsidiary and U.S. headquarters. Not only did the company cut down on decision time but it gained two other benefits from the program: Japanese staff members were assimilated more quickly into Intel's organizational culture, and the lower turnover rates cut personnel costs.[73]

Managers also face cultural differences at home. Employees who consider English a second language are increasingly shaping the U.S. work force.[74] Don Ackerman owns the Economy Color Card Company, a maker of swatch sample books that textile salespeople carry on sales calls, and he estimates that about 30 percent of his 900 employees speak little or no English. To recruit new employees, the company's director of human resources, Dot Mandl, runs ads in Ukrainian-, Russian-, German-, and Portuguese-language newspapers.[75]

To be successful communicators, managers must avoid projecting their own culture onto others and assuming that certain behaviors mean the same thing to everyone. **Stereotyping** is the attempt to neatly categorize individuals by trying to predict their behavior or character based on their membership in a particular class or group. However, such assumptions can be inaccurate and deceptively simple, placing limits on people in certain groups based on false or generally held assumptions. For example, a manager might wrongly assume that Korean employees will act the way Japanese employees do simply because they are both Asian.[76]

stereotyping The process of trying to categorize individuals by predicting their behavior or character according to their membership in a particular class or group

Inconsistent Nonverbal Cues

Because nonverbal cues communicate so much of the meaning and feeling derived from a message, cues that are inconsistent with the verbal message cause communication distortion. Effective managers are careful to avoid nonverbal cues that are inconsistent with the message they want to convey. Moreover, careful observation of how individuals in the organization tend to use language, facial expression, and body language can provide managers with clues to what these individuals mean when they send a message.

Organizational Barriers

Some characteristics of the organization itself can distort messages. When managers are aware of these barriers, they can redesign organizational structures, develop organizational procedures, and establish organizational goals to relieve distortion and promote effective communication.

information overload The condition that exists when message volume or rate exceeds the capacity of receivers to deal with it

Information Overload

The volume and rate of messages can exceed the capacity of receivers, causing **information overload.** Individuals facing overload cope with it in various ways: by ignoring some of the messages, by delaying responses to messages they deem unimportant, by answering only parts of some messages, by responding inaccurately to certain messages, by taking less time with each message, or by reacting only superficially to all messages.[77]

Managers can help overcome information overload by realizing that some information is not necessary (or is needed by only a few people) and by making information accessible through appropriate filing systems, distribution procedures, and information-handling equipment. Further, they can give information meaning rather than merely passing it on, and they can help employees set priorities to deal with the flow of information.[78]

For instance, the Workers' Compensation Board in Ontario, Canada, found itself drowning in a flood of paper. Its quarter of a million files on injured employees took up a mile and a half of shelf space, and it received another 20,000 pieces of mail every day. Computerizing the system to get rid of paper and to make information more accessible benefited the organization in two ways: it saved money by using fewer couriers, temporary clerks, and office supplies; and it allowed employees to spend more time serving their customers with faster claim handling.[79]

Message Complexity

When managers send messages, they are communicating both as individuals and as representatives of their organizations. Formulating business messages can sometimes be difficult, considering the adjustment of personal ideas and style to organizational standards. The complexity of messages can also be affected by the technical level of the material and the working conditions (such as time constraints and interruptions). To keep messages clear and easy to understand, managers must remember to create them carefully.[80]

Before starting, effective managers think clearly about the purpose of the message and about who will be receiving it. When creating the message, they guide receivers through it by telling them what to expect, by using language that is concrete and specific, and by sticking to the point. They connect new information to existing ideas by showing receivers how new information relates to familiar concepts, and they make sure to emphasize and review key points. Finally, effective managers ask for feedback so that they can clarify and improve their message.[81]

Message Competition

Managers are constantly faced with the problem of two or more messages competing for their attention. If someone is talking on the phone while reviewing a report, neither message gets the attention required for successful communication. If conversations or interviews are frequently interrupted, the noise distorts much of the message.

Effective managers try to eliminate potential sources of interference. Written documents should be visually appealing and easy to comprehend, and if possible, they should be delivered when the receiver has time to read them. Oral messages are most effective when message competition is at a minimum, when senders can speak directly to receivers (rather than to intermediaries or to answering machines), and when the location for a presentation or an interview is comfortable and quiet, is adequately lighted, has good acoustics, and offers few distractions.

Differing Status and Task Orientation

People tend to avoid communicating with other organization members who have differing status or task responsibility. Employees may be overly cautious when sending messages to managers, talking only about subjects they think the manager is interested in. Similarly, managers may distort messages by refusing to discuss anything that would tend to undermine their authority in the organization. Moreover, belonging to a particular department or being responsible for a particular task can narrow a manager's or an employee's point of view so that it differs from the attitudes, values, and expectations of people who belong to other departments or who are responsible for other tasks. To offset the effects of status and task responsibility, effective managers deemphasize differences and reward employees for keeping managers and colleagues well informed.[82]

Lack of Trust

When strict status differences are enforced, employees and managers alike have trouble developing high levels of trust. Trusting can be risky because other organization members may not respond in a supportive or responsible way. But trust between individuals and among group members is a critical ingredient for the stability of an organization and of its members (see Chapter 16). No matter how clearly managers express their ideas, clarity alone is not enough; organizational communication must encourage and reinforce an atmosphere of trust. For managers to build and maintain trust, they must be both visible and accessible rather than insulated behind assistants or secretaries. Employees want to know that managers are out in front leading the way. To build trust, effective managers share key information, communicate honestly, and include employees in decision making.[83]

Limitations of Communication Structures

Organizational communication is affected by formal restrictions on who may communicate with whom and who is authorized to make decisions. The process of organizing subdivides work tasks vertically and horizontally, which delineates the basic formal communication network. However, these divisions are focused on work specialization, not on creating communication relationships. Thus the resulting communication structures are rarely the most efficient.

Designing too few formal channels prevents effective communication. Strongly centralized organizations, especially those with a high degree of formalization, reduce communication capacity, and they decrease the tendency of managers and employees to communicate horizontally—thus limiting the ability to coordinate activities and decisions. Tall organizations tend to provide too many vertical communication links, so messages may become distorted as they move through the organization's levels.[84]

Managers must offer opportunities for communication upward, downward, and horizontally, using such techniques as employee surveys, open-door policies, newsletters, memos, task groups, and liaison roles. Many organizations, such as Pacific Gas & Electric in San Francisco, are restructuring to reduce hierarchical levels, to increase coordination, and to encourage two-way communication. In addition, effective managers make sure that the communication flow matches the tasks to be done; centralized structures are emphasized for routine, simple tasks, and decentralized structures are encouraged for nonroutine or technical tasks.[85]

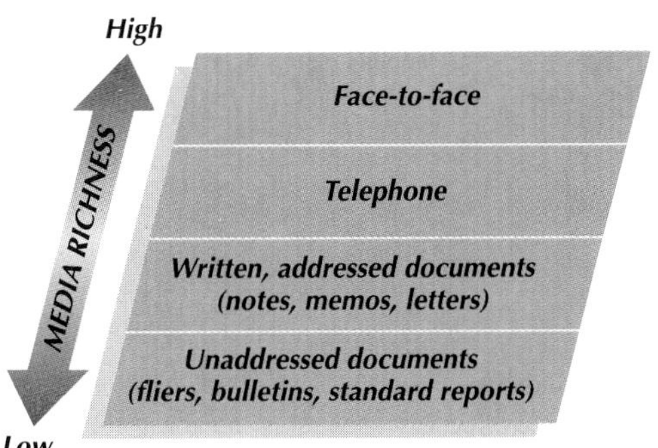

EXHIBIT 17.9
Hierarchy of Media Richness

Managers should remember that the more ambiguous the message, the richer the medium must be in order to ensure effective communication.

Incorrect Choice of Medium

Not every medium suits a given communication situation. Inappropriate communication media can distort messages so that the intended meaning cannot be effectively communicated. Effective managers carefully select the most appropriate communication media by matching the choice with the nature of the message and with the group or the individual who will receive the message.[86] A medium's richness—its value in a given communication situation—is determined by (1) its ability to convey a message using more than one informational cue (visual, verbal, vocal), (2) its ability to facilitate feedback, and (3) its ability to establish personal focus (see Exhibit 17.9).

Face-to-face communication is the richest medium because it is personal, it provides immediate feedback, it transmits information from both verbal and nonverbal cues, and it conveys the emotion behind the message. Telephones and other interactive electronic media rank lower on the richness scale; although they allow immediate feedback, they don't provide visual nonverbal cues such as facial expressions, eye contact, and body movements. Written media can be personalized through addressed memos, letters, and reports, but they lack the immediate feedback and the visual and vocal nonverbal cues that contribute to the meaning of a message. The leanest media are generally impersonal written messages such as bulletins, fliers, and standard reports. They not only lack the ability to transmit nonverbal cues and to give feedback but also eliminate any personal focus.[87]

Nonroutine, complex messages require rich media to counteract the potential for misunderstanding. Effective managers use rich media to extend and to humanize their presence throughout the organization, to communicate caring and personal interest to the employees, and to gain employee commitment to organizational goals. Simple, routine messages can be communicated through leaner media. Information such as statistics, facts, figures, and conclusions can be sent efficiently through a note, memo, or written report.[88]

A Closed Communication Climate

Management style heavily influences the organizational culture. In the past, managers were often guarded about sharing information, which created a closed communication climate. However, the current trend is toward a communication climate that is open, positive, and nonthreatening. To achieve such an open climate, managers spend more time listening than issuing orders. They respond constructively to employees and encourage them to risk communicating personal as well as work-related information. Employees are thus encouraged to

SOCIAL RESPONSIBILITY AND ETHICS

Electronic Communication Raises New Privacy Issues

Most people would not be able to read someone else's mail or tap into phone conversations with a clear conscience. Such practices are widely considered unethical. In fact, they are against the law. But as telephone calls, the U.S. mail, and paper and pencil give way to high-tech equivalents such as automated telephones, facsimile transmissions, electronic mail, and personal computers, a whole new set of ethical and legal concerns about communication privacy is emerging.

Current privacy laws were written in 1968. They protect the privacy of mail and telephone conversations. But that was well before anyone could foresee the advances in technology that began in the 1970s. As a result, messages sent via electronic mail, computer networks, and cellular telephones remain unprotected.

Alana Shoars found this out when she worked at Epson America, the U.S. arm of the Japanese computer maker. The company hired her to train employees in the use of electronic mail (or e-mail, as it is commonly called), which is the process that speeds messages and documents from computer to computer. Shoars discovered that her boss placed an "unauthorized and illegal" tap on the system so that the company could read electronic messages and memos that employees exchanged with outsiders. Shortly after she questioned the practice, she was fired for insubordination. Although she has filed suit against the company for invasion of privacy, legal experts believe she faces a difficult challenge trying to apply existing privacy laws to new technology.

For example, some privacy issues encompass conventional communication methods. These usually center on the question of who owns what in a typical office. Some argue that because office equipment such as telephones, desks, file cabinets, and computers are provided for conducting business in the organization, anything in them or sent through them is the organization's property. Others argue that employees deserve the same rights to privacy and confidentiality they have at home. In Alana Shoars's situation, this issue becomes even more complex because the communication that was intercepted by the employer was made on behalf of that same employer.

Privacy issues surrounding e-mail differ from those of conventional communication methods because of the nature of the new medium. Unlike a telephone conversation, which ends when the communicating parties hang up, e-mail can be stored for later retrieval. And even though most e-mail systems require a password to access messages and documents (which provides some sense of privacy), the messages are often stored on a centralized computer that is accessible to system technicians and perhaps to others in authority.

In 1986 Congress took some steps to protect the privacy of e-mail communication. The Office of Technology Assessment, the congressional fact-finding agency that specializes in examining technology matters, found that government agencies such as the Drug Enforcement Administration, the Federal Bureau of Investigation, the U.S. Customs Service, and the Internal Revenue Service frequently intercepted high-tech communications of individuals and corporations. They intercepted electronic mail, picked up satellite transmissions, tapped into cellular radio frequencies, and monitored computer usage. But the government was not the only culprit; individuals and corporations were also spying through electronic eavesdropping.

The 1986 act that Congress passed protects electronic communications from eavesdropping by the government or by any other unauthorized third party. However, the legislation does not make clear whether e-mail has any protection from interception or disclosure by a private employer, as in Alana Shoars's case. And as the use of electronic communications increases, this issue promises to be a hot topic for the 1990s.

What's Your Opinion?

1. What are the benefits and limitations of assuring employees maximum confidentiality and privacy in their organizational communication?
2. What can managers do to prevent what might be considered invasion of privacy with regard to the organization's electronic communications?

offer suggestions, to help set goals, to participate in solving problems, and to help make decisions.

For example, General Motors' NDH Bearings subsidiary in Sandusky, Ohio, became a world-class supplier of bearings to GM, Chrysler, and other auto manufacturers thanks in part to an emphasis on open communication. Sharing information has become a tradition at NDH, and when asked whether management could share too much, one manager replied that he would rather err on the side of overcommunicating. Several times a year, top managers and union officials join forces in an all-day meeting devoted to dissecting all aspects of the business; information from these meetings is shared with all NDH employees and managers in a series of follow-up meetings. The company also shares information through newsletters and through 24-hour broadcasting of business data through a network of television monitors in NDH plants and offices. Because of the open communication climate and the trust that has developed between union and management and between management and employees, NDH's profitability increased nearly 50 percent within two years.[89]

Unethical Communications

The ethical and legal aspects of communication center on such issues as honesty, full disclosure of information, and support of human dignity and worth. An organization cannot create illegal or unethical messages and still be credible or successful in the long run. Relationships within the organization and between the organization and the external environment depend on trust, honesty, and fairness. Organizational communication is considered ethical when its messages include all the information that ought to be there, when that information is adequate and relevant to the situation, when it is completely truthful, and when it isn't deceptive in any way.[90]

Inefficient Communication

Producing letters and memos takes time and resources, and all companies are concerned about holding down costs while maximizing the benefits of their communication activities. Only about 13 percent of the mail a manager receives is of immediate value, so managers can help reduce the number of messages by thinking twice before sending a message. The value of information depends on its timeliness. One way to speed up the process is for managers to make sure that written messages are prepared correctly the first time around. If people don't understand their writing assignment, they should ask for more guidance—and they should be as clear as possible when making writing assignments themselves. Also, standardizing written communication can reduce writing time and can save the reader's time (because the familiar format enables people to absorb the information quickly).[91]

Employees and managers can learn efficient oral and writing skills in classes, workshops, and seminars on dealing with customers, managing employees, and getting along with co-workers. Learning what not to do is just as important as learning what to do, and the expense of training employees saves the cost of wasted, ambiguous, or ill-prepared messages.[92]

SUMMARY

Managers rely on communication to carry out their managerial functions of planning, organizing, leading, and controlling. To be effective, they must understand the importance of nonverbal communication in getting meaning across, they must be fluent in both oral and written media, and they must understand the benefits and drawbacks of electronic media.

Communication falls into two basic categories: nonverbal and verbal. Nonverbal communication transmits information through behavior, appearances, and gestures. The effects of nonverbal communication are often unintentional and may conflict with verbal communication, such as when a manager professes to be concerned with what an employee says but continues to read while the employee is talking. Verbal communication, in contrast, relies on language, and it can appear in two basic forms: oral and written.

The communication process involves five steps: (1) the sender has an idea, (2) the idea becomes a message, (3) the message is transmitted to the receiver, (4) the receiver gets the message, and (5) the receiver gives feedback to the sender. Effective organizational communication requires managers to consider both interpersonal communication, which involves communication between two people, and group communication, which involves communication within or among groups. Managers who use interpersonal communication effectively maintain their objectivity, focus on working together, communicate honestly, express a belief in employee competence, and remain open to questioning. For effective group communication, managers should support group goals by preparing for member participation, valuing diversity, contributing ideas and seeking information, stressing group productivity, using diverse communication roles, avoiding self-interest roles, easing tensions, building group pride, and taking responsibility for group results.

Effective communication requires managers to be familiar with group communication networks, which are patterns of communication among group members. Centralized networks such as the wheel, the Y, and the chain work best in groups that must solve simple, routine problems quickly and efficiently. Decentralized networks such as the pinwheel and the circle usually work best in groups that must solve complex, nonroutine problems.

Organizations rely on both formal and informal communication. The organization's structure and hierarchy dictate formal communication channels that funnel information both vertically and horizontally. External communication with stakeholders such as suppliers, the media, and other groups influences the way these outside groups perceive and react to the organization. To use external communication effectively, managers can assign formal contacts such as marketers, public relations people, and crisis communication managers. They can also cultivate informal contacts with people outside the organization. Without regard for organization structure or hierarchy, the informal channels evolve from employees' interpersonal and social interaction. The grapevine has its own structures, including the single-strand chain, the gossip chain, the probability chain, and the cluster chain, and it is a powerful source of unofficial information.

To improve organizational communication, managers need to recognize and overcome communication barriers. Interpersonal barriers include differences in perception, incorrect filtering, language problems, poor listening, differing emotional states, cultural diversity, and inconsistent nonverbal cues. Organizational barriers include information overload, message complexity, message competition, differing status and task orientation, lack of trust, limitations of communication structures, incorrect choice of medium, closed communication climate, unethical communications, and inefficient communication.

MEETING A MANAGEMENT CHALLENGE AT

General Motors entered the 1980s faltering under the attack of Japanese automakers with their well-built, fuel-efficient cars. GM's efforts to compete with the Japanese had produced a series of daunting setbacks, and GM's top managers called for an unprecedented reorganization of the company to restore its competitive position. But their attempts misfired because they failed to communicate the new goals to employees. So top managers called on Alvie Smith, director of corporate communication, to open new channels of communication and to marshall support for the sweeping reorganization.

Smith began by improving communication between headquarters and the field. He beefed up established media (such as the company's monthly publication for employees and retirees, *GM Today*), and he started the bimonthly *GM Management*

GM's state-of-the-art Saturn plant in Spring Hill, Tennessee

Journal to keep field managers informed about corporate thinking and strategy. He also experimented with new channels of communication, such as making extensive use of video. *Issue Update,* a six-program yearly video series for GM's 60,000 managers and supervisors, conveyed the company's position on such issues as product quality, customer satisfaction, and target markets. Then Smith compiled and distributed video highlights of a key top-level management conference. The video left its viewers with no doubt about the serious nature of GM's problems.

Smith found that electronic media could also be used to promote direct contact between headquarters and the field. All GM locations have satellite receivers, and many conversations between corporate executives and field management are carried live on interactive satellite television. By hooking up its 9,700 dealers to a new satellite system GM had established what it said was the world's largest private satellite network.

Having improved two-way communication between headquarters and the field, Smith turned his attention to bolstering communication within each field office and factory. Plants and offices throughout GM were producing 350 employee newsletters, and Smith began by boosting their effectiveness. He encouraged their editors to improve their visual appeal, and he provided graphic and editorial materials to supplement local efforts. Smith also met with local managers to enlist their support for these publications.

Having gained their attention, Smith convinced these local managers to improve their speaking skills. GM's own research had revealed that the closer the source of information was to the employee, the greater its relevance and its credibility—and, therefore, its effectiveness. But GM's middle managers had traditionally been poor communicators. Smith organized workshops to improve the speaking skills of GM plant managers and to impress these executives with the importance of their role as the leading GM communicator in each location.

GM realized that effective employee communication is a fundamental part of good management and can contribute to an organization's performance. By 1989 GM's quality had improved but the company continued to lose market share. GM faces tough times in the 1990s. The firm reported a record $4.45 billion loss in 1991 and is again reorganizing to compete locally and globally. The communications lessons GM learned in the 1980s will surely play a major role in the company's strategies as it drives into the twenty-first century.[93]

***You're the Manager*:** Robert Stempel, GM's chairman, has renewed GM's focus on car quality and cost reduction. Stempel is determined to enlist the support of all GM employees. As the newly appointed director of employee communication at GM's Saginaw division, your job is to encourage better communication within the division and between the division and people in other areas of GM. Your goal is to get the *right* message to the *right* audience at the *right* time using the *right* media.

Ranking Questions

1. Saginaw's general manager realizes that her personal communication style is important, for several reasons: as the division's top manager she holds primary responsibility for successful communication within the division, she needs to communicate with the managers who report to her, and her style sets an example for other managers. She asks you to sit in on one-on-one meetings for several days to observe any nonverbal messages that she may be sending. You observe the following four habits; rank them from most negative to most positive.
   a. She rarely comes out from behind her massive desk when meeting with people in her office; at one point she gave an employee a congratulatory handshake, and the employee had to lean way over her desk to reach her.
   b. When an employee hands her a report and then sits down to discuss it, she alternates between making eye contact and making notes on the report.
   c. She is consistently pleasant, even if the person she is meeting is delivering bad news.

d. She interrupts meetings to answer her phone, then apologizes to the people in her office for the interruption.

2. GM managers learn that some Japanese companies are working on a steering column that collapses on impact. Stempel believes this new steering column design will give competitors an additional edge with safety-conscious consumers. He assigns the Saginaw division to beat the Japanese companies to market with GM's version of the collapsible steering column. Your general manager has assembled a 40-member cross-functional team including designers, engineers, production specialists, and outside suppliers. She calls you for advice on organizing the team for the most effective communication. She offers four alternatives and asks you to rank them.
   a. This group needs a leader to focus its efforts. The wheel pattern is ideal because it ensures that all activity will be coordinated by a single person.
   b. The general manager is concerned that GM's suppliers may gain access to sensitive inside information. One way to isolate them while simplifying GM's own lines of communication would be to use a Y pattern with the leader at the center, the suppliers at the top, and GM personnel at the base.
   c. Designing a steering column is a complicated task that requires the free interchange of ideas. The pinwheel network is the best communication pattern for the job.
   d. Divide the team into five subteams, each structured as a pinwheel network. Have these subteams report to a leader according to the wheel pattern.

Multiple-Choice Questions

3. Stempel has ordered layoffs that will release 10 percent of Saginaw's employees. The general manager asks you to recommend the best way to break the news to those who will lose their jobs.
   a. Soften the blow by writing an article for the division newsletter, *The Saginaw Scene,* describing GM's plans to lay off 10 percent of the Saginaw work force.
   b. It is the managers' responsibility to tell the employees who report to them. However, the general manager should send a brief personal letter to all laid-off employees, noting their accomplishments and expressing support for their job-seeking efforts.
   c. The general manager owes it to the employees to meet with them individually and break the news.
   d. Post a list of employees to be laid off on divisional bulletin boards.

4. Employees have grown to trust the division grapevine more than they trust formal communication from division management. Although the grapevine is normally very accurate, a blatantly false rumor concerning the division's future has been circulating for several days. What's the first step you should take to handle this?
   a. Identify the opinion leaders throughout the division—employees who are known to be good sources of inside information—and invite them to a private session with management. Explain why the rumor is false, giving them complete data on the issue. Ask them to share the information with their colleagues.
   b. Publish a memorandum to all employees, insisting that the rumor is false and stating the facts.
   c. Instruct all managers to tell their departments that the rumor is false.
   d. Call a divisionwide meeting at which the general manager can explain the facts and publicly state that the rumor is false.

Analysis Questions

5. What risks does GM run by increasingly relying on teleconferences and video productions to meet its communication needs?
6. Explain how GM's efforts to improve communication can prevent stereotyping.
7. What points should GM trainers emphasize to help senders improve the effectiveness of their communication?

Special Project

A GM facility in California has called on you for help. This plant hired a large number of recent immigrants from the same country, but the immigrants don't seem to have integrated into the mainstream life of the factory. All the immigrants speak some English, but all have a heavy accent and none is particularly fluent in English. Some employees born in the United States are starting to complain that the immigrants don't understand instructions; the immigrants complain that they have to read their colleagues' minds in order to figure out what to do. Draft a two-page memo suggesting how the California facility can overcome the issues to encourage better communication between immigrants and those born in the United States.[93]

KEY TERMS

channel (538)
communication (532)
communication network (540)
decoding (538)
downward communication (543)
electronic communication (537)
encoding (537)
external communication (546)
feedback (538)
filtering (550)
formal communication (542)
grapevine (545)
horizontal communication (544)
informal communication (545)
information overload (552)
internal communication (541)
message (537)
noise (549)
nonverbal communication (533)
oral communication (535)
perception (550)
perceptual organization (550)
selective perception (550)
stereotyping (552)
upward communication (543)
verbal communication (535)
vertical communication (542)
written communication (536)

QUESTIONS

For Review

1. What are the stages in the communication process and how do they interrelate?
2. What is noise and what is its effect on the message in the communication process?
3. In what ways can people communicate nonverbally?
4. How does formal communication differ from informal communication?
5. What are the different directions in which communication can flow in an organization? Describe the purposes of each.

For Analysis

1. In what ways would managers' communication skills affect their relationships with others in the organization?
2. What may be some of the positive and negative implications as electronic communication continues to replace traditional media such as face-to-face meetings, telephone calls, and paper-based mail (letters and memos)?
3. What can managers do to control the grapevine?
4. Some organizations have their own jargon or slang that is unique to their environment. What are some of the communication benefits and some of the pitfalls that could result from using such jargon?
5. How does upward, downward, and horizontal communication work in a college or university?

For Application

1. Suppose you wanted to respond to a job listing in the paper. What would be the most appropriate method of communication? Why?
2. How can the night-shift manager at a Denny's restaurant who must fire a popular cook for poor performance communicate this news to the rest of the crew?
3. As an entry-level employee, what communication steps would you take if you discovered that your company had been falsifying safety records?
4. If a CEO uncovered falsified safety records, what communication steps could he or she take?
5. How might the general manager of a large division of General Foods get "plugged into" the division's grapevine?

KEEPING CURRENT IN MANAGEMENT

From recent magazines and newspapers, select a profile of a manager who seems to be successful because of good communication skills. One example might be a teacher whose students excel because they are encouraged to ask questions and to think creatively. Another example might be a business or not-for-profit executive who regularly seeks contact with the organization's stakeholders to determine how the organization can better serve their needs.

1. How does the manager facilitate communication? Does this manager use formal or informal communication or both? Does the organization have a grapevine, and does the manager use it to convey information?
2. How well does communication flow upward, downward, and horizontally in the organization? Are communication patterns best described as centralized or

decentralized? Is there any evidence of message distortion?
3. How does the manager encourage two-way communication? Is the manager an active listener? How would you evaluate this manager's internal and external communication skills?

SHARPEN YOUR MANAGEMENT SKILLS

In publicly owned companies, communicating with securities analysts is one of top management's most important tasks. These analysts make recommendations to current and prospective shareholders about buying, selling, or holding stocks, and the information they gather from company leaders can greatly influence their recommendations.

Oracle Systems, a software developer that had previously enjoyed spectacular earnings growth, announced in April 1990 that earnings for the preceding quarter were flat. This wasn't terribly bad news, nor are such announcements at all uncommon. But Wall Street pounded the company, sending its stock price down by 31 percent. Why such a severe reaction to mildly bad news? The reason is that stock analysts had gotten into the habit of making rosy projections about the company's growth. This was unrealistic, but Oracle Systems didn't do anything to dampen their enthusiasm. As a result, when reality finally arrived, the stock market was shocked and reacted wildly.[94]

- *Decision:* You're the chief financial officer of a midsized manufacturer of medical supplies. A securities analyst is on the phone, asking about a rumor that some of your biggest customers are switching to a competitor with lower prices. You know that the reality is even worse than the rumor; the new competitor will probably take a large share of the market before your company can respond. Decide whether you should confirm only as much as the analyst already knows, or explain that things will get worse before they get better.
- *Communication:* Based on your decision, respond to the analyst's query by writing a paragraph or two that would represent your oral response.

CASE

Allstate Ensures Good Communication

Maturation of the baby-boom generation has ended the era of easy growth for insurance companies. Larry Williford, Allstate's senior vice president for corporate communications, knows that insurers must now try to take business from each other. Williford is making sure Allstate stays in touch with its employees to make them more productive and to make the company more competitive.

HISTORY

Allstate grew up with the American automobile industry. Sears president Robert E. Wood convinced his board of directors to put up $700,000 to start a company that would sell auto insurance by mail. Sears named the company Allstate, after the brand name of its tires. It sold automobile policies through Sears mail-order catalogs until 1933, when it installed its first agents in Sears stores. By the end of World War II, Allstate was collecting $12 million a year in auto policy premiums; then the demand for both cars and insurance exploded. Allstate added life and property insurance in the 1950s, and today it insures 1 in 10 homes and 1 in 10 automobiles. Annual premiums total $8 billion for auto insurance plus $8 billion for life and property insurance, and Allstate accounts for half of Sears's profits. Allstate still has offices in every Sears store, but 70 percent of its agents now work in branch offices all around the country.

ENVIRONMENT

Allstate makes its far-flung system cohesive by using both technology and a personal touch to foster employee communications. Communication with its 55,000 employees has been part of Allstate's strategic planning process since 1982, when then-CEO Donald F. Craib, Jr., asked employees at all levels, often face-to-face, to tell him how to restructure the company. The company has installed a video-conferencing system that connects all 26 regional offices with headquarters in Northbrook, Illinois. Top management uses the system to discuss policy issues, and it has greatly enhanced executive productivity. Allstate also uses communications technology to give its 4,000 insurance agents a marketing edge. By linking them with a computer network that has access to a huge database, Allstate provides agents with information about Sears customers, such as average incomes in certain neighborhoods, what customers buy, and when they buy it.

Allstate also uses computers to help the 5,000 employees at company headquarters calculate their individual profit-sharing and retirement benefits. At several kiosks, computers using video disks put beginners at ease by humorously giving basic benefit information through an animated Sherlock Holmes story. Experienced users can skip the story and go straight to the calculations. All employees can use the system at their convenience without assistance from a human resource officer.

Allstate also communicates with employees through several publications. An annual report, *Perspectives,* explores issues affecting the company and communicates the company's perspective. A recent edition sought to stimulate conversation among employees about how external environments and outside opinions affect the company. It showed a photograph of the CEO posing casually at home with his wife to communicate the idea that Allstate wants employees to balance work and home life and to have the best of both worlds.

GOALS AND CHALLENGES

Williford's goals include improving communications by direct contact with employees and by harnessing new technology. A major focus for the 1990s is educating employees about AIDS. Williford hopes that company literature will encourage employees to discuss the AIDS problem at home and educate employees about the safety of working alongside someone with HIV. Allstate is improving its computer network by consolidating its large mainframe computer systems and adding more personal computers to give users better access to more information. The company is spending $20 million to make its Management Information System software more flexible, faster, and more productive.

1. How does Allstate use verbal communication to improve organizational performance?
2. How has Allstate minimized organizational barriers to effective communications about its employee benefits?
3. How can Williford get feedback from employees about their reaction to the AIDS education program?
4. What degree of centralized control over information in Allstate's own customer database should be designed into Allstate's new computer network to ensure both productivity and sufficient access to information among insurance agents?

PART FOUR INTEGRATIVE CASE

Herman Miller Leads the Way with Participation

No one can accuse the people at Herman Miller of sitting down on the job. This multinational maker of contemporary office furniture has grown spectacularly over the years. Annual sales hit $50 million in 1976, skyrocketed to $255 million in 1981, then climbed to $829 million in 1989. But as the 1980s closed, Herman Miller's growth potential seemed more limited. Recession had dulled customer demand, and company income had remained nearly flat for several years. Competitors were also stepping up their efforts: market leader Steelcase was unveiling new products and BIF Korea, based in Seoul, was aggressively moving into the United States.

Chairman Max DePree was determined to keep quality and customer satisfaction high, but he also had to deliver financial results. DePree had to decide whether to continue Herman Miller's tradition of encouraging employees and managers to participate in business decisions, or whether to deemphasize participation and instead guide the firm's activities directly from the top during difficult periods. Which path would be best for Herman Miller's long-term performance?

HERMAN MILLER'S GOAL: TO PROVIDE QUALITY, SERVICE, AND GOOD FINANCIAL RETURNS IN THE CONTEXT OF CORPORATE VALUES

→ *Maintain the tradition of encouraging managers and employees to participate in decisions*

→ *Reduce participation and apply top-down leadership during difficult times to steer managers and employees in more profitable directions*

HISTORY

D. J. DePree joined Star Furniture in Zeeland, Michigan, in 1909, became president in 1919, and bought the firm in 1923. He changed the company name to Herman Miller in honor of his father-in-law, who funded the purchase. Herman Miller emphasized classical home furniture until the 1930s, when the Depression and heated competition drove the business to the brink of ruin. Then designer Gilbert Rohde proposed a line of simpler, more functional furniture he argued was better suited to the smaller space of modern homes. DePree decided to gamble on Rohde's contemporary designs. He won: by 1945, contemporary furniture designs had all but banished classical designs from the marketplace, and Herman Miller had earned a reputation for design innovation that endures today.

Next, Rohde began to think about the design of office furniture. Although the desk was typically seen as a status symbol as well as a functional work surface, Rohde wanted to redefine the desk as a more productive work tool. He designed a series of desk components that could be mixed and matched according to the user's needs. So successful was this new line that Herman Miller soon dropped home furnishings to concentrate on office furniture. Over the next 25 years, DePree's openness to new ideas attracted talented designers who developed such innovations as the award-winning Eames chair and the Noguchi table, both of which remain in the Herman Miller line today.

In the 1960s, Herman Miller introduced the Action Office, a pioneering concept in the move away from permanently walled-in offices and toward flexible, open floor plans. The Action Office was conceived as a system of movable wall panels, work surfaces, and storage units that can easily be rearranged as the space requirements or the work needs of the office change. Individual workstations have some privacy, but the layout is open and encourages communication between occupants. In the mid-1980s, Herman Miller introduced Ethospace, a system of furniture and partition components that allows users to blend private and open offices, solid and see-through wall panels, built-in and freestanding furniture, all in a functional, flexible, and attractive way.

Two generations of DePrees have headed Herman Miller. D. J. DePree, the first CEO, was succeeded by his son Hugh D. DePree. In turn, Hugh DePree was followed by his younger brother, Max O. DePree. Max DePree became chairman in 1988, and the next two CEOs have been nonfamily members. To ensure that up-and-coming managers have a chance to earn the top slot, DePree has announced that he will be the last family member to lead the company.

ENVIRONMENT

Herman Miller's achievements are due, in large part, to the influence of its participatory management philosophy on the internal environment. The roots of this philosophy go back to the 1930s, when D. J. DePree paid a condolence call on the widow of a company millwright who had died on the job. The widow read several beautiful passages of poetry and DePree, touched, asked the poet's name. He was surprised when the woman replied that her husband had written the poems. As he left, DePree wondered whether he had employed a millwright who wrote poetry or a poet who did millwright's work. He came away convinced that he had to recognize the personal abilities of all company members. By providing an environment that enabled people to develop their talents and skills, he would also be encouraging individuals to contribute to the enterprise. DePree reasoned that this valuable diversity of viewpoint and ability would help Herman Miller grow and prosper.

In keeping with DePree's vision, Herman Miller's 5,400 employees worldwide participate in everyday decisions and activities. Each department is organized into small teams, and every team member is expected to suggest ways of achieving monthly departmental goals. Once a month, team leaders meet to share these ideas and to review results. Team leaders evaluate team members' performance twice a year, and team members also evaluate their leaders. In addition, teams elect representatives who caucus with management to discuss performance and grievances. People at every level are encouraged to communicate upward, downward, and even diagonally when they have a concern or an idea. To keep everyone abreast of corporate goals and results, the company circulates videotapes of monthly management discussions.

Since 1950, Herman Miller employees have been covered by a profit-sharing program known as the Scanlon plan. Management designed this program to encourage interest and participation in company decisions, to reinforce how individual effort contributes to company performance, and to ensure that employees share in the results. Employees receive a quarterly bonus check based on several measures, including cost-cutting suggestions, productivity, and corporate results. Moreover, managers and employees are covered by a "silver parachute" that guarantees payment of up to 2½ years' salary if Herman Miller is acquired in a hostile takeover that affects employee jobs by reducing salary, eliminating bonuses, changing responsibilities, or moving the worksite far away. The company also fixes management salaries as a ratio of the average pay of its factory employees; the CEO's pay is capped at 20 times the average factory pay.

GOALS AND CHALLENGES

One of Herman Miller's biggest challenges has been to maintain market share and profitability in an increasingly competitive market. Many organizations downsized in the late 1980s, so the market for office furniture was barely growing. Herman Miller was particularly hard-hit by a slump in the electronics industry, which accounted for 30 percent of its business. Even as competitors cut their prices to maintain market share, Herman Miller was trying to sell its premium-priced Ethospace system, and sales and earnings stalled. Rather than dismantle the participatory programs and direct decisions and actions from the top to improve profits, Herman Miller executives fine-tuned the existing system to put more emphasis on external elements such as customer satisfaction and financial returns. Managers also pushed harder on cost reduction goals, and employees offered ideas that saved the company $12 million annually. The company pursued new industry segments to replace the sagging sales in existing customer industries and explored new areas such as residential furniture for the elderly and office systems for clinics. Another priority was building closer ties with dealers who agreed to focus almost exclusively on Herman Miller products.

These changes nudged sales higher, but Herman Miller isn't out of the woods quite yet. Hobbled by economic recession, sales in 1991 topped $878 million, only 1.6 percent higher than in 1990. Even with this small increase, Herman Miller gained market share because industry sales of office furniture dropped 2.2 percent during the year. Although the company recently shelved its plan to make residential furniture for seniors, citing inadequate return, sales in the health-care market are growing. As he meets the challenges of this tough environment, Max DePree plans to continue relying on the participatory approach that has served his company for decades.

1. Discuss how Alderfer's ERG theory of motivation can be seen in the workplace at Herman Miller. In terms of satisfaction–progression and frustration–regression, how might employees react if DePree were to switch to a more autocratic leadership approach?
2. How are contingency theories of leadership reflected in Herman Miller's management approach? How might a low-scoring LPC leader fare at Herman Miller? A high-scoring LPC leader?
3. Identify the formal groups at Herman Miller. How do company norms contribute to group cohesiveness?
4. How does effective communication contribute to Herman Miller's ability to achieve its corporate goals? What types of verbal and nonverbal communication can DePree use to reinforce the company's belief in helping employees and managers develop their own abilities?

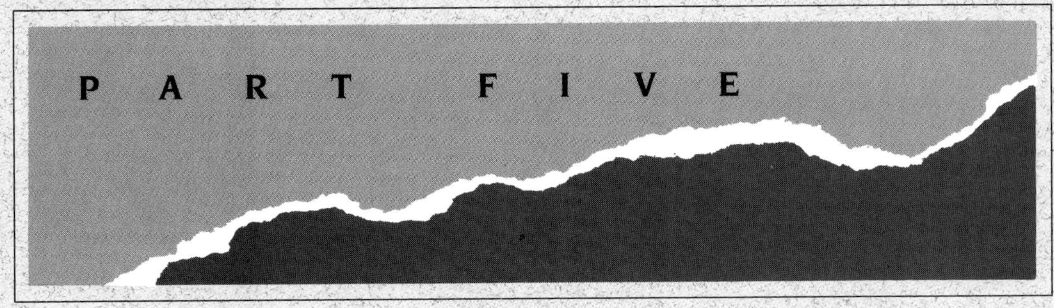

Controlling

CHAPTER OUTLINE

18

Information Resource Management

After studying this chapter, you will be able to

1. Differentiate between data and information and explain the criteria necessary for information to be useful
2. Explain the importance of information as a strategic resource
3. Outline the ways managers use information to plan, organize, lead, and control
4. Identify the major types of information systems and their applications
5. List the five most common categories of computers
6. Distinguish data processing from data communications
7. Discuss the benefits and limitations of centralized and decentralized data processing

FACING A MANAGEMENT CHALLENGE AT

AMERICAN EXPRESS

Charging through the Information Age

Day after day, more than 30 million people were telling James D. Robinson III all about themselves: what they ate, where they traveled, when they bought luxuries, and a host of other facts. That was the problem; they were giving him facts—tons of them. More than three million charge card receipts were arriving at American Express offices each day, so much paper that CEO Robinson and his managers were having a difficult time managing the masses of data. As he was pushing every employee to provide high-quality service to customers, Robinson was watching his company's slow burial beneath a mountain of paper. The torrent of data was creating problems and obscuring opportunities.

First, the problem. Processing the millions of pieces of paper for return to cardholders was inefficient and quite prone to errors. Hundreds of employees were required to film receipts for storage, to enter charge amounts into a mainframe computer for billing, to sort receipts and match them with others from the same accounts, to process billing statements, and to insert the receipts and their corresponding statements into envelopes for mailing. Mistakes were made, and time was wasted. Some receipts were mangled. Account numbers were misread. Nearly 200 people were employed just to resolve errors that had been made during the initial processing, and answering a cardholder's query about a single transaction sometimes took hours.

The sluggish process cost American Express in another important way. The company pays merchants when it receives transaction receipts from them, then it turns around and bills cardholders. The longer it takes to process receipts and bill cardholders, the longer it takes for American Express to get paid. And while it is waiting for customers to pay, the company has to set aside enough money (called a "float") to pay merchants for new transactions. The longer it takes to get paid, the more money the company has to set aside in its float—money that can't be used for other purposes.

One possible solution for these problems was to stop returning receipts to cardholders with their statements, a step already taken by Visa and MasterCard. But Robinson demanded a high level of service for his customers. Most American Express cardholders used their cards for business purposes, and they needed their receipts for business and tax records. Not returning receipts would profoundly affect customer satisfaction.

Second, the missed opportunities. Even if the paper mountain were blasted away with a more efficient system, that would still leave the question of how to manage all of those data describing the wants and needs of American Express cardholders. Robinson's goal was to make American Express into a service-industry giant by offering a wide variety of services, from charge cards to financial planning to travel to entertainment. Those 30 million customers were telling Robinson a lot about themselves. Now he had to use their data to gain a competitive advantage, to build customer loyalty, and to enter new markets. Would he be better off by just not sending the receipts back to cardholders? Or should he invest millions of dollars and several years in new technology? How could all the data be transformed into information that could be used to market new goods and services? How could he avoid the trap of generating so much information that confusion would be the only result?[1]

CHAPTER OVERVIEW

James Robinson was grappling with the two sides of information. The right information at the right time can make an organization dramatically more effective and more competitive. On the other hand, masses of unstructured data can obscure important phenomena, clog decision-making channels, and hinder efforts to improve productivity and quality. This chapter explores the management of information as a strategic resource for an organization. Differentiating

Walgreens, the largest drugstore chain in the United States, created a satellite communication network to speed the flow of information between stores and headquarters, boosting productivity and customer satisfaction. Using the network, Walgreens's pharmacists can instantly look up all customer prescriptions in the main computer in Des Plaines, Illinois, so customers can buy refills at any of the chain's 1,600 stores.

between data and useful information is the first topic covered, followed by discussions of how information can be used strategically and how information affects managerial decisions. The chapter then focuses on the use of computers to manage information systems that handle transactions, provide information, and assist decision making. Finally, information technology is described, and current issues in information technology are discussed.

MANAGEMENT AND INFORMATION

Just as they value human, technological, and financial resources, successful organizations also put a premium on information resources. All four key functions of management rely on the effective use of information. Planning requires information about the environment and the organization's capabilities. Leading relies on information, from giving employees feedback to communicating strategic goals. Organization structure and information are closely linked; in fact, one of the biggest problems with an inappropriate organization design is poor information flow. And managers can't achieve effective control without accurate, timely information about the organization's performance. Information about the economy, customers and their needs, competitors, the work force, and new technologies are all vital to the survival and success of an organization.[2]

The effective use of information streamlined the market-analysis efforts at San Francisco-based Chevron Chemical Company when it implemented a computer system to organize and process marketing data. According to John Hanlon, coordinator of systems development and operations in the company's information systems group, productivity and information quality soared. Before implementation of the new system, analysts spent four to five days creating month-end reports on market conditions. With the new system, creation of month-end reports comparing sales forecast with actual sales takes just a half day. More important, having the data organized and easily accessible has allowed more sophisticated analysis of data, resulting in better information.[3]

Transforming Data into Information

data Facts, ideas, or concepts that are collected and stored in raw, unprocessed form

information The result of processing, correlating, or summarizing raw data to create useful insights

One of the most important steps in information management is recognizing just what constitutes information. **Data** are facts, ideas, or concepts that are collected and stored in raw form. An organization's data can include everything from sales figures to customer names to product brochures from competitors. By themselves, data don't offer much meaning or insight. For data to have meaning, they must be converted into a format that communicates knowledge or conclusions.

Information is the result of processing, correlating, or summarizing raw data to create knowledge (see Exhibit 18.1).[4] Data can provide the facts, but it is the analysis of those facts that gives managers the information they need to make better decisions. Social scientist Gregory Bateson provided a succinct summary of the value of information when he described it as "a difference that makes a difference."[5] In other words, information tells a manager something that he or she didn't know before ("a difference"), and that knowledge enables the manager to make decisions or take action ("makes a difference").

Thomas Stephens, the vice president of finance at Lever Brothers Food Division, recently installed a computer system aimed at providing summarized infor-

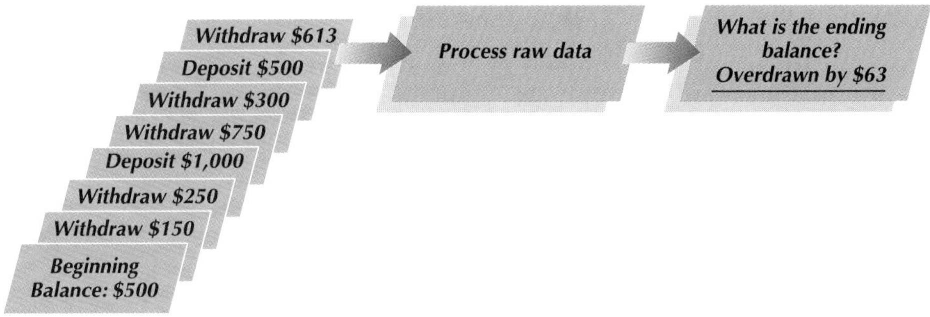

EXHIBIT 18.1

Transforming Data into Information

By themselves, the transaction data shown here don't provide much insight into the account's current status. But by processing the data, the bank can extract a key piece of information—the account is overdrawn—and it can then take action.

mation to upper management. Formerly, an inch-thick document filled with data was distributed to (and usually ignored by) the management team. With the new computerized reporting system, executives can quickly trace a problem back to its cause by initiating a computer search through the layers of divisional results. Instead of asking why profits are down, executives at Lever Brothers are likely to ask why Imperial margarine sales are below target on the West Coast. Converting data to usable information has given the management team a better understanding of their operations, which enables executives to make faster, better-informed decisions.[6]

Distilling data into meaningful information isn't always an easy or obvious task. Knowing what is meaningful to each decision maker in an organization requires a thorough understanding of the organization's internal and external environments. Because managing strategic information can be challenging, and doing so is critical to an organization's success, many large organizations now have a top-level executive, often called the *chief information officer (CIO),* who focuses on information and information systems. These executives do a lot more than just keep an eye on computers. James Marston, CIO of American President Companies, manages a wide variety of projects and systems for the California-based shipping company. For instance, one of American President's competitive advantages is its ability to let customers on both sides of the Pacific monitor the progress of their shipments. To deliver this capability, the company uses a sophisticated satellite communications system that constantly tracks the location and progress of each ship on its way across the ocean. Customers can tap into the system and find out exactly where their shipments are and when they are expected in port. It is the CIO's job to manage the design and operation of this and many other advanced information systems.[7]

Before managers can benefit from information, however, the information must meet several criteria, as the following section points out.

Making Information Useful

As James Robinson, James Marston, and other managers concerned with information could certainly attest, information is helpful only if it is useful. Managers can have a never-ending supply of interesting and amusing information, but if it's not useful, it won't help them manage more effectively. For information to be useful, it must meet five criteria:[8]

- *It must be accurate.* Just how accurate information needs to be depends on the situation. If a manager is trying to size up the market for toothpaste in Indonesia, getting a population figure that is within a few hundred thousand people will probably be just fine. On the other hand, when processing invoices, accounting managers need information that is precise down to the last penny.

- *It must be timely.* Managers frequently encounter decisions that simply can't wait, decisions that have to be made, with or without the "necessary" information. When a manager has to make a decision within a finite period of time, information that sheds light on the decision a week or a month later is of little use. On the other hand, information that arrives too early might not help unless the manager has a good storage and retrieval system.
- *It must be complete.* Information should cover everything a manager has to consider in making a decision. If a manager is studying employee records in order to choose a new production supervisor, he or she needs to see the records of all qualified employees in order to make the optimum decision.
- *It must be relevant.* Every college student is familiar with exam questions in which some of the information provided is irrelevant. Managers and their employees face the same situation every day, and one of the most difficult aspects of information management is deciding what is relevant and then providing decision makers with only the relevant information. John Whiteside, a software engineer at Digital Equipment Corporation, was inundated with so many electronic mail messages that he took matters into his own hands and programmed his computer to sort incoming mail and automatically toss out irrelevant and unimportant messages. By doing so, he is now able to focus on the information that he specifically needs to make the decisions that are part of his job.[9]
- *It must be concise.* Information must be in a form that the decision maker can use efficiently. A mayor looking for a single budget figure doesn't want to dig through stacks of reports or computer printouts to find it.

Of course, information in the real world is rarely perfect, and managers must often make do with whatever information they can get. But the closer information comes to meeting these five criteria, the more it will improve the management process and the more valuable it will be as a strategic resource.

Information as a Strategic Resource

Whether an organization manufactures goods, delivers services, or puts laws into effect, it must acquire and analyze information, disseminate it, and take action based on the interpretation of that information (see Exhibit 18.2). When the right information is provided to the key decision makers in an organization, it can be used in strategic decision making. For example, William Smithburg, CEO at Quaker Oats, was the driving force behind the development of the Executive Support System (ESS), a system used to computerize all the information that had been coming into the Quaker Oats offices on paper. The system provides access to company performance data, internal communications, and environmental scanning information. According to Smithburg, "I use the ESS more for environmental scanning than for management control. In days of drought in farming areas, for example, I can get into the ESS and quickly find agricultural information that will influence our costs for raw materials."[10] Information used in strategic decision making affects organizational efficiency, competitive advantage, customer loyalty, and an organization's ability to find new markets.

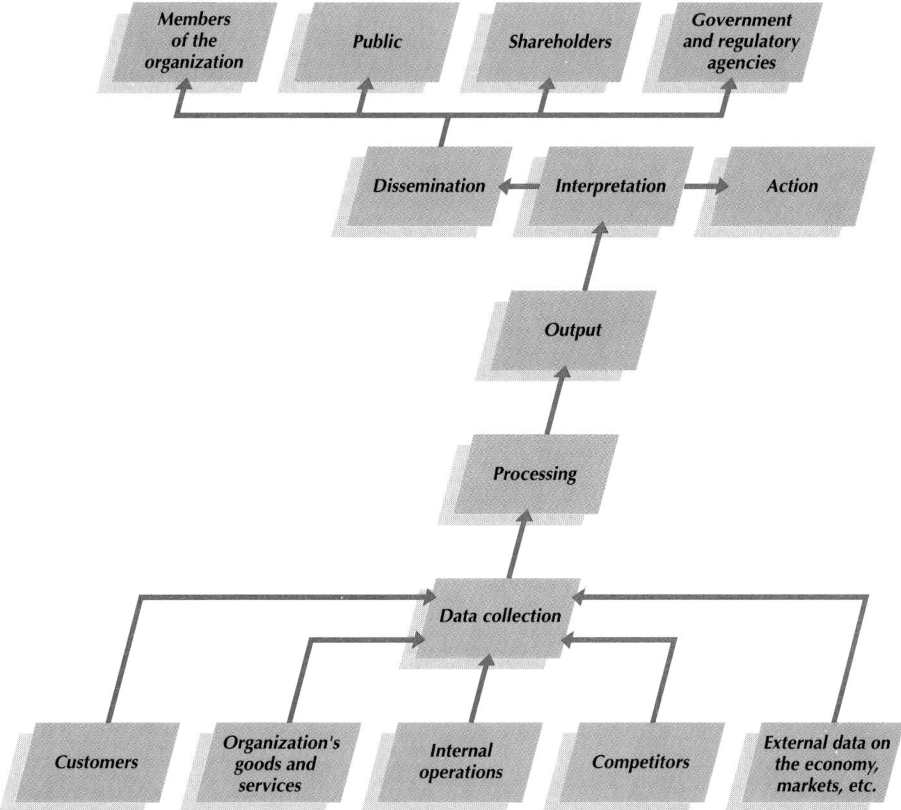

EXHIBIT 18.2

Organizational Information Flows

Every organization collects data from a number of sources, including its own internal operations, its customers, and its competitors. These data flow through the organization and are processed into information that supports managerial decision making. Some information is then disseminated to members of the organization, the public, government agencies, or other stakeholders.

Increasing Organizational Efficiency

Information summarized from complex data can reduce labor requirements, increase quality, and provide a better understanding of an organization's operations. For example, Reebok increased sales from $13 million to $308 million in just three years. With an all-manual system controlling inventory, shipping, and receiving, Reebok lacked adequate information to process customer orders in a timely fashion. At times, customers received back-order notices because Reebok couldn't find the inventory. To revamp its distribution system, Reebok built an automated warehouse and implemented computer systems to match inventory with customer orders. With better information, inventory accuracy at Reebok is now greater than 99 percent.[11]

Similarly, the government of Singapore implemented the Tradenet System to manage the world's largest port. The $50 million system links brokers (such as freight forwarders, shipping companies, banks, and insurance companies) with relevant government agencies (such as customs and immigration officials), so a vessel that used to take two to four days to clear the port can now take care of its business in as little as 10 minutes. By increasing the port's efficiency, Tradenet helps ensure that ships will continue to make Singapore a port of choice in the Far East.[12]

Staying Ahead of Competitors

Having information about the external environment is essential for organizations to get ahead and stay ahead of their competitors. Managers can identify their information needs and institute ongoing work activities aimed at capturing

MANAGERIAL DECISION MAKING

Fidelity Invests in Information Technology

Strong customer service and the outstanding performance of its investment products have made Fidelity Investments the largest mutual fund company in the world. Chairman and CEO Edward C. Johnson III focuses on computer technology to keep Fidelity ahead of its competitors in providing customers with excellent service.

Mutual fund companies such as Fidelity pool money from investors to buy stocks, bonds, and other investment products. Fidelity is the largest of these companies, with over $165 billion in assets. Investors can choose from more than 100 Fidelity funds, with options that include retirement accounts, company pension plans, college savings plans, and general investing.

Information technology plays a key role in Fidelity's continuing success. In fact, the company maintains its own technology research department, the Fidelity Technologies Group, to look for ways that emerging technologies can help the company grow and serve its customers better. One of the more exotic options the group is looking into is the talking workstation, for instance.

Two recent Fidelity information-management innovations are Fidelity On-line Xpress (FOX), a microcomputer software package, and Fidelity TouchTone Trader, which lets customers buy and sell using touch-tone telephones. FOX connects individual investors directly to the financial markets, and it also supplies them with research reports, statistics, and other information needed to make informed investment decisions. TouchTone Trader doesn't offer the additional information services of FOX, but it does allow customers to buy and sell from any touch-tone telephone, which is perfect for busy people on the move.

But Johnson knows that there is more to information management than breakthroughs such as FOX. The basic transaction-processing and customer service systems that handle the flow of data into and out of the company must be accurate and reliable. For Fidelity, this includes a telephone system that can handle the millions of calls the company gets every year. The firm maintains more than 20 toll-free numbers for customers and potential customers to access accounts, ask questions, and request information.

Johnson is intimately familiar with the consequences of inadequate information-management capabilities: the company's systems were strained past the

the necessary data. For example, Xerox saw its world market share for copiers drop from 82 percent to 41 percent in just six years, a result of Japanese competitors entering the copier business. To avoid losing market share in the midsize copier market where it still dominates, Xerox routinely gathers competitive product data. Competing products are taken apart by Xerox engineers to see how the copiers are made and to estimate their production cost. Xerox uses this competitive benchmarking (see Chapter 3, "Meeting a Management Challenge") as one technique in its quest to build higher-quality copiers at lower cost.[13]

In addition to ongoing programs like Xerox's benchmarking, organizations occasionally have one-time needs for information gathering as well. For example, ABB Asea Brown Boveri, the Swiss multinational with interests in electrical power plants, power distribution, public transportation, environmental controls, and other related holdings, gathered competitor intelligence to research and plan the acquisition of the U.S. firm Combustion Engineering. A senior staff member of ABB's U.S. arm was able to compile a detailed analysis in a very short period of time without alerting the press or other firms in the industry. The analyst utilized professional organizations, government agencies, major publications, and most important, a variety of on-line databases such as Dow Jones News Retrieval, Investext, and Nexis. Six weeks after beginning the intelligence-gathering project, ABB management made an offer and Combustion Engineering accepted it. Clearly, the quality of the information and the speed with which it was collected played a crucial role in the company's ability to make the proper offer without risking competitive involvement.[14]

limits when the stock market crashed in 1987. Fidelity, like every investment firm, was flooded with calls from customers who wanted to sell. Disconcerted by its inability to handle the calling volume, Fidelity decided to redesign its information systems in order to boost capacity. A combination of hardware, software, well-organized data, motivated people, and efficient procedures ensures that Fidelity will never be caught short again.

Fidelity's first step was to replace its limited-capacity phone system. Capable of handling 672 callers simultaneously on its toll-free lines, the upgraded system has enabled Fidelity operators to leave customers on hold no more than 15 seconds. A master console in Boston is at the heart of the efficient phone system, routing calls to available operators in Fidelity facilities throughout the country. The system typically handles 120,000 calls a day now. Realizing that its 1,000 operators are personally responsible for much of the information transmitted to customers, Fidelity gives these people an extensive amount of training regarding the company's product lines. The college-educated operators spend 60 hours in initial study, and they are required to attend more training sessions when new products are introduced.

The company's next step was to develop a computer-based information system to give operators immediate access to customer account information. The computer workstations must access six separate mainframe computers in order to display customer account information on one screen. In the words of Fidelity executive John Cook, "Fidelity has spent more on developing systems in the last five years than anyone else and probably more on enhancing systems than most firms spend to develop them."

Fidelity is aware of its dependence on computers and manages its vulnerability carefully. To keep its systems up and running in case of an electrical blackout, there are five backup generators. And its own fiber optic telephone system protects Fidelity from problems with local service. By carefully maintaining its existing information systems and constantly looking for ways to apply new technologies, Fidelity plans to keep its customers satisfied and its competitors on the run.

Apply Your Knowledge

1. How has Fidelity used information-management technology to improve customer service?
2. What are the risks and drawbacks of installing enough information-handling capacity to address even the biggest load peaks, such as the 1987 crash?

Building Customer Loyalty

Information can be used to identify customers and to increase their product loyalty. The frequent flyer programs used by many airlines are good examples of a technique that builds customer loyalty. If customers fly a certain number of miles on United Airlines, for instance, they are given award checks that can be used for free flights or for upgrades to first class. Without information about the customer and the miles flown, this program would never work.

Similarly, customer information is key to the success of Staples, the office-supplies discounter (see Chapter 8). Founder Tom Stemberg targeted small companies that were unable to receive large discounts from other office suppliers because of their relatively low volumes. His major problem was finding those customers. Stemberg knew his success or failure hinged on his ability to get and maintain information about his potential customer base. Relying on computers and databases, Staples's system uses telemarketing to find the customers, attract them to the store for the first time, and then gather information about their needs and buying patterns. This information is used to offer special promotions and discounts again and again to convert these first-time buyers into loyal customers. Staples has enjoyed incredible success with its direct-marketing techniques, all of which are based on high-quality information.[15]

Finding New Markets

Information can be used to help organizations identify new opportunities, as American Express was hoping to do by analyzing the data it received about cardholders and their purchase patterns. By capturing data on products and customers and converting those data into information, managers can find new markets for existing products as well as new product opportunities with existing customers. For example, 3M scientists recently developed a drag-reduction coating for aerospace applications. While testing the new coating for Boeing, engineers from 3M and Boeing decided to test the material on rowing shells in Puget Sound—just for the fun of it. Information on the impressive results was reported to 3M managers, who recognized the unexpected opportunity. After continued testing, the new coating was used on the hull of the Stars and Stripes in its successful bid for the 1988 America's Cup. 3M now sells the coating to sailors, a market completely unanticipated during initial development of the product.[16]

At times, information and information technologies developed to increase internal efficiency may themselves become new products aimed at entirely new markets. The salespeople at American Hospital Supply (AHS), which buys medical supplies from manufacturers and sells them to hospitals, categorized their customers by purchasing habits. Managers at AHS realized that this information would be valuable to the manufacturers as well, and they opened another business area by selling information to the manufacturers. This by-product of the selling process is the basis for a new business opportunity.[17]

HOW MANAGERS USE INFORMATION

Information plays a central role in every aspect of management. Here's a brief look at the ways managers use information in the four managerial functions of planning, organizing, leading, and controlling.

Using Information to Plan

In the planning process, managers use information to develop goals and to allocate the organizational resources needed to attain those goals. Sandy Sigiloff, former CEO of The Wickes Companies, earned a reputation for being able to "consume information and make decisions on a dime." He gave much of the credit for his reputation to Wickes's information system, which allowed him to get the right information at the right time. When Wickes was struggling back from bankruptcy and a massive debt burden, Sigiloff used information to keep lenders closely informed about the company's financial health, which boosted the lenders' confidence and willingness to help the company get back on its feet.[18]

A significant amount of crucial information is also necessary for the strategic decision involved in developing and introducing a new product.[19] Information regarding customers, current and emerging competitors, market opportunities, threats, and economic factors is necessary to successfully launch new products. Strategic insight gained from pertinent information allowed Nintendo to re-energize the U.S. home video-game market, a market that had collapsed in the early 1980s (the pre-Nintendo days). Most experts had written off home video games, saying that they were a passing fad and that young people were no longer interested. But Minoru Arakawa, head of Nintendo of America, observed that people were still playing arcade video games, which offered much better sound and graphics than early home systems. From this, Nintendo surmised that there was still a market for home games; but to be successful, home games would have to be as challenging and as exciting as arcade games. With this strategic information, Nintendo planned and launched the original Nintendo Entertainment System, one of the best-selling toys of all time.[20]

Using Information to Organize

Information also plays a key role in the design of organization structure. The information system at Mrs. Fields Cookies (see "Cooking Up a Competitive Information System" at the end of this chapter) allows Debbi and Randy Fields to manage hundreds of stores with an unusually flat organization structure. The company's fully integrated information system keeps executives in such close contact with employees and customers that their spans of management are many times wider than the typical executive's.[21]

In order to staff the organization correctly, managers must have information about the needs of the organization and the skills of its employees. If managers fail to properly assess the skills needed for specific positions, the organization will fail to achieve its goals. Excelan, a $39 million marketer of circuitboards and software in San Jose, California, uses a database system to collect data and analyze the buying behavior of current and potential customers. Excelan's customers had traditionally based purchase decisions on technical product features and specifications, but analysis of buying behavior began to show that more and more customers were basing decisions on overall business criteria such as productivity. Marketing and sales managers are using this information to hire employees with more business knowledge and to provide additional training in this area.[22]

Using Information to Lead

Information is an important part of leadership and motivation. Informational power, the ability to release or withhold vital information, is one of the six types of managerial power, and it can be used both positively and negatively. Bob Sloss, president of metal-spring manufacturer Connor Spring, designed his company's information system around the notion that all employees should have access to company information, even sensitive profitability figures. By doing so, Sloss used his informational power to enable all his managers and employees to make better decisions.[23] On the other hand, when managers keep information away from employees (intentionally or not), or when the company's information system doesn't provide the right information, then decision making, productivity, and quality will likely suffer.

The innovative use of data and information drives the success of Visible Changes, a hair salon chain headquartered in Houston, Texas. At the heart of the company's people management system is a computer system that tracks sales volume, the productivity of each haircutter, the popularity of each hair-care product, and the number of repeat customers. Compensation for haircutters is based on performance, and since the company wants to build repeat business, haircutters are paid a 35 percent commission each time they are requested by a returning client, as opposed to a 25 percent commission for walk-in customers. Visible Changes also wants to increase its profitability by selling hair-care products, so haircutters earn health-care benefits by selling $120 worth of products each week, and they earn a 15 percent cut of product sales above $120 a week. Profit sharing ties employees to the company and gives them a stake in its future. These and many other incentive programs established by the company are aimed

Mrs. Paul's uses a computerized information system to control the production of frozen fish meals. Using the weight of the fish before it is processed, the weight of any scraps, and the weight of the finished products, the computer calculates the production yield. If the actual yield drops below the expected yield at any point during the day, production managers can immediately adjust the equipment to improve the yield.

at increasing performance by motivating and rewarding employees. Visible Changes even includes employees in the decision making. Recently, employees agreed that every haircutter must achieve a request rate of 25 percent within three months and 50 percent within six months—or leave. Without the ability to collect and analyze data, these reward programs would not be possible.[24]

Using Information to Control

Information is the key to implementing effective management control systems (see Chapter 19 for an in-depth discussion of control). The control process is defined as setting standards, measuring actual performance, comparing actual performance with standards, and acting on the results. For instance, the comparison of actual performance with standards yields information. Without information, managers cannot accurately evaluate a situation or take the appropriate action. The implementation of new control systems often occurs because management receives new information. For example, in the airline industry, a critical standard is overall seat utilization. In the past, airlines were conservative when it came to overbooking flights because bumping passengers created bad publicity. However, new information from market experiments indicated that bumped customers would sell their tickets back to the airline for various combinations of free flights and cash. This gave the airlines a way to handle passenger overflow. By utilizing computer modeling, the airlines booked flights more aggressively, knowing that they had a way to handle potential overflows.[25]

Connor Springs's information system allows employees at any stage of a product's design and production to insert special instructions, recommend changes, or stop production entirely until problems can be worked out. If an employee knows that only one firm can provide special services for a particular part (such as surface grinding), he or she can make a note in the information system, and when the part is ready for grinding, the employee handling that phase will know where to send it. Because the system gives employees vital information, they can improve quality and productivity by taking action when they see problems or opportunities.[26]

Mrs. Fields, Connor Springs, and other companies that benefit from information are able to do so because they have systems that process information efficiently and effectively. The following section describes the components of a typical information system, compares several common types, and explains the approaches that managers can take when designing information systems.

INFORMATION SYSTEMS

information systems Procedures and equipment that support the timely use, management, and processing of data or information regarding an organization's operations

computer-based information system (CBIS) An information system in which the computer plays a significant role

Information systems are manual or computerized systems that support the timely use, management, and processing of data and information concerning an organization's operations. An information system supports the activities of key people in the organizational environment, including employees, managers, customers, owners, and shareholders. Information systems can be completely computerized, completely manual, or some combination of the two.[27] A system that relies on computers for most or all of its operation is called a **computer-based information system (CBIS)**.

A CBIS can range from a single employee with his or her computer to global systems that link dozens of computers in many different countries. When considering the design and operation of information systems, it is helpful to divide them into three classes: personal, work-group, and organizationwide information systems.[28] As the name indicates, a personal system benefits a single employee or manager. Work-group systems coordinate the computing operations for a department, team, or other group of people. Such systems enable the people involved to share information (when several people edit copies of a report, for example) and information resources (when several people have access to a single expensive printer). Organizationwide systems encompass many people and departments throughout the organization; such systems frequently involve a variety of large and small computers serving people in different locations.

Information systems can be costly to develop and maintain, and the implementation of a system can dramatically change the way an organization conducts its operations. Because of the risks involved, it is important for managers to follow a careful process when developing new systems. For instance, the design of an organizationwide system usually involves five phases: (1) preliminary investigation to determine the nature and scope of the project, (2) requirements analysis to assess the needs of people who will use the system, (3) design of the system to identify and map out the various components, (4) purchase of the components, and (5) implementation of the system.[29] Exhibit 18.3 shows the major steps involved in each phase.

Regardless of the specific approach they take in designing a system, managers should keep four important points in mind. First, an information system should support the efforts of the people who will use it. In other words, the system should work for the people, not the other way around. Careful analysis of user needs is the best way to ensure that this happens. If a system doesn't help users, or if it adds to the complexity of their jobs, they aren't likely to use it.

Second, blindly automating existing organizational procedures is often a mistake. Before turning any procedure over to the computer, whether it's recording

Phase	Major Steps
Preliminary investigation	Determine nature of problem and scope of project Determine possible solutions Assess project feasibility Report to management
Requirements analysis	Collect facts relating to user and technical requirements Analyze facts Report to management
System design	Review requirements Conceptualize system Design physical system Finalize benefits and costs Report to management
System acquisition	Review design Prepare specifications for suppliers Evaluate and select suppliers Purchase components Report to management
System implementation	Schedule implementation Program, debug, and test software Train personnel Convert operations to new system Conduct postimplementation review Perform ongoing system maintenance

EXHIBIT 18.3

Developing an Organizationwide Information System

This table lists the major steps involved in designing and implementing an organizationwide information system. In some cases, the organization will do all these steps itself; in other cases, it will hire an outside contractor to do some or all of the steps.

customer orders or managing a warehouse, managers need to ask themselves whether the existing way is really the best way, now that a computer system is part of the picture. Automating a faulty or inappropriate procedure will only lead to more efficient mistakes—in other words, it will make the organization more efficient but not more effective. Ted Standish, director of information systems for Gillette's North Atlantic Group, says it well: "The way a job was done in the past may not be the way we want it done in the future."[30] And referring to sales force automation technologies, consultant Peter Perera points out that a "computer will not substitute for basic selling techniques and sound management. If you have a problem, a computer will only aggravate it."[31]

Third, managers must be committed to using their new information systems if they want to dramatically alter and improve the organization's operations.[32] If they don't throw their support behind the design, implementation, and continuing maintenance of the system, managers will inadvertently send a message to employees that the system isn't important to the organization's success.

Fourth, information systems must grow and evolve as the organization itself grows and evolves. When an organization increases the number of customers or clients it serves, moves into new markets, faces new competitors, or responds to any of a variety of other internal and external changes, its information systems must adapt as well.

Components of an Information System

The term *information system* conjures images of hardware and software components, but CBISs actually contain five basic components: hardware, software, data, procedures, and people. It's important for managers to understand all five components in order to communicate with and support information system developers.[33]

hardware Computerized machinery used to process transactions and convert data to information

software The collection of computer programs that control the processing of data in a computer

- *Hardware.* The machinery used to process data and convert them to information is considered **hardware.** This includes the computer itself, input and output devices, data storage devices, and communications devices such as modems, which connect computers to telephone lines.
- *Software.* The computer programs that control the processing of data in a computer are called **software.** Software consists of instructions that guide the circuitry within the computer, and the term *software* is applied to commercially prepared computer programs (such as operating systems, word processors, and spreadsheets) as well as to custom-written programs that address specific organizational tasks.[34]
- *Data.* The facts used to create information constitute the system's data. These facts are generally stored on tape, disc, or compact disc until the computer requires them. Sales figures, salary amounts, part numbers, and economic measures are examples of the data used in typical information systems. Organized collections of data constitute a *database;* a database is analogous to a library in that it contains organized, collected information and some means of accessing that information.[35]
- *Procedures.* To utilize a computer-based information system effectively, managers rely on well-defined policies and procedures to guide the operation of computer systems in order to satisfy the needs of all users. Standard operating procedures guide daily computer use, and disaster recovery procedures describe the steps to be taken in the event of a hardware failure, fire, or some

other emergency. Because information systems have to work within organizations' managerial context, system designers need to understand management expectations when implementing procedures.

- *People.* Often overlooked as a critical element, people have the most impact on the success or failure of an information system. People develop, implement, and update the computer programs; operate and maintain the computer hardware; and use the information created by the computer system. The implementation of a new system can affect employees, suppliers, and customers, so managers need to address these changes through training and attention to the human element.

Types of Information Systems

Computers are tackling problems faced by all levels of employees and management within organizations. First the computer transformed operational management of organizations' day-to-day transactions (such as order processing, accounting, and inventory control). Then computers were applied to the information needs of middle managers with the advent of management information systems and personal computers to support planning and budgeting. And, more recently, computers have been used to support strategic decision-making needs.[36] These computer systems are characterized as transaction-processing systems, management information systems, and decision support and executive information systems.[37]

Transaction-Processing Systems

When an organization encounters well-structured, routine processes that have traditionally been handled manually, efficiency can be significantly increased by implementing a **transaction-processing system (TPS)**, a computerized system that automates data collection and processing. American Express uses TPSs to accept charges and to bill cardholders, for instance. As American Express's situation illustrates, a TPS can be called on to handle thousands or even millions of transactions during a single day.

transaction-processing system (TPS) An information system that supports the collection and processing of an organization's transactions

Sometimes a TPS interacts directly with another computer system, as when a drugstore's computers transmit orders to a drug wholesaler's computers. In most cases, however, people are involved. When a passenger checks in for a flight and the airline representative checks with the computer to assign a seat, a TPS is the type of system at work. When the seat is assigned, the computer updates its database, taking that seat off the available list and confirming the customer's name on the passenger log.

Management Information Systems

Unlike a transaction-processing system, which automates recordkeeping, a *management information system (MIS)* collects, processes, and transmits information that supports routine, predictable decisions that managers confront. The goal of an MIS is the collection and distribution of information to managers so they can evaluate situations using their own judgment and then make the appropriate decisions.

An MIS usually supplies reports and statistics, such as monthly sales figures, employee records, and factory production schedules. In doing so, an MIS often takes data from a transaction-processing system and transforms them into useful information. In addition, in cases involving routine decision making, such as decision support system (DSS) An information system that helps higher-level managers solve unstructured and nonroutine problems

deciding how many tires are needed in order to manufacture a certain number of cars, an MIS can go beyond simple report generation and provide automated answers to management questions.

Decision Support and Executive Information Systems

Whereas management information systems provide structured, routine information for managerial decision making, a **decision support system (DSS)** assists managers in solving nonroutine problems. A related type of system is the *executive information system (EIS),* which is designed to meet the information and decision needs of the most senior executives in the organization (see Exhibit 18.4). Managers use DSSs and EISs to model various sets of data to answer a series of "what if" questions. For both types of systems to be useful for managers, they should support semistructured or unstructured decision making, should be flexible to changing needs, and should be easy to learn and use.[38]

Many decision support systems use the power of desktop computers for analysis while retrieving data from larger computers. For example, Hertz has implemented a DSS to give its managers access to marketing information. By storing data and information on the mainframe computer and using the personal computer to do the data analysis, Hertz managers are able to analyze mountains of demographic data and make immediate marketing decisions in the dynamic car-rental market. The system allows managers to keep track of and respond to current market conditions, and it also utilizes historical performance data to help managers predict future performance. Models in the system can suggest special rates and unlimited mileage promotions to boost sales when performance is predicted to be slow. The greatest advantage of the system has been providing managers with instant access to information directly related to their decision-making needs.[39]

Types of Computers

Organizations first put computers to use in the early 1950s. To get an idea of how far the computer has come since those days, if automobiles had advanced as

EXHIBIT 18.4

Decision Support System for Executives

Comshare's Commander program enables executives to dig deeper for detail. Here executives touch the "briefing book" (*first screen*) and then choose "financial performance" (*second screen*), which highlights in red the decrease in electronic sales in July (*third screen*). After checking trends for the year (*fourth screen*), executives can get more detail on the troubled electronics division (*fifth and sixth screens*), such as information about how badly switch sales have slumped. By touching a figure, they can call more screens to probe further.

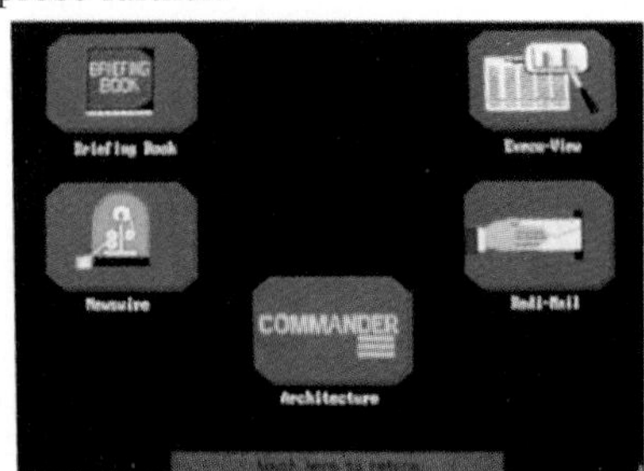

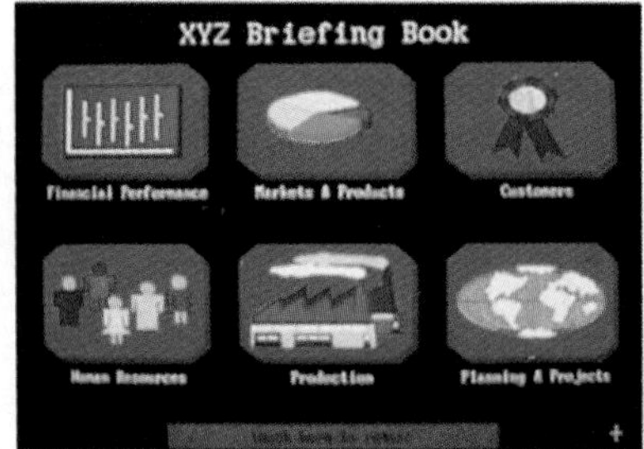

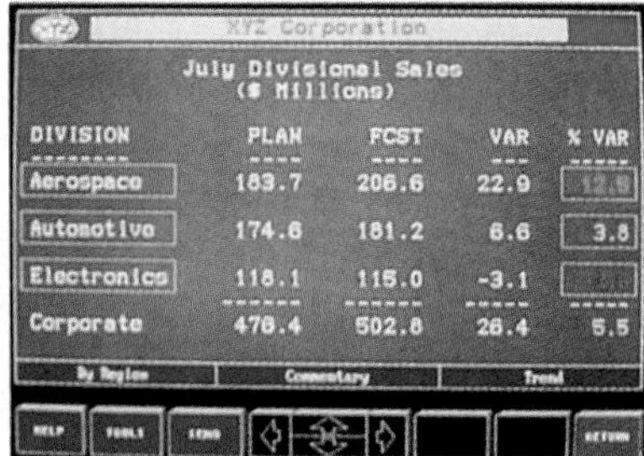

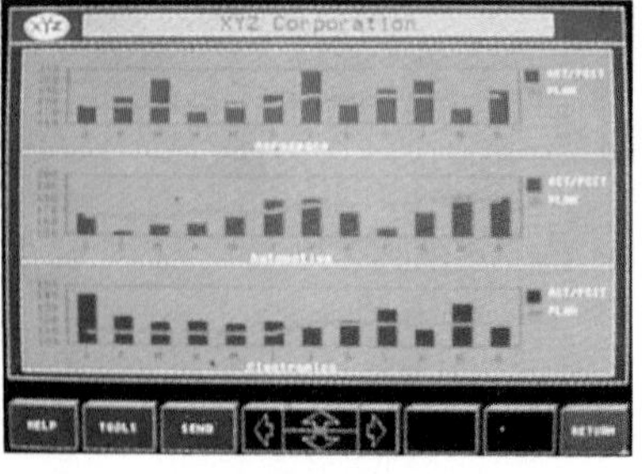

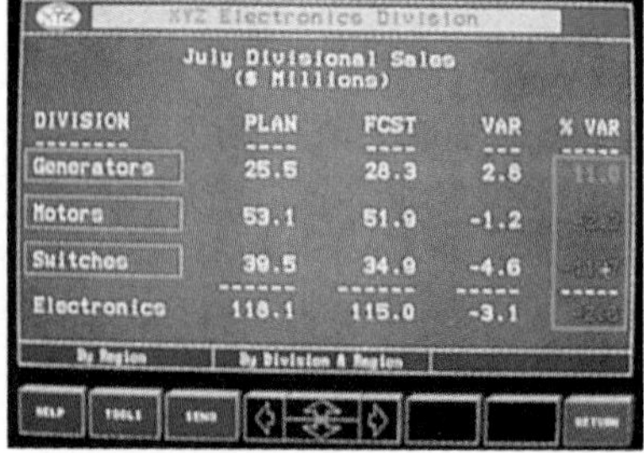

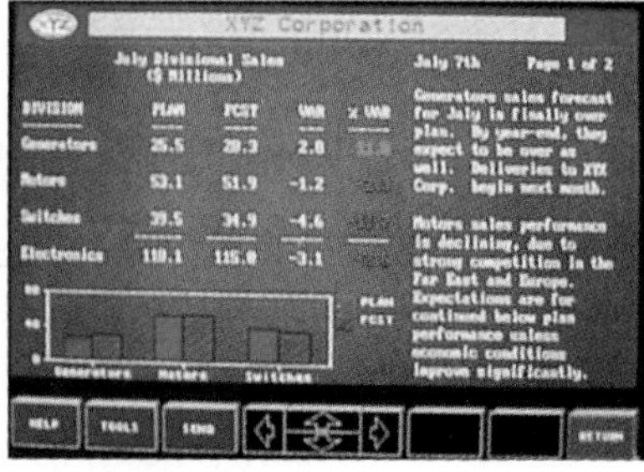

much in the last four decades as computers have, consumers would be able to buy a Rolls-Royce for less than $3, and it would get something like 3 million miles on a gallon of gas.[40] This is more than just an amusing piece of trivia, however. If computers hadn't made the mind-boggling advances they've made since the 1950s, they would not be much of a force in management today. Few organizations would have the budget—or the patience—for a computer that would fill a large room, dim city lights when it was operating, last an average of only a few hours between failures, and have less computing power than today's cheapest pocket calculator.[41]

A computer-based information system can be as simple as a single personal computer or as complex as a multiple-computer network that spans several continents. Technological advances in the last few decades have produced quite a range of computer types, from micro units that fit in the palm of the hand to multimillion-dollar supercomputers. In increasing order of processing power, today's computers can be grouped into five classes: microcomputers, workstations, minicomputers, mainframes, and supercomputers. Many information systems contain two or more types; a typical example is the system in which a mainframe computer performs complex tasks and data storage for a number of microcomputers.

- *Microcomputers* are the computers that most people are familiar with; the Apple Macintosh and the IBM Personal Computer (PC) are among the best-known products. A microcomputer, often referred to generically as a *personal computer,* represents the smallest and least-expensive class of computers. Computers in this category are now available in several sizes, designated by *desktop, laptop, notebook,* and even *palmtop.* The leading manufacturers of microcomputers include IBM, Apple, and Compaq, but hundreds of companies are fighting for a share of this market.
- *Workstations* are a relatively recent development, merging the speed of minicomputers with the desktop convenience of microcomputers. Workstations are used primarily by designers, engineers, scientists, and others who need fast computing and powerful graphics capabilities to solve mathematically intense problems. A typical application in this segment is computer-aided design (CAD). An engineer for Rockwell International, for instance, might use a CAD system to design a part for the space shuttle; the system could perform such tasks as predicting response to stresses and calculating the amount of steel required to make the part. Three of the leading manufacturers of workstations are Sun Microsystems, Hewlett-Packard, and Digital Equipment Corporation (DEC). (A note on terminology: workstations are just as "personal" as microcomputers, in that they are typically used by a single person, but the term *workstation* is needed to separate this more powerful class of computers. Also, any terminal at which a computer user works has traditionally been called a workstation, but increasingly the computer industry is using the term solely to describe this particular class of computers.)
- *Minicomputers* emerged in the 1960s at the same time as the modern mainframe. Minicomputers have the same general capabilities as mainframes, such as supporting multiple users simultaneously, but they are smaller, cheaper, and less powerful. Typical applications of minicomputers include controlling a manufacturing process in a factory, managing a company's payroll, and helping a wholesaler keep track of sales and inventory. Some important applications that traditionally fell in the minicomputer category,

particularly in scientific research and engineering, have been largely taken over by workstations as the power of those machines has increased in recent years. Leading makers of minicomputers include Hewlett-Packard, DEC, and IBM.

- *Mainframe computers* are large and powerful systems capable of handling vast amounts of data. These systems embodied the popular image of computers until the arrival of the microcomputer in the late 1970s and early 1980s. Mainframes handle a variety of business tasks, particularly finance and accounting activities that require lots of repetitive calculations. The traditional way of giving people access to mainframe computing power is through a series of *dumb terminals,* devices that look a lot like desktop computers but don't have enough processing power to operate on their own. Today's major mainframe manufacturers include IBM, Control Data, Hitachi, Siemens, Unisys, and Amdahl.[42]
- *Supercomputers* represent the leading edge in computer performance. A supercomputer is capable of handling the most complex processing tasks, with speeds in excess of a billion calculations per second. A Cray Research Y-MP, one of the best-known supercomputers, can process in one minute the work that a typical mainframe would take several hours to accomplish. It carries an equally breathtaking price tag, in the neighborhood of $20 million to $25 million.[43] For certain engineering and scientific problems, however, a supercomputer is the only tool that can do the job. Seismic analysis, weather forecasting, complex engineering modeling, and genetic research are among the common uses of supercomputers. As one might expect, only a handful of companies compete in this market, including the leader Cray Research, IBM, Fujitsu, Hitachi, and NEC.[44]

The Impact of Information Systems

Managers who implement new information systems must confront the ways in which information systems can affect an organization. The availability of cost-effective information technology has caused many changes in both organization structure and organization-to-organization linkages.[45]

New external linkages can occur when organizations use computer technology to cement working partnerships. For example, Otis Elevator has implemented an integrated database of customer and service history. Sophisticated technology detects faults in a customer's elevator and transmits this information automatically to Otis's centralized system. A repair technician is then directed to repair the elevator.[46] This changes the relationship between Otis and its customers by using information to forge closer links.

Information systems are altering the relationship between consumer goods producers such as Procter & Gamble and supermarket retailers. Before the days of computerized checkout scanners, retailers relied on the producers for market information to make decisions about merchandising, pricing, and advertising. Today, however, retailers can collect a prodigious amount of data with their checkout scanners, and they have a much better idea of what sells when and why. This new level of information-processing capability allows retailers to make better decisions without relying on producers.[47]

Inside the organization, information systems support managers' efforts to flatten the organization structure, partly by giving employees more information

With the help of 1,000 personal computers linked to a mainframe computer, Coca-Cola personnel can now avoid the frustration of missing telephone messages or vital company memos. Cheryl Currid, Coca-Cola's director of applied-information technology, has seen this information system improve communication among managers, employees, and work groups, boosting the company's responsiveness and helping decision makers more quickly get the information they need to solve pressing problems.

and thus more power to solve problems on their own. For example, the home electronics division of Thorn EMI, a diversified British company, implemented extensive information systems to support its organizational strategy. As a result, management layers have been reduced from 13 to 4, making information flow throughout the division more efficient and effective.[48]

Information systems can also improve an organization's responsiveness. At a General Electric dishwasher plant that has made extensive use of information technology, top management gets information about problems at the lowest levels that have significant impact on operations. One GE manager remembers that before the plant made a serious commitment to information technology by implementing a highly automated factory, inventory management was so poor that minor parts would be depleted. The problem would go undetected for weeks until work came to a standstill. With their new "factory of the future," top management knows about potential problems in hours or minutes, and people in the plant can correct problems immediately.[49]

Limitations of Information Systems

Information systems can bring innumerable benefits to the organization, but with these advances come a host of issues that did not exist before the information revolution. As organizations become more dependent on computers, their vulnerability increases as well. Without computers, says G. N. Simonds, executive director of management information systems at Chrysler, "We cannot run our plants, we cannot schedule, we cannot bill or collect money for our product, we can't design our product. In essence, we very quickly shut the company down."[50]

Organizations must consider the consequences of computer crime (such as "hackers" breaking into a phone company's computers and stealing long-distance time), power outages, fires, earthquakes, sabotage, and software bugs that could damage their computer systems and cripple their organizations. For example, a recent software glitch resulted in a massive shutdown of AT&T's

Advanced data communications technology allows Gannett to prepare its *USA Today* International Edition in Arlington, Virginia, then beam the text and photos via satellite to printing plants around the world. To distribute an issue of *USA Today* in London on a Wednesday morning, Gannett transmits materials to the printer in Zurich, Switzerland, on Tuesday afternoon; the newspapers are printed and then shipped to England overnight.

long-distance telephone network, affecting tens of millions of customers throughout the nation.[51] Organizations need to take steps to avoid such problems, of course, but managers don't have complete control over circumstances inside and outside the organization. To minimize the impact of system shutdowns and other problems, managers need to outline detailed disaster recovery and backup procedures before problems occur.[52] For example, GE safeguards its worldwide communications network by using 500 small computers around the world to route traffic between its three mainframe computer centers. These small computers have the ability to automatically reroute traffic when lines go down. Extensive backup power alternatives to the three mainframe computers allow GE to keep network availability above its goal of 99.85 percent.[53]

Technologically advanced organizations must use computers wisely and guard against information overload. The depersonalization that can result from an extensive reliance on computers intimidates many employees and customers. And, with information so easily transmitted and altered, organizations, governments, and societies are vulnerable to the misinterpretation of information. Erroneous information can cause inappropriate and damaging responses. For example, a test message was sent out from the International Atomic Energy Agency in Vienna to weather centers in 25 countries. Clearly marked as a test, the message referred to a buildup of radiation over Eastern Europe and the former Soviet Union. As the test message spread, it was misinterpreted as an actual event. Stock markets from Tokyo and Hong Kong to the Middle East, Europe, and Wall Street reacted erratically to the rumors of another Chernobyl.[54]

INFORMATION SYSTEM TECHNOLOGY

The ever-increasing demands from users for more power and capability continue to drive advances in information-processing technology. New technologies enter the marketplace regularly, offering organizations many choices, and the successful organizations utilize technology to become more efficient and effective. Consider the extent to which information-processing technologies have enhanced the field of law enforcement. Police departments use automated records systems to maintain large databases for immediate search and retrieval capabilities. Computer-aided dispatch systems utilize communications technology to improve allocation of officers to patrol duties. Mobile digital terminals link patrol officers with local, county, state, and federal criminal justice information systems, giving them remote access to the automated records systems. And an automated fingerprint identification system uses sophisticated algorithms to check one fingerprint against all the fingerprints on file.[55] The two major categories of information technology are data processing and data communications. In addition, the emerging technology of expert systems offers a great deal of promise to organizations faced with complex decision-making processes.

Data Processing

data processing Collecting, sorting, and storing data with the goal of converting them into useful information

At the core of any information system is the **data-processing** function, the collection and sorting of data and the conversion of those data into useful information. As computers have evolved in the last several decades, so have the ways that organizations approach data processing. Up until the 1960s (and for many years after that in some organizations), one didn't just walk up to the computer and go to work. Computer use at the time was characterized by **batch processing,** in which users prepared data and programs, then submitted their "jobs" to the computer center, where operators collected the jobs and fed them to the computer in "batches" at regular intervals. Users had no choice but to sit and wait for the results. It isn't hard to imagine the impact that such delays would have on organizational performance.

batch processing A method of data processing in which transactions are collected in a file and then processed as a group, usually at night when there is little demand for computer resources

Batch processing is the appropriate choice for many computing applications, including payrolls, customer billings, and marketing research. In many data-processing situations, however, anything more than a modest amount of delay is intolerable. What if a bank's customers tried to get cash from an ATM, and the machine responded with the message, "I'm working on your request; please come back tomorrow for your cash"? Or what if the computers processing radar data for an air-traffic control system were so slow that they couldn't keep up with the movement of all the planes? In cases such as these, the computer has to respond nearly instantaneously in order for the information it provides to be useful. This leads to the idea of **on-line processing,** in which the user is connected directly to the transaction-processing system, and the system acts on each input as it is entered.[56]

on-line processing A method of data processing in which users interact directly with the transaction-processing system; the computer's files, therefore, are updated as soon as new information is available

Even though these issues may seem too technical to be of much use to managers, they can have a profound impact on an organization's success or failure. Mrs. Fields would not be able to operate with such a lean management structure if it weren't for computer technology. And American Express knew it would not be able to satisfy customers if it didn't make major changes to its information-handling abilities. In both cases, managers at all levels had to become familiar with at least the basics of data processing in order to effectively integrate computers into their organizations.

Data Communications

Just as data processing is a key function in most organizations, so is an organization's ability to communicate electronically, both inside the organization and out. Data-processing power can be multiplied many times over by linking two or more computers, using technology for transmission of data between computers, known as **data communications.** In the broadest sense, data communications is used to fax documents, authorize credit card purchases, print newspapers simultaneously in separate locations, receive cash from automatic teller machines, speak on the telephone, and watch live television broadcasts from the other side of the world. Voice and video aren't normally considered part of the realm of data communications, but with advances in digital telephones and television, computers increasingly handle voice and video in the same way they handle text and numerical data.

data communications The technology for transmitting data between computers

A **computer network** is a form of data communication in which two or more computers are linked together. For instance, mainframe computer networks run automatic teller machines and airline reservation systems. Today, personal computers linked in *local area networks (LANs)* are beginning to solve business problems that once required their larger counterparts. Donald F. Tuline, president of Richmond Savings Credit Union located in British Columbia, was faced with a huge number of bad loans (as a result of a slump in the fishing industry and the collapse of Vancouver real estate). Tuline decided to solve the financial crisis by attracting new business with a sliding-scale pricing scheme that gave

computer network A form of data communication in which hardware devices such as computers, workstations, printers, and data disk drives are linked together increasing discounts to higher-volume customers. Because the bank's existing minicomputer was unable to handle the financial analysis needed for the sliding scale, Tuline implemented a personal computer network connecting 250 employees in six offices. Using the linked personal computers to calculate the new pricing scheme has increased annual revenues by close to $500,000. Moreover, the networked PCs allow employees to write their own custom software, to help customers with tax returns, and to execute their own direct-mail promotions. The flexibility afforded by the network has given the credit union a unique competitive advantage.[57]

Similarly, Mrs. Fields uses its network to feed business data back and forth between corporate headquarters and each store. Aside from required government forms, paperwork has virtually been eliminated. Moreover, employees are encouraged to use the electronic mail system made possible by the network to send complaints and suggestions directly to top management. In addition to the flat organization structure described earlier in this chapter, using the network for transmission of business data and electronic mail has significantly reduced the number of employees needed at headquarters and allowed top management to react immediately to problems and new ideas.[58]

electronic data interchange (EDI) A form of data communication that allows automatic transmission of preformatted business transaction data between organizations with little or no human interaction

Electronic data interchange (EDI) is a form of data communications that allows computer-to-computer transmission of business transaction data between organizations using standard formats (see Exhibit 18.5).[59] Because computers transmit data directly to other computers, without much human interaction, EDI cuts down on processing costs and decreases transaction times. The textile company Milliken buys fibers from suppliers such as Du Pont and then weaves the fabric for delivery to customers such as Levi Strauss. The finished garment is then shipped to Nordstrom, The Gap, and other retailers. By using EDI to transmit orders, shipment dates, and inventory data, Milliken has linked its 55 plants and warehouses with its suppliers and customers. The order turnaround time for Milliken has been reduced from six weeks to one week.[60] EDI is having a substantial impact on organizational computing because it strengthens the bonds between organizations, their suppliers, and their customers while increasing efficiency and lowering costs for participating business partners.

teleconferencing The use of communications technology to conduct meetings among people in separate locations

With the advances in data communications technology, many organizations are changing the way they conduct business. As communication between entities becomes easier and faster, trends such as teleconferencing and telecommuting are commonplace. **Teleconferencing** refers to meetings that take place with peo-

EXHIBIT 18.5

Electronic Data Interchange

Electronic data interchange (EDI) links business organizations with their customers and suppliers and allows preformatted business transactions to be exchanged electronically with little or no human intervention.

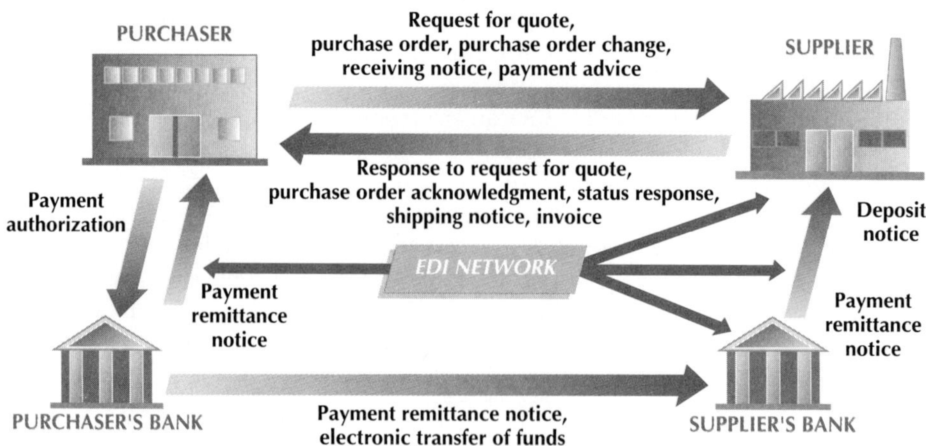

ple who are in physically separated sites. For example, the retail chain Wal-Mart utilizes a form of teleconferencing called videoconferencing to enable headquarters staff and store employees to both see and hear each other on television. Wal-Mart uses teleconferencing to broadcast urgent messages, to handle situations in which many stores must converse with headquarters to solve a critical problem, to share merchandising and display information between stores, and to implement training. The satellite technology used by Wal-Mart for teleconferencing also gathers sales and inventory data from stores for the central computer, transmits credit card authorizations, and tracks the company's complex distribution system.[61]

Other forms of teleconferencing include computer conferencing (involving electronic mail) and audio teleconferencing (using telephones). With computer conferencing, conference members transmit electronic messages to each other. Often, an electronic bulletin board is used to post a topic for discussion. With audio teleconferencing, conference participants use the telephone to discuss important topics. Referred to as conference calling, this technology allows participants to have a discussion with more than two people on the telephone.[62]

Since data communications tools are available at a reasonable cost, there has been an increase in home-based employment. Communications tools such as the telephone, computers with modems, and fax machines link **telecommuters** to their co-workers, suppliers, and clients.[63] The number of people telecommuting is expected to top 33 million in the coming years.[64] Telecommuters are spared the physical commute and some of the office politics; the organizations that employ them bypass the expense of establishing physical office space. However, telecommuting cannot work for every job, such as many management, personal-service, and manufacturing positions. Organizations must also consider the motivation and initiative of each employee before giving him or her the opportunity to work from home.[65]

Steve Roberts may be the ultimate telecommuter: a computer consultant and author, he has outfitted his bicycle with four computers, and he communicates with clients via an electronic-mail hookup beamed by satellite. The bicycle serves as his office, and Roberts consults for companies such as Sun Microsystems that want to explore mobile computing and telecommunication.

telecommuters Employees and managers who use communications technology to accomplish work from home

Expert Systems

An **expert system** is a computer system that attempts to replicate the decisions of a human expert in a specific subject area. It uses stored facts and rules to mimic human decision making (see Exhibit 18.6). Expert systems are part of a broader field known as **artificial intelligence,** or the ability of computers to accomplish tasks that human observers would consider intelligent. Expert systems are the area of artificial intelligence most frequently applied to organizational management situations.[66] For example, selling computer systems involves a complex step known as configuration, in which the right pieces of hardware and software must be selected to meet each customer's needs. Massachusetts-based Digital Equipment uses an expert system called the Expert Configurator (XCON) to configure almost every computer system it sells. A pioneering effort in expert system technology, XCON ensures that components of computer systems can work together and that all necessary components are included in the configuration. Digital now uses more than 50 expert systems, saving the company more than $200 million a year in increased efficiency.[67] Other companies with successful expert systems include Westinghouse, Imperial Chemical Industries, and Du Pont, which now has over 600 expert systems in place.[68]

expert system A computerized system designed to replicate the decisions of a human expert about a specific subject

artificial intelligence The use of computers to mimic human thought

Managers may consider developing expert systems to capture the expertise of seasoned employees, to minimize the risk of error in decision making, or to

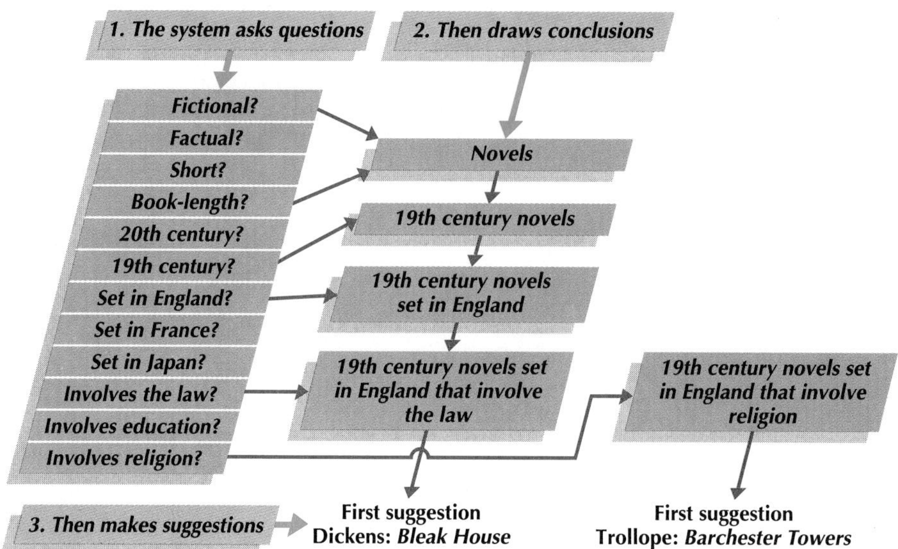

EXHIBIT 18.6

Dialogue with a Simple Expert System

This simplified expert system helps readers select books by asking about their preferences, then drawing conclusions based on their responses. Rules (for example, if the answers to "Fictional?" and "Book-length?" are yes, then the reader wants a novel) and stored data allow the system to draw these conclusions.

interrelate large volumes of essential information. When organizations develop expert systems to capture expertise, they minimize the risk of losing key employees in specific jobs who can make decisions quickly and effectively. Such systems record the rules that experienced employees rely on in their own decision making, and then give other employees access to this accumulated knowledge. Expert systems developed to minimize risk of error are aimed at reducing financial loss, decision-making time, and loss of life, and they cover far-reaching applications in medicine, manufacturing, and aviation. Managers who use expert systems to process large volumes of information utilize the ability of expert systems to reach conclusions by uncovering linkages and relationships buried in masses of data.[69]

The accounting firm Coopers & Lybrand developed an expert system that does all three. Called ExperTAX, the system helps accountants provide better tax advice and better tax returns for corporate clients; ExperTAX minimizes the risk of error because it never forgets to ask the client a question, and it always checks tax information against the client's financial statistics. Updating all the users in a timely fashion to reflect tax code changes or new strategies for corporate tax planning is accomplished quickly in the expert system. And since ExperTAX incorporates the detailed tax rules, junior accountants can perform more complete and accurate tax planning while being trained by the expert system.[70]

ISSUES IN INFORMATION RESOURCE MANAGEMENT

As the management of information resources becomes increasingly important to the success of organizations, the widespread use of computers forces managers to face some new and often controversial issues.

Computer Literacy and Computer Phobia

One of the most important information-management issues that today's managers face is educating employees to accept the new procedures and skills necessary for working with computers. Computer phobia (an unreasonable fear of working with computers) can occur when managers fail to prepare and educate their employees for new computer systems and procedures. Without adequate training, an individual with little or no computer background might find a new computer system daunting. And first impressions have a lasting impact.

To develop a computer-literate work force, managers should introduce computers and computer systems with as much guidance, training, and support as possible. For example, Chevron took several steps to overcome possible resistance to its new computerized human resource system. First, the computer system was designed to be easy to learn and easy to use. Next, modular training programs were developed for various categories of users, such as front-line managers, human resource managers and professionals, and system operators. Finally, Chevron trained its field representatives to handle problems and questions. By making the system easy to use and by providing training and support, Chevron successfully implemented the new system and overcame the fears of the new users.[71]

Centralized versus Distributed Processing

Distributed processing is a good example of how technology interacts with the art and science of management. Just as an organization can lean toward centralized control or toward decentralized control, so too can an information system. **Centralized data processing** is an approach to data processing in which computer power—and control of that computer power—is concentrated in one part of the organization. This is analogous to a centralized organization structure, in which power and decision-making authority are concentrated in the hands of a few top managers. Many of the electronic cash registers used by supermarkets, on the other hand, are examples of **distributed data processing,** in which data are processed on two or more computers.[72] In these systems, each register is actually a small computer that performs selected data processing by reading the bar code from the product purchased, storing the data, and calculating the customer's total. The data are then transmitted to a central computer where they are used to manage inventory, initiate promotions, and calculate profitability. This system would also be considered a batch-processing system since sales data are accumulated throughout the day and then processed at night on the central computer.

centralized data processing An approach to data processing in which control is concentrated in one central part of the organization

distributed data processing A method of processing data in which the transformation process occurs on two or more computers

Organizations traditionally performed data processing on central computers and passed out printed reports to appropriate employees and managers. For companies with a large number of transactions, centralization does provide attractive economies of scale. A central information systems department can be economical and can provide a great degree of control over the integrity and security of the data. However, with advances in information technology, users of personal computers and workstations have a formidable amount of processing power on their desks—and an increasing awareness of how their own computers can help them create information.

While distributed processing allows computer users to have more control over their information, the integrity of the data becomes a major concern. When the processing is distributed, the data are also distributed. This makes the data difficult to consolidate, and it causes concern for the accuracy of the data. For instance, the marketing manager might use a personal computer to increase next month's revenue projection based on sales force optimism, while at the same

SOCIAL RESPONSIBILITY AND ETHICS

Your Right to Privacy vs. the Marketing Databases

Right now, even as you're reading this, your name and your life are part of dozens and dozens of databases. Your school knows the courses you take, the grades you get, and your home address. Your bank knows your account balance, where you used to bank, maybe even your mother's maiden name (it's requested on most account applications). Your government knows how much money you made last year, the kind of car you own, and how many speeding tickets you've received. The list goes on and on: video stores, libraries, doctors, dentists, insurance companies, and many others keep records on your behavior and activities.

There is nothing unethical about maintaining a database, and there is certainly nothing unethical about using a computer to manage the database. The ethical dilemmas arise when companies buy, borrow, rent, or exchange information, usually without your knowledge or permission. Most of the time, you will probably never know that your records are being seen or used by others, people you never imagined would or should be able to put together a big file on your life.

That's dilemma number one: Who should have the right to see your records? Should the government have the right to ask your employer to turn over your employment records? Should a company selling low-cost long-distance telephone service be allowed to look at your telephone records? In the 1980s, the Selective Service Administration wanted to find men of draft age who hadn't yet registered. Among other databases, they bought a list of names and birthdays from an ice cream parlor, a list developed as a promotion to recognize children's birthdays in some special way. In the outcry that followed, the Selective Service gave back the list. But the dilemma remains: Who should see your records?

Dilemma number two: Should you have the right to know who wants your records and be able to refuse access? Say you've been getting all kinds of unsolicited mailings lately, and you're tired of having your mailbox filled with offers to buy magazine subscriptions, computer software, or ski parkas. You can ask that mailers not use your name and address by writing to the Direct Marketing Association. But that's the easy

time the manufacturing manager, sitting at another personal computer, is decreasing the revenue projection based on a shortage of materials. Without a mechanism for reconciling these differences, the organization would end up with conflicting information.

One attractive compromise between centralized and distributed processing is called an integrated network. Houston-based American General decided to link the various distributed systems used by its subsidiaries, Life and Casualty Insurance and National Life and Accident. By linking minicomputers at the subsidiaries to a centralized mainframe computer, American General managers gained centralized control of top-level data while still allowing the district sites to maintain control over their own systems and data.[73]

The Paperless Office

A major issue in the management of information is the reduction of paper in the workplace. With sophisticated computer and communications equipment, electronic pulses are replacing paper in offices and factories around the globe, at least in theory. The key goal of the paperless office is to slash operating costs by improving the efficiency of storing and retrieving business communications as well as increasing the accuracy of data and information.[74] In reality, however, many organizations find that achieving the paperless office is easier said than done, largely because computers can generate paper reports so quickly and easily.

The U.S. Department of Defense's nerve center, the Pentagon, found itself drowning in paper. For instance, the manuals that show naval technicians how part. What happens when you apply for health insurance and you are asked to sign a statement that allows the insurer to search a medical records database for your history and to provide information on you to others? In some cases, such as when the government wants to verify your eligibility for welfare, you must be notified for a response before the government makes a move on a negative decision. Should you have the right to know when people want your records? Should you have the right to allow some people to see your records and to refuse others?

Dilemma number three: What information should or should not be disclosed? In the United States, there are at least five major federal laws on privacy, dealing with credit data, governmental data, bank files, videotape movie rentals, and computerized matching of government data. Despite these federal laws and some additional ones in selected states, a lot of personal information about U.S. citizens can still be disclosed, information that may embarrass people or in some other way have a negative impact on their lives. Denmark, in contrast, has strict laws that prohibit marketers from exchanging information about substance abuse, criminal activities, or sexual inclinations; other countries have similar restrictions. But who decides what should or should not be allowed to be disclosed?

A debate is raging between companies that compile, use, and sell marketing databases and people who are concerned about privacy. On the one hand, privacy advocates argue that people should have the right to be left alone. On the other hand, companies argue that they should have the right to freedom of speech, specifically the right to inform customers about their offers. Thus the ultimate dilemma: Does a company's freedom of speech outweigh the consumer's right to privacy? Some argue that although the freedom of speech is guaranteed in the U.S. Constitution, the right to privacy is not. As the number of comprehensive databases continues to grow, this issue promises to be a central topic in information management.

What's Your Opinion?

1. Should companies be allowed to collect, store, or sell information about you or your company?
2. Are the voluntary ethical guidelines adopted by companies sufficient, or are laws necessary to protect consumers' privacy?

to maintain a 9,600-ton Navy Ticonderoga-class cruiser weigh approximately 26 tons. On average, the cost of operating and maintaining a weapon is nearly seven times its purchase price, due in large part to the huge cost of managing so much paper. In response, the Defense Department has mounted a $1 billion program called Computer-aided Acquisitions & Logistics Support (CALS) aimed at creating a paperless environment by storing and organizing its vast data and information in computers. Even though only 15 percent of the existing paper at the Defense Department will be stored electronically by the turn of the century, even that modest start should save more than $100 million annually.[75]

The goal of the paperless office carries two drawbacks, however. First, many clerical and support jobs in the contemporary organization are based on the creation and handling of printed documents. The paperless office will presumably displace these people. In response, organizations reducing their paper burdens are reassigning displaced clerical employees to more productive assignments. The second drawback concerns vulnerability to all the phenomena that can afflict any information system, from power failure to data piracy.[76]

MANAGEMENT AROUND THE WORLD

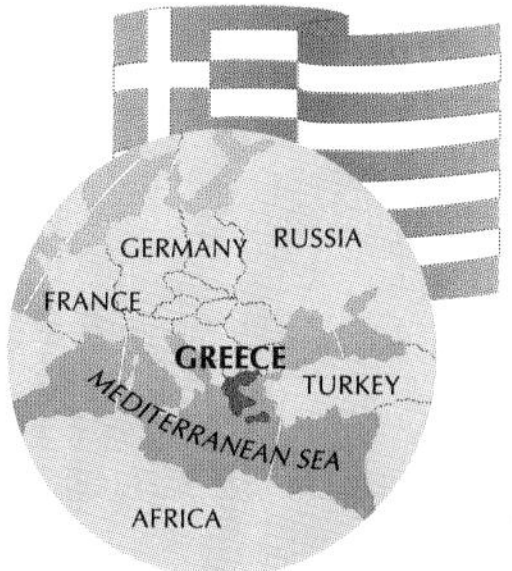

Now that the European Community is a unified market, information systems regulations are a key issue. Although EC members France and the U.K. have laws preventing computer hacking, Greece is one of several members without such laws. Authorities fear that countries without antihacking laws will attract hackers who feel they can operate without impunity.

Security

Data management is a complex responsibility made even more complicated by the threat of a security breach. Computer crime and attacks by computer viruses are key vulnerabilities for organizations with inadequate security provisions. In the United States alone, high-tech thieves steal $3 billion to $5 billion worth of services annually through computer hacking. And computer viruses, like contagious diseases, can spread through a computer network, debilitating all the com-

This computer center in Paris, France, operated by CTL Telematique, provides data processing and communications capabilities for the Minitel network of home shopping and bill-paying terminals that blankets France. To protect the integrity of the data that are processed in this computer system, the company restricts access to the computer room and has contingency plans to deal with the potential loss of data or other security problems.

puter systems linked to that network. IBM's massive internal network was recently invaded by a self-replicating Christmas greeting. Initiated as a prank by a law student hacker in West Germany, the virus found its way into computers on five continents. Many viruses are more vicious, wiping out whole databases and erasing disc drives.[77] The Michaelangelo virus, for instance, is programmed to permanently erase data from disc drives every year on March 6 (the artist's birthday).

To protect computer systems and networks from virus programs, experts recommend that computer users make backup copies of their data regularly, regulate access to computers and networks by using passwords, and restrict downloading of unauthorized software from bulletin boards.[78] However, even restricting access to only organization members may not be enough; many computer crimes are perpetrated by insiders. Sometimes security comes down to simple luck. A $70 million electronic embezzlement scheme attempted by two employees of the First National Bank of Chicago failed when the accounts they were stealing from were overdrawn.[79]

Some organizations are reacting to security threats against their information systems by analyzing their risks and taking defensive action. Aetna, the insurance company located in Hartford, Connecticut, has combined information systems security with business risk analysis activities. Under the heading Corporate/Security Risk Management, information systems security receives more attention because it is combined with broad business risk management. The loss of computer systems or data would completely halt operations, so comparing information system risk with other corporate risks emphasizes Aetna's dependence on computers and motivates management to proactively protect its vulnerable computer systems and networks.[80]

SUMMARY

Data are facts, ideas, or concepts that are collected and stored in raw form; information is the result of processing, correlating, or summarizing raw data to create knowledge. Daily sales receipts, raw demographic information, and inventory figures are examples of data. It is the task of information-management and information-processing systems to convert those data into meaningful information. Information is most useful to managers if it is accurate, timely, complete, relevant, and concise.

The chapter described four ways in which information can contribute as a strategic resource. The first is increasing organizational efficiency by getting information to decision makers sooner, reducing labor requirements, increasing quality, and providing a better understanding of an organization's operations. The second way supports the effort to stay ahead of competitors; information plays a key role by keeping managers informed about their internal and external environments. The third way is in helping to build customer loyalty. This can be done in a variety of ways, including identifying customers and their needs and encouraging repeat purchases. The fourth way is in identifying new markets by finding opportunities for new products and new opportunities for existing products.

In the planning process, managers use information to develop goals and to allocate the organizational resources needed to attain those goals. Information affects organizing decisions such as span of management and work-force requirements. Information is a key component of leadership, since informational power is one of the six types of managerial power. And information is the lifeblood of managerial control, keeping managers informed about organizational performance and providing the means to apply corrective measures when needed.

The three major types of information systems include transaction-processing systems, management information systems, and decision support and executive information systems. Transaction-processing systems are information systems that support the daily flow of data into and out of the organization, including sales receipts, orders, and customer reservations. Management information systems are aimed at supporting the routine decisions managers confront, often by analyzing data from transaction-processing systems. Decision support systems assist managers in solving nonroutine problems; executive information systems are similar to decision support systems, but they are designed specifically to meet the needs of top-level executives.

Computers can be divided into five general categories. Microcomputers make up the low end of the performance spectrum, with desktop, laptop, notebook, and palmtop machines designed to make individual users more productive. Workstations are the next step up in performance, offering the same basic functions as personal computers but with greater speed and processing power. Minicomputers bridge the gap between workstations and mainframes, offering multiuser capabilities at lower prices than mainframes. Many large computing problems are handled by mainframe computers, which have the ability to process and store enormous amounts of data. The top of the performance spectrum is occupied by supercomputers, which provide the power needed for extremely complex problems such as weather forecasting. Of these five, microcomputers, workstations, and mainframes represent the majority of modern computing applications.

Data processing involves collecting, sorting, and analyzing data to produce meaningful information. Data processing falls into two general categories: batch processing (in which data are stored and processed not when they are entered, but at some later time, as when a company sends bills to customers at the end of the month) and on-line processing (in which inputs are acted on immediately, such as when a customer requests cash from an ATM). The related topic of data communications covers the methods used to link two or more computers into networks.

Centralized data processing can provide economies of scale, and it generally decreases the risk of sabotage or corrupted data. On the other hand, keeping important information away from employees who need it to make on-the-job decisions can hurt an organization's effectiveness.

MEETING A MANAGEMENT CHALLENGE

AMERICAN EXPRESS

James D. Robinson III is not a man who shies away from innovation—indeed, he encourages it. So when confronted with an avalanche of paper that was threatening to bury his company, he chose to have a system designed that would copy, store, analyze, sort, and mail the millions of receipts the company received every day. He wanted a system that would reduce costs, increase productivity, enhance customer service, and give American Express a competitive edge by using the information derived from the data contained on those receipts. He got what he wanted—six years and $80 million later.

Today the millions of charge receipts received every day at American Express are sent through a unique transaction-processing system that stores images of the receipts on optical computer disks. (All of those paper receipts are then shredded and buried in secret locations for security.) Computers

Mail-order catalogs for American Express cardholders

index and sort the images according to customer billing cycle and zip code, collate the images with the appropriate billing statements, print more legible and useful copies of the images on perforated paper, and insert those sheets of paper with billing statements into envelopes that are then presorted for mailing. All of this is done so quickly that 100,000 pages of billing statements are printed in only one hour at each of two processing sites in the United States. Customer queries can be processed within minutes now that the receipt images are stored on computers.

Nearly 400 people who were employed to process, correct, and retrieve the millions of paper receipts received every day have been replaced by the transaction-processing system, which is operated by three people who do more work in less time and with greater accuracy. Billing costs have been reduced by 25 percent, with nearly half of that savings coming from a reduction in the money American Express needs to keep available to pay merchants for charged purchases. Because the bills are processed and mailed in a shorter period, the company receives payments from cardholders more quickly.

The system has enabled the company to gain a competitive advantage in two ways. The first advantage is rather subtle: of the three major card companies, American Express is the only one that still returns copies of receipts to its customers for record-keeping—a service that is especially useful for businesspeople. The second advantage is more crucial. Robinson can honestly say that he knows his customers very well, because the purchasing data on each receipt are transformed into information that is used tactically and strategically. Cardholders are categorized by income and life-style and then profiled according to 450 attributes derived from their purchasing patterns, age, sex, and other data. These continually updated portraits are augmented with surveys that are targeted to that cardholder's income and life-style. All this information has allowed American Express to enter a booming business: direct-mail merchandising, which is its fastest-growing subsidiary. The company now sells more by mail order than L. L. Bean. The information is also used to find new subscribers for magazines owned by the company's publishing subsidiary—periodicals that, again, are appropriate to each cardholder's life-style.

What began with a transaction-processing system has been expanded into an important decision-making tool so that Robinson is better able to make strategic decisions. He now has at his fingertips a wealth of information useful in making decisions about new products and services, new markets, and ways to further innovate for a competitive advantage.

You're the Manager: American Express is considered an industry leader in its use of technology, as evidenced by its transaction-processing system. You work for the vice president of information management as a planner, considering how to ensure the best use of information throughout American Express subsidiaries. The corporation owns Shearson Lehman (the second-largest securities company on Wall Street), IDS Financial Services (the financial-planning firm), and Travel Related Services (traveler's checks, credit cards, and other travel-related services).

Ranking Questions

1. You know that organizing the right data is crucial to providing useful information to decision makers in the company. Assume that each of the following pieces of data is available to the people who make approval decisions for new customers for the classic green American Express card. In addition to providing the right data, you don't want to overload the decision makers with irrelevant or unnecessary data. Assuming that you've already identified people who are above a minimum income threshold, how important would the following pieces of data regarding applicants be for card-approval decisions?
   a. Credit history, specifically on-time payment records
   b. Family size, because larger families are likely to use their cards more often, which increases American Express's revenue
   c. Age, because older people are likely to make more money
   d. Educational background, so that you can pick the people who've graduated from the best universities
2. Like nearly all credit customers, American Express cardholders are concerned about database privacy. Their worries range from outsiders getting access to their card numbers to the fear that companies are building profiles on them that say more than the customers are comfortable revealing, such as what kind of videos they like to rent or which hotels they prefer to stay in. How could American Express best calm the fears of its customers?
   a. The company should explain its security measures to cardholders and give them the option of not releasing their financial data to other businesses.
   b. To be completely secure, the company should never sell data to anyone, and it should restrict access to the data to only a handful of trusted executives.
   c. The problem is much larger than American Express; thousands of companies build databases, so there is little that American Express can do to allay the fears of its customers.
   d. Simply by using their cards, American Ex-

press customers forfeit the right to privacy, since there is no way to process a transaction without the customer's name being involved; if customers are worried about their privacy, they should use cash instead.

Multiple-Choice Questions

3. Suppose that several dozen customers called to complain about the new system that delivers processed images of their receipts, not the actual receipts themselves. Your customer service staff tried to convince them the processed images contain the same data and information as the original, and in fact, they offer even more. These customers are adamant, however; if they can't get the receipts back, they'll cancel their cards. Your calculations show that circumventing the system for these few customers will cost you more than the revenue that these customers represent. What should you do?
   a. Explain to the customers that American Express needs to use the new system in order to stay competitive.
   b. Explain to the customers that the new system is better for them because it provides better records of their transaction; keep trying to convince them of that fact.
   c. For these customers only, circumvent the new system and provide them with their actual receipts.
   d. You hate to lose customers, but thank them graciously for their past use of American Express cards, explain that you won't be able to cater to their particular needs, and convey your hope they'll reconsider along with your understanding if they want to go ahead and turn in their cards.
4. Because so much of Travel Related Services's business involves information, and because Robinson has taken such an aggressive stance on quality and customer service, TRS has developed a formidable competitive strength in its ability to manage information. In fact, the ability to leverage its information-processing capabilities is a key factor when the company considers expanding into new business areas. From this perspective, which of the following moves makes the most sense?
   a. Setting up a division that processes credit-card transactions for other companies
   b. Publishing a finance magazine, similar to *Worth* or *Money*
   c. Expanding Travel Related Services into actual travel services by purchasing a hotel chain or rental-car firm
   d. Moving into the credit-reporting business, collecting credit information on consumers and selling it to credit grantors

Analysis Questions

5. What impact has this information system had on American Express?
6. Could American Express possibly lose customer loyalty through the overuse of information collected on its cardholders—for example, through its direct-mail marketing? If so, how could this be prevented?
7. Has American Express invested too much time and money to create its image-transaction-processing system, especially since technology changes so rapidly? Why or why not?

Special Project

Fostering customer loyalty can be one of the key benefits of a good information system. An automobile dealer who keeps track of customers and the mileage on their cars, for instance, can mail them reminders concerning periodic maintenance shortly before the maintenance is due. This information system provides a service for customers and allows the dealer to build closer ties with its customers. Considering the types of customer data that American Express collects and the needs, wants, and behaviors of its customers, identify ways in which American Express's information system could be used to build customer loyalty.[81]

KEY TERMS

artificial intelligence (589)
batch processing (587)
centralized data processing (591)
computer-based information system (CBIS) (578)
computer network (587)
data (570)
data communications (587)
data processing (586)
decision support system (DSS) (582)
distributed data processing (591)
electronic data interchange (EDI) (588)
expert system (589)
hardware (580)
information (570)
information systems (578)
on-line processing (587)
software (580)
telecommuters (589)
teleconferencing (588)
transaction-processing system (TPS) (581)

QUESTIONS

For Review

1. What is the difference between data and information?
2. How is information used as a strategic resource?
3. What are the three main types of information systems?
4. What are the five major types of computers?
5. What two major trends have resulted from advances in data communications technology?

For Analysis

1. Why might a company's CIO be reluctant to let employees use home computers to tap into centralized databases while working at home?
2. A retail drugstore has developed a computer-based information system to provide customers with a detailed accounting of all purchases of prescription drugs for a given year. Customers may request this report at any time, and it is particularly useful in preparing their income tax returns. How is the information generated by this system used as a competitive advantage?
3. How might a shortage of useful information affect the strategic management process?
4. Why are people considered to be a fundamental part of information systems?
5. What effect might a new information system have on employee motivation?

For Application

1. How might your college or university take advantage of expert system technology?
2. Centex, a large home-construction company, continually looks for new plots of land that it can develop into residential communities. In terms of managerial planning, what are some of Centex's information needs?
3. How can Burger King use information to build customer loyalty?
4. Why does a consumer-electronics manufacturer such as Yamaha enclose warranty registration cards with its stereo equipment?
5. A senior investment counselor has just advised his company he plans to retire in one year. This will be a great loss to the company since the senior investment counselor has the greatest knowledge of how to sell investments to customers considering their tendency toward risk and current financial position. In fact, the counselor has been responsible for training employees for the last few years. How can the organization utilize technology to capture the unique abilities of the investment counselor?

KEEPING CURRENT IN MANAGEMENT

From recent magazines or newspapers, select an article that discusses a manager who implemented a new computer system to utilize information as a strategic resource. One example might focus on a manager who implemented a system to increase organizational efficiency. Another example might involve a manager who implemented an information system aimed at building customer loyalty.

1. What strategic information is the manager expecting from the system? Has the organization increased sales or reduced costs as a result of the new information generated by the computer system?
2. What data are being collected? Why?
3. Did the manager acknowledge any limitations to this information system? What did the company do to help employees adjust to the new system?

SHARPEN YOUR MANAGEMENT SKILLS

Donald Elitzer wants to push the information revolution another step. Here's his idea: offer people the use of a fax machine and up to 20 free transmissions per month, in exchange for providing some information about themselves and agreeing to receive two fax advertisements a day. Called HomeFax, this service (if Elitzer finds enough financial backing to get started, that is) will benefit advertisers who know they'll be reaching accurately identified target customers. In short, Elitzer is looking to build a new kind of information system, one in which customers willingly tell advertisers about themselves and their product needs.

- *Decision:* Identify the type of person who is likely to respond to such an offer, using such criteria as age, sex, occupation, education, and income.
- *Communication:* Once you've identified a likely target audience, draft a one-page sales letter that introduces the idea and persuades people to give it a try.

CASE

Cooking Up a Competitive Information System

Computers helped build Mrs. Fields into an international retail cookie empire. The company later suffered multimillion-dollar losses, but founder Debbi Fields has improved profits through retrenchment and is still relying on computers to control quality, costs, and personnel.

HISTORY

Debbi Fields's newlywed husband loved her big, chewy, homebaked chocolate chip cookies so much that in 1977 he loaned her $25,000 to open a store and sell them in Palo Alto, California. Within three years the couple had 15 stores, and in 1981 they moved their home and headquarters to Park City, Utah, believing that computers and communications satellites would let them operate far from major commercial centers. By 1983 sales reached $30 million from 160 stores in 17 states, and the next year Mrs. Fields opened its first foreign outlet in Sydney, Australia. The company expanded into Hong Kong, Tokyo, and Singapore, and it gobbled up rival cookie seller Famous Amos to become the largest chain in the $400 million cookie market.

Mrs. Fields grew to 650 stores, tried unsuccessfully to extend its brand name to ice cream and macadamia nut soda, and bought the unprofitable 110-store La Petite Boulangerie chain. This aggressive expansion led to a loss of $19 million in 1988, when the chain was forced to close the weakest fifth of its cookie stores and cut the headquarters staff from 160 to 130. Mrs. Fields moved back into profitability as sales rose 8 percent in 1989 to $130 million for a net income of $1.5 million, and the profit picture continues to improve in the 1990s.

ENVIRONMENT

Debbi Fields controls and leads her company through a computer system that links all outlets with headquarters. The system continuously tracks sales through each cash register. Every night sales data from each store stream into Park City for tabulation and every morning Fields calls to congratulate her best performers. Personal computers in each store are programmed on the basis of Fields's business philosophy of keeping products fresh (nothing is sold that is more than two hours old) and sales high. Each computer charts hourly sales versus projections, updates projections on the basis of the day's experience, spits out an hour-by-hour baking schedule, and makes sales suggestions; if sales are slow, for example, it may tell the most vivacious employee to go outside with samples to woo customers.

The system also has reduced by 60 percent both the need for administrative personnel and the time managers spend on paperwork. It can schedule a crew, interview and test job applicants, order supplies, make sales reports and projections, transmit memos, and train employees. The system allows the company to hire employees who would rather sell to customers than sit behind a desk doing paperwork, and its electronic mail system lets employees ask specific questions of anyone in the company, even Fields, with a promised response within 48 hours.

GOALS AND CHALLENGES

Mrs. Fields decided to recapture the growth of its glory days by focusing on bakeries, and computers are again at the heart of the effort. The company plans to convert its La Petite bakeries to Mrs. Fields Bakeries and then to open 100 more (mostly in grocery stores) resulting in 520 freestanding cookie stores and 260 bakeries. Combining bakery items with cookie store menus could also give cookie stores a full day of sales, from bread and croissants in the morning to cookies in the afternoon. The bakery business is more complex than cookie retailing, but it can also be more stable, and Fields thinks her company's expertise with computers will help everyone handle the complexities of the new business. Computers have already helped make the struggling La Petite bakery chain profitable within 14 months of its purchase. Mrs. Fields installed personal computers and scheduling software within three days of buying the chain, fired bakery managers who didn't accept the computer-based management style, and cut La Petite's staff at headquarters from 63 to 4.

1. How does Mrs. Fields transform data into information? To what extent is this information useful?
2. How does Mrs. Fields use its information system to plan, organize, lead, and control?
3. If Debbi Fields buys another bakery chain, what type of information system should she use to maintain the same level of control as she has over her cookie stores?
4. What influence has information technology had on the design and growth of Mrs. Fields's organization structure?

CHAPTER OUTLINE

19 Foundations of Management Control

After studying this chapter, you will be able to

1. Discuss the importance of management control and outline the steps in the management control process
2. List the three levels of control and the three types of control; identify the most important contemporary trend regarding types of control
3. Contrast bureaucratic and clan control and explain their implications for managers
4. Identify characteristics of effective control programs
5. Explain how managers use financial statements and ratio analysis to improve the effectiveness of management control
6. Differentiate among expense centers, revenue centers, profit centers, and investment centers
7. Discuss two types of budgets and identify examples of each

FACING A MANAGEMENT CHALLENGE AT

TOYS 'R' US

Playing for Keeps with a "Killer" Instinct for Control

Charles Lazarus became king of toy and game retailing in rapid fashion, in the process becoming one of a handful of retail pioneers who developed a phenomenon known as "category killers"—specialty stores that dominate sales in a class of products. Lazarus, founder and chairman of Toys 'R' Us, created a company so powerful that it could make or break a new toy—or even, in some cases, a toy manufacturer. Feared by his competitors and adored by investors, Lazarus was intent on extending his reach both at home and abroad. He counted 220 million potential customers in the United States alone, and he estimated another 320 million in the rest of the developed world. To become the top toy seller in Europe and Japan and to maintain leading status in North America while staying profitable would require very high performance in three important areas: finance, operations, and human resources.

As Lazarus expanded Toys 'R' Us in the United States, he raced past hundreds of stumbling retailers—department stores, discounters, and specialty chains that had collapsed beneath the weight of debt. These struggling chains had attempted to expand too quickly, taking out huge bank loans that they had difficulty repaying. Lazarus knew he would need tight financial controls to avoid overburdening his company with debt—not an easy task considering his ambitious plans for global expansion. It wouldn't be just a matter of controlling costs. A positive cash flow would have to be generated at each store, which would mean ringing up high and rising sales. Lazarus had already scored big with impressive sales, to be sure, but his international vision could be financed only by controlling the company's resources so that expansion would be paid for out of current sales revenues and the sale of stock to shareholders. He would thus avoid the path of debt chosen by so many of his competitors.

Lazarus knew he was in a high-volume business: his stores needed to be fully stocked with large numbers of toys and games, and timely marketing campaigns were necessary to push products. But doing all of this to the extent required for international expansion and dominance meant that Lazarus would have to institute tight controls at three operational points: when products were bought from suppliers, when they were held in inventory, and when they were presented and sold to customers. In the first case, buyers had to be farsighted enough to select toys and games that would sell, and they had to receive the necessary information to buy more of the items that were going fast. Inventory would have to be controlled precisely so that empty shelves wouldn't hamper sales. Finally, stores would have to be designed and managed in such a way that customers would want to buy more than just the few toys at the top of the popularity ladder.

Making it all work, of course, would require setting standards for all employees, from buyers to warehouse workers and from store managers to sales clerks. The danger would be enforcing an overly strict, top-down management system that would alienate employees, reduce morale, and damage employee motivation and productivity so that actual sales would never reach projected sales. How much control could Lazarus and his corporate staff exert over frontline employees without losing their dedication? Could he apply technological advances throughout the Toys 'R' Us chain to achieve high degrees of control? Could he control finances sufficiently to grow aggressively without being burdened by debt?[1]

CHAPTER OVERVIEW

Charles Lazarus and his team at Toys 'R' Us face substantial challenges as they try to keep their growing organization under control. Establishing appropriate control systems can provide managers of all organizations with timely information to keep their operations running smoothly. This chapter explores both the

Well-designed controls can improve product quality and enhance profit. Managers at Heinz's Ore-Ida potato processing plants discovered that high-speed slicing machines were cutting potatoes too fine, changing the taste of Tator Tots. Once managers slowed the equipment and controlled consistency so that Tator Tots tasted chunkier, sales improved, which more than paid for the slower speed.

theoretical aspects of control and the practical application of financial controls. A definition of control and a discussion of its importance begin the chapter. Next, implementation of the control process is described, and organizational control theories are examined. The final part of the chapter focuses on financial and budgetary controls.

UNDERSTANDING MANAGEMENT CONTROL

The traditional role of control in the United States is based on the work of Frederick W. Taylor, the turn-of-the-century father of scientific management (see Chapter 2). Taylor emphasized establishing order through strict management control to achieve efficiency in the work force. Work was divided into small, standardized jobs for which individuals could be held accountable, and a hierarchical management structure existed to exert control over employees and to increase labor efficiency.[2] Taylor advocated the separation of planning and implementation. Because managers were responsible for planning and employees were responsible for implementation, Taylor thought managers therefore lacked hands-on knowledge of the organization's operational processes.[3]

Over the years, many U.S. businesses adopted Taylor's concept of control. But this traditional notion of control is under siege as aggressive global competitors in Japan, South Korea, and other countries set increasingly high standards for world-class products and performance. Whereas Taylor viewed control as a process imposed on employees by managers, the need to compete more effectively has spurred more organizations to rethink the control process.[4]

A growing number of companies recognize that they should focus on controlling processes, not on controlling people. Furthermore, these companies are achieving major productivity and quality gains by involving their employees in the control function, broadening the scope of jobs, and giving self-managing teams the opportunity to address problems. Rather than performing limited tasks, employees are encouraged to monitor and improve their own work activities. Several years ago, at the Kodak division that makes x-ray cassettes, spools, canisters, and cartons for Kodak film, Daniel Cardinale did nothing but operate a punch press eight hours a day. Now Cardinale coaches fellow members of his quality team, meets with suppliers to boost the quality of incoming parts, interviews prospective employees, and helps manage inventory. More effective use of human resources to better control processes has enabled Cardinale's unit to do in one shift nearly the same amount of work that used to take three.[5]

Management Control Defined

control The regulatory process directing the activities an organization conducts to achieve anticipated goals and standards

Control is the regulatory process that directs the activities an organization conducts to achieve anticipated goals and standards.[6] The control function requires managers to establish appropriate performance standards, compare actual performance with the predetermined standards, and remedy problem areas. For example, William Walsh, founder of the not-for-profit organization Project Hope, sends volunteer doctors from the West to train local physicians and nurses in developing nations. To achieve his goal, Walsh established a performance standard—to spend 85 percent of Project Hope revenues on its programs. If overhead eats up more than 15 percent, then Project Hope will be less successful in meeting its philanthropic goals. On the other hand, the organization knows that it must spend a certain amount on overhead and staff support if the people in the organization are to be as productive as possible—hence the 15/85 percent standard.[7] Program spending as a percentage of revenue (a financial control) is one vital statistic Walsh monitors regularly to help Project Hope efficiently meet its goals. If the numbers stray from the standard in either direction, the problem must be remedied.

Controls are required to successfully manage every organizational function. Financial, budgetary, and human resource controls are used by managers of every department, whereas R&D, marketing, and operations management controls are specific to their functions.

- *Financial and budgetary control.* Financial control enables top-level managers to assess the overall functioning of the organization. The classic and definitive financial measure in for-profit firms is of course profit. Middle managers in all departments use budgetary control to keep spending on target. On a monthly basis, most organizations compare actual spending with the budget, and they require managers to analyze and explain any significant deviations.
- *Operations control.* Managers use operations control to regulate the process of producing goods and services. Many companies use operations control to help them reduce the amount of time it takes to produce a product and to increase the amount of time that critical machines are operational.
- *Marketing control.* Marketing control is the process used to evaluate how effectively pricing, promotion, distribution, and products meet the customers' expectations. Thus, marketing controls must monitor internal and competitive sales performance as well as internal and competitive pricing, promotion, and distribution. Many companies use marketing controls to monitor sales by region, competitors' prices, and competitive product introductions.
- *R&D control.* R&D control is the process of regulating the development of new products. Such controls could include the formal ranking and selection of development projects based on customer needs or the management of development projects.[8]
- *Human resource control.* Human resource control is the process of regulating employee behavior. Human resource controls include both improving the capabilities of employees (through stricter hiring policies or better training opportunities) and implementing rewards, bonuses, or incentive programs aimed at encouraging employees to focus on those activities necessary for the organization to achieve its goals.[9]

The Importance of Control

The control function is closely linked with the planning function. Managers use the planning process to prepare courses of action to achieve organizational goals. The control function is the ongoing process used to determine if an organization is meeting its goals. By tracking progress toward meeting the organizational goals and using the feedback on performance wisely, the control function provides managers with a method to improve their plans and keep their organizations on course in the face of changing conditions. For example, Craig Tysdal, vice president of sales for Network Equipment Technologies, had an organizational goal to keep the collection of customer payments timely. Tysdal, faced with a high frequency of overdue customer payments, implemented a control process in which sales managers receive bonuses based on their ability to collect customer payments in a timely fashion. According to Tysdal, in only one year the number of accounts overdue more than 90 days was cut in half.[10]

The need for controls can best be understood by looking at what happens in their absence (see Exhibit 19.1). Without information to indicate when disturbing trends start to develop, organizations lack the ability to respond. If an organization does not perceive environmental changes or internal problems that affect its ability to achieve goals, then it could be faced with a major crisis. Routine feedback gives managers time to respond to problems while they are still small, thus preventing a major organizational tragedy.[11]

Control systems themselves are not capable of directly controlling organizational performance. Rather, they provide information to managers who are in a position to exercise control. If managers use the information well, the control system works. If they use it poorly, the system may produce unintended results.[12] For example, Pittsburgh-based H.J. Heinz received feedback from its marketing control systems that the tuna operation was no longer the low-cost operator in that market. In response to the tough competition from low-wage rivals in Thailand, Heinz reduced the work force at its StarKist canning factories in Puerto Rico and American Samoa by 5 percent. The remaining fish cleaners were so overworked, they were leaving literally tons of meat on the bone every day. Operations control systems alerted management to the high amount of waste. StarKist managers reacted by slowing the production lines, hiring 400 hourly workers and 15 supervisors, and retraining the work force. StarKist increased labor costs by $5 million but reduced waste by $15 million. Feedback

EXHIBIT 19.1

The Impact of Inadequate Controls

An organization lacking adequate controls will experience a self-feeding cycle of competitive decay. By implementing controls throughout the organization, costs can be reduced, reversing this cycle of decay.

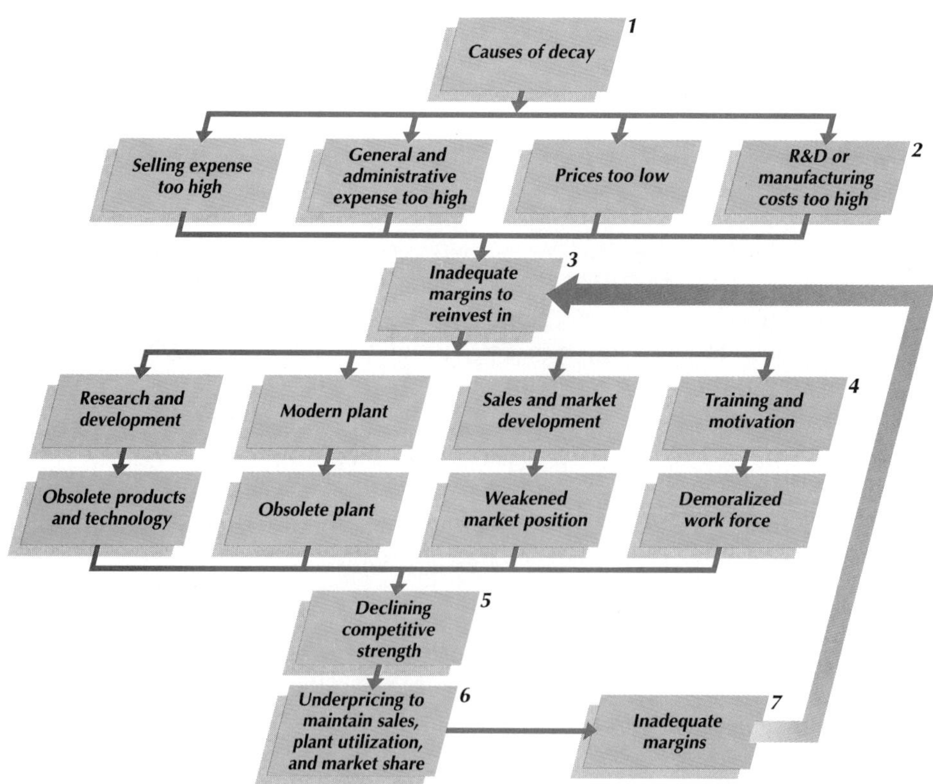

from the control systems allowed management to react quickly, which resulted in a savings of $10 million.[13]

Control can assist organizations in their endeavors to improve quality both in their work activities and in the end product delivered to the customer. By meeting customers' expectations for product, price, support, distribution, and reliability, an organization becomes more competitive. Quality is a function of an organization's ability to develop and produce the product, distribute the product, and support the product. All are based on effective internal processes. World-class quality relies on the dual foundations of top-management support and *continual process improvement,* which is an effort to improve the performance of every process in the organization, with the idea that things are never "good enough" and can always be improved. Top management sets the goal of higher quality, and continual process improvement is the control function that guides all members of the organization toward improving quality.[14]

A Japanese company well known for quality and cost control, Toyota controls its processes using continual process improvement. In one innovative department, machine uptime (a measure of equipment utilization) averages 90 percent; uptime at comparable U.S. competitors hovers around 50 percent. What is most disturbing for the competition is that Toyota's overhead cost in this process is the lowest in the industry.[15] Organizations that adopt continual process improvement as a primary control mechanism can, over time, increase quality while decreasing costs, thus increasing competitiveness.[16]

Controls are a vital part of an organization's ability to increase its productivity over time and remain competitive. The term *experience curve* means that the inflation-adjusted costs of doing business decrease as organizations learn how to do things better. Companies further along the experience curve gain a competitive advantage because they have had more time to lower their costs through productivity gains. Lowering costs increases profitability. However, continual cost reductions require constant management control to be able to isolate and manage costs effectively. As chairman and CEO of Abbott Laboratories, Robert Schoellhorn notes that "to simply raise prices along with the [health-care] industry is not the Abbott way. You must develop an attitude throughout the company that you can always find a better and lower-cost way to do things."[17]

THE CONTROL PROCESS

Managers follow four steps to implement an effective control process. These steps, generally followed in order, are (1) establishing standards, (2) measuring performance, (3) comparing performance to standards, and (4) taking action (see Exhibit 19.2). By properly implementing the control process, managers receive control feedback guiding them to recognize employee performance, improve the control function by changing standards and measures, or alter the plans due to changing conditions. In essence, the control process is the ongoing system that keeps an organization moving in the direction of its goals.[18]

Step 1: Establish Standards

Standards are specific criteria against which future performance will be measured. Managers are responsible for translating organizational goals and plans into measurable and appropriate standards for monitoring the ongoing perfor-

standards Explicit criteria against which future performance will be measured

EXHIBIT 19.2

The Control Process

The control process consists of four steps: establishing standards, measuring performance, comparing performance to standards, and taking action.

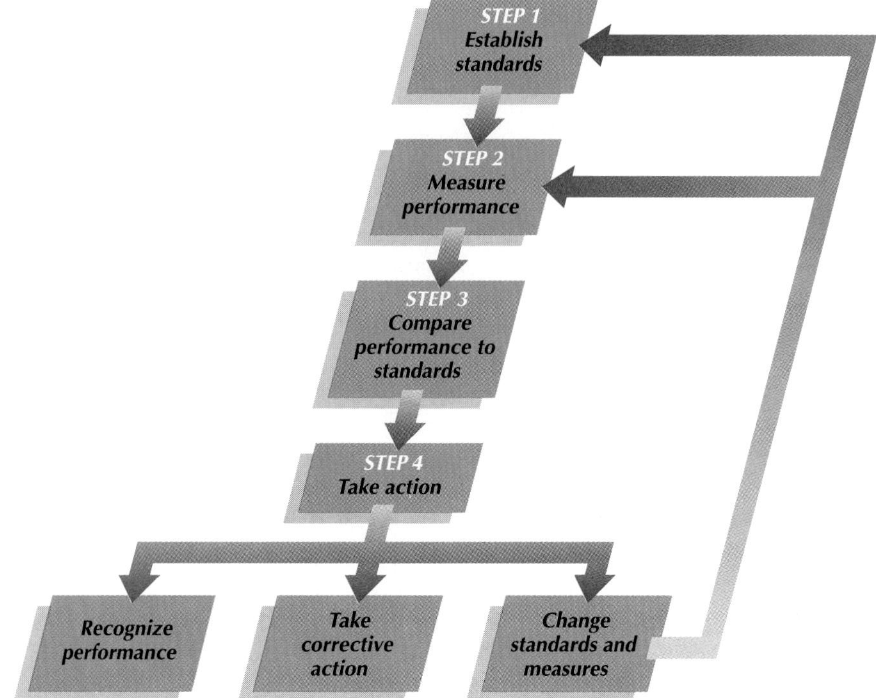

mance of the organization. When managers identify and monitor the key measurements essential for organizational success, they are actually communicating performance expectations to their employees. So defining performance standards is critical both to measuring performance and to motivating employees. In the automotive and computer industries, customer satisfaction surveys done by third parties are important measures of success. For example, Honda Motor Company's Acura division may establish a performance standard of being number one in the J. D. Powers customer satisfaction survey (a widely respected measure of performance in the auto industry). This standard clearly communicates the company's goal of customer satisfaction to all employees. In Virginia, the health department established a goal of reducing infant mortality. The performance standards included statistics relating to prenatal care, teenage pregnancy, and birth weight.[19]

Step 2: Measure Performance

Once standards have been defined, managers must establish a process to measure performance on a regular basis. Most managers strive to report performance based on quantitative data, since such data tend to be relatively objective and easy to evaluate. For Honda, the measurement process would be as simple as getting a copy of the latest J. D. Powers survey. Fairfield Inn, the chain of economy inns operated by Marriott, strives to offer its road-weary customers the cleanest rooms and friendliest staff. To provide this excellent customer service, Fairfield management created standards to measure the level of service its guests received. Managers developed and implemented Scorecard, an evaluation system. Scorecard uses a computer-administered touch screen at checkout to measure guest responses to four service-related questions.[20]

Managers must also decide how often the data will be collected and reported. The ideal frequency for measuring performance depends on the type of organization, the importance of the standard to organizational effectiveness, and the likelihood that performance would change dramatically. For example, growing cities are often concerned with air quality. Since air quality is important to the quality of life of their citizens, and since it is likely to change quickly (due to the combination of weather and pollution), cities may choose to measure and report air quality daily.

MANAGEMENT AROUND THE WORLD

In efforts to combat inflation, various nations have at times implemented control systems for wages and prices. Government officials in Argentina, for instance, recently lowered the tariff on imported cigarettes, anticipating that the lower prices on imported products would force domestic suppliers to keep their own prices down as well.

Step 3: Compare Performance to Standards

Managers must exercise judgment when comparing performance to standards. If performance falls short of the standard, how far off must it be before a manager should react? (Statistical process control, covered in Chapter 20, can provide the answer in many cases.) Managers must understand the causes both of failing to meet standards and of exceeding standards. Comparing performance to standards often identifies symptoms of a much deeper problem, so managers must use their analytical and diagnostic skills when evaluating objective and subjective data in order to unearth problems. At Honda, extensive evaluation of the J. D. Powers survey might lead managers to many different conclusions. Customers may be very satisfied with the car while less satisfied with the service, for instance. At Fairfield Inn, guest responses to the service-related questions collected by the Scorecard system are correlated with data indicating which employees were responsible for a particular guest, allowing management to keep track of individual performance.[21]

Step 4: Take Action

After managers have compared performance to standards, they usually must take some form of action. One of the following three actions is generally appropriate.

Take Corrective Action

Corrective action is taken to modify organizational practices in an effort to get performance in line with standards. For example, a manager may measure the daily output of a production process and discover that output recently decreased. To bring output levels back in line with standards, the manager might establish employee incentive programs or participate with employees to solve the problems that are slowing the production process. At Toys 'R' Us, corrective action might include putting an item on sale to get rid of inventory that is piling up or ordering more of an item that is starting to look like a hit. Managers have the difficult job of choosing the best alternative for each situation.[22]

General Electric has demonstrated how fast corrective action can ward off disaster. GE opened a state-of-the-art factory in Columbia, Tennessee, to manufacture a new rotary compressor. Within two years, the compressor's failure rate (a preestablished performance measure) approached 1 percent. The control system alerted management to the higher-than-expected failure rate. Warranty information showed that the failures occurred in warm-weather states for customers using the bigger refrigerators with the larger compressors. In other words,

SOCIAL RESPONSIBILITY AND ETHICS

Cost-Cutting at the Expense of Employee Privacy

Many U.S. companies are faced with soaring medical costs yet still must provide adequate medical benefits to attract and retain employees. Analyzing employee use of medical benefits and making decisions based on trends has become a critical cost-control practice for corporate personnel departments. Increasingly, personal health records of employees are analyzed for possible opportunities to reduce medical costs. Is employee privacy being sacrificed?

Dr. J. C. Bisgard, Pacific Bell's medical director, recently found that employees enrolled in health maintenance organizations (HMOs) filed more mental health–related workers' compensation and disability claims. Bisgard recommended a new program to provide professional treatment for troubled employees within 24 hours, regardless of their health plan. By providing immediate care to employees diagnosed as depressed, Pacific Bell reduced disability costs by getting the employees back to work sooner.

In a similar investigation, First Chicago found that pregnant women who were not members of an HMO were more likely to have cesarean sections than women who were members of such organizations. By requiring a second opinion on nonemergency cesareans, First Chicago has reduced the overall number of cesarean sections and, since cesarean sections are more expensive, has reduced its medical costs. Similar analyses based on employee medical and disability records is one reason First Chicago's medical costs per employee are rising at 3 percent per year, compared with an average increase of 15 percent for companies its size. According to Dr. Wayne Burton, medical director of First Chicago, "The only way to do more to control health-care costs is with more information."

James Perkins, senior vice president and chief personnel officer of Federal Express, agrees. FedEx administers its own health and disability programs using a database that integrates personnel, medical, and dis-

when the compressors were working the hardest, they failed. Concern for product reliability and customer satisfaction prompted Roger W. Schipke, senior vice president for appliances, to make some quick decisions. First, he formed a team of engineers to diagnose the problem. The team discovered that a lubrication problem was causing one of the compressor's smaller parts to wear more quickly than expected, but redesigning the lubrication device would take months. Schipke approved the redesign and implemented a plan for GE to replace free any compressor that broke down. The most painful and expensive decision was to purchase compressors from abroad while the engineering team redesigned the product. By reacting immediately with both short-term and long-term remedies, Schipke maintained the company's reputation for product reliability and customer satisfaction.[23]

Recognize Performance

If performance meets or exceeds standards, managers should recognize the achievement. By applauding employees and departments that have achieved specific goals, managers reinforce positive performance and motivate their employees to continue working diligently. Recognizing performance can range from a handshake to a raise or promotion. The California bank Wells Fargo pays its people significantly more than competitor banks while maintaining low operating costs. It currently has over 45 distinct merit reward plans. Chairman Carl Reichardt says, "You can see that our people are being rewarded because they're productive. And that to me is the right way to go."[24]

Fairfield Inn uses the individual performance feedback from its Scorecard system to complement competitive base pay with monthly bonuses of up to 10 percent of base pay. Employees of Fairfield Inn praise the system that allows them to be compensated for their performance, while customers enjoy the excellent service encouraged by the Scorecard human resource control system. Fair-

ability records. Recent feedback from this control system showed that 16 percent of its 74,000 U.S. workers account for 80 percent of the health-care bills. FedEx's system enables it to spot doctors who do too many tests as well as employees who overuse medical services. Corrective action has reduced medical costs per claim by 8.5 percent.

Although analyzing use and controlling misuse of medical benefits has paid off by reducing medical and disability costs, the privacy of employees is at risk. In fact, the American Civil Liberties Union (ACLU) is concerned that computerized personnel, medical, and disability records may be accessed by supervisors and co-workers, denying employees the right to confidentiality. Analysis of the computerized data is distressing to employees with current or past mental health problems, chronic diseases, AIDS, and other physical or mental handicaps. Employees and the ACLU worry that knowledge of medical records could influence hiring, promotion, performance, and firing decisions.

To allay such fears, Pacific Bell does its analyses using files stripped of all names, while Federal Express and First Chicago use secure computer systems, accessible only to medical personnel. But the data still exist. As companies relentlessly pursue a reduction in skyrocketing medical costs, will the day come when private records are used to weed out less healthy employees? Concern for privacy is demonstrated by the recently passed Americans with Disabilities Act, which makes it illegal for employers to refuse to hire people with certain health problems. Even though companies have no choice but to manage their health-care costs and to control increasing medical bills, employees have a right to confidential medical information, and managers will need to strike a careful balance between cost control and privacy.

What's Your Opinion?

1. Is it ethical for organizations to use employee medical information in their pursuit of cost control?
2. Aside from medical cost control, what are some examples of ethical issues faced by designers of control systems in other areas?

field Inn has staked out a successful position in an extremely crowded market segment.[25]

Change Standards and Measures

If an organization consistently exceeds or fails to meet standards, managers should consider changing the standards and associated performance measures. Standards and measures may be unrealistic either because they were set up incorrectly or because conditions affecting them have changed. Changing conditions that could affect standards are increased employee productivity (causing the output standard to be too low) and increased competition in the marketplace (causing the sales standard to be too high).

For example, Whistler, the radar detector manufacturer, was faced with a manufacturing process that was out of control. When 25 percent of the detectors failed final inspection at two Massachusetts plants, the parent company, Massachusetts-based Dynatech, called in consultants to significantly reduce the defect rate. The consultants emphasized building quality in rather than inspecting for quality, and they helped Whistler restructure the production line and form quality teams to improve the production process. Within two years, the defect rate was down to 1 percent and still falling.[26]

CONTROL IN THE ORGANIZATION

Understanding the organization is critical to the successful implementation of control systems. For example, the U.S. government is composed of hundreds of separate agencies as diverse as the Social Security Administration and the National Security Council. A major struggle in the U.S. government is the imposition of governmentwide rules to control hiring, pay, and promotion on agencies that differ so vastly.[27] To effectively implement control systems, managers of government agencies, corporations, and not-for-profit organizations must understand levels of control, types of control methods, and organizational forms of control.

Levels of Control

The planning and controlling functions are interdependent processes that together guide an organization toward performance. First, managers generate a plan; then they create control systems to monitor the effectiveness of their plan. Strategic, tactical, and operational controls are put in place to monitor strategic, tactical, and operational plans. For these controls to be effective, managers at various levels in the organization have the primary responsibility for establishing and evaluating strategic, tactical, and operational controls.[28] For example, the company president is responsible for strategic controls, a production supervisor is responsible for operational controls, and a manufacturing manager focuses on tactical controls.

Strategic Control

strategic control The regulatory process ensuring successful implementation of an organization's long-range strategic plans, emphasizing environmental effects and internal strategic directions

Strategic control is a regulatory process that ensures successful implementation of an organization's long-range strategic plans, specifically emphasizing the impact of broad environmental effects and internal strategic directions.[29] For instance, Charles Lazarus at Toys 'R' Us stays intimately involved with financial matters (such as long-term debt) and strategic decisions (such as the move into the Japanese market) that have major effects on the company, but he is likely to leave lower-level control issues to individual store managers. Strategic control is the responsibility of top management and is characterized by long time frames in which the control window could stretch from one quarter to one decade, based on the nature of the business. By monitoring both the environment and the critical internal work activities, strategic controls continually determine whether strategic plans need to be altered. Environmental factors such as competitive actions, political changes, volatility in customer needs, economic shifts, and technological change present threats and opportunities. Monitoring internal work activities could affect the attainment of strategic plans. Internal activities that can profoundly influence an organization's ability to reach its goals include the selection of R&D projects and the implementation of new transformation processes. Consequently, top managers may become involved with tactical and operational controls to ensure they are in synch with strategic controls.[30]

Tactical Control

tactical control The regulatory process aimed at successful implementation of department-level tactical plans, emphasizing specific internal and external forces affecting them

Tactical control is a regulatory process that ensures successful implementation of department-level plans, focusing on specific internal and external forces that affect such tactical plans.[31] Middle management is responsible for tactical control, focusing on shorter time frames, such as weekly, monthly, or quarterly. Tactical control focuses primarily on meeting department goals and budgets, both of which may be affected by internal forces or by external issues. Examples of internal practices that could have an impact on tactical plans in an R&D department include excessive spending and slipping project schedules. Examples of specific environmental controls that could affect tactical plans for a marketing department include monitoring competitors' prices and evaluating market share. Middle managers may be involved in strategic and operational controls by providing information to top-level management and by reviewing critical aspects of the operational controls.[32]

Operational Control

Operational control is a regulatory process that ensures successful implementation of day-to-day operational plans by monitoring specific and focused internal activities.[33] First-line managers are responsible for operational control, which provides short-term feedback, usually daily, hourly, or weekly. At Toys 'R' Us, for example, store managers need to keep informed of employee work load, inventory levels, and other details that affect the operation of their stores. Higher-level managers would be interested in operational controls if they had an impact on tactical or strategic plans. For example, a performance standard in many manufacturing environments is cycle time, or the length of time necessary to produce a product. Although the production supervisor may be interested in cycle time as a daily measure of production performance, the manufacturing manager and president may be interested in cycle time as a monthly or quarterly measure that supports the strategic goal of increasing manufacturing productivity to gain a competitive advantage.[34]

operational control The regulatory process ensuring successful implementation of day-to-day operational plans by monitoring specific and focused internal activities

The three levels of control must be integrated. If the strategic plan emphasizes cycle time reduction as a competitive advantage, then both the tactical and operational plans should stress cycle time reduction. Additionally, strategic, tactical, and operational controls should be put in place to evaluate the organization's ability to meet key performance standards. Motorola, for example, has formally included cycle time reduction, together with quality improvement, in its corporate strategic plans.[35] Every level in the organization has to work in concert to achieve these goals, since each level supports and affects the levels above and below it.

Types of Control Methods

All managers, whether focused on strategic, tactical, or operational controls, must understand the various types of control methods in order to determine appropriate application. The three types of control methods can be distinguished according to where they are applied in the process. Controls placed before, during, and after a given process are needed to regulate performance and meet organizational goals (see Exhibit 19.3).

Preliminary Control

Preliminary control, also known as *precontrol* or *feedforward,* is the regulation of inputs to a transformation process, ensuring that the inputs meet estab-

preliminary control The regulation of a process's inputs to ensure they meet established standards

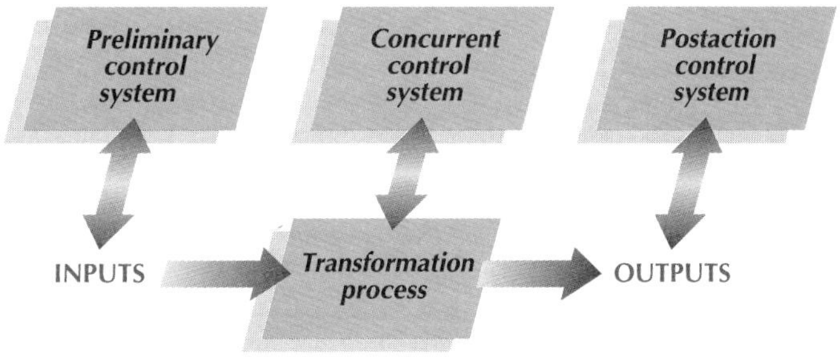

EXHIBIT 19.3

Types of Controls

Preliminary control measures the quality of inputs to the transformation process; concurrent control measures the quality of the process itself; and postaction control measures the quality of outputs.

Preliminary control system

Concurrent control system

Postaction control system

INPUTS → *Transformation process* → OUTPUTS

lished standards for eventual success of the process. An organization should employ preliminary control only on those resources that are critical to the process. For instance, one of the preliminary controls important in service organizations is hiring the right employees and training them to handle the special nature of service production and delivery. In a manufacturing organization, working with suppliers to increase the quality of incoming raw materials would be considered a preliminary control.[36]

North American Lighting in Flora, Illinois, uses concurrent control to check automobile headlamp quality during the production process. Assembly-line employees examine the quality of each lens and test each reflector assembly before they are attached and finished, ensuring that problems are uncovered and corrected before the headlamps are incorporated into new cars.

Pinellas County, Florida, has no insurance for its government vehicles since it handles all its own claims. With cost reduction as its incentive, the county government instituted a number of controls to improve the driving performance of its employees. In two years, the county government recorded a 47 percent reduction in vehicle accidents. Preliminary controls are used to train employees to drive more effectively and safely. Also, sophisticated equipment measures drivers' reaction time, depth perception, and peripheral vision before they operate a government vehicle, which helps managers ensure that employees are ready to drive.[37]

Concurrent Control

concurrent control The regulation of ongoing processes to ensure they adhere to established standards

Concurrent control, also known as *screening control,* regulates ongoing organizational activities and transformation processes to ensure that those processes adhere to established standards. Concurrent control inserts checkpoints during the process so that a decision can be made either to continue the process or to correct an observed problem. When transforming an idea to a product design, many organizations involve manufacturing engineers and suppliers in product-design checkpoints to improve the manufacturability of the design and to lower the production cost.[38]

When Harley-Davidson began to produce a new model of motorcycle called the Café Racer, its quality inspectors discovered an average of $1,000 worth of defects in each of the first 100 finished bikes. The company realized that it needed to insert concurrent control checkpoints throughout the manufacturing process to catch problems as they occurred—when there was still time to fix them.[39]

Postaction Control

postaction control The regulation of a process's outputs to ensure they comply with established standards

Postaction control, also known as *feedback,* regulates the outputs of the organization to ensure they comply with established standards. Postaction controls provide management with useful information to solve quality problems and to reward employees for good performance. In Pinellas County, Florida, postaction controls contribute to the reduction of the accident rate for county-owned automobiles. A significant postaction control involves reviewing the driving records of all employees who drive county vehicles. Depending on the feedback, corrective action may be required, including individual counseling for the employee and suspension or revocation of driving privileges.[40]

An important trend in management control regarding quality is shifting the control emphasis from postaction control to concurrent and preliminary controls. In the traditional view of quality, control is applied as an inspection activity, to see how effective each process is at producing quality output. However, more and more organizations now realize that they cut down on waste and rework by assuring that inputs to the process and the process itself are properly managed, which builds quality *into* the process rather than simply checking for it once the process is finished. Chapter 20 explores this distinction in detail.

Integrating Types of Control

To successfully monitor all aspects of their processes, organizations typically integrate preliminary, concurrent, and postaction controls. Control systems that make use of these three types of controls focus managers' attention on the quality of the inputs, the process itself, and the outputs. For example, General Mills established strict control systems for its Red Lobster restaurants located around the country. Preliminary controls are utilized to ensure quality for the 60 million pounds of seafood consumed each year. General Mills purchases fish worldwide, delivers it to warehouses around the country (where it is inspected), and flies it fresh daily to Red Lobster restaurants. Frozen shrimp from Ecuador and Thailand arrives at the General Mills processing plant in St. Petersburg, Florida, where it is loaded onto a conveyor belt, peeled, cleaned, cooked, quick frozen, and packed. This preliminary control system saves about 25 cents per pound over the average restaurant's seafood cost, and it ensures consistent quality. At the restaurant, meals are prepared to precise specifications. Cooking times for each fish, standard placement of food on the plate, and serving temperatures for heated foods are established standards, and managers employ concurrent controls by doing regular spot checks. In fact, managers even carry thermometers in their shirt pockets. A computer assists Red Lobster in implementing postaction control. Each customer order is recorded by the computer system, and the data are used to inform the manager what fish to defrost and what dishes to prepare for the next day. Red Lobster and General Mills are using preliminary, concurrent, and postaction controls in an ongoing effort to cut costs and offer customers the best food and service possible.[41]

Cybernetic and Noncybernetic Control Systems

Managers can use two types of control systems to regulate the transformation process. **Cybernetic control systems** are self-regulating control systems that, once implemented, can automatically measure, evaluate, and correct a process. With the increased use of computers, cybernetic control systems are on the rise.[42] A control system of this sort is what Charles Lazarus of Toys 'R' Us implemented to manage inventory levels. A simple example of a cybernetic con-

cybernetic control systems Self-regulating control systems capable of automatically measuring, evaluating, and correcting a process

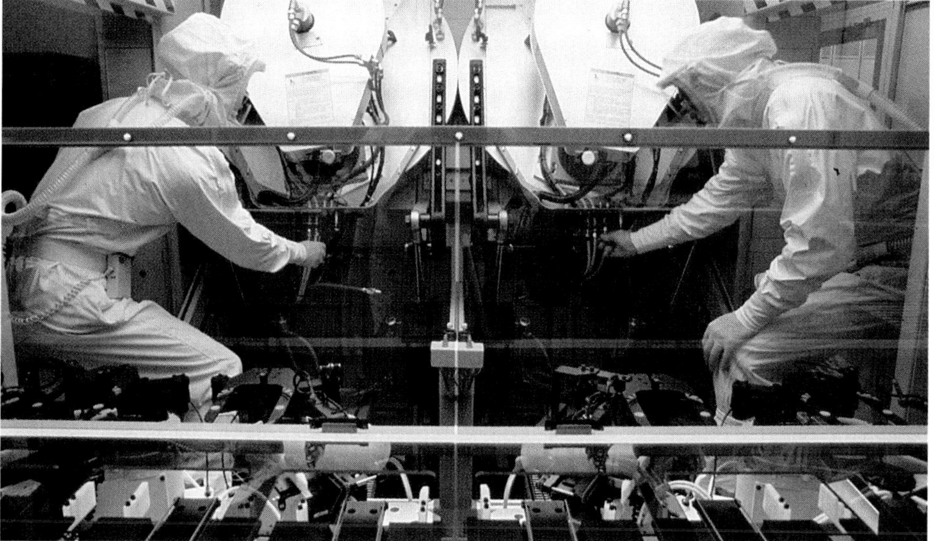

Intel, maker of sophisticated computer chips, uses cybernetic controls to maintain an absolutely clean environment throughout the manufacturing process in its Albuquerque, New Mexico, plant. Even a speck of dust can ruin an entire batch of chips, so the cybernetic control system is critical to helping managers pinpoint and quickly correct any problems. As a result of these self-regulating controls, this plant loses fewer than 20 percent of its chips to contamination.

trol system is the thermostat designed to maintain the appropriate temperature. A sensor determines when the temperature is above or below the desired level. When the temperature drops below the indicated level, the heat is turned on. The heater is turned off when the temperature rises above the indicated level.[43]

Manufacturing companies that have long-term contracts with suppliers are implementing computer systems that automatically pay a supplier on receipt of goods. In the past, goods would be shipped, and an invoice would be issued by the supplier. An accounting employee at the manufacturing company would receive the invoice and would then check to see if the goods had been both ordered and received. If so, a check would be issued. Implementing a cybernetic control system for a well-defined process can eliminate a lot of routine work for employees, freeing human resources and thus increasing productivity.

noncybernetic control systems Control systems that rely on human intervention for the measurement, evaluation, or correction of a control process

Noncybernetic control systems rely on human intervention in the measurement, evaluation, or correction of a control process. The more complex a control system is, the more likely it is to use a noncybernetic control system. Although the computer can be used to automate the measurement phase of a control system, managerial judgment is often required for the evaluation and action phases.

bureaucratic control The regulation of organizational activities in a formal and inflexible manner, designed to achieve employee compliance

clan control The regulation of organizational activities in a flexible and informal manner, designed to achieve employee commitment

Organizational Forms of Control

Once managers have decided on the appropriate mix of preliminary, concurrent, and postaction controls, they need to decide what form those controls will take. The two organizational forms of control are bureaucratic and clan control (see Exhibit 19.4).[44] Typically, large organizations that have existed for a long time are more likely to operate with bureaucratic control, but the choice depends in part on the organizational culture.[45]

Bureaucratic control regulates organizational activities by using a formal and generally inflexible style aimed at achieving compliance with performance standards. Organizations that exercise primarily bureaucratic control are usually characterized by a tall hierarchical structure with limited, formal employee participation. The top-down controls are enforced using rules, regulations, and policies to ensure that employees meet minimally acceptable levels of performance.[46]

Clan control, on the other hand, regulates organizational activities by using a flexible and informal style aimed at achieving employee commitment. Organizations using the clan control approach are characterized by a flat hierarchical structure with employee participation in all facets of operations. Controls developed with employees are aimed at continually increasing levels of employee and group performance. A major benefit of involving employees in the development and implementation of control is the feeling of ownership and subsequent commitment to performance that usually results.[47]

Clan control helps Compaq maintain flexible but effective control over the computer manufacturing process. At the Houston plant, production employees work on a U-shaped assembly line that allows employees at the beginning and the end to monitor quality, discuss operations, and agree on any needed adjustments to the production process.

Top-level managers of many large bureaucratic companies are beginning to understand the cost of bureaucratic control. In an effort to reduce paperwork and gain employee commitment, many organizations have moved toward clan controls. Motorola's radio-telephone plant in Illinois trimmed its management hierarchy from seven tiers to four and gave employees a greater opportunity to participate in decision making. At Eastman Kodak, cross-functional teams are encouraged to work together to resolve problems rather than gain management approval at each step, as previously required. And at General Electric's appliance division, the number of managers needed to sign off on product design

EXHIBIT 19.4 Bureaucratic versus Clan Control

Organizations with clan controls can be differentiated from those with bureaucratic controls by their approaches to job design, performance expectations, organization climates, compensation policies, employment assurances, employee participation, and labor–management relations.

	Bureaucratic Control	Clan Control
Job design principles	Individual attention limited to performing individual job.	Individual responsibility extended to upgrading system performance.
	Job design fragments work and separates doing and thinking.	Job design enhances content of work, emphasizes whole task, and combines doing and thinking.
	Accountability focused on individual.	Accountability focused on teams.
	Fixed job definition.	Flexible definition of duties, contingent on changing conditions.
Performance expectations	Measured standards define minimum performance; stability seen as desirable.	Emphasis placed on "stretch goals," higher goals that tend to be dynamic and oriented to the marketplace.
Organization climates: structure, systems, and style	Structure tends to be layered, with top-down controls.	Flat organization structure with mutual influence systems.
	Coordination and control rely on rules and procedures.	Coordination and control based more on shared goals, values, and traditions.
	More emphasis placed on prerogatives and positional authority.	More emphasis placed on problem solving, relevant information, and expertise.
	Status symbols distributed to reinforce hierarchy.	Status minimized to deemphasize inherent hierarchy.
Compensation policies	Variable pay used where feasible to provide individual incentive.	Variable rewards used to create equity and to reinforce group achievements (gain sharing, profit sharing).
	Individual pay geared to job evaluation.	Individual pay geared to skills and mastery.
	In downturn, cuts concentrated on hourly payroll.	In downturn, cuts focus on equality of sacrifice.
Employment assurances	Employees regarded as variable costs.	Employees assured that participation will not result in loss of job; commitment to avoiding job cuts and assisting in reemployment; priority placed on training and retaining existing work force.
Employee participation	Employee input allowed on relatively narrow agenda; attendant risks emphasized; methods include open-door policy, attitude surveys, grievance procedures, and collective bargaining in some organizations.	Employee participation encouraged on wide range of issues; attendant benefits emphasized; new methods include concepts of corporate governance.
	Business information distributed on strictly defined "need to know" basis.	Business data shared widely.
Labor–management relations	Adversarial relations emphasized; focus on interest conflict.	Mutuality in labor relations emphasized; joint planning and problem solving placed on expanded agenda; unions, managers, and employees redefine their respective roles.

GLOBAL MANAGEMENT

Using Control to Encourage Innovation

Although creativity and innovation are critical elements for success in today's competitive marketplace, how global managers use control to develop new ideas into new products differs from organization to organization and from country to country. In the past, strict or overly cost-conscious controls often forced employees to work within narrow guidelines or with limited resources, which could hamper their creative talents. But in an increasing number of companies around the world, managers are reexamining how they can use control to actively encourage innovation. Many Japanese companies, for example, are establishing control processes to systematically reuse new or improved technologies to create innovative new products. In contrast, many United States firms are using controls to insulate creative groups from bureaucratic controls and to provide incentives for creative thinkers. Both approaches can be effective if carefully planned and implemented.

In Japan, companies often establish control procedures that encourage the development of new technology and the transfer of technology from one business unit to another. In fact, the control system at many Japanese companies requires cross-functional teams to review every aspect of the business as a method of identifying opportunities and resources for innovative products. For example, Sharp sponsors a program encouraging all employees to submit ideas for new products. Cross-functional teams analyze the best ideas to see how they fit with Sharp's worldwide technological base. Over the past few years, nearly 150 teams have investigated a variety of ideas, leading to a steady stream of promising new-product concepts that range from electronic organizers to liquid-crystal display projection televisions.

Canon takes a slightly different approach. Its controls are geared toward recycling technology throughout the organization to spur innovation around existing resources. Using this approach to control, Canon was able to improve its laser printers and plain-paper

changes has been reduced by more than 15 (from an all-time high of 21).[48] Moving away from bureaucratic control enables employees to take on more decision-making responsibility and thus be more involved in the organization and committed to the successful achievement of its goals.

However, organizations usually don't rely exclusively on one form of control or the other, and a degree of each is appropriate for all organizations. Bureaucratic and clan control, therefore, should be viewed as two parts of an overall picture of control. Too much bureaucratic control can stifle creativity and discourage employees. Not enough bureaucratic control can cause an organization to place too little emphasis on budgeting, cost control, and other fundamentals that are necessary to organizational success.

MANAGING EFFECTIVE CONTROL

Effective organizations are capable of meeting their established goals even though changes occur in the environment, and managerial control is the mechanism they use to detect environmental changes and to monitor organizational performance. However, control systems aren't automatically effective and helpful; dysfunctional control systems can actually work against the organization's objectives.

Characteristics of Dysfunctional Control Systems

In some organizations, control systems fail to provide management with the correct signals and directions. Managers who receive incorrect control feedback take courses of action that are inappropriate to the situation and may cause serious damage to the organization. Common pitfalls in establishing or manag-

facsimile machines by adapting a version of the toner cartridge originally developed for the firm's personal copiers. This transfer of technology improved all the products and enabled Canon to make the most of its original investment in innovation.

Some U.S. firms, including Corning, use controls to actively encourage technology transfer. But many long-established firms in the United States find that their regular control systems are too rigid to support creativity and innovation. For this reason, some companies are forming special new-product teams or units that are allowed to operate outside the usual control processes or with modified controls that differ from those used in the rest of the company. For example, Colgate-Palmolive has established Colgate Venture, a unit insulated from its parent's regimented control systems. Staffed with creative, risk-taking personnel, Colgate Venture encourages innovative product development by applying more flexible controls and rewarding creativity. Similarly, General Foods's Culinova Group operates separately from its mainstream businesses and is developing innovative ways of leading the parent into the refrigerated take-out food business. Scott Paper has also carved out a special business unit, with its own control systems, to tackle the entrepreneurial idea of selling its products to do-it-yourself home owners.

Designing and implementing effective controls can be a delicate balancing act under any circumstances. But managers who want to nurture innovation need to be particularly sensitive to the ways their control systems may unintentionally hurt or derail the creative process. Whether they follow the path favored by many Japanese firms or choose the approach favored by many U.S. firms, the global manager must carefully adapt control systems to the individual organization's goals, environment, and culture.

Apply Your Knowledge

1. How might control systems limit creativity and innovation in a government agency?
2. How might a firm with subsidiaries in the United States and in Japan use control to spur creativity in both countries?

ing control systems include overcontrol and undercontrol, inconsistent controls, and failure to differentiate controls.[49]

Overcontrol and Undercontrol

Managers may find that their controls are either too strict or too lenient. **Overcontrol** is the excessive regulation of work activities, which restricts individual autonomy. **Undercontrol** is poor or nonexistent regulation of work activities; employees may be granted too much individual autonomy. Both overcontrol and undercontrol can hurt performance. Too much control can stifle innovation, create morale problems, and lead to an abundance of red tape, slowing decision making and implementation. Too little control can hurt internal coordination and lead to excessive spending and other inefficient uses of resources. The key is to find the right balance of controls to support performance. Companies that issue credit cards, for example, try to strike a balance between setting application standards that are so strict that the firm can't sign up enough cardholders (overcontrol) and setting standards that are so loose that the firm signs up people who turn out to be credit problems (undercontrol).

overcontrol Excessive regulation of work activities, restricting individual autonomy and causing ineffective organizational performance

undercontrol Unregulated work activities, granting employees too much individual autonomy and causing ineffective organizational performance

When organizations acquire or merge with other organizations, differences in managerial control can affect overall performance. When managers purchase or merge with an organization that has loose controls, they can often improve performance by tightening those controls. However, joining two organizations with differing degrees of control can contribute to culture clash and may hurt performance. For instance, A&P has expanded in recent years by purchasing family-owned regional supermarket chains—such as Waldbaum's, Shopwell, and Borman's—and instituting stricter financial, budgetary, and inventory controls to improve profits. But Borman's executives found A&P's control systems too strict, and as a result of this overcontrol, the first year of combined operations fell short of profit projections. To boost performance, A&P had to review its control procedures and look for ways of creating more synergy in the future.[50]

Inconsistent Controls

Control systems, if designed inappropriately, can send mixed messages to employees. Managers must design control systems that induce the appropriate employee behaviors to assure organizational success in the long term. A common example of the mixed-messages problem is employee compensation that is not well integrated with the control systems. Consider a group of product designers who have been asked by their manager to spend a portion of their time thinking about future project ideas. If these employees then see that their compensation is based strictly on performance relative to current projects, they aren't likely to spend much time on the future projects.

Failure to Differentiate Controls

Control strategies often mirror organizational structure. For instance, a centralized organization is likely to have a single, centralized control system that imposes the same set of standards and actions across all divisions and departments. However, failure to distinguish control needs among various parts of an organization is a common source of control problems.

Consider an organization such as the National Park Service, which oversees 355 parks and monuments in 49 states (all except Delaware) and the District of Columbia, Puerto Rico, the U.S. Virgin Islands, Saipan, American Samoa, and Guam. Some of these sites possess primarily scenic interest, others are historical, and still others are scientific. They range in size from less than 1,000 square feet to more than 13 million acres. And the sites are extremely diverse, from wild rivers to the White House, from the Grand Canyon to the Statue of Liberty.[51] Clearly, the Park Service faces a huge variety of control situations at these sites, and it would be a mistake to impose consistent standards, performance measures, and corrective actions across the entire park system.

In contrast, a single control system does work well for companies like Toys 'R' Us, in which all the operating units are in similar businesses and in similar circumstances. In fact, one of Charles Lazarus's keys to success is ensuring consistency from store to store so that centralized control systems are effective. In the case of Toys 'R' Us, it would be a mistake *not* to impose control consistency because this is one of the company's key competitive strengths.

Characteristics of Effective Control Systems

Just as it helpful to identify the characteristics of a dysfunctional control system, it is important to identify and understand what makes a control system effective and successful. One crucial attribute is the manager's personal style of control (see Exhibit 19.5). Selecting a personal style that is consistent with the organization and its level of clan control is critical in implementing a control system that will fit the culture of the organization.[52]

In addition to requiring that managers have an appropriate personal control style, effective control systems are characterized by strong links with the organization's planning system, and they are accurate, timely, relevant, and objective and measurable.[53]

- *Linked with planning.* When the control function is linked closely with planning, control systems can provide feedback about progress toward goals and

EXHIBIT 19.5

Selecting a Management Control Style

Managers should ask themselves several questions about their personal control style.

1. In general, what kind of managerial style do I have?	
Participative	***Directive***
I frequently consult my employees on decisions, encourage them to disagree with my opinion, share information with them, and let them make decisions whenever possible.	**I usually take most of the responsibility for my employees, make most of the major decisions for them, pass on only the most relevant job information to them, and provide detailed and close direction for them.**
2. In general, what kind of climate, structure, and reward system does my organization have?	
Participative	***Nonparticipative***
Employees at all levels of the organization are urged to participate in decisions and influence the course of events. Managers are clearly rewarded for developing employee skills and decision-making capacities.	**Most important decisions are made by a few people at the top of the organization. Managers are not rewarded for developing employee competence or for encouraging employees to participate in decision making.**
3. How accurate and reliable are the measures of key areas of subordinate performance?	
Accurate	***Inaccurate***
All major aspects of performance can be adequately measured; changes in measures accurately reflect changes in performance; measures cannot be easily sabotaged or faked by subordinates.	**Not all critical aspects of performance can be measured; measures often do not pick up on important changes in performance; good performance cannot be adequately defined to establish measurements; measures can be easily sabotaged.**
4. Do my subordinates desire to participate and respond well to opportunities to take responsibility for decision making and performance?	
High desire to participate	***Low desire to participate***
Employees are eager to participate in decisions, are involved in the work itself, can make a contribution to decision making, and want to take more responsibility.	**Employees do not want to be involved in decisions, do not want additional responsibility, have little to contribute to decisions being made, and are not involved in the work itself.**

can communicate organizational goals through performance measures. For example, Digital Equipment Corporation (DEC) recently installed a new information system to help managers customize a business plan for each division. A strategic plan is developed on the basis of factors such as the maturity of the business and the state of the competition; this plan then generates appropriate performance standards for each division. Like DEC, many organizations require their managers to establish performance standards during the planning process in order to measure ongoing progress.[54]

- *Accurate.* Effective control systems depend on gathering and disseminating reliable and valid information. If control data are inaccurate, managers will draw incorrect conclusions and take inappropriate actions. When managers implement control systems, they must be sure to capture valid data and transform them into accurate information.[55] For instance, it isn't hard to imagine the problems that would result if stores in the Toys 'R' Us chain failed to provide accurate sales data to the company's forecasting system; the system would misjudge consumer demand and probably end up overordering some items and underordering others.
- *Timely.* Control data should be provided to the responsible managers frequently enough to allow them to react to problems while there is still time to take decisive action. Without timely control information, problem situations

turn into major disasters. If product managers are unaware of a competitive product introduction, they may find their market share dropping radically and find themselves without a plan to counter the competition. However, if the competitive entry is detected early enough, promotions and pricing could be altered to address the competitor's new product. This is why companies usually spend a great deal of time visiting trade shows, listening to customers, analyzing patents, and engaging in other activities that try to uncover signs of future competitive products. At the extreme, control data can be worthless if they arrive late.

- *Relevant.* To provide the appropriate data for controlling the transformation process, managers must identify specific areas that should be monitored. Often, managers can improve performance by changing or influencing portions of the transformation process that are particularly important.[56] Once these key areas have been identified, managers will be able to measure results and consider whether to take action. But if they have too many irrelevant data or too few of the right data, managers may be distracted or mislead and therefore unable to exert effective control.
- *Objective and measurable.* Control data that are subjective and qualitative can't easily provide managers with the ability to compare employees, departments, time frames, and other elements. Assume that a manager at Microsoft receives status reports from two project managers. The first manager provides vague, subjective information and reports that the project is slightly behind schedule and that the number of software defects is as expected. The second project manager provides objective, measurable information and reports that the project is five days behind schedule and that the number of software defects exceeds performance standards by 2 percent. If both product managers reported their control information objectively and quantitatively, the R&D manager could easily compare the situations and act accordingly. Without objective and measurable feedback, the R&D manager has to work harder to understand and correct problems.

financial statement A summary of the overall financial status of an organization

balance sheet A financial statement detailing an organization's assets, liabilities, and shareholder equity at a specific point in time

MANAGING FINANCIAL CONTROLS

Financial controls provide managers and stakeholders with a common language for evaluating organizational performance. For example, stakeholders can use financial data to evaluate the effectiveness of companies when making decisions about purchasing or selling stock. Top-level managers use financial controls to monitor the overall health of the organization. Feedback from financial controls is also used by managers throughout the planning process. Knowing how well an organization performed financially in the previous year is essential for determining the plans and controls necessary for the coming year.

Financial statements summarize the overall financial status of an organization, and they fall into two basic categories.[57] The **balance sheet** is a time-specific statement of an organization's assets and claims against those assets, including liabilities and shareholder equity (see Exhibit 19.6). A balance sheet summarizes the financial worth of an organization on a particular date. Assets are shown at cost, or the price the company paid for those assets, whereas liabilities indicate the amount the company owes. Shareholders' equity is the net worth of the company or the claim the owners (shareholders) have on the assets of the firm. Shareholder's equity is equal to the difference between the assets and liabilities.[58]

Manville's CEO W. Thomas Stephens uses a laptop computer to stay on top of his firm's financial situation even while he's traveling. By examining the company's financial statements and by scrutinizing budgetary controls, Stephens has been able to monitor Manville's recovery from bankruptcy. He has also evaluated potential acquisition targets by analyzing their financial statements.

EXHIBIT 19.6 Macro Toy Company Balance Sheet as of December 31, 1993

The balance sheet states the company's assets, liabilities, and shareholder's equity at a particular point in time.

Assets		Liabilities	
Cash	$ 70,000	Accounts payable	$ 150,000
Marketable securities	30,000	Notes payable to bank (8%)	200,000
Accounts receivable, net	450,000	Accruals	20,000
Inventories	350,000	Federal income taxes payable	80,000
Total current assets	$ 900,000	Total current liabilities	$ 450,000
Gross plant and equipment	$2,100,000	Mortgage bonds (6%)	150,000
Allowance for depreciation	(500,000)	Debentures (7%)	400,000
Net plant and equipment	$1,600,000	Total liabilities	$1,000,000
		Shareholders' equity	
		Common stock	$ 500,000
		Retained earnings	1,000,000
		Shareholders' equity	$1,500,000
Total assets	$2,500,000	Liabilities plus equity	$2,500,000

An **income statement** summarizes the company's financial performance over a particular period of time, such as a year or a quarter (see Exhibit 19.7). Revenues and expenses are the key elements of an income statement. *Revenues* originate from the sale of goods and services. *Expenses* are costs incurred in the production or sale of the goods and services. The difference between revenues and expenses is *income*.[59]

Ratio analysis is a process for comparing organizational performance with historical, competitive, or industry performance. **Ratios** are indexes derived

income statement A summary of an organization's revenues, expenses, and profits over a particular period of time

ratio analysis A managerial process used to compare organizational performance with historical, competitive, or industry performance

EXHIBIT 19.7 Macro Toy Company Income Statement for Year Ended December 31, 1993

The income statement summarizes the performance of the company over a particular period of time.

Net Sales		$5,400,000
Cost of goods		4,400,000
Gross margin on sales		$1,000,000
Operating expenses:		
Selling	$200,000	
General and administrative	330,000	
Lease payments	20,000	
Total operating expenses		$ 550,000
Operating income		$ 450,000
Add: Other revenues (interest on marketable securities plus royalties)		3,000
Operating income plus other revenues		$ 453,000
Less other expenses:		
Interest on bank note	$ 16,000	
Interest on mortgage	9,000	
Interest on debentures	28,000	
Total interest expense		53,000
Income before taxes		$ 400,000
Federal income taxes (at 40%)		160,000
Net income (net profit)		240,000
Dividends		$ 70,000
Increase in retained earnings		170,000

ratios Indexes derived from comparing one financial measure to another

from comparing one financial measure to another. Used in ratio analysis, ratios are tools for comparing one organization's performance with a competitor's performance or with the performance of the entire industry. Managers also use ratios to track company performance over time, highlighting any significant financial deviations. Liquidity ratios, leverage ratios, activity ratios, and profitability ratios are critical tools used by top managers and investors to evaluate the financial performance of an organization.[60]

liquidity ratios Indexes used to analyze an organization's ability to meet short-run obligations with current assets

current ratio An index used to measure an organization's ability to cover current liabilities with current assets

Liquidity ratios indicate the company's capacity to meet short-term obligations with current assets. A commonly used liquidity ratio is the **current ratio,** which measures the ability of a company to meet short-term debts (current liabilities) with its liquid assets (current assets). The current ratio listed for Macro Toy Company (see Exhibit 19.8) indicates the company might have more trouble meeting short-term debt obligations than other companies within the industry. Short-term creditors would probably be wary about extending additional credit to Macro, although there might be extenuating circumstances that would explain Macro's ratio.

leverage ratios Indexes used to analyze an organization's ability to meet its long-term and short-term debt obligations

debt ratio The extent to which total company assets are financed through both short-term and long-term debt

Leverage ratios indicate the company's capacity to meet its long-term and short-term debt obligations. These ratios indicate the extent to which the company uses debt to finance investments. Since debt requires the company to repay the loan with interest, excessive debt may increase bankruptcy risk. One of the more important leverage ratios is the **debt ratio,** which measures the extent to which total company assets are financed through both short-term and long-term debt. Macro's debt ratio is slightly less than the industry average, and company managers might want to consider taking on more long-term debt to pay off current liabilities. This action would bring the current ratio more in line with the industry average and the debt ratio would remain unchanged since total debt would remain the same. Of course, decisions regarding this and all other financial matters require more information than just these ratios; the ratios serve only as broad indicators.

activity ratios Indexes used to analyze an organization's effectiveness in using its assets to generate sales

inventory turnover A measure of how inventory is managed to meet sales

Activity ratios indicate how effectively the company is using its assets to generate sales. Two commonly used activity ratios are inventory turnover and average collection period ratio. **Inventory turnover** measures how effectively inventory is managed to meet sales. Inventory exists to absorb fluctuations in material deliveries and in customer demand. Low inventory turnover may indicate a large investment in inventory relative to the amount needed to fill orders. High inventory turnover often signals that inventory is too small and that the firm frequently is unable to meet customer orders. While inventory turnover for Macro indicates a low level of inventory, further investigation would establish whether Macro was simply understocked or using inventory extremely efficiently.

average collection period A measure of how many days from the sales date it takes to receive a customer payment

profitability ratios Indexes used to analyze an organization's effectiveness in earning a net return on sales and investments

net profit margin A measure of the percentage of sales left after deducting expenses

Average collection period ratio measures how many days it takes to receive customer payment from the sales date. A high average collection period may indicate slow billing procedures, ineffective incentives for customers to pay on time, or poor selection of customers when extending credit. A low average collection period may indicate customers are not extended enough credit, causing them to purchase from the competition for better credit terms. The average collection period for Macro is rather low and indicates management should investigate whether strict credit terms are driving customers away.

Profitability ratios measure the success of the organization in earning a net return on sales and investments. Three important profitability ratios are net profit margin, return on investment, and return on equity. **Net profit margin**

EXHIBIT 19.8 Ratio Definitions and Values for Macro Toy Company

Ratios are used to compare current performance with past performance and industry averages.

Ratio	Ratio Formula	Industry Average	Appropriate Ratio Level for Macro Toy Company	Actual Macro Toy Company Ratios
Liquidity ratios				
Current	Current assets / Current liabilities	2.4	2.6	2.0
Quick	(Current assets − inventory) / Current liabilities	1.2	1.7	1.22
Leverage ratios				
Debt	Total debt / Total assets	0.45	0.4	0.4
Debt equity[a]	Long-term debt / Shareholders' equity	0.48	0.43	0.37
Times interest earned	(Earnings before taxes + interest) / Interest charges	6.0	6.5	8.55
Fixed-charges coverage	Income available for meeting fixed charges / Fixed charges	3.2	3.5	4.19
Activity ratios				
Inventory turnover (per year)	Cost of goods sold / Average inventory	5.0	9.0	11.0
Average collection period, days	Average accounts receivable / Average credit sales per day	56.0	46.0	30.0
Fixed-assets turnover	Sales / Fixed assets	11.0	10.0	3.375
Total assets turnover	Sales / Total assets	7.0	6.5	2.16
Profitability ratios				
Gross profit margin, %	(Sales − cost of goods sold) / Sales	12.0	14.0	18.5
Net operating margin, %	Operating income / Sales	5.0	6.0	8.33
Profit margin on sales, %	Net income / Sales	3.5	4.0	4.44
Return on total assets, %[b]	(Net income + interest) / Total assets	9.6	10.5	11.72
Return on equity, %	Net income / Shareholders' equity	13.5	15.0	16.0

[a] Sometimes current debt or total debt, rather than long-term debt, is used in computing this ratio.

[b] Return on total assets as defined here [(net income + interest)/total assets] is sometimes referred to as the "operating return on total assets." Also, the term "return on total assets" is often used to refer to net income/total assets; however, the ratio (net income/total assets) is not very meaningful.

(also called net operating margin) indicates the percentage of sales left after deducting expenses. For Macro Toy Company, the net profit margin indicates that Macro is adept at generating sales, reducing expenses, or both. **Return on investment (ROI)** measures a firm's effectiveness in generating returns on the money that has been invested in it. One common way of expressing ROI is *return on total assets,* which is net income plus interest divided by total assets. This indicates how effectively the company is using its assets. Another way of looking at ROI is **return on equity,** which is net income divided by shareholders' equity (the total value of the stock owned by the company's shareholders). This indicates how effectively the company is using the money that shareholders have invested in it by purchasing stock. As Exhibit 19.8 shows, Macro is outperforming the industry average on both measures.

return on investment (ROI) A measure of an organization's effectiveness in generating returns from its investment in assets

return on equity A measure of an organization's effectiveness in generating returns on the shareholders' investments

MANAGING BUDGETARY CONTROLS

Budgeting is the process that allocates organizational resources to units within the organization in order to support organizational plans and strategies.[61] A **budget** is defined as the quantitative expression of a plan, whether for an organization or for a unit within the organization.[62] Budgets are generally created at the beginning of each year, whereas actual performance is compared to the standards expressed in the budget on a monthly or quarterly basis. Managers are held accountable for deviations from budget standards.

budgeting An allocation of organizational resources to units within the organization in order to support organizational plans and strategies

budget A financial plan for an organization or for a unit within the organization

Budgetary control must be considered a component of an organization's total control system. Consequently, its purpose should be limited and specific. Budgets can be used to evaluate performance, motivate employees, or plan for future events. If motivation is the budgetary goal, targets should be difficult but attainable and fairly rigid. Use of budgets for planning implies that they should be based on the "most likely" scenario. If performance is to be evaluated from budgetary control information, adjustments are made after the fact for unforeseen events. Since these budget characteristics are in conflict, the purpose of budgetary control must be clearly defined to effectively influence behavior (see Exhibit 19.9).[63]

At Daihatsu Motor Company, a medium-sized Japanese automobile producer, budgetary control is used to motivate personnel to implement and measure continual process improvement. Managers in production receive monthly reports that compare budgeted and actual costs only for the expenses that can be reduced through employees' continual efforts and through process improvement activities. In addition, the budgeted production costs are tightened monthly to encourage cost reduction for as long as a given model is in production.[64] Budgetary control, if properly designed and implemented, can motivate employees to focus on activities that enhance the effectiveness of the organization.

Responsibility Centers

A **responsibility center** is a component of a larger organization headed by a manager who is held accountable for achieving specific financial goals. ("Center" in this sense refers to a part of the organization, such as a division or a department, not to a specific physical location or facility.) These financial goals can include profit, revenues, costs, or investments.[65] By defining responsibility centers, top managers are delegating responsibility for middle and lower-level

responsibility center A discrete organization unit headed by a manager responsible for achieving specific goals

EXHIBIT 19.9 Budget Design Choices

Some budget design decisions are related to planning; others are related to control. Effective managers are aware of the purpose of each decision in designing budgets that encourage the right kind of behavior in the organization.

Planning Decisions	Control Decisions	
• **Initiation and participation** Should the budget be prepared primarily from the bottom up or from the top down? • **Implementation** How can a company blend the overview of top management with the depth of knowledge of operations found in operating units? • **Timing** When does a company start and when does it complete the budget process? How is the budget linked to the strategic planning process?	• **Rolling budgets and revision** Should the budget period be for 12 months followed by another 12-month budget a year later, or should a calendar quarter be added each time a calendar quarter expires? Should the budget remain fixed for the budget period, or should it be revised periodically during the period? • **Fixed or flexible budgets** Should performance be evaluated against the original budget or against a budget that incorporates the actual activity level of the business?	• **Bonuses based on budgets** Should incentive compensation, if any, be based on actual versus budgeted performance or on actual performance against some other standard? • **Evaluation criteria** Should the budget used to evaluate performance include only those items over which the evaluated manager has control, or should it include all unit costs and revenues appropriate to the managerial unit? • **Budget tightness** What degree of "stretch" should there be in the budget?

managers to make short-term and long-term decisions. Responsibility centers decentralize organizational decision making, giving managers both more control and more responsibility.

A **profit center** is a responsibility center whose performance is based on profit, or the difference between revenue and cost. For a unit of an organization to be a profit center, it must have significant control over its major revenues and costs. Profit centers give those decision makers who are closest to customers the responsibility for the revenue-versus-cost trade-offs that determine profitability. An example of a decentralized profit center is the loan production offices (LPOs) used by many large banks, such as Citibank and BankAmerica. LPOs give banks the ability to expand beyond their home states to new markets while maintaining the responsibility of providing excellent customer service. Each profit center has a manager who is responsible for all costs and revenues associated with the LPO's activities.[66]

profit center A responsibility center headed by a manager who is held accountable for achieving profit targets

An **expense center** is a responsibility center whose performance is based on control over spending. An expense center is appropriate when a manager has no responsibility for generating revenues. Personnel and accounting departments are two examples of expense centers; these functional areas can't directly generate revenue, so their financial performance is instead based on how much they cost the organization.

expense center A responsibility center headed by a manager who is held accountable for achieving expense targets

A **revenue center** is a responsibility center whose performance is based on generating revenues. A revenue center is appropriate for divisions or departments that have sole responsibility for sales. A sales or marketing department may be defined as a revenue center. These units typically aren't considered profit centers, however, since they rarely have control over the total costs of doing business and thus cannot control profit.

revenue center A responsibility center headed by a manager who is held accountable for achieving revenue targets

An **investment center** is a responsibility center whose performance is based on ROI. Top managers establish investment centers to delegate the responsibility for investing in plant, equipment, and other assets critical to organizational performance.

investment center A responsibility center headed by a manager who is held accountable for achieving return-on-investment targets

Types of Budgets

Various types of budgets provide managers with differing methods for controlling the financial health of the organization. When establishing budgetary control, managers must determine the financial elements critical to the success of their organizations. These key financial elements must then be measured and evaluated. Operating and financial budgets provide methods to measure completely different elements of financial effectiveness.

Operating Budgets

operating budget A financial plan allocating resources to responsibility centers in order to support organizational plans and strategies

profit budget A projection of profits for the coming year, made by comparing anticipated revenues to anticipated expenses

An **operating budget** is a financial plan that allocates resources to responsibility centers in order to support organizational plans and strategies. Three common types of operating budgets are used by the responsibility centers: profit budgets, revenue budgets, and expense budgets.

A **profit budget** is an operating budget that projects profits for the coming period by comparing anticipated revenues and anticipated expenses. Profit budgets typically exist for each profit center as well as for the organization as a whole. NBC News is a profit center of NBC owned by General Electric. Unable to meet expected profit levels, NBC News cut satellite and communication expenses and increased revenues by selling news programming to other countries.[67] Mystic Seaport Museum, a not-for-profit organization located in Mystic, Connecticut, organized its retail store both as a for-profit corporation, wholly owned by the Seaport, and as a profit center, complete with a profit budget.[68]

revenue budget A projection of anticipated revenues for the coming period

A **revenue budget** is an operating budget that projects anticipated revenues for the coming period. Revenue budgets are developed by each revenue center. The Big Apple Circus, a not-for-profit circus serving the New York metropolitan area, estimates revenues as the total of ticket sales, fundraising, and grants.[69]

expense budget A projection of anticipated expenses for the coming period

An **expense budget** is an operating budget that projects anticipated expenses for the coming period. Expense budgets are created by each expense center. For example, Wayne Harvey, business manager of the Big Apple Circus, divided the organization into nine expense centers and he manages each using a detailed expense budget.[70]

Financial Budgets

financial budget A projection of cash inflows and cash outflows for the coming period

A **financial budget** summarizes the organization's sources and uses of cash for the coming period. Sources of cash can include revenues, newly issued stock, loans, or the sale of company assets. Cash is used to pay operating expenses, purchase new assets, pay off loans, issue dividends to shareholders, or supplement retained earnings. For example, Chrysler was faced with a $2 billion negative cash flow for its auto operations at the end of fiscal year 1990. To boost its cash, Chrysler furiously slashed operating costs, halved the March 1991 quarterly dividend, and renegotiated loan terms.[71]

cash budget A financial plan showing the sources and uses of cash for a specific period, such as daily, weekly, monthly, or yearly

capital expenditures budget Cash sources and cash uses associated with the future purchase of large assets, including buildings, land, and machinery

A **cash budget,** or *cash-flow budget,* projects the detailed sources and uses of cash for a specific period, such as daily, weekly, monthly, or yearly (see Exhibit 19.10). The main goal of the cash budget is to detail a plan for having enough cash on hand to cover an organization's cash obligations for a specific day, week, month, or year. Since Chrysler was in a cash-poor situation, the cash budget provided a framework for managers to discuss how to free up more cash for coming periods.

A **capital expenditures budget** is a plan for the purchase of large assets, including buildings, land, and machinery. Because major expenditures often re-

EXHIBIT 19.10

Macro Toy Company Cash-Flow Statement, 1993

Cash-flow statements enumerate the sources and uses of cash over a particular time period, in this case for the year.

Sources of Funds (cash in 000s)		
Assets	Decrease in cash	$ 30
	Decrease in accounts receivable	150
	Increase in allowance for depreciation	60
Liabilities	Increase in accruals	5
	Increase in income taxes payable	15
Shareholder's equity	Sales of additional common stock	20
	Increase in retained earnings	170
		$450

Uses of Funds (cash in 000s)		
Assets	Purchase of marketable securities	$ 10
	Increase in inventories	70
	Increase in gross fixed assets	310
Liabilities	Decrease in accounts payable	10
	Decrease in mortgage bonds	25
	Decrease in debentures	25
		$450

quire loans (which of course involve interest and principal payments), the capital expenditures budget is critical in assessing how a planned capital expenditure will affect cash flow in current and in future years.[72]

Approaches to Budget Development

After management has decided on the critical financial variables for an organization and has chosen the types of budgets to be used, the budgets must be developed. The budget-development process varies based on the amount of managerial participation, and many organizations use a combination of approaches.

Managers of the General Electric plant in Greenville, South Carolina, prepare capital expenditures budgets to plan the current and future cash-flow impact of constructing plant extensions. Since the plant opened in 1968, managers have periodically added capacity to take advantage of forecasted increases in demand for the gas turbines produced at this facility.

Managers can have budgets imposed on them by higher-level managers, or they might develop budgets themselves. The three approaches to budget development are top-down, bottom-up, and zero-base.[73]

Top-Down Budgeting

top-down budgeting A process by which top managers impose budgets on lower-level managers

Top-down budgeting is a budget-development process in which budget targets are imposed by top managers in the company. The top-down approach to budgeting allows high-level managers to put forward their comprehensive views of the organization and of its economic and competitive environments. In a small company, the owner may be the only manager with knowledge of the company's goals, strategies, and available resources.

The top-down budgeting process is used appropriately in many situations. Business unit managers may be given explicit performance objectives by top managers in times of economic crisis. When the nature of the business requires close coordination between units, top-down budgeting can effectively set financial objectives. And if managers lack a global perspective, top managers may choose to dictate the budget. The major limitations of top-down budgeting are that the executives involved might not have the frontline perspective needed to apportion the organization's resources most effectively and that lower-level managers might be less committed to budgets that they had no control in formulating. For these reasons, many organizations combine top-down and bottom-up approaches.

Bottom-Up Budgeting

bottom-up budgeting A process in which the lower-level managers directly responsible for operations develop individual budgets that are combined to create an overall organizational budget

Bottom-up budgeting is a process in which the lower-level managers directly responsible for operations develop individual budgets that are combined to create an overall organizational budget. The bottom-up approach to budgeting makes use of the operating managers' detailed knowledge of the environment and the marketplace, knowledge that is available only to those who are involved on a daily basis. Managers are more likely to adhere to budgets that they were responsible for preparing. For example, Jean-Marie Descarpentries, head of the Franco-British CMB Packaging, uses budgets to make managers stretch for the unreachable. Each year he asks the heads of 94 profit centers to project their best possible performance if everything, including product demand, goes just right. Bottom-up budgeting is used by Descarpentries to motivate his managers to exceed the previous year's performance and industry averages.[74]

Bottom-up budgeting has two major drawbacks. The first is that middle- and lower-level managers might not have the perspective needed to appropriately balance resource demands across the entire organization. For instance, a marketing manager and a manufacturing manager might both push for an additional $1,000,000 in their budgets for the following year, when the division manager to whom both report knows that there is only $1,500,000 to divide across the departments and that the organization needs to invest most of that in manufacturing. The second disadvantage of bottom-up budgeting is that it can consume a lot of time as the organization tries to reconcile the often conflicting and overlapping demands presented by lower-level managers.

Zero-Base Budgeting

zero-base budgeting A process by which managers calculate resource requirements based on the coming year's priorities, rather than on the past year's requirements

Zero-base budgeting is a process in which managers calculate resource requirements based on the coming year's priorities rather than on the past year's requirements. This method forces managers to base their budget on strategic plans and to justify their need for resources accordingly. This is in stark contrast to the budgeting situation in most organizations, in which next year's budget is largely a reflection of this year's figures, perhaps with incremental changes. This keeps organizational spending fairly stable but fails to give organizations the flexibility to adapt to changes in the environment.[75] Zero-base budgeting is also helpful in identifying programs or activities that are being continued automatically from year to year, when in fact they should be modified or perhaps curtailed entirely.

THE FINANCIAL AUDIT

The accuracy of financial and budgetary information is based on the effectiveness of the internal financial control system. The goal of an audit is to ensure that financial reports accurately reflect the condition of the company. According to the United States General Accounting Office, an **audit** can include the independent review of financial reports, compliance with applicable laws and regulations, efficiency and economy of operations, and effectiveness of achieving program results. An audit, then, is an independent appraisal of an organization's financial and operational efficiency and effectiveness.[76] The results of an audit provide key control information to managers, enabling them to see whether corrective action is required anywhere in the organization.

audit An independent appraisal of an organization's financial and operational efficiency and effectiveness performed by an accountant

An **external audit** is an appraisal of an organization's financial statements by an independent certified public accountant for reporting to shareholders, the Internal Revenue Service, and other interested parties. The independent expert focuses only on whether the financial reports of the organization conform to generally accepted accounting principles. Publicly held corporations are required by law to have regular external audits to assure investors that financial reports are reliable.

external audit An appraisal of an organization's financial statements performed by independent certified public accountants for reporting to shareholders, the Internal Revenue Service, and other interested parties

The **internal audit** evaluates the accuracy of financial and accounting controls as well as the overall review of operation efficiency. The internal audit is aimed at helping managers improve their operations through the use of better controls.

internal audit An appraisal performed by an employee of the organization to evaluate the accuracy of financial and accounting controls as well as the efficiency of operations

Although audits can be intrusive, they are also a tool that managers can use to continually improve their operations. Internal audits, especially, can help organizations identify control problems and poor managerial decision making. When an independent expert identifies areas for improvement, the successful manager uses this constructive feedback to tighten up the system.

SUMMARY

Control is the regulatory process that directs an organization's activities toward anticipated goals and standards. Effective organizations monitor activities through financial and budgetary controls, operations control, marketing control, R&D control, and human resource control. Control systems highlight significant performance problems throughout the organization on an ongoing basis. To implement control systems, managers must define standards, measure performance, compare performance with standards, and, finally, take action. Managerial action might be to correct the problem, recognize employee performance, or change the standards and measurement process.

Levels of controls are strategic, tactical, or operational. Strategic controls are used by top management to ensure successful implementation of an organization's long-range strategic plans, specifically emphasizing the impact of broad environmental effects and internal strategic directions. Tactical controls, implemented by middle managers, are aimed at successful implementation of department-level tactical plans, focusing on internal and external forces that affect them. Operational controls are used by lower-level managers and focus on successful implementation of day-to-day operational plans by monitoring specific and focused internal activities.

Types of controls include preliminary, concurrent, and postaction. Preliminary control focuses on the inputs to an organizational process to ensure that they meet established standards for eventual success of the process. Concurrent control regulates ongoing organizational processes to ensure that the processes adhere to established standards. Postaction control monitors the outputs of the organization to ensure that they comply with established standards. Organizations that utilize the three types of controls in their systems will increase the quality of inputs, transformations, and outputs. The significant trend regarding types of control is that more organizations are shifting from postaction control to concurrent and preliminary control.

Control systems can be defined as cybernetic or noncybernetic, based on the level of human interaction necessary for control systems. Cybernetic control systems are self-regulating and can automatically measure, evaluate, and correct a process. Noncybernetic control systems rely on human intervention in the measurement, evaluation, or correction of a control process. Simpler, well-defined processes are likely candidates for cybernetic control systems, whereas more complex control systems generally require human judgment for evaluation and action phases.

Organizational forms of control include bureaucratic control, characterized by a formal and inflexible structure, and clan control, which is informal and flexible. Control systems that are dysfunctional suffer from overcontrol, undercontrol, inconsistent controls, or the failure to differentiate controls. Effective control systems are generally linked with planning, and they should be accurate, timely, relevant, and objective and measurable.

Financial control is used by managers to assess the overall health of the organization. Analysis of the balance sheets, income statements, and ratios of an organization are methods for assessing effectiveness. The balance sheet lists assets, liabilities, and shareholder equity in order to summarize the financial worth of an organization on a specific date. An income statement summarizes the company's financial performance over a particular period of time by detailing revenues, expenses, and profit. Ratio analysis is a process for indexing one financial measure relative to another for evaluating company performance over time and for comparing it with industry averages.

Budgetary control involves a financial commitment to the organization's strategies and plans. The budget contains the organization's detailed revenue and expense accounts, grouped either by operating units such as divisions and departments or by products and product lines. Responsibility centers, such as profit, revenue, expense, and investment centers, specify financial goals for managers to achieve. An operating budget is the numerical plan that allocates resources to responsibility centers in order to support organizational plans and strategies. A financial budget defines the sources and the uses of cash for the coming period.

Budgets can be developed by top management or by low-level managers. Top-down budgeting calls for top managers to define budget numbers for their managers, whereas bottom-up budgeting allows budgets to be developed by the responsible managers and approved by top management. Zero-base budgeting is a form of bottom-up budgeting that requires responsible managers to calculate resource requirements based on the coming year's priorities, rather than on the past year's requirements.

The audit process is an independent appraisal of an organization's financial and operational efficiency and effectiveness. An external audit focuses on the financial controls that could affect the accuracy of financial statements, and an internal audit reviews the entire control system for efficiency and effectiveness.

MEETING A MANAGEMENT CHALLENGE AT

TOYS 'R' US

Charles Lazarus *(third from left)*, CEO, Toys 'R' Us, with President Bush and dignitaries at a new store opening

What Charles Lazarus has accomplished at Toys 'R' Us is nothing short of a revolution—not just in toy sales, but in retailing as a whole. He is showing the retail industry how to use controls throughout a business to achieve low-debt growth and to sustain market dominance. Toys 'R' Us is approaching 700 stores globally, and although 70 percent of those stores are in the United States, the company's international outlets—particularly in Canada, Japan, Germany, and Spain—have shown stunning growth. Lazarus has accomplished this while holding long-term debt quite low. Not only does the company have more stores than its competitors, but the low debt enables Toys 'R' Us to pay its bills on time, a capability that is especially appreciated in lean times and gives it unrivaled influence with toy manufacturers.

All of the control systems that Lazarus has implemented are interrelated, so their individual success in meeting standards has contributed dramatically to the company's fortunes. Indeed, without all of the control systems in place, Lazarus would probably never have been able to keep the company's debt so low. The control systems begin with the first part of the Toys 'R' Us operation: buying from manufacturers. Company buyers are not held to unachievable standards in what is essentially a fashion industry—they buy new toys and games in small quantities so that the poor sellers can be eliminated quickly and so that the company doesn't overcommit itself to a toy that never reaches its projected success.

Making such limited buying work, though, has required the development of an inventory control system. Bar-code scanning technology feeds sales information into a central corporate computer, which then routes inventory to stores and automatically determines when—and in what quantities—to order more toys and games from manufacturers. Moreover, Toys 'R' Us is able to place electronic orders directly with the computers of about 80 percent of its suppliers. This inventory control system has done more than keep shelves stocked: hot sellers are spotted quickly so that store displays can be modified to take advantage of buying trends. It has also made Toys 'R' Us into a year-round retailer in an industry that once lived on the success of the Christmas shopping season.

The systems have also enabled Lazarus to succeed on low profit margins. High volume pushes up sales per square foot, which reduces costs as a percentage of sales, which lowers prices to customers. And that has kept sales high year-round—the system Lazarus needed to avoid debt.

Lazarus has also maintained strict corporate control over store design so that every store is virtually identical in size, color scheme, floor layout, and product display. This has not only contributed to customer loyalty but has also helped corporate management sustain inventory and sales efficiency throughout the chain. Stores are designed functionally so that they are convenient to shoppers and employees alike.

The only control system at Toys 'R' Us that is not strictly of the top-down variety is concerned with human resources, namely, the store managers, upon whose shoulders much of the corporation's fortunes rest. Lazarus has shifted more of the day-to-day decision making down to the store managers because it helps morale, reduces employee turnover, and improves customer service. Moreover, Lazarus has instituted this control system in a notably Toys 'R' Us style: information collected daily on each store's sales and inventory is fed electronically back to managers, who have the authority to work with warehouse staffs to achieve even greater efficiencies in inventory and retail sales management. It's the most personal twist to a series of control systems that has helped Lazarus build a category-killing chain that spans the globe.

You're the Manager: Charles Lazarus wants to focus his attention on long-term strategic issues, so he recently appointed you to the position of chief operating officer. In this position, you are responsible for guiding day-to-day operations and generally seeing that the organization stays on track toward meeting its short-term goals.

Ranking Questions

1. The inventory control system tracks sales and uses that information to control buying and inventory processing. Some store managers, however, are still concerned that the computer doesn't always make the best choices for their individual stores. Rank from best to worst the ways you can improve the system.
   a. Let store managers override computer buying and inventory decisions when their judgment conflicts with the computer.
   b. Encourage store managers who aren't always satisfied with the computer's choices to point out instances where the computer forecast was incorrect (by comparing forecasts with actual sales). Then ask the information systems experts to refine the forecasting model based on this information.
   c. Let store managers set standards for sales, based on local markets.
   d. Remove store managers completely from inventory control decisions.
2. Even though much of the company's operations are under computer control, the performance of individual employees is still key to the company's success. After all, it is employees, not computers, who stock the shelves, help customers, and move shoppers through checkout lines. If you could immediately apply the following control options, how would you rank them in terms of their ability to ensure employee performance?
   a. Rely on preliminary control; the most effective step to take is to carefully interview potential employees. This will help you get the best people into the organization and reduce performance problems later on.
   b. People are individuals and perform best when treated as such; let frontline managers in the stores identify the performance measures that are more appropriate for their employees.
   c. Sales and profits are the final measure of performance, so you should wait to see if employee performance is affecting sales before taking any action.
   d. Identify the appropriate measures of employee performance (e.g., customer satisfaction, checkout efficiency, shelf stocking time), then institute these performance standards in three stages: first as postaction control, then as concurrent control, then as preliminary control.

Multiple-Choice Questions

3. Costs of entry and expansion in Japan are greater than expected, primarily because of changing regulatory constraints and local politics. What's the best way for the company to control the start-up and development costs for these stores?
   a. Set tougher budgeting standards before each store is built and opened.
   b. Don't try to apply the control system used in other countries; the stores in these countries need their own systems.
   c. Recognize that some markets are more expensive to conduct business in, and keep applying the same controls the company uses elsewhere.
   d. Start with the same recognition as in (c), then challenge store managers in Japan to reduce costs as much as possible, coupling this request with some sort of motivational incentive.
4. Corporate managers have redesigned layouts within all stores, reducing the shelf space devoted to certain toys and games at each store. Which of the following is the most appropriate next step, in terms of the sales performance expected of each store manager relative to the products?
   a. Never make any changes in performance standards because doing so might set a precedent.
   b. For the products now held in lower quantities, reduce the sales standards for each store manager.
   c. For each of the products in question, ask each manager to estimate sales for his or her store, then average these answers and make that number the new performance standard for each product.
   d. Keep all standards the same until new sales trends resulting from the design change can be determined.

Analysis Questions

5. How has centralized control contributed to the company's financial performance?
6. How do the looser human resources controls, particularly those on store managers, help or hinder the company's global expansion?
7. What if the company reaches a point where it

can't sustain expansion without taking on more long-term debt? Should it stop growing until it has enough money to build new stores, even if delaying gives competitors a chance to grow?

Special Project

An independent toy manufacturer has hit tough times, but it doesn't expect its troubles to last long. Its toys have been some of the most innovative that Toys 'R' Us sells, attracting a loyal group of customers willing to spend money on these items year-round. To get through tough times, the manufacturer's management has come to Lazarus, you, and the chief financial officer in an effort to get a cash advance on toys and games. Toys 'R' Us has the money to prepay large orders, and Lazarus is more than willing to help out a valued, independent manufacturer whose designers could well think up a huge hit someday. Now it is up to you to design a control system to make sure that Toys 'R' Us doesn't end up giving money away for nothing; that is, you not only have to make sure that the prepaid toys and games are sold but also that Toys 'R' Us can help the manufacturer get onto a more solid financial footing for the long run. Write a one-page outline of how you can meet these goals through the use of controls.[77]

KEY TERMS

activity ratios (622)
audit (629)
average collection period (622)
balance sheet (620)
bottom-up budgeting (628)
budget (624)
budgeting (624)
bureaucratic control (614)
capital expenditures budget (626)
cash budget (626)
clan control (614)
concurrent control (612)
control (602)
current ratio (622)
cybernetic control systems (613)
debt ratio (622)
expense budget (626)
expense center (625)
external audit (629)
financial budget (626)
financial statement (620)
income statement (621)
internal audit (629)
inventory turnover (622)
investment center (625)
leverage ratios (622)
liquidity ratios (622)
net profit margin (622)
noncybernetic control systems (614)
operating budget (626)
operational control (611)
overcontrol (617)
postaction control (612)
preliminary control (611)
profitability ratios (622)
profit budget (626)
profit center (625)
ratio analysis (621)
ratios (622)
responsibility center (624)
return on equity (624)
return on investment (ROI) (624)
revenue budget (626)
revenue center (625)
standards (605)
strategic control (610)
tactical control (610)
top-down budgeting (628)
undercontrol (617)
zero-base budgeting (628)

QUESTIONS

For Review

1. What are the four steps in implementing a control system?
2. How does bureaucratic control differ from clan control?
3. What are the types of control systems and how are they related?
4. What are the three tools used in financial analysis?
5. What are the differences among the four responsibility centers?

For Analysis

1. Considering levels of control, what controls are the responsibility of top managers?
2. How is the control process implemented for budgetary control?
3. How are financial budgets used by companies with high amounts of debt?
4. Explain the relationship between budget-development approaches and organizational forms of control.
5. How are the four types of ratios used to evaluate the performance of a company?

For Application

1. How might a professor implement a control system to evaluate students in a college course?
2. How might McDonald's use preliminary control, concurrent control, and postaction control to regulate dishes prepared in a restaurant kitchen?

3. How might the Field Museum of Natural History in Chicago use the concept of responsibility centers to manage results?
4. What kind of budget-development process might the owner of a chain of ice cream stores adopt?
5. What kind of control style should a police captain adopt?

KEEPING CURRENT IN MANAGEMENT

From recent magazines or newspapers select an article that discusses a manager who has used controls to manage the organization. One example might focus on a manager who failed to implement effective controls and caused serious damage to the company. Another example might involve a manager who increased profits or lowered costs by effectively implementing or improving an organization's controls.

1. What controls did the manager implement or fail to implement? Has the organization become more successful?
2. What levels in the organization were affected by the control issues? What functional areas were affected by the controls? Are the four steps for implementing control systems recognizable in the article?
3. What impact did the organization structure have on the control systems? Does bureaucratic or clan control seem appropriate, given the organization's situation?

SHARPEN YOUR MANAGEMENT SKILLS

If you've traveled on a commercial airline flight, you probably know the true meaning of boredom, both on the ground and in the air. Northwest Airlines thinks it has the answer. The carrier is currently installing an individual interactive video system in each seat of its planes, starting with its fleet of 747s. These systems let passengers select movies (free in first class; passengers in coach pay $6 for the first movie and $3 for each one after that), play video games (about $4 an hour), shop for products, or listen to music. In the future, the systems might provide live news and sports broadcasts, phone services, and other features. And to the consternation of some observers, the systems will carry advertising from various companies.

Understandably, Northwest thinks the idea has potential, but industry experts don't agree among themselves. Some think the flying public won't take to the new gadgets at all; others are of mixed opinion; and some are quite positive.

- *Decision:* This project is obviously an expensive undertaking, with eventual success uncertain at best. Figure out a method for Northwest to control its investment in the project to maximize potential return while minimizing risk (to the greatest possible extent, anyway).
- *Communication:* Prepare a brief article for the company's next annual report to shareholders, describing the systems and the company's plan for investing in it. Keep in mind that investors want to know what you're doing with their money and why. (Feel free to make up any details you need to complete this exercise.)

CASE

Benetton's Organization Is Well Knit

Benetton is one of the world's largest knitting manufacturers and retailers because it has embraced the constant change at the heart of fashion. President Luciano Benetton made his company responsive to consumers' ever-changing whims by building both flexibility and control into the entire production cycle. But he can't control the economy, and profits are slipping.

HISTORY

The death of their father forced Luciano Benetton and his 13-year-old sister to quit school and go to work in Treviso, Italy. Fifteen-year-old Luciano got a job in a clothing store and later became a wholesaler; his sister entered a knitting shop and in her spare time knit brightly colored sweaters that Luciano sold both on the streets and to shops.

In 1965 the family opened a small sweater-knitting mill in Treviso. The company still concentrates on colorful, moderately priced apparel, but today it has three factories producing 50 million pieces of clothing a year for 6,300 Benetton retail store franchises in 92 countries. Benetton diversified by licensing companies to produce cosmetics and other nonapparel items under the Benetton name, by purchasing ski equipment manufacturer Nordica for $150 million, and by entering a joint insurance venture with Britain's Prudential Corporation (it has since sold its interest in the joint venture for $300 million).

Meanwhile, even though costs for raw materials have risen, Benetton has not raised prices; the entire retail industry is in a slump and the company needs to stay competitive. Total revenues increased 13 percent in 1989 to $1 billion, but net profits fell 12 percent to $73.5 million. As the company enters the 1990s, sales are flat, profits per share are down, and Benetton stock is close to a record low.

ENVIRONMENT

Benetton keeps service quality high and costs low through a computerized order, production, and distribution system that links franchises with the company's factories and warehouse. To order a sweater, a store contacts a Benetton sales agent, who then calls the company's main computer, which relays the order to the warehouse if the sweater is in stock or to the knitting mill if it is not. Sweaters can be delivered halfway around the world within a week from the warehouse or within a month from the factory—far faster than competitors can deliver. Only eight people are needed to ship 230,000 items of clothing daily from the company's single warehouse, where computers address packages and robots put them on trucks. Data generated in the ordering process help Benetton forecast production needs and help it make fast purchasing decisions on raw materials.

Also, Benetton tries to forecast fashion trends by sending new styles and colors first to a few Benetton-owned stores in Italy, where point-of-sale information systems tell the company what's hot and what's not; sales agents are informed of which styles and colors sell best, so that they can help franchisees make purchasing decisions. But Benetton does not have control of its entire production system. Although its global competitors shift nimbly from one low-cost manufacturer to another, 85 percent of Benetton's production remains inside Italy; much of that work is done by small subcontractors who sometimes delay orders for U.S. and Canadian franchises by 10 months.

GOALS AND CHALLENGES

Luciano Benetton believes that his company must continually expand to remain healthy. To advance this goal, he plans to open 1,000 more stores, concentrating on Eastern Europe, the Far East, and South America. He plans to gain market share in the United States, where Benetton has 600 stores, by wholesaling more nonapparel items to such retailers as J. C. Penney and by introducing a wider variety of fabrics. Luciano Benetton also plans to use money from sale of the insurance venture to expand Nordica into sportswear production, which (unlike subcontractors) would have the advantage of being under the company's direct control. These moves will complicate his business, but Benetton believes that his information system will allow him to maintain control.

1. How does Benetton ensure the quality of its apparel items and service to customers?
2. How does Benetton use strategic, operational, and tactical controls? What types of control methods does it use?
3. How could Benetton use the control process to achieve the same quality of performance at Nordica that it has from its knitting mill?
4. What type of responsibility center should managers create at the Nordica factory?

CHAPTER OUTLINE

Operations Management

After studying this chapter, you will be able to

1. Explain the role of operations management in both manufacturing and service environments
2. Classify the strategic roles played by operations management
3. Identify the unique aspects of services and their relation to operations management
4. Categorize operations management efforts into the design or redesign of systems and the management of ongoing operations
5. Contrast just-in-time management with traditional operations management philosophies
6. Distinguish between quality control and quality assurance
7. Describe the two major techniques used to measure and control quality

FACING A MANAGEMENT CHALLENGE AT

HARLEY-DAVIDSON

Getting Harley Back on the Road

When Japanese companies began selling heavyweight motorcycles in the United States in the early 1970s, Harley-Davidson management remained calm. They controlled 99.7 percent of the market, and they had few doubts that they would retain much of it. After all, they argued, if your customers love your product so much they tattoo your logo on their chests, you can count on their loyalty.

But Harley management was mistaken. The Harley was no longer the superb machine that Lee Marvin drove across the screen in *The Wild One*. (Contrary to popular myth, Marvin's co-star Marlon Brando rode a Triumph in the movie, not a Harley.) Harleys leaked puddles of engine oil, vibrated like jackhammers, and broke down frequently. Harley's older customers patiently pulled them apart and rebuilt them correctly, but younger riders were not so forgiving. They increasingly chose the trouble-free, smooth-riding imports from Honda, Yamaha, Suzuki, and Kawasaki. By the time Harley's market share had slipped to 23 percent, the company was leaking red ink along with engine oil.

Harley's newly appointed chairman Vaughn Beals had never ridden a motorcycle, but he recognized a company with a serious problem. If Harley couldn't make its existing line of bikes correctly, how was it going to introduce new, well-built models to compete with the Japanese?

At the heart of Harley's difficulties were its outmoded manufacturing methods and systems, which were devised during the era when Harley was a small family-owned company. When Harley tried to increase production to meet the Japanese threat, its production systems collapsed, and quality skidded off the road.

One source of trouble was bloated, disorganized inventory. Parts at Harley's assembly plant in York, Pennsylvania, were made in large batches for long production runs, stored until needed, and then loaded onto the 3.5-mile conveyer that clattered endlessly around the plant. In Harley's cavernous inventory storage, it sometimes took hours to find the right parts, and when they were found, they were often rusty or damaged. Even though Harley spent $25 million a year to maintain its inventory, over half its cycles came off the line missing parts.

Switching Harley's manufacturing machinery from one bike model to another was so time-consuming that the company had to produce large numbers of a single model at a time, which resulted in large inventory costs. When one piece of machinery broke down, hundreds of parts piled up behind it. And to make matters worse, Harley plants were labyrinths of poorly organized workstations. In the 72 days it took to build each frame, Harley workers had to cart components from one corner of the plant to the other.

When Beals introduced the Cafe Racer, a new model meant to signal Harley's return to quality, he established an ad hoc team to inspect the first 100 bikes off the assembly line. The news was terrible. The group uncovered $100,000 worth of defects. Beals expanded his inspection teams to cover all Harley cycles, and the quality of cycles leaving the factory improved. But Beals realized that the Quality Audit Program was an expensive, time-consuming Band-Aid that simply identified defects after the products were made.

Beals's experience with the Cafe Racer convinced him that the only way to save Harley was to stop mistakes before they occurred. But where should he start? How could Beals reduce the time it took to set up machinery for production runs, cut back on costly inventory, and streamline the factory layout? How could he revamp the entire operations system without adding to Harley's steadily mounting losses?[1]

CHAPTER OVERVIEW

Vaughn Beals and his management team at Harley-Davidson grew to realize that the solution to their problems could be found in improved operations manage-

Levi Strauss is using operations management techniques to streamline its apparel sewing operations. In the Roswell, New Mexico plant, conventional sewing processes *(left)* are giving way to the more efficient methods used by a self-managing team *(right)*. Because team members can perform many functions and can manage the production schedule, 13 operators are now able to complete the work once handled by 25.

ment. This chapter explores the foundations of operations management, starting with a discussion of the vital importance that this field of study plays in today's organizations, and it explores the unique nature of services production. The next two sections address the tasks of designing operations, then managing ongoing operations once all the necessary systems are in place. The coverage of operations design includes such topics as capacity planning, site selection, process layout, and technologies that can be used in operations management. The section on the management of ongoing operations covers production planning and scheduling, inventory control, and purchasing management. The chapter concludes with a look at quality control and quality assurance in operations management, and Chapter 21 continues the coverage of quality, productivity, and customer satisfaction.

UNDERSTANDING OPERATIONS MANAGEMENT

operations management The collection of planning and control activities that managers use to produce goods and services

Operations management is the collection of planning and control activities that managers use to produce goods and services.[2] To improve an organization's ability to produce quality goods and services, operations management focuses on three areas: inputs, outputs, and the processes that transform inputs to outputs. Inputs include labor, raw materials, and money; outputs are the result of the transformation process and include assembled goods (such as automobiles or televisions), services (such as the delivery of a package or the repair of an automobile), or a combination of the two (such as a restaurant where the food is prepared and served to customers). In manufacturing TV sets, Sony employs operations management techniques to purchase materials, plan labor requirements, assemble TVs, and distribute them. At Supercuts, operations management is used to schedule appointments, to order hair products, and to wash, cut, and dry customers' hair.

Harley-Davidson and other organizations have been seriously challenged by Japanese competitors producing higher-quality, more reliable, less costly products. Effective, efficient operations management is at the heart of the Japanese success story, and given the intensity of global competition, managers everywhere must strive for continual improvement in their operations if they hope to remain competitive.[3]

Much of the emphasis in operations management is necessarily on technologies and techniques, but it is important to realize that, as in every other aspect of management, people make or break the system. Then again, people rely on the organization's systems, whether the system is as simple as a telephone or as complex as an automated production facility. Motivation and effort can't compensate for inadequate operations systems. It is the *combination* of people and technology that makes Harley-Davidson, Federal Express, Nordstrom, Frito-Lay, and other world-class companies successful.[4]

Before considering the elements involved in designing an efficient and effective operation, it is helpful to consider two important issues that affect operations management. The first is the relationship between operations management and organizational strategy. The second involves the special nature of operations management in service organizations.

MANAGEMENT AROUND THE WORLD

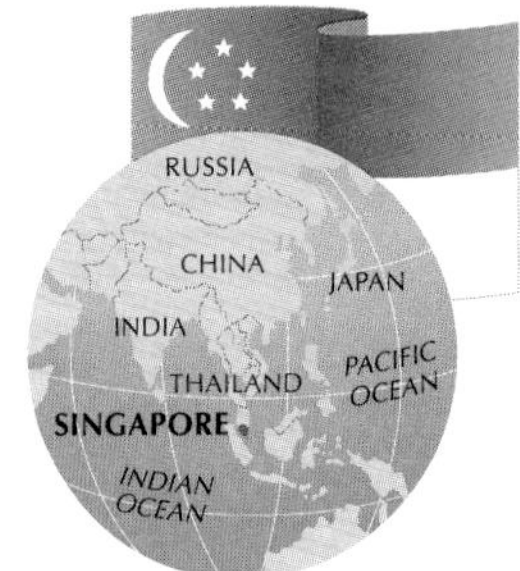

Companies operating in and based in Singapore have used advanced operations management techniques to transform the nation into one of the world's leading centers of high-technology manufacturing. With its highly educated work force and modern factories, Singapore is ready to challenge Japan, Taiwan, and other manufacturing countries in Asia.

Operations Management and Organizational Strategy

Operations management is at the core of the organization's ability to meet the needs of customers as well as other stakeholders; consequently, operations management has close ties with organizational strategy. For instance, Harley-Davidson's lapses in operations management turned the company's strategy upside down, from playing market leader to playing catch-up with overseas competitors. Conversely, when McDonald's decided to open its first restaurant in Moscow, the company had to do extensive groundwork to establish an operation that would support this strategic initiative.

Operations management does not receive the same level of strategic attention in every organization. Manufacturing experts Steven C. Wheelwright and Robert H. Hayes identified four strategic roles that operations management can play in the organization. They refer to roles as stages, with the implication that organizations can and should progress from one to the next:[5]

- *Stage 1: Internally neutral.* At this basic stage, management views operations as something that has to be done in order to get on with the organization's business, but not as something that actively contributes to strategic success. As a result, managers approach operations with an eye toward reducing costs and other organizational burdens. Not surprisingly, organizations with Stage 1 operations generate little or no competitive strength from their production facilities.
- *Stage 2: Externally neutral.* At this stage, managers are also looking for "neutral" operations, but in comparison to the organization's competition. Managers look at major competitors in the same industry and try to do as they do in terms of work-force policies, technology, and other operational elements. The key objective of a Stage 2 operation is to stay on par with competitors without unduly disrupting the organization.
- *Stage 3: Supportive.* At this stage, operations shift from being a neutral element to being a force for positive contribution. Operations in a Stage 3 organization support and strengthen the organization's strategy, and production managers watch for developments such as new technologies that might be able to increase the organization's competitiveness. Operations are generally responsible for 75 percent of an organization's investment, 80 percent of

its personnel, and 85 percent or more of its material and equipment expenses.[6] Thus, without input from operations, strategic revisions could result in economic disaster for the organization. If operations management policies are consistent with organizational strategy, operations management can improve the long-term quality, productivity, and competitiveness of the organization.[7]

- *Stage 4: Strategic.* At the most advanced stage, operations play a key role in planning and strategy development. World-class manufacturers with technologically advanced products are the firms most likely to exhibit Stage 4 operations. Stage 4 organizations view operations as an integral part of the organization, and they expect operations to contribute at the same level as research, marketing, and other functions.

As organizations face increasing competitive pressure, both at home and abroad, the significance of operations management will continue to grow. Companies such as Nucor, Motorola, and McDonald's provide ample evidence that U.S. companies can succeed in global markets by relying to a significant degree on effective operations management.

Operations Management in Service Organizations

Although many people associate production and operations management with factories, the principles discussed in this chapter apply not only to manufacturing facilities but to service firms, not-for-profit organizations, and government agencies. Applying effective operations management techniques to the production of services is a critical issue for U.S. business because services are such an important part of the U.S. economy. In fact, roughly three-quarters of the U.S. work force is now employed in service-sector jobs.[8]

Service organizations have experienced much lower productivity growth than manufacturing organizations, due in part to the difficulty of producing some services (particularly those services in which people play a central role in product quality, such as haircutting, legal representation, and medicine) and in part to the lower level of attention that operations management has received in most service organizations. However, some services are developing creative strategies to boost productivity. For example, Tokyo's Seiyu Supermarkets has developed a prototype supermarket aimed at dramatically improving supermarket productivity. Technological innovations that have boosted productivity include a computer-driven robotic system for unloading delivery trucks, a programmable robot for stocking the shelves, a self-serve cold-cut dispenser (that allows the customer to select the type of meat, thickness, and quantity desired), LCD displays of merchandise prices, and automatic audio descriptions of products and recipes. As a result of implementing these innovations, the company has been able to significantly boost productivity while using 20 percent fewer employees. In addition to the increased productivity, customer service has improved as well.[9]

Automation and other applications of technology are only part of the answer, however. In many cases, simply redesigning and simplifying processes results in higher service quality and productivity. When Nordstrom allows its salespeople to issue exchanges and refunds on the spot, without going to management for approval, the company not only makes its customers happier but also makes the process more efficient.

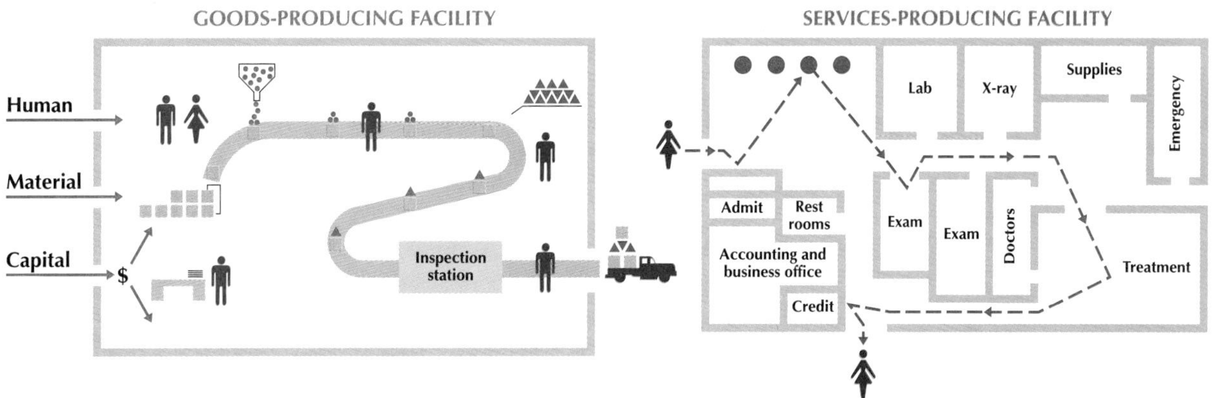

EXHIBIT 20.1

Goods- and Services-Producing Facilities

In a goods-producing facility, materials travel through the system on the way to becoming finished products. In contrast, in many services facilities, customers move through the system as the product is delivered to them.

To remain competitive, service organizations must continue to strive for improvement in their operations, just as manufacturers must. Consolidated Freightways, a trucking firm, now provides its customers with precisely timed deliveries to help the customers achieve their goals of reducing inventory. Nynex not only offers telephone service to customers but also offers to engineer a customer's network and select the necessary hardware and software. And J.B. Hunt Transport, of Lowell, Arkansas, another trucking company, is experimenting with a satellite system to track and communicate with its fleet. All these firms have gone beyond the traditional services they offer to form stronger relationships with customers and increase their competitive strengths.[10]

Both goods and services are created using production systems; that is, both transform input resources into higher-valued outputs (see Exhibit 20.1).[11] Services, however, exhibit four distinct characteristics that disinguish them from manufactured goods and that need to be considered in operations management:[12]

- *Services are intangible.* The intangibility of services creates a number of challenges. One of the most important is the difficulty of measuring product quality. For instance, it's fairly easy to measure the quality of wheat, steel, and stereo amplifiers, but how does one measure the quality of legal services, haircuts, education, or legislative representation? (Chapter 21 explores techniques for measuring service quality.)
- *It is usually impossible to separate the service from the service provider.* Services don't follow the normal model of production-sale-consumption; they are sold first, then produced and consumed simultaneously. Because services can't be stored, it is usually impossible to separate the production from the consumption. One area of operations management in which this has a major impact is facility location. Within the limits of cheap transportation, labor, and a few other factors, goods can be produced just about anywhere and then shipped to customers. Service facilities, on the other hand, must be located close to customers in most instances. In addition, customers usually enter service-production facilities, but they rarely enter goods-production facilities. Thus, managers of service facilities have to concern themselves with such issues as physical atmosphere and visitor safety.
- *Services usually cannot be stored in anticipation of sales.* A baker can make six loaves of bread and sell them one at a time, but a barber can't make six haircuts and sell them one at a time. Consider the challenge this presents the

The design of operational systems is a key aspect of managing a service business. Managers of the Silver Queen Gondola at Little Nell in Aspen, Colorado, must consider such issues as capacity planning, the gondola car design, and the layout of waiting areas. They must also ensure that skiers receive the same fast, safe passage to the top of the mountain regardless of variations in the weather or in the number of people riding the gondola.

managers at a ski resort such as Sun Valley, Idaho. They can sell skiing time only when customers are available, weather conditions are cooperating, the lifts are operating, and the staff is trained and on the job. If any one of these pieces of the puzzle is missing, they can't sell skiing—and they can't store their capacity to sell skiing for some later date when they've got all the pieces together. They can train employees all summer long, tune up the lift engines, hope for snow, and use effective marketing to pull in a steady stream of customers, but they are still at the mercy of service perishability.

- *Consistency and quality can be major challenges in service operations.* Consistency and quality need close attention with all products, but they are of particular concern with services, for three reasons. First, customers often play a role in the quality of services. Jenny Craig Weight Loss Centres can't promise the same results to everyone because the customer has as much or more control over the outcome of this service as the provider has. Second, the performance of individual employees usually has a big impact on service quality. The best technical system in the world for delivering quality service will fall apart if employees aren't motivated to serve customers. A delicious restaurant meal just isn't quite as special if customers have to tangle with a waiter who's in a bad mood. Third, because services usually can't be stored, fluctuations in production volume can affect quality. Anyone who has tried to place a long-distance phone call on a major holiday only to be greeted by a recorded message about circuit overloads knows all about this problem. A manufacturer of goods can anticipate periods of high demand and build extra products ahead of time, but service providers don't have that luxury.

Even with these profound differences, however, many aspects of goods and services production are similar. Both goods and services must be designed with customer needs in mind, and production facilities must be developed with an eye on costs, quality, and capacity. The application of technology and process-flow designs can simplify production of both types of products. Techniques to determine consumer demand, schedule production, and manage inventory are also critical to both. For all of these issues, operations management offers the techniques needed to plan and control the production of both types of products.[13]

DESIGNING OPERATIONS

Operations management efforts fall into two categories: (1) designing or redesigning the sytems that will produce the organization's goods or services, and (2) managing those systems once they are up and running. This section addresses the first topic, which covers product design, capacity planning, facilities location and layout, and several important operations technologies. The first step is that the product, a tangible good or an intangible service (or a combination thereof), must be designed. In both cases, development activities ensure the product meets customer expectations and can be produced and sold at a profit. Once the organization has designed the product, management must consider capacity issues, facilities location, layout of production, and production technology, as Vaughn Beals and his management team at Harley-Davidson learned when they set about the task of returning Harley to a position of competitiveness.

When developing Teddy Grahams, Nabisco had the idea that a small uniquely shaped graham cracker would be a big hit with children. After testing many cracker shapes with prospective customers, Nabisco confirmed that the bear-shaped graham cracker was the big winner. During development, Nabisco did a thorough analysis, from the cost of the ingredients to the size of the market, to get a good picture of the profit potential for Teddy Grahams and Teddy Graham Bearwiches. The snack crackers utilized ingredients and technology that Nabisco already employed, so manufacturing would be easy. Nabisco managers determined that their production facility had enough capacity, but the assembly line had to be modified for the smaller Bearwiches. They reconfigured existing technology to pick up a cookie smaller than half the size of most sandwich cookies, slather it with filling, and position it so that the front and back sides of the bear were aligned. Even with detailed planning, the first run on the assembly line backed up, and the factory floor wound up ankle deep in cookies and fillings. Once Nabisco managers fine-tuned their operations, Bearwiches went on to become the number two sandwich cookie, second only to Nabisco's own Oreos.[14]

Product Design

Product design is a systematic process for the development of new goods and services or for the improvement of existing goods or services.[15] This process is just as important for service organizations as it is for manufacturing organizations. For example, Wendy's was faced with a choice between using fresh or frozen french-fried potatoes. Using fresh potatoes would require employees at each restaurant to peel, cut, cook, and serve the potatoes. Using frozen potatoes would reduce the labor required because the preprocessed potatoes would simply have to be cooked and served. The preprocessed potatoes were also more uniform. Wendy's management chose the frozen potatoes, reducing the number of employees and limiting the amount of quality control required at each facility.[16] At the U.S. Postal Service, product design activities have increased the level of service to postal customers. By researching and initiating programs encouraging high-volume postal customers to place bar codes on letters, by instituting nine-digit zip codes, and by presorting the mail by zip code, the Postal Service has significantly increased its volume with fewer employees.[17]

Research-and-development (R&D) or product engineering departments are usually responsible for creating and improving products. In many companies, the people in these departments have historically enjoyed a great deal of freedom to pursue their designs, often with little regard for the difficulties that those designs might present during production. In today's hotly competitive markets, however, organizations realize that competitive advantage results from the overall ability to bring new products to market and to satisfy customers, and not necessarily from the ability to design the most-elegant or most-sophisticated products. And bringing competitive new products to market quickly requires communication and cooperation between designers and the people in manufacturing, finance, marketing, and other departments.

To improve the process, organizations are employing a technique called **design for manufacturability and assembly (DFMA)**.[18] The goal of DFMA is to make sure that new products can be produced and delivered to customers quickly and cost-efficiently. Results of DFMA efforts can include such moves as changing the placement of components in a product in order to cut the number of steps needed for assembly or simply using fewer parts. The trend toward

design for manufacturability and assembly (DFMA) A design philosophy that tries to develop new products that can be produced and delivered to customers quickly and efficiently

A&P uses information from its checkout scanners to assist in capacity planning. By monitoring hourly customer volume, weekly shopping peaks, and seasonal variations, the managers of this A&P supermarket in New Jersey can schedule checkout, packing, service desk, and deli counter coverage. They can also use scanner data to support longer-term capacity planning for store expansion.

simplifying product designs by using fewer parts has led to striking increases in productivity rates. Philips reduced the number of parts in its compact disc players by 75 percent. Swatch, the Swiss manufacturer, slashed the number of components in its watches from 150 to 51.[19] In both cases, operations productivity soared because the products were designed for greater manufacturability and easier assembly.

DFMA restructures the product-development process by creating design teams that include R&D engineers, manufacturing engineers, assemblers, and buyers. The payback can be outstanding. For example, when Ford implemented DFMA, in one year it trimmed manufacturing costs by more than $1.2 billion and became Detroit's most profitable automaker.[20] Ford's DFMA efforts included reducing the average number of components in its cars from 30,000 to 22,000.[21] NCR (now part of AT&T) used DFMA for its latest electronic point-of-sale cash register. William R. Sprague, a senior manufacturing engineer, says that even with a blindfold on, he can assemble the register in less than two minutes.[22] And Hewlett-Packard used DFMA to develop its new super-minicomputers produced at its manufacturing operation in Cupertino, California. HP's design team consisted of R&D engineers, manufacturing engineers, and purchasing managers. As a result, failures at a prototype stage where failure rates were typically as high as 30 percent were reduced to a mere handful.[23]

Capacity Planning

capacity planning The process of determining and adjusting an organization's resources to meet customer demand

Once products have been designed, organizations must address their ability to produce the goods or services. The term *capacity* refers to the volume of manufacturing or service delivery that an organization possesses. **Capacity planning,** then, is the process of outlining and adjusting the organization's resources to meet customer demand. The neighborhood convenience store needs to consider traffic volume throughout the day and night in order to plan staffing levels appropriately. At the other extreme of complexity, when it plans for the production of an airliner, Boeing has to consider not only the staffing of thousands of people, but factory floor space, material flows from hundreds of suppliers, internal deliveries, cash flow, tools and equipment, and dozens of other factors. Because of the potential impact on finances, customers, and employees, capacity planning involves some of the most difficult decisions that managers have to make.

Long-Term Capacity Planning

Capacity planning involves both long-term and short-term decisions. Top management uses long-term capacity planning to make significant decisions about an organization's capacity, such as expanding existing facilities, constructing new facilities, or phasing out unneeded ones. Firms may choose to expand facilities, perhaps to handle new products or product lines or perhaps to enable the organization to utilize new technology in the production process.[24]

Long-term capacity planning usually involves a great deal of risk, for two reasons. First, large shifts in demand are difficult to predict accurately. In some cases, a company needs to build an entire factory to manufacture a new product that has yet to prove itself in the market. Managers face the dilemma of creating too much capacity or not creating enough to satisfy customer demand. Second, long-term capacity decisions can be difficult or impossible to undo. What if

General Motors builds a plant to produce a new car model, only to discover that consumers don't like the car? On the other hand, what if GM sells or tears down a factory because demand for the product built there has dropped off, only to watch demand later pick back up?

Short-Term Capacity Planning

In contrast, short-term capacity planning focuses on how an organization needs to alter capacity to handle short-term fluctuations in customer demand. **Capacity requirements planning (CRP)** examines the organization's production plans in order to determine and modify the labor and equipment resources needed to meet short-term demand. Managers have three sets of options for dealing with short-term demand fluctuations: absorbing fluctuations, changing production rates, or changing the size of the work force.[25] Each option has benefits and limitations, as Exhibit 20.2 indicates. (Short-term capacity planning actually falls into the management of ongoing operations, but it is addressed in this section in order to compare it with long-term capacity planning.)

capacity requirements planning (CRP) The process of translating forecasts of customer demand into the labor and equipment resources needed to meet short-term demand

Managers can absorb demand fluctuations in three ways. First, they can produce extra goods in advance of demand peaks. Of course, this option isn't available for services, since they usually have to be consumed as they are produced. Second, managers can increase order lead time, which is the time between receipt of a customer order and delivery of the product. This shifts some of the demand to times when capacity is available. Third, managers can employ marketing efforts to shift demand to times when capacity is more readily available. This is why movie theaters offer discount tickets for daytime shows; they are trying to shift demand away from the busier evening shows to make better use of their capacity during the day.

Similarly, production managers have several options for changing the rate of production. The first is to change the number of hours that the production staff works, increasing employees' hours to cover demand peaks. An alternative to asking people to work longer is to permanently staff the production team with more people. An increasingly popular option is hiring outside subcontractors when demand increases. Companies now hire computer programmers, writers, security staff, and a wide variety of other personnel on temporary assignments to help with demand fluctuations. And in some cases, more production equipment is the answer to short-term capacity problems, although like increasing staff size, buying equipment that will be used only during peak times can be a wasteful approach.

Finally, managers may be forced to change the size of their work forces. This is usually the most expensive and potentially disruptive set of options. The two choices in this case are hiring more employees or permanently reducing the size of the work force through layoffs. Increasing the number of employees must be considered carefully because it can burden the organization with excess personnel if the demand slips back to its previous level. And layoffs put former employees and their families in difficult situations, while frequently decreasing the morale and productivity of those that are still employed.

The Metropolitan Museum of Art, a not-for-profit organization located in New York City, has succeeded in planning for both long-term and short-term capacity requirements. To house additional art exhibits donated to the museum, the Met recently increased its capacity by completing a 1.5-million-square-foot expansion. This long-term expansion allows more space for both exhibits and

EXHIBIT 20.2 Strategies to Deal with Uneven Demand

When customer demand fluctuates, managers can employ a variety of strategies to meet the changing demand.

Strategy	Methods	Costs	Remarks
Absorb demand fluctuations by varying inventory level, backordering, or shifting demand	Produce in earlier period and hold until product is demanded	Cost of holding inventory	Service operations cannot hold service inventory; they must staff for peak levels of shift demand
	Offer to deliver the product or service later, when capacity is available	Delay in receipt of revenue, at the least; may result in lost customers	Manufacturing companies with perishable products are often prevented from using this method
	Exert special marketing efforts to shift the demand to slack periods	Costs of advertising, discounts, or promotional programs	This is another example of the interrelationship between functions within a business
Change only the production rate in accordance with the nonuniform demand pattern	Work additional hours without changing the work-force size	Overtime premium pay	Reduces the time available for maintenance work without interrupting production
	Staff for high production levels so that overtime is not required	Excess personnel wages during periods of slack demand	Sometimes work force can be utilized for deferred maintenance during periods of low demand
	Subcontract work to other firms	Continuing company overhead plus subcontractors' overhead and profit	Utilizes the capacity of other firms but provides less control of schedules and quality levels
	Revise make-or-buy decisions to purchase items when capacity is fully loaded	Waste of company skills, tooling, and equipment not utilized in slack periods	All of these methods require capital investments sufficient for the peak production rate, which will be underutilized in slack periods
Change the size of the work force to vary the production level in accordance with demand	Hire additional personnel as demand increases	Employment costs for advertising, travel, interviewing, training, etc.; shift premium costs if additional shift is added	Skilled workers may not be available when needed; they are likely to seek employment elsewhere
	Lay off personnel as demand subsides	Cost of severance pay and increases in unemployment insurance costs; loss of efficiency due to decline in morale as high-seniority workers are moved into jobs for which they are inexperienced, "bumping" workers with less seniority	The company must have adequate capital investment in equipment for the peak work-force level

museumgoers. To handle short-term demand peaks, the museum has also increased its viewing hours to better accommodate both local and out-of-town viewers. And by staying open on Friday and Saturday evenings, the facility caters to a younger, more diverse audience.[26]

Facilities Location

The choice of a location for a plant, warehouse, or service facility is crucial because geographic position affects the success of the organization.[27] Location can determine an organization's ability to hire employees, to buy materials, to distribute products, or to attract customers. An organization that depends on trucks to deliver raw materials or transport finished goods would locate close to a major highway. To lure customers, a service organization would choose a convenient location for its customers. Management must consider the organization's mission and goals when considering the location of production facilities.

For example, Warren Handler of CWII of California, a small-scale garment manufacturer, located his company's factory in downtown Los Angeles. The garment industry transferred much of its production offshore to keep labor costs low, but Handler decided to keep his production facility close to his designers, fabric suppliers, and customers in order to respond quickly to the fashion changes that drive the industry. If a particular item is suddenly the rage, Handler works with his in-house designer and production chief to design, order and receive the fabric, cut, sew, and ship the garments within four weeks. A similar process for a company with a factory located in Hong Kong or Taiwan could take as long as three months. Thus, facility location is a competitive advantage for CWII, allowing it to respond more quickly to the ever-changing demands of fashion.[28]

To provide airport employees with convenient child-care services, the Dade County Aviation Department decided to locate a day-care center on the premises of Miami International Airport. This on-site location enables parents to check on their children during the day, an important consideration for working parents.

Facilities Layout

Another crucial facilities design decision is **work-flow layout,** the arrangement of production work centers and other facilities (such as material, equipment, and support departments) needed for the processing of goods and services. Work-flow layout affects the amount of on-hand inventory, the efficiency of handling materials, equipment utilization, and the productivity and morale of employees. A key factor in work-flow layout is whether the operation involves *make-to-order products* (which are created in response to specific orders from customers) or *make-to-stock products* (which are created before orders are received, then held in inventory until sold).[29]

work-flow layout The arrangement of production facilities, including equipment, material flows, and personnel

Work-flow layout is applicable to the production of both goods and services. In the manufacturing of goods, the primary concern is the efficient movement of resources and inventory. In the production of services, work-flow layout controls the flow of customers through the system and influences the customer's satisfaction with the service.[30] For example, Wertkauf, a privately owned German retailer, customizes aesthetically pleasing layouts for each store, in a way that maximizes sales in each individual store. On the other hand, K Mart uses a standardized layout for all its stores. A customer who goes to a new K Mart is not inconvenienced by a different store layout. K Mart management believes this approach simplifies store operations while providing maximum convenience for customers.[31]

Three typical work-flow layouts include process layout, product layout, and fixed-position layout (see Exhibit 20.3).[32]

Process Layout

The **process layout** is a work-flow configuration in which the production centers are arranged according to the function provided. Specific functions, such

process layout A work-flow configuration in which the production centers are arranged according to the function provided, such as painting, welding, or filing

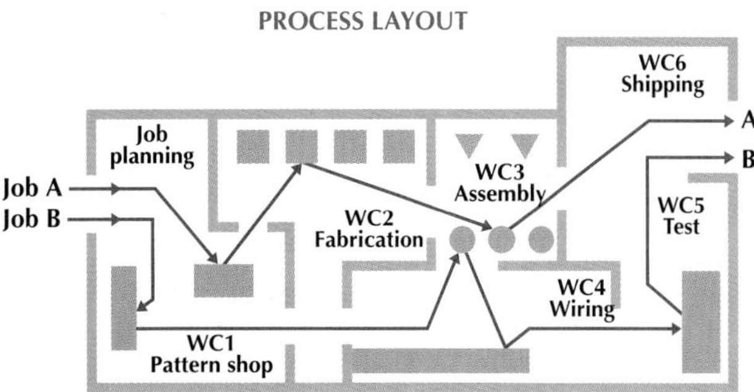

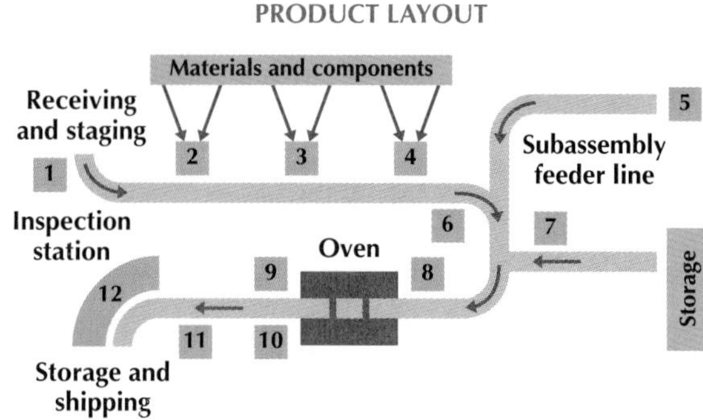

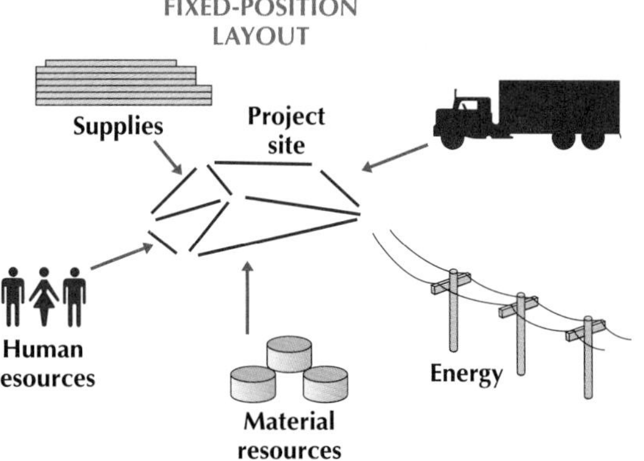

EXHIBIT 20.3

Work-flow Layouts

Work-flow layout is often determined by the type of product an organization is producing. Typically, a process layout is used for an organization producing made-to-order products. A product layout is used when an organization is producing large quantities of just a few products. A fixed-position layout is used when the product is too large to move.

as drilling or x-raying, are performed in one location for different products or customers. Process layouts can be found in machine shops and medical clinics.

Process layouts have distinct benefits and limitations. They are flexible enough to allow custom work, they tend to provide employees with a sense of satisfaction in the varied and challenging tasks, and they limit the amount of specialized, expensive equipment that an organization needs to purchase. For instance, a dental center that houses several dentists might dedicate one room to x-rays and purchase one x-ray unit for that room, rather than purchasing a machine for each dentist. On the other hand, the control of production in process layouts is more complex because each job must be individually routed, thereby driving up the cost of material handling. Labor costs are also likely to be higher because skilled workers are usually needed to operate the various production centers.[33]

Product Layout

product layout A work-flow configuration in which the production centers are arranged according to the specific sequences required by each type of good or service being produced

The **product layout** is a work-flow configuration in which the production centers are arranged according to specific sequences for each type of good or service. Product layouts are often called *line layouts* since each product moves along a specialized line of operations. Often, conveyers and robots are used to minimize the amount of materials handling. Product layouts can be found in automobile assembly plants and cafeterias.

Although the product layout reduces materials handling and simplifies production control, it might require a large investment in specialized equipment for each line and result in substantial interdependence of production centers on the line. In fact, the breakdown of a single machine can halt the entire production line. Although labor costs are low (because unskilled labor often suffices), the jobs are highly monotonous.

Fixed-Position Layout

The **fixed-position layout** is a work-flow layout in which labor, materials, and equipment are brought to the location where the good is being produced or the customer is being served. Home, road, and bridge construction are typical examples of a fixed-position layout. Other large goods, such as airplanes and ships, must also be built in a fixed-position layout. Repair services often utilize fixed-position layouts as well: a plumber, for example, goes to a job site bringing the tools, material, and expertise needed to repair a broken pipe.

fixed-position layout A work-flow layout in which inputs are brought to the location where the good is being produced or where the customer is being served

Although the cost of moving the product during production is usually minimal, the costs of moving material, equipment, and labor to the product or site in a fixed-position layout can be high. However, managers usually don't have much choice when the fixed-position layout is required, as they might with product or process layouts.

Operations Management Technology

With recent advances in computer capability and applications, the opportunity to employ technology to revamp the production process is enormous. Computers now control production processes, guide machinery, and bring robots to life. The value to the organization of new systems and technologies can be assessed on several dimensions:[34]

- *Cost.* Technology can dramatically reduce not only the labor costs directly associated with manufacturing the product but also the supporting labor costs, materials costs, inventory carrying costs (such as warehouse fees), and space costs.
- *Quality.* Technology can provide a more consistent manufacturing process, reducing the defect level and boosting quality. Also, with the enhanced process capabilities afforded by new technology, new performance characteristics may be possible.
- *Time.* Technology can reduce production time in two important ways. First, computers and various kinds of automation equipment can reduce the time required to transform inputs into outputs, such as the increased speed with which a robot can paint a car. Second, technology can lead to reduced setup times and changeover times on a production line. An organization can also save time by implementing technologies that speed up the design process and link to the manufacturing process.

When the designers of production systems use technology effectively, they can reduce costs, improve quality, and lower manufacturing and development time. For example, the fast-food industry is implementing technology to respond to a shortage of available workers. A variety of technological applications are under development, and many labor-saving devices have already been introduced. McDonald's recently installed a grill that cooks hamburgers simultaneously on both sides. Kentucky Fried Chicken has developed microprocessor-based controllers that keep temperatures in ovens and fryers at a consistent level to assure accurate cooking. Previously, employees had to painstakingly adjust the ovens and fryers daily. Pizza Hut has installed personal computers in each restaurant to assist with work schedules and to manage inventory.[35] Each of

GLOBAL MANAGEMENT

The Price of Offshore Manufacturing

Offshore manufacturing has a powerful appeal to many companies. With cheaper labor costs as the magnet, companies sacrifice local jobs to reduce manufacturing costs by building factories in countries with developing economies. Although reduced expenses are inviting, labor costs will eventually equalize over time. For instance, Japan used to have significantly lower labor costs than the United States, but as the Japanese economy grew, labor costs became more comparable to those in the United States. Increasingly, however, Japanese companies themselves are moving offshore in pursuit of lower costs, just as U.S. manufacturers have moved their factories to Taiwan and Singapore. For example, Toyota makes dies and jigs for pressing autobody panels in Thailand at roughly 40 percent of Japanese costs, and Sony has located consumer product factories in seven other Asian nations.

Access to local markets is another reason manufacturers shift their factories to other countries. According to a recent survey of 200 large and medium-sized firms, 56 percent of the companies that manufacture offshore said they were doing so primarily because of market access, whereas only 32 percent cited labor cost and quality issues as the main reason. For example, General Motors and Ford have joint ventures with Korean automakers to build subcompact cars for the growing local market as well as for export to the United States. For Digital Equipment Corporation (DEC), labor costs are no longer the prime consideration in plant location decisions. Clifford Clarke, manager of international trade and policy at DEC, concludes that their number one priority is "to manufacture where markets are growing."

Moving factories offshore often means there is less control over quality and productivity, and in today's marketplace, where quality is a competitive advantage, losing control could mean losing market share. Keeping factories at home and tackling quality and productivity problems is a long-term strategy for sustained performance. For example, in the T-shirt industry,

these uses of technology allows the organization to produce more in less time and at higher quality.

Computer-Aided Design and Manufacturing

computer-aided design (CAD) The use of computer graphics and mathematical modeling in the design of new products

Computers have become an important part of the product design phase in many organizations. **Computer-aided design (CAD)** is the use of computer graphics and mathematical modeling in the design of products. A related technology is *computer-aided engineering (CAE),* in which three-dimensional images and calculations performed on the computer allow engineers to test products without ever building preliminary models. With CAD and CAE, new ideas can be subjected electronically to temperature variations, various stresses, and even simulated accidents at great savings in time and money. For example, Boeing and other aircraft makers can subject a new aircraft design to the stresses that the actual plane will experience during landing, without building anything. Now such products can be perfected—or bad ideas abandoned—before they are put into production. Boeing, in fact, made extensive use of CAD in the development of the Boeing 767, where CAD systems helped the design team improve the quality of the design, reduce prototype development time, and lower the cost of later design alterations.[36]

computer-aided manufacturing (CAM) The use of computers to control conveyers, machine tools, inspection devices, and other production equipment

The use of computers to control production machines (such as robots, inspection devices, and measurement instrumentation) is called **computer-aided manufacturing (CAM)**. CAM systems increase the output, speed, accuracy, and dependability of production lines. Combinations of CAD and CAM are rapidly becoming significant factors in a variety of industries. Microdynamics is a Dallas manufacturer of CAD/CAM systems for manufacturers of clothing, shoes, and other products made from fabric or leather. The system lays out patterns in order to use material efficiently, saving clients 2 to 4 percent annually on the

U.S. manufacturers have fended off imports by implementing automation in their domestic factories to increase quality and productivity.

Offshore manufacturing has lost some of its glitter lately, causing some manufacturers to come back home and persuading others to stay at home. Although advances in U.S. manufacturing capability and cost-effectiveness are part of the draw, problems with offshore manufacturing such as lower quality, unsatisfactory vendor relationships, hidden costs, and culture clashes have slowed the offshore exodus. Some companies, seeing the United States make major gains in quality and productivity through better management and increased use of automation, are bringing their factories back home.

For example, in the past, Liz Claiborne had difficulty convincing U.S. textile mills to produce small batches of custom fabrics used in 80 percent of Claiborne's high-fashion apparel. In order to find the appropriate fabrics in small lot sizes, Claiborne had to go abroad, usually to Asia. And since the material was there it made sense to go ahead and locate factories there as well. Recently, however, new trade agreements that limit growth in Asian clothing imports spurred Claiborne to set up two factory locations in New York and to work with domestic suppliers. Although the company originally brought the factories home to get around the import restrictions, it now believes the New York location allows both better quality control and faster turnaround.

Another eye-opener for U.S. firms is that the attractiveness of low wages can be outweighed by other costs, such as import duties, shipping, currency fluctuations, and the cost of having inventory tied up during long ocean voyages. Because of these factors, Tandy moved its computer production from South Korea back to Texas and cut costs by 7.5 percent.

Apply Your Knowledge

1. When does it make sense for an organization to locate factories overseas?
2. How might the management of operations be more complex when a manufacturing facility is located overseas?

cost of materials. By linking the system directly to the knives, lasers, and water jets that cut the material, customers improve manufacturing precision. Microdynamics' systems now supervise the manufacture of Liz Claiborne clothing, Bally shoes, Levi Strauss jeans, and La-Z-Boy recliners.[37]

Computer-Integrated Manufacturing

A new level of computerization in operations management is **computer-integrated manufacturing (CIM)**, in which all of the elements of design, engineering, and production, including CAD and CAM, are integrated in computer networks that communicate across departments. For some companies, CIM is proving to be a better route to competitive success than the massive automation schemes attempted in the last several decades.[38]

computer-integrated manufacturing (CIM) The highest level of computerization in operations management, in which all elements of design and production are integrated in computer networks

CIM is a key component in "factories of the future," such as the Fanuc plant in Japan where a small crew works by day with machines to manufacture parts for robots and machine tools. But by night, the factory works alone. Robots click and whir as they solder circuitboards, inspect their work with camera eyes, and hand boards to the next robot down the line. Other robots unload raw materials, while still others work metal into simple shapes that can be used by the computer-controlled machining center—a machine that can change its tools, reposition the part, and cut away unwanted portions of the work piece like a sculptor forming a figure. One person monitors the plant's activity on closed-circuit television screens, and this person can correct production problems simply by typing commands on a computer keyboard.[39]

Flexible Manufacturing Systems

Flexible manufacturing systems (FMSs) are automated production systems that can be easily switched from producing one product to producing the next.

flexible manufacturing systems (FMSs) Automated production systems that can easily switch between product types

MANAGERIAL DECISION MAKING

World-Class Manufacturing at NeXT

Steve Jobs, co-founder of Apple Computer, is widely recognized as a visionary designer of new products. However, visit him at his current company, NeXT, and he'll tell you that he is as proud of the factory as he is of the innovative NeXT computer system.

Jobs and his team were determined from the beginning to build a world-class manufacturing facility. However, they didn't just blindly apply the latest high-tech automation. They started by developing a product that was easy to build, and they designed a simplistic yet fast and efficient manufacturing process. Then they judiciously applied automation technologies wherever doing so would make the most sense.

The results were indeed impressive. A NeXT computer grows from start to finish in about 20 minutes, compared to the days or even weeks that competitive products can take using old-style manufacturing techniques. The manufacturing time is so short that engineers can make design changes and implement them almost instantaneously, making the NeXT computers quite free of the patches and fixes found in many electronic products. In addition, the NeXT factory is surprisingly small, since there is no need to store vast supplies of parts or collections of half-finished computers waiting at overtaxed work centers. And, perhaps more significant, defect rates in NeXT computers are one-tenth the industry average.

Why does the NeXT factory work so well, when so many advanced automation projects haven't lived up to their promises? First, as a relatively new company, NeXT had the advantage of not being tied down to decades-old factories and entrenched methods and mindsets. It created the operations management systems from the ground up, taking advantage of the industry's accumulated knowledge and experience. Second, Jobs gave manufacturing a higher priority than it often gets in other U.S. companies. At one point, more Ph.D.s worked in production than on product design. Third, the NeXT computers are designed for fast, easy manufacturing. Since manufacturability is a key design goal, there aren't any unpleasant surprises when a new product moves from design into production. And finally, machines and people do the work that each is best suited for; the machines take care of the repetitive, boring assembly work, and the people monitor the process, analyze results, and make adjustments as necessary, all the while applying generous doses of creativity and ingenuity.

Apply Your Knowledge

1. How did Steve Jobs use operations management as a competitive advantage?
2. What operations management concepts were employed by NeXT in designing a product that was fast and easy to build and in implementing a production process that uses minimal inventory?

An FMS includes a computer that is responsible for controlling the production process and that is linked to automated machine tools and materials-handling equipment.[40]

For example, Northrop's Aircraft Division at Hawthorne, California, has an FMS for producing small metal parts that become the hundreds of brackets, clips, and spacers in an airplane. The system controls 25 production stations including punch presses, press brakes, and tanks for chemical treatments such as anodizing. Up to 2,000 unique parts can be produced in random sequence by the FMS. Previously, the parts took 8 to 12 weeks to work their way through the factory. Using the flexible manufacturing system, the 2,000 parts are finished in a week, saving Northrop 70 hours of manufacturing time per plane.[41]

MANAGING ONGOING OPERATIONS

The second category of operations management tasks covers the management of production systems once they are set up and running. This category is closely linked to design operations, however. The systems have to be designed to meet the ongoing needs of the organization, and as the organization's needs change

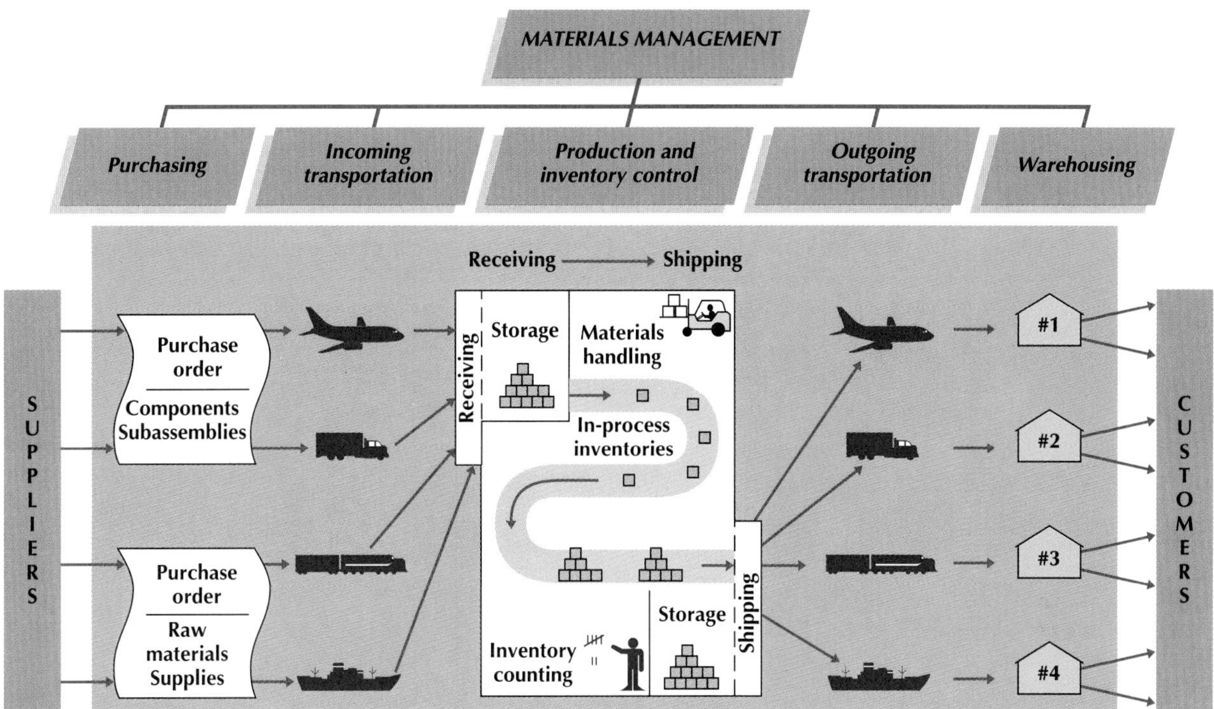

EXHIBIT 20.4

Major Elements of Materials Management

Materials managers oversee a wide variety of systems in the typical organization.

(when new products or existing production equipment becomes obsolete, for instance), operations systems must often be redesigned.

A significant part of managing ongoing operations is the process of **materials management:** planning, organizing, and controlling the flow of materials from the initial purchase of raw materials through the transformation process to the distribution of finished goods (see Exhibit 20.4). The goal of materials management is to have the right material in the right place at the right time. **Inventory management** is the control of all inventory in the production facility, including the functions of receiving, storing, shipping, materials handling, and inventory counting. Managing inventory means balancing the risks of having too much inventory against the risks of having too little inventory. High inventory levels tie up cash and increase materials-handling costs, interest costs, and costs associated with storing inventory. In addition, excessive inventories can hide problems in the production process, such as assembly delays. On the other hand, insufficient inventories impede the production process and restrict sales. Organizations can use the following operations management techniques to alter capacity, schedule production, and manage inventory.[42]

materials management The planning, organizing, and controlling of the flow of materials from purchase of raw materials through final distribution

inventory management The control of inventory in operations management, including such functions as shipping and receiving, storage, and internal materials handling

The Aggregate Production Plan and the Master Schedule

The **aggregate production plan** matches overall product demand with production capacity over a period of one year.[43] By comparing demand forecasts with the capacity requirement plan, the aggregate production plan helps managers identify potential resource mismatches and other circumstances that will need their attention throughout the year. By combining both demand and capacity information, the aggregate production plan provides an overall "build plan" for

aggregate production plan A plan that, over one year, matches product demand with the production capacity needed to produce those products the coming year. Generally updated quarterly, this production plan is termed aggregate because it is usually stated in broad output units, such as the total number of cars (rather than the number of each specific model).

The two basic approaches to aggregate production planning are top-down and bottom-up. In using the top-down approach, the aggregate production plan is developed at the product-line or product-category level; this approach is used in manufacturing compact disc players. With the bottom-up approach, the plan is developed at the level of specific product types, such as portable, car, and home CD players. The individual plans would then be consolidated to arrive at the aggregate plan, specifying overall output and the capacity needed to achieve the plan. As computer capability has become more economical, the bottom-up approach has come to be more widely used, since the computer can now easily take over the time-consuming task of compiling all the individual plans.[44]

master production schedule (MPS) A specific plan derived from the aggregate production plan, identifying the number of products to be produced and the specific capacity requirements necessary over the short term

The **master production schedule (MPS)** is derived from the aggregate production plan and is a specific plan identifying the number of products to be produced and the specific capacity requirements necessary over the short term. The master schedule is more detailed than the aggregate production plan because it breaks down specific model numbers or types of services. To keep the MPS accurate, changing conditions must be reflected in the master production schedule. For instance, if products cannot be produced due to a shortage in material, the MPS should be adjusted to reflect the change.[45]

Operations Control Systems

dependent demand Demand for a given product or component that is influenced by the demand for another product

independent demand Demand that is not directly dependent on the demand for another item

Operations control systems are aimed at regulating the production process and keeping production costs and delays to a minimum. To manage these systems successfully, managers first need to understand the nature of demand. **Dependent demand** occurs when the number of required units of an item is derived from the demand of another item. **Independent demand** occurs when the demand for one item is not dependent on the demand for another item. For example, the components of an automobile (such as wheels, engines, and frames) exhibit dependent demand, whereas the cars for which these components are made exhibit independent demand. Dependent demand can often be calculated, whereas independent demand is generally forecast.[46] For instance, demand for automobile components can be calculated directly from the demand for cars. If Toyota is going to produce 12,000 units of a particular model next month, it will need 48,000 wheels, 12,000 engines, and 12,000 frames for that model. For the cars themselves, however, there is no way to calculate demand since the demand for cars is independent of the demand for any other products. Consequently, the demand for cars must be forecast using consumer surveys, extrapolations of sales histories, and other predictive methods.

The following operations management systems, used appropriately, enable operations to effectively manage the production of both independent- and dependent-demand products.

Economic Order Quantity and Reorder Point

economic order quantity (EOQ) The most economical order size, which minimizes both the cost of ordering new inventory and the cost of holding excess inventory

A key decision in materials management is the number of parts or products to order at a given time. When demand for inventory items is independent, management must decide how many items to order and when to place the order to avoid running out of inventory. The **economic order quantity (EOQ)** calculation is an inventory management technique designed to minimize both the cost of ordering new inventory and the cost of carrying excess inventory by determining the optimal number of units per order. *Ordering costs* are the costs related to placing a specific order, such as shipping, receiving, and inspecting the incoming inventory. *Holding costs,* also known as carrying costs, are the costs associated with having inventory on hand, such as storing, insuring, financing, and moving raw materials, work-in-process, and finished goods.

To minimize these costs, the EOQ formula includes the ordering cost C_o, the holding cost for each unit C_h, and the annual unit demand for the inventory item D. The EOQ formula, then, is

$$EOQ = \sqrt{\frac{2DC_o}{C_h}}$$

Managers can use this formula to calculate the optimal number of units per order to meet the yearly, known demand.[47] For example, assume a small manufacturer of bicycles expects to build 5,000 bicycles per year. The annual demand for wheels would be 10,000. The ordering cost is $125 per order and the average holding cost per unit per year is $10. Using these figures, EOQ is calculated as follows:

$$EOQ = \sqrt{\frac{2(10{,}000 \text{ units})(\$125)}{\$10}} = 500 \text{ units}$$

This calculation shows that the optimal number of wheels per order is 500.

Once the order quantity has been calculated, the next decision is when to order the unit. A different calculation, called **reorder point (ROP)**, is used to determine when the order should be placed considering the amount of time between order placement and delivery. To determine the inventory level at which the order should be placed, the ROP formula includes the daily demand for the item d and the lead time for the new order in days L. The ROP formula is

$$\text{ROP} = d \times L$$

If an order is placed when the inventory level reaches the calculated ROP, the new inventory arrives when the inventory on hand is approaching 0. For example, the bicycle manufacturer with a yearly demand for 10,000 wheels has a daily demand of about 40 wheels (assuming 250 work days per year). On average, the delivery of an order takes 3 days. The reorder point for wheels is calculated as follows:

$$\text{ROP} = d \times L = 40 \text{ units per day} \times 3 \text{ days} = 120 \text{ units}$$

When the inventory stock of wheels drops to 120, an order should be placed. The order would arrive 3 days later, just as the on-hand stock is depleted.[48] In a typical manufacturing plant, however, lead time is not always precise, and demand cannot always be predicted. To avoid a *stockout,* a situation in which inventory is completely depleted, many organizations use safety stock. *Safety stock* is additional inventory that is kept on hand in the event that demand is higher than predicted.[49]

To be sure that the 33 Sears department stores in Mexico have the optimal inventory level, managers use a computer program to calculate the economic order quantity for every item in every branch. This calculation is important because managers want to avoid a stockout on popular items, but they also want to avoid the expense of storing large quantities of safety stock as a hedge against unanticipated demand.

reorder point (ROP) A calculation that determines when orders should be placed to avoid stockouts

Material Requirements Planning

A more complex inventory calculation is required when the demand for inventory items is dependent. **Material requirements planning (MRP)** is an inventory planning and control system (generally computer-based) that uses the mas-

material requirements planning (MRP) A computer-based control system that uses the master production schedule to identify the materials needed in production ter production schedule to identify the specific components and materials needed for the creation of the end product or service (see Exhibit 20.5).[50] The MRP system is usually responsible for initiating the purchasing process (for raw materials) and for outlining the assembly plans to ensure completion of the product at the specified date. In transforming a product from input raw materials into output goods or services, raw material must be delivered on time, and subcomponents must be completed at a specific time in the production process for input into the final product.

MRP was devised in the late 1960s to replace tedious and time-consuming manual systems and continues to help many companies to improve their operations. For example, Black & Decker has greatly improved its operations by implementing MRP. With yearly sales of over $1 billion, Black & Decker manufactures nearly 20,000 units. By introducing MRP, the company improved its materials handling and reduced the number of engineering change orders, inventory levels, and past-due receipts from suppliers. MRP effectively prodded Black & Decker to improve its recordkeeping, thereby reducing inventory and improving customer service.[51]

Manufacturing Resources Planning

manufacturing resource planning (MRPII) A computer-based control system that integrates financial, accounting, personnel, engineering, and marketing information with MRP production control activities

Manufacturing resource planning (MRPII) is a computer-based control system that integrates financial, accounting, personnel, engineering, and marketing information with MRP production planning and control activities.[52] In essence, MRPII systems are traditional MRP systems linked with management information systems from other functions to effectively plan and control every organizational resource.[53] For example, financial information is provided by MRPII in the form of cash flow needed to support the master schedule. Cash outflows calculated by MRPII include payments to suppliers and shippers of material and payment of wages and other costs associated with building the products. Cash inflows are calculated based on the forecast orders combined with firm orders. Similarly, personnel information is provided by adding the bill of labor, stating labor needs by skill category. Labor shortages can then be projected, giving the personnel department advance notice to plan to hire, train, and reassign employees.[54]

just-in-time (JIT) systems Operational control systems designed to run production facilities with a minimum level of inventory

Just-in-Time Management

Just-in-time (JIT) systems are operational control systems designed to run production facilities using the smallest level of inventory possible. But JIT is

EXHIBIT 20.5

The MRP Process

The material requirements plan (MRP) process combines information from the inventory, the master schedule, and the bill of materials (a list of the parts in each product). MRP outputs include inventory updates, assembly plans, and various performance reports.

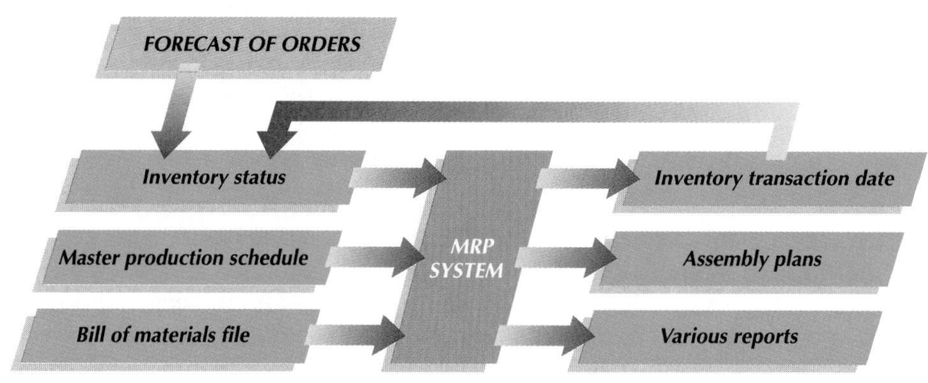

Coleman, maker of lanterns, ice coolers, and camping stoves, adopted just-in-time management as a way of reducing holding costs and eliminating storage for work-in-process. As a result of implementing JIT systems, the Wichita, Kansas, plant where Paul Grimes works now turns out more products with the same number of employees, and safety stock has been virtually eliminated. In turn, this increased efficiency has helped improve Coleman's customer service, cash flow, and profitability.

more than just an inventory control technique; it is a "philosophy of manufacturing based on planned elimination of all waste and continuous improvement of productivity."[55] Traditional operations systems such as MRP are built around "push systems," in which batches of materials are "pushed" into production systems. Inevitably, one work center will get overtaxed, forcing batches to wait in front of this bottleneck, causing work-in-process inventory to increase and lengthening cycle time, or the total time to manufacture a product. In contrast, JIT systems, also known as *kanban, zero-inventory,* and *stockless systems,* are "pull systems" that pull work in process through production systems by downstream production demand and that pull raw materials from suppliers when needed.[56]

JIT systems reduce cycle time by lowering inventory levels throughout the factory and by allowing material to flow through without waiting. Finished-goods inventory is reduced because products are built only to meet sales demand. Since a work center performs its operation at the request of the next work center downstream, work-in-process inventory is minimized. Moreover, the need for a stockroom to hold raw material is eliminated because suppliers deliver material only when it is needed.[57]

The successful implementation of JIT relies on the careful scheduling of work, on-time delivery of high-quality supplies, and skilled employees who are capable of handling problems that may arise during production (such as shortages or breakdowns). In the absence of unnecessary inventory, JIT systems must be flexible. Teamwork and close cooperation are vital. Production employees work in teams and learn all the functions of the team so that they can fill any position. Suppliers also cooperate by delivering parts several times per day, just as if they were extensions of the main production plan.[58]

Saturn is General Motors's showcase manufacturing plant, where the latest operations controls, including JIT, are applied to keep costs low and quality high. At the $1.9 billion Saturn complex located in Tennessee, JIT manufacturing is a fundamental organizational change being implemented on Saturn's factory floor with the full commitment of production employees. Rather than being stockpiled during work in process, parts are fabricated or purchased just in time for the next production step. In fact, the Saturn factory has 101 doors, so that parts can be delivered quickly to the factory floor when needed.[59]

Many companies are beginning to use JIT for shop-floor control while continuing to use MRP for controlling material purchases and the master schedule.[60] Often, the shop-floor control portion of JIT (the part that focuses just on the production line) is easier for an organization to implement because it exists within the confines of the organization. Extending JIT to suppliers with the expectation that material will be delivered when needed is difficult without long-standing relationships with suppliers. Moreover, suppliers may not be flexible enough if the organization is not a prime customer. So, JIT for shop-floor control can allow a company to keep work-in-process and finished-goods inventories to a minimum while using MRP to keep raw material inventory low yet available. In this case, a stockroom would still exist.

JIT concepts can be used to reduce inventory and cycle time for service organizations as well. Koley's Medical Supply illustrates this principle with its program of "stockless distribution" for hospitals. With this system, Koley's takes over the function of the traditional stockroom found in hospitals. Rather than making large, general deliveries to the stockroom, the company delivers specific items in just the right quantities directly to the various floors and rooms in the hospital. (This isn't always simple, either. At one hospital, Koley's has to make deliveries to 168 individual receiving points.) Omaha's Bishop Clarkson Memorial Hospital was Koley's first customer under the stockless program, and it managed to reduce annual inventory costs from $500,000 to just $7,000. The remaining $7,000 is used to keep a small stock of critical supplies needed in emergencies. In addition to the direct financial savings, Clarkson also has reduced the administrative costs associated with supplies. Through such innovative programs, Koley's manages to serve its customers better and increase its own profits.[61]

Purchasing Management

purchasing The acquisition of the raw materials, parts, components, supplies, and finished products needed in operations

Purchasing is the acquisition of the raw materials, parts, components, supplies, and finished products that an organization needs to produce its own goods and services. Effective management of the purchasing process can ensure better quality and conformity of raw materials, lower prices, dedicated supplier bases, and more effective delivery.[62]

By understanding operations management strategies, buyers can establish long-term supplier relationships. Steady relationships can assure suppliers of steady orders, which gives them more incentive to increase the quality of raw materials and to be more responsive to the delivery requirements dictated by JIT manufacturing. For example, Warren Norquist, purchasing and materials management director for Polaroid, eliminated the need for a stockroom and its staff of five by altering the process of purchasing and delivering office supplies. Prior to the change, office supplies were ordered and delivered in large quantities and stored in a stockroom. Now, L. E. Muran of Billerica, Massachusetts, supplies Polaroid with all its office products. Muran created a catalog especially for Polaroid and gave a copy to each secretary. The secretaries then check off the office products they need. A Muran representative picks up the orders daily, and Muran delivers individual packages for each location within 48 hours.[63]

In the past, buyers collected bids from multiple suppliers in order to get the lowest price, and a single part might have been purchased from several suppliers.

Increasingly, organizations are reducing the number of suppliers they use, and they are purchasing specific parts and services under long-term contracts from just a few suppliers who are considered part of the overall team. For example, IBM management has changed the goals of the purchasing department from buying parts from the lowest bidders to establishing long-term contracts with a small set of trusted suppliers.[64] Better relationships with fewer suppliers helps an organization maintain quality and uninterrupted supplies.

Global sourcing, or purchasing of materials and services from worldwide suppliers, is a fact of life in today's economy. Although global sourcing has the advantage of lowering costs, boosting quality, avoiding trade barriers, and securing technically superior components, organizations must consider the political situation in the supplier's country, the logistics involved, the increased lead times, and the currency-exchange rates. Combining the goals of global sourcing with just-in-time purchasing is a nightmare for purchasing departments, but many companies are devising creative solutions to conquer the conflicts. For example, Honeywell's Residential Building Controls Division, located in Golden Valley, Minnesota, has implemented a JIT program with some of its international suppliers. The suppliers set up a U.S. warehouse, and Honeywell pays for the stock after it leaves the warehouse. This compromise allows Honeywell to pursue its JIT purchasing goals while continuing to utilize global sourcing.[65]

MANAGING QUALITY AND PRODUCTIVITY IN OPERATIONS

Operations management plays a key role in two of today's most important management issues: quality and productivity. This section introduces the concept of quality, contrasts quality assurance and quality control, and examines two common techniques for measuring quality in a production operation.

Quality is a measure of how closely a good or service conforms to predetermined standards, especially the needs and expectations of customers.[66] Product quality can be achieved by improving product design with techniques such as DFMA and with technologies such as CAD/CAM and FMS, by increasing the quality of raw materials through long-term relationships with suppliers, and by improving the production processes for both goods and services. Many organizations are finding success in quality endeavors by simplifying their production processes. When implementing JIT to reduce inventory, for example, organizations often uncover and solve process problems, thus streamlining their operations as well. Some organizations focus on reducing the complexity of operations in order to decrease defects. For example, Norman Garrity, senior vice president of manufacturing and engineering at Corning Glass Works, has set goals for reducing product defects and cutting inventories at the dozen plants he supervises. At two factories that manufacture pollution-control devices, the Corning, New York, company eliminated 115 unnecessary operations to cut production time from four weeks to three days. Says Garrity, "If you just simplify the process, you don't need to spend a lot of money in automating."[67]

quality A measure of how closely a product conforms to predetermined standards and customer expectations

Quality Assurance and Quality Control

Quality assurance is a system of policies, procedures, and guidelines that managers can use to ensure that goods and services conform to specified standards of product quality.[68] By developing quantifiable standards of product quality and

quality assurance Policies, procedures, and guidelines that managers can use to ensure that products conform to specified standards of quality; unlike quality control, quality assurance seeks to build quality into the product, rather than simply inspecting for it at the end of the assembly line comparing them with actual measurements, managers have the information they need to make decisions to accept, reject, or correct the product.

Quality assurance focuses on building quality in, rather than merely checking for its existence at the end of the transformation process. In this respect, quality assurance differs from the traditional notion of **quality control,** which focuses on end-of-the-line inspection to make sure that products meet quality standards. Harley-Davidson's Vaughn Beals discovered the limitations of traditional quality control when his inspection team uncovered an abundance of errors at the end of the production line but were powerless to do anything more than simply report them. By adopting a quality assurance focus, Harley-Davidson and other leading manufacturers go beyond mere inspection to adjust and redesign their processes to make sure tasks are done right the first time.

quality control A traditional approach to quality management that focuses on final inspection to make sure that products meet quality standards

Techniques for Measuring Quality

Managers can use two major statistical methods to mathematically assess product quality: acceptance sampling and process control (see Chapter 21 for more information on quality management). **Acceptance sampling** is a statistical tool to control the quality of input material or output products. In acceptance sampling, portions of incoming or outgoing material are tested, and if the number of defects in the sample exceeds a predetermined standard, known as the **acceptable quality level,** management takes corrective action. If the material that does not meet the acceptable quality level is received from an outside supplier, the inspection group might have to reject the entire batch. If it was produced internally, the inspection group may send it back to the production work centers for rework.[69]

acceptance sampling A statistical tool in which portions of incoming or outgoing material are tested to determine defect rates

acceptable quality level A predetermined level of defects that is considered acceptable

Managers use **statistical process control** (SPC) to monitor and control the transformation process itself. All processes exhibit some degree of variability, whether it's the amount of salt applied to a batch of french fries or the number of blemishes in a car's paint job. The goal in SPC is to reduce the variation of process performance characteristics. For instance, one of the process performance characteristics for a bolt is length. If a bolt is supposed to be 3 inches long, control limits (which define the shortest acceptable length and longest acceptable length) indicate the acceptable variation in bolt length, such as 2.95 inches and 3.05 inches (see Exhibit 20.6). If measurements taken on samples of the bolt indicate that the length consistently falls outside the control limits, the process is out of control and managers must look for the cause of the quality problem.[70]

statistical process control (SPC) A system of measurement that monitors the quality of the transformation process in order to reduce performance variations

Operations managers use statistical process control to improve product quality by building quality in rather than inspecting for quality at the end of the production process. In other words, SPC supports the concept of quality assurance, rather than quality control. Although operations managers may employ acceptance sampling for incoming products, chances are they are encouraging their suppliers to adopt SPC so that the incoming inspections can be eliminated. Many companies, in fact, are moving to formally certify their suppliers' ability to provide quality parts and materials. This is particularly important in JIT operations.

SPC provides information to fix process problems while the product is still in production. This not only increases quality but also decreases costs, since less time and energy are spent on final inspection and rework. General Electric makes compressors for its refrigerators at a factory in Columbia, Tennessee.

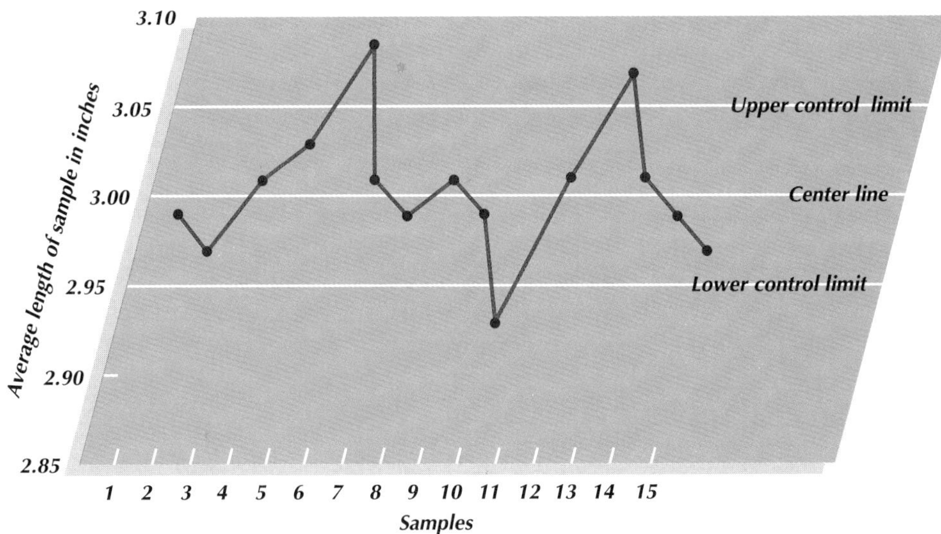

EXHIBIT 20.6

Control Charts in Statistical Process Control

In this example of a control chart, the acceptable length of the bolt being manufactured ranges from 2.95 to 3.05 inches. The chart shows that two samples were unacceptably long, one sample was too short, and the rest were clustered around the center line of 3.00 inches.

The tolerance on the diameter of the crankshaft in the compressor is a mere 50 millionths of an inch; if the crankshaft is smaller or larger by more than this amount, the compressor won't operate correctly. Using SPC, the people at GE can check for quality at 1,000 points along the assembly line. If they see a problem, the partially completed crankshaft is fixed immediately. And if the technicians see the same problem repeatedly, they know that some aspect of the process needs attention, and because they know precisely where along the production line the problem is occurring, they can quickly locate and solve the problem. If the technicians waited until the end of the production line and then did simple quality control inspections, they would have to scrap the problem crankshafts, and they would encounter a much more complicated job of finding the process problem. By checking quality during the manufacturing process, GE ensures lower costs and higher quality.[71]

Techniques for Measuring Productivity

Productivity measures the efficiency of the production process in transforming input resources into output goods and services.[72] Although productivity is primarily a measure of efficiency, increasing the effectiveness of an organization's operations can lead to increased efficiency and thus increased productivity. However, as Chapter 1 pointed out, if an organization is able to increase its efficiency but is not working on the right set of activities, performance will suffer.[73]

productivity A measure of a production process's efficiency in transforming input resources into output goods and services

Two productivity measures are often used to measure the efficient use of an organization's resources:[74]

- *Total factor productivity.* Managers can measure organizational productivity by computing **total factor productivity,** which relates total outputs to total inputs in the production of goods and services. The following equation is used:

total factor productivity The ratio of total outputs to total inputs

$$\text{Total factor productivity} = \frac{\text{Goods and Services (outputs)}}{\text{Labor + Capital + Energy + Technology + Materials (inputs)}}$$

partial factor productivity The ratio of total outputs to one particular input

- *Partial factor productivity.* To help them understand the individual components of overall organizational productivity, managers often measure productivity using one significant input resource. **Partial factor productivity** relates total outputs to one critical input, such as labor, using the following equation:

$$\text{Partial factor productivity} = \frac{\text{Goods and Services (outputs)}}{\text{Labor (input)}}$$

  Harley-Davidson, for instance, might choose to measure partial factor productivity for labor costs, capital expenditures, and facilities expenses, each of which would provide an important insight into overall productivity.

The successful management of any operation requires attention to more than just quality and productivity. Such other factors as the time required to get new products to market and relationships with customers are major factors as well. However, an increasing number of organizations have discovered that without concentrated efforts directed toward increasing quality and productivity they will be unable to remain competitive and reach organizational goals. Chapter 21 continues this discussion, with more details on managing for quality and productivity, as well as the all-important concept of customer satisfaction.

SUMMARY

Operations management is the collection of planning and control activities that managers use to produce goods and services. Operations management focuses on three areas: inputs (labor, raw materials, and money), outputs (finished goods and services), and the transformation processes themselves. Both goods and services production can benefit from effective operations management techniques because both transform input resources into higher-valued outputs. Both can use operations management techniques to design and manage ongoing operations for increased quality, productivity, and competitiveness.

Operations management can play one of four strategic roles in the organization. An organization in Stage 1 treats operations almost as a necessary evil, in which the emphasis is on minimizing costs and headaches associated with production. In Stage 2, management seeks to keep production capability on a par with the organization's competitors, but not to actively build competitive advantage through operations. When an organization is in Stage 3, it assigns operations a key role in supporting organizational strategy and goals, including developing new capabilities if that is necessary to add competitive strengths in line with the organization's strategic direction. At the most advanced level, Stage 4, operations play an active and integral role in the formulation and execution of strategy, and operations are expected to contribute to competitiveness to the same degree that other functional areas contribute.

Four unique attributes distinguish services from goods: (1) services are intangible; (2) it is usually impossible to separate the service provider from the service itself; (3) services are perishable, which means that they usually can't exist after they are delivered; and (4) consistency of quality is a big challenge in services because customers often play a role in service quality, because individual employee motivation and performance can dramatically affect product quality, and because fluctuations in demand can strain an organization's ability to produce quality services.

Operations management efforts fall into two major categories: designing or redesigning operations and managing those operations from one day to the next. In terms of operations design, the chapter addressed the issues of product design and manufacturability, capacity planning for smooth and profitable operations, decisions regarding the location of an organization's facilities, the layout of the facilities themselves and how layout affects quality and productivity, and several important operations management technologies, including computer-aided design (CAD), computer-aided manufacturing (CAM), computer-integrated manufacturing (CIM), and flexible manufacturing systems (FMS). The ongoing management of operations, in contrast, involves production planning and scheduling; a number of operations control systems, including economic order quantity (EOQ) and reorder point (ROP) calculations, material requirements planning, manufacturing resource planning, and just-in-time management philosophies; and purchasing management.

Just-in-time (JIT) is a management philosophy that strives to eliminate waste, in terms of both materials and time. One dominant aspect of JIT is production facilities that are designed to run using as little inventory as possible. JIT "pulls" materials through the system, so that they are made available just at the moment they are needed. This contrasts sharply with traditional "push" systems, in which a batch of materials flows through the system, often creating backups and excess stockpiles wherever problems occur.

On the surface, quality control and quality assurance seem quite similar, but there is a fundamental difference between the two. Quality control inspects for quality at the end of the transformation process, whereas quality assurance builds quality in the products by checking at points throughout the process. If a problem shows up, it is fixed immediately, without waiting for it to filter to the end of the process.

Two key statistical methods used in operations quality control are acceptance sampling, which focuses on the quality of input material or output products, and statistical process control (SPC), which addresses the quality of the transformation process. Acceptance sampling is primarily a quality control technique, whereas SPC is a quality assurance technique because it gives managers tools to build quality into their products.

MEETING A MANAGEMENT CHALLENGE AT HARLEY-DAVIDSON

Harley-Davidson saw its commanding lead in heavyweight motorcycles falter when powerful Japanese bikes appeared in the U.S. market. If Harley was to stay on the road, CEO Vaughn Beals had to uncover the key elements of Japanese success and put them to work for his own company. Initially, he was baffled. Honda's motorcycle plant, at Marysville, Ohio (which had begun to build motorcycles for sale in the U.S. market), was staffed by American workers, just as Harley's plants were. It bought parts from American suppliers, just as Harley did. And Honda had no clear technological advantage that Beals could identify. In fact, Honda didn't own a PC, whereas Harley used a complex, computerized MRP system.

Given the opportunity to tour the Marysville plant, Beals gathered his senior managers and engineers and set off to learn. And he found the answer to his question: Honda turned out better motorcycles because the Honda managers were simply doing a better job of managing. If Harley was to make a comeback, it would have to adopt some of the operations management systems that the Japanese used so effectively.

Richard Teerlink, Vaughn Beals's successor as CEO of Harley-Davidson

Beals set his staff to work installing a version of just-in-time inventory control. Switching to JIT was not easy. Some employees laughed when management announced that Harley was replacing its computer-based control system, its overhead conveyers, and its high-rise part storage with a manual system that used simple pushcarts. But within two months, the employees were converts. Switching to JIT almost immediately reduced Harley's investment in inventory, which freed funds to design and engineer new models. Even more important, making JIT work forced Harley to rethink every aspect of its operations systems.

JIT forced Harley to change its purchasing practices. Suppliers were no longer adversaries; they were partners. Harley forged cooperative relationships with a select group of suppliers who could deliver high-quality parts according to Harley's demanding JIT schedule. Paradoxically, this approach allowed Harley to cut costs as well as increase quality. Because Harley used fewer suppliers, it could place larger orders that qualified for bulk discounts.

To keep stocks of its own work in progress low, the company reduced machine-tool setup times so that components could be made in smaller quantities. One way it cut setup time was to standardize components for various product lines. For instance, working closely with production engineers, Harley's designers reworked the crankpins used in two different models, lowering the time it took to switch from making one crankpin to the other from two hours to three minutes.

The reductions in setup time improved productivity, and they enabled Harley to switch from a product layout to a process layout, which is better suited to the small production runs that Harley needed in order to keep inventory down. Small runs also helped Harley introduce product upgrades more quickly, and they boosted quality, because with small runs, defects are limited to fewer parts.

These changes (along with a hefty temporary tariff on imported heavyweights) helped Harley roar back into the motorcycle business. It has beaten back competition from Japanese firms while demonstrating that it's possible for a U.S. firm to be a low-cost, high-quality producer. Harley no longer has stockrooms; all the materials are on the floor. It no longer relies on inspection programs such as Quality Audit, and production-control staff has been slashed from 22 to 2. It no longer buys parts from 820 companies; the number of suppliers has been cut more than 50 percent. Harley's share of the U.S. heavyweight market is back up to 60 percent, well ahead of second-place Honda's 19 percent.

***You're the Manager*:** Since 1986 Harley-Davidson's sales have nearly doubled, and its earnings have grown at an annual rate of 57 percent. Such success, critics say, has bred complacency. Sensing that there might be some truth in these remarks, Richard Teerlink, who replaced Vaughn Beals as CEO, has hired you as an operations management consultant to evaluate the company's manufacturing systems and to help plot its course for the future.

Ranking Questions

1. During the winter, the market for motorcycles is dormant. But even before the slush melts off the road, Harley-Davidson dealerships are crowded with customers eager to roar down the highway on one of Harley's famous hogs. The spring rush invariably leads to delays in delivery because Harley's JIT philosophy doesn't permit the company to accumulate finished goods during the winter. Teerlink has jotted down a list of approaches that Harley could use to meet this seasonal fluctuation without building up inventory. He asks you to rank them.
   a. Hire additional employees in the spring and lay them off in the fall.
   b. Subcontract more subassembly operations.
   c. Ask employees to put in overtime during the spring rush.
   d. Bend the no-inventory rule and accumulate one or two months' worth of finished bikes over the winter, in preparation for spring.
2. Teerlink is a firm believer in continuous improvement. Harley-Davidson has established itself as a low-cost, high-quality producer in the United States, has steadily recovered market share, and is ready to expand into new markets and new industries. But Teerlink worries that Harley will achieve growth at the expense of productivity. He has drawn up a list of four methods for increasing productivity and asks you to rank them. Important considerations are their appropriateness and Harley's ability to introduce them quickly.
   a. Cross-train staff so that each employee is certified to perform several jobs.
   b. Install an MRPII system.
   c. Trim the labor force further.
   d. Increase R&D spending on motorcycle designs.

Multiple-Choice Questions

3. Harley-Davidson has recovered its lead in the U.S. heavyweight motorcycle market, but sales of heavyweight motorcycles are dropping. Harley has decided to diversify and has investigated four companies that it would like to acquire. As an operations management consultant, which company would you recommend for a first pur-

chase, in terms of fitting with Harley's operations management experience?
   a. A company that produces small corporate jets
   b. A fast-food franchise
   c. A company that makes recreational vehicles
   d. A company that makes spark plugs
4. The demand for Harleys continues to increase, outstripping the capacity of Harley's motorcycle factories in York, Pennsylvania, and Milwaukee, Wisconsin. Teerlink called senior management together to address this problem, and they decided to build a new state-of-the-art factory. In addition to expanding capacity, they hope to perfect new production processes that will end the Japanese threat in U.S. markets and that will enable the company to compete in Southeast Asia. Ultimately, Teerlink hopes to introduce these new methods in Harley's older facilities. The decision to open a new plant brings with it a host of questions. One of the most important is location. Teerlink asks you to recommend one of four site choices:
   a. Adjacent to the York factory.
   b. Adjacent to the Milwaukee factory.
   c. In Santa Cruz, California.
   d. In Kyoto, Japan.

Analysis Questions

5. Harley-Davidson uses an MRP system to complement its JIT system. How does MRP ensure that Harley's JIT works smoothly?
6. How did changes in operations management improve quality at Harley-Davidson?
7. Harley-Davidson has used JIT successfully to revitalize its operations systems. What liabilities of JIT must Harley guard against?

Special Project

It's finally happened. Harley enthusiasts have begun to question the company's continued reliance on push rods for operating engine valves. Most imports have overhead cams, a configuration that yields more power. Making a transition to overhead cams will not be simple. Teerlink has called you into his office and asked you to make a presentation to the board of directors on how the switch to overhead cams will affect Harley's operations systems. Your job is to help the board understand the kinds of operations systems issues the company must address before it can make the change. Prepare an outline for a half-hour presentation.[75]

KEY TERMS

acceptable quality level (660)
acceptance sampling (660)
aggregate production plan (653)
capacity planning (644)
capacity requirements planning (CRP) (645)
computer-aided design (CAD) (650)
computer-aided manufacturing (CAM) (650)
computer-integrated manufacturing (CIM) (651)
dependent demand (654)
design for manufacturability and assembly (DFMA) (643)
economic order quantity (EOQ) (654)
fixed-position layout (649)
flexible manufacturing systems (FMSs) (651)
independent demand (654)
inventory management (653)
just-in-time (JIT) systems (656)
manufacturing resource planning (MRPII) (656)
master production schedule (MPS) (654)
material requirements planning (MRP) (655)
materials management (653)
operations management (638)
partial factor productivity (662)
process layout (647)
productivity (661)
product layout (648)
purchasing (658)
quality (659)
quality assurance (659)
quality control (660)
reorder point (ROP) (655)
statistical process control (SPC) (660)
total factor productivity (661)
work-flow layout (647)

QUESTIONS

For Review

1. What are the five issues that operations managers consider when designing operations?
2. What are the benefits and limitations of the three work-flow layouts?
3. What is the relationship between the aggregate production plan and the master production schedule?
4. What are the four stages of operations management, relative to organizational strategy?
5. How do the two ratios of productivity differ?

For Analysis

1. How is operations management affected when products are designed by engineers with little input from other functional areas?
2. What are the implications of using technology to correct poor process quality?
3. How might an organization currently using a material requirements planning system move to a just-in-time inventory system?
4. What is the long-term impact of pursuing the lowest-cost supplier for raw materials and components?
5. What quality control techniques would be used to inspect for quality? What tools would be used to build in quality?

For Application

1. How might an operations manager describe the process of designing operations for a car wash?
2. The president of a computer manufacturing firm read an article describing the operations of a competitor. The competitor's product used one-half the parts but its work force was twice as productive. Concerned with competitiveness, how might the president achieve these results?
3. What inventory control system would a toy store implement and why?
4. What inventory control system would minimize raw material, work-in-process inventory, and finished goods inventory for a toy manufacturer?
5. What operations management techniques would be employed by an Alaskan fish cannery plant to measure and increase productivity?

KEEPING CURRENT IN MANAGEMENT

From recent magazines or newspapers, find an article that discusses a manager who implemented a new operations management technique to improve the quality, productivity, or competitiveness of the organization. One example might focus on a manager who modified the design of a product or who implemented new production technology. Another example might involve a manager who implemented a new production-and-inventory control system, such as JIT, MRP, or MRPII.

1. Was the manager redesigning the operations, improving the ongoing production, or both? Explain. Has the organization become more profitable through quality or productivity gains?
2. Who was most affected by the change? Why? What functional areas were affected? How?
3. Explain the operations management techniques used to increase the quality of the product or the productivity of the employees. What additional steps can they take to increase quality and productivity?

SHARPEN YOUR MANAGEMENT SKILLS

The late Sam Walton used a number of retailing innovations to take his company, Wal-Mart, from obscurity in Arkansas to its current position as the nation's largest retailer. Wal-Mart owes a large part of its success to its highly efficient, low-cost operating system, particularly its innovative distribution system that keeps stores supplied at significantly lower cost than competitors are able to manage.

However, a new operations wrinkle is causing current CEO David Glass some concern. As he visits stores around the country, he is noticing an increasing number of employees staffing "the back office." In other words, these employees aren't out on the sales floor helping customers. As he watched Wal-Mart grow in his later years, the legendary Walton used to say things like "We're gettin' just like Sears, Roebuck in some ways. We got so many back office people workin' off the floor." In the realm of retailing efficiency and cost control, comparing one's company to Sears is about the sharpest criticism imaginable.

- *Decision:* Devise a set of operating guidelines that will satisfy Sam Walton's desire to keep "back office" employment to a minimum. This can include anything from automation systems that eliminate some of the demand for support staff to job rotation schemes that let back office staffers contribute to sales and customer support more directly.
- *Communication:* Assume that you're sitting next to Glass on an airplane and that you have his attention. Explain your plan to him.

CASE

Black & Decker Operates on the Cutting Edge

Just when Black & Decker CEO Nolan D. Archibald seemed to have achieved another corporate turnaround, he stumbled over a multibillion-dollar acquisition. Black & Decker has recovered market share and revenues are rising, but loan interest is devouring profits, and the company must become more efficient to stay healthy.

HISTORY

S. Duncan Black's $1,200 partnership with Alonzo G. Decker to manufacture candy dippers in 1910 has evolved into the world's largest power-tool and home-improvements company, with more than 60 factories serving 100 countries. Black & Decker found its niche in 1916 when it introduced its first major tool, the half-inch electric drill with patented pistol grip and trigger switch. It built a factory the next year in Towson, Maryland; quickly moved into international markets; and issued a steady stream of products, including the world's first portable screwdriver in 1922 and the Dustbuster hand-held vacuum in 1979—a year when revenues topped $1 billion and profits hit $85 million.

But B&D bogged down in the 1980s, losing market share for five straight years to Makita of Japan, Bosch of West Germany, and Emerson Electric's Skil. Archibald was hired away from Beatrice to become B&D president in 1985 and was elevated to chairman and CEO six months later. Archibald turned the company around by slashing overhead, eliminating 3,000 jobs, and redesigning B&D's power-tool and appliance lines. But his decision to purchase miniconglomerate Emhart Corporation for $2.8 billion in 1989 saddled B&D with huge interest payments that soon devoured 60 percent of its operating income, and the recession prevented B&D from selling the Emhart assets, which would have made the deal profitable. Annual net income fell from $97 million the year before the purchase to $51 million as the company entered the 1990s.

ENVIRONMENT

Archibald is trying to control costs and solidify customer relationships by coordinating all facets of management. Before he arrived, B&D's corporate structure was a confederation of nearly sovereign fiefdoms; British, French, and German managers sold their own products in their own countries without regard for global strategy. Today, Archibald insists that managers see the big picture, and he has integrated purchasing, marketing, production, distribution, and customer service functions. Purchasing managers must now consider quality as well as the cost of materials, and distribution managers can't look at transportation costs without weighing customer service. Teams made up of sales, research, and production employees have a say in product development and, as a result, new power tools are being introduced more quickly.

B&D is improving production processes. For example, its factory in Spennymoor, England, traditionally built power-tool motors as part of the tool's plastic case, which prevented the motors from being tested until the tool was fully assembled. Now, motors are built separately, and each element can be tested as it is assembled, improving quality and efficiency. B&D also is making just-in-time deliveries to customers, providing them with the right product at the right time so that they no longer need to stock much inventory.

GOALS AND CHALLENGES

Archibald's top goal is to reduce the company's debt. He has cut $100 million in annual expenses by closing Emhart's headquarters and combining its manufacturing operations with B&D's. He is also trying to sell some Emhart operations, but otherwise he wants to squeeze out more profits by focusing on new products, better quality, and higher productivity. B&D is introducing new cordless drills and screwdrivers for the do-it-yourself crowd and is working to coordinate the marketing of Emhart locks, faucets, glue guns, and bolts with B&D power tools. The company is seeking to improve customer service by halving its order cycle times, which currently run three to five days. And it is trying to improve productivity and quality control by using fewer separate types of motors for its various power-tool models.

1. How have Archibald and Black & Decker improved the company's use of inputs, outputs, and transformation processes? Has Archibald's decision to purchase Emhart Corporation affected operations management?
2. What implications would just-in-time delivery of raw materials and just-in-time distribution of finished goods have for capacity planning at one of B&D's power-tool factories?
3. What operations management methods would Archibald use in designing a delivery service for Emhart's locks, faucets, glue guns, and bolts?
4. Black & Decker's size enables it to purchase raw materials for its power tools globally and to achieve low prices by buying in volume. What operations management methods would managers of such a program use?

CHAPTER OUTLINE

21 Quality, Productivity, and Customer Satisfaction

After studying this chapter, you will be able to

1. Describe the management imperatives for organizational performance
2. Explain the relationship among quality, productivity, and customer satisfaction
3. Identify the eight dimensions of quality
4. Discuss the five ways in which managers can improve quality
5. Explain how managers can improve productivity
6. Relate product value to customer satisfaction
7. Discuss the steps managers can take to improve customer satisfaction

FACING A MANAGEMENT CHALLENGE AT

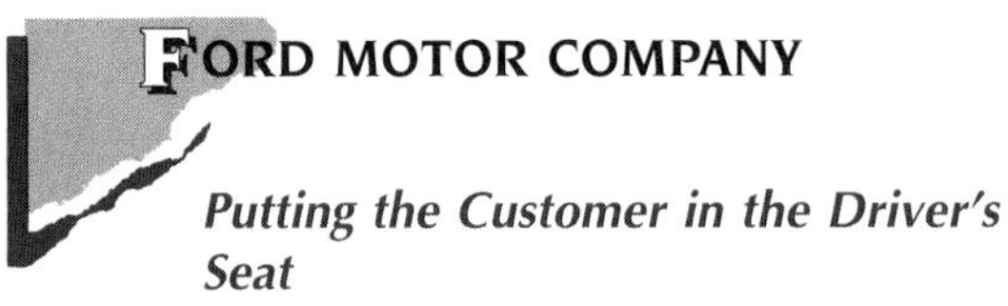

FORD MOTOR COMPANY

Putting the Customer in the Driver's Seat

Ford has been a household name since the early days of the auto industry, but in the 1970s and 1980s, its automobiles were in a dwindling percentage of U.S. garages. Long one of the proudest corporations in the United States, Ford was facing a battle for survival. Inroads from overseas automobile makers had depressed earnings and shaved market share so badly that in a single year the nation's second-largest automaker lost $1.5 billion—a company record. New chairman Donald E. Petersen took scant comfort in realizing that his company was not alone in its misery. He couldn't return Ford to profitability by blaming an industrywide slump.

Part of the problem was that overseas auto production was more efficient than domestic production. But a more serious challenge, Petersen saw, was that consumers perceived Ford and other U.S.-made automobiles as being of inferior quality because they had a large number of defects. Petersen decided the only way to get Ford out of the breakdown lane was to improve productivity in the factory and satisfy the customer on the highway. That meant increasing quality.

In plotting his strategy Petersen identified a number of weak links in Ford's organizational performance. First, there was no thorough, systematic method in place to measure customer reaction to the company's automobiles and to quickly redesign products to satisfy buyers. Second, the company's design process and production lines were inefficient. Individuals in departments such as engineering, finance, and design worked in isolation from each other as new cars came into being. The lack of coordination resulted in expensive backtracking late in the production game. That depressed productivity. Outmoded production lines meant it took too many hours to bring an automobile to market and changes in design could not be quickly made. In addition, employees weren't cross-trained to do each other's jobs; this caused additional costs and delays when work backed up behind any group that was behind schedule. Third, the company was not as quality-conscious as it needed to be in order to compete in the global market. Employees and managers needed more motivation to work together on products that would satisfy customer needs. The components in Ford cars just broke down too often, especially when compared with the low defect rate in the overseas competition.

Petersen knew that the solution would require a fundamental change in Ford's corporate culture. Thanks to competition from overseas, the days had passed when a company could get away with making whatever products it chose. Everyone at Ford had to adopt a new mental posture of meeting the customer's needs with quality products. Above all, everyone had to cooperate in turning out quality products.

That was more than a quick tune-up. It was a major overhaul. How could Petersen meet the competitive challenge by improving the quality of Ford's automobiles and responding efficiently to customer needs? How could he increase the productivity of the design and production processes? And how could he motivate employees and managers to work as a team? [1]

CHAPTER OVERVIEW

As Ford's Donald Petersen and his successor Harold Poling recognized, customers care passionately about quality, and when quality improves, productivity and customer satisfaction are both enhanced. This chapter explores quality, productivity, and customer service, three closely related concepts that hold the key to organizational performance now and in the future. The chapter opens with a discussion of management imperatives for performance and then examines quality, including the eight dimensions of quality and the ways that managers can improve quality. Next is a look at productivity trends and the ways organizations can improve productivity. The chapter closes with a discussion of customer satisfaction, including the connection between product value and customer satisfaction, and of the ways managers can increase customer satisfaction.

ORGANIZATIONAL PERFORMANCE TODAY AND TOMORROW

As the twentieth century draws to a close, forward-thinking managers are already reflecting on the challenges of the next millennium. Although it is impossible to accurately predict the cause, the nature, or the impact, changes will inevitably occur in the internal and external environments, influencing every organization's current and future performance. Against this backdrop of change, managers of all organizations need to prepare for the problems and opportunities ahead. Even managers who have a reputation for high personal performance and for consistent contributions to organizational performance cannot be assured that their achievements will be sustainable into the future, so it is important for them to focus their efforts on the areas having the greatest impact.[2]

Management Imperatives

How can managers identify the decisions and activities most likely to have a significant influence on current and future organizational performance and on an organization's abilities to meet its strategic goals? Despite the diversity among organizations and their missions, goals, and plans, managers at all levels can achieve better performance by concentrating their efforts on four key imperatives: (1) meeting customer needs, (2) increasing efficiency and effectiveness, (3) meeting competitive challenges, and (4) differentiating products.

Meeting Customer Needs

The first management imperative for organizational performance involves meeting customer needs. Although managers often take into account the interests and desires of other stakeholders, their top priority is to find out what

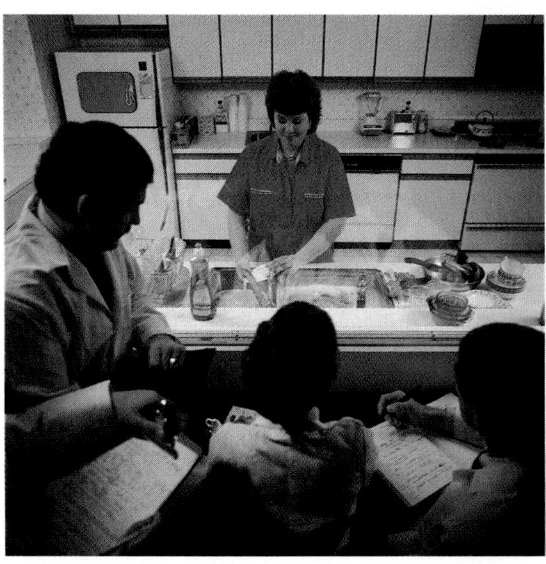

Colgate-Palmolive stays tuned to customer needs by conducting extensive market research. Here, Colgate technical specialists watch how a customer uses dishwashing detergent so they can continue to improve the product and its packaging. Using feedback from such research, Colgate introduces as many as 200 new products every year, including household cleaners, soaps, laundry detergents, and dental care products.

customers need and then meet those needs. After all, without customers or constituents for their goods or services, organizations have no reason for being. However, customer needs can, and do, change, so organizations must be flexible and responsive if they are to maintain an ongoing relationship with current customers as well as attract new customers. By keeping their sights on the moving target of customer needs, managers can cultivate a level of customer loyalty that translates into long-term organizational performance.[3]

Consider how David M. Clarke, president of Regis University in Denver, has met his customers' needs. Looking beyond the needs of 18- to 22-year-olds, Clarke found another group whose needs were not being met: adults. He reasoned that working adults needed new skills to further their careers, so he set out specifically to meet those needs. Clarke scheduled evening classes and set up 10 community locations for student convenience, and he established classrooms at IBM and Coors to accommodate their employees. By treating students as customers and meeting their needs, Clarke increased enrollment from 1,000 to 8,000 and turned heavy losses into budget surpluses.[4]

Increasing Efficiency and Effectiveness

As Chapter 1 pointed out, personal and organizational performance consists of efficiency (doing things right) and effectiveness (doing the right things). If managers sacrifice efficiency for effectiveness, then they are wasting resources but achieving organizational goals; if, on the other hand, they sacrifice effectiveness for efficiency, they are using the fewest possible resources but failing to achieve their goals. Neither extreme is healthy for an organization over the long term. For current and future performance, managers must find ways of using resources more efficiently while improving goods and services to better achieve their goals.[5]

C&J Industries in Meadville, Pennsylvania, supplies specialized components such as fuse units to Ford, NCR, and other manufacturers. Founder Harold Corner recently streamlined his plant for maximum efficiency. He utilizes computer-aided design and manufacturing to speed new-product development and production, and customers transmit their specifications electronically instead of on traditional paper blueprints, saving both time and effort. Corner's increased efficiency has also increased his company's effectiveness: customers receive higher-quality products more quickly than before.[6]

Meeting Competitive Challenges

Traditional assumptions about who is and who is not a competitor are being shattered every day as organizations confront competition both locally and globally, from organizations large and small. Long-established cookie makers Nabisco and Pepperidge Farm now have to look over their shoulders at brash newcomers such as R.W. Frookies; credit card giants American Express, Visa, and MasterCard have to react to the U.S. invasion of JCB, Japan's mightiest charge card. Moreover, not-for-profit organizations now face competition from for-profit organizations (and vice versa in some cases). One example is the for-profit corporation Education Alternatives, which operates private schools in two cities (Eagan, Minnesota, and Paradise Valley, Arizona) and manages a public school (in Dade County, Florida), competing with public and private educational systems for students and for contracts to operate schools.[7]

In this highly charged competitive environment, more organizations are finding that they must move beyond simply meeting the customer's basic needs.

Consider Intuit, a fast-growing software company in Menlo Park, California, whose flagship product is Quicken, a PC program that helps customers manage their finances. Scott Cook, Intuit's president, knows his product meets customer needs, but he keeps the improvements coming. Although most people expect to struggle when learning a new program, Cook has designed Quicken so that users are up and running within six minutes after opening the box, or they get their money back, an approach that has helped Quicken capture a 60 percent share of its market. Other organizations meet competitive challenges by forging closer relationships with suppliers so that they can better manage the quality, timing, availability, and cost of resources. For example, stereo speaker maker Bose has brought seven supplier representatives into its Framingham, Massachusetts, office on a full-time basis. Representing parts, packaging, office supplies, printing, and delivery service suppliers, these on-site reps attend production and marketing meetings, offer suggestions, and customize their products to meet Bose's needs. Bose benefits from its suppliers' expertise and fast response, and the suppliers get more business with less time and trouble.[8]

Cleveland-based Premier differentiates its electronics and industrial parts business in three ways. First, the company offers fast delivery: most orders, even small orders, are shipped within a day. Second, Premier specializes in hard-to-find and discontinued parts that few firms stock. Third, Premier believes in service. Sales representative Suzanne Spagnoletti travels to customer factories or offices to learn firsthand about customer needs.

Differentiating Products

So many organizations have figured out how to meet customer needs that an increasing number of goods and services are startlingly similar. Relatively few differences might be perceived among department stores, banks, cat foods, cereals, and other product categories; even a gilt-edged brand name no longer automatically sets the product apart or guarantees customer loyalty. More than ever before, managers need to find ways of differentiating their products so that customers have a reason to choose theirs rather than a competing product. Products can be differentiated in a variety of ways, but an increasingly popular and compelling method is time-based competition, delivering goods and services significantly faster than any competitor and still offering competitive costs and quality. For example, Citicorp has used time-based competition to successfully build a $15 billion business in home mortgages. Other providers' customers may wait up to 45 days to learn if their loans have been approved, but Citicorp's MortgagePower customers get decisions within 15 days, and some are approved in 15 minutes.[9]

Another way to differentiate products is through superior customer service. Even the most mundane product, one ordinarily seen as a commodity, can draw customer attention if the right kind of service is provided. For instance, textile producer Milliken has a thriving business selling shop towels, a product more popularly known as rags. Milliken sells its shop towels to commercial laundries, who in turn rent them to factories, hospitals, and other bulk users. To differentiate its shop towels, Milliken offers sales skills workshops, electronic order entry, market research assistance, and other services that help the laundries identify and service their shop towel customers more efficiently.[10]

Quality, Productivity, and Customer Satisfaction

To address the issues raised by these four management imperatives, managers must understand and apply three closely related concepts. The first is the concept of quality, defined in Chapter 20 as a measure of how closely a product conforms to predetermined standards, especially the needs and expectations of customers. Generally, managers improve quality so that they can better meet customer needs, compete more effectively, and differentiate their products. But when an organization makes quality a top priority, its managers and employees find that they redo their work less often, they reduce wasted time and materials, and they experience fewer delays in completing their work. One study at Merrill Lynch, for instance, revealed that the overall cost of service errors, including corrections, was $210 million per year. Some experts put the cost of organizational waste as high as 50 percent of net sales. Although top managers may spend heavily to improve quality (conducting employee training and installing new equipment are two examples), these investments generally reduce the cost of errors over the long run and help organizations use resources more efficiently.[11]

The quest for quality leads directly to the second concept that managers need to understand and apply when they address the issues raised by the management imperatives. Improved quality means fewer errors, so the organization runs more efficiently, thereby increasing its productivity. Productivity was defined in Chapter 20 as a measure of the efficiency of the process by which input resources are transformed into output goods and services. Productivity rises when mistakes go down, but improved quality also increases productivity in another way. Higher-quality products help an organization achieve higher market share, and when more units are sold, the per-unit cost drops, yielding a further increase in productivity.[12]

However, the cycle does not end there. Once quality improves, leading to productivity increases, organizations can offer an improved product at a reasonable price. Thus, improved quality and productivity contribute directly to **customer satisfaction,** fulfilling customer needs and expectations by providing the appropriate product with the appropriate service delivery before, during, and after the transaction. Customers themselves judge their satisfaction with goods and services by comparing the overall performance of the product and service package to both their needs and their expectations. If the performance meets or exceeds their needs and expectations, they are more satisfied than if the performance falls short. Further, if they are satisfied with a product, they will return for more and, in many cases, may even be willing to pay a premium for it. This increases the organization's profitability and provides the financial resources for a new round of quality and productivity enhancements. And customers tend to share their experiences with friends and colleagues, making word-of-mouth one of an organization's most important promotional channels. Taken as a whole, this cycle of quality, productivity, and customer satisfaction enables organizations to meet all four of the management imperatives that affect performance today and tomorrow (see Exhibit 21.1).[13]

customer satisfaction Fulfillment of customer needs and expectations by offering the appropriate product with the appropriate service delivery before, during, and after the transaction

EXHIBIT 21.1 The Quality, Productivity, and Customer Satisfaction Cycle

When organizations improve their quality, they set off a chain reaction that leads to improved productivity and to improved customer satisfaction, which, in turn, lead to higher organizational performance. Now because the organization has more resources to use for improving quality, the cycle starts again.

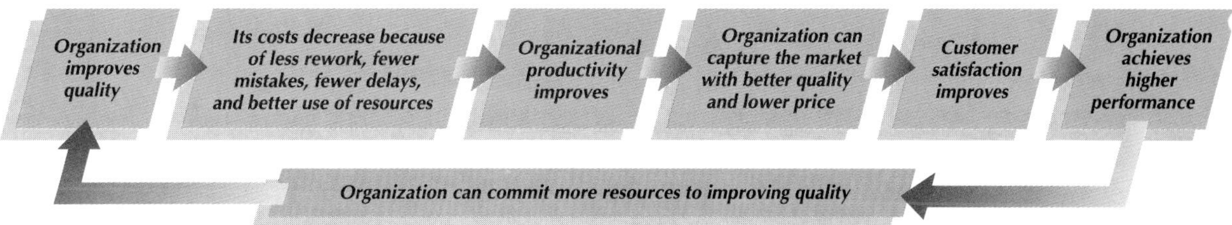

MANAGEMENT AND QUALITY

Perhaps no other management issue has received as much attention in recent years as quality, although it is hardly a new issue. In the 1950s, Japanese companies turned to the quality teachings of W. Edwards Deming and J. M. Juran, both of the United States, to rebuild industrial strength by reversing the country's former reputation for making cheap, inferior products. At the time, U.S. industry generally set the worldwide standard for quality, but within 20 years, Japanese firms had snatched the title of quality leader and were rapidly widening the gap. The proof of Japan's quality achievements was evident all around the world, as people drove Japanese cars, listened to Japanese stereos, and squeezed the shutter on Japanese cameras. Stung by the defection of customers rushing to buy Japanese products, manufacturers in the United States, in Europe, and elsewhere realized that good quality was a necessity, rather than a luxury, for effective global competition. Today, managers of service firms, government agencies, school systems, hospitals, and a wide variety of other organizations are also examining how they can improve quality to meet the needs of customers and constituents. Further, organizations of all types are spreading the responsibility for defining and delivering quality throughout the organization, making quality everyone's job.[14]

Dimensions of Quality

What is quality? Although the quality of goods and services can be judged in a variety of ways, Harvard professor David A. Garvin identified eight broad dimensions that describe quality from the customer's viewpoint: performance, features, reliability, conformance, durability, serviceability, aesthetics, and perceived quality.[15]

- *Performance* relates to the product's primary operating characteristics. In a manufactured product such as a car, performance would include traits such as braking, steering, and speed; in a service such as banking, performance would include traits such as accurate recording of deposits and prompt mailing of account statements. Not-for-profit Intermountain Health Care operates hospitals in Idaho, Wyoming, and Utah. Intermountain is boosting the quality of its performance by identifying and eliminating variations in medical care so that all patients receive uniformly high-quality attention in surgical procedures as well as in preoperative and postoperative care.[16] This increase in performance quality is important to Intermountain customers.
- *Features* are the characteristics that supplement the product's basic functionality. In a manufactured product such as an upholstered sofa, features include choice of color and fabric; in a service such as airline transportation, features include complimentary soft drinks and reserved seating. Sulzer Brothers, a Zurich-based producer of industrial weaving and papermaking equipment, has added features such as electronic ordering and customer training to boost quality.[17]
- *Reliability* refers to the probability that the product will not malfunction or fail within a specific, reasonable period. In a manufactured product such as an electronic cash register, reliability allows continuous use without time lost for repair; in a service such as car repair, reliability means that the repair corrects the original problem and does not lead to other repairs. This dimen-

sion of quality applies to products that are used for some time rather than to products such as hamburgers and haircuts that are instantly consumed. In Germany, for instance, customers who buy BMW cars enjoy the reliability of driving thousands of miles at 120 miles per hour without a breakdown.[18]

- *Conformance* is the degree to which a product's design and operating characteristics conform to established standards and specifications. In a manufactured product such as paper, conformance involves meeting standards of size and thickness; in a service such as tax accounting, conformance means accurately applying the appropriate statutes. Unprecedented conformance to high standards has helped Lanxide, a tiny materials company in Delaware, capture the market for reinforced ceramics and metals used in mining and in airplane engines. Lanxide's secret is a new way of avoiding the surface blemishes that formerly plagued these materials.[19]
- *Durability* is a measure of product life or the amount of use received from a product (including necessary repairs) before it deteriorates to the point where it must be replaced. In a manufactured product such as a light bulb, durability refers to the length of time the bulb gives off light before it burns out; in a service such as a certificate of deposit, durability refers to the period a customer can leave money on deposit before the rate becomes so unattractive that the customer must switch to another investment to receive a better rate. The durability of A.T. Cross's pens and pencils is legendary: although they are backed with a lifetime guarantee, fewer than 2 percent ever need repair.[20]
- *Serviceability* relates to the speed, courtesy, proficiency, and ease of repair associated with servicing a product. In a manufactured product such as a washing machine, serviceability involves rapid, competent repair; in a service such as payroll processing, serviceability relates to the prompt and courteous resolution of errors. The United States Automobile Association (USAA), an insurance firm, enhances serviceability by promoting a toll-free phone number for customer inquiries and by using an electronic imaging system that stores policies, letters, and other documents so that representatives can quickly call them up when resolving customer problems.[21]
- *Aesthetics* refers to the look, feel, sound, smell, and taste of a product. This dimension of quality is subjective and varies from customer to customer. In a processed food such as orange juice, aesthetics include color, consistency, acidity, and aroma; in a service such as a retail store, aesthetics involves the physical look and the furnishings of the store. For example, the Tiroler Schmuckkastl, a jewelry store in Seefeld, Austria, displays its merchandise interspersed with handpainted Tirolean decorations, creating an ambience that conveys high quality.[22]
- *Perceived quality* relates to customers' subjective judgments of the quality of goods and services, even though these judgments are sometimes based on incomplete or undocumented information. In a manufactured product such as a stereo amplifier, perceived quality can mean brand image and past experience with a similar product; in a service such as a dental clinic, perceived quality might relate to neighborhood reputation and the advice of friends. Consider the perceived quality of Federal Express's service: loyal customers are sold on the company's ability to absolutely, positively deliver a package overnight.[23] On the other hand, Ford and the other U.S. automakers will continue to battle perceived quality concerns for years, even after they reach technical parity with international competitors, because of bad experiences buyers had with their cars in the past.

Motorcycle owners are concerned with several dimensions of product quality, but the most important dimension is performance, including such primary operating characteristics as speed, braking, handling, and gas mileage. Yamaha and other manufacturers sponsor racers as a way of demonstrating their motorcycles' superior performance.

EXHIBIT 21.2

Competing on the Basis of Quality

Organizations can choose to compete on the basis of one or more of the eight dimensions of quality. Motorola promotes the quality of its cellular telephones by emphasizing their durability.

Although all eight dimensions contribute to the customer's overall assessment of a product's quality, a product does not have to be the best in every dimension to be considered better quality than competing products. In fact, improving quality in one dimension may cause a deterioration in quality in another dimension. For instance, adding features to a television set may lower reliability, because the set now contains more parts and more connections that can potentially malfunction or fail. Therefore, managers must consider which dimensions are most important to their customers and then compete only on the basis of those key dimensions, being sure to consistently deliver what they promise (see Exhibit 21.2). For example, Chrysler has decided to emphasize performance, conformance, and aesthetics in its sporty Viper model. The car boasts a powerful V-10 engine and handles like a race car, able to accelerate to 100 miles per hour and then come to a stop, all within 15 seconds. The sleek lines enhance the car's aesthetics. However, the two-seater was not designed to compete on features; it lacks all-wheel drive and other features typically found on expensive sports cars.[24]

Improving Quality

Once managers have determined the appropriate quality dimensions for their goods and services, they next consider how their organizations will consistently deliver this quality. Methods of quality assurance and quality control are generally used to establish and monitor quality standards throughout operational areas, but an increasing number of organizations are working to improve quality throughout the organization. To do so, they can apply a wide variety of approaches that extend beyond traditional operations management techniques and that involve managers and employees inside as well as outside the operations function. Among these approaches are quality circles and quality-improvement teams, total quality management, and benchmarking. In addition, organizations can apply for national quality awards or use award standards to improve quality.

Quality Circles and Quality-Improvement Teams

A **quality circle** (QC) is a small group of employees from one organizational unit who meet regularly to discuss and find solutions to quality problems in their area of responsibility. Quality circles typically consist of 4 to 12 volunteers (employees and often one or more managers) who meet on a continuing basis to identify quality problems, collect and analyze data, and then consider alternatives and implement solutions. Many organizations support QCs by providing members with special training in group dynamics, decision making, and statistical techniques for quality control. Quality circles have been popular in Japan since 1962, but they were not introduced in the United States until the 1970s, when Lockheed executives visited Japan and observed QCs in operation. Bringing the technique back to the United States, Lockheed later reported that its 15 QCs not only improved quality but saved the company nearly $3 million at the same time.[25]

quality circle (QC) A group of people from a single organizational unit who meet regularly to find solutions to quality problems in their area of responsibility

However, not every organization is successful with the QC technique. QCs are less effective when top managers see QCs as a quick fix, stand-alone solution to quality problems, or when organizations rush to start QCs without first laying a foundation of training and trust among employees and managers. Employees weary from management's previous well-intentioned but often short-lived attempts to improve quality may be unenthusiastic. Middle managers may also balk, unwilling to invite employee participation or to implement employee suggestions. Without guidance or goals, QCs sometimes focus on inappropriate or trivial problems, and they can wither from lack of management attention. To have a long-term effect, QCs must be seen as a top-management priority, and they must be integrated into the organization's structure, strategy, culture, and decision-making processes.[26]

For example, although CEO James Humphrey set quality priorities and paved the way for QCs by holding several meetings with employees to explain the process, QCs got off to a rocky start at Nelson Metal Products in Grandville, Michigan. The company did not train all its managers and employees in the technique, so some were unsupportive. Also, Humphrey started too many circles at once, so when many requested help from maintenance and other support units, those units became overwhelmed and could not immediately respond, leaving the QCs feeling ignored. Undaunted, Nelson managers revamped the process, demonstrated their support by personally participating in QCs, and empowered QCs to go after problems throughout the company. Ultimately, QCs helped Nelson cut its defect rate from 2,500 per million to fewer than 10 per million.[27]

quality-improvement team (QIT) A group of people from several departments who meet to solve quality problems that cut across functional or departmental lines

In some organizations, the quality circle has been supplanted by the **quality-improvement team** (QIT), a small group of employees and managers drawn from several departments who meet to discuss and solve quality problems that cut across functional or departmental lines. Federal Express, Xerox, and other organizations use QITs to find and solve a variety of quality problems. These QITs may be formed spontaneously to tackle specific quality issues, or they may serve on an ongoing basis. In contrast to quality circles, which focus on solving quality problems within a single work unit or area of responsibility, QITs work on quality issues that involve more than one work unit or function.[28]

Total Quality Management

total quality management (TQM) A comprehensive approach that involves building quality into every organizational process

Total quality management (TQM), also known as *total quality control,* is a comprehensive approach that involves building quality into every organizational process (see Exhibit 21.3). As such, TQM often involves quality circles and quality-improvement teams. Top managers who adopt the TQM approach recognize that quality is the responsibility of every organization member and should be built into all internal processes that directly or indirectly relate to customer satisfaction. Customer satisfaction comes at the end of a chain of internal transformation processes in which one department provides output that serves as input for the next department; for instance, purchasing provides raw materials to the production department, which in turn provides the finished goods that marketers sell to customers. TQM instills quality in every link of this chain by making each person responsible for supplying the next person in the process with quality output, whether it is an accurate cost accounting, a compelling sales brochure, or a sturdy product package.[29]

EXHIBIT 21.3 Total Quality Management: 14 Points

These 14 points, based on the work of W. Edwards Deming, can help managers improve their goods and services through total quality management.

1. Create constancy of purpose for the improvement of goods and services. **The organization should constantly strive to improve quality, productivity, and customer satisfaction to improve performance today and tomorrow.**
2. Adopt a new philosophy to reject mistakes and negativism. **Customers, managers, and employees all need to change their attitudes toward unacceptable work quality and sullen service.**
3. Cease dependence on mass inspection. **Instead of inspecting products after production to weed out bad quality, improve the process to build in good quality.**
4. End the practice of awarding business on price alone. **Create long-term relationships with suppliers who can deliver the best quality.**
5. Improve constantly and forever the system of production and service. **Improvement is not a one-time effort; managers must lead the way to continuous improvement of quality, productivity, and customer satisfaction.**
6. Institute training. **Train all organization members to do their jobs consistently well.**
7. Institute leadership. **Managers must provide the leadership to help employees do a better job.**
8. Drive out fear. **Create an atmosphere in which employees are not afraid to ask questions or to point out problems.**
9. Break down barriers between units. **Ensure that people in organizational departments or units do not have conflicting goals and are able to work as a team to achieve overall goals.**
10. Eliminate slogans, exhortations, and targets for the work force. **These alone cannot help anyone do a better job, and they imply that employees could do better if they tried harder; instead, management should provide methods for improvement.**
11. Eliminate numerical quotas. **Quotas count only finished units, not quality or methods, and they generally lead to defective goods, wasted resources, and demoralized employees.**
12. Remove barriers to pride in work. **Most people want to do a good job but are prevented from doing so by misguided management, poor communication, faulty equipment, defective materials, and other barriers that managers must remove to improve quality.**
13. Institute a vigorous program of education and retraining. **Both managers and employees have to be educated in the new quality methods.**
14. Take action to accomplish the transformation. **With top-management commitment, have the courage to make the changes throughout the organization that will improve quality.**

J. M. Juran defines TQM as three processes: quality planning, quality control, and quality improvement; he refers to these processes as the *Juran Trilogy.* In Juran's model, quality planning involves identifying the organization's customers and their needs, developing products to meet those needs, and developing processes that can produce the products. Quality control is the process of comparing actual product performance to desired performance and taking action on any discrepancies. Quality improvement aims to continually raise performance through, for example, improving the organization's infrastructure so that it can more easily produce quality results and diagnosing, then solving, recurring quality problems.[30]

Rosetta Riley, director of continuous improvement processes with General Motors, helped Cadillac implement total quality management to boost quality and responsiveness to customer needs. Under TQM, executives call five Cadillac buyers every week to learn more about their likes and dislikes; this feedback is then incorporated into car design plans. Cadillac's TQM system earned the Malcolm Baldrige National Quality Award in 1990.

W. Edwards Deming and Walter Shewhart also stressed the need for continuous quality improvement in their model, which became known as the *Deming cycle,* or the *PDCA cycle,* where PDCA stands for "plan, do, check, act and analyze." The steps represent planning a product that will meet customer needs, making it, checking it during manufacturing to be sure that it will meet customer needs, marketing the product, then analyzing how effectively the product met those customer needs. The cycle starts over again when insights gained from the analysis are fed back into the planning process.[31]

TQM is spreading around the world. Among the international devotees are Ciba-Geigy, Toyota, Fiat, and Four Seasons Hotels; in the United States, TQM users include Ford, H.J. Heinz, Procter & Gamble, the city of Portland (Oregon), and many branches of the U.S. government. In fact, the U.S. Navy's commitment to TQM covers a wide range of installations, from shipyards to ships at sea. At Cherry Point, a naval aviation depot in North Carolina that maintains and repairs Navy aircraft, TQM has replaced traditional quality-control inspections. By building in quality throughout the maintenance and repair process, Cherry Point has reduced the number of defects from as many as ten per aircraft to as few as one for every two planes. However, to implement TQM in every installation, commanding officers will have to foster closer collaboration between officers and enlisted personnel by breaking down some of the communication barriers in the Navy's rigid hierarchical structure.[32]

A related quality-improvement process that is gaining momentum is **quality function deployment (QFD)**, a powerful tool for designing directly into products those features that meet customer needs and expectations. Quality function deployment allows organizations to translate customer wants (as identified by salespeople, marketing research, and customer communications) into product specifications, ensuring that the product meets quality standards set by customers, not by managers. In Japan, chipmaker NEC IC Microcomputer Systems applies QFD by charting customer needs, relating those needs to quality specifications, and then engineering the chips to meet those specifications. As a result, NEC chips function exactly as customers expect.[33]

quality function deployment (QFD) The process of designing customer needs and expectations directly into product quality

Although specific quality goals may vary, an increasing number of organizations are using TQM to target *six sigma,* a measure of quality equivalent to 99.9997 percent defect-free products, or just 3.4 defects per million products made. George M. C. Fisher, chairman of Motorola, is using TQM to pursue six-sigma quality in processes and products throughout the company. He has made manufacturing quality 150 times better by applying TQM, and he has also used TQM to reduce the number of errors in Motorola service manuals to a quality level of 5.8 sigma, or only 10 defects per million manuals. Fisher may soon declare a more challenging goal: quality equivalent to only 60 defects per *billion.*[34]

zero defects Being completely defect-free

continuous-improvement process A continuous cycle of improvements that result in ever-higher levels of quality

As close to perfect as six sigma may be, the ultimate quality goal is to achieve **zero defects,** completely defect-free products. After all, if 99.9 percent quality were acceptable, then 16,000 pieces of mail would be lost every hour by the U.S. Postal Service; 22,000 checks would be deducted from the wrong bank accounts every hour; and people would suffer nearly an hour's worth of unsafe drinking water every month. In search of zero defects, many organizations adopt an approach known as a **continuous-improvement process,** an unending cycle of improvements that result in ever-higher levels of quality. Even when organizations have achieved virtually defect-free quality, they can continue to improve in other areas by slashing production or delivery times or by providing customers with more choices for the same price or for a lower price. Consider how Mac Connection, a mail-order retailer selling software and parts for Macintosh computers, uses the continuous-improvement process approach. First the company cut its time for shipping customer orders from three days to overnight. Next, it improved its order-processing system to allow customers who order by 3 a.m. to receive their orders by 4 p.m. the same day. Then the firm revamped its telephone ordering system to speed the time needed to place an order; now customers spend only 60 seconds calling in a telephone order.[35]

Benchmarking

benchmarking Comparing an organization's processes and products to the world's best and then matching or exceeding that quality

Another way that managers can improve quality is through **benchmarking,** the process of comparing an organization's processes and products to the standards of the world's best and then working to match or exceed those standards. Managers who apply quality benchmarks seek out and emulate the best anywhere in the world, not just in their own industry or their own country, so that they can gain competitive superiority, not just competitive parity. This means rating the manufacturing process, product development, distribution, and other key functions against those of acknowledged leaders; analyzing how these role models achieve their outstanding results; and then applying that knowledge to make quality improvements. Among the world-class organizations frequently cited as benchmarks are Toyota, IBM, and Hewlett-Packard for production; L.L. Bean and Federal Express for distribution; American Express and Nordstrom for customer service; and Xerox for benchmarking programs themselves.[36]

By going outside their own industry for key benchmarks, organizations can often identify and emulate quality practices that far exceed those of competitors. For example, when GTE's customers complained that the firm's telephone-service billing system was confusing, GTE managers used benchmarks to identify the performance leader in billing, American Express. As a result, the company developed a billing system so superior that competitors are paying GTE to help them with similar installations.[37]

An effective benchmarking program starts with the measurement and analysis of the organization's own processes, practices, and products, providing a basis for comparison. Once managers understand their organization's performance, they can seek out the quality leaders. In addition, they may make site visits to gain an in-depth understanding of the benchmark processes, and they may share ideas and expertise in exchange for this help. However, benchmarking doesn't end once the role model's processes have been adapted to fit the organization's unique situation. The standards of quality performance never stand still—customers expect quality to get better and better—so organizations cannot rest even when they have achieved their targets. Therefore, benchmarking is most effective when applied as part of a continuous-improvement process.[38]

National Quality Awards

Following the guidelines of various national quality awards is another way organizations can improve quality. In Japan, the Deming Prize is a highly regarded industrial quality award named in honor of quality pioneer W. Edwards Deming. In the United States, the Malcolm Baldrige National Quality Award honors the quality achievements of U.S. companies. Another coveted quality award is the Shingo Prize for Excellence in Manufacturing, named for Dr. Shigeo Shingo, who helped Toyota develop its renowned production system and JIT controls. The Shingo Prize is open to North American companies and to researchers and students who further the knowledge of quality manufacturing techniques.[39]

Applying for one of these quality awards can spur an organization to achieve higher quality levels; even when an organization doesn't win, its managers can learn how to improve by measuring their performance against the rigorous award requirements. Electronics supplier Solectron, based in San Jose, California, applied three times for the Baldrige, using the application process to gauge its quality achievements and to chart a path for improved quality. Feedback from Baldrige examiners helped Solectron executives pinpoint specific areas for improvement and, on its third try, Solectron won a Baldrige for quality improvement in manufacturing. Many organizations request award applications solely to guide their efforts in quality improvement, not because they plan to apply. Because the Baldrige emphasizes such values as integration of quality into daily operations, superior customer satisfaction, and concrete results such as market share gains, those who use the guidelines as a blueprint for quality can make dramatic improvements.[40]

Despite the many benefits, competing for a national quality award can be expensive, time-consuming, and stressful. Xerox estimates it spent roughly $800,000 applying for the Baldrige; Marlow Industries, a $13 million company, spent far less ($140,000) but invested much time installing quality procedures and preparing to apply. Applying for the Deming Prize put enormous pressure on nearly everyone working for NEC Tohoku in Japan. This maker of telephone switches and computer accessories prepared 244,000 pages of quality improvement and measurement plans and reports in its quest for the Deming. Hisaei Kikuchi, NEC Tohoku's president, also set a six-month deadline for filling all orders on time, improving financial measures, and reducing defect costs; employees and managers worked feverishly to achieve these goals. Using TQM, the company reduced product defects, improved production processes, and increased customer satisfaction. In the end, Kikuchi, like many national quality award winners, found that his firm had achieved more than just a medal: the company had earned national acclaim, had impressed current and potential customers, and, above all, had made better quality the cornerstone of an aggressive, profitable new growth strategy.[41]

MANAGEMENT AROUND THE WORLD

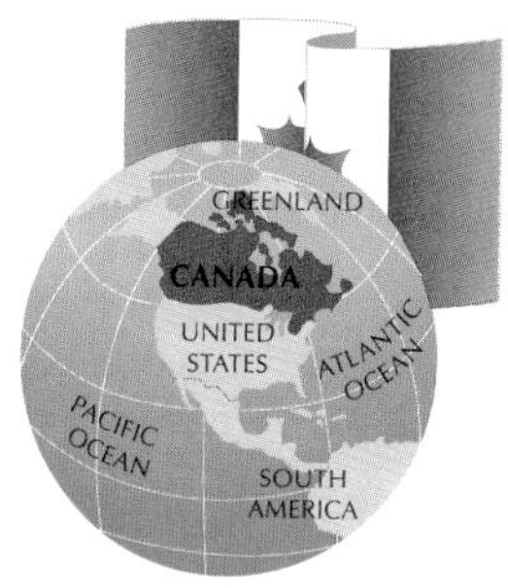

The Canadian government added a "quality" category to the Canada Awards for Business Excellence, thus joining a growing list of countries that sponsor national quality awards to stimulate increased efforts toward quality throughout the business community.

MANAGEMENT AND PRODUCTIVITY

When managers focus on improving quality, they often wind up with better productivity because their costs go down and their efficiency goes up. But pro-

MANAGERIAL DECISION MAKING

Winning Isn't Everything

Since the Malcolm Baldrige National Quality Award was established in 1987, hundreds of companies have applied, but only a handful have been chosen, including corporate giants such as Motorola and Federal Express. So when John Wallace accepted the Baldrige in 1990, his Houston-based Wallace Company basked in the acclaim. This $90 million distributor of pipes, valves, and fittings had proven that even a small firm can implement a world-class quality-management program.

Wallace's quality journey took five years and an investment of nearly $2 million. The firm reaped rewards in functions ranging from delivery to billing. On-time deliveries climbed from 75 percent to 92 percent, new safety procedures yielded $500,000 in savings, and market share climbed from 10 percent to 18 percent. Despite these impressive accomplishments, Wallace lost $690,000 the year it received the award and, within months, laid off 25 percent of the work force. Ultimately, the cash-flow squeeze became so severe that Wallace was forced to file for bankruptcy. How could this happen to a firm so recently honored for its quality management?

Although there are no easy answers, Wallace believes that the quality campaign did help the company: "Without the quality program, we wouldn't have made it this far." His quest for quality started in 1985, when two struggling competitors were acquired by new owners with the financial resources to compete more aggressively. Wallace saw quality as a good way to differentiate his firm, but his decision was also influenced by Celanese, a Wallace customer that had cut back on the number of suppliers it used and asked its remaining suppliers to become involved in the quality movement.

At first, Wallace executives ran the program themselves, but they soon turned to specialists to plan and conduct the in-depth training that helped employees gain the skills needed for quality management. Top managers taught some of the training sessions, demonstrating their commitment to the program. After training, associates formed cross-functional teams to tackle a variety of company problems. Every department was scrutinized, and the teams found 72 methods to improve quality, including standardizing the billing procedure and finding new ways to load delivery trucks.

ductivity alone is also an important issue for managers everywhere. In today's global marketplace, where organizations increasingly cross national borders to compete for resources and for customers, managers must find ways of using their inputs more efficiently to produce outputs.[42] Managers in government and not-for-profit organizations face ever-increasing pressures to improve productivity, since the demand for many such services continues to grow while budgets remain tight.

Productivity can be measured in national, organizational, and individual terms. At the national level, industrial productivity is often calculated using measures such as total domestic product output per employed person (which focuses on the overall production per person employed within that country) or output per hour of labor (which focuses on the overall production achieved during one hour's work within that country). National productivity is one of the key factors in a country's standard of living: when companies produce more from the same resources, they can make more products available to the nation's citizens; and when they produce enough to export to other countries, they earn more financial resources, which can be used to hire more employees and to attract more resources to further increase output. Thus, an upward productivity cycle raises the nation's standard of living, whereas a downward trend in productivity dampens the standard of living. Moreover, if another nation holds a productivity advantage, it can generally offer products of the same or better quality for lower prices, attracting trade at the expense of other nations.[43]

At the organizational level, productivity is generally measured according to

With the program under way, Wallace managers decided to try for the coveted Baldrige Award. The application process was a grueling exercise—applicants must submit 75 pages of data—and after Wallace had been named a finalist, the company had to submit to an on-site inspection. Once Wallace received the award, the company's commitment of time and money didn't end, because winners are required to help spread the word about quality. Thus, while some Wallace managers crisscrossed the country making presentations, others fielded as many as 80 inquiries per day and conducted plant tours for would-be Baldrige contenders.

Meanwhile, Wallace hiked its prices, and the recessionary economy took its toll. As sales started to sag throughout the industry, the company lost its share of orders, although it did retain its customers. Then its only lender started experiencing difficulties and so, just months after winning, Wallace had to scramble for financing. Even as its executives preached the glories of quality, the company was fending off creditors. Looking back, the drive to win the Baldrige and the requirement to tell the story over and over again seem to have distracted the company and added to its problems. "We were so busy doing the presentations that we weren't following up and getting the sales," admits the chairman. At this point, the firm is positive about its future and confident that a return from bankruptcy is just around the corner.

Wallace and other firms have realized that winning the Baldrige is no guarantee that a company has solved all its problems or that it can compete more effectively. The award assesses only the quality-management process; it does not review financial performance, product quality, or customer satisfaction. However, the General Accounting Office studied 20 high-scoring applicants and concluded that most have benefited from the experience. In these firms, customer complaints have decreased, order-processing time has improved, and market share has increased. For Baldrige aspirants, winning isn't everything; the discipline of applying a formal quality-management process may well be the most important reward of all.

Apply Your Knowledge

1. If required to do so, how could Wallace prove to Baldrige examiners that its product quality and customer satisfaction were top-notch?
2. How might Wallace use benchmarking to improve the quality of its nonproduction procedures?

standards such as sales per employee or product output per square foot, and measures can also be used to compare the productivity of units within the organization. Similar to the way the productivity cycle works for nations, a highly productive organization can offer more goods and services, and at lower prices, and can therefore earn more profits to reinvest in resource inputs and to fuel continued growth, thus competing effectively against its rivals. Finally, individual productivity is the basic building block for organizational and national productivity, and it is calculated according to such measures as daily production output or number of forms processed per hour.[44]

Productivity is no longer confined to the factory floor: service businesses, government agencies, hospitals, and other nonmanufacturing organizations are actively seeking productivity improvements, and manufacturing organizations are looking for new efficiencies in finance, in accounting, in marketing, in human resources, and in other nonproduction departments. However, when managers try to boost productivity quickly by cutting costs, they must take care to preserve both quality and customer satisfaction, or they risk losing customers and profits. Managers of the Japanese theme park SpaResort Hawaiians once tried to boost efficiency through money-saving actions such as lowering the room temperature in an indoor swimming area. Customer complaints about that and other cost-cutting measures went largely unanswered until top management began to question the dropoff in visitors. Only by identifying customer needs and then setting and meeting quality and productivity goals could SpaResorts reverse the slide. The company has since won a Deming Prize for its

Advanced-technology infant monitoring equipment has improved productivity and the quality of health care at Stanford Hospital's newborn intensive care unit. The nurses are freed from routinely checking infants' vital signs; sensors automatically detect any changes in the infants' vital signs and alert nurses so they can respond.

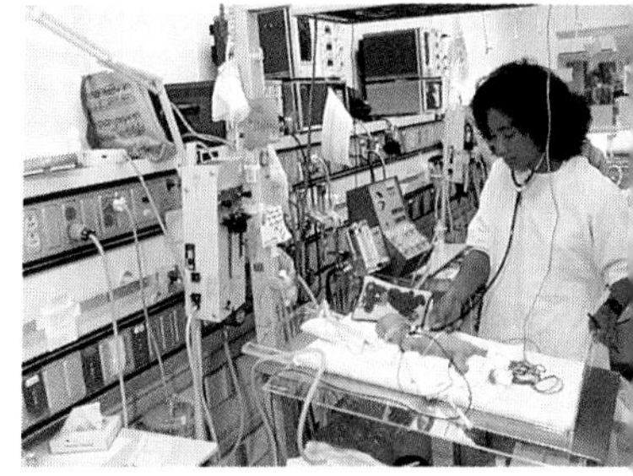

exacting attention to quality, and its productivity and customer satisfaction levels have also improved.[45]

Productivity Trends

Although U.S. productivity remains high in absolute terms, growth in productivity has been lagging. Since 1950, national productivity as measured by hourly manufacturing output has improved very slowly in the United States, compared with the dramatic increases scored by Japan (see Exhibit 21.4). In just 16 years, from 1973 to 1989, United States productivity (as measured by average annual increase in output per hour) rose only 2.6 percent, less than half the 5.5 percent increase attained by Japan. Consider how productivity relates to automobile manufacturing. A recent survey found that a plant in Japan takes an average of 19.1 hours to manufacture a car. The same car requires 19.5 hours to build in a Japanese-managed plant in the United States, but it requires nearly 40 percent more time, a total of 26.5 hours, to build in a U.S.-managed plant in the United States. Further, U.S. productivity lags not just in manufacturing but also in product development: compared with Japanese industry, U.S. firms take nearly twice as long to design, produce, and market a product, and they require more engineers, too. Clearly, these disparities affect the ability of U.S. manufacturers to compete in world markets.[46]

Service productivity in the United States has also been growing, but more slowly than manufacturing. U.S. government figures show that productivity in services barely achieved an annual increase of 1 percent from 1979 to 1988. The greatest service productivity gains were achieved by telecommunications, securities, and retailing, whereas health services and legal services fared worst. Some of the gains in service productivity can be attributed to automation: in the securities industry, for example, computerization has allowed businesses to keep up with a fivefold increase in stock market transactions during the 1980s.[47]

EXHIBIT 21.4

International Productivity Trends

Growth in manufacturing productivity in the United States has lagged behind other countries. Although U.S. manufacturing productivity has increased since 1950, productivity gains in Japan and in West Germany (prior to unification) have been more dramatic.

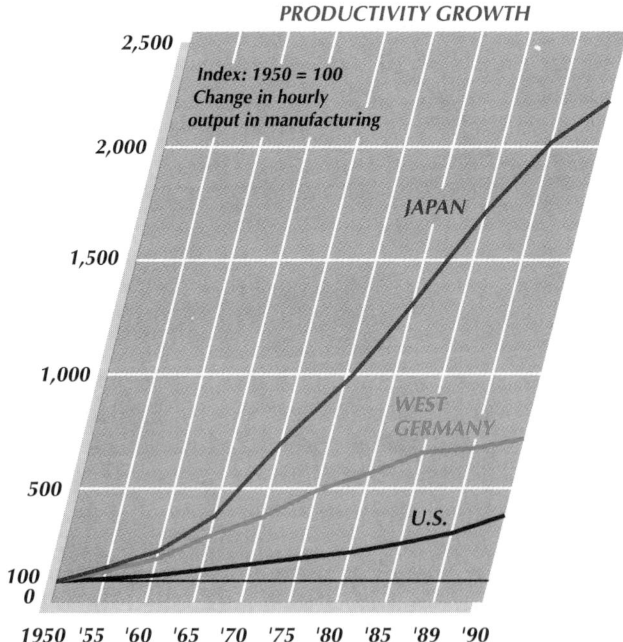

Although productivity improvements are as important to service providers as they are to manufacturers, the reported slow growth in service productivity may not reflect the impact of needed quality and customer service improvements. For instance, many self-service supermarkets in the United States are adding full-service deli counters, salad bars, and other services that require more employee attention, so their productivity as measured by the number of employee hours (input) per sales dollar (output) looks worse. In actuality, these supermarkets are offering a higher level of quality and service, which is not reflected in established productivity measures but contributes to higher customer satisfaction, ultimately affecting profitability. Therefore, managers should understand the quality as well as the quantity represented by productivity figures.[48]

Improving Productivity

Given current trends in productivity and their potential impact on organizational performance, how can managers improve productivity? They can start by designing and applying productivity measurements and goals that are appropriate for their organization's inputs, transformation processes, and outputs. Once managers have determined what to measure and how to measure it, they can set meaningful goals and use both operational and human resource approaches to improve productivity.

Meaningful Productivity Measurements and Goals

National-level measures of productivity, such as the ratio of countrywide production output to employee hours invested, are helpful when economists and public policy officials want an overview of the current health of an industry or of a nation as compared with prior periods. But on the organizational, divisional, or departmental level, managers have to gear their productivity measurements to the specific activities and results that affect their own organization's efficiency. Many organizations use the total factor productivity ratio (see Chapter 20) as a gauge of overall productivity; then they apply partial factor productivity ratios to a range of individual activities. For example, Beatrice Foods applies partial factor productivity measurements to a wide range of organizational activities. To measure employee productivity, the firm uses ratios such as sales per employee and sales per payroll dollar; to analyze energy productivity, it uses such measures as units of goods produced per cubic foot of gas consumed and units of goods produced per kilowatt hour of electricity consumed. At Pemex, the Mexican state-owned oil producer, Director-General Francisco Rojas uses productivity measures to compare efficiency among its various geographic units as well as with outside competitors. Such comparisons have helped Rojas identify numerous productivity improvements, saving $1 billion over four years.[49]

To properly gauge productivity, managers must be sure that their measures are valid, complete, comparable, inclusive, timely, and cost-effective (see Exhibit 21.5). With meaningful productivity measures in place, managers can go ahead and set productivity goals for their key activities to improve productivity on an organizationwide basis as well as within individual organizational units. For instance, citing global competition, General Electric is pushing for overall annual productivity increases of 5 to 6 percent from its various businesses; division and department managers at Beatrice Foods and Honeywell are required to set productivity goals for their own units. As with any goals, productivity goals must be challenging, attainable, specific and measurable, time defined, and rele-

EXHIBIT 21.5

Meaningful Productivity Measures

The only effective way for managers to monitor their productivity and track improvements over time is by constructing meaningful measures. These key questions help managers create the measures they need.

Characteristic	Key Management Question
Validity	Does the measure accurately reflect fluctuations in productivity?
Completeness	Does the measure cover all the appropriate components of output and input rather than a select few?
Comparability	Can the measure be used to accurately compare productivity between various periods so that changes can be detected?
Inclusiveness	Are separate measures being used to examine all the significant activities of an organization, not just strictly operational processes?
Timeliness	Can data for each measure be gathered and analyzed in time for management to take action to solve productivity problems?
Cost-effectiveness	Does the value of the measurement outweigh the cost of measuring and reporting?

vant (see Chapter 7). When AT&T started developing a new cordless telephone for the consumer market, company executives realized that they had to use time more efficiently if the phone was to reach the market ahead of competitors. Managers set the ambitious productivity goal of slashing product-development time by 50 percent, and they delegated design, production, and marketing authority to a series of cross-functional teams but set strict deadlines for accomplishing each task. As a result, AT&T cut development time from two years to one, reduced product costs, and improved quality, all at the same time.[50]

Operational Approaches to Improved Productivity

To meet productivity improvement goals, managers can apply one or more operational approaches that focus on production techniques, process refinements, and new technology. Such approaches can take a variety of forms, including automating standardized manufacturing or service processes, decreasing changeover time (the time required to switch a factory from producing one product to producing another), and reducing the number of steps necessary to create or deliver a product. An important way of uncovering new ideas for improving operational productivity is to invest in research and development. But using R&D to develop incremental improvements to existing processes is only the first step. To maintain a competitive edge, effective managers look beyond short-term productivity improvements to nurture research into advanced technology that can potentially revolutionize operations in the future.[51]

Automation and new technology often promise dramatic productivity improvements, but by themselves they cannot achieve productivity goals; the underlying operational processes must be streamlined and free from trouble spots first. Moreover, automation is not always practical or even necessary when simplifying or reconfiguring the existing operations can boost productivity. William P. Conlin, president of CalComp, demonstrated this when he was struggling to stay afloat making graphics plotters that create engineering drawings. A bigger competitor brought out a faster, cheaper plotter, hammering CalComp's sales and its profits. To fight back, Conlin had to boost productivity and raise profits, all on a strict budget. He dispensed with his traditional straight-line assembly arrangement and installed a series of small U-shaped assembly areas. Less time is now lost in moving goods between stations, and because employees work so closely, they can more easily communicate to resolve quality and production issues as they arise. Conlin spent $300,000 but raised CalComp's productivity by 50 percent and lowered production costs by 30 percent.[52]

Time has become an increasingly important element in managers' efforts to improve productivity through operational efficiencies. Simply put, compressing the operational cycle by speeding the planning, ordering, production, and delivery of products promotes more efficient use of resources. One benefit of shorter total cycle time is faster feedback about sales, so the organization can quickly adjust its resources and production to meet expected demand. Another benefit is that managers receive early warnings about quality so that they can quickly find and correct any problems early in the production cycle, before large batches of products have been completed. Finally, when organizations do not need long lead times to make new products or to switch from making one to making another, they can react more quickly and flexibly to changes in customer needs.[53]

For maximum productivity, organizations should investigate the entire process, from supplier to customer, to implement improvements that unclog supply, production, and distribution bottlenecks, pare unneeded inventory, and assure a continuous flow of products. For example, GM's Inland-Fisher Guide division in Grand Rapids, Michigan, makes automotive seat covers. It is the center link in a transformation process that starts with inputs from yarn producers and fabric manufacturers and ends when the plant's seat covers are shipped to other facilities to be fitted onto seats and installed in new cars. At one time, the cycle from yarn manufacture to seat installation required 71 days, including waiting time when materials sat in inventory until used. Inland-Fisher managers made internal changes to compress their portion of the cycle from 18 days to 7. They cut more time by working with suppliers and with employees at the facilities who receive the seat covers to coordinate production schedules, ordering, and shipping, slicing a total of 40 days from the cycle.[54]

Human Resource Approaches to Improved Productivity

No single factor has as much potential for improving productivity as human resources. The effect of human resources on productivity is dramatically illustrated by General Motors' experience with its assembly plant in Fremont, California. Under GM management, productivity and quality were the lowest of any plant in the corporation, absenteeism among the 5,000 employees ran a dismal 20 percent, costs were 30 percent above those of Far East competitors, and the plant suffered several wildcat strikes every year. On the basis of this performance, GM decided to shut the plant and lay off employees. Several years later, Toyota and GM started a joint venture and Toyota reopened the Fremont plant, rehiring 2,500 of the laid-off employees. Within a year, the plant's quality and productivity had become the best in the corporation, absenteeism had dropped to 2 percent, costs were on a par with those of overseas competitors, and no wildcat strikes occurred. In the same plant with essentially the same work force, stunning productivity and quality gains had been achieved solely through a change in management.[55]

As GM's experience shows, more effective management of organization members can be a powerful way of improving productivity. Therefore, in an increasing number of organizations, more attention is paid to recruiting, staffing, and training people, for both management and nonmanagement jobs. Managers want to hire and develop those people who are capable of finding and implementing productivity boosters and other improvements. Savvy top managers actively invite the involvement of employees and of managers at all levels because the people closest to the process, whether in manufacturing, marketing, or any other function, are generally the most knowledgeable about how to make it more efficient. And when people are empowered to offer suggestions, to make decisions, and to take action to improve organizational productivity, they can make the vital difference between average and superior performance. For example, the top managers of Dana, a maker of truck and car parts headquartered in Toledo, Ohio, encourage their machine operators, materials handlers, and other hands-on employees to search out and implement ways of moving products more quickly and efficiently through the manufacturing process. Dana managers meet twice a year to exchange productivity improvement ideas and to compare results so that all facilities can benefit. Employee involvement has helped push Dana's productivity well above industry standards.[56]

The opportunity to make a significant contribution in the workplace motivates many organization members, whether they work individually or in teams to tackle productivity problems, and managers can encourage and reward these contributions in a variety of ways. At Florida Power & Light, employee teams are energized by having their best ideas shared at company expositions. Some organizations honor productivity champions at ceremonial dinners, and still others pay cash awards for implemented ideas. For example, city employees in Phoenix earn a reward of 10 percent of the money their productivity suggestions save, up to a maximum of $2,500, and the larger cash awards are handed out in a ceremony attended by the mayor and the city council. Another way to motivate managers and employees is through gain sharing, the method of rewarding productivity gains in which organization members receive a share of the value of productivity increases (see Chapter 14). Square D, a manufacturer of electrical equipment, bases its gain sharing on improvements in the number of quality units shipped to fill customer orders, so employees are rewarded for volume increases and for sustained quality levels.[57]

MANAGEMENT AND CUSTOMER SATISFACTION

Quality and productivity are two related paths to customer satisfaction, which is the ultimate goal and the real test of any organization's performance. Unfortunately, many businesses fail the test, according to a comprehensive study of customer satisfaction conducted for the U.S. government. About one-third of all households report having been dissatisfied with a purchase, but many don't bother complaining because they don't think it's worth the trouble. Moreover, many who do complain are not satisfied with the response. When customers are dissatisfied and when they receive unsatisfactory responses to their complaints, they defect to competitors. Over time, the potential revenue loss from defections can be considerable (see Exhibit 21.6). On the positive side, the survey showed that understanding and responding to customer dissatisfaction can dramatically increase a company's market share and profitability.[58] Of course, customer satisfaction isn't limited to the for-profit sector; not-for-profit organizations must also be concerned about customer satisfaction because their future vitality is threatened when customers are dissatisfied and seek other alternatives. To start, managers need to understand how product value relates to customer satisfaction.

If you lose	One customer per day	Five customers per day	Ten customers per day
Spending $5 weekly	$94,900	$474,500	$949,000
Spending $10 weekly	$189,800	$949,000	$1,898,000
Spending $50 weekly	$949,000	$4,745,000	$9,490,000
Spending $100 weekly	$1,898,000	$9,490,000	$18,980,000

Potential annual revenue loss from dissatisfied buyers

EXHIBIT 21.6

The High Cost of Customer Dissatisfaction

If an organization lost just one customer a day, and if each lost customer had been spending $5 per week, the possible revenue loss over a single year could be as much as $94,900—a figure that rises dramatically as the number of lost customers and the amount of their spending increase.

Product Value and Customer Satisfaction

In a sense, customers do not buy goods and services; they buy solutions to problems and the fulfillment of needs and wants. If a product doesn't solve a problem or fulfill a need or desire, it has no value to customers. A product that minimally satisfies customers is known as a **generic product** (see Exhibit 21.7). When customers can choose among many generic products that satisfy their needs, managers may differentiate their products according to **added value,** the increased worth of their products compared with that of the generic product.[59]

generic product A basic product that minimally satisfies customer needs

added value The increased worth of a product compared with the generic product

The added value may be extra features that deliver desirable benefits, special services that enhance the generic product, or distinctive feelings that the product generates in its users, such as feeling important, pampered, or entertained. Tom Wilson, CEO of the Detroit Pistons basketball organization, realizes that fans have many sports choices, so he adds value to the games with live entertainment, including celebrity free-throw contests, jugglers, and a nine-foot-high video screen flashing short animated films. Similarly, Tom Vitacco, CEO of PrintMasters, reflects the situation in many industries when he says, "The equipment is the same in most print shops. What makes you different in this business is how you treat customers." Vitacco knows that his customers have many generic product choices, so he must add value by going the extra mile in service.[60]

Wilson and Vitacco recognize the distinction between expected products and augmented products. An **expected product,** as the name implies, delivers the basic value that customers expect beyond the generic product. For PrintMasters, the expected value is transforming a customer's original document into a speci-

expected product A product that delivers the basic value that customers expect beyond the generic product

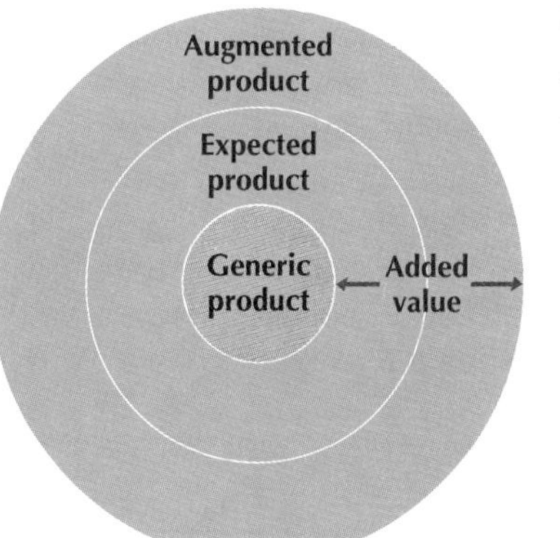

EXHIBIT 21.7

Adding Value to the Basic Product

The generic product is the minimally acceptable product that organizations must offer to be in the market. The expected product adds value that the customer has come to expect, and the augmented product adds even more value.

fied number of copies, on schedule and at the right price, which any print shop can do. An **augmented product** enhances the expected product by adding more value. PrintMasters creates an augmented product by offering delivery, graphic design advice, protective packaging, easy payment plans, and a host of other measures that increase the value received by the customer. However, augmentation is not a one-time event; as with the ongoing process used to improve quality, managers must continually reevaluate the way they augment products to be sure that the added value remains meaningful to customers and that it is sufficiently differentiated from competitors.[61]

To augment the basic product, Lerner's stores offer a multitude of payment options, a variety of fashions and accessories, and even the ambience of live in-store music. These augmentations, which vary according to local needs and competition, increase the value that Lerner's customers perceive and serve to differentiate the store from its competitors.

augmented product A product with more added value than the expected product

Improving Customer Satisfaction

To improve customer satisfaction by defining, developing, marketing, and augmenting products with the package of added value that customers desire, managers follow a five-step process: (1) understand customer expectations, (2) define and communicate customer satisfaction goals, (3) establish or upgrade the infrastructure, (4) measure customer satisfaction, and (5) evaluate results and take corrective action.

Understand Customer Expectations

The first and last measure of customer satisfaction is whether or not a product lives up to customer expectations, so the logical place to start is by understanding just what those expectations are. Through customer interviews, questionnaires, and other means, managers need to uncover what customers expect so that they can see how their products measure up. Customers have expectations about a variety of product elements, including the value/price ratio, product quality, features and benefits, warranties and guarantees, problem resolution, and the buying experience.

value/price ratio A measure of the value that customers receive as a function of the product price

- *Value/price ratio.* Naturally, customers like to get as much value as possible in return for the prices they pay. The **value/price ratio** measures the value that customers receive as a function of the product price. Organizations can increase this ratio for their products either by raising the value or by lowering the price. For example, high-style retailer Neiman-Marcus adds value by offering personalized service and other extras; discounter Sam's Warehouse improves its ratio through lower prices.[62]
- *Product quality.* Products should provide a level of quality as defined by customer needs and usage. If a customer buys a paper clip, quality might be defined as the ability to hold papers together until the clip is removed. If a customer makes a telephone call, quality would be defined as a connection that allows both parties to converse clearly and for as long as they choose without static or interruption. Quality that falls below customer needs and usage will not meet customer expectations.
- *Features and benefits.* Every customer has some minimum level of required product features, together with the benefits those features provide, and this level generally rises as more products add value to compete with the augmented products of competitors. If a product doesn't meet the minimum feature and benefit expectations of customers, it will not lead to customer satisfaction. For example, a remote control was once considered added value for a television set, but today it is part of the expected product, and customers are generally not satisfied without one.

- *Warranties and guarantees.* Nobody wants to purchase a product without some reassurance that it will live up to its promised performance and quality. A common technique is to offer to refund the purchase price or to replace or repair a defective product in the event that a product fails after purchase or does not meet customer expectations. Beyond the legal assurances they give customers, warranties and guarantees are powerful competitive tools when advertised as added value.[63]
- *Problem resolution.* How an organization responds to problems is an important point of evaluation for customers, and smart companies know that a dissatisfied customer presents an opportunity to improve. Studies show that a customer who has a problem and is satisfied with the resolution is likely to be even more loyal than a customer who routinely uses the product without trouble. When customers point out problems, managers have an opportunity to demonstrate their commitment to customer satisfaction.[64]
- *Buying experience.* Another important measure of customer satisfaction is the experience of selecting and purchasing goods and services. Making the process fast, convenient, trouble-free, and as enjoyable as possible can add value to any product. Direct Tire in Massachusetts sells tires and automotive services, and it is dedicated to making the purchase experience as fast and painless as possible, by offering loaner cars, ferrying customers whose cars are being serviced, and keeping fresh-brewed coffee in its clean, quiet waiting room.[65] Not-for-profit organizations and government agencies have their equivalents of the purchase experience, whether it's processing passport applications faster or making tax return forms easier to understand.

Define and Communicate Customer Satisfaction Goals

Once managers have determined what their customers' expectations are, they can define customer satisfaction goals. The specific goals depend on each organization's unique situation, but all customer satisfaction goals should have four attributes:

- They should be specific and meaningful statements of the organization's intentions. A goal of "fast delivery" is less specific and less meaningful than targeting "next-day delivery by 10:30 a.m."
- They should differentiate the product from its competitors. If everyone offers next-day delivery by 10:30 a.m., then an organization's customer satisfaction goals have to add value by beating that time.
- They should add value that customers want. An airline that targets "the best airline food in the world" will probably satisfy customers less than promising "five-minute check-in and boarding."
- They should be challenging but achievable. An airline cannot set a goal of "no delayed flights" because it cannot control the weather, the major reason for delays. Moreover, an organization that promises more than it can deliver will only upset its customers and frustrate its employees, but by setting high goals that are achievable, organizations encourage higher performance.[66]

When managers set and communicate ambitious customer satisfaction goals, they create expectations that their products will perform as promised. To avoid overselling or making unrealistic promises, it is important to carefully consider the specific goals and the way they are communicated to customers and to organization members. If an organization adds product value and sets goals that reflect that value, it should communicate these capabilities to customers.[67]

Establish or Upgrade the Infrastructure

Once top management has made a commitment to improving customer satisfaction, the next step is to plan how to achieve the goals. Long-term customer satisfaction is not a program, a project, or a slogan; managers need a systematic way to consistently deliver the added value and satisfy customers on an ongoing basis. This is accomplished by establishing or upgrading the *infrastructure,* which encompasses the people, training, organization structure, communication, and equipment needed to ensure customer satisfaction. An infrastructure may involve training employees to handle every service situation, or it may include an international network of sophisticated diagnostic equipment, teams of technicians, or delivery mechanisms for spare parts. Even though it already has a service infrastructure in place, Northwest Airlines announced a five-year plan to spend $422 million to improve customer satisfaction. This effort includes more flight attendants, better food, fewer canceled flights, and fewer lost bags. In fiercely competitive industries such as air travel, it makes sense for companies to differentiate themselves on customer satisfaction, justifying an investment in the infrastructure.[68]

Measure Customer Satisfaction

Once the goals, plans, and infrastructure have been established, the next step is to measure customer satisfaction. Rather than wait for dissatisfied customers to complain, managers can proactively measure satisfaction and search out existing problems as well as opportunities to improve. Similar to the way they uncover expectations, managers can measure customer satisfaction by holding personal meetings with customers, sending out questionnaires, reading complaint letters, and answering customer service hot lines (see Exhibit 21.8). For example, to measure customer satisfaction with its service and support, electronics giant Hewlett-Packard mails surveys to 40,000 customers each year, and it also contacts customers right after their equipment has been serviced. Granite Rock, a producer of concrete, asphalt, sand, and gravel, conducts an extensive customer satisfaction survey every three years. But every year, Granite Rock asks all customers to complete a short survey that rates company performance and compares it with competitors so that managers can pinpoint problems.[69]

What should be measured, of course, are elements that are important to customers. Federal Express, for instance, found through research that 12 elements are critical to customer satisfaction. It now measures performance on these indicators daily: abandoned calls (hangups before customer service agents

EXHIBIT 21.8

Measuring Customer Satisfaction

In addition to measuring customer satisfaction directly, managers can also rely on satisfaction surveys conducted by outside research firms. This table, for instance, shows how major airlines in the United States and around the world compare in terms of customer satisfaction.

U.S. Airlines	Rank	Points	International Airlines	Rank	Points
American	1	18.62	Singapore	1	25.14
Delta	2	18.12	Swissair	2	23.95
United	3	16.61	JAL	3	22.57
Midway*	4	16.54	SAS	4	22.33
Piedmont	5	15.11	Qantas	5	22.08
TWA	6	14.91	Lufthansa	6	22.05
Pan Am*	7	14.69	KLM	7	21.34
Northwest	8	13.95	British Airways	8	20.54
US Air	9	13.73	Air France	9	20.50
Continental	10	12.62	Varig	10	19.94

*No longer in business.

SOCIAL RESPONSIBILITY AND ETHICS

Employee Monitoring: Coaching or Spying?

How can organizations be sure their employees are providing service that satisfies customers? An increasing number are using monitoring techniques, either silent monitoring (where managers can record or listen in on telephone or computer contacts with customers at any time) or direct monitoring (where managers or experienced employees sit with service employees to offer assistance during the actual customer contact). Monitoring allows managers to observe how service employees deal with customers and then offer feedback to improve their performance. For example, more than 200 service specialists at the General Electric Answer Center answer over 14,000 daily telephone inquiries about GE appliances. Ten managers listen in, then play back some of the conversations to coach employees on better responses. As a result, the customer satisfaction rate for Answer Center contacts is an impressive 96 percent, and GE racks up $16 per call in appliance sales or service savings.

Monitoring is not new; AT&T, for one, has been using it for almost 100 years. In recent years, many airlines, appliance manufacturers, car-rental firms, banks, and other service firms have started using monitoring as a way of improving or maintaining customer satisfaction. However, to those whose performance is being scrutinized, monitoring may feel more like spying than coaching. Should organizations have the right to monitor employees at any time, even when those being monitored are unaware that their behavior is being studied? Not knowing when someone is watching or listening in can be stressful. As one recent study showed, the telephone operators being silently monitored reported significantly more stress-related health problems than unmonitored operators, so the way silent monitoring is used can be cause for concern among employees.

Should organizations have the right to monitor employees without their permission? Where is the line between legitimate monitoring and invasion of privacy? These are fast becoming key issues because the increasing sophistication of electronic monitoring tools multiplies the opportunities for abuse. One software program, called Peek, lets managers electronically view an employee's computer screen, but only with the employee's permission each time. Another program from the same manufacturer, called Spy, has no such restrictions; the manager can view the employee's computer screen at any time, without notice or permission. When managers cannot monitor their employees' computer screens, they may be tempted to secretly read the correspondence that employees send through the company's electronic mail system. Already, several lawsuits have been filed by employees who charge they were fired because of their electronic mail messages, despite company assurances that personal privacy would be respected.

Few laws address the specific issues raised by silent monitoring. Congress is currently considering legislation that would force organizations to give employees advance notice of silent monitoring and to use a distinctive sound or a visible cue that signals employees when they are being monitored. However, despite the potential for unethical and unauthorized usage, many experts believe that monitoring, when properly conducted, can improve the quality of customer contact and enhance customer satisfaction. Here are some guidelines for setting up a fair but effective program:

- Disclose to employees specifically why and how monitoring is being used.
- Use monitoring data to counsel employees rather than to discipline them.
- Invite seasoned employees to help develop guidelines and to coach employees with less experience.
- Measure employees by the quality, not the quantity, of their customer contacts.

What's Your Opinion?

1. Should organizations that record interactions between employees and customers advise customers that their calls are being recorded?
2. How can government agencies improve the service provided by employees such as welfare caseworkers without monitoring their professional interactions or their telephone conversations with clients?

can take a call), reopened complaints (any complaint reactivated because a customer is not satisfied with the original response), damaged packages, international services (including customs delays), requested billing adjustments, lost packages, missed pickups, missing proofs of delivery (which are promised with every bill), packages without identification, right-day late deliveries (deliveries delivered even one minute later than promised), traces (searches for proof of performance), and wrong-day late deliveries (deliveries made later than the promised date). By measuring and comparing performance against satisfaction goals, the firm uncovers problems so that it can take action to improve satisfaction.[70]

Evaluate Results and Take Corrective Action

Measurement alone cannot improve customer satisfaction; effective managers use what they learn to make the necessary changes. This means comparing performance and complaints with customer satisfaction goals to identify shortfalls, to uncover causes, and to take corrective action to eliminate the sources of dissatisfaction. For example, Federal Express received many complaints about the surcharge it once added for Saturday service, a surcharge that applied even if the customer brought the package to a Federal Express location. However, some company officials were reluctant to remove the surcharge because it provided needed revenue to cover the costs of this weekend service. After hearing the complaints and weighing the costs, Federal Express managers decided the customers were right and removed the surcharge. Within six months, Saturday service was so popular that it generated a healthy return.[71] As Federal Express proved, and as many other organizations now know, increased customer satisfaction often leads to improved financial performance.

SUMMARY

Organizations can achieve better performance today and tomorrow by focusing on four management imperatives. The first, meeting customer needs, involves attracting and retaining customers by finding out what they want and providing it. The second, increasing efficiency and effectiveness, involves using resources more efficiently while improving products to better achieve organizational goals. The third, meeting competitive challenges, relates to the organization's ability to compete with a wide variety of organizations on the local and global levels. The fourth management imperative, differentiating products, refers to the challenge of setting an organization's products apart from the competition.

Quality, productivity, and customer satisfaction are closely related. When organizations improve quality, they reduce waste, spend less time on rework, and complete tasks more quickly. This higher level of quality helps an organization use its resources more productively. Better quality also leads to higher market share, and when more units are sold, the unit cost drops, further improving productivity. The increased efficiency allows the organization to offer a better product at a reasonable price, contributing to customer satisfaction. And as more customers are satisfied, they buy more, thus increasing profitability and providing the financial resources for another round of quality and productivity improvements.

Eight broad dimensions describe quality from the customer's viewpoint: performance, features, reliability, conformance, durability, serviceability, aesthetics, and perceived quality. Organizations can improve quality by using quality circles, small groups of people from one organizational unit who meet to resolve quality problems in their area of responsibility, and by using quality-improvement teams, groups of people from several departments who meet to resolve quality problems that cut across functional or departmental lines. Another way to improve quality is through total quality management, a comprehensive approach in which quality is built into every organizational process. Managers can also improve quality through benchmarking, comparing the organization's processes and products to the world's best and then matching or exceeding those quality standards. Finally, the process of applying for national quality awards can also help managers improve quality.

To improve organizational productivity, managers first design and apply productivity measurements and goals that are appropriate for their organizational inputs, transformation processes, and outputs. Next, they use both operational and human resource approaches to improve productivity. Operational approaches focus on production techniques, process refinements, and new technology. Human resource approaches involve effective recruitment, selection, training, and management of organization members, employee and management involvement, and motivation.

Customers select products according to the product's value in fulfilling a need or solving a problem, so the degree of product value directly relates to customer satisfaction levels. A product that satisfies only minimally is a generic product, but a product that provides added value such as desirable benefits leads to higher customer satisfaction. From an expected product, customers expect basic value beyond the generic product, and from an augmented product, customers receive even more value than from an expected product. To improve customer satisfaction, managers follow a five-step process: (1) understand customer expectations, (2) define and communicate customer satisfaction goals, (3) establish or upgrade the infrastructure, (4) measure customer satisfaction, and (5) evaluate results and take corrective action.

MEETING A MANAGEMENT CHALLENGE AT FORD MOTOR COMPANY

The Ford Motor Company entered the 1980s with two years of losses totaling over $1.6 billion, and then-chairman Donald E. Petersen grew to realize that consumers were disappointed in the performance of automobiles built in the United States. He had to restore customer satisfaction by improving quality and put the company back into overdrive by increasing productivity.

One of Petersen's first moves was an appeal for help from quality guru W. Edwards Deming, who started by focusing management attention on processes and the people involved in those processes. (Petersen would later give much of the credit for Ford's turnaround to Deming.) Next, under the banner "Quality is Job 1," Petersen instituted an array of programs designed to increase quality and productivity by obtaining greater input from customers, employees, and suppliers. New consumer surveys, dubbed competitive new vehicle quality (CNVQ) studies, are reviewed twice a month at meetings that typically involve 100 Ford people and last from four to seven hours. Consumer comments are used to tune the design and performance standards of Ford cars to better provide what customers want.

An employee involvement (EI) program was designed to obtain as much input as possible from the company's employees. In the spirit of participative management, managers and employees are now expected to share power in the workplace, solving problems jointly. Every week, more than 30 of these EI teams meet to discuss new ideas for improving Ford cars. In the company's new design for a Lincoln Town Car, over 2,600 suggestions from employees were incorporated into the final product.

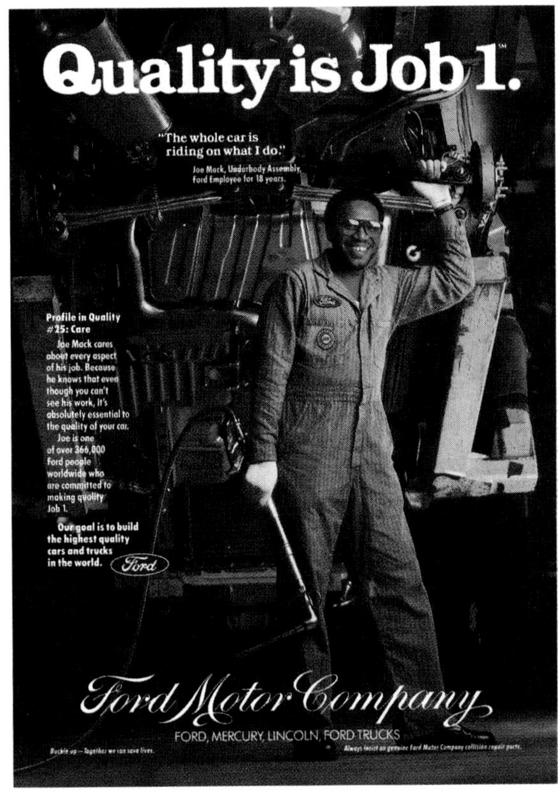

Joe Mack, underbody assembly specialist, featured in Ford ads

To improve productivity, Ford increased employees' job responsibilities. Strict union rules that prohibited workers from correcting problems outside their assigned areas have been scuttled. With the idea of fostering employee initiative as well as boosting productivity by cutting bureaucratic red tape, Petersen told managers to allow decisions to be made "at the lowest level at which expert knowledge is to be found."

Prior to the changes wrought by Petersen, Ford's relationships with its suppliers were strained. The company would play one component maker against another in a continuing effort to get lower prices. Quality suffered. Under Petersen's new philosophy, however, Ford began signing five-year contracts with single sources for nearly 90 percent of the components making up its cars, instead of engaging in short-term, adversarial relationships. And now Ford trains its key suppliers in areas such as product engineering, inventory control, quality, and productivity.

Ford began to let its suppliers design as well as manufacture the parts. Product quality improved as Ford benefited from outside expertise. Farming out the design work also cut the average time required to produce a car. That hiked productivity. So did a new round of robotics and flexible construction techniques at Ford's assembly plants.

Petersen's programs paid off handsomely. By the end of the 1980s the $84 billion corporation was reporting the best profits in the industry. Its share of the U.S. market increased from 16.6 percent to 22.3 percent. Average defects per vehicle plummeted from 6.7 to fewer than 1.5 in 10 years, very close to the Japanese average of 1.2. Productivity has increased to the point where Ford can now build its Taurus model as fast as Toyota can build a similar car.

However, challenge once again faces Ford and Petersen's successor, Harold Poling. After weathering several years in a recession that gripped the U.S. auto market, Ford lost $2.3 billion in 1991, its worst financial performance ever. Poling and his team are confident, however, that the company is back on track and will return to profitability when the auto market picks up again.

You're the Manager: You have joined the Ford team as assistant to the vice president for quality assurance. You are there to offer suggestions on how the company can fine-tune its new efforts to boost productivity, quality, and customer satisfaction.

Ranking Questions

1. You recognize that employee involvement plays a central role in Ford's pursuit of quality. Rank the following methods in terms of their ability to get employees involved and to ensure that decisions are made as far down the organizational chart as possible.
   a. Establish a quality circle in each of the following departments: design, manufacturing, marketing, accounting. Each QC is directed to identify and resolve quality challenges. Employees in the QC that achieves the lowest rate of defects will receive a substantial bonus.
   b. Start a quality-improvement team to consist of employees from design, manufacturing, marketing, research and development, and other areas. Representatives from each department will trade information and avoid making decisions in isolation.
   c. For the next car that is developed, launch a campaign that will reward all of the employees working on the project with a substantial bonus, if they achieve six sigma, when the product rolls off the assembly line.
   d. Carry out a detailed consumer survey. Identify what car buyers liked least and best about Ford cars in the past. Process these answers into design criteria for new cars.
2. One veteran manufacturer of brake drums supplies the vast majority of the brake drums that Ford buys. While it has consistently underbid competitors to get Ford business, it has unfortunately maintained its low pricing by failing to invest in quality. As a result, the products have defect rates that are too high for Ford's new standards. Rank these solutions to the problem.
   a. Establish strict new quality guidelines for suppliers. Insist that Ford be reimbursed specific amounts when defect rates go above defined limits.
   b. Switch to a better-quality brake drum supplier.
   c. Have the supplier design as well as manufacture the brake drums so that it has a better idea of what kind of product will work best.
   d. Arrange for Ford experts to work on-site with the supplier to train its people, upgrade its facilities, and reduce defect rates.

Multiple-Choice Questions

3. The minivan market has been one of the few bright spots in the auto industry in recent years. Not surprisingly, this segment quickly filled with a variety of products from the top manufacturers. The name of the game now is to provide the most attractive total product package to consumers. Which of the following product augmentations would likely be the biggest hit with young families?

a. A high-end sound system, complete with multiple-disc CD player, six or eight speakers, and a powerful amplifier.
b. A cargo-hauling system that makes it easy to carry the variety of toys, baby supplies, sports equipment, and other things that families need to haul around.
c. Extensive chrome plating on bumpers, fender trim, door handles, and other external components, designed to prevent corrosion for 10 years or more.
d. Structural improvements that provide a greater level of survivability in the event of accidents. These improvements would go far beyond the level currently required by the government.

4. Customer satisfaction goals provide the standards by which Ford can measure its progress, and they also provide a rallying point for employees and dealers. Which of the following represents the best goal, in terms of the criteria described in the chapter?
   a. The most attractive cars and trucks made in the United States.
   b. Perfect design and manufacturing processes, with zero product defects and 200,000-mile reliability.
   c. Annual 10 percent decreases in new-product defects and top-five ranking in the J. D. Powers customer satisfaction survey.
   d. The most sophisticated research, engineering, and testing facilities in the industry.

Analysis Questions

5. In what way did Ford employ human resource approaches to improving productivity?
6. What role is played by the biweekly meetings at which competitive new vehicle quality studies are reviewed by Ford personnel?
7. Is there any risk in letting employees have so much input into car designs?

Special Project

Efforts to improve quality and customer satisfaction too often fall prey to sloganeering, particularly with phrases such as "where quality is king" and "total customer satisfaction." For Ford's efforts to be successful over the long haul, you know that the company must start with a strong statement of goals. Using the four characteristics of customer satisfaction goal statements outlined in the chapter, write a brief goal statement to guide Ford's customer satisfaction efforts.[72]

KEY TERMS

added value (689)
augmented product (690)
benchmarking (680)
continuous-improvement process (680)
customer satisfaction (673)
expected product (689)
generic product (689)
quality circle (QC) (677)
quality function deployment (QFD) (679)
quality-improvement team (QIT) (677)
total quality management (TQM) (678)
value/price ratio (690)
zero defects (680)

QUESTIONS

For Review

1. How do quality, productivity, and customer satisfaction relate to organizational performance?
2. What steps can managers take to improve customer satisfaction?
3. What are the eight dimensions of quality?
4. Why are meaningful productivity measures and goals important for improving organizational productivity?
5. What is benchmarking, and how can managers use it to improve quality?

For Analysis

1. Would a Baldrige award–winning company be likely to benefit from applying for the Shingo or the Deming Prize? Why or why not?
2. What are the benefits and limitations of compressing the operational cycle in a health-care organization such as a dental clinic?
3. What product values might differentiate the generic, the expected, and the augmented products that business customers consider when shopping for an electric typewriter?

4. Why is measuring the productivity of salespeople as important as measuring the productivity of manufacturing output?
5. Is there an upper limit to the quality improvements achievable through continuous-improvement processes? Why or why not?

For Application

1. How can a provider of SAT study courses such as Princeton Review measure customer satisfaction?
2. What productivity goals and measures might the manager of a local shoe store establish?
3. How might a bank use added value to enhance the generic checking account product and create an augmented product?
4. Who might be invited to join a quality-improvement team charged with solving quality problems with mail delivery on your campus?
5. What expectations about product value might be held by store owners who buy milk from a local dairy wholesaler?

KEEPING CURRENT IN MANAGEMENT

Find a recent newspaper or magazine article in which a manager discusses how improving quality has helped the organization improve customer satisfaction. Examples might include a manufacturer that is initiating a quality drive to improve product reliability, a mail-order business that is speeding up its customer ordering or delivery methods, or a car dealer that is training its service technicians to diagnose and repair engine problems on the first try.

1. What organizations directly compete with this organization? How does this organization differentiate its goods and services from those offered by competitors? Why did the organization decide to improve quality as a way of improving customer satisfaction?
2. What steps did the manager take to improve quality? Which of the eight dimensions of quality were affected? How did management uncover customer needs and expectations in relation to these eight dimensions?
3. How was quality measured before and after the improvement? What changes were visible to customers? How is the organization searching for problems and taking corrective action to keep customers satisfied?

SHARPEN YOUR MANAGEMENT SKILLS

Discount stockbrokers have made quite a splash in the financial services industry in recent years. Investors who don't need the advice and research services of traditional brokerage firms such as Merrill Lynch—and who don't want to pay the high fees that higher levels of service carry—can buy and sell stock through discounters such as Charles Schwab and save up to 50 percent or more on commissions. And in addition to lower fees, Schwab offers a level of service automation not found in traditional brokerage companies. For instance, Schwab customers can buy and sell via their personal computers or their telephones, using a system that responds to key presses.

New customer-satisfaction technologies don't come without a price, however. In addition to the purchase price, there is employee training, installation and maintenance fees, and the potential for disrupting business while the transition to new equipment takes place. Schwab needs to make sure that the total costs (both financial and nonfinancial) of any new equipment will not exceed the benefits.

- *Decision:* Draw up a list of criteria for Schwab to use when it considers the purchase of new equipment, specifically new equipment that is intended to improve or maintain customer satisfaction.
- *Communication:* Write a brief memo in which you share your suggested criteria with Schwab's top management. Assume that the memo will be transmitted via electronic mail, which means you have limited control over the format of the text and no opportunity for graphics; the words themselves will have to get your point across.

Caterpillar Transforms Itself

Caterpillar, the world's leading manufacturer of earth-moving equipment, has climbed back to the top of the industry by modernizing its factories. Sales revenues are rising, but a changing economy is devastating profits. In an effort to find a solution, Caterpillar has chosen as CEO Donald Fites, a civil engineer with 35 years at the company.

HISTORY

Caterpillar was founded in 1928 in Peoria, Illinois, when Best Tractor merged with the California company of Benjamin Holt, who modified farming tractors in 1904 by replacing iron wheels with crawler tracks. In the 1930s the company expanded overseas and shifted its focus to construction and road equipment. Volume tripled during World War II as Caterpillar sold earth-moving equipment to the military, and demand remained high during postwar reconstruction.

Sales reached $8.6 billion in 1980, but falling demand for large equipment combined with intense competition from Komatsu and other overseas producers led to three straight years of losses totaling $953 million by 1984. The next year Caterpillar launched a major program to reduce costs, find new customers, and improve efficiency. It improved production methods, doubled its product line, shifted its focus to smaller equipment, cut its work force by a third, and recovered market share by keeping prices low. Earnings shot to $497 million to end the 1980s, but the next decade opened with profits of only $210 million, despite record sales of $11.4 billion, and economic conditions were expected to deteriorate.

ENVIRONMENT

Caterpillar management has given each of the company's 30 factories around the world responsibility for finding its own way to meet the corporate goals of improving competitiveness and quality. Results have been dramatic. For example, a plant near headquarters has reduced the time it takes to turn raw steel bars into crawler tracks from five months to five days by using robots and computer-integrated, flexible, pull-through production. The plant can also produce any size lot without retooling. A few blocks away computerized cells, taking up no more than 15 square feet, produce tractor gears that formerly traveled an entire mile down the production line; each gear had to be picked up, machined, and put back 20 times. Other plants save labor by using automatically guided vehicles to move products through the assembly process and by using robots to preassemble, wash, and paint items.

But there were problems with Caterpillar's structure. The company had long been organized into engineering, manufacturing, marketing, and finance divisions. That functional structure worked fine when the company had only a few plants, but it was too inflexible in a complex international marketplace. Decisions were made only at the top of each division, and as information moved through the hierarchy it sometimes became distorted. Activities were duplicated throughout the company, and few employees felt any true sense of responsibility for their own jobs, much less the organization's products.

GOALS AND CHALLENGES

Fites is trying to improve decision making and response to customers by reorganizing the company into a matrix structure of 13 profit centers and 4 service divisions spread around the globe. The new structure makes Caterpillar's 60,000 employees more directly responsible for the quality and level of their output, and it ties them more directly to dealers and customers, who can now find help with a single telephone call instead of several. Fites also is endeavoring to meet and exceed customers' ever-increasing expectations for quality and value while lessening product development time and costs. He is involving customers in product development from the beginning, and he is using teams that can design products and manufacturing processes simultaneously. Finally, the company will continue modernizing its factories throughout the decade to improve quality, productivity, and customer service with continuous work-flow technologies, just-in-time delivery, and flexible manufacturing.

1. What has Caterpillar done to increase efficiency and effectiveness?
2. What has the company done to better meet customer needs and competitive challenges?
3. How has Caterpillar used operational approaches to achieve its goal of improved productivity?
4. In what ways is Fites likely to improve customer satisfaction by including customers in the product development process?

PART FIVE INTEGRATIVE CASE

Levi Strauss Buttons Up Quality Operations

Who can build a company on a 140-year-old product? Levi Strauss, that's who. Since 1853, when the founder fashioned work pants from tent canvas, Levi Strauss has been dedicated to making and selling quality apparel. Over the years, Levi's plants have turned out more than 2 billion pairs of jeans, but the ups and downs of fashion trends have taken their toll on sales and profits. Levi's 1981 sales hit \$2.8 billion but bounced between \$2.5 billion and \$2.8 billion for the next few years. Net income gyrated but began to stabilize as the company methodically cut its costs by trimming the work force during the 1980s. CEO Robert D. Haas led the company through a leveraged buyout, to return it from publicly held to private control in 1985, then refocused Levi's attention on casual apparel.

After the buyout, Haas saw that domestic demand for jeans was fading and international profits were falling despite Levi's global reputation for quality. How could Haas preserve the company's commitment to quality while building future sales and profits? He could pressure managers and employees to slash costs and find new ways of boosting productivity. Or he could couple new information and manufacturing systems with employee involvement to pursue more efficient operations. Haas knew that either path would affect Levi's long-term outlook.

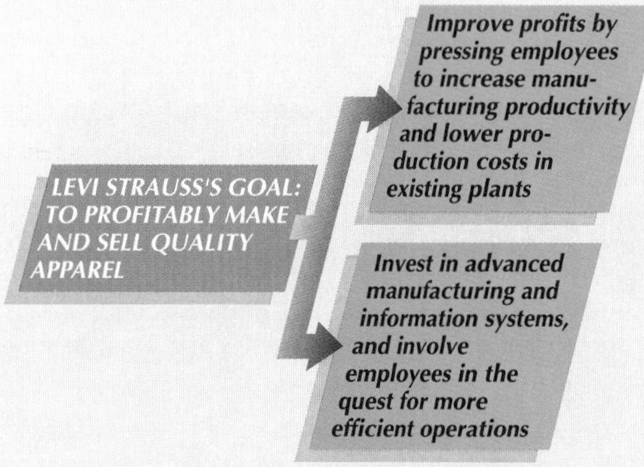

LEVI STRAUSS'S GOAL: TO PROFITABLY MAKE AND SELL QUALITY APPAREL

Improve profits by pressing employees to increase manufacturing productivity and lower production costs in existing plants

Invest in advanced manufacturing and information systems, and involve employees in the quest for more efficient operations

HISTORY

When dry goods merchant Levi Strauss moved to San Francisco in 1853, gold rush miners were looking for pants that could withstand their rugged outdoor life. Strauss made pants out of canvas he had planned to sell for tents, and word quickly spread about these sturdy "waist-high overalls." He soon switched to colorfast blue denim, and in 1873 Strauss teamed up with tailor Jacob W. Davis to file a patent for pants reinforced with copper rivets at key stress points. This pants model, dubbed 501, appealed to prospectors, cowboys, and others in need of durable britches.

When Strauss died in 1904, the clothing manufacturing and wholesaling business he had built passed to his four nephews, who kept up the tradition of quality. After World War II, family members Walter Haas, Jr., and Peter Haas were named to top management spots. The Haases decided to take the company out of wholesaling and concentrate exclusively on apparel manufacturing. During the 1950s and 1960s, jeans became increasingly popular, and Levi's created a women's clothing unit and an international division to take advantage of the growth potential. In 1971 the company sold shares to the public and diversified into sportswear and career clothing. By the time Robert Haas became CEO in 1984, blue jeans sales—and profits—were fading fast.

Haas recognized that the company needed some alterations. A former Peace Corps volunteer and a great-great-grandnephew of the founder, Haas had held senior management positions in corporate planning and in operations before assuming the CEO position. He and his family decided that they could build both sales and profits if they held tighter control, so they arranged a leveraged buyout, which returned Levi's to private ownership in 1985. Today, family members own more than 90 percent of the company; employees in the ESOP own the remainder.

ENVIRONMENT

During the 1970s, global jeans demand was riding high, and Levi's expanded to 70 countries. But when jeans fell out of fashion in the 1980s, demand in overseas markets dropped even faster than demand in the United States. By the mid-1980s, the foreign exchange equation had shifted against Levi's, which also hurt international profits. Management considered pulling back from many overseas markets, until Lee C. Smith, head of the international division, proposed that Levi's streamline by closing some factories, selling selected assets, and narrowing sales territories and product lines. With those changes, and a snappy new advertising campaign stressing the company's all-American image, Levi's overseas sales rebounded. The foreign exchange rate slowly became more favorable, boosting the division's profits.

By 1988, the Eastern European market was becoming more attractive, and Levi's opened a plant in Hungary. The plant used computerized cutting machines to prepare the denim for the sewing machine operators, who were able to complete a pair of jeans in less than 11 minutes. A pair of 501 jeans cost nearly two weeks' salary in Hungary, but Levi's couldn't keep up with the demand.

In the United States, Levi's was also searching for higher performance by shuttering plants, downsizing the work force, and putting the emphasis back on clothing for the casual life-style. Levi's successfully relaunched the company's first product, button-fly 501 jeans. The company also took a second look at the baby boomers who had originally worn jeans in the 1960s. As they aged and gained weight, the boomers needed looser-fitting clothing, but they also wanted a more tailored look. Levi's answer: Dockers, a new line of casual clothing as comfortable as jeans but with updated fashion appeal. Designers used computer-aided design systems to develop Levi's Dockers designs, and backed by a $10 million advertising campaign, Dockers quickly became a hit.

Levi's also believes in making a social contribution. The company has a Community Involvement Team Program that supports employees' volunteer efforts by offering donations, grants, and matching contributions, and it sponsors programs that champion the interests of low-income people, minorities, and disadvantaged people. In 1987, Levi's established an "Aspirations Statement" that explains the company's goals for team-oriented leadership, a diverse work force, performance recognition, ethical management, clear communications, and employee empowerment.

GOALS AND CHALLENGES

Although the company offers 7,000 products at any given time, Haas is determined not to compromise on quality. Before production, Levi's tests its raw materials for durability, colorfastness, and other characteristics. In-process quality inspectors check for quality before the product is complete, quality control inspectors check after the product has been sewn, and two additional checks verify that the finished quality meets Levi's standards before the product is shipped to the store. Producing one pair of jeans requires over 40 separate steps; only a few, such as the decorative stitching on the rear pockets, are completely automated, so some variations can occur during assembly.

However, after the downsizing of the 1980s, employee morale was low. Applying the values emphasized in Levi's Aspirations Statement, managers soon found ways to involve employees in the search for higher efficiency and effectiveness. For example, at the Blue Ridge, Georgia plant, morale improved when managers introduced a gain-sharing program. Employees receive bonuses based on the savings from lower costs, lower absenteeism, higher quality, and better safety. Managers of the Roswell, New Mexico, plant switched from assembly-line production to modular manufacturing, and they organized plant employees into self-managing teams. Each team was given responsibility for all the tasks needed to complete the type of jeans made in the factory. Now 13 employees can do the work that 25 once handled, the defect rate is down, and production is much speedier. Moreover, one team suggested a change that reduced the number of wrist movements needed to sew a pocket, which made the operation safer and lowered labor costs at the same time.

Even before the leveraged buyout, management teams were investigating how to establish closer ties with the retailers selling Levi's products. The teams fanned out to ask retailers about what they needed from apparel manufacturers, then crafted a collection of information services they dubbed LeviLink. LeviLink's electronic data interchange capabilities allows merchants to order merchandise, receive advance shipping notices, be billed, and even pay for goods via computer links. Retailers also receive merchandise preticketed with bar-coded price tags that can be read by the scanners attached to their electronic cash registers; this speeds customer checkout and helps merchants track their inventory levels. LeviLink helps determine the appropriate inventory levels of Levi's merchandise for individual retailers by analyzing their past and present Levi's sales, then suggesting recommended order levels for each product. Ultimately, Haas wants to create a direct information link between store and factory so that as existing goods are sold, replacements are produced. This tight control over Levi's operations helped push 1991 sales to $5 billion, and it promises to support even higher growth—and profits—in the years ahead.

1. How does Levi's use preliminary, concurrent, and postaction controls to maintain product quality? Is the firm moving toward bureaucratic or clan control? Why?
2. What impact does LeviLink have on its merchants' inventory management? Will LeviLink ultimately become a just-in-time management system? Why or why not?
3. What types of information systems does Levi's operate? How might Levi's help smaller merchants overcome computer phobia so they can take advantage of LeviLink?
4. Does Levi's consider consumers to be its customers? Does Levi's consider retailers to be its customers? Explain your answers.

Integrated Video Exercises

CHAPTER 1

THE FOUNDATIONS OF MANAGEMENT

SYNOPSIS

VIDEO EXERCISE

Like any profession, management requires certain skills and abilities. The manager in this video was having difficulty functioning effectively in his position, especially with regard to prioritizing his work and delegating tasks to employees. He missed deadlines and immersed himself in details that others could handle. His secretary and his assistant were both interested in taking on more responsibility and more challenging assignments, but the manager was reluctant to delegate. By working with a more experienced manager and by practicing the new methods he was shown, this manager was able to learn and ultimately master the skills he needed to plan, organize, lead, and control more effectively and more efficiently.

EXERCISES

Analysis

1. The manager's inability to set priorities might signal a deficiency in which of the three managerial skills: conceptual, interpersonal, or technical?
2. What reasons might the less-experienced manager in this video give for being reluctant to ask for help from a mentor?
3. What reasons might the more-experienced manager give for acting as a mentor?
4. According to the video, what demands did this manager face? What choices did he face?
5. How did this manager play the role of disseminator? Of leader?

Application

Training programs can help managers learn specific managerial skills and better apply the skills they have. If you were designing a training program for first-line managers who are being considered for promotion into middle management, which of the three managerial skills would you emphasize? Describe some of the ways you would help first-line managers develop the appropriate set of managerial skills.

Decision

Assume that you're the middle manager to whom the manager in this video reports. If he could not change his approach and never learned to delegate or to prioritize his tasks, how would you react? You know this manager is knowledgeable and hard-working, but you can't afford to let his department miss important deadlines again and again. What are your options and how would you evaluate each?

Ethics

It's never easy to tell a manager that his or her performance doesn't meet expectations. But without feedback, the manager's performance may continue to deteriorate and, ultimately, he or she may be fired. Considering the potential consequences for the low-performing manager, is it ethical for a higher-level manager to refrain from mentioning any performance deficiencies?

Teamwork

Team up with one or two other students and identify specific sources of help that this manager can tap in his quest to improve his managerial capabilities, including finding a mentor and other sources. Then role play a scene in which one student, portraying the higher-level manager, reviews the steps the other student (as the lower-level manager) is planning to take to become a more efficient and more effective manager.

CHAPTER 2

MANAGEMENT THEORIES AND PERSPECTIVES

SYNOPSIS

VIDEO EXERCISE

The development of contemporary management practices has been influenced by three broad management perspectives: classical management, behavioral management, and quantitative management. All three perspectives are being applied today in one form or another. In the first video segment, the Du Pont plant manager expresses concerns that echo those of the classical management theorists, who focused on waste, efficiency, and costs, as well as the need to scientifically investigate methods for improving work flow. In the second segment, Donald Petersen, retired CEO of Ford, discusses practices and issues that are at the core of the behavioral management perspective, including the need for employee involvement and the realization that people can make a difference. And in the third segment, Federal Express managers are shown applying a range of quantitative management tools at the Memphis distribution hub.

EXERCISES

Analysis

1. Does the Du Pont manager's interest in scientific management principles preclude his using any behavioral management techniques? Why or why not?
2. What are the inputs and outputs of a Ford Taurus plant? How do assembly-line employees relate to the transformation process?
3. If he wanted management advice, would Donald Petersen be more likely to read a book by Frederick Taylor or a book by Douglas McGregor? Why?
4. Considering Federal Express's use of sophisticated quantitative management tools, how could entropy affect the Memphis superhub?
5. How could an MIS help Du Pont determine the level of yield and waste in its transformation process?

Application

Drawing on the ideas of Harrington Emerson and Henri Fayol, list at least 10 classical management practices that would help Federal Express achieve its goal of delivering all customer shipments on time.

Decision

Assume you're a Du Pont plant manager who wants to find the most efficient method of handling raw materials. You are thinking about using time-and-motion studies to determine how employees are currently handling raw materials, but you know that some people object to that approach. As you consider your decision, what arguments can you make for and against using time-and-motion studies?

Ethics

Federal Express is known for standing behind its promise of guaranteed on-time delivery, no matter what the weather. But should the company's pilots be expected to fly in bad weather? Assume that you manage Federal Express's superhub. How would you outline the ethical issues raised by this question?

Teamwork

Imagine that you and three other students have asked assembly-line employees at a Ford plant about the management approaches they've seen in the past decade. Break into two teams. One team should list typical statements Ford employees might make as they describe Theory X management; the second team should list some typical employee statements about Theory Y management. Compare the lists. How do the statements differ? Which management approach do you think the Ford employees would say they prefer? Why?

CHAPTER 3

THE COMPLEX ORGANIZATIONAL ENVIRONMENT

SYNOPSIS

VIDEO EXERCISE

The organizational environment, which consists of all the forces that influence the organization, can have a powerful effect on individual decisions and actions. The external forces in the general environment have a more general influence, and the external forces in the task environment have a more direct impact on the organization. The internal environment contains all forces inside the organization, including owners and shareholders, the board of directors, employees, and the organizational culture. This video examines the shift in attitude and behavior at the Alameda Naval Aviation Depot that came about as a result of changes in the external environment and in the organizational culture, demonstrating how the environment (and organizational culture in particular) can influence performance.

EXERCISES

Analysis

1. What influence do technological forces in the general environment have on the Alameda Naval Aviation Depot?
2. What guiding beliefs seem to be underlying the Depot's new culture?
3. Identify one or more stories that communicate the new values of the Depot's culture. What values are being communicated in these stories?
4. Could the Depot use rationing to adapt to the environment? Why or why not?
5. What competition does the Depot face in the task environment?

Application

According to the video, the 1970s slogan for a facility such as the Depot might have been: "It's good enough for government." What slogan(s) might the Depot adopt in the 1990s to communicate the guiding values of quality, safety, and accountability?

Decision

Would you recommend that Captain William Tinston, Jr., the Depot's commanding officer, create a board of directors to supervise management and organizational performance? Although the Depot isn't a corporation, top managers can establish a group to function like a board of directors by supervising the Depot's management, goals, and plans. What decision would you recommend? Why?

Ethics

The need for the Alameda Naval Aviation Depot and five other Naval Air Systems rework facilities is likely to be reduced because the Cold War is over. If any of these rework facilities is closed because of budget cuts, many people will be out of work, and people who have specialized skills that relate only to military equipment may face a long period of unemployment. In light of such human and economic costs, is it ethical for the U.S. government to close facilities such as the Depot and put people out of work? Is it ethical to continue operating the Depot simply to avoid layoffs and damage to the local economy? How would you resolve this ethical question?

Teamwork

You and two other students have been asked to help the Depot conduct forecasting. Captain Tinston would like you to recommend which external elements should be examined to predict future conditions. With your classmates, identify at least six areas in which forecasting would help the commanding officer prepare for environmental shifts.

CHAPTER 4

SOCIAL RESPONSIBILITY AND ETHICS

SYNOPSIS

VIDEO EXERCISE

Managerial decisions and actions have increasingly come under scrutiny as academics, social activists, and managers debate the ideal relationship between the organization and society. The concept of social responsibility argues that every organization has obligations that go beyond pursuing its own goals; organizations should act in a manner that benefits society as well. Although both law and company policy have an influence, it is the managers' sense of right and wrong that ultimately determines how each organization will respond to the needs of society, so social responsibility can be seen as rooted in managerial ethics. In the first video segment, the ethics of David Butler's actions in buying and misusing a savings and loan company's assets are examined. In the second segment, Robert Sweeney of the National Association of Accountants discusses how organizations can guide employees and managers toward ethical behavior.

EXERCISES

Analysis

1. Must an organizational code of ethics always be in writing? What might happen if the code were unwritten but discussed with newly hired employees and managers on their first day of work?
2. Why should ethical standards be periodically reexamined? Identify some of the problems an organization might face if its ethics code is never updated.
3. Can the question of David Butler's S&L paying for improvements to his home be seen as an ethical dilemma or an ethical lapse? Why?
4. Imagine that a manager transfers from the U.S. plant of an international corporation to its plant in Africa. He finds that local officials have been demanding (and receiving) small bribes for handling routine customs inspections; however, his company's international ethical code (enforced globally) forbids such payments. Is this an ethical dilemma or an ethical lapse? What are the legal and ethical implications of this situation?
5. Can a manager who behaves unethically be expected to take the initiative and find ways to benefit society? Where on the continuum of social responsibility would you expect to position this manager's actions? Explain.

Application

Assume you manage a hardware store. Develop a five-point code of ethics to guide your employees through the ethical issues they face daily on the job.

Decision

Teenagers found guilty of ethical lapses such as shoplifting are sometimes sentenced to volunteer their time for some social cause. If you were making this decision, which area(s) of social responsibility would you recommend?

Ethics

Many not-for-profits hire professional fundraising firms to help raise money for their cause, and a portion of the money raised is used to pay the fundraisers. Is it ethical for an organization to avoid telling contributors about such an arrangement? Should contributors be told how much of their donation goes to this fee? If so, how and when should this be disclosed?

Teamwork

You head a not-for-profit clinic that uses professional fundraisers to elicit donations. A major donor (played by a classmate) is angry about the ethics of your clinic "wasting money" on a fundraising firm. How can you explain your clinic's actions using one or more of the tools for resolving ethical dilemmas? Use role playing to resolve this situation.

CHAPTER 5

MANAGEMENT AND THE GLOBAL ORGANIZATION

SYNOPSIS

VIDEO EXERCISE

Because of the high speed and low cost of today's communication, transportation, and information systems, an increasing number of organizations are crossing national borders to acquire resources or to sell products. As the first video segment shows, many firms successfully enter the international marketplace through exporting, which requires (1) the development of a quality product needed in another country, (2) a long-term commitment to selling abroad, and (3) a clear understanding of their overseas markets. In the second segment, Dr. Joseph Duncan of Dun & Bradstreet discusses the long-term market opportunity in Eastern Europe and examines the political, legal, and economic barriers to international trade.

EXERCISES

Analysis

1. Roger Johnson of Western Digital says that if your firm's competitors are involved in international trade, you have no choice but to enter the global marketplace. How would you support his statement? How would you rebut it?
2. According to Sid Swartz, selling Timberland shoes in Italy is a way to draw fashion-conscious U.S. retailers' attention to these made-in-America products. Is this an example of multidomestic or transnational management? Why?
3. Dr. Joseph Duncan notes that changes to contract law are necessary to encourage trade in Eastern Europe. How would such changes affect firms exporting to Eastern Europe or considering direct investment?
4. Discuss how the blocked currency of Eastern European nations affects local companies that want to start exporting products to Western Europe.
5. Why is quality an important criterion for successful exporting?

Application

If people in the Eastern European countries shun locally made products in favor of goods imported from the West, what types of laws and regulations are government officials likely to impose to protect local industry?

Decision

Imagine that Timberland is considering whether to use direct investment to open an off-shore production plant to serve its Asian markets. What alternatives can you suggest? What are the pros and cons of each?

Ethics

You're the head of a U.S. drug company facing an ethical dilemma. One of your drugs hasn't yet been approved for sale in the United States because the Food and Drug Administration has raised serious questions about its safety. However, other countries have not raised any objections. What arguments can you make for and against selling this drug overseas, where it has been approved?

Teamwork

Assume that Western Digital is building a state-of-the-art factory in Asia. In a team of four students, identify the issues to consider and the ways that Roger Johnson can respond to the host government's requests to share Western Digital's manufacturing technology with local firms. You may choose to break into two groups, with one group outlining the issues to be considered and the other group identifying Johnson's possible responses.

CHAPTER 6

DECISION MAKING

SYNOPSIS

VIDEO EXERCISE

Group decision making has many benefits, including the availability of more knowledge, a broader perspective on the problem and potential solutions, and the likelihood that group members will more readily accept the decision. But group decision making also has limitations: it can be slow; it can prevent managers from acting quickly and decisively; and it can be dominated by one or two individuals. As the video explains, one of the most serious limitations is the potential for groupthink, which can result in compromises that are not in the organization's best interest—and may have disastrous consequences. But Dr. Irving Janis, who coined the term *groupthink,* suggests in the video that managers can counteract groupthink by (1) maintaining an open group climate, (2) avoiding insulation, (3) asking each member to critically evaluate the issues and assumptions, and (4) taking care not to unduly influence the group's decision-making process.

EXERCISES

Analysis

1. How does brainstorming avoid some of the problems of groupthink?
2. How do the devil's advocate technique and the dialectic process overcome the potential for groupthink?
3. Why are members of a group more likely to feel satisfied with a decision they have collectively made and more likely to support its implementation?
4. Can a nominal group get caught up in groupthink? Why or why not?
5. Is a Delphi group exempt from groupthink because the members never personally meet to discuss their viewpoints? Explain.

Application

How can the officers of your college's student government avoid groupthink as they consider how to solve the problem of excessive noise in dormitories during the weekend? List at least four specific steps they might take.

Decision

You are the student government president. Several students are confronting you about the student government's decision concerning weekend dormitory noise, which resulted in a rule forbidding students from playing stereos or televisions without headphones after 9 p.m. on the weekend. These students say no one asked for their ideas or consulted them about the decision, so they do not have to comply. Controversial decisions in which both sides have a valid case crop up frequently; list ways in which you might handle such decisions in the future.

Ethics

Is it ethical for a college scholarship to be awarded solely on the basis of financial need, without regard to academic ability or other criteria? Outline the arguments for and against this practice, and write a paragraph discussing how college administrators might resolve this question.

Teamwork

In a team of five students, identify rules of thumb that you use to make decisions during your college career (example: an instructor who doesn't take attendance in one course will not take attendance in others, so if you must cut classes, you want to enroll in this instructor's courses). Once the heuristics have been identified, list the advantages and disadvantages of each, either by assigning one or more to each team member or by discussing the advantages and disadvantages as a group. Then outline several rules for applying these heuristics appropriately.

CHAPTER 7

ORGANIZATIONAL GOALS AND PLANNING

SYNOPSIS

VIDEO EXERCISE

The planning process includes developing the organizational mission, setting goals, and devising plans to achieve the goals. The mission is the topmost goal and describes the organization's purpose. It also incorporates top management's vision of where the organization should be in the future, what it should be, and whom it will serve. Next, managers use the mission to guide the development of goals at three levels: the strategic, the tactical, and the operational. In this video, Richard Mahoney, CEO of Monsanto, discusses the global chemical company's strategic goals, which stretch beyond traditional profitability targets to include nine nonfinancial goals such as improved safety and protection for the natural environment.

EXERCISES

Analysis

1. How might Monsanto use the MBO process to link the strategic goal of eliminating toxic air emissions to the daily activities of the people who work in each Monsanto chemical plant?
2. Imagine that Mahoney has set a strategic goal of eliminating all employee safety hazards within one year. List two tactical goals and two operational goals that would support this strategic goal.
3. Each time Monsanto acquires a firm, it must bring that firm's planning process into line with the parent's planning process, so that goals and plans are coordinated. Should Mahoney send planning specialists to teach each newly acquired firm Monsanto's methods? Why or why not?
4. If the Canadian government passes environmental protection laws more stringent than similar U.S. laws, Monsanto may have to spend more than expected to comply with the new rules. What types of plans should Mahoney prepare for dealing with the possibility that such a situation may occur?
5. Would Monsanto use a standing plan or a single-use plan to pursue a nonfinancial goal such as cutting all air emissions by the end of the year?

Application

You are the head of a Monsanto project team making plans to reduce water pollution around your plant. Which forecasting tools would be most useful as you start the planning process?

Decision

Assume that Canada has passed an environmental protection law that seems to be more stringent than that of any country in which Monsanto operates. Because Canada represents less than 10 percent of the firm's sales, Mahoney is considering making plans to withdraw from the market. Should he use the jury of executive opinion, a sales force composite, or leading indicators to support this decision? Why?

Ethics

Monsanto's environmental and safety goals are admirable, but the company must make a significant investment to achieve those goals. If the company passes those costs on in the form of higher prices, is it ethical to expect customers to bear those costs?

Teamwork

You and three classmates have been asked to join Monsanto's planning task force as community representatives who can suggest specific strategic goals the company might set for protecting the natural environment. As a team, draw up a list of four or more strategic goals for Monsanto's consideration.

CHAPTER 8

STRATEGIC MANAGEMENT AND IMPLEMENTATION

SYNOPSIS

VIDEO EXERCISE

Strategic management is the process of formulating, implementing, and controlling broad plans—strategies—to guide the organization in achieving its strategic goals. Strategies set the organization's direction and provide the general framework that management will use to achieve its goals. Managers develop strategy at three levels: the corporate level, the business level, and the functional level. One model that managers can use as a framework for developing business-level strategy was developed by Michael Porter. Cost leadership, differentiation, and focus are Porter's three generic competitive strategies for attaining competitive advantage. The video shows how Elliot Wadsworth, owner of the White Flower Farm, combines quality, service, breadth of selection, and gardening expertise to form a unique and effective differentiation strategy.

EXERCISES

Analysis

1. Why is White Flower Farm's business-level strategy considered a differentiation strategy and not a focus strategy?
2. How might Wadsworth gather information about White Flower Farm's competitors for the external assessment portion of his situation analysis?
3. Does White Flower Farm seem to be pursuing a concentration or diversification growth strategy? Defend your answer.
4. Now that White Flower Farm has grown to $10 million in annual sales, under what conditions should management consider switching to a grand strategy of stability?
5. Considering White Flower's direct-mail and telephone sales operation, what role does the functional-level strategy for information resources play?

Application

Assume that Wadsworth has set a strategic goal of a 2 percent annual market share gain in the direct-mail gardening industry. In maintaining strategic control, what critical areas should be monitored to ensure that actual results measure up to expected results?

Decision

As more competitors enter the mail-order gardening business, Wadsworth will have to decide whether to change the company's strategy. Which element of strategy (scope, distinctive competence, resource deployment, or synergy) would be easiest to change? Why?

Ethics

Is it ethical to advertise a sale on products that are in extremely short supply? If Wadsworth had planned a tulip bulb sale but received less than half the number of bulbs he ordered from overseas suppliers, would he be acting ethically if he advertised the sale without disclosing the limited supply of bulbs?

Teamwork

Working in a team of six, identify three strengths, three weaknesses, three opportunities, and three threats that Wadsworth might consider as he starts the strategic management process. Three students can work on listing the organizational strengths and weaknesses while three students work on the environmental opportunities and threats. Compare lists and determine how White Flower Farm might best use its strengths to overcome the threats.

CHAPTER 9

FOUNDATIONS OF ORGANIZATION STRUCTURE

SYNOPSIS

VIDEO EXERCISE

Organization structure is the formal system of interaction and coordination that links the tasks of individuals and groups to achieve organizational goals. This structure is used to distribute the authority to make decisions and take actions. Although top managers distribute some authority throughout the organization, they also retain a certain amount of authority. Centralization is the extent to which authority remains concentrated at top management levels, while decentralization is the extent to which authority is delegated to lower levels. New United Motors Manufacturing Inc. (NUMMI), a joint venture between General Motors and Toyota, has moved toward the decentralized end of the structural spectrum. NUMMI's employees are responsible for controlling their own work processes, and they have the authority to solve problems and take actions that improve quality and productivity while reducing costs.

EXERCISES

Analysis

1. How does the decentralization of authority at NUMMI affect accountability for the quality of cars produced in the plant?
2. Bill Borton, NUMMI's assistant general manager, says that the plant's managers now function as trainers and facilitators. Can the managers still be considered to have line authority? Or do they now have staff authority?
3. How does delegation contribute to NUMMI's performance?
4. Does NUMMI's decentralized structure violate the scalar principle? Why or why not?
5. How can NUMMI managers use direct contact to resolve problems that arise between interdependent work teams?

Application

In a decentralized structure such as NUMMI, managers are generally encouraged to contact anyone in the organization who can help solve a problem. What effect would you expect this level of decentralization to have on the informal organization?

Decision

Borton recommends that every organization decentralize to improve quality and productivity while cutting costs. What issues should the top manager of a company that produces snack foods in seven factories consider when deciding whether to decentralize authority to the managers and employees who operate the various plants?

Ethics

Imagine that Borton has received an employee suggestion about a new process that will save NUMMI $500,000 per year—but will also displace the five employees responsible for the previous process. Is it ethical for Borton to reward the employee for a suggestion that displaces other employees? How could Borton best resolve this situation?

Teamwork

Assume that NUMMI wants to give new employees a brief written explanation of how decentralization will affect their everyday decisions and activities. Team up with another student and draft a paragraph that can be included in NUMMI's employee handbook.

CHAPTER 10

ORGANIZATION DESIGN

SYNOPSIS

VIDEO EXERCISE

Over the years, scholars and practitioners have explored the principles of organization design and considered how they can be applied to achieve organizational goals. Researcher Rensis Likert proposed a continuum of four types of organization design. At one extreme is the traditional organization that relies on formal authority and the hierarchical chain of command, an organization he called System 1. At the other extreme is the organization that relies on manager-employee collaboration and encourages freer interaction, an organization he called System 4. This video shows how North American Tool and Die (NATD) applied System 4 principles to boost employee satisfaction and company performance.

EXERCISES

Analysis

1. Would you characterize the organization structure at NATD as mechanistic or organic? Why?
2. NATD operations use unit and small-batch technology. What are the implications for organization design?
3. Would NATD be able to operate effectively in a highly changeable environment if it used the traditional bureaucratic structure suggested by Max Weber? Why or why not?
4. Given that NATD's environment is complex and changeable, would you expect to see a low or high degree of differentiation? Explain.
5. Do you think NATD's organization design is more like the network or the lattice? Support your answer.

Application

Imagine that NATD changes its strategy and decides to mass produce standardized metal components for car engines. How would you expect this change in strategy and technology to affect the firm's organization design?

Decision

What kind of organization design would be appropriate if NATD diversified by buying a high-technology ceramics plant, which is unrelated to its current metal stamping business? Assume that the design is for the overall organization (not the individual plant), and that the ceramics plant uses a functional design and is located 100 miles from the nearest NATD facility.

Ethics

A switch from unit and small-batch technology to mass production and large-batch technology often means that skilled technicians are now responsible for only a small piece of the process, rather than being responsible for making each individual product from beginning to end. As a result, technicians may feel less motivated because they lose the satisfaction of crafting a complete product. Do you think it is ethical for managers to make such a switch, knowing how technicians are likely to react? Why or why not?

Teamwork

In a two-student team, determine whether your college's structural configuration is a professional bureaucracy or a machine bureaucracy. Each student should analyze the college's characteristics in terms of one of these two configurations and prepare a brief (one-page) report of the results. Then get together, compare reports, and agree on which type of structural configuration the college exemplifies.

CHAPTER 11

ORGANIZATIONAL CHANGE AND INNOVATION

SYNOPSIS

VIDEO EXERCISE

Achieving large-scale, comprehensive change—especially in people's behavior and in culture—isn't easy, but it can be critical when the health and performance of the entire organization are at stake. To accomplish such massive change, top managers sometimes turn to a specialized approach known as organizational development (OD), a long-term, organizationwide change effort that is managed from the top and that uses behavioral science techniques to intervene in organizational processes as a way of improving the organization's effectiveness and health. Team building is a commonly used OD technique, and the video shows how this team building can help work groups improve communication, collaboration, and effectiveness.

EXERCISES

Analysis

1. Who is the change agent in the video, and how does this person gather information to diagnose the problem?
2. Was the change in the video planned or reactive? Support your answer.
3. How did the manager in the video unfreeze and move group members' attitudes and behavior?
4. Identify the driving forces for change that appeared in the video.
5. Which of the six methods for overcoming resistance to change did the manager in the video use? Do you agree with his choice of method(s)?

Application

Imagine that Xerox is planning to move its headquarters from Stamford, Connecticut, to Boston, Massachusetts, but top managers anticipate that many headquarters managers and employees will resist the change because of uncertainty and differing perceptions. How might Jules E. Cochoit, training and operations manager for Xerox, use education and communication to overcome this resistance?

Decision

Put yourself in the shoes of Susan Zuanich, manager of organizational development and training for Johnson & Johnson's Iolab. If Iolab's performance were declining and she wanted to find out why, would she be more likely to uncover the reasons if she decided to use the OD technique of survey feedback or the technique of third-party intervention?

Ethics

Assume that the team-building efforts featured in the video have been successfully extended to the factory floor, where a group of production employees have become so committed to the performance goals that they have developed a revolutionary new technique to speed shipbuilding. The technique is based on one team member's original idea that was then perfected by the group. If Bounty wants to reward this achievement, is it ethical to reward only the idea's originator? Or is it ethical to reward the team only as a group? How can this dilemma be resolved?

Teamwork

Team up with five other students to complete a nine-cell matrix analysis of the possible educational courses your college might offer for three markets: the undergraduate market, the graduate market, and the adult education market. The various course categories you will be considering are music, business, and writing. Suggest at least one course in each category for each market.

CHAPTER 12

ORGANIZING NEW VENTURES

SYNOPSIS

VIDEO EXERCISE

Entrepreneurs and intrapreneurs share some key traits for success, including the ability to create new products or new ways of getting things done and the desire to see their ideas carried through to fruition. Tom Monaghan, founder of Domino's Pizza, explains in this video the thought process he went through in establishing his successful company. He particularly emphasizes the role of imagination and intuition. The second part of the video highlights the intrapreneurial successes of the 3M Corporation, widely recognized as one of the world's most creative and innovative organizations. In fact, you'll meet the inventor of the Post-it Note, which was one of the earliest examples of intrapreneurial success. The final segment discusses an incentive plan that gives managers a sense of ownership in their organizations, with the goal of stimulating higher performance.

EXERCISES

Analysis

1. Which entrepreneurial strategy did Tom Monaghan pursue when he established Domino's Pizza?
2. Which of the entrepreneurial characteristics described in the chapter contributed to Monaghan's success?
3. How did Monaghan handle the crises of entrepreneurial growth?
4. Monaghan mentions a key performance measure; what is this measure and how does it help him lead the organization to peak performance?
5. Why does a sense of ownership usually lead people to higher levels of performance?

Application

The 3M segment notes that 3M employees are encouraged to "see things in new ways." What steps could managers take to help employees think creatively?

Decision

Tom Monaghan points out that he did no formal marketing research to test his idea of 30-minute delivery. However, many entrepreneurs fail precisely because they don't test their ideas before implementing them. Was Monaghan simply lucky? If you had been in Monaghan's shoes when Domino's was being launched, would you have made the same decision not to conduct research or would you have relied on intuition as well? Why?

Ethics

The compensation plan discussed in the third segment of the video is designed to emphasize both risks and rewards. Are there any potential ethical questions with this plan? Is it fair to the people whose pay is determined in this manner?

Teamwork

In a team of five people, two students, playing the role of entrepreneurs with an idea, are seeking equity financing from three investors, played by the other students. The two entrepreneurs need to have an idea for a new business (any kind will do), and they need to present their plan to the three investors. As part of the presentation, the entrepreneurs should explain not only why the product or business idea is good but also why they are the right people to implement it (the entrepreneurs can make up any personal qualifications they may need for this exercise). The investors then need to judge whether the entrepreneurs have the necessary characteristics to succeed, whether the entrepreneurial strategy chosen is appropriate, and whether they will invest in the new enterprise.

CHAPTER 13

HUMAN RESOURCE MANAGEMENT

SYNOPSIS

VIDEO EXERCISE

The U.S. work force is becoming quite diverse, with more women than ever working outside the home, a steady stream of people from around the globe moving into positions in U.S. organizations, and ethnic minorities fulfilling widespread professional opportunities. Diversity, as this video points out, implies differences, and these differences present both a challenge and an opportunity. The challenge is to create organizational environments in which all employees can succeed; the opportunity lies in utilizing a wider pool of talent and perspective. This video highlights the problems of not recognizing and responding to diversity, and it outlines steps that managers can take to ensure the success of a diverse work force.

EXERCISES

Analysis

1. What is the difference between stereotyping people based on culture and being sensitive to cultural differences?
2. As you listen to your instructor's next lecture, watch for slang that may impede communication with non-native English speakers, then find workable alternatives to the slang phrases.
3. What is likely to happen to organizations that don't accommodate the increasingly diversified work force?
4. Aside from population shifts, what external forces are making diversity an important issue for today's managers?
5. How can organizations benefit from a diverse work force?

Application

What steps might you take to ensure effective communications in a work force that includes a significant number of non-native speakers of English?

Decision

Although disappointing examples to the contrary still abound, the United States does a better job of accommodating a diverse work force than many other countries do. Assume you're the CEO of a U.S. company establishing a division in Japan, where women executives are rare. You're looking for a person to head the new division, and the top candidate for the job is a woman. Should she get the job, when you know that some of the people she'll have to work with won't easily accept women executives? Support your answer.

Ethics

Many people consider affirmative action to be a fair and helpful mechanism for giving underrepresented work-force groups equal employment opportunities. Opponents and skeptics, however, question whether affirmative action is fair to those who aren't in such groups. In addition, some people from traditionally underrepresented groups don't appreciate the stigma that they say affirmative action attaches to their careers. Do you agree with the principle of affirmative action?

Teamwork

Watch a TV show (any variety) or movie with three or four other students. As you're watching, keep an eye out for cultural stereotyping or any uses of slang that may inhibit communication in a multicultural environment. Take notes individually, then meet afterward to see if everyone identified the same things. If not, discuss why.

CHAPTER 14

MANAGEMENT AND MOTIVATION

SYNOPSIS

VIDEO EXERCISE

Motivation is one of the most important responsibilities a manager has. Unfortunately, it can also be one of the most difficult to understand and to implement. This video illustrates the thoughts of three of the most influential thinkers in the field of motivation: Abraham Maslow, David McClelland, and B. F. Skinner. These theorists agree on some important questions concerning motivation, but they don't always agree on others. For instance, all agree behavior can be changed through motivation, but they don't necessarily agree on the most effective ways to accomplish this. The second part of the video points out another difficulty in motivating employees: no two employees have the same motivational "hot buttons," and with a work force becoming increasingly diverse, the motivational challenges grow increasingly complex.

EXERCISES

Analysis

1. Why do managers need to motivate their employees? Won't good employees naturally do a good job?
2. Are Maslow's higher-order needs important to low-income employees who are living from paycheck to paycheck? What about the successful sales representative shown in the video; is self-actualization more important than money?
3. Many CEOs have multimillion-dollar compensation packages; is money still a motivator when you're making five or ten million dollars a year?
4. Will pay-for-knowledge systems motivate all employees equally? Why or why not?
5. Why are there so many different theories regarding motivation? How should managers deal with the varied and sometimes conflicting theories as they try to motivate employees?

Application

Assume you have the task of designing a gain-sharing program for an oil-exploration team; what features would your program have? If you like, do some library research to understand the nature of oil exploration before designing your program.

Decision

Would you recommend that the owner of a professional sports team implement a performance-based merit pay system? Why or why not? Are you aware of any performance-based pay components in the contracts of today's athletes? Would pay for performance work better in some sports than in others?

Ethics

Are company motivation programs simply ways to manipulate people? Why or why not?

Teamwork

In a team of four or five students, pick a job that one of you now holds or has held (a friend or family member's job will do as well). First make sure everyone in the group understands the job and the performance issues involved, then design a pay-for-knowledge system for this job. When you've completed the design, have each team member comment on whether the system would motivate him or her.

CHAPTER 15

LEADERSHIP IN ORGANIZATIONS

VIDEO EXERCISE

SYNOPSIS

Many of the behavioral and contingency theories of leadership share a common feature: some sort of distinction between leaders who emphasize people and interpersonal relationships and leaders who emphasize results, goals, tasks, or production output. This video shows two managers in action with their teams of employees; one places more importance on the relationships in the group, and the other seems to consider goals and results most important.

EXERCISES

Analysis

1. Which leadership style leads to higher performance: a concern for people and relationships, or a concern for goals, tasks, and production levels? Explain your answer.
2. What are the risks of putting too much emphasis on either extreme (i.e., too much emphasis on relationships or too much emphasis on tasks)? Is it possible to emphasize both people and production simultaneously?
3. What are the similarities between the dichotomy shown in the video (a relationship orientation versus a results orientation) and the various leadership models and theories described in this chapter?
4. Should a team operating without direct supervision place more emphasis on its own internal relations or on its assigned team goals? Explain your answer.
5. What difficulties might managers experience when trying to apply Fiedler's contingency model of leadership?

Application

In practice, managers often find themselves having to adjust their emphasis from people to goals and back again as the situation demands. Assume you've been given the task of drawing up guidelines for project managers at Borland International, a leading developer of personal computer software. These managers are looking for guidance in terms of how much emphasis to put on goals throughout the various stages of a project and how much to put on people. Outline the advice you would give these managers.

Decision

Now put yourself in the shoes of one of those project managers at Borland. Your team's new product is late, but three of your seven programmers have scheduled vacations in the next few weeks. What should you consider before deciding whether to ask the three people to cancel their vacations?

Ethics

How much responsibility does a manager have for the happiness and quality of life of his or her employees? Defend your answer in terms of the ethical decision-making tools presented in Chapter 4.

Teamwork

In a team of four to eight students, complete one or more of the other exercises associated with this video. When you've finished, discuss how leaders emerged in the group and whether those leaders seemed to be concerned more with goals or more with the various relationships in the group. If the group was unable to complete the task in a reasonable amount of time, try to understand why and identify things you as a group member might do differently next time.

CHAPTER 16

GROUPS IN ORGANIZATIONS

SYNOPSIS

VIDEO EXERCISE

Conflict is a key issue in the management of organizational groups. As an expert in this video points out, conflict can be good in some cases and bad in others, depending on the nature of the conflict and its effect on group performance. Conflict can arise because of differences in goals, perspectives, or motivations of group members. Ironically, conflict results because the people involved care about the issue at hand. This caring can form the basis of conflict resolution, provided managers understand the source of the conflict and then help the opposing parties channel their emotions into finding mutually acceptable solutions.

EXERCISES

Analysis

1. What does the professor in the video mean when he says that caring is the source of all conflict? If everyone cared, why would there be any conflicts to resolve?
2. Should managers always intervene when they observe conflict in their organizations? If not, under what circumstances should they intervene, and under what circumstances should they take a hands-off approach?
3. Does an absence of conflict mean that a group is functioning well? Can you give a general answer to this question that applies to all organizational situations?
4. Can you envision a situation in which a command group (a personnel department, for instance) could not be functioning as a group, according to the definition presented in the chapter?
5. Describe a group situation (one from your own experiences or one that you've made up) in which there is healthy conflict and compare that to a situation in which conflict is not healthy for the group. Why is conflict good for the group in one situation but not in the other?

Application

Assume you've just joined a group that has been functioning together with the same set of members for over a year. Using what you know about groups, how could you as a newcomer best contribute to this group's performance?

Decision

Put yourself in the shoes of a grocery store manager. In one case, you encounter two assistant managers who are arguing about the most efficient way to unload produce trucks. In another case, two accountants are arguing whether the way the store reports revenues to the state government is accurate. Would you intervene in either case? Why or why not?

Ethics

What aspect of group behavior might create pressure that leads to ethical lapses? How might this pressure be avoided or reduced?

Teamwork

Put together a team of four or five students with the assumption that you have a major homework project to complete by next Monday. It's now Thursday, and one member of the group is pushing everyone else to set aside time on the weekend to doublecheck the group's work for accuracy. Another member has previous plans to go away for the weekend and doesn't want to change those plans. As a group, try to resolve the conflict, then discuss how you were able (or unable) to resolve it.

CHAPTER 17

MANAGEMENT AND COMMUNICATION

SYNOPSIS

VIDEO EXERCISE

Communication is a key managerial responsibility, affecting all areas of management from planning through controlling. Even a seemingly minor miscommunication can create major headaches for the people in an organization, as this video points out. The importance of communication—and the ease with which it can fall apart—prompts successful managers to take extra care when formulating and transmitting their messages. The second segment of the video highlights another key communication issue, the realm of nonverbal communication. In some cases, the nonverbal message supports and enhances the verbal message, but in others, nonverbal signals can conflict with or even overwhelm the verbal message.

EXERCISES

Analysis

1. Is it possible for a manager to overcommunicate? Explain your answer.
2. How can the sender of a message be sure that the message was received and decoded as the sender intended? Can the sender ever be totally sure?
3. Would an electronic mail exchange, rather than a face-to-face conversation, have avoided the communication breakdown between the editor and the reporter who didn't finish the article when the editor expected him to?
4. Who was at fault in the communication breakdown between the editor and the reporter? Explain your answer.
5. Did the budget overrun in the second part of the video result from a communication breakdown, or was a different sort of managerial problem involved? Explain your answer.

Application

One way to avoid communication breakdowns such as the one over schedules and priorities (involving the editor and the reporter) is to formalize the goal-setting process using various control mechanisms so that communication problems can be minimized. Design such a system for the editor and point out its benefits and limitations.

Decision

If you were the manager leading the meeting in the second part of the video (the woman who discovered the budget overrun), would you have handled the problem with George, the accounting manager, in the same way? Why or why not?

Ethics

What obligations in terms of job-related communication privacy do employees and their employers have to each other?

Teamwork

Divide into groups of four students. In each group, the first member reads a short passage from a book or magazine, rephrases it in his or her own words, and passes it on to the second and third students. However, the first student should tell the second and third students separately, so one can't hear what the other hears, and so the first student has to repeat the message. Next, the second and third students relay what they were told, in their own words, to the fourth student, again at different times so neither can hear what the other is telling the fourth student. Lastly, the fourth student relays what he or she heard back to the first student. The group reconvenes and the first student assesses whether the original thought survived the trip intact. If not, the group should figure out where and how the original message got corrupted.

CHAPTER 18

INFORMATION RESOURCE MANAGEMENT

SYNOPSIS

VIDEO EXERCISE

Information is a key strategic resource for any organization, and the computer represents a powerful means for making the most of that resource. The law firm shown in this video demonstrates the dramatic impact that a well-designed information system can have on individual and organization performance. These results apply to the field of law, of course, but the concepts they employ can be applied to virtually any organization. The capabilities shown in the video, which include word processing, graphics, database retrieval, and electronic mail, help employees and managers make better use of their information resources—and of their own time and talents.

EXERCISES

Analysis

1. Can you think of any dangers in relying on a computer in a high-pressure situation such as a courtroom? How might computer users lessen the risks that you're able to identify?
2. How do the personal computers in this video improve the quality of the information that these people are dealing with?
3. How does the single personal computer you saw in the courtroom constitute an information system? How does it convert data into information?
4. Would you call the courtroom computer a management information system (MIS) or a decision support system (DSS)? Defend your answer.
5. The text identified four strategic uses of information; which of these four did you see represented in the scenarios shown in this video?

Application

How might the managing partner of this law firm use personal computers to help with managerial control? If necessary, do some quick research into the basic operation of a law office and the information-processing products available to lawyers before outlining your answer.

Decision

Assume that you're the managing partner of this law firm, and a computer training firm is offering a one-week training course in computer use for lawyers. You've heard from other lawyers that the course is really quite good, but you're concerned about the amount of time that the training might involve. What should you consider before asking all the lawyers in the office to attend?

Ethics

Is it fair for one side in a court proceeding to use computers as shown in this video if the other side doesn't have similar capabilities?

Teamwork

With a team of three or four other students, research the products available today for word processing in a small office. Relying on product reviews in magazines, product literature from manufacturers, and whatever insight you can glean through interviews or other sources, outline the hardware and software components that would make an effective solution for a five-person office.

CHAPTER 19

FUNDAMENTALS OF CONTROL

SYNOPSIS

VIDEO EXERCISE

The company you'll see in this video faces a classic control problem: product quality has slipped below standards, and no one is completely sure why it happened or how the problem can be fixed. The managers move into action when a major customer rejects products because of poor quality, and they begin to identify the multiple reasons for the disappointing performance. This company's efforts involve all three phases of the control process, and they emphasize the importance of clear performance standards and timely feedback. (Product quality is just one of many aspects of organizational control, of course, but it is relatively easy to demonstrate and discuss, so it provides a perfect illustration of control concepts.)

EXERCISES

Analysis

1. Why is it important for this company to redesign its financial reporting system in an effort to fix a purely technical problem with one of its products?
2. Based on what you've learned so far about the distinction between quality control and quality assurance (i.e., whether the emphasis is on post-action control or preliminary and concurrent controls), would you say that this company now exhibits a quality control approach or a quality assurance approach? Is this different from its approach before the problem was discovered and fixed?
3. What role did people play, both in the control problem and in its resolution? Did the solution involve controlling people more carefully? Explain your answer.
4. Did the company have a problem with performance standards? If so, how did the managers resolve this particular problem?
5. The top manager in the manufacturing company became closely involved in the quality improvement effort. Since top managers are primarily concerned with strategic issues, does his involvement constitute strategic control, or is it tactical or operational control?

Application

What preliminary control steps should this manufacturer take to help improve the quality of its products? How would these steps help?

Decision

Assume you're the CEO of the manufacturing company shown in the video, and your company has fixed the quality problem. Should you approach the key customer who returned the defective products and explain the steps you've taken to improve quality, even if this involves sharing some embarrassing past performance and managerial problems? Explain your answer.

Ethics

Is this manufacturer obligated to tell customers about potential quality problems in its products, even if there is no certainty that the problems will actually appear?

Teamwork

In a team of four or five students, select a not-for-profit organization that one student belongs to or is aware of and assume that this organization continually has problems paying its monthly bills. The overall amount of cash available each year seems like enough to pay all the bills, but there never seems to be enough on hand when the bills are due. Design a simple budgetary control system that would alleviate this problem.

CHAPTER 20

OPERATIONS MANAGEMENT

SYNOPSIS

VIDEO EXERCISE

The principles of successful operations management apply whether the product in question is a giant piece of earth-moving equipment or a precision laser videodisk. This video provides a quick look at both kinds of operations, first at a Caterpillar plant and then at Pioneer's laserdisk production facility. Both segments show how the organizations address a wide variety of operations management issues, from control concepts to the latest in design and production technology. In addition, you can sense from the video how important operations management is to the success of both of these companies, even though one is considered high technology and the other is in the vastly different field of heavy equipment. Lastly, you'll see how both facilities, even with the latest technological systems in place, rely on people to make it all happen.

EXERCISES

Analysis

1. What examples did you see of testing for quality at the Caterpillar and Pioneer plants?
2. Is Caterpillar's worldwide dealer network part of its operations? Why or why not?
3. How is technology used in the Caterpillar plant to improve quality and productivity? Has this technology eliminated the need for human interaction in the manufacturing process?
4. Why does Caterpillar want its customers to know about such details as the fact that it uses a flexible manufacturing system? Why should customers care about anything other than getting good equipment at a good price?
5. Does the facilities layout in the Pioneer videodisk plant fall into the process, product, or fixed-position category? Why?

Application

In a complex, multistage process such as the one described in the Pioneer plant, handling demand fluctuations can be a major operational challenge. If you were the manager of the Pioneer plant, what steps would you take to handle temporary periods of unusually high demand?

Decision

Introducing new processes and new equipment into any kind of operation creates some special management challenges. These can range from employee displacement to training to simply finding space to put everything. Assume you're the manager of the Caterpillar plant; draw up a list of general issues you should consider before deciding to make any significant changes to the plant's operations.

Ethics

How might a quality control or quality assurance system be a source of ethical pressure on the employees and managers involved?

Teamwork

With three or four other students, research the process used to manufacture mountain bikes, personal computers, or another product that interests you. Based on what you can learn from the research, sketch a production facility that uses a product, process, or fixed-position layout, whichever you think is best for the product you've chosen.

CHAPTER 21

QUALITY, PRODUCTIVITY, AND CUSTOMER SATISFACTION

SYNOPSIS

VIDEO EXERCISE

The interrelated issues of quality, productivity, and customer satisfaction create a two-edged sword. Managed well, they build on each other, and improvements in one area often lead to improvements in one or both of the other areas. Managed poorly, they can feed off each other in a downward spiral, such as when poor quality leads to productivity and customer satisfaction problems, which in turn dampen the organization's ability to fix the quality problems, which creates more productivity and satisfaction problems. This video highlights the importance of these issues and their interrelatedness. It also points out that quality is just as important in service-producing organizations as it is in goods-producing organizations.

EXERCISES

Analysis

1. Should the same process used to define quality standards for tangible goods also be used to define standards for intangible services? Why or why not?
2. Would this delivery company's facilities be of any concern to customers? After all, the customers care only whether they get good service and a good price, so do the facilities really matter?
3. Is there anything wrong with the performance goals listed early in the video (the group of goals that included 98 percent on-time deliveries)? What effect might these goals have on customer satisfaction?
4. How will the quality improvements identified in the video help the company cut costs? Is it safe to say that quality improvements always result in cost cuts? Why or why not?
5. Which of the steps taken to improve quality and productivity were in the realm of operations? Which involved human resources?

Application

How could this company have used benchmarking to help improve its quality, productivity, and customer satisfaction? Did you see any cases of benchmarking in the video?

Decision

Once employees realize that management wants to improve all aspects of quality, productivity, and customer satisfaction, suggestions are bound to start rolling in from all directions. Propose a set of guidelines that will help the company choose which ideas should be implemented, including the people who should make the decisions.

Ethics

Do organizations have an ethical responsibility to provide quality goods and services? Do for-profit and not-for-profit organizations have the same type of responsibility?

Teamwork

Join up with a team of five or six students and assume that together you'll be working on a semester-long project in one of your classes. Assume further that your performance on this project constitutes one-half of your final grade. (You can use a real course if it helps identify particular issues and concerns.) What steps can you take to ensure that the quality of your work will meet the instructor's expectations?

REFERENCES

NOTES

CHAPTER 1

1. Adapted from Brenton R. Schlender, "Bill Gates Sets a New Target," *Fortune,* 25 February 1991, 12–13; Fred Moody, "Mr. Software," *New York Times Magazine,* 25 August 1991, 26–30, 54, 56, 59; Microsoft Corporation 1990 Annual Report, 1–18; Evelyn Richards, "A Hard-Nosed Businessman with a Certain Boyish Charm," *Washington Post,* 30 December 1990, H3; Carrie Tuhy and Greg Couch, "Software's Old Man Is 30," *Money,* July 1986, 54–55; Brenton R. Schlender, "How Bill Gates Keeps the Magic Going," *Fortune,* 18 June 1990, 82–86, 88–89; G. Pascal Zachary, "Operating System: Opening of 'Windows' Shows How Bill Gates Succeeds in Software," *Wall Street Journal,* 21 May 1990, A1, A4; Mary Jo Foley, "Boy Wonder: Microsoft's Bill Gates," *Electronic Business,* 15 August 1988, 54–56; D. Ruby, S. Kanzler, R. Glitman, and T. Pompili, "Can Microsoft Blend Blue Jeans and Gray Flannel?" *PC Week,* 21 October 1986, 57, 59, 72–74; Daniel Ruby and Stephen Kanzler, "Is IBM–Microsoft Relationship Near Its End?" *PC Week,* 21 October 1986, 57, 74; Dan Ruby, "Microsoft's Network Is a Model for Corporate Communications Systems," *PC Week,* 21 October 1986, 73; Richard A. Shaffer, "The Growth of Microsoft," *Personal Computing,* June 1986, 29; Jonathan B. Levine, "Microsoft: Recovering from Its Stumble over 'Windows,'" *Business Week,* July 22, 1985, 107–108; "Microsoft Splits Up Presidency," *Los Angeles Times,* 4 February 1992, D5.
2. Randy Hodson and Teresa A. Sullivan, *The Social Organization of Work* (Belmont, Calif.: Wadsworth, 1990), 288.
3. E. B. Knauft, Renee A. Berger, and Sandra T. Grey, *Profiles of Excellence* (San Francisco: Jossey-Bass, 1991), 92–93; Mark Maremont, "The Brit Invasion That Could Rock Tower Records," *Business Week,* 3 December 1990, 41; Lisa Cross, "Swim with Sharks," *Graphic Arts Monthly,* April 1988, 116–118; Adrienne S. Harris, "Management: Second to One," *Black Enterprise,* June 1990, 282.
4. Michael Janofsky, "Hard Days for Sports in Eastern Europe," *New York Times,* 10 March 1991, sec. 8, 5.
5. Edwin A. Gerloff, *Organizational Theory and Design* (New York: McGraw-Hill, 1985), 6–7.
6. James L. Perry and Hal G. Rainey, "The Public–Private Distinction in Organization Theory: A Critique and Research Strategy," *Academy of Management Review* 13, no. 2 (April 1988): 182–201.
7. Alex Taylor III, "Can GM Remodel Itself?" *Fortune,* 13 January 1992, 26–29, 32–34.
8. Judith Manfredo Legorreta and Dennis R. Young, "Why Organizations Turn Nonprofit: Lessons from Case Studies," in *The Economics of Nonprofit Institutions: Studies in Structure and Policy,* edited by Susan Rose-Ackerman (New York: Oxford University Press, 1986), 199–200; Burton A. Weisbrod, *The Nonprofit Economy* (Cambridge, Mass.: Harvard University Press, 1988), 84.
9. Courtland L. Bovée and John V. Thill, *Marketing* (New York: McGraw-Hill, 1992), 5–6.
10. *Handbook for Professional Managers,* edited by Lester R. Bittel and Jackson E. Ramsey (New York: McGraw-Hill, 1985), 518.
11. Gail E. Schares, "You Think Your Job Is Tough, Try Turning East Germany Around," *Business Week,* 3 December 1990, 51; "Private Hands May Save Zoo a State Abandoned," *New York Times,* 14 April 1991, 18.
12. Hal G. Rainey, "Public Management: Recent Research on the Political Context and Managerial Roles, Structures, and Behaviors," *Journal of Management* 15, no. 2 (1989): 229–250.
13. Robert D. Pritchard, Steven D. Jones, Philip L. Roth, and Karla K. Steubing, "Effects of Group Feedback, Goal Setting, and Incentives on Organizational Productivity," *Journal of Applied Psychology* 73, no. 2 (1988): 337–358.
14. Peter F. Drucker, *Management: Tasks, Responsibilities, Practices* (New York: Harper & Row, 1974), 45–46.
15. John Templeman, "Bertelsmann: When Being a Giant Isn't Enough," *Business Week,* 12 November 1990, 72–75; Fremont E. Kast and James E. Rosenzweig, *Organization and Management: A Systems and Contingency Approach* (New York: McGraw-Hill, 1985), 400.
16. Drucker, *Management,* 401.
17. Peter F. Drucker, *The New Realities* (New York: Harper & Row, 1989), 230.
18. Laxmi Nakarmi, "At Lucky-Goldstar, the Koos Loosen the Reins," *Business Week,* 18 February 1991, 72.
19. Nakarmi, "At Lucky-Goldstar, the Koos Loosen the Reins," 72.
20. Stephen Phillips, "Just Don't Get in Joe Gorman's Way," *Business Week,* 12 November 1990, 88, 90.
21. Joyce Anne Oliver, "Motivating People to Succeed Is His Greatest Joy," *Marketing News,* 18 March 1991, 16.
22. Leslie Brokaw, "Putting the House in Order," *Inc.,* March 1991, 102.
23. Henry Mintzberg, *The Nature of Managerial Work* (New York: Harper & Row, 1973), 4; Stephen J. Carroll and Dennis J. Gillen, "Are the Classical Management Functions Useful in Describing Managerial Work?" *Academy of Management Review* 12, no. 1 (1987): 38–51.
24. Henry Mintzberg, "The Manager's Job: Folklore and Fact," *Harvard Business Review,* July–August 1975, 49–61.
25. Mintzberg, "The Manager's Job," 50.
26. Rosemary Stewart, "A Model for Understanding Managerial Jobs and Behavior," *Academy of Management Review* 7, no. 1 (1982): 7–13.
27. Roy Serpa and Donald W. Jackson, Jr., "Top Management's Selling Role," *Chief Executive,* June 1990, 36.
28. Andrew Kupfer, "How to Be a Global Manager," *Fortune,* 14 March 1988, 52–54, 58.
29. Jane Pickard, "Michael Osbaldeston: Chief Executive, Ashridge Management College," *Personnel Management,* January 1990, 26–27.
30. John Kotter, *The General Managers* (New York: Free Press, 1982), 60–76.
31. Clifton Brown, "Now the Hard Part for Riley: Coaching Knicks," *New York Times,* 1 June 1991, 29, 31; Ira Berkow, "New Coach, with Old Problems," *New York Times,* 1 June 1991, 29; Sam Goldaper, "The Once, Future and Present Coach," *New York Times,* 1 June 1991, 31.
32. Rosemary Stewart, *Choices for the Manager* (Englewood Cliffs, N.J.: Prentice Hall, 1982), 5; Stewart, "A Model for Understanding Managerial Jobs and Behavior," 7–13.
33. Thomas M. Rohan, "Keeping the Boss Happy—Four Times," *Industry Week,* 16 July 1990, 50–52.
34. Colin P. Hales, "What Do Managers Do? A Critical Review of the Evidence," *Journal of Management Studies,* January 1986, 88–115; Mintzberg, "The Manager's Job," 49–61; Stewart, "A Model for Understanding Managerial Jobs and Behavior," 12.
35. Tom Peters, *Thriving on Chaos* (New York: Harper & Row, 1987), 521–522.
36. Wal-Mart 1989 Annual Report, 29.
37. Rosabeth Moss Kanter, "The New Managerial Work," *Harvard Business Review,* November–December 1989, 92; John Teresko, "Speeding the Product Development Cycle," *Industry Week,* 18 July 1988, 41.
38. Kast and Rosenzweig, *Organization and Management,* 244–245; Ron Zemke, "Putting the Squeeze on Middle Managers," *Training,* December 1988, 41–46; Hodson and Sullivan, *The Social Organization of Work,* 296.
39. Samuel C. Certo and J. Paul Peter, *Strategic Management: Concepts and Applications* (New York: McGraw-Hill, 1991), 7.
40. Gerald d'Amboise and Marie Muldowney, "Management Theory for Small Business: Attempts and Requirements," *Academy of Management Review* 13, no. 2 (1988): 226–240.
41. Louis E. Boone and David L. Kurtz, "CEOs: A Group Profile," *Business Horizons,* July–August 1988, 38–42; Ford S. Worthy, "How CEOs Manage Their Time," *Fortune,* 18 January 1988, 88; Andrall E. Pearson, "Tough-Minded Ways to Get Innovative," *Harvard Business Review,* May–June 1988, 99–106; Harry S. Jonas III, Ronald E. Fry, and Suresh Srivastva, "The Office of the CEO: Understanding the Executive Experience," *Academy of Management Executive* 4, no. 3 (1990): 36–48; Andrall E. Pearson, "Six Basics for General Managers," *Harvard Business Review,* July–August 1989, 94–101; Jerome M. Rosow, ed., *Views from the Top: Establishing the Foundation for the Future of Business* (New York: Facts on File, 1985), xi.
42. Peter F. Drucker, "Tomorrow's Restless Managers," *Industry Week,* 18 April 1988, 25–

27; Zemke, "Putting the Squeeze on Middle Managers," 41–46; Kenneth Labich, "Making over Middle Managers," *Fortune,* 8 May 1989, 58–64.

43. Anne Scott Daughtrey and Betty Roper Ricks, *Contemporary Supervision* (New York: McGraw-Hill, 1989), 41.

44. Lester B. Korn, "How the Next CEO Will Be Different," *Fortune,* 22 May 1989, 157–161.

45. Robert L. Katz, "Skills of an Effective Administrator," *Harvard Business Review,* September–October 1974, 90–102.

46. Katz, "Skills of an Effective Administrator," 90–102.

47. Gregory L. Miles, "Heinz Ain't Broke, But It's Doing a Lot of Fixing," *Business Week,* 11 December 1989, 84–88.

48. Katz, "Skills of an Effective Administrator," 90–102.

49. Mark Stevens, "Turnaround Tricks: Getting a Company Back on Its Feet," *Working Woman,* December 1990, 45–48.

50. Katz, "Skills of an Effective Administrator," 90–102.

51. "Just One Rider Holds the Reins," *Business Week,* 26 March 1990, 70.

52. Ann M. Morrison, Randall P. White, Ellen Van Velsor, and the Center for Creative Leadership, "Women with Promise: Who Succeeds, Who Fails?" *Working Woman,* June 1987, 79–84.

53. Robert Mims and Ephraim Lewis, "A Portrait of the Boss," *Business Week,* 19 October 1990, 8–14; Patricia M. Carey, "The Making of a Global Manager," *North American International Business,* June 1990, 36–41; Lyman W. Porter and Lawrence E. McKibbin, *Management Education and Development: Drift or Thrust into the 21st Century?* (New York: McGraw-Hill, 1988), 64, 77, 93.

54. Porter and McKibbin, *Management Education and Development,* 217, 224–226.

55. Barbara Block, "Intuition Creeps out of the Closet and into the Boardroom," *Management Review,* May 1990, 59; Lise M. Saari, Terry R. Johnson, Steven D. McLaughlin, and Denise M. Zimmerle, "A Survey of Management Training and Education Practices in U.S. Companies," *Personnel Psychology,* 1988, 741; David J. Cherrington, *The Management of Human Resources* (Boston: Allyn & Bacon, 1991), 369; A. Nicholas Komanecky, "Developing New Managers at GE," *Training and Development Journal,* June 1988, 62; Ken Bowman, "The Organic Way to Grow Managers," *Personnel Management,* October 1990, 50–55.

56. Terence R. Mitchell and James R. Larson, Jr., *People in Organizations: An Introduction to Organizational Behavior* (New York: McGraw-Hill, 1987), 539–540; Morrison et al., "Women with Promise," 80; Joseph Weber, "'I Am Intense, Aggressive, and Hard-Charging,'" *Business Week,* 30 April 1990, 58; Ellen Fagenson, "The Power of a Mentor," *Group & Organization Studies* 13, no. 2 (June 1988): 182–194.

57. Stephen D. Solomon, "The Entrepreneurial Age," *Career Futures,* 1 July 1988, 9; Mims and Lewis, "A Portrait of the Boss," 11.

58. Norm Alster, "Henri Termeer's Orphan Drug Strategy," *Forbes,* 27 May 1991, 202, 204, 207.

59. Thomas J. Peters and Robert H. Waterman, Jr., *In Search of Excellence* (New York: Warner Books, 1982), 223–229; Perry Pascarella and Mark A. Frohman, *The Purpose-Driven Organization: Unleashing the Power of Direction and Commitment* (San Francisco: Jossey-Bass, 1990), 107–118.

60. Jenny C. McCune and Don Wallace, "Never Say Die," *Success,* July–August 1990, 35–44.

61. Kotter, *The General Managers,* 47.

62. Michael L. Dertouzos, Richard K. Lester, and Robert M. Solow, *Made in America: Regaining the Productive Edge* (New York: Harper Perennial, 1990), 26–29; Karen Pennar, "Yes, We're Down. No, We're Not Out," *Business Week,* 17 December 1990, 62; Thomas A. Stewart, "The New American Century: Where We Stand," *Fortune,* Spring–Summer 1991, 12–23.

63. Peters, *Thriving on Chaos,* 81; Stewart, "The New American Century," 12–23.

64. George S. Day, *Market Driven Strategy* (New York: Free Press, 1990), 18.

65. Rosabeth Moss Kanter, *The Change Masters* (New York: Touchstone Books, 1984), 20–23; W. Jack Duncan, Peter M. Ginter, and Stuart A. Capper, "Excellence in Public Administration: Four Transferable Lessons from the Private Sector," *Public Productivity & Management Review* 14, no. 3 (Spring 1991): 227–236.

66. Richard I. Kirkland, Jr., "Entering a New Age of Boundless Competition," *Fortune,* 14 March 1988, 40–48.

67. Peters, *Thriving on Chaos,* 474.

68. Drucker, *The New Realities,* 86–88.

69. Stephen C. Harper, "How to Prevent the Rude Awakening of Management Shock," *Industrial Management,* July–August 1990, 11–14, 32.

70. See note 1.

CHAPTER 2

1. Adapted from Bo Burlingham, "This Woman Has Changed Business Forever," *Inc.,* June 1990, 34–46; "The Body Shop: Brave New Markets," *European Cosmetic Markets,* July 1991, 199–201; Anne Ferguson, "Soapworks' Good Works," *Management Today,* May 1989, 94–100; David Oates, "Keeping Body and Soul Together," *Director,* June 1988, 64–67; Jon Steinberg, "The Body Biz," *Ms.,* September 1988, 50–53; John Barnes, "A 'Natural' Formula for Success," *U.S. News & World Report,* 12 December 1988, 70; Dana Longstreet, "Saving Faces," *American Health,* July–August 1990, 54–55; Mark Maremont, "A Cosmetics Company with a Conscience," *Business Week,* 23 May 1988, 136; Anita Roddick, "Anita Roddick: Eco-business," *Utne Reader,* September–October 1990, 47; Deborah Cowley, "The Woman from the Body Shop," *Reader's Digest,* September 1989, 159–164; Lisa Distelheim, "The Entrepreneur," *Life,* November 1988, 21–23; Connie Wallace, "Lessons in Marketing from a Maverick," *Working Woman,* October 1990, 81–84; Rachel Simpson, "How Body Shop Stays on Its Toes," *Marketing,* September 1986, 24–27; Vicki Woods, "The Beauty Queens," *Vogue,* January 1990, 190–195, 240.

2. Nordstrom 1989 Annual Report, 7, 11.

3. Lisa Gubernick, "Making History Pay," *Forbes,* 13 May 1991, 132; Alan M. Kantrow, ed., "Why History Matters to Managers," *Harvard Business Review,* January–February 1986, 81–88; Claude S. George, Jr., *The History of Management Thought,* 2nd ed. (Englewood Cliffs, N.J.: Prentice Hall, 1972), 181.

4. Harold Koontz, "The Management Theory Jungle Revisited," in *Contemporary Readings in Organizational Behavior,* edited by Fred Luthans and Kenneth R. Thompson (New York: McGraw-Hill, 1981), 355–372; Fred Luthans and Todd I. Stewart, "A General Contingency Theory of Management," in *Contemporary Readings in Organizational Behavior,* edited by Fred Luthans and Kenneth R. Thompson (New York: McGraw-Hill, 1981), 373.

5. Elizabeth M. Fowler, "Educating Managers in Hungary," *New York Times,* 3 January 1989, sec. d, 8.

6. Joseph W. McGuire, "Management Theory: Retreat to the Academy," *Business Horizons,* July–August 1982, 31–37; John P. Kotter, *The General Managers* (New York: Free Press, 1982), 147; Koontz, "The Management Theory Jungle Revisited," 355–372; Raymond E. Miles, *Theories of Management: Implications for Organizational Behavior and Development* (New York: McGraw-Hill, 1975), 2–3.

7. George, *The History of Management Thought,* 170–171; Daniel A. Wren, *The Evolution of Management Thought,* 2nd ed. (New York: Wiley, 1979), 560–561; Daniel A. Wren, "Management History: Issues and Ideas for Teaching and Research," *Journal of Management* 13, no. 2 (1987): 339–350.

8. Wren, "Management History," 339–350.

9. Alvin Toffler, *The Third Wave* (New York: Morrow, 1980), 17–23.

10. Wren, *The Evolution of Management Thought,* 6–7.

11. Wren, *The Evolution of Management Thought,* 5–6; Toffler, *The Third Wave,* 20–23; Alfred D. Chandler, Jr., *Strategy and Structure: Chapters in the History of the American Industrial Enterprise* (Cambridge, Mass.: MIT Press, 1962), 19.

12. Wren, *The Evolution of Management Thought,* 8–9; Toffler, *The Third Wave,* 62–67.

13. George, *The History of Management Thought,* 3–22; Wren, *The Evolution of Management Thought,* 16, 18, 23–24; Chester I. Barnard, *The Functions of the Executive* (1938; reprint Cambridge, Mass.: Harvard University Press, 1968), 5; Peter F. Drucker, *Management: Tasks, Responsibilities, Practices* (New York: Harper & Row, 1974), 21.

14. Stephenson O. Unyimadu, "Management and Industrial Revolution in Europe, United States of America and Japan," *Engineering Management International* 5 (1989): 209–218.

15. Drucker, *Management,* 22–23; George, *The History of Management Thought,* 62–63; Wren, *The Evolution of Management Thought,* 70–75.

16. Steven L. Mandell, *Computers and Data Processing Today* (St. Paul, Minn.: West Publishing, 1986), 39–41; George, *The History of Management Thought,* 75–77; Wren, *The Evolution of Management Thought,* 78–81.

17. George, *The History of Management Thought,* 84–85; Drucker, *Management,* 23; Allen C. Bluedorn, ed., "Special Book Review Section on the Classics of Management," *Academy of Management Review,* 11 April 1986, 442.

18. George, *The History of Management Thought,* 75, 82–83, 85; Chandler, *Strategy and Structure,* 21–22; Wren, *The Evolution of Management Thought,* 81–84, 94–96, 98–101.

19. Sudhir Kakar, *Frederick Taylor: A Study in Personality and Innovation* (Cambridge, Mass.: MIT Press, 1970), 20–21, 41, 87–97; Frederick Winslow Taylor, *Shop Management,* reprinted in Frederick Winslow Taylor, *Scientific Management* (New York: Harper & Brothers,

1947), 9, 28–29, 32–33; George, *The History of Management Thought,* 90–94.

20. Bluedorn, "Special Book Review Section on the Classics of Management," 443–447; George, *The History of Management Thought,* 90–94; Herbert J. Davis and Richard O. Blalack, "From Scientific Management to Management Science: An Integrative Effort," *Industrial Management,* November 1975, 10–14; Anne Scott Daughtrey and Betty Roper Ricks, *Contemporary Supervision: Management People and Technology* (New York: McGraw-Hill, 1989), 6–7.

21. Henri Fayol, *General and Industrial Management,* trans. Constance Storrs (London: Pitman & Sons, 1949, reprint 1954), 67; Peter F. Drucker, *The Practice of Management* (New York: Harper & Row, 1982), 284; Taylor, *Shop Management,* 98–99.

22. Drucker, *Management,* 24; Bluedorn, "Special Book Review Section on the Classics of Management," 443–447; George, *The History of Management Thought,* 90–94; Fremont E. Kast and James E. Rosenzweig, *Organization & Management: A Systems and Contingency Approach,* 4th ed. (New York: McGraw-Hill, 1985), 59–62.

23. Frederick Winslow Taylor, *Principles of Scientific Management,* reprinted in *Scientific Management* (New York: Harper & Brothers, 1947), 7.

24. Edwin A. Locke, "The Ideas of Frederick W. Taylor: An Evaluation," *Academy of Management Review* 7, no. 1 (1982): 14–24; David Halpern, Stephen Osofsky, and Myron I. Peskin, "Taylorism Revised and Revised for the 1990s," *Industrial Management,* January–February 1989, 20–23.

25. Thomas A. Stewart, "Do You Push Your People Too Hard?" *Fortune,* 22 October 1990, 124.

26. W. Jack Duncan, *Great Ideas in Management* (San Francisco: Jossey-Bass, 1989), 58.

27. George, *The History of Management Thought,* 99–101; Bluedorn, "Special Book Review Section on the Classics of Management," 448–451; Wren, *The Evolution of Management Thought,* 169; Frank B. Gilbreth and Lillian M. Gilbreth, "Classifying the Elements of Work," in *Management Classics,* 2nd ed., edited by Michael T. Matteson and John M. Ivancevich (Santa Monica, Calif.: Goodyear Publishing, 1981), 142; *Taylor's Testimony before the Special House Committee,* reprinted in *Scientific Management* (New York: Harper & Brothers, 1947), 68–71.

28. George, *The History of Management Thought,* 99–101.

29. Frank B. Gilbreth, Jr., and Ernestine Gilbreth Carey, *Cheaper by the Dozen* (New York: Crowell, 1948); George, *The History of Management Thought,* 99–101; Gilbreth and Gilbreth, "Classifying the Elements of Work," 142–151.

30. Pamela B. Blake, "Central Sterile Supply Productivity and Time Study Analysis," *Hospital Material Management Quarterly,* November 1990, 1–8.

31. Alex W. Rathe, ed., *Gantt on Management: Guidelines for Today's Executive* (New York: American Management Association and American Association of Mechanical Engineers, n.d.), 22, 97–106; George, *The History of Management Thought,* 103–105.

32. Michael Schroeder and Walecia Konrad, "Nucor: Rolling Right into Steel's Big Time," *Business Week,* 19 November 1990, 76–80; Lawrence R. Jauch and James B. Townsend, *Cases in Strategic Management and Business Theory,* 2nd ed. (New York: McGraw-Hill, 1990), 276; Rathe, *Gantt on Management,* 135–137.

33. George, *The History of Management Thought,* 107–109; Duncan, *Great Ideas in Management,* 30, 36, 40.

34. Wren, *The Evolution of Management Thought,* 226–248; Bertram M. Gross, *The Managing of Organizations: The Administrative Struggle,* Vol. 1 (London: Free Press of Glencoe, 1964), 128–136; Fayol, *General and Industrial Management,* x.

35. Fayol, *General and Industrial Management,* 3–6.

36. Fayol, *General and Industrial Management,* 19, 41–42; Bluedorn, "Special Book Review Section on the Classics of Management," 454–456; George, *The History of Management Thought,* 110–115; Drucker, *Management,* 24; Wren, *The Evolution of Management Thought,* 226–234.

37. Max Weber, "The Ideal Bureaucracy," in *Management Classics,* 2nd ed., edited by Michael T. Matteson and John M. Ivancevich (Santa Monica, Calif.: Goodyear Publishing, 1981), 152–158; Wren, *The Evolution of Management Thought,* 249–254; Richard M. Weiss, "Weber on Bureaucracy: Management Consultant or Political Theorist?" *Academy of Management Review* 8, no. 2 (1983): 242–248; Kast and Rosenzweig, *Organization & Management,* 67.

38. Wren, *The Evolution of Management Thought,* 249–254; Gross, *The Managing of Organizations,* 136–143; Charles Perrow, "The Short and Glorious History of Organizational Theory," in *Contemporary Readings in Organizational Behavior,* edited by Fred Luthans and Kenneth R. Thompson (New York: McGraw-Hill, 1981), 412; James A. Gazell and Darrlee L. Pugh, "Administrative Theory and Large Organizations of the Future: Whither Bureaucracy?" *International Journal of Public Administration* 13, no. 6 (1990): 827–858.

39. Jon Connole, "Bureaucracy Even Surprises Centerior CEO," *Crain's Cleveland Business,* 30 April 1990, 22; Ellen Wojahn, "Reebok Wants Respect," *CFO,* February 1988, 28–36.

40. Chester I. Barnard, "The Theory of Authority," in *Management Classics,* 2nd ed., edited by Michael T. Matteson and John M. Ivancevich (Santa Monica, Calif.: Goodyear Publishing, 1981), 228–235; Perrow, "The Short and Glorious History of Organizational Theory," 410; William B. Wolf, *The Basic Barnard: An Introduction to Chester I. Barnard and His Theories of Organization and Management* (Ithaca, N.Y.: New York State School of Industrial and Labor Relations, 1974), 7–16, 82–83, 111–114; Barnard, *The Functions of the Executive,* 3–7, 65–75.

41. James G. March and Herbert A. Simon, *Organizations* (New York: Wiley, 1958), 28.

42. L. Urwick, *The Elements of Administration* (New York: Harper & Brothers, n.d.), 66, 82–84; Gross, *The Managing of Organizations,* 120–121, 142–148; George, *The History of Management Thought,* 142–143.

43. Perrow, "The Short and Glorious History of Organizational Theory," 409; Y. K. Shetty, "Contingency Management: Current Perspective for Managing Organizations," *Management Review* 14, no. 4 (1974): 27–34.

44. Perrow, "The Short and Glorious History of Organizational Theory," 410–411.

45. George, *The History of Management Thought,* 138–139, 152–153; Bluedorn, "Special Book Review Section on the Classics of Management," 451–454; Wren, *The Evolution of Management Thought,* 324–334; Gross, *The Managing of Organizations,* 150–160; Mary Parker Follett, "Management as a Profession," in *Management Classics,* 2nd ed., edited by Michael T. Matteson and John M. Ivancevich (Santa Monica, Calif.: Goodyear Publishing, 1981), 9–18.

46. L. D. Parker, "Control in Organizational Life: The Contribution of Mary Parker Follett," *Academy of Management Review* 9, no. 4 (1984): 736–745.

47. George, *The History of Management Thought,* 105–106; Drucker, *Management,* 24; Wren, *The Evolution of Management Thought,* 211–213.

48. Drucker, *Management,* 181; Wren, *The Evolution of Management Thought,* 299–300; George, *The History of Management Thought,* 136.

49. F. J. Roethlisberger and William J. Dickson, *Management and the Worker* (Cambridge, Mass.: Harvard University Press, 1939), 14–18; Elton Mayo, *The Human Problems of an Industrial Civilization* (New York: Macmillan, 1933), 55–76.

50. Roethlisberger and Dickson, *Management and the Worker,* 3–4, 57–59; Berkeley Rice, "The Hawthorne Defect; Persistence of a Flawed Theory," *Psychology Today,* February 1982, 70–74; Alex Carey, "The Hawthorne Studies: A Radical Criticism," *American Sociological Review,* 32, no. 3 (1967): 403–416; John G. Adair, "The Hawthorne Effect: A Reconsideration of the Methodological Artifact," *Journal of Applied Psychology* 69, no. 2 (1984): 334–345.

51. Roethlisberger and Dickson, *Management and the Worker,* 412–426; Wren, *The Evolution of Management Thought,* 307–313; George, *The History of Management Thought,* 137; Bluedorn, "Special Book Review Section on the Classics of Management," 461–463.

52. George, *The History of Management Thought,* 136–137; Wren, *The Evolution of Management Thought,* 318–323; Elton Mayo, "The Seamy Side of Progress," in *Management Classics,* 2nd ed., edited by Michael T. Matteson and John M. Ivancevich (Santa Monica, Calif.: Goodyear Publishing, 1981), 208–215.

53. Michael T. Matteson and John M. Ivancevich, eds., *Management Classics,* 2nd ed. (Santa Monica, Calif.: Goodyear Publishing, 1981), 236; Paul Hersey and Kenneth H. Blanchard, *Management of Organizational Behavior: Utilizing Human Resources,* 5th ed. (Englewood Cliffs, N.J.: Prentice Hall, 1988), 32–35; A. H. Maslow, "A Theory of Human Motivation," in *Readings in Managerial Psychology,* 3rd ed., edited by Harold J. Leavitt, Louis R. Pondy, and David M. Boje (Chicago: University of Chicago Press, 1980), 5–22; Hugh J. Arnold and Daniel C. Feldman, *Organizational Behavior* (New York: McGraw-Hill, 1986), 52–55.

54. Adapted from Gazell and Pugh, "Administrative Theory and Large Organizations of the Future," 827–858; Wren, *The Evolution of Management Thought,* 482–486; Douglas McGregor, *The Human Side of Enterprise* (New York: McGraw-Hill, 1960), 33–57; Raymond W. Smith, "Five Misconceptions about Big Business: Counterproductive Rules of Thumb," *Vital Speeches of the Day,* 1 August 1988, 631–634.

55. Toffler, *The Third Wave,* 78.
56. Wren, *The Evolution of Management Thought,* 475–476; John J. Morse and Jay W. Lorsch, "Beyond Theory Y," in *Readings in Managerial Psychology,* 2nd ed., edited by Harold J. Leavitt and Louis R. Pondy (Chicago: University of Chicago Press, 1973), 399–412.
57. Hersey and Blanchard, *Management of Organizational Behavior,* 15; Arnold and Feldman, *Organizational Behavior,* 4.
58. Shetty, "Contingency Management," 27–34; Jay W. Lorsch, "Making Behavioral Science More Useful," *Harvard Business Review,* March–April 1979, 171–180; T. F. Gautschi, "Hawthorne Studies: A Workplace Classic," *Design News,* 23 October 1989, 180.
59. Drucker, *Management,* 11–12; Gross, *The Managing of Organizations,* 214–215; Davis and Blalack, "From Scientific Management to Management Science," 10–14; George, *The History of Management Thought,* 158–160.
60. George, *The History of Management Thought,* 158–163; Wren, *The Evolution of Management Thought,* 508–517.
61. Gross, *The Managing of Organizations,* 215; Gregory P. White, "A Survey of Recent Management Science Applications in Higher Education Administration," *Interfaces* 17, no. 2 (March–April 1987): 97–108; Thomas M. Cook and Robert A. Russell, *Introduction to Management Science* (Englewood Cliffs, N.J.: Prentice Hall, 1977), 1–24.
62. Robert R. Love, Jr., and James M. Hoey, "Management Science Improves Fast-Food Operations," *Interfaces* 20, no. 2 (March–April 1990): 21–29.
63. Ronald L. Coccari, "How Quantitative Business Techniques Are Being Used," *Business Horizons,* July–August 1989, 70–74; Cook and Russell, *Introduction to Management Science,* 5, 111, 209, 271.
64. Emily T. Smith, "Doing It for Mother Earth," *Business Week Quality 1991,* 25 October 1991, 44, 46, 49.
65. Cook and Russell, *Introduction to Management Science,* 434, 447–448.
66. The Reader's Digest Association, Inc., 1990 Annual Report, 4, 6–7.
67. Shetty, "Contingency Management," 27–34; Coccari, "How Quantitative Business Techniques Are Being Used," 70–74; Satish Mehra, "Applying MS/OR Techniques to Small Businesses," *Interfaces* 20, no. 2 (March–April 1990): 38–41; Cook and Russell, *Introduction to Management Science,* 181–196.
68. Jerry Banks and Frederick A. Rossini, "Management Science Failures in the Public Sector," *Public Productivity Review,* no. 42 (Summer 1987): 15–23.
69. Fremont E. Kast and James E. Rosenzweig, "General Systems Theory: Applications for Organizations and Management," *Academy of Management Journal* 15, no. 4 (December 1972): 447–463; John B. Miner, *The Management Process: Theory, Research, and Practice* (New York: Macmillan, 1973), 18–19.
70. Wren, *The Evolution of Management Thought,* 464–465, 523–524; Donde P. Ashmos and George P. Huber, "The Systems Paradigm in Organizational Theory: Correcting the Record and Suggesting the Future," *Academy of Management Review* 12, no. 4 (1987): 607–621; Kast and Rosenzweig, "General Systems Theory," 447–463; Ludwig von Bertalanffy, "General System Theory: A New Approach to Unity of Science," *Human Biology,* December 1951, 344; Koontz, "The Management Theory Jungle Revisited," 360–362.
71. Kast and Rosenzweig, "General Systems Theory," 447–463.
72. Daniel R. Denison, *Corporate Culture and Organizational Effectiveness* (New York: Wiley, 1990), 137–141.
73. McGuire, "Management Theory: Retreat to the Academy," 31–37; Meme Drumwright, "Contingency Theories of Leadership: A Review," *Baylor Business Studies* 12, no. 3 (August–October 1981): 29–43; Shetty, "Contingency Management," 27–34; Sang M. Lee, Fred Luthans, and David L. Olson, "A Management Science Approach to Contingency Models of Organizational Structure," *Academy of Management Journal* 25, no. 3 (September 1982): 553–566.
74. Henry L. Tosi, Jr., and John W. Slocum, Jr., "Contingency Theory: Some Suggested Directions," *Journal of Management* 10, no. 1 (1984): 9–26; Shetty, "Contingency Management," 27–34; J. Benjamin Forbes, "The Relationship between Management Styles and Functional Specialization," *Group and Organization Studies* 10, no. 1 (March 1985): 95–111; McGuire, "Management Theory: Retreat to the Academy," 31–37.
75. William G. Ouchi and Alfred M. Jaeger, "Type Z Organization: Stability in the Midst of Mobility," *Academy of Management Review* 3 (1978): 305–314; William Ouchi, *Theory Z: How American Business Can Meet the Japanese Challenge* (Reading, Mass.: Addison-Wesley, 1981), 69.
76. "Panel 3: The Applicability of the Japanese Model to U.S. Public Sector Organizations," *Public Productivity Review,* Summer 1984, 127–147.
77. Jeremiah J. Sullivan, "A Critique of Theory Z," *Academy of Management Review* 8, no. 1 (1983): 132–142; Stephen C. Harper, "Now That the Dust Has Settled: Learning from Japanese Management," *Business Horizons,* July–August 1988, 43–51; John Lie, "Is Korean Management Just Like Japanese Management?" *Management International Review* 3, no. 2 (second quarter 1990): 113–118.
78. Thomas J. Peters and Robert H. Waterman, Jr., *In Search of Excellence* (New York: Harper & Row, 1982), 1–26.
79. Peters and Waterman, *In Search of Excellence,* 1–26; John Case, "Why 'Fixes' Fail," *Inc.,* January 1989, 25–26; Earnest R. Archer, "Toward a Revival of the Principles of Management," *Industrial Management,* January–February 1990, 19–22.
80. See note 1.

CHAPTER 3

1. Adapted from Shari Caudron, "How Xerox Won the Baldrige," *Personnel Journal,* April 1991, 98, 100–102; Michael Schrage, "A Challenge to Conventional Notions of What Corporate R&D Is All About," *Washington Post,* 25 January 1991, F3; Michael A. Verespej, "Gutsy Decisions of 1990," *Industry Week,* 18 February 1991, 23–24, 26–30, 32, 34; Xerox Corporation 1990 Annual Report; David Altany, "Copycats: Once Obscure, 'Benchmarking' Is Fast Becoming the Buzzword of the Year," *Industry Week,* 5 November 1990, 11, 12, 14, 18; Beverly Geber, "Benchmarking: Measuring Yourself against the Best," *Training: The Magazine of Human Resource Development,* November 1990, 36–38, 40, 42, 44; John H. Sheridan, "Suppliers: Partners in Prosperity; Forging Close Bonds with Suppliers Can Provide a Competitive Edge, but the Relationship Is a Two-Way Street," *Industry Week,* 19 March 1990, 12–14, 16, 18–19; Derek Hornby, "Battle for Britain," *Management Today,* January 1990, 5; Sana Siwolop, "Man of the Year (Xerox Chairman and CEO David T. Kearns)," *Financial World,* 12 December 1989, 56–59; Anne Ferguson, "Mitcheldean Is Run on a Zero-Defects Basis," *Management Today,* November 1989, 92–93; H. Garrett DeYoung, "Back from the Brink: Xerox Redefines Its Notion of Quality," *Electronic Business,* 16 October 1989, 50–54; David Kearns, "Xerox: Satisfying Customer Needs with a New Culture," *Management Review,* February 1989, 61–63; Carol Kennedy, "Xerox Charts a New Strategic Direction," *Long Range Planning,* February 1989, 10–17; Michael A. Verespej, "Partnership in the Trenches; Managers and Workers Are Finding That Cooperation Can Spawn Competitiveness," *Industry Week,* 17 October 1988, 56–57, 60, 62, 64; Lee O. Smith, "The Cuomo Commission's 'New Realism,'" *Challenge,* September–October 1988, 37–43; Maurice F. Holmes, "Xerox: Leading through Technology," *Black Enterprise,* February 1988, 100, 102; John G. Belcher, Jr., "The Role of Unions in Productivity Management," *Personnel,* January 1988, 54–58.
2. Adapted from Philip S. Thomas, "Environmental Analysis for Corporate Planning," *Business Horizons,* October 1974, 27–38; Richard L. Daft, Juhani Sormunen, and Don Parks, "Chief Executive Scanning, Environmental Characteristics, and Company Performance: An Empirical Study," *Strategic Management Journal* 9 (1988): 123–139.
3. Donde P. Ashmos and George P. Huber, "The Systems Paradigm in Organization Theory: Correcting the Record and Suggesting the Future," *Academy of Management Review* 12, no. 4 (1987): 607–621; Fremont E. Kast and James E. Rosenzweig, *Organization and Management: A Systems and Contingency Approach,* 4th ed. (New York: McGraw-Hill, 1985), 132; Fremont E. Kast and James E. Rosenzweig, "General Systems Theory: Applications for Organization and Management," *Academy of Management Journal* 15, no. 4 (December 1972): 447–463.
4. Dinah Lee, "India Waits for a Lotus to Blossom," *Business Week,* 15 June 1990, 155.
5. Thomas R. Horton, *"What Works for Me"* (New York: Amacom, 1989), 326–329.
6. John Naisbitt and Patricia Aburdene, *Reinventing the Corporation* (New York: Warner Books, 1985), 271.
7. Kast and Rosenzweig, *Organization and Management,* 106, 132–135; Edwin A. Gerloff, *Organizational Theory and Design* (New York: McGraw-Hill, 1985), 24.
8. Sue Greenfeld, Robert C. Winder, and Gregory Williams, "The CEO and the External Environment," *Business Horizons,* November–December 1988, 20–25; George A. Steiner, *The New CEO* (New York: Macmillan, 1983), 87–88.
9. Greenfeld, Winder, and Williams, "The CEO and the External Environment," 20–25; Thomas, "Environmental Analysis for Corporate Planning," 27–38.
10. Jennifer Lawrence and Steven W. Colford, "Green Guidelines Are the Next Step," *Advertising Age,* 29 January 1991, 28, 30; John Holusha, "Packaging and Public Image: McDonald's Fills a Big Order," *New York Times,* 2 November 1990, sec. a, 1, sec. d, 5; Patricia Leigh Brown, "A Symbol of the Fast-Food Cul-

ture," *New York Times,* 2 November 1990, sec. d, 5.

11. Horton, *"What Works for Me,"* 341–346; Dean Foust, "Bill Marriott," *1991 Business Week 1000,* 1991, 58.

12. Rochelle Kass, "Approaching ATM Equality," *Bank Systems and Technology,* July 1990, 56–60; Amal Kumar Naj, "Clouds Gather over the Biotech Industry," *Wall Street Journal,* 30 January 1989, B1, B5.

13. Tim Frasca, "Codelco Seen Burdened by Past Policies," *American Metal Market,* 21 August 1990, 1, 16.

14. Fred G. Steingraber, "Managing in the 1990s," *Business Horizons,* January–February 1990, 50–61.

15. Michael E. Porter, *Competitive Advantage: Creating and Sustaining Superior Performance* (New York: Free Press, 1985), 286; Dinah Lee, "Rebuilding a Tiger: Who'll Get the Lion's Share?" *Business Week,* 25 March 1991, 46–47.

16. William C. Frederick, Keith Davis, and James E. Post, *Business and Society: Corporate Strategy, Public Policy, Ethics,* 6th ed. (New York: McGraw-Hill, 1988), 139–141; Michael Kublin, "The Soviet Factory Director: A Window on Eastern Bloc Manufacturing," *Industrial Management,* March–April 1990, 21–26.

17. John Naisbitt and Patricia Aburdene, *Megatrends 2000* (New York: William Morrow, 1990), 95–103; Alvin Toffler, *Powershift* (New York: Bantam Books, 1990), 413–422.

18. Barry Keating and J. Holton Wilson, *Managerial Economics* (Orlando, Fla.: Academic Press, 1986), 494; Peter Drucker, "Making Managers of Communism's Bureaucrats," *Wall Street Journal,* 15 August 1990, A8; Richard I. Kirkland, Jr., "Who Gains from the New Europe," *Fortune,* 18 December 1989, 83–88.

19. John S. McCallum, "Of Self-Interest, Economic Policy and Influencing the Government," *Business Quarterly,* Spring, 1990, 54–57; Ralph E. Winter, "Many Businesses Blame Governmental Policies for Productivity Lag," *Wall Street Journal,* 28 October 1980, 1; Ted Holden, "A Tsunami of Red Ink Sweeps across Japan," *Business Week,* 25 February 1991, 52–53; Joan C. Szabo, "Small Firms' Credit Crunch," *Nation's Business,* July 1990, 25–27; "British Business Failures," *Wall Street Journal,* 1 July 1991, A6.

20. Peter F. Drucker, *The Age of Discontinuity* (New York: Harper Torchbooks, 1978), xxv; Jonathan P. Hicks, "Steelmakers' Inferiority Syndrome," *New York Times,* 7 August 1989, sec. d, 1, 7; Robert H. Hayes and Ramchandran Jaikumar, "Manufacturing's Crisis: New Technologies, Obsolete Organizations," *Harvard Business Review,* September–October 1988, 77.

21. John Diebold, *Making the Future Work* (New York: Simon & Schuster, 1984), 350–352.

22. Gene Bylinsky, "Technology in the Year 2000," *Fortune,* 18 July 1988, 92–98; "A New B-School Mission: Teaching High-Tech Savvy," *Business Week,* 19 November 1984, 170, 172; Toffler, *Powershift,* 54–55; James E. Ellis, "H & R Block Expands Its Tax Base," *Business Week,* 22 April 1991, 52.

23. Tom Peters, *Thriving on Chaos* (New York: Harper & Row, 1987), 241–244; Michael L. Tushman and Philip Anderson, "Technological Discontinuities and Organizational Environments," *Administrative Science Quarterly* 31 (1986): 439–465; Michael A. Verespej, "Gutsy Decisions of 1989," *Industry Week,* 19 February 1990, 34.

24. Kevin J. Clancy, "Hurtling toward the Millennium: A Twenty-Year Perspective on Social Change in America," paper presented at the 37th Annual Conference of the Advertising Research Foundation, New York, New York, 9 April 1991; Malcolm Wheatley, "The Best of Both Worlds," *Management Today,* October 1989, 24; Roger Feather, "Internal Communication in Canada," *IABC Communication World,* December 1990, 36–37; James W. McKie, ed., *Social Responsibility and the Business Predicament* (Washington, D.C.: The Brookings Institution, 1974), 1–3; "Arby's to Test Light Menu," *Adweek's Marketing Week,* 15 April 1991, 6.

25. Judith Waldrop, "You'll Know It's the 21st Century When . . . ," *American Demographics,* December 1990, 23–27; Kate Ballen, "How America Will Change over the Next 30 Years," *Fortune,* 17 June 1991, 12; Robert S. Menchin, *The Mature Market* (Chicago: Probus, 1989), 147.

26. "Colleges Conquer the Baby Bust," *American Demographics,* September 1987, 30; Curtis Hartman, "Redesigning America," *Inc.,* June 1988, 58–74; Harry Bacas, "Desperately Seeking Workers," *Nation's Business,* February 1988, 16; Peter F. Drucker, *Managing the Non-Profit Organization* (New York: HarperCollins, 1990), 29–31, 68.

27. Kenichi Ohmae, *The Borderless World* (New York: HarperBusiness, 1990), 8–9; Otis Port, "Why the U.S. Is Losing Its Lead," *Business Week,* 15 June 1990, 35–39; Toffler, *Powershift,* 206, 460.

28. William J. Holstein, "The Stateless Corporation," *Business Week,* 14 May 1990, 98–105; George Rabstejnek, "Let's Get Back to the Basics of Global Strategy," *Journal of Business Strategy,* September–October 1989, 32–35.

29. Daft, Sormunen, and Parks, "Chief Executive Scanning, Environmental Characteristics, and Company Performance," 123–139.

30. Theodore Levitt, *The Marketing Imagination* (New York: Free Press, 1986), 5.

31. Richard C. Heydinger, "Consumerism: A Force To Be Reckoned With?" *Risk Management,* February 1990, 48; Thomas J. Peters and Robert H. Waterman, Jr., *In Search of Excellence* (New York: Harper & Row, 1982), 156.

32. Michael Schrage, "Customers May Be Your Best Collaborators," in *The Wall Street Journal on Managing,* edited by David Asman (New York: Doubleday Currency, 1990), 22.

33. Philip R. Thomas, *Competitiveness Through Total Cycle Time* (New York: McGraw-Hill, 1990), 7–15; George Stalk, Jr., "Time—The Next Source of Competitive Advantage," *Harvard Business Review,* July–August 1988, 41–51.

34. Steingraber, "Managing in the 1990s," 50–61; Porter, *Competitive Advantage,* 71–73.

35. "A Lean, Mean Subcontracting Machine," *Business Tokyo,* December 1990, 40–41.

36. John H. Sheridan, "Betting on a Single Source," *Industry Week,* 1 February 1988, 31–36.

37. Robert B. Reich, "Metamorphosis of the American Worker," *Business Month,* November 1990, 58–66; Patricia Sellers, "What Customers Really Want," *Fortune,* 4 June 1990, 58–68.

38. Kenneth R. Sheets, "Labor's Agenda for the '90s," *U.S. News & World Report,* 19 March 1990, 37–38; William J. Hampton, "GM Bets an Arm and a Leg on a People-Free Plant," *Business Week,* 12 September 1988, 72–73.

39. Gary Weiss, "William Donaldson," *The 1991 Business Week 1000,* 1991, 78.

40. Xavier Vives, "Deregulation and Competition in Spanish Banking," *European Economic Review* 34 (1990): 403–411.

41. George A. Steiner and John F. Steiner, *Business, Government, and Society: A Managerial Perspective,* 6th ed. (New York: McGraw-Hill, 1991), 152.

42. Leslie W. Rue and Phyllis G. Holland, *Strategic Management: Concepts and Experiences* (New York: McGraw-Hill, 1989), 48.

43. David Lei, "Building U.S. Presence in European Markets," *Journal of Business Strategy,* July–August 1990, 32–36.

44. Dean Foust, "Who's In Charge Here?" *Business Week,* 19 March 1990, 38–39; Judith H. Dobrzynski, "If Stockholders Bang on Boardroom Doors, Open 'Em," *Business Week,* 3 December 1990, 149; Richard B. Schmitt, "Toy-Firm Investor Gripes He Ventured but Didn't Gain," *Wall Street Journal,* 28 August 1989, B2; "Discovery Toys Announces Settlement," *Business Wire,* 15 June 1990, 1.

45. Mayer N. Zald, "The Power and Functions of Boards of Directors: A Theoretical Synthesis," in *Concepts for Corporate Strategy,* edited by John W. Bonge and Bruce P. Coleman (New York: Macmillan, 1972), 66–67; Paula L. Rechner, "Corporate Governance: Fact or Fiction?" *Business Horizons,* July–August 1989, 11–15; Richard J. Umbdenstock, Winifred M. Hageman, and Bruce Amundson, "The Five Critical Areas for Effective Governance of Not-for-Profit Hospitals," *Hospital & Health Services Administration* 35, no. 4 (Winter 1990): 481–492; James Kristie, "The Chairman and the Board: Daniel E. Gill, Bausch & Lomb," *Directors & Boards* 14, no. 3 (Spring 1990): 58, 59–60.

46. Tracy E. Benson, "Empowered Employees," *Industry Week,* 19 February 1990, 12–20.

47. Daniel R. Denison, *Corporate Culture and Organizational Effectiveness* (New York: Wiley, 1990), 2, 33; Frank Petrock, "Corporate Culture Enhances Profits," *HR Magazine,* November 1990, 64–66; Meinolf Dierkes and Ariane Berthoin Antal, "Creative Management in a Changing Environment," in *Handbook for Creative and Innovative Managers,* edited by Robert L. Kuhn (New York: McGraw-Hill, 1988), 606.

48. Alan L. Wilkins and Nigel J. Bristow, "For Successful Organization Culture, Honor Your Past," *Academy of Management Executive* 1, no. 3 (1987): 221–229; Denison, *Corporate Culture and Organizational Effectiveness,* 95–108.

49. Guy S. Saffold III, "Culture Traits, Strength, and Organizational Performance: Moving Beyond 'Strong' Culture," *Academy of Management Review* 13, no. 4 (1988): 546–558; Petrock, "Corporate Culture Enhances Profits," 64–66.

50. Adapted from Stanley M. Davis, *Managing Corporate Culture* (New York: Harper & Row, 1984), 3–5; Yoash Wiener, "Forms of Value Systems: A Focus on Organizational Effectiveness and Cultural Change and Maintenance," *Academy of Management Review* 13, no. 4 (1988): 534–545; Kenneth Labich, "Big Changes at Big Brown," *Fortune,* 18 January 1988, 56–64.

51. Saffold, "Culture Traits, Strength, and Organizational Performance," 546–558; Denison, *Corporate Culture and Organizational Effectiveness,* 176, 179–183.

52. Harrison M. Trice and Janice M. Beyer, "Studying Organizational Cultures through

Rites and Ceremonials," *Academy of Management Review* 9, no. 4 (1984): 653–669.

53. Michael Elmes and David Wilemon, "Organizational Culture and Project Leader Effectiveness," *Project Management Journal,* September 1988, 54–63; Claudia H. Deutsch, "The Parables of Corporate Culture," *New York Times,* 13 October 1991, sec. 3, 25.

54. Robert Neff and Laxmi Nakarmi, "How Chung Ju-Yung Is Trying to Reunite Korea," *Business Week,* 13 May 1991, 110–111.

55. Kathleen MacKay, "Making a Difference," *Executive Female,* July–August 1988, 52–53, 66–67.

56. Karl Albrecht and Ron Zemke, *Service America!* (1985; reprint New York: Warner Communications, 1990), 143–144.

57. John Markoff, "A 'Gunslinger's' Growing Pains," *New York Times,* 13 January 1991, sec. 3, 23.

58. Trice and Beyer, "Studying Organizational Cultures through Rites and Ceremonials," 653–669.

59. Linda Smircich, "Concepts of Culture and Organizational Analysis," *Administrative Science Quarterly* 28 (1983): 339–358.

60. Brian Dumaine, "Those Highflying PepsiCo Managers," *Fortune,* 10 April 1989, 78–86; PepsiCo Annual Report 1989, 4.

61. Mark M. Nelson and E. S. Browning, "GE's Culture Turns Sour at French Unit," *Wall Street Journal,* 31 July 1990, A8.

62. R. T. Lenz, "'Determinants' of Organizational Performance: An Interdisciplinary Review," *Strategic Management Journal* 2 (1981): 131–154.

63. Robert Duncan, "What Is the Right Organization Structure?" *Organizational Dynamics,* Winter 1979, 59–80; Thomas H. Naylor, "The Reeducation of Soviet Management," *Across the Board,* February 1988, 28–37; Gregory G. Dess and Donald W. Beard, "Dimensions of Organizational Task Environments," *Administrative Science Quarterly* 29 (1984): 52–73.

64. Duncan, "What Is the Right Organization Structure?" 59–80; Larry Light and Leah Nathans Spiro, "The War of the Plastic," *Business Week,* 15 April 1991, 28–29.

65. Duncan, "What Is the Right Organization Structure?" 59–80.

66. Alan D. Meyer, Geoffrey R. Brooks, and James B. Goes, "Environmental Jolts and Industry Revolutions: Organizational Responses to Discontinuous Change," *Strategic Management Journal* 11 (1990): 93–110; Thierry C. Pauchant and Ian I. Mitroff, "Crisis Management: Managing Paradox in a Chaotic World," *Technological Forecasting and Social Change* 38 (1990): 117–134; Asra Q. Nomani, "Global Dogfight: World's Major Airlines Scramble to Get Ready for Competitive Battle," *Wall Street Journal,* 14 January 1992, A1, A8, A9.

67. Barbara W. Keats and Michael A. Hitt, "A Causal Model of Linkages among Environmental Dimensions, Macro Organizational Characteristics, and Performance," *Academy of Management Journal* 31, no. 3 (1988): 570–598; Dess and Beard, "Dimensions of Organizational Task Environments," 52–73.

68. Brian Dumaine, "How to Manage in a Recession," *Fortune,* 5 November 1990, 58–72.

69. Frances J. Milliken, "Perceiving and Interpreting Environmental Change: An Examination of College Administrators' Interpretation of Changing Demographics," *Academy of Management Journal* 33, no. 1 (1990): 42–63; Dess and Beard, "Dimensions of Organizational Task Environments," 52–73; David Ulrich and Jay B. Barney, "Perspectives in Organizations: Resource Dependence, Efficiency, and Population," *Academy of Management Review* 9, no. 3 (1984): 471–481; Keith G. Provan, "Interorganizational Linkages and Influence over Decision Making," *Academy of Management Journal* 25, no. 2 (1982): 443–451.

70. Ronald Henkoff, "Turning Water into Gold," *Fortune,* 6 May 1991, 98.

71. Milliken, "Perceiving and Interpreting Environmental Change," 42–63.

72. Marc J. Dollinger, "Environmental Boundary Spanning and Information Processing Effects on Organizational Performance," *Academy of Management Journal* 27, no. 2 (1984): 351–368.

73. "The 500: David Fern and Jack Knight, Knight Floor Covering," *Inc.,* December 1990, 85.

74. Kast and Rosenzweig, *Organization and Management,* 107–108; Lawrence G. Hrebiniak and William F. Joyce, "Organizational Adaptation: Strategic Choice and Determinism," *Administrative Science Quarterly* 30 (1985): 336–349.

75. John P. Kotter, "Managing External Dependence," *Academy of Management Review* 4, no. 1 (1979): 87–92; Duncan, "What Is the Right Organization Structure?" 59–80; Peters, *Thriving on Chaos,* 28, 34.

76. Carol Hymowitz, "Upscale Look for Limited Puts Retailer Back on Track," *Wall Street Journal,* 24 February 1989, B1, B5; The Limited 1989 Annual Report, 1–23.

77. Yvan Allaire and Mihaela E. Firsirotu, "Coping with Strategic Uncertainty," *Sloan Management Review,* Spring 1989, 7–16; Thomas A. Stewart, "The New American Century: Where We Stand," *Fortune,* Spring–Summer 1991, 12–23.

78. Allaire and Firsirotu, "Coping with Strategic Uncertainty," 7–16; Anthony Ramirez, "A Warming World: What It Will Mean," *Fortune,* 4 July 1988, 102–107.

79. Steve Weiner, "Staying on Top in a Tough Business in a Tough Year," *Forbes,* 27 May 1991, 46–48.

80. Kotter, "Managing External Dependence," 87–92.

81. Allaire and Firsirotu, "Coping with Strategic Uncertainty," 7–16; Gary Slutsker, "Look Out for the Taxi Dispatchers," *Forbes,* 20 August 1990, 86–87; Kathleen Killette, "Cellular Competitor—FCC Gives the Nod to Service Provider for Enhancement of Mobile Radio Service," *CommunicationsWeek,* 18 February 1991, 8.

82. Gary Hamel, Yves L. Doz, and C. K. Prahalad, "Collaborate with Your Competitors—And Win," *Harvard Business Review,* January–February 1989, 133–139; Peter Fuchs, "Strategic Alliances," *Business Tokyo,* April 1991, 22–27.

83. "Too Big to Ignore," *Forbes,* 13 May 1991, 136.

84. Kotter, "Managing External Dependence," 87–92.

85. Gary Hoover, Alta Campbell, and Patrick J. Spain, eds., *Hoover's Handbook 1991: Profiles of Over 500 Major Corporations* (Austin, Tex.: The Reference Press, 1990), 270.

86. See note 1.

CHAPTER 4

1. Adapted from Mark Bittman, "Ben & Jerry's Caring Capitalism," *Restaurant Business,* 20 November 1990, 132; Jim Castelli, "Management Styles: Finding the Right Fit," *HR Magazine,* September 1990, 38; Steven S. Ross, "Green Groceries," *Mother Jones,* February–March 1989, 48; Bill Kelley, "The Cause Effect," *Food and Beverage Marketing,* March 1990, 20; Ellie Winninghoff, "Citizen Cohen," *Mother Jones,* January 1990, 12; Erik Larson, "Forever Young," *Inc.,* July 1988, 50; Jeanne Wegner, "This Season, Sharp-dressed Dairy Products Are Wearing Green," *Dairy Foods,* September 1990, 72; "Soda, Milk Bottles Lead the Way," *Plastics World,* 22 April 1990, 7; Therese R. Welter, "Industry and the Environment: A Farewell to Arms," *Industry Week,* 20 August 1990, 36; Daniel Seligman, "Ben & Jerry Save the World," *Fortune,* 3 June 1991, 247.

2. Peter F. Drucker, *The Practice of Management* (New York: Harper & Row, 1982), 381–388; Peter F. Drucker, *Management: Tasks, Responsibilities, Practices* (New York: Harper & Row, 1974), 312–314, 324–325.

3. Donna J. Wood, "Social Issues in Management: Theory and Research in Corporate Social Performance," *Journal of Management* 17, no. 2 (1991): 383–406; Archie B. Carroll, "A Three-Dimensional Conceptual Model of Corporate Performance," *Academy of Management Review* 4, no. 4 (1979): 497–505; Van R. Wood, Lawrence B. Chonko, and Shelby D. Hunt, "Social Responsibility and Personal Success: Are They Incompatible?" *Journal of Business Research* 14 (1986): 193–212; Jean B. McGuire, Alison Sundgren, and Thomas Schneeweis, "Corporate Social Responsibility and Firm Financial Performance," *Academy of Management Journal* 31, no. 4 (1988): 854–872; Drucker, *Management,* 344–345.

4. Wood, "Social Issues in Management," 383–406; Carroll, "A Three-Dimensional Conceptual Model of Corporate Performance," 497–505.

5. Carroll, "A Three-Dimensional Conceptual Model of Corporate Performance," 497–505; Wood, "Social Issues in Management," 383–406.

6. Carroll, "A Three-Dimensional Conceptual Model of Corporate Performance," 497–505; Kenneth E. Goodpaster, "Business Ethics and Stakeholder Analysis," *Business Ethics Quarterly* 1, no. 1 (January 1991): 53–73; Thomas Donaldson, "Ethically, 'Society Expects More from a Corporation,'" *U.S. News & World Report,* 6 September 1982, 30.

7. Patrick E. Roche and Scott Boyer, presentation made to the Business Marketing Communications Association, Bellevue, Washington, 22 August 1991; Richard E. Wokutch, "Corporate Social Responsibility Japanese Style," *Academy of Management Executive,* May 1990, 56–74.

8. James J. Chrisman and Archie B. Carroll, "SMR Forum: Corporate Responsibility—Reconciling Economic and Social Goals," *Sloan Management Review,* Winter 1984, 59–65; Wokutch, "Corporate Social Responsibility Japanese Style," 56–74.

9. Chrisman and Carroll, "SMR Forum: Corporate Responsibility," 59–65; Wokutch, "Corporate Social Responsibility Japanese Style," 56–74; Wood, "Social Issues in Management," 383–406; Steven L. Wartick and Philip L. Cochran, "The Evolution of the Corporate Social Performance Model," *Academy of Management Review* 10, no. 4 (1985): 758–769.

10. George A. Steiner and John F. Steiner, *Business, Government, and Society: A Managerial Perspective,* 6th ed. (New York: McGraw-Hill,

1991), 14–15; Goodpaster, "Business Ethics and Stakeholder Analysis," 53–73.

11. Michael Rion, *The Responsible Manager* (San Francisco: Harper & Row, 1990), 46; Wokutch, "Corporate Social Responsibility Japanese Style," 58–59; Nancy C. Roberts and Paula J. King, "The Stakeholder Audit Goes Public," *Organizational Dynamics,* Winter 1989, 63–79; Samuel C. Certo and J. Paul Peter, *Strategic Management: Concepts and Applications* (New York: Random House, 1988), 205; Milton R. Moskowitz, "Company Performance Roundup," *Business and Society Review,* Summer 1989, 66–72; Janice Castro, "Home Is Where the Heart Is," *Time,* 3 October 1988, 46–49.

12. William Celis III, "College Tries to Aid Its Neighborhood," *New York Times,* 21 August 1991, sec. a, 18.

13. Marc J. Epstein, "What Shareholders Really Want," *New York Times,* 28 April 1991, sec. 3, 11.

14. Kenneth E. Aupperle, Archie B. Carroll, and John D. Hatfield, "An Empirical Examination of the Relationship between Corporate Social Responsibility and Profitability," *Academy of Management Journal* 28, no. 2 (1985): 446–463; Arieh A. Ullmann, "Data in Search of a Theory: A Critical Examination of the Relationships among Social Performance, Social Disclosure, and Economic Performance of U.S. Firms," *Academy of Management Review* 10, no. 3 (1985): 540–557; Tad Tuleja, *Beyond the Bottom Line,* as summarized in *Soundview Executive Book Summaries,* January 1987, 2.

15. Tad Tuleja, "Beyond the Bottom Line," *Soundview Executive Book Summaries,* January 1987, 1–8.

16. Jo David and Karen File, "Saintly Companies That Make Heavenly Profits," *Working Woman,* October 1989, 72–78, 122–124, 126; Ronald Grzywinski, "The New Old-Fashioned Banking," *Harvard Business Review,* May–June 1991, 87–98.

17. Elizabeth Kolbert, "An 'Inspirational' Ice Cream Factory," *New York Times,* 11 September 1991, sec. a, 10; Ross, "Green Groceries," 48–49.

18. Ruth Behrens, "Companies and Communities Share Healthy Causes," *Business and Health,* September 1988, 30–32, 34–35.

19. Nancy J. Perry, "Saving the Schools: How Business Can Help," *Fortune,* 7 November 1988, 42, 44–46, 50, 52, 54, 56; Nancy J. Perry, "The Education Crisis: What Business Can Do," *Fortune,* 4 July 1988, 71–73, 76–77, 80–81.

20. Christine Gorman, "The Literacy Gap," *Time,* 19 December 1988, 56–57; Joel Keehn, "How Business Helps the Schools," *Fortune,* 21 October 1991, 161.

21. Perry, "Saving the Schools," 46; Nancy J. Perry, "Where We Go from Here," *Fortune,* 21 October 1991, 114–115, 118, 120, 124, 129; Perry, "The Education Crisis," 71–73, 76–77, 80–81; "Where the Money Is Going," *Fortune,* 21 October 1991, 162, 164, 166, 168, 170, 172, 174, 176, 178, 180.

22. Moskowitz, "Company Performance Roundup," 70.

23. Jonathan P. Hicks, "Black Businesses Work in Schools," *The New York Times Education Life,* 7 April 1991, sec. 4A, 36–37.

24. Cyndee Miller, "Reebok Pays Cost of Human Rights Concert Tour," *Marketing News,* 12 September 1988, 6, 13.

25. David Kirkpatrick, "Environmentalism: The New Crusade," *Fortune,* 12 February 1990, 44–48, 50–52; Maggie Mentel Schaver, "Nonprofits Looking Out for the Environment," *Nonprofit World,* January–February 1991, 23–25; Frank Edward Allen, "Environment: Odds and Ends," *Wall Street Journal,* 30 December 1991, B1.

26. Carolyn Lesh, "Loblaws," *Advertising Age,* 29 January 1991, 38.

27. John Strahinich, "This Devil's Advocate Means Business," *Readers Digest,* April 1987, 123–124, 126, 128.

28. Sheryl Flatow, "A Chorus Line," *Public Relations Journal,* November 1986, 44, 46–50.

29. Flatow, "A Chorus Line," 44, 46–50.

30. William Glaberson, "Auditor Says Contractor Tried to Impede Search," *New York Times,* 21 October 1988, sec. d, 4.

31. David and File, "Saintly Companies That Make Heavenly Profits," 124, 126, 143.

32. Connie Wallace, "Lessons in Marketing from a Maverick," *Working Woman,* October 1990, 81–82, 84; Rahul Jacob, "Body Shop International: What Selling Will Be Like in the '90s," *Fortune,* 13 January 1992, 63–64; Eben Shapiro, "The Sincerest Form of Rivalry," *New York Times,* 19 October 1991, sec. b, 1.

33. Steiner and Steiner, *Business, Government, and Society,* 178; Roberts and King, "The Stakeholder Audit Goes Public," 67; Philip James, "Holding Managers to Account on Safety," *Personnel Management,* April 1990, 54, 56–58; Wayne Tusa, "Developing an Environmental Audit Program," *Risk Management,* August 1990, 24, 26, 28–29.

34. Ben & Jerry's Homemade, Inc., 1989 Annual Report, 4.

35. William C. Frederick, Keith Davis, and James E. Post, *Business and Society* (New York: McGraw-Hill, 1988), 117–119.

36. Eileen Norris, "Getting the Message Out," *Electronic Media,* 6 February 1988, 14.

37. David L. Kirp, "Uncommon Decency: Pacific Bell Responds to AIDS," *Harvard Business Review,* May–June 1989, 140–151.

38. Frederick, Davis, and Post, *Business and Society,* 356; Kirkpatrick, "Environmentalism," 44.

39. Steiner and Steiner, *Business, Government, and Society,* 173–175; Frederick, Davis, and Post, *Business and Society,* 353; Meg Cox, "Corporate Giving Is Flat, and Future Looks Bleaker," *Wall Street Journal,* 17 October 1988, B1; Claudia H. Deutsch, "When Employees Choose a Charity," *New York Times,* 11 August 1991, sec. 3, 25.

40. Cox, "Corporate Giving Is Flat," B1; "Where the Money Is Going," 162; Michael Schroeder, "Charity Doesn't Begin at Home Anymore," *Business Week,* 25 February 1991, 91.

41. P. Rajan Varadarajan and Anil Menon, "Cause-Related Marketing: A Coalignment of Marketing Strategy and Corporate Philanthropy," *Journal of Marketing,* July 1988, 58–74.

42. Peter Goldberg, "A Dangerous Trend in Corporate Giving," *New York Times,* 29 March 1987, sec. 3, 2; Fritz Jellinghaus, "Profits Have a Place in Philanthropy," *New York Times,* 29 March 1987, sec. 3, 2.

43. Joshua Levine, "I Gave at the Supermarket," *Business Week,* 25 December 1989, 138, 140; Goldberg, "A Dangerous Trend in Corporate Giving," 2; Jellinghaus, "Profits Have a Place in Philanthropy," 2.

44. Rogene A. Buchholz, *Fundamental Concepts and Problems in Business Ethics* (Englewood Cliffs, N.J.: Prentice Hall, 1989), 13, 30–32; Goodpaster, "Business Ethics and Stakeholder Analysis," 53–73.

45. Raziel Abelson and Kai Nielsen, "History of Ethics," in *Encyclopedia of Philosophy,* Vol. 3, edited by Paul Edwards (New York: Macmillan, 1967, reprint 1972), 81–82.

46. Kai Nielsen, "Problems of Ethics," in *Encyclopedia of Philosophy,* Vol. 3, edited by Paul Edwards (New York: Macmillan, 1967, reprint 1972), 117–118.

47. Brian O'Reilly, "Drugmakers," *Fortune,* 29 July 1991, 48; Courtland L. Bovée and John V. Thill, *Marketing* (New York: McGraw-Hill, 1992), 358–359.

48. Philip R. Cateora, *International Marketing,* 7th ed. (Homewood, Ill.: Irwin, 1990), 127.

49. Richard M. Hodgetts and Fred Luthans, *International Management* (New York: McGraw-Hill, 1991), 461; James E. Austin, *Managing in Developing Countries* (New York: Free Press, 1990), 181–182; Jere W. Morehead and Sandra G. Gustavson, "Complying with the Amended Foreign Corrupt Practices Act," *Risk Management,* April 1990, 76–78, 80, 82.

50. Ford S. Worthy, "When Somebody Wants a Payoff," *Fortune Pacific Rim 1989,* 117–118, 120, 122; Hodgetts and Luthans, *International Management,* 461; Morehead and Gustavson, "Complying with the Amended Foreign Corrupt Practices Act," 76–78, 80, 82.

51. Robert Jackall, "Moral Mazes: Bureaucracy and Managerial Work," *Harvard Business Review,* September–October 1983, 118–130.

52. Andrew Pollack, "Issue of Deceit in Electronics," *New York Times,* 31 March 1983, sec. d, 2.

53. Patrick E. Murphy, "Creating Ethical Corporate Structures," *Sloan Management Review,* Winter 1989, 81–87.

54. LaRue Tone Hosmer, "Adding Ethics to the Business Curriculum," *Business Horizons,* July–August 1988, 14.

55. Hosmer, "Adding Ethics to the Business Curriculum," 13.

56. William D. Hitt, *Ethics and Leadership: Putting Theory into Practice* (Columbus, Ohio: Battelle Press, 1990), 99–107; Buchholz, *Fundamental Concepts and Problems in Business Ethics,* 49–50.

57. LaRue Tone Hosmer, *The Ethics of Management* (Homewood, Ill.: Irwin, 1991), 109–111; Donald Robin, Michael Giallourakis, Fred R. David, and Thomas E. Moritz, "A Different Look at Codes of Ethics," *Business Horizons,* January–February 1989, 66–73; Buchholz, *Fundamental Concepts and Problems in Business Ethics,* 50–52.

58. Buchholz, *Fundamental Concepts and Problems in Business Ethics,* 52–55; Hitt, *Ethics and Leadership,* 107–112.

59. Hosmer, *The Ethics of Management,* 111–113; Robin, Giallourakis, David, and Moritz, "A Different Look at Codes of Ethics," 66–73.

60. Hosmer, "Adding Ethics to the Business Curriculum," 14; W. Edward Stead, Dan L. Worrell, and Jean Garner Stead, "An Integrative Model for Understanding and Managing Ethical Behavior in Business Organizations," *Journal of Business Ethics,* March 1990, 233–342.

61. Hosmer, *The Ethics of Management,* 116–117, 126.

62. Frederick, Davis, and Post, *Business and Society,* 60.

63. Peter Laslett, "Social Contract," in *Encyclopedia of Philosophy,* Vol. 7, edited by Paul Edwards (New York: Macmillan, 1967, reprint 1972), 465–467; Thomas W. Dunfee, "Business Ethics and Extant Social Contracts," *Business*

Ethics Quarterly 1, no. 1 (January 1991): 23–51; Hitt, *Ethics and Leadership,* 114–121.
64. Rene Sacasas and Anita Cava, "Law, Ethics and Management: Toward an Effective Audit," *Business Forum,* Winter 1990, 18–21.
65. Bernice Kanner, "Saving Salomon," *New York,* 9 December 1991, 40–48.
66. Murphy, "Creating Ethical Corporate Structures," 81.
67. Kenneth R. Andrews, "Ethics in Practice," *Harvard Business Review,* September–October 1989, 99–104; Michael R. Hyman, Robert Skipper, and Richard Tansey, "Ethical Codes Are Not Enough," *Business Horizons,* March–April 1990, 15–22; Stead, Worrell, and Stead, "An Integrative Model for Understanding and Managing Ethical Behavior in Business Organizations," 238; "Executive Suite: Unbecoming an Officer," *Time,* 30 September 1991, 52.
68. Stead, Worrell, and Stead, "An Integrative Model for Understanding and Managing Ethical Behavior in Business Organizations," 239.
69. Hyman, Skipper, and Tansey, "Ethical Codes Are Not Enough," 16.
70. Stead, Worrell, and Stead, "An Integrative Model for Understanding and Managing Ethical Behavior in Business Organizations," 239.
71. Rita Kay Meyer, "Chemical's Executive Training Emphasizes Ethics," *American Banker,* 17 June 1988, 16; Murphy, "Creating Ethical Corporate Structures," 83–84; Karin Ireland, "The Ethics Game," *Personnel Journal,* March 1991, 72, 74–75.
72. Hosmer, *The Ethics of Management,* 190.
73. James Hirsch, "Singer Case Whistle-Blower Says a Reward Was Motive," *New York Times,* 16 March 1989, sec. d, 1, 4; Tim Smart, "The 1863 Law That's Haunting Business," *Business Week,* 21 January 1991, 68; Fremont E. Kast and James E. Rosenzweig, *Organization and Management: A Systems and Contingency Approach,* 4th ed. (New York: McGraw-Hill, 1985), 170–172.
74. John A. Byrne, "Businesses Are Signing Up for Ethics 101," *Business Week,* 15 February 1988, 56–57; Frederick, Davis, and Post, *Business and Society,* 70; Stead, Worrell, and Stead, "An Integrative Model for Understanding and Managing Ethical Behavior in Business Organizations," 241.
75. Murphy, "Creating Ethical Corporate Structures," 84.
76. John A. Byrne, "The Best-Laid Ethics Programs . . . ," *Business Week,* 9 March 1992, 67–69.
77. Byrne, "The Best-Laid Ethics Programs . . . ," 67–69.
78. Sharyn Rosenbaum, "Market News: Companies' Hopes Deflated," *Health Industry Today,* February 1992, 12–13; Evelyn Gilbert, "RM Braces for Breast Implant Suits," *National Underwriter,* 27 January 1992, 3, 44.
79. See note 1.
80. Based on information from Gary Weiss, "The Salomon Shocker: How Bad Will It Get?" *Business Week,* 26 August 1991, 54–57.

CHAPTER 5

1. Adapted from Anthony J. F. O'Reilly, "Leading a Global Strategic Charge," *Journal of Business Strategy,* July–August 1991, 10–13; Anthony J. F. O'Reilly, "Heinz and the Year of the Operator," *Review of Business,* Fall 1985, 27–30; Claudia H. Deutsch, "At Heinz, a Bottom-Line Leader," *New York Times,* 8 May 1988, sec. 3, 1; Gregory Stricharchuk, "Heinz Splits Up Star-Kist in Move to Raise World's Canned Fish Sales," *Wall Street Journal,* 2 November 1988, B6; Ford S. Worthy, "Why There's Still Promise in China," *Forbes,* 27 February 1989, 95–101; Walter G. Schmid, "Heinz Covers the Globe," *Journal of Business Strategy,* March–April 1989, 17–20; Annabella Gabb, "Heinz Meanz Brandz," *Management Today,* July 1989, 64–70; Chriss Swaney, "Heinz Poised for Growth into Next Century," *Pittsburgh Business Times & Journal,* 19 March 1990, 1; Patrice Duggan, "Feeding China's 'Little Emperors,'" *Forbes,* 6 August 1990, 84–85; "H.J. Heinz Co.," *Advertising Age,* 26 September 1990, 80–84; Tom Lester, "The Unique Problems of Heinzight," *Marketing,* 1 November 1990, 26–27; H.J. Heinz Company Annual Meeting, 1990, 3–20; H.J. Heinz Company: Quarterly Report of Earnings and Activities, 1991 Third Quarter–Nine Months.
2. C. K. Prahalad and Yves L. Doz, *The Multinational Mission* (New York: Free Press, 1987), 1–2; Richard M. Hodgetts and Fred Luthans, *International Management* (New York: McGraw-Hill, 1991), 5–6.
3. Michael E. Porter, "Changing Patterns of International Competition," in *Global Strategic Management: The Essentials,* 2nd ed., edited by Heidi Vernon-Wortzel and Lawrence H. Wortzel (New York: Wiley, 1991), 111–135; Hodgetts and Luthans, *International Management,* 3–5, 105; Christopher A. Bartlett and Sumantra Ghoshal, "Organizing for Worldwide Effectiveness: The Transnational Solution," in *Global Strategic Management: The Essentials,* 2nd ed., edited by Heidi Vernon-Wortzel and Lawrence H. Wortzel (New York: Wiley, 1991), 513–528.
4. Bartlett and Ghoshal, "Organizing for Worldwide Effectiveness," 513–528; Alan M. Rugman, Donald J. Lecraw, and Laurence D. Booth, *International Business: Firm and Environment* (New York: McGraw-Hill, 1985), 7; Porter, "Changing Patterns of International Competition," 111–135; Lawrence H. Wortzel, "Global Strategies: Standardization versus Flexibility," in *Global Strategic Management: The Essentials,* 2nd ed., edited by Heidi Vernon-Wortzel and Lawrence H. Wortzel (New York: Wiley, 1991), 135–149.
5. James F. Bolt, "Global Competitors: Some Criteria for Success," *Business Horizons,* January–February 1988, 34–41; Rugman, Lecraw, and Booth, *International Business,* 7; George S. Day, *Market Driven Strategy: Processes for Creating Value* (New York: Free Press, 1990), 254; Robert Collison, "How Bata Rules the World," *Canadian Business,* September 1990, 28–34.
6. Peter J. Dowling and Randall S. Schuler, *International Dimensions of Human Resource Management* (Boston: PWS-Kent, 1990), 32; Kenichi Ohmae, *The Borderless World* (New York: HarperBusiness, 1990), 82–98; Bolt, "Global Competitors," 34–41; Bartlett and Ghoshal, "Organizing for Worldwide Effectiveness," 513–528; Jack Egan, "Business without Borders," *U.S. News & World Report,* 16 July 1990, 29–31.
7. Lois Therrien, "Honeywell Is Finally Tasting the Sweet Life," *Business Week,* 3 June 1991, 34; Clemens P. Work, "If This Is Belgium, It Must Be Tuesday," *U.S. News & World Report,* 16 July 1990, 31–32.
8. Michael E. Porter, *The Competitive Advantage of Nations* (New York: Free Press, 1990), 14; Yves Doz, "International Industries: Fragmentation versus Globalization," in *Global Strategic Management: The Essentials,* 2nd ed., edited by Heidi Vernon-Wortzel and Lawrence H. Wortzel (New York: Wiley, 1991), 20–34.
9. Mark L. Fagan, "A Guide to Global Sourcing," *Journal of Business Strategy,* March–April 1991, 21–25; Porter, *The Competitive Advantage of Nations,* 609–610; Doz, "International Industries," 20–34; "Red Lobster's Global Reach," *U.S. News & World Report,* 26 November 1990, 56.
10. Porter, *The Competitive Advantage of Nations,* 609–610; Doz, "International Industries," 20–34; Robert J. Allio, "Formulating Global Strategy," *Planning Review,* March–April 1989, 22–23, 26–28; Fagan, "A Guide to Global Sourcing," 21–25; British Petroleum 1990 Annual Report, 8–11.
11. Jeremy Main, "How to Go Global—And Why," *Fortune,* 28 February 1989, 70–73, 76; Mike McNamee and Paul Magnusson, "Think Globally, Survive Locally," *Business Week,* 26 November 1990, 50–51; Igor Reichlin, "Where Nike and Reebok Have Plenty of Running Room," *Business Week,* 11 March 1991, 56, 60; Donald G. Halper and H. Chang Moon, "Striving for First-Rate Markets in Third-World Nations," *Management Review,* May 1990, 20–22.
12. Theodore Levitt, *The Marketing Imagination* (New York: Free Press, 1986), 20–21; Ohmae, *The Borderless World,* 3–26; Porter, *The Competitive Advantage of Nations,* 97–99; Sylvia Nasar, "World's Appetite for U.S. Products Is Still Increasing," *New York Times,* 11 November 1991, sec. a, 1, sec. c, 2; Phil Hall, "The 'What?' Card," *ABA Banking Journal,* March 1990, 39–40.
13. John S. McClenahen, "Thinking Globally," *Industry Week,* 21 August 1989, 12–14, 18; Louis Uchitelle, "Small Companies Going Global," *New York Times,* 27 November 1989, sec. c, 1, 5; Leslie Brokaw, "Foreign Affairs," *Inc.,* November 1990, 92–94, 98, 100, 102, 104.
14. Michael E. Porter, "The Competitive Advantage of Nations," *Harvard Business Review,* March–April 1990, 73–93; Porter, *The Competitive Advantage of Nations,* 71.
15. Michael E. Porter, "Why Nations Triumph," *Fortune,* 12 March 1990, 94–95, 98, 102, 104, 108; Allio, "Formulating Global Strategy," 22–23, 26–28.
16. James E. Austin, *Managing in Developing Countries* (New York: Free Press, 1990), 22–23, 46–48; Hodgetts and Luthans, *International Management,* 16–18.
17. Hodgetts and Luthans, *International Management,* 16–18; Austin, *Managing in Developing Countries,* 22–23, 46–48.
18. Austin, *Managing in Developing Countries,* 53–55; Porter, *The Competitive Advantage of Nations,* 637–638.
19. Jeffrey Ryser and Robert Neff, "Boiling Heat, Isolation—and 300 Multinationals," *Business Week,* 22 February 1988, 22D–22H.
20. Rugman, Lecraw, and Booth, *International Business,* 152–158; Christopher Farrell, Michael J. Mandel, Keith Hammonds, Dori Jones Yang, and Paul Magnusson, "At Last, Good News," *Business Week,* 3 June 1991, 24–25; Jonathan Weil, "U.S. Exports Fell 2.2% in December, Reflecting Global Economic Slowdown," *Wall Street Journal,* 21 February 1992, A2; Nasar, "World's Appetite for U. S. Products Is Still Increasing," A1, C2.
21. Steven Greenhouse, "A Freer, But Shrink-

ing, Market," *New York Times,* 12 March 1990, sec. d, 1, 8.
22. Rugman, Lecraw, and Booth, *International Business,* 158–160.
23. Robert W. Casey, "Should You Be Competing in the Global Marketplace?" *Working Woman,* October 1988, 58–66.
24. Jay N. Nisberg, *The Random House Handbook of Business Terms* (New York: Random House, 1988), 139; Robert Williams, Mark Teagan, and Jose Beneyto, *The World's Largest Market: A Business Guide to Europe 1992* (New York: Amacom, 1990), 158–159.
25. Austin, *Managing in Developing Countries,* 248–263.
26. Peter Smith Ring, Stefanie Ann Lenway, and Michele Govekar, "Management of the Political Imperative in International Business," *Strategic Management Journal* 11 (1990): 141–152; Hodgetts and Luthans, *International Management,* 118–121; Austin, *Managing in Developing Countries,* 57–58, 179; Stephen J. Kobrin, "Political Risk: A Review and Reconsideration," in *Global Strategic Management: The Essentials,* 2nd ed., edited by Heidi Vernon-Wortzel and Lawrence H. Wortzel (New York: Wiley, 1991), 179–193; Benjamin Weiner, "What Executives Should Know About Political Risk," *Management Review,* January 1992, 19–22.
27. Robert L. Rose, "Brazil Turns Chillier for Multinationals," *Wall Street Journal,* 4 February 1991, A8; Robert L. Rose, "Latin Squeeze: Brazil's Moves to Curb Its Inflation Also Curb U.S. Concerns' Profits," *Wall Street Journal,* 25 July 1990, A1, A9.
28. Rose, "Latin Squeeze," A1, A9.
29. Kevin Kelly, "Going Global? You'll Need Lawyers, Lobbyists—And Luck," *Business Week,* 21 March 1988, 146; Ooi Guat Tin, "Weapons against Bureaucracy," *Asian Business,* December 1990, 24–30.
30. Austin, *Managing in Developing Countries,* 180–182.
31. Williams, Teagan, and Beneyto, *The World's Largest Market,* 43–50; Rugman, Lecraw, and Booth, *International Business,* 51–66; Heinz Weihrich, "Europe 1992: What the Future May Hold," *Academy of Management Executive* 4, no. 2 (1990): 7–18; Keith Brasher, "As U.S. Urges Free Markets, Its Trade Barriers Are Many," *New York Times,* 7 February 1992, sec. a, 1, sec. d, 4; Paul Magnusson, "Did Washington Lose Sight of the Big Picture?" *Business Week,* 2 December 1991, 38–39; G. Pascal Zachary, "Claim Is Made for Improving Display Screens," *Wall Street Journal,* 10 January 1992, B1, B11.
32. Rugman, Lecraw, and Booth, *International Business,* 51–66; Weihrich, "Europe 1992: What the Future May Hold," 7–18; Williams, Teagan, and Beneyto, *The World's Largest Market,* 43–50.
33. Porter, *The Competitive Advantage of Nations,* 665–667; Rahul Jacob, "Export Barriers the U.S. Hates Most," *Fortune,* 27 February 1989, 88–89; Rugman, Lecraw, and Booth, *International Business,* 68; Williams, Teagan, and Beneyto, *The World's Largest Market,* 256; Jacqueline Mitchell, "Growing Movement to 'Buy American' Debates the Term," *Wall Street Journal,* 24 January 1992, A1, A7.
34. Shawn Tully, "Now the New New Europe," *Fortune,* 2 December 1991, 136–142; Sara Hammes, "Europe's Growing Market," *Fortune,* 2 December 1991, 144–145; Donald N. Thompson, "The Triad, Reciprocity, and Alliances: New Realities for Trade," *Business Quarterly,* Summer 1990, 25–29; Rugman, Lecraw, and Booth, *International Business,* 245–246.
35. Tully, "Now the New New Europe," 136–142; Hammes, "Europe's Growing Market," 144–145; Eric G. Friberg, "1992: Moves Europeans Are Making," *Harvard Business Review,* May–June 1989, 85–89; Eckart E. Goette, "Europe 1992: Update for Business Planners," *Journal of Business Strategy,* March–April 1990, 10–13; Thompson, "The Triad, Reciprocity, and Alliances," 25–29; Williams, Teagan, and Beneyto, *The World's Largest Market,* xv, 1–22, 254–262.
36. John Templeman and Patrick Oster, "One Big Currency—And One Big Job Ahead," *Business Week,* 23 December 1991, 40–42; Tully, "Now the New New Europe," 136–142; Goette, "Europe 1992," 10–13; Thompson, "The Triad, Reciprocity, and Alliances," 25–29; Williams, Teagan, and Beneyto, *The World's Largest Market,* xv, 1–22, 254–262; Daniel Oliver, "Antitrust as a 1992 Fortress," *Wall Street Journal,* 24 April 1989, A14; Tully, "Now the New New Europe," 136–142; Richard A. Melcher, "Europe, Too, Is Edgy about Imports—From America," *Business Week,* 27 January 1992, 48–49.
37. Paul Magnusson and Stephen Baker, "The Mexico Pact: Worth the Price?" *Business Week,* 27 May 1991, 32–35; William J. Holstein and Amy Borrus, "Inching toward a North American Market," *Business Week,* 25 June 1990, 40–41; Chuck Hawkins and William J. Holstein, "The North American Shakeout Arrives Ahead of Schedule," *Business Week,* 17 April 1989, 34–35.
38. Ellen F. Jackofsy, John W. Slocum, Jr., and Sara J. McQuaid, "Cultural Values and the CEO: Alluring Companions?" *Academy of Management Executive* 11, no. 1 (1988): 39–49.
39. Graham Practice, "Adapting Management Style to the Organisation of the Future," *Personnel Management,* June 1990, 58–62; Jackofsy, Slocum, and McQuaid, "Cultural Values and the CEO," 39–49.
40. Jackofsy, Slocum, and McQuaid, "Cultural Values and the CEO," 39–49; Practice, "Adapting Management Style to the Organisation of the Future," 58–62; Hodgetts and Luthans, *International Management,* 46–47.
41. Practice, "Adapting Management Style to the Organisation of the Future," 58–62; Hodgetts and Luthans, *International Management,* 51; Jackofsy, Slocum, and McQuaid, "Cultural Values and the CEO," 39–49.
42. Jackofsy, Slocum, and McQuaid, "Cultural Values and the CEO," 39–49; Practice, "Adapting Management Style to the Organisation of the Future," 58–62; Hodgetts and Luthans, *International Management,* 47–48.
43. Jackofsy, Slocum, and McQuaid, "Cultural Values and the CEO," 39–49.
44. Robert T. Keller and Ravi R. Chinta, "International Technology Transfer: Strategies for Success," *Academy of Management Executive* 4, no. 2 (1990): 33–43; Ben L. Kedia and Rabi S. Bhagat, "Cultural Constraints on Transfer of Technology across Nations: Implications for Research in International and Comparative Management," *Academy of Management Review* 13, no. 4 (1988): 559–571; Rugman, Lecraw, and Booth, *International Business,* 286–288; Austin, *Managing in Developing Countries,* 56.
45. Jacob, "Export Barriers the U.S. Hates the Most," 88–89.
46. Arnoud de Meyer and Atsuo Mizushima, "Global R&D Management," in *Global Strategic Management: The Essentials,* 2nd ed., edited by Heidi Vernon-Wortzel and Lawrence H. Wortzel (New York: Wiley, 1991), 439–451; Austin, *Managing in Developing Countries,* 234–236.
47. Hodgetts and Luthans, *International Management,* 103–104; Ronaleen R. Roha, "Taking Your Small Business Global," *Changing Times,* December 1989, 103–109.
48. Rugman, Lecraw, and Booth, *International Business,* 93; Hodgetts and Luthans, *International Management,* 102–103; Rose Brady, "U.S. Exporters That Aren't American," *Business Week,* 29 February 1988, 70–71.
49. Rugman, Lecraw, and Booth, *International Business,* 93; Hodgetts and Luthans, *International Management,* 102–103; Christopher Knowlton, "The New Export Entrepreneurs," *Fortune,* 6 June 1988, 87–102; Jorge Ribeiro, "Invasion of the Theme Parks," *Business Tokyo,* March 1991, 46–48.
50. Edward Cundiff and Marye Tharp Hilger, *Marketing in the International Environment* (Englewood Cliffs, N.J.: Prentice Hall, 1988), 70–71; Rugman, Lecraw, and Booth, *International Business,* 94; *Statistical Abstract of the United States: 1990* (Washington, D.C.: GPO, 1990), 778.
51. Lowell Steele, "Managing Joint International Development," *Research Technology Management,* July–August 1990, 16–26; Deepak K. Datta, "International Joint Ventures: A Framework for Analysis," in *Global Strategic Management: The Essentials,* 2nd ed., edited by Heidi Vernon-Wortzel and Lawrence H. Wortzel (New York: Wiley, 1991), 149–158; Benjamin Gomes-Casseres, "Joint Ventures in the Face of Global Competition," *Sloan Management Review,* Spring 1989, 17–26; Allen R. Myerson, "Setting Up an Island in the Soviet Storm," *New York Times,* 30 December 1990, sec. 3, 1, 6; "Ideas for the 1990s," *Fortune,* 26 March 1990, 128.
52. Jerry Flint, "Ingenuity," *Forbes,* 23 December 1991, 54, 57.
53. Oded Shenkar and Yoram Zeira, "International Joint Ventures: A Tough Test for HR," *Personnel,* January 1990, 26–31; Constance Mitchell, "Partnerships Have Become a Way of Life for Corning," *Wall Street Journal,* 12 July 1988, 6; George Fields, "Marry at the Risk of Divorce when Entering Japan's Market," *Tokyo Business Today,* October 1990, 16; Joshua Hyatt, "The Partnership Route," *Inc.,* December 1988, 145–148.
54. Jeff Shear, "Foreign Investment Is Making a Borderless Corporate World," *Insight,* 2 July 1990, 40–42; Roger Thurow, "Seeing the Light," *Wall Street Journal,* 20 September 1991, R1, R2; Steve Dryden, "Investing in Eastern Europe," *Europe,* January–February 1990, 24–26.
55. Hodgetts and Luthans, *International Management,* 99–100; Day, *Market Driven Strategy,* 272; John Marcom, Jr., "Blue Blazers and Guacamole," *Forbes,* 25 November 1991, 64–68; "Brooks Brothers Suits M&S's U.S. Taste," *Chain Store Age Executive,* December 1988, 20–21.
56. Austin, *Managing in Developing Countries,* 231–234; Constantinos C. Markides and Norman Berg, "Manufacturing Offshore Is Bad Business," *Harvard Business Review,* Sep-

tember–October 1988, 113–120; Gary Taylor, "Maquilas at the Crossroads," *International Business,* October 1991, 32–36; Joel Millman, "Bienvenidos, Tigers!" *Forbes,* 27 May 1991, 190–192; Edmund Faltermayer, "U.S. Companies Come Back Home," *Fortune,* 30 December 1991, 106–112.

57. Balaji S. Chakravarthy and Howard V. Perlmutter, "Strategic Planning for a Global Business," in *Global Strategic Management: The Essentials,* 2nd ed., edited by Heidi Vernon-Wortzel and Lawrence H. Wortzel (New York: Wiley, 1991), 74–85; "Corporate Culture and Human Resource Management," in *Global Strategic Management: The Essentials,* 2nd ed., edited by Heidi Vernon-Wortzel and Lawrence H. Wortzel (New York: Wiley, 1991), 479–481.

58. Andrew Kupfer, "How to Be a Global Manager," *Fortune,* 14 March 1988, 52–58.

59. "Corporate Culture and Human Resource Management," 479–481; Chakravarthy and Perlmutter, "Strategic Planning for a Global Business," 74–85.

60. Chakravarthy and Perlmutter, "Strategic Planning for a Global Business," 74–85; "Corporate Culture and Human Resource Management," 479–481.

61. Klaus E. Agthe, "Managing the Mixed Marriage," *Business Horizons,* January–February 1990, 37–43.

62. See Note 1.

63. Information on Fang family from Phyllis Berman and Jean Sherman Chatzky, "Closer to the Consumer," *Forbes,* 20 January 1992, 56–57. © Forbes Inc., 1992.

CHAPTER 6

1. Stephen Kreider Yoder, "A 1990 Reorganization at Hewlett-Packard Already Is Paying Off," *Wall Street Journal,* 22 July 1991, A1, A5; Kathleen K. Wiegner, "Good-bye to the HP Way?" *Forbes,* 26 November 1990, 36–37; Lance Knobel, "Hewlett-Packard's Culture Shock," *Management Today,* June 1988, 100–106; J. A. Savage, "Changing of Guard, Sharper Customer Focus in Store at HP," *Computerworld,* 24 December 1990, 23; J. A. Savage and Nell Margolis, "Analysts: HP Reorg Puts Young on Hot Seat," *Computerworld,* 8 October 1990, 133; G. Pascal Zachary, "Hewlett-Packard Revises Its Game Plan," *Wall Street Journal,* 12 October 1990, A4.

2. Edwin McDowell, "Penguin to Raise Prices Next Year by 4 Cents a Book," *New York Times,* 19 October 1990, sec. d, 17.

3. Charles H. Kepner and Benjamin B. Tregoe, *The New Rational Manager* (New York: Princeton Research Press, 1981), viii, 83; Fremont A. Shull, Jr., Andre L. Delbecq, and L. L. Cummings, *Organizational Decision Making* (New York: McGraw-Hill, 1970), 12–14, 30–31.

4. Irving L. Janis, *Crucial Decisions* (New York: Free Press, 1989), 143; Gerald F. Smith, "Defining Managerial Problems: A Framework for Prescriptive Theorizing," *Management Science* 35, no. 8 (August 1989): 963–981.

5. Judy Temes, "Milk Trade Creamed by No-Fat Margins," *Crain's New York Business,* 6 May 1991, 11.

6. David A. Cowan, "Developing a Process Model of Problem Recognition," *Academy of Management Review* 11, no. 4 (1986): 763–776; Henry Mintzberg, Duru Raisinghani, and Andre Theoret, "The Structure of 'Unstructured' Decision Processes," *Administrative Science Quarterly* 21 (June 1976): 246–275.

7. H. Kuklan, "Crisis Confrontation in International Management: Consequences and Coping Actions," *Management International Review* 28, no. 3 (1988): 21–30.

8. A. J. Robinson, "Will Business Ever Get Back to Usual in China?" in *Wall Street Journal on Managing,* edited by David Asman (New York: Doubleday Currency, 1990), 226–229.

9. James L. Sheedy, "Retooling Your Workers along with Your Machines," in *Wall Street Journal on Managing,* edited by David Asman (New York: Doubleday Currency, 1990), 76–79.

10. Janis, *Crucial Decisions,* 143.

11. Mintzberg, Raisinghani, and Theoret, "The Structure of 'Unstructured' Decision Processes," 246–275; Paul C. Nutt, "Types of Organizational Decision Processes," *Administrative Science Quarterly* 29 (1984): 414–450.

12. "Inc. 500: Resource Conservation Services," *Inc.,* December 1990, 80.

13. Fremont E. Kast and James E. Rosenzweig, *Organization and Management: A Systems and Contingency Approach,* 4th ed. (New York: McGraw-Hill, 1985), 424–425.

14. C. H. Chung, J. R. Lang, and K. N. Shaw, "An Approach for Developing Support Systems for Strategic Decision Making in Business," *Omega International Journal of Management Science* 17, no. 2 (1989): 135–146; Peter G. W. Keen and Michael S. Scott Morton, *Decision Support Systems: An Organizational Perspective* (Reading, Mass.: Addison-Wesley, 1978), 67–68, 85–86.

15. Margaret A. Gilliam, "Wal-Mart Stores, Inc.," *First Boston Equity Research* (investment analysis), 3 December 1990, 11.

16. Mintzberg, Raisinghani, and Theoret, "The Structure of 'Unstructured' Decision Processes," 246–275; Keen and Morton, *Decision Support Systems,* 67–68, 85–86.

17. Ted Holden, "A Retail Rebel Has the Establishment Quaking," *Business Week,* 1 April 1991, 39–40.

18. Kast and Rosenzweig, *Organization and Management,* 429; Paul E. Moody, *Decision Making: Proven Methods for Better Decisions* (New York: McGraw-Hill, 1983), 4–5, 44.

19. Keith H. Hammonds, "Ronald Jackson," *The 1991 Business Week 1000,* 1991, 80.

20. N. S. Fagley and Paul M. Miller, "The Effects of Decision Framing on Choice of Risky vs. Certain Options," *Organizational Behavior and Human Decision Process* 39 (1987): 264–277.

21. Percy H. Hill, Hugo A. Bedau, Richard A. Chechile, William J. Crochetiere, Barbara L. Kellerman, Daniel Ounjian, Stephen G. Pauker, Susan P. Pauker, and Jeffrey Z. Rubin, *Making Decisions* (Reading, Mass.: Addison-Wesley, 1979), 14; Kenneth R. MacCrimmon and Donald A. Wehrung, *Taking Risks: The Management of Uncertainty* (New York: Free Press, 1986), 9–11; James G. March and Zur Shapira, "Managerial Perspectives on Risk and Risk Taking," *Management Science* 33, no. 11 (November 1987): 1404–1417.

22. Monsanto 1990 Annual Report, 3.

23. James W. Frederickson, "The Comprehensiveness of Strategic Decision Process: Extension, Observations, Future Directions," *Academy of Management Journal* 27, no. 3 (1984): 445–466; Paul C. Nutt, *Making Tough Decisions: Tactics for Improving Managerial Decision Making* (San Francisco: Jossey-Bass, 1989), 4; MacCrimmon and Wehrung, *Taking Risks,* 14–15.

24. Michael A. Verespej, "Gutsy Decisions of 1990," *Industry Week,* 18 February 1990, 26.

25. Patricia M. Fandt and Gerald R. Ferris, "The Management of Information and Impressions: When Employees Behave Opportunistically," *Organizational Behavior and Human Decision Processes* 45 (1990): 140–158; Nutt, *Making Tough Decisions,* 6–7.

26. Robert McClory, "Playing to a Full House in Florida," *Nonprofit World,* July–August 1989, 14–17.

27. Herbert A. Simon, *Administrative Behavior,* 3rd ed. (New York: Free Press, 1976), 5–7; Moody, *Decision Making,* 182.

28. John H. Taylor, "Risk Taker," *Forbes,* 14 November 1988, 108.

29. Simon, *Administrative Behavior,* 80.

30. Max H. Bazerman, *Judgment in Managerial Decision Making,* 2nd ed. (New York: Wiley, 1990), 4–5.

31. Simon, *Administrative Behavior,* 79–81; Janis, *Crucial Decisions,* 28–31.

32. Simon, *Administrative Behavior,* 79–109; Bazerman, *Judgment in Managerial Decision Making,* 4–5; Janis, *Crucial Decisions,* 28–31; Michael J. Prietula and Herbert A. Simon, "The Experts in Your Midst," *Harvard Business Review,* January–February 1989, 120–124; Ronald A. Heiner, "Imperfect Decisions in Organizations," *Journal of Economic Behavior and Organization* 9 (1988): 25–44.

33. James G. March and Herbert A. Simon, *Organizations* (New York: Wiley, 1958), 140; Simon, *Administrative Behavior,* xxvii–xxxi; Katherine Weisman, "Safe Harbor," *Forbes,* 4 September 1989, 58–60.

34. Bazerman, *Judgment in Managerial Decision Making,* 4–5; Laurence Paquette and Thomas Kida, "The Effect of Decision Strategy and Task Complexity on Decision Performance," *Organizational Behavior and Decision Processes* 41 (1988): 128–142.

35. Hill et al., *Making Decisions,* 21–22; Smith, "Defining Managerial Problems," 963–981; Benjamin B. Tregoe, "Decision-Making Process," in *Handbook for Professional Managers,* edited by Lester R. Bittel and Jackson E. Ramsey (New York: McGraw-Hill, 1985), 219.

36. "Nonprofits Respond to Competition," *Nonprofit World,* September–October 1990, 11–12.

37. Peter F. Drucker, *The Practice of Management* (New York: Harper & Row, 1982), 351–355; "Nonprofits Respond to Competition," 11–12; Hill et al., *Making Decisions,* 23.

38. Richard M. Morris, "From T. G. Rose to Robert Ludlum: Conquering Operational Myths," *Industrial Management,* July–August 1990, 4–5.

39. "Nonprofits Respond to Competition," 11–12.

40. Nutt, *Making Tough Decisions,* 397–398; Larry L. Barker, Kathy J. Wahlers, Kittie W. Watson, and Robert J. Kibler, *Groups in Process* (Englewood Cliffs, N.J.: Prentice Hall, 1987), 113; R. Jeffery Ellis, *Managing Strategy in the Real World* (Lexington, Mass.: Lexington Books, 1988), 17; "Making Fast Strategic Decisions in High-Velocity Environments," *Academy of Management Journal* 32, no. 3 (1989): 543–576.

41. Echo Montgomery Garrett, "My Catalog Is My Showroom," *Venture,* November 1988, 32–33.

42. Ben Heirs, "Managing a Thinking Team," *Industry Week,* 2 November 1987, 111; Barker et al., *Groups in Process,* 113–114; Drucker, *The Practice of Management,* 353–356; Ann Langley, "Patterns in the Use of Formal Analy-

sis in Strategic Decisions," *Organization Studies* 11, no. 1 (1990): 17–45.
43. Seth Lubove, "Over the Line Extension," *Forbes,* 22 July 1991, 64–65.
44. Drucker, *The Practice of Management,* 362–363; Thomas P. Ference, "Organizational Communications and the Decision Process," *Management Science* 17, no. 2 (October 1970): B83–B96.
45. Joel Millman, "Bienvenidos, Tigers!" *Forbes,* 27 May 1991, 190–192.
46. Drucker, *The Practice of Management,* 364–365; Nutt, *Making Tough Decisions,* 27; Janis, *Crucial Decisions,* 333.
47. Brian Dumaine, "What the Leaders of Tomorrow See," *Fortune,* 3 July 1989, 48–62.
48. Tregoe, "Decision-Making Process," 219.
49. Theodore Levitt, *Thinking about Management* (New York: Free Press, 1991), 7.
50. Edwin A. Gerloff, *Organizational Theory and Design* (New York: McGraw-Hill, 1985), 24; Moody, *Decision Making,* 3–6; L. J. Bourgeois III and Kathleen M. Eisenhardt, "Strategic Decision Processes in High-Velocity Environments: Four Cases in the Microcomputer Industry," *Management Science* 34, no. 7 (July 1988): 816–835.
51. Moody, *Decision Making,* 9; Fagley and Miller, "The Effects of Decision Framing," 264–277.
52. Bazerman, *Judgment in Managerial Decision Making,* 5–6, 11–39; Nutt, *Making Tough Decisions,* 303.
53. Bazerman, *Judgment in Managerial Decision Making,* 72; Jerry Ross and Barry M. Staw, "Expo 86: An Escalation Prototype," *Administrative Science Quarterly* 31 (1986): 274–297; Barry M. Staw and Jerry Ross, "Good Money after Bad," *Psychology Today,* February 1988, 30; Shlomo Maital, "Do Economists Know Anything a Manager Wants to Know?" *Across the Board,* July–August 1990, 7.
54. Melissa Travis, "Saved by Sony," *Business Tokyo,* January 1991, 34–38.
55. Nutt, *Making Tough Decisions,* 303; Anna Grandori, "A Prescriptive Contingency View of Organizational Decision Making," *Administrative Science Quarterly* 29 (1984): 192–209; Boris Yavitz and William H. Newman, *Strategy in Action* (New York: Free Press, 1982), 107–108, 118–121.
56. Peter F. Drucker, *Management: Tasks, Responsibilities, Practices* (New York: Harper & Row, 1974), 475–476.
57. Bill Leonard, "Taking a Big Risk," *HR Magazine,* January 1990, 53.
58. Ference, "Organizational Communications Systems and the Decision Process," B83-B96; Max D. Richards, *Setting Strategic Goals and Objectives* (St. Paul, Minn.: West Publishing, 1986), 18.
59. K. Michael Haywood, "Thoughts on Thinking: A Critical Human-Resource Skill," *Cornell H.R.A. Quarterly,* August 1987, 51–55; Heirs, "Managing a Thinking Team," 109; Stephen D. Brookfield, *Developing Critical Thinkers* (San Francisco: Jossey-Bass, 1987), 7–9.
60. J. Frank Yates, *Judgment and Decision Making* (Englewood Cliffs, N.J.: Prentice Hall, 1990), 372–375; Nutt, *Making Tough Decisions,* 20; Douglas McGregor, *The Human Side of Enterprise* (New York: McGraw-Hill, 1960), 216–217.
61. Richard Phalon, "The Big Money in Bitter Berries," *Forbes,* 10 June 1991, 77–79.
62. Prietula and Simon, "The Experts in Your Midst," 120–124; Herbert A. Simon, "Making Management Decisions: The Role of Intuition and Emotion," *Academy of Management Executive,* February 1987, 57–63.
63. Subrata N. Chakravarty, "A Tale of Two Companies," *Forbes,* 27 May 1991, 86–95.
64. Guisseppi A. Forgionne, "Corporate Management Science Activities: An Update," *Interfaces,* 3 June 1983, 20–23; Harvey M. Wagner, "Operations Research: A Global Language for Business Strategy," *Operations Research* 36, no. 5 (September–October 1988): 797–803; Kast and Rosenzweig, *Organization and Management,* 444.
65. Hill et al., *Making Decisions,* 120, 127.
66. William J. Stevenson, *Business Statistics: Concepts and Applications,* 2nd ed. (New York: Harper & Row, 1985), 561–563; Kast and Rosenzweig, *Organization and Management,* 444–447.
67. F. Hutton Barron, "Payoff Matrices Pay Off at Hallmark," *Interfaces,* July–August 1985, 20–25.
68. Charles L. Olson and Mario J. Picconi, *Statistics for Business Decision Making* (Glenview, Ill.: Scott, Foresman, 1983), 840; Hill et al., *Making Decisions,* 136–137.
69. Stevenson, *Business Statistics,* 574–577; Edward A. McCreary, "How to Grow a Decision Tree," in *Readings in Management,* 5th ed., edited by Max D. Richards (Cincinnati: South-Western Publishing, 1978), 122–130.
70. Kast and Rosenzweig, *Organization and Management,* 436–439.
71. James L. Webster, William E. Reif, and Jeffrey S. Bracker, "The Manager's Guide to Strategic Planning Tools and Techniques," *Planning Review,* November–December 1989, 4–13, 48.
72. Wagner, "Operations Research," 797–803.
73. Hill et al., *Making Decisions,* 178–179.
74. Jean E. Weber, *Mathematical Analysis: Business and Economic Applications,* 4th ed. (New York: Harper & Row, 1982), 675.
75. Robert E. Shannon, "Operations Research and Mathematical Modeling," in *Handbook for Professional Managers,* edited by Lester R. Bittel and Jackson E. Ramsey (New York: McGraw-Hill, 1985), 634.
76. Hill et al., *Making Decisions,* 188.
77. Kast and Rosenzweig, *Organization and Management,* 95.
78. Victor H. Vroom, "A New Look at Managerial Decision Making," in *Readings in Management,* 5th ed., edited by Max D. Richards (Cincinnati: South-Western Publishing, 1978), 105–121; Victor H. Vroom and Arthur G. Jago, *The New Leadership: Managing Participation in Organizations* (Englewood Cliffs, N.J.: Prentice Hall, 1988), 101–105, 107–116.
79. John L. Cotton, David A. Vollrath, Kirk L. Froggatt, Mark L. Lengnick-Hall, and Kenneth R. Jennings, "Employee Participation: Diverse Forms and Different Outcomes," *Academy of Management Review* 13, no. 1 (1988): 8–22; Edwin A. Locke, David M. Schweiger, and Gary P. Latham, "Participation in Decision Making: When Should It Be Used?" *Organizational Dynamics,* Winter 1986, 65–79.
80. George A. Steiner, John B. Miner, and Edmund R. Gray, *Management Policy and Strategy* (New York: Macmillan, 1982), 262–263.
81. Joseph F. McKenna, "A Republic United," *Industry Week,* 15 October 1990, 69.
82. William Fulmer and Robert Fulmer, "Strategic Group Technique: Involving Managers in Strategic Planning," *Long Range Planning* 23 (April 1990): 79–84; D. Kent Zimmerman, "Nominal Group Technique," in *Handbook for Professional Managers,* edited by Lester R. Bittel and Jackson E. Ramsey (New York: McGraw-Hill, 1985), 604–605; Kast and Rosenzweig, *Organization and Management,* 472–473.
83. Curtis J. Tompkins, "Forecasting Business Conditions," in *Handbook for Professional Managers,* edited by Lester R. Bittel and Jackson E. Ramsey (New York: McGraw-Hill, 1985), 337–338; Forest Woody Horton, Jr., and John S. Pruden, "Benefit: Cost Analysis—A Delphi Approach," *Information Management Review* 3, no. 4 (1988): 47–54.
84. Terence R. Mitchell and James R. Larson, Jr., *People in Organizations: An Introduction to Organizational Behavior* (New York: McGraw-Hill, 1987), 371–372; Larry K. Michaelsen, Warren E. Watson, and Robert H. Black, "A Realistic Test of Individual Versus Group Consensus Decision Making," *Journal of Applied Psychology* 74, no. 5 (1989): 834–839; William Ouchi, *Theory Z: How American Business Can Meet the Japanese Challenge* (Reading, Mass.: Addison-Wesley, 1981), 42–46; Drucker, *Management,* 468.
85. Mitchell and Larson, *People in Organizations,* 371–372; Barker et al., *Groups in Process,* 177; Janis, *Crucial Decisions,* 58–59; Hill et al., *Making Decisions,* 97–98.
86. Laura Jereski, "Can Paul Fireman Put the Bounce Back in Reebok?" *Business Week,* 18 June 1990, 181–182.
87. Russell L. Ackoff and Elsa Vergara, "Creativity in Problem Solving and Planning," in *Handbook for Creative and Innovative Managers,* edited by Robert L. Kuhn (New York: McGraw-Hill, 1988), 81–82; Andrew E. Schwartz, "When Good Ideas Are Needed Fast," *Nonprofit World,* November–December 1989, 22–23; Charles S. Whiting, "Operational Techniques of Creative Learning," in *Readings in Management,* 5th ed., edited by Max D. Richards (Cincinnati: South-Western Publishing, 1978), 131–142.
88. David M. Schweiger and Phyllis A. Finger, "The Comparative Effectiveness of Dialectical Inquiry and Devil's Advocacy: The Impact of Task Biases on Previous Research Findings," *Strategic Management Journal* 5 (1984): 335–350.
89. Ackoff and Vergara, "Creativity in Problem Solving and Planning," 87; Steiner, Miner, and Gray, *Management Policy and Strategy,* 273–274.
90. David M. Schweiger and William R. Sandberg, "The Utilization of Individual Capabilities in Group Approaches to Strategic Decision-Making," *Strategic Management Journal* 10 (1989): 31–43; David M. Schweiger, William R. Sandberg, and Paula L. Rechner, "Experiential Effects of Dialectical Inquiry, Devil's Advocacy, and Consensus Approaches to Strategic Decision Making," *Academy of Management Journal* 32, no. 4 (1989): 745–772; David M. Schweiger, William R. Sandberg, and James W. Ragan, "Group Approaches for Improving Strategic Decision Making: A Comparative Analysis of Dialectical Inquiry, Devil's Advocacy, and Consensus," *Academy of Management Journal* 29, no. 1 (1986): 51–71.
91. See note 1.
92. Based on information from Joseph Weber and Brian Bremner, "The Screws Are Tightening at Black & Decker," *Business Week,* 23 September 1991, 61, 64.

CHAPTER 7

1. Joseph F. McKenna, "Secretary Martin SCANS the Skills Horizon," *Industry Week,* 19 August 1991, 63, 66; Robert J. Samuelson, "Gibberish on Job Skills," *Washington Post,* 11 July 1991, A15; Frank Swoboda, "U.S. Graduates Seen Ill-Prepared on Workplace 'Thinking Skills,'" *Washington Post,* 3 July 1991, A12; Frank Swoboda, "Job Skills Gap Looms, Panel Finds; High School Students Seen as Unprepared," *Washington Post,* 30 May 1991, B10; "Preparing Young People for the Workforce: Commission, in Report Released Today, Defines New Skills to Meet New Demands," *USA Today,* 2 July 1991, 11A; Karen Ball, "50% of Teens Not Ready for Work, U.S. Panel Says," *Philadelphia Inquirer,* 3 July 1991, D9; Jennifer Toth, "Study Gives High Schools 'F' in Preparing Students for Jobs," *Los Angeles Times,* 8 August 1991, A5; Aleta Watson, "Job Skills Standard to Be Set for Students," *San Jose Mercury News,* 6 April 1990, A12.

2. Peter F. Drucker, *Management: Tasks, Responsibilities, Practices* (New York: Harper & Row, 1974), 48, 75, 101–102; John C. Camillus, *Strategic Planning and Management Control* (Lexington, Mass.: Lexington Books, 1986), 3.

3. Russell L. Ackoff, *A Concept of Corporate Planning* (New York: Wiley-Interscience, 1970), 23; Peter F. Drucker, *The Practice of Management* (New York: Harper & Row, 1982), 88.

4. Pete Engardio, "Look, Up in the Sky—It's Taiwan's Shipping Tycoon," *Business Week,* 8 July 1991, 45.

5. Lawrence R. Jauch and William F. Glueck, *Business Policy and Strategic Management,* 5th ed. (New York: McGraw-Hill, 1988), 65; Leslie W. Rue and Phyllis G. Holland, *Strategic Management: Concepts and Experiences,* 2nd ed. (New York: McGraw-Hill, 1989), 6–7.

6. George A. Steiner, *Strategic Planning: What Every Manager Must Know* (New York: Free Press, 1979), 20, 346–347; Ackoff, *A Concept of Corporate Planning,* 1–4; Fremont E. Kast and James E. Rosenzweig, *Organization and Management: A Systems and Contingency Approach,* 4th ed. (New York: McGraw-Hill, 1985), 478–479.

7. Kast and Rosenzweig, *Organization and Management,* 480–481.

8. Camillus, *Strategic Planning and Management Control,* 15–18.

9. Drucker, *Management,* 77–90; James A. Belasco, "This Vision Thing," *Executive Excellence,* January 1990, 3–4; Jesse Stoner-Zemel, "Realizing Your Vision," *Executive Excellence,* July 1990, 16–17; George L. Morrisey, "Who Needs a Mission Statement? You Do," *Training and Development Journal,* March 1988, 50–52; Laura Nash, "Mission Statements—Mirrors and Windows," *Harvard Business Review,* March–April 1988, 155–156; Jerome H. Want, "Corporate Mission," *Management Review,* August 1986, 46–50; Thomas F. Crum, "Clarity of Vision," *Executive Excellence,* January 1990, 5–6; Fred R. David, "How Companies Define Their Mission," *Long Range Planning* 22, no. 1 (1989): 90–97.

10. Yasuo Inoue, "Management Challenges for the Dai-Ichi Kangyo Bank Ltd.," *Business Japan,* October 1990, 32–33.

11. Drucker, *Management,* 88–89; Tom Ruddell and Lloyd Pettegrew, "The Best Companies Have and Heed Codes/Creeds," *IABC Communication World,* September 1988, 30–31; E. B. Knauft, Renee A. Berger, and Sandra T. Gray, *Profiles of Excellence: Achieving Success in the Nonprofit Sector* (San Francisco: Jossey-Bass, 1991), 125.

12. Knauft, Berger, and Gray, *Profiles of Excellence,* 33–41.

13. David, "How Companies Define Their Mission," 90–97; Morrisey, "Who Needs a Mission Statement?" 50–52; Jauch and Glueck, *Business Policy and Strategic Management,* 59; Steiner, *Strategic Planning,* 156–162.

14. Drucker, *Management,* 99–102; Max D. Richards, *Setting Strategic Goals and Objectives* (St. Paul, Minn.: West Publishing, 1986), 2–3.

15. Jauch and Glueck, *Business Policy and Strategic Management,* 78; Richards, *Setting Strategic Goals and Objectives,* 30–31; Drucker, *Management,* 100–101; Canadian National 1990 Annual Report, inside front cover.

16. Richards, *Setting Strategic Goals and Objectives,* 34–35; Canadian National 1990 Annual Report, 8, 16.

17. Richards, *Setting Strategic Goals and Objectives,* 39–40; Canadian National 1990 Annual Report, 5–12.

18. Kast and Rosenzweig, *Organization and Management,* 186–187; Richards, *Setting Strategic Goals and Objectives,* 24–43; Anthony P. Raia, *Managing by Objectives* (Glenview, Ill.: Scott, Foresman, 1974), 29.

19. Raia, *Managing by Objectives,* 57; Gilbert Fuchsberg, "Gurus of Quality Are Gaining Clout," *Wall Street Journal,* 27 November 1990, B1, B12.

20. Charles H. Granger, "The Hierarchy of Objectives," in *Executive Skills: A Management by Objectives Approach,* edited by George Odiorne, Heinz Weihrich, and Jack Mendleson (Dubuque, Iowa: Brown, 1980), 38; Raia, *Managing by Objectives,* 57; Henry L. Tosi, John R. Rizzo, and Stephen J. Carroll, "Setting Goals in Management by Objectives," in *Executive Skills: A Management by Objectives Approach,* edited by George Odiorne, Heinz Weihrich, and Jack Mendleson (Dubuque, Iowa: Brown, 1980), 70; Robert Albanese, "Objectives and Goals," in *Handbook for Professional Managers,* edited by Lester R. Bittel and Jackson E. Ramsey (New York: McGraw-Hill, 1985), 619; Richard Brandt, "The Selling Frenzy That Nearly Undid Oracle," *Business Week,* 3 December 1990, 156–157.

21. Tosi, Rizzo, and Carroll, "Setting Goals in Management by Objectives," 70; Raia, *Managing by Objectives,* 57; John Hillidge, "Planning for Growth in a Small Company," *Long Range Planning* 23, no. 3 (1990): 76–81.

22. Steiner, *Strategic Planning,* 164–165; Raia, *Managing by Objectives,* 57; Carla Rapoport, "The World's Most Valuable Company," *Fortune,* 10 October 1988, 92–104.

23. Raia, *Managing by Objectives,* 57; Granger, "The Hierarchy of Objectives," 38; Steiner, *Strategic Planning,* 164; Alaska Air Group 1989 Annual Report, 2–3, 14.

24. Jack L. Mendleson, "Goal Setting: An Important Management Tool," in *Executive Skills: A Management by Objectives Approach,* edited by George Odiorne, Heinz Weihrich, and Jack Mendleson (Dubuque, Iowa: Brown, 1980), 56–61; Robert D. Pritchard, Philip L. Roth, Steven D. Jones, Patricia J. Galgay, and Margaret D. Watson, "Designing a Goal-Setting System to Enhance Performance: A Practical Guide," *Organizational Dynamics,* Summer 1988, 69–78.

25. David W. Ewing, *The Practice of Planning* (New York: Harper & Row, 1968), 26–29; Drucker, *Management,* 117–119; Granger, "The Hierarchy of Objectives," 36; Richards, *Setting Strategic Goals and Objectives,* 16–17; Albanese, "Objectives and Goals," 620.

26. Edwin A. Locke, Gary P. Latham, and Miriam Erez, "The Determinants of Goal Commitment," *Academy of Management Review* 13, no. 1 (1988): 23–29; Steiner, *Strategic Planning,* 279–281; Pritchard et al., "Designing a Goal-Setting System to Enhance Performance," 69–78; Edwin A. Locke, "The Ubiquity of the Technique of Goal Setting in Theories of and Approaches to Employee Motivation," *Academy of Management Review,* July 1978, 594–601.

27. Locke, Latham, and Erez, "The Determinants of Goal Commitment," 23–29; Gary P. Latham, Miriam Erez, and Edwin A. Locke, "Resolving Scientific Disputes by the Joint Design of Crucial Experiments by the Antagonists: Application to the Erez-Latham Dispute Regarding Participation in Goal Setting," *Journal of Applied Psychology* 73, no. 4 (1988): 753–772; Richards, *Setting Strategic Goals and Objectives,* 21.

28. Ackoff, *A Concept of Corporate Planning,* 4–5; Theodore A. Andersen, "Coordinating Strategic and Operational Planning," in *Concepts for Corporate Strategy,* edited by John W. Bonge and Bruce P. Coleman (New York: Macmillan, 1972), 274–275; Raia, *Managing by Objectives,* 33–34; Snap-on Tools 1990 Annual Report, 4–18.

29. Ackoff, *A Concept of Corporate Planning,* 4–5; Snap-on Tools 1990 Annual Report, 4–18.

30. Kast and Rosenzweig, *Organization and Management,* 490–493; Andersen, "Coordinating Strategic and Operational Planning," 275; Snap-on Tools 1990 Annual Report, 12–13.

31. William K. Fallon, ed., *AMA Management Handbook,* 2nd ed. (New York: Amacom, 1983), 1–56; Dale D. McConkey, *How to Manage by Results* (New York: Amacom, 1983), 38; L. J. Bourgeois III and Kathleen M. Eisenhardt, "Strategic Decision Processes in High-Velocity Environments: Four Cases in the Microcomputer Industry," *Management Science* 34, no. 7 (July 1988): 816–835; Kast and Rosenzweig, *Organization and Management,* 499–500; Michael A. Verespej, "Gutsy Decisions of 1990," *Industry Week,* 18 February 1991, 23–34; James R. Norman, "Xerox on the Move," *Forbes,* 10 June 1991, 70–71.

32. McConkey, *How to Manage by Results,* 38; BP 1990 Annual Report, 9–17.

33. John J. Curran, "Companies That Rob the Future," *Fortune,* 4 July 1988, 84–89; Stephen C. Harper, "How to Prevent the Rude Awakening of Management Shock," *Industrial Management,* July–August 1990, 11–14, 32; Gary Hector, "Yes, You Can Manage Long Term," *Fortune,* 21 November 1988, 64–76.

34. Kast and Rosenzweig, *Organization and Management,* 498–499.

35. Kast and Rosenzweig, *Organization and Management,* 498–499; Peter T. Kilborn, "In Coal Country, a Home-Grown Clinic," *New York Times,* 15 March 1991, sec. a, 1, 22.

36. Kast and Rosenzweig, *Organization and Management,* 498–499; Kilborn, "In Coal Country, a Home-Grown Clinic," sec. a, 1, 22.

37. Kast and Rosenzweig, *Organization and Management,* 498–499.

38. Ackoff, *A Concept of Corporate Planning,* 42–43; Peter Coy, "Twin Engines," *Business Week,* 20 January 1992, 56–59, 62–63.

39. Susan Caminiti, "If It's Hot, They've Got

It," *Fortune,* 3 June 1991, 103.
40. Katarzyna Wandycz, "Turning a Rag into Riches," *Forbes,* 27 May 1991, 350–353.
41. Steiner, *Strategic Planning,* 229–230; Stephen A. Rutty, David A. Deluca, and John K. Jackson, "Advance Planning for Emergencies Minimizes Outage Time," *Transmission & Distribution,* November 1989, 36–40.
42. Samuel C. Certo and J. Paul Peter, *Strategic Management,* 2nd ed. (New York: McGraw-Hill, 1991), 12; John Thackray, "Planning's Future Shock," in *Modern Management: Ideas and Issues,* 2nd ed., edited by David R. Hampton (Encino, Calif.: Dickenson Publishing, 1975), 101–112.
43. Arie P. de Geus, "Planning as Learning," *Harvard Business Review,* March–April 1988, 70–74; Christopher Knowlton, "Shell Gets Rich by Beating Risk," *Fortune,* 26 August 1991, 79–82.
44. McConkey, *How to Manage by Results,* 57; Rue and Holland, *Strategic Management,* 25–26.
45. Rosabeth Moss Kanter, *The Change Masters* (New York: Simon & Schuster, 1983), 304–306.
46. Scott Jaschik, "In Tight Economy, Tougaloo Shows How Black Institutions Can Use Strategic Planning to Aid Their Special Missions," *Chronicle of Higher Education,* 2 October 1991, A1, A33-A35.
47. Jauch and Glueck, *Business Policy and Strategic Management,* 52.
48. Drucker, *The Practice of Management,* 119, 121; Raia, *Managing by Objectives,* 22; George S. Odiorne, *Management by Objectives* (New York: Pitman, 1965), 55–56; Richards, *Setting Strategic Goals and Objectives,* 104–107.
49. John A. Byrne, "Profiting from the Nonprofits," *Business Week,* 26 March 1990, 66–74; Dale D. McConkey, "Applying Management by Objectives to Nonprofit Organizations," in *Managing Nonprofit Organizations,* edited by Diane Borst and Patrick J. Montana (New York: Amacom, 1977), 141–154.
50. Mendleson, "Goal Setting: An Important Management Tool," 56–67; John Humble, "Avoiding the Pitfalls of the MBO Trap," in *Executive Skills: A Management by Objectives Approach,* edited by George Odiorne, Heinz Weihrich, and Jack Mendleson (Dubuque, Iowa: Brown, 1980), 113–125; Raia, *Managing by Objectives,* 17, 55; Drucker, *The Practice of Management,* 128–129.
51. Raia, *Managing by Objectives,* 17, 19, 73–75; Ronald G. Greenwood, "Management by Objectives: As Developed by Peter Drucker, Assisted by Harold Smiddy," *Academy of Management Review* 6, no. 2 (1981): 225–230.
52. Humble, "Avoiding the Pitfalls of the MBO Trap," 113–125; Drucker, *The Practice of Management,* 130–133; Raia, *Managing by Objectives,* 92.
53. Raia, *Managing by Objectives,* 108–112, 115–120; Harold Koontz, "Making Managerial Appraisal Effective," in *Executive Skills: A Management by Objectives Approach,* edited by George Odiorne, Heinz Weihrich, and Jack Mendleson (Dubuque, Iowa: Brown, 1980), 202–216; Mark L. McConkie, "A Clarification of the Goal Setting and Appraisal Processes in MBO," *Academy of Management Review* 4, no. 1 (1979): 29–40.
54. Jan P. Muczyk, "Dynamics and Hazards of MBO Applications," *Personnel Administrator,* May 1979, 51–62.
55. William B. Werther, Jr., and Heinz Weihrich, "Refining MBO through Negotiations," in *Executive Skills: A Management by Objectives Approach,* edited by George Odiorne, Heinz Weihrich, and Jack Mendleson (Dubuque, Iowa: Brown, 1980), 85; Humble, "Avoiding the Pitfalls of the MBO Trap," 113–125; Odiorne, *Management by Objectives,* 55.
56. Richards, *Setting Strategic Goals and Objectives,* 123–124; Raia, *Managing by Objectives,* 149–151; Humble, "Avoiding the Pitfalls of the MBO Trap," 121; David Halpern and Stephen Osofsky, "A Dissenting View of MBO," *Public Personnel Management* 19, no. 3 (Fall 1990): 321–330; David R. Hampton, "The Planning-Motivation Dilemma," in *Modern Management: Ideas and Issues,* 2nd ed., edited by David R. Hampton (Encino, Calif.: Dickenson Publishing, 1975), 56–57.
57. Humble, "Avoiding the Pitfalls of the MBO Trap," 113–125.
58. Steven C. Wheelwright and Spyros Makridakis, *Forecasting Methods for Management,* 4th ed. (New York: Wiley, 1985), 20–25; Percy H. Hill, Hugo A. Bedau, Richard A. Chechile, William J. Crochetiere, Barbara L. Kellerman, Daniel Ounjian, Stephen G. Pauker, Susan P. Pauker, and Jeffrey Z. Rubin, *Making Decisions* (Reading, Mass.: Addison-Wesley, 1979), 188; Drucker, *Management,* 124; Curtis J. Tompkins, "Forecasting Business Conditions," in *Handbook for Professional Managers,* edited by Lester R. Bittel and Jackson E. Ramsey (New York: McGraw-Hill, 1985), 335–347; Amar Bhide, "Why Not Leverage Your Company to the Hilt?" *Harvard Business Review,* May–June 1988, 92–98.
59. Hisao Okuzumi, "Taisei Corporation Plans for the Year 2000," *Long Range Planning* 23 (February 1990): 53–65.
60. Wheelwright and Makridakis, *Forecasting Methods for Management,* 10–14.
61. Wheelwright and Makridakis, *Forecasting Methods for Management,* 10–14; Charles L. Olson and Mario J. Picconi, *Statistics for Business Decision Making* (Glenview, Ill.: Scott, Foresman, 1983), 635–636.
62. Olson and Picconi, *Statistics for Business Decision Making,* 637; Knauft, Berger, and Gray, *Profiles of Excellence,* 102–108.
63. Martin K. Starr, *Operations Management* (Englewood Cliffs, N.J.: Prentice Hall, 1978), 247; Wheelwright and Makridakis, *Forecasting Methods for Management,* 49; Olson and Picconi, *Statistics for Business Decision Making,* 637; Irving Abramowitz, *Production Management* (New York: Ronald Press, 1967), 28; Joshua Hyatt, "The Next Big Thing," *Inc.,* July 1990, 44–54.
64. Wheelwright and Makridakis, *Forecasting Methods for Management,* 49; Vicky Cahan, "When the Rivers Go Dry and the Ice Caps Melt," *Business Week,* 13 February 1989, 95–98.
65. Olson and Picconi, *Statistics for Business Decision Making,* 640.
66. Wheelwright and Makridakis, *Forecasting Methods for Management,* 3, 26.
67. Wheelwright and Makridakis, *Forecasting Methods for Management,* 11, 140, 192.
68. Starr, *Operations Management,* 250–251; Wheelwright and Makridakis, *Forecasting Methods for Management,* 165–180.
69. Wheelwright and Makridakis, *Forecasting Methods for Management,* 192–200; Stanley W. Angrist, "Believers in One Wave Theory See U.S. in Deep Trough Soon," *Wall Street Journal,* 8 August 1991, C1, C9.
70. Wheelwright and Makridakis, *Forecasting Methods for Management,* 200–201; Dana Milbank, "Machine Tool Orders Lose Their Punch as an Indicator of Economic Activity," *Wall Street Journal,* 29 July 1991, A4.
71. J. Scott Armstrong, "The Ombudsman: Research on Forecasting: A Quarter-Century Review, 1960–1984," *Interfaces* 16, no. 1 (January–February 1986): 89–109.
72. Wheelwright and Makridakis, *Forecasting Methods for Management,* 11, 279.
73. Wheelwright and Makridakis, *Forecasting Methods for Management,* 304–309.
74. Gene Bylinsky, "The Marvels of 'Virtual Reality,'" *Fortune,* 3 June 1991, 138–142.
75. Abramowitz, *Production Management,* 27; Wheelwright and Makridakis, *Forecasting Methods for Management,* 311–312.
76. Wheelwright and Makridakis, *Forecasting Methods for Management,* 312–314.
77. Jean E. Weber, *Mathematical Analysis: Business and Economic Applications,* 4th ed. (New York: Harper & Row, 1982), 48–49.
78. Sarah Stiansen, "Breaking Even," *Success,* November 1988, 16.
79. "Feet First," *Executive Female,* May–June 1991, 71; Stride Rite 1990 Annual Report.
80. Arnoldo C. Hax and Dan Candea, *Production and Inventory Management* (Englewood Cliffs, N.J.: Prentice Hall, 1984), 259; Starr, *Operations Management,* 134–140.
81. Starr, *Operations Management,* 134–140; Donald G. Malcolm and Lawrence S. Hill, "Graphical and Network Planning Techniques," in *Industrial Engineering Handbook,* 3rd ed., edited by H. B. Maynard (New York: McGraw-Hill, 1971), 8-57–8-58.
82. Hax and Candea, *Production and Inventory Management,* 325–327; Malcolm and Hill, "Graphical and Network Planning Techniques," 8-58–8-59.
83. Hax and Candea, *Production and Inventory Management,* 325–344; Starr, *Operations Management,* 150–156; Malcolm and Hill, "Graphical and Network Planning Techniques," 8-60–8-63.
84. See note 1.

CHAPTER 8

1. Adapted from Michael Selz, "Office Supply Firms Take Different Paths to Success," *Wall Street Journal,* 30 May 1991, B2; Stephen D. Solomon, "Born to Be Big," *Inc.,* June 1989, 94; Burr Leonard, "Ballpoint Pens 'R' Us," *Forbes,* 6 April 1987, 172; Robert E. Charm, "Thomas G. Stemberg of Staples Inc.," *New England Business,* 2 May 1988, 17, 66; Steven Flax, "Perils of the Paper Clip Trade," *New York Times Magazine,* 11 June 1989, 65, 83–85; Roger C. Lanctot, "Homing In on the Office," *HFD—The Weekly Home Furnishings Newspaper,* 25 April 1988, 1, 88–90; Susan Caminiti, "Seeking Big Money in Paper and Pens," *Fortune,* 31 July 1989, 173–174; David Rottenberg, "Staples' Top Gun," *Boston Magazine,* December 1987, 91–95; Michael Barrier, "Tom Stemberg Calls the Office," *Nation's Business,* July 1990, 42–44; Rowland T. Moriarty and Ursula Moran, "Managing Hybrid Marketing Systems," *Harvard Business Review,* November–December 1990, 146–155; Nancy Brumback, "'New Retailer, Staples, Out to Build Mass Chain of 'Office Superstores,'" *HFD—The Weekly Home Furnishings Newspaper,* 28 December 1987, 57–58; Udayan Gupta, "Retail Start-Up Decides to Start Out Big," *Wall Street Journal,* 14 May 1987, 34; "The Toys 'R' Us of Office Supplies," *Adweek's Marketing*

Week, 15 August 1988, 44–45; Kathy Sizemore, "Office Supply 'Supermarkets' Heading to N.Y.," *Crain's New York Business,* 2 February 1987, 3, 21; "Staples Inc.," *Boston Business Journal,* 8 October 1990; Staples 1990 Annual Report, 1–9.

2. John W. Bonge and Bruce P. Coleman, eds., *Concepts for Corporate Strategy: Readings in Business Policy* (New York: Macmillan, 1972), 1–3; Leslie W. Rue and Phyllis G. Holland, *Strategic Management: Concepts and Experiences,* 2nd ed. (New York: McGraw-Hill, 1989), 3; Robert Boyden Lamb, ed., *Competitive Strategic Management* (Englewood Cliffs, N.J.: Prentice Hall, 1984), ix–x; Raymond E. Miles, Charles C. Snow, Alan D. Meyer, and Henry J. Coleman, Jr., "Organizational Strategy, Structure, and Process," *Academy of Management Review* 3 (July 1978): 546–562.

3. Samuel C. Certo and J. Paul Peter, *Strategic Management: Concepts and Applications,* 2nd ed., (New York: McGraw-Hill, 1991), 17; Kenneth R. Andrews, *The Concept of Corporate Strategy,* 2nd ed. (Homewood, Ill.: Irwin, 1980), vi.

4. Benjamin B. Tregoe and Peter M. Tobia, "Strategy versus Planning: Bridging the Gap," *Journal of Business Strategy,* November–December 1991, 14–19.

5. Boris Yavitz and William H. Newman, *Strategy in Action: The Execution, Politics, and Payoff of Business Planning* (New York: Free Press, 1982), 22–23.

6. Edwin A. Gerloff, *Organizational Theory and Design* (New York: McGraw-Hill, 1985), 44; C. K. Prahalad and Gary Hamel, "The Core Competence of the Corporation," *Harvard Business Review,* May–June 1990, 79–91.

7. Lisle Carter, Jr., "United Way at the Workplace: Coping with America's Needs," *Fund Raising Management,* March 1985, 20–24.

8. William H. Newman, "Shaping the Master Strategy of Your Firm," in *Concepts for Corporate Strategy: Readings in Business Policy,* edited by John W. Bonge and Bruce P. Coleman (New York: Macmillan, 1972), 131–147; Rue and Holland, *Strategic Management,* 135–136; H. Igor Ansoff, *Implanting Strategic Management* (Englewood Cliffs, N.J.: Prentice Hall, 1984), 80–81; Yavitz and Newman, *Strategy in Action,* 46.

9. Arnoldo C. Hax and Nicolas S. Majluf, "The Concept of Strategy and the Strategy Formation Process," *Interfaces* 18, no. 3 (May–June 1988): 99–109; Rue and Holland, *Strategic Management,* 8–10; Yavitz and Newman, *Strategy in Action,* 223–236; Richard G. Hamermesh, *Making Strategy Work: How Senior Managers Produce Results* (New York: Wiley, 1986), 32–36, 47–49; James Brian Quinn, "Managing Strategies Incrementally," in *Competitive Strategic Management,* edited by Robert Boyden Lamb (Englewood Cliffs, N.J.: Prentice Hall, 1984), 57.

10. William E. Rothschild, "How to Ensure the Continued Growth of 'Strategic Planning,'" in *Competitive Strategic Management,* edited by Robert Boyden Lamb (Englewood Cliffs, N.J.: Prentice Hall, 1984), 200–201; Andrews, *The Concept of Corporate Strategy,* vii.

11. Lee W. Sargeant, "Strategic Planning in a Subsidiary," *Long Range Planning,* April 1990, 43–54; Gary McWilliams, "'Open Systems' May Be DEC's 'Open Sesame,'" *Business Week,* 24 June 1991, 101–103.

12. Henry Mintzberg, "Crafting Strategy," *Harvard Business Review,* July–August 1987, 66–75; Henry Mintzberg, "The Design School: Reconsidering the Basic Premises of Strategic Management," *Strategic Management Journal* 11 (1990): 171–195; Daniel H. Gray, "Uses and Misuses of Strategic Planning," *Harvard Business Review,* January–February 1986, 89–97.

13. Lawrence R. Jauch and William F. Glueck, *Business Policy and Strategic Management,* 5th ed. (New York: McGraw-Hill, 1988), 18–20; Mintzberg, "The Design School," 171–195; Yvan Allaire and Mihaela Firsirotu, "Strategic Plans as Contracts," *Long Range Planning* 23, no. 1 (1990): 102–115.

14. Quinn, "Managing Strategies Incrementally," 56; Tregoe and Tobia, "Strategy versus Planning," 14–19.

15. Dale D. McConkey, *How to Manage by Results* (New York: Amacom, 1983), 110–111.

16. John M. Bryson, "A Strategic Planning Process for Public and Non-profit Organizations," *Long Range Planning* 21, no. 1 (1988): 73–81; Certo and Peter, *Strategic Management,* 97; Elmer H. Burack and Nicholas J. Mathys, "Environmental Scanning Improves Strategic Planning," *Personnel Administrator,* April 1989, 82, 84, 87.

17. John C. Camillus, *Strategic Planning and Management Control* (Lexington, Mass.: Lexington Books, 1986), 67–69; Andrews, *The Concept of Corporate Strategy,* 65.

18. Merritt L. Kastens, *Long-Range Planning for Your Business: An Operating Manual* (New York: Amacom, 1976), 51–62; G. J. Medley, "Strategic Planning for the World Wildlife Fund," *Long Range Planning* 21, no. 1 (1988): 46–54.

19. Michael E. Porter, *Competitive Strategy: Techniques for Analyzing Industries and Competitors* (New York: Free Press, 1980), 368–382; Susan E. Jackson and Jane E. Dutton, "Discerning Threats and Opportunities," *Administrative Science Quarterly* 33 (1988): 370–387; R. T. Lenz and Jack L. Engledow, "Environmental Analysis Units and Strategic Decision-making: A Field Study of Selected 'Leading-Edge' Corporations," *Strategic Management Journal* 7 (1986): 69–89; Medley, "Strategic Planning for the World Wildlife Fund," 46–54.

20. Certo and Peter, *Strategic Management,* 97.

21. John A. Pearce II, "Selecting among Alternative Grand Strategies," *California Management Review* 24, no. 3 (Spring 1982): 23–31.

22. Pearce, "Selecting among Alternative Grand Strategies," 23–31; Certo and Peter, *Strategic Management,* 100–101.

23. John A. Pearce II and James W. Harvey, "Concentrated Growth Strategies," *Academy of Management Executive* 4, no. 1 (1990): 61–68; Pearce, "Selecting among Alternative Grand Strategies," 23–31; Peter F. Drucker, *Management: Tasks, Responsibilities, Practices* (New York: Harper & Row, 1974), 104–105.

24. Andrews, *The Concept of Corporate Strategy,* 31; Ted Kumpe and Piet T. Bolwijn, "Manufacturing: The New Case for Vertical Integration," *Harvard Business Review,* March–April 1988, 75–81; Chiquita Brands International 1990 Annual Report, 2–4.

25. Pearce, "Selecting among Alternative Grand Strategies," 23–31; Certo and Peter, *Strategic Management,* 100; Joseph Weber, "Seizing the Dark Day," *Business Week,* 13 January 1992, 26–28.

26. Pearce, "Selecting among Alternative Grand Strategies," 23–31; Raphael Amit and Joshua Livnat, "A Concept of Conglomerate Diversification," *Journal of Management* 14, no. 4 (1988): 593–604; Rothschild, "How to Ensure the Continued Growth of Strategic Planning," 217–218.

27. Pearce, "Selecting among Alternative Grand Strategies," 23–31; Certo and Peter, *Strategic Management,* 101; Bruce Kogut, "Joint Ventures: Theoretical and Empirical Perspectives," *Strategic Management Journal* 9 (1988): 319–332.

28. Judann Dagnoli, "Philip Morris Tilts to Food," *Advertising Age,* 1 April 1991, 1, 36; Gary Hoover, Alta Campbell, and Patrick J. Spain, eds., *Hoover's Handbook 1991: Profiles of Over 500 Major Corporations* (Austin, Tex.: The Reference Press, 1990), 430; PepsiCo 1989 Annual Report, 16; Andrea Rothman, "Can Wayne Calloway Handle the Pepsi Challenge?" *Business Week,* 27 January 1992, 90–92, 94–95, 98.

29. Jauch and Glueck, *Business Policy and Strategic Management,* 204–206; John Case and Elizabeth Conlin, "Second Thoughts on Growth," *Inc.,* March 1991, 46–57.

30. Jauch and Glueck, *Business Policy and Strategic Management,* 204–206; Desmond Smith, "Plane Truths," *Canadian Business,* June 1990, 30–38, 142.

31. Rue and Holland, *Strategic Management,* 51–52; Donald H. Thain and Richard L. Goldthorpe, "Turnaround Management: How to Do It," *Business Quarterly,* Winter 1990, 39–47; Philip S. Scherer, "The Turnaround Consultant Steers Corporate Renewal," *Journal of Management Consulting* 5, no. 1 (1989): 17–24; Michael Maren, "Rebound!" *Success,* June 1990, 48–51.

32. Porter, *Competitive Strategy,* 254–255, 267–270.

33. Rue and Holland, *Strategic Management,* 52–53; Pearce, "Selecting among Alternative Grand Strategies," 23–31; Ron Grover, "Armand Hammer Wouldn't Recognize This Oxy," *Business Week,* 28 January 1991, 58.

34. Donald C. Hambrick and Richard A. D'Aveni, "Large Corporate Failures as Downward Spirals," *Administrative Science Quarterly* 33 (1988): 1–23; Mark Ivey and Michael Oneal, "Continental: Writing the Book on Chapter 11," *Business Week,* 18 March 1991, 35.

35. Andrews, *The Concept of Corporate Strategy,* 30; Rue and Holland, *Strategic Management,* 54; Rick Tetzeli, "Corporate Boot Hill Makes Room for One More Cadaver," *Fortune,* 30 December 1991, 9.

36. Pearce, "Selecting among Alternative Grand Strategies," 23–31; "Conglomerateurs Par Excellence," *The Economist,* 16 June 1990, 82.

37. Frederick W. Gluck, "A Fresh Look at Strategic Management," *Journal of Business Strategy* 6 (Fall 1985): 4–19; Certo and Peter, *Strategic Management,* 102; Rue and Holland, *Strategic Management,* 9, 152–153; Kenichi Ohmae, *The Mind of the Strategist* (New York: McGraw-Hill, 1982), 137, 140–142; Michael E. Porter, *Competitive Advantage: Creating and Sustaining Superior Performance* (New York: Free Press, 1985), 317–320, 364–365.

38. Rue and Holland, *Strategic Management,* 9, 156–157; Certo and Peter, *Strategic Management,* 102–107; Porter, *Competitive Strategy,* 362–364; Leila J. Gainer, "Frameworks for Organizational Strategy," *Training and Development Journal,* September 1989, S7–S10.

39. Hamermesh, *Making Strategy Work,* 132–

144; Certo and Peter, *Strategic Management,* 102–107; Porter, *Competitive Strategy,* 362–364.
40. Philip Kotler and Gary Armstrong, *Principles of Marketing,* 4th ed. (Englewood Cliffs, N.J.: Prentice Hall, 1989), 33–34; Rue and Holland, *Strategic Management,* 153–157; Porter, *Competitive Strategy,* 365–367.
41. Rothschild, "How to Ensure the Continued Growth of Strategic Planning," 203–204.
42. Certo and Peter, *Strategic Management,* 107–110; Rue and Holland, *Strategic Management,* 153–157; Porter, *Competitive Strategy,* 365–367.
43. Gluck, "A Fresh Look at Strategic Management," 4–19; Porter, *Competitive Strategy,* 365–367; Rue and Holland, *Strategic Management,* 157–158; Hamermesh, *Making Strategy Work,* 130–147.
44. Rigoberto Tiglao, "Flour Power in Manila," *Far Eastern Economic Review,* 22 March 1990, 47–48.
45. Vijay Govindarajan, "A Contingency Approach to Strategy Implementation at the Business-Unit Level: Integrating Administrative Mechanisms with Strategy," *Academy of Management Journal* 31, no. 4 (1988): 828–853.
46. Miles et al., "Organizational Strategy, Structure, and Process," 546–562.
47. Miles et al., "Organizational Strategy, Structure, and Process," 546–562; Jauch and Glueck, *Business Policy and Strategic Management,* 240.
48. Miles et al., "Organizational Strategy, Structure, and Process," 546–562; Donald C. Hambrick, "Some Tests of the Effectiveness and Functional Attributes of Miles and Snow's Strategic Types," *Academy of Management Journal* 26, no. 1 (1983): 5–26; 3M 1990 Annual Report, 3.
49. Miles et al., "Organizational Strategy, Structure, and Process," 546–562; Anthony Vandyk, "EgyptAir: New Planes, Broader Horizons," *Air Transport World,* June 1989, 66–71.
50. Miles et al., "Organizational Strategy, Structure, and Process," 546–562; Hambrick, "Some Tests of the Effectiveness and Functional Attributes of Miles and Snow's Strategic Types," 5–26.
51. Miles et al., "Organizational Strategy, Structure, and Process," 546–562.
52. Porter, *Competitive Advantage,* 4–12; Porter, *Competitive Strategy,* 34–35, 40–42.
53. Porter, *Competitive Advantage,* 12–14, 21; Porter, *Competitive Strategy,* 35–37; Danny Miller and Peter H. Friesen, "Porter's (1980) Generic Strategies and Performance: An Empirical Examination with American Data. Part I: Testing Porter," *Organization Studies* 7, no. 1 (1986): 37–55; Ian C. MacMillan, "Controlling Competitive Dynamics by Taking Strategic Initiative," *Academy of Management Executive* 2, no. 2 (1988): 111–118; Bill Saporito, "Is Wal-Mart Unstoppable?" *Fortune,* 6 May 1991, 50–59.
54. Porter, *Competitive Advantage,* 14, 21; Porter, *Competitive Strategy,* 37–38.
55. Porter, *Competitive Strategy,* 38–40; Porter, *Competitive Advantage,* 15–16, 21; Matthew Grimm, "White Castle at 70: Still the Value King," *Adweek's Marketing Week,* 28 January 1991, 24.
56. Porter, *Competitive Strategy,* 41–42; Danny Miller and Peter H. Friesen, "Porter's (1980) Generic Strategies and Performance: An Empirical Examination with American Data. Part II: Performance Implications," *Organization Studies* 7, no. 3 (1986): 255–261; Alan I. Murray, "A Contingency View of Porter's 'Generic Strategies,'" *Academy of Management Review* 13, no. 3 (1988): 390–400; James J. Chrisman, Charles W. Hofer, and William R. Boulton, "Toward a System for Classifying Business Strategies," *Academy of Management Review* 13, no. 3 (1988): 413–428; Peter Wright, Mark Kroll, Ben Kedia, and Charles Pringle, "Strategic Profiles, Market Share, and Business Performance," *Industrial Management,* May–June 1990, 23–28; Govindarajan, "A Contingency Approach to Strategy Implementation at the Business-Unit Level," 828–853; Gareth R. Jones and John E. Butler, "Costs, Revenue, and Business-Level Strategy," *Academy of Management Review* 13, no. 2 (1988): 202–213; Charles W. L. Hill, "Differentiation versus Low Cost or Differentiation and Low Cost: A Contingency Framework," *Academy of Management Review* 13, no. 2 (1988): 401–412.
57. Kotler and Armstrong, *Principles of Marketing,* 289–294; Courtland L. Bovée and John V. Thill, *Marketing* (New York: McGraw-Hill, 1992), 271–272; Rue and Holland, *Strategic Management,* 160–161.
58. Kotler and Armstrong, *Principles of Marketing,* 289–294; Rue and Holland, *Strategic Management,* 160–161.
59. Subrata N. Chakravarty, "Queen Anne at the Mall," *Forbes,* 24 June 1991, 78–80.
60. Charles W. Hofer, Edwin A. Murray, Jr., Ram Charan, and Robert A. Pitts, *Strategic Management: A Casebook in Policy and Planning,* 2nd ed. (St. Paul, Minn.: West Publishing, 1984), 17; Richards, *Setting Strategic Goals and Objectives,* 39–41; Certo and Peter, *Strategic Management,* 115; Derek F. Abell, *Defining the Business: The Starting Point of Strategic Planning* (Englewood Cliffs, N.J.: Prentice Hall, 1980), 189–190.
61. Abell, *Defining the Business,* 189–190; Certo and Peter, *Strategic Management,* 117; Rue and Holland, *Strategic Management,* 179–180; Kenichi Ohmae, *The Borderless World* (New York: HarperBusiness, 1990), 28.
62. Certo and Peter, *Strategic Management,* 117; Rue and Holland, *Strategic Management,* 181–182; Jack Burton, "Just in Time," *International Management,* October 1989, 46–48; "Saab 2000 Moves Ahead," *Interavia Aerospace Review,* December 1989, 1213.
63. Rue and Holland, *Strategic Management,* 181–182; Certo and Peter, *Strategic Management,* 117; Patricia L. Nemetz and Louis W. Fry, "Flexible Manufacturing Organizations: Implications for Strategy Formulation and Organization Design," *Academy of Management Review* 13, no. 4 (1988): 627–638; Gerhard Johannes Plenert, *International Management and Production* (Blue Ridge Summit, Pa.: Tab Professional and Reference Books, 1990) 26–27.
64. Rue and Holland, *Strategic Management,* 183–184; Certo and Peter, *Strategic Management,* 117–118; William H. Miller, "Zero Absenteeism, Gentle People," *Industry Week,* 18 June 1990, 78.
65. Tamara J. Erickson, John F. Magee, Philip A. Roussel, and Kamal N. Saad, "Managing Technology as a Business Strategy," *Sloan Management Review,* Spring 1990, 73–78; John J. Quinn, "Brief Case: Strategic Management of R&D," *Long Range Planning* 23 (February 1990): 147–150; Certo and Peter, *Strategic Management,* 115–116; Rue and Holland, *Strategic Management,* 183; Keith H. Hammonds, "Corning's Class Act," *Business Week,* 13 May 1991, 68–76.
66. Tom Richman, "The Best of Intentions," *Inc.,* April 1991, 109–110.
67. Rue and Holland, *Strategic Management,* 176; Bonge and Coleman, eds., *Concepts for Corporate Strategy,* 267.
68. Jauch and Glueck, *Business Policy and Strategic Management,* 331–334; Theodore A. Anderson, "Coordinating Strategic and Operational Planning," in *Concepts for Corporate Strategy: Readings in Business Policy,* edited by John W. Bonge and Bruce P. Coleman (New York: Macmillan, 1972), 273–288.
69. Alfred D. Chandler, Jr., *Strategy and Structure* (Cambridge, Mass.: MIT Press, 1962), 13–14; Danny Miller, Cornelia Droge, and Jean-Marie Toulouse, "Strategic Process and Content as Mediators between Organizational Context and Structure," *Academy of Management Journal* 31, 3 (September 1988): 544–569; Andrews, *The Concept of Corporate Strategy,* 113–121; Craig R. Hickman and Michael A. Silva, *Creating Excellence* (New York: New American Library, 1984), 77–82, 85–86.
70. Anil K. Gupta and V. Govindarajan, "Business Unit Strategy, Managerial Characteristics, and Business Unit Effectiveness at Strategy Implementation," *Academy of Management Review* 27, no. 1 (1984): 25–41; Paul F. Buller, "For Successful Strategic Change: Blend OD Practices with Strategic Management," *Organizational Dynamics* 16 (Winter 1988): 42–55; Benjamin B. Tregoe and Peter M. Tobia, "A Point of View: Let's Hear It for Strategic Commitment," *National Productivity Review* 9, no. 3 (Summer 1990): 253–256; Rue and Holland, *Strategic Management,* 198–202.
71. Donald K. Yee, "Pass or Fail? How to Grade Strategic Progress," *Journal of Business Strategy,* May–June 1990, 10–14; Jauch and Glueck, *Business Policy and Strategic Management,* 375–378; Andrews, *The Concept of Corporate Strategy,* 123.
72. Joan Delaney, "Not Just Another Food Shop," *Executive Female,* July–August 1991, 58–61; Sylvia Carter, "An Adriana's Salvation Party," *New York Newsday,* 18 March 1992, 56.
73. Charles J. Bodenstab, "Keeping Tabs on Your Company," *Inc.,* August 1989, 131–132; Andrews, *The Concept of Corporate Strategy,* 133–134; J. Scott Armstrong, "The Value of Formal Planning for Strategic Decisions: Review of Empirical Research," *Strategic Management Journal* 3 (1982): 197–211; Hofer et al., *Strategic Management,* 22–26.
74. Michael Goold and John J. Quinn, "The Paradox of Strategic Controls," *Strategic Management Journal* 11 (1990): 43–57; Peter Lorange, "Strategic Control: Some Issues in Making It Operationally More Useful," in *Competitive Strategic Management,* edited by Robert Boyden Lamb (Englewood Cliffs, N.J.: Prentice Hall, 1984), 247–271; Rue and Holland, *Strategic Management,* 218–219; C. K. Prahalad and Yves L. Doz, "An Approach to Strategic Control in MNCs," *Sloan Management Review,* Summer 1981, 5–13; V. Govindarajan and Joseph Fisher, "Strategy, Control Systems, and Resource Sharing: Effects on Business-Unit Performance," *Academy of Management Journal* 33, no. 2 (1990): 259–285.
75. Christopher Knowlton, "Europe Cooks Up a Cereal Brawl," *Fortune,* 3 June 1991, 175–179.

76. See note 1.
77. Adapted from James L. Morrison, "The Continuing Seminar on Organizational Planning and Policy Analysis: Implications for Community College Planning Offices," Educational Resources Information Center report no. ED 305120 (1989): 1–10; Ty J. Handy, "The Necessity of Environmental Scanning Prior to Long-Range Planning Activities at Higher Education Institutions," paper presented at the Conference of the Mid-South Educational Research Association, 13 November 1990, New Orleans, Louisiana.

CHAPTER 9

1. Adapted from Milton Moskowitz, Robert Levering, and Michael Katz, *Everybody's Business* (New York: Doubleday, 1990), 133–137; Gary Hoover, Alta Campbell, and Patrick J. Spain, *Hoover's Handbook 1991* (Austin, Tex.: The Reference Press, 1990), 447; Jolie Solomon and Carol Hymowitz, "P&G Makes Changes in the Way It Develops and Sells Its Products," *Wall Street Journal,* 11 August 1987, 1, 12; Brian Dumaine, "P&G Rewrites the Marketing Rules," *Fortune,* 6 November 1989, 35–48; Zachary Schiller, "The Marketing Revolution at Procter & Gamble," *Business Week,* 25 July 1988, 72–76; Richard Koenig, "P&G Creates New Posts in Latest Step to Alter How Firm Manages Its Brands," *Wall Street Journal,* 12 October 1987, 8; Bob Messenger, "Procter & Gamble: A Tradition in Transition," *Prepared Foods,* April 1989, 46–50; Kevin T. Higgins, "Firms Tune-Up Their Management," *Marketing News,* 25 September 1989, 2, 26.
2. Lawrence G. Hrebiniak, "Implementing Strategy," *Chief Executive,* April 1990, 74–77; Peter F. Drucker, *Management: Tasks, Responsibilities, Practices* (New York: Harper & Row, 1974), 523–526; Jay R. Galbraith, *Organization Design* (Reading, Mass.: Addison-Wesley, 1977), 5–6; Danny Miller, "Configurations of Strategy and Structure: Towards a Synthesis," *Strategic Management Journal* 7 (1986): 233–249; Fremont E. Kast and James E. Rosenzweig, *Organization and Management: A Systems and Contingency Approach,* 4th ed. (New York: McGraw-Hill, 1985), 234–235.
3. Robert Duncan, "What Is the Right Organization Structure?" *Organizational Dynamics,* Winter 1979, 59–80; Herbert A. Simon, *Administrative Behavior,* 3rd ed. (New York: Free Press, 1976), 220; William G. Scott and Terence R. Mitchell, *Organization Theory: A Structural and Behavioral Analysis,* 3rd ed. (Homewood, Ill.: Irwin, 1976), 19, 34–36; Ernest Dale, *Organization* (New York: American Management Association, 1967), 57.
4. David R. Hampton, Charles E. Summer, and Ross A. Webber, *Organizational Behavior and the Practice of Management,* 5th ed. (Glenview, Ill.: Scott, Foresman, 1987), 489; Alfred D. Chandler, Jr., "Origins of the Organization Chart," *Harvard Business Review,* March–April 1988, 156–157; R. M. Cyert and J. G. March, "Organizational Design," in *New Perspectives in Organization Research,* edited by W. W. Cooper, H. J. Leavitt, and M. W. Shelly II (New York: Wiley, 1964), 557.
5. Dale, *Organization,* 233–238; Tom Peters, *Thriving on Chaos* (New York: Harper & Row, 1987), 444–446.
6. Ricardo Semler, "Managing without Managers," *Harvard Business Review,* September–October 1989, 76–84; "Bubble Chart Sends Message," *The Pryor Report,* July 1990, 4.
7. Henry Mintzberg, *The Structuring of Organizations* (Englewood Cliffs, N.J.: Prentice Hall, 1979), 69–71; Galbraith, *Organization Design,* 13–14.
8. Scott and Mitchell, *Organization Theory,* 31; Adam Smith, *Wealth of Nations* (New York: Collier, 1909), 9–13.
9. Howard Schlossberg, "Even amid Controversy, Bryant Finds Census Work Enjoyable," *Marketing News,* 1 April 1991, 2; Cyndee Miller, "Census Decision Seen as Unlikely to Hurt Marketing Researchers," *Marketing News,* 19 August 1991, 2, 22.
10. Dale, *Organization,* 46–47; Scott and Mitchell, *Organization Theory,* 20, 31–33; Joseph A. Litterer, *The Analysis of Organizations* (New York: Wiley, 1965), 162–173; Simon, *Administrative Behavior,* 20–22, 137–138; Peter F. Drucker, *The Practice of Management* (New York: Harper & Row, 1982), 293–296; Elliott Jacques, "In Praise of Hierarchy," *Harvard Business Review,* January–February 1990, 127–133.
11. Paul R. Lawrence and Jay W. Lorsch, *Organization and Environment* (Boston: Harvard Business School, 1986), 169; Scott and Mitchell, *Organization Theory,* 35–37; Dale, *Organization,* 28–31; Simon, *Administrative Behavior,* 22; Drucker, *Management,* 524–526.
12. Mintzberg, *The Structuring of Organizations,* 9; Galbraith, *Organization Design,* 16.
13. Simon, *Administrative Behavior,* 125–135; Peter Miller and Ted O'Leary, "Hierarchies and American Ideals, 1900–1940," *Academy of Management Review* 14, no. 2 (1989): 250–265; William Glasgall, "Ready, Set, Merge," *Business Week,* 29 July 1991, 24–27.
14. Chester I. Barnard, *The Functions of the Executive* (1938; reprint Cambridge, Mass.: Harvard University Press, 1968), 163–175; Chester I. Barnard, "The Theory of Authority," in *Management Classics,* 2nd ed., edited by Michael T. Matteson and John M. Ivancevich (Santa Monica, Calif.: Goodyear Publishing, 1981), 228–235; Scott and Mitchell, *Organization Theory,* 274–277; Simon, *Administrative Behavior,* 125–142.
15. Dale D. McConkey, *How to Manage by Results* (New York: Amacom, 1983), 203; Robert W. Moorman, "Lean, Mean Leisure Machine," *Air Transport World,* March 1991, 86–89.
16. Carrie R. Leana, "Predictors and Consequences of Delegation," *Academy of Management Journal* 29, no. 4 (1986): 754–774; McConkey, *How to Manage by Results,* 148–150; John B. Miner, *The Management Process* (New York: Macmillan, 1973), 211; Dale, *Organization,* 29–30.
17. Miner, *The Management Process,* 211–212; McConkey, *How to Manage by Results,* 148–152; Edward J. Mayo and Lance P. Jarvis, "Delegation 101: Lessons from the White House," *Business Horizons,* September–October 1988, 2–12; Anne Scott Daughtrey and Betty Roper Ricks, *Contemporary Supervision: Managing People and Technology* (New York: McGraw-Hill, 1989), 150–152.
18. Jay T. Knippen and Thad B. Green, "Delegation," *Supervision,* March 1990, 7–9, 17; Daughtrey and Ricks, *Contemporary Supervision,* 154–155.
19. McConkey, *How to Manage by Results,* 148–152; Robert B. Nelson, "Mastering Delegation," *Executive Excellence,* January 1990, 13–14; Mayo and Jarvis, "Delegation 101," 2–12; Daughtrey and Ricks, *Contemporary Supervision,* 154–155; Tess Kirby, "Delegating: How to Let Go and Keep Control," *Working Woman,* February 1990, 32, 37.
20. Douglas Harbrecht, Amy Borrus, and Bill Javetski, "Managing the War," *Business Week,* 4 February 1991, 34–37.
21. Galbraith, *Organization Design,* 17–18; Mintzberg, *The Structuring of Organizations,* 181–191.
22. Paul Kaestle, "A New Rationale for Organizational Structure," *Planning Review,* July–August 1990, 20–22, 27; Drucker, *Management,* 572–576; Stephanie Anderson Forest, "Chipping Away at Frito-Lay," *Business Week,* 22 July 1991, 26; Laurie M. Grossman, "Frito-Lay Chief Aims to Cut Unit's Fat and Give Snack Food a Spicier Image," *Wall Street Journal,* 11 July 1991, B1, B4; "PepsiCo's Frito-Lay Appoints 4 Presidents of Regional Divisions," *Wall Street Journal,* 12 August 1991, B6; Clay Chandler and Paul Ingrassia, "Just as U.S. Firms Try Japanese Management, Honda Is Centralizing," *Wall Street Journal,* 11 April 1991, A1, A4.
23. Drucker, *Management,* 572–580; Mintzberg, *The Structuring of Organizations,* 182–186.
24. Robert E. Levinson, *The Decentralized Company* (New York: Amacom, 1983), 13–17; Drucker, *Management,* 572–580; Mintzberg, *The Structuring of Organizations,* 182–186; Kaestle, "A New Rationale for Organizational Structure," 20–22, 27.
25. Mintzberg, *The Structuring of Organizations,* 182–186; Kaestle, "A New Rationale for Organizational Structure," 20–22, 27; Drucker, *Management,* 572–580; James A. Gazell and Darrell L. Pugh, "Administrative Theory and Large Organizations of the Future: Whither Bureaucracy?" *International Journal of Public Administration* 13, no. 6 (1990): 827–858.
26. Dan R. Dalton, William D. Todor, Michael J. Spendolini, Gordon J. Fielding, and Lyman W. Porter, "Organization Structure and Performance: A Critical Review," *Academy of Management Review* 5, no. 1 (1980): 49–64; Mintzberg, *The Structuring of Organizations,* 134–135; Kast and Rosenzweig, *Organization and Management,* 239–240; Allan Cox, "Managing without Hierarchy: Even 'Flat' Companies Need Leaders," *New York Times,* 20 August 1989, sec. 3, 3.
27. David D. Van Fleet and Arthur G. Bedeian, "A History of the Span of Management," *Academy of Management Review,* July 1977, 356–372; Galbraith, *Organization Design,* 17, 47; Mintzberg, *The Structuring of Organizations,* 134–135; Robert R. Bell and Frank S. McLaughlin, "Span of Control in Organizations," *Industrial Management,* September–October, 1977, 23–26; David D. Van Fleet, "Span of Management Research and Issues," *Academy of Management Journal,* September 1983, 546–552; John S. McClenahen, "Managing More People in the '90s," *Industry Week,* 20 March 1989, 30–38.
28. Bell and McLaughlin, "Span of Control in Organizations," 23–26; Van Fleet and Bedeian, "A History of the Span of Management," 356–372; McClenahen, "Managing More People in the '90s," 30–38; Edward E. Lawler III, "Substitutes for Hierarchy," *Organizational Dynamics,* Summer 1988, 4–15; Paul D. Collins and Frank Hull, "Technology and Span of Control: Woodward Revisited," *Journal of Management Studies* 23, no. 2 (March 1986): 143–164;

Frank M. Hull and Paul D. Collins, "High-Technology Batch Production Systems: Woodward's Missing Type," *Academy of Management Journal* 30, no. 4 (1987): 786–797.
29. Rocco Carzo, Jr., and John N. Yanouzas, "Effects of Flat and Tall Organization Structure," *Administrative Science Quarterly,* June 1969, 178–191.
30. Carzo and Yanouzas, "Effects of Flat and Tall Organization Structure," 178–191; Carol Hymowitz, "When Firms Cut Out Middle Managers, Those at Top and Bottom Often Suffer," *Wall Street Journal,* 5 April 1990, B1, B4; Mintzberg, *The Structuring of Organizations,* 136; Gazell and Pugh, "Administrative Theory and Large Organizations of the Future," 827–858.
31. Robert M. Tomasko, *Downsizing: Reshaping the Corporation for the Future* (New York: Amacom, 1987), 2–29; Rosabeth Moss Kanter, *When Giants Learn to Dance* (New York: Simon & Schuster, 1989), 57.
32. Peters, *Thriving on Chaos,* 425–430.
33. Galbraith, *Organization Design,* 18; Dale, *Organization,* 61–67; Litterer, *The Analysis of Organizations,* 332–348.
34. Dale, *Organization,* 61–67; Galbraith, *Organization Design,* 18.
35. Hillel Schmid, "Staff and Line Relationships Revisited: The Case of Community Service Agencies," *Public Personnel Management* 19, no. 1 (Spring 1990): 71–83; Edwin A. Gerloff, *Organizational Theory and Design* (New York: McGraw-Hill, 1985), 253; Dale, *Organization,* 61–68.
36. Rensis Likert, *The Human Organization: Its Management and Value* (New York: McGraw-Hill, 1967), 50–51, 160–161; Gerloff, *Organizational Theory and Design,* 224; Galbraith, *Organization Design,* 23; Litterer, *The Analysis of Organizations,* 316–317.
37. Simon, *Administrative Behavior,* 28–34; Scott and Mitchell, *Organization Theory,* 134–136; Gerloff, *Organizational Theory and Design,* 228.
38. Gerloff, *Organizational Theory and Design,* 228–229; Scott and Mitchell, *Organization Theory,* 242–243; Norman Ridley, "Resource Management in the United Kingdom Customs and Excise," *Optimum,* Summer 1989, 21–37; Alex Taylor III, "How Buick Is Bouncing Back," *Fortune,* 6 May 1991, 83–88.
39. Hrebiniak, "Implementing Strategy," 74–77; Drucker, *Management,* 559–563; Litterer, *The Analysis of Organizations,* 177–181; Gerloff, *Organizational Theory and Design,* 228–230.
40. Barbara N. Berkman, "Ericsson Is Restructuring to Adapt to a Deregulated Global Market," *Electronic Business,* 21 January 1991, 34–37.
41. Gerloff, *Organizational Theory and Design,* 231.
42. Scott and Mitchell, *Organization Theory,* 175–176; Toys 'R' Us 1989 Annual Report, 16–17.
43. Gerloff, *Organizational Theory and Design,* 230; Scott and Mitchell, *Organization Theory,* 175–176.
44. Miner, *The Management Process,* 243–244; Scott and Mitchell, *Organization Theory,* 175–176; Gerloff, *Organizational Theory and Design,* 231–232; Howard Banks, "Running Ahead, But Running Scared," *Forbes,* 13 May 1991, 38–40.
45. Gerloff, *Organizational Theory and Design,* 231–232.
46. Scott and Mitchell, *Organization Theory,* 180–182; Archer Daniels Midland 1990 Annual Report, 4–7.
47. Scott and Mitchell, *Organization Theory,* 180–182; Gerloff, *Organizational Theory and Design,* 230.
48. Drucker, *Management,* 566–567; Brian Dumaine, "Bureaucracy Busters," *Fortune,* 17 June 1991, 36–50.
49. Drucker, *Management,* 566–568.
50. Scott and Mitchell, *Organization Theory,* 182; Gerloff, *Organizational Theory and Design,* 229.
51. "Why a Big Steelmaker Is Mimicking the Minimills," *Business Week,* 27 March 1989, 92; John Naisbitt and Patricia Aburdene, *Reinventing the Corporation* (New York: Warner Books, 1985), 240–241.
52. Andrew H. Van de Ven, Andre L. Delbecq, and Richard Koenig, Jr., "Determinants of Coordination Modes within Organizations," *American Sociological Review* 41 (April 1976): 322–338; Paul R. Lawrence and Jay W. Lorsch, "Differentiation and Integration in Complex Organizations," *Administrative Science Quarterly* 9 (March 1967): 1–47; Jay Galbraith, *Designing Complex Organizations* (Reading, Mass.: Addison-Wesley, 1973), 3–4, 91–93.
53. James D. Thompson, "Technology and Structure," in *Organizations by Design: Theory and Practice,* edited by Mariann Jelinek, Joseph A. Litterer, and Raymond E. Miles (Plano, Tex.: Business Publications, 1981), 207–218; Mintzberg, *The Structuring of Organizations,* 22; Robert M. Tomasko, *Downsizing* (New York: Amacom, 1987), 160; Steve Lohr, "The Best Little Bank in America," *New York Times,* 7 July 1991, sec. 3, 1, 4.
54. Thompson, "Technology and Structure," 207–218; Tomasko, *Downsizing,* 160–162; Mintzberg, *The Structuring of Organizations,* 22; Keith H. Hammonds, "The Trashmaster That's Top of the Heap," *Business Week,* 27 May 1991, 80.
55. Thompson, "Technology and Structure," 207–218; Mintzberg, *The Structuring of Organizations,* 22; Tomasko, *Downsizing,* 162.
56. Galbraith, *Designing Complex Organizations,* 17–18; Hampton, Summer, and Webber, *Organizational Behavior,* 526–527.
57. Galbraith, *Organization Design,* 113–114; Hampton, Summer, and Webber, *Organizational Behavior and the Practice of Management,* 524–525; Galbraith, *Designing Complex Organizations,* 15–16.
58. Rita Pappens, "From Trucks to Pulp to Paper to Boxes," *Pulp and Paper International,* November 1990, 59–61.
59. Mintzberg, *The Structuring of Organizations,* 161–162; Hampton, Summer, and Webber, *Organizational Behavior and the Practice of Management,* 527–528; Galbraith, *Designing Complex Organizations,* 18–19.
60. Galbraith, *Designing Complex Organizations,* 18; Hampton, Summer, and Webber, *Organizational Behavior and the Practice of Management,* 527; Galbraith, *Organization Design,* 113–114.
61. Galbraith, *Organization Design,* 115–116, 141; Brenton R. Schlender, "How Fujitsu Will Tackle the Giants," *Fortune,* 1 July 1991, 78–82.
62. Mintzberg, *The Structuring of Organizations,* 163–164; Galbraith, *Organization Design,* 116–117.
63. Dumaine, "The Bureaucracy Busters," 36–50.
64. Paul R. Lawrence and Jay W. Lorsch, "New Management Job: The Integrator," *Harvard Business Review,* November–December 1967, 142–150; Lawrence and Lorsch, "Differentiation and Integration in Complex Organizations," 1–47; Mintzberg, *The Structuring of Organizations,* 165–168.
65. Joseph M. Winski, "Brand Builders," *Advertising Age,* 20 August 1987, 92, 96, 98; Laurie Petersen, "Brand Managing's New Accent," *Adweek's Marketing Week,* 15 April 1991, 18–20.
66. Hampton, Summer, and Webber, *Organizational Behavior and the Practice of Management,* 528.
67. Mintzberg, *The Structuring of Organizations,* 9, 81–84; Kast and Rosenzweig, *Organization and Management,* 235; Simon, *Administrative Behavior,* 334.
68. Galbraith, *Organization Design,* 99–100; Kast and Rosenzweig, *Organization and Management,* 235; Mintzberg, *The Structuring of Organizations,* 9, 81–84.
69. E. B. Knauft, Renee A. Berger, and Sandra T. Gray, *Profiles of Excellence* (San Francisco: Jossey-Bass, 1991), 56–57.
70. Dumaine, "The Bureaucracy Busters," 36–50.
71. Simon, *Administrative Behavior,* 147–149; Kast and Rosenzweig, *Organization and Management,* 235; Mintzberg, *The Structuring of Organizations,* 36–37; Mintzberg, *Management,* 527.
72. Barnard, *The Functions of the Executive,* 120–123; Mintzberg, *The Structuring of Organizations,* 36–37; Barnard, *The Functions of the Executive,* 115–123; Galbraith, *Designing Complex Organizations,* 47; Simon, *Administrative Behavior,* 147–149.
73. See note 1.

CHAPTER 10

1. Adapted from Larry Carpenter, "How to Market to Regions," *American Demographics,* November 1987, 44–45; Barbara Hetzer, "Pushing Decisions Down the Line at Campbell Soup," *Business Month,* July 1989, 62–63; David Wellman, "Campbell: The Next Generation," *Food & Beverage Marketing,* August 1990, 16–19; Joseph Weber, "Campbell Is Bubbling, But for How Long?" *Business Week,* 17 June 1991, 56–57; Tom Peters, "There Are No Excellent Companies," *Fortune,* 27 April 1987, 341–344, 352; Kevin T. Higgins, "Firms Tune Up Their Management," *Marketing News,* 25 September 1989, 2, 26.
2. Adapted from Jay R. Galbraith, *Organization Design* (Reading, Mass.: Addison-Wesley, 1977), 4–5, 11–12; Edwin A. Gerloff, *Organizational Theory and Design* (New York: McGraw-Hill, 1985), 127–143.
3. Peter F. Drucker, *Management: Tasks, Responsibilities, Practices* (New York: Harper & Row, 1974), 529–545.
4. Michael W. Stebbins and Abraham B. Shani, "Organization Design: Beyond the 'Mafia' Model," *Organizational Dynamics* 17 (Winter 1989): 18–30.
5. Max Weber, "The Ideal Bureaucracy," in *Management Classics,* 2nd ed., edited by Michael T. Matteson and John M. Ivancevich (Santa Monica, Calif.: Goodyear, 1981), 152–158; Charles Perrow, "The Short and Glorious History of Organizational Theory," in *Contemporary Readings in Organizational Behavior,* 3rd ed., edited by Fred Luthans and Kenneth R.

Thompson (New York: McGraw-Hill, 1981), 412; Daniel A. Wren, *The Evolution of Management Thought,* 2nd ed. (New York: Wiley, 1979), 249–254.
6. Max Weber, *Economy and Society,* Vol. 3, edited by Guenther Roth and Claus Wittich (New York: Bedminster Press, 1968), 956–963; Peter M. Blau, "Weber's Theory of Bureaucracy," in *Max Weber,* edited by Dennis Wrong (Englewood Cliffs, N.J.: Prentice Hall, 1970), 141–142; Wren, *The Evolution of Management Thought,* 249–254.
7. Blau, "Weber's Theory of Bureaucracy," 143–145; David Silverman, *The Theory of Organizations* (New York: Basic Books, 1971), 73–75.
8. Blau, "Weber's Theory of Bureaucracy," 143–145; Warren G. Bennis, "The Coming Death of Bureaucracy," in *Management Classics,* 2nd ed., edited by Michael T. Matteson and John M. Ivancevich (Santa Monica, Calif.: Goodyear, 1981), 159–167.
9. William G. Scott and Terence R. Mitchell, *Organization Theory,* 3rd ed. (Homewood, Ill.: Irwin, 1976), 308–309; Silverman, *The Theory of Organizations,* 109–111.
10. Rensis Likert, *The Human Organization: Its Management and Value* (New York: McGraw-Hill, 1967), 4–10, 14–25, 46–55; William Dowling, ed., *Effective Management and the Behavioral Sciences* (New York: Amacom, 1978), 52–74.
11. Likert, *The Human Organization,* 4–10, 14–25, 47–60; Dowling, *Effective Management,* 52–74.
12. Dowling, *Effective Management,* 52–74; Likert, *The Human Organization,* 36–46.
13. Stebbins and Shani, "Organization Design," 18–30; Silverman, *The Theory of Organizations,* 109–124; Scott and Mitchell, *Organization Theory,* 308–313; Edgar H. Schein, *Organizational Psychology,* 2nd ed. (Englewood Cliffs, N.J.: Prentice Hall, 1970), 106–108.
14. Scott and Mitchell, *Organization Theory,* 308–313; Silverman, *The Theory of Organizations,* 109–124; Stebbins and Shani, "Organization Design," 18–30; Thomas G. Cummings, "Self-Regulating Work Groups: A Socio-Technical Synthesis," in *Organization Development: Theory, Practice, and Research,* 3rd ed., edited by Wendell L. French, Cecil H. Bell, Jr., and Robert A. Zawacki (Homewood, Ill.: BPI Irwin, 1989), 311–319.
15. Bill Saporito, "Campbell Soup Gets Piping Hot," *Fortune,* 9 September 1991, 142–148.
16. James D. Thompson, "Technology and Structure," in *Organizations by Design: Theory and Practice* (Plano, Tex.: Business Publications, 1981), 207–208; Richard H. Hall, *Organizations: Structure and Process,* 3rd ed. (Englewood Cliffs, N.J.: Prentice Hall, 1982), 63–64; Silverman, *The Theory of Organizations,* 109–124.
17. Paul R. Lawrence and Jay W. Lorsch, *Organization and Environment* (Boston: Harvard Business School Press, 1986), 185–186, 209–210; Galbraith, *Organization Design,* 28–31.
18. Gannett 1990 Annual Report, 1–15, 24–31, 60; Cary Peyton Rich, "They Don't Teach This at Harvard," *Folio,* May 1991, 60–65.
19. Hall, *Organizations: Structure and Process,* 53; Harold J. Leavitt, *Managerial Psychology,* 4th ed. (Chicago: University of Chicago Press, 1978), 328–336; Saul W. Gellerman, "In Organizations, as in Architecture, Form Follows Function," *Organizational Dynamics,* Winter 1990, 57–68.
20. Arthur D. Chandler, Jr., *Strategy and Structure* (Cambridge, Mass.: MIT Press, 1962), 13–16.
21. Chandler, *Strategy and Structure,* 17–51.
22. Andy Pasztor, "Strategic Air Command to Be Eliminated in Sweeping Reorganization of Air Force," *Wall Street Journal,* 18 September 1991, A5; Robert Pear, "Soviet Union's Demise Spurs Upheaval in U.S. Heartland," *New York Times,* 29 December 1991, sec. 1, 12.
23. Lawrence E. Fouraker and John M. Stopford, "Organizational Structure and the Multinational Strategy," in *Organizations by Design: Theory and Practice,* edited by Mariann Jelinek, Joseph A. Litterer, and Raymond E. Miles (Plano, Tex.: Business Publications, 1981), 46–58; William G. Egelhoff, "Strategy and Structure in Multinational Corporations: A Revision of the Stopford and Wells Model," *Strategic Management Journal* 9 (1988): 1–14.
24. Henry Mintzberg, *The Structuring of Organizations* (Englewood Cliffs, N.J.: Prentice Hall, 1979), 281–282; Peter Nulty, "America's Toughest Bosses," *Fortune,* 27 February 1989, 40–54.
25. Tom Burns and G. M. Stalker, "Management Structures and Systems," in *Organizations by Design: Theory and Practice,* edited by Mariann Jelinek, Joseph A. Litterer, and Raymond E. Miles (Plano, Tex.: Business Publications, 1981), 140–152; Tom Burns and G. M. Stalker, "Mechanistic and Organic Systems," in *Management Classics,* 2nd ed., edited by Michael T. Matteson and John M. Ivancevich (Santa Monica, Calif.: Goodyear, 1981), 390–395; Gerloff, *Organizational Theory and Design,* 51–58.
26. Burns and Stalker, "Mechanistic and Organic Systems," 390–395; Galbraith, *Organization Design,* 28; Lawrence and Lorsch, *Organization and Environment,* 187–189.
27. Burns and Stalker, "Mechanistic and Organic Systems," 390–395; Lawrence and Lorsch, *Organization and Environment,* 187–189; Galbraith, *Organization Design,* 28.
28. Gene Bylinsky, "The Hottest High-Tech Company in Japan," *Fortune,* 1 January 1990, 83–88.
29. Lawrence and Lorsch, *Organization and Environment,* 9–11, 15–17, 19–20; R. Rothwell and T. G. Whiston, "Design, Innovation and Corporate Integration," *R&D Management* 20, no. 3 (1990): 193–201; Gerloff, *Organizational Theory and Design,* 58–63.
30. Lawrence and Lorsch, *Organization and Environment,* 137–140, 239–242; Rothwell and Whiston, "Design, Innovation and Corporate Integration," 193–201; Paul R. Lawrence and Jay W. Lorsch, "Differentiation and Integration in Complex Organizations," *Administrative Science Quarterly* 12, no. 1 (June 1967): 1–47; Arthur H. Walker and Jay W. Lorsch, "Organizational Choice: Product Versus Function," in *Organizations by Design: Theory and Practice,* edited by Mariann Jelinek, Joseph A. Litterer, and Raymond E. Miles (Plano, Tex.: Business Publications, 1981), 265–278.
31. John F. Rockart and James E. Short, "IT in the 1990s: Managing Organizational Interdependence," *Sloan Management Review* 7 (Winter 1989): 7–17.
32. Mariann Jelinek, Joseph A. Litterer, and Raymond E. Miles (Plano, Tex.: Business Publications, 1981), 170–171; Mintzberg, *The Structuring of Organizations,* 249–251.
33. Joan Woodward, *Industrial Organization: Theory and Practice,* 2nd ed. (London: Oxford University Press, 1980), 9, 40–41, 50–67; Gerloff, *Organizational Theory and Design,* 84–86; Mintzberg, *The Structuring of Organizations,* 251–258.
34. Woodward, *Industrial Organization,* 40–42, 50–67; David R. Hampton, Charles E. Summer, and Ross A. Webber, *Organizational Behavior and the Practice of Management,* 5th ed. (Glenview, Ill.: Scott, Foresman, 1987), 494–495; Gerloff, *Organizational Theory and Design,* 84–86.
35. Mintzberg, *The Structuring of Organizations,* 251–258; Gerloff, *Organizational Theory and Design,* 84–86.
36. John R. Emshwiller, "Building an International Business on Man-Made Rocks," *Wall Street Journal,* 10 September 1991, B2.
37. Woodward, *Industrial Organization,* 123–153; Hampton, Summer, and Webber, *Organizational Behavior and the Practice of Management,* 494–495; Mintzberg, *The Structuring of Organizations,* 251–258.
38. Woodward, *Industrial Organization,* 71; Mintzberg, *The Structuring of Organizations,* 251–258; Frank M. Hull and Paul D. Collins, "High-Technology Batch Production Systems: Woodward's Missing Type," *Academy of Management Journal,* December 1987, 786–797.
39. Woodward, *Industrial Organization,* 31; Dennis S. Mileti, David F. Gillespie, and J. Eugene Hass, "Size and Structure in Complex Organizations," *Social Forces,* September 1977, 208–217; John B. Cullen, Kenneth S. Anderson, and Douglas D. Baker, "Blau's Theory of Structural Differentiation Revisited: A Theory of Structural Change or Scale?" *Academy of Management Journal* 29 (1986): 203–229; Hall, *Organizations: Structure and Process,* 56–63.
40. Eric G. Flamholtz, *Growing Pains: How to Make the Transition from an Entrepreneurship to a Professionally Managed Firm* (San Francisco: Jossey-Bass, 1990), 197–211; W. Graham Astley, "Organizational Size and Bureaucratic Structure," *Organization Studies* 6, no. 3 (1985): 201–228; Joseph A. Litterer, *The Analysis of Organizations* (New York: Wiley, 1965), 403–411.
41. Astley, "Organizational Size and Bureaucratic Structure," 201–228; Richard T. Pascale, "Fit or Split?" *Across the Board,* June 1990, 48–52; Hall, *Organizations: Structure and Process,* 56–63; Mintzberg, *The Structuring of Organizations,* 138–143; Litterer, *The Analysis of Organizations,* 403–411.
42. John A. Byrne, "Is Your Company Too Big?" *Business Week,* 27 March 1989, 84–94.
43. Robert E. Quinn and Kim Cameron, "Organizational Life Cycles and Shifting Criteria of Effectiveness: Some Preliminary Evidence," *Management Science* 29, no. 1 (January 1983): 33–51; Larry E. Greiner, "Evolution and Revolution as Organizations Grow," *Harvard Business Review,* July–August 1972, 37–46; Bill T. Meyer and David W. Merrell, "The Life Cycle of the Organization—Part 1," *The Journal of Commercial Bank Lending,* January 1984, 19–37; Bill T. Meyer and David W. Merrell, "The Life Cycle of the Organization—Part 2," *The Journal of Commercial Bank Lending,* February 1984, 39–57; Joan Delaney, "Getting the Right Start," *Executive Female,* September–October 1991, 54–56.
44. Greiner, "Evolution and Revolution as

Organizations Grow," 37–46; Meyer and Merrell, "The Life Cycle of the Organization—Part 1," 19–37; Meyer and Merrell, "The Life Cycle of the Organization—Part 2," 39–57; Quinn and Cameron, "Organizational Life Cycles," 33–51; Leslie Brokaw, "The Truth about Start-Ups," *Inc.*, April 1991, 52–67.
45. Steven B. Kaufman, "The Goal System That Drives Cypress," *Business Month*, July 1987, 30–32; "Cypress Semiconductor," *Standard & Poor's Corporate Descriptions*, accessed on-line 21 November 1991.
46. Meyer and Merrell, "The Life Cycle of the Organization—Part 1," 19–37; Meyer and Merrell, "The Life Cycle of the Organization—Part 2," 39–57; Quinn and Cameron, "Organizational Life Cycles," 33–51; Flamholtz, *Growing Pains*, 37–40, 208–210, 350–351; Greiner, "Evolution and Revolution as Organizations Grow," 37–46; Andrew Tanzer, "Bobo Wang's Midlife Crisis," *Forbes*, 24 June 1991, 110–111.
47. Flamholtz, *Growing Pains*, 37–40, 208–210, 350–351; Greiner, "Evolution and Revolution as Organizations Grow," 37–46; Meyer and Merrell, "The Life Cycle of the Organization—Part 1," 19–37; Meyer and Merrell, "The Life Cycle of the Organization—Part 2," 39–57; Mintzberg, *The Structuring of Organizations*, 244–247; Quinn and Cameron, "Organizational Life Cycles," 33–51; Stuart Gannes, "America's Fastest-Growing Companies," *Fortune*, 23 May 1988, 28–40; Rick Wartzman, "Hughes Aircraft Will Undergo a Restructuring," *Wall Street Journal*, 23 July 1991, A4.
48. Flamholtz, *Growing Pains*, 186; Hugh J. Arnold and Daniel C. Feldman, *Organizational Behavior* (New York: McGraw-Hill, 1986), 242–243; E. B. Knauft, Renee A. Berger, and Sandra T. Gray, *Profiles of Excellence* (San Francisco: Jossey-Bass, 1991), 77–84.
49. Arnold and Feldman, *Organizational Behavior*, 242–243; Flamholtz, *Growing Pains*, 187; Gerloff, *Organizational Theory and Design*, 248–249.
50. Charles W. L. Hill, Michael A. Hitt, and Robert E. Hoskisson, "Declining U.S. Competitiveness: Reflections on a Crisis," *Academy of Management Executive* 11, no. 1 (1988): 51–60; Flamholtz, *Growing Pains*, 186; Arnold and Feldman, *Organizational Behavior*, 242–243; Flamholtz, *Growing Pains*, 187; Gerloff, *Organizational Theory and Design*, 248–249.
51. Flamholtz, *Growing Pains*, 189; Robert E. Hoskisson and Michael A. Hitt, "Strategic Control Systems and Relative R&D Investment in Large Multiproduct Firms," *Strategic Management Journal* 9 (1988): 605–621; Barbara W. Keats and Michael A. Hitt, "A Causal Model of Linkages among Environmental Dimensions, Macro Organizational Characteristics, and Performance," *Academy of Management Journal* 31, no. 3 (September 1988), 570–598.
52. Chandler, *Strategy and Structure*, 2–13; Gerloff, *Organizational Theory and Design*, 238; Flamholtz, *Growing Pains*, 189–190.
53. Motorola 1990 Annual Report, 37; Motorola 1989 Annual Report, 2–5.
54. Hill, Hitt, and Hoskisson, "Declining U.S. Competitiveness," 51–60; Keats and Hitt, "A Causal Model of Linkages among Environmental Dimensions," 570–598; Arnold and Feldman, *Organizational Behavior*, 245–252; Flamholtz, *Growing Pains*, 189–192; Gerloff, *Organizational Theory and Design*, 248–249.
55. Gerloff, *Organizational Theory and Design*, 231, 238; Flamholtz, *Growing Pains*, 189–192; Arnold and Feldman, *Organizational Behavior*, 249–252.
56. Jeffrey R. Williams, Betty Lynn Paez, and Leonard Sanders, "Conglomerates Revisited," *Strategic Management Journal* 9 (1988): 403–414; Mintzberg, *The Structuring of Organizations*, 412–414.
57. Stewart Toy and Mark Maremont, "Meet Monsieur Luxury," *Business Week*, 30 July 1990, 48–52.
58. Williams, Paez, and Sanders, "Conglomerates Revisited," 403–414; Mintzberg, *The Structuring of Organizations*, 412–430.
59. Lawton R. Burns, "Matrix Management in Hospitals: Testing Theories of Matrix Structure and Development," *Administrative Science Quarterly* 34 (1989): 349–368; Robert Duncan, "What is the Right Organization Structure?" *Organizational Dynamics*, Winter 1979, 59–79; Christopher A. Bartlett and Sumantra Ghoshal, "Matrix Management: Not a Structure, a Frame of Mind," *Harvard Business Review*, July–August 1990, 138–145; Jay R. Galbraith, "Matrix Organization Designs," in *Organizations by Design: Theory and Practice*, edited by Mariann Jelinek, Joseph A. Litterer, and Raymond E. Miles (Plano, Tex.: Business Publications, 1981), 295–307.
60. Duncan, "What Is the Right Organization Structure?" 59–79; Galbraith, "Matrix Organization Designs," 295–307; Tom Peters, *Thriving on Chaos* (New York: Harper & Row, 1987), 428; Thomas H. Naylor, "Gorbachev's Management Style," *Across the Board*, July–August 1990, 28–33.
61. Mintzberg, *The Structuring of Organizations*, 168–175; Galbraith, "Matrix Organization Designs," 295–307; Duncan, "What Is the Right Organization Structure?" 59–79.
62. Galbraith, "Matrix Organization Designs," 295–307; Mintzberg, *The Structuring of Organizations*, 168–175; Duncan, "What Is the Right Organization Structure?" 59–79.
63. Bartlett and Ghoshal, "Matrix Management," 138–145; Mintzberg, *The Structuring of Organizations*, 168–175; Galbraith, "Matrix Organization Designs," 295–307; Duncan, "What Is the Right Organization Structure?" 59–79.
64. Bryan Borys and David B. Jemison, "Hybrid Arrangements as Strategic Alliances: Theoretical Issues in Organizational Combinations," *Academy of Management Review* 14, no. 2 (1989): 234–249; Mintzberg, *The Structuring of Organizations*, 278, 395, 398, 410.
65. Champion International 1990 Annual Report, 7–53.
66. Mintzberg, *The Structuring of Organizations*, 299–300; Hall, *Organizations: Structure and Process*, 44–45.
67. Mintzberg, *The Structuring of Organizations*, 305–313.
68. Mintzberg, *The Structuring of Organizations*, 314–347.
69. Mintzberg, *The Structuring of Organizations*, 348–379.
70. Mintzberg, *The Structuring of Organizations*, 380–430.
71. Mintzberg, *The Structuring of Organizations*, 431–467; James A. Gazell and Darrell L. Pugh, "Administrative Theory and Large Organizations of the Future: Whither Bureaucracy?" *International Journal of Public Administration* 13, no. 6 (1990): 827–858; Robert H. Waterman, Jr., "'Adhocracy': Lessons from the Changemasters," *Hospitals*, 5 January 1991, 56.
72. Danny Miller, "Configurations of Strategy and Structure: Towards a Synthesis," *Strategic Management Journal* 7 (1986): 233–249.
73. See note 1.

CHAPTER 11

1. Adapted from "Reality Intrudes into the Magic Kingdom," *The Economist*, 21 April 1990, 71–72; The Walt Disney Company 1990 Annual Report; "Muttonchops Need Not Apply," *Harper's Magazine*, June 1990, 40–41; Paul L. Blocklyn, "Making Magic: The Disney Approach to People Management," *Personnel*, December 1988, 28–35; Brian Dumaine, "Creating a New Corporate Culture," *Fortune*, 15 January 1990, 127–131; Ronald Grover, Larry Armstrong, Jonathan Levine, and Todd Mason, "Disney's Magic," *Business Week*, 9 March 1987, 62–69; Christopher Knowlton, "How Disney Keeps the Magic Going," *Fortune*, 4 December 1989, 111–132; Stephen Koepp, "Do You Believe in Magic," *Time*, 25 April 1988, 66–73; Rita Koselka, "Mickey's Midlife Crisis," *Forbes*, 13 May 1991, 42–43; Myron Magnet, "Putting Magic Back in the Magic Kingdom," *Fortune*, 5 January 1987, 65; Charlene Marmer Solomon, "How Does Disney Do It?" *Personnel Journal*, December 1989, 50–57.
2. Robert L. Kuhn, ed., *Handbook for Creative and Innovative Managers* (New York: McGraw-Hill, 1988), 1–2; Abraham Zaleznick, "Making Managers Creative: The Psychodynamics of Creativity and Innovation," in *Handbook for Creative and Innovative Managers*, edited by Robert L. Kuhn (New York: McGraw-Hill, 1988), 35–42; Peter F. Drucker, *Management: Tasks, Responsibilities, Practices* (New York: Harper & Row, 1974), 787–788; Teresa M. Amabile, "A Model of Creativity and Innovation in Organizations," *Organizational Behavior* 10 (1988): 123–167.
3. Mike McNamee, "The Justice Dept. Flexes—And the Banks Cringe," *Business Week*, 7 October 1991, 126; Ylonda Gault, "Buyers Riding Coach," *Crain's New York Business*, 6 May 1991, 3, 25.
4. Gail DeGeorge, "Wackenhut Is Out to Prove That Crime Doesn't Pay," *Business Week*, 17 December 1990, 95–96.
5. Peter Fuhrman, "You Think Pan Am's Got Problems?" *Forbes*, 10 June 1991, 82–83.
6. E. B. Knauft, Renee A. Berger, and Sandra T. Gray, *Profiles of Excellence* (San Francisco: Jossey-Bass, 1991), 94–101.
7. Susan Carey, "Holiday Inn Hotel Perseveres in Battle to Be Constructed in Heart of Mongolia," *Wall Street Journal*, 16 September 1991, A11A.
8. Robert Chin and Kenneth D. Benne, "General Strategies for Effecting Changes in Human Systems," in *Organization Development: Theory, Practice, and Research*, 3rd ed., edited by Wendell L. French, Cecil H. Bell, Jr., and Robert A. Zawacki (Homewood, Ill.: BPI Irwin, 1989), 88.
9. David Woodruff and Thane Peterson, "The Greening of Detroit," *Business Week*, 8 April 1991, 54–60.
10. Jay R. Galbraith, *Organization Design* (Reading, Mass.: Addison-Wesley, 1977), 4–5; Stanley M. Davis, "Future Perfect," *Small Business Reports*, April 1990, 48–57; James A. Belasco, *Teaching the Elephant to Dance: Em-*

powering Change in Your Organization (New York: Crown, 1990), 28.
11. Paul Hersey and Kenneth H. Blanchard, *Management of Organizational Behavior,* 5th ed. (Englewood Cliffs, N.J.: Prentice Hall, 1988), 334–336; Jerome H. Want, "Managing Change in a Turbulent Business Climate," *Management Review,* November 1990, 38–41; Richard M. Morris III, "Going with the Flow," *Industrial Management,* January–February 1990, 2–3; Ernest C. Huge, "Developing Vision and Strategy for Change," *Executive Excellence,* January 1990, 6–7.
12. Eric Morgenthaler, "A 19th-Century Firm Shifts, Reinvents Itself and Survives 100 Years," *Wall Street Journal,* 9 May 1989, A1, A6.
13. Kurt Lewin, *Field Theory in Social Science* (New York: Harper & Row, 1951), 228–229; Hersey and Blanchard, *Management of Organizational Behavior,* 347; Edgar H. Schein, *Organizational Psychology,* 2nd ed. (Englewood Cliffs, N. J.: Prentice Hall, 1970), 120.
14. Lynn A. Isabella, "Evolving Interpretations as a Change Unfolds: How Managers Construe Key Organizational Events," *Academy of Management Journal* 33, no. 1 (1990): 7–41; "The Foundations of OD: Theory and Practice on Change in Organizations," in *Organization Development: Theory, Practice, and Research,* 3rd ed., edited by Wendell L. French, Cecil H. Bell, Jr., and Robert A. Zawacki (Homewood, Ill.: BPI Irwin, 1989), 80–82.
15. John A. Kotter and Leonard A. Schlesinger, "Choosing Strategies for Change," *Harvard Business Review,* March–April 1979, 106–114; Mark Frohman, "Lower-Level Management: The Internal Customers of Change," *Industry Week,* 5 November 1990, 28–34; Paul R. Lawrence, "How to Deal with Resistance to Change," *Harvard Business Review,* January–February 1969, 4–12, 166–176; Bill Saporito, "The Revolt against 'Working Smarter,'" *Fortune,* 21 July 1986, 58–65; Robert D. Gilbreath, "The Myths about Winning Over Resisters to Change," *Supervisory Management,* January 1990, 1–2; Nancy K. Austin, "Just Do It," *Working Woman,* April 1990, 78–80, 126.
16. Arnold S. Judson, *Changing Behavior in Organizations: Minimizing Resistance to Change* (Cambridge, Mass.: Blackwell, 1991), 32–33; Saporito, "The Revolt against 'Working Smarter,'" 58–65; Gilbreath, "The Myths About Winning Over Resisters to Change," 1–2; Kotter and Schlesinger, "Choosing Strategies for Change," 106–114; Lawrence, "How to Deal with Resistance to Change," 4–12, 166–176.
17. Frohman, "Lower-Level Management: The Internal Customers of Change," 28–34; Saporito, "The Revolt against 'Working Smarter,'" 58–65; Gilbreath, "The Myths about Winning Over Resisters to Change," 1–2; Kotter and Schlesinger, "Choosing Strategies for Change," 106–114; Lawrence, "How to Deal with Resistance to Change," 4–12, 166–176; Stuart Feldman, "Boulevard Bancorp: A Good Rate of Return," *Personnel,* September 1991, 11.
18. Lawrence, "How to Deal with Resistance to Change," 4–12, 166–176; Kotter and Schlesinger, "Choosing Strategies for Change," 106–114; Frohman, "Lower-Level Management: The Internal Customers of Change," 28–34; Saporito, "The Revolt against 'Working Smarter,'" 58–65; Gilbreath, "The Myths about Winning Over Resisters to Change," 1–2; Daniel Valentino and Bill Christ, "Teaming Up for Market: Cheaper, Better, Faster," *Management Review,* November 1989, 46–49.
19. Lewin, *Field Theory in Social Science,* 172–174; "The Foundations of OD: Theory and Practice on Change in Organizations," in *Organization Development: Theory, Practice, and Research,* 3rd ed., edited by Wendell L. French, Cecil H. Bell, Jr., and Robert A. Zawacki (Homewood, Ill.: BPI Irwin, 1989), 80–81; Alfred J. Marrow, *The Practical Theorist: The Life and Work of Kurt Lewin* (New York: Basic Books, 1969), 151–152; Hersey and Blanchard, *Management of Organizational Behavior,* 135–136, 336–339.
20. Kotter and Schlesinger, "Choosing Strategies for Change," 106–114; Judson, *Changing Behavior in Organizations,* 85–86, 108–113; Lawrence, "How to Deal with Resistance to Change," 4–12, 166–176; John Lawrie, "The Differences between Effective and Ineffective Change Masters," *Supervisor Management,* June 1991, 9–10; Michael A. Verespej, "People: The Only Sustainable Edge," *Industry Week,* 1 July 1991, 19–21; Lois Therrien, "The Rival Japan Respects," *Business Week,* 13 November 1989, 108–118.
21. Kotter and Schlesinger, "Choosing Strategies for Change," 106–114; Arnold S. Judson, "Invest in a High-Yield Strategic Plan," *Journal of Business Strategy,* July–August 1991, 34–39; Lawrence, "How to Deal with Resistance to Change," 4–12, 166–176; Judson, *Changing Behavior in Organizations,* 94–96, 116–129; Lawrence, "How to Deal with Resistance to Change," 4–12, 166–176.
22. Sharon Nelton, "Cultural Changes in a Family Firm," *Nation's Business,* January 1989, 62–65.
23. Tom Terez, "A Manager's Guidelines for Implementing Successful Operational Changes," *Industrial Management,* July–August 1990, 18–20; Kotter and Schlesinger, "Choosing Strategies for Change," 106–114.
24. David Evans, "IBM Canada Rediscovers Its Customers," *Canadian Business,* November 1990, 36–47.
25. Kotter and Schlesinger, "Choosing Strategies for Change," 106–114; Belasco, *Teaching the Elephant to Dance,* 95.
26. Yumiko Ono, "Toys 'R' Us Learns Give-and-Take Game of Discounting with Japanese Suppliers," *Wall Street Journal,* 8 October 1991, A18.
27. Kotter and Schlesinger, "Choosing Strategies for Change," 106–114.
28. Judson, *Changing Behavior in Organizations,* 78–81; Kotter and Schlesinger, "Choosing Strategies for Change," 106–114.
29. Vaune Davis, "Bureaucracy Busting: How Management Buy-ins Changed Royal Trustco," *Canadian Business,* March 1990, 89–93.
30. Harold J. Leavitt, "Applied Organization Change in Industry: Structural, Technical, and Human Approaches," in *New Perspectives in Organization Research,* edited by W. W. Cooper, H. J. Leavitt, and M. W. Shelly II (New York: Wiley, 1964), 55–71.
31. Olle Stiwenius, "Planning for a Rapidly Changing Environment in SAS," *Long Range Planning* 18, no. 2 (1985): 22–29.
32. Leavitt, "Applied Organization Change in Industry," 55–71; Robert B. Horton, "Planning for Surprise," *Industry Week,* 6 August 1990, 27.
33. Leavitt, "Applied Organization Change in Industry," 55–71; Marc H. Meyer and Edward B. Roberts, "Focusing Product Technology for Corporate Growth," *Sloan Management Review* 7 (Summer 1988): 7–16; Sharon Efroymson First, "All Systems Go: How to Manage Technological Change," *Working Woman,* April 1990, 47–54.
34. Thomas H. Fitzgerald, "Can Change in Organizational Culture Really Be Managed?" *Organizational Dynamics,* August 1988, 5–15; Yoash Wiener, "Forms of Value Systems: A Focus on Organizational Effectiveness and Cultural Change and Maintenance," *Academy of Management Review* 13, no. 4 (1988): 534–545; Courtenay J. Culp, "Shaping Your Corporate Culture," *Association Management,* August 1988, 77–79.
35. Beckhard, *Organization Development,* 7, 9–13; Michael Beer and Anna Elise Walton, "Organization Change and Development," in *Organization Development: Theory, Practice, and Research,* 3rd ed., edited by Wendell L. French, Cecil H. Bell, Jr., and Robert A. Zawacki (Homewood, Ill.: BPI Irwin, 1989), 58–78.
36. Beer and Walton, "Organization Change and Development," 58–78; Kim S. Cameron, David A. Whetten, and Myung U. Kim, "Organizational Dysfunctions of Decline," *Academy of Management Journal* 30, no. 1 (1987): 126–138; William Weitzel and Ellen Jonsson, "Decline in Organizations: A Literature Integration and Extension," *Administrative Science Quarterly* 34 (1989): 91–109; Leonard Greenhalgh, Anne T. Lawrence, and Robert I. Sutton, "Determinants of Work Force Reduction Strategies in Declining Organizations," *Academy of Management Review* 13, no. 2 (1988): 241–254; Willem Mastenbroek, "A Dynamic Concept of Revitalization," *Organizational Dynamics,* Spring 1988, 52–61.
37. "The Foundations of OD: Theory and Practice on Change in Organizations," in *Organization Development: Theory, Practice, and Research,* 3rd ed., edited by Wendell L. French, Cecil H. Bell, Jr., and Robert A. Zawacki (Homewood, Ill.: BPI Irwin, 1989), 80–82; W. Warner Burke, "Organization Development," in *AMA Management Handbook,* 2nd ed., edited by William K. Fallon (New York: Amacom, 1983), 1-65–1-73; Hugh J. Arnold and Daniel C. Feldman, *Organizational Behavior* (New York: McGraw-Hill, 1986) 523–534; Matthew B. Miles and Richard A. Schmuck, "The Nature of Organization Development," in *Organization Development: Theory, Practice, and Research,* 3rd ed., edited by Wendell L. French, Cecil H. Bell, Jr., and Robert A. Zawacki (Homewood, Ill.: BPI Irwin, 1989), 37–38.
38. "The Foundations of OD," 80–82; Miles and Schmuck, "The Nature of Organization Development," 38.
39. Arnold and Feldman, *Organizational Behavior,* 524–525.
40. Burke, "Organization Development," 1-70–1-71; Arnold and Feldman, *Organizational Behavior,* 525–530.
41. Miles and Schmuck, "The Nature of Organization Development," 38.
42. "The Foundations of OD," 80–82; Arnold and Feldman, *Organizational Behavior,* 533.
43. Paul S. Goodman and James W. Dean, Jr., "Why Productivity Efforts Fail," in *Organization Development: Theory, Practice, and Research,* 3rd ed., edited by Wendell L. French, Cecil H. Bell, Jr., and Robert A. Zawacki (Homewood, Ill.: BPI Irwin, 1989), 400–407; "The Foundations of OD," 80–82.

44. Burke, "Organization Development," 1–72.
45. "OD Interventions: An Overview," in *Organization Development: Theory, Practice, and Research,* 3rd ed., edited by Wendell L. French, Cecil H. Bell, Jr., and Robert A. Zawacki (Homewood, Ill.: BPI Irwin, 1989), 139–142; Arnold and Feldman, *Organizational Behavior,* 533–539.
46. David G. Bowers and Jerome L. Franklin, "Survey-Guided Development: Using Human Resources Measurement in Organizational Change," in *Organization Development: Theory, Practice, and Research,* 3rd ed., edited by Wendell L. French, Cecil H. Bell, Jr., and Robert A. Zawacki (Homewood, Ill.: BPI Irwin, 1989), 244–253.
47. Beckhard, *Organization Development,* 40–41, 108–109; Arnold and Feldman, *Organizational Behavior,* 533–539; Belasco, *Teaching the Elephant to Dance,* 186–187.
48. Arnold and Feldman, *Organizational Behavior,* 534.
49. Beckhard, *Organization Development,* 27–29; Arnold and Feldman, *Organizational Behavior,* 533–539; Chet Borucki and Carole K. Barnett, "Restructuring for Self-Renewal: Navistar International Corporation," *Academy of Management Executive* 4, no. 1 (1990): 36–49.
50. Richard E. Walton, "Interpersonal Confrontation and Basic Third-Party Functions: A Case Study," in *Organization Development: Theory, Practice, and Research,* 3rd ed., edited by Wendell L. French, Cecil H. Bell, Jr., and Robert A. Zawacki (Homewood, Ill.: BPI Irwin, 1989), 221–234.
51. Belasco, *Teaching the Elephant to Dance,* 139–148.
52. Christian F. Paul and Albert C. Gross, "Increasing Productivity and Morale in a Municipality: Effects of Organization Development," in *Organization Development: Theory, Practice, and Research,* 3rd ed., edited by Wendell L. French, Cecil H. Bell, Jr., and Robert A. Zawacki (Homewood, Ill.: BPI Irwin, 1989), 574–586.
53. Frank Friedlander and L. Dave Brown, "Organization Development," in *Organization Development: Theory, Practice, and Research,* 3rd ed., edited by Wendell L. French, Cecil H. Bell, Jr., and Robert A. Zawacki (Homewood, Ill.: BPI Irwin, 1989), 41–57; Beckhard, *Organization Development,* 9–14; Arnold and Feldman, *Organizational Behavior,* 540–541; Yoram Zeira and Joyce Avedisian, "Organizational Planned Change: Assessing the Chances for Success," *Organizational Dynamics,* Spring 1989, 31–45.
54. Alfred M. Jaeger, "Organization Development and National Culture: Where's the Fit?" in *Organization Development: Theory, Practice, and Research,* 3rd ed., edited by Wendell L. French, Cecil H. Bell, Jr., and Robert A. Zawacki (Homewood, Ill.: BPI Irwin, 1989), 660–672; Beckhard, *Organization Development,* 26–27; Richard Dunford, Dexter C. Dunphy, and Doug A. Stace, "Strategies for Planned Change: An Exchange of Views between Dunford, Dunphy and Stace," *Organization Studies* 11, no. 1 (1990): 131–136.
55. Otis Port, "Back to Basics," *Business Week Innovation 1989,* 14–18; Kenneth Labich, "The Innovators," *Fortune,* 6 June 1988, 50–64; Vilma Barr, "The Process of Innovation: Brainstorming and Storyboarding," *Mechanical Engineering,* November 1988, 42–46; Russell Mitchell, "Masters of Innovation," *Business Week,* 10 April 1989, 58–63; Kevin Kelly, "3M Run Scared? Forget about It," *Business Week,* 16 September 1991, 59–62.
56. Perry Pascarella and Mark A. Frohman, *The Purpose-Driven Organization* (San Francisco: Jossey-Bass, 1990), 1–3; Labich, "The Innovators," 50–64.
57. Andrall E. Pearson, "Tough-Minded Ways to Get Innovative," *Harvard Business Review,* May–June 1988, 99–106; W. J. Vrakking, "The Innovative Organization," *Long Range Planning* 23, no. 2 (1990): 94–102.
58. Tom Brown, "Andy Van de Ven: Why Companies Don't Learn," *Industry Week,* 19 August 1991, 36–43; Amabile, "A Model of Creativity and Innovation in Organizations," 123–167; Richard E. Walton, *Innovating to Compete* (San Francisco: Jossey-Bass, 1987), 17–24; Sandra Salmans, "Thou Shalt Create," *Business Month,* June 1990, 52–55.
59. Amabile, "A Model of Creativity and Innovation in Organizations," 123–167; Brown, "Andy Van de Ven," 36–43; Walton, *Innovating to Compete,* 271–272; Winston Fletcher, "Blessed Be the New Creation," *Director,* March 1990, 72–76.
60. Russell L. Ackoff and Elsa Vergara, "Creativity in Problem Solving and Planning," in *Handbook for Creative and Innovative Managers,* edited by Robert L. Kuhn (New York: McGraw-Hill, 1988), 77–89.
61. Barr, "The Process of Innovation," 42–46.
62. William C. Miller, "Techniques for Stimulating New Ideas: A Matter of Fluency," in *Handbook for Creative and Innovative Managers,* edited by Robert L. Kuhn (New York: McGraw-Hill, 1988), 116–118.
63. Rosabeth Moss Kanter, "When a Thousand Flowers Bloom: Structural, Collective, and Social Conditions for Innovation in Organization," *Organizational Behavior* 10 (1988): 169–211; Mitchell, "Masters of Innovation," 58–63; Giovanni Grossi, "Promoting Innovation in a Big Business," *Long Range Planning* 23 (February 1990): 41–52.
64. Gareth Morgan, "Endangered Species: New Ideas," *Business Month,* April 1989, 75–77; Labich, "The Innovators," 50–64; Ray Wise, "The Boom in Creativity Training," *Across the Board,* June 1991, 38–42; Lois Therrien, "McRisky," *Business Week,* 21 October 1991, 114–122.
65. Dayr A. Reis and John H. Betton, "Bureaucracy and Innovation: An Old Theme Revisited," *Industrial Management,* November–December 1990, 21–24; Kanter, "When a Thousand Flowers Bloom," 169–211; Betty A. Velthouse, "Creativity and Empowerment: A Complementary Relationship," *Review of Business,* Fall 1990, 13–18; Alfred A. Marcus, "Responses to Externally Induced Innovation: Their Effects on Organizational Performance," *Strategic Management Journal* 9 (1988): 387–402.
66. Joshua Hyatt, "Ideas at Work," *Inc.,* May 1991, 59–66.
67. Kanter, "When a Thousand Flowers Bloom," 169–211; Rosabeth Moss Kanter, *When Giants Learn to Dance* (New York: Touchstone Simon & Schuster, 1989), 205–214; Charles W. Hucker, "A Place for Creativity: The Hallmark Innovation Center," in *Handbook for Creative and Innovative Managers,* edited by Robert L. Kuhn (New York: McGraw-Hill, 1988), 271–276.
68. Rosabeth Moss Kanter, *Change Masters* (New York: Touchstone Simon & Schuster, 1983), 28–36; Andrew H. Van de Ven, "Central Problems in the Management of Innovation," *Management Science* 32, no. 5 (May 1986): 590–607; David Woodruff, "GM: All Charged Up over the Electric Car," *Business Week,* 21 October 1991, 106–108.
69. See note 1.

CHAPTER 12

1. Adapted from Joe Mullich, "Worth It!" *Business Journal of New Jersey,* September 1991, 32–37; Paul B. Brown, "Cookie Monsters," *Inc.,* February 1989, 55–59; Leslie Brokaw, "Snack Attack," *Inc.,* April 1990, 69; Jenny C. McCune, "Cooking Up a Sales Strategy," *Success,* May 1990, 27; Alyssa A. Lappen, "Meet the Frookie Man," *Forbes,* 1 October 1990, 191, 193.
2. Ralph M. Gaedeke and Dennis H. Tootelian, *Small Business Management* (Needham Heights, Mass.: Allyn & Bacon, 1991), 2–3.
3. Richard I. Kirkland, Jr., "Pile 'Em High and Sell 'Em Cheap," *Fortune,* 29 August 1988, 91–92.
4. Janice Castro, "She Calls All the Shots," *Time,* 4 July 1988, 54–57; S&P Million Dollar Directory (on-line).
5. Tom Richman, "The Entrepreneur of the Year," *Inc.,* January 1990, 43–62.
6. Charles R. Kuehl and Peggy A. Lambing, *Small Business Planning and Management* (Orlando, Fla.: Dryden Press, 1990), 26.
7. Elizabeth A. Conlin and Louise Washer, "They Tried to Steal My Business . . . ," *Working Woman,* October 1988, 43–46.
8. Kuehl and Lambing, *Small Business Planning and Management,* 26.
9. Howard H. Stevenson and David E. Gumpert, "The Heart of Entrepreneurship," *Harvard Business Review,* March–April 1985, 85–94.
10. Michael Oneal and Gail DeGeorge, "Why Startups Can't Wait to Fly the Risky Skies," *Business Week,* 8 July 1991, 35; Michael Derchin, "Analyzing American's Bold Gambit," *Travel Weekly,* 7 February 1985, 1, 4; Dennis J. H. Kraft, Tae H. Oum, and Michael W. Tretheway, "Airline Seat Management," *Logistics and Transportation Review,* June 1986, 115–130; Jane Levere, "The Pricing Game," *Travel Weekly,* 30 January 1985, 132–133; Bill Poling, "USAir's Malin Hits Airline Pricing System," *Travel Weekly,* 23 January 1986, 70; Jerry Brown, "USAir Official Assails Pricing Departments' Low-Fare Advocates," *Travel Weekly,* 11 April 1988, 17.
11. Gaedeke and Tootelian, *Small Business Management,* 11.
12. Brent Bowers, "Pain Can Be an Impetus for a Problem-Solving Business: Emotional and Physical Survivors Market Their Own Antidotes," *Wall Street Journal,* 6 November 1991, B2.
13. Dan Steinhoff and John F. Burgess, *Small Business Management Fundamentals* (New York: McGraw-Hill, 1989), 5.
14. Gaedeke and Tootelian, *Small Business Management,* 12.
15. Jeanne Saddler, "Fears Mount That Small-Business Sector Is in a State of Permanent Retrenchment," *Wall Street Journal,* 14 February 1992, B1–B2; "The 1990 Guide to Small Business," *U.S. News & World Report,* 23 October 1989, 72–86.
16. William O'Hare and Jan Larson, "Women

in Business, Where, What, and Why," *American Demographics,* July 1991, 34–38.
17. Dorothy J. Gaiter, "Equal Opportunities," *Wall Street Journal,* 22 November 1991, R14.
18. "The 1990 Guide to Small Business," 72–86.
19. Thomas P. Cullen and Timothy J. Dick, "Tomorrow's Entrepreneur and Today's Hospitality Curriculum," *The Cornell H.R.A. Quarterly,* August 1990, 54–57.
20. Murray B. Low and Ian C. MacMillan, "Entrepreneurship: Past Research and Future Challenges," *Journal of Management,* June 1988, 139–161; William B. Gartner, "'Who Is an Entrepreneur?' Is the Wrong Question," *American Journal of Small Business,* Spring 1988, 11–32; Kuehl and Lambing, *Small Business Planning and Management,* 29–39.
21. Arnold C. Cooper, Carolyn Y. Woo, and William C. Dunkelberg, "Entrepreneur's Perceived Chances for Success," *Journal of Business Venturing,* 3 (1988): 97–108.
22. Selwyn Feinstein, "Nonprofit Venture Aimed at Helping the Homeless Learns About Cash Flow," *Wall Street Journal,* 14 April 1989, B3A.
23. Peter F. Drucker, *Innovation and Entrepreneurship* (New York: Harper & Row, 1986), 209–232.
24. David Churbuck, "Success Formula," *Forbes,* 27 May 1991, 334; Larry Armstrong, "Now, It's No Sweat to Set the VCR," *Business Week,* 17 November 1990, 124; Larry Armstrong, "The Geniuses Who Made VCRs Simple Enough for a 50-Year-Old," *Business Week,* 31 December 1990, 54.
25. Joseph Anthony, "Your Own Business," *Sylvia Porter's Personal Finance,* March 1989, 32–47.
26. Gaedeke and Tootelian, *Small Business Management,* 97–143.
27. Anthony, "Your Own Business," 42.
28. Kuehl and Lambing, *Small Business Planning and Management,* 89; Gaedeke and Tootelian, *Small Business Management,* 121.
29. *Franchise Opportunities Handbook* (Washington, D.C.: GPO, 1988), xxix.
30. John P. Hayes and Gregory Matusky, "Goodbye to the Small Fries, Hello to the Big Guys," *Inc.,* September 1989, 102–113.
31. Leslie Brokaw, "The Truth about Start-Ups," *Inc.,* April 1991, 52–67.
32. Kuehl and Lambing, *Small Business Planning and Management,* 164–175.
33. Jim Carland and JoAnn Carland, *Small Business Management: Tools for Success* (Boston: PWS-Kent, 1990), 246–268.
34. Roger Thompson, "Business Plans: Myth and Reality," *Nation's Business,* August 1988, 16–20.
35. Gaedeke and Tootelian, *Small Business Management,* 248–264.
36. Russell Mitchell, "As Exports Rise, Big Companies Rev Up Hiring," *Business Week,* 10 April 1988, 91.
37. Gaedeke and Tootelian, *Small Business Management,* 248–264.
38. Gaedeke and Tootelian, *Small Business Management,* 248–264.
39. Gaedeke and Tootelian, *Small Business Management,* 248–264.
40. Lisa J. Moore and Sharon F. Golden, "You Can Plan to Grow or You Can Just Let It Happen to You," *U.S. News & World Report,* 23 October 1989, 73–77.
41. Steven Greenhouse, "In Poland, a Small Capitalist Miracle," *New York Times,* 19 December 1989, sec. d, 1, 3.
42. Bradford McKee, "Using Incubators as Steppingstones to Growth," *Nation's Business,* October 1991, 8.
43. Moore and Golden, "You Can Plan to Grow or You Can Just Let It Happen to You," 76.
44. Brokaw, "The Truth about Start-Ups," 60.
45. Neil C. Churchill and Virginia L. Lewis, "The Five Stages of Small Business Growth," *Harvard Business Review,* May–June 1983, 30–50.
46. Ret Autry, "Companies to Watch, International Dairy Queen," *Fortune,* 29 July 1991, 110.
47. Cynthia Rigg, "Starting Over in America, Nicaraguan Cooks Up Successful Food Stores," *Crain's New York Business,* 29 July 1991, 25.
48. Carland and Carland, *Small Business Management, Tools for Success,* 29.
49. Jeffrey Lener, "The Vital Steps To a Successful Start-Up," *Success,* October 1988, 67–80.
50. Carland and Carland, *Small Business Management, Tools for Success,* 31–35; Brokaw, "The Truth about Start-Ups," 52–67.
51. Gifford Pinchot III, *Entrepreneuring* (New York: Harper & Row, 1985), 12.
52. Pinchot, *Entrepreneuring,* 6–7.
53. Pinchot, *Entrepreneuring,* 181–192.
54. Christopher K. Bart, "New Venture Units: Use Them Wisely to Manage Innovation," *Sloan Management Review,* Summer 1988, 35–43.
55. Don L. Boroughs, "Smart Moves for Small Businesses," *U.S. News & World Report,* 3 June 1991, 57–58.
56. Boroughs, "Smart Moves for Small Businesses," 57–58.
57. Boroughs, "Smart Moves for Small Businesses," 57–58.
58. Boroughs, "Smart Moves for Small Businesses," 57–58.
59. Adapted in part from Larry Greiner, "Evolution and Revolution as Organizations Grow," *Harvard Business Review,* July–August 1972, 37–46.
60. See note 1.

CHAPTER 13

1. Adapted from "Changing a Corporate Culture," *Business Week,* 14 May 1984, 130–138; Johnson & Johnson 1990 Annual Report; "Shrinking, Changing Labor Force Prompts Johnson & Johnson Family Issues," *Employee Benefits Plan Review,* September 1989, 57–60; "What Makes Sales Forces Run?" *Sales & Marketing Management,* 3 December 1984, 24–26; Susan Dentzer, "Excessive Claims," *Business Month,* July 1990, 52–63; Evelyn Gilbert, "Benefits No 'Soft' Issue: J&J Official," *National Underwriter,* 10 December 1990, 15, 21; Christopher Power, "At Johnson & Johnson, a Mistake Can Be a Badge of Honor," *Business Week,* 26 September 1988, 126–128; Lee Smith, "J&J Comes a Long Way from Baby," *Fortune,* 1 June 1981, 58–56; Neal Templin, "Johnson & Johnson 'Wellness' Program for Workers Shows Healthy Bottom Line," *Wall Street Journal,* 21 May 1990, B1, B6; Barbara Scherr Trenk, "Corporate Fitness Programs Become Hearty Investments," *Management Review,* August 1989, 33–37; Michael A. Verespej, "A Ticket to Better Health," *Industry Week,* 4 February 1991, 24–25; Joseph Weber, "No Band-Aids for Ralph Larsen," *Business Week,* 28 May 1990, 86–87.
2. Annette A. Hartenstein, "Human-Resource Management Practices in the Federal Government," *National Productivity Review,* Winter 1987–1988, 45–53.
3. Hartenstein, "Human-Resource Management Practices in the Federal Government," 45–53.
4. Randall H. Schuler, "Repositioning the Human Resource Function: Transformation or Demise?" *Academy of Management Executive,* August 1990, 49–60.
5. A. Nicholas Komanecky, "Developing New Managers at GE," *Training and Development Journal,* June 1988, 62–64; *Harvard Business Review,* "Manage People, Not Personnel," *Soundview Executive Book Summaries,* November 1990, 1–8.
6. Robert H. Hayes and Ramchandran Jaikumar, "Manufacturing's Crisis: New Technologies, Obsolete Organizations," *Harvard Business Review,* September–October 1988, 77–85.
7. Wm. G. Thomas, "Training and Development Do Make Better Managers!" *Personnel,* January 1988, 52–53; Gerald T. Gabris, "Innovative Approaches to Public-Sector Management Development and Training," *Public Productivity & Management Review,* Winter 1989, 155–160.
8. Robert M. Tomasko, *Downsizing; Reshaping the Corporation for the Future* (New York: Amacom, 1990), 227.
9. David J. Jefferson, "Boeing, Facing Delays in 747 Deliveries, Turns to Lockheed for Loan of Workers," *Wall Street Journal,* 3 August 1987, A3, A9.
10. Dyan Machan, "Cultivating the Gray," *Forbes,* 4 September 1989, 126, 128.
11. Rhiannon Chapman, "Personnel Management in the 1990s," *Personnel Management,* January 1990, 28–32; Terry E. Hedrick, "New Challenges for Government Managers," *The Bureaucrat,* Spring 1990, 17–20; John Maxwell, "Managing Human Resources in the 1990s: International Perspectives," *Practising Manager,* Winter 1990, 9–14; Jon L. Pierce and Candace A. Furo, "Employee Ownership: Implications for Management," *Organizational Dynamics,* Winter 1990, 32–43.
12. Robert L. Mathis and John H. Jackson, *Personnel/Human Resource Management* (St. Paul: West Publishing Company, 1988), 86, 598.
13. "Manage People, Not Personnel," 1–8.
14. Mathis and Jackson, *Personnel/Human Resource Management,* 87.
15. "Manage People, Not Personnel," 1–8.
16. Jeanne Saddler, "Money, Morale Problems Are Making Top Managers Say No to Federal Jobs," *Wall Street Journal,* 26 April 1988, 60.
17. Jeanne M. Brett, "Why Employees Want Unions," *Organizational Dynamics,* Spring 1980, 47–59.
18. Redwood Anthony, "Human Resources Management in the 1990s," *Business Horizons,* January–February 1990, 74–80.
19. Gregory Gordon and Ronald E. Cohen, *Down to the Wire: UPI's Fight for Survival* (New York: McGraw-Hill, 1990), 186, 316.
20. Richard N. Current, T. Harry Williams, Frank Freidel, and W. Elliot Brownlee, *The Essentials of American History* (New York: Alfred A. Knopf, 1972), 97–98.

21. David J. Cherrington, *The Management of Human Resources* (Boston: Allyn & Bacon, 1991), 525–528.
22. Marilyn Loden and Judy B. Rosener, *Workforce America! Managing Employee Diversity as a Vital Resource* (Homewood, Ill.: Business One Irwin, 1991), 206, 207.
23. Kristine E. Daynes, "Disabilities Act in Action," *Personnel,* October 1990, 11, 12.
24. Leon E. Wynter and Jolie Solomon, "A New Push to Break the 'Glass Ceiling,'" *Wall Street Journal,* 15 November 1989, B1, B12.
25. Peter Waldman, "Affirmative Action Faces Likely Setback," *Wall Street Journal,* 30 November 1988, B1.
26. Lura K. Romei, "No Handicap to Hiring," *Modern Office Technology,* September 1991, 86, 88, 90.
27. Susan G. Richer and David M. Weiss, "Employee Suggestion Programs in Nonprofit Hospitals," *Health Care Management Review,* 1988, 59–65.
28. Anthony A. Gruebl III, "The Managers Guide to the Worker Adjustment and Retraining Notification Act," *Advanced Management Journal,* Spring 1990, 12–15.
29. Richard B. McKenzie, "Fraud Law Could Shield Workers from Surprise Closings," *Wall Street Journal,* 27 April 1988, 11.
30. Michael E. Verespej, "Partnership in the Trenches," *Industry Week,* 17 October 1988, 56, 57, 60, 62, 64; Lance E. Hazzard, "A Union Says Yes to Attendance," *Personnel Journal,* November 1990, 47–49.
31. Clare Ansberry, "Workplace Injuries Proliferate as Concerns Push People to Produce," *Wall Street Journal,* 16 June 1989, A1, A5; R. Henry Moore, "OSHA: What's Ahead for the 1990s," *Personnel,* June 1990, 66–69.
32. "Pinups Are Ruled Harassment," *Independent Record,* 24 January 1991, 7B.
33. Kenneth M. York, "Defining Sexual Harassment in Workplaces: A Policy-Capturing Approach," *Academy of Management Journal,* December 1989, 830–850.
34. Gretchen Morgenson, "Watch That Leer, Stifle That Joke," *Forbes,* 15 May 1989, 69–72.
35. Daniel A. Thomann and Donald E. Strickland, "Line Managers and the Daily Round of Work: The Front-Line Defense against Sexual Harassment," *Industrial Management,* May–June 1990, 14–16.
36. Amy Saltzman, "Hands Off at the Office," *U.S. News & World Report,* 1 August 1988, 56–58.
37. Marlene C. Piturro, "HR Policies Give Companies New Direction," *Management Review,* April 1989, 16–18.
38. Joseph Duffey, "Competitiveness and Human Resources," *California Management Review,* Spring 1988, 92–100.
39. "Medical Spending Grows at an 'Alarming' Rate," *Independent Record,* 21 December 1990, 2A.
40. Emily T. Smith, Alice Cuneo, and Jo Ellen Davis, "Stress: The Test Americans Are Failing," *Business Week,* 18 April 1988, 74–76.
41. Carol A. Perkin, "Help for Workers Who Care for Their Parents," *New York Times,* 4 June 1989, sec. 3, F19.
42. Kenneth A. Kovach and John A. Pearce II, "HR Strategic Mandates for the 1990s," *Personnel,* April 1990, 50–55.
43. Joel Dreyfuss, "Get Ready for the New Work Force," *Fortune,* 23 April 1990, 165, 168, 172, 176, 180, 181.
44. Randall H. Schuler, "Repositioning the Human Resource Function: Transformation or Demise?" *Academy of Management Executive,* August 1990, 49–60.
45. William H. Wagel, "On the Horizon: HR in the 1990s," *Personnel,* January 1990, 11–16.
46. "Is Business Bungling Its Battle with Booze?" *Business Week,* 25 March 1991, 76; Pallab Ghosh, "Employers Crack Down," *Management Today,* August 1990, 92.
47. Jack Kelley, "Poll: On-Job Drug Use Is Significant," *USA Today,* 13 December 1988, 1A.
48. Joseph E. McKendrick, Jr., "Latest AMS Survey Finds: One-Third of Nation's Employers Have or Are Considering Drug Testing," *Management World,* March–April 1990, 3–4.
49. Tim W. Ferguson, "Motorola Aims High, So Motorolans Won't Be Getting High," *Wall Street Journal,* 26 June 1990, A17.
50. Allan Hanson, "What Employees Say about Drug Testing," *Personnel,* July 1990, 32–36.
51. Lewis B. Maltby, "Put Performance to the Test," *Personnel,* July 1990, 30, 31.
52. Joan O'C. Hamilton, "A Video Game That Tells if Employees Are Fit for Work," *Business Week,* 3 June 1991, 36.
53. "U.S. AIDS Deaths Hit 100,000," *Independent Record,* 25 January 1991, 3C.
54. Joseph F. Coates, Jennifer Jarratt, and John B. Mahaffie, *Future Work* (San Francisco: Jossey-Bass, 1990), 354.
55. Joseph G. Ormsby, Garalyn McClure Franklin, Robert K. Robinson, and Alicia B. Gresham, "AIDS in the Workplace: Implications for Human Resource Managers," *Advanced Management Journal,* Spring 1990, 23–27; George E. Stevens, "Understanding AIDS," *Personnel Administrator,* August 1988, 84–87.
56. Smothers, "Survey Finds a Clash on AIDS in Workplace," *New York Times,* 7 February 1988, 29.
57. Tom St. George, "Quality of Work Life: Why Things Get Tougher as You Go," *Training,* January 1984, 70–72.
58. Mathis and Jackson, *Personnel/Human Resource Management,* 87.
59. Coates, Jarratt, and Mahaffie, *Future Work,* 241.
60. Coates, Jarratt, and Mahaffie, *Future Work,* 241, 242.
61. William B. Werther, Jr., and Keith Davis, *Personnel Management and Human Resources* (New York: McGraw-Hill, 1985), 241, 603; David E. DeCenzo and Stephen P. Robbins, *Personnel/Human Resource Management* (Englewood Cliffs, N.J.: Prentice Hall, 1988), 618.
62. Marc G. Singer, *Human Resource Management* (Boston: PWS-Kent, 1990), 541.
63. Jonathan Kapstein and John Hoerr, "Volvo's Radical New Plant: 'The Death of the Assembly Line'?" *Business Week,* 28 August 1989, 92, 93.
64. Kovach and Pearce, "HR Strategic Mandates for the 1990s," 52.
65. Steven M. Darien, "Father Flanagan Meets Conan the Barbarian," *Personnel,* October 1990, 9.
66. Barney Olmsted and Suzanne Smith, *Creating a Flexible Workplace* (New York: Amacom, 1989), 130.
67. Deirdre Fanning, "The Executive Life: Japanese Families, Alone in America," *New York Times,* 12 December 1990, sec. 3, 23; Bob Hagerty, "Companies in Europe Seeking Executives Who Can Cross Borders in a Single Bound," *Wall Street Journal,* 25 January 1991, B1–B2; Jennifer J. Laabs, "The Global Talent Search," *Personnel Journal,* August 1991, 38–44; Luis R. Gomez-Mejia and Theresa Welbourne, "Compensation Strategies in a Global Context," *Human Resources Planning,* 14 (1991): 29–41.
68. James W. Walker, *Human Resource Planning* (New York: McGraw-Hill, 1980), 5, 355, 356.
69. David J. Cherrington, *The Management of Human Resources* (Boston: Allyn & Bacon, 1991), 144–152.
70. Singer, *Human Resource Management,* 546; Cherrington, *The Management of Human Resources,* 157–158.
71. Richard A. Melcher and Jonathan Levine, "Fired! Now, Europe Is Singing the White-Collar Blues," *Business Week,* 26 November 1990, 70, 71.
72. Cherrington, *The Management of Human Resources,* 141.
73. Mathis and Jackson, *Personnel/Human Resource Management,* 162.
74. Roy Hill, "Nissan and the Art of People Management," *Director,* March 1990, 46–49.
75. Mathis and Jackson, *Personnel/Human Resource Management,* 163.
76. Singer, *Human Resource Management,* 541.
77. Juliette Walker, "New Tactics for New Recruits," *Japan Times Weekly International Edition,* 15–21 April 1991, 17.
78. William J. Hampton, "How Does Japan Inc. Pick Its American Workers?" *Business Week,* 3 October 1988, 84, 88.
79. Steven L. Premack and John P. Wanous, "A Meta-Analysis of Realistic Job Preview Experiments," *Journal of Applied Psychology* 70 (1985): 706–719.
80. Claudia H. Deutsch, "Psst! References Are Sneaking Back, for Real," *New York Times,* 2 December 1990, sec. 3, 25.
81. Thomas J. Burns, "Tests to Target Dependability," *Nation's Business,* March 1989, 26, 28, 29.
82. Eugene B. McGregor, "The Public Sector Human Resource Puzzle: Strategic Management of a Strategic Resource," *Public Administration Review,* November–December 1989, 941–950.
83. Hampton, "How Does Japan Inc. Pick Its American Workers?" 84, 88.
84. Aaron M. Cohen, "Can 'Japanese Management' Help East Europe?" *Management Japan,* Autumn 1990, 15, 16.
85. Myron E. Weiner, *Human Services Management: Analysis and Applications* (Belmont, Calif.: Wadsworth, 1990), 349.
86. Singer, *Human Resource Management,* 525.
87. "Manage People, Not Personnel," 1–8.
88. J. D. Dunn and Frank M. Rachel, *Wage and Salary Administration: Total Compensation Systems* (New York: McGraw-Hill, 1971), 277.
89. Richer and Weiss, "Employee Suggestion Programs in Nonprofit Hospitals," 60.
90. Paul Neuberg, "Shock Treatment in Hungary," *Business,* July 1990, 58–63.
91. Anne E. Preston, "The Nonprofit Worker in a For-Profit World," *Journal of Labor Economics* 7(1989): 438–462.
92. Cherrington, *The Management of Human Resources,* 402.
93. Cherrington, *The Management of Human Resources,* 406.
94. Arnold H. Wensky and Robin J. Legendre, "Incentive Training at First Service Bank," *Personnel Journal,* April 1989, 102, 107.

95. Ken Bowman, "The Organic Way to Grow Managers," *Personnel Management,* October 1990, 50–52, 55.
96. Edgar Wille, "Should Management Development Just Be for Managers?" *Personnel Management,* August 1990, 34–37.
97. J. E. Osburne, "Upward Evaluations: What Happens when Staffers Evaluate Supervisors," *Supervisory Management,* March 1990, 1–2.
98. David M. Slipy, "Anthropologist Uncovers Real Workplace Attitudes," *HR Magazine,* October 1990, 76–77.
99. Lin Grensing, "Don't Let Them Out the Door without an Exit Interview," *Management World,* March–April 1990, 11–13.
100. See note 1.

CHAPTER 14

1. Adapted from Thomas M. Rohan, "Maverick Remakes Old-Line Steel," *Industry Week,* 21 January 1991, 26–30; "Nucor's Ken Iverson on Productivity and Pay," *Personnel Administrator,* October 1986, 46–52, 106–108; John Merwin, "People, Attitudes and Equipment," *Forbes,* 8 February 1988, 68–72; "Empowering Employees," *Chief Executive,* March–April 1989, 44–49; Michael A. D'Amato and Jeremy H. Silverman, "How to Make Money in a Dull Business," *Across the Board,* December 1990, 54–59; Richard Preston, "Annals of Enterprise; Hot Metal-I," *The New Yorker,* 25 February 1991, 43–71.
2. Keith Davis and John W. Newstrom, *Human Behavior at Work,* 8th ed. (New York: McGraw-Hill, 1989), 16.
3. Richard M. Steers and Lyman W. Porter, *Motivation and Work Behavior,* 5th ed. (New York: McGraw-Hill, 1991), 6–8.
4. Steers and Porter, *Motivation and Work Behavior,* 5–6.
5. Dennis Faust, "Innkeepers Beware: Kemmons Wilson Is Checking In Again," *Business Week,* 1 February 1988, 79–80.
6. Carl M. Cannon, "Golden Shackles," *Business Month,* September 1988, 56, 60–61, 63.
7. Mary Williams, "Managing Workplace Diversity . . . the Wave of the '90s," *IABC Communications World,* January 1990, 16–19; Michael A. Verespej, "Without a New Rx: Warfare," *Industry Week,* 8 January 1990, 88, 92, 97.
8. Robert M. Tomasko, *Downsizing: Reshaping the Corporation for the Future* (New York: Amacom, 1990), 49–52.
9. Brian Bremner, "Among Restaurateurs, It's Dog Eat Dog," *Business Week,* 9 January 1989, 86; Verespej, "Without a New Rx: Warfare," 88, 92, 97; Williams, "Managing Workplace Diversity," 16–19.
10. Janice Castro, "Where Did the Gung-ho Go?" *Time,* 11 September 1989, 52–54, 56; Stanley J. Modic, "Motivating without Promotions," *Industry Week,* 19 June 1989, 24–27; "Plateaued Workers Cause Big Damage," *Wall Street Journal,* 17 August 1988, 23.
11. Steers and Porter, *Motivation and Work Behavior,* 5–6.
12. Steers and Porter, *Motivation and Work Behavior,* 6–8.
13. Edward L. Deci and Richard M. Ryan, "Intrinsic Motivation and Self-Determination in Human Behavior," in *Motivation and Work Behavior,* 5th ed., edited by Richard M. Steers and Lyman W. Porter (New York: McGraw-Hill, 1991), 44–51; Steers and Porter, *Motivation and Work Behavior,* 478–479.
14. Dennis P. Slevin, *The Whole Manager* (New York: Amacom, 1989), 209–211; Gregory Moorhead and Ricky W. Griffin, *Organizational Behavior,* 2nd ed. (Boston: Houghton Mifflin, 1989), 108; L. M. Gilbreth, *The Psychology of Management* (Easton, Pa.: Hive, 1980), 271–301; Victor H. Vroom and Arthur G. Jago, *The New Leadership* (Englewood Cliffs, N.J.: Prentice Hall, 1988), 13.
15. Saul W. Gellerman, *Motivation and Productivity* (New York: American Management Association, 1963), 32–47.
16. Douglas McGregor, *The Human Side of Enterprise* (New York: McGraw-Hill, 1960), 33–57; Joseph W. McGuire, "Management Theory: Retreat to the Academy," *Business Horizons,* July–August 1982, 31–37; Gellerman, *Motivaton and Productivity,* 83–92.
17. David J. Cherrington, "Need Theories of Motivation," in *Motivation and Work Behavior,* 5th ed., edited by Richard M. Steers and Lyman W. Porter (New York: McGraw-Hill, 1991), 32–33; Donald P. Schwab, "Motivation in Organizations," in *Handbook for Professional Managers,* edited by Lester R. Bittel and Jackson E. Ramsey (New York: McGraw-Hill, 1985), 584–585.
18. A. H. Maslow, "A Theory of Human Motivation," in *Readings in Managerial Psychology,* 3rd ed., edited by Harold J. Leavitt, Louis R. Pondy, and David M. Boje (Chicago: University of Chicago Press, 1980), 5–22; Herbert L. Petri, *Motivation: Theory, Research, and Applications,* 3rd ed. (Belmont, Calif.: Wadsworth, 1991), 322–326.
19. Alan Deutschman, "What 25-Year-Olds Want," *Fortune,* 27 August 1990, 42–47, 50.
20. Abraham H. Maslow, "A Theory of Human Motivation," *Psychological Review* 50 (1943): 370–396; Mahmoud A. Wahba and Lawrence G. Bridwell, "Maslow Reconsidered: A Review of Research on the Need Hierarchy Theory," *Organizational Behavior and Human Performance* 15 (1976): 212–240; Cherrington, "Need Theories of Motivation," 37–39; J. D. Dunn and Elvis C. Stephens, *Management of Personnel: Manpower Management and Organizational Behavior* (New York: McGraw-Hill, 1972), 167–169.
21. Cherrington, "Need Theories of Motivation," 36–37; John P. Campbell and Robert D. Pritchard, "Motivation Theory in Industrial and Organizational Psychology," in *Handbook of Industrial and Organizational Psychology,* edited by Marvin D. Dunnette (Chicago: Rand McNally, 1976), 97–98.
22. Moorhead and Griffin, *Organizational Behavior,* 114; Cherrington, "Need Theories of Motivation," 37.
23. Moorhead and Griffin, *Organizational Behavior,* 114; Campbell and Pritchard, "Motivation Theory in Industrial and Organizational Psychology," 97–98.
24. Suzanne Alexander, "For Some Students, the Value of Learning Lies in Dance Tickets and Parking Passes," *Wall Street Journal,* 29 January 1992, B1, B9.
25. Fred Luthans, *Organizational Behavior,* 5th ed. (New York: McGraw-Hill, 1989), 245; Tom Richman, "Reorganizing for Growth," *Inc.,* January 1991, 110.
26. Frederick Herzberg, "New Approaches in Management Organization and Job Design," in *Management Classics,* 2nd ed., edited by Michael T. Matteson and John M. Ivancevich (Santa Monica, Calif.: Goodyear, 1981), 281–288; Davis and Newstrom, *Human Behavior at Work,* 109–112.
27. Frederick Herzberg, "One More Time: How Do You Motivate Employees?" *Harvard Business Review,* September–October 1987, 109–120; Herzberg, "New Approaches in Management Organization and Job Design," 281–288.
28. Herzberg, "One More Time: How Do You Motivate Employees?" 109–120; Kevin Maney, "Soviet McDonald's Tastes Success," *USA Today,* 22 November 1991, 8B.
29. Robert J. House and Lawrence A. Wigdor, "Herzberg's Dual-Factor Theory of Job Satisfaction and Motivation: A Review of the Evidence and a Criticism," *Personnel Psychology,* Winter 1967, 369–389.
30. Cherrington, "Need Theories of Motivation," 39.
31. David C. McClelland, "That Urge to Achieve," in *Readings in Management,* 5th ed., edited by Max D. Richards (Cincinnati: Southwestern Publishing, 1978), 403–411; Gellerman, *Motivation and Productivity,* 122–132; David C. McClelland, "Business Drive and National Achievement," in *Readings in Managerial Psychology,* 2nd ed., edited by Harold J. Leavitt and Louis R. Pondy (Chicago: University of Chicago Press, 1973), 179–202.
32. David C. McClelland and David H. Burnham, "Power Is the Great Motivator," *Harvard Business Review,* March–April 1976, 100–110; Kathy Rebello, "Microsoft: Bill Gates' Baby Is on the Top of the World. Can It Stay There?" *Business Week,* 24 February 1992, 60–64; Kathy Rebello, "How Microsoft Makes Offers People Can't Refuse," *Business Week,* 24 February 1992, 65; Charles A. Jaffe, "Management by Fun," *Nation's Business,* January 1990, 58–60; Anne R. Field, "Managing Creative People," *Success,* October 1988, 85–87.
33. Moorhead and Griffin, *Organizational Behavior,* 122; Cherrington, "Need Theories of Motivation," 41–42; "Peer Recognition Key to Motivation," *Productivity,* October 1991, 6.
34. McClelland and Burnham, "Power Is the Great Motivator," 100–110; Cherrington, "Need Theories of Motivation," 41–43.
35. McClelland, "That Urge to Achieve," 408–410; Petri, *Motivation: Theory, Research, and Applications,* 258.
36. Victor H. Vroom, *Work and Motivation* (New York: Wiley, 1964), 14–29, 262–264; Daniel R. Ilgen, Delbert M. Nebeker, and Robert D. Pritchard, "Expectancy Theory Measures: An Empirical Comparison in an Experimental Simulation," *Organizational Behavior and Human Performance* 28 (1981): 189–223; Craig C. Pinder, "Valence-Instrumentality-Expectancy Theory," in *Motivation and Work Behavior,* 5th ed., edited by Richard M. Steers and Lyman W. Porter (New York: McGraw-Hill, 1991), 144–145, 151.
37. Vroom, *Work and Motivation,* 262–263; Edward E. Lawler III, "The Design of Effective Reward Systems," in *Handbook of Organizational Behavior,* edited by Jay W. Lorsch (Englewood Cliffs, N.J.: Prentice Hall, 1987), 255–257; Schwab, "Motivation in Organizations," 586–588.
38. Vroom, *Work and Motivation,* 14–18, 262–263; Lawler, "The Design of Effective Reward Systems," 256–257; Schwab, "Motivation in Organizations," 586–588.
39. Dawn Gunsch, "Award Programs at Work," *Personnel Journal,* September 1991, 85–89.

40. Vroom, *Work and Motivation,* 15–16; Schwab, "Motivation in Organizations," 586–588; Lawler, "The Design of Effective Reward Systems," 256–257.
41. Walter B. Newsom, "Motivate, Now," *Personnel Journal,* February 1990, 51–55.
42. Lawler, "The Design of Effective Reward Systems," 256–257.
43. Lynn E. Miller and Joseph E. Grush, "Improving Predictions in Expectancy Theory Research: Effects of Personality, Expectancies, and Norms," *Academy of Management Journal* 31, no. 1 (1988): 107–122; Douglas D. Baker, Ramarathnam Ravichandran, and Donna M. Randall, "Exploring Contrasting Formulations of Expectancy Theory," *Decision Sciences* 20 (1989): 1–13; Steers and Porter, *Motivation and Work Behavior,* 150–154; Terence R. Mitchell, "Expectancy Theories of Job Satisfaction, Occupational Preference, and Effort: A Theoretical, Methodological, and Empirical Appraisal," *Psychological Bulletin* 81, no. 12 (1974): 1053–1077.
44. Pinder, "Valence - Instrumentality - Expectancy Theory," 151–154; J. G. Hunt and J. W. Hill, "The New Look in Motivational Theory for Organizational Research," in *Readings in Managerial Psychology,* 2nd ed., edited by Harold J. Leavitt and Louis R. Pondy (Chicago: University of Chicago Press, 1973), 43–59.
45. Pinder, "Valence - Instrumentality - Expectancy Theory," 151–153; Campbell and Pritchard, "Motivation Theory in Industrial and Organizational Psychology," 78–79.
46. J. Stacey Adams, "Toward an Understanding of Inequity," *Journal of Abnormal and Social Psychology* 67 (1963): 422–436; J. Stacey Adams, "Inequity in Social Exchange," in *Advances in Experimental Social Psychology,* vol. 2, edited by L. Berkowitz (New York: Academic Press, 1965), 267–299.
47. Adams, "Toward an Understanding of Inequity," 422–436; Adams, "Inequity in Social Exchange," 267–299.
48. Richard C. Huseman, John D. Hatfield, and Edward W. Miles, "A New Perspective on Equity Theory: The Equity Sensitivity Construct," *Academy of Management Review* 12, no. 2 (1987): 222–234; Richard A. Cosier and Dan R. Dalton, "Equity Theory and Time: A Reformulation," *Academy of Management Review* 8, no. 2 (1983): 311–319; Amanda Bennett, "Paying Workers to Meet Goals Spreads, But Gauging Performance Proves Tough," *Wall Street Journal,* 10 September 1991, B1, B2.
49. Michael A. Verespej, "Merit Raises: 'A Joke,'" *Industry Week,* 19 February 1990, 73–74; Joani Nelson-Horchler, "The Pay Revolt Brews," *Industry Week,* 18 June 1990, 28–30, 32–36; Amanda Bennett, "Caught in the Middle," *Wall Street Journal,* 18 April 1990, R9–R10.
50. Campbell and Pritchard, "Motivation Theory in Industrial and Organizational Psychology," 109–110.
51. Steers and Porter, *Motivation and Work Behavior,* 59; Robert C. Beck, *Motivation: Theories and Principles,* 3rd ed. (Englewood Cliffs, N.J.: Prentice Hall, 1990), 153; Moorhead and Griffin, *Organizational Behavior,* 44; Judith L. Komaki, Timothy Coombs, and Stephen Schepman, "Motivational Implications of Reinforcement Theory," in *Motivation and Work Behavior,* 5th ed., edited by Richard M. Steers and Lyman W. Porter (New York: McGraw-Hill, 1991), 87–106.
52. W. Clay Hamner, "Reinforcement Theory and Contingency Management in Organizational Settings," in *Motivation and Work Behavior,* 5th ed., edited by Richard M. Steers and Lyman W. Porter (New York: McGraw-Hill, 1991), 61–87; Komaki, Coombs, and Schepman, "Motivational Implications of Reinforcement Theory," 87–106.
53. Jolie Solomon, "Managers Focus on Low-Wage Workers," *Wall Street Journal,* 9 May 1989, B1.
54. Adi Ignatius, "Now If Ms. Wong Insults a Customer, She Gets an Award," *Wall Street Journal,* 24 January 1989, A1, A17.
55. Richard D. Avery and John M. Ivancevich, "Punishment in Organizations: A Review, Propositions, and Research Suggestions," *Academy of Management Review* 5 (1980): 123–132; Janice M. Beyer and Harrison M. Trice, "A Field Study of the Use and Perceived Effects of Discipline in Controlling Work Performance," *Academy of Management Journal* 4 (1984): 743–764.
56. Ferdinand F. Fournies, "Why Employees Don't Do What They're Supposed to Do," *Success,* April 1990, 42–43.
57. Hamner, "Reinforcement Theory and Contingency Management in Organizational Settings," 74–75; Gunsch, "Award Programs at Work," 85–89.
58. Hamner, "Reinforcement Theory and Contingency Management in Organizational Settings," 74–77.
59. Hamner, "Reinforcement Theory and Contingency Management in Organizational Settings," 75.
60. Hamner, "Reinforcement Theory and Contingency Management in Organizational Settings," 76.
61. Hamner, "Reinforcement Theory and Contingency Management in Organizational Settings," 75–76.
62. Hamner, "Reinforcement Theory and Contingency Management in Organizational Settings," 75–77.
63. Moorhead and Griffin, *Organizational Behavior,* 175.
64. Lawler, "The Design of Effective Reward Systems," 255–265; Nancy J. Perry, "Here Come Richer, Riskier Pay Plans," *Fortune,* 19 December 1988, 50–52, 54, 58.
65. Earl Ingram II, "The Advantages of Knowledge-Based Pay," *Personnel Journal,* April 1990, 138–140; Lawler, "The Design of Effective Reward Systems," 255–265; Perry, "Here Come Richer, Riskier Pay Plans," 50–52, 54, 58.
66. Michael Schroeder, "Watching the Bottom Line Instead of the Clock," *Business Week,* 7 November 1988, 134, 136.
67. Perry, "Here Come Richer, Riskier Pay Plans," 52, 54.
68. Kevin M. Paulsen, "Gain Sharing: A Group Motivator," *MW,* May–June 1989, 24–25.
69. Perry, "Here Come Richer, Riskier Pay Plans," 52.
70. William K. Sayers, "ESOPs Are No Fable," *Small Business Reports,* June 1990, 57–60; John Case, "Collective Effort," *Inc.,* January 1992, 32–35, 38, 42–43.
71. Lance D. Tane and Michael E. Treacy, "Benefits That Bend with Employees' Needs," *Nation's Business,* April 1984, 80–82.
72. Bruce G. Posner, "If at First You Don't Succeed," *Inc.,* May 1989, 132, 134.
73. Gunsch, "Award Programs at Work," 87; Dennis T. Jaffe and Cynthia D. Scott, "Bridging Your Workers' 'Motivation Gap,'" *Nation's Business,* March 1989, 30–32.
74. See Note 1.

CHAPTER 15

1. Adapted from James C. Hyatt and Amal Kumar Naj, "GE Is No Place for Autocrats, Welch Decrees," *Wall Street Journal,* 3 March 1992, B1, B10; Noel Tichy and Ram Charan, "Speed, Simplicity, Self-Confidence: An Interview with Jack Welch," *Harvard Business Review,* September-October 1989, 112–120; John S. McClenahen, "Training Americans for Work," *Industry Week,* 19 September 1988, 52–60; Stratford P. Sherman, "The Mind of Jack Welch," *Fortune,* 27 March 1989, 39–50; Amal Kumar Naj, "GE's Latest Invention: A Way to Move Ideas from Lab to Market," *Wall Street Journal,* 14 June 1990, A1, A9; Stratford P. Sherman, "Today's Leaders Look to Tomorrow," *Fortune,* 26 March 1990, 30–32; Martha H. Peak, "Anti-manager Named Manager of the Year," *Management Review,* October 1991, 7.
2. John P. Kotter, *The Leadership Factor* (New York: Free Press, 1988), 11–15.
3. Gary A. Yukl, *Leadership in Organizations,* 2nd ed. (Englewood Cliffs, N.J.: Prentice Hall, 1989), 5, 12–13, 37; Bernard M. Bass, *Bass & Stogdill's Handbook of Leadership* (New York: Free Press, 1990), 11–18; Peter F. Drucker, "Leadership: More Doing than Dash," *Wall Street Journal,* 6 January 1988, 14.
4. Henry Mintzberg, *Power In and Around Organizations* (Englewood Cliffs, N.J.: Prentice Hall, 1983), 4–5; Yukl, *Leadership in Organizations,* 14; Gary Yukl, "Managerial Leadership: A Review of Theory and Research," *Journal of Management* 15, no. 2 (1989): 251–289.
5. Richard Poe, "A Winning Spirit," *Success,* July–August 1990, 60–72.
6. Paul Hersey and Kenneth H. Blanchard, *Management of Organizational Behavior,* 5th ed. (Englewood Cliffs, N.J.: Prentice Hall, 1989), 207; Gary Yukl and Tom Taber, "The Effective Use of Managerial Power," *Personnel,* March–April 1987, 37–44; Philip M. Podsakoff and Chester A. Schriesheim, "Field Studies of French and Raven's Bases of Power: Critique, Reanalysis, and Suggestions for Future Research," *Psychological Bulletin* 97, no. 3 (1985): 387–411; Yukl, *Leadership in Organizations,* 44–52; Thomas A. Stewart, "New Ways to Exercise Power," *Fortune,* 6 November 1989, 52–64.
7. Podsakoff and Schriesheim, "Field Studies of French and Raven's Bases of Power," 387–411; Yukl, *Leadership in Organizations,* 44–52; E. B. Knauft, Renee A. Berger, and Sandra T. Gray, *Profiles of Excellence* (San Francisco: Jossey-Bass, 1991), 42–50.
8. Bass, *Bass & Stogdill's Handbook of Leadership,* 236–238; Yukl, *Leadership in Organizations,* 17–18; Podsakoff and Schriesheim, "Field Studies of French and Raven's Bases of Power," 387–411; Knauft, Berger, and Gray, *Profiles of Excellence,* 42–50.
9. Yukl, *Leadership in Organizations,* 18–19; Podsakoff and Schriesheim, "Field Studies of French and Raven's Bases of Power," 387–411; Knauft, Berger, and Gray, *Profiles of Excellence,* 42–50.
10. Yukl, *Leadership in Organizations,* 20–21; Hersey and Blanchard, *Management of Organizational Behavior,* 210; Knauft, Berger, and Gray, *Profiles of Excellence,* 42–50.
11. Bass, *Bass & Stogdill's Handbook of Leadership,* 233–234; Yukl, *Leadership in Organiza-*

tions, 22–23; Podsakoff and Schriesheim, "Field Studies of French and Raven's Bases of Power," 387–411; Hersey and Blanchard, *Management of Organizational Behavior,* 210–211; Knauft, Berger, and Gray, *Profiles of Excellence,* 42–50.

12. Podsakoff and Schriesheim, "Field Studies of French and Raven's Bases of Power," 387–411; Bass, *Bass & Stogdill's Handbook of Leadership,* 234–235; Yukl and Taber, "The Effective Use of Managerial Power," 37–44; Knauft, Berger, and Gray, *Profiles of Excellence,* 42–50.

13. Patti Reid, "Student Takes His Recycling Drive Straight to the Top," *New York Times,* 1 March 1992, sec. 12, 1, 6; Nancy Marx Better, "Green Teens," *New York Times Magazine,* 8 March 1992, 44, 66, 68.

14. Yukl, *Leadership in Organizations,* 13.

15. Yukl and Taber, "The Effective Use of Managerial Power," 37–44; Yukl, *Leadership in Organizations,* 43–52; Bass, *Bass & Stogdill's Handbook of Leadership,* 247–250.

16. Stewart, "New Ways to Exercise Power," 52–64; Thomas A. Stewart, "CEOs See Clout Shifting," *Fortune,* 6 November 1989, 66; Peter Block, "How to Be the New Kind of Manager," *Working Woman,* July 1990, 51–54; Jay A. Conger, "Leadership: The Art of Empowering Others," *Academy of Management Executive* 3, no. 1 (1989): 17–24.

17. Patrick Houston, "High Anxiety," *Business Month,* June 1990, 32–41; Stewart, "New Ways to Exercise Power," 52–64.

18. William D. Hitt, *Ethics and Leadership: Putting Theory into Practice* (Columbus, Ohio: Battelle Press, 1990), 1–4, 140–141; Yukl, *Leadership in Organizations,* 50.

19. Mintzberg, *Power In and Around Organizations,* 171; Robert W. Allen, Dan L. Madison, Lyman W. Porter, Patricia A. Renwick, and Bronston T. Mayes, "Organizational Politics: Tactics and Characteristics of Its Actors," in *Contemporary Readings in Organizational Behavior,* edited by Fred Luthans and Kenneth R. Thompson (New York: McGraw-Hill, 1981), 297–304; Bass, *Bass & Stogdill's Handbook of Leadership,* 231–257, 290–291; Yukl, *Leadership in Organizations,* 25–26; Abraham Zaleznik, *The Managerial Mystique: Restoring Leadership in Business* (New York: Harper & Row, 1990), 150–151, 243–244.

20. Yukl, *Leadership in Organizations,* 25–27; Mintzberg, *Power In and Around Organizations,* 187–210; Allen et al., "Organizational Politics," 297–304.

21. Bill Saporito, "Campbell Soup Gets Piping Hot," *Fortune,* 9 September 1991, 142–148.

22. Robert G. Lord, Christy L. De Vader, and George M. Alliger, "A Meta-Analysis of the Relation between Personality Traits and Leadership Perceptions: An Application of Validity Generalization Procedures," *Journal of Applied Psychology* 71, no. 3 (1986): 402–410; Arthur G. Jago, "Leadership Perspectives in Theory and Research," *Management Science* 28, no. 3 (1982): 315–336.

23. Yukl, "Managerial Leadership," 251–289; Yukl, *Leadership in Organizations,* 174–175; Bass, *Bass & Stogdill's Handbook of Leadership,* 59–88.

24. Bass, *Bass & Stogdill's Handbook of Leadership,* 59–88; Lord, De Vader, and Alliger, "A Meta-Analysis of the Relation between Personality Traits and Leadership Perceptions," 402–410; Yukl, *Leadership in Organizations,* 175–176.

25. Jago, "Leadership Perspectives in Theory and Research," 315–336; Lord, De Vader, and Alliger, "A Meta-Analysis of the Relation between Personality Traits and Leadership Perceptions," 402–410; Yukl, *Leadership in Organizations,* 175–176; Bass, *Bass & Stogdill's Handbook of Leadership,* 59–88.

26. Jago, "Leadership Perspectives in Theory and Research," 315–336; Yukl, "Managerial Leadership," 251–289; Bass, *Bass & Stogdill's Handbook of Leadership,* 419–420.

27. Robert Tannenbaum and Warren H. Schmidt, "How to Choose a Leadership Pattern," *Harvard Business Review,* May–June 1973, 162–180.

28. Tannenbaum and Schmidt, "How to Choose a Leadership Pattern," 162–180.

29. Thomas R. Horton, *"What Works for Me"* (New York: Amacom, 1986), 37–56.

30. Yukl, *Leadership in Organizations,* 81–82; Hersey and Blanchard, *Management of Organizational Behavior,* 92–98.

31. "Conversation . . . with Rensis Likert," in *Likert's System 4,* rev. ed. (New York: Amacom, 1975), 6–12; Hersey and Blanchard, *Management of Organizational Behavior,* 92–98; Yukl, *Leadership in Organizations,* 81–82.

32. Bass, *Bass & Stogdill's Handbook of Leadership,*511–524; Yukl, *Leadership in Organizations,* 74–80.

33. Yukl, *Leadership in Organizations,* 74–80; Bass, *Bass & Stogdill's Handbook of Leadership,* 511–524.

34. Patricia O'Toole, "How Do You Build a $44 Million Company? By Saying 'Please,'" *Working Woman,* April 1990, 88–92.

35. Paul C. Nystrom, "Managers and the Hi-hi Leader Myth," *Academy of Management Journal* 21, no. 2 (1978): 325–331; Jago, "Leadership Perspectives in Theory and Research," 315–336; Yukl, "Managerial Leadership," 251–289; Bass, *Bass & Stogdill's Handbook of Leadership,* 511–524.

36. Robert R. Blake and Jane Srygley Mouton, "A Comparative Analysis of Situationalism and 9,9 Management by Principle," *Organizational Dynamics,* Spring 1982, 20–43; Robert R. Blake and Jane S. Mouton, *The Versatile Manager: A Grid Profile* (Homewood, Ill.: Dow Jones-Irwin, 1980), 10–12; Robert R. Blake and Jane Srygley Mouton, *The Managerial Grid* (Houston: Gulf, 1964), 8–9.

37. Blake and Mouton, *The Versatile Manager,* 10–12; Blake and Mouton, *The Managerial Grid,* 8–9; Blake and Mouton, "A Comparative Analysis of Situationalism and 9,9 Management by Principle," 20–43.

38. Bass, *Bass & Stogdill's Handbook of Leadership,* 494–500; Yukl, *Leadership in Organizations,* 194–197; Jago, "Leadership Perspectives in Theory and Research," 315–336; Yukl, "Managerial Leadership," 194–197, 251–289.

39. Meme Drumwright, "Contingency Theories of Leadership: A Review," *Baylor Business Studies* 12, no. 3 (August–October 1981): 29–43.

40. Yukl, *Leadership in Organizations,* 194–198; Bass, *Bass & Stogdill's Handbook of Leadership,* 495–500; Jago, "Leadership Perspectives in Theory and Research," 315–336.

41. Jago, "Leadership Perspectives in Theory and Research," 315–336; Yukl, *Leadership in Organizations,* 194–198; Bass, *Bass & Stogdill's Handbook of Leadership,* 495–500.

42. Bass, *Bass & Stogdill's Handbook of Leadership,* 495–500; Jago, "Leadership Perspectives in Theory and Research," 315–336; Yukl, *Leadership in Organizations,* 194–198.

43. Yukl, *Leadership in Organizations,* 194–198; Bass, *Bass & Stogdill's Handbook of Leadership,* 495–500; Jago, "Leadership Perspectives in Theory and Research," 315–336.

44. Drumwright, "Contingency Theories of Leadership," 29–43; Jago, "Leadership Perspectives in Theory and Research," 315–336; Yukl, *Leadership in Organizations,* 194–198; Bass, *Bass & Stogdill's Handbook of Leadership,* 495–500; Lawrence H. Peters, Daniel D. Hartke, and John T. Pohlmann, "Fiedler's Contingency Theory of Leadership: An Application of the Meta-Analysis Procedures of Schmidt and Hunter," *Psychological Bulletin* 97 (1985): 274–285.

45. Bass, *Bass & Stogdill's Handbook of Leadership,* 495–508; Peters, Hartke, and Pohlmann, "Fiedler's Contingency Theory of Leadership," 274–285; Drumwright, "Contingency Theories of Leadership," 29–43; Jago, "Leadership Perspectives in Theory and Research," 315–336.

46. Martin G. Evans, "The Effects of Supervisory Behavior on the Path–Goal Relationship," *Organizational Behavior and Human Performance* 5 (1970): 277–298; Robert J. House, "A Path Goal Theory of Leader Effectiveness," *Administrative Science Quarterly* 16 (1971): 321–338; Robert J. House and Terrence R. Mitchell, "Path–Goal Theory of Leadership," *Journal of Contemporary Business,* Autumn 1974, 81–97.

47. House, "A Path Goal Theory of Leader Effectiveness," 321–338; House and Mitchell, "Path-Goal Theory of Leadership," 81–97.

48. House and Mitchell, "Path-Goal Theory of Leadership," 81–97; Drumwright, "Contingency Theories of Leadership," 29–43.

49. House, "A Path Goal Theory of Leader Effectiveness," 321–338; House and Mitchell, "Path-Goal Theory of Leadership," 81–97.

50. House and Mitchell, "Path-Goal Theory of Leadership," 81–97; House, "A Path Goal Theory of Leader Effectiveness," 321–338.

51. Yukl, *Leadership in Organizations,* 101–102; Jago, "Leadership Perspectives in Theory and Research," 315–336.

52. John Holusha, "Grace Pastiak's 'Web of Inclusion,'" *New York Times,* 5 May 1991, sec. 3, 1, 6.

53. Bass, *Bass & Stogdill's Handbook of Leadership,* 628–633; Yukl, *Leadership in Organizations,* 102–104; Drumwright, "Contingency Theories of Leadership," 29–43.

54. Victor H. Vroom and Arthur G. Jago, "On the Validity of the Vroom-Yetton Model," *Journal of Applied Psychology* 63 (1978): 151–162; Yukl, "Managerial Leadership," 251–289.

55. Jago, "Leadership Perspectives in Theory and Research," 315–336; Yukl, *Leadership in Organizations,* 112–117; Vroom and Jago, "On the Validity of the Vroom-Yetton Model," 151–162.

56. Victor H. Vroom and Arthur G. Jago, *The New Leadership: Managing Participation in Organizations* (Englewood Cliffs, N.J.: Prentice Hall, 1988), 19–20, 117–122; Bass, *Bass & Stogdill's Handbook of Leadership,* 465–470; Vroom and Jago, "On the Validity of the Vroom-Yetton Model," 151–162; Yukl, *Leadership in Organizations,* 112–117; Drumwright, "Contingency Theories of Leadership," 29–43.

57. Vroom and Jago, *The New Leadership,* 25–26, 136–138; Yukl, *Leadership in Organiza-*

tions, 112–117; Vroom and Jago, "On the Validity of the Vroom-Yetton Model," 151–162; Bass, *Bass & Stogdill's Handbook of Leadership,* 465–470.
58. Vroom and Jago, *The New Leadership,* 26–27; Vroom and Jago, "On the Validity of the Vroom-Yetton Model," 151–162.
59. Vroom and Jago, *The New Leadership,* 28–29; Jago, "Leadership Perspectives in Theory and Research," 315–336; Vroom and Jago, "On the Validity of the Vroom-Yetton Model," 151–162.
60. Vroom and Jago, *The New Leadership,* 180–181; Yukl, "Managerial Leadership," 251–289; Bass, *Bass & Stogdill's Handbook of Leadership,* 465–470.
61. Hersey and Blanchard, *Management of Organizational Behavior,* 171–177.
62. Hersey and Blanchard, *Management of Organizational Behavior,* 172–179.
63. Hersey and Blanchard, *Management of Organizational Behavior,* 172–182.
64. Jane R. Goodson, Gail W. McGee, and James F. Cashman, "Situational Leadership Theory," *Group & Organization Studies* 14, no. 4 (December 1989): 446–461; Robert P. Vecchio, "Situational Leadership Theory: An Examination of a Prescriptive Theory," *Journal of Applied Psychology* 72, no. 3 (1987): 444–451; Claude L. Graeff, "The Situational Leadership Theory: A Critical View," *Academy of Management Review* 8, no. 2 (1983): 285–291.
65. Bass, *Bass & Stogdill's Handbook of Leadership,* 683–686; Yukl, *Leadership in Organizations,* 108–112.
66. Yukl, *Leadership in Organizations,* 108–112; Bass, *Bass & Stogdill's Handbook of Leadership,* 683–686.
67. Brian Dumaine, "Who Needs a Boss?" *Fortune,* 7 May 1990, 54–55; Yukl, *Leadership in Organizations,* 108–112; Bass, *Bass & Stogdill's Handbook of Leadership,* 683–686.
68. William D. Hitt, *Ethics and Leadership* (Columbus, Ohio: Battelle, 1990), 160–161; John J. Hater and Bernard M. Bass, "Superiors' Evaluations and Subordinates' Perceptions of Transformational and Transactional Leadership," *Journal of Applied Psychology* 73, no. 4 (1988): 695–702; Allan R. Cohen and David L. Bradford, "Influence without Authority: The Use of Alliances, Reciprocity, and Exchange to Accomplish Work," *Organizational Dynamics,* 17, no. 3 (1989): 5–17.
69. Cohen and Bradford, "Influence without Authority," 5–17; Bernard M. Bass, *Leadership and Performance beyond Expectations* (New York: Free Press, 1985), 11–20, 26–27; Yukl, *Leadership in Organizations,* 210–211.
70. Jay A. Conger, *The Charismatic Leader* (San Francisco: Jossey-Bass, 1989), 25–34; Hitt, *Ethics and Leadership* 161–167; Bernard M. Bass, "Leadership: Good, Better, Best," *Organizational Dynamics* 13 (Winter 1985): 26–40; Noel M. Tichy and David O. Ulrich, "SMR Forum: The Leadership Challenge—A Call for the Transformational Leader," *Sloan Management Review,* Fall 1984, 59–68; Bernard M. Bass, "From Transactional to Transformational Leadership: Learning to Share the Vision," *Organizational Dynamics* 18, no. 3 (Winter 1990): 19–31.
71. Bass, "From Transactional to Transformational Leadership," 19–31.
72. Bo Burlingham, "This Woman Has Changed Business Forever," *Inc.,* June 1990, 34, 36–38, 41–42, 44–46.
73. Knauft, Berger, and Gray, *Profiles of Excellence,* 10, 33–41.
74. Zaleznik, *The Managerial Mystique,* 240–241; Bass, *Leadership and Performance,* 27–31.
75. See note 1.

CHAPTER 16

1. Adapted from Tracy E. Benson, "Empowered Employees Sharpen the Edge," *Industry Week,* 19 February 1990, 12–20; David J. Dent, "Overnight Sensation," *Black Enterprise,* June 1988, 308–314; Brian Dumaine, "Who Needs a Boss?" *Fortune,* 7 May 1990, 52–60; Dean Foust, Jonathan Kapstein, Pia Farrell, Peter Finch, and Chris Power, "Mr. Smith Goes Global," *Business Week,* 13 February 1989, 66–72; Eric Olsen, "Control through Chaos: Build a Team that Never Drops the Ball," *Success,* November 1990, 40–44; Daniel Pearl, "Federal Express Finds Its Pioneering Formula Falls Flat Overseas," *Wall Street Journal,* 15 April 1991, A1, A6; Frederick W. Smith, "Empowering Employees," *Small Business Reports,* January 1991, 15–20; Todd Vogel, "Can UPS Deliver the Goods in a New World?" *Business Week,* 4 June 1990, 80–82; Therese R. Welter, "New-Collar Workers," *Industry Week,* 15 August 1988, 36–39.
2. John J. Gabarro, "The Development of Working Relationships," in *Handbook of Organizational Behavior,* edited by Jay W. Lorsch (Englewood Cliffs, N.J.: Prentice Hall, 1987), 172–189.
3. Clayton P. Alderfer, "An Intergroup Perspective on Group Dynamics," in *Handbook of Organizational Behavior,* edited by Jay W. Lorsch (Englewood Cliffs, N.J.: Prentice Hall, 1987), 190–222; Stephen P. Robbins, *Organizational Behavior,* 4th ed. (Englewood Cliffs, N.J.: Prentice Hall, 1989), 226.
4. John Case, "The Change Masters," *Inc.,* March 1992, 58–61, 64, 66, 70.
5. "Pluralism," NBC Nightly News, hosted by Tom Brokaw, 23 October 1991; The Conference Board, "Heard at the Annual Quality Conference: Innovation, Transformation, Customer Focus," *Quality Briefing,* Fall 1991, 2; "Taking Lessons from the Dance," *New York Times,* 8 September 1991, sec. 3, 23.
6. B. Aubrey Fisher and Donald G. Ellis, *Small Group Decision Making,* 3rd ed. (New York: McGraw-Hill, 1990), 10.
7. Fisher and Ellis, *Small Group Decision Making,* 20–21.
8. Paul S. Goodman, Elizabeth C. Ravlin, and Linda Argote, "Current Thinking about Groups: Setting the Stage for New Ideas," in *Designing Effective Work Groups,* edited by Paul S. Goodman and Associates (San Francisco: Jossey-Bass, 1986), 1–33; Fisher and Ellis, *Small Group Decision Making,* 20–22.
9. Fred Moody, "Mr. Software," *New York Times Magazine,* 25 August 1991, 26, 28–31, 54, 56, 59; "Microsoft Plans for 3 to Succeed Michael Hallman," *Wall Street Journal,* 4 February 1992, A9.
10. Hugh J. Arnold and Daniel C. Feldman, *Organizational Behavior* (New York: McGraw-Hill, 1986), 187; Fisher and Ellis, *Small Group Decision Making,* 21–22; Goodman, Ravlin, and Argote, "Current Thinking about Groups," 1–33; Bernard M. Bass, *Bass & Stogdill's Handbook of Leadership* (New York: Free Press, 1990), 612.
11. John E. Hocking, Duane C. Margreiter, and Cal Hylton, "Intra-audience Effects: A Field Test," *Human Communication Research* 3 (1977): 243–249; Fisher and Ellis, *Small Group Decision Making,* 21.
12. John S. McClenahen, "Not Fun in the Sun," *Industry Week,* 15 October 1990, 22–24; Olsen, "Control through Chaos," 40, 42, 44; Alex Prud'homme, "Executive Retreats: Let's Get Physical," *Business Month,* March 1990, 61–66.
13. Anthony DePalma, "How Undergraduates Can Succeed: Study Together, and in Small Classes," *New York Times,* 6 November 1991, sec. b, 9.
14. Robbins, *Organizational Behavior,* 226–227; Gregory Moorhead and Ricky W. Griffin, *Organizational Behavior,* 2nd ed. (Boston: Houghton Mifflin, 1989), 261–262.
15. Joseph Weber, "With This Lifeguard, It's Sink or Swim," *Business Week,* 18 February 1991, 56, 58.
16. Sara Lee 1990 Annual Report, 46.
17. Arnold and Feldman, *Organizational Behavior,* 182.
18. "NAFE Bulletin Board," *Executive Female,* November–December 1991, 58.
19. John Hoerr, "The Payoff from Teamwork," *Business Week,* 10 July 1989, 56–62; George S. Odiorne, "The New Breed of Supervisor: Leaders in Self-Managed Work Teams," *Supervision,* August 1991, 14–17.
20. Hoerr, "The Payoff from Teamwork," 58.
21. Russel Mitchell, "How Ford Hit the Bull's-Eye with Taurus," *Business Week,* 30 June 1986, 69–70.
22. Thomas Owens, "The Self-Managing Work Team," *Small Business Report,* February 1991, 53–65; Hoerr, "The Payoff from Teamwork," 62; Dumaine, "Who Needs a Boss?" 52–55, 58, 59; "Keep an Eye Off Your Workers," *Business Ethics* 5, no. 5, September–October 1991, 9; Joann S. Lublin, "Trying to Increase Worker Productivity, More Employers Alter Management Style," *Wall Street Journal,* 13 February 1992, B1, B3.
23. John B. Miner, *Organizational Behavior: Performance and Productivity* (New York: Random House, 1988), 280–281; John Hoerr, "Work Teams Can Rev Up Paper-Pushers, Too," *Business Week,* 28 November 1988, 64, 68, 72; John Hoerr, "Benefits for the Back Office, Too," *Business Week,* 10 July 1989, 59.
24. Kenneth D. Benne and Paul Sheats, "Functional Roles of Group Members," *Journal of Social Issues* 4 (1948): 41–49; Fisher and Ellis, *Small Group Decision Making,* 210–213.
25. Terence R. Mitchell and James R. Larson, Jr., *People in Organizations: An Introduction to Organizational Behavior,* 3rd ed. (New York: McGraw-Hill, 1987), 265–266; C. D. Fisher and R. Gitelson, "A Meta-Analysis of the Correlates of Role Conflict and Ambiguity," *Journal of Applied Psychology* 68 (1983): 320–333; R. S. Schuler, "Role Perceptions, Satisfaction, and Performance: A Partial Reconciliation," *Journal of Applied Psychology* 60 (1975): 683–687.
26. Norm Alster, "What Flexible Workers Can Do," *Fortune,* 13 February 1989, 62–64, 66.
27. Arthur G. Bedeian, Beverly G. Burke, and Richard Moffett, "Outcomes of Work–Family Conflict among Married Male and Female Professionals," *Journal of Management* 14, no. 3 (1988): 475–491.
28. Mitchell and Larson, *People in Organizations,* 265.

29. Fisher and Gitelson, "A Meta-Analysis of the Correlates of Role Conflict and Ambiguity," 320–333.
30. Mitchell and Larson, *People in Organizations,* 266–267; R. D. Caplan, "Organizational Stress and Individual Strain: A Socio-Psychological Study of Risk Factors in Coronary Heart Disease among Administrators, Engineers, and Scientists" (Doctoral Dissertation, University of Michigan, 1971), *Dissertation Abstracts International,* 32, 6706b–6707b (University Microfilms No. 72-14822); M. Friedman, R. H. Rosenman, and V. Carrol, "Changes in Serum Cholesterol and Blood Clotting Time in Men Subjected to Cyclic Variation of Occupational Stress," *Circulation* 17 (1958): 852–861.
31. Daniel C. Feldman, "The Development and Enforcement of Group Norms," *Academy of Management Review* 9, no. 1 (1984): 47–53; Patricia H. Andrews, "Group Conformity," in *Small Group Communication,* 5th ed., edited by Robert Cathcart and Larry Samovar (Dubuque, Iowa: Brown, 1988), 225–235; Mitchell and Larson, *People in Organizations,* 268–269.
32. Stephanie Strom, "Harassment Rules Often Not Pushed," *New York Times,* 20 October 1991, sec. a, 1, 22.
33. Feldman, "The Development and Enforcement of Group Norms," 47–53.
34. Strom, "Harassment Rules Often Not Pushed," 22.
35. "Keep an Eye Off Your Workers," 9.
36. Feldman, "The Development and Enforcement of Group Norms," 47–53; Barnaby J. Feder, "Helping Corporate America Hew to the Straight and Narrow," *New York Times,* 3 November 1991, sec. 3, 5.
37. Martha E. Mangelsdorf, "Managing the New Work Force," *Inc.,* January 1990, 78–81, 83.
38. Feldman, "The Development and Enforcement of Group Norms," 47–53.
39. Bass, *Bass & Stogdill's Handbook of Leadership,* 600–605; Fisher and Ellis, *Small Group Decision Making,* 38–40; Mitchell and Larson, *People in Organizations,* 246–249.
40. Fisher and Ellis, *Small Group Decision Making,* 38–40; Mitchell and Larson, *People in Organizations,* 246–249; Ferdinand Protzman, "Keeping in Step in a Free Market," *New York Times,* 15 October 1991, sec. d, 1, 8.
41. Mitchell and Larson, *People in Organizations,* 246–249; Fisher and Ellis, *Small Group Decision Making,* 38–40; Daniel R. Denison, *Corporate Culture and Organizational Effectiveness* (New York: Wiley, 1990), 95–108.
42. Claudia Deutsch, "To Sell a New Idea, Vary the Pitch," *New York Times,* 31 March 1991, sec. 3, 19.
43. E. B. Knauft, Renee A. Berger, and Sandra T. Gray, *Profiles of Excellence* (San Francisco: Jossey-Bass, 1991), 106–107.
44. Robbins, *Organizational Behavior,* 256–257.
45. Robbins, *Organizational Behavior,* 227–230.
46. Dumaine, "Who Needs a Boss?" 55.
47. Bruce W. Tuckman and Mary Ann C. Jensen, "Stages of Small-Group Development Revisited," *Group & Organization Studies* 2, no. 4 (1977): 419–427.
48. Robbins, *Organizational Behavior,* 227–231.
49. Mitchell and Larson, *People in Organizations,* 229–230; Hoerr, "The Payoff from Teamwork," 56–58; Wendy Zellner, "For Auto Workers, It's Team Spirit vs. Suspicion," *Business Week,* 10 July 1989, 60–61.
50. W. Barnett Pearce, "Trust in Interpersonal Communications," *Speech Monographs* 41 (1974): 236–244; Fisher and Ellis, *Small Group Decision Making,* 28–29.
51. Moody, "Mr. Software," 56; Peter Kilborn, "Worker Takeover Opens a New Path for Industry," *New York Times,* 22 November 1991, A24.
52. Hoerr, "The Payoff from Teamwork," 56–58.
53. Agis Salpukas, "How Railroads Cut Jobs without Drawing Blood," *New York Times,* 13 October 1991, sec. 3, 9.
54. Feder, "Helping Corporate America Hew to the Straight and Narrow," 5.
55. Fisher and Ellis, *Small Group Decision Making,* 28–29.
56. Lorraine P. Holden, "Teamwork: A Delicate Balance," *Managers Magazine,* June 1990, 12–19, 65.
57. Marilyn E. Gist, "Organizational Behavior: Group Structure, Process, and Effectiveness," *Journal of Management* 13, no. 2 (1987): 237–257; Fisher and Ellis, *Small Group Decision Making,* 23.
58. Anne B. Fisher, "Morale Crisis," *Fortune,* 18 November 1991, 70–72, 76, 80.
59. J. Richard Hackman and Richard E. Walton, "Leading Groups in Organizations," in *Designing Effective Work Groups,* edited by Paul S. Goodman and Associates (San Francisco: Jossey-Bass, 1986), 72–119; J. Richard Hackman, "The Design of Work Teams," in *Handbook of Organizational Behavior,* edited by Jay W. Lorsch (Englewood Cliffs, N.J.: Prentice Hall, 1987), 315–342.
60. Dumaine, "Who Needs a Boss?" 59.
61. David Gonzalez, "An Immigrant's Field of Dreams Transforms a Dingy Patch of the Bronx," *New York Times,* 12 November 1991, sec. b, 3.
62. Celia Kuperszmid Lehrman, "Just Tell Her She Can't," *Executive Female,* March–April 1990, 41–43.
63. Thomas C. Hayes, "Compaq Ousts Its Legendary Chief," *New York Times,* 26 October 1991, 33, 34.
64. M. Kamil Kozan, "Cultural Influences on Styles of Handling Interpersonal Conflicts: Comparisons among Jordanian, Turkish, and U.S. Managers," *Human Relations* 42, no. 9 (1989): 787–799.
65. Fisher and Ellis, *Small Group Decision Making,* 256–257; Amanda Bennett, "Personalizing the Conflict at Eastern Air," *Wall Street Journal,* 9 March 1989, B1.
66. Aimee L. Stern, "Converse in Adland, Playing Catch-Up Ball," *New York Times,* 24 March 1991, sec. 3, 5.
67. Dean Tjosvold, "Making Conflict Productive," *Personnel Administrator,* June 1984, 121–130; Kenneth Thomas, "Conflict and Conflict Management," in *Handbook of Industrial and Organizational Psychology,* edited by Marvin D. Dunnette (Chicago: Rand McNally, 1976), 889–935; Fisher and Ellis, *Small Group Decision Making,* 256–257; Stern, "Converse in Adland," 5.
68. L. R. Hoffman and N. R. F. Maier, "Quality and Acceptance of Problem Solutions by Members of Homogeneous and Heterogeneous Groups," *Journal of Abnormal and Social Psychology* 62 (1961): 401–407; Richard E. Walton and John M. Dutton, "The Management of Interdepartmental Conflict: A Model and Review," *Administrative Science Quarterly,* March 1969, 73–84; Thomas, "Conflict and Conflict Management," 889–935.
69. Mitchell and Larson, *People in Organizations,* 415–419; Arnold and Feldman, *Organizational Behavior,* 212–217; Robbins, *Organizational Behavior,* 371–374; Robert H. Doktor and Marvin D. Loper, "Interpersonal Relationships," in *Handbook for Professional Managers,* edited by Lester R. Bittel and Jackson E. Ramsey (New York: McGraw-Hill, 1985), 424–425.
70. Arnold and Feldman, *Organizational Behavior,* 227; Stern, "Converse in Adland," 5.
71. Fisher and Ellis, *Small Group Decision Making,* 276; Arnold and Feldman, *Organizational Behavior,* 227–228.
72. See note 1.
73. Information on the Olympic Job Opportunities Program and the companies and athletes involved based on information from Stephanie Anderson Forest and Julia Flynn Siler, "To Go for the Gold, You Gotta Have Green," *Business Week,* 17 February 1992, 137.

CHAPTER 17

1. Adapted from "An Interview with General Motors' Alvie Smith," *Communication World,* June 1984, 19–21; Jerry Flint, "A Year for Living Dangerously," *Forbes,* 4 March 1991, 84–85; Paul Ingrassia and Joseph B. White, "GM Posts Record '91 Loss of $4.45 Billion, Sends Tough Message to UAW on Closings," *Wall Street Journal,* 25 February 1992, A3, A6; Andrea Gabor, "General Motors Reinvents the Wheel," *U.S. News & World Report,* 21 August 1989, 40–41; Bruce Goodsite, "General Motors Attacks Its Frozen Middle," *Communication World,* October 1987, 20–23; S. C. Gwynne, "The Right Stuff," *Time,* 29 October 1990, 74–84; S. C. Gwynne, "Two Sides of a Giant," *Time,* 19 February 1990, 68–70; Michelle Krebs, "Satellite System to Link GM, Dealers," *Automotive News,* 21 May 1990, 1, 55; Patrick McKeand, "GM Division Builds a Classic System to Share Internal Information," *Public Relations Journal,* November 1990, 24–26, 41; M. M. Petty, James Cashman, Anson Seers, Robert Stevenson, Charles Barker, and Grady Cook, "Better Communication at General Motors," *Personnel Journal,* September 1989, 40–49; John H. Sheridan, "A Star in the GM Heavens," *Industry Week,* 18 March 1991, 50–54; Alex Taylor III, "The New Drive to Revive GM," *Fortune,* 9 April 1990, 52–61; James B. Treece, "Will GM Learn from Its Own Role Models?" *Business Week,* 9 April 1990, 62.
2. Ruth G. Newman, "Polaroid Develops a Communication System—But Not Instantly," *Management Review,* January 1990, 34–38.
3. Eugene F. Finkin, "Controlling Costs through Effective Communication," *The Journal of Business Strategy,* November–December 1991, 59–61.
4. Gary L. Kreps, *Organizational Communication,* 2nd ed. (New York: Longman, 1990), 12.
5. Courtland L. Bovée and John V. Thill, *Business Communication Today,* 3rd ed. (New York: McGraw-Hill, 1992), 4.
6. Allan D. Frank and Judi L. Brownell, *Organizational Communication and Behavior: Communicating to Improve Performance* (New York: Holt, Rinehart and Winston, 1989), 271.
7. Frank and Brownell, *Organizational Communication and Behavior,* 272.
8. Pauline E. Henderson, "Communication:

Communication without Words," *Personnel Journal,* January 1989, 22–29.
9. Frank and Brownell, *Organizational Communication and Behavior,* 272.
10. Kreps, *Organizational Communication,* 42–45.
11. Bovée and Thill, *Business Communication Today,* 29.
12. Alan Farnham, "The Trust Gap," *Fortune,* 4 December 1989, 56–58, 62, 66, 70, 74, 78.
13. Bovée and Thill, *Business Communication Today,* 32.
14. Kreps, *Organizational Communication,* 38.
15. Kreps, *Organizational Communication,* 39.
16. James Suchan and Clyde Scott, "Unclear Contract Language and Its Effect on Corporate Culture," *Business Horizons,* January–February 1986, 20–25.
17. Raymond W. Smith, "Interdependence via Communications for First Global Civilization," *The Journal of Private Sector Policy,* March 1991, 31–36.
18. Jeff B. Copeland, Vern E. Smith, Karen Springen, and Jodi Stewart, "Broadcast News, Inc.," *Newsweek,* 4 January 1988, 34–35; Robert Johansen and Christine Bullen, "Thinking Ahead: What to Expect from Teleconferencing," *Harvard Business Review,* March–April 1985, 164–166, 168, 170, 172, 174.
19. Kreps, *Organizational Communication,* 25.
20. Pamela Shockley-Zalabak, *Fundamentals of Organizational Communication* (New York: Longman, 1991), 25; Bovée and Thill, *Business Communication Today,* 35.
21. Shockley-Zalabak, *Fundamentals of Organizational Communication,* 26.
22. Bovée and Thill, *Business Communication Today,* 37.
23. Kreps, *Organizational Communication,* 35.
24. Gloria Gordon, "EXCEL Winner Talks Communication," *IABC Communication World,* April 1990, 13–15.
25. Kreps, *Organizational Communication,* 149; R. Wayne Pace and Don F. Faules, *Organizational Communication,* 2nd ed. (Englewood Cliffs, N.J.: Prentice Hall, 1989), 197; Shockley-Zalabak, *Fundamentals of Organizational Communication,* 133–134; Charles Conrad, *Strategic Organizational Communication,* 2nd ed. (Fort Worth, Tex.: Holt, Rinehart and Winston, 1990), 166.
26. Conrad, *Strategic Organizational Communication,* 165–166.
27. Kreps, *Organizational Communication,* 162.
28. Pace and Faules, *Organizational Communication,* 198.
29. Anthony P. Carnevale, Leila J. Gainer, Ann S. Meltzer, and Shari L. Holland, "Workplace Basics: The Skills Employers Want," *Training & Development Journal,* October 1988, 22–26, 28–30.
30. Shockley-Zabalak, *Fundamentals of Organizational Communication,* 183, 201.
31. Conrad, *Strategic Organizational Communication,* 251, 258; Kreps, *Organizational Communication,* 173, 175–176, 187.
32. Frank and Brownell, *Organizational Communication and Behavior,* 47; Conrad, *Strategic Organizational Communication,* 258.
33. Louis Kraar, "Japan's Gung-Ho U.S. Car Plants," *Fortune,* 30 January 1989, 98–100, 104, 106, 108.
34. Kreps, *Organizational Communication,* 20–21.
35. Frank K. Sonnenberg, "Internal Communication: Turning Talk into Action," *The Journal of Business Strategy,* November–December 1991, 52–55.
36. Thomas R. Horton, *"What Works for Me"* (New York: Amacom, 1989), 112–115.
37. Faye Rice, "Champions of Communication," *Fortune,* 3 June 1991, 111–112, 116, 120.
38. Kreps, *Organizational Communication,* 201.
39. Jitendra Mishra, "Managing the Grapevine," *Public Personnel Management,* Summer 1990, 213–228.
40. Frank and Brownell, *Organizational Communication and Behavior,* 348.
41. Kreps, *Organizational Communication,* 203; Frank and Brownell, *Organizational Communication and Behavior,* 49; Pace and Faules, *Organizational Communication,* 99–100.
42. Nell Withers Thomas, "Just What Do Employees Want? Communication Is the Key to Finding Out," *Management Quarterly,* Summer 1990, 29–34.
43. Kreps, *Organizational Communication,* 203–204; Frank and Brownell, *Organizational Communication and Behavior,* 49; Pace and Faules, *Organizational Communication,* 105–106.
44. David J. Dent, "Overnight Sensation," *Black Enterprise,* June 1988, 308, 310, 312, 314.
45. Kreps, *Organizational Communication,* 207; Pace and Faules, *Organizational Communication,* 109–110.
46. Kreps, *Organizational Communication,* 204; Frank and Brownell, *Organizational Communication and Behavior,* 51; Pace and Faules, *Organizational Communication,* 111–112.
47. "Training: A Key to Achieving Quality," *Small Business Report,* December 1987, 54–56, 58, 61.
48. Kreps, *Organizational Communication,* 210; Frank and Brownell, *Organizational Communication and Behavior,* 260; Pace and Faules, *Organizational Communication,* 115–116.
49. Jitendra Mishra, "Managing the Grapevine," *Public Personnel Management,* Summer 1990, 213–228.
50. Tom Richman, "Seducing the Customer: Dale Ballard's Perfect Selling Machine," *Inc.,* April 1988, 96–98, 100, 102, 104.
51. Kreps, *Organizational Communication,* 201; Frank and Brownell, *Organizational Communication and Behavior,* 260.
52. Kreps, *Organizational Communication,* 209.
53. Horton, *"What Works for Me,"* 113–114; Frank and Brownell, *Organizational Communication and Behavior,* 260.
54. Kreps, *Organizational Communication,* 21–22.
55. Patricia Sellers, "How to Handle Customers' Gripes," *Fortune,* 24 October 1988, 88–89, 92, 96, 100.
56. Bovée and Thill, *Business Communication Today,* 13; Kreps, *Organizational Communication,* 235–236.
57. Kreps, *Organizational Communication,* 230–240.
58. Laurence Barton, "Coping with Crisis: Teaching Students Managerial and Ethical Constraints," *The Bulletin,* September 1990, 27–32.
59. Lawrence R. Werner, "When Crisis Strikes, Use a Message Action Plan," *Public Relations Journal,* August 1990, 30–31.
60. Stuart Elliott, "Public Angry at Slow Action on Oil Spill," *USA Today,* 21 April 1989, 1B–2B; E. Bruce Harrison and Tom Prugh, "Assessing the Damage: Practitioner Perspectives on the Valdez," *Public Relations Journal,* October 1989, 40–45; Allanna Sullivan and Amanda Bennett, "Critics Fault Chief Executive of Exxon on Handling of Recent Alaskan Oil Spill," *Wall Street Journal,* 31 March 1989, B1; Tom Eisenhart, "The King of Public Relations Talks Damage Control," *Business Marketing,* September 1990, 86–87; Ben Yagoda, "Cleaning Up a Dirty Image," *Business Month,* April 1990, 48–51.
61. Clare Ansberry, "Oil Spill in the Midwest Provides Case Study in Crisis Management," *Wall Street Journal,* 8 January 1988, 21; Jay Stuller, "When the Crisis Doctor Calls," *Across the Board,* May 1988, 45–51.
62. Bovée and Thill, *Business Communication Today,* 12–13; Fred Luthans, "Successful vs. Effective Real Managers," *Academy of Management Executive* 2, no. 2 (1988): 127–132.
63. Kreps, *Organizational Communication,* 29; Frank and Brownell, *Organizational Communication and Behavior,* 8.
64. Pace and Faules, *Organizational Communication,* 150–151; Kreps, *Organizational Communication,* 31.
65. Conrad, *Strategic Organizational Communication,* 127; Shockley-Zalabak, *Fundamentals of Organizational Communication,* 57; Pace and Faules, *Organizational Communication,* 160.
66. Pace and Faules, *Organizational Communication,* 152; Shockley-Zalabak, *Fundamentals of Organizational Communication,* 57; Frank and Brownell, *Organizational Communication and Behavior,* 269.
67. John Stoltenberg, "See the Big Picture? Now Show Your Staff . . . ," *Working Woman,* April 1990, 84–86, 126.
68. Shockley-Zalabak, *Fundamentals of Organizational Communication,* 156; Bovée and Thill, *Business Communication Today,* 33.
69. Shockley-Zalabak, *Fundamentals of Organizational Communication,* 157–158.
70. Michelle Osborn, "Products and Morale Get a Boost," *USA Today,* 2 October 1991, 1B–2B.
71. Shockley-Zalabak, *Fundamentals of Organizational Communication,* 156; Bovée and Thill, *Business Communication Today,* 41.
72. W. Jack Duncan, Larry R. Smeltzer, and Terry L. Leap, "Humor and Work: Applications of Joking Behavior to Management," *Journal of Management* 16, no. 2 (1990): 255–278; James Krohe, Jr., "Take My Boss—Please," *Across the Board,* February 1987, 31–35.
73. Michael Berger, "Building Bridges over the Cultural Rivers," *International Management,* July–August 1987, 61–62.
74. Don Oldenburg, "What Do You Say? Making American Idioms as Clear as Day," *Washington Post,* 23 August 1989, C5.
75. Ron Scherer, "America's Factory Workers: Immigrants Turn the Shop Floor into a 'Mini-U.N.,'" *Christian Science Monitor,* 1 June 1988, 1, 6.
76. Shockley-Zalabak, *Fundamentals of Organizational Communication,* 153; Jesus Sanchez, "The Art of Deal Making," *Los Angeles Times,* 15 February 1988, 3.
77. Pace and Faules, *Organizational Communication,* 158; Shockley-Zalabak, *Fundamentals of Organizational Communication,* 56.
78. Jerie McArthur and D. W. McArthur, "The Pitfalls (and Pratfalls) of Corporate Communications," *Management Solutions,* December 1987, 15–21.

79. Gordon Graham, "End of the Paper Chase?" *Canadian Business,* May 1990, 73–74.
80. Bovée and Thill, *Business Communication Today,* 45–46.
81. Bovée and Thill, *Business Communication Today,* 45–46.
82. Pace and Faules, *Organizational Communication,* 157–158; Conrad, *Strategic Organizational Communication,* 130–132; Shockley-Zalabak, *Fundamentals of Organization,* 57; McArthur and McArthur, "The Pitfalls (and Pratfalls) of Corporate Communications," 15–21.
83. John Cook and Toby Wall, "New Work Attitude Measures of Trust, Organizational Commitment and Personal Need Non-Fulfilment," *Journal of Occupational Psychology,* 53 (Great Britain, 1980): 39–51; Kreps, *Organizational Communication,* 164; Conrad, *Strategic Organizational Communication,* 132; Robert L. Dilenschneider, "Communication: The Ultimate Exercise of Power—A Briefing for Leaders," *Soundview Executive Book Summaries* 13, no. 10, part 2 (October 1991): 1–8; Frank and Brownell, *Organizational Communication and Behavior,* 340.
84. Shockley-Zalabak, *Fundamentals of Organizational Communication,* 57; Pace and Faules, *Organizational Communication,* 158; Frank and Brownell, *Organizational Communication and Behavior,* 42–43, 101; Conrad, *Strategic Organizational Communication,* 130.
85. Kreps, *Organizational Communication,* 219; Anne B. Fisher, "CEOs Think That Morale Is Dandy," *Fortune,* 18 November 1991, 83–84.
86. Shockley-Zalabak, *Fundamentals of Organizational Communication,* 161; Frank and Brownell, *Organizational Communication and Behavior,* 261.
87. Robert H. Lengel and Richard L. Daft, "The Selection of Communication Media as an Executive Skill," *Academy of Management Executive,* August 1988, 225–231.
88. Shockley-Zalabak, *Fundamentals of Organizational Communication,* 54.
89. Sheridan, "A Star in the GM Heavens," 50–54.
90. Jules Harcourt, "Developing Ethical Messages: A Unit of Instruction for the Basic Business Communication Course," *The Bulletin,* September 1990, 17–20.
91. Bovée and Thill, *Business Communication Today,* 22–23.
92. Bovée and Thill, *Business Communication Today,* 22–23.
93. See note 1.
94. Oracle Systems material based on information from Lynn Brenner, "Biting the Bullet," *The Marketer,* June 1990, 34–38.

CHAPTER 18

1. Adapted from Dennis Livingston, "American Express Reins in the Paper," *Systems Integration,* May 1990, 52–58; James A. Rothi and David C. Yen, "Why American Express Gambled on an Expert Data Base," *Information Strategy,* Spring 1990, 16–22; Patrick Lyons and Anthony Fabiano, "Using Expert System Technology to Foster Innovation," *Review of Business,* Fall 1990, 33–38; John Paul Newport, Jr., "American Express: Service that Sells," *Fortune,* 20 November 1989, 80–94; Steve Fluty, "American Express Goes the Distance," *Inform,* January 1987, 34–36; Eva Kiess-Moser, "Customer Satisfaction," *Canadian Business Review,* Summer 1989, 43–45; "American Express: Focus on Management," *Incentive Marketing,* January 1989, 32–33; Jill Andresky Fraser, "James D. Robinson III: Member since 1969," *Inc.* September 1990, 159.
2. A. V. Knight and D. J. Silk, *Managing Information, Information Systems for Today's General Manager* (New York: McGraw-Hill, 1990), 3–10.
3. Tom Eisenhart, "After 10 Years of Marketing Decision Support Systems, Where's the Payoff?" *Business Marketing,* June 1990, 46–51.
4. James A. Senn, *Information Systems in Management* (Belmont, Calif.: Wadsworth, 1990), 62.
5. David Kroenke, *Management Information Systems,* 2nd ed. (New York: McGraw-Hill, 1992), 18.
6. William M. Bulkeley, "Special Systems Make Computing Less Traumatic for Top Executives," *Wall Street Journal,* 20 June 1988, 17.
7. Paul Kondstadt, "Ship 54—Where Are You?" *CIO,* May 1990, 80–81, 84, 86.
8. Adapted in part from Senn, *Information Systems in Management,* 64.
9. James S. Hirsch, "Flood of Information Swamps Managers, But Some Are Finding Ways to Bail Out," *Wall Street Journal,* 12 August 1991, B1-B2.
10. Lou Wallis, "Power Computing at the Top," *Across the Board,* January–February 1989, 42–51.
11. Clyde E. Witt, "Reebok's Distribution on Fast Track," *Material Handling Engineering,* March 1989, 43–48.
12. Benn R. Konsynski and F. Warren McFarlan, "Information Partnerships—Shared Data, Shared Scale," *Harvard Business Review,* September–October 1990, 114–120.
13. Christopher Knowlton, "What America Makes Best," *Fortune,* 28 March 1988, 40–53.
14. Jack B. Rochester, "Using Information Systems for Business and Competitor Intelligence," *I/S Analyzer,* May 1990, 1–12.
15. Stephen D. Solomon, "Born to Be Big," *Inc.,* June 1989, 94–100.
16. Knowlton, "What America Makes Best," 43.
17. Michael S. Scott Morton, *The Corporation of the 1990s, Information Technology and Organizational Transformation* (New York: Oxford University Press, 1991), 16–17.
18. Mary E. Boone, *Leadership and the Computer* (Rocklin, Calif.: Prima Publishing, 1991), as summarized in *Soundview Executive Summaries,* November 1991, 3–4.
19. Henry C. Lucas, Jr., *Information Systems Concepts for Management* (New York: McGraw-Hill, 1990), 33.
20. Raymond Roel, "The Power of Nintendo," *Direct Marketing,* September 1989, 24–26, 28–29; Michael Major, "Can Nintendo Bring Video Games Back?" *High-Tech Marketing,* July 1986, 48–49; Joe Mandese, "Power Plays," *Marketing & Media Decisions,* March 1989, 101–103, 106; Stewart Wolpin, "How Nintendo Revived a Dying Industry," *Marketing Communications,* May 1989, 36–38, 40.
21. Jack Schember, "Mrs. Fields' Secret Weapon," *Personnel Journal,* September 1991, 56–58.
22. Roland T. Moriarty and Gordon S. Swartz, "Automation to Boost Sales and Marketing," *Harvard Business Review,* January–February 1989, 100–108.
23. John Case, "The Knowledge Factory," *Inc.,* October 1991, 54–59.
24. Bruce G. Posner and Bo Burlingham, "The Hottest Entrepreneur in America," *Inc.,* January 1988, 44–58.
25. Morton, *The Corporation of the 1990s, Information Technology and Organizational Transformation,* 86–87.
26. Case, "The Knowledge Factory," 54–59.
27. Charles S. Parker, *Management Information Systems, Strategy and Action* (New York: McGraw-Hill, 1989), 813.
28. Kroenke, *Management Information Systems,* 7–8.
29. Parker, *Management Information Systems,* 584.
30. Joanne Kelleher, "Gillette Information Systems Stays Close to the Business," *ComputerWorld,* 8 October 1990, 52–53.
31. Eric J. Adams, "Stalking the Global Sale," *World Trade,* June–July 1991, 34–36.
32. Senn, *Information Systems in Management,* 644–646.
33. Kroenke, *Management Information Systems,* 22–24.
34. Senn, *Information Systems in Management,* 139–141, 206–210.
35. Kroenke, *Management Information Systems,* 123–124.
36. Knight and Silk, *Managing Information, Information Systems for Today's General Manager,* 11–13.
37. Senn, *Information Systems in Management,* 446–449.
38. Parker, *Management Information Systems,* 432–437.
39. Meghan O'Leary, "Putting Hertz Executives in the Driver's Seat," *CIO,* February 1990, 62–69.
40. Donald H. Sanders, *Computers Today,* 3rd ed. (New York: McGraw-Hill, 1988), 27.
41. Adapted in part from Sanders, *Computers Today,* 27; Timothy Trainor and Diane Krasnewich, *Computers!* (New York: McGraw-Hill, 1989), 32.
42. Gary Hoover, Alta Campbell, and Patrick J. Spain, *Hoover's Handbook 1991* (Austin, Tex.: The Reference Press, 1990), 67.
43. Hoover, Campbell, and Spain, *Hoover's Handbook,* 193.
44. Hoover, Campbell, and Spain, *Hoover's Handbook,* 193.
45. Morton, *The Corporation of the 1990s, Information Technology and Organizational Transformation,* 83–86.
46. John F. Rockart and James E. Short, "IT in the 1990s: Managing Organizational Interdependence," *Sloan Management Review,* Winter 1989, 7–17.
47. Jolie Solomon and Carol Hymowitz, "Team Strategy: P&G Makes Changes in the Way It Develops and Sells Its Products," *Wall Street Journal,* 11 August 1987, 1, 12.
48. Daniel Goleman, "Why Managers Resist Machines," *New York Times,* 7 February 1988, sec. 3, 4.
49. Goleman, "Why Managers Resist Machines," sec. 3, 4.
50. Katherine M. Hafner, Geoff Lewis, Kevin Kelly, Maria Shao, Chuck Hawkins, and Paul Angiolillo, "Is Your Computer Secure?" *Business Week,* 1 August 1988, 64–72.
51. John J. Keller, "Software Glitch at AT&T Cuts Off Phone Service for Millions," *Wall Street Journal,* 16 January 1990, B1, B4.
52. Paul Tate, "Risk! The Third Factor," *Datamation,* 15 April 1988, 58–64.

53. Alyssa A. Lappen, "Messenger of the Gods," *Forbes,* 21 March 1988, 150–151.
54. Tate, "Risk! The Third Factor," 59.
55. Lori Beckman, "Taking the Byte Out of Crime," *PC Today,* May 1991, 66–71.
56. Kroenke, *Management Information Systems,* 44.
57. Richard Brandt, Deidre A. Depke, Geoff Lewis, Keith H. Hammonds, and Chuck Hawkins, "The Personal Computer Finds Its Missing Link," *Business Week,* 5 June 1989, 120–128.
58. Brandt et al., "The Personal Computer Finds Its Missing Link," 122.
59. Gary Forger, "Slashing Lead Times with Quick Response," *Modern Materials Handling,* July 1989, 77–78; Senn, *Information Systems in Management,* 611–615.
60. Forger, "Slashing Lead Times with Quick Response," 77–78.
61. Faye Rice, "Why K Mart Has Stalled," *Fortune,* 9 October 1989, 79; John Huey, "Wal-Mart: Will It Take Over the World?" *Fortune,* 30 January 1989, 52–61.
62. Parker, *Management Information Systems,* 518–519.
63. Parker, *Management Information Systems,* 516–517.
64. Donna Whittingham-Barnes, "Making Your Office User Friendly," *Black Enterprise,* April 1990, 57–62.
65. Parker, *Management Information Systems,* 518–519.
66. Senn, *Information Systems in Management,* 586–589.
67. Eugene Linden, "Putting Knowledge to Work," *Time,* 28 March 1988, 60–63; Senn, *Information Systems in Management,* 590; C. Lawrence Meador and Ed G. Mahler, "Choosing an Expert Systems Game Plan," *Datamation,* 1 August 1990, 64–69.
68. Meador and Mahler, "Choosing an Expert Systems Game Plan," 64–69; Della Bradshaw, "The Computer Learns from the Experts," *Financial Times,* 27 April 1989, Technology section, 26.
69. Senn, *Information Systems in Management,* 589–590.
70. Dorothy Leonard-Barton and John J. Sviokla, "Putting Expert Systems to Work," *Harvard Business Review,* March–April 1988, 91–98; Patrick Lyons and Anthony Fabiano, "Using Expert System Technology to Foster Innovation," *Review of Business,* Fall 1990, 33–38, 48.
71. Jay F. Stright, Jr., "An EPIC Tale," *Personnel Journal,* June 1990, 72–81.
72. Parker, *Management Information Systems,* 810.
73. "Insurance Company Builds Mini-Mainframe Network," *Administrative Management,* December 1986, 7.
74. Warren Brown, "Electronic Pulses Replacing Paper in Workplace," *Washington Post,* 2 September 1988, F1, F2.
75. Frances Seghers, "A Search and Destroy Mission—Against Paper," *Business Week,* 6 February 1989, 91, 95.
76. Brown, "Electronic Pulses Replacing Paper in Workplace," F1, F2.
77. Hafner et al., "Is Your Computer Secure?" 65–66; Tate, "Risk! The Third Factor," 59.
78. "Fighting Parasites," *The Futurist,* July–August 1988, 2.
79. Hafner et al., "Is Your Computer Secure?" 66.
80. Tate, "Risk! The Third Factor," 61.
81. See note 1.

CHAPTER 19

1. Adapted from "Why Toys 'R' Us Will Succeed in Japan," *Discount Store News,* 6 May 1991, 6; Laura Liebeck, "Toys 'R' Us Blazes Path for Overseas Discounters," *Discount Store News,* 6 May 1991, 1–2; Danny Biederman, "Kids 'R' Us Takes Manhattan," *Children's Business,* April 1991, 6; Laura Liebeck, "Toys 'R' Us Gives '90s Consumers More," *Discount Store News,* 15 April 1991, 53–54; "Toys 'R' Us to Open 4 Stores in Japan on Schedule," *Japan Economic Newswire,* 24 October 1990; Susan Caminiti, "The New Champs of Retailing," *Fortune,* 24 September 1990, 85–90; John Wirebach, "How Retailers Reach the New Consumers," *Automotive Marketing,* August 1990, 41–43; "Toys 'R' Us Still Going Strong while Competitors Falter," *Discount Store News,* 16 July 1990, 85; Walter F. Loeb, "Toys 'R' Us Takes Manhattan," *HFD—The Weekly Home Furnishings Newspaper,* 3 December 1990, 14; Peter N. Ylvisaker, "Retailing: Survival of the Fittest," *Buildings,* May 1990, 52–54; "People Come before Technology," *Chain Store Age Executive,* October 1990, 18A; Faye Rice, "Superelf Plans for Xmas," *Fortune,* 11 September 1989, 151; "A Fascination with Speed," *CIO,* 22 February 1988, 37–39; Amy Dunkin, Keith H. Hammonds, and Mark Maremont, "How Toys 'R' Us Controls the Game Board," *Business Week,* 19 December 1988, 58–60; "Toys 'R' Us: King of the Hill," *Dun's Business Month,* December 1985, 40–41.
2. Richard E. Walton, "From Control to Commitment in the Workplace," *Harvard Business Review,* March–April 1985, 77–84.
3. Dean M. Schroeder and Alan G. Robinson, "America's Most Successful Export to Japan: Continuous Improvement Programs," *Sloan Management Review,* Spring 1991, 67–79.
4. Gerhard Johannes Plenert, *International Management and Production* (Blue Ridge Summit, Pa.: Tab Books, 1990), xiii–xiv; Walton, "From Control to Commitment," 79.
5. Ronald Henkoff, "Cost-Cutting: How to Do It Right," *Fortune,* 9 April 1990, 40–49.
6. Stephen G. Green and M. Ann Welsh, "Cybernetics and Dependence: Reframing the Control Concept," *Academy of Management Review* 13, no. 2 (1988): 287–301.
7. Gwen Kinkead, "America's Best-Run Charities," *Fortune,* 9 November 1987, 145–149.
8. Mark F. Blaxill and Thomas M. Hout, "The Fallacy of the Overhead Quick Fix," *Harvard Business Review,* July–August 1991, 95–96.
9. Kenneth A. Merchant, "The Control Function of Management," *Sloan Management Review,* Summer 1982, 43–55.
10. Teri Lammers, Leslie Brokaw, Jay Finegan, Susan Greco, and Martha E. Mangelsdorf, "Timely Sales Incentive," *Inc.,* April 1991, 107.
11. Charles J. Bodenstab, "Keeping Tabs on Your Company," *Inc.,* August 1989, 131–132.
12. Cortlandt Cammann and David A. Nadler, "Fit Control Systems to Your Managerial Style," *Harvard Business Review,* January–February 1976, 65–72.
13. Henkoff, "Cost-Cutting," 46.
14. Schroeder and Robinson, "America's Most Successful Export to Japan," Spring 1991, 77–79.
15. Mark F. Blaxill and Thomas M. Hout, "The Fallacy of the Overhead Quick Fix," *Harvard Business Review,* July–August 1991, 93–101.
16. A. Donald Stratton, "Kaizen and Variability," *Quality Progress,* April 1990, 44–45.
17. B. Charles Ames and James D. Hlavacek, "Vital Truths about Managing Your Costs," *Harvard Business Review,* January–February 1990, 140–147.
18. R. B. Chase and D. A. Tansik, "The Customer Contact Model for Organization Design," *Management Science* 29 (1983): 1037–1050.
19. Joseph L. Fisher, "Helping the Governor to Manage," *The Council of State Governments* 62 (1989): 131–135.
20. Leonard A. Schlesinger and James L. Heskett, "Breaking the Cycle of Failure in Services," *Sloan Management Review,* Spring 1991, 17–28.
21. Schlesinger and Heskett, "Breaking the Cycle of Failure in Services," 24–27.
22. Philip B. Crosby, *Quality Is Free* (New York: McGraw-Hill, 1984), 106–124.
23. Ira C. Magaziner and Mark Patinkin, "Cold Competition: GE Wages the Refrigerator War," *Harvard Business Review,* March–April 1989, 114–124; Zachary Schiller and Karen Wolman, "The Refrigerator That Has GE Feeling the Heat," *Business Week,* 25 April 1988, 65–66.
24. Schlesinger and Heskett, "Breaking the Cycle of Failure in Services," 19.
25. Schlesinger and Heskett, "Breaking the Cycle of Failure in Services," 24–27.
26. Joel Dreyfuss, "Victories in the Quality Crusade," *Fortune,* 10 October 1988, 80–88.
27. David Kirkpatrick, "It's Simply Not Working," *Fortune,* 19 November 1990, 179–196.
28. Lawrence G. Hrebiniak and William F. Joyce, "The Strategic Importance of Managing Myopia," *Sloan Management Review,* Fall 1986, 5–13.
29. Richard L. Daft and Norman B. Macintosh, "The Nature and Use of Formal Control Systems for Management Control and Strategy Implementation," *Journal of Management* 10, no. 1 (1984): 43–66.
30. Georg Schreyogg and Horst Steinmann, "Strategic Control: A New Perspective," *Academy of Management Review* 12, no. 1 (1987): 91–103.
31. Daft and Macintosh, "The Nature and Use of Formal Control Systems for Management Control and Strategy Implementation," 43–66.
32. J. H. Horovitz, "Strategic Control: A New Task for Top Management," *Long Range Planning,* June 1979, 2–7.
33. Daft and Macintosh, "The Nature and Use of Formal Control Systems for Management Control and Strategy Implementation," 43–66.
34. Eric G. Flamholtz, "Accounting, Budgeting and Control Systems in Their Organizational Context: Theoretical and Empirical Perspectives," *Accounting, Organizations and Society* 8, no. 2–3 (1983): 153–169.
35. Roger W. Schmenner, "The Merit of Making Things Fast," *Sloan Management Review,* Fall 1988, 11–17.
36. Harold Koontz and Robert W. Bradspies, "Managing through Feedforward Control: A Future-Directed View," *Business Horizons,* June 1972, 25–36.
37. Nancy L. Reppert, "Instilling Employee Pride through a Loss Control Program," *Risk Management,* July 1988, 36–41.
38. Otis Port, Zachary Schiller, and Resa W. King, "A Smarter Way to Manufacture," *Business Week,* 30 April 1990, 110–117.
39. Vaughn Beals, "Operation Recovery," *Success,* January–February 1989, 16.

40. Reppert, "Instilling Employee Pride through a Loss Control Program," 36–41.
41. John Harris, "Dinnerhouse Technology," *Forbes,* 8 July 1991, 98–99.
42. Flamholtz, "Accounting, Budgeting and Control Systems," 154.
43. John J. D'Azzo and Constantine H. Houpis, *Feedback Control System Analysis of Synthesis,* 2nd ed. (New York: McGraw-Hill, 1966), 1–3.
44. Walton, "From Control to Commitment," 77–84.
45. William G. Ouchi, "The Transmission of Control through Organizational Hierarchy," *Academy of Management Journal* 21, no. 2 (1978): 191.
46. Daft and Macintosh, "The Nature and Use of Formal Control Systems," 43–66; Mark F. Blaxill and Thomas M. Hout, "The Fallacy of the Overhead Quick Fix," *Harvard Business Review,* July–August 1991, 93–101.
47. Blaxill and Hout, "The Fallacy of the Overhead Quick Fix," 95–96.
48. Port, Schiller, and King, "A Smarter Way to Manufacture," 112.
49. Scott S. Cowen and J. Kendall Middaugh II, "Designing an Effective Financial Planning and Control System," *Long Range Planning* 21, no. 6 (1988): 83–92.
50. Bill Saporito, "A&P: Grandma Turns a Killer," *Fortune,* 23 April 1990, 207–214.
51. Gary Hoover, Alta Campbell, and Patrick J. Spain, *Hoover's Handbook* (Austin, Tex.: The Reference Press, 1990), 393.
52. Cammann and Nadler, "Fit Control Systems to Your Managerial Style," 69–72.
53. Kenneth A. Merchant, "The Control Function of Management," *Sloan Management Review,* Summer 1982, 43–47.
54. Thomas A. Stewart, "Why Budgets Are Bad for Business," *Fortune,* 4 June 1990, 179–190.
55. Ouchi, "The Transmission of Control," 191.
56. William H. Sihler, "Toward Better Management Control Systems," *California Management Review* 14, no. 2 (1971): 33–39.
57. Lawrence D. Schall and Charles W. Haley, *Introduction to Financial Management* (New York: McGraw-Hill, 1988), 397–398.
58. Schall and Haley, *Introduction to Financial Management,* 397.
59. Schall and Haley, *Introduction to Financial Management,* 397.
60. Schall and Haley, *Introduction to Financial Management,* 399–422.
61. Daft and Macintosh, "The Nature and Use of Formal Control Systems," 59.
62. Sverre Hogheim, Norvald Monsen, Rignor H. Olsen, and Olov Olson, "The Two Worlds of Management Control," *Financial Accountability & Management,* Autumn 1989, 163–178.
63. J. Kendall Middaugh II, "Management Control in the Financial-Services Industry," *Business Horizons,* May–June 1988, 79–86.
64. ToshiroHiromoto,"AnotherHiddenEdge—Japanese Management Accounting," *Harvard Business Review,* July–August 1988, 22–26.
65. Middaugh, "Management Control in the Financial-Services Industry," 84–85.
66. Middaugh, "Management Control in the Financial-Services Industry," 85.
67. David Lieberman, "As NBC News Cuts Costs Will It Clobber Quality?" *Business Week,* 5 December 1988, 137–138.
68. Nancy Jackson, "Mystic Seaport Museum," *CFO,* November 1989, 71–72.
69. Julia Homer, "Big Apple Circus," *CFO,* August 1989, 55–56.
70. Homer, "Big Apple Circus," 56.
71. James B. Treece and David Woodruff, "Crunch Time Again for Chrysler," *Business Week,* 5 March 1991, 92–94.
72. Schall and Haley, *Introduction to Financial Management,* 478–479.
73. Neil C. Churchill, "Budget Choice: Planning vs. Control," *Harvard Business Review,* July–August 1984, 150–164.
74. Shawn Tully, "The CEO Who Sees beyond Budgets," *Fortune,* 4 June 1990, 186.
75. Flamholtz, "Accounting, Budgeting and Control Systems," 153–169.
76. Joel G. Siegel and Marvin F. Milich, "Auditing Corporate Management," *Managerial Planning,* March–April 1985, 8–10.
77. See note 1.

CHAPTER 20

1. Adapted from James B. Shuman, "Easy Rider Rides Again," *Business Tokyo,* July 1991, 26–30; Vaughn Beals, "Harley-Davidson: An American Success Story," *Journal for Quality and Participation,* June 1988, A19–A23; Vaughn Beals, "Quality and Productivity: The Harley-Davidson Experience," *Survey of Business,* Spring 1986, 9–11; Sharon Brady, "School of Hard Knocks," *Software Magazine,* April 1988, 37–44; Shirley Cayer, "Harley's New Manager-Owners Put Purchasing Out Front," *Purchasing,* 13 October 1988, 50–54; Claudia H. Deutsch, "Now Harley-Davidson Is All Over the Road," *New York Times,* 17 April 1988, sec. 3, 12; Holt Hackney, "Easy Rider," *Financial World,* 4 September 1990, 48–49; Roy L. Harmon and Leroy D. Peterson, "Reinventing the Factory," *Across the Board,* March 1990, 30–38; John Holusha, "How Harley Outfoxed Japan with Exports," *New York Times,* 12 August 1990, sec. 3, 5; Peter C. Reid, "How Harley Beat Back the Japanese," *Fortune,* 25 September 1989, 155–164.
2. Richard B. Chase and Eric L. Prentis, "Operations Management: A Field Rediscovered," *Journal of Management,* Summer 1987, 351–366.
3. John N. Pearson, Jeffrey S. Bracker, and Richard E. White, "Operations Management Activities of Small, High Growth Electronics Firms," *Journal of Business Management,* January 1990, 20–29.
4. Tom Peters, *Thriving on Chaos* (New York: Harper & Row, 1987), 128.
5. Steven C. Wheelwright and Robert H. Hayes, "Competing through Manufacturing," *Harvard Business Review,* January–February 1985, 99–109.
6. Wickham Skinner, *Manufacturing: The Formidable Competitive Weapon* (New York: Wiley, 1985), 4.
7. Chase and Prentis, "Operations Management, A Field Rediscovered," 353.
8. Jagannath Dubashi and Robert McGough, "Computers: A Global Report—In Search of Productivity," *Financial World,* 21 January 1992, 52–53.
9. Saeed Samiee, "Productivity Planning and Strategy in Retailing," *California Management Review,* Winter 1990, 61–62.
10. Jerry Flint and William Heuslein, "An Urge to Service," *Forbes,* September 1989, 172, 176.
11. Joseph G. Monks, *Operations Management, Theory and Problems* (New York: McGraw-Hill, 1987), 2–3.
12. Information on service characteristics adapted from Courtland L. Bovée and John V. Thill, *Marketing* (New York: McGraw-Hill, 1992), 694–697.
13. Chase and Prentis, "Operations Management: A Field Rediscovered," 353.
14. Jon Berry, "Inside Nabisco's Cookie Machine," *Adweek's Marketing Week,* 18 March 1991, 22–24.
15. Pearson, Bracker, and White, "Operations Management Activities of Small, High Growth Electronics Firms," 23.
16. James B. Dilworth, *Production and Operations Management: Manufacturing and Nonmanufacturing* (New York: Random House, 1989), 63.
17. Jacqueline Trescott, "The Man in the Postmaster's Hot Seat," *Washington Post,* 18 December 1989, D1, D8-D9.
18. Nan S. Langowitz, "Managing New Product Design and Factory Fit," *Business Horizons,* May–June 1989, 76–79.
19. Ted Kumpe and Piet T. Bolwijn, "Manufacturing: The New Case for Vertical Integration," *Harvard Business Review,* March–April 1988, 75–81.
20. Otis Port and Wendy Zellner, "Pssst! Want a Secret for Making Super Products?" *Business Week,* 2 October 1989, 106–110.
21. Kumpe and Bolwijn, "Manufacturing: The New Case for Vertical Integration," 75–81.
22. Otis Port, "A New Vision for the Factory," *Business Week,* 16 June 1989, 146; Port and Zellner, "Pssst! Want a Secret for Making Super Products?" 106, 110.
23. Timothy D. Schellhardt and Carol Hymowitz, "U.S. Manufacturers Face Big Changes in the Years Ahead," *Wall Street Journal,* 2 May 1989, A2, A8.
24. Monks, *Operations Management, Theory and Problems,* 77–78.
25. Information on short-term capacity planning adapted in part from Dilworth, *Production and Operations Management,* 149.
26. Pamela Bayless, "Fine Art: Coping with Cuts at the Met," *Crain's New York Business,* 20 May 1991, 1, 30.
27. Pearson, Bracker, and White, "Operations Management Activities of Small, High Growth Electronics Firms," 23.
28. Joel Kotkin, "The Great American Revival," *Inc.,* February 1988, 52–63.
29. American Production and Inventory Control Society, *APICS Dictionary,* 1992, 27.
30. Monks, *Operations Management, Theory and Problems,* 122–124.
31. Samiee, "Productivity Planning and Strategy in Retailing," 54–76.
32. Monks, *Operations Management, Theory and Problems,* 122–135.
33. Monks, *Operations Management, Theory and Problems,* 125.
34. Paul S. Adler, "Managing Flexible Automation," *California Management Review,* Spring 1988, 34–56.
35. Calvin Sims, "Robots to Make Fast Food Chains Still Faster," *New York Times,* 24 August 1988, D5.
36. Edward G. Krubasik, "Customize Your Product Development," *Harvard Business Review,* November–December 1988, 46–52.
37. Kotkin, "The Great American Revival," 62.
38. Stephen Kreider Yoder, "Putting It All Together," *Wall Street Journal,* 4 June 1990, R24-R24.
39. Fred Hiatt, "Japanese Robots Reproducing Like Rabbits," *Washington Post,* 2 January 1990, A1, A13; Gene Bylinsky, "The Race to

the Automatic Factory," *Fortune,* 21 February 1983, 51.

40. Monks, *Operations Management, Theory and Problems,* 128–129.

41. Thomas M. Rohan, "Factories of the Future," *Industry Week,* 21 March 1988, 33–66.

42. Monks, *Operations Management, Theory and Problems,* 358–359.

43. Dilworth, *Production and Operations Management,* 146–151.

44. Dilworth, *Production and Operations Management,* 146–160.

45. Monks, *Operations Management, Theory and Problems,* 330–341.

46. Chase and Prentis, "Operations Management: A Field Rediscovered," 353; Monks, *Operations Management, Theory and Problems,* 367, 393–394, 438–442.

47. Barry Render and Ralph M. Stair, Jr., *Quantitative Analysis for Management* (Needham Heights, Mass: Allyn and Bacon, 1991), 274–276.

48. Render and Stair, *Quantitative Analysis for Management,* 277–278.

49. Render and Stair, *Quantitative Analysis for Management,* 305–307.

50. Peter Duchessi, Charles M. Schaninger, and Don R. Hobbs, "Implementing a Manufacturing Planning and Control Information System," *California Management Review,* Spring 1989, 75–90.

51. Sumer C. Aggarwal, "MRP, JIT, OPT, FMS? Making Sense of Production Operations Systems," *Harvard Business Review,* September–October 1985, 8–16.

52. Monks, *Operations Management, Theory and Problems,* 435–437.

53. Duchessi, Schaninger, and Hobbs, "Implementing a Manufacturing Planning and Control Information System," 76.

54. Richard J. Schonberger and Edward M. Knod, Jr., *Operations Management: Improving Customer Service* (Boston: Irwin, 1991), 387–388.

55. APICS, *APICS Dictionary,* 1992, 24.

56. Chase and Prentis, "Operations Management: A Field Rediscovered," 351–366.

57. Charles O'Neal and Kate Bertrand, "Developing a Winning J.I.T. Marketing Strategy," *Soundview Executive Book Summaries,* May 1991, 1–8.

58. Cook, "Ringing in Saturn," 53; Monks, *Operations Management, Theory and Problems,* 416–417.

59. Cook, "Ringing in Saturn," 53.

60. Robert F. Lundrigan, "How to Get a Head Start on Synchronized Manufacturing," *P&IM Review with APICS News,* January 1988, 38–39.

61. "Changing Markets Demand 'Value-Added Services,'" *Traffic Management,* August 1989, 79, 81, 83, 85.

62. Joseph J. Klock, "How to Manage 3,500 (or Fewer) Suppliers," *Quality Progress,* June 1990, 43–47.

63. Flint and Heuslein, "An Urge to Service," 172–176.

64. Cook, "Ringing in Saturn," 53.

65. John S. McClenahen, "Sources of Frustration," *Industry Week,* 1 October 1990.

66. Monks, *Operations Management, Theory and Problems,* 582.

67. Schellhardt and Hymowitz, "U.S. Manufacturers Face Big Changes in the Years Ahead," A1.

68. Monks, *Operations Management, Theory and Problems,* 583–584.

69. Schonberger and Knod, *Operations Management,* 637–650; Monks, *Operations Management, Theory and Problems,* 583–617.

70. Schonberger and Knod, *Operations Management,* 637–650; Monks, *Operations Management, Theory and Problems,* 583–617.

71. Rohan, "Factories of the Future," 44.

72. Schonberger and Knod, *Operations Management,* 55.

73. Peter F. Drucker, *Management: Tasks, Responsibilities, Practices* (New York: Harper & Row, 1974), 44–46.

74. Norman Gaither, *Production and Operations Management: A Problem-Solving and Decision-Making Approach* (Orlando, Fla.: Dryden, 1990), 627–637: W. Bruce Chew, "No-Nonsense Guide to Measuring Productivity," *Harvard Business Review,* January–February, 1988, 110–118; Michael L. Dertouzos, Richard K. Lester, Robert M. Solow, and the MIT Commission on Industrial Productivity, *Made in America: Regaining the Productivity Edge* (New York: HarperPerennial, 1989), 26–42.

75. See note 1.

CHAPTER 21

1. Adapted from David Woodruff and Stephen Phillips, "Ford Has a Better Idea: Let Someone Else Have the Idea," *Business Week,* 30 April 1990, 116–117; Steve Salerno, "Formula for Success," *American Legion Magazine,* August 1989, 24–25, 55; John H. Sheridan, "America's Best Plants," *Industry Week,* 15 October 1990, 27–64; Ellis Pines, "From Top Secret to Top Priority: The Story of TQM," *Aviation Week & Space Technology,* 21 May 1990, S5–S17, S24; Joseph F. McKenna, "Take the 'A' Training," *Industry Week,* 21 May 1990, 22–29; Donald E. Petersen, "Ford Has a Lesson for America," *Industry Week,* 19 February 1990, 55; Neal E. Boudette, "Give Me a T . . . ," *Industry Week,* 8 January 1990, 62–65; Andrea Gabor, *The Man Who Discovered Quality* (New York: Times Books/Random House, 1990), 3–4; Andrew Kupfer, "How America Stacks Up," *Fortune,* 9 March 1992, 30–34, 38, 42, 46.

2. Ross E. Robson and Karen S. Richards, "The Quality and Productivity Equation for the Future," in *The Quality and Productivity Equation: American Corporate Strategies for the 1990s,* edited by Ross E. Robson (Cambridge, Mass.: Productivity Press), 323–328.

3. D. Keith Denton, "Customer-Focused Management," *HR Magazine,* August 1990, 62–67; Chip R. Bell and Ron Zemke, "The Performing Art of Service Management," *Management Review,* July 1990, 42–45; Tom Peters, *Thriving on Chaos* (New York: Harper & Row, 1987), 58–59; Milind M. Lele, *The Customer Is Key* (New York: Wiley, 1987), 1–5.

4. Marj Charlier, "Ailing College Treats Student as Customer, and Soon Is Thriving," *Wall Street Journal,* 17 July 1991, A1, A5.

5. Peter F. Drucker, *Management: Tasks, Responsibilities, Practices* (New York: Harper & Row, 1974), 44–46.

6. Jeremy Main, "Manufacturing the Right Way," *Fortune,* 21 May 1990, 54–64.

7. Nancy Dreicer, "1990s: The Work Force of a New Age," in *The Quality and Productivity Equation: American Corporate Strategies for the 1990s,* edited by Ross E. Robson (Cambridge, Mass.: Productivity Press, 1990), 213–219; Judith Rawnsley and Matt Rothman, "Charged Up," *Business Tokyo,* July 1991, 44–46; Gail DeGeorge, "The Green in the Little Red Schoolhouse," *Business Week,* 14 October 1991, 68–69.

8. Peters, *Thriving on Chaos,* 474–475; Daniel P. Finkelman and Anthony R. Goland, "Customers Once Can Be Customers for Life," *Information Strategy: The Executive's Journal,* Summer 1990, 5–9; John Case, "Customer Service: The Last Word," *Inc.,* April 1991, 89–93; George Stalk, Jr., and Thomas M. Hout, *Competing against Time* (New York: Free Press, 1990), 267; John S. McClenahen, "So Long, Salespeople," *Industry Week,* 18 February 1991, 48–51.

9. Theodore Levitt, *The Marketing Imagination* (New York: Free Press, 1986), 72–73; Amanda Bennett, "Many Customers Expect Better Service—And Say They Are Willing to Pay for It," *Wall Street Journal,* 12 November 1990, B1, B10; Gretchen Morgenson, "The Trend Is Not Their Friend," *Forbes,* 16 September 1991, 114–119; Philip R. Thomas, *Competitiveness through Total Cycle Time* (New York: McGraw-Hill, 1990), 7–15; Stalk and Hout, *Competing against Time,* 31, 35–37, 98–101.

10. Peters, *Thriving on Chaos,* 67–69.

11. W. Edwards Deming, *Out of the Crisis* (Cambridge, Mass.: MIT CAES, 1986), 1–17; Valarie A. Zeithaml, A. Parasuraman, and Leonard L. Berry, *Delivering Quality Service* (New York: Free Press, 1990), 8–12; Philip B. Crosby, *The Eternally Successful Organization* (New York: McGraw-Hill, 1988), 25–36; William E. Conway, "Work, Waste, and Quality," in *The Quality and Productivity Equation: American Corporate Strategies for the 1990s,* edited by Ross E. Robson (Cambridge, Mass.: Productivity Press, 1990), 121–129.

12. Deming, *Out of the Crisis,* 1–17; Zeithaml, Parasuraman, and Berry, *Delivering Quality Service,* 11–13.

13. Lele, *The Customer Is Key,* 82–84, 139; Howard Schlossberg, "Author: Consumers Just Can't Wait to Be Satisfied," *Marketing News,* 4 February 1991, 13; Wolfgang Muller, "European Firms Set Management Principles for Customer Satisfaction," *Marketing News,* 4 February 1991, 6; Bennett, "Many Customers Expect Better Service," B1, B10.

14. J. M. Juran, *Juran on Leadership for Quality: An Executive Handbook* (New York: Free Press, 1989), 7–9; Otis Port, "Dueling Pioneers," *Business Week Quality 1991,* 25 October 1991, 17; Keki R. Bhote, *World Class Quality: Using Design of Experiments to Make It Happen* (New York: Amacom, 1991), 27–29; Deming, *Out of the Crisis,* 1–17; Otis Port, "Questing for the Best," *Business Week Quality 1991,* 25 October 1991, 8–16.

15. David A. Garvin, "Competing on the Eight Dimensions of Quality," *Harvard Business Review,* November–December 1987, 101–109.

16. Garvin, "Competing on the Eight Dimensions of Quality," 101–109; Paul E. Plsek, "Defining Quality at the Marketing/Development Interface," *Quality Progress,* June 1987, 28–36; Julia Flynn Siler and Sandra Atchison, "The R~ at Work in Utah," *Business Week Quality 1991,* 25 October 1991, 113.

17. Garvin, "Competing on the Eight Dimensions of Quality," 101–109; Plsek, "Defining Quality at the Marketing/Development Interface," 28–36; Gail E. Schares, "A Swiss Athlete Gets in Fighting Trim," *Business Week Quality 1991,* 25 October 1991, 29.

18. Garvin, "Competing on the Eight Dimensions of Quality," 101–109; Plsek, "Defining

Quality at the Marketing/Development Interface," 28–36; John Templeman, "Grill-to-Grill with Japan," *Business Week Quality 1991,* 25 October 1991, 39.

19. Garvin, "Competing on the Eight Dimensions of Quality," 101–109; Plsek, "Defining Quality at the Marketing/Development Interface," 28–36; John Carey, "He's a Materials Boy," *Business Week Quality 1991,* 25 October 1991, 162.

20. Garvin, "Competing on the Eight Dimensions of Quality," 101–109; Plsek, "Defining Quality at the Marketing/Development Interface," 28–36; Louis S. Richman, "What America Makes Best," *Fortune 1991,* Spring–Summer 1991, 81.

21. Garvin, "Competing on the Eight Dimensions of Quality," 101–109; Plsek, "Defining Quality at the Marketing/Development Interface," 28–36; Wendy Zellner, "Premium Treatment," *Business Week Quality 1991,* 25 October 1991, 124; Thomas Teal, "Service Comes First: An Interview with USAA's Robert F. McDermott," *Harvard Business Review,* September–October 1991, 117–127.

22. Garvin, "Competing on the Eight Dimensions of Quality," 101–109; Plsek, "Defining Quality at the Marketing/Development Interface," 28–36; Linda M. Lash, *The Complete Guide to Customer Service* (New York: Wiley, 1989), 87–88.

23. Garvin, "Competing on the Eight Dimensions of Quality," 101–109; Plsek, "Defining Quality at the Marketing/Development Interface," 28–36.

24. Plsek, "Defining Quality at the Marketing/Development Interface," 28–36; Garvin, "Competing on the Eight Dimensions of Quality," 101–109; Port, "Questing for the Best," 8–16; David Woodruff, "The Racy Viper Is Already a Winner for Chrysler," *Business Week,* 4 November 1991, 36–38.

25. Harry Katzan, Jr., *Quality Circle Management: The Human Side of Quality* (Blue Ridge Summit, Pa.: Tab Books, 1989), 21–26; Howard H. Greenbaum, Ira T. Kaplan, and William Metlay, "Evaluation of Problem-Solving Groups: The Case of Quality Circle Programs," *Group & Organization Studies* 13, no. 2 (June 1988): 133–147; Thomas Li-Ping Tang, Peggy Smith Tollison, and Harold D. Whiteside, "Quality Circle Productivity as Related to Upper-Management Attendance, Circle Initiation, and Collar Color," *Journal of Management* 15, no. 1 (1989): 101–113; James S. Bowman, "Quality Circles: Promise, Problems, and Prospects in Florida," *Public Personnel Management* 18, no. 4 (Winter 1989): 375–403.

26. Juran, *Juran on Leadership for Quality,* 284–295; Peter Burrows, "Corporate Culture Is the Next Quality Frontier," *Electronic Business,* 7 October 1991, 64–66; Peter Burrows, "Power to the People," *Electronic Business,* 7 October 1991, 96–100; Thomas M. Rohan, "A New Culture," *Industry Week,* 17 April 1989, 43–55; Ricky W. Griffin, "Consequences of Quality Circles in an Industrial Setting: A Longitudinal Assessment," *Academy of Management Journal* 31, no. 2 (1988): 338–358.

27. Claudia H. Deutsch, "A Revival of the Quality Circle," *New York Times,* 26 May 1991, sec. 3, 23.

28. Juran, *Juran on Leadership for Quality,* 215; Aaron Bernstein, "Quality Is Becoming Job One in the Office, Too," *Business Week,* 29 April 1991, 52–56.

29. Leopold S. Vansina, "Total Quality Control: An Overall Organizational Improvement Strategy," *National Productivity Review* 9, no. 1 (Winter 1989–90): 59–73; Danny A. Samson and Amrik Sohal, "The Strategic Status of Quality: An Australian Perspective," *International Journal of Technology Management* 5, no. 3 (1990): 293–307; Port, "Questing for the Best," 8–16; Juran, *Juran on Leadership for Quality,* 176–184; John Gilks, "Total Quality: A Strategy for Organizational Transformation," *Canadian Manager,* Spring 1990, 23–25.

30. Juran, *Juran on Leadership for Quality,* 20–21.

31. Gabor, *The Man Who Discovered Quality,* 20–21.

32. Amy Borrus, "The Navy Tries to Get Its Ship in Shape," *Business Week Quality 1991,* 25 October 1991, 134; Mary Walton, *Deming Management at Work* (New York: G.P. Putnam's Sons, 1990), 166–178.

33. Port, "Questing for the Best," 9; Robert Neff, "No. 1—And Trying Harder," *Business Week Quality 1991,* 25 October 1991, 20–24.

34. Bhote, *World Class Quality,* xv; Charles A. Sengstock, Jr., "Pursuing the Not-So-Elusive Goal of Perfection," *Public Relations Journal,* August 1991, 22–23; Brian M. Cook, "In Search of Six Sigma: 99.9997% Defect-Free," *Industry Week,* 1 October 1990, 60–65.

35. "Why 99.9% Just Won't Do," *Inc.,* April 1989, 26; Port, "Questing for the Best," 9; Thane Peterson, "Top Products for Less Than Top Dollar," *Business Week Quality 1991,* 25 October 1991, 66–68; Gary McWilliams, "Mail-Order Madness," *Business Week Quality 1991,* 25 October 1991, 128.

36. Port, "Questing for the Best," 8–16; A. Steven Walleck, "A Backstage View of World-Class Performers," *Wall Street Journal,* 26 August 1991, A10; Rick Whiting, "Benchmarking: Lessons from the Best-in-Class," *Electronic Business,* 7 October 1991, 128–134.

37. Whiting, "Benchmarking: Lessons from the Best-in-Class," 128–134; Claudia H. Deutsch, "Emulating the Best of the Best," *New York Times,* 30 December 1990, sec. 3, 23.

38. Walleck, "A Backstage View of World-Class Performers," A10; Whiting, "Benchmarking: Lessons from the Best-in-Class," 128–134.

39. Karen S. Richards and Ross E. Robson, "Corporate Strategies for the Quality and Productivity Equation," in *The Quality and Productivity Equation: American Corporate Strategies for the 1990s,* edited by Ross E. Robson (Cambridge, Mass.: Productivity Press, 1990), 3–11; Christopher Farrell and Amy Borrus, "Even Uncle Sam Is Starting to See the Light," *Business Week Quality 1991,* 25 October 1991, 132–137.

40. Quang Bao and Elizabeth B. Baatz, "How Solectron Finally Got in Touch with Its Workers," *Electronic Business,* 7 October 1991, 47–48; Howard Schlossberg, "Director of Baldrige Award Spreads Gospel of Quality," *Marketing News,* 1 April 1991, 2; Gilbert Fuchsberg, "Three Small Firms Beat Out Big-Timers for Baldrige Award," *Wall Street Journal,* 10 October 1991, A3; John Carey, "The Prize and the Passion," *Business Week Quality 1991,* 25 October 1991, 58–59; Art Durity, "Everyone's a Winner in the Baldrige Stakes," *Management Review,* November 1991, 36–39.

41. Jeremy Main, "Is the Baldrige Overblown?" *Fortune,* 1 July 1991, 62–65; "Quality Fever at Florida Power," *Fortune,* 1 July 1991, 65; Kevin G. Drayton, "Are You Ready to Apply for the Award?" *Management Review,* November 1991, 40–43; Robert Neff, "Going for the Glory: Prestige—And Plumper Profits, Too," *Business Week Quality 1991,* 25 October 1991, 61; Elizabeth B. Baatz, "Who Says Small-Fry Can't Compete for the Baldrige?" *Electronic Business,* 7 October 1991, 50.

42. Wickham Skinner, "The Productivity Paradox Explained," in *The Quality and Productivity Equation: American Corporate Strategies for the 1990s,* edited by Ross E. Robson (Cambridge, Mass.: Productivity Press, 1990), 147–157; Michael L. Dertouzos, Richard K. Lester, and Robert M. Solow, *Made in America: Regaining the Productive Edge* (New York: HarperPerennial, 1990), 26–29; Karen Pennar, "Yes, We're Down. No, We're Not Out," *Business Week,* 17 December 1990, 62; Thomas A. Stewart, "The New American Century: Where We Stand," 12–23.

43. Kevin F. F. Quigley, "U.S. Government and Productivity: Problems and Prospects," in *The Quality and Productivity Equation: American Corporate Strategies for the 1990s,* edited by Ross E. Robson (Cambridge, Mass.: Productivity Press, 1990), 169–178; Pennar, "Yes, We're Down," 62; Sidney L. Jones, "Economic Policies in a Changing Global Society," in *The Quality and Productivity Equation: American Corporate Strategies for the 1990s,* edited by Ross E. Robson (Cambridge, Mass.: Productivity Press, 1990), 35–57.

44. Quigley, "U.S. Government and Productivity," 169–178; Pennar, "Yes, We're Down," 62.

45. Skinner, "The Productivity Paradox Explained," 147–157; Eric Anschutz, "The Star-Spangled Toyota," *The Bureaucrat,* Winter 1989–90, 27–31; Neff, "No. 1—And Trying Harder," 20–24.

46. Pennar, "Yes, We're Down," 62; Stewart, "The New American Century," 12–23; Quigley, "U.S. Government and Productivity," 169–178.

47. Michael J. Mandel, "There's a Silver Lining in the Service Sector," *Business Week,* 4 March 1991, 60–61.

48. Mandel, "There's a Silver Lining in the Service Sector," 60–61.

49. Y. K. Shetty, "Key Elements of Productivity Improvement Programs," *Business Horizons,* March–April 1982, 15–22; George W. Grayson, "Mexico's Pemex Begins to Act Like a Competitor," *Wall Street Journal,* 27 September 1991, A11.

50. David Bain, *The Productivity Prescription* (New York: McGraw-Hill, 1982), 54–75, 157–161; Shetty, "Key Elements of Productivity Improvement Programs," 15–22; Brian Dumaine, "How Managers Can Succeed through Speed," *Fortune,* 13 February 1989, 54–59; Jeffrey Lener, "The Right Tool for the Right Job," *Business Month,* April 1990, 62–65.

51. Robert Buderi, "The Brakes Go On in R&D," *Business Week,* 1 July 1991, 24–26; John A. White, "Productivity: Who Cares," in *The Quality and Productivity Equation: American Corporate Strategies for the 1990s,* edited by Ross E. Robson (Cambridge, Mass.: Productivity Press, 1990), 159–168.

52. Patrick E. Cole, "Simpler Designs, Simpler Factories," *Business Week Innovation 1989,* 16 June 1989, 150; Patrick E. Cole, "How CalComp Streamlined Itself," *Business Week,* 6 June 1988, 108.

53. Stalk and Hout, *Competing against Time,* 61–67; John H. Sheridan, "Racing against Time," *Industry Week,* 17 June 1991, 22–28; Otis Port, "How the New Math of Productivity

Adds Up," *Business Week,* 6 June 1988, 103–114.
54. Cole, "Simpler Designs, Simpler Factories," 150; Sheridan, "Racing against Time," 22–28.
55. Kim S. Cameron, "The Critical Role of Management Skills in America's Future," in *The Quality and Productivity Equation: American Corporate Strategies for the 1990s,* edited by Ross E. Robson (Cambridge, Mass.: Productivity Press, 1990), 189–204.
56. Thomas J. Peters and Robert H. Waterman, Jr., *In Search of Excellence* (New York: Warner, 1982), 248–251.
57. Lorraine Dusky, "Bright Ideas: Anatomy of a Corporate Revolution," *Working Woman,* July 1990, 58–63; "A New Culture," *Industry Week,* 17 April 1989, 43–55; Tracy E. Benson, "Empowered Employees Sharpen the Edge," *Industry Week,* 19 February 1990, 13–20; Richard J. Schonberger and Edward M. Knod, Jr., *Operations Management: Improving Customer Service* (Boston: Irwin, 1991), 695–696; Ronald Henkoff, "Some Hope for Troubled Cities," *Fortune,* 9 September 1991, 121–128.
58. Technical Assistance Research Programs Institute, "Consumer Complaint Handling in America: An Update Study," 1 April 1986, executive summary, 2–4.
59. Drucker, *Management,* 79–80; Levitt, *The Marketing Imagination,* 74–78.
60. Levitt, *The Marketing Imagination,* 74–78; James B. Treece, "Sometimes the Game Is the Dull Moment," *Business Week,* 18 February 1991, 122; "Treat Them Right," *Inc.,* October 1989, 131.
61. Levitt, *The Marketing Imagination,* 78–82; Frank Sonnenberg, "Customer Satisfaction: The Strategic Edge for the 1990s," *Adweek's Marketing Week,* 3 September 1990, 20–23.
62. Courtland L. Bovée and John V. Thill, *Marketing* (New York: McGraw-Hill, 1992), 774–775.
63. Lash, *The Complete Guide to Customer Service,* 139–140; Charles A. Jaffe, "Guaranteed Results," *Nation's Business,* February 1990, 62–65.
64. Lash, *The Complete Guide to Customer Service,* 154.
65. Paul B. Brown, "The Real Cost of Customer Service," *Inc.,* September 1990, 49–50, 54, 58, 60.
66. Ron Zemke and Dick Schaaf, *The Service Edge: 101 Companies that Profit from Customer Care* (New York: New American Library, 1989), 39–40; Lele, *The Customer Is Key,* 58–61.
67. Lele, *The Customer Is Key,* 64–65; Zemke and Schaaf, *The Service Edge,* 61–62.
68. Judith Valente, "Northwest to Invest in Service," *Wall Street Journal,* 31 January 1990, B1–B2.
69. Valerie Rice, "The Art and Science of Customer Surveys," *Electronic Business,* 7 October 1991, 141–144; Edward O. Welles, "How're We Doing?" *Inc.,* May 1991, 80–83.
70. *Blueprints for Service Quality: The Federal Express Approach* (New York: American Management Association, 1991), 55–58.
71. Zemke and Schaaf, *The Service Edge,* 34–35.
72. See note 1.

ILLUSTRATION AND TEXT CREDITS

CHAPTER 1

8 Exhibit 1.3, from U.S. Bureau of the Census, *Statistical Abstract of the United States, 1990* (Washington, D.C.: GPO, 1990), 786.
8 Exhibit 1.4, adapted from Anthony J. Michels and Tricia Welsh, "The Service 500," *Fortune,* 3 June 1991, 253–268. © 1991 Time Inc. All rights reserved; and Alison Rogers and Ricardo Sookdeo, "The Fortune 500," *Fortune,* 20 April 1992, 211–312. © 1991 Time Inc. All rights reserved.
13 From *Social Responsibility and the Business Predicament,* edited by James W. McKie, Brookings Institution, 1974, pp. 22–40. Reprinted by permission; Lisa Berger, "Digging In," reprinted from *Across The Board,* October 1990, 27–31, The Conference Board, New York City by permission of the Council of Foundations.
14 Exhibit 1.5, adapted from *The Nature of Managerial Work* by Henry Mintzberg. Copyright © 1973 by Henry Mintzberg. Reprinted by permission of HarperCollins Publishers, 92–93.
17 Exhibit 1.6, adapted from Rosemary Stewart, *Choices for the Manager,* © 1982, p. 3. Reprinted by permission of Prentice Hall, Englewood Cliffs, New Jersey; and McGraw-Hill Book Co. Ltd., Berkshire, England.
21 Exhibit 1.8, adapted from Lester B. Korn, "How the Next CEO Will Be Different," *Fortune,* 22 May 1989, 157. © 1989 Time Inc. All rights reserved.
24–25 Sarah Smith, "America's Most Admired Corporations," *Fortune,* 29 January 1990, 58–92; Ellen Schultz, "America's Most Admired Corporations," *Fortune,* 18 January 1988, 32–52; Bill Saporito, "Let's Hear It from the Winner—And from a Loser," *Fortune,* 18 January 1988, 38; Joseph Weber, "Merck Needs More Gold from the White Coats," *Business Week,* 18 March 1991, 102–104; Gary Hoover, Alta Campbell, and Patrick J. Spain, eds., *Hoover's Handbook 1991: Profiles of Over 500 Major Corporations* (Austin, Tex.: The Reference Press, 1990), 374; "The Best of 1987: Public Service," *Business Week,* 11 January 1988, 156.
27 Adapted from James E. Austin, *Managing in Developing Countries: Strategic Analysis and Operating Techniques* (New York: Free Press, 1990), 10–11, 24, 85–86.
34 Adapted from Sotheby's 1990 Annual Report, inside cover, 6; Judith H. Dobrzynski, "A Bigger Canvas for Sotheby's," *Business Week,* 21 May 1990, 134–136; *The Art of Buying and Selling at Auction* (New York: Sotheby's, 1990) 1, 10, 15; Katrine Ames, Maggie Malone, and Donna Foote, "Sold! The Art Auction Boom," *Newsweek,* 18 April 1988, 65, 68, 73; Judith H. Dobrzynski, "What Am I Bid for a Fast-Climbing Auction House?" *Business Week,* 11 April 1988, 86, 87, 90.

CHAPTER 2

41 Adapted from Randy Hodson and Teresa A. Sullivan, *The Social Organization of Work* (Belmont, Calif.: Wadsworth, 1990), 18–22.
42 Exhibit 2.2, from Claude S. George, Jr., *The History of Management Thought,* Second Edition, © 1972, pp. vii–viii. Adapted by permission of Prentice Hall, Englewood Cliffs, New Jersey.
44 Exhibit 2.3, Courtesy Stevens Institute of Technology.
45 Exhibit 2.4, Courtesy of Frank B. Gilbreth, Charleston, SC.
47 Exhibit 2.5, from Claude S. George, Jr., *The History of Management Thought,* Second Edition, © 1972, p. 108. Adapted by permission of Prentice Hall, Englewood Cliffs, New Jersey.
47 Exhibit 2.6, adapted from *The Evolution of Management Thought,* by Daniel A. Wren, 234. Copyright © 1979. Reprinted by permission of John Wiley & Sons, Inc. and from Henri Fayol, *General and Industrial Management,* translated by Constance Storrs, 3–6. Copyright © 1984 by IEEE and Lake Publishing Company, Belmont, CA 94002.
48 Exhibit 2.7, adapted from Henri Fayol, *General and Industrial Management,* trans. Constance Storrs, 97. Copyright © 1984 by IEEE and Lake Publishing Company, Belmont, CA 94002; and Claude S. George, Jr., *The History of Management Thought,* 2nd ed. (Englewood Cliffs, N.J.: Prentice Hall, 1972), 113.
50–51 Bob Hagerty, "Unilever Profit Edged Higher in 2nd Quarter," *Wall Street Journal,* 12 August 1991, B4A; Walecia Konrad, "The New, Improved Unilever Aims to Clean Up in the U.S.," *Business Week,* 29 November 1989, 102, 106; Gary Hoover, Alta Campbell, and Patrick J. Spain, eds., *Hoover's Handbook 1991: Profiles of Over 500 Major Corporations* (Austin, Tex.: The Reference Press, 1990), 549.
54 Exhibit 2.8, adapted from Douglas M. McGregor, "The Human Side of Enterprise," in *Management Classics,* 2nd ed., edited by Michael T. Matteson and John M. Ivancevich (Santa Monica, Calif.: Goodyear Publishing, 1981), 256–264.
58–59 "Brunswick's Dramatic Turnaround," *Journal of Business Strategy,* January–February 1988, 4–7; "The Corporate Elite," *Business Week,* 19 October 1990, 88; Gary Hoover, Alta Campbell, and Patrick J. Spain, eds., *Hoover's Handbook 1991: Profiles of Over 500 Major Corporations* (Austin, Tex.: The Reference Press, 1990), 143.
63 Exhibit 2.10, adapted from William Ouchi, *Theory Z,* © 1981, by Addison-Wesley Publishing Company, Inc. Reprinted with permission of the publisher; and William G. Ouchi and Alfred M. Jaeger, "Type Z Organization: Stability in the Midst of Mobility," *Academy of Management Review,* Vol. 3, 1978, pp. 308 and 311. Reprinted by permission of the Academy of Management.
69 Adapted from Todd Vogel and Chuck Hawkins, "Can UPS Deliver the Goods in a New World?" *Business Week,* 4 June 1990, 80–82; Simon Caulkin, "UPS's USP," *Management Today,* November 1989, 116–121; Amy Cortese, "Erbrick Delivers for United Parcel Service," *Computerworld,* 27 February 1989, 97, 101; Resa W. King, "UPS Isn't About to Be Left

Holding the Parcel," *Business Week,* 13 February 1989, 69; Peter Truell, "UPS to Control Its Jet Fleet, Ending Management Pacts," *Wall Street Journal,* 25 August 1987, A24.

CHAPTER 3

78 Exhibit 3.3, adapted from Kate Ballen, "How America Will Change over the Next 30 Years," *Fortune,* 17 June 1991, 12. © 1991 Time Inc. All rights reserved.
79 Exhibit 3.4, adapted from Milton Moskowitz, Robert Levering, and Michael Katz, *Everybody's Business* (New York: Doubleday Currency, 1990), 218–219; Michael Salter, "Big Stores, Bigger Sales: Canada," *McLean's,* 15 December 1986, 42–43; "Toys 'R' Us Goes Overseas—And Finds that Toys 'R' Them, Too," *Business Week,* 26 January 1987, 71–72.
82 Exhibit 3.5, from T. G. Herrick, *Bank Analysts Handbook,* 1978, p. 266. Copyright © 1978 by Tracy G. Herrick, successor to John Wiley & Sons. Reprinted by permission; and Alan Gart, *The Insider's Guide to the Financial Services Revolution* (New York: McGraw-Hill, 1984), 23. Copyright © 1948.
84–85 Adapted from Theresa Agovino, "School Plans to Toe Fiscal Bottom Line," *Crain's New York Business,* 29 April 1991, 13.
87 Exhibit 3.6, from The Reader's Digest Association 1990 Annual Report, 8–9. Courtesy Reader's Digest.
89 Rose Brady and Peter Galuszka, "Let's Make a Deal—But a Smaller One," *Business Week,* 20 January 1992, 44–45.
90 Exhibit 3.7, adapted from Robert Duncan, "What Is the Right Organization Structure?" *Organizational Dynamics,* Winter 1979, 59–80. Reprinted, by permission of the publisher, from *Organizational Dynamics,* Winter 1979 © 1979. American Management Association, New York. All rights reserved.
92–93 Adapted from Adrian Waller, "Progressive Governor Brings Oita to the Fore," *Japan Times* 31, no. 8 (25 February–3 March 1991): 1, 5. Reprinted by permission of Japan Times Ltd.
95 Exhibit 3.8, Courtesy Ad Council.
101 Gary Hoover, Alta Campbell, and Patrick J. Spain, eds., *Hoover's Handbook 1991: Profiles of Over 500 Major Corporations* (Austin, Tex.: The Reference Press, 1990), 309; Joe Queenan, "Big Blue Is Back," *Barron's* 28 May 1990, 10–11, 24–26; Jagannath Dubashi, "Old Elephant, New Tricks," *Financial World,* 27 November 1990, 24–25; Carol J. Loomis, "Can John Akers Save IBM?" *Fortune,* 15 July 1991, 40–56; IBM 1990 Annual Report, 1–26; "It's Official: IBM and Apple Tie the Knot," *Business Week,* 14 October 1991, 54.

CHAPTER 4

105 Exhibit 4.1, from Archie B. Carroll, "A Three-Dimensional Conceptual Model of Corporate Performance," *Academy of Management Review* 4, no. 4 (1979): 497–505. Reprinted by permission of the Academy of Management.
106 Exhibit 4.2, adapted from "SMR Forum: Corporate Responsibility—Reconciling Economic and Social Goals," by James J. Chrisman and Archie B. Carroll, *Sloan Management Review,* Winter 1984, pp. 59–65, by permission of the publisher. Copyright 1984 by the Sloan Management Review Association. All rights reserved.
108–109 Milton R. Moskowitz, "Company Performance Roundup," *Business and Society,* Summer 1989, 66–72; Kathleen Teltsch, "Japanese in U.S. Aiding Charities as Volunteers," *New York Times,* 2 May 1991, sec. b, 1, 7; Michael Schroeder, "Charity Doesn't Begin at Home Anymore," *Business Week,* 25 February 1991, 91; Richard E. Wokutch, "Corporate Social Responsibility Japanese Style," *Academy of Management Executive,* May 1990, 56–74.
112 Adapted from Robert Williams, Mark Teagan, and Jose Beneyto, *The World's Largest Market: A Business Guide to Europe 1992* (New York: Amacom, 1990), 76.
118 Exhibit 4.5, Courtesy McGraw-Hill.
119 Kenneth A. Macke, ". . . With Some Attendant Risks," *New York Times,* 30 December 1990, sec. 3, 11; Adam Snyder, "Do Boycotts Work?" *Adweek's Marketing Week,* 8 April 1991, 16–18; Kervin Kelly, "Dayton Hudson Finds There's No Graceful Way to Flip-Flop," *Business Week,* 24 September 1990, 50; Tamar Lewin, "Ending Aid to Family Planning, Large Retailer Is Caught in Storm," *New York Times,* 15 September 1990, 7.
122 Exhibit 4.6, adapted from Michael R. Hyman, Robert Skipper, and Richard Tansey, "Ethical Codes Are Not Enough," *Business Horizons,* March–April 1990, 15–22.
126 Exhibit 4.7, Courtesy Raytheon Company.
133 Adapted from Howard L. Siers, "Doing the Right Thing at Monsanto," *Management Accounting,* June 1991, 24; William H. Miller, "Those Stingy American Companies," *Industry Week,* 21 January 1991, 48, 50–53; Monsanto Company's Environmental Annual Review, July 1991, 1–3, 9, 10; Monsanto 1990 Annual Report, 1, 7, 8, 15–17; Patricia Baird, "New Fat Substitutes," *Restaurant Business,* 1 September 1990, 64; "Monsanto's Marketing Woes; Show Me," *Economist,* 10 March 1990, 74, 76; "Monsanto Muscles into Fat Substitute Market," *Chemical & Engineering News,* 5 March 1990, 5, 6; Gary Hoover, Alta Campbell, and Patrick J. Spain, eds., *Hoover's Handbook 1991; Profiles of Over 500 Major Corporations* (Austin, Tex.: The Reference Press, 1990), 384; Milton Moskowitz, Robert Levering, and Michael Katz, *Everybody's Business* (New York: Doubleday, 1990), 527–529; Laurie Freeman, "The Day When 'Fat' Won't Be Sinful," *Advertising Age,* 13 November 1989, 513; Rick Reiff, "Blood, Sweat and Profits," *Forbes,* 6 March 1989, 110, 112.

CHAPTER 5

137 Exhibit 5.1, adapted from "The 'Stateless' World of Manufacturing." Reprinted from the May 14, 1990 issue of *Business Week* by permission. Copyright © 1990 McGraw-Hill, Inc.
140 Exhibit 5.2, adapted from James Beeler, "Exports: Ship 'Em Out," *Fortune,* Spring–Summer 1991, 58–59. Reprinted by permission of Time, Inc.
142 Adapted from Monua Janah, "Rating Risk in the Hot Countries," *Wall Street Journal,* 20 September 1991, R4.
143 Exhibit 5.3, adapted from Philip R. Cateora, *International Marketing,* Richard D. Irwin, Inc., © 1987, p. 300.
146–147 Adapted from Matt Schaffer, *Winning the Countertrade War* (New York: Wiley, 1989), 73; Warren J. Keegan, *Global Marketing Management* (Englewood Cliffs, N.J.: Prentice Hall, 1989), 548; Alan M. Rugman, Donald J. Lecraw, and Laurence D. Booth, *International Business: Firm and Environment* (New York: McGraw-Hill, 1985), 72–73; Karen Benezra, "Soviets Say 'Da' to Pepsi in a Trade for Vodka," *Gannett Westchester Newspapers,* 20 January 1991, Commerce and Industry section part 1, 30; Monsanto 1989 Annual Report, 8; John S. DeMott, "Soviet Promise: Bets on a Bartering Revival," *International Business,* October 1991, 17–19.
152 Exhibit 5.5, adapted from Ellen F. Jackofsy, John W. Slocum, Jr., and Sara J. McQuaid, "Cultural Values and the CEO: Alluring Companions?" *Academy of Management Executive* 11, no. 1 (1988): 39–49. Reprinted by permission of the Academy of Management.
156 Adapted from Constance Mitchell, "Partnerships Have Become a Way of Life for Corning," *Wall Street Journal,* 12 July 1988, 6. Reprinted by permission of *The Wall Street Journal,* © 1988 Dow Jones & Company, Inc. All Rights Reserved Worldwide.
158 Exhibit 5.6, adapted from Gary Taylor, "Maquilas at the Crossroads," *International Business,* October 1991, 33. Reprinted by permission of American International Publishing Co.
165 Adapted from Maryfran Johnson, "DEC's Purchase of Philips Wins Praise," *Computerworld,* 29 July 1991, 88; "Whirlpool in Europe; But Will It Wash?" *Economist,* 13 July 1991, 70; "Philips Failing," *World Press Review,* June 1991, 39; Geoffrey Foster, "Hanging on the Fate of Philips," *Management Today,* June 1991, 31; Mat Toor, "Philips Gambles on High-Tech," *Marketing,* 11 April 1991, 2, 3; Gary Hoover, Alta Campbell, and Patrick J. Spain, eds., *Hoover's Handbook of World Business 1992* (Austin, Tex.: The Reference Press, 1991), 259; Milton Moskowitz, Robert Levering, and Michael Katz, *Everybody's Business* (New York: Doubleday, 1990), 279, 280; Jonathan Kapstein, Jonathan Levine, and Gail E. Schares, "A Chilling New Era for Philips—And Europe," *Business Week,* 12 November 1990, 58, 59; Jonathan Kapstein and Jonathan B. Levine, "European High Tech Is Sinking Mighty Low," *Business Week,* 17 September 1990, 52; Jonathan Kapstein and Jonathan Levine, "A Would-Be World-Beater Takes a Beating," *Business Week,* 16 July 1990, 40, 41; "The New Boss at Philips: Timmer the Timorous," *Economist,* 7 July 1990, 68, 69; Jonathan B. Levine, Jonathan Kapstein, and Stanley Reed, "What's Behind the Bombshell at Philips?" *Business Week,* 28 May 1990, 38, 39.
166–167 Adapted from Marriott 1990 Annual Report, 2–5, 22–27, 29, 46–47; Marriott 1989 Annual Report, 2– 5; Dean Foust, "Marriott Is Smoothing Out the Lumps in Its Bed," *Business Week,* 1 April 1991, 74–75; Christopher Muller, "The Marriott Divestment: Leaving the Past Behind," *Cornell Hotel and Restaurant Administration Quarterly,* February 1990, 7–13; Carol Kennedy, "How Marriott Corporation Grew Five-Fold in Ten Years," *Long Range Planning* 21, no. 2 (1988): 10–14; Howard Riell, "Marriott Taps Service Synergy: A Period of Adaptation," *Restaurant Business,* 10 February 1988, 182–183; Bill Gillette, "Conservative Approach Fuels Marriott Success," *Hotel and Motel Management,* 19 June 1989, 3, 58–59, 91; Megan Rowe, "Marriott Sets the Standard," *Lodging Hospitality,* June 1989, 22, 24–26, 28; Charlene Marmer Solomon, "Marriott's Family Matters," *Personnel Journal,* October 1991, 40–42; Judith Hudnutt Sawyer, "Bill Marriott, Jr.: In the Driver's Seat," *Meetings & Conventions,* August 1986, 60, 62, 64; "Rooms at the

Inn," *Fortune,* 2 January 1989, 62; Faye Rice, "Hotels Fight for Business Guests," *Fortune,* 23 April 1990; Frank E. Camacho, "Meeting the Needs of Senior Citizens Through Lifecare Communities: Marriott's Approach to the Development of a New Service Business," *Journal of Services Marketing* 2, no. 1 (Winter 1988): 49–53; "Biography: J. W. Marriott, Jr.," Marriott, May 1991.

CHAPTER 6

178 Exhibit 6.4, adapted from *Administrative Behavior,* Third Edition, by Herbert A. Simon. New York: The Free Press, 1976, pp. 80–81.
180–181 Based on information from Steven Waldman, "Putting a Price Tag on Life," *Newsweek,* 11 January 1988, 40.
186 Adapted from Richard M. Hodgetts and Fred Luthans, *International Management* (New York: McGraw-Hill, 1991), 28–29.
188 Exhibit 6.6, adapted from *Business Statistics: Concepts and Applications,* Second Edition by William J. Stevenson. Copyright © 1985 by Harper & Row, Publishers, Inc. Reprinted by permission of HarperCollins Publishers.
189 Exhibit 6.7, adapted from *Business Statistics: Concepts and Applications,* Second Edition by William J. Stevenson. Copyright © 1985 by Harper & Row, Publishers, Inc. Reprinted by permission of HarperCollins Publishers.
190–191 Gerry Blackwell, "Damage Control: Why Honesty and Speed Are Key in a Product Recall," *Canadian Business,* August 1990, 62–63. Reprinted by permission of C. B. Media.
194 Exhibit 6.8, adapted from Terence R. Mitchell and James R. Larson, Jr., *People in Organizations: An Introduction to Organizational Behavior* (New York: McGraw-Hill, 1987), 371. Copyright © 1987. Reprinted by permission of McGraw-Hill, Inc.
201 "Kellogg's LaMothe to Retire; Langbo Named Chairman and CEO,"PR Newswire, 18 October 1991; David Woodruff, "Winning the War of Battle Creek," *Business Week,* 13 May 1991, 80; Claudia H. Deutsch, "Has Kellogg Lost Its Snap?" *New York Times,* 24 September 1989, sec. 3, 1, 6; Patricia Sellers, "How Kellogg Beat the Blahs," *Fortune,* 29 August 1988, 54, 55, 58, 60, 64; Alan J. Zakon, "It's Just Not Good Enough!" *Management Review,* January 1988, 20, 21; Russell Mitchell, "The Health Craze Has Kellogg Feeling G-r-r-reat," *Business Week,* 30 March 1987, 52, 53.

CHAPTER 7

206 Exhibit 7.2, CSX 1990 Annual Report, 3.
207 Exhibit 7.3, adapted from Peter F. Drucker, *Management: Tasks, Responsibilities, Practices* (New York: Harper & Row, 1974), 100, 105–117.
208 Adapted from James E. Austin, *Managing in Developing Countries* (New York: Free Press, 1990), 87.
216–217 Adapted from Nancy Jeffrey, "Preparing for the Worst: Firms Set Up Plans to Help Deal with Corporate Crises," *Wall Street Journal,* 7 December 1987, 23. Reprinted by permission of *The Wall Street Journal,* © 1987 Dow Jones & Company, Inc. All Rights Reserved Worldwide.
219 Exhibit 7.5, adapted from George Odiorne, Heinz Weihrich, and Jack Mendleson, *Executive Skills: A Management by Objectives Approach* (Dubuque, Iowa: Brown, 1980), 24; Anthony P. Raia, *Managing by Objectives* (Glenview, Ill.: Scott, Foresman, 1974), 16.
222 Exhibit 7.6, adapted from Irving Abramowitz, *Production Management* (New York: Ronald Press, 1967), 28–29. Copyright © 1967. Reprinted by permission of John Wiley & Sons, Inc.
224–225 Adapted from Carol Kennedy, "How Marriott Corporation Grew Fivefold in Ten Years," *Long Range Planning* 21, no. 2 (1988): 10–14; Faye Rice, "Hotels Fight for Business Guests," *Fortune,* 23 April 1990, 265–274; Marriott 1989 Annual Report, 2–5, 12.
227 Exhibit 7.7, adapted from *Mathematical Analysis: Business and Economic Applications,* Fourth Edition, by Jean E. Weber. Copyright © 1982 by Jean E. Weber. Reprinted by permission of HarperCollins Publishers.
235 Kevin Kelly, "3M Run Scared? Forget about It," *Business Week,* 16 September 1991, 59, 62; 3M 1990 Annual Report, 1–7; Dale Kurschner, "Troubled Economy Puts 3M in a Sticky Situation," *Minneapolis–St. Paul City Business,* 6–12 May 1991, 1, 18, 19; "5 Companies with Star Potential," *Business Month,* December 1989, 44, 45, 48; "Masters of Innovation," *Business Week,* 10 April 1989, 58–63.

CHAPTER 8

243 Exhibit 8.2, adapted from Samuel C. Certo and J. Paul Peter, *Strategic Management: Concepts and Applications,* 2nd ed. (New York: McGraw-Hill, 1991), 99.
244–245 Janice McCormick and Nan Stone, "From National Champion to Global Competitor: An Interview with Thomson's Alain Gomez," *Harvard Business Review,* May–June 1990, 126–135; Jonathan B. Levine, "The Heat on Alain Gomez," *Business Week,* 11 March 1991, 66–67; Gary Hoover, Alta Campbell, and Patrick J. Spain, eds., *Hoover's Handbook 1991: Profiles of Over 500 Major Corporations* (Austin, Tex.: The Reference Press, 1990), 532.
248 Adapted from James Austin, *Managing in Developing Countries* (New York: Free Press, 1990), 272–274; U.S. Department of Commerce, *Statistical Abstract of the United States* (Washington, D.C.: GPO, 1990), 831, 836.
251 Exhibit 8.4, adapted with the permission of The Free Press, a Division of Macmillan, Inc. from *Competitive Strategy: Techniques for Analyzing Industries and Competitors* by Michael E. Porter, p. 362. Copyright © 1980 by The Free Press.
252 Exhibit 8.5, adapted with the permission of The Free Press, a Division of Macmillan, Inc. from *Competitive Strategy: Techniques for Analyzing Industries and Competitors* by Michael E. Porter, p. 365. Copyright © 1980 by The Free Press.
254 Exhibit 8.6, adapted from Raymond E. Miles, Charles C. Snow, Alan D. Meyer, and Henry J. Coleman, Jr., "Organizational Strategy, Structure, and Process," *Academy of Management Review* 3 (July 1978): 546–562. Reprinted by permission of the Academy of Management.
255 Exhibit 8.7, adapted with the permission of The Free Press, a Division of Macmillan, Inc. from *Competitive Strategy: Techniques for Analyzing Industries and Competitors* by Michael E. Porter, pp. 40–41. Copyright © 1980 by The Free Press.
258 Exhibit 8.8, adapted from Courtland L. Bovée and John V. Thill, *Marketing* (New York: McGraw-Hill, 1992), 271. Copyright © 1992. Reprinted by permission of McGraw-Hill, Inc.
256–257 Andrew Pollack, "An Appetite for Mergers," *New York Times,* 18 August 1991, sec. 3, 10; A. W. Clausen, "Strategic Issues in Managing Change: The Turnaround at BankAmerica Corporation," *California Management Review* 32, no. 2 (Winter 1990): 98–105; Joan O'C. Hamilton, "Will BankAmerica Have the Last Laugh?" *Business Week,* 26 November 1990, 148–150; Gary Hector, "It's Banquet Time for BankAmerica," *Fortune,* 3 June 1991, 69–74; BankAmerica 1990 annual report; Gary Hoover, Alta Campbell, and Patrick J. Spain, eds., *Hoover's Handbook 1991: Profiles of Over 500 Major Corporations* (Austin, Tex.: The Reference Press, 1990), 111.
267 "Nissan Motor: New Information System Gives Customers Firm Delivery Dates," *Business Japan,* September 1991, 22, 23; Jean S. Bozman, "Nissan Motors with AS/400s," *Computerworld,* 26 August 1991, 31; William J. Fife, "The Automation Imperative," *Chief Executive,* May 1991, 34–37; Gary S. Vasilash, "Listening, Believing, and Transnationalizing," *Production,* March 1991, 70, 71; Yasuhiro Ishizuna, "The Transformation of Nissan—The Reform of Corporate Culture," *Long Range Planning,* June 1990, 9–15; Larry Armstrong, "The American Drivers Steering Japan through the States," *Business Week,* 12 March 1990, 98, 99; Stewart Toy and David Castellon, "How Nissan Plans to Shift Out of Reverse," *Business Week,* 18 July 1988, 120, 121; Jeffrey Ryser, "Japanese Car Wars Have Nissan Biting the Bullet," *Business Week,*; 8 December 1988, 52, 53; Andrew Tanzer and Marc Beauchamp, "Confession Time at Nissan," *Forbes,* 3 November 1986, 48, 51.
268–269 E. S. Ely, "Some High Hurdles Loom for Pepsico's Fast-Food Hotshots," *New York Times,* 16 February 1992, sec. 3, 5; PepsiCo 1990 Annual Report, 2–35, 50–51, inside back cover; "Domino's, Pizza Hut Make a Run for the Border, Continue Their War," *Marketing News,* 11 November 1991, 5; James Scarpa, "Company of the Year: PepsiCo's the Right One, Baby," *Restaurant Business,* 10 October 1991, 129–131, 134–137, 140; Gary Hoover, Alta Campbell, and Patrick J. Spain, eds., *Hoover's Handbook of American Business 1992* (Austin, Tex.: The Reference Press, 1991), 432; Jeffrey A. Trachtenberg, "Succession Game," *Forbes,* 11 February 1985, 169, 172; "A Different Brand of Leader," *Chief Executive,* July–August 1991, 40–43, 46, 48; Paul Frumkin and Theresa Howard, "The Future of Pizza Hut: Diversification," *Nation's Restaurant News,* 18 November 1991, 70; John Marcom, Jr., "Cola Attack," *Forbes,* 26 November 1990, 48–49; Gary A. Hemphill, "Pepsi Rallies Bottlers for Global Push," *Beverage Industry,* May 1990, 15, 19; Milford Prewitt and Peter O. Keegan, "PepsiCo Blazes International Trail," *Nation's Restaurant News,* 18 November 1991, 58, 62; Scott Hume and Bradley Johnson, "'Value' Trend Nibbles at Fast-Food Profits," *Advertising Age,* 6 May 1991, 20; Stephanie Anderson Forest, "Chipping Away at Frito-Lay," *Business Week,* 22 July 1991, 26; Mark Landler, "Shoppers Squeeze Nickels—And Consumer-Goods Makers," *Business Week,* 30 September 1991, 26.

CHAPTER 9

277 Exhibit 9.2, from Henry Mintzberg, *The Structuring of Organizations,* © 1979, p. 27.

Adapted by permission of Prentice Hall, Englewood Cliffs, New Jersey.
282 Exhibit 9.3, from Henry Mintzberg, *The Structuring of Organizations,* © 1979, p. 136. Adapted by permission of Prentice Hall, Englewood Cliffs, New Jersey.
282–283 Adapted from Robert M. Tomasko, *Downsizing: Reshaping the Corporation for the Future* (New York: Amacom, 1987), 28–32, 46–68; Thomas R. Horton and Peter C. Reid, *Beyond the Trust Gap* (Homewood, Ill.: Irwin, 1991), 6–7, 9–10, 22–24, 47, 58–65, 100–103; Norm Alster, "It's Still a Difficult Environment," *Forbes,* 5 August 1991, 42–44; Stephen Kreider Yoder, "Quick Change: A 1990 Reorganization at Hewlett-Packard Already Is Paying Off," *Wall Street Journal,* 22 July 1991, A1, A4; Barbara Buell and Robert D. Hof, "Hewlett-Packard Rethinks Itself," *Business Week,* 1 April 1991, 76–79; George Bailey and David Sherman, "Downsizing: The Alternatives May Be Cheaper," *Management Review,* April 1988, 54–55; George Bailey and Julia Szerdy, "Is There Life after Downsizing?" *Journal of Business Strategy,* January–February 1988, 8–11.
285 Exhibit 9.5, from Henry Mintzberg, *The Structuring of Organizations,* © 1979, p. 23. Adapted by permission of Prentice Hall, Englewood Cliffs, New Jersey; adapted from Rensis Likert, *The Human Organization: Its Management and Value* (New York: McGraw-Hill, 1967), 50. Copyright © 1967. Reprinted by permission of McGraw-Hill, Inc.
286 Exhibit 9.6, adapted from Herbert A. Simon, *Administrative Behavior,* 3rd ed. (New York: Free Press, 1976), 28–34; Edwin A. Gerloff, *Organizational Theory and Design* (New York: McGraw-Hill, 1985), 228. Copyright © 1985. Reprinted by permission of McGraw-Hill, Inc.
290 Exhibit 9.7, adapted from Henry Mintzberg, *The Structuring of Organizations* (Englewood Cliffs, N.J.: Prentice Hall, 1979), 23.
294 Adapted from Stuart Rock, "Swissair: New Routes to Staying on Top," *Director,* November 1988, 185–188, by kind permission of Director Publications, London SW1, England.
295 Philip R. Cateora, *International Management,* 7th ed. (Homewood, Ill.: Irwin, 1990), 110.
301 Andrew Kupfer, "Ma Bell and the Seven Babies Go Global," *Fortune,* 4 November 1991, 118–120, 124, 128; "AT&T Sets Global Goals for International Units," *Report on AT&T,* 8 July 1991, 1–10; Gary Hoover, Alta Campbell, and Patrick J. Spain, eds., *Hoover's Handbook 1991: Profiles of Over 500 Major Corporations* (Austin, Tex.: The Reference Press, 1990), 83; AT&T 1990 Annual Report, 1, 18; Milton Moskowitz, Robert Levering, and Michael Katz, *Everybody's Business* (New York: Doubleday, 1990), 626–630; Carol Kennedy, "The Transformation of AT&T," *Long Range Planning,* June 1989, 10–17; John J. Keller, "AT&T: The Making of a Comeback," *Business Week,* 18 July 1988, 56–59; "Attuned to the Way You Do Business," *Modern Office Technology,* May 1985, 9, 10, 13–15, 20.

CHAPTER 10

307 Exhibit 10.1, adapted from Rensis Likert, *The Human Organization: Its Management and Value,* 3rd ed. (New York: McGraw-Hill, 1967), 197–211. Copyright © 1967. Reprinted by permission of McGraw-Hill, Inc.
311 Exhibit 10.2, adapted from Tom Burns and G. M. Stalker, "Mechanistic and Organic Systems," in *Management Classics,* 2nd ed., edited by Michael T. Matteson and John M. Ivancevich (Santa Monica, Calif.: Goodyear, 1981), 391–392.
312 Adapted from Paul Klebnikov, "The Powerhouse," *Forbes,* 2 September 1991, 46–52. © Forbes Inc., 1991; Jules Arbose, "ABB The New Energy Powerhouse," *International Management,* June 1988, 24–30. Reprinted by kind permission of International Management, © Reed Business Publishing, 1992.
314 Exhibit 10.3, adapted from Joan Woodward, *Industrial Organization: Theory and Practice,* 2nd ed. (London: Oxford University Press, 1980), 50–80. Reprinted by permission of Oxford University Press.
315 Exhibit 10.4, adapted from Eric G. Flamholtz, *Growing Pains: How to Make the Transition from an Entrepreneurship to a Professionally Managed Firm* (San Francisco: Jossey-Bass, 1990), 197–211; W. Graham Astley, "Organizational Size and Bureaucratic Structure," *Organization Studies* 6, no. 3 (1985): 201–228; Joseph A. Litterer, *The Analysis of Organizations* (New York: Wiley, 1965), 403–411.
320 T. W. Kang, *Is Korea the Next Japan?* (New York: Free Press, 1989), 30.
322 Adapted from Robert L. Kuhn, ed., *Handbook for Creative and Innovative Managers* (New York: McGraw-Hill, 1988), 263–270; Raymond E. Miles and Charles C. Snow, "Organizations: New Concepts for New Forms," *California Management Review* 28, no. 3 (Spring 1986): 62–73; Alvin Toffler, "Breaking with Bureaucracy," *Across the Board,* January–February 1991, 17–21; Tom Peters, "Restoring American Competitiveness: Looking for New Models of Organizations," *Academy of Management Executive* 2, no. 2 (May 1988): 103–109; Jan Shaw, "Galoob Regroups after President Leaves Toymaker," *San Francisco Business Times,* 5 July 1991, 3; John W. Wilson, "And Now, the Post-Industrial Corporation," *Business Week,* 3 March 1986, 64–71; Standard & Poor's Register—Corporate, on-line 29 March 1992.
324 Exhibit 10.9, from Henry Mintzberg, *The Structuring of Organizations,* © 1979, pp. 466–467. Adapted by permission of Prentice Hall, Englewood Cliffs, New Jersey.
331 Adapted from Peter Nulty, "Behind the Mess at Westinghouse," *Fortune,* 4 November 1991, 93-94, 98-99; Milton Moskowitz, Robert Levering, and Michael Katz, *Everybody's Business* (New York: Doubleday, 1990), 449-451; Gary Hoover, Alta Campbell, and Patrick J. Spain, eds., *Hoover's Handbook 1991* (Austin, Tex.: The Reference Press, 1990), 586.
333 Adrienne Linsenmeyer, "Kodak Gets Back into Focus," *Financial World,* 14 May 1991, 18; Gary Hoover, Alta Campbell, and Patrick J. Spain, eds., *Hoover's Handbook 1991: Profiles of Over 500 Major Corporations* (Austin, Tex.: The Reference Press, 1990), 218; Milton Moskowitz, Robert Levering, and Michael Katz, *Everybody's Business* (New York: Doubleday, 1990), 305–307; Eastman Kodak Company 1990 Annual Report, inside cover; Seth Lubove, "Aim, Focus and Shoot," *Forbes,* 26 November 1990, 67, 68, 70; Keith H. Hammonds, "A Moment Kodak Wants to Capture," *Business Week,* 27 August 1990, 52, 53; Wes Iversen, "Information Systems: Tying It All Together," *Industry Week,* 20 August 1990, 20, 21, 24–27, 30; Jay Palmer, "The Picture Brightens; At Eastman Kodak, Things Are Looking Up at All Divisions," *Barron's,* 25 June 1990, 8, 9, 57–59; John W. Boroski, "Putting It Together: HR Planning in '3D' at Eastman Kodak," *Human Resource Planning* 13 (1990): 45–57.

CHAPTER 11

337 Information on Toro adapted from Brian Dumaine, "Closing the Innovation Gap," *Fortune,* 2 December 1991, 56-59, 62. © 1991 Time Inc. All rights reserved.
337 Bob Savic, "The Fallout from Unification," *Asian Finance,* 15 September 1991, 93–96.
338–339 Exhibit 11.1, ©Visa U.S.A. Inc. 1991. All Rights Reserved. Reproduced with the permission of Visa U.S.A. Inc.
341 Exhibit 11.2, adapted from Kurt Lewin, *Field Theory in Social Science* (New York: Harper & Row, 1951), 228–229. Reprinted by permission of Miriam Lewin, Ph.D.
343 Exhibit 11.3, from Paul Hersey and Kenneth H. Blanchard, *Management of Organizational Behavior: Utilizing Human Resources,* Fifth Edition, © 1988, p. 338. Adapted by permission of Prentice Hall, Englewood Cliffs, New Jersey.
344 Exhibit 11.4, adapted from and reprinted by permission of *Harvard Business Review.* An exhibit from "Choosing Strategies for Change" by John A. Kotter and Leonard A. Schlesinger, March–April 1979, p. 111. Copyright © 1979 by the President and Fellows of Harvard College; all rights reserved.
346–347 Adapted from Thomas A. Stewart, "GE Keeps Those Ideas Coming," *Fortune,* 12 August 1991, 40–49; Bernard C. Reimann, "Corporate Strategies that Work," *Planning Review,* January–February 1992, 41–42; James Braham, "Creativity: Eureka!" *Machine Design,* 6 February 1992, 32–36; "GEA: Making Things Happen—Productivity Driven," *Appliance Manufacturer,* January 1992, GEA6–GEA10.
354–355 Adapted from Christina Elnora Garza, "Studying the Natives on the Shop Floor," *Business Week,* 30 September 1991, 74–78; Christina Elnora Garza, "The Touchy Ethics of Corporate Anthropology," *Business Week,* 30 September 1991, 78; Louis P. White and Kevin C. Wooten, "Ethical Dilemmas in Various Stages of Organizational Development," in *Organization Development: Theory, Practice, and Research,* 3rd ed., edited by Wendell L. French, Cecil H. Bell, Jr., and Robert A. Zawacki (Homewood, Ill.: BPI Irwin, 1989), 650–659.
357 Exhibit 11.6, from Vilma Barr, "The Process of Innovation: Brainstorming and Storyboarding," *Mechanical Engineering,* November 1988, 42.
357 Exhibit 11.7, adapted from William C. Miller, "Techniques for Stimulating New Ideas: A Matter of Fluency," in *Handbook for Creative and Innovative Managers,* edited by Robert L. Kuhn (New York: McGraw-Hill, 1988), 117. Copyright © 1988. Reprinted by permission of McGraw-Hill, Inc.
365 Laura Zinn, "Why 'Business Stinks' at Woolworth," *Business Week,* 25 November 1991, 72, 76; "Woolworth Corporation," *Wall Street Transcript,* 15 July 1991, 101, 840–841, 841; Robert Spector, "Woolworth Maps Out Bold Expansion Plan," *Footwear News,* 24 June 1991, 2, 8; Harlan S. Byrne, "Woolworth Corp.; Specialty Stores Earn Big Bucks for the Old Five-and-Dime Retailer," *Barron's,* 17 June 1991, 49–50; Lee Tom Perry, "Strategic Improvising: Formulate and Implement Competitive

Strategies in Concert," *Organizational Dynamics,* Spring 1991, 51–64.

CHAPTER 12

369 Exhibit 12.1, adapted from Ralph M. Gaedeke and Dennis H. Tootelian, *Small Business Management* (Needham Heights, Mass.: Allyn & Bacon, 1991), 4.
370 Adapted from Marilyn Johnson, "Here's a Business Tip: Bulgaria," *Arizona Business Gazette,* 7 February 1992, 20.
370–371 Adapted from Elizabeth Conlin, "Educating the Market," *Inc.,* July 1991, 62–67. Reprinted with permission, *Inc.* magazine, July 1991. Copyright © 1991 by Goldhirsh Group, Inc., 38 Commercial Wharf, Boston, MA 02110.
374 Exhibit 12.2, adapted from *Small Business: Planning and Management,* Second Edition, by Charles R. Kuehl and Peggy A. Lambing, copyright © 1990 by The Dryden Press, reprinted by permission of the publisher, p. 29.
377 Exhibit 12.3, adapted from Sally Saville Hodge, "Buying a Business," *Sylvia Porter's Personal Finance,* March 1989, 41–47.
378 Exhibit 12.4, adapted from Joseph Anthony, "Your Own Business," *Sylvia Porter's Personal Finance,* March 1989, 32–47.
380 Exhibit 12.5, adapted from Mark Mehler and Judy Lyon Davis, "Money." First appeared in *Success,* December 1989, 35–42. Written by Mark Mehler and Judy Lyon Davis. Reprinted with permission of *Success* Magazine. Copyright © 1989 by Hal Holdings, Inc.
382 Exhibit 12.6, adapted from John B. Hinge, "Small Businesses, Big Numbers," *Wall Street Journal,* 22 November 1991, R18. Reprinted by permission of *The Wall Street Journal,* © 1991 Dow Jones & Company, Inc. All Rights Reserved Worldwide.
384–385 Adapted from Tom Richman, "Not for Profit." Reprinted with permission, *Inc.* magazine, November 1990, pp. 108–117. Copyright © 1990 by Goldhirsch Group, Inc., 38 Commercial Wharf, Boston, MA 02110; and Leslie Brokaw, "The Truth about Start-Ups." Reprinted with permission, *Inc.* magazine, April 1991 pp. 52–67. Copyright © 1991, by Goldhirsch Group, Inc., 38 Commercial Wharf, Boston, MA 02110.
387 Exhibit 12.7, from *Intrapreneuring* by Gifford Pinchot III, p. 31. Copyright © 1985 by Gifford Pinchot III. Reprinted by permission of HarperCollins Publishers.
390 Exhibit 12.8, reprinted from "New Venture Units: Use Them Wisely to Manage Innovation," by Christopher K. Bart, *Sloan Management Review,* Summer 1988, p. 39, by permission of the publisher. Copyright 1988 by the Sloan Management Review Association. All rights reserved.
397 Robert D. Hof, "Why Sun Can't Afford to Shine Alone," *Business Week,* 9 September 1991, 87, 88; Jonathan Fuerbringer, "Learning to Dance with a Bouncy Dollar," *New York Times,* 8 September 1991, sec. 3, 1, 6; Stan Davis and Bill Davidson, "The Myth of the Immortal Corporation," *Across the Board,* June 1991, 24–27; Julie Pitta, "The Trojan Horse Approach," *Forbes,* 15 April 1991, 110, 112; Gary Hoover, Alta Campbell, and Patrick J. Spain, eds., *Hoover's Handbook 1991: Profits of Over 500 Major Corporations* (Austin, Tex.: The Reference Press, 1991), 524; John Markoff, "A 'Gunslinger's' Growing Pains," *New York Times,* 13 January 1991, sec. 3, 23; Robert Wrubel, "Top Gun Once More," *Financial World,* 2 October 1990, 56, 57.

CHAPTER 13

400 Exhibit 13.1, adapted from Eugene B. McGregor, Jr., "The Public Sector Human Resource Puzzle," *Public Administration Review,* November–December 1988, 941–950. Reprinted with permission from *Public Administration Review,* © by the American Society for Public Administration (ASPA), 1120 G Street NW, Suite 500, Washington, DC 20005. All rights reserved.
404 Daniel Quinn Mills, *Labor-Management Relations,* 4th ed. (New York: McGraw-Hill, 1989), 295.
405 Exhibit 13.3, from *The Labor Relations Process,* Third Edition, by William H. Holley and Kenneth M. Jennings, p. 293, copyright © 1988 by The Dryden Press, reprinted by permission of the publisher.
406 Exhibit 13.4, adapted from James W. Walker, *Human Resource Planning* (New York: McGraw-Hill, 1980), 34, 35, 42; Robert L. Mathis and John H. Jackson, *Personnel/Human Resource Management* (St. Paul: West Publishing, 1988), 108, 213, 528, 529; Barbara Berish Brown, "The Civil Rights Act of 1991," *Employment Relations Today,* Winter 1991/1992, 491–495.
412 Adapted from Audrey Edwards, Suzanne B. Laporte, and Abby Livingston, "Cultural Diversity in Today's Corporations." First appeared in *Working Woman,* November 1991. Written by Audrey Edwards. Reprinted with permission of *Working Woman* Magazine. Copyright © 1991 by W. W. T. Partnership.
417 Exhibit 13.7, Myron E. Weiner, *Human Services Management* (Belmont, Calif.: Wadsworth, 1990), 353. Reprinted by permission of Wadsworth, Inc.
420 Adapted from Johnnie L. Roberts, "Araskog Confronted by ITT Holders, Defends $11.4 Million '90 Compensation," *Wall Street Journal,* 8 May 1991, B8; Dana Wechsler Linden and Vicki Contavespi, "Incentivize Me, Please," *Forbes,* 27 May 1991, 208–212; John A. Byrne, "The Flap over Executive Pay," *Business Week,* 6 May 1991, 90–96; Michael Moore, "Compensation: The Million-Dollar-a-Year CEO Is Fast Becoming a Public Enemy. It's Now Time for America's Executives to Ask, How Much Is Enough?" *Business Month,* October 1990, 36–37.
422 Exhibit 13.8, J. D. Dunn and Frank M. Rachel, *Wage and Salary Administration: Total Compensation Systems* (New York: McGraw-Hill, 1971), 172. Copyright © 1971. Reprinted by permission of McGraw-Hill, Inc.
428 Information regarding TBS policy from Marilyn Loden and Judy B. Rosener, *Workforce America! Managing Employee Diversity as a Vital Resource,* Business One Irwin, © 1991, p. 188.
429 Merck & Company, Inc., 1990 Annual Report, 2, 7–13, 38, 40; Gary Hoover, Alta Campbell, and Patrick J. Spain, eds., *Hoover's Handbook 1991: Profiles of Over 500 Major Corporations* (Austin, Tex.: The Reference Press, 1990), 374; Milton Moskowitz, Robert Levering, and Michael Katz, *Everybody's Business* (New York: Doubleday, 1990), 162–165; Bill Leonard, "Trosin Discovers the Right Mix at Merck," *HRMagazine,* December 1990, 56–58; Steven M. Darien, "Father Flanagan Meets Conan the Barbarian," *Personnel,* October 1990, 9; Allen I. Kraut, "Some Lessons on Organizational Research Concerning Work and Family Issues," *Human Resource Planning* 13, no. 2 (1990): 109–118; Stephanie Lawrence, "Merck & Co.," *Personnel Journal,* April 1989, 64–66; Cathy Trost, "Boss's Backing Vital to Family Benefits," *Wall Street Journal,* 10 January 1989, B1.
430–431 Adapted from Dana Milbank, "Changes at Alcoa Point Up Challenges and Benefits of Decentralized Authority," *Wall Street Journal,* 7 November 1991, B1, B7; Alcoa 1990 Annual Report, 2–15; Michael Schroeder, "The Recasting of Alcoa," *Business Week,* 4 September 1991, 62, 64; Michael Schroeder, "The Quiet Coup at Alcoa," *Business Week,* 27 June 1988, 58–61, 64–65; Thomas F. O'Boyle and Peter Pae, "O'Neill Recasts Alcoa with His Eyes Fixed on a Decade Ahead," *Wall Street Journal,* 9 April 1990, A1, A4; "Alcoa, the Microcosm," *Financial World,* 25 June 1991, 76–80; Thomas A. Stewart, "A New Way to Wake Up a Giant," *Fortune,* 22 October 1990, 90–91, 94, 98, 102, 103; Gary Hoover, Alta Campbell, and Patrick J. Spain, eds., *Hoover's Handbook of American Business 1992* (Austin, Tex.: The Reference Press, 1991), 87; Tracy E. Benson, "Beyond Niche Marketing," *Industry Week,* 17 September 1990, 12–14, 16–19; George David Smith and Bettye H. Pruitt, "When Industrial Research Was Young: The Rise of Alcoa Laboratories," *Research Management,* March–April 1987, 24–33; Sue Kapp, "Alcoa's 'Natural Leader,'" *Business Marketing,* January 1987, 12–13; Karen Bemowski, "The Benchmarking Bandwagon," *Quality Progress,* January 1991, 19–24.

CHAPTER 14

436 Exhibit 14.1, adapted from Keith Davis and John W. Newstrom, *Human Behavior at Work,* p. 16. Copyright © 1989. Reprinted by permission of McGraw-Hill, Inc.
438 Exhibit 14.2, adapted from J. L. Gibson, J. M. Ivancevich, and J. H. Donnelly, *Organizations: Behavior, Structure, Processes,* Seventh Edition, p. 102. © 1991, 1973, 1976, 1979, 1982, 1985, 1988. Reprinted by permission of Richard D. Irwin, Inc.; and Richard M. Steers and Lyman W. Porter, *Motivation and Work Behavior,* Fifth Edition, p. 33. Copyright © 1991. Reprinted by permission of McGraw-Hill, Inc.
439 Rosalie L. Tung, "Motivation in Chinese Industrial Enterprises," in *Motivation and Work Behavior,* edited by Richard M. Steers and Lyman W. Porter (New York: McGraw-Hill, 1991), 342–351.
440 Exhibit 14.3, adapted from Richard M. Steers and Lyman W. Porter, *Motivation and Work Behavior,* 5th ed. (New York: McGraw-Hill, 1991), 35. Copyright © 1991. Reprinted by permission of McGraw-Hill, Inc.
443 Exhibit 14.4, adapted from John B. Miner, *Organizational Behavior* (New York: Random House, 1988), 199. Copyright © 1988. Reprinted by permission of McGraw-Hill, Inc.
446 Exhibit 14.5, from Gregory Moorhead and Ricky W. Griffin, *Organizational Behavior,* Second Edition, p. 124. Copyright © 1989 by Houghton Mifflin Company. Adapted with permission.
447 Exhibit 14.6, from Gregory Moorhead and Ricky W. Griffin, *Organizational Behavior,* Third Edition, p. 161. Copyright © 1992 by Houghton Mifflin Company. Adapted with permission.
448–449 Adapted from Stephen Baker, "If

You're Lucky, Your Next Car Will Be Made in Mexico," *Business Week,* 25 October 1991, 72–73; Mariah E. DeForest, "Managing a Maquiladora," *Automotive Industries,* May 1989, 72–73; Thomas M. Rohan, "Mexican Border Boom: Salvation or Slavery?" *Industry Week,* 15 August 1988, 46–49; Jeff Stinson, "Maquiladoras Challenge Human Resources," *Personnel Journal,* November 1989, 90–93; Todd Vogel, "The One-Minute Manager Meets the $4-a-Day Worker," *Business Week,,* 4 July 1988, 24a, 24d; Christopher Wilson, "Maquiladoras: Benefits for U.S. Manufacturers," *Business America,* 13 October 1986, 14; R. Andrew Rathbone, "Maquiladoras Demand More Mexican Managers," *San Diego Business Journal,* 2 July 1990, 25–26.

453 Exhibit 14.7, adapted from Richard M. Steers and Lyman W. Porter, *Motivation and Work Behavior* (New York: McGraw-Hill, 1991), 65–72. Copyright © 1991. Reprinted by permission of McGraw-Hill, Inc.

456–457 Adapted from Joseph G. Newlin and G. Jonathan Meng, "The Public Sector Pays for Performance," *Personnel Journal,* October 1991, 110, 112–114. Copyright 1991. Reprinted with permission of *Personnel Journal,* Costa Mesa, CA. All rights reserved. Albert C. Hyde, "The New Environment for Compensation and Performance Evaluation in the Public Sector," *Public Personnel Management,* Winter 1988, 351–357. Reprinted with permission of Public Personnel Management, International Personnel Management Assoc., Alexandria, VA.

465 Robert McGough, "Changing Course," *FW,* 23 July 1991, 42–45; Erika Penzer, "The Power of Empowerment," *Incentive,* May 1991, 97–99, 138; "American Agrees to Change Flight Attendant Weight Policy," *Aviation Daily,* 14 March 1991, 484; Lawrence Kaufman, "It Takes Good People to Have a Good Firm," *AirCommerce,* 25 March 1991, S2; AMR Corporation 1990 Annual Report, 1; Gary Hoover, Alta Campbell, and Patrick J. Spain, eds., *Hoover's Handbook 1991* (Austin, Tex.: The Reference Press, 1990), 87; Milton Moskowitz, Robert Levering, and Michael Katz, *Everybody's Business* (New York: Doubleday, 1990), 587–589; Kenneth Labich, "American Takes On the World," *Fortune,* 24 September 1990, 40–42, 44, 46, 48; Michael Gates, "American Airlines: Do People Make the Difference?" *Incentive,* May 1989, 16–18, 138, 139; Aaron Sugarman, "Success through People," *Incentive,* May 1988, 20–22, 24, 26, 28, 30, 32, 34, 38, 40, 43, 156, 157.

CHAPTER 15

471 Exhibit 15.1, from Gary A. Yukl, *Leadership in Organizations,* Second Edition, © 1989, p. 44. Adapted by permission of Prentice Hall, Englewood Cliffs, New Jersey.

472–473 Adapted from David C. Limerick, "Managers of Meaning: From Bob Geldof's Band Aid to Australian CEOs." Reprinted, by permission of the publisher, from *Organizational Dynamics,* Spring 1990 © 1990. American Management Association, New York. All rights reserved; and excerpts from *Is That It?* by Bob Geldof copyright © 1986 by Bob Geldof. Used by permission of Grove Press, Inc.

475 Exhibit 15.2, from Gary A. Yukl, *Leadership in Organizations,* Second Edition, © 1989, p. 176. Adapted by permission of Prentice Hall, Englewood Cliffs, New Jersey.

477 Exhibit 15.3, adapted from and reprinted by permission of *Harvard Business Review.* An exhibit from "How to Choose a Leadership Pattern," by Robert Tannenbaum and Warren H. Schmidt, May–June 1973, p. 164. Copyright © 1973 by the President and Fellows of Harvard College; all rights reserved.

479 Exhibit 15.4, from Paul Hersey and Kenneth H. Blanchard, *Management of Organizational Behavior: Utilizing Human Resources,* Fifth Edition, © 1988, p. 92. Reprinted by permission of Prentice Hall, Englewood Cliffs, New Jersey.

480 Exhibit 15.5, from Robert R. Blake and Jane S. Mouton, "A Comparative Analysis of Situationalism and 9,9 Management by Principle," *Organizational Dynamics,* Spring 1982, 23.

482 Exhibit 15.6, from Gary A. Yukl, *Leadership in Organizations,* Second Edition, © 1989, p. 196. Adapted by permission of Prentice Hall, Englewood Cliffs, New Jersey.

484 Exhibit 15.7, from Gary A. Yukl, *Leadership in Organizations,* Second Edition, © 1989, p. 101. Adapted by permission of Prentice Hall, Englewood Cliffs, New Jersey.

486 Exhibit 15.8, reprinted from *The New Leadership: Managing Participation in Organizations* by Victor H. Vroom and Arthur G. Jago, 1988, Prentice Hall, Englewood Cliffs, New Jersey. Copyright 1987 by V. H. Vroom and A. G. Jago. Used with permission of the authors.

487 Exhibit 15.9, from Paul Hersey and Kenneth H. Blanchard, *Management of Organizational Behavior: Utilizing Human Resources,* Fifth Edition, © 1988, p. 171. Adapted by permission of Prentice Hall, Englewood Cliffs, New Jersey.

489 Adapted from Richard M. Hodgetts and Fred Luthans, *International Management* (New York: McGraw-Hill, 1991), 409–415.

490–491 Adapted from Herbert Burkholz, "A Shot in the Arm for the F.D.A.," *New York Times Magazine,* 30 June 1991, 15–44; Bruce Ingersoll, "FDA's Kessler Moves Swiftly on Food Labels," *Wall Street Journal,* 16 May 1991, B1, B12; John Carey, "The FDA Is Growling at Drugmakers, Too," *Business Week,* 1 July 1991, 34–35; Ronald M. Schwartz and Sandra M. Rifkin, "No More Paper Tigers," *American Druggist,* June 1991, 26–34.

496 Information on T. J. Rogers and Cypress Semiconductor adapted from Richard Brandt, "The Bad Boy of Silicon Valley," *Business Week,* 9 December 1991, 64-68.

497 Jonna Crispens, "Stew's Second Store," *Supermarket News,* 23 September 1991, 1, 50, 51; Matthew L. Wald, "Stew Leonard's, Believe It or Not!" *New York Times,* 25 May 1989, C1; Judith Springer, "Stew Leonard's Builds Sales from Scratch," *Supermarket News,* 27 February 1989, 35; "In-Store Disneyland," *Incentive,* January 1989, 26, 30; Bruce Bolger, "Stew Leonard; Unconventional Wisdom," *Incentive,* November 1988, 36, 38–40; Patricia Natschke, "Stew Leonard: Each Patron Is Investment Worth $50G," *Supermarket News,* 11 April 1988, 12; Lisa McGurrin, "Hillbilly Music in the Frozen Peas at Stew Leonard's," *New England Business,* 17 February 1986, 38, 39, 41; William F. Doescher, "Caring for Customers = Success," *D&B Reports,* July–August 1985, 8, 9.

CHAPTER 16

502 Exhibit 16.2, adapted from Paul S. Goodman, Elizabeth C. Ravlin, and Linda Argote, "Current Thinking about Groups: Setting the Stage for New Ideas," in *Designing Effective Work Groups,* edited by Paul S. Goodman and Associates (San Francisco: Jossey-Bass, 1986), 16.

506 Exhibit 16.4, adapted from John Hoerr, "The Payoff from Teamwork," reprinted from the July 10, 1989 issue of *Business Week* by permission. Copyright © 1989 McGraw-Hill, Inc.

506 Fremont E. Kast and James E. Rosenzweig, *Organization & Management: A Systems and Contingency Approach,* 4th ed. (New York: McGraw-Hill, 1985), 343; John B. Miner, *Organizational Behavior: Performance and Productivity* (New York: Random House, 1988), 280–281.

508 Exhibit 16.5, adapted from Kenneth D. Benne and Paul Sheats, "Functional Roles of Group Members," *Journal of Social Issues* 4 (1948): 41–49; B. Aubrey Fisher and Donald G. Ellis, *Small Group Decision Making,* 3rd ed. (New York: McGraw-Hill, 1990), 210–212. Copyright © 1990. Reprinted by permission of McGraw-Hill, Inc.

510–511 Adapted from Erik Larson, "Forever Young," *Inc.,* July 1988, 50–53, 56, 58, 60, 62; Howard Kurtz, "Ben & Jerry: Premium Ice Cream Sprinkled with Liberal Ideology," *Washington Post,* 29 November 1989, A3; "Ben & Jerry's Chief to Quit at Year End; Lacy to be President," *Wall Street Journal,* 7 February 1990, B5; N. R. Kleinfield, "Wntd: C.F.O. with 'Flair for Funk,'" *New York Times,* 26 March 1989, sec. 3, 4.

515 Exhibit 16.7, adapted from Bruce W. Tuckman and Mary Ann C. Jensen, "Stages of Small Group Development Revisited," *Group & Organization Studies* 2, no. 4 (1977): 419–427. Reprinted by permission of Sage Publications, Inc.

517 Exhibit 16.8, adapted from Marsha Sinetar, "Building Trust into Corporate Relationships," pp. 73–79. Reprinted, by permission of the publisher, from *Organizational Dynamics,* Winter 1988 © 1988. American Management Association, New York. All rights reserved.

518–519 Adapted from Louis Kraar, "Japan's Gung-Ho U.S. Car Plants," *Fortune,* 30 January 1989, 98–100, 104, 106, 108; S. C. Gwynne, "The Right Stuff," *Time,* 29 October 1990, 74–77, 81, 84; John Hoerr, "The Payoff from Teamwork," *Business Week,* 10 July 1989, 56–62; Marguerite Michaels, "Hands across the Workplace," *Time,* 26 December 1988, 14, 15, 17; Doron P. Levin, "At Saturn Plant, a Vote on Innovation," *New York Times,* 14 November 1991, sec. d, 1, 9.

529 Corning 1990 Annual Report, 1; James R. Houghton, "Quality: Beyond the Corporate Walls," *Executive Speeches,* March 1991, 19–24; Gary Hoover, Alta Campbell, and Patrick J. Spain, eds., *Hoover's Handbook 1991* (Austin, Tex.: The Reference Press, 1990), 189; John Hoerr, "Sharpening Minds for a Competitive Edge," *Business Week,* 17 December 1990, 72, 74, 78; John H. Sheridan, "America's Best Plants," *Industry Week,* 15 October 1990, 27, 37, 40; Chris Lee, "Beyond Teamwork," *Training,* June 1990, 25–32.

CHAPTER 17

533 Exhibit 17.1, adapted from Courtland L. Bovée and John V. Thill, *Business Communication Today,* 3rd ed. (New York: McGraw-Hill, 1992), 7. Copyright © 1992. Reprinted by per-

mission of McGraw-Hill, Inc.
534 Brigham Young University, David M. Kennedy Center for International Studies, "Culturgram for the '90s," Republic of Ecuador, December 1990.
535 Exhibit 17.2, adapted from G. Michael Barton, "Communication: Manage Words Effectively," *Personnel Journal*, January 1990, 36. Copyright © 1990. Reprinted with permission *Personnel Journal*, Costa Mesa, CA. All rights reserved.
536 Exhibit 17.3, adapted from Sally Solo, "Japanese Comics Are All Business," *Fortune*, 9 October 1989, 144.
538 Exhibit 17.4, from Courtland L. Bovée and John V. Thill, *Business Communication Today*, 3rd ed. (New York: McGraw-Hill, 1992), 34. Copyright © 1992. Reprinted by permission of McGraw-Hill, Inc.
541 Exhibit 17.5, figure adapted from *Strategic Organizational Communication*, Second Edition, by Charles Conrad, copyright © 1990 by Holt, Rinehart and Winston, reprinted by permission of the publisher.
544 Exhibit 17.6, from R. Wayne Pace and Don F. Faules, *Organizational Communication*, Second Edition, © 1989, p. 98. Adapted by permission of Prentice Hall, Englewood Cliffs, New Jersey.
545 Exhibit 17.7, from Jitendra Mishra, "Managing the Grapevine," *Public Personnel Management*, Summer 1990, 220. Reprinted with permission of *Public Personnel Management*, International Personnel Management Assoc., Alexandria, VA.
548–549 Adapted from Keith Denton, "Improving Community Relations," *Small Business Reports*, August 1990, 33–34, 36–41.
550 Exhibit 17.8, adapted from Pamela Shockley-Zalabak, *Fundamentals of Organizational Communication* (New York: Longman, 1991), 25.
555 Exhibit 17.9, from Richard L. Daft, Robert H. Lengel, and Linda Klebe Trevino, "Message Equivocality, Media Selection, and Manager Performance: Implications for Information Systems," *MIS Quarterly*, September 1987, 358. Reprinted by special permission from the *MIS Quarterly*, Volume 11, Number 3, September 1987. Copyright 1987 by the Society for Information Management and the Management Information Systems Research Center at the University of Minnesota.
556 Adapted from Evelyn Richards, "Privacy at the Office: Is There a Right to Snoop?" *Washington Post*, 9 September 1990, H1, H6; Jeffrey Rothfeder, "Putting Electronic Eavesdroppers Outside the Law," *Business Week*, 29 September 1986, 87; Rob Kolstad, "Ethics in Electronic Mail," *UNIX Review*, November 1989, 89–91, 93–95.
563 John Desmond, "LANs in This Network Will Answer to the Mainframe; Sears Technology Manages One (Massive) Logical, SNA Network," *Software Magazine*, July 1991, 68, 69; Ruth Kastrud, "Invigorating Company Operations with Technology," *Best's Review*, July 1991, 110–112; Barbara Reynolds, "AIDS at Work—Employers' Challenge: Educate Their Workers," *USA Today*, 2 April 1990, 11A; Milton Moskowitz, Robert Levering, and Michael Katz, *Everybody's Business* (New York: Doubleday, 1990), 665, 666; Laurie Sue Brockway, "Employee Annual Reports; Thriving Amidst Corporate Change," *Public Relations Journal*, July 1989, 21–24; Karen B. Greenbaum, "Innovative Communication Techniques," *Employee Benefits Journal*, December 1988, 30–33; William H. Miller, "More Than Fish Stories Now," *Industry Week*, 24 August 1987, 39–41; Lad Kuzela, "Zooming In On Decisions," *Industry Week*, 2 September 1985, 46–48.
564–565 Source: Herman Miller 1991 Annual Report, 1, 8–9; Joani Nelson-Horchler, "The Magic of Herman Miller," *Industry Week*, 18 February 1991, 11–12, 14, 17; Andrew Tanzer, "'I Want to Be the Toyota of Furniture,'" *Forbes*, 16 May 1988, 92, 96; Dana Wechsler, "A Comeback in Cubicles," *Forbes*, 21 March 1988, 54, 56; Kenneth Labich, "Hot Company, Warm Culture," *Fortune*, 27 February 1989, 74–76, 78; "A Brief History of Herman Miller," Herman Miller (unpaged, 1991); "Herman Miller Is Built on Its People, Research, and Designs," Herman Miller news release, 16 October 1991, 1–14; Steven Prokesch, "Employees Go To the Rescue: Labor Policy Aids Miller Furniture," *New York Times*, 14 August 1986, D1, D5; Robert J. McClory, "The Creative Process at Herman Miller," *Across the Board*, May 1985, 8–22; Richard H. Ruch, "Make Participation a Way of Life," *Working Woman*, July 1990, 52; Fern Schumer Chapman, "Sitting Pretty," *CFO*, March 1987, 46–48, 50, 52, 54–55; Bob Daily, "Multiple Pay, Multiple Problems," *Business Month*, June 1990, 76–77; Judith Ramquist, "SMR Forum: Labor–Management Cooperation: The Scanlon Plan at Work," *Sloan Management Review*, Spring 1982, 49–55.

CHAPTER 18

571 Exhibit 18.1, adapted from James A. Senn, *Information Systems in Management* (Belmont, Calif.: Wadsworth, 1990), 63. Reprinted by permission of Wadsworth, Inc.
573 Exhibit 18.2, adapted from Henry C. Lucas, Jr., *Information Systems Concepts for Management* (New York: McGraw-Hill, 1990), 18–19. Copyright © 1990. Reprinted by permission of McGraw-Hill, Inc.
574–575 Source: Adapted from Fidelity Investments, *Fidelity Focus*, Summer 1991, 20–25; PR Newswire, "Fidelity Announces FOX and TouchTone Trader," 20 February 1992; PR Newswire, "Fidelity Reports Surge in IRA Accounts," 10 February 1992; Julie Rohrer, "Money Management's Brave New World," *Institutional Investor*, March 1991, 39–44; Jaclyn Fierman, "Fidelity's Secret: Faithful Service," *Fortune*, 7 May 1990, 86–92; David Churbuck, "Watch Out, Citicorp," *Forbes*, 16 September 1991, 38–39; Hank Gilman, "Fidelity's 2d Round of Layoffs Removes 5000 Jobs in City Office," *Boston Globe*, 1 March 1988, C 1.
579 Exhibit 18.3, adapted from Charles S. Parker, *Management Information Systems* (New York: McGraw-Hill, 1989), 584. Copyright © 1989. Reprinted by permission of McGraw-Hill, Inc.
582 Exhibit 18.4, from Jeremy Main, "At Last, Software CEOs Can Use," *Fortune*, 13 March 1989, 78. Photos reprinted by permission of James Schnept.
588 Exhibit 18.5, adapted from James A. Senn, *Information Systems in Management* (Belmont, Calif.: Wadsworth, 1990), 612. Copyright © 1990. Reprinted by permission of Wadsworth, Inc.
592–593 Adapted from R. C. Baker, Roger Dickinson, and Stanley Hollander, "Big Brother 1994: Marketing Data and the IRS," *Journal of Public Policy & Marketing* 5 (1986): 231; "Is Nothing Private?" *Business Week*, 4 September 1989, 74–82; "Privacy vs. Free Speech," *Direct Marketing*, May 1989, 42; Robert J. Posch, Jr., "Can We Have à la Carte Constitutional Rights?" *Direct Marketing*, July 1989, 76.
593 Joanne Kelleher, Elisabeth Horwitt, Michael Alexander, and Ellis Booker, "Adventures in the New Europe," *Computerworld*, 12 August 1991, S5–S29.
598 Information on HomeFax from Esther Dyson, "Who Pays for Data?" *Forbes*, 3 February 1992, 96. © Forbes Inc., 1992.
599 Jack Schember, "Mrs. Fields' Secret Weapon," *Personnel Journal*, September 1991, 56–58; Bob Garrison, "Mrs. Fields' Green Fields," *Prepared Foods*, August 1990, 39, 40; Stephen D. Solomon, "Use Technology to Manage People," *Inc.*, May 1990, 124–126; Judith Springer, "Mrs. Fields Plans to Open in Stores," *Supermarket News*, 30 April 1990, 37; Bradley Johnson, "Mrs. Fields Sells Name for Dough," *Advertising Age*, 23 April 1990, 75; Grace Lichtenstein, "Fortune Cookie," *Savvy Woman*, June 1989, 59, 60, 62, 108; Don Steinberg, "Crumbling Mrs. Fields Puts Its Chips on PCs in Bakeries," *PC Week*, 20 February 1989, 1, 8, 61; "Mrs. Fields Automates the Way the Cookie Sells," *Chain Store Age Executive*, April 1988, 73, 74, 76.

CHAPTER 19

604 Exhibit 19.1, adapted from and reprinted by permission of *Harvard Business Review*. An exhibit from "Vital Truths about Managing Your Costs," by B. Charles Ames and James D. Hlavacek, January–February 1990, p. 144. Copyright © 1990 by the President and Fellows of Harvard College; all rights reserved.
607 Philip R. Cateora, *International Marketing* (Homewood, Ill.: Irwin, 1990), 554.
608–609 Adapted from Janet Novack, "Abuse Control," *Forbes*, 10 June 1991, 98, 102–103. © Forbes Inc., 1991.
615 Exhibit 19.4, adapted from and reprinted by permission of *Harvard Business Review*. An exhibit from "From Control to Commitment in the Workplace," by Richard E. Walton, March–April 1985, p. 81. Copyright © 1985 by the President and Fellows of Harvard College; all rights reserved.
616–617 Adapted from G. David Hughes, "Managing High-Tech Product Cycles," *Academy of Management Executive* 4, no. 2 (1990): 44–55; Ronald Alsop, "Consumer-Product Giants Relying On 'Intrapreneurs' in New Ventures," *Wall Street Journal*, 22 April 1988, 35; Gary Hamel and C. K. Prahalad, "Corporate Imagination and Expeditionary Marketing," *Harvard Business Review*, July–August 1991, 81–92; W. Alan Randolph and Barry Z. Posner, "What Every Manager Needs to Know about Project Management," *Sloan Management Review*, Summer 1988, 65–73.
619 Exhibit 19.5, adapted from and reprinted by permission of *Harvard Business Review*. An exhibit from "Fit Control Systems to Your Managerial Style," by Cortlandt Cammann and David A. Nadler, January–February 1976, p. 70. Copyright © 1976 by the President and Fellows of Harvard College; all rights reserved.
621 Exhibit 19.6, adapted from Lawrence D. Schall and Charles W. Haley, *Introduction to Financial Management* (New York: McGraw-Hill, 1988), 398. Copyright © 1988. Reprinted by permission of McGraw-Hill, Inc.
621 Exhibit 19.7, adapted from Lawrence D.

Schall and Charles W. Haley, *Introduction to Financial Management* (New York: McGraw-Hill, 1988), 401. Copyright © 1988. Reprinted by permission of McGraw-Hill, Inc.
623 Exhibit 19.8, adapted from Lawrence D. Schall and Charles W. Haley, *Introduction to Financial Management* (New York: McGraw-Hill, 1988), 410. Copyright © 1988. Reprinted by permission of McGraw-Hill, Inc.
625 Exhibit 19.9, adapted from and reprinted by permission of *Harvard Business Review*. An exhibit from "Budget Choice: Planning vs. Control," by Neil C. Churchill, July–August 1984, p. 151. Copyright © 1984 by the President and Fellows of Harvard College; all rights reserved.
627 Exhibit 19.10, adapted from Lawrence D. Schall and Charles W. Haley, *Introduction to Financial Management* (New York: McGraw-Hill, 1988), 424. Copyright © 1988. Reprinted by permission of McGraw-Hill, Inc.
634 Adapted in part from Rick Wartzman, "Interactive Video Means Jet Set Need Never Come Down to Earth," *Wall Street Journal*, 7 January 1992, B1-B2. Reprinted by permission from *The Wall Street Journal*, © 1992, Dow Jones & Company, Inc. All Rights Reserved Worldwide.
635 Gary Levin, "Benetton Gets the Kiss-off: Magazines Say No to Retailer's Ads," *Advertising Age*, 22 July 1991, 1, 40; David Moin and Chuck Struensee, "Benetton's New Beat: Minding the Merchandise," *Women's Wear Daily*, 5 September 1990, 6, 7; William A. Ruch, "A Point of View: Putting Time on Your Side," *National Productivity Review*, Autumn 1990, 391–394; Lory Zottola, "The United Systems of Benetton," *Computerworld*, 2 April 1990, 70; John Rossant, "Benetton Strips Down to Sportswear," *Business Week*, 5 March 1990, 42; Yezdi Pavri, "Working Wonders," *CA Magazine*, August 1989, 32–39; Janette Martin, "Benetton's IS Instinct," *Datamation*, 1 July 1989, 68-15, 68-16; Curtis Bill Pepper, "Fast Forward," *Business Month*, February 1989, 25–30.

CHAPTER 20

639 Mike Van Horn, *Pacific Rim Trade* (New York: Amacom, 1989), 318–321.
641 Exhibit 20.1, from Joseph G. Monks, *Operations Management, Theory and Problems* (New York: McGraw-Hill, 1987), 2. Copyright © 1987. Reprinted by permission of McGraw-Hill, Inc.
646 Exhibit 20.2, adapted from James B. Dilworth, *Production and Operations Management* (New York: Random House, 1989), 149. Copyright © 1989. Reprinted by permission of McGraw-Hill, Inc.
648 Exhibit 20.3, adapted from Joseph G. Monks, *Operations Management, Theory and Problems* (New York: McGraw-Hill, 1987), 124–126. Copyright © 1987. Reprinted by permission of McGraw-Hill, Inc.
650–651 Adapted from Karen Pennar, "Manufacturing: The Key to Growth," *Business Week*, 11 January 1988, 70–73; Isadore Barmash, "The T-Shirt Industry Sweats It Out," *New York Times*, 30 December 1990, F6; William H. Miller, "U. S. Manufacturing on Whose Turf?" *Industry Week*, 5 September 1988, 53–81; Louis Kraar, "The New Powers of Asia," *Fortune*, 28 March 1988, 126–132.
652 Adapted from "NeXT Touts 86% Increase in Sales of Its Computers," *San Jose Mercury News*, 1 August 1991, C3; Mark Alpert, "The Ultimate Computer Factory," *Fortune*, 26 February 1990, 75–79; Neal E. Boudette, "Creating the Computer-Integrated Enterprise," *Industry Week*, 18 June 1990, 62, 65–66.
653 Exhibit 20.4, from Joseph G. Monks, *Operations Management, Theory and Problems* (New York: McGraw-Hill, 1987), 358–359. Copyright © 1987. Reprinted by permission of McGraw-Hill, Inc.
656 Exhibit 20.5, adapted from *Production and Operations Management: A Problem-Solving and Decision-Making Approach*, Fourth Edition by, Norman Gaither, copyright © 1990 by The Dryden Press, reprinted by permission of the publisher.
666 Adapted in part from John Huey, "America's Most Successful Merchant," *Fortune*, 23 September 1991, 46-59. © 1991 Time, Inc. All rights reserved.
667 Joseph Weber and Brian Bremner, "The Screws Are Tightening at Black & Decker," *Business Week*, 23 September 1991, 61, 64; Black & Decker 1990 Annual Report, 1, 3, 4; Gary Hoover, Alta Campbell, and Patrick J. Spain, eds., *Hoover's Handbook 1991* (Austin, Tex.: The Reference Press, 1990), 129; Milton Moskowitz, Robert Levering, and Michael Katz, *Everybody's Business* (New York: Doubleday, 1990), 119–120; Steve Paloncy, "Team Approach Cuts Costs," *HRMagazine*, November 1990, 61, 62; Brian S. Moskal, "Logistics Gets Some R-e-s-p-e-c-t," *Industry Week*, 18 June 1990, 14–16, 18, 19, 22; Joseph Weber, "Black & Decker Cuts a Neat Dovetail Joint," *Business Week*, 31 July 1989, 52, 53; Kevin T. Higgins, "Firms Tune-Up Their Management," *Marketing News*, 25 September 1989, 2, 26; James Fallon, "'Manufacturability' Focus Turns Around B&D Facility," *Metalworking News*, 17 April 1989, 1, 26; B. H. Lawrence, "Retooling: Black & Decker's Plan to Buy Emhart Is Latest Step in Its Expansion Strategy," *Washington Post*, 27 March 1989, B1, B22; John Huey, "The New Power in Black & Decker," *Fortune*, 2 January 1989, 89–91, 94.

CHAPTER 21

673 Exhibit 21.1, adapted from pages 1–17. Reprinted from *Out of the Crisis* by W. Edwards Deming by permission of MIT and W. Edwards Deming. Published by MIT, Center for Advanced Engineering Study, Cambridge, MA 02139. Copyright 1986 by W. Edwards Deming.
676 Exhibit 21.2, Courtesy Motorola.
678 Exhibit 21.3, adapted from pages 23–24. Reprinted from *Out of the Crisis* by W. Edwards Deming by permission of MIT and W. Edwards Deming. Published by MIT, Center for Advanced Engineering Study, Cambridge, MA 02139. Copyright 1986 by W. Edwards Deming.
681 Adapted from David R. McCamus, "Performance Measurement and the Quality Voyage," *CMA Magazine*, December 1990–January 1991, 8–12.
682–683 Adapted from Laurie Kretchmar, "Oh, the Pity of a Baldrige Award," *Fortune*, 9 March 1992, 153; Mark Ivey, "The Ecstasy and the Agony," *Business Week*, 21 October 1991, 40; Jeremy Main, "Is the Baldrige Overblown?" *Fortune*, 1 July 1991, 62–65; Peter Burrows, "Past Baldrige Applicants Begin to See Their Efforts Pay Off," *Electronic Business*, 7 October 1991, 11; Don Nichols, "The Company That Quality Built," *Management Review*, August 1991, 34–35; John Carey, "The Prize and the Passion," *Business Week Quality 1991*, 25 October 1991, 58–59.
684 Exhibit 21.4, adapted from Thomas A. Stewart, "The New American Century: Where We Stand," *Fortune's New American Century*, Spring–Summer 1991, 21. © 1991 Time Inc. All rights reserved. *Handbook of Economic Statistics* (Washington, D.C.: Central Intelligence Agency, 1991).
686 Exhibit 21.5, adapted from David Bain, *The Productivity Prescription* (New York: McGraw-Hill, 1982), 62–75, 171. Copyright © 1986. Reprinted by permission of McGraw-Hill, Inc.
689 Exhibit 21.6, adapted from Adrienne S. Harris, "The Customer's Always Right," *Black Enterprise*, June 1991, 234. Copyright June 1991, The Earl G. Graves Publishing Co., Inc., 130 Fifth Avenue, New York, NY 10011. All rights reserved.
689 Exhibit 21.7, adapted from and reprinted by permission of *Harvard Business Review*. An exhibit from "Marketing Success Through Differentiation—of Anything" by Theodore Levitt, January/February 1980. Copyright © 1980 by the President and Fellows of Harvard College; all rights reserved.
692 Exhibit 21.8, from Courtland L. Bovée and John V. Thill, *Marketing* (New York: McGraw Hill, Inc., 1992), 731. Copyright © 1992. Reprinted by permission of McGraw-Hill, Inc.
693 Adapted from Gene Bylinsky, "How Companies Spy on Employees," *Fortune*, 4 November 1991, 131–134; Glenn Rifkin, "Do Employees Have a Right to Electronic Privacy?" *New York Times*, 8 December 1991, sec. 3, 8.
698 Information on Charles Schwab from Jason Zweig, "A Touch of Class," *Forbes*, 3 February 1992, 82, 84. © Forbes Inc., 1992.
699 Tracy E. Benson, "Caterpillar Wakes Up," *Industry Week*, 20 May 1991, 33, 36, 37; Bob Gilligan, "Caterpillar Grades Up Based on Broadband LAN," *Manufacturing Systems*, March 1991, 18–22; Caterpillar Inc. 1990 Annual Report, 1–6; Gary Hoover, Alta Campbell, and Patrick J. Spain, eds., *Hoover's Handbook 1991* (Austin, Tex.: The Reference Press, 1990), 157; Milton Moskowitz, Robert Levering, and Michael Katz, *Everybody's Business* (New York: Doubleday, 1990), 253–254.
700–701 Robert Howard, "Values Make the Company: An Interview with Robert Haas," *Harvard Business Review*, September–October 1990, 132–144; Gary Hoover, Alta Campbell, and Patrick J. Spain, eds., *Hoover's Handbook of American Business 1992* (Austin, Tex.: The Reference Press, 1991), 341; Lee Branst, "Quality Wears Well for Levi Strauss," *Quality*, March 1983, 16–17; "A Comfortable Fit," *Economist*, 22 June 1991, 67–68; Brenton R. Shlender, "How Levi Strauss Did an LBO Right," *Fortune*, 7 May 1990, 105–107; Maria Shao, "For Levi's, A Flattering Fit Overseas," *Business Week*, 5 November 1990, 76–77; Tracy E. Benson, "Robert Haas' Vision Scores 20/20," *Industry Week*, 2 April 1990, 19, 22–23; Nancy J. Perry, "The Workers of the Future," *Fortune 1991, The New American Century*, Spring–Summer 1991, 68; Philip Revzin, "Progress in Work: Ventures in Hungary Test Theory That West Can Uplift East Bloc," *Wall Street Journal*, 5 April 1990, A1, A18; "Fashion Houses Turn to the Electronic Drawing Board," *Infoworld*, 14 May 1990, 46; Wayne Eckerson, "Levi's Net Strategy Pays Big Dividends," *Network World*, 4 September 1989, 19–20; "Levi Strauss Associates Inc.," *Wall Street Journal*, 21 February 1992, B3.

PHOTO CREDITS

CHAPTER 1

2 Tim Brown/Tony Stone Worldwide
6 Bill Ray
10 S. Dorantes/Sygma
12 Courtesy Pizza Hut
16 T. Michael Keza
25 Ken Kerbs
28 Courtesy Commonwealth Edison
30 Rich Frishman, Everett, WA

CHAPTER 2

36 Bruce Ayres/Tony Stone Worldwide
38 Courtesy King Features Syndicate
49 Brian Yablonsky/Duomo
56 Courtesy NASA
57 Courtesy Federal Express
58 Mark Zemnick
61 Ted Streshinsky/Photo 20-20
62 William Strode/Woodfin Camp & Associates
65 Christopher Pillitz/Network-Matrix

CHAPTER 3

70 Bob Daemmrich/Stock, Boston
73 Chris Niedenthal/Black Star
77 Courtesy Boeing Commercial Airplane Group
79 Shelly Katz/Black Star
80 Courtesy US Postal Service
81 Mike Maple/Woodfin Camp & Associates
88 Mark Tuschman
97 Courtesy Xerox Corporation

CHAPTER 4

102 Tony Stone Worldwide
104 Courtesy DuPont World Magazine
110 Phil Matt
111 Z. Cavaricci/Amnesty International USA
115 A Borden Contribution, courtesy Berwick Hospital Center, Berwick, PA
116 Courtesy Community Food Bank of New Jersey
120 Gary Newkirk/Allsport
121 Michael Abramson/Woodfin Camp & Associates
129 E. J. Camp/Outline Press

CHAPTER 5

134 Joe Carini/Image Works
136 Courtesy Pillsbury Company
139 Jeffrey Aaronson, Aspen, CO
144 Pascal Le Segretain/Sygma
149 Chris Davies/Network-Matrix
153 Michael Abrahams/Network-Matrix
154 Jeffrey MacMillan/U.S. News & World Report
157 Russ Gilbert/The San Diego Union
161 Courtesy H. J. Heinz Company

CHAPTER 6

170 Courtesy American Red Cross
173 James Skovmand/The San Diego Union
175 Tony Freeman/PhotoEdit
179 Wesley Allison
183 Courtesy Hyatt International Corporation
190 Robbie McClaran
192 Dan Ford Connolly/Picture Group
195 Anthony Tarantino
197 Courtesy Hewlett-Packard Company

CHAPTER 7

202 Zephyr Pictures
205 Bevil Knapp
209 David Young-Wolff/PhotoEdit
210 Kevin Horan/Picture Group
212 Bob Daemmrich/Image Works
214 Julie A. Lopez/Habitat for Humanity International
221 Philip Saltonstall
231 AP/Wide World Photos

CHAPTER 8

236 Jim Baird/The San Diego Union
239 Charles Thatcher/Woodfin Camp & Associates
241 Sandra Johnson/Retna
242 Sean M. Haffey/The San Diego Union
246 Courtesy Larry Peplin, The University of Michigan-Dearborn
256 Reuters/Bettmann
258 Photo reprinted courtesy of NTID Focus magazine, published by the National Technical Institute of Technology, photo by A. Sue Weisler
260 Richard Petty
263 Richard Howard

CHAPTER 9

272 Tom Tracy/Stock Market
274 Thomas Muscionico/Contact Press/Woodfin Camp & Associates
276 Dirck Halstead/TIME Magazine
280 Mark Richards
288 Andy Sacks/Tony Stone Worldwide
292 Charlie Archambault
295 Louis Psihoyos/Matrix
297 Mary Beth Camp/Matrix

CHAPTER 10

302 Superstock
305 Michael L. Abramson
308 Steven Pumphrey
314 Bob Daemmrich/The Image Works
316 Michael Newman/Photo Edit
321 Steve Smith/Onyx
326 Courtesy United States Surgical Corporation
328 Jonathan Levine

CHAPTER 11

334 Alan Levenson/TIME Magazine
337 Reuters/Bettmann
339 Courtesy San Diego County Water Authority
345 Courtesy Solidarity Magazine, photo by Karl Mantyla
348 Louis Psihoyos/Matrix
349 Breton Littlehales
359 Louis Psihoyos/Matrix
361 Peter Stachiw/Picture Group

CHAPTER 12

366 Mary Beth Camp/Matrix
368 Courtesy Lisa Conte, Shaman Pharmaceuticals
373 Bruce Zake
375 © 1991 Nora Feller
377 Courtesy ACN Franchise Systems
381 David Hiser/Photographers, Aspen
389 Dana Fineman/Sygma
393 Courtesy R. W. Frookies

CHAPTER 13

398 Doug Menuez/Reportage
401 Courtesy The Institute for Effective Education
409 Will van Overbeek
410 Jackson Hill/Southern Lights
411 Max Aguilera-Hellweg
414 Peter Freed
418 Mark Richards Photography
425 Courtesy Johnson & Johnson

CHAPTER 14

434 David Perry Lawrence
437 Jim Harrison/Stock, Boston
441 Dennis Bud Gray
447 Louis Psihoyos/Matrix
450 Michael Melford
452 Bob Daemmrich/Stock, Boston
459 M. Abramson/Woodfin Camp & Associates
461 Charles Gupton

CHAPTER 15

466 John Abbott
469 Bruce McAllister
470 John R. McCutchen/The San Diego Union
476 Kevin Horan
481 Rick Browne/Stock, Boston
483 Will van Overbeek
490 Chris Davies/Network-Matrix
493 Courtesy General Electric

CHAPTER 16

498 Courtesy Rockwell International
501 Brian Moody
505 Courtesy Avon Products

507 Forest McMullin/Black Star
513 Mitsutaka Kurashina, Tokyo
516 Red Thai/TIME Magazine
518 David Austen/Picture Group
524 Robbie McClaran

CHAPTER 17

530 Robert McElroy/Woodfin Camp & Associates
532 Mark Richards/PhotoEdit
534 Bob Daemmrich/Image Works
535 Tom Sobolik/Black Star
537 Frank Siteman/Stock, Boston
542 John S. Abbott
552 Paul Chesley/Photographers/Aspen
559 Dan Dry/Dan Dry & Associates

CHAPTER 18

568 Peter Vadnai/Stock Market
570 Mark M. Lawrence
578 Eli Albalancy, Wynnewood, PA
585 Steven Pumphrey. All Rights Reserved
586 Courtesy USA TODAY International
589 NEWSWEEK, James D. Wilson
594 Philippe Gontier/Image Works
595 Courtesy American Express

CHAPTER 19

600 Frank Herholdt/Tony Stone Worldwide
602 Glenn Oakley
612 Holt Confer/Image Works
613 Courtesy Intel Corporation
614 Jay Brousseau
620 Nina Barnett
627 Will & Deni McIntyre
631 Charlie Archambault/U.S. News & World Report

CHAPTER 20

636 Ira Wexler/Folio
638 Left & right, Eric Draper
642 David Hiser/Photographers/Aspen
644 Jonathan Levine
647 Brian Smith
655 Keith Dannemiller/SABA
657 Paul Chesley/Photographers/Aspen
663 Chris Sanders

CHAPTER 21

668 Tom Tracy/Stock Market
670 John S. Abbott
672 Bruce Zake
675 Pascal Rondeau/Tony Stone Worldwide
679 Peter Yates
683 Peter Menzel/Stock, Boston
690 Ken Kerbs Photography
695 Courtesy Ford Motor Company

GLOSSARY

A

Acceptable quality level A predetermined level of defects that is considered acceptable

Acceptance sampling A statistical tool in which portions of incoming or outgoing material are tested to determine defect rates

Acceptance theory of authority The notion that authority is meaningful only when employees accept the manager's legitimate right to direct their activities

Accountability The requirement that managers achieve the expected results or justify any deviation to managers higher in the chain of command

Acquired-needs theory A need theory suggesting that needs are acquired or learned through life and that some people are more oriented to certain needs than to other needs

Activity ratios Indexes used to analyze an organization's effectiveness in using its assets to generate sales

Adaptation model A strategy analysis tool based on the relationship of business-level strategy to the internal and external environments

Added value The increased worth of a product compared with the generic product

Adhocracy An organization design characterized by a matrix organization, relatively decentralized authority, considerable work specialization, and little formalization

Adjourning The fifth stage of group development, during which the group disbands after completing its work

Administrative management A management approach that stresses the functional aspects of the organization and management by planning, organizing, leading, and controlling

Administrative model of decision making A model that assumes managers cannot always approach decision making logically and rationally

Advocacy An organization's support of a particular cause, through financial, material, and human resource backing

Affirmative action A process of active steps to hire and retain members of minority groups that are underrepresented in the work force

Agenda A set of goals and plans that a manager develops to address short-term and long-term responsibilities

Aggregate production plan A plan that, over one year, matches product demand with the production capacity needed to produce those products

Artificial intelligence The use of computers to mimic human thought

Audit An independent appraisal of an organization's financial and operational efficiency and effectiveness performed by an accountant

Augmented product A product with more added value than the expected product

Authority The right to make decisions, to perform or supervise activities, and to allocate resources in order to achieve organizational goals

Autocratic leader A manager who tends to centralize authority and to make unilateral decisions

Average collection period A measure of how many days from the sales date it takes to receive a customer payment

Avoidance learning Strengthening one behavior by allowing people to avoid the negative consequences of not exhibiting that behavior

B

Balance of payments A financial measure of the difference between the outflow and the inflow of a nation's products and funds

Balance of trade A financial measure of the difference between the value of a country's imports and the value of its exports

Balance sheet A financial statement detailing an organization's assets, liabilities, and shareholder equity at a specific point in time

Bankruptcy A retrenchment strategy in which an organization unable to meet its obligations seeks court protection to gain time and opportunity to attempt a turnaround

Batch processing A method of data processing in which transactions are collected in a file and then processed as a group, usually at night when there is little demand for computer resources

BCG growth-share matrix A four-cell matrix that categorizes SBUs in the organizational portfolio according to market growth and market share

Behavior modification The deliberate use of techniques to change human behavior

Behavioral management A management perspective that focuses on the nature and impact of individual and group behavior in organizations

Behavioral science movement A school of management thought that stresses scientific research about human behavior to guide management practices

Benchmarking Comparing an organization's processes and products to the world's best and then matching or exceeding that quality

Benefits Parts of the compensation package provided by the employer other than direct wages, such as health insurance

Blocked currency A currency that cannot be redeemed in the international financial marketplace

Bottom-up budgeting A process in which the lower-level managers directly responsible for operations develop individual budgets that are combined to create an overall organizational budget

Boundary spanning Organizational roles that link and coordinate the organization's plans and activities with the environment

Bounded rationality The idea that a manager's ability to make objective decisions is restricted by time constraints and by cognitive limitations

Brainstorming An informal interactive group technique in which members generate many alternatives without passing judgment on their value

Break-even analysis A quantitative tool that helps managers understand the relationship among costs, sales volume, and sales revenues

Break-even point The point at which sales volume produces sales revenues equal to total costs

Budget A financial plan for an organization or for a unit within the organization

Budgeting An allocation of organizational resources to units within the organization in order to support organizational plans and strategies

Buffering Either building a reserve or releasing resources and finished goods as a way of adapting to environmental uncertainty

Bureaucracy A management approach that emphasizes a structured organization in which positions and authority are defined according to formal rules

Bureaucratic control The regulation of organizational activities in a formal and inflexible manner, designed to achieve employee compliance

Business-level strategy The level of strategy that determines how a company will compete in each of its business units

Business plan A document detailing business strategies and tactics prepared by an entrepreneur prior to opening a new business

C

Capacity planning The process of determining and adjusting an organization's resources to meet customer demand

Capacity requirements planning (CRP) The process of translating forecasts of customer demand into the labor and equipment resources needed to meet short-term demand

Capital expenditures budget Cash sources and cash uses associated with the future purchase of large assets, including buildings, land, and machinery

Career development Preparing key employees for present and future jobs

Cash budget A financial plan showing the sources and uses of cash for a specific period, such as daily, weekly, monthly, or yearly

Causal model A quantitative forecasting tool that helps managers predict the behavior of one variable on the basis of past interaction with other variables

Cause-related marketing An activity in which the company contributes a specified amount to a social cause when customers buy its products

Centralization The extent to which authority is concentrated at the top management levels

Centralized data processing An approach to data processing in which control is concentrated in one central part of the organization

Chain of command The unbroken line of authority that extends from the bottom to the top of the organization and defines reporting relationships

Change Any alteration in the organization's existing situation

Change agents Specialists with the behavioral science skills to guide organizational change

Channel The means of transferring a message from the sender to the receiver

Clan control The regulation of organizational activities in a flexible and informal manner, designed to achieve employee commitment

Classical management A set of management theories that focus on increasing the efficiency of the organization as a whole

Classical model of decision making A model that assumes managers always approach decision making rationally and objectively

Classical organization theory A management approach that emphasizes the total organization and ways to improve overall effectiveness and efficiency

Closed system A system that is self-sufficient, with little or no interaction within its environment

Coaching A one-on-one relationship in which supervising managers or more experienced employees give other employees continual guidance and feedback about their performance

Code of ethics A formal statement of the organization's values, ethical principles, and ethical rules

Coercive power Power derived from the ability to penalize others

Cohesiveness The extent to which members are loyal and committed to a group and its goals

Collective bargaining The process by which representatives of employees negotiate an employment agreement with the employer

Command group A group composed of a manager and all employees who report directly to the manager

Communication The exchange and comprehension of information

Communication network The pattern of communication within a group and among groups

Comparative advantage The benefit to nations of specializing in the export of products they can produce more cheaply because of their natural and human resources

Compensation The direct wages, benefits, and incentives given to employees in exchange for their work

Competitors Rival organizations that provide goods or services to the same set of customers or that vie for the same resources

Compliance Adherence to laws and regulations

Computer-aided design (CAD) The use of computer graphics and mathematical modeling in the design of new products

Computer-aided manufacturing (CAM) The use of computers to control conveyers, machine tools, inspection devices, and other production equipment

Computer-based information system (CBIS) An information system in which the computer plays a significant role

Computer-integrated manufacturing (CIM) The highest level of computerization in operations management, in which all elements of design and production are integrated in computer networks

Computer network A form of data communication in which hardware devices such as computers, workstations, printers, and data disk drives are linked together

Concentration A growth strategy that involves focusing organizational resources on the growth of one product or on a small group of related products

Conceptual skills Abilities enabling people to understand the complex interrelationships between the organization's component parts and to see the organization within the context of its environment

Concurrent control The regulation of ongoing processes to ensure they adhere to established standards

Condition of ambiguity A situation in which the manager has little or no information about the problem, the alternatives, or the consequences of each alternative

Condition of certainty A situation in which the manager has complete information about the problem, the alternatives, and the consequences of a decision

Condition of risk A situation in which the manager understands the problem and the alternatives and has only enough information to estimate the probability that the available alternatives will lead to the desired outcome

Condition of uncertainty A situation in which the manager understands the problem but has incomplete information about the alternatives and the probable consequences of each alternative

Conflict Disagreement resulting from differences between two or more individuals or groups

Conglomerate organization An organization design in which the divisions are largely unrelated

Consideration The extent to which leaders show concern and respect for employees

Constituents Individuals and organizations that are served by organizations in the public sector

Contingency plans Alternative courses of action to be followed if unforeseen environmental shifts occur

Contingency theory A management approach emphasizing that appropriate management behavior should be adapted to the unique circumstances of the organization and the specific situation

Continuous-flow-process technology A type of technology in which products are manufactured through a continually linked series of transformation processes

Continuous-improvement process A continuous cycle of improvements that result in ever-higher levels of quality

Control The regulatory process directing the activities an organization conducts to achieve anticipated goals and standards

Controlling The process of monitoring and regulating the organization's progress toward achieving goals

Core job dimensions According to job characteristics theory, the job aspects (skill variety, task identity, task significance, autonomy, and feedback) that are necessary for employees to be motivated, satisfied, and effective

Corporate-level strategy The level of strategy that guides the organization's overall direction, defines the businesses in which a company competes, and specifies how resources are allocated

Corporate social performance A business's degree of integration of the principles of social responsibility, the process of responsiveness to social issues, and the development of policies to address social problems

Corporation A form of business ownership in which a legal entity, chartered by the state, has an existence separate and apart from that of its owners

Cost leadership strategy A generic competitive strategy that keeps costs as low as possible to attract a broad market and to yield high profits

Creative imitation An entrepreneurial strategy that aims to do a better job of bringing an existing idea to market and satisfying customers

Creativity The process of generating novel ideas

Crisis problem A situation that urgently requires an immediate decision

Current ratio An index used to measure an organization's ability to cover current liabilities with current assets

Customer departmentalization Grouping of jobs that meet the unique needs of customers or constituents

Customer satisfaction Fulfillment of customer needs and expectations by offering the appropriate product with the appropriate service delivery before, during, and after the transaction

Customers Individuals and organizations that buy the goods or services produced by an organization

Cybernetic control systems Self-regulating control systems capable of automatically measuring, evaluating, and correcting a process

D

Data Facts, ideas, or concepts that are collected and stored in raw, unprocessed form

Data communications The technology for transmitting data between computers

Data processing Collecting, sorting, and storing data with the goal of converting them into useful information

Debt capital A form of financing in which the funds received by an organization must be repaid

Debt ratio The extent to which total company assets are financed through both short-term and long-term debt

Decentralization The extent to which authority is delegated to lower management levels

Decision The choice made from among available alternatives that is expected to lead to a favorable solution to a problem

Decision making The process of recognizing a problem, generating and weighing alternatives, coming to a decision, taking action, and assessing the results

Decision support system (DSS) An information system that helps higher-level managers solve unstructured and nonroutine problems

Decision tree An analytical tool that graphically portrays the logical series of actions and decisions in a problem situation

Decisional roles Four managerial roles in which managers make choices and commitments: the manager as entrepreneur, the manager as disturbance handler, the manager as resource allocator, and the manager as negotiator

Decoding The process of interpreting a message to arrive at the sender's meaning

Delegation The process of transferring to others a part of a manager's total work load, including the appropriate authority and responsibility

Delphi group A consulting group of experts who respond to circulated questionnaires and offer ideas about a problem until a consensus has been reached

Demassing Flattening the organization structure by widespread cutbacks of managers in nearly all departments and at several levels

Democratic leader A manager who tends to delegate authority and to encourage participation in decision making

Demotion Changing an employee's job to a lower-status position

Deontology A theory that judges the intentions of the person's decision or activities, rather than the consequences

Departmentalization The arrangement of individual jobs and activities into logical units and then combining these units to form the total organization

Dependent demand Demand for a given product or component that is influenced by the demand for another product

Design for manufacturability and assembly (DFMA) A design philosophy that tries to develop new products that can be produced and delivered to customers quickly and efficiently

Developed countries Nations with a relatively high per capita income and a high degree of industrialization

Devil's advocate A technique in which one or more group members deliberately challenge the group's view of the problem, the alternatives, and their evaluation

Dialectic process A technique in which individuals or groups present and defend opposing solutions to a particular problem to derive an improved solution

Differentiation The degree of variation in structure, behavior, and orientation among organizational units

Differentiation strategy A generic competitive strategy in which an organization crafts a product that customers perceive to be distinctly different from those offered by the competition

Direct investment An arrangement in which an organization acquires an ownership interest in an overseas company or invests in production and marketing facilities in another country

Distinctive competence An organization's competitive superiority in a given skill

Distributed data processing A method of processing data in which the transformation process occurs on two or more computers

Diversification A growth strategy that involves the acquisition of organizations in other industries or in other lines of business

Divestiture A retrenchment strategy that involves selling all or part of an organization

Divisional organization An organization design in which separate but related units are established according to product, geography, customer, or other departmentalization method

Divisionalized form An organization design characterized by relatively decentralized authority, divisional or conglomerate organization, standardized outputs, and high formalization

Domain shift A change in the organization's products and services to avoid unfavorable environmental forces or to interact with favorable environmental elements

Domestic business Organizational activities that take place within the borders of one country

Downsizing Flattening the organization structure selectively by cutting middle management layers, expanding spans of management, and reducing the size of the work force

Downward communication A flow of information from higher to lower levels in the organization's hierarchy

E

Econometric model A quantitative forecasting tool comprising a series of regression equations that together predict how interrelated variables will affect the economy, the organization, and the organization's industry

Economic forces The availability of resources and the broad economic trends that affect the organization

Economic order quantity (EOQ) The most economical order size, which minimizes the organization's cost of ordering new inventory and its cost of holding excess inventory

Effectiveness The ability to accomplish the organization's goals

Efficiency The ability to minimize waste of the organization's available resources

Effort-performance expectancy The perceived relationship between the effort required and the performance that is likely to result

Electronic communication The transmission of information using advanced techniques such as computer modems, facsimile machines, voice mail, electronic mail, teleconferencing, videocassettes, and private television networks

Electronic data interchange (EDI) A form of data communication that allows automatic transmission of preformatted business transaction data between organizations with little or no human interaction

Employee-centered leader behavior A behavior pattern emphasizing interpersonal relationships, strong teamwork, and employee participation

Employee stock ownership plan (ESOP) A reward system in which managers encourage employees to own stock in their own companies, providing an incentive for employees to increase the value of that stock through higher performance

Empowerment Giving employees discretion, authority, and some powers of self-management

Encoding The process of putting an idea into a message form that the receiver will understand

Entrepreneur A person who takes initiative for a business project, organizes the resources it requires, and assumes the risks it entails

Entrepreneurial judo An entrepreneurial strategy in which an idea is aimed at filling holes left by others in the industry

Entrepreneurship The process of launching a new venture, organizing the resources it requires, and assuming the risks it entails

Entropy The tendency of systems to deteriorate over time

Environmental change The degree to which an organization's environment is stable or shifting

Environmental complexity The number of elements in the organizational environment and the extent to which the organization understands these elements and their impact

Environmental munificence The level of resources available in the organizational environment to support prolonged growth and stability

Environmental uncertainty How much change and complexity influence the organization and its performance

Equity capital A form of financing in which the funds received by an organization are exchanged for part-ownership in the organization

Equity theory A process theory suggesting that people are motivated to seek equitable treatment compared with others in similar situations

ERG theory A need theory that refines the hierarchy of needs by reducing the number of categories to three: existence needs, relatedness needs, and growth needs

Esteem needs The need for self-respect and for personal recognition

Ethical behavior Conduct that is considered "right" or "good" in the context of a governing moral code

Ethical dilemma An unresolved ethical question in which each of the conflicting sides has an arguable case to make

Ethical lapse A situation that occurs when a manager makes an unethical decision or engages in unethical behavior

Ethical standards Guidelines governing moral conduct of a particular group

Ethics The study of decision making within the framework of a system of moral standards

Ethnocentric management A management approach in which the values and interests of the parent company in its home country guide the decisions and actions of operations outside the home country

Exchange rate The price at which one country's currency can be exchanged for another country's currency

Exit interview A formal conversation with a departing employee to learn why the employee is leaving the organization

Expectancy theory A process theory suggesting that before people act, they consider whether they have the ability and whether their effort will bring about the desired results

Expected product A product that delivers the basic value that customers expect beyond the generic product

Expense budget A projection of anticipated expenses for the coming period

Expense center A responsibility center headed by a manager who is held accountable for achieving expense targets

Expert power Power derived from the manager's personal skills, technical knowledge, and experience

Expert system A computerized system designed to replicate the decisions of a human expert about a specific subject

Exporting Selling products outside the country in which they are produced

Expropriation The seizure of business assets by a host government, with little or no payment to organizational owners

External audit An appraisal of an organization's financial statements performed by independent certified public accountants for reporting to shareholders, the Internal Revenue Service, and other interested parties

External communication A flow of information between the organization and outside individuals or groups

External environment Forces outside the organization that influence the ability to achieve organizational goals

Extinction Decreasing a specific behavior by withholding positive consequences that were once associated with that behavior

Extrinsic rewards Rewards that are provided by others as a consequence of a particular behavior

F

Feedback In systems theory, information about the status and results of organizational activities; in communication, a response from the receiver that cues the sender as to how the message is being interpreted and how the communication is being received in general

Fiedler contingency model A model that relates leadership style (as determined by manager reaction to the least preferred co-worker) to the favorability of situational variables to determine the appropriate leadership approach

Filtering The process of screening out or abbreviating information before passing a message to someone else

Financial budget A projection of cash inflows and cash outflows for the coming period

Financial statement A summary of the overall financial status of an organization

First-line manager A manager at the first level of management who supervises and coordinates the work of nonmanagerial employees

Fixed-position layout A work-flow layout in which inputs are brought to the location where the good is being produced or where the customer is being served

Flat structure An organization structure characterized by a wide span of management and few hierarchical levels

Flexible manufacturing systems (FMSs) Automated production systems that can easily switch between product types

Flexible reward system A reward system that offers employees the option of selecting the rewards they consider most valuable

Focus strategy A generic competitive strategy in which an organization concentrates on a limited part of the market, a limited product line, or a confined geographic area

For-profit organization An organization that sets as its primary goal the achievement of profit

Force-field analysis A technique for analyzing the overall impact of the various forces that work for and against change

Forecast A prediction or an estimate of future events or conditions

Forecasting The process of predicting future environmental conditions based on current data, research, and past experience

Formal communication A flow of information that is dictated by the organization's official structure

Formal group A group created by the organization to carry out specific tasks related to organizational goals

Formal organization The planned structure and relationships officially established by top managers

Formalization The use of written documents to systematize, link, and control the activities of organization members

Forming The first stage of group development, during which group members meet and lay the foundation for the group's purpose, structure, and tasks

Franchising A licensing arrangement in which the licensor supplies a complete package of goods, services, and materials to the licensee

Friendship group An informal group that forms spontaneously in response to a social attraction among members

Functional departmentalization Grouping of jobs dedicated to a single organizational function

Functional-level strategy The level of strategy that determines how activities in each of the organization's functional areas will support business-level strategy

Functional manager A manager who supervises the activities of one organizational department

Functional organization An organization design based on employee function or specialized skill

G

Gain sharing A reward system in which employees receive bonuses based on their unit's performance

Gantt chart A project planning tool developed by scientific management theorist Henry L. Gantt to show the planned duration and current status of all activities in a project

GE business screen A nine-cell matrix that classifies SBUs according to industry attractiveness and business strength

General environment The part of the external environment composed of forces that have a general influence on the organization

General manager A manager who oversees all the functions and activities in a single organizational unit

Generic product A basic product that minimally satisfies customer needs

Geocentric management A management approach in which managers take a global view of the organization's international operations

Geographical departmentalization Grouping of jobs by defined locations

Goal A target or future state that an organization strives to achieve

Grand strategy A comprehensive general strategy formulated to direct the major actions that will help the organization achieve long-term goals

Grapevine An informal interpersonal channel of information not officially sanctioned by the organization

Group Two or more people who interact interdependently in the pursuit of a common goal

Groupthink The tendency of members deeply involved in a group to pursue harmony and agreement rather than realistically considering the problem and the alternatives

Growth strategy A grand strategy involving expanding the organization along one or more dimensions

H

Hardware Computerized machinery used to process transactions and convert data to information

Harvest A retrenchment strategy that involves minimizing investment and maximizing short-term profits while planning to sell or liquidate in the long term

Hersey-Blanchard situational leadership theory A contingency theory of leadership that contends that leader behavior should be altered according to the employees' readiness to perform tasks

Heuristics Rules of thumb that managers use to simplify the decision-making process

Hierarchy of needs theory Abraham Maslow's theory that people are motivated to fulfill a sequence of five categories of human needs: physiological, safety, social, esteem, and self-actualization needs

Home country A country where the company has its headquarters

Horizontal communication A flow of information across departmental boundaries, either laterally or diagonally

Horizontal coordination The linking of activities across departments so that organizational goals can be achieved

Horizontal integration A growth strategy that involves the acquisition of one or more competitors

Host country Any nation outside the home country where an organization conducts business activities

Human relations movement A management perspective that views employees as responding to the interpersonal processes within the work unit

Human resource management A comprehensive, integrated system for effectively managing the work force in the effort to achieve organizational goals

Human resource planning The process of analyzing an organization's needs for various employees in accord with its goals, and devising activities to meet those needs

Hygiene factors Factors that influence dissatisfaction

I

Import quotas Legal restrictions on the amount of a particular product that can be shipped into a country

Importing Purchasing products from a supplier in another country

Income statement A summary of an organization's revenues, expenses, and profits over a particular period of time

Incrementalism Deciding on an alternative that differs only slightly from the existing situation

Incubators Business-development facilities designed to help young companies grow beyond the start-up phase

Independent demand Demand that is not directly dependent on the demand for another item

Individualism The degree to which people expect to take care of themselves and their own families

Informal communication A flow of information without regard for organizational structure, hierarchical levels, or reporting relationships

Informal group A group formed voluntarily by its members rather than by the organization

Informal organization The unofficial, unwritten system of relationships that develops spontaneously within the organization

Information The result of processing, correlating, or summarizing raw data to create useful insights

Information overload The condition that exists when message volume or rate exceeds the capacity of receivers to deal with it

Information systems Procedures and equipment that support the timely use, management, and processing of data or information regarding an organization's operations

Informational power Power derived from the ability to control access to important information

Informational roles Three roles in which managers receive and transmit information: the manager as monitor, the manager as disseminator, and the manager as spokesperson

Infrastructure The network of transportation, utilities, housing, education, highways, communication, and other facilities that serve fundamental personal and organizational needs

Initiating structure The extent to which leaders define their own roles and their employees' roles to achieve organizational goals

Innovation The transformation of creative ideas into goods or services that meet customer needs or solve customer problems

Inputs The human, physical, financial, and information resources used to produce goods and services

Integration The degree of coordination and collaboration exhibited among organizational units

Interacting group A decision-making group in which people meet personally to solve a problem

Interest group An informal group created by members with a common purpose, agenda, or concern

Internal audit An appraisal performed by an employee of the organization to evaluate the accuracy of financial and accounting controls as well as the efficiency of operations

Internal communication The exchange of messages among organization members

Internal environment Forces inside the organization that can influence the organization and its performance

International business Organizational activities that take place across national borders in more than one country

International forces Factors originating outside the organization's home country that can affect how the organization interacts with people and organizations

Interpersonal roles Three roles in which managers develop and maintain relationships: the manager as figurehead, the manager as leader, and the manager as liaison

Interpersonal skills Abilities enabling people to work well with and through other people, to communicate effectively, and to work cooperatively within a group

Intrapreneur A person who promotes innovation and creativity within a larger organization

Intrinsic rewards Internally experienced rewards that result directly from a person's behavior

Inventory management The control of inventory in operations management, including such functions as shipping and receiving, storage, and internal materials handling

Inventory turnover A measure of how inventory is managed to meet sales

Investment center A responsibility center headed by a manager who is held accountable for achieving return-on-investment targets

J

Job The array of tasks and responsibilities given to an employee in order to meet organizational goals

Job analysis A systematic process of collecting information about jobs, including the purpose of each job, its duties, its place in the organizational hierarchy, its working conditions and environment, and employee requirements

Job-centered leader behavior A behavior pattern emphasizing the job's technical aspects and the completion of the tasks to achieve group goals

Job characteristics The theory that employees will be satisfied if they can assume adequate responsibility, can believe their jobs are meaningful, and can receive feedback regarding their performance

Job description A list of duties, working conditions, relationships, equipment, and other requirements that define a particular job

Job design The effort to organize and specify the tasks, duties, and responsibilities of a job in order to advance organizational goals

Job enlargement The horizontal expansion of employee tasks to offer variety and to make the job more challenging

Job enrichment The vertical expansion of jobs by increasing employee responsibilities associated with the positions

Job evaluation A process of ascertaining how much each job is worth to the organization and assuring that the pay level for each job is fair

Job rotation The lateral transfer of employees to various jobs to broaden their focus and increase their knowledge

Job satisfaction The positive emotional state resulting from performance in a job

Job specifications A list of the knowledge, skills, and abilities needed by an employee to successfully perform each job

Joint venture An arrangement in which two or more organizations cooperate to develop, produce, or sell products

Jury of executive opinion A qualitative forecasting technique in which organizational executives meet and decide as a group on their best estimate for the forecast

Just-in-time (JIT) systems Operational control systems designed to run production facilities with a minimum level of inventory

L

Labor relations The conduct of relations between management and labor unions

Labor supply The people who may potentially be employed by an organization

Labor union A group of employees that collectively bargains on behalf of employees and oversees their interests in the workplace

Layoffs Terminations of employees for strategic reasons that are not connected with employee performance

Leader Someone who advances organizational goals by influencing the attitudes and actions of others

Leadership The ability to influence and to motivate others to achieve organizational goals

Leading The process of using influence to motivate others to work toward accomplishing goals

Leading indicators Variables that are correlated with the movements of a broad economic phenomenon but that tend to occur in advance of the phenomenon

Least preferred co-worker (LPC) scale A questionnaire that scores managers' descriptions of the one person they have least enjoyed working with

Legitimate power Power derived from a specific position in the organization structure and the formal authority vested in it

Less-developed countries (LDCs) Nations with a relatively low per capita income and a low degree of industrialization

Leverage ratios Indexes used to analyze an organization's ability to meet its long-term and short-term debt obligations

Licensing An arrangement in which one organization sells a second organization the rights to a patent, a brand name, or a product

Line authority Formal authority based on the hierarchical positions in the chain of command

Line position A position in which managers and employees make decisions and supervise activities that directly contribute to the organization's performance

Liquidation A retrenchment strategy that involves dissolving or selling an entire organization

Liquidity ratios Indexes used to analyze an organization's ability to meet short-run obligations with current assets

M

Machine bureaucracy An organization design characterized by relatively centralized authority, narrow and precise work specialization, functional departmentalization, and high formalization

Management The process of attaining organizational goals by effectively and efficiently planning, organizing, leading, and controlling the organization's human, physical, financial, and information resources

Management by objectives (MBO) A collaborative process in which managers and employees set mutually agreeable goals, define the responsibility for results, and determine the means of evaluating individual and group performance

Management information systems (MIS) Management tools that focus on the collection, processing, and transmission of information to support management functions

Management science A quantitative management perspective that applies mathematical models to management situations

Manager Someone who participates in the management process by planning, organizing, leading, or controlling the organization's resources

Managerial grid A method developed by Blake and Mouton to analyze leader behavior and style using a grid with two axes, concern for people and concern for production

Manufacturing resource planning (MRPII) A computer-based control system that integrates financial, accounting, personnel, engineering, and marketing information with MRP production control activities

Masculinity The degree to which assertiveness, competitiveness, and materialism dominate a society

Mass-production and large-batch technology A type of technology in which products are manufactured in large quantities, frequently on an assembly line

Master production schedule (MPS) A specific plan derived from the aggregate production plan, identifying the number of products to be produced and the specific capacity requirements necessary over the short term

Material requirements planning (MRP) A computer-based control system that uses the master production schedule to identify the materials to be used in production

Materials management The planning, organizing, and controlling of the flow of materials from purchase of raw materials through final distribution

Matrix analysis A technique to stimulate creativity and innovation in which managers use a two- or three-dimensional matrix to identify new-product ideas

Matrix organization An organization design that overlays a divisional organization design onto a functional organization design, forming two chains of command

Mechanistic structure A relatively inflexible organization structure characterized by centralized decision making, narrow work specialization, and hierarchical delegation and communication

Mentor An experienced manager who helps someone with less experience develop better managerial skills, learn specific job functions, and gain an understanding of the organization

Merit system A system in which employees receive rewards as their performance improves

Meritocracy An organization that rewards individual performance through merit pay or advancement

Message The symbolic representation of an idea the sender wants to communicate

Middle manager A manager who executes the strategies established by top management and who supervises and coordinates the activities of first-line managers

Mission The basic purpose for and driving force behind an organization's existence

Mission statement A declaration of the organization's purpose and scope of operations

Motivation The force that moves people to initiate, direct, and sustain behavior and action

Motivators Factors that influence satisfaction

Multidomestic management A management approach in which a company operating in several countries allows its local units to act independently and does not coordinate its various operations on a global basis

Multinational corporation (MNC) A company that produces goods or services in several countries and manages its global activities from one organizational headquarters

N

National competitive advantage The ability of a country's industries to innovate and upgrade to the next level of technology and productivity

Nationalization The appropriation of one company's operations or an entire industry's operations by a host government for the benefit of the nation

Need A perceived deficiency

Need for achievement The desire to reach goals, to assume challenges, and to excel

Need for affiliation The desire to form personal bonds with others

Need for power The desire to influence or to control others

Need theories Theories of motivation that focus on the needs that cause people to act in certain ways

Negative entropy The capacity to obtain new inputs from the environment to keep the system from falling into decline

Net profit margin A measure of the percentage of sales left after deducting expenses

Network building Management activities that help build relationships with people inside and outside the organization

Neutralizers Situational variables that negate leader behavior or prevent leaders from exhibiting particular behaviors

New-market leadership An entrepreneurial strategy that aims to create and implement products faster and better than anyone else, thereby leading and dominating the new market

New venture An organization still in its formative stages

Noise Any interference in the communication process that distorts the meaning intended by the sender

Nominal group A decision-making group that uses a formal structure to facilitate individual thinking and active group participation

Noncrisis problem A problem that requires a decision but less urgently than a crisis problem

Noncybernetic control systems Control systems that rely on human intervention for the measurement, evaluation, or correction of a control process

Nonprogrammed decision A decision made in a situation where predetermined decision rules cannot be applied because the situation is less structured, occurs rarely, or is unique

Nonrational escalation of commitment Staying committed to a previous decision after it should be abandoned

Nonverbal communication The expression of information through gesture and behavior

Norming The third stage of group development, during which members come to understand and to accept their roles and responsibilities

Norms Informal standards of behavior that govern member actions in a group

Not-for-profit organization An organization that does not have profit-making as its primary goal but focuses on social, cultural, or political goals

O

Offshore production Establishing manufacturing or assembly plants in other countries where labor and resource costs are relatively low

Ombudsmanship A system of review and evaluation that provides employees with an avenue for airing concerns about ethical conflicts

On-line processing A method of data processing in which users interact directly with the transaction-processing system; the computer's files, therefore, are updated as soon as new information is available

On-the-job training A training method in which a manager trains employees while they are at their work assignments

Open system A system that interacts with its environment and receives feedback

Operating budget A financial plan allocating resources to responsibility centers in order to support organizational plans and strategies

Operational control The regulatory process ensuring successful implementation of day-to-day operational plans by monitoring specific and focused internal activities

Operational goals Targets to be achieved by departments and individuals

Operational plans The means of pursuing operational goals

Operations management A management approach that uses quantitative techniques to improve the productivity and efficiency of goods or services production; the collection of planning and control activities that managers use to produce goods and services

Opportunity problem A situation that can be dealt with in a way that has a positive effect on the organization and its performance

Oral communication The expression of ideas through the spoken word

Organic structure A relatively flexible organization structure characterized by decentralized decision making, fluid work definition, and horizontal and vertical communication

Organization A group of two or more people who work together in a consciously structured setting to achieve group goals

Organization chart A diagram of the positions and relationships within the organization structure

Organization design The process of developing and implementing an appropriate organization structure

Organization structure A formal system of interaction and coordination that links the tasks of individuals and groups to effectively achieve organizational goals

Organizational behavior The study of the effect that organizations have on their members and of the effect that members have on their organizations

Organizational culture The values and norms shared by members of an organization

Organizational development (OD) A long-term, organization-wide planned change effort that is managed from the top and that aims to improve organization effectiveness and health by using behavioral science techniques to intervene in organizational processes

Organizational environment All forces with the potential to influence the organization and its performance

Organizational life cycle A series of four developmental stages through which every organization passes

Organizational politics The pursuit, protection, and use of power to achieve individual or group goals not necessarily directly related to organizational goals

Organizing The process of creating a framework for developing and assigning tasks, obtaining and allocating resources, and coordinating work activities to achieve goals

Orientation A short-term process of introducing employees to their jobs, their supervisors, the organization's structure, and its hierarchy

Outputs The results, goods, and services produced by an organization

Overcontrol Excessive regulation of work activities, restricting individual autonomy and causing ineffective organizational performance

P

Partial factor productivity The ratio of total outputs to one particular input

Partners Two or more organizations that work together in a formal or informal arrangement that helps them achieve goals effectively

Partnership A form of business ownership in which the organization is owned by two or more individuals

Path-goal theory A contingency theory of leadership which holds that leader effectiveness depends on the ability to motivate and to satisfy employees so they will perform

Pay-for-knowledge system A system in which employees receive rewards as they learn to perform additional tasks or acquire new skills

Payoff matrix A quantitative tool that compares probable outcomes of two or more alternatives, which can differ depending on various future conditions

Perception The way individuals process information to comprehend the world around them

Perceptual organization The process of organizing selected details into some meaningful order and filling in the gaps with assumptions

Performance The degree to which individuals and organizations achieve the organization's goals with effectiveness and efficiency

Performance appraisal The process of evaluating employee performance in relation to expectations and providing feedback

Performance-outcome expectancy The perceived relationship between a person's performance and the possibility that various outcomes will result

Performing The fourth group development stage, in which the group is fully functional and able to move ahead toward its goals

Philanthropy Gifts of money, time, goods, or services to charitable, humanitarian, or educational institutions

Physiological needs The lowest-level needs in Maslow's hierarchy, including the elements that ensure basic human survival

Plan The means of pursuing goals

Planned change Change that is deliberately designed and implemented in anticipation of future environmental threats and opportunities

Planning The process of formulating goals and developing ways to achieve them

Policy A standing plan that provides broad guidelines for directing managerial activities in pursuit of organizational goals

Political risk The likelihood that an organization's international goals, operations, or investments will be threatened by a host government's political, legal, or regulatory policies or actions

Politicolegal forces Governmental policies, legal policies, laws, and institutions that influence people and organizations

Polycentric management A management approach in which managers in the home country allow managers in other countries to make their own decisions in response to local needs and environmental pressures

Porter's generic competitive strategies Three business-level strategies—cost leadership, differentiation, and focus—that help organizations attain competitive advantage

Portfolio strategy An approach to corporate-level strategy that involves analyzing the relationships and positions of an organization's SBUs to create the mix that will best support organizational goals

Positive reinforcement Strengthening behavior by offering pleasant consequences for a particular action

Postaction control The regulation of a process's outputs to ensure they comply with established standards

Power The capacity to affect the decisions, attitudes, and behavior of others

Power distance The extent to which people in the society accept the often unequal distribution of power

Preliminary control The regulation of a process's inputs to ensure they meet established standards

Private sector Organizations under private control

Private stock offering Equity financing in which shares in the company are offered only to selected investors

Problem A situation in which the existing circumstances differ significantly from the preferred situation

Procedure A standing plan encompassing a series of detailed steps to be followed in particular recurring situations

Process departmentalization Grouping of jobs dedicated to a single operational process or technique

Process layout A work-flow configuration in which the production centers are arranged according to the function provided, such as painting, welding, or filing

Process-oriented innovation Incremental improvements to existing products and production or other organizational processes

Process theories Theories of motivation focusing on the thought processes that guide people as they act to satisfy their needs

Product departmentalization Grouping of jobs according to the products offered by the organization

Product layout A work-flow configuration in which the production centers are arranged according to the specific sequences required by each type of good or service being produced

Product life cycle The passage of goods and services through a progression of market acceptance stages

Product-oriented innovation The development of goods and services that incorporate novel breakthrough advances

Productivity A measure of a production process's efficiency in transforming input resources into output goods and services

Products Goods or services

Professional bureaucracy An organization design characterized by decentralized authority, functional or hybrid departmentalization, a large core of skilled professionals, a technical support staff, and little formalization

Profit budget A projection of profits for the coming year, made by comparing anticipated revenues to anticipated expenses

Profit center A responsibility center headed by a manager who is held accountable for achieving profit targets

Profit sharing A reward system in which employees receive bonuses based on the organization's profitability

Profitability ratios Indexes used to analyze an organization's effectiveness in earning a net return on sales and investments

Program A complex single-use plan consisting of a set of interrelated actions aimed at achieving a one-time major goal

Program Evaluation and Review Technique (PERT) A project planning tool that helps managers identify the optimal sequencing of activities, the expected time for project completion, and the best use of resources within a complex project

Programmed decision A decision made when the situation occurs frequently enough or is sufficiently well-structured to be resolved by applying predetermined decision rules

Project A single-use plan that is narrower in scope than a program and that is aimed at achieving a specific one-time goal

Project departmentalization Grouping of jobs according to the skills needed to complete a specific project

Project manager A manager who is responsible for a specific project that involves coordinating people and activities in several departments

Promotion The elevation of an employee to a different job that pays better or is higher in the chain of command

Public sector Organizations under governmental control

Public stock offering Equity financing in which shares in the company are offered for sale to the general public

Punishment Decreasing a behavior by providing unpleasant consequences

Purchasing The acquisition of the raw materials, parts, components, supplies, and finished products needed in operations

Q

Qualitative forecasting A forecasting method based on individual judgments or committee agreements about future events or conditions

Quality A measure of how closely a product conforms to predetermined standards and customer expectations

Quality assurance Policies, procedures, and guidelines that managers can use to ensure that products conform to specified standards of quality; unlike quality control, quality assurance seeks to build quality into the product, rather than simply inspecting for it at the end of the assembly line

Quality circle (QC) A group of people from a single organizational unit who meet regularly to find solutions to quality problems in their area of responsibility

Quality control A traditional approach to quality management that focuses on final inspection to make sure that products meet quality standards

Quality function deployment (QFD) The process of designing customer needs and expectations directly into product quality

Quality-improvement team (QIT) A group of people from several departments who meet to solve quality problems that cut across functional or departmental lines

Quality of work life A philosophy of improving productivity by providing employees with the opportunity to use their individual abilities, pursue self-improvement, and identify with the organization

Quantitative forecasting A mathematical method of analyzing historical data to determine a pattern that can be projected into the future

Quantitative management A management perspective that applies mathematical techniques, statistical tools, and information aids to management situations

R

Ratio analysis A managerial process used to compare organizational performance with historical, competitive, or industry performance

Rationing Deliberately limiting production of goods and services during times of peak demand

Ratios Indexes derived from comparing one financial measure to another

Reactive change Change that is undertaken piecemeal to resolve specific problems as they occur

Realistic job preview A recruiting technique in which a representative of the organization tells job applicants both the good and bad aspects of the organization and the jobs they seek

Recruiting The process of attracting qualified people to apply for positions with an organization

Referent power Power derived from the ability to inspire respect, admiration, and loyalty

Regression analysis A quantitative forecasting tool that uses mathematical equations to predict the behavior of one variable on the basis of the fluctuation of one or more known variables

Regulators Governmental agencies, their representatives, and groups who influence or enforce guidelines that affect the organization's actions

Reinforcement The use of techniques that cause a behavior to be repeated or abandoned

Reinforcement theories Motivation theories that suggest that people's behavior is directly related to the consequences of their actions

Reorder point (ROP) A calculation that determines when orders should be placed to avoid stockouts

Replacement chart An organization chart showing each key management position, who occupies it, when a vacancy may occur, and the potential replacements

Resource dependence The degree to which the organization depends on resources from the environment

Resource deployment The way the organization apportions its human, physical, financial, and information resources

Responsibility The obligation to perform assigned tasks or activities

Responsibility center A discrete organization unit headed by a manager responsible for achieving specific goals

Retrenchment strategy A grand strategy that involves reducing organizational operations

Return on equity A measure of an organization's effectiveness in generating returns on the shareholders' investments

Return on investment (ROI) A measure of an organization's effectiveness in generating returns from its investment in assets

Revenue budget A projection of anticipated revenues for the coming period

Revenue center A responsibility center headed by a manager who is held accountable for achieving revenue targets

Reward power Power derived from the ability to provide valued rewards to others

Role A set of behaviors expected of a member who holds a particular position within a group

Role ambiguity The uncertainty created by lack of understanding of a role or how to perform it

Role conflict A conflict caused by contradictory or incompatible expectations associated with a particular role

Role overload The inability of an individual to perform up to the expectations of a particular role

Rule A standing plan specifying the circumstances in which certain activities can or cannot be performed

S

S corporation A special form of a corporation that allows the profits and losses of the company to be taxed at personal tax rates while still providing the advantages of a corporation, notably limited liability

Safety needs Needs related to a safe, secure life

Sales force composite A qualitative forecasting method that combines estimates provided by salespeople, sales managers, and distributors in order to derive a prediction about future sales

Satisficing Searching for alternatives only until a satisfactory, not an optimal, solution is found

Scientific management A management perspective that focuses on the rational, scientific study of work situations to improve employee efficiency

Scope The spectrum of products offered, operations performed, markets served, or supplier relationships specified in a strategy

Selection The process of choosing the applicants who best suit vacant positions and organizational needs

Selective perception The process of focusing only on details that are pertinent to an individual's present circumstances and consistent with personal views and preferences

Self-actualization needs The highest-level needs in Maslow's hierarchy, reflecting the need to realize one's full potential

Self-managing team A team in which members are responsible for virtually all aspects of an operation or a process

Simple structure An organization design characterized by centralization of authority, minimal work specialization, minimal differentiation, and minimal formalization

Simulation model A mathematical representation of a problem that reflects the relationships between the elements and is used to project the results of certain actions under various circumstances

Single-use plan A plan designed to fit a one-time situation

Skills inventory A list of each employee's skills, knowledge, and other job-related personal information

Slack resources A cushion of resources that help departments cope with environmental changes

Small business An independently owned business, generally employing fewer than 500 people

Smoothing Making internal adjustments in anticipation of expected environmental fluctuations

Social audit A systematic evaluation and reporting of the organization's performance in the area of social responsibility

Social contract theories Theories that suggest that individuals as members of communities and of groups agree implicitly to conform to the goals and rules of these groups

Social contribution The behavior of an organization that actively looks for ways to help stakeholders, above and beyond what is normally expected of it

Social needs The need for love, affection, acceptance, and a sense of belonging

Social obligation The behavior of an organization that voluntarily conforms with legal and ethical standards but goes no further

Social opposition The behavior of an organization that must be forced to comply with legal and ethical standards

Social responsibility The argument that an organization has a greater obligation to society beyond the pursuit of its own goals

Social responsiveness The behavior of an organization that goes beyond legal and ethical standards to respond to some stakeholder needs

Socialization A relatively long-term process of making an employee aware of the organizational culture

Sociocultural forces The values, attitudes, needs, and demographic characteristics of the societies in which the organization operates

Sociotechnical systems theory The concept that organization design must take into account the interaction of the organization members, the technological system, and the degree of environmental interaction

Software The collection of computer programs that control the processing of data in a computer

Sole proprietorship A form of business ownership in which the organization is owned by one individual

Span of management The number of people who report directly to one manager

Special interest groups Groups of people who band together to influence the actions of organizations

Stability strategy A grand strategy that involves maintaining the status quo by continuing to offer the same goods or services and continuing to serve the same markets

Staff authority The authority to provide advice and to direct activities within a particular functional area of expertise

Staff position A position in which managers and employees assist line positions by providing information and guidance or performing specialized tasks

Staffing The process of attracting and selecting employees for positions in accordance with organizational goals

Stakeholders Any group inside or outside the organization that can affect or be affected by the organization's activities

Standards Explicit criteria against which future performance will be measured

Standing plan A plan for guiding management decisions and activities in situations that recur repeatedly

Start-up A new venture created by an entrepreneur

Statistical process control (SPC) A system of measurement that monitors the quality of the transformation process in order to reduce performance variations

Stereotyping The process of trying to categorize individuals by predicting their behavior or character according to their membership in a particular class or group

Storming The second stage of group development, during which members clarify their roles and responsibilities and come to terms with group issues

Storyboarding A technique that stimulates creativity and innovation by asking participants to focus on a well-defined problem, jot down their ideas, and then combine and reorder the ideas to uncover promising solutions

Strategic business unit (SBU) A separate business, with its own set of managers, products, resources, customers, and competitors, that is managed independently of a company's other organizational units

Strategic control The regulatory process ensuring successful implementation of an organization's long-range strategic plans, emphasizing environmental effects and internal strategic directions

Strategic goals Broadly defined targets for the organization's overall future results

Strategic management The ongoing process of formulating, implementing, and controlling broad plans to guide the organization in achieving its strategic goals, given its internal and external environment

Strategic plans The means of pursuing strategic goals

Strategy A comprehensive plan aimed at helping the organization achieve its goals

Substitutes Situational variables that make leader behavior unnecessary or redundant

Substitutes for leadership theory A contingency theory of leadership that argues that certain situational variables can substitute for leader behavior or can render leader behavior ineffective

Subsystem A system within a system, as in the work units within an organization

Succession Filling the vacancy created by the departure of an employee

Superordinate goal A goal whose achievement requires the cooperation of all group members

Suppliers People and organizations who furnish the resources that other organizations use to produce goods and services

SWOT analysis A situation analysis tool that helps managers identify internal strengths and weaknesses, external opportunities and threats, and the potential impact of these factors on organizational performance

Synectics A technique for stimulating creativity and innovation in which participants consider a broadly worded problem, generate ideas using analogies and metaphors, and agree on a single, radically new solution

Synergy The combined activity of two or more subsystems that results in better performance than when the units work in isolation

System A group of interrelated components that function as a whole to achieve common goals

System 1 A traditional organization design that relies heavily on formal authority and the hierarchical chain of command

System 4 An ideal form of organization design that relies on manager-employee collaboration, uses a wide array of motivational processes, and encourages freer interaction among organization members

Systems theory A contemporary management perspective that views organizations as functioning systems within the environment

T

Tactical control The regulatory process aimed at successful implementation of department-level tactical plans, emphasizing specific internal and external forces affecting them

Tactical goals Targets to be achieved by the divisions or units of the organization

Tactical plans The means of pursuing tactical goals

Tall structure An organization structure with a narrow span of management and many hierarchical levels

Tariffs Duties or taxes collected by a government on products imported into the country

Task environment The part of the external environment that includes forces with a direct effect on the organization

Task group A group created to handle a narrow range of tasks related to a specific issue or goal

Team A formal group characterized by relative autonomy and active employee participation in management and decision-making activities

Technical skills Abilities enabling people to use knowledge, methods, techniques, and equipment to perform specialized tasks

Technological forces The knowledge, techniques, and activities that lead to profound changes in products or processes

Technological forecasting A qualitative forecasting method that focuses on long-term predictions of the environment and technology

Technology The skills, equipment, and procedures used by organizations to transform inputs into outputs

Telecommuters Employees and managers who use communications technology to work from home

Teleconferencing Using communications technology to hold meetings among people in separate locations

Termination Any dismissal of an employee

Theories of justice Theories that contend that decisions must be based on equity, fairness, and impartiality

Theories of rights Theories that contend that the most ethical decisions are those that best maintain the rights of the people affected

Theory A An idealized management perspective that views U.S. management of organizations as characterized by short-term employment, individual responsibility, and individual decision making

Theory J An idealized management perspective that views Japanese management of organizations as characterized by lifetime employment, collective responsibility, and consensual decision making

Theory X A management philosophy in which employees are seen as lazy, unambitious, and in need of coercion to complete work tasks

Theory Y A management philosophy in which employees are seen as interested in assuming responsibility, capable of innovative approaches to work problems, and having no inherent distaste for work

Theory Z An idealized blend of U.S. and Japanese management approaches characterized by long-term employment, individual responsibility, and consensual decision making

Time-and-motion study The study of the physical movements and the time involved in completing a task

Time departmentalization Grouping of jobs according to the time of day they are performed

Time-series method A quantitative forecasting tool used to identify patterns in historical data and predict how these are likely to recur in the future

Top-down budgeting A process by which top managers impose budgets on lower-level managers

Top manager A manager who is part of the small group of people at the highest level of management who bear overall responsibility for the organization

Total factor productivity The ratio of total outputs to total inputs

Total quality management (TQM) An approach that builds quality into every organizational process

Training The process of teaching employees the behaviors, knowledge, and skills necessary for performing their jobs successfully or of reinforcing existing abilities to improve job performance

Traits An individual's personal characteristics

Transaction-processing system (TPS) An information system that supports the collection and processing of an organization's transactions

Transactional leadership An approach in which managers motivate employees to perform by clarifying task requirements and by providing rewards in return for employee efforts to achieve the goals

Transfer A lateral move to a different job of similar pay and responsibility within the organization

Transformation process The management, technological, and production operations performed by the organization to convert inputs to outputs

Transformational leadership An approach in which leaders motivate employees to do more than is expected to achieve superior performance

Transnational management A management approach in which an organization uses an integrated strategy for achieving organizational goals on a worldwide level while stressing local flexibility in host countries

Turnaround A retrenchment strategy intended to reverse a negative trend and regain profitability

Two-factor theory A need theory arguing that job dissatisfaction and lack of motivation are derived from factors separate from those that affect satisfaction and motivation

U

Uncertainty avoidance The degree to which people feel threatened when confronted with ambiguity or uncertainty

Undercontrol Unregulated work activities, granting employees too much individual autonomy and causing ineffective organizational performance

Unethical behavior Conduct that is considered "wrong" or "bad" in the context of a moral code

Unit and small-batch technology A type of technology in which products are custom-produced to customer specifications or produced in small quantities by skilled employees

Upward communication A flow of information from lower to higher levels in the organization's hierarchy

Utilitarian theories Theories that evaluate the ethics of decisions and actions according to the greatest amount of good they generate

V

Valence The value of the anticipated satisfaction that each possible outcome of an action represents

Value/price ratio A measure of the value that customers receive as a function of the product price

Venture capitalists Individuals or companies that invest in new or expanding businesses

Verbal communication The expression of information through language, using words and grammar

Vertical communication A flow of information up and down the organization's hierarchy

Vertical integration A growth strategy that involves the acquisition of one or more organizations that are suppliers, distributors, or customers of the firm's products

Voluntary export restraints Voluntary restrictions in which one nation agrees to limit exports of certain types of products to another nation

Vroom-Yetton-Jago model A contingency theory of leadership that examines how situational factors affect the degree of employee participation in decision making

W

Whistle-blowing An employee's public disclosure of illegal, unethical, wasteful, or harmful practices by his or her own organization

Work-flow layout The arrangement of production facilities, including equipment, material flows, and personnel

Work specialization The degree to which an organization's work is divided into smaller parts that constitute separate jobs

Written communication The expression of ideas through words that are meant to be read

Z

Zero-base budgeting A process by which managers calculate resource requirements based on the coming year's priorities, rather than on the past year's requirements

Zero defects Being completely defect-free

Author Index

Subject Index

Organization/Brand/ Company Index